Studies in American Tort Law

Studies in American Tort Law

SEVENTH EDITION

Vincent R. Johnson
SOUTH TEXAS DISTINGUISHED PROFESSOR OF LAW
ST. MARY'S UNIVERSITY

Chenglin Liu
PROFESSOR OF LAW
ST. MARY'S UNIVERSITY

CAROLINA ACADEMIC PRESS
Durham, North Carolina

LCCN: 2022934381
ISBN: 978-1-5310-2126-9
eISBN: 978-1-5310-2127-6

Carolina Academic Press
700 Kent Street
Durham, North Carolina 27701
(919) 489-7486
www.cap-press.com

Printed in the United States of America

To the happy memory of my parents,
Anna Ruth Johnson and Harry P. Johnson,
who provided a world of care and inspiration
—VRJ

To Xue, Jennie, and Vincent
—CL

Summary of Contents

Contents

Table of Cases

Table of Books and Articles

Abraham, Kenneth S., Individual Action and Collective Responsibility: The Dilemma of Mass Tort Reform, 73 Va. L. Rev. 845 (1987), 437

Ackerman, Robert M., Mitigating Disaster: A Communitarian Response, 9 Cardozo J. Conflict Resol. 283 (2008), 437

American Law Institute, Restatement, Second, of Agency, 722, 723, 725

American Law Institute, Restatement, Third, of Agency, 722, 723, 726, 746

American Law Institute, Restatement of Torts (various drafts and editions), cited throughout

American Law Institute, Restatement, Second, of Contracts (1981), 1122

American Law Institute, Restatement, Third, of Restitution & Unjust Enrichment (2011), 1021

American Law Institute, Restatement, Third, of the Law Governing Lawyers (2000), 305, 739

American Law Institute, Restatement, Third, of Unfair Competition Law (1995), 1161

Anderson, David, Is Libel Law Worth Reforming?, 140 U. Pa. L. Rev. 487 (1991), 1124

Antolini, Denise E., Modernizing Public Nuisance: Solving the Paradox of the Special Injury Rule, 28 Ecology L.Q. 755 (2001), 997

Austin, Regina, Employer Abuse, Worker Resistance, and the Tort of Intentional Infliction of Severe Emotional Distress, 41 Stan. L. Rev. 1 (1988), 85

Bender, Leslie, A Lawyer's Primer on Feminist Theory and Tort, 38 J. Legal Educ. 3 (1988), 327

Boston, Gerald W., Strict Liability for Abnormally Dangerous Activity: The Negligence Barrier, 36 San Diego L. Rev. 597 (1999), 759

Calvert, Robert W., "...In the Interest of Justice," 4 St. Mary's L. J. 291 (1972), 665

Campbell, John, Bernard Cho, & Christopher Robertson, Time Is Money: An Empirical Assessment of Non-Economic Damages Arguments, 95 Wash. U. Lev. Rev. 1, 33 (2017), 204

Cantu, Charles E., A New Look at an Old Conundrum: The Determinative Test for the Hybrid Sales/Service Transaction Under Section 402A of the Restatement (Second) of Torts, 45 Ark. L. Rev. 913 (1993), 777

Cantu, Charles, Assault and Battery, in Texas Torts and Remedies (1987), 62

Chamallas, Martha, The Architecture of Bias: Deep Structures in Tort Law, 146 U. Pa. L. Rev. 463 (1998), 225

Chamallas, Martha, & Jennifer B. Wriggins, The Measure of Injury (2010), 100

Coase, Ronald, The Problem of Social Cost, 3 J. L. & Econ. 1 (1960), 989, 992

Dobbs, Dan B., Paul T. Hayden, and Ellen M. Bublick, The Law of Torts (2d ed. 2016) (various editions), 7, 175

Eldredge, L., Law of Defamation 5 (1978), 1111

Feeley, Andrew, Kayla Horan, & David Schap, Statutory Modification of the Collateral Source Rule, 23 J. Leg. Econ. 81, 90 (April 2017), 213-14

Fischer, David A., Fraudulently Induced Consent to Intentional Torts, 46 U. Cinn. L. Rev. 71 (1977), 161

Geier, Peter, Score One for "Hedonic" Damages, Nat'l L.J., July 24, 2006, at 7, 210

Gifford, Donald G., Public Nuisance as a Mass Products Liability Tort, 71 U. Cinn. L. Rev. 743 (2003), 994

Grady, Mark F., Better Medicine Causes More Lawsuits, and New Administrative Courts Will Not Solve the Problem, 86 Nw. U. L. Rev. 1068 (1992), 275

Grady, Mark F., Why Are People Negligent? Technology, Nondurable Precautions, and the Medical Malpractice Explosion, 82 Nw. U. L. Rev. 293 (1988), 275

Harper, Fowler V., Fleming James, Jr., & Oscar S. Gray, The Law of Torts (3d ed. 2006), 61

Holliday, Wyatt, Comment, "The Answer to Criminal Aggression is Retaliation": Stand-Your-Ground Laws and the Liberalization of Self-Defense, 43 U. Tol. L. Rev. 407 (2012), 167

Johnson, Vincent R., Advanced Tort Law: A Problem Approach 6-16 (3d ed. 2020), 809

Johnson, Vincent R., "Absolute and Perfect Candor" to Clients, 34 St. Mary's L.J. 737 (2003), 1030

Johnson, Vincent R., Americans Abroad: International Education Programs and Tort Liability, 32 J.C.U.L. 309 (2006), 364

Johnson, Vincent R., Comparative Defamation Law: England and the United States, 24 U. Miami Intl. & Comp. L. Rev. 1, 4-10 (2016), 1126

Johnson, Vincent R., Credit-Monitoring Damages in Cybersecurity Tort Litigation, 19 Geo. Mason L. Rev. 113 (2011), 210

Keating, Patrick J., Kevin R. Sutherland, Gerald V. Cleary III, & Timothy J. Walsh, Recent Developments in Aviation and Space Law, 38 Tort Trial & Ins. Prac. L.J. 205 (2003), 437

Keeton, W. Page, Fraud—Concealment and Non-Disclosure, 15 Tex. L. Rev. 1 (1936), 1025

Keeton, W. Page, et al., Prosser and Keeton on Torts (5th ed. 1984), cited throughout

King, Joseph H., Jr.,Causation, Valuation, and Chance in Personal Injury Torts Involving Preexisting Conditions and Future Consequences, 90 Yale L.J. 1353 (1981), 414

Kutner, Peter B, The Prosser Myth of Transferred Intent, 91 Ind. L.J. 1105, 1107 (2016), 56

Lambert, Wesley B., The Price of Life: A Prediction of South Carolina's Approach to Expert Testimony on Hedonic Damages Using the Willingness-to-Pay Method, 64 S.C.L. Rev. 1037, 1062 (2013), 203

Love, Jean C., Discriminatory Speech and the Tort of Intentional Infliction of Emotional Distress, 47 Wash. & Lee L. Rev. 123 (1990), 77, 99

Magruder, Calvert, Mental and Emotional Disturbance in the Law of Torts, 49 Harv. L. Rev. 1033 (1936), 81

Mathews, Benjamin D., Potential Tort Liability for Personal Use of Drone Aircraft, 46 St. Mary's L.J. 573, 592-93 (2015), 971

McClurg, Andrew J., Dead Sorrow: A Story About Loss and a New Theory of Wrongful Death Damages, 85 B.U. L. Rev. 1 (2005), 227

McNamara, John W., Note, Murder and the Tort of Intentional Infliction of Emotional Distress, 1986 Duke L.J. 572, 105

Miller, Ted R., Willingness to Pay Comes of Age: Will the Tort System Survive?, 83 Nw. U. L. Rev. 876 (1989), 230

Mullenix, Linda, Mass Tort Litigation: Cases and Materials (2d ed. 2008), 436

Pedrick, Willard H., Intentional Infliction: Should Section 46 Be Revised?, 13 Pepperdine L. Rev. 1 (1985), 85

Poplar, D., Tolling the Statute of Limitations for Battered Women After Giovine v. Giovine: Creating Equitable Exceptions for Victims of Domestic Abuse, 101 Dick. L. Rev. 161 (1996), 94

Prosser, William L., Palsgraf Revisited, 52 Mich. L. Rev. 1 (1953), 259

Prosser, William L., Privacy, 48 Cal. L. Rev. 383 (1960), 1129

Prosser, William L., Private Action for Public Nuisance, 52 Va. L. Rev. 997, 996

Prosser, William L., Transferred Intent, 45 Texas L. Rev. 650 (1967), 55, 970

First Edition Preface

Tort law is a prime battleground in the ongoing debate over social policy. This book attempts to illuminate that debate through the use of cases and materials that clearly reflect not only the current rules on injury compensation, but also the policy choices underlying those rules.

Lawyers must know what the law is now, and how to apply it to the facts of a client's case. But they must also understand public policy, if they are to effectively participate in the important (and inevitable) legal processes through which existing rules are continually challenged, reaffirmed, discarded, and replaced.

As an instructional text, Studies in American Tort Law (SATL) does not speak from an ideological perspective. In that sense, the book is intended to be both "balanced" and "mainstream." Within a clear doctrinal framework (which is undoubtedly influenced by the work of the late William Prosser), a range of views is presented, reflecting dominant themes and issues in tort law, such as fault, proportionality, deterrence, internalization of costs, and distribution of losses. These views are then linked, juxtaposed, and explored with the purpose of assisting students in the task of assessing the merits and limitations of these positions. In the end, however, the evaluation of the public policies which have shaped the current tangle of rules on liability for personal injury and property damage is left to the reader. This book attempts to promote a better understanding of the values advanced and the interests sacrificed by the adoption or application of particular rules in given contexts.

In terms of organization, SATL moves from simple concepts and elementary rules to ones that are more complex or elusive. The book has a strong doctrinal framework and strives for clarity, to the extent that clarity is possible, on the assumption that if simple points are dealt with efficiently, time can then be profitably spent on difficult or uncertain questions.

In selecting or writing material for the book, students and professors have been foremost in mind. At each juncture, the test has been whether the selection is both readable and teachable. The goal has been to include material that is vivid, provocative, and worthy of the reader's time.

A few features of SATL deserve mention. First, although cases are used as the principal vehicle for teaching torts, a special effort has been made to integrate statutory law into the text. In particular, careful attention has been paid to the give-and-take process through which judge-made law and legislation influence one another. Second, the significance of liability insurance is highlighted, for students must come to appreciate the critical role that insurance (or the lack of it) plays in the resolution of real cases. Third, "ethics notes" have been included throughout the book for the purpose of sensitizing students to the difficult ethical questions that practicing lawyers face each day. These notes demonstrate, in part, that lawyers are subject to higher standards than persons in other callings. Fourth, the materials in SATL explore a number of issues associated with the law and feminism movement. These issues raise questions of social justice that should be of concern to all lawyers.

SATL introduces students to—but is careful not to overwhelm them with—law and economics. At appropriate junctures in SATL, economic issues are explored, as in connection with the negligence balancing test and the materials discussing computation of damages, liability for nuisance, and strict liability. The goal is not to view all of tort law through an economic lens, but to employ economic analysis when it is particularly useful. This approach allows professors from the law-and-economics "school" to use the materials in the text as a starting point for classroom discussions; those faculty members who eschew economic analysis can allow the economic commentary to stand on its own, without need for in-class elaboration.

By emphasizing doctrinal clarity and the role of public policy, SATL seeks to afford professors maximum flexibility in teaching the law of torts. At the same time, it endeavors to ensure that all students develop a firm foundation in both what the law is and what it can be. We hope that SATL will prove to be a book that can be productively taught by professors and readily grasped by students.

VINCENT R. JOHNSON
San Antonio, Texas

Seventh Edition Preface and Acknowledgments

The seventh edition of Studies in American Tort Law reflects the highly dynamic nature of the torts field. It includes several new principal cases, scores of citations to recent judicial opinions and statutes, and many references to the Restatement, Third, of Torts.

My PowerPoint file for Studies in American Tort Law is available to law professors adopting the book. Contact: vjohnson@stmarytx.edu. Students may wish to use the companion volume: Vincent R. Johnson, *Mastering Torts: A Student's Guide to the Law of Torts* (Carolina Academic Press, 7th ed. 2022).

Alan Gunn was my excellent co-author on the first three editions of Studies in American Tort Law. Following the completion of the third edition, he assumed emeritus status at the University of Notre Dame. Alan's contributions to the text are still very much a part of this book. His language informs the discussion of virtually every important topic. In particular, Studies in American Tort Law continues to be enriched by Alan's lucid explorations of how law-and-economics scholarship sometimes illuminates the study of tort issues. Many of those discussions are now setoff as separate notes on "Economic Analysis" bearing his name.

Chenglin Liu, my colleague at St. Mary's University, has been my co-author since the sixth edition of Studies in American Tort Law. Educated in China, Sweden, and the United States, Liu is an outstanding teacher and the author of influential articles published in journals at Harvard, Stanford, Penn, Hastings, Texas, Arizona, Cornell, Virginia, Washington (in St. Louis), and other fine universities. Liu is one of the leading American scholars on Chinese tort law, and has published two books on Chinese law, including most recently *Chinese Law in Context* (2020 Carolina Academic Press).

Work on the seventh edition was ably assisted by several law students at St. Mary's University. In particular, Professor Chenglin Liu thanks his research assistants for their excellent work. That talented group included: RJ Ruiz, Kathryn L. Cantu, Meghan L. Rockwell, Falak A. Momin, Jamie I. Weber, Hannah E. Ward, and Daisy J. Ramirez.

I had the pleasure of working with Sherack Malokwu, Griffin Farney, Ross Potter, Joseph Wolfgang Villarreal-Snydelaar, Maximiliano S. Lerma, Margaret Ford, Christiana Segura, Pablo Medina, and Lucas James Orlando. These promising young members of the legal profession improved the draft for this book in many ways.

I am grateful to Dean Patricia Roberts for her leadership of the law school and her support of a wide range of scholarly endeavors. St. Mary's University School of Law provided generous support for this work.

Excerpts from the various Restatements of the Law cited in the book are reproduced with the permission of the American Law Institute, which holds the copyrights to those works.[1]

The photograph of William J. Brennan, Jr. (p. 1083) is from Harris & Ewing, Collection of the Supreme Court of the United States. The photograph of the portrait of William H. Rehnquist (p. 1110) is by Thomas Lepp, Collection of the Supreme Court of the United States. The New York State Court of Appeals provided the portraits of William S. Andrews (p. 262) and Charles D. Breitel (p. 637). The photograph of Benjamin N. Cardozo (p. 261) is by Harris & Ewing, photographer, Public domain, via Wikimedia Commons. The photograph of Learned Hand (p. 272) is from the Harvard Law Art Collection. Other photographs were supplied by the individuals pictured or by law schools or courts with which they were associated.

Omissions within quoted material are denoted by the insertion of ellipses. An ellipsis at the beginning or end of a paragraph sometimes also denotes the omission of one or more preceding or subsequent paragraphs. In excerpts from articles and cases, footnotes have been omitted, unless otherwise indicated.

VINCENT R. JOHNSON
St. Mary's University School of Law
San Antonio, Texas
February 13, 2022

1. Those works include: Restatement, Second, Torts, copyright 1965, 1977, and 1979 by The American Law Institute; Restatement, Third, Torts: Liability for Physical and Emotional Harm, copyright 2010, 2012 by The American Law Institute; Restatement, Third, of Torts, Liability for Economic Harm, copyright 2020 by The American Law Institute; Restatement, Third, Torts: Apportionment of Liability, copyright 2000 by The American Law Institute; Restatement, Third, Torts: Products Liability, copyright 1998 by The American Law Institute; Restatement, Second, Agency, copyright 1959 by The American Law Institute; Restatement, Third, Agency, copyright 2006 by The American Law Institute; Restatement, Third, Restitution & Unjust Enrichment, copyright 2011 by The American Law Institute; Restatement, Third, Unfair Competition, copyright 1995 by The American Law Institute. Excerpts from these works are reprinted with permission. All rights are reserved by the American Law Institute.

Studies in American Tort Law

Chapter 1

An Overview of Modern Tort Liability: Intentional Injury, Failure to Exercise Care, and Strict Liability

Personal Injury and Property Damage. Tort law is a dynamic field not easily described. Its rules are nowhere set down in a single comprehensive code, and indeed they continually evolve in response to the felt needs of society.

In general, tort law is a vehicle of legal redress for victims of physical injury or damage to tangible property. It also, on occasion, provides compensation or other relief for such diverse forms of harm as emotional distress, impairment of reputation, and non-tangible economic injuries.

The disputes which fall within the bounds of tort law are as broad as the range of human activities. Litigants include individuals and corporations, governmental bodies and non-profit institutions, professionals and volunteers. Indeed, every person whose conduct or inaction precipitates a result which another perceives as harmful is a potential tort defendant.

Tort law encompasses many distinct causes of action — including, for example, claims for defamation, invasion of privacy, negligence, and false imprisonment, to mention but a few. Some torts (such as trespass to land) are ancient in origin, while others (such as strict products liability) have emerged only recently; a number of actions (for example, fraud) are well-defined and consistently recognized, though others (for example, wrongful birth and wrongful life) are only loosely understood or are the subject of little consensus.

New Rights and Remedies. New torts are elevated to legal status as ideas change concerning the duties persons owe to one another. In fact, that process has been underway since not long after William defeated Harold at the Battle of Hastings in 1066. Thus, early in the twentieth century, an English writer reflecting on his country's contribution to Anglo-American tort jurisprudence aptly remarked:

> [I]t has never been of much use to contend that *merely* because an action is new it cannot be brought. . . . If the judges thought that a new remedy was necessary, they invented it, unless the invention of it would have shocked public opinion, in which event they left . . . [the task] to Parliament. . . .

> .... Torts of a specific character have increased steadily in number throughout our legal history, and the courts can even now, if they think fit, enlarge the list....
>
> [At times, the willingness of English courts to recognize new remedies was so great that it] was more difficult for jurists to state this branch of the law scientifically than for judges to make the law itself. Writers on the law were like map-makers whose rulers conquer territory so rapidly that the bounds of their realms cannot be traced.

Percy H. Winfield, *The Foundation of Liability in Tort*, 27 Colum. L. Rev. 1, 4–5 (1927). This is not to suggest that judges are indiscriminate in recognizing new rights. As one tribunal explained:

> This Court treads cautiously when deciding whether to recognize a new tort.... While the law must adjust to meet society's changing needs, we must balance that adjustment against boundless claims in an already crowded judicial system.

Trevino v. Ortega, 969 S.W.2d 950, 951–52 (Tex. 1998).

Common Law and Statutory Law. In large measure, tort law is a "common law" subject, meaning that its principles often have been articulated not by legislatures, but by courts. Indeed, for centuries—beginning long before legislative lawmaking was popularized by the leaders of the Progressive Era and the New Deal—judges have defined standards of civil liability as part of the process of deciding the disputes that come before them. It is well recognized that when *A* sues *B*, alleging that a wrong has been committed, the court may decide that the complaint states a cause of action in tort entitling *A* to relief *either* because *B's* conduct violates a command of the legislature *or* because *B's* conduct transgresses the common (non-statutory) law of the jurisdiction. When a court rests its decision on the latter ground, it must necessarily state, either expressly or implicitly, what the common law is. Non-statutory common-law principles articulated by courts impose legal obligations which are binding upon all members of the community, notwithstanding the absence of legislation. Where applicable, common-law rules govern not only the instant dispute, but similar future cases as well.

"Making" Versus "Finding" Law. Earlier generations might have described the judge's role in common-law adjudication as that of merely "finding" the law through a disciplined process of legal analysis and reasoning. Today, however, most members of the legal profession candidly acknowledge that the process involves considerable discretion. At times, judges are in fact engaged in a process of making law, rather than in the scientific discovery of preordained principles. Contrary, perhaps, to contemporary public opinion, such law-making by courts is not a new encroachment by activist judges upon established prerogatives of the legislature. Rather, common-law adjudication antedates the ascendancy of statutes; it is a time-honored process the origins of which can be traced back for the better part of a millennium.

Increasing Importance of Statutes. Today's tort law is significantly shaped by legislative intervention into what was once almost exclusively the domain of the judiciary. Statutes are an increasingly present feature of the legal landscape. When they speak to an issue, whether directly or indirectly, they cannot be ignored. Tort lawyers must be as familiar with statutes as with court opinions. Note, however, that many judges are wary of legislative intrusions into the field of torts, and they have sometimes reacted by holding statutes invalid, often on state constitutional grounds.

Primarily State Law. For the most part, tort law is a creature of the state, rather than the national, government. Under America's federal system, each state has broad leeway to define the conditions under which a person will be subject to tort liability for causing harm to another. This state power is restricted only by the relatively limited demands of the federal constitution (*e.g.*, with respect to free speech or due process) and, more importantly, by federal legislative enactments that preempt contrary state provisions pursuant to the Supremacy Clause of the U.S. Constitution. Because reasonable persons may differ on issues of individual responsibility and social accountability for personal injury or property damage, the principles of tort law governing a particular issue may vary from one jurisdiction to the next.

Re-forming Tort Law. Not only do state lawmakers (courts and legislatures) sometimes diverge on questions of accident compensation, but attitudes shift with the passage of time. Rules once thought to strike a sound balance between competing interests may come to be regarded as out of step with changed circumstances. Not surprisingly, the standards of tort law are regularly subject to re-examination. Interest groups urge legislatures to "re-form" the law governing accidents. Moreover, each court case involving a common law issue presents a potential occasion for the judiciary to decide whether to follow an existing rule. To be sure, there is a strong presumption — embodied in the doctrine of "*stare decisis*" — that courts should stand by their earlier decisions. However, not infrequently, a point is reached where the reasoning underlying an old rule is insufficiently persuasive to justify its continued application. In such instances, the only intelligent course is for the rule to be abandoned in favor of a new, sounder standard — whether through judicial decision or legislative action.

Litigation Follows Innovation. Consider the following:

> Innovation is frequently followed by litigation because new or expanded practices often cause harm. When losses occur as a result of such developments, lawsuits offer a public mechanism for compensating injured persons, forcing innovators to internalize the costs of their endeavors, and creating incentives for measures that minimize future harm by reducing activity levels or increasing precautions. Within proper limits, litigation can, and frequently does, provide a healthy check on market excesses by requiring persons who benefit from selling goods or services to bear the burden of incidental losses or at least spread those losses broadly among those who

> enjoy the goods or services. In the early and mid-twentieth century, mass production of automobiles was soon followed by car-accident lawsuits, and mass-marketing of consumer goods gave rise to products-liability litigation. More recently, the widespread use of computerized databases has produced lawsuits related to data security and identity theft, and the expansion of international education programs is now generating claims by students injured while studying in foreign countries. It is entirely natural, from the perspective of more than a century of American legal history, for the recent vast expansion of standardized testing to be followed by lawsuits [on behalf of the thousands who have been harmed by the erroneous scoring of standardized tests].

Vincent R. Johnson, *Standardized Tests, Erroneous Scores, and Tort Liability*, 38 Rutgers L.J. 655, 668–70 (2007).

The Restatement, the Hornbooks, and Mastering Torts. It is not surprising that over the years there have been efforts to articulate in simple but comprehensive terms the mass of tort law that has emerged from the courts. In this regard, one authority has achieved preeminence: the Restatement of Torts by the American Law Institute. Respected for its clarity, as well as its wisdom in identifying the "best" view in areas where there are competing positions, the Restatement of Torts has been widely influential. The "blackletter" provisions of the Restatement of Torts, and the reasoning advanced by the Restatement commentary in support of those rules, have been cited in judicial decisions more than 88,000 times.

Founded early in the twentieth century, the American Law Institute is an organization of highly respected judges, professors, and practitioners. A principal focus of the ALI's work has been to "restate" the principles governing torts, contracts, agency, and other fields of law. The first Restatement of Torts was completed in four volumes in 1939. That work was replaced by the Second Restatement, another four-volume treatise, the various books of which were published between 1965 and 1979. Today, portions of the Second Restatement remain in effect, but much of the work on the Third Restatement of Torts has been completed.

The volume on harm caused by defective products (called the Restatement, Third, of Torts: Products Liability) was finalized in 1998, and the volume on comparative principles (called the Restatement, Third, of Torts: Apportionment of Liability) was completed in 2000. The work on basic principles of liability for physical and emotional harm is also complete, and was published in two volumes called the Restatement, Third, of Torts: Liability for Physical and Emotional Harm. Those books were issued in 2010 (§§1 to 36) and 2012 (§§37 to 65). In 2020, the Restatement, Third, of Torts: Liability for Economic Harm was completed. Other topics, including liability for defamation and basic intentional torts, are now being addressed.

Thus, on most matters, the Third Restatement has superseded the Second Restatement, and on other matters that is not yet true. Until the work on the Third Restatement is finished, one must exercise care in citing Restatement provisions. Of course,

William L. Prosser

the Restatement is merely a guide—albeit a very persuasive guide—for students, scholars, practitioners, and courts. However, the Restatement is not the law anywhere until its provisions, one by one, are adopted by judicial decision or legislation. Courts are free to endorse the Restatement or reject it. States that follow the Restatement on one subject may embrace divergent positions on others.

There are two other important works of tort scholarship that should be noted, namely the hornbooks (single-volume treatises) on tort law published by West Academic Publishing. Dean William L. Prosser's hornbook on the law of torts was first published in 1941, and before his death in the early 1970s the book, in various editions, achieved legendary status among law students, professors, judges, and the bar. It was cited in thousands of decisions and was probably the single most influential law book written in America during the twentieth century. The Prosser hornbook was last published under the editorship of other scholars (W. Page Keeton, Dan B. Dobbs, Robert E. Keeton, and David G. Owen), with the revised title of "Prosser and Keeton on Torts" (5th ed. 1984), and is now mainly of historical interest. A more up-to-date source of guidance is a newer hornbook by three eminent scholars, professors Dan B. Dobbs, Paul T. Hayden, and Ellen M. Bublick, The Law of Torts (2d ed. 2016).

Users of this textbook will find it useful to consult its companion study guide which provides a clear, condensed narrative treatment of the 23 chapters covered in this book: Vincent R. Johnson, Mastering Torts: A Student's Guide to the Law of Torts (7th ed. 2022). Mastering Torts references more than 200 cases—including all of the "principal" cases in this text—to illustrate the meaning and limits of the most important features of American tort law.

Tort Law and Public Policy. The substantive content of tort law cannot be explained by reference to a single objective or goal. Rather, the contours of the field have been shaped by the pursuit of a variety of ends, each of which has commanded some degree of support as being a socially desirable objective. It is useful to identify these sometimes-congruent, sometimes-conflicting public policies. A clear understanding of them does much to explain the content of particular rules. It also makes possible the evaluation of tort standards by clarifying the interests advanced or sacrificed through adherence to a given position.

To be sure, there is no comprehensive list of relevant public policy considerations. Yet some arguments have been invoked with such regularity that their historical significance cannot be ignored. What follows is a brief, introductory sketch of several important public-policy arguments.

It has often been urged that:

Liability should be based on "fault." The fault principle has been strongly influential for more than a century, and it accounts for much of the law of negligence, and other tort rules as well. In part, it is intended to allow individuals a maximum sphere of action free of the risk of tort liability. According to the fault principle, only if the defendant's conduct is blameworthy should liability be imposed. In general, the term "fault" is used in torts to encompass situations where harm is the product of intentionally tortious conduct or failure to exercise care.

Liability should be proportional to fault. The proportionality principle seeks to limit or refine application of the fault principle. In part, it holds that liability should not be levied on an individual tortfeasor, even if fault is shown, if doing so would expose the defendant to a burden that is disproportionately heavy or perhaps unlimited. In addition, the principle of proportionality holds that where the tortious conduct of two or more persons contributes to the production of harm, liability for the loss should be allocated among the actors in accordance with the degree to which their conduct caused the damage.

Liability should be used to deter accidents. The deterrence principle recognizes that tort law is concerned not only with fairly allocating past losses, but also with minimizing the costs of future accidents. According to this principle, tort rules should discourage persons from engaging in those forms of conduct which pose an excessive risk of personal injury or property damage. In some cases, this means nothing more than that liability should be imposed on those who deliberately inflict injury or cause harm by ignoring foreseeable risks. In other situations, such as those where a risk of harm is foreseeable to more than one person, the policy of deterrence may favor placing the threat of liability on the party best situated to avoid the loss, or, as some might say, the cheapest cost avoider, or taking fault on the part of all such persons into account in determining damages, so that all relevant actors have an incentive to avoid causing losses.

The costs of accidents should be spread broadly. The idea underlying the "spreading" rationale is that the financial burden of accidents may be diminished by spreading losses broadly so that no person is forced to bear a large share of the damages. For example, some argue that when a defective product unforeseeably causes injury to a consumer, it is best to place the loss on the manufacturer, even in the absence of fault, for unlike the unfortunate consumer, the manufacturer can distribute the loss to a large segment of the public by incrementally adjusting the price of its products. Losses can be spread not only through increases in the costs of goods and services, but through other devices such as taxation and insurance. Though controversial, the spreading principle revolutionized the law of products liability and has catalyzed other changes in tort doctrine.

The costs of accidents should be shifted to those best able to bear them. The "shifting" rationale is closely related to the spreading principle insofar as it seeks to use the process of loss allocation to minimize the economic burden of accidents. According to this view, a loss will be less severely felt if it is placed on one with substantial resources than on one with limited wealth, and therefore losses should be shifted to those financially able to bear them. Proponents of this view argue, for example, that it is undesirable to force an accident victim with only $100 in assets to bear the full amount of a $100 loss, for doing so means that the accident will have a devastating financial impact. In contrast, shifting that same loss to a defendant with a million dollars in assets may be desirable, for then the loss will not really be felt by either the plaintiff or the defendant. To be sure, the law has never held that a poor person should always be able to recover from a rich one, or that a wealthy person is precluded from seeking damages from one financially less well to do. Indeed, there is great reluctance to applying one law to the rich and another to the poor. Yet, the shifting rationale—sometimes pejoratively referred to as the search for the "deep pocket"—has not been without influence. However, its impact on tort doctrine has been more covert than the impact of many other policy considerations.

Those who benefit from dangerous activities should bear resulting losses. Certain activities—*e.g.*, owning a dog that may bite or using explosives—entail a serious risk of harm to third persons even if care is exercised by the actor. According to this principle, fairness requires that those who benefit from engaging in such conduct should bear resulting losses, even in the absence of fault. Thus, it is sometimes said that an activity "must pay its own way." What this means is that the law should force actors to "internalize" the costs that their endeavors inflict on third persons. Only when those costs are taken into account, it is argued, are actors likely to make decisions about activities and precautions that are not only personally beneficial, but socially responsible.

Tort law should foster predictability in human affairs. The idea here is that persons should not be forced to act at their peril, uncertain as to what the law requires of them or what they may expect of others. Depending on how this principle is interpreted, it can be used to support a variety of views, including those holding that tort rules should provide clear notice of the type of conduct that is expected in particular circumstances; that standards should not be unnecessarily subjective, if objective standards are feasible; that tort rules prospectively enacted by the legislature are preferable to those retroactively created by the judiciary; or even that bright-line rules are preferable to flexible norms which require a jury to second-guess the propriety of an actor's conduct after it has occurred.

Tort law should facilitate economic growth and the pursuit of progress. In the late nineteenth century, this principle held great sway, and many rules were crafted to limit the tort liability of commercial enterprises. The theory was that a greater benefit for the community would be produced by freeing the engines of industrialization and economic expansion from the specter of tort liability than by requiring such concerns to compensate those injured by their products or activities. In the twentieth century, there was growing recognition that the pursuit of progress was not an unqualified good, and increased support for holding businesses accountable for the losses they cause. However, the policy in favor of promoting growth and progress has been resurgent in recent years. There is continuing concern that tort liability not be so readily imposed that industrial creativity is stifled, that entrepreneurship is chilled, that professionals are unwilling to render important services, or that American businesses are globally uncompetitive.

Tort law should be administratively convenient and efficient, and should avoid intractable inquiries. Only a limited amount of resources can be devoted to the administration of justice in any society. This principle holds that tort rules should be shaped so that the dollars spent on accident compensation are efficiently employed. Thus, legal standards should not be so complex or uncertain that their application entails an undue expenditure of judicial resources or imposes unnecessarily high litigation costs on parties. So, too, the convenience and efficiency principles discourage the pursuit of what might be called intractable inquiries, matters where the facts are such that even after expenditure of considerable time and money, there is a substantial risk that an erroneous result will be reached.

Tort law should promote individual responsibility and discourage the waste of resources. According to this view, tort law should encourage individuals to employ available resources to protect their own interests, rather than depend upon others to save them from harm. Some would argue that this policy has been on the wane in recent years, as changes in tort doctrine have made it easier for accident victims to lay responsibility for their losses at the doorstep of others. Yet, the continued vitality of the anti-waste or self-protection principle can be seen in various areas of the law, including those defenses based on the plaintiff's conduct which limit the plaintiff's ability to recover damages even when the defendant is shown to have engaged in tortious conduct. There is a continuing struggle to define how much one must do for oneself, and how much one can expect from others.

Courts should accord due deference to co-equal branches of government. Although courts have traditionally created and updated the common law, there are occasions when the judiciary should eschew action in favor of other branches of government. Thus, it is often urged that certain questions are best left to the legislature because of its ability to gather facts through the legislative hearing process, to craft comprehensive solutions to broad-ranging questions, or to represent the will of the public on highly controversial issues. Presumably, the policy favoring deference to co-equal branches of government has less force where legislative or executive action is likely to be distorted by the lobbying of special interest groups, the under-representation of victims in the decision-making process, or lack of adequate funding.

Accident victims should be fully compensated. There is a strong public interest in ensuring that accident victims obtain the financial resources needed to overcome the injuries they have sustained. Proponents of this view argue that tort rules should be crafted and applied with an eye toward this goal, even if that means diminished respect for the fault or proportionality principles or other tort policies. A corollary to the compensation principle is the argument that a system that awards compensation on a regular, predictable, and consistent basis is preferable to one in which doctrinal and administrative vicissitudes render the availability of compensation a matter of chance.

These various perspectives on public policy are sometimes antagonistic. Adherence to the fault principle may mean that an actor will not be held liable for an unforeseeable injury, but also that the victim of that accident will not be compensated. Yet, it is often possible for a decision on issues of accident compensation to advance more than one tort goal. For example, a court may hold that a driver who causes an auto accident by exceeding the prescribed speed limit is liable to an injured pedestrian for all resulting damages. In that case, it may be said that the decision bases liability on fault (because the conduct was unreasonable and the harm was foreseeable), deters future accidents by this driver or others (by showing that violators will be held liable), fully compensates the victim (by imposing liability for resulting damages), embraces a predictable standard (namely the posted speed limit), and defers to the legislature's judgment as to the maximum reasonable speed on the road (by holding that violation of the speed limit constitutes actionable negligence).

Much of tort law can be understood in terms of the congruence and competition between the policies identified above.

An Alternative to "Policy Analysis." Until the middle of the twentieth century, very few judges explicitly justified their decisions by invoking policy arguments. Instead, the common law of torts was seen as redressing wrongs caused by those who violated accepted standards of conduct in the community. The defendant who had behaved acceptably was not liable (save in a handful of cases involving "strict liability"); the defendant whose misbehavior caused harm to the plaintiff had to make amends. The rules of tort law grew from decisions reached in particular cases, with novel situations being dealt with largely by analogy.

Much can be said for the older view. For one thing, the body of tort law that emerged over the course of several hundred years of decisions that were largely indifferent (at least explicitly) to policy concerns was quite satisfactory: much of it survives today. Furthermore, as some of the opinions reproduced in this book will show, judges are not necessarily very good at making decisions about public policy: they receive no training in disciplines relevant to policymaking (such as economics and statistics); they are not selected for their offices on the basis of their past success as policymakers; and they have no facilities for conducting even the most basic empirical research on the factual questions relevant to policy issues. Nor does our system of government explicitly charge judges with responsibility for policymaking; that function is assigned to legislatures and administrative agencies.

The judicial opinions that make up most of this book were written by judges with a variety of approaches to the law. Some rest explicitly on policy grounds; some apply existing rules more or less just because they are there; some seem to rest on policy considerations that have not been spelled out; some rely on convention; some apply (explicitly or otherwise) accepted community standards. Whatever else it may be, the common law is diverse.

Three Categories of Liability. In modern tort law, there are three overarching categories of tort liability: actions for intentionally inflicted injury (including a diverse array of intentional torts); actions based on failure to exercise care (including claims under the doctrines of negligence and recklessness); and actions in which liability is imposed without regard to the actor's state of mind or exercise of care (strict liability). A given course of injurious conduct may give rise to claims falling within one or more of these categories. Outside of these three categories there is no tort liability.

A. Intentionally Inflicted Injury

Garratt v. Dailey

Supreme Court of Washington
279 P.2d 1091 (Wash. 1955)

HILL, Justice.

The liability of an infant for an alleged battery is presented to this court for the first time. Brian Dailey (age five years, nine months) was visiting with Naomi Garratt, an adult and a sister of the plaintiff, Ruth Garratt, likewise an adult, in the back yard of the plaintiff's home, on July 16, 1951. It is plaintiff's contention that she came out into the back yard to talk with Naomi and that, as she started to sit down in a wood and canvas lawn chair, Brian deliberately pulled it out from under her. The only one of the three persons present so testifying was Naomi Garratt. (Ruth Garratt, the plaintiff, did not testify as to how or why she fell.) The trial court, unwilling to accept this testimony, adopted instead Brian Dailey's version of what happened, and made the following findings:

> III.... that while Naomi Garratt and Brian Dailey were in the back yard the plaintiff, Ruth Garratt, came out of her house into the back yard. Sometime subsequent thereto defendant, Brian Dailey, picked up a lightly built wood and canvas lawn chair which was then and there located in the

> back yard of the above described premises, moved it sideways a few feet and seated himself therein, at which time he discovered the plaintiff, Ruth Garratt, about to sit down at the place where the lawn chair had formerly been, at which time he hurriedly got up from the chair and attempted to move it toward Ruth Garratt to aid her in sitting down in the chair; that due to the defendant's small size and lack of dexterity he was unable to get the lawn chair under the plaintiff in timc to prevent her from falling to the ground....
>
> IV.... that when the defendant, Brian Dailey, moved the chair in question ... *he did not have any intent to injure the plaintiff, or any intent to bring about any unauthorized or offensive contact with her person or any ... purpose, intent or design to perform a prank or to effect an assault and battery upon the person of the plaintiff.*

(Italics ours, for a purpose hereinafter indicated.)

It is conceded that Ruth Garratt's fall resulted in a fractured hip and other painful and serious injuries. To obviate the necessity of a retrial in the event this court determines that she was entitled to a judgment against Brian Dailey, the amount of her damage was found to be $11,000. Plaintiff appeals from a judgment dismissing the action and asks for the entry of a judgment in that amount or a new trial.

....

It is urged that Brian's action in moving the chair constituted a battery. A definition (not all-inclusive but sufficient for our purpose) of a battery is the intentional infliction of a harmful bodily contact upon another. The rule that determines liability for battery is given in 1 Restatement, Torts, 29, § 13, as:

> An act which, directly or indirectly, is the legal cause of a harmful contact with another's person makes the actor liable to the other, if
>
> (a) the act is done with the intention of bringing about a harmful or offensive contact or an apprehension thereof to the other or a third person, and
>
> (b) the contact is not consented to by the other or the other's consent thereto is procured by fraud or duress, and
>
> (c) the contact is not otherwise privileged.

We have in this case no question of consent or privilege. We therefore proceed to an immediate consideration of intent and its place in the law of battery. In the comment on clause (a), the Restatement says:

> *Character of actor's intention.* In order that an act may be done with the intention of bringing about a harmful or offensive contact or an apprehension thereof to a particular person, either the other or a third person, the act must be done for the purpose of causing the contact or apprehension or with knowledge on the part of the actor that such contact or apprehension is substantially certain to be produced....

We have here the conceded volitional act of Brian, i.e., the moving of a chair. Had the plaintiff proved to the satisfaction of the trial court that Brian moved the chair while she was in the act of sitting down, Brian's action would patently have been for the purpose or with the intent of causing the plaintiff's bodily contact with the ground, and she would be entitled to a judgment against him for the resulting damages....

The plaintiff based her case on that theory, and the trial court held that she failed in her proof and accepted Brian's version of the facts rather than that given by the eyewitness who testified for the plaintiff....

A battery would be established if, in addition to plaintiff's fall, it was proved that, when Brian moved the chair, he knew with substantial certainty that the plaintiff would attempt to sit down where the chair had been. If Brian had any of the intents which the trial court found, in the italicized portions of the findings of fact quoted above, that he did not have, he would of course have had the knowledge to which we have referred. The mere absence of any intent to injure the plaintiff or to play a prank on her or to embarrass her, or to commit an assault and battery on her would not absolve him from liability if in fact he had such knowledge....

While a finding that Brian had no such knowledge can be inferred from the findings made, we believe that before the plaintiff's action in such a case should be dismissed there should be no question but that the trial court had passed upon that issue; hence, the case should be remanded for clarification of the findings to specifically cover the question of Brian's knowledge, because intent could be inferred therefrom. If the court finds that he had such knowledge the necessary intent will be established and the plaintiff will be entitled to recover, even though there was no purpose to injure or embarrass the plaintiff....

.... The only circumstance where Brian's age is of any consequence is in determining what he knew, and there his experience, capacity, and understanding are of course material.

....

Costs on this appeal will abide the ultimate decision of the superior court....

Remanded for clarification.

[Following the remand, which resulted in a judgment for plaintiff in the amount of $11,000, there was a second appeal, 304 P.2d 681 (Wash. 1956).]

ROSELLINI, Justice.

.... [O]n remand, the judge who heard the case stated that ... [i]n order to determine whether the defendant knew that the plaintiff would sit in the place where the chair had been, it was necessary for him to consider carefully the time sequence, as he had not done before; and this resulted in his finding that the arthritic woman had begun the slow process of being seated when the defendant quickly removed the chair and seated himself upon it, and that he knew, with substantial certainty, at that time that she would attempt to sit in the place where the chair had been. Such a conclusion, he stated, was the only reasonable one possible. . . . [T]he record . . . is sufficient to charge the defendant with intent to commit a battery.

The judgment is affirmed.

Note

1. ***Vosburg v. Putney.*** The famous case of Vosburg v. Putney, 50 N.W. 403 (Wis. 1891), was an action for assault and battery. "The injury complained of was caused by a kick inflicted by defendant upon the leg of the plaintiff, a little below the knee. The transaction occurred in a school-room . . . during school hours, both parties being pupils in the school. . . ." The evidence showed that the defendant reached across an aisle with his foot and touched the shin of the plaintiff's right leg. The plaintiff did not feel the kick, either because it was so slight or because it produced a loss of sensation. However, moments later the plaintiff experienced severe pain.

Despite various treatments and a subsequent operation, plaintiff lost the use of his limb. Several weeks before the kicking incident, plaintiff had injured the same leg above the knee in a coasting accident. At least one medical expert opined at trial that the limb was in a diseased condition when the kick was given and that the kick had aggravated the condition. There was medical agreement that the kick was the exciting cause of the destruction of the bone in plaintiff's leg. The Supreme Court of Wisconsin wrote that:

> Had the parties been upon the play-grounds of the school, engaged in the usual boyish sports, the defendant being free from malice, wantonness, or negligence, and intending no harm to plaintiff in what he did, we should hesitate to hold . . . that he could be held liable in this action. Some consideration is due to the implied license of the play-grounds. But it appears that the injury was inflicted in the school, after it had been called to order by the teacher, and after the regular exercises of the school had commenced. Under these circumstances, no implied license to do the act complained of existed. . . .

Today, would the defendant child of *Vosburg* be held liable for battery? Keep in mind what Garratt v. Dailey says about the meaning of intent. *See also* McElhaney v. Thomas, 405 P.3d 1214, 1219 (Kan. 2017) (holding that "'intent to bump' another person with a Ford F-150 truck, if proved, can establish the legally requisite culpable state of mind to sustain both a battery and a punitive damages claim").

2. ***Intent and Culpability.*** According to Professors David Jung and David Levine:

> "Knowledge intent" is the Restatement's creation. Until the Reporter for the first Restatement, Professor Francis Bohlen, drawing on the criminal law and the scholarly literature, introduced the concept, it did not appear at all under that name in the torts cases. Yet, once introduced, the definition gained prominence, and it is the most frequently cited definition of intent.
>
> . . . .

> For Professor Bohlen and the drafters of the first Restatement . . . [a]cting with knowledge that harm was certain to follow was the same as acting for the purpose of causing that harm because both reflected culpable states of mind. "One who embarks upon a particular course of action with knowledge that it involves as a necessary result an invasion of another's legally protected interest is as culpable as though the act were done for the very purpose of invading the interest." . . .

David J. Jung & David I. Levine, *Whence Knowledge Intent? Whither Knowledge Intent?*, 20 U.C. Davis L. Rev. 551, 554–55 (1987).

3. ***Why sue a child?*** See the notes beginning at p. 57, *infra*.

B. Actions Based on Lack of Care

Negligence is the breach of a duty to exercise reasonable care on behalf of another. Put differently, conduct which foreseeably subjects another to an unreasonable risk of harm is negligent.

Doe v. Roe

Court of Appeal of California
267 Cal. Rptr. 564 (Ct. App. 1990)

SMITH, Acting Presiding Justice.

. . . .

Defendant Richard Roe[1] appeals from a judgment after a court trial finding him liable to plaintiff Jane Doe for $150,000 in damages based on negligent transmittal of the virus herpes simplex II (hereafter herpes) sometime in early 1985. Defendant does not contest the court's finding that he transmitted the disease to plaintiff or the amount of damages assessed. Rather he argues that he had no duty to . . . [protect plaintiff from the disease] as a matter of law because the risk of asymptomatic transmission was unforeseeable in 1985.

. . . .

Defendant and plaintiff became acquainted in early 1985. . . . Soon after he asked her out, the subject of venereal disease came up. Plaintiff told defendant that she and her boyfriend were "clean," and that she would not want to put herself in a position where she could possibly contract a sexual disease. Defendant replied, "I don't blame you, I wouldn't want one either," but did not tell her he had previously contracted herpes.

1. [Fn. 1:] By stipulation of the parties and order of this court the parties have been designated by fictitious names to protect their privacy.

In fact, defendant had suffered three prior outbreaks of herpes. . . . Each time the lesions healed by themselves.

Defendant and plaintiff began dating. . . . Over a four-month period, they had sex once or twice a week. Defendant never disclosed the existence of his herpes condition, nor did he ever wear a condom during sexual relations. Up to that time, he made no attempt to educate himself about the disease, nor did he tell plaintiff about it because he didn't think he could give it to anybody.

. . . . [P]laintiff contracted genital herpes from defendant. Unlike defendant, who experienced only mild manifestations of the illness, plaintiff suffered greatly. She came down with 102-degree fever, swollen lymph glands, a sore throat and painful lesions on her genitalia which lasted three weeks. Since the onset of disease, she suffers outbreaks on the average of twice a month, each of which lasts about 10 days. She has undergone humiliation, severe physical discomfort and emotional distress. . . .

. . . . The [trial] court found . . . that defendant was negligent in either not disclosing that he was infected with herpes or taking precautions such as the use of a condom, to prevent its transmission. The court found the total damages to plaintiff to be $200,000, but it reduced that figure by 25 percent due to contributory negligence on her part[2]. . . .

Defendant contends . . . that as a matter of law he was relieved of a duty to plaintiff to disclose his condition or take measures to prevent its spread because he believed that he could not transmit the disease unless he had an active manifestation of the infection. Defendant cites several medical articles and pamphlets . . . in an attempt to show that as of 1985 the existence of asymptomatic shedding (transmission without lesions) was not well known. . . . Since the risk of harm was unforeseeable, defendant argues, there can be no duty of care. . . .

In determining whether a duty should be imposed, the courts are guided by the basic principle expressed in Civil Code section 1714 that everyone is responsible for injury occasioned to another by his own want of ordinary care or skill. . . . Departures from this rule are warranted only by balancing a number of policy considerations, including the foreseeability of the harm suffered, the degree of certainty the plaintiff suffered injury, the closeness of the connection between defendant's conduct and the injury suffered, the moral blame attached to the defendant's conduct and the consequences to the community of imposing a duty to exercise care. . . . With the exception of foreseeability, defendant does not dispute that *all* of them substantially weigh in favor of the imposition of a duty of care on his part to warn . . . or at least take precautions. . . .

---

2. [Fn. 2:] The court cited evidence that midway through the relationship plaintiff discovered that defendant's female roommate (who plaintiff suspected might have a venereal disease) was romantically interested in defendant. The court held that once she obtained this knowledge, plaintiff should have either ended the relationship or required that precautions be taken during intercourse.

Since the court's judgment implied a finding that defendant exposed plaintiff to a foreseeable risk, we must view the record in the light most favorable to the judgment to determine whether a reasonable trier of fact could have found the risk of harm foreseeable. . . . "Ordinarily foreseeability is a question of fact. . . . It may be decided as a question of law only if 'under the undisputed facts there is no room for a reasonable difference of opinion.'" . . . . "'The degree of foreseeability necessary to warrant the finding of a duty will . . . vary from case to case. For example, in cases where the burden of preventing future harm is great, a high degree of foreseeability may be required. . . . On the other hand, in cases *where there are strong policy reasons for preventing the harm, or the harm can be prevented by simple means, a lesser degree of foreseeability may be required*.'" . . . . In the present case, it is beyond question that our state's policy of preventing the spread of venereal disease is great and that the burden of warning a prospective sex partner is small. Thus, only a slight degree of foreseeability was needed to warrant the imposition of a duty of due care in the present case.

The evidence shows defendant knew he had herpes and that it could be transmitted by sexual contact. Although he had several outbreaks of the virus prior to 1985, defendant did absolutely nothing to find out about its contagiousness or what steps could be taken to prevent his giving it to a prospective partner. Defendant also testified that his lesions would appear at times without warning. Knowing that he had this infectious condition and that plaintiff was concerned about contracting venereal disease, defendant entered into a sexual liaison with plaintiff and continued to have intercourse with her on a regular basis for four months without revealing to her this material fact, electing to gamble with her health rather than inform her of his condition or educate himself about the disease. Under these facts, the record supports the court's implied finding that the risk of harm was foreseeable and that defendant unreasonably failed to exercise due care to guard against this risk. . . .

Our conclusion is not altered by the fact that defendant did not have an active outbreak of the disease during the relationship. There is no evidence in the record to support defendant's repeated assertion that he "relied on his doctors," in failing to disclose the condition or take precautionary measures during sex. No one, much less a physician, told plaintiff that he could not transmit herpes as long as he did not have lesions; defendant simply made up his mind that such was the case. Dr. Norman, whom defendant consulted in 1987, testified that, as of 1985 he believed that asymptomatic transmission was *improbable*, not impossible; moreover, defendant did not hear this as a medical opinion until after he was served with the lawsuit. On the other hand, there was evidence at trial that the phenomenon of asymptomatic transmission was not only known in the medical community but reported in lay literature long before defendant commenced his affair with plaintiff.

Kozup v. Georgetown University (D.D.C. 1987) 663 F. Supp. 1048 (*affd. in pertinent part* (D.C. Cir. 1988) 851 F.2d 437), relied on by defendant as controlling, is inapposite. In that case, a blood bank was held not liable for negligently transmitting AIDS to a blood donor recipient because as of October 1982, it was not known that AIDS could be transmitted by blood. . . . Here, defendant admittedly had *actual knowledge* that herpes was sexually transmissible. . . . Finally, plaintiff testified that if such a disclosure had been made to her, she would never have consented to sexual relations. We therefore find substantial evidence to support the trial court's finding that there was a duty of care and that defendant's breach of that duty proximately resulted in plaintiff's injuries.

. . . .

The judgment is affirmed.

Notes

1. ***Other Precedent. See also*** John B. v. Superior Court, 137 P.3d 153, 161 (Cal. 2006) (holding that "the tort of negligent transmission of HIV does not depend solely on actual knowledge of HIV infection and would extend at least to those situations where the actor, under the totality of the circumstances, has reason to know of the infection"); Chester v. Deep Roots Alderwood, LLC, 371 P.3d 113, 117 (Wash. App. 2016) (holding that a tattoo parlor and artist were not negligent in failing to use sterile ink to prevent contamination because the plaintiff failed to show "that sterile ink was widely available at the time in question, that claims of sterility were reliable, or that tattoo artists had the means to test ink for contamination and sterilize it on site").

2. ***Negligence.*** According to the Third Restatement:

> A person acts negligently if the person does not exercise reasonable care under all the circumstances. Primary factors to consider in ascertaining whether the person's conduct lacks reasonable care are the foreseeable likelihood that the person's conduct will result in harm, the foreseeable severity of any harm that may ensue, and the burden of precautions to eliminate or reduce the risk of harm.

Restatement, Third, of Torts: Liab. for Physical & Emotional Harm § 3 (2010).

3. ***Recklessness and Gross Negligence.*** Recklessness is a more-blameworthy variety of tortious conduct than negligence, and according to many authorities the difference between the two is a matter of degree. Both depend upon failure to exercise care. Negligence is the failure to use that degree of care which an ordinary, reasonable, prudent person would use under similar circumstances; recklessness involves something more, and it has been defined at least two ways. Objectively defined, recklessness consists of an extreme lack of care; subjectively defined, recklessness is carelessness accompanied by conscious indifference to a known risk of serious harm. Some authorities employ the objective definition; others, the subjective definition; and still others, both definitions, either interchangeably or in combination. According to the Third Restatement:

> A person acts recklessly in engaging in conduct if:
>
> (a) the person knows of the risk of harm created by the conduct or knows facts that make that risk obvious to another in the person's situation, and

> (b) the precaution that would eliminate or reduce that risk involves burdens that are so slight relative to the magnitude of the risk as to render the person's failure to adopt the precaution a demonstration of the person's indifference to the risk.

Restatement, Third, of Torts: Liab. for Physical and Emotional Harm § 2 (2010).

The manner in which recklessness is defined may determine whether it can be proved under the facts in a particular case. For example, suppose that a school requires a student to play dodge ball despite knowing that a doctor had sent a note indicating that the student should not participate in any sport involving side-to-side movement. It may be easier to establish that the defendant knew of an unreasonable danger and disregarded it, than to show that the defendant's conduct fell so far below what was required as to amount to an extreme departure from acceptable conduct.

Recklessness is viewed as more blameworthy than negligence, but less blameworthy than intentionally harmful conduct. Whether it is more akin to intentional wrongdoing than to negligence, or vice versa, depends upon the matter at issue. Recklessness serves just as well as intent in satisfying the "*scienter*" requirement in an action for fraud (*see* Chapter 21); in proving "actual malice" in a defamation action by a public official or public figure (*see* Chapter 22); and (in some states) as a predicate for imposition of punitive damages (*see* Chapter 4). Conduct that is merely negligent fulfills none of those purposes. In contrast, recklessness generally stands with negligence, rather than intent, when it comes to defenses based on misconduct by the plaintiff. As discussed below, many states hold that a plaintiff's carelessness (contributory negligence) or venturesomeness (assumption of the risk) will reduce or bar a plaintiff's recovery in an action based on negligence or recklessness, but not in an action based on intentional wrongdoing.

As defined in Texas, "gross negligence" is roughly equivalent to the level of wrongdoing which other jurisdictions refer to as recklessness. *See* Tex. Civ. Prac. & Rem. Code § 41.001(11) (Westlaw 2022) ("'Gross negligence' means an act or omission: (A) which when viewed objectively from the standpoint of the actor at the time of its occurrence involves an extreme degree of risk, considering the probability and magnitude of the potential harm to others; *and* (B) of which the actor has actual, subjective awareness of the risk involved, but nevertheless proceeds with conscious indifference to the rights, safety, or welfare of others" (emphasis added)).

4. ***Wilfulness and Wantonness.*** It is important to be attentive to terminology. Some authorities use the terms "wilful," "wanton," and "reckless" interchangeably. *See* Restatement, Second, of Torts § 282 cmt. e (Special Note). Other authorities say that "'[w]ilful misconduct' sometimes refers to conduct involving an intent to cause harm; but 'wanton misconduct' is commonly understood to mean recklessness." Restatement, Third, of Torts: Liab. for Physical and Emotional Harm § 2 cmt. a (2010).

Note that the "word 'negligent' is often used [imprecisely] to include all conduct [including recklessness and mere negligence] which, although not intended to invade any legally protected interest, has the element of social fault." Restatement, Second, of Torts § 282 cmt. e (Special Note) (brackets added).

5. ***Contributory Negligence, Comparative Negligence, and Comparative Fault.*** At common law, there were two major defenses, either of which totally defeated a claim based on negligence: contributory negligence and assumption of the risk. Contributory negligence existed wherever the plaintiff's failure to exercise care for personal safety or self-protection contributed to the plaintiff's injury or loss. This defense could be raised at common law only in a negligence action, but if it was proved, it had a dramatic effect. Any contributory negligence on the part of the plaintiff, however small, absolved the defendant from all liability for negligence, however great. *See* Restatement, Second, of Torts § 467. (Under a related rule, "contributory recklessness" fully defeated an action based on recklessness. *See* Restatement, Second, of Torts § 482(2).)

In recent years, the harsh common law rule on contributory negligence has been modified by two developments, the first of which means that such conduct is no longer always a total bar to recovery, and the second of which holds that contributory negligence can be raised as a defense not only in negligence cases, but in certain other actions as well.

(a) The First Stage of Change: Comparative Negligence. The first development, the replacement of contributory negligence by comparative negligence, in many states took place during the late 1960s or 1970s. In general, there are two basic schemes for comparative negligence, "pure" and "modified."

In states adopting *pure comparative negligence*, a contributorily negligent plaintiff is not barred from recovery, but damages are reduced in proportion to the plaintiff's fault. Thus, a plaintiff 65% responsible for an accident can recover compensation for 35% of any damages sustained.

In states adopting *modified comparative negligence*, there is normally a 50% threshold. If the plaintiff's contributory negligence exceeds (some jurisdictions say "equals or exceeds") 50% of the total negligence in the case, there can be no recovery. If the plaintiff's contributory negligence is below that threshold, the plaintiff can recover from a negligent defendant, but damages will be proportionally reduced. Thus, typically, in a state with a modified comparative negligence system, a plaintiff 65% responsible for an accident can recover nothing, but a plaintiff 49% responsible can recover 51% of any losses suffered. *See, e.g.*, State v. Tidwell, 735 S.W.2d 629 (Tex. Ct. App. 1987) (where game wardens stopped their vehicle to allow an intoxicated hunter in their custody to attempt to catch a rattlesnake, the hunter's recovery from the State for snake-bite injuries was reduced by 40%); Wager v. Moore, 220 A.3d 48, 56 (Conn. App. 2019) (holding that a pedestrian's negligence exceeded that of the motorist driving the vehicle that struck her, and therefore recovery was barred).

Courts and others sometimes continue to refer to the plaintiff's failure to exercise care as "contributory negligence," even though in most jurisdictions the common law rule of contributory negligence has been supplanted by a comparative approach.

In such instances, the better practice may be to refer to the plaintiff's failure to exercise care as "comparative negligence," but old habits die hard and not everyone conforms to that usage.

(b) The Second Stage of Change: Comparative Fault. The second stage in modification of the traditional rules on plaintiff negligence was the adoption of comparative fault. This approach is sometimes termed "comparative causation," "comparative responsibility," or "proportionate responsibility."

Under the doctrine of comparative fault, which replaced comparative negligence in many jurisdictions beginning in the 1980s, negligence on the part of the plaintiff may be invoked to offset liability for recklessness or strict liability, as well as liability for negligence, on either a pure or a modified basis. Other forms of fault on the part of the plaintiff, such as recklessness or unreasonable post-accident failure to mitigate damages, are treated similarly under most comparative fault systems. Under comparative fault, negligence or recklessness by the plaintiff is not a defense to intentionally tortious conduct.

Without adopting comparative fault, some—but not all—comparative negligence states permit negligence by the plaintiff to be raised as a defense to recklessness. This is logical since negligence and recklessness both involve lack of care and there is nothing difficult about comparing an ordinary lack of care by the plaintiff (comparative negligence) to an extreme lack of care by the defendant (recklessness).

To better understand the idea of comparative fault, read sections 1 and 2 of the Uniform Comparative Fault Act. They can be found in the notes in Chapter 16, Part D.

(c) Three Regimes Today. Today, some jurisdictions[3] still follow the common law rule on contributory negligence, others have comparative negligence, and yet others adhere to comparative fault. *See* Chapter 16. Lawyers therefore need to understand all three regimes in order to be able to understand court opinions or represent clients whose claims may be governed by the law of other jurisdictions.

6. ***Assumption of the Risk.*** The second major defense to negligence at common law—assumption of the risk—existed when a person (a) subjectively appreciated a danger, (b) voluntarily chose to confront it, and (c) either manifested a willingness to relieve the defendant of any obligation to exercise care or had no expectation that care would be exercised. This defense, which totally barred recovery, could be raised at common law not only in suits based on negligence, but also in actions predicated on recklessness or strict liability. In addition, consent, a doctrine jurisprudentially related to assumption of the risk, likewise precluded actions based on intentional wrongdoing.

Today, in jurisdictions subscribing to comparative negligence or comparative fault, assumption of the risk, like contributory negligence, is often treated as only a

3. Maryland, District of Columbia, Virginia, North Carolina, and Alabama.

partial defense in actions based on recklessness, negligence, or strict liability. However, in certain situations it survives as a complete defense. *See* Chapter 16. Consent is still a total bar to recovery for an intentionally perpetrated tort. *See* Chapter 3.

Students tend to overestimate the applicability of assumption of the risk, thinking that the defense is established anytime one suffers injury after confronting a known danger. That is not the case—at least with respect to dangers that are not inherently part of an activity. With respect to special (rather than inherent) risks, the courts have been diligent in requiring convincing proof of each of the defense's three elements. Not only must the plaintiff have been subjectively aware of the danger, but the decision to confront the danger must have been voluntary, rather than coerced. In addition, the facts must show that the plaintiff either agreed to absolve the defendant of the need to exercise care on the plaintiff's behalf or had no reasonable expectation that care would be exercised. Those demanding requirements will often not be met.

Cohen v. Petty

Court of Appeals of the District of Columbia
65 F.2d 820 (D.C. Cir. 1933)

GRONER, Associate Justice.

Plaintiff's declaration alleged that on December 14, 1930, she was riding as a guest in defendant's automobile; that defendant failed to exercise reasonable care in its operation, and drove it at a reckless and excessive rate of speed so that he lost control of the car and propelled it off the road against an embankment on the side of the road, as the result of which plaintiff received permanent injuries. The trial judge gave binding instructions, and the plaintiff appeals.

There were four eyewitnesses to the accident, namely, plaintiff and her sister on the one side, and defendant and his wife on the other. All four were occupants of the car. Defendant was driving the car, and his wife was sitting beside him. Plaintiff and her sister were in the rear seat.... They had known one another for a number of years, and plaintiff and her sister frequently drove out in the country with defendant and his wife.... After passing the Country Club ..., the automobile suddenly swerved out of the road, hit the abutment of a culvert, and ran into the bank, throwing plaintiff and her sister through the roof of the car onto the ground.

.... Plaintiff testified that just before the accident, perhaps a minute, she heard the defendant, who, as we have said, was driving the car, exclaim to his wife, "I feel sick," and a moment later heard his wife exclaim in a frightened voice to her husband, "Oh, John, what is the matter?" Immediately thereafter the car left the road and the crash occurred.... Plaintiff, when she heard defendant's wife exclaim, "What is the matter?" instead of looking at the driver of the car, says she continued to look down the road, and as a result she did not see and does not know what subsequently occurred, except that there was a collision with the embankment.

Defendant's evidence as to what occurred just before the car left the road is positive and wholly uncontradicted. His wife, who was sitting beside him, states that they were driving along the road at a moderate rate of speed when all of a sudden defendant said, "Oh, Tree, I feel sick" — defendant's wife's name is Theresa, and he calls her Tree. His wife looked over, and defendant had fainted. "His head had fallen back and his hand had left the wheel, and I immediately took hold of the wheel with both hands, and then I do not remember anything else until I waked up on the road in a strange automobile." The witness further testified that her husband's eyes were closed when she looked, and that his fainting and the collision occurred in quick sequence to his previous statement, "Oh, Tree, I feel so sick." The defendant himself testified that he had fainted just before the crash, that he had never fainted before, and that so far as he knew he was in good health, that on the day in question he had breakfast late, and had no luncheon, but that he was not feeling badly until the moment before the illness and the fainting occurred. He explained the incident as follows: "I was going along, just casually along, and I said 'My, Tree, I feel awfully sick,' and with that I went back like that [indicating]. I just remember my hands getting away from the wheel. I did not have time to think of any danger or anything else. I just fainted out and passed out."

....

The sole question is whether . . . the trial court was justified in taking the case from the jury. We think its action was in all respects correct.

It is undoubtedly the law that one who is suddenly stricken by an illness, which he had no reason to anticipate, while driving an automobile, which renders it impossible for him to control the car, is not chargeable with negligence. . . .

In the present case the positive evidence is all to the effect that defendant did not know and had no reason to think he would be subject to an attack such as overcame him. Hence negligence cannot be predicated in this case upon defendant's recklessness in driving an automobile when he knew or should have known of the possibility of an accident from such an event as occurred.

....

Affirmed.

Notes

*1. **Other Precedent.*** In Amoako-Okyere v. Church of the Messiah United Methodist Church, 41 N.E.3d 1275, 1285 (Ohio App. 2015), the court held that a church was not liable for negligent supervision related to the death of a teenager who died as the result of a "choking game" prank. There was no evidence "that anyone at the youth retreat knew of the choking game or could have anticipated that any of the retreat attendees would have participated in the choking game" while at the camp.

2. ***Contingent Fees.*** Many injured persons could not afford to hire an attorney if they had to pay money up front. To address that reality, the American legal system embraces the type of contingent fee system that many other countries have rejected.

A cornerstone of the American tort system is the contingent fee contract. This arrangement for financing legal services enables anyone who is seriously injured and has a plausibly meritorious claim to obtain a lawyer—often a very good lawyer—even if that person has no money to pay for representation.

A contingent fee contract gives a lawyer a financial interest in the client's case that is dependent upon its success. If the lawyer wins the case and recovers money for the client, the lawyer gets to keep a percentage of the recovery—often something on the order of 30 to 35%, depending on the terms of the contract. In contrast, if the case is unsuccessful and the client recovers nothing, the lawyer receives no payment for the services rendered. Thus, if the client wins, the lawyer wins; if the client loses, the lawyer loses. Needless to say, a lawyer whose fee is contingent on success has an incentive to work hard, for if the client does not prevail, the lawyer is denied compensation for the work performed.

The contingent fee arrangement provides not only a device for financing legal services, but a mechanism for screening the merits of potential claims. A lawyer ordinarily will be unwilling to accept a contingent fee for working on a case that lacks merit. Only suits that have a reasonable basis in law and in fact are likely to be undertaken on such terms. Consequently, contingent fees help to ensure both that meritorious cases reach the courts and that legally or factually frivolous claims do not.

Although it is possible, and sometimes desirable, for a lawyer and client to agree to a different form of fee arrangement, virtually all plaintiffs in American [personal injury] tort litigation are represented on a contingent fee basis. In contrast, the defendants in tort actions typically pay their lawyers by the hour for the services they perform. Hourly billing, like contingent fees, creates an incentive for thoroughness in the preparation of a case. The more hours worked, the greater the fee earned by the lawyer. So long as the defendant (or the defendant's insurance company) is willing to pay the bill, there is little reason for a lawyer to forgo steps which reasonably should be undertaken for the purpose of mounting a robust defense.

Consequently, as presently structured, the financing of attorney's fees in the American tort system tends to ensure that the claims decided in litigation are thoroughly investigated, well prepared, and vigorously asserted. That, of course, is appropriate in the American adversarial system of justice, which depends for its success on the clash of competing interests as a vehicle for learning the truth about the facts and fairly resolving claims.

Vincent R. Johnson, *Tort Law in America at the Beginning of the 21st Century*, 1 Renmin Univ. of China L. Rev. 237 (2000).

3. ***The "American Rule" on Attorney's Fees.*** Under the "American rule" on attorney's fees, each side bears its own costs of legal representation. However, plans are

frequently put forth to discard the American approach in favor of the "English rule," the "loser pays" principle. Under that approach, the loser in litigation must pay the winner's attorney's fees. Needless to say, if many persons cannot afford to pay the fees of their own lawyer, except on a contingent basis, those same persons, when unsuccessful in litigation, can hardly afford to pay the fees charged by their opponent's attorney. Rather than risk incurring liability for the fees of one's opponent, many persons would simply forgo bringing claims, at least in the large range of cases in which the issue of liability is less than clear. Loser-pays proposals continue to be a common element in proposed tort-reform legislation.

4. ***Statutory Attorney's Fees.*** At both the state and federal levels, many statutes dealing with particular types of actions—including some relating to the field of torts—permit the prevailing party to recover, in addition to money damages, reimbursement for their attorney's fees.

5. ***Frivolous Litigation and Attorney's Fees.*** In Texas, an award of attorney's fees is available where a cause of action is dismissed because it has no basis in law or fact.

Texas Civil Practice and Remedies Code § 30.021 (Westlaw 2022)

> In a civil proceeding, on a trial court's granting or denial, in whole or in part, of a motion to dismiss filed under the rules adopted by the supreme court under Section 22.004(g), Government Code, the court shall award costs and reasonable and necessary attorney's fees to the prevailing party. This section does not apply to actions by or against the state, other governmental entities, or public officials acting in their official capacity or under color of law.

C. Strict Liability Conduct

Harris v. Anderson County Sheriff's Office

Supreme Court of South Carolina.
673 S.E.2d 423 (S.C. 2009)

Justice KITTREDGE.

. . . .

Deputy Todd Caron of the Anderson County Sheriff's Office kenneled his police dog (Sleuber) at the Happistance Veterinary Clinic (clinic) . . . , while he was on vacation. Sleuber had a recent history of multiple unprovoked attacks, a history well known to Deputy Caron and the sheriff's office. Jennifer Harris worked at the clinic as a veterinary assistant. While kenneled at the clinic, Sleuber attacked Harris, severely injuring her. . . . Harris did not provoke the attack.

Harris pursued workers' compensation benefits from her employer, the clinic. Harris subsequently filed this lawsuit against the sheriff's office, asserting claims under section 47-3-110 and negligence. . . . The circuit court reasoned that the sheriff's office was no longer in control of its police dog (and should not be held responsible) once care of the dog was relinquished to the clinic. In granting the sheriff's office summary judgment, the circuit court held that when a dog owner leaves his dog in the care of another, section 47-3-110 only permits a claim against the "other person having the dog in his care or keeping." Harris appealed....

... [In Hossenlopp v. Cannon, 285 S.C. 367, 329 S.E.2d 438 (1985)], the Court was presented with a common law negligence claim arising from injuries caused by a dog. At the time, South Carolina adhered to what was commonly referred to as the "one free bite" rule. The "one free bite" rule imposed common law liability against a dog owner only when the owner knew or should have known of the dog's vicious propensities, that is, there was no liability for the first bite. In *Hossenlopp*, under our policy-making role in the common law, we rejected the "one free bite" rule and imposed quasi-strict liability on dog owners by adopting the "California Rule" for dog bite liability. This shift in the common law is reflected in the *Hossenlopp* Court's adoption of the following jury instruction:

> The law of California provides that the owner of any dog which bites a person while such person is on or in a public place or is lawfully on or in a private place, including the property of the owner of such dog, is liable for such damages as may be suffered by the person bitten regardless of whether or not the dog previously had been vicious, regardless of the owner's knowledge or lack of knowledge of any such viciousness, and regardless of whether or not the owner has been negligent in respect to the dog, provided, however, that if a person knowingly and voluntarily invites attack upon himself [herself], or if, when on the property of the dog owner, a person voluntarily, knowingly, and without reasonable necessity, exposes himself [herself] to the danger, the owner of the dog is not liable for the consequences.
>
> .... The following year, 1986, the [South Carolina] Legislature enacted section 47-3-110:
>
> Whenever any person is bitten or otherwise attacked by a dog while the person is in a public place or is lawfully in a private place, including the property of the owner of the dog or other person having the dog in his care or keeping, the owner of the dog or other person having the dog in his care or keeping is liable for the damages suffered.... If a person provokes a dog into attacking him then the owner of the dog is not liable.

.... Section 47-3-110 retained *Hossenlopp*'s strict liability against dog owners and additionally imposed liability on any other persons having the dog in their "care or keeping."

To construe the term "or" in an atypical manner, limiting the statutory claim of Harris to the clinic, would be inconsistent with the remedial and strict liability underpinnings of the statute. With the singular exception for the circumstance where the injured person provokes the attack, the Legislature has chosen to impose strict liability against dog owners and others having "the dog in [their] care or keeping."....

Strict liability is a policy decision to impose liability regardless of fault. Relieving the dog owner of liability where the dog was in the care or keeping of another would be contrary to the statutory language and run counter to the manifest legislative intent of strict liability. . . .

The Legislature's use of the phrase "care or keeping" clearly requires that the "other person" act in a manner which manifests an acceptance of responsibility for the care or keeping of the dog. . . . An example of this . . . is illustrated in the case of *Nesbitt v. Lewis,* 335 S.C. 441, 517 S.E.2d 11 (Ct. App. 1999).

Nesbitt involved an unprovoked attack by dogs on a child who was lawfully on private property. The property was owned by three persons, a mother and her two adult children, a son and a daughter. The mother owned the dogs, and she lived on the property with her son. The mother was liable under the statute simply as a result of owning the dogs. . . .

The son was liable under the statute as a property owner who exercised control over the premises. As concerns the statutory element of "care or keeping," the son "lived with [his mother] at the time of the attack and . . . tended [to] the dogs, taking them to the veterinarian, feeding them, and playing with them on occasion." . . . .

The daughter was the third property owner. She "had lived elsewhere for over five years." The daughter "did not take care of the dogs . . . [and she did] not exercise control over the premises. . . ." *Id.* The *Nesbitt* court reversed a jury verdict against the daughter. . . .

Nesbitt, thus, presents three scenarios. . . . First, the dog owner is strictly liable and common law principles are not implicated. Second, a property owner is liable when he exercises control over, and assumes responsibility for, the care and keeping of the dog. Third, a property owner is not liable under the statute when he has no control of the premises and provides no care or keeping of the dog. . . .

. . . [W]e hold that a person injured by a dog may pursue a claim against the owner of the dog when the injury occurs while the dog is in the care or keeping of another. . . .

Reversed and Remanded.

Notes

1. ***Strict Liability for Harm Caused by Animals.*** Statutes have frequently abolished the traditional common-law fault requirement and imposed strict liability for all harm caused to human beings and livestock by dogs. *See* Restatement, Third, of Torts: Liab. for Physical & Emotional Harm § 23 cmt. d (2010) ("half of all jurisdictions"). In Indiana, a dog-bite statute renders dog owners strictly liable if their dogs bite a postal delivery worker or other public servant without provocation, but otherwise a plaintiff must prove negligence. *See* Cook v. Whitsell-Sherman, 796 N.E.2d 271 (Ind. 2003). Why would a legislature draw that distinction?

2. ***Defenses to Strict Liability and Absolute Liability.*** In cases based on strict liability, the defendant ordinarily may assert the defenses of assumption of the risk

and comparative fault (if the latter has been adopted) for the purpose of precluding or limiting recovery by the plaintiff. However, in some strict-liability cases, such defenses may not be raised. This may be true where strict liability is imposed by a statute that is intended to protect a vulnerable class of persons from harm or otherwise allocate full responsibility to persons in the position of the defendant. In such instances, which are rare, the statute is sometimes said to impose "absolute liability." *See* Seim v. Garavalia, 306 N.W.2d 806 (Minn. 1981) (holding that a dog bite statute imposed not merely strict, but absolute, liability).

3. ***Examples of Strict Liability.*** Strict liability has frequently been applied to cases involving harm caused by defective products, abnormally dangerous activities, or dangerous animals, and employers are held strictly liable for torts committed by employees within the scope of their employment. *See* Chapters 14 & 15. The policy basis for strict liability varies somewhat from field to field. In some instances, strict liability is used to ensure maximum deterrence by increasing the likelihood that an actor will be held liable. In other cases, the doctrine is an instrument for simplifying or making more dependable the compensation process. In yet other situations, strict liability serves as a vehicle for allocating losses to those persons best able to bear or spread the losses. Finally, in some cases, strict liability tends to ensure that those who benefit from hazardous activities bear the costs arising therefrom. Of course, any given application of strict liability may be intended to further more than one of these objectives.

In Nebraska, a statute makes a city strictly liable for injuries or death to innocent third persons caused by police motor vehicle pursuits. *Cf.* Jurs v. City of Omaha, 727 N.W.2d 735 (Neb. Ct. App. 2007). What is the policy basis for the Nebraska rule?

4. ***The No-fault National Vaccine Injury Compensation Program.*** Just as courts sometimes dispense with proof of fault in accident cases, some legislative schemes provide for no-fault compensation. Under the National Vaccine Injury Compensation Program persons are entitled to compensation for vaccine-caused injuries without the necessity of proving that the manufacturer or administrator was at fault. Victims may reject an award under the program and sue in tort, but the doctrinal limitations imposed by federal law often make that an undesirable course. As Justice Antonin Scalia explained in Bruesewitz v. Wyeth LLC, 131 S. Ct. 1068 (2011):

> The Act establishes a no-fault compensation program "designed to work faster and with greater ease than the civil tort system." . . . . A person injured by a vaccine, or his legal guardian, may file a petition for compensation in the United States Court of Federal Claims, naming the Secretary of Health and Human Services as the respondent. A special master then makes an informal adjudication of the petition within (except for two limited exceptions) 240 days. The Court of Federal Claims must review objections to the special master's decision and enter final judgment under a similarly tight statutory deadline. At that point, a claimant has two options: to accept the

court's judgment and forgo a traditional tort suit for damages, or to reject the judgment and seek tort relief from the vaccine manufacturer.

Fast, informal adjudication is made possible by the Act's Vaccine Injury Table, which lists the vaccines covered under the Act; describes each vaccine's compensable, adverse side effects; and indicates how soon after vaccination those side effects should first manifest themselves. Claimants who show that a listed injury first manifested itself at the appropriate time are prima facie entitled to compensation. No showing of causation is necessary; the Secretary bears the burden of disproving causation. A claimant may also recover for unlisted side effects, and for listed side effects that occur at times other than those specified in the Table, but for those the claimant must prove causation. Unlike in tort suits, claimants under the Act are not required to show that the administered vaccine was defectively manufactured, labeled, or designed.

Successful claimants receive compensation for medical, rehabilitation, counseling, special education, and vocational training expenses; diminished earning capacity; pain and suffering; and $250,000 for vaccine-related deaths. Attorney's fees are provided, not only for successful cases, but even for unsuccessful claims that are not frivolous. These awards are paid out of a fund created by an excise tax on each vaccine dose.

The *quid pro quo* for this, designed to stabilize the vaccine market, was the provision of significant tort-liability protections for vaccine manufacturers. The Act requires claimants to seek relief through the compensation program before filing suit for more than $1,000. Manufacturers are generally immunized from liability for failure to warn if they have complied with all regulatory requirements (including but not limited to warning requirements) and have given the warning either to the claimant or the claimant's physician. They are immunized from liability for punitive damages absent failure to comply with regulatory requirements, "fraud," "intentional and wrongful withholding of information," or other "criminal or illegal activity." And . . . , the Act expressly eliminates liability for a vaccine's unavoidable, adverse side effects. . . .

In *Bruesewitz*, the Supreme Court held that all design-defect tort claims against vaccine manufacturers were preempted by the Act.

5. ***Consequences of Classification***. Important legal consequences flow from classification of the defendant's conduct as intentional, reckless, negligent, or strict liability. Those consequences concern, among other matters:

(a) ***Scope of Liability***. Typically, the law is willing to extend liability to a larger class of persons and award greater compensatory damages in cases involving high culpability, such as intentional or reckless conduct, than in cases predicated upon mere negligence or strict liability. *See generally* Restatement, Third, of Torts: Liab.

for Physical & Emotional Harm § 33(b) (2010). In part, the reason here is that where conduct is highly blameworthy there is a reduced risk of imposing liability disproportionate to fault.

Consider suits for harm done by misrepresentation. An action based on intentional misrepresentation of a material fact (fraud) may often be commenced by a person who expectedly relies upon the false communication, regardless of whether its content reaches that person directly or indirectly. *See* Restatement, Second, of Torts § 531. However, in many jurisdictions, a similar suit may not be maintained by one who foreseeably relies on a negligently made misstatement, unless the evidence establishes that there have been direct dealings or the equivalent between the plaintiff and the defendant. So, too, many courts hold that proof of an intentional misrepresentation in a business transaction entitles the victim to compensation for not only out-of-pocket losses and expected consequential damages, but, to the extent that they can be proved, damages sufficient to give the plaintiff the benefit of the contract which was entered into with the defendant. *See* Restatement, Second, of Torts § 549. However, benefit-of-the-bargain damages cannot normally be recovered in an action for negligent misrepresentation, and compensation is limited to out-of-pocket losses and consequential damages. *See* Restatement, Second, of Torts § 552B. Chapter 21 discusses misrepresentation.

(b) ***Punitive or Exemplary Damages.*** Punitive or exemplary damages are awarded to punish or make an example of the defendant, but only if the defendant's conduct is highly culpable. Accordingly, cases based on ordinary negligence will never support an assessment of punitive damages. However, on appropriate facts, reckless or intentional conduct may justify such an award. *See, e.g.*, Micari v. Mann, 481 N.Y.S.2d 967 (Sup. Ct. 1984) (involving an acting teacher who induced students to engage in various sexual acts).

In an action based on strict liability, punitive damages are available where the evidence establishes a high degree of blameworthiness on the part of the defendant. *See* Smith v. Brown & Williamson Tobacco Corp., 410 S.W.3d 623, 631 (Mo. 2013) (deception about the dangerous and addictive qualities of cigarettes). Punitive damages are discussed in detail in Chapter 4.

(c) ***Defenses.*** As indicated earlier in this chapter, defenses based on the plaintiff's own failure to exercise care may be invoked to reduce or preclude liability in actions based on recklessness, negligence, or, if comparative fault has been adopted, strict liability. However, negligence on the part of the plaintiff is not a defense in suits predicated on intentional conduct.

(d) ***Respondeat Superior.*** *Respondeat superior*—meaning "let the master answer" or "look to the one higher up"—is a legal doctrine under which one person, who is without fault, is vicariously held liable for the tortious actions of another. In traditional work settings, an employer will be held liable for the torts of an employee occurring within the "scope of employment." The issue of whether harmful conduct is within that scope frequently turns upon such facts as the time and place of the tort and whether the employee's conduct was actuated, at least in part, by a desire to serve the business purposes of the employer. *See generally* Chapter 14.

An employer is less readily held liable for an employee's intentional wrongdoing than for negligent conduct. *See* Medlin v. Bass, 398 S.E.2d 460, 464 (N.C. 1990) (noting that "[i]ntentional tortious acts are rarely considered to be within the scope of an employee's employment" and rejecting a *respondeat superior* claim based on sexual assault). Predictably, vicarious liability for recklessness falls between those two extremes. Of course, an employee's strict liability conduct may be imputed to an employer, if the acts occur within the scope of the employment.

The imputation of vicarious liability to an employer does not absolve the employee from liability. The employee ordinarily remains subject to suit by the victim, and if the employer is forced to pay a judgment based on the agent's tort, the employer may normally seek reimbursement ("indemnity") from the agent. *See* Chapter 17.

(e) ***Insurance.*** The nature of the defendant's tortious conduct may determine whether resulting losses will be compensated by the defendant's insurance. Intentional harm, generally, is not covered. *See* 7A Couch on Insurance § 103:25 (2017 ed.). Otherwise a liability policy could be used as a license to wreak havoc at will.

Policy language varies, but the operative question is ordinarily whether the damage falls within the terms of a provision excluding coverage for harm "expected or intended from the standpoint of the insured." The facts surrounding many intentional torts are such that it is possible to conclude that injury or damage was "intended" by the insured, as that term is used in insurance contracts. *See* Allstate Ins. Co. v. Mugavero, 589 N.E.2d 365, 370 (N.Y. 1992) (holding that injuries to children as a result of alleged sodomy and sexual abuse were "intentionally caused" within the meaning of an insurance coverage exclusion). However, not all intentional torts are so characterized—which is not surprising in view of the many cases holding that intent to do harm is not a prerequisite to intentional tort liability.

The most that can be said is that insurance coverage will be denied for many, but not all, intentional torts. In Garrett v. Dailey, *supra*, the insurance company paid the judgment, even though Brian Dailey committed an intentional battery when he pulled the chair from behind the elderly plaintiff.

Many decisions interpreting the intentional-harm exclusion in insurance contracts hold that for coverage to be denied, subjective intent to cause harm must be proven. The reluctance of some courts to find that harm was "intended from the standpoint of the insured" probably reflects their "desire to aid the innocent victim" inasmuch as "application of the exclusionary clause may limit . . . [the victim's] recovery to a tortfeasor whose pocket is less deep than the insurer's." Kersh v. Heffner, 542 So. 2d 1118, 1120 (La. Ct. App. 1989).

The term "expected injury," as used in an insurance policy provision denying coverage for harm "expected or intended from the standpoint of the insured," is not synonymous with foreseeable injury. Otherwise few persons would find purchasing insurance worthwhile. Consequently, harm foreseeably resulting from the defendant's negligent, reckless, or strict-liability conduct may be covered under the defendant's liability insurance, subject of course to the many limitations of the law of insurance.

(f) ***Immunities***. At common law, a wide array of immunities barred litigation of certain categories of tort actions. For example, sovereign immunity precluded suits against the government; spousal immunity forbade claims between spouses; parental immunity prevented suits by children against parents; and charitable immunity foreclosed actions against charities. For varying reasons, these kinds of litigation were viewed as detrimental to the common good.

Beginning around 1940, there was a marked trend toward abrogating immunities in whole or in part on the theory that, except in extraordinary circumstances, all persons should be held accountable for the harm they tortiously cause. In jurisdictions retaining immunities in diminished form, the line was sometimes drawn with reference to the forms of tort liability. For example, Maryland initially abolished spousal immunity only in negligence actions (*see* Boblitz v. Boblitz, 462 A.2d 506 (Md. 1983)).

Under the Federal Tort Claims Act, it is possible to sue the federal government for injuries resulting from negligence (*see* 28 U.S.C. § 1346(b) (Westlaw 2022)), but not for claims arising out of such intentional torts as battery, assault, false imprisonment, and deceit (*see* 28 U.S.C. § 2680(h) (Westlaw 2022)). Some state tort claims acts draw similar distinctions. *See* Durbin v. City of Winnsboro, 135 S.W.3d 317 (Tex. App. 2004) (holding that an action by the parents of a son who died in a motorcycle accident while being pursued by a police officer was not a claim for an intentional tort, and therefore was not barred by the Texas Tort Claims Act, which permits certain suits for negligence). As these examples suggest, it is difficult to generalize about the legal contours of partial immunities.

In recent years, some persons have argued that the widespread abrogation of common law immunities left important endeavors vulnerable to ruin via tort litigation. To address that risk, some immunities have been legislatively restored or newly created to protect non-profit organizations and individuals who assist their efforts. *See* Chapter 18. In these areas, too, the scope of immunity may be defined with reference to the nature of the defendant's tortious conduct. *See* Conn. Gen. Stat. Ann. § 52-557m (Westlaw 2022) (providing that uncompensated directors, officers, and trustees of certain nonprofit organizations are immune from liability, except where damage or injury is caused by "reckless, wilful, or wanton misconduct"); N.Y. Not-for-Profit Corp. Law § 720-a (Westlaw 2022) (immunizing uncompensated directors, officers, and trustees of certain not-for-profit corporations from liability, except where the conduct constitutes "gross negligence or was intended to cause the resulting harm").

(g) ***Workers' Compensation***. Under workers' compensation laws, persons injured in on-the-job accidents are compensated pursuant to special statutory schemes, rather than via the traditional tort system. A covered employee whose injury arises "out of and in the course of employment" is entitled to an insurance award without proof that the injury resulted from tortious conduct of the employer. The amount of the award is computed according to schedules, which typically take into account the nature of the injury and the resulting degree of disability. The size of the payout is generally much less than what might be recovered in tort litigation.

To encourage employers to participate in workers' compensation systems by paying insurance premiums, statutes immunize participating employers and co-employees from suit in tort based upon work-related accidents. The immunity bars actions based on negligence, but does not preclude claims predicated on intentional wrongdoing. *See* Sitzman v. Schumaker, 718 P.2d 657, 659 (Mont. 1986) (otherwise, by participating in the workers' compensation system, the employer "would have bought the right to hit his employees"); Kissinger v. Mannor, 285 N.W.2d 214, 217 (Mich. Ct. App. 1979) (an action for intentional infliction of severe mental distress was not barred where plaintiff's foreman disclosed to 40 co-workers that plaintiff had "crapped [in] his pants"); Caudle v. Betts, 512 So. 2d 389 (La. 1987) (an action for battery was not barred where the defendant's C.E.O. intentionally shocked the plaintiff with an auto condenser as a practical joke).

Actions based on recklessness and other forms of tortious behavior falling short of intentional injury are also typically precluded by workers' compensation immunity. *See* Gantt v. Security, USA, 356 F.3d 547 (4th Cir. 2004) (holding that workers' compensation barred a tort suit for reckless infliction of emotional distress, and that the plaintiff failed to prove intent to injure); *but see* Stringer v. Minnesota Vikings Football Club, LLC, 705 N.W.2d 746 (Minn. 2005) (recognizing that a co-employee may be sued for gross negligence under limited circumstances, but denying recovery for a heat stroke related death).

(h) ***Statutes of Limitations***. A statute of limitations bars commencement of a suit after expiration of a certain period of time. *See generally* Chapter 19. The length of the period is determined by the nature of the claim or the type of damage alleged. Consequently, a suit framed as an action based on one variety of tortious conduct may be subject to a different period of limitations than might apply if the suit were framed differently. The provisions applicable in New York under its Civil Practice Law and Rules, N.Y. C.P.L.R. § 215(3) (Westlaw 2022) provide a useful illustration. A personal-injury claim litigated as an intentional battery will be subject to a one-year period of limitations under the terms of C.P.L.R. § 215, which provides in relevant part:

> The following actions shall be commenced within one year:
>
> ....
>
> (3) an action to recover damages for assault, battery, false imprisonment, malicious prosecution, libel, slander, false words causing special damages, or a violation of the right of privacy....

A suit for negligence, rather than for battery, would fall within the broad provisions of N.Y. C.P.L.R. § 214 (Westlaw 2022), which require the following actions to be commenced within three years:

> 3. an action to recover a chattel or damages for the taking and detaining of a chattel;
>
> 4. an action to recover damages for injury to property except as provided in § 214-c [dealing with toxic torts];
>
> 5. an action to recover damages for a personal injury except as provided in §§ 214-b [dealing with "Agent Orange" cases], 214-c [toxic torts] and 215 [certain intentional torts];
>
> 6. an action to recover damages for malpractice, other than medical, dental or podiatric malpractice, regardless of whether the underlying theory is based on contract or tort. . . .

So too, while an action for negligent misrepresentation resulting in property damage might fall within the three-year rule imposed by § 214 quoted above, an action for fraud — which normally requires a showing of intentional or reckless misrepresentation — would be subject to a longer period of limitations under N.Y. C.P.L.R. § 213(8) (Westlaw 2022). That section provides that actions based upon fraud must be commenced within six years of "the time the plaintiff . . . discovered the fraud, or could with reasonable diligence have discovered it."

(i) ***Discharge in Bankruptcy.*** Like other debts, tort liability generally may be discharged through bankruptcy proceedings. *See* Burnam v. Patterson, 119 S.W.3d 12 (Tex. App. 2003) (barring continuation of a negligence lawsuit). Thus, potentially thousands of tort claims against Chrysler and General Motors were extinguished when those auto manufacturers went bankrupt in 2009.

There are at least two important exceptions to the discharge rule. If either exception applies, bankruptcy protection does not erase the tort claim, and collection of damages may later be pursued when the defendant acquires assets.

First, it is not possible to discharge a debt "for willful and malicious injury by the debtor to another entity or to the property of another entity." *See* 11 U.S.C.A. § 523 (a)(6) (Westlaw 2022). Ordinary negligence will never fall within this nondischargeable category, but many intentional torts will. *See* W.J.A. v. D.A., 43 A.3d 1148, 1151 (N.J. 2012) (describing a judgment based on defamation and frivolous litigation that was nondischargeable).

Second, bankruptcy will not discharge a debt for "money, property, [or] services . . . obtained by . . . actual fraud." *See* 11 U.S.C.A. § 523 (a)(2)(A) (Westlaw 2022). Tort actions for fraud are discussed in Chapter 21 and normally require proof of an intentionally or recklessly false misstatement.

D. An Introduction to Insurance

Although courts seldom mention insurance in explaining their decisions in tort cases, the importance of insurance to the tort system should not be underestimated. An award of damages means little or nothing to a plaintiff who cannot collect the judgment. Unless the defendant is wealthy, the existence of liability insurance which will cover a judgment for the plaintiff may determine whether it is worthwhile for the plaintiff to sue. When the defendant does have liability insurance that will cover the plaintiff's claim, the insurance company is usually solely responsible for defending the action and for deciding whether to settle.

Insurance, Deterrence, and Risk-Spreading. Two of the major policy concerns which shape the law of torts — deterrence and risk-spreading — implicate insurance. With respect to deterrence, the availability and cost of liability insurance will sometimes determine whether one undertakes an activity that may cause harm, and liability insurers often insist that their insureds take particular kinds of precautions. As for risk-spreading, the availability of first-party insurance (insurance that covers the insured's own loss) provides a method by which those who may suffer losses can spread their risks. This means that a court's decision to impose a particular kind of liability to promote "risk-spreading" should, in principle, be based not simply upon a belief that risk-spreading is good, but upon a showing that first-party insurance does not already provide adequate risk-spreading.

1. Liability Insurance

Liability insurance pays amounts which the insureds (the owner of the policy and others specified in the policy) become liable to pay to accident victims. No liability-insurance policy covers all potential claims. Automobile liability insurance, which in some states is mandatory for car owners, covers claims against the owner or driver for damages arising out of automobile accidents. Homeowners' insurance often covers homeowners and their family members for liability arising from causes not involving the use of an automobile. (Liability coverage under most homeowners' policies is not limited to accidents sustained in the insured's home.) Many businesses carry liability insurance covering claims arising out of their business activities.

"Underlitigating" Cases. Almost all liability insurance excludes coverage for harms inflicted intentionally by the insured, so in many, if not most, intentional-tort cases, the insurance company need not defend the claim or pay damages if they are awarded. This puts some pressure on plaintiffs — as well as defendants — to characterize claims as arising out of negligence, recklessness, or strict liability, rather than as intentional torts, such as battery. For a heroic but unsuccessful attempt at this, see Saba v. Darling, 575 A.2d 1240 (Md. 1990), in which someone who had been punched by a drunkard sued, not for battery, but for the drunkard's "negligence" in becoming intoxicated.

Liability insurance is always limited in amount; it is therefore desirable for a seriously injured victim to hold as many persons as possible liable for the injury. A million-dollar judgment against someone whose liability insurance covers damages only up to $50,000 may be worth only $50,000.

Why Buy Insurance? Insurance companies are businesses, not charities. They must earn more from premiums and from investing those premiums than they pay out in claims. This means that insureds must, in the aggregate, pay more for insurance than they would pay in damages if they were not insured. Why, then, does anyone buy insurance? One answer is that some kinds of liability insurance are compulsory—automobile liability insurance in some states, for example. Another answer is that many insureds are "risk averse"—they would rather pay a relatively small sum each year than take a chance (even a very small chance) of having to pay a much larger amount as damages. Finally, most liability insurance covers not only damages assessed against the insured but also the costs of the defense, and the defense is usually handled by the insurance company. Some insureds therefore buy liability insurance as a way of hiring an insurance company to handle claims.

Conflicts Between Insurer and Insured. Cases in which the plaintiff sues for more than the amount of the defendant's liability insurance can create serious conflict-of-interest problems. Suppose, for example, that an insured who has coverage for $100,000 of liability is sued for $300,000. Suppose further that there is a 50-50 chance that the plaintiff will win the suit. If the plaintiff offers to settle the suit for the policy limit of $100,000, the insured would want to accept the offer: the settlement is within the policy limits, so the insurer would pay the entire amount and the insured would pay nothing. For the insurer, however, taking the case to trial looks attractive: settlement means that the company will have to pay $100,000; going to trial means that the company will pay the cost of the trial but will face only a 50-percent chance of having to pay $100,000 in damages (with the insured liable for the rest if the plaintiff wins). The language of most policies gives the right to decide whether to settle to the insurer, but the courts, noting the conflict between the interests of the insurer and the insured, have created a cause of action for "bad-faith" conduct in settling. Under this cause of action, an insurer who negligently (unreasonably) rejects a settlement offer within policy limits has a duty to pay the full amount of a subsequent verdict that exceeds policy limits.

For example, in Crisci v. Security Insurance Co. of New Haven, 426 P.2d 173 (Cal. 1967), the court held that an insurance company breached its duty to consider the interests of the insured in proposed settlements. The company had rejected offers within the limits of a $10,000 policy even though it knew that an award at trial might exceed $100,000. The company did so because it assertedly believed that the plaintiff had no chance of winning on a critical mental suffering issue. That belief was unreasonable because the insurance company knew that the accident could have caused the plaintiff's psychosis, that its own agents had told it that without evidence of prior mental defects (which it did not have) a jury was likely to believe that the plaintiff's fall precipitated her psychosis, and that the plaintiff had reputable experts on her side of what was a clearly debatable issue. The company was held liable for the amount of the judgment (a total of $101,000) in excess of policy limits, and for mental distress damages suffered by the insured.

An insurer becomes liable for amounts in excess of policy limits only if its rejection of an offer to settle a claim within policy limits was negligent (unreasonable). What the law of negligence requires on a given set of facts will become clearer after you read Chapter 5, which sets out the basic principles of negligence. In many jurisdictions, there is a well-developed body of law that charts the twists and turns of the rules governing liability for negligent failure to settle a claim within policy limits.

Notes

1. ***Settlement.*** The vast majority of tort cases are resolved through settlement rather than litigation; the percentage is often put at 95% or higher. Settlement may come at any stage: before suit is filed; after filing, but before the trial; during trial; or even after a verdict has been returned. Whether a case settles prior to judgment is to some extent a function of whether the parties agree, at least generally, on what the result will be if the case is tried to a final judgment. If the law or the facts are so uncertain that the parties significantly differ in their predictions of the outcome, there is a good chance that the case will not settle—at least if the amount in controversy is worth fighting over.

2. ***Confidential Settlements Versus Open Records.*** Sometimes the terms of a settlement are confidential and the related court records are sealed. However, secrecy can contribute to dangerous products remaining on the market. In some states, court records are presumptively open and can be sealed only for compelling reasons. For example:

Texas Rules of Civil Procedure Rule 76(a) (Westlaw 2022)

> 1. . . . No court order or opinion issued in the adjudication of a case may be sealed. Other court records, as defined in this rule, are presumed to be open to the general public and may be sealed only upon a showing of all of the following:
>
> (a) a specific, serious and substantial interest which clearly outweighs: (1) this presumption of openness; (2) any probable adverse effect that sealing will have upon the general public health or safety;
>
> (b) no less restrictive means than sealing records will adequately and effectively protect the specific interest asserted. . . .

3. ***Ethics in Law Practice: Settlement Offers.*** A "lawyer who receives from opposing counsel an offer of settlement in a civil controversy . . . must promptly inform the client of its substance unless the client has previously indicated that the proposal will be acceptable or unacceptable or has authorized the lawyer to accept or to reject the offer." Model Rules of Professional Conduct Rule 1.4 cmt. 2 (2022).

4. ***Settlement Incentives.*** "Tort reform" efforts sometimes try to discourage litigation and encourage settlement. *See, e.g.,* Tex. Civ. Prac. & Rem. Code § 42.001 *et seq.* (Westlaw 2022).

Under Texas law, if a settlement offer is made and rejected and the judgment ultimately rendered is "significantly less favorable" (which essentially means 20% less favorable) to the rejecting party than was the settlement offer, the offering party may recover litigation costs from the rejecting party.

"'Litigation costs' means money actually spent and obligations actually incurred that are directly related to the case in which a settlement offer is made . . . [including]: . . . court costs; . . . reasonable fees for not more than two testifying expert witnesses; and . . . reasonable attorney's fees." The recoverable amount is limited to those litigation costs incurred by the offering party after the date the rejecting party declined the settlement offer. More important, litigation costs may not be greater than the sum of 50% of the economic damages plus 100% of non-economic and exemplary damages awarded to the claimant (with certain other adjustments). This means that recovery of litigation costs is available only to the extent that the plaintiff wins something and not where the defense prevails on summary judgment or a take-nothing judgment. Thus, if the defendant is the rejecting party, the plaintiff may rely on these provisions to enhance the plaintiff's recovery; if the plaintiff is the rejecting party, the defendant can take away part of the plaintiff's recovery.

"The settlement procedures . . . apply only to claims for monetary relief," and only after a declaration has been filed with the court. The rules expressly do not apply to "a class action; . . . a shareholder's derivative action; . . . an action by or against a governmental unit; . . . an action brought under the Family Code; . . . an action to collect workers' compensation benefits . . . ; or an action filed in a justice of the peace court," so presumably they affect a wide range of tort cases that do not fall within those exceptions.

In Smith v. Baptiste, 694 S.E.2d 83, 85 (Ga. 2010), the court upheld against constitutional attack a "tort reform" statute creating liability for certain attorney's fees and expenses of litigation in tort actions in cases where settlement offers had been made.

5. ***Duty to Defend and Duty to Pay.*** The standard liability insurance policy imposes two duties on an insurer: a duty to defend and a duty to pay. These duties are separate, so the duty to defend a suit seeking covered damages may exist even if, on the facts as eventually established, the insurer has no duty to pay. This would be the case, for instance, if *A* ran over *B* and *B* sued *A*, alleging battery and negligence. Because the suit alleges negligence (which is typically a covered claim) the insurer would have a duty to defend it. This is true even though the insurer will have no duty to pay if the factfinder determines that *A* ran *B* down on purpose (because intentional harm is normally excluded from coverage).

The duties to defend and to pay arise at different points in time. The duty to defend attaches when the insured is sued, even though the facts are yet to be determined. The duty to pay does not arise until the litigation has terminated through adjudication or settlement.

6. ***Reservation of Rights.*** An insurance company unsure of whether the policy covers the loss in question will often proceed with a defense under a "reservation of

rights" so that, if the insured loses the case, the company can assert that the policy does not cover the award.

7. ***Ethics in Law Practice: Coverage Disputes.*** Suppose that the lawyer retained by an insurance company to defend the insured in an auto accident case learns, in the course of the representation, that the insured may have run down the plaintiff deliberately. The policy does not require the company to defend or pay claims for intentional injuries. The plaintiff offers to settle with the insurance company for a sum well within the policy limits. The insured would like to have the settlement accepted; the company would, if it knew the facts, disclaim coverage. The lawyer, who represents the insured but is hired and paid by the insurance company, must respect the confidences of the client (the insured) and so cannot inform the company of the facts giving rise to the dispute without the insured's consent. *See* Model Rules of Professional Conduct Rule 1.6 (2018) (stating the general rule on confidentiality of client information). However, if the facts showed that the policy *clearly* did not cover the injury, the lawyer could not help the insured persist in a course of conduct that would lead to the company's settling the case, as doing that would help the insured perpetrate a fraud against the company. *See* Model Rules of Professional Conduct Rule 1.2(d) (2018) ("A lawyer shall not counsel a client to engage, or assist a client, in conduct that the lawyer knows is criminal or fraudulent").

A complex body of law has emerged to address these and other difficult ethical questions in insurance defense practice. Because the rules differ from state to state, it is essential to consult the law of the jurisdiction. At some point the conflict may be so severe as to require the attorney to withdraw from the case. *See, e.g.*, Employers Casualty Co. v. Tilley, 496 S.W.2d 552 (Tex. 1973).

8. ***Automobile Liability Insurance and Deterrence.*** Many drivers, particularly young drivers, have assets insufficient to pay large judgments, and so the prospect of a large judgment does not create much of a deterrent effect. In theory, a system of compulsory liability insurance could enhance automobile safety. Persons without insurance could not drive, and insurance companies would charge the most dangerous kinds of drivers (those with convictions for drunken driving, for example) premiums so large that many of them would give up driving.

In practice, things have not worked out so tidily. For one thing, drivers in most states can meet compulsory-insurance requirements by buying policies that provide coverage much lower than that needed to satisfy even routine judgments for death or serious injuries. Furthermore, "assigned-risk" pools provide insurance at a relatively low cost even to very dangerous drivers. Finally, considerations other than safety play an important role in insurance rate regulation. To take but one example, some states prohibit insurance companies from charging young male drivers higher premiums than young female drivers, even though it is well established that young male drivers are, statistically, much worse risks than young female drivers. By insisting that men and women pay the same premiums, these states make insurance more expensive for women and cheaper for men, thus discouraging women from driving and encouraging men to do so. This may well contribute to equality of the sexes in some sense, at the cost of making the roads more dangerous.

2. First-Party Insurance

Common examples of first-party insurance include life insurance, medical insurance, fire insurance, and collision and comprehensive coverage for automobiles. This kind of insurance creates a form of loss-spreading. All of those who buy the insurance pay for the losses that occur; without insurance like this, the losses would fall upon fewer people. The existence of insurance does not, of course, make losses go away; it just shifts the financial burdens of the losses from the few people who would bear them if there were no insurance to all policy holders. Indeed, because some people whose losses will be covered by insurance will act more carelessly than if they did not have insurance,[4] the institution of insurance probably causes the total amount of losses to increase.

First-party insurance does not play the same direct role in the tort process as liability insurance. Its existence does have some effect on the law of torts, however. For example, in New York, damages caused by a fire started by the defendant's negligence are quite limited; one reason is the courts' belief that most property owners will have fire insurance, and that holding a defendant whose negligence has burned down 50 houses liable to all 50 owners would unduly concentrate the loss on the defendant. *See* Ryan v. New York Central R. Co., 35 N.Y. 210 (1866), a decision which has not generally been accepted in other jurisdictions.

"No-Fault" Automobile Insurance. One form of first-party insurance—"no-fault" automobile insurance—has in many states displaced a portion of the tort system. Under most no-fault plans, automobile owners give up the right to sue others for certain kinds of harms (typically property damage, up to a specified dollar limit, and in many states minor personal injuries as well). In exchange, the victim's own insurance company pays for the damage. An important idea behind no-fault insurance was to reduce the role of lawyers and claims adjusters and so to allow a larger portion of the money paid as insurance premiums to go to accident victims. This would reduce the cost of insurance considerably. Studies have shown that, in cases

---

4. Some people deny this at first, but it is almost certainly true. Consider, for example, how knowledge that the theft insurance on a new $50,000 car had lapsed would affect the owner's willingness to leave the car parked at a mall while attending a movie. Or imagine the owner of a $700,000 house: would that person not seriously consider installing a sprinkler system if unable to get fire insurance? Even if some people's behavior would be the same with or without insurance, losses will increase because of insurance even if only a few insureds act more carelessly than if they did not have coverage.

The tendency of insurance to make insureds somewhat more willing to engage in risky behavior is called "moral hazard" in the insurance business. Some features of first-party insurance exist largely to limit the effects of moral hazard. For example, a "deductible" in an automobile-insurance policy may require the owner to pay for part of any damage sustained; this encourages owners to take precautions (as well as to refrain from submitting a claim for every little scratch).

which go through the tort system, victims end up with about half of the money spent by the insurance companies and defendants: the rest goes toward resolving disputes. Furthermore, no-fault benefits are usually paid promptly; litigation of a tort case may not be over until years after the accident. Another advantage of no-fault, with respect to "compensation," is that no-fault systems cover all victims, not just those who can convince a factfinder that someone else was at fault.

No-fault was originally proposed as a complete substitute for the tort system for auto-accident cases, but political forces have squelched that. (In New Zealand, by contrast, a no-fault system run by the government has replaced almost all of the law of torts.) A few of today's no-fault systems provide benefits (subject to stringent limits) to an accident victim without affecting the victim's right to sue whoever caused the accident. Most no-fault laws limit tort actions to cases in which the victim's medical expenses exceed an amount specified by statute, or to cases in which the victim suffers disfiguring injuries.

Chapter 2

Basic Intentional Torts

A. The Concept of Intent

Focus on Consequences. Intent is a state of mind about consequences or results, and exactly what must be intended varies with the tort in issue. For example, false imprisonment requires intent to confine; trespass to land, intent to be present at the place in question; and conversion, intent to exercise dominion and control over personal property.

Purpose and Knowledge. As indicated in Garratt v. Dailey, 279 P.2d 1091 (Wash. 1955), *supra* at 12, there are two varieties of intent. The first—purpose—depends upon the defendant's subjective wishes and exists whenever the defendant acts with the purpose of causing the consequence which the law forbids. The other variety of intent—knowledge—is present if the defendant, regardless of subjective purposes, knows with substantial certainty that the act in question will cause the prohibited result. While substantial certainty does not mean absolute certainty, it means certainty for all practical purposes.

See generally Restatement, Third, of Torts: Liab. for Physical & Emotional Harm §1 (2010) (discussing purpose and knowledge).

As the following cases indicate, many questions can be raised about intent. Must the alleged tortfeasor intend to injure or harm the plaintiff? How does a mistake about the surrounding facts affect a finding of intent? Can liability be based on intent produced by insanity or some other mental deficiency? Should a defendant who intends to cause one kind of harm escape liability if a different kind of harm results?

1. Intent to Injure

Lambertson v. United States

United States Court of Appeals for the Second Circuit
528 F.2d 441 (2d Cir. 1976)

VAN GRAAFEILAND, Circuit Judge.

....

Appellant, an employee of Armour & Co., sustained serious injuries to his mouth as a result of the actions of one William Boslet, a meat inspector for the United States Department of Agriculture....

On August 30, 1972, a truck shipment of beef arrived at the receiving dock of Armour's Syracuse plant. Plaintiff was one of the employees assigned to unload this truck. While he was so engaged, he was suddenly and without warning jumped by Boslet who, screaming "boo," pulled plaintiff's wool stocking hat over his eyes and, climbing on his back, began to ride him piggyback. As a result of this action, plaintiff fell forward and struck his face on some meat hooks located on the receiving dock[1] suffering severe injuries to his mouth and teeth.

It is apparently agreed by all witnesses that the mishap was the result of one-sided horseplay and with no intention on Boslet's part to injure plaintiff. Indeed, immediately after the incident Boslet apologized to plaintiff, telling him that he was only playing around and meant no harm.

Seeking redress for his injuries, plaintiff commenced the instant action against the United States pursuant to the Federal Tort Claims Act, 28 U.S.C. § 1346(b).

Traditionally, the sovereign has always been immune from suit. To alleviate the harshness of this rule, Congress enacted the Federal Tort Claims Act which permits civil actions against the United States for personal injury and property damage caused by the "negligent or wrongful act or omission of any employee of the Government while acting within the scope of his office or employment." 28 U.S.C. § 1346(b). 28 U.S.C. § 2680, however, lists several claims expressly excepted from the purview of the Act, among which are any claims arising out of an assault or battery.[2] Since the United States has not consented to be sued for these torts, federal courts are without jurisdiction to entertain a suit based on them....

1. [Fn. 2:] These meat hooks were no more than six inches away from plaintiff's head when Boslet jumped on his back.

2. [Fn. 3:] Section 2680 reads in pertinent part as follows:

> The provisions of this chapter and section 1346(b) of this title shall not apply to
>
> ....
>
> (h) Any claim arising out of assault, battery, false imprisonment, false arrest, malicious prosecution, abuse of process, libel, slander, misrepresentation, deceit, or interference with contract rights.

. . . [T]he parties agree that the sole basis for Judge Port's dismissal was his conclusion that Boslet's actions constituted a battery. Appellant contests this conclusion and steadfastly maintains that his complaint sounds in negligence.

. . . .

It is hornbook law in New York, as in most other jurisdictions, that the intent which is an essential element of the action for battery is the intent to make contact, not to do injury. . . . As the court stated in Masters [v. Becker, 254 N.Y.S.2d 633, 635 (App. Div. 1964)]:

> A plaintiff in an action to recover damages for an assault founded on bodily contact must prove only that there was bodily contact; that such contact was offensive; and that the defendant intended to make the contact. The plaintiff is not required to prove that defendant intended physically to injure him. Certainly he is not required to prove an intention to cause the specific injuries resulting from the contact.

Harper and James put it that "it is a battery for a man . . . to play a joke upon another which involves a harmful or offensive contact." Prosser says that a "defendant may be liable where he has intended only a joke." *Accord* Restatement (Second) of Torts § 13, comment c (1965). Since there is not the remotest suggestion that Boslet's leap onto plaintiff's back, his piggy back ride and his use of plaintiff's hat as a blindfold might have been accidental, there was no error in the District Court's determination that it was a battery.

To say that plaintiff's claim was not one "arising out of" a battery would be to blink at the exclusionary provisions of § 2680. . . .

We would find it much more pleasant to reach a decision based on what we wish Congress had said, rather than what it did say. However, to permit plaintiff to recover by "dressing up the substance" of battery in the "garments" of negligence would be to "judicially admit at the back door that which has been legislatively turned away at the front door." . . . .

Affirmed.

[The concurring opinion of Judge Oakes has been omitted.]

Notes

1. *See also* Ryan v. Napier, 425 P.3d 230, 233 (Ariz. 2018). In *Ryan*, a negligence claimant was permitted to recover damages for dog-bite injuries he received when a law enforcement officer intentionally released a police dog against him. On appeal, the court reversed the judgment, holding that "plaintiffs cannot assert a negligence claim based solely on an officer's intentional use of physical force." *Id.* at 233.

2. ***Degrees of Probability.*** To some extent, the difference between knowledge, recklessness, and negligence is a matter of degree. According to the Restatement:

> If the actor knows that the consequences are certain, or substantially certain, to result from his act, and still goes ahead, he is treated by the law

> as if he had in fact desired to produce the result. As the probability that the consequences will follow decreases, and becomes less than substantial certainty, the actor's conduct loses the character of intent, and becomes mere recklessness.... As the probability decreases further, and amounts only to a risk that the result will follow, it becomes ordinary negligence....

Restatement, Second, of Torts § 8A cmt. b.

3. ***Motive.*** An individual's motivation is not dispositive of whether a particular result was intended. For example, in Ruple v. Brooks, 352 N.W.2d 652, 655 (S.D. 1984), the victim of a series of obscene telephone calls sued the caller for intentional infliction of severe emotional distress, a tort which, as its name suggests, requires proof of intent to cause emotional anguish. In affirming a judgment for the plaintiff, the court wrote:

> Defendant claims that the directed verdict on the issue of liability at the close of plaintiff's case foreclosed him from presenting evidence of his motivations for making the obscene telephone calls. He alleges that his motives were anger and frustration over the difficulties his wife encountered in working with plaintiff, and that such motives would show a lack of intent to cause emotional distress.... No matter what defendant's specific motivation may have been, such motivation does not negate the fact that the act was done intentionally. In fact, defendant's admitted anger when making the telephone calls greatly strengthens a finding of intent to cause emotional harm....

4. ***"Intentional Acts."*** The *Ruple* court's suggestion that the defendant was liable because his "act was done intentionally" is extremely misleading. The law almost never holds someone liable simply for performing an "intentional act" which caused harm. For example, suppose that the defendant intentionally fires a rifle at a target. Unknown to the defendant, the plaintiff is sleeping in tall grass near the target and is hit by the bullet. Is the defendant, having intentionally done an act that caused harm to the plaintiff, liable for the intentional tort of battery? Certainly not: the defendant did not intend to inflict any contact—let alone a harmful or offensive one—on the plaintiff or anyone else. (If the defendant's shooting was careless under the circumstances, the plaintiff may have a negligence claim.) Similarly, someone who intentionally drives at ten miles an hour over the speed limit and who, as a result, accidentally crashes into another car, may be liable for *negligence*, but has certainly not committed an intentional tort. Intention has to do with results, not just with "acts." A competent lawyer should never argue that a defendant committed an intentional tort on the sole ground that the defendant "acted intentionally." What should the court in *Ruple* have said instead of "the act was done intentionally"?

5. ***Problem: Trickery at the Cliff.*** The plaintiff's boyfriend deliberately tricked her into jumping from a cliff. He did this by leading her to the top of a hill, "disappearing" by jumping into the lake below, and having his nephew urge the plaintiff to jump into the lake to "save" him. Because of her love and concern for her boyfriend,

the plaintiff jumped and was severely injured when she landed. Can the plaintiff sue her boyfriend for negligence, or has she been the victim of an intentional tort (or perhaps no tort at all)?

2. Intent and Mistake

Ranson v. Kitner

Appellate Court of Illinois
31 Ill. App. 241 (1888)

CONGER, J.

This was an action brought by appellee against appellants to recover the value of a dog killed by appellants, and a judgment [was] rendered for $50.

The defense was that appellants were hunting for wolves, that appellee's dog had a striking resemblance to a wolf, that they in good faith believed it to be one, and killed it as such.

Many points were made, and a lengthy argument failed to show that error in the trial below was committed, but we are inclined to think that no material error occurred to the prejudice of appellants.

The jury held them liable for the value of the dog, and we do not see how they could have done otherwise under the evidence. Appellants are clearly liable for the damages caused by their mistake, notwithstanding they were acting in good faith.

We see no reason for interfering with the conclusion reached by the jury, and the judgment will be affirmed.

Notes

1. ***Mistake and Intent.*** *See also* La Bruno v. Lawrence, 166 A.2d 822 (N.J. Super. Ct. 1960) (mistake as to a boundary line was no defense to an action for intentional trespass to land). These cases do not mean, however, that mistake is never relevant to the question whether the defendant intended to interfere with the person or property of another. Consider again the example (at p. 46, n.4, *supra*) of the defendant who shoots at a target and hits the plaintiff, sleeping nearby. This is not an intentional tort, even though the case might be described as one in which the defendant made a "mistake" about whether anyone was in a position to be shot. How is this case to be distinguished from Ranson v. Kitner?

2. ***Mistake and Privilege.*** While a mistake as to the surrounding facts will not necessarily preclude a finding of tortious intent, the existence of a mistake may bear upon whether the defendant can assert a privilege (*e.g.*, self-defense, defense of property, recapture of chattels, etc.) that will defeat the plaintiff's action, notwithstanding proof of intent. *See generally* Chapter 3.

3. ***Induced Mistake.*** Conduct based upon a mistake induced by the plaintiff does not ordinarily give rise to liability. *See, e.g.*, Tousley v. Board of Education,

40 N.W. 509 (Minn. 1888) (plaintiff was not allowed to recover for the conversion of wood where his words and conduct had caused the defendant to believe that the wood belonged to a third person). The best explanation may be that the plaintiff is "estopped" from denying the truth of his or her earlier assertions. Estoppel is a widely recognized legal doctrine.

4. ***Volitional-Act Requirement.*** There is no tort liability for an involuntary act. *See* Henrickson v. Sebanc, 336 P.2d 201 (Cal. Ct. App. 1959) (the touching of a boy's face was not an actionable battery where it was caused by the boy's abrupt movement and was not intentional). What if, while the defendant is yelling at the plaintiff, spit flies from the defendant's mouth and strikes the plaintiff? Battery?

If a third person takes hold of the defendant's hand and strikes plaintiff with it, the only voluntary act is that of the third person, and thus the third person, not the defendant, will be liable for battery. *Cf.* Reynolds v. Pierson, 64 N.E. 484 (Ind. Ct. App. 1902) (*A* jerked *B's* arm, causing *C*, who was leaning on *B*, to fall).

3. Intent and Insanity

McGuire v. Almy

Supreme Judicial Court of Massachusetts
8 N.E.2d 760 (Mass. 1937)

QUA, Justice.

This is an action of tort for assault and battery. [At trial, the jury returned a verdict for plaintiff in the amount of $1,500.] The only question of law reported is whether the judge should have directed a verdict for the defendant.

The following facts are established by the plaintiff's own evidence: In August, 1930, the plaintiff was employed to take care of the defendant. The plaintiff was a registered nurse.... The defendant was an insane person. Before the plaintiff was hired she learned that the defendant was a "mental case and was in good physical condition,".... During the period of "fourteen months or so" while the plaintiff cared for the defendant, the defendant "had a few odd spells," when she showed some hostility to the plaintiff and said that "she would like to try and do something to her."....

On April 19, 1932, the defendant, while locked in her room, had a violent attack. The plaintiff heard a crashing of furniture and then knew that the defendant was ugly, violent and dangerous. The defendant told the plaintiff and a Miss Maroney, "the maid,"... that if they came into the defendant's room, she would kill them. The plaintiff and Miss Maroney looked into the defendant's room, "saw what the defendant had done," and "thought it best to take the broken stuff away before she did any harm to herself with it." They sent for a Mr. Emerton, the defendant's brother-in-law. When he arrived the defendant was in the middle of her room about ten feet from the door, holding upraised the leg of a low-boy as if she were going to strike. The plaintiff stepped into the room and walked toward the defendant, while Mr. Emerton and Miss Maroney remained in the doorway. As the plaintiff approached the defendant and tried to take hold of the defendant's hand which held the leg, the defendant struck the plaintiff's head with it, causing . . . [injuries].

The extent to which an insane person is liable for torts has not been fully defined in this Commonwealth. . . .

Turning to authorities elsewhere, we find that courts in this country almost invariably say in the broadest terms that an insane person is liable for his torts. . . . Thus it is said that a rule imposing liability tends to make more watchful those persons who have charge of the defendant and who may be supposed to have some interest in preserving his property; that as an insane person must pay for his support, if he is financially able, so he ought also to pay for the damage which he does; that an insane person with abundant wealth ought not to continue in unimpaired enjoyment of the comfort which it brings while his victim bears the burden unaided; and there is also a suggestion that courts are loath to introduce into the great body of civil litigation the difficulties in determining mental capacity which it has been found impossible to avoid in the criminal field.

The rule established in these cases has been criticized severely by certain eminent text writers both in this country and in England, principally on the ground that it is an archaic survival of the rigid and formal medieval conception of liability for acts done, without regard to fault, as opposed to what is said to be the general modern theory that liability in tort should rest upon fault. Notwithstanding these criticisms, we think, that as a practical matter, there is strong force in the reasons underlying these decisions. . . . Fault is by no means at the present day a universal prerequisite to liability, and the theory that it should be such has been obliged very recently to yield at several points to what have been thought to be paramount considerations of public good. . . .

. . . [W]here an insane person by his act does intentional damage to the person or property of another he is liable for that damage in the same circumstances in which a normal person would be liable. This means that in so far as a particular intent would be necessary in order to render a normal person liable, the insane person, in order to be liable, must have been capable of entertaining that same intent and must have entertained it in fact. But the law will not inquire further into his peculiar mental condition with a view to excusing him if it should appear that delusion or other consequence of his affliction has caused him to entertain that intent or that a normal person would not have entertained it.

. . . .

Coming now to the application of the rule to the facts of this case, it is apparent that the jury could find that the defendant was capable of entertaining and that she did entertain an intent to strike and to injure the plaintiff and that she acted upon that intent. . . .

The defendant further argues that she is not liable because the plaintiff, by undertaking to care for the defendant with knowledge of the defendant's condition and by walking into the room in spite of the defendant's threat under the circumstances shown, consented to the injury, or, as the defendant puts it, assumed the risk, both contractually and voluntarily.... [W]e think that the defendant was not entitled to a directed verdict on this ground. Although the plaintiff knew when she was employed that the defendant was a mental case, and despite some show of hostility and some violent and unruly conduct, there was no evidence of any previous attack or even of any serious threat against anyone. The plaintiff had taken care of the defendant for "fourteen months or so." We think that the danger of actual physical injury was not, as matter of law, plain and obvious up to the time when the plaintiff entered the room on the occasion of the assault. But by that time an emergency had been created. The defendant was breaking up the furniture, and it could have been found that the plaintiff reasonably feared that the defendant would do harm to herself. Something had to be done about it. The plaintiff had assumed the duty of caring for the defendant. We think that a reasonable attempt on her part to perform that duty under the peculiar circumstances brought about by the defendant's own act did not necessarily indicate a voluntary consent to be injured. Consent does not always follow from the intentional incurring of risk. "The degree of danger, the stress of circumstances, the expectation or hope that others will fully perform the duties resting on them, may all have to be considered."....

Judgment for the plaintiff on the verdict.

Notes

1. ***Famous Case.*** *McGuire* is the leading case on whether an insane person can be held liable for an intentional tort, and its holding is consistent with the great weight of authority. *See* Restatement, Second, of Torts § 895J ("One who has deficient mental capacity is not immune from tort liability solely for that reason"); Wagner v. State, 122 P.3d 599 (Utah 2005) (finding that an attack by a mentally disabled patient was a battery).

In Williams v. Kearbey, 775 P.2d 670, 672 (Kan. Ct. App. 1989), an insane 14-year-old was held liable for injuries he inflicted during a shooting spree at a junior high school. The *Williams* court quoted Seals v. Snow, 254 P. 348 (Kan. 1927):

> "Undoubtedly, there is some appearance of hardship, even of injustice, in compelling one to respond for that which, for want of the control of reason, he was unable to avoid; that it is imposing upon a person already visited with the inexpressible calamity of mental obscurity an obligation to observe the same care and precaution respecting the rights of others that the law demands of one in the full possession of his faculties. But the question of liability in these cases . . . is a question of policy; and it is to be disposed of as would be the question whether the incompetent person should be supported at the expense of the public, or of his neighbors, or at the expense of his own estate. If his mental disorder makes him dependent, and at the same time prompts him to commit injuries, there seems to be no greater reason for imposing upon the neighbors or the public one set of

> these consequences, rather than the other; no more propriety or justice in making others bear the losses resulting from his unreasoning fury, when it is spent upon them or their property, than there would be in calling upon them to pay the expense of his confinement in an asylum, when his own estate is ample for the purpose.". . . .
>
> Although the above language is somewhat dated, the reasoning is still well grounded in sound public policy. Someone must bear the loss and, as between the tortfeasor, the injured party, and the general public, sound public policy favors placing the loss on the person who caused it, whether sane or not.

A similar result was reached in Goff v. Taylor, 708 S.W.2d 113, 115 (Ky. Ct. App. 1986), another shooting case, in which the defendant argued unsuccessfully that liability should turn upon whether the actor could distinguish right from wrong and was able to conform his conduct to the law. The court wrote:

> That the subjective standard would afford fairer treatment of a defendant afflicted with a mental disability cannot be disputed. The question the commentators [favoring that standard] do not attempt to reach is the fairness to the victim of the wrongful conduct. Is a victim any less entitled to compensation for his loss because of the mental deficiencies of his tortfeasor? We believe that the answer is no. . . .

2. ***Avoiding Intractable Inquiries.*** The rule that insanity and lesser degrees of mental incompetency create no immunity from tort liability is accounted for, in part, by the reluctance of courts to embark upon intractable inquiries into the workings of the mind. Among the factors contributing to that reluctance, the Restatement has noted:

> [T]he unsatisfactory character of the evidence of mental deficiency in many cases, together with the ease with which it can be feigned, the difficulty of estimating its existence, nature and extent; and some fear of introducing into the law of torts the confusion that has surrounded the defense of insanity in the criminal law.

Restatement, Second, of Torts § 895J cmt. a.

3. ***Mental Deficiencies That Preclude Intent.*** Although a mental deficiency does not, by itself, confer an immunity from liability in tort, the condition may bear upon the matter of whether the defendant acted with the necessary intent. For example, a mental condition may deprive the defendant of the intent to deceive that is essential to an action for deceit. Or suppose that an insane delusion causes a defendant to think that if he throws a knife at the plaintiff the knife will disintegrate in the air before striking the victim. The defendant throws the knife and the plaintiff is hurt. The defendant has not intentionally injured the plaintiff. In this case, the defendant is not using insanity as a *defense* to an intentional tort; he is using it to show that he lacked the intent necessary for that tort.

4. ***Related Legislation.*** In some jurisdictions, the common-law rule holding insane persons liable for their intentional torts has been echoed in legislation. *See, e.g.*, Cal. Civ. Code § 41 (Westlaw 2022) ("A person of unsound mind, of whatever degree, is civilly liable for a wrong done by the person, but is not liable in exemplary damages unless at the time of the act the person was capable of knowing that the act was wrongful").

5. ***Minority Rule.*** In Anicet v. Gant, 580 So. 2d 273 (Fla. Dist. Ct. App. 1991), the court described the issues as "straight from a difficult exam question in Torts I." In a rare departure from the majority rule, the court held that an insane resident confined in a hospital ward designed "for the lowest functioning and most dangerous patients" was not liable for injuries sustained by an attendant who was struck by a heavy ashtray thrown by the resident. The court recognized that imposing liability on an insane person is normally justified on the grounds that "as between an innocent injured person and an incompetent injuring one, the latter should bear the loss," and that "imposition of liability . . . encourage[s] the utmost restriction of the insane person so that he may cause no unnecessary damage to the innocent." However, the court found those rationales inapplicable to the case before it. The court wrote:

> [The defendant,] . . . his relatives, and society did as much as they could do . . . [to prevent harm] by confining him in the most restricted area of a restricted institution that could be found. Hence, it would serve no salutary purpose to impose the extra financial burden of a tort recovery.
>
> As to the "fairness" issue, it is likewise clear that the imposition of liability would in fact counter our notions of what would be just to [a defendant] who has no control over his actions and is thus innocent of any wrongdoing in the most basic sense of that term. . . .
>
> In sum, we revert to the basic rule that where there is no fault, there should be no liability. . . .

The *Anicet* court distinguished McGuire v. Almy on the ground that there the defendant was being cared for at home, making "encouragement of further restriction" possible.

6. ***Duties to Caregivers.*** Under the doctrine of primary assumption of the risk (discussed in Chapter 16), persons accept the inherent risks of their callings and activities, and are barred from suing others for negligence related to those risks. Thus, a firefighter who is injured by an inherent risk of fighting fires — such as the risk that a burning structure might collapse — cannot sue the person who negligently started the fire.

Some cases have applied this line of analysis to suits by professionals injured by patients for whom they are employed to care. *See, e.g.*, Berberian v. Lynn, 845 A.2d 122, 129 (N.J. 2004) (holding, in a negligence action, "that a mentally disabled patient, who does not have the capacity to control his or her conduct, does not owe his or her caregiver a duty of care"). It is useful to remember that primary assumption of the risk ordinarily bars only negligence claims, not suits based on reckless or intentional conduct. An injured firefighter can still sue an arsonist. *McGuire* involved a claim for intentional battery.

However, there is some authority that interprets the scope of primary assumption of the risk more broadly. In Gregory v. Cott, 176 Cal. Rptr. 3d 1, 8 (Cal. 2014), the California Supreme Court held that primary assumption of the risk barred an in-home aide's suit against an Alzheimer's patient and her husband, even if patient's violent conduct was intentional.

7. ***Intoxication.*** Courts have been unwilling to allow persons charged with intentional wrongdoing to raise a defense based on intoxication. If the defendant was able to form a tortious intent, it is irrelevant that the intent would not have existed but for the intoxication. *Cf.* Saba v. Darling, 575 A.2d 1240 (Md. 1990) (the defendant "was able to form a conscious intent to punch" the plaintiff).

4. Transferred Intent

Keel v. Hainline

Supreme Court of Oklahoma
331 P.2d 397 (Okla. 1958)

WILLIAMS, Justice.

In this action [for assault and battery], Patricia Ann Burge, a minor, hereinafter referred to as plaintiff, obtained a judgment against ... [six minors], for damages for personal injury. Defendant Keel alone appeals.

As his first proposition of error defendant asserts that ... there was no evidence that the injury was willfully or intentionally inflicted or that the injury was the proximate result of wrongful and unlawful activity on the part of Keel and the other defendants.

The evidence reveals that on February 1, 1956, some thirty five to forty students ... went to a class room for instruction in music. The class met at the hour of 10:30 a.m., but, for some unknown reason, their instructor did not make an appearance until some thirty or forty minutes later. During the absence of the instructor, several of the male students indulged in what they termed "horse play." This activity consisted of throwing wooden blackboard erasers, chalk, cardboard drum covers, and, in one instance, a "coke" bottle, at each other. It appears that two or three of the defendants went to the north end of the class room and the remaining defendants went to the south end of the room. From vantage points behind the blackboard on the north end and the piano on the south end, they threw the erasers and chalk back and forth at one another. This activity was carried on for a period of some 30 minutes, and terminated only when an eraser, thrown by defendant Jennings, struck plaintiff in the eye, shattering her eye glasses, and resulting in the loss of the use of such eye. Plaintiff was sitting in her chair near the center of the room engaged in studying her lessons at the time she was struck by the eraser, and had not been participating in the so called "horse play" in any manner. None of the defendants intended to strike or injure plaintiff. They were, however, throwing at each other, with the intention of striking each other, although in sport and apparently without intent to cause injury.

The case of Peterson v. Haffner, 59 Ind. 130, 26 Am. Rep. 81, involved a situation in which the defendant, between 13 and 14 years of age, was playing in the street with some boys, and in sport threw a piece of mortar at another boy, and the mortar hit a third boy in the eye, putting it out. In the opinion affirming the judgment for the plaintiff, the court held that it was clear that an assault and battery had been committed. In the body of the opinion it is stated:

> He did not intend to inflict the injury, but he intended to do the wrongful act from which the injury resulted and he is answerable for that result....

The case of Singer v. Marx, 144 Cal. App. 2d 637, 301 P.2d 440, 442, involved a situation in which a 9 year old boy threw a rock which struck and injured an 8 year old girl.... [The court stated:]

> While throwing rocks at trees or into the street ordinarily is an innocent and lawful pastime, that same act when directed at another person is wrongful. The evidence at bar... warrants an inference that Tim threw at Barbara and inadvertently struck Denise. In such circumstances the doctrine of 'transferred intent' renders him liable to Denise.

Defendant strenuously argues that the class had not been called to order by the teacher and that the defendants were merely playing until the teacher arrived, and therefore could not be said to have been engaged in any wrongful or unlawful acts. We do not agree. We do not believe and are not willing to hold that the willful and deliberate throwing of wooden blackboard erasers at other persons in a class room containing 35 to 40 students is an innocent and lawful pastime, even though done in sport and without intent to injure. Such conduct is wrongful, and we so hold....

[The court then held that Keel aided and abetted the wrongful activity, though his participation was limited to retrieving erasers and handing them to others for further throwing.]

.... As is well stated at 52 Am. Jur. 454, Torts, § 114:

> One who commands, directs, advises, encourages, procures, instigates, promotes, controls, aids, or abets a wrongful act by another has been regarded as being as responsible as the one who commits the act so as to impose liability upon the former to the same extent as if he had performed the act himself.

Judgment affirmed.

Notes

1. ***Writs at Early Common Law.*** Following the Norman conquest, justice in England was administered by many local courts. Gradually, the King began to permit some cases to come before his Council, usually for a fee. The formal document commencing this litigation was called a "writ." Bearing the royal seal, the writ

directed the King's judges to hear the matter. Because the exercise of royal jurisdiction interfered with and impaired the income of local courts, it was strongly resisted. Writs were available to cover only a limited, though ever-expanding, number of situations. *See generally* Charles A. Keigwin, *Cases in Common Law Pleading* 1–10, 15–16 (2d ed. 1934).

Two writs of a distinctly tortious nature emerged: "trespass" and "trespass on the case" (the latter sometimes called simply "case"). In general, the writ of trespass lay for injuries directly inflicted (e.g., where a person was struck by a rock thrown by defendant or a dog was given poison); whereas case would lie for harm caused indirectly (e.g., where a person was injured by tripping over an object left in the road or a dog ate poison left for it to find). The intricate complexities attending the development of these writs and their influence on the law of torts has been chronicled elsewhere and need not be repeated here. *See generally* W. Page Keeton, Dan B. Dobbs, Robert E. Keeton, and David G. Owen, Prosser and Keeton on Torts § 6 (5th ed. 1984). However, two features of today's law should be linked to the writ of trespass: nominal damages and transferred intent.

2. ***Nominal Damages.*** First, because the writ of trespass was quasi-criminal in nature, it did not require proof of actual damages. Case, in contrast, necessitated a showing of actual loss on the part of the plaintiff. Even today, those torts descended from the writ of trespass—battery, assault, false imprisonment, trespass to land, and trespass to chattels—still do not require proof of actual damages.[3] In cases involving no actual harm, the plaintiff will receive judgment for a nominal sum, typically one dollar, to vindicate the plaintiff's technical right. In virtually all other areas of tort law, the plaintiff must prove that the defendant caused harm.

3. ***Transferred Intent.*** The history of the writ of trespass is thought by some to determine the scope of the doctrine of transferred intent. In the simplest of terms, that doctrine holds that if the defendant intended to cause any one of the five trespassory torts, then the defendant "intended" to cause any invasion within that range of actions that befalls either the intended victim or a third party. Thus, if the defendant shoots to frighten *A* (assault), but actually strikes *A*, there is an intentional battery. The same is true if the bullet fired to frighten *A* misses *A* and strikes *B*. This is true even if *B*'s presence was wholly unexpected. Indeed, under the doctrine, if the bullet fired to scare *A* passes through *A* and also strikes *B*, whose presence was unknown, there are *two* intentional batteries. As Prosser said, the "intention follows the bullet." William L. Prosser, *Transferred Intent*, 45 Texas L. Rev. 650, 661–62 (1967).

The concept of transferred intent originally took root in a world of all-or-nothing compensation before the theory of negligence liability was well established and long before the advent of comparative fault principles. Does the doctrine of transferred intent still make sense?

---

3. Except for trespass to chattels, in some circumstances. *See* Glidden v. Syzbiak, 63 A.2d 233 (N.H. 1949).

To answer this question it is useful to distinguish unexpected injuries to intended victims from unexpected injuries to third parties. Treating unintended injury to an intended victim as an intentional tort is hardly shocking. The defendant intended to invade the interests of the plaintiff, and in that sense the resulting harm was not accidental, even if unexpected. To call that type of invasion an intentional tort appeals to common sense. It also alleviates some of the difficulties of proving exactly what the defendant intended.

In contrast, in cases involving unexpected harm to third parties (particularly third parties not known to be present), the defendant never intended to harm the plaintiff, and it is purely fictional to treat the case as if the defendant did. Why should the law do this? Could not the unexpected victim simply sue for negligence or recklessness? Is an intentional-tort suit preferable to those actions? Recall the consequences of classification (relating to insurance, bankruptcy, *respondeat superior*, and the like) discussed in Chapter 1. In some cases, the innocent plaintiff *is worse off* if the fiction of transferred intent is applied to a case. For example, in Baska v. Scherzer, 156 P.3d 617 (Kan. 2007), a hostess was injured when she attempted to break up a fight between guests. The court held that, in light of the doctrine of transferred intent, her claim was time-barred because the one-year statute of limitations for intentional torts applied to the case, rather than the two-year statute of limitations for negligence.

See generally Vincent R. Johnson, *Transferred Intent in American Tort Law*, 87 Marquette L. Rev. 903 (2004) (arguing that transferred intent should not be applied to cases involving unintended victims because actions based on lack of care (negligence and recklessness) provide such plaintiffs a viable and often preferable route to recovery); Peter B. Kutner, *The Prosser Myth of Transferred Intent*, 91 Ind. L.J. 1105, 1107 (2016) ("despite Prosser's great influence on American tort law, Prosser's position on transferred intent is not the law now and should not be").

Virtually all of the modern transferred-intent cases have involved assault and battery. Prosser said it could also apply with respect to false imprisonment, trespass to land, and trespass to chattels. The Third Restatement says transferred intent may also apply to the tort of outrage, but seems to suggest that these will be "rare cases." *See* Restatement, Third, of Torts: Liab. for Physical & Emotional Harm § 46 cmt. i (2012).

In the Second Restatement, the sections defining assault and battery are crafted so that either tort will lie if there is intent to commit an assault or a battery involving the same person or a different person. *See* Restatement, Second, of Torts §§ 13 and cmt. b, 16, 18, 20 and 21 (1965). And the section on false imprisonment is drafted so that liability is imposed if there was intent to confine either the plaintiff or a third person. *Id.* at § 35(1). *See also* Restatement, Third, of Torts: Liab. for Physical & Emotional Harm § 1 cmt. b & § 33 cmt. c (2010).

4. ***No Transferred Negligence***. The doctrine of transferred intent has no counterpart in negligence. *Cf.* Palsgraf v. Long Island R.R. Co., 162 N.E. 99 (N.Y. 1928)

(there is no liability in negligence unless a danger to the plaintiff was reasonably to be anticipated, regardless of whether a risk was posed to others). To that extent, the doctrine illustrates a general tendency of the law to extend liability more readily if the defendant's conduct rises to the level of intentional wrongdoing.

5. ***Children and Intent.*** The general rule at common law is that children are liable for their torts, whether they are committed intentionally, negligently, or as a matter of strict liability. However, the immaturity of the child is taken into account in determining whether, in the first instance, a tort has been committed. For example, with battery, a child may be of such tender years, and so unaware of surrounding circumstances, as to be incapable of forming the required intent to make a harmful or offensive contact. If so, there is no tort even if the child pokes someone in the eye: only an unfortunate accident.

A few states treat a child below a certain age as incapable of forming a tortious intent. *See, e.g.*, De Luca v. Bowden, 329 N.E.2d 109 (Ohio 1975) (children under the age of seven cannot be held liable for intentional torts); *cf.* Hatch v. O'Neill, 202 S.E.2d 44 (Ga. 1973) (minor under the age of criminal responsibility is immune from suit in tort). Other states have declined to do so. *See* Bailey v. C.S., 12 S.W.3d 159 (Tex. App. 2000) (holding that minority, standing alone, was insufficient to prove that a four-year-old child lacked intent to commit a battery when he struck his babysitter in the throat when she delayed playing a game).

See also Chapter 5, discussing the negligence liability of minors.

6. ***Why Sue a Minor Child?*** There are several reasons to sue a minor child. To begin with, a tort judgment against a minor may be satisfied out of the personal holdings of the child, if any, or periodically renewed at statutorily prescribed intervals until such time as the child obtains sufficient assets to cover the judgment. However, upon reaching the age of legal majority, the child may discharge the debt through bankruptcy proceedings, unless the underlying conduct was "wilful and malicious" within the meaning of the Bankruptcy Code, or involved procurement of money, property, or services by fraud. *See* 11 U.S.C.A. §§ 523(a)(6) and 523(a)(2)(A) (Westlaw 2022).

Of much greater practical importance today is the possibility that a judgment against a minor may be covered by liability insurance. The parent's homeowner's policy may include children living at home within the definition of an "insured." However, liability-insurance policies generally exclude coverage for harm "expected or intended from the standpoint of the insured."

In some cases, it may be best, for the purpose of reaching insurance proceeds, for the plaintiff to style the action as one for accidental wrongdoing (negligence), rather than intentional battery, if the facts support that characterization. Not all cases afford the plaintiff that kind of flexibility. *See, e.g.*, Clark v. Allstate Ins. Co., 529 P.2d 1195 (Ariz. Ct. App. 1975) (an insured high school student admitted that he intended to strike the victim in the face; the liability-insurance policy did not apply even though the defendant claimed that he did not mean to injure the victim).

7. ***Common-Law Parental Liability for the Torts of Minor Children.*** In the absence of statute, a parent is not liable for the torts of a minor child by the mere fact of parentage. *See* Ross v. Souter, 464 P.2d 911 (N.M. 1970).

However, vicarious liability — meaning liability for the wrongs of another — may arise in some cases. For example, if a child is an employee of the parent, the parent will be liable for torts committed in the course of the employment because employers are liable for their employees' torts. *See* Chapter 14. Similarly, liability under agency law principles may sometimes extend to non-business settings. *See* Butler v. Moore, 188 S.E.2d 142, 144 (Ga. Ct. App. 1972) (child acted as the agent of the parent in making home repairs); De Anda v. Blake, 562 S.W.2d 497, 499 (Tex. Civ. App. 1978) (minor operated a car at the insistence of her mother for her mother's benefit). So, too, vicarious liability may be imposed if a parent subsequently ratifies a child's independent tortious conduct. *See* Hower v. Ulrich, 27 A. 37 (Pa. 1893) (father accepted corn after learning that his children had stolen it).

Liability of a personal (rather than vicarious) nature — that is, liability for one's own wrongdoing — will be found if a parent directs a child to commit a tortious act or knowingly assists in tortious conduct. *See* Harrington v. Hall, 63 A. 875, 876 (Del. 1906) (parent instructed child to shoot a foxhound); Langford v. Shu, 128 S.E.2d 210 (N.C. 1962) (parent participated in a practical joke that her children played on a neighbor, who jumped with fright and was injured when a furry object sprang out of a box said to contain a snake-eating mongoose). And a parent may be liable for failure to control a child with specifically known dangerous tendencies. *See* Chapter 9.

8. ***Parental-Liability Statutes.*** Prompted by juvenile vandalism, virtually all states have enacted laws which modify the common law and make parents vicariously liable for some harms inflicted by their minor children. Parental-liability statutes vary widely in their coverage. Among the most important differences concern the basis of liability and the limits, if any, on maximum dollar recovery. While many statutes limit a parent's exposure to a relatively small amount (perhaps $7,500 or less), some allow much higher recoveries. *See* Fla. Stat. Ann. § 741.24 (Westlaw 2022) (recovery for malicious or willful destruction or theft of property "shall be limited to the actual damages in addition to taxable court costs"). Indeed, the Hawaii statute appears to completely reverse the common law rule of no vicarious liability by providing that "The father and mother of unmarried minor children shall jointly and severally be liable in damages for tortious acts committed by their children. . . ." Haw. Rev. Stat. Ann. § 577-3 (Westlaw 2022); *see also* La. Civ. Code Ann. art. 2318 (Westlaw 2022) (similar).

Contrast the following civil-liability provisions from Oregon and Texas:

Oregon Revised Statutes § 30.765 (Westlaw 2022)

(1) In addition to any other remedy provided by law, the parent or parents of an unemancipated minor child shall be liable for actual damages to person or property caused by any tort intentionally or recklessly committed by such child. However, a parent who is not entitled to legal custody of the

minor child at the time of the intentional or reckless tort shall not be liable for such damages.

(2) The legal obligation of the parent or parents of an unemancipated minor child to pay damages under this section shall be limited to not more than $7,500, payable to the same claimant, for one or more acts.

Texas Family Code §§ 41.001–.002 (Westlaw 2022)

§ 41.001 Liability

A parent or other person who has the duty of control and reasonable discipline of a child is liable for any property damage proximately caused by . . . the wilful and malicious conduct of a child who is at least 10 years of age but under 18 years of age.

§ 41.002 Limits of Damages

Recovery for damage caused by wilful and malicious conduct is limited to actual damages, not to exceed $25,000 per occurrence, plus court costs and reasonable attorney's fees.

The legislative compromises that attend the enactment of parental-liability laws may lead to anomalous results. For example, under the Texas statute, if a teenager fires a gun across the street toward a neighbor's house, intentionally blowing a hole through the front door, there will be parental liability for the property damage. If the bullet kills or wounds someone standing by the door, the parent will not be liable for death or personal injury.

Many parental liability tort statutes impose a "living with" or "residing with" requirement; others refer to "custody and control" or use similar language; and still others have no control, custody, or residence restrictions at all. *See* Canida v. Canida, 751 So. 2d 647, 649 n.1 (Fla. Dist. Ct. App. 1999) (overnight visiting every other weekend did not constitute "living with" the father for purposes of imposing liability).

Some, but not all, losses under parental-liability statutes may be covered by the parent's liability insurance policy.

Brudney v. Ematrudo

United States District Court for the District of Connecticut
414 F. Supp. 1187 (D. Conn. 1976)

ZAMPANO, District Judge.

The plaintiff, Karen Brudney, a former student at Yale University, commenced this action against Peter Ematrudo, a member of the New Haven Police Department, to recover damages . . . for assault and battery. . . .

After a careful review of the evidence, the Court accepts neither of the parties' complete version of the facts and finds as follows. On May 11, 1972, at approximately 11:00 A.M., a peaceful anti-war demonstration held in front of the Yale-in-China building in New Haven turned into a serious physical encounter between students and police. Scuffles and fights occurred. The defendant, observing that detective Giannotti had been knocked to the ground and was under attack by several students, left his post on the steps of the building and rushed to assist his fellow officer. After issuing a verbal warning that went unheeded, he lashed out with his blackjack in order to subdue a male demonstrator (probably Cruz) who was assaulting Giannotti. As the blackjack descended and hit the head of the demonstrator, it accidentally glanced the head of the plaintiff, causing a mild injury. Because the blackjack struck its intended target, the defendant did not realize the weapon also touched the plaintiff's body as it came down in and among a pushing, shoving, fighting group of persons. The plaintiff, on the other hand, feeling an unexpected, sharp and sudden force against her head, reasonably assumed she was the object of the defendant's blackjack.

.... There is not a scintilla of credible evidence to support an inference that the action of any other person caused the injury to the plaintiff. But, contrary to the plaintiff's allegation, the Court concludes she was not the victim of an unprovoked act of police brutality....

.... The defendant resorted to the use of force to aid another policeman under assault only after his verbal warning was ignored. His use of a blackjack was necessary, reasonable, limited and relatively controlled under the circumstances. Due to the crush of the crowd and the plaintiff's close proximity to the demonstrators who were attacking the officer, the blackjack accidentally grazed the plaintiff's head. Immediately after the release of the fallen officer by the protestors, the defendant ceased using the blackjack and retreated to call for assistance from uniformed police. It seems evident, therefore, that the defendant's application of force was restricted to a good faith effort to extricate a fellow police officer from great potential harm and to restore order and discipline within the crowd. Finally, the minor nature of the injury inflicted negates any suggestion by the plaintiff and her witnesses that the defendant acted maliciously or sadistically.

... [T]he Court is impelled to the conclusion that the defendant did not commit an actionable assault and battery against the plaintiff. It is evident that the defendant acted within reasonable limits in determining the type and amount of force required in order to rescue officer Giannotti during the altercation with the demonstrators.... It is unfortunate that the plaintiff received an injury through no fault on her part, yet the record fails to convince the Court that she proved her claims by a preponderance of the evidence.

Accordingly, judgment may enter for the defendant.

Notes

1. ***Why the Difference?*** Is *Brudney* inconsistent with *Keel*? Did the plaintiff's attorney forget to argue the doctrine of transferred intent, or is the doctrine inapplicable?

2. ***Wrongfulness.*** In *Keel*, the court took pains to point out that the deliberate throwing of the erasers, in a classroom containing 35 to 40 students, not all of whom

participated in the battle, was not an innocent pastime. Rather, the court found, the conduct constituted a "wrongful act." Would *Keel* have turned out differently if all of the persons in the room had been consensual participants in the horseplay? Would the act have still been wrongful? Or, what if *A* and *B* were the only participants in the eraser battle, both had consented to the risks, and an eraser somehow struck *C*, whose presence could not possibly have been anticipated?

B. Battery and Assault

Two Distinct Actions. The torts of assault and battery are conceptually distinct. Battery is the intentional infliction of unconsented bodily contact that is harmful or offensive, whereas assault is the intentional creation of apprehension of imminent battery.

A tort victim unaware of an offer of physical contact prior to its infliction suffers a battery without an assault. And if the victim is cognizant of an imminent threat, but the perpetrator desists before the blow is struck, there is an assault without a battery. Thus, either tort may exist independently of the other, although the two actions frequently co-exist, as where, during a dispute, the defendant grabs the plaintiff by the throat and physically prepares to strike. *See generally* Restatement, Second, of Torts §§13–34; *see also* Bowie v. Murphy, 624 S.E.2d 74 (Va. 2006) (holding that completion of a battery by making contact did not negate an assault claim based on anticipation of the battery).

Policy Basis. The existence of the tort of assault, even when no battery follows, shows that the law sometimes redresses purely emotional injury, not just physical harm. In an action for assault, the loss of mental tranquility is treated as a significant injury.

The actions for assault and battery serve deterrence functions. Assault penalizes intentional conduct that is likely to result in a breach of the peace, whether because once a threat of contact is made the actor is apt to carry through, or because the endangered victim may resort to force in self-defense. Battery deters the purposeful infliction of unnecessary harm.

Historical Development. The torts of assault and battery are ancient in origin. This is not surprising, for "[o]ne of the first functions of orderly government is the maintenance of peace and order in the community." Fowler V. Harper, Fleming James, Jr., and Oscar S. Gray, The Law of Torts § 3.1 (3d ed. 2006). The earliest known case of assault dates back to the mid-fourteenth century, where, in I de S et ux. v. W de S, YB Lib. Assis, Edw. III, f. 99, pl. 60 (1348), a tavern keeper's wife who dodged a hatchet swung at her by an irate customer recovered half a mark.

Requirement of Intent. Most authorities opine that battery requires a showing of intent to cause contact and that assault requires proof of intent to cause apprehension of contact. However, the doctrine of transferred intent may apply.

Terminology. Criminal law has frequently used the terms "assault" and "battery" interchangeably (often in the same breath) to denote the unconsented infliction of bodily harm. Perhaps for that reason, civil courts have not always employed these terms correctly. *See* O'Brien v. Cunard S.S. Co., 28 N.E. 266 (Mass. 1891) (incorrectly referring to injection of a smallpox vaccine as assault, rather than battery). One jurisdiction has abandoned efforts to distinguish the two torts. *See* Charles E. Cantu, *Assault and Battery*, Texas Torts and Remedies (1987) (indicating that the state Penal Code, which has combined assault and battery into the criminal offense of assault, is controlling in civil suits). Thus, in Texas, the tort of assault covers contact, as well as apprehension of contact.[4]

Noble v. Louisville Transfer Co.

Court of Appeals of Kentucky
255 S.W.2d 493 (Ky. Ct. App. 1952)

MILLIKEN, Justice.

....

Marcella Noble and her five year old daughter, Sherry, arrived at Union Station, Louisville, about 1:45 a.m. . . . The mother hired the defendant's taxicab to take them to their home. . . . Mrs. Noble, a young woman, was pregnant at the time and her little daughter, Sherry, was nauseated. Sherry vomited in the defendant's taxicab on their way home, and this became the *casus belli* of this litigation.

Mrs. Noble avers that the driver of the cab, appellee, James Wood, Sr., ordered her to clean up the vomit, and that she went into her dark house to get a rag for that purpose while Wood detained Sherry just outside the cab. The street was dark, slumbering neighbors were near, Wood was a big man (6 feet 1 and 1/2 inches, 210 pounds), Sherry was sick, and Mrs. Noble "was not feeling very well. . . ."

According to Mrs. Noble she cleaned up the floor of the cab because she was afraid of Wood, who still held Sherry. According to Wood when Sherry got out of the cab "the little tot started to heave again and she vomited against my leg where I was standing by the side of the door and I reached down and touched this little baby on her shoulder, and I said: 'Why, honey, you are not through vomiting yet, are you?'". . . . Mrs. Noble construed Wood's holding of Sherry to be a detention of the child. On the other hand, Wood, when asked, "When did you have her (Sherry) in your arms—when she was vomiting over there?" answered: "I never had her in my

4. In Texas, "The elements of assault are the same in both criminal and civil cases. . . . 'A person commits assault if the person: (1) intentionally, knowingly, or recklessly causes bodily injury to another, including the person's spouse; (2) intentionally or knowingly threatens another with imminent bodily injury, including the person's spouse; or (3) intentionally or knowingly causes physical contact with another when the person knows or should reasonably believe that the other will regard the contact as offensive or provocative.' Tex. Penal Code § 22.01(a)." Jones v. Shipley, 508 S.W.3d 766, 768–69 (Tex. App. 2016).

arms. I got more sense than that. . . . I touched her with my little finger to keep her from falling over."

. . . .

[Suits were filed alleging battery, assault, and false imprisonment of Sherry and assault of Mrs. Noble. On appeal, the court found the false imprisonment and assault claims to be without merit.]

. . . . When Wood placed his hand on Sherry his manifest intention was to help the sick child and not to harm her. There was neither the harmful or offensive physical contact with Sherry nor the manifest intention to harm her which are required to constitute a battery. Restatement of the Law of Torts, Sections 13 through 20.

We concur with the view of the trial judge that there was not sufficient evidence of any conduct on the part of Wood to constitute an offense. We conclude that the evidence given at the trial, with all inferences that the jury could justifiably draw from it, is insufficient to support a verdict for the plaintiffs, so that such a verdict, if returned, would have to be set aside. As a consequence, the court was correct in directing verdicts for the defendants. . . .

Notes

1. ***Harmfulness.*** To be actionable as battery, contact must be harmful or offensive. "Harmful" is a term of art denoting any unconsented alteration of a structure or function of the body, even if the change does not affect the plaintiff's health. However, some courts have declined to embrace this broad formulation of the rule. *See* Rhodes v. E.I. du Pont de Nemours & Co., 636 F.3d 88 (4th Cir. 2011) (rejecting the plaintiffs' argument that the tort of battery under West Virginia law includes any chemical exposure that results in a potentially dangerous, detectable level of a chemical in a person's body, even if the person has not become ill).

2. ***Offensiveness and Presumed Consent.*** Contact is offensive if it would offend a reasonable person's sense of personal dignity. Contacts which are ordinarily and necessarily incident to the conduct of everyday affairs do not meet this requirement. A tap on the shoulder to obtain information will not give rise to liability. *See* Coward v. Baddeley, 4 H. & N. 478, 157 Eng. Rep. 927 (1859). Nor will the rendering of assistance to an intoxicated person, *see* Hoffman v. Eppers, 41 Wis. 251 (1866), or the casual jostling of another to clear a passage through congested quarters, *see* Cole v. Turner, 6 Mod. Rep. 149, 90 Eng. Rep. 958 (1709).

To some extent, the question is one of what should reasonably be expected, for by engaging in particular forms of conduct, one knowingly runs certain risks. Some bodily contact may be inevitable where a patron frequents a crowded bar, but an action for battery will still lie where one patron gives another a hard elbow to the stomach. Similarly, if the defendant excitedly grasps the plaintiff's shoulder, it may make a difference whether the two are spectators at a football game or users of a public library. The issue is whether the "conduct is unwarranted by the social usages prevalent at the time and place." Restatement, Second, of Torts § 19 cmt. a.

In Gerber v. Veltri, 702 Fed. Appx. 423, 425–36 (6th Cir. 2017), a law professor (Gerber) "had a tense argument with another professor over a student research assistant." Later, when the dean saw Gerber "pass by in the hallway, he attempted to stop Gerber so they could discuss the incident." The dean placed "his left non-dominant hand on Gerber's right shoulder," saying "Scott, we need to talk," and directing "Gerber with his other hand toward the nearby faculty lounge." Gerber "reacted very suddenly," and said "[t]ake your hands off me." The dean "did so immediately." In affirming a judgment that the dean had not committed a battery, the court wrote, "Touching a colleague on the shoulder to get his attention is well within the ordinary 'social usages prevalent' in the workplace."

3. ***Intent to Harm or Offend.*** An occasional case holds that intent to harm or offend is a prerequisite to liability for battery. *See* Mullins v. Parkview Hosp., Inc., 865 N.E.2d 608 (Ind. 2007). However, the great weight of authority is to the contrary.

4. ***Battery and Consent.*** Contact is a battery only if it is unconsented or exceeds the scope of consent. *See* Murphy v. Implicito, 920 A.2d 678 (N.J. Super. Ct. App. Div. 2007) (involving a battery claim against a physician who exceeded the scope of consent by implanting a "cadaver bone").

Normally, consent to contact cannot be implied in the face of another's express assertions to the contrary. *See* Restatement, Second, of Torts § 892 cmt. c; Childers v. A.S., 909 S.W.2d 282, 293 (Tex. App. 1995) (evidence that, during "sexual games" between children, the plaintiff told the defendant "to stop" precluded summary judgment for the defendant child).

Can a sensitive person render generally permitted contacts tortious merely by manifesting an objection and refusing to consent? Perhaps. *See* Cohen v. Smith, 648 N.E.2d 329 (Ill. App. Ct. 1995) (patient stated a cause of action against a male nurse and a hospital for battery and intentional infliction of emotional distress by alleging that she informed them of her religious beliefs against being seen unclothed by a man and that the male nurse was nonetheless present during her cesarean delivery and touched the patient's naked body).

5. ***Good Intentions and Important Goals.*** If the evidence establishes an intentional, unconsented touching that is harmful or offensive, it is irrelevant to the issue of liability that defendant sought merely to advance the plaintiff's interests or acted in furtherance of some other important goal. The "Good Samaritan" who insists, over objection, on setting the plaintiff's fracture will be subject to a claim for damages. *See* Clayton v. New Dreamland Roller Skating Rink, 82 A.2d 458 (N.J. Super. Ct. App. Div. 1951).

6. ***Damages for Battery and Unanticipated Consequences.*** In an action for battery, the plaintiff may obtain an award for compensatory damages for losses actually suffered, including physical and mental harm. If no losses are established, nominal damages (traditionally one dollar) may be awarded to vindicate the plaintiff's technical right. In cases involving highly culpable conduct (for example, sexual abuse of a child), punitive damages may be awarded.

If the elements of battery are shown, it is irrelevant that the resulting injuries are more extensive than might reasonably have been anticipated. *See* White v. University of Idaho, 768 P.2d 827 (Idaho Ct. App. 1989) (a touch on the back "in a movement later described as one a pianist would make in striking and lifting the fingers from a keyboard" required removal of a rib); Saba v. Darling, 575 A.2d 1240 (Md. 1990) (unintended broken jaw). This is commonly called the "eggshell skull" principle, though there is really no such thing as an "eggshell skull." *See* Chapter 8.

Picard v. Barry Pontiac-Buick, Inc.

Supreme Court of Rhode Island
654 A.2d 690 (R.I. 1995)

LEDERBERG, Justice.

[After having difficulties with a garage over whether her brakes needed to be repaired, plaintiff contacted a television news reporter, who was described as a "troubleshooter." Thereafter, the plaintiff took a picture of the defendant, "presumably as evidence for the troubleshooter reporter." The photograph clearly showed the defendant fully facing the camera, standing upright while pointing his index finger at the plaintiff.]

. . . .

The defendant testified that as he was looking at the car, plaintiff had come up behind him and aimed the camera toward him. He then pointed at plaintiff and said, "who gave you permission to take my picture?" then walked around the car to plaintiff, placed his index finger on the camera and again asked, "who gave you permission to take my picture?" The defendant denied grabbing plaintiff, touching her body, threatening her or making any threatening gestures, scuffling with her or reaching for the photograph. He also testified that he did not intend to cause plaintiff any bodily harm.

[In a subsequent action for assault and battery, the jury awarded compensatory and punitive damages.]

. . . . The defendant appealed the judgment. . . .

The plaintiff testified that she was frightened by defendant's actions. A review of the attendant circumstances attests that such a reaction was reasonable. The defendant admitted approaching plaintiff, and the photograph taken that day clearly showed defendant pointing his finger at plaintiff as defendant approached her. Because plaintiff's apprehension of imminent bodily harm was reasonable at that point, plaintiff has established a prima facie case of assault.

. . . [D]efendant contended that a battery did not occur because defendant did not intend to touch or injure plaintiff. Rather, defendant argued, the evidence showed that he intended to touch plaintiff's camera, not plaintiff's person, and therefore the contact was insufficient to prove battery. With this contention we must disagree. Even if this court were to accept defendant's characterization of the incident, a battery had nonetheless occurred. The defendant failed to prove that his actions ... were accidental or involuntary. Therefore, defendant's offensive contact with an object attached to or identified with plaintiff's body was sufficient to constitute a battery. As noted in the comments to the Restatement (Second) Torts § 18, cmt. c at 31 (1965):

> Unpermitted and intentional contacts with anything so connected with the body as to be customarily regarded as part of the other's person and therefore as partaking of its inviolability is actionable as an offensive contact with his person. *There are some things such as clothing or a cane or, indeed, anything directly grasped by the hand which are so intimately connected with one's body as to be universally regarded as part of the person* (Emphasis added).

The defendant's contact with the camera clutched in plaintiff's hand was thus sufficient to constitute a battery....

[The court found that the award of compensatory damages was grossly excessive and that the facts would not support an award of punitive damages.]

.... We remand the case to the Superior Court for a new trial on ... [damages].

Notes

1. ***Other Precedent.*** *See also* Fisher v. Carrousel Motor Hotel, Inc., 424 S.W.2d 627 (Tex. 1967) (plate grabbed from hand); S.H. Kress & Co. v. Brashier, 50 S.W.2d 922 (Tex. Civ. App. 1932) (book grabbed from hand).

2. ***Personal Effects.*** At some point the connection between the plaintiff's body and the item which is struck becomes so slight that an action for battery will not lie. The line of distinction is difficult to draw and depends upon the emotional reaction of a reasonable person. "The ordinary man might well regard a horse upon which he is riding as part of his personality but, a passenger in a public omnibus or other conveyance would clearly not be entitled so to regard the vehicle merely because he was seated in it." *See* Restatement, Second, of Torts § 18 cmt. c.

3. ***Ethics in Law Practice: Assault and Battery.*** An attorney who commits an assault or battery is subject not merely to tort liability and criminal prosecution, but to professional discipline in the form of reprimand, suspension, or removal from practice. *See* Matter of Hickox, 57 P.3d 403 (Colo. 2002) (six-month suspension based, in part, on domestic violence); Matter of Runyon, 491 N.E.2d 189 (Ind. 1986) (attorney disbarred based, in part, on evidence that he struck his ex-wife with a club and held her at gunpoint).

Moore v. El Paso Chamber of Commerce

Court of Civil Appeals of Texas
220 S.W.2d 327 (Tex. Civ. App. 1949)

SUTTON, Justice.

[To promote its annual rodeo and Livestock Show, the El Paso Chamber of Commerce encouraged residents to go "Western" for a week by wearing some sort of distinguishing regalia. People on the street who were not attired in western wear were roped and lifted into wagons and conveyed to "corrals" where many of them were invited or caused to occupy a "hot seat," a chair wired with hot wires, wherein they were lightly "shocked." Persons subjected to the horseplay were released when they purchased rodeo tickets or handkerchiefs which, when worn about the neck, satisfied the attire requirement.]

... [D]uring the rodeo week, plaintiff and her mother had been down town shopping.... They were approached by three young ropers, who, plaintiff said, had their eyes on her, and [were] about forty feet away. One of them said: "let's get that girl," or "let's get that one," or something to that effect. Plaintiff was a young woman just past seventeen and married for some two months. The young woman said to her mother "Let's duck in here," and ran into the drug store. One of the young men with his rope followed her. She said she was frightened and not interested in the play and sought to escape from the drug store into the lobby of the Hilton where she thought she would be safe from the apprehension. To do so she had to pass through a door connecting the drug store and the lobby. The door had a glass panel. She ran against the door and pushed her left hand through the glass and received very severe cuts....

Plaintiff... charged the Chamber of Commerce, acting through its agents, servants and representatives, with the responsibility and liability for the injuries received.... She charged ... that the defendant, its agents, servants and employees negligently, carelessly, recklessly and wilfully, in violation of the laws of the State, assaulted plaintiff by chasing her for the purpose of roping her and imprisoning her without her consent....

[Following the submission of special issues, the jury returned findings that Claude Weaver, the young man who chased the plaintiff in the drug store was acting at the direction of one "Shorty"; that Shorty was within the actual or implied scope of his authority from the Chamber of Commerce; that Weaver caused Plaintiff to push the glass and was negligent; that Plaintiff was negligent in failing to properly care for her own safety; and that Plaintiff had been damaged in the sum of $6,163.00. The trial court granted judgment for the Defendant.]

Apparently the trial court considered contributory negligence a defense in this case and that the findings of the jury on the issues of contributory negligence defeated her right to recover on the verdict otherwise favorable to her. In our opinion this is not a negligence case. All that young Weaver did he willed or purposed to do, save to become responsible for the serious injury inflicted as a consequence of what he did that led to it. He intended to do exactly what he did do, except the infliction of the injury. What he did then was an intentional and not a negligent wrong. . . . [C]ontributory negligence is no defense to an intentional wrong. . . . We conclude, therefore, the findings of contributory negligence do not defeat the right of recovery.

. . . . [P]laintiff had the legal right to make a lawful use of the streets of the city without hindrance, interference and molestation, and that right was violated by young Weaver in his pursuit or chase of her in an effort to restrain her and compel her submission to the "horse-play" of the day and in doing so he caused her "to push the glass in the door between the Hilton Hotel Drug Store and the lobby in the Hilton Hotel and to be injured thereby." . . . .

It is clear to us the Chamber of Commerce must be liable for the acts of Claude Weaver. The corrals were set up and maintained by the Chamber of Commerce through its Livestock Committee in the interest of and as a part of the rodeo and Livestock Show. It is true the Chamber of Commerce employed no one in the sense people were engaged for hire to do the things that were done in the operation of the corrals but "one good fellow after another would just go ahead and take a hand at it." Their services to that extent were voluntary and gratuitous, but nevertheless all they did was for and in the interest of the Chamber of Commerce in furthering its projects. What Claude Weaver did was the chief activity of the corrals — the matter of going out and bringing in the people. The Chamber of Commerce had a representative in charge all the time and Weaver worked there, using the rope and bringing in people along with the others for more than a day and a half. The Chamber of Commerce may not permit him to openly engage in those activities peculiarly their own until an unfortunate accident and injury happens and then say he was not acting for them but that he was a mere volunteer and acting for himself. . . .

"The relation of agency does not depend upon an express appointment and acceptance thereof, but it may be, and frequently is, implied from the words and conduct of the parties and circumstances of the particular case. It may be implied from a single transaction. . . . It is often difficult to determine upon general principles whether any agency exists; rather it must be determined from the facts and circumstances of the particular case, and if it appears from such facts and circumstances that there was at least an implied intention to create the relation, it will by implication be held to exist." . . . .

It is difficult to find, we think, stronger facts than the facts of the instant case from which agency may be implied and held to exist.

. . . . The judgment of the trial court will be accordingly reversed and judgment here rendered for the plaintiff for her damages and costs.

Notes

1. ***Indirect Force.*** Indirect contact may give rise to battery. The defendant who throws water or sets a dog upon the plaintiff, or drives a truck fast, knowing that the

plaintiff will be thrown from its bed, commits a battery. *See* Restatement, Second, of Torts § 18 cmt. c. *See also* Field v. Philadelphia Elec. Co., 565 A.2d 1170 (Pa. Super. Ct. 1989) (release of radioactive steam); Lambrecht v. Schreyer, 152 N.W. 645 (Minn. 1915) (defendant whipped a horse which the plaintiff was driving).

2. ***Knowledge of Contact.*** The plaintiff's lack of awareness of the contact at the time it occurs — for example, because plaintiff is asleep or under anesthetic — will not defeat an action for battery. *See* Restatement, Second, of Torts § 18 cmt. d.

Western Union Telegraph Co. v. Hill

Court of Appeals of Alabama
150 So. 709 (Ala. Ct. App. 1933)

SAMFORD, Judge.

The action in this case is based upon an alleged assault on the person of plaintiff's wife by one Sapp, an agent of defendant in charge of its office in Huntsville, Ala. The assault complained of consisted of an attempt on the part of Sapp to put his hand on the person of plaintiff's wife coupled with a request that she come behind the counter in defendant's office, and that, if she would come and allow Sapp to love and pet her, he "would fix her clock."

.... Was there such an assault as will justify an action for damages?

....

While every battery includes an assault, an assault does not necessarily require a battery to complete it. What it does take to constitute an assault is an unlawful attempt to commit a battery, incomplete by reason of some intervening cause; or, to state it differently, to constitute an actionable assault there must be an intentional, unlawful, offer to touch the person of another in a rude or angry manner under such circumstances as to create in the mind of the party alleging the assault a well-founded fear of an imminent battery, coupled with the apparent present ability to effectuate the attempt, if not prevented....

What are the facts here? .... Defendant was under contract with plaintiff to keep in repair and regulated an electric clock in plaintiff's place of business. When the clock needed attention, that fact was to be reported to Sapp, and he in turn would report to a special man, whose duty it was to do the fixing. At 8:13 o'clock p.m. plaintiff's wife reported to Sapp over the phone that the clock needed attention, and, no one coming to attend the clock, plaintiff's wife went to the office of defendant about 8:30 p.m. There she found Sapp in charge and behind a desk or counter, separating the public from the part of the room in which defendant's operator worked. The counter is four feet and two inches high, and so wide that, Sapp standing on the floor, leaning against the counter and stretching his arm and hand to the full length, the end of his fingers reaches just to the outer edge of the counter. The photographs in evidence show that the counter was as high as Sapp's armpits. Sapp had had two or three drinks and was "still slightly feeling the effects of whisky; I felt all right; I felt good and amiable." When plaintiff's wife came into the office, Sapp came from towards the rear of the room and asked what he could do for her. She replied: "I asked him if he understood over the phone that my clock was out of order and when he was going to fix it. He stood there and looked at me a few minutes and said: 'If you will come back here and let me love and pet you, I will fix your clock.' This he repeated and reached for me with his hand, he extended his hand toward me, he did not put it on me; I jumped back. I was in his reach as I stood there. He reached for me right along here (indicating her left shoulder and arm)." The foregoing is the evidence offered by plaintiff tending to prove an assault.

Per contra, aside from the positive denial by Sapp of any effort to touch Mrs. Hill, the physical surroundings as evidenced by the photographs of the locus tend to rebut any evidence going to prove that Sapp could have touched plaintiff's wife across that counter even if he had reached his hand in her direction unless she was leaning against the counter or Sapp should have stood upon something so as to elevate him and allow him to reach beyond the counter. However, there is testimony tending to prove that, notwithstanding the width of the counter and the height of Sapp, Sapp could have reached from six to eighteen inches beyond the desk in an effort to place his hand on Mrs. Hill. The evidence as a whole presents a question for the jury. This was the view taken by the trial judge, and in the several rulings bearing on this question there is no error.

The next question is, Was the act of Sapp towards Mrs. Hill, plaintiff's wife, such as to render this defendant liable under the doctrine of *respondeat superior*? It is admitted that at the time of the alleged assault Sapp was the manager of defendant's office . . . [and] that he was in and about his master's business incident to that office. . . .

The defendant is a public service corporation, maintaining open offices for the transaction of its business with the public. . . . People entering these offices are entitled to courteous treatment, and if, while transacting the business of the corporation with the agent, an assault is made growing out of, or being related to the business there in hand, the corporation would be liable. . . . But the assault in this case, if committed, was clearly from a motive or purpose solely and alone to satisfy the sensuous desires of Sapp, and not in furtherance of the business of defendant. In such case the liability rests with the agent and not the master. . . . [W]hile Sapp was the agent of defendant, in the proposal and technical assault made by him on plaintiff's wife he stepped aside wholly from his master's business to pursue a matter entirely personal. Where this is so, the doctrine of *respondeat superior* does not apply. . . .

The rulings of the trial court with reference to this question were erroneous. . . .

Reversed and remanded.

Notes

1. ***Present Apparent Ability.*** Assault is actionable only if the defendant's actions in fact put the plaintiff in apprehension of an immediate contact. Thus, there is no

assault if the defendant's attempt to inflict contact was unknown to the plaintiff before battery was accomplished or the effort was abandoned. *See* Restatement, Second, of Torts § 22. Nor is there an assault if the plaintiff believes—even mistakenly—that the defendant lacks the ability to commit a battery.

> Thus, if the actor, believing a revolver to be loaded, points it at another and threatens to shoot him, the actor is not liable . . . if the other believes that the revolver is unloaded. This is true though the other is mistaken in his belief, the revolver is in fact loaded, and the actor is only prevented from carrying out his purpose by a bystander snatching the revolver from him.

Restatement, Second, of Torts § 24 cmt. a. Of course, once the plaintiff has been placed in apprehension, the defendant is subject to liability, even though the defendant's acts are thereafter terminated or frustrated. Restatement, Second, of Torts § 23. In a similar vein, liability for assault does not depend upon the defendant's actual ability or intention to carry out the threat:

> The actor may know that he is incapable of carrying out the threat of harm of which he intends to put the other in apprehension. It is only necessary that the other believe that the actor have the ability and that the actor intend to bring about such belief on the part of the other.

Restatement, Second, of Torts § 33 cmt. a.

2. ***Apprehension of Contact.*** Apprehension is not equivalent to fear. According to the Restatement:

> It is enough that . . . [the plaintiff] believes that the act is capable of immediately inflicting the contact upon him unless something further occurs. Therefore, the mere fact that he can easily prevent the threatened contact by self-defensive measures which he feels amply capable of taking does not prevent the actor's attempt to inflict the contact upon him from being an actionable assault. . . .

Restatement, Second, of Torts § 24 cmt. b.

Whether the plaintiff was placed in apprehension is normally an issue for the fact finder to resolve. *See* Lesser v. Neosho County Comm. Coll., 741 F. Supp. 854, 866 (D. Kan. 1990) (where a student-athlete doubted assurances from other students that the coach would not strike him in the genitals during a "cup check," the issue of reasonable apprehension was a jury question sufficient to preclude summary judgment).

In Saucier *ex rel.* Mallory v. McDonald's Restaurants, 179 P.3d 481 (Mont. 2008), the limited guardian of a mentally disabled employee brought a tort action against a fast-food restaurant and its manager arising out of the manager's sexual relationship with the employee. The court held that there was no basis for an assault claim because there was no evidence the manager "ever communicated a *threat* of harmful or offensive contact" or that the employee was "ever put in fear of such contact." However, the allegations and evidence supported a claim for battery because the mentally disabled employee lacked capacity to consent to the sexual relationship, which requires "the capability to appreciate the nature, extent, and probable consequences of the conduct." Consent is discussed in Chapter 3.

3. ***Reasonableness of Reaction.*** There is some dispute as to whether the plaintiff's apprehension of contact must be reasonable or merely genuine. According to the Restatement, if the defendant succeeds in intentionally placing the plaintiff in apprehension of imminent contact, it is irrelevant that the defendant's acts would not have placed a person of ordinary courage in such apprehension. Restatement, Second, of Torts § 27. In that situation, the actor has intentionally invaded the legally protected interests of the plaintiff, and "the mere fact that the actor succeeds in accomplishing his purpose by conduct which ordinarily would not accomplish it, is no basis for an immunity. . . ." *Id.* at cmt. a.

However, some cases have reached a different conclusion. For example, in Bouton v. Allstate Ins. Co., 491 So. 2d 56 (La. Ct. App. 1986), the court held that a homeowner was not assaulted by trick-or-treaters, one of whom wore military fatigues and another of whom flashed a camera in the homeowner's face, for a "reasonable person expects to see an endless array of ghouls, beasts, and characters" on Halloween.

In Jones v. Shipley, 508 S.W.3d 766, 770 (Tex. App. 2016), "while chaperoning a school field trip, . . . Shipley allegedly rushed toward a second grader, John Doe, and shook her finger at him while stating she would 'get him.'" The appellate court held that the resulting claim for assault by threat of bodily injury was properly dismissed, stating:

> The act of walking "aggressively" toward John Doe and shaking her finger at him, together with the vague verbal threat to "get" him, does not support a reasonable inference in the mind of a reasonable person that Shipley made an objective threat to inflict imminent bodily injury on the second grader during a school-sponsored field trip to the zoo. This is particularly true given the Joneses' allegation that what Shipley had threatened a week earlier, when she spoke more precisely, was expulsion from the school, which is neither bodily injury nor imminent. . . .

4. ***Imminent versus Future Threats.*** A threat of future harm will not support an action for assault:

> The apprehension created must be one of imminent contact, as distinguished from any contact in the future. "Imminent" does not mean immediate, in the sense of instantaneous contact, as where the other sees the actor's fist about to strike his nose. It means rather that there will be no significant delay. It is not necessary that one shall be within striking distance of the other, or that a weapon pointed at the other shall be in a condition for instant discharge. It is enough that one is so close to striking distance that he can reach the other almost at once, or that he can make the weapon ready for discharge in a very short interval of time.

Holbert v. Noon, 260 P.3d 836, 848 (Or. App. 2011) (Armstrong, J., dissenting).

In S & F Corporation v. Daley, 376 N.E.2d 699 (Ill. App. Ct. 1978), Buchta and Gomez, customers at a bar called the "Candy Store," were told by a waitress to pay for drinks they had not ordered for women they did not know. According to the court:

> When the customers objected to paying for these "drinks" the waitress pointed to two men at the bar and said "They're not going to like it." She told the customers to pay or else, and made a motion to the two men at the bar, approximately 15 feet away. Buchta and Gomez then paid the waitress $20 each . . . [and] left the premises. . . .

In finding that an assault had been committed, the court wrote:

> The threat to Buchta was an immediate one, and not merely a threat to act in the future. . . . The necessity of a "present ability" to inflict a battery upon the victim . . . is satisfied by the immediate presence of these bouncers, especially when coupled with the waitress' gestures toward them.

What if the bouncers had been outside in the parking lot, or in another room, or 50 feet away, or not scheduled to come on duty for a half hour?

5. ***Conditional Threats.*** Whether a conditional threat to commit a battery constitutes an assault depends upon whether the condition is one which the defendant is privileged to enforce through physical contact or a threat to inflict the same. Thus, an action for assault may lie where the defendant screams "Get right out of my house or I will shoot you dead," but not where the defendant heatedly states "I will give you one minute to leave my house. If you don't, I will put you out." The difference is that there is a privilege to use physical force, but not deadly force, to eject an unwanted guest, and one may threaten only that degree of force that it would be permissible to use. *See* Restatement, Second, of Torts § 30 and illus. 1 & 2.

6. ***Verbal Nuances.*** Words accompanying conduct provide a basis for determining whether the plaintiff was placed in apprehension of imminent contact. Such language may reveal, for example, that despite appearances to the contrary, the defendant had no intention of striking the plaintiff, as where the defendant raises a whip, exclaiming, "If you were not an old man, I would knock you down." State v. Crow, 23 N.C. 375 (1841); *cf.* Restatement, Second, of Torts § 31 cmt. b and illus. 2 ("If it were not assize time, I would not take such language from you").

Words may also clarify the significance of ambiguous conduct. Whether an actor causes an assault by reaching into his coat pocket during a quarrel may depend upon whether he simultaneously states, "'I will blow out your brains,' or 'Wait a minute; I need a handkerchief.'" Restatement, Second, of Torts § 31 illus. 3.

7. ***Threatening Gestures Versus Words Alone.*** Words unaccompanied by some form of threatening gesture are generally said to be insufficient to support an action for assault. *See* Bollaert v. Witter, 792 P.2d 465 (Or. Ct. App. 1990) (no assault where the defendant stated, without an overt act, "I'm a Vietnam Vet . . . let's duke it out. . . . I wouldn't be surprised if my wife . . . took a gun and shot you").

> Apparently the origin of this rule [that words alone are not enough] lay in nothing more than the fact that in the early days the King's courts had their hands full when they intervened at the first threatening gesture, or in other words, when the fight was about to start; and taking cognizance of all the belligerent language which the foul mouths of merrie England could dispense was simply beyond their capacity.

W. Page Keeton, Dan B. Dobbs, Robert E. Keeton, and David G. Owen, Prosser and Keeton on Torts § 10, at 45 (5th ed. 1984). Constraints based on limited judicial resources still obtain. However, the Restatement opines:

> [T]here may be . . . situations in which . . . words themselves, without any accompanying gesture, are sufficient under the circumstances to arouse a reasonable apprehension of imminent bodily contact. . . . An entirely motionless highwayman, standing with a gun in his hand and crying "Stand and deliver!" creates quite as much apprehension as one who draws the gun; and any rule which insists upon such a gesture as essential to liability is obviously quite artificial and unreasonable.

Restatement, Second, of Torts § 31 cmts. a & d.

In Castiglione v. Galpin, 325 So. 2d 725 (La. Ct. App. 1976), the plaintiffs went to the defendant's residence to turn off the water because the bill had not been paid. The court held that there was an assault when the defendant, after stating, "I'll get a gun and shoot you if you dare to close that water," retrieved his gun and either placed it on his lap or pointed it at the plaintiffs. Would the case have turned out differently, if the gun was on the defendant's lap when the plaintiffs arrived and remained there at all times? What if the gun was in the house and the defendant never moved to retrieve it after making his threat?

Some gestures are deemed too slight to support a cause of action for assault. *See* Okoli v. Paul Hastings, LLC., No. 152536/2012 (N.Y. Sup. Ct. 2012) (finger wagging and yelling during a deposition did not constitute an assault).

8. ***Sexual Advances.*** Because words unaccompanied by a threatening gesture are normally insufficient to constitute an assault, some cases have held that no action will lie where one person does nothing more than *verbally* solicit another to engage in sexual relations. *See, e.g.*, Davis v. Richardson, 89 S.W. 318 (Ark. 1905). However, times are changing, and verbal advances, especially if repeated or vulgar, may become actionable on some tort theory.

An unwanted, *physical* sexual advance is a battery, and the threat of such an advance can be an assault. In McDonald v. Ford, 223 So. 2d 553 (Fla. Dist. Ct. App. 1969), plaintiff and defendant spent an evening together, then returned to defendant's home. While plaintiff was putting records on the stereo, defendant came up behind her, laughingly embraced her, and, though she resisted, "kissed her hard." A violent struggle ensued. The court held that, although the initial stages of the struggle did not constitute an assault and battery, the latter stages did.

9. ***Damages for Assault.*** In an action for assault, the plaintiff can recover compensatory damages for mental disturbance, including fright, humiliation, and the like, as well as damages for resulting physical illness. In the absence of proof of harm, the jury can award nominal damages to vindicate the plaintiff's legal right to be safe from apprehension of battery. Punitive damages may be recovered for an assault involving egregious facts.

10. ***Battery by Smoke?*** Can contact with smoke be a battery? *See* Leichtman v. WLW Jacor Comm., Inc., 634 N.E.2d 697 (Ohio Ct. App. 1994) (antismoking advocate sufficiently alleged that a radio talk show host committed "battery" by intentionally blowing cigar smoke in the advocate's face when the advocate was in the studio to discuss the harmful effects of smoking and breathing secondary smoke).

11. ***Battery, Assault, and Domestic Violence.*** Do actions for assault and battery offer effective avenues of relief for victims of domestic violence? Perhaps not.

> People who commit domestic violence generally are, in theory, liable under intentional tort theories.... But despite the frequency with which people are injured by "domestic violence torts," very few tort suits are brought.... This underenforcement is caused by several factors. First, standard liability insurance policies generally do not cover domestic violence torts. Second, many defendants have limited or no assets. Third, statutes of limitations are typically shorter for intentional torts than for negligence.
>
> A consequence of the dearth of lawsuits is that one of the key aims of the tort system—deterrence—is failing....

Jennifer Wriggins, *Domestic Violence Torts*, 75 S. Cal. L. Rev. 121, 122–23 (2001).

C. Intentional or Reckless Infliction of Severe Emotional Distress

1. In General

Historical Development. Although threats of future harm or words alone generally cannot sustain an action for assault, they may, on appropriate facts, support a claim for intentional or reckless infliction of severe emotional distress (sometimes called the "tort of outrage"). Most jurisdictions now recognize this action, and its elements are well established.

Viewed broadly, "[e]motional harm encompasses a variety of mental states, including fright, fear, sadness, sorrow, despondency, anxiety, humiliation, depression (and other mental illnesses), and a host of other detrimental—from mildly unpleasant to disabling—mental conditions." Restatement, Third, of Torts: Liab. for Physical & Emotional Harm § 45 cmt. a (2012).

In contrast to the relatively ancient lineage of assault and battery, the tort of outrage is a modern judicial development. As recently as 1934, the first Restatement explained the tort of assault as an historical anomaly, boldly stating that:

> The interest in mental and emotional tranquility and, therefore, in freedom from mental and emotional disturbance[,] is not, *as a thing in itself*, regarded as of sufficient importance to require others to refrain from conduct intended or recognizably likely to cause such a disturbance.

(Emphasis added.) However, even at that date, courts permitted recovery of emotional-distress damages in at least two situations. First, in cases of tortiously inflicted physical injury, damages for pain and suffering could be recovered in addition to compensation for physical harm. Second, certain other traditional torts not involving physical harm (such as assault, libel, slander, and false imprisonment) permitted an award of damages for mental anguish, as well as compensation for more-tangible losses. Consequently, the doctrinal question posed during the middle years of the twentieth century was not whether emotional distress damages could ever be recovered, but whether a claim for emotional anguish was actionable absent proof of physical injury or some other tort. Eventually, the courts relented and recognized an independent cause of action. Recounting the history of this development, one court wrote:

> Traditionally, at common law an action for mental distress alone could not be brought.... This reluctance to fashion a direct remedy reflected a policy consideration that because these damages were difficult to assess and prove[,] a flood of fictitious and trivial claims might result if an independent tort were recognized....
>
> This narrow approach was gradually eroded as courts reflected society's increasing valuation of an individual's interest in privacy and emotional well-being. This culminated in 1948 when the American Law Institute recognized as an independent cause of action outrageous conduct causing severe emotional distress....

Sheltra v. Smith, 392 A.2d 431, 432 (Vt. 1978). Over the years, the doctrinal contours of the tort of outrage have shifted. As Professor Jean C. Love explained:

> In 1948 the American Law Institute adopted the following proposition as section 46: "One who, without a privilege to do so, intentionally causes severe emotional distress to another is liable (a) for such emotional distress and (b) for bodily harm resulting from it."
>
> Ten years later, Professor [William] Prosser, as the Reporter for the Restatement (Second) of Torts, announced that there were over one hundred cases dealing with the question of liability for intentional infliction of emotional distress. Professor Prosser redrafted section 46 "to keep the courts from running wild on this thing" and added numerous comments designed to "spell out some boundaries, qualifications and limitations" to the new tort. As a result, section 46 of the Restatement (Second) of Torts

> imposes liability for damages on a defendant who "by extreme and outrageous conduct intentionally or recklessly causes severe emotional distress to another. . . ."

Jean C. Love, *Discriminatory Speech and the Tort of Intentional Infliction of Emotional Distress*, 47 Wash. & Lee L. Rev. 123, 126–27 (1990).

The current formulation of the tort of outrage is found in Restatement, Third, of Torts: Liab. for Physical & Emotional Harm § 46 (2012) ("An actor who by extreme and outrageous conduct intentionally or recklessly causes severe emotional harm to another is subject to liability for that emotional harm and, if the emotional harm causes bodily harm, also for the bodily harm").

The Problem of Genuineness. In an attempt to assure that the plaintiff had in fact suffered emotional distress, some jurisdictions initially required proof that the alleged suffering resulted in physical harm to the plaintiff, such as a miscarriage, a heart attack, or a less-serious physical illness. Eventually, courts questioned the soundness of that approach, and today most permit recovery even though the emotional distress is unaccompanied by physical illness or other tangible consequences. In a typical opinion, the Supreme Judicial Court of Massachusetts wrote:

> There is a fear that "[i]t is easy to assert a claim of mental anguish and very hard to disprove it." . . . .
>
> While we are not unconcerned with these problems, we believe that "the problems presented are not . . . insuperable" and that "administrative difficulties do not justify the denial of relief for serious invasions of mental and emotional tranquility. . . ." . . . . "That some claims may be spurious should not compel those who administer justice to shut their eyes to serious wrongs and let them go without being brought to account. It is the function of courts and juries to determine whether claims are valid or false. This responsibility should not be shunned merely because the task may be difficult to perform." . . . .
>
> Furthermore, the distinction between the difficulty which juries may encounter in determining liability and assessing damages where no physical injury occurs and their performance of that same task where there has been resulting physical harm may be greatly overstated. "The jury is ordinarily in a better position . . . to determine whether outrageous conduct results in mental distress than whether that distress in turn results in physical injury. From their own experience jurors are aware of the extent and character of the disagreeable emotions that may result from the defendant's conduct, but a difficult medical question is presented when it must be determined if emotional distress resulted in physical injury. . . . Greater proof that mental suffering occurred is found in the defendant's conduct designed to bring it about than in physical injury that may or may not have resulted therefrom." . . . .

Agis v. Howard Johnson Co., 355 N.E.2d 315, 317–18 (Mass. 1976).

Relationship to Negligent Infliction of Emotional Distress. In recent years, some courts have recognized an independent tort action for *negligent* infliction of severe emotional distress. That tort differs from the tort of outrage in several respects, the most important of which is that it may be predicated on conduct that is merely unreasonable, rather than extreme and outrageous. Consequently, the negligence-based action raises heightened concerns about the genuineness of the alleged emotional loss and the risk of imposing liability disproportionate to fault—concerns which are less weighty in cases involving highly egregious conduct. Negligent infliction of emotional distress is examined in Chapter 11.

Four Avenues for Recovery. In summary, compensation for emotional distress is potentially recoverable in at least four different ways: (1) as a "parasitic"[5] claim incidental to a tort involving physical injury; (2) as one element of recovery in an action for certain non-physical-injury torts other than the "tort of outrage" or negligent infliction (*e.g.*, libel, slander, malicious prosecution,[6] assault, false imprisonment, bad faith insurance practices,[7] and others); (3) in an independent action for intentional or reckless infliction of severe emotional distress; or (4) in an independent action for negligent infliction of severe emotional distress.

Harris v. Jones

Court of Appeals of Maryland[8]
380 A.2d 611 (Md. 1977)

MURPHY, Chief Judge.

In Jones v. Harris, 35 Md. App. 556, 371 A.2d 1104 (1977), a case of first impression in Maryland, the Court of Special Appeals . . . recognized intentional infliction of emotional distress as a new and independent tort in this jurisdiction. . . . We granted certiorari to review the decision of the Court of Special Appeals and to decide whether, if intentional infliction of emotional distress is a viable tort in Maryland, the court erred in reversing judgments entered on jury verdicts for the plaintiff. . . .

---

5. "Some . . . authorities [discussing personal injury cases] refer to damages for thought-based suffering as 'parasitic' damages in that the right to recover them is dependent upon liability for another independent or separate tort that acts as host to the damage claims." Fortes v. Ramos, 2001 WL 1685601, *7, n.6 (R.I. Super.). "Damages for emotional distress with a host cause of action, known as 'parasitic' damages, have been recovered even in cases where the independent action giving rise to emotional distress damages is trivial." *See* Sacco v. High Country Independent Press, Inc., 896 P.2d 411, 418 (Mont. 1995).

6. *See* Bhatia v. Debek, 948 A.2d 1009 (Conn. 2008) (affirming a $2.5 million award of emotional distress damages based on malicious prosecution in a case where the plaintiff's former girlfriend had initiated a prosecution of him for allegedly sexually assaulting their child).

7. *See* Dickerson v. Lexington Ins. Co., 556 F.3d 290 (5th Cir. 2009) (allowing an award for mental anguish under a bad faith statute based on untimely payment of a homeowner's policy claim following Hurricane Katrina).

8. In Maryland, the highest state court is the Court of Appeals. The intermediate appellate court is the Court of Special Appeals.

The plaintiff, William R. Harris, a 26-year-old, 8-year employee of General Motors Corporation (GM), sued GM and one of its supervisory employees, H. Robert Jones.... The declaration alleged that Jones, aware that Harris suffered from a speech impediment which caused him to stutter, and also aware of Harris' sensitivity to his disability, and his insecurity because of it, nevertheless "maliciously and cruelly ridiculed ... [him]." It was also alleged in the declaration that Jones' actions occurred within the course of his employment with GM and that GM ratified Jones' conduct.

The evidence at trial showed that Harris stuttered throughout his entire life. While he had little trouble with one syllable words, he had great difficulty with longer words or sentences....

.... Harris worked under Jones' supervision at a GM automobile assembly plant. Over a five-month period, between March and August of 1975, Jones approached Harris over 30 times at work and verbally and physically mimicked his stuttering disability. In addition, two or three times a week during this period, Jones approached Harris and told him, in a "smart manner," not to get nervous. As a result of Jones' conduct, Harris was "shaken up" and "felt like going into a hole and hide."

On June 2, 1975, Harris asked Jones for a transfer to another department; Jones refused, called Harris a "troublemaker" and chastised him for repeatedly seeking the assistance of his committeeman, a representative who handles employee grievances. On this occasion, Jones, "shaking his head up and down" to imitate Harris, mimicked his pronunciation of the word "committeeman," which Harris pronounced "mmitteeman."....

Harris had been under the care of a physician for a nervous condition for six years prior to the commencement of Jones' harassment. He admitted that many things made him nervous, including "bosses." Harris testified that Jones' conduct heightened his nervousness and his speech impediment worsened. He saw his physician on one occasion during the five-month period that Jones was mistreating him; the physician prescribed pills for his nerves.

Harris admitted that other employees at work mimicked his stuttering.... He said that a bad day at work caused him to become more nervous than usual. He admitted that he had problems with supervisors other than Jones, that he had been suspended or relieved from work 10 or 12 times, and that after one such dispute, he followed a supervisor home on his motorcycle, for which he was later disciplined.

Harris' wife testified that her husband was "in a shell" at the time they were married, approximately seven years prior to the trial. She said that it took her about a year to get him to associate with family and friends and that while he still had a difficult time talking, he thereafter became "calmer."....

.... The jury awarded Harris $3,500 compensatory damages and $15,000 punitive damages against both Jones and GM.

In concluding that the intentional infliction of emotional distress, standing alone, may constitute a valid tort action, the Court of Special Appeals relied upon [the] Restatement (Second) of Torts ..., which provides, in pertinent part:

§ 46. Outrageous Conduct Causing Severe Emotional Distress

> (1) One who by extreme and outrageous conduct intentionally or recklessly causes severe emotional distress to another is subject to liability for such emotional distress, and if bodily harm to the other results from it, for such bodily harm.

. . . .

Illustrative of the cases which hold that a cause of action will lie for intentional infliction of emotional distress, unaccompanied by physical injury, is Womack v. Eldridge, 215 Va. 338, 210 S.E.2d 145 (1974). There, the defendant was engaged in the business of investigating cases for attorneys. She deceitfully obtained the plaintiff's photograph for the purpose of permitting a criminal defense lawyer to show it to the victims in several child molesting cases in an effort to have them identify the plaintiff as the perpetrator of the offenses, even though he was in no way involved in the crimes. While the victims did not identify the plaintiff, he was nevertheless questioned by the police, called repeatedly as a witness and required to explain the circumstances under which the defendant had obtained his photograph. As a result, plaintiff suffered shock, mental depression, nervousness and great anxiety as to what people would think of him and he feared that he would be accused of molesting the boys. The court, in concluding that a cause of action had been made out, . . . identified four elements which must coalesce to impose liability for intentional infliction of emotional distress:

> (1) The conduct must be intentional or reckless;
>
> (2) The conduct must be extreme and outrageous;
>
> (3) There must be a causal connection between the wrongful conduct and the emotional distress;
>
> (4) The emotional distress must be severe.

. . . . We agree that the independent tort of intentional infliction of emotional distress should be sanctioned in Maryland, and that by closely adhering to the four elements outlined in *Womack*, two problems which are inherent in recognizing a tort of this character can be minimized: (1) distinguishing the true from the false claim, and (2) distinguishing the trifling annoyance from the serious wrong. . . .

. . . . Section 46 of the Restatement, comment d, states that "Liability has been found only where the conduct has been so outrageous in character, and so extreme in degree, as to go beyond all possible bounds of decency, and to be regarded as atrocious, and utterly intolerable in a civilized community." The comment goes on to state that liability does not extend, however:

> to mere insults, indignities, threats, annoyances, petty oppressions, or other trivialities. The rough edges of our society are still in need of a good deal of filing down, and in the meantime plaintiffs must necessarily be expected and required to be hardened to a certain amount of rough language, and to occasional acts that are definitely inconsiderate and unkind. . . .

Comment f states that the extreme and outrageous character of the conduct "may arise from the actor's knowledge that the other is peculiarly susceptible to emotional distress, by reason of some physical or mental condition or peculiarity." The comment continues:

> The conduct may become heartless, flagrant, and outrageous when the actor proceeds in the face of such knowledge, where it would not be so if he did not know. It must be emphasized . . . that major outrage is essential to the tort. . . .

In his now classic article, *Mental and Emotional Disturbance in the Law of Torts*, 49 Harv. L. Rev. 1033 (1936), Professor Calvert Magruder warned against imposing liability for conduct which is not outrageous and extreme; he observed . . . that "Against a large part of the frictions and irritations and clashing of temperaments incident to participation in a community life, a certain toughening of the mental hide is a better protection than the law could ever be," and . . . he said:

"‥ . . No pressing social need requires that every abusive outburst be converted into a tort; upon the contrary, it would be unfortunate if the law closed all the safety valves through which irascible tempers might legally blow off steam."

In determining whether conduct is extreme and outrageous, it should not be considered in a sterile setting, detached from the surroundings in which it occurred. . . . The personality of the individual to whom the misconduct is directed is also a factor. "There is a difference between violent and vile profanity addressed to a lady, and the same language to a Butte miner and a United States marine." . . . .

. . . [C]ases decided by other courts reflect an application of these principles. For example, in Pakos v. Clark, . . . [453 P.2d 682 (Or. 1969)], the court held that the conduct of a police officer who told the plaintiff that he was crazy as a bedbug and would be put back in an asylum and his children taken from him, and the conduct of another official who puffed up his cheeks and bulged his eyes 7 or 8 times at the plaintiff, was not extreme and outrageous conduct. In Paris v. Division of State Compensation Ins. Funds, 517 P.2d 1353 (Colo. App. 1973), a supervisor delivered a letter of reprimand to the plaintiff, a paraplegic, which contained the statement: "You must realize that your job was created for you because of your handicap." The court there affirmed the trial court's ruling that this conduct was not so outrageous as to support an action for the intentional infliction of emotional distress. . . .

It is for the court to determine, in the first instance, whether the defendant's conduct may reasonably be regarded as extreme and outrageous; where reasonable men may differ, it is for the jury to determine whether, in the particular case, the conduct has been sufficiently extreme and outrageous to result in liability. . . .

In cases where the defendant is in a peculiar position to harass the plaintiff, and cause emotional distress, his conduct will be carefully scrutinized by the courts. . . . Thus, in Alcorn [v. Anbro Engineering, Inc., 468 P.2d 216 (Cal. 1970),] . . . the court referred to comment e of the Restatement, *supra*, § 46, i.e., that the extreme and outrageous character of the defendant's conduct may arise from his abuse of a position, or relation with another person, which gives him actual or apparent authority over him, or power to affect his interests. In that case, the Supreme Court of California said that a plaintiff's status as an employee should entitle him to a greater degree of protection from insult and outrage than if he were a mere stranger. . . .

The Court of Special Appeals found that Jones' conduct was intended to inflict emotional distress and was extreme and outrageous. As to the other elements of the tort, it concluded that the evidence was legally insufficient to establish either that a causal connection existed between Jones' conduct and Harris' emotional distress, or that Harris' emotional distress was severe.

While it is crystal clear that Jones' conduct was intentional, we need not decide whether it was extreme or outrageous, or causally related to the emotional distress which Harris allegedly suffered. The fourth element of the tort—that the emotional distress must be severe—was not established by legally sufficient evidence justifying submission of the case to the jury. That element of the tort requires the plaintiff to show that he suffered a severely disabling emotional response to the defendant's conduct. The severity of the emotional distress is not only relevant to the amount of recovery, but is a necessary element to any recovery. . . . Comment j of § 46 of the Restatement, *supra*, elaborates on this requirement:

> Emotional distress passes under various names, such as mental suffering, mental anguish, mental or nervous shock, or the like. It includes all highly unpleasant mental reactions, such as fright, horror, grief, shame, humiliation, embarrassment, anger, chagrin, disappointment, worry, and nausea. It is only where it is extreme that the liability arises. . . . The intensity and the duration of the distress are factors to be considered in determining its severity. Severe distress must be proved; but in many cases the extreme and outrageous character of the defendant's conduct is in itself important evidence that the distress has existed. . . .
>
> . . . [T]here is no liability where the plaintiff has suffered exaggerated and unreasonable emotional distress, unless it results from a peculiar susceptibility to such distress of which the actor has knowledge.
>
> . . . .

Thus, in Johnson v. Woman's Hospital, 527 S.W.2d 133 (1975), the Court of Appeals of Tennessee found that severe emotional distress was established by evidence showing nervous shock sustained by a mother whose newly born deceased infant was displayed to her in a jar of formaldehyde. *See also* Reeves v. Melton, 518 P.2d 57 (Okl. Ct. App. 1973). In Swanson v. Swanson, 121 Ill. App.2d 182, 257 N.E.2d 194 (1970), the court held that severe emotional distress was not shown by evidence of plaintiff's nervous shock resulting from the deliberate refusal of his brother to inform him of their mother's death, or to publish her obituary.

. . . [W]e find no evidence, legally sufficient for submission to the jury, that the distress was "severe". . . . The evidence that Jones' reprehensible conduct humiliated Harris and caused him emotional distress, which was manifested by an aggravation of Harris' pre-existing nervous condition and a worsening of his speech impediment, was vague and weak at best. It was unaccompanied by any evidentiary particulars other than that Harris, during the period of Jones' harassment, saw his physician on one occasion for his nerves, for which pills were prescribed — the same treatment which Harris had been receiving from his physician for six years prior to Jones' mistreatment. The intensity and duration of Harris' emotional distress is nowhere reflected in the evidence. All that was shown was that Harris was "shaken up" by Jones' misconduct and was so humiliated that he felt "like going into a hole and hide." While Harris' nervous condition may have been exacerbated somewhat by Jones' conduct, his family problems antedated his encounter with Jones and were not shown to be attributable to Jones' actions. Just how, or to what degree, Harris' speech impediment worsened is not revealed by the evidence. Granting the cruel and insensitive nature of Jones' conduct toward Harris, and considering the position of authority which Jones held over Harris, we conclude that the humiliation suffered was not, as a matter of law, so intense as to constitute the "severe" emotional distress required to recover for the tort of intentional infliction of emotional distress.

Judgment affirmed; costs to be paid by appellant.

Notes

1. ***Unendurable-Distress Requirement.*** The Maryland high court is not alone in demanding convincing proof of emotional distress. The plaintiff in Russo v. White, 400 S.E.2d 160 (Va. 1991), alleged that over a period of about two months she had received 340 "hang-up" calls from the defendant. The calls were particularly threatening because of their frequency, because the plaintiff was a single parent of a young child, and because the plaintiff had little basis for judging the defendant's proclivity for violence. The majority held that even if the defendant's conduct rose to the level of outrageousness, liability should be denied. Opining that independent actions for infliction of mental distress are "'not favored' in the law," the court said that "liability arises only when the emotional distress is extreme, and *only where the distress is so severe that no reasonable person could be expected to endure it.*" Applying that standard to the facts of the case, the court wrote:

> The plaintiff has alleged that she was nervous, could not sleep, experienced stress and "its physical symptoms," withdrew from activities, and was unable to concentrate at work. There is no claim, for example, that she had any objective physical injury caused by the stress, that she sought medical attention, that she was confined at home or in a hospital, or that she lost income. Consequently, we conclude that the alleged effect on the plaintiff's sensitivities is not the type of extreme emotional distress that is so severe that no reasonable person could be expected to endure it.

See also Alderson v. Bonner, 132 P.3d 1261 (Idaho Ct. App. 2006) (a woman who was surreptitiously videotaped in various stages of undress by her mother's former supervisor, and who alleged that as a result, she was "embarrassed, ashamed and angry and felt physically ill . . . , will change clothes only in a windowless room, away from windows, or in the dark . . . [and] experienced difficulty trusting males and is fearful walking alone at night," did "not demonstrate the sort of emotional turmoil from which liability can arise"). *But see* Czajkowski v. Meyers, 172 P.3d 94 (Mont. 2007) (permitting recovery where the plaintiff produced evidence that, as a result of extensive verbal abuse and surveillance by a neighbor, she "was fearful, lost countless hours of sleep, lost weight . . . and her hands would shake").

In some states, a claim for intentional infliction of emotional distress must be supported by "competent medical evidence." *See* Cruz *ex rel.* Alvarez v. City of Philadelphia, 2008 WL 4347529, *12 (E.D. Pa. 2008) (discussing Pennsylvania law).

2. ***The Importance of Evidentiary Particulars.*** The severity of the plaintiff's distress must be shown by evidentiary particulars. In Serv. Corp. Int'l v. Guerra, 348 S.W.3d 221 (Tex. 2011), a man was buried at a cemetery in a plot that had been sold to someone else. When his family refused the cemetery's request that it be allowed to move the body to another burial plot, the cemetery did so anyway. In reversing a substantial award of emotional distress damages to the decedent's daughters, in a suit alleging intentional infliction of emotional distress and other claims, the court wrote:

> [The] witnesses generally acknowledged that the Guerra family members experienced very strong emotional reactions that would be expected from the unauthorized moving of a loved one's body. But none of the witnesses, including the daughters themselves, identified a specific "high degree of mental pain and distress" experienced by particular family members, or a substantial disruption of any particular family member's daily routine. The witnesses agreed with the Guerras' attorney that the family generally suffered "devastation," but generalized, conclusory descriptions of how an event affected a person are insufficient evidence on which to base mental anguish damages. . . .

3. ***Egregious-Conduct Requirement.*** Like the requirement that distress be severe, the requirement of "extreme and outrageous conduct" has often been read as imposing an exceptionally demanding standard. In Hamilton v. Ford Motor Credit Co., 502 A.2d 1057 (Md. Ct. Spec. App. 1986), the evidence showed that a debt collector had engaged in a "wide array of objectionable and harassing conduct," including persistent telephone calls and a variety of threats. In holding that the conduct failed to qualify as extreme and outrageous, the court wrote:

> To satisfy that element, conduct must completely violate human dignity. "[E]xtreme and outrageous conduct exists only if 'the average member of the community must regard the defendant's conduct . . . as being a complete denial of the plaintiff's dignity as a person.'" . . . The conduct must strike to the very core of one's being, threatening to shatter the frame upon which one's emotional fabric is hung.

4. ***Compensation versus Deterrence.*** Why should proof of severe harm be required in an action based on the tort of outrage, but not in an action for battery

or assault? The difference is difficult to justify, unless there is reason to deter battery or assault unaccompanied by actual harm, but no similar reason to deter extreme and outrageous conduct unaccompanied by severe emotional distress. Put differently, the emotional distress action, by requiring proof of harm in all cases, seems to be animated more by the goal of compensation than by deterrence. In *Intentional Infliction: Should Section 46 Be Revised?*, 13 Pepperdine L. Rev. 1 (1985), Professor Willard H. Pedrick argued that because deterrence of anti-social conduct is a major objective of the law, a plaintiff should not be required to prove "severe mental distress" in an action based on extreme and outrageous conduct.

A similar argument addressed to workplace harassment was made in Regina Austin, *Employer Abuse, Worker Resistance, and the Tort of Intentional Infliction of Severe Emotional Distress*, 41 Stan. L. Rev. 1, 55 (1988):

> The severe harm requirement of section 46 insulates outrageous supervisory conduct from attack and penalizes those workers who, because of their own personal or social resources, have the strength to withstand abuse.... The emphasis must be on the conduct of the employer, not on the suffering and misery of the aggrieved workers....

5. ***The Role of Motive.*** The defendant's motivation may play a role in the assessment of whether liability will be imposed for intentional or reckless infliction of severe emotional distress. For example, in Burgess v. Perdue, 721 P.2d 239 (Kan. 1986), a doctor failed to relay the plaintiff's statement that she refused permission for an autopsy on her son's brain, and thereafter the procedure was performed. When a second doctor, the plaintiff's son's regular physician, learned what had happened, she contacted the plaintiff and told her that the State hospital had "her son's brain in a jar" and asked what should be done with it. In denying liability for the resulting emotional distress, the court said:

> While the statements made to the mother were probably shocking, they were not outrageous.... The doctor called the mother because she knew the mother had not wanted the brain autopsied. The doctor was concerned that any impropriety be resolved. She did not intend to harass or intimidate or otherwise abuse the mother. No malice was involved.

A similar result was reached, on different grounds, in Ruth v. Fletcher, 377 S.E.2d 412 (Va. 1989). There, Ted alleged that Patty intentionally convinced him that she was pregnant with his child, fostered the development of a bond of love and affection between Ted and the child, caused Ted to pay monthly child support in return for visitation rights, and then, when it suited her purposes, cut off Ted's visitation rights and proved that he was not the child's father, causing Ted severe emotional distress. In reversing a judgment for the plaintiff, the court focused on testimony relating to the defendant's motivation:

> Ted was asked whether he thought Patty had told him he was the father of the child in order deliberately to hurt him. He replied, "I don't think so, not deliberately to hurt me." He also said that when she called to advise him

> of the adoption, she was crying. As she talked to him, she asked him why he was not yelling and screaming. He replied, "Because I can hear in your voice, Patty, this is the hardest thing you have ever done." According to Ted, she answered "You are right. You are absolutely right."
>
> . . . .
>
> We fail to discern from this record any proof that Patty's conduct was "intentional or reckless." . . . .

Arguably, the plaintiff intended to cause Ted's suffering because she "knew" that her revelation of nonpaternity would cause severe emotional distress. A better justification for the *Ruth* court's holding is that, without proof of a scheme to deceive, the defendant's conduct was not shown to have been extreme and outrageous.

6. ***Outrageousness Established.*** Conduct has been found to be extreme and outrageous where:

- A 13-year-old girl who was drugged and raped by an employee of a nonprofit corporation was blamed and abused by the director of the corporation to whom she reported the incident, Crouch v. Trinity Christian Ctr. of Santa Ana, Inc., 253 Cal. Rptr. 3d 1, 13 (Cal. App. 2019) (damages reduced to $900,000);
- An automobile club wrongfully denied a life insurance claim after altering an autopsy report falsely to reflect that plaintiff's wife, who never consumed alcohol during their 46-year marriage, was drunk when she died in a one-car accident, Tidelands Automobile Club v. Walters, 699 S.W.2d 939 (Tex. App. 1985);
- An obstetrician delegated responsibility for a complex premature delivery to an inexperienced resident, resulting in decapitation of the child, Lucchesi v. Frederic N. Stimmell, M.D., Ltd., 716 P.2d 1013 (Ariz. 1986);
- A woman recovering from a miscarriage was falsely informed that an arrest warrant had been issued for her husband, Neufeldt v. L.R. Foy Constr. Co., 693 P.2d 1194 (Kan. 1985); and
- A neighbor harassed an elderly couple by making frequent telephone calls, sending them 1,400 pieces of nuisance mail, operating a strobe light and a lawn mower at night, hanging obscene signs near their property line, placing sharp objects on their driveway, and setting fire to their woods, Welty v. Heggy, 429 N.W.2d 546 (Wis. 1988).

There are also many cases where courts have found alleged facts sufficiently extreme and outrageous as to escape a motion to dismiss. This was true in cases where the defendant allegedly:

- Falsely accused the plaintiff of making a bomb threat, Baez v. JetBlue Airways 745 F. Supp. 2d 214 (E.D. N.Y. 2010) ("as an airline employee in post-9/11 America, . . . [the defendant] knew or should have known that her false accusations would, at the very least, likely subject . . . [the plaintiff] to extensive police interrogation and potentially serious criminal charges");

- Intentionally subjected the plaintiff "to exercises and manipulations intended to render him vulnerable, exploited those vulnerabilities, and, as a result, . . . [the plaintiff] required 'deprogramming' by an expert in cult dynamics," Myers v. Lee, 2010 WL 2757115, *7 (E.D. Va. 2010);
- Made an extremely low settlement offer in a case involving serious damages, Young v. Allstate Ins. Co., 198 P.3d 666 (Hawaii 2008); and
- Harassed the plaintiff with death threats and gunshots near the plaintiff's property line, Levy v. Franks, 159 S.W.3d 66 (Tenn. Ct. App. 2004).

7. ***Outrageousness Wanting***. Extreme and outrageous conduct has been found wanting where:

- Neighbors trapped the plaintiff's cat, which was roaming on their property; turned the cat over to animal control, which exterminated it; and denied knowledge of the cat's whereabouts when the plaintiff inquired about the animal, which she thought was lost, Alvarez v. Clasen, 946 So. 2d 181 (La. Ct. App. 2006);
- A university failed to deal with an employee dispute where one coworker accused another of being fat and said that she did not have children because her husband was "shooting blanks," Morrissey v. Yale University, 844 A.2d 853 (Conn. 2004);
- An employee made false reports to the police about an employer's alleged scalping of professional football tickets and called the police to report that the employer was preventing her from leaving his office, Langeslag v. KYMN, Inc., 664 N.W.2d 860 (Minn. 2003);
- Feuding neighbors retaliated by painting religious slogans on their roof facing the plaintiffs' property, Lybrand v. Trask, 31 P.3d 801 (Alaska 2001);
- A newspaper published a picture of the plaintiff's deceased wife in her coffin, Cox Texas Newspapers v. Wootten, 59 S.W.3d 717 (Tex. App. 2001);
- An employer, in a severe and curt manner, questioned an employee about possible theft, Randall's Food Markets, Inc. v. Johnson, 891 S.W.2d 640 (Tex. 1995);
- A known non-smoker was forced to work in one part of an 1,100-square-foot room in which smoking by two co-workers was permitted, Bernard v. Cameron and Colby Co. Inc., 491 N.E.2d 604 (Mass. 1986); and
- A nuclear power plant was allegedly slow in detecting problems with contradictory dosimeter readings and in reporting the aberrational readings to the Nuclear Regulatory Commission, Caputo v. Boston Edison Co., 924 F.2d 11 (1st Cir. 1991).

8. ***Interference with Child Custody***. Interference with the plaintiff's right to child custody can give rise to an outrage action. *See* In re S.K.H., 324 S.W. 3d 156 (Tex. Ct. App. 2010) (affirming a judgment for intentional infliction of emotional distress against grandparents who had taken possession of their grandchild and concealed the child's whereabouts from the child's mother).

Even if the plaintiff cannot show that the defendant's interference with custody constituted "extreme and outrageous conduct" which caused the plaintiff "severe mental distress," an action may be available under the terms of Restatement, Second, of Torts § 700:

> One who, with knowledge that the parent does not consent, abducts or otherwise compels or induces a minor child to leave a parent legally entitled to its custody or not to return to the parent after it has been left him, is subject to liability to the parent.

9. ***Workplace Distress.*** In GTE Southwest, Inc. v. Bruce, 998 S.W.2d 605 (Tex. 1999), the court opined that an action for intentional infliction of emotional distress will not lie for ordinary employment disputes, which include at "a minimum such things as criticism, lack of recognition, and low evaluations," and that in the workplace "extreme conduct exists only in the most unusual of circumstances." The court, nevertheless, found that demanding standard satisfied where a supervisor's acts of harassment, intimidation, and humiliation, and daily obscene and vulgar behavior, continued over a two-year period. The employer was held liable for the supervisor's actions because they were closely connected to the supervisor's authorized duties.

Interestingly, an employer or supervisor may be in a weaker position than an employee when it comes to asserting a tort of outrage claim. In Langeslag v. KYMN Inc., 664 N.W.2d 860 (Minn. 2003), the court found that, during a 3-year period, Langeslag (an employee) frequently shouted at Eddy (the principal owner of a radio station), used vulgar language, invaded his personal space, threatened to sue him, and filed false reports with the police. In finding that the conduct did not rise to the level of being extreme and outrageous, the court noted that "Eddy could have terminated Langeslag's employment at any time, and thereby put an end to Langeslag's offensive conduct and prevented or mitigated his emotional distress."

2. Abusive Language

The Restatement opines that "liability clearly does not extend to mere insults, indignities, threats, annoyances, petty oppressions, or other trivialities. . . . There must still be freedom to express an unflattering opinion. . . ." Restatement, Second, of Torts § 46 cmt. d. While most courts would probably agree, abusive language may at some point go beyond the "mere[ly] insult[ing]" and warrant liability. This is especially likely if the abusive language is coupled with harmful action.

Slocum v. Food Fair Stores of Florida, Inc.

Supreme Court of Florida
100 So. 2d 396 (Fla. 1958)

DREW, Justice.

This appeal is from an order dismissing a complaint for failure to state a cause of action. Simply stated, the plaintiff sought money damages for mental suffering or emotional distress, and an ensuing heart attack and aggravation of pre-existing heart disease, allegedly caused by insulting language of the defendant's employee directed toward her while she was a customer in its store. Specifically, in reply to her inquiry as to the price of an item he was marking, he replied: "If you want to know the price, you'll have to find out the best way you can . . . you stink to me." She asserts, in the alternative, that the language was used in a malicious or grossly reckless manner, "or with intent to inflict great mental and emotional disturbance to said plaintiff."

. . . [T]he central problem in this case, . . . [is] whether . . . the use of insulting language under the circumstances described, constituted an actionable invasion of a legally protected right. . . .

. . . [I]t is uniformly agreed that the determination of whether words or conduct are actionable in character is to be made on an objective rather than subjective standard, from common acceptation. The unwarranted intrusion must be calculated to cause "severe emotional distress" to a person of ordinary sensibilities, in the absence of special knowledge or notice. There is no inclination to include all instances of mere vulgarities, obviously intended as meaningless abusive expressions. . . .

A broader rule has been developed in a particular class of cases, usually treated as a distinct and separate area of liability originally applied to common carriers. Rest. Torts, per. ed., § 48. The courts have from an early date granted relief for offense reasonably suffered by a patron from insult by a servant or employee of a carrier, hotel, theater, and most recently, a telegraph office. The existence of a special relationship, arising either from contract or from the inherent nature of a non-competitive public utility, supports a right and correlative duty of courtesy beyond that legally required in general mercantile or personal relationships. . . .

. . . [T]here is no impelling reason to extend the rule of the latter cases. . . .

Affirmed.

Notes

1. *See also* Hilton v. Mish, 720 Fed. Appx. 260, 267 (6th Cir. 2018). The court found that "portions of the email calling EH a 'crack and heroin whore'" were "the closest statements to 'extreme and outrageous conduct,'" but were nonactionable "they were only intended to be seen by a single unrelated third party through a private email, and the Hiltons only became aware of the statements by chance roughly a year after they were made." *Id.* at 257.

2. ***Carriers, Innkeepers, and Utilities.*** An exception to the rule on "mere insults" was traditionally recognized in cases involving common carriers, innkeepers, and utilities. During the formative days of tort law, such entities often enjoyed monopoly status, *de jure* (by reason of law) or *de facto* (as a matter of fact). Accordingly, the law held them to a higher standard of care. For example, in Lipman v. Atlantic Coast Line R. Co., 93 S.E. 714 (S.C. 1917), the court ruled that a cause of action was stated where, with intent to cause emotional distress, a train conductor allegedly addressed a passenger "in a rude and angry manner, in the presence of other passengers, [and told him] that he [the passenger] was a lunatic . . . and that he [the conductor] would be glad to give him two black eyes if he were off duty."

This exception to the "mere insult" rule was described in section 48 of the Restatement, Second, of Torts:

> A common carrier or other public utility is subject to liability to patrons utilizing its facilities for gross insults which reasonably offend them, inflicted by the utility's servants while otherwise acting within the scope of their employment.

The drafters of the Third Restatement concluded that few cases had cited this section. Reasoning that "[t]he circumstances of the insult, including the fact that the actor was a servant of a public utility, are factors in determining whether the conduct was extreme and outrageous," the Restatement no longer recognizes an independent rule applicable to carriers and utilities. Restatement, Third, of Torts: Liab. for Physical & Emotional Harm § 46 Reporters' Note cmt. a (2012).

The higher duties sometimes imposed on carriers, innkeepers, and utilities are not limited to protection from insults. *See* Taboada v. Daly Seven, Inc., 626 S.E.2d 428 (Va. 2006) (holding that the "special relationship between an innkeeper and a guest, . . . imposes on the innkeeper . . . [an] elevated duty of 'utmost care and diligence' to protect a guest from . . . the criminal conduct of a third person on the innkeeper's property").

"Common carriers" are businesses which transport persons, goods, or messages for a fee. In California, the term has sometimes been broadly construed. *See* McIntyre v. Smoke Tree Ranch Stables, 23 Cal. Rptr. 339 (Cal. Dist. Ct. App. 1962) (guided tour mule ride); Squaw Valley Ski Corp. v. Superior Ct., 3 Cal. Rptr. 2d 897 (Cal. Ct. App. 1992) (chair lift); Neubauer v. Disneyland, Inc., 875 F. Supp. 672 (C.D. Cal. 1995) ("Pirates of the Caribbean" amusement ride); *but see* Grotheer v. Escape Adventures, Inc., 14 Cal. App. 5th 1283 (2017) (a hot air balloon operator is not a common carrier subject to a higher duty of care).

3. ***Known Sensitivity.*** A second exception to the rule that abusive language is generally not actionable exists where the defendant exploits a known sensitivity of the plaintiff. For example, in LaBrier v. Anheuser Ford, Inc., 612 S.W.2d 790 (Mo. Ct. App. 1981), the evidence showed that the defendant's employees knew that the plaintiff was easily distraught and had previously suffered severe emotional problems. Notwithstanding that knowledge, they appeared at her residence in the presence

of two neighbors and, in a loud and threatening voice, attempted to humiliate and harass the plaintiff, asking the whereabouts of her husband (a salesman for defendant) and his demonstrator automobile, and threatening to have her husband arrested by issuing an "all-points bulletin." The court held that in determining whether the defendant's conduct was extreme and outrageous and whether mental distress was intentionally or recklessly inflicted, the jury could take into account the employees' knowledge of the plaintiff's past emotional problems.

Other cases include: Liberty Mut. Ins. Co. v. Steadman, 968 So. 2d 592 (Fla. Dist. Ct. App. 2007) (finding that the defendants' "nine-month delay in authorizing lung transplant surgery" that a judge had previously directed the corporate defendant to authorize could be found to be extreme and outrageous because the defendants knew that the plaintiff had a very limited life expectancy and that additional distress could hasten her demise); Archer v. Farmer Bros., 70 P.3d 495 (Colo. Ct. App. 2002) (liability imposed where, five days after an employee suffered a heart attack, two supervisors barged into the house where he was staying and fired the employee while he lay partially clothed in bed).

4. ***Ethics in Law Practice: Rudeness by Lawyers and the Litigation Privilege***. The judicial proceedings privilege (discussed in Chapter 22) normally insulates lawyers from civil liability for statements uttered incidental to litigation. *See* Rabinowitz v. Wahrenberger, 966 A.2d 1091 (N.J. Super. A.D. 2009) (rejecting an outrage claim based on questions asked in a deposition).

However, if the lawyer's statements were not, even in a broad sense, pertinent to the issues before the court, or were accompanied by odious in-court or out-of-court conduct, it may be possible to state a claim. *See* Danjczek v. Spencer, 156 F. Supp. 3d 739, 761 (E.D. Va. 2016) (holding that a defense lawyer adequately pled facts from which a jury could conclude that a prosecutor engaged in a "prolonged, vindictive, and multifaceted campaign of misconduct [that] rose to the level of 'outrageous and intolerable' conduct").

Of course, a lawyer's use of extreme language may have consequences other than civil liability. In Mobley Law Firm PA v. Lisle Law Firm PA, 120 S.W.3d 537 (Ark. 2003), a lawyer who neglected a client's case responded to the client's anxiety about the apparent lack of progress by stating "I don't have a speedometer up my ass." The court found that statement "shocking" and relied on it as a reason for holding that the attorney was fired for cause and was not entitled to his full contractual fee.

In Comuso v. National Railroad Passenger Corp., 2000 WL 502707 (E.D. Pa.), an attorney who threatened to kill the defendant and uttered various profanities in the courtroom was disqualified from further participation in the matter, assessed fees and costs, and reported to disciplinary authorities.

5. ***Statutory Relief for Insults***. Even if insulting language is insufficient to support an action under the tort of outrage, relief may be available pursuant to statute. In a few jurisdictions, statutes create a civil remedy for insulting words tending to provoke a breach of the peace. For example:

Virginia Code Annotated § 8.01-45 (Westlaw 2022)

> All words shall be actionable which from their usual construction and common acceptance are construed as insults and tend to violence and breach of the peace.

See also Miss. Code Ann. § 95-1-1 (Westlaw 2022) (similar); W. Va. Code § 55-7-2 (Westlaw 2022) (similar). Such an action is subject to the constitutional limitations which have been imposed in recent years on suits for defamatory libel or slander. *See* Chapter 22.

3. Domestic Violence and Harassment

If spouse abuse does not amount to battery or assault, should it be actionable under the tort of outrage?

Feltmeier v. Feltmeier

Supreme Court of Illinois
798 N.E.2d 75 (Ill. 2003)

Justice RARICK delivered the opinion of the court:

Plaintiff, Lynn Feltmeier, and defendant, Robert Feltmeier, were married on October 11, 1986, and divorced on December 16, 1997. The judgment for dissolution of marriage incorporated the terms of a December 10, 1997, marital settlement agreement. On August 25, 1999, Lynn sued Robert for the intentional infliction of emotional distress. According to the allegations contained in the complaint, Robert engaged in a pattern of domestic abuse, both physical and mental in nature, which began shortly after the marriage and did not cease even after its dissolution.

.... The [intermediate] appellate court concluded that Lynn, as plaintiff, could "maintain an action at law to recover monetary damages...." ....

The first matter ... is whether Lynn's complaint states a cause of action for intentional infliction of emotional distress....

According to the ... complaint, since the parties' marriage in October 1986, and continuing for over a year after the December 1997 dissolution of their marriage: ... [Robert entered into a continuous and outrageous course of conduct toward Lynn] ..., including ... on repeated occasions: battering Lynn by striking, kicking, shoving, pulling hair and bending and twisting her limbs and toes; preventing Lynn from leaving the house to escape the abuse; yelling insulting and demeaning epithets at Lynn; engaging in verbal abuse which included threats and constant criticism of Lynn in such a way as to demean, humiliate, and degrade her; throwing items at Lynn with the intent to cause her harm; attempting to isolate Lynn from her family and friends; getting very upset if Lynn would show the marks and bruises resulting from Robert's abuse to others; and, since the divorce, engaging in stalking behavior.

... Robert first contends that the allegations ... do not sufficiently set forth conduct which was extreme and outrageous when considered "[i]n the context of the subjective and fluctuating nature of the marital relationship." ... Robert cites several cases from other jurisdictions.... In Pickering v. Pickering, 434 N.W.2d 758, 761 (S.D.1989), the Supreme Court of South Dakota held that the tort of intentional infliction of emotional distress should be unavailable as a matter of public policy when predicated on conduct which leads to the dissolution of a marriage. However, unlike the case at bar, the conduct serving as the basis for the tort in *Pickering* was the wife's extramarital affair, and the court noted that South Dakota law already provided a remedy for this type of claim in the form of an action against the paramour for alienation of affections.... Next, Robert cites Hakkila v. Hakkila, ... [812 P.2d 1320, 1327 (N.M. Ct. App.1991)], in which the Court of Appeals of New Mexico found that a husband's insults and occasional violent outbursts over the course of the parties' 10-year marriage were insufficiently outrageous to establish liability for intentional infliction of emotional distress....

Finally, Robert cites a Texas case, Villasenor v. Villasenor, 911 S.W.2d 411, 415 n. 2 (Tex. App. 1995), wherein the court, in *dicta,* noted that because the marital relationship "'is highly subjective and constituted by mutual understandings and interchanges which are constantly in flux[,]' ... [f]or purposes of determining outrageous conduct, the insults, indignities, threats, annoyances, petty oppressions, or other trivialities associated with marriage and divorce must be considered upon the individual facts of each case." .... [W]hile we agree that special caution is required in dealing with actions for intentional infliction of emotional distress arising from conduct occurring within the marital setting, our examination of both the law ... and the most commonly raised policy concerns leads us to conclude that no valid reason exists to restrict such actions or to require a heightened threshold for outrageousness in this context.

One policy concern that has been advanced is the need to recognize the "mutual concessions implicit in marriage," and the desire to preserve marital harmony. *See* Henriksen v. Cameron, 622 A.2d 1135, 1138–39 (Me.1993). However, in this case, brought after the parties were divorced, "there is clearly no marital harmony remaining to be preserved." .... Moreover, we agree with the Supreme Judicial Court of Maine that "behavior that is 'utterly intolerable in a civilized society' and is intended to cause severe emotional distress is not behavior that should be protected in order to promote marital harmony and peace." ....

Indeed, the Illinois legislature, in creating the Illinois Domestic Violence Act of 1986 (Act) (750 ILCS 60/101 *et seq.* (West 2002)), has recognized that domestic violence is "a serious crime against the individual and society" and that "the legal system has ineffectively dealt with family violence in the past, allowing abusers to escape effective prosecution or financial liability." .... However, ... while the Act created the crime of domestic battery and "provides a number of remedies in an effort to protect abused spouses and family members, it did not create a civil cause of action to remedy the damages done." .... Thus, it would seem that the public policy of this state would be furthered by recognition of the action at issue.

A second policy concern is the threat of excessive and frivolous litigation if the tort is extended to acts occurring in the marital setting.... However, we believe that the showing required of a plaintiff in order to recover damages for intentional infliction of emotional distress provides a built-in safeguard against excessive and frivolous litigation....

Another policy consideration ... is that a tort action for compensation would be redundant. However, ... [a]n action for dissolution of marriage also provides no compensatory relief for domestic abuse.... In Illinois, as in most other states, courts are not allowed to consider marital misconduct in the distribution of property when dissolving a marriage. *See* 750 ILCS 5/503(d) (West 2002).

After examining case law from courts around the country, we find the majority have recognized that public policy considerations should not bar actions for intentional infliction of emotional distress between spouses or former spouses based on conduct occurring during the marriage....

... Illinois cases in which the tort of intentional infliction of emotional distress has been sufficiently alleged have very frequently involved a defendant who stood in a position of power or authority relative to the plaintiff.... While these past cases have generally involved abuses of power by employers, creditors, or financial institutions, we see no reason to exclude the defendant at issue here, a spouse/former spouse, from the many types of individuals who may be positioned to exercise power over a plaintiff. *See* D. Poplar, *Tolling the Statute of Limitations for Battered Women After Giovine v. Giovine: Creating Equitable Exceptions for Victims of Domestic Abuse,* 101 Dick. L. Rev. 161, 170, 175 (1996) (many battered women remain in an abusive relationship because they are economically dependent upon their spouses, they fear for the well-being of their children, or fear that leaving will only encourage their spouses to commit more severe violence; indeed, constant physical and mental abuse causes a battered woman to develop a belief in the strength and omnipotence of her abuser).

....

In the instant case, ... when the ... allegations of the complaint are viewed in their entirety, they show a type of domestic abuse that is extreme enough to be actionable....

It is equally clear ... that Robert either intended to inflict, or knew that his conduct was likely to inflict, severe emotional distress upon Lynn. However, Robert does contest the adequacy of the complaint as to the third necessary element, that his conduct in fact caused severe emotional distress. He argues that Lynn's complaint "contains no factual allegations from which the level of severity of the emotional distress could be inferred." We must disagree.

Lynn's complaint specifically alleges that, "[a]s a direct and proximate result of the entirety of [Robert's] course of conduct, [she] has sustained severe emotional distress including, but not limited to[,] loss of self-esteem and difficulty in forming other relationships, and a form of Post Traumatic Stress Disorder sustained by battered and abused women as a result of being repeatedly physically and verbally abused and harassed over a long period of time." The complaint also alleges that Lynn has suffered depression and a "fear of being with other men," and that her enjoyment of life has been substantially curtailed. Finally, it is alleged that Lynn has incurred, and will continue to incur, medical and psychological expenses in an effort to become cured or relieved from the effects of her mental distress.

. . . .

The second certified question we examine is whether Lynn's claim for intentional infliction of emotional distress based on conduct prior to August 25, 1997, is barred by the applicable statute of limitations. Robert contends that each separate act of abuse triggered a new statute of limitations so that "all claims by Lynn based upon incidents occurring prior to August 25, 1997," or more than two years before the date on which Lynn filed her complaint, would be time-barred. Lynn responds that Robert's actions constitute a "continuing tort" for purposes of the statute of limitations and that her complaint, filed within two years of the occurrence of the last such tortious act, is therefore timely. . . .

. . . . We agree that the applicable statute of limitations for intentional infliction of emotional distress is two years, because the tort is a form of personal injury. . . . The ultimate question, however, is when the statute of limitations began to run in the instant case.

Generally, a limitations period begins to run when facts exist that authorize one party to maintain an action against another. . . . However, under the "continuing tort" or "continuing violation" rule, "where a tort involves a continuing or repeated injury, the limitations period does not begin to run until the date of the last injury or the date the tortious acts cease." . . . .

. . . Robert . . . maintains that "each of the alleged acts of abuse inflicted by Robert upon Lynn over a 12 year period are separate and distinct incidents which give rise to separate and distinct causes of action, rather than one single, continuous, unbroken, violation or wrong which continued over the entire period of 12 years." We must disagree. While it is true that the conduct set forth in Lynn's complaint could be considered separate acts constituting separate offenses of, *inter alia,* assault, defamation and battery, Lynn has alleged, and we have found, that Robert's conduct *as a whole* states a cause of action for intentional infliction of emotional distress. . . .

. . . [W]e find the case of Pavlik v. Kornhaber, . . . [761 N.E.2d 175 (Ill. App. Ct. 2001)], to be instructive. In *Pavlik,* the court first found that plaintiff's complaint stated a cause of action for intentional infliction of emotional distress, where the defendant's persistent notes, sexually explicit comments, insistence on meetings to discuss his desire for sexual contact and lewd behavior in their employer-employee relationship were such that a reasonable person would perceive them to be sufficiently offensive and sinister to rise to the level of extreme and outrageous behavior.... The court in *Pavlik* then found that the trial court had erred in dismissing the plaintiff's claim as untimely. While the defendant argued that his sexual advances took place outside the two-year statute of limitations for personal injury, the plaintiff had alleged an ongoing campaign of offensive and outrageous sexual pursuit that established a continuing series of tortious behavior, by the same actor, and of a similar nature, such that the limitations period did not commence until the last act occurred or the conduct abated....

We find the following passage, wherein the *Pavlik* court explains its reasons for applying the continuing tort rule to the plaintiff's action for intentional infliction of emotional distress, to be particularly cogent:

> Illinois courts have said that in many contexts, including employment, repetition of the behavior may be a critical factor in raising offensive acts to actionably outrageous ones.... It may be the pattern, course and accumulation of acts that make the conduct sufficiently extreme to be actionable, whereas one instance of such behavior might not be.... It would be logically inconsistent to say that each act must be independently actionable while at the same time asserting that often it is the cumulative nature of the acts that give rise to the intentional infliction of emotional distress. Likewise, we cannot say that cumulative continuous acts may be required to constitute the tort but that prescription runs from the date of the first act.... Because it is impossible to pinpoint the specific moment when enough conduct has occurred to become actionable, the termination of the conduct provides the most sensible place to begin the running of the prescriptive period.

....

The purpose behind a statute of limitations is to prevent stale claims, not to preclude claims before they are ripe for adjudication....

Therefore, ... the continuing tort rule should be extended to apply in cases of intentional infliction of emotional distress.

... [E]mbracing the concept of a continuing tort in the area of intentional infliction of emotional distress "does not throw open the doors to permit filing these actions at any time." .... As with any continuing tort, the statute of limitations is only held in abeyance until the date of the last injury suffered or when the tortious acts cease. Thus, we find that the two-year statute of limitations for this action began to run in August 1999, because Lynn's complaint includes allegations of tortious behavior by Robert occurring as late as that month. Applying the continuing tort rule to the instant case, Lynn's complaint, filed August 25, 1999, was clearly timely and her claims based on conduct prior to August 25, 1997, are not barred by the applicable statute of limitations.

....

The third certified question is whether Lynn's claim against Robert for intentional infliction of emotional distress has been released by the language of their marital settlement agreement. Robert argues that two provisions within the agreement operate to release him from liability.[9] . . . [W]e believe, as did the appellate court, that "the question can be simply answered in the negative in light of our holding on the continuing-tort theory." . . . .

The marital settlement agreement was executed by the parties on December 11, 1997. We have found that Lynn's cause of action did not accrue until the date of the last tortious act, in August 1999. It is clear that a contractual release cannot be construed to include claims not within the contemplation of the parties, and it will not be extended to cover claims that may arise in the future. . . . *See also* Farm Credit Bank of St. Louis v. Whitlock, 581 N.E.2d 664 (Ill. 1991) (a general release is inapplicable to an unknown claim). Indeed, "a release covering all claims that might later arise between the parties 'would constitute a consent to the foregoing of legal protection for the future and would plainly be against public policy.'". . . . Thus, we agree with the appellate court's conclusion that "[a] release with very general boilerplate language, such as the two provisions at issue, cannot be construed to release future causes of action between the parties." . . . .

. . . . The appellate court's judgment is . . . affirmed.

Notes

1. ***Continuing Tort Doctrine.*** In Harvey v. Merchan, 860 S.E.2d 561 (Ga. 2021), the plaintiff alleged that the "continuing tort" theory should apply to her cause of action because she was subjected to continuous and repeated sexual abuse on a weekly, if not daily, basis from birth until she left the family home at the age of 22. The Supreme Court of Georgia disagreed because "every instance of alleged abuse constituted a discrete tort, and the continuing tort doctrine does not apply to situations in which each injury is known to the victim at the time the wrong was inflicted." *Id.* at 568.

---

9. Paragraph 8(a) of the agreement provided in part:

"To the fullest extent by law permitted to do so, . . . each of the parties does hereby forever . . . waive . . . all . . . tort claims . . . by reason of the marital relations existing between the parties hereto, under any present or future law, . . . and each party further . . . agrees . . . that neither of them will at any time hereafter sue the other . . . for the purpose of enforcing any of the rights . . . relinquished under this paragraph 8(a), and further agrees that in the event any suit shall be commenced, this release, when pleaded, shall be and constitute a complete defense. . . .

Paragraph 8(d) provided in part:

"[Except as herein otherwise provided, and to the fullest extent that they may lawfully do so, all the rights, claims, and demands of every kind, nature, and description which each party has, or may hereafter have, or claim to have against the other shall be and the same hereby are forever discharged . . . and all matters and charges whatsoever, and any and all . . . causes of actions, . . . which each party ever had or now has or which he or she . . . hereafter can, shall, or may have against the other . . . for . . . any cause . . . whatsoever, from the beginning of the world to the effective date hereof, shall be and the same are extinguished.]" — Ed. (*see* 777 N.E.2d at 1044–45 (Ill. App. Ct. 2000).

In Pierce v. Cook, 992 So. 2d 612 (Miss. 2008), an attorney represented a husband, wife, and son on a medical malpractice claim. During the course of the representation, the attorney had an adulterous affair with the wife. The husband then sued on a variety of theories and won a judgment for $1.5 million. In affirming the award, the Mississippi Supreme Court held that the outrage claim was not time-barred because the defendant attorney had committed a continuing tort. The majority wrote:

> "A 'continuing tort' is one inflicted over a period of time; it involves a wrongful conduct that is repeated until desisted, and each day creates a separate cause of action. . . ."
>
> . . . . Cook [the aggrieved former client] testified to several wrongful acts by Pierce [the defendant attorney], that occurred until the divorce, which constituted repeated wrongful conduct, causing Cook emotional distress. Not only did Pierce take Kathleen on a trip to New Orleans during which they had sexual relations, but Pierce flaunted his involvement with Kathleen in front of Cook at a local restaurant in Jackson. Furthermore, there is tape-recorded evidence in which Pierce's voice is in the background clearly "coaching" Kathleen concerning what to say to Cook. Pierce himself called Cook on his birthday, allegedly apologizing for the situation with Kathleen. Based on this evidence, the Court finds there was repeated wrongful contact by Pierce. We thus find that the trial court did not err in tolling the statute of limitations until the date of the divorce decree. . . .

2. ***Spouse Abuse.*** *See* Christians v. Christians, 637 N.W.2d 377 (S.D. 2001) (permitting an outrage action based on a husband's conduct after the filing of a divorce, which included accusing his wife of child abuse, having the child repeatedly examined by law enforcement authorities, and causing his wife to lose her job); McCulloh v. Drake, 24 P.3d 1162 (Wyo. 2001) (holding that "extreme and outrageous conduct by one spouse which results in severe emotional distress to the other spouse should not be ignored by virtue of the marriage of the victim to the aggressor and . . . that such behavior can create an independent cause of action"); Twyman v. Twyman, 855 S.W.2d 619, 620 n.1 (Tex. 1993) (permitting an action incidental to divorce where the husband subjected his wife to sadomasochistic bondage activities, knowing that she feared such activities because she had been raped at knife-point before their marriage).

At least one state has opted to recognize a separate tort for "battered woman's syndrome." *See* Giovine v. Giovine, 663 A.2d 109 (N.J. Super. Ct. App. Div. 1995).

The law's abhorrence for domestic violence is reflected in the fact that, in some states, such actions enjoy a longer statute of limitations.

MICHIGAN STATUTES ANNOTATED § 600.5805 (Westlaw 2022)

. . . .

(2) The period of limitations is 2 years for an action charging assault, battery, or false imprisonment.

> (3) The period of limitations is 5 years for an action charging assault or battery brought by a person who has been assaulted or battered by his or her spouse or former spouse, an individual with whom he or she has had a child in common, or a person with whom he or she resides or formerly resided. . . .
>
> (4) The period of limitations is 5 years for an action charging assault and battery brought by a person who has been assaulted or battered by an individual with whom he or she has or has had a dating relationship. . . .

Until the recent rise of feminist legal theory, the law often ignored domestic violence. *See* Jennifer B. Wriggins, *Toward a Feminist Revision of Torts*, 13 J. Gender, Soc. Pol'y & L. 139, 155 (2005) (reporting that a review of thousands of cases revealed only 34 tort cases dealing with domestic violence).

3. ***Racial and Ethnic Harassment.*** In Contreras v. Crown Zellerbach Corp., 565 P.2d 1173 (Wash. 1977), a case involving the use of ethnic epithets, the court held that the plaintiff's membership in a particular ethnic group could be taken into account in determining whether the defendant's conduct was extreme and outrageous. Nevertheless, it may be difficult to succeed on an outrage claim predicated mainly on racial or ethnic slurs. *See* Walker v. Thompson, 214 F.3d 615 (5th Cir. 2000) (racist remarks did not amount to intentional infliction of emotional distress).

It may make a difference whether racial or ethnic abuse occurs on one occasion or on many. *Compare* Colon v. Wal-Mart Stores, Inc., 703 N.Y.S.2d 863 (Sup. Ct. 1999) ("isolated ethnic epithet"), *with* Weathers v. Marshalls of MA, Inc., 2002 WL 1770927 (E.D. La.) (constant racial epithets).

Should the question whether the words are extreme and outrageous be judged under an objective standard or a subjective standard? That is, should the issue be whether an ordinary member of the community would regard the conduct as extreme and outrageous, or whether a person in the plaintiff's position would have regarded the language as extreme and outrageous? *See* Jean C. Love, *Discriminatory Speech and the Tort of Intentional Infliction of Emotional Distress*, 47 Wash. & Lee L. Rev. 123, 147–53 (1990) ("there are reported cases of racial, ethnic, and religious epithets in which the victim's claim has been dismissed, even though members of the minority community to which the plaintiff belongs surely would have exclaimed, 'Outrageous'!").

4. ***Sexual Assault and Harassment.*** Evidence of sexual assault may be sufficient to form the basis of an action for intentional or reckless infliction of severe emotional distress. *See* Chancellor v. Pottsgrove School Dist., 501 F. Supp. 2d 695 (E.D. Pa. 2007) (holding that a band teacher's ten-month sexual relationship with a student could support a claim); K.M. v. Alabama Dept. of Youth Services, 360 F. Supp. 2d 1253 (M.D. Ala. 2005) (insertion of a finger into juvenile detainee's vagina was actionable).

However, sexual harassment not involving an assault is often not actionable under the tort of outrage. *See* Capriotti v. Chivukula, 2005 WL 83253 (E.D. Pa. 2005) (stating that "[s]exual harassment alone does not generally rise to the level of outrageousness necessary to constitute intentional infliction of emotional distress" and finding that no claim was stated based on allegations of a sexually hostile work environment); Bailey v. Fed. Home Loan Bank of Topeka, 1998 WL 982900 (D. Kan.) (conduct was not outrageous where a supervisor referred to the female workers as "gals," occasionally stared inappropriately at female workers, and took female workers to a restaurant called "Hooters"); Lahr v. Fulbright & Jaworski, L.L.P., 1996 WL 673438 (N.D. Tex.) (even if conduct can be said to constitute sexual harassment, the standard for intentional infliction of emotional distress is higher).

In Dillard Dept. Stores v. Gonzalez, 72 S.W.3d 398 (Tex. App. 2002), the court held that the evidence was insufficient to support a finding that the actions of a male employee's former supervisor constituted intentional infliction of emotional distress where the supervisor hugged the employee, called him pet names, made off-color remarks implying homosexuality, and leaned against the employee.

However, there is precedent that an employer who fosters a corporate culture that allows a manager to sexually harass employees is subject to liability. *See* Manning v. Metropolitan Life Ins., 127 F.3d 686 (8th Cir. 1997) (whether employer's alleged acts of tolerating various forms of sexual harassment by a supervisor and coworker constituted the tort of outrage, under Arkansas law, was a question for the jury); *but see* Hoffman-La Roche, Inc. v. Zeltwanger, 144 S.W.3d 438 (Tex. 2004) (a handful of instances of off-color jokes being told among a large number of employees over a period of several years was legally insufficient to show that an employer fostered a corporate culture that allowed managers to sexually harass employees).

Today, claims of sexual harassment in the workplace are often litigated under Title VII of the Civil Rights Act of 1964, which creates a federal statutory action for sex-based discrimination. In Creditwatch, Inc. v. Jackson, 157 S.W.3d 814 (Tex. 2005), the Texas Supreme Court held that availability of state statutory remedies for sexual harassment precluded an emotional distress claim for such conduct. The difficulty of successfully suing for the tort of outrage is suggested by the fact that the opinion in *Creditwatch* began by noting "[f]or the tenth time in little more than six years, we must reverse an intentional infliction of emotional distress claim for failing to meet the exacting requirements of that tort."

Decisions like *Creditwatch* have been criticized by scholars who argue that the boundary between torts and civil rights laws needs to be re-thought in order to compensate the recurrent injuries that are experienced disproportionately by marginalized groups. *See* Martha Chamallas & Jennifer B. Wriggins, The Measure of Injury: Race, Gender, and Tort Law 20–21 (2010), *reviewed in* Vincent R. Johnson, *On Race, Gender, and Radical Tort Reform*, 17 Wm. & Mary J. Women & Law 591 (2011).

Does failure to investigate and respond promptly to an employee's complaint of sexual harassment itself constitute outrageous conduct? Probably not. *See* Martin v. Baer, 928 F.2d 1067 (11th Cir. 1991) (holding that failure to investigate rumors of sexual harassment was at most a negligent omission); Ammon v. Baron Automotive Group, 270 F. Supp. 2d 1293 (D. Kan. 2003) (not extreme and outrageous).

Is it extreme and outrageous to make false allegations of sexual harassment? Henderson v. Wellman, 43 S.W.3d 591 (Tex. App. 2001), held that false allegations and other conduct failed to rise to the required level of egregiousness.

5. ***Stalking.*** On appropriate facts, stalking might support an action for the tort of outrage. However, in some states there are statutory remedies. *See* Veile v. Martinson, 258 F.3d 1180 (10th Cir. 2001) (affirming a judgment in a statutory action where a funeral home owner was stalked by a competitor).

6. ***Debt Collection.*** A creditor may take reasonable steps to collect a debt, even though the effort is likely to cause the debtor severe emotional distress. *See* MacDermid v. Discover Financial Services, 342 Fed. Appx. 138 (6th Cir. 2009) (holding that because probable cause existed to prosecute a credit card applicant for unauthorized use and possession of a credit card, which she had requested be issued in her husband's name without his consent, a credit card company's threats of criminal prosecution against the applicant were justified and could not amount to outrageous conduct, even though the applicant committed suicide allegedly due to the company's harassing debt collection efforts).

In some cases, however, unwarrantedly oppressive debt collection practices have supported successful actions under the tort of outrage. *See, e.g.*, Turman v. Central Billing Bureau, 568 P.2d 1382 (Or. 1977) (a blind woman was subjected to repeated telephone calls).

Nevertheless, as a remedy for debt collection abuses, the tort of outrage has been largely superseded by the terms of the federal Fair Debt Collection Practices Act, 15 U.S.C. §§1692A–1692K (Westlaw 2022) (FDCPA). The Act provides for administrative enforcement of its provisions and also permits persons injured by an intentional violation of its terms to maintain a civil cause of action against an offending debt collector for actual damages (including emotional distress), costs and attorney fees, and, in the case of an individual plaintiff, additional damages not exceeding $1,000. *Id.* at §1692k. By proceeding under the civil remedy provisions of the FDCPA, rather than under the tort of outrage, a plaintiff can avoid the necessity of proving "extreme and outrageous conduct" or intolerably "severe mental distress." In cases falling outside of the statute, it is still possible to sue for outrage. *See* MacDermid v. Discover Financial Services, 488 F.3d 721 (6th Cir. 2007) (action stated against a credit card company that "threatened criminal prosecution, without a proper basis, to collect a purely *civil* debt").

The Fair Debt Collection Practices Act is a good example of the law's tendency to replace common-law developments with statutory "solutions." Some states have also enacted debt-collection laws. *See* Hamilton v. Ford Motor Credit Co., 502 A.2d 1057 (Md. Ct. Spec. App. 1986) (holding that an action was stated under the Maryland statute even though the facts failed to establish a claim for intentional or reckless infliction of severe emotional distress).

7. ***Ethics in Law Practice: Collections Work.*** The requirements of the Fair Debt Collection Practices Act apply to any attorney or law firm that "regularly" collects debts on behalf of third parties. *See* Heintz v. Jenkins, 514 U.S. 291 (1995); *see also* Eads v. Wolpoff & Abramson, LLP, 538 F. Supp. 2d 981 (W.D. Tex. 2008) (finding that a debtor stated claims against a law firm under the FDCPA); Nielsen v. Dickerson, 307 F.3d 623 (7th Cir. 2002) (attorney liable for misleading nature of debt collection letters sent on creditor's behalf).

In mandating fair treatment of third persons, the FDCPA is consistent with state rules of attorney ethics patterned on the American Bar Association's Model Rules of Professional Conduct (Westlaw 2022). Rule 4.4 provides:

> In representing a client, a lawyer shall not use means that have no substantial purpose other than to embarrass, delay, or burden a third person, or use methods of obtaining evidence that violate the legal rights of such a person.

Amplifying this provision, the comment to Rule 4.4 says that "Responsibility to a client requires a lawyer to subordinate the interests of others to those of the client, but that responsibility does not imply that a lawyer may disregard the rights of third persons."

Section 1692c(a)(2) of the FDCPA prohibits a debt collector from communicating with a debtor who is represented by an attorney, unless the attorney fails to respond to the collector within a reasonable period of time, or unless the attorney permits direct communications with the debtor. A similar obligation is imposed on attorneys by most state ethics codes. *See* Model Rules of Professional Conduct Rule 4.2 (Westlaw 2022). Consequently, an attorney who engages in impermissible communication with a represented debtor may be subject both to an action for damages under the FDCPA and to professional discipline, such as reprimand, suspension, or disbarment.

4. Bystanders and Third Persons

Extraordinarily difficult questions can arise with respect to whether a plaintiff may recover for outrageous conduct not "directed at" the plaintiff, but at someone else. For example, can a parent state a claim against the person who sexually abuses the parent's young child? What about a girl whose boyfriend is murdered? Or family members who discover father's mutilated body dumped on the front porch? Or a person who unexpectedly receives an alarming phone message intended for another?

Courts are often reluctant to recognize "third-party" claims. For example, in Bettis v. Islamic Republic of Iran, 315 F.3d 325 (D.C. Cir. 2003), the court held that the nieces and nephews of a victim who was kidnapped and tortured by a state-sponsored terrorist group could not recover on a tort of outrage claim because the conduct was not directed at them and they were not members of the victim's immediate family.

In Alderson v. Bonner, 132 P.3d 1261 (Idaho Ct. App. 2006), the defendant was apprehended outside the plaintiff's residence with a video camera containing surreptitiously made tapes of the plaintiff's mother and sister in various stages of undress, which were filmed at a different residence. The court rejected the plaintiff's outrage claim, noting that the defendant's act of standing on the plaintiff's front porch, looking through an uncovered window, was not so extreme or outrageous as to state a claim, and that the plaintiff had failed to prove that the filming at a different location was a violation of *her* rights.

In thinking about bystanders and third parties, it is essential to focus on the culpability requirement of an outrage action. The tort may be intentionally *or recklessly* committed. Therefore, it is useful to ask whether the defendant acted with a purpose of causing the plaintiff emotional distress, with substantial certainty that such distress would occur, or with reckless indifference to circumstances highly likely to precipitate distress for the plaintiff (or at least for the class of persons of which the plaintiff is a member). If any of those types of culpability is established, an argument can be made that liability should be imposed.

In Dragna v. New Orleans La. Saints, L.L.C., 2018 WL 4997670, at *1 (La. App.), the plaintiff filed suit against the Saints, seeking rescission of his season ticket sale and other damages. The court rejected a claim for intentional infliction of emotional distress, because the plaintiff alleged merely that some players refused to take the field until after the National Anthem was played, causing many fans to boo and curse the Saints players. What was the strongest ground for ruling against the plaintiff? Lack of culpability? Lack of extreme and outrageous conduct? Lack of intolerably severe emotional distress?

Purpose. If another person is seriously harmed *for the purpose* of causing the plaintiff emotional distress, establishing liability should not be difficult. In that case, the defendant acted with the purpose variety of intent. Thus, a mother who disfigures her child for the purpose of torturing the child's father is subject to liability to the father for his emotional distress (and, of course, to the child, too). *See* Restatement, Third, of Torts: Liab. for Physical & Emotional Harm § 46 illus. 12 (2012).

Knowledge. If a person is physically harmed when the plaintiff is known to be present, it might reasonably be urged that the attacker was substantially certain that the plaintiff would suffer emotional distress and should be held responsible. This would seem to be true at least in cases where the victim and the plaintiff are related. The Third Restatement says that "[c]ourts generally have limited the potential scope of liability for emotional harm to bystanders present at the time of the tortious conduct who are also close family members of the victim." Restatement, Third, of Torts: Liab. for Physical & Emotional Harm § 46 cmt. i (2012). Allowing recovery in such situations is generally consistent with the law of negligent infliction of emotional distress (*see* Chapter 11). Many jurisdictions (but not all) recognize a claim for emotional distress based on negligence if a (1) family member, (2) in close proximity, (3) witnesses the death or serious physical injury of a loved one.

A question can be raised as to whether the Third Restatement goes too far in limiting recovery to close family members. Suppose that a gang leader enters a grade school classroom and stabs the teacher numerous times in front of the teacher's impressionable young students. It is hard to believe that students who suffer severe emotional distress as a result of the attack would be denied recovery on the ground that they were not related to the teacher. The Second Restatement clearly allowed the possibility of recovery by non-family members. It stated:

> [T]here appears to be no essential reason why a stranger who is asked for a match on the street should not recover when the man who asks for it is shot down before his eyes. . . .
>
> Illustration:
>
> 21. In the presence of A, a bystander, B quarrels violently with C, draws a pistol, and threatens to kill C. B knows that A is pregnant, and that it is highly probable that his conduct will cause severe emotional distress to A. A suffers severe emotional distress, which results in a miscarriage. B is subject to liability to A.

Restatement, Second, of Torts § 46 cmt. l.

Recklessness. In Taylor v. Vallelunga, 339 P.2d 910 (Cal. Dist. Ct. App. 1959), a young girl who watched her father being brutally beaten by attackers on Christmas day was denied recovery. At the time, the result arguably made sense because the tort of outrage was still defined in exclusively intentional terms, and the attacker had been unaware of the girl's presence. Without knowledge of the plaintiff's presence, it was probably impossible to show that the girl was substantially certain (certain for all practical purposes) to suffer emotional distress. (Indeed, as far as the opinion in *Taylor* reflects, the defendant was unaware that the victim even had a daughter.)

The tort of outrage now encompasses recklessness, as well as intentionally tortious conduct. "Courts uniformly hold that reckless conduct . . . can support a claim." Restatement, Third, of Torts: Liab. for Physical & Emotional Harm § 46 cmt. h (2012). Thus, it is reasonable to suggest that the result in *Taylor* would be different today. The cases that allow parents to recover for the sexual abuse of their children often can be explained on the ground that the abuser acted with reckless indifference in causing them emotional distress. *Cf.* Gibson v. Brewer, 1996 WL 364795 (Mo. Ct. App. 1996), *rev'd in relevant part on other grounds*, 952 S.W.2d 239 (Mo. 1997).

Marlene F. v. Affiliated Psychiatric Med. Clinic, 770 P.2d 278 (Cal. 1989), involved a mother and child who were patients of a therapist. Outside of the presence of the mother, the therapist sexually molested the child. The court held that the mother could sue for the tort of *negligent* infliction of severe emotional distress. In a separate concurrence, Justice Arguelles argued that the facts were sufficient to make out an action for *intentional* infliction of emotional distress.

Other cases support the view that in an action by a third person neither presence nor knowledge of presence is essential if other factors, such as the nature of the defendant's conduct, or the relationship between the victim and the plaintiff, establish a high probability that the plaintiff would suffer emotional distress. *See, e.g.*, Papieves v. Lawrence, 263 A.2d 118 (Pa. 1970) (permitting parents to recover where their 14-year-old son was struck by a motor vehicle driven by the defendant, and the defendant, without attempting to obtain medical assistance, removed the body from the scene of the accident, stored it in his garage, and a few days later buried it in a field); Cahalin v. Rebert, 10 Pa. D. & C.3d 142, 150 (Pa. Dist. Ct. 1979) (holding that a custodial parent who was not present when his former spouse kidnapped their daughter stated an action for outrage).

In John W. McNamara, Note, *Murder and the Tort of Intentional Infliction of Emotional Distress*, 1986 Duke L.J. 572, 572–85, a student author argued that a presence requirement is insupportable in cases involving the murder of an immediate family member.

Courts rarely engage in a detailed discussion of liability for "reckless infliction of emotional distress." However, that subject was considered in Doe 1 *ex rel.* Doe 1 v. Roman Catholic Diocese of Nashville, 154 S.W.3d 22 (Tenn. 2005), an action by victims of child molestation against a church based on the conduct of a former priest. The court concluded that reckless infliction of emotional distress need not be directed at a specific individual. The court wrote:

> We acknowledge that our holding herein eliminates the distinction between direct claims and bystander claims when the infliction of emotional distress claim is predicated upon recklessness....
>
> .... Three elements are required: first, the conduct complained of must have been reckless; second, the conduct must have been so outrageous that it is not tolerated by civilized society; third, the conduct complained of must have caused serious mental injury....

Transferred Intent. The Third Restatement, without citation to any supporting case law, says that the concept of transferred intent applies to the tort of outrage. *See* Restatement, Third, of Torts: Liab. for Physical & Emotional Harm § 46 cmt. i (2012). The Restatement offers this illustration:

> 6. Caryn wants to take revenge on her ex-boyfriend, Mike. She calls his home one night with a false story that his daughter has been murdered, employing a horrific account of the events leading to her death. Unknown to Caryn, Mike's roommate, Gordie, who has a very close relationship with Mike's daughter, answers her call and suffers severe emotional harm at the news. Caryn is subject to liability under this Section even though she acted with a purpose to cause emotional harm to Mike and not to Gordie.

Id. at illus. 6. A better reason than the fiction of transferred intent for imposing liability on the stated facts is that Caryn acted with reckless indifference to the interests of the class of persons who might answer the phone.

The fiction of transferred intent should be avoided in this context because it does little to clarify the difficult culpability issues relating to the tort of outrage. The

Third Restatement itself acknowledges that "difficulty with the use of transferred intent does arise in a context where an actor's conduct may be substantially certain to cause emotional harm to a large group of individuals ('bystanders'), such as when a beloved national leader is assassinated." *Id.* § 46 cmt. i. A review of cases citing § 46 fails to reveal any tort of outrage action relying on transferred intent.

Notes

1. ***Punitive Damages.*** Although a large majority of courts say that the tort of outrage will support an award of punitive damages, a few courts have reached a contrary result. *See* Knierim v. Izzo, 174 N.E.2d 157 (Ill. 1961) (denying punitive damages on the ground that the outrageous conduct of the defendant forms the basis of the action and thus an award of compensatory damages is sufficiently punitive); Hall v. May Stores Co., 637 P.2d 126 (Or. 1981) (an award of punitive damages was precluded by the free expression provision of the Oregon constitution).

2. ***Constitutional Restrictions Relating to Speech and Press.*** Conduct that would otherwise be outrageous may be protected under the First Amendment. However, the cases often appear to be disconcertingly inconsistent.

The constitutional guarantees of free speech and free press sometimes bar recovery. *See* Hustler Magazine v. Falwell, 485 U.S. 46 (1988) (holding that a defendant who published a parody describing a fictitious incestuous affair between the plaintiff (a minister) and his mother during a rendezvous in an outhouse was not liable for the tort of outrage because no one would have believed the depiction to be true, and the First Amendment prohibits states from imposing liability for statements that are not provably false); Citizen Publishing Co. v. Miller, 115 P.3d 107 (Ariz. 2005) (holding that a newspaper could not be held liable to Islamic-Americans under the tort of outrage for publishing a letter to the editor stating that American forces in Iraq should execute five Muslims at random whenever an atrocity occurred because the material did not fall within one of the narrow exceptions to First Amendment protection for political speech).

However, in Esposito-Hilder v. SFX Broadcasting, Inc., 665 N.Y.S.2d 697 (App. Div. 1997), a radio station was liable for holding an "Ugliest Bride" contest, in which they made derogatory comments about the plaintiff's appearance after her bridal photograph appeared in a local newspaper and invited their audience to do the same. The court held that the allegations stated a claim for intentional infliction, even though the statements were opinion protected by the First Amendment, and thus could not form the basis for a defamation action.

The Restatement says that "publication of truthful information obtained lawfully may not ordinarily be the basis for an award of damages in tort, regardless of the emotional harm that might occur to, for example, a rape victim whose identity is lawfully discovered by a reporter and revealed in a newspaper article." Restatement, Third, of Torts: Liab. for Physical & Emotional Harm § 46 cmt. f (2012).

3. ***Constitutional Restrictions Relating to Religion.*** The constitutional guarantee of free exercise of religion sometimes means that an outrage claim will fail. *See* Tran v. Fiorenza, 934 S.W.2d 740 (Tex. App. 1996) (holding that excommunication is an ecclesiastical matter and therefore claims for defamation and intentional infliction of emotional harm were not subject to judicial review); Paul v. Watchtower Bible and Tract Society, 819 F.2d 875 (9th Cir. 1987) (finding that the free-exercise clause barred an action for intentional infliction of emotional distress by a former Jehovah's Witness who was "shunned" pursuant to church doctrine); *see also* Pleasant Glade Assembly of God v. Schubert, 264 S.W.3d 1 (Tex. 2008) (holding that the defendants were entitled to Free Exercise protection from liability for emotional damages that arose from "laying hands" on a former church member to combat "evil forces").

Nevertheless, other cases have held churches or their leaders liable for the tort of outrage. *See* Doe v. Corporation of Pres. of Church of Jesus Christ of Latter-Day Saints, 167 P.3d 1193 (Wash. App. 2007) (affirming a jury verdict for the plaintiff on an outrage claim where there was evidence that the plaintiff child, a victim of domestic sexual abuse, consulted her bishop for aid and protection, and the bishop told her that if the abuse were reported to Child Protective Services, she (the child), rather than her stepfather abuser, would be the cause of her family's break up and would be at the center of church gossip); Guinn v. Church of Christ of Collinsville, Okla., 775 P.2d 766 (Okla. 1989) (allowing an action for invasion of privacy and intentional infliction of severe emotional distress where the plaintiff's sexual activities were publicly disclosed to church members by the elders of her church).

4. ***Criminal Conversation and Alienation of Affections.*** Koestler v. Pollard, 471 N.W.2d 7 (Wis. 1991), illustrates a statutory barrier to an action for outrage. At common law, a spouse could bring an action for "criminal conversation" against a third party who engaged in adultery with the spouse's marriage partner. However, these claims were legislatively abolished in Wisconsin, as in many other states. Koestler sued for intentional infliction of severe emotional distress, alleging that Pollard had intentionally concealed from him the fact that Pollard was the biological father of a child born to Koestler's wife and revealed that fact only after Koestler developed a bond of affection with the child. The court held that the plaintiff's claim was legislatively barred because it was, in substance, a claim for criminal conversation. Compare Figueiredo-Torres v. Nickel, 584 A.2d 69 (Md. 1991), in which the complaint alleged that the defendant, a psychologist, had inflicted emotional distress upon the plaintiff by seducing his wife while treating the couple for marital problems. The court held that the claim was not barred by the abolition of actions for criminal conversation and alienation of affections.

At common law, an action for alienation of affections would lie if wrongful conduct of a third party, perhaps involving conferral of gifts or other benefits, caused one spouse to lose the affection or consortium of the other spouse. The action is still recognized in a few states. *See* Gorman v. McMahon, 792 So. 2d 307 (Miss. Ct. App. 2001).

D. False Imprisonment

One of the earliest torts known to the common law, the action for false imprisonment protects the plaintiff's interest in freedom of movement. Sometimes called "false arrest," the action is available to a plaintiff who suffers an unconsented, intentional confinement within fixed boundaries as a result of the defendant's unlawful use of force, threat of force, or assertion of legal authority. The plaintiff must be aware of the confinement or must suffer harm as a result of it. *See generally* Restatement, Second, of Torts §§ 35–45A.

1. Unconsented Intentional Confinement within Boundaries

Bird v. Jones

Queen's Bench 7 A. & E. 742
115 Eng. Rep. 668 (1845)

[In an action for false imprisonment, plaintiff had a verdict, and thereafter defendant obtained a rule nisi[10] for a new trial.]

COLERIDGE, J.

. . . .

A part of a public highway was enclosed, and appropriated for spectators of a boat race paying a price for their seats. The plaintiff was desirous of entering this part, and was opposed by the defendant, but after a struggle, during which no momentary detention of his person took place, he succeeded in climbing over the enclosure. Two policemen were then stationed by the defendant to prevent, and they did prevent him from passing onwards in the direction in which he declared his wish to go; but he was allowed to remain unmolested where he was, and was at liberty to go, and was told that he was so, in the only other direction by which he could pass. This he refused for some time, and during that time, remained where he had thus placed himself. . . .

. . . [A]lthough thus obstructed, the plaintiff was at liberty to move his person and go in any other direction, at his free will and pleasure. . . .

I am of opinion that there was no imprisonment. To call it so appears to me to confound partial obstruction and disturbance with total obstruction and detention. A prison may have its boundary large or narrow, visible or tangible . . . ; it may itself be movable or fixed, but a boundary it must have; and that boundary the party

10. A "rule nisi" is a device in English law for securing review of a verdict. It is a court order obtained by the losing party stating that it shall have a new trial unless the prevailing party shows good cause why the verdict should stand. If good cause is not shown, the rule is made "absolute" by striking the conditional language ("unless . . ."), in which case there will be a new trial. If good cause is established, the rule is "discharged" and the verdict stands. — Ed.

imprisoned must be prevented from passing; he must be prevented from leaving that place, within the ambit of which the party imprisoning would confine him, except by prison-breach. Some confusion seems to me to arise from confounding imprisonment of the body with mere loss of freedom; it is one part of the definition of freedom to be able to go wheresoever one pleases; but imprisonment is something more than the mere loss of this power; it includes the notion of restraint within some limits defined by a will or power exterior to our own....

If, in the course of a night, both ends of a street were walled up, and there was no egress from the house but into the street, I should have no difficulty in saying that the inhabitants were thereby imprisoned; but, if only one end were walled up, and an armed force stationed outside to prevent any scaling of the wall or passage that way, I should feel equally clear that there was no imprisonment. If there were, the street would obviously be the prison; and yet, as obviously, none would be confined to it.

[Rule absolute.]

[The concurring opinions of WILLIAMS, J. and PATTERSON, J. are omitted.]

LORD DENMAN, C.J. [dissenting]:

.... A Company unlawfully obstructed a public way for their own profit, extorting money from passengers, and hiring policemen to effect this purpose. The plaintiff, wishing to exercise his right of way, is stopped by force, and ordered to move in a direction which he wished not to take....

... I consider these acts as amounting to imprisonment. That word I understand to mean any restraint of the person by force....

I had no idea that any person in these times supposed any particular boundary to be necessary to constitute imprisonment, or that the restraint of a man's person from doing what he desires ceases to be an imprisonment because he may find some means of escape.

It is said that the party here was at liberty to go in another direction.... But this liberty to do something else does not appear to me to affect the question of imprisonment. As long as I am prevented from doing what I have a right to do, of what importance is it that I am permitted to do something else?

....

Notes

1. ***Partial Interference with Freedom of Movement.*** In addition to *Bird*, see Randall's Food Markets, Inc. v. Johnson, 891 S.W.2d 640, 645–46 (Tex. 1995) (employer's request that employee stay away from a particular area of the business premises during work hours did not constitute "false imprisonment").

2. ***Intent Requirement.*** False imprisonment is an intentional tort; confinement resulting from negligence or even recklessness is not redressable by this action.

However, someone injured by a lack of care which leads to confinement may have a negligence or recklessness claim, subject to defenses like contributory negligence, which are not available in cases of intentional torts.

The intent required to support an action for false imprisonment is intent to confine, not just an intent to do something wrong. For a creative (if not plainly erroneous) effort to find the necessary intent, see Oviatt v. Pearce, 954 F.2d 1470 (9th Cir. 1992). A jail's lack of internal procedures for keeping track of whether inmates attended scheduled court appearances led to the plaintiff's detention for 114 days without arraignment, in violation of a law requiring trial or release within 60 days. The defendant's decision to maintain the procedures, which were known to be defective, was held to be "tantamount to an intent to confine."

The defendant in Green v. Donroe, 440 A.2d 973 (Conn. 1982), shot himself, then called the police. Embarrassed to admit that he had inflicted his own wound, he described a fictitious person who he said had tried to rob him. The plaintiff, who resembled the description, was picked up. When the defendant refused to identify the plaintiff, plaintiff was released from custody, after being detained for about ten minutes. In an action by plaintiff for false imprisonment, the court wrote:

> "A person is not liable for false imprisonment unless his act is done for the purpose of imposing a confinement, or with knowledge that such confinement will, to a substantial certainty, result from it." . . . . The facts found by the trial court . . . negate any intention on the part of the defendant to bring about the detention of the plaintiff, or, indeed, of anybody. . . . His contrivance of the bogus robbery was found to have been motivated solely by his embarrassment over shooting himself. The trial court was not compelled to infer from the description he gave to the police that he intended or expected any arrest to result. . . .
>
> . . . "It is not enough that the actor realizes or should realize that his actions involve a risk of causing a confinement, so long as the likelihood that it will do so falls short of a substantial certainty." . . . .

3. ***Transferred Intent.*** The Restatement says that the rule of transferred intent applies to false imprisonment actions. Restatement, Second, of Torts § 43. However, there are few cases.

4. ***Reasonable Means of Escape.*** Confinement is not complete, and there is no false imprisonment, if the plaintiff knows of a reasonable means of escape. *See* Restatement, Second, of Torts § 36 and cmt. a. An avenue of escape that poses a risk of substantial harm to the person or property of the plaintiff or others, or which would otherwise offend a normal sense of decency or personal dignity, is not "reasonable." False imprisonment cannot be maintained by one who fails to take advantage of a means of escape which would entail only "slight inconvenience" or a mere "technical invasion" of another's property interests. *Id.*

In Hester v. Brown, 512 F. Supp. 2d 1228 (M.D. Ala. 2007), the court held that a mother who accompanied her daughter to a hospital in an ambulance was not falsely imprisoned because, in contrast to her daughter who was physically restrained to a stretcher and screamed for treatment to stop, the mother sat in the front seat of the ambulance, was never restrained, and had an "uninhibited ability to exit the ambulance."

The plaintiff in Davis & Alcott Co. v. Boozer, 110 So. 28 (Ala. 1926), took ill at work and was denied permission by her supervisor to go home. The court held that, although the door through which the plaintiff had entered the plant had been locked, there was no false imprisonment because another door to which workers had access was unlocked, as it normally was during the day. Would the case have turned out differently if the second door had regularly been locked and plaintiff had simply failed to discover that it was open on that occasion?

5. ***Modes of Confinement.*** Confinement may be caused by:

- Imposition of physical barriers (e.g., locking a door, taking the plaintiff's crutches, or removing a ladder);
- Use of force (e.g., grabbing the plaintiff's person or garments);
- Threatening the immediate application of force to the plaintiff's person, to members of plaintiff's family, or to plaintiff's property (e.g., threatening to shoot plaintiff's child or keep plaintiff's laptop); or
- Assertion of legal authority (e.g., purporting to place the plaintiff under arrest, or falsely informing an accident victim that the law requires the victim to complete a report before leaving the scene).

See Restatement, Second, of Torts §§ 38, 39, 40, 40A, and 41; Whittaker v. Sanford, 85 A. 399 (Me. 1912) (refusal to provide a boat to go ashore after an ocean voyage).

6. ***Being Forced to Follow.*** According to Restatement, Second, of Torts § 36 cmt. c:

> If the actor by force or threats of force, or by exerting legal authority, compels another to accompany him from place to place, he has effectively confined the other as though he had locked him in a room.

7. ***Retention of Property.*** False imprisonment may result from the defendant's exercise of control over the plaintiff's property if the plaintiff elects to remain with the property. For example, in Fischer v. Famous-Barr Co., 646 S.W.2d 819 (Mo. Ct. App. 1982), the defendant's employee seized the plaintiff's package and told her that she would "have to come back up on the fourth floor" to have a security device, which had set off an alarm, removed from clothing plaintiff had purchased. *See also* Restatement, Second, of Torts § 40A illus. 2 (retention of a customer's purse to keep her from leaving the store is actionable).

Some decisions appear to embrace a contrary rule, taking the view that "not every inducement to remain can rise to the level of false imprisonment." Marcano v. Northwestern Chrysler-Plymouth Sales, Inc., 550 F. Supp. 595, 603 (N.D. Ill. 1982) (plaintiff remained with a repossessed automobile for hours before leaving defendant's premises without interference; no false imprisonment).

8. ***Consent.*** Consent will bar a suit for false imprisonment if the defendant's actions are within the scope of the consent. *See* Morgan v. Greenwaldt, 786 So. 2d 1037 (Miss. 2001) (plaintiff's voluntary signing of a consent-to-treatment form precluded her suit against those treating her for psychiatric problems).

However, consent can expire or be revoked. The plaintiff in Noguchi v. Nakamura, 638 P.2d 1383 (Haw. Ct. App. 1982), was injured when she fell from the open door of her boyfriend's car when he suddenly drove off. A claim of false imprisonment was not barred by the plaintiff's having voluntarily entered the car. The court wrote:

> . . . [Plaintiff] had refused to go anywhere on the day in question with the appellee but to the store and back. She was back; she was in front of her parents' house, and she had the car door open when appellee suddenly started off. A jury could well have found . . . that her consent . . . had expired. . . .

2. Unlawful Force, Threat of Force, or Assertion of Legal Authority

Morales v. Lee

Court of Appeals of Texas
668 S.W.2d 867 (Tex. App. 1984)

CADENA, Chief Justice.

Defendant, Dr. Cesar Morales, appeals from a judgment following trial to a jury, granting actual damages and exemplary damages to the plaintiff, Linda Lee, for alleged false imprisonment. . . .

Plaintiff was a part-time employee in Dr. Morales' office. . . . The incident of which plaintiff complained occurred in Dr. Morales' medical office on . . . the day on which she was fired.

At 6:00 p.m. . . . Linda Lee was called into Dr. Morales' private office, in the presence of a co-worker, Mrs. Lydia Martinez, and the doctor's son, Guillermo. Five dollars was missing: he asked her if she took the money. She replied "no." By her testimony, the doctor then "got mad . . . just went crazy. . . . He got all mad and he had a chart in his hand and he slammed the chart down on the desk . . . he was screaming and hollering and he was cussing at me and he was threatening me. He told me 'don't leave.' He said, 'If you leave, I'll call the police and the police will be here in a minute.'" Later she testified: "I was scared of him, I thought he was going to hit me." When asked whether she was subsequently allowed to leave the office, she answered "yes . . . after he decided to let me go, he said, 'get the hell out of here. I don't want to see you anymore.'" The plaintiff then left the doctor's private office, but waited outside in the waiting room to get her paycheck before going home. A co-worker testified that she was shaking and crying, and couldn't talk after the incident. Linda Lee testified that she couldn't sleep at night, that she had nightmares, couldn't eat, and

Carlos C. Cadena

would throw up afterwards. She stated that she consulted a doctor for these problems, and that she was out of work for five or six months afterwards because she was upset, confused, and unable to work. Linda's mother testified that her daughter had been in excellent health prior to this incident, but afterwards was depressed, unable to sleep at night, unable to eat, and lost twenty pounds.

We agree that there is no evidence supporting a finding of false imprisonment.

False imprisonment consists of a willful detention of another without his consent without legal justification. . . .

. . . . Threats of future action, such as to call the police and have the plaintiff arrested, are not ordinarily sufficient in themselves to effect an unlawful imprisonment. W. Prosser, Torts, § 11. . . .

The judgment of the trial court is reversed and judgment is here rendered that plaintiff take nothing.

TIJERINA, Justice, dissenting.

". . . . *A wrongful detention may be effected by acts alone or by words alone*, or by both operating together, if the effect thereof is to operate on the will of the individual so as to prevent his free motion." . . . .

The majority is correct in saying that a threat to call the police, standing alone, is not sufficient to conclude that the complainant was unlawfully detained. But, the jury, as the fact finder, heard, observed and weighed all the other factors such as the age, sex, relative size of the parties, demeanor of the witnesses, employer-employee relationship, and susceptibility of the complainant to intimidation.... It is settled that the imprisonment need not be for more than an appreciable length of time and that it is not necessary that any damage result from it other than the confinement itself, since the tort is complete with even a brief restraint of the plaintiff's freedom. Prosser, Torts § 11 at 43 (4th ed. 1971). Thus, in the instant case, the jury could have found or reasonably inferred that the angry outburst of hollering and threats by appellant was calculated to operate upon the mind of appellee and inspire fear of injury to her person.... We should not substitute our judgment for that of the jury....

I ... would affirm....

Notes

1. ***Future Harm***. A threat is a future threat if it proposes the use of force at an "appreciably later" time. Restatement, Second, of Torts § 40 cmt. b.

Compare Morales with Marcus v. Liebman, 375 N.E.2d 486, 489 (Ill. App. Ct. 1978). The plaintiff, suffering mental difficulties, had voluntarily entered one hospital. She later requested her release within five days by signing a form. The defendant doctor threatened to have the plaintiff involuntarily committed to a second hospital unless she signed another paper revoking her earlier request for discharge; she signed this paper. The court found a present threat establishing a cause of action for false imprisonment:

> The defendant could have initiated commitment procedures immediately. The fact that these procedures could not have been concluded immediately does not change the threat to one in the future. At the time the alleged threat was made plaintiff was already confined. It was certainly reasonable for the plaintiff to believe that before her release commitment procedures could have been concluded.

2. ***Moral Pressure and Economic Coercion***. Moral pressure and economic coercion are normally insufficient predicates for false imprisonment.

In Faniel v. Chesapeake & Potomac Telephone Co., 404 A.2d 147 (D.C. 1979), plaintiff alleged that she was falsely imprisoned in a car when she accompanied her superiors and a security officer to her home to recover an unauthorized company telephone which she had admitted using. Plaintiff testified that she was told that "a trip to her home would be necessary to recover the equipment," that she "just assumed that [she] had to go," and that she feared discipline if she did not cooperate. The court rejected the claim:

> ... [I]t is not enough for plaintiff to feel "mentally restrained" by the actions of the defendant.... The evidence must establish a restraint against the plaintiff's will, as where she yields to force, to the threat of force or to the assertion of authority.... Although plaintiff may submit to a confinement without resistance, if the submission is voluntary, as where an accused

voluntarily accompanies his accusers to vindicate himself, then no false imprisonment occurs....

... [F]ear of losing one's job, although a powerful incentive, does not render involuntary the behavior induced....

3. ***Confinement of the Elderly.*** An action for false imprisonment can be used to redress involuntary confinement of senior citizens in nursing homes or hospitals. *See* Covenant Care, Inc. v. Superior Court, 11 Cal. Rptr. 3d 222 (Cal. 2004) (affirming punitive damages awarded to the estate of a decedent based on multiple torts, including false imprisonment, inflicted by a nursing facility).

Enright v. Groves

Court of Appeals of Colorado
560 P.2d 851 (Colo. Ct. App. 1977)

SMITH, Judge.

Defendants Groves and City of Ft. Collins appeal from judgments entered against them upon jury verdicts awarding plaintiff $500 actual damages and $1,000 exemplary damages on her claim of false imprisonment, $1,500 actual damages and $3,000 exemplary damages on her claim of intentional infliction of mental distress, also referred to as outrageous conduct, and $500 actual damages and $1,000 exemplary damages on her claim of battery....

The evidence at trial disclosed that on August 25, 1974, Officer Groves, while on duty as a uniformed police officer of the City of Fort Collins, observed a dog running loose in violation of the city's "dog leash" ordinance. He observed the animal approaching what was later identified as the residence of Mrs. Enright, the plaintiff. As Groves approached the house, he encountered Mrs. Enright's eleven-year old son, and asked him if the dog belonged to him. The boy replied that it was his dog, and told Groves that his mother was sitting in the car parked at the curb by the house. Groves then ordered the boy to put the dog inside the house, and turned and started walking toward the Enright vehicle.

Groves testified that he was met by Mrs. Enright with whom he was not acquainted. She asked if she could help him. Groves responded by demanding her driver's license. She replied by giving him her name and address. He again demanded her driver's license, which she declined to produce. Groves thereupon advised her that she could either produce her driver's license or go to jail. Mrs. Enright responded by asking, "Isn't this ridiculous?" Groves thereupon grabbed one of her arms, stating, "Let's go!"

One eyewitness testified that Mrs. Enright cried out that Groves was hurting her. Her son who was just a few feet away at the time of the incident testified that his mother also screamed and tried to explain that her arm dislocated easily. Groves refused to release her arm, and Mrs. Enright struck him in the stomach with her free hand. Groves then seized both arms and threw her to the ground. With her lying on her stomach, he brought one of her arms behind her in order to handcuff her. She continued to scream in pain and asked him to stop hurting her. Groves pulled her up and propelled her to his patrol car where, for the first time, he advised her that she was under arrest.

She was taken to the police station where a complaint was signed charging her with violation of the "dog leash" ordinance and bail was set. Mrs. Enright was released only after a friend posted bail. She was later convicted of the ordinance violation.

....

Appellants contend that Groves had probable cause to arrest Mrs. Enright, and that she was in fact arrested for and convicted of violation of the dog-at-large ordinance. They assert, therefore, that her claim for false imprisonment or false arrest cannot lie, and that Groves' use of force in arresting Mrs. Enright was permissible. We disagree.

False arrest arises when one is taken into custody by a person who claims but does not have proper legal authority. W. Prosser, Torts § 11 (4th ed.). Accordingly, a claim for false arrest will not lie if an officer has a valid warrant or probable cause to believe that an offense has been committed and that the person who was arrested committed it. Conviction of the crime for which one is specifically arrested is a complete defense to a subsequent claim of false arrest....

Here, however, the evidence is clear that Groves arrested Mrs. Enright, not for violation of the dog leash ordinance, but rather for refusing to produce her driver's license. This basis for the arrest is exemplified by the fact that he specifically advised her that she would either produce the license or go to jail. We find no statute or case law in this jurisdiction which requires a citizen to show her driver's license upon demand, unless, for example, she is a driver of an automobile and such demand is made in that connection....

We conclude that Groves' demand for Mrs. Enright's driver's license was not a lawful order and that refusal to comply therewith was not therefore an offense in and of itself. Groves was not therefore entitled to use force in arresting Mrs. Enright. Thus Groves' defense based upon an arrest for and conviction of a specific offense must, as a matter of law, fail.

....

Judgment affirmed.

Notes

1. ***Probable Cause and Reasonable Suspicion***. Probable cause for an arrest exists when the apparent state of facts would induce a reasonably intelligent and prudent person to believe that a crime has been, or is being, committed. As noted in *Enright*, an officer who makes an arrest based on probable cause normally has an absolute defense to a claim of false imprisonment.

Supreme Court precedent allows something less than probable cause—"reasonable suspicion"—as a basis for investigative detention. If that standard has been satisfied, an action for false arrest will be barred. *See also* Fulk v. Roberts, 517 N.E.2d 1098 (Ill. App. Ct. 1987) (conservation officers had a specific and articulable basis for conducting an investigatory stop on first day of hunting season).

An action involving an arrest by a law enforcement officer may be barred by the doctrines of official immunity (if the suit is against the officer) or sovereign immunity (if the suit is against the government). *See* Chapter 18.

2. ***Relevance of Guilt.*** Some authorities hold that "regardless of the unreasonableness of a party's arrest, if he actually committed the crime . . . , he cannot maintain an action for false arrest. . . ." Taco Bell, Inc. v. Saleme, 701 S.W.2d 78 (Tex. App. 1985). The unlawful conduct defense is discussed in Chapter 3.

3. ***Knowledge of Confinement or Damage.*** Liability for false imprisonment requires that the plaintiff know of the confinement or be harmed by it. *See* Parvi v. City of Kingston, 362 N.E.2d 960 (N.Y. 1977) (although the plaintiff's recollection was wiped out as a result of the alcohol he had consumed and the injuries he sustained, the plaintiff's awareness of the confinement was established circumstantially by the testimony of arresting officers who said that plaintiff had asked to be let out of the car).

Absent proof of actual damages, nominal damages may be recovered to vindicate the plaintiff's right to freedom of movement. Punitive damages may be awarded in a case involving egregious conduct. *See* Haryanto v. Saeed, 860 S.W.2d 913 (Tex. App. 1993) (affirming an award of $2 million in punitive damages, on top of $1 million in compensatory damages, where an aide to a Saudi prince took a hotel employee hostage and threatened to kill him).

In Dayton Hudson Corp. v. Altus, 715 S.W.2d 670 (Tex. App. 1986), a customer was arrested for shoplifting and jailed for nine to eleven hours in a dirty, noisy cell, with filthy prisoners, including apparent drug users. She later stopped teaching Sunday school because her children were teased about the event. In the customer's suit for false imprisonment against the store owner, the court held that evidence of jail conditions, as well as length of confinement and resulting public embarrassment, could be taken into account in determining actual and exemplary damages.

Johnson v. Barnes & Noble Booksellers, Inc.

United States Court of Appeals for the Eleventh Circuit
437 F.3d 1112 (11th Cir. 2006)

PER CURIAM:

.... At trial, Johnson testified that after purchasing a compact disk, he asked a female clerk for assistance in locating the book. As the store clerk stooped down to retrieve a book from the bottom of the shelf, she, or her shirt, was touched by Johnson. Johnson claimed that he was merely trying to help the store clerk with her shirt, which she was trying to reach in order to tuck it in, while the store clerk maintained that Johnson inappropriately grabbed her buttocks. The store clerk left Johnson and reported to her supervisors that Johnson had touched her inappropriately. Although not having observed the incident, two store managers and a security guard approached Johnson, accused him of having touched the store employee inappropriately, which Johnson adamantly denied, and then escorted Johnson to an office where he was detained for one to two hours. During this detention, he was interrogated, photographed and subjected to racially discriminatory remarks. When the police arrived, they questioned Johnson about the incident, returned his ID and driver's license, which had been taken from him by the Barnes & Noble employees, and told him to leave the store. Johnson was not arrested.

....

In this case, the district court instructed the jury on the Florida law of false imprisonment ... as follows:

> The issue for your determination on the false imprisonment claim of plaintiff against defendant is whether the defendant intentionally caused the plaintiff to be restrained against his will.

Barnes & Noble argued at trial that it was additionally entitled to an instruction that ...:

> ... [T]he first issue for your determination is whether the defendants had the legal authority to restrain the Plaintiff under the rules governing a citizen's arrest. A citizen's arrest can occur on the basis of misdemeanor if it was committed in the presence of the citizen or involved a breach of the peace....
>
> If you find that the conduct of the Plaintiff constituted a breach of the peace, thus giving the defendants lawful authority to detain the Plaintiff, then you must determine if the detention was conducted in a reasonable manner and for a reasonable amount of time.

The district court refused to give the instruction....

.... Section 877.03, Florida Statutes defines a breach of the peace as occurring when a person commits "such acts as are of a nature to corrupt the public morals, or outrage the sense of public decency, or affect the peace and quiet of persons who may witness them, or engages in brawling or fighting[.]" Fla. Stat. § 877.03. Florida courts have narrowly interpreted the meaning of this statute . . . and have required a showing that a breach of the peace presents an imminent threat to the public security or morals to justify a citizen taking immediate action. State v. Furr, 723 So. 2d 842, 844 (Fla. Dist. Ct. App.1999) (finding drunk driving amounts to a breach of the peace because of the immediate threat to life involved in driving while intoxicated). . . . Moreover, Florida law requires that in order to effectuate a citizen's arrest, the breach must "be committed in the presence of the private citizen." . . . Indeed, pursuant to Florida law, not even a police officer can effectuate a warrantless arrest for a misdemeanor, if the misdemeanor was not committed in his presence. . . .[11]

. . . [I]t is undisputed that the store clerk's allegation of Johnson's conduct, if true, would constitute a misdemeanor. Fla. Stat. § 784.03. Johnson was detained, however, by Barnes & Noble employees who had been told, but had not witnessed, the alleged misdemeanor. Moreover, there were no allegations that Johnson had continued this behavior or was at the time of the detention disruptive or committing other "such acts as are of a nature to corrupt the public morals, or outrage the sense of public decency, or affect the peace and quiet of persons who may witness them." Under the facts presented here — showing no imminent threat and actions not committed in the presence of those detaining Johnson — we find that the district court did not err in denying the requested instruction for breach of the peace. . . .

Alternatively, Barnes & Noble argues that the damages award of $117,000 is excessive and should be reversed. This Court cannot disturb a jury award stemming from a Florida state law claim where the trial court refused to alter the amount, unless the verdict is "so inordinately large as obviously to exceed the maximum limit of a reasonable range within which the jury may properly operate." . . .

. . . . Johnson argues that the verdict was reasonable under Florida law. He testified at trial that he suffered embarrassment when he had to explain the incident to his wife and children, that he developed a facial twitch, which he attributes to the incident, that he has significantly altered his shopping habits, that he has lost weight, that he has been unable to sleep, and that he was barred from entering a Barnes & Noble store for the rest of his life. In addition, plaintiff's expert witness testified at trial that Barnes & Noble had no policies and procedures in place that would have

11. [Fn. 3:] Under common law: "A private person may arrest for a misdemeanor only if it was committed in his presence and it involved a breach of the peace." Moll v. United States, 413 F.2d 1233, 1236 (5th Cir. 1969) (citing 4 Wharton, Criminal Law and Procedure §§ 1601–03; 5 Am. Jur. 2d, Arrest §§ 34–36; 6 C.J.S. Arrest § 8); *see also* Restatement 2d of Torts, § 141 ("[A] private person is privileged . . . to impose confinement upon [another] for the purpose of terminating or preventing the renewal of an affray or an equally serious breach of the peace which is being or has been committed in the actor's presence or of preventing such other from participating therein, if (a) the other is or the actor reasonably believes him to be participating or about to participate in the affray, and (b) the confinement or force is not intended or likely to cause death or serious bodily harm, and (c) the actor reasonably believes that the force or confinement is necessary to prevent the other from participating in the affray or other equally serious breach of the peace.").

prevented the unlawful detention of individuals and that employees were permitted to exercise unbridled discretion when handling situations with customers.

.... [W]e find that the award of $117,000 ... was within the range of permissible awards.... [T]he jury's verdict is AFFIRMED.

Notes

1. ***Shoplifters.*** A false imprisonment action by a suspected shoplifter may be barred by the privilege a merchant has to detain, for purposes of investigation, one reasonably suspected of theft. *See* Chapter 3.

2. ***Liability for Instigating an Arrest.*** Can a person be held liable for false imprisonment merely because the person provided information to the police that led to the arrest of an innocent individual? Generally not. This result makes sense because society wants to encourage citizens to assist law enforcement efforts. According to many courts, the line is drawn between intentionally providing false information to the police (which may give rise to liability) and merely providing inaccurate information (which does not give rise to liability). *See, e.g.*, Dangerfield v. Ormsby, 264 S.W.3d 904 (Tex. App. 2008) (no liability based on erroneous identification of the plaintiff in photo line-up). Although some decisions speak in terms of whether the informant has "caused" the arrest, it is probably better to analyze such cases in terms of privilege. That is, there is a privilege to disclose to law enforcement officers potentially useful information reasonably believed to be true; there is no privilege to supply information that is known to be false.

3. ***Negligent Identification.*** Similar issues arise in cases where a plaintiff sues not for false imprisonment, but on some other ground, such as negligence. *See* Brunson v. Affinity Federal Credit Union, 972 A.2d 1112 (N.J. 2009) (declining to recognize a cause of action against a bank for negligent investigation of purported fraud arising from an imposter's misuse of the plaintiff's identity to cash counterfeit payroll checks).

In Davis v. Equibank, 603 A.2d 637, 638 (Pa. Super. Ct. 1992), a bank teller, reviewing a police display of photographs, misidentified the plaintiff as the perpetrator of a robbery. Thereafter, the plaintiff was held in police custody for 17 days until the teller testified at a preliminary hearing that she believed the robber was taller than the plaintiff. In a negligence action against the teller and bank, the court held that, despite the seriousness of the plaintiff's loss of freedom, sound public policy precluded recognition of a cause of action for "negligent identification." "[T]he efficient enforcement of criminal law requires that a private person who renders aid to the police by giving honest, even if mistaken, information about crimes should be protected." Jaindl v. Mohr, 661 A.2d 1362, 1364 (Pa. 1995).

The weight of authority is consistent with *Davis*, so long as the misidentification is made in good faith. Some decisions go even further. *See* Hagberg v. California Federal Bank FSB, 81 P.3d 244 (Cal. 2004) (holding that "when a citizen contacts law enforcement personnel to report suspected criminal activity and to instigate law enforcement personnel to respond, the communication . . . enjoys an unqualified privilege").

4. ***Malicious Prosecution Distinguished.*** A private person who initiates or procures the institution of criminal proceedings against someone not guilty of the offense commits the tort of malicious prosecution if:

> (a) the accuser initiates, procures, or continues a criminal proceeding against another;
>
> (b) the accuser acts without probable cause;
>
> (c) the accuser acts for an improper purpose; and
>
> (d) the proceeding terminates in favor of the party against whom it was brought.

Restatement (Third) of Torts: Liab. for Economic Harm § 21 (2020).

3. Defenses

Peterson v. Sorlien

Supreme Court of Minnesota
299 N.W.2d 123 (Minn. 1980)

SHERAN, Chief Justice.

This action by plaintiff Susan Jungclaus Peterson for false imprisonment and intentional infliction of emotional distress arises from an effort by her parents, in conjunction with other individuals . . . , to prompt her disaffiliation from an organization known as The Way Ministry.

. . . . The jury returned a verdict exonerating Mr. and Mrs. Jungclaus and the other remaining defendants of the charge of false imprisonment; however, the jury found defendants Veronica Morgel and Kathy Mills liable for intentional infliction of emotional distress, assessing against each of them $1 compensatory damages and $4,000 and $6,000 respectively as punitive damages.

. . . . [T]his case marks the emergence of a new cultural phenomenon: youth-oriented religious or pseudo-religious groups which utilize the techniques of what has been termed "coercive persuasion" or "mind control" to cultivate an uncritical and devoted following . . .

At the time of the events . . . , Susan Jungclaus Peterson was 21 years old. . . . In 1973, she graduated with honors from high school, ranking second in her class. She matriculated that fall at Moorhead State College. A dean's list student during her first year, her academic performance declined and her interests narrowed after she joined the local chapter of . . . The Way. . . .

. . . . As her sophomore year began, Susan committed herself significantly, selling the car her father had given her and working part-time as a waitress to finance her contributions to The Way. Susan spent the following summer in South Dakota, living in conditions described as appalling and overcrowded, while recruiting, raising money and conducting training sessions for The Way.

As her junior year in college drew to a close, the Jungclauses grew increasingly alarmed by the personality changes they witnessed in their daughter; overly tired, unusually pale, distraught and irritable, she exhibited an increasing alienation from family, diminished interest in education and decline in academic performance. The Jungclauses, versed in the literature of youth cults and based on conversations with former members of The Way, concluded that through a calculated process of manipulation and exploitation Susan had been reduced to a condition of psychological bondage.

. . . [D]efendant Norman Jungclaus, father of plaintiff, arrived at Moorhead to pick up Susan following the end of the third college quarter. Instead of returning to their family home, defendant drove with Susan to Minneapolis to the home of Veronica Morgel. . . . Susan was greeted by Kathy Mills and several young people who wished to discuss Susan's involvement in the ministry. Each of these present had been in some way touched by the cult phenomenon. Kathy Mills, the leader of the group, had treated a number of former cult members, including Veronica Morgel's son. . . .

The avowed purpose of deprogramming is to break the hold of the cult over the individual through reason and confrontation. Initially, Susan was unwilling to discuss her involvement; she lay curled in a fetal position, in the downstairs bedroom where she first stayed, plugging her ears and crying while her father pleaded with her to listen. . . . This behavior persisted for two days during which she intermittently engaged in conversation, at one point screaming hysterically and flailing at her father. But by Wednesday Susan's demeanor had changed completely; she was friendly and vivacious and that night slept in an upstairs bedroom. Susan spent all day Thursday reading and conversing with her father and on Saturday night went roller-skating. On Sunday she played softball at a nearby park, afterwards enjoying a picnic lunch. The next week Susan spent in Columbus, Ohio, flying there with a former cult member who had shared with her the experiences of the previous week. While in Columbus, she spoke every day by telephone to her fiancé who, playing tapes and songs from the ministry's headquarters in Minneapolis, begged that she return to the fold. Susan expressed the desire to extricate her fiancé from the dominion of the cult.

Susan returned to Minneapolis. . . . Unable to arrange a controlled meeting so that Susan could see her fiancé outside the presence of other members of the ministry, her parents asked that she sign an agreement releasing them from liability for their past weeks' actions. Refusing to do so, Susan stepped outside the Morgel residence with the puppy she had purchased in Ohio, motioned to a passing police car and shortly thereafter was reunited with her fiancé in the Minneapolis headquarters of The Way. Following her return to the ministry, she was directed to counsel and initiated the present action.

.... Plaintiff seeks a judgment notwithstanding the verdict on the issue of false imprisonment, alleging that defendants unlawfully interfered with her personal liberty by words or acts which induced a reasonable apprehension that force would be used against her if she did not otherwise comply.... The jury, instructed that an informed and reasoned consent is a defense to an allegation of false imprisonment and that a nonconsensual detention could be deemed consensual if one's behavior so indicated, exonerated defendants with respect to the false imprisonment claim.

The period in question ... [covered] 16 days. The record clearly demonstrates that Susan willingly remained in the company of defendants for at least 13 of those days. During that time she took many excursions into the public sphere, playing softball and picnicking in a city park, roller-skating at a public rink, flying aboard public aircraft and shopping and swimming while relaxing in Ohio. Had Susan desired, manifold opportunities existed for her to alert the authorities of her allegedly unlawful detention; in Minneapolis, two police officers observed at close range the softball game in which she engaged; en route to Ohio, she passed through the security areas of the ... airports in the presence of security guards and uniformed police; in Columbus she transacted business at a bank, went for walks in solitude and was interviewed by an F.B.I. agent who sought assurances of her safety. At no time during the 13-day period did she complain of her treatment or suggest that defendants were holding her against her will. If one is aware of a reasonable means of escape that does not present a danger of bodily or material harm, a restriction is not total and complete and does not constitute unlawful imprisonment. Damages may not be assessed for any period of detention to which one freely consents....

.... The central issue for the jury, then, was whether Susan voluntarily participated in the activities of the first three days. The jury concluded that her behavior constituted a waiver.

... [T]he behavior Susan manifested during the initial three days at issue must be considered in light of her actions in the remainder of the period. Because, it is argued, the cult conditioning process induces dramatic and non-consensual change giving rise to a new temporary identity on the part of the individuals whose consent is under examination, Susan's volitional capacity prior to treatment may well have been impaired. Following her readjustment, the evidence suggests that Susan was a different person, "like her old self." As such, the question of Susan's consent becomes a function of time. We therefore deem Susan's subsequent affirmation of defendants' actions dispositive.

.... [T]he method of cult indoctrination ... is predicated on a strategy of coercive persuasion that undermines the capacity for informed consent. While we acknowledge that other social institutions may utilize a degree of coercion in promoting their objectives, none do so to the same extent or intend the same consequences. Society, therefore, has a compelling interest favoring intervention. The facts in this case support the conclusion that plaintiff only regained her volitional capacity to consent after engaging in the first three days of the deprogramming process. As such, we hold that when parents, or their agents, acting under the conviction that the judgmental capacity of their adult child is impaired, seek to extricate that child from what they reasonably believe to be a religious or pseudo-religious cult, and the child at some juncture assents to the actions in question, limitations upon the child's mobility do not constitute meaningful deprivations of personal liberty sufficient to support a judgment for false imprisonment. But . . . we do not endorse self-help as a preferred alternative. . . .[12]

[The court further held that plaintiff's other arguments, relating in part to her intentional infliction of mental distress claim, did not warrant reversal.]

WAHL, Justice (dissenting in part, concurring in part).

I must respectfully dissent. In every generation, parents have viewed their children's religious and political beliefs with alarm and dismay if those beliefs were different from their own. Under the First Amendment, however, adults in our society enjoy freedoms of association and belief. In my view, it is unwise to tamper with those freedoms and with longstanding principles of tort law out of sympathy for parents seeking to help their "misguided" offspring, however well-intentioned and loving their acts may be. . . .

The unrebutted evidence shows that defendant Norman Jungclaus, the father of the 21-year-old plaintiff in this case, took his adult daughter, kicking and screaming, to a small bedroom in the basement of the Morgel home. . . . Norman Jungclaus admitted that she did not go with him willingly. . . . Defendant Perkins testified that plaintiff screamed and cried and pleaded with several people to let her go, but her pleas were ignored. This situation continued until 3 a.m. Tuesday. At one point that morning, plaintiff flew at her father, and he held her arms around her from the back, in his words, "for maybe a half an hour, until she calmed down again." . . . .

The majority opinion finds, in plaintiff's behavior during the remainder of the 16 day period of "deprogramming," a reasonable basis for acquitting defendant Jungclaus of the false imprisonment charge for the initial three days, during which time he admittedly held plaintiff against her will. Under this theory, plaintiff's "acquiescence" in the later stages of deprogramming operates as consent which "relates back" to the events of the earlier three days, and constitutes a "waiver" of her claims for those days. Cases cited by the majority do not lend support to this proposition. . . .

Certainly, parents who disapprove of or disagree with the religious beliefs of their adult offspring are free to exercise their own First Amendment rights in an attempt, by speech and persuasion without physical restraints, to change their adult children's minds. But parents who engage in tortious conduct in their "deprogramming" attempts do so at the risk that the deprogramming will be unsuccessful and the adult children will pursue tort remedies against their parents. To allow parents' "conviction

12. [Fn. 2:] . . . [S]ome courts have permitted the creation of temporary guardianships to allow the removal of cult members to therapeutic settings. If the individuals desire, at the end of the conservatorship they may return to the cult. . . .

that the judgmental capacity of their [adult] child is impaired [by her religious indoctrination]" to excuse their tortious conduct sets a dangerous precedent.

Here, the evidence clearly supported a verdict against Norman Jungclaus on the false imprisonment claim.... The trial court's holding in this regard should be reversed.

....

OTIS, Justice (dissenting in part).

I join in the views expressed by Justice Wahl, and particularly take issue with a rule which authorizes what is euphemistically described as "limitations upon the adult child's mobility" whenever a parent, or indeed a stranger acting for a parent, subjectively decides, without the benefit of a professional opinion or judicial intervention, that the adult child's "judgmental capacity" is impaired and that she should be "extricated" from what is deemed to be a religious or pseudo-religious cult.

....

We furnish no guidelines or criteria for what constitutes "impaired judgmental capacity" other than the fact that the adult child has embraced an unorthodox doctrine with a zeal which has given the intervenor cause for alarm, a concern which may be well-founded, ill-founded or unfounded.

....

At age 21, a daughter is no longer a child.... Susan Peterson was not only an adult... but she was a bright, well-educated adult.... [T]o hold that for seeking companionship and identity in a group whose proselyting tactics may well be suspect, she must endure without a remedy the degrading and humiliating treatment she received at the hands of her parents, is, in my opinion, totally at odds with the basic rights of young people to think unorthodox thoughts, join unorthodox groups, and proclaim unorthodox views. I would reverse the denial of recovery as to that cause of action.

Notes

1. ***Alternative Rationales.*** One finds in the majority opinion threads of at least four different arguments:

> (1) that plaintiff waived her right to sue for false imprisonment that occurred during the initial three-day confinement by failing to object or commence suit during the subsequent 13-day period;
>
> (2) that during the three-day period plaintiff lacked the capacity either to consent or not consent, and therefore the confinement was not unconsented;
>
> (3) that the confinement was not a "meaningful deprivation of liberty": *de minimis non curat lex*; and
>
> (4) that the parents had a privilege to engage in otherwise tortious conduct, perhaps on the ground that one may inflict lesser harm to prevent greater harm from occurring.

Which of these rationales is the most persuasive? The defenses of consent and private necessity are examined in Chapter 3.

2. ***Actions by Minor Children.*** Parents enjoy some degree of latitude in exercising control over their minor children because there is a privilege to discipline. *See* Restatement, Second, of Torts § 147 (stating that "A parent is privileged to apply such reasonable force or to impose such reasonable confinement upon his child as he reasonably believes to be necessary for its proper control, training, or education"). In determining whether force or confinement is reasonable, the following factors are relevant: the age, sex, and physical and mental condition of the child; the nature of the offense and the child's apparent motive; the influence of the child's example upon other children of the same family; whether the force or confinement is reasonably necessary and appropriate to compel obedience to a proper command; and whether it is disproportionate to the offense, unnecessarily degrading, or likely to cause serious or permanent harm.

Courts may also be reluctant to impose liability on persons who assist parents in their efforts to discipline or control an unemancipated minor child. *See* R.D.J. v. Vaughan Clinic, P.C., 572 So. 2d 1225 (Ala. 1990) (holding that the trial court did not err in finding that none of the defendants "unlawfully detained" R.D.J. in treating her, because each defendant provided treatment in reliance upon her mother's consent).

3. ***Tort Liability of Religious "Cults."*** A religious organization which engages in indoctrination through brainwashing, or other forms of coercive conduct, may be subject to tort liability. *See* Eilers v. Coy, 582 F. Supp. 1093 (D. Minn. 1984) (false imprisonment proved); Lewis v. Holy Spirit Ass'n for Unification, 589 F. Supp. 10, 12 (D. Mass. 1983) (an outrage action was "conceivable," but adequate facts were not alleged).

However, courts are reluctant to review the indoctrination practices, initiation procedures, or conditions of membership in religious organizations, in part because of the free-exercise-of-religion and free-association guarantees of the First Amendment.

E. Trespass to Land

On, Under, or Above. The tort of trespass to land ("trespass *quare clausum fregit*" or "trespass q.c.f.") protects a possessor's interest in exclusive possession of real property. A person who intentionally and without consent or privilege enters on, under, or above the land of another commits a trespass. Taking an unauthorized shortcut across the plaintiff's lot, tunneling under it, stringing utility lines above it, or building a structure on it, all may be trespasses.

Direct or Indirect. Indirect invasions, like throwing trash onto property without personally crossing the boundary, are also actionable. If *A* deliberately pushes *B* onto *C's* land, *A* commits a trespass. Because *B* had no intent to enter, *B* will not be held liable unless *B* fails to leave the property with reasonable dispatch. In addition, one who enters property with the permission of the possessor commits a trespass by failing to leave after the consent has expired.

Nominal Damages are Presumed. If the defendant's entry causes no harm, nominal damages will be awarded to vindicate the plaintiff's legal right to exclusive possession of the land. In Boring v. Google Inc., 362 Fed. Appx. 273 (3d Cir. 2010), the plaintiffs, "who live on a private road in Pittsburgh, discovered that Google had taken 'colored imagery of their residence, including the swimming pool, from a vehicle in their residence driveway months earlier without obtaining any privacy waiver or authorization.'" They alleged "that their road is clearly marked with a 'Private Road, No Trespassing' sign," and sued on a variety of theories. The Third Circuit held that the plaintiffs stated a cause of action for trespass to land.

Mistake is No Defense. It is no defense to liability that the defendant was mistaken about the ownership of the property. All that is required is the intent to be present (or transferred intent); intent to be present *on someone else's land* is not necessary.

Trespass to land is best considered in tandem with the tort of private nuisance, an action which protects a possessor from non-trespassory interference with the use or enjoyment of land (such as the discomforts that result from bright lights, noise, and odors). Trespass q.c.f. and nuisance are considered in Chapter 20.

F. Trespass to Chattels and Conversion

Two Tort Actions. The intentional exercise of dominion or control over another's personal property may give rise to an action for conversion or for trespass to chattels. (The latter tort is also known as trespass *de bonis asportatis*, or trespass d.b.a., and although the Latin means "for goods taken away," a "taking" is no longer essential to the tort.) In general, conversion will lie in cases of major interference with the plaintiff's rights; trespass to chattels applies to relatively minor interference.

Conversion Justifies a Forced Judicial Sale. The distinction between conversion and trespass to chattels is important because of the way in which damages are calculated. Conversion uses an unusual measure of damages, as explained in this excerpt from Pearson v. Dodd, 410 F.2d 701 (D.C. Cir. 1969):

> Conversion is the substantive tort theory which underlay the ancient common law form of action for trover. A plaintiff in trover alleged that he had lost a chattel which he rightfully possessed, and that the defendant had found it and converted it to his own use. With time, the allegations of losing and finding became fictional, leaving the question of whether the defendant had "converted" the property the only operative one.
>
> The most distinctive feature of conversion is its measure of damages, which is the value of the goods converted. The theory is that the "converting" defendant has in some way treated the goods as if they were his own,

> so that the plaintiff can properly ask the court to decree a forced sale of the property from the rightful possessor to the converter.
>
> Because of this stringent measure of damages, it has long been recognized that not every wrongful interference with the personal property of another is a conversion. Where the intermeddling falls short of the complete or very substantial deprivation of possessory rights in the property, the tort committed is not conversion, but the lesser wrong of trespass to chattels.
>
> The Second Restatement of Torts has marked the distinction by defining conversion as: "[A]n intentional exercise of dominion or control over a chattel which so seriously interferes with the right of another to control it that the actor may justly be required to pay the other the full value of the chattel."
>
> Less serious interferences fall under the Restatement's definition of trespass [d.b.a.]. . . .

The difference is more than a semantic one. The measure of damages in trespass is not the whole value of the property interfered with, but rather the actual diminution in its value caused by the interference.

Kinds and Degrees of Interference. "While the tort of conversion originally required a separate showing that the converter made some use of the property that amounted to a total deprivation of that property to its owner, by the twentieth century common-law conversion more broadly encompassed any conduct inconsistent with the owner's property rights." Aroma Wines & Equip., Inc. v. Columbian Distrib. Services, Inc., 871 N.W.2d 136, 145 (Mich. 2015) (discussing a parallel state conversion statute with different "use" requirements).

A person may interfere with a chattel by taking possession of it, using it, moving it from one place to another, transferring possession to a third person, withholding possession, or destroying or otherwise altering the chattel. Section 222A(2) of the Restatement, Second, of Torts provides that:

> In determining the seriousness of the interference and the justice of requiring the actor to pay the full value, the following factors are important:
>
> (a) the extent and duration of the actor's exercise of dominion and control;
>
> (b) the actor's intent to assert a right in fact inconsistent with the other's right of control;
>
> (c) the actor's good faith;
>
> (d) the extent and duration of the resulting interference with the other's right of control;
>
> (e) the harm done to the chattel;
>
> (f) the inconvenience and expense caused to the other.

"No one factor is always predominant in determining the seriousness of the interference . . . ," nor is the proffered list "intended to be exclusive." *Id.* at cmt. d.

Intent Required. Conversion and trespass to chattels are intentional torts; the intent necessary is intent to affect the chattel. Good motives are no defense, and, while a mistake of fact or law will not preclude a finding of intent, mistake may bear upon whether the actor can establish a privilege *See id.* at §§ 217 and 244; privileges, such as public and private necessity, are discussed in Chapter 3. Unintentional harmful interference with personal property may be actionable under the principles of negligence, recklessness, or strict liability.

Superior Possessory Rights. A plaintiff is not required to prove ownership of the property, merely possessory rights superior to the defendant. *See* Community Voice Line, L.L.C. v. Great Lakes Commun. Corp., 18 F. Supp. 3d 966, 982 (N.D. Iowa 2014) (involving alleged conversion of telephone numbers that were "ported" by the defendant to another company).

CompuServe, Inc. v. Cyber Promotions, Inc.

United States District Court for the Southern District of Ohio
962 F. Supp. 1015 (S.D. Ohio 1997)

GRAHAM, District Judge.

....

Plaintiff CompuServe Incorporated ("CompuServe") is one of the major national commercial online computer services.... CompuServe ... provides its subscribers with a link to the much larger resources of the Internet. This allows its subscribers to send and receive electronic messages, known as "e-mail," by the Internet. Defendants Cyber Promotions, Inc. and its president Sanford Wallace are in the business of sending unsolicited e-mail advertisements on behalf of themselves and their clients to hundreds of thousands of Internet users, many of whom are CompuServe subscribers. CompuServe has notified defendants that they are prohibited from using its computer equipment to process and store the unsolicited e-mail and has requested that they terminate the practice. Instead, defendants have sent an increasing volume of e-mail solicitations....

In an effort to shield its equipment from defendants' bulk e-mail, CompuServe has implemented software programs designed to screen out the messages and block their receipt. In response, defendants have modified their equipment and the messages they send in such a fashion as to circumvent CompuServe's screening software....

The Restatement § 217(b) states that a trespass to chattel may be committed by intentionally using or intermeddling with the chattel in possession of another. Restatement § 217, Comment e defines physical "intermeddling" as follows:

... intentionally bringing about a physical contact with the chattel....

Electronic signals generated and sent by computer have been held to be sufficiently physically tangible to support a trespass cause of action. Thrifty-Tel, Inc., v. Bezenek, ... [54 Cal. Rptr.2d 468 (Cal. Ct. App. 1996)]; State v. McGraw, 480 N.E.2d 552, 554 (Ind.1985) (... recognizing in dicta that a hacker's unauthorized access to a computer was more in the nature of trespass than criminal conversion).... It is undisputed that plaintiff has a possessory interest in its computer systems. Further, defendants' contact with plaintiff's computers is clearly intentional. Although electronic messages may travel through the Internet over various routes, the messages are affirmatively directed to their destination.

Defendants, citing Restatement (Second) of Torts § 221, which defines "dispossession," assert that not every interference with the personal property of another is actionable and that physical dispossession or substantial interference with the chattel is required. Defendants then argue that they did not, in this case, physically dispossess plaintiff of its equipment or substantially interfere with it. However, the Restatement (Second) of Torts § 218 defines the circumstances under which a trespass to chattels may be actionable:

> One who commits a trespass to a chattel is subject to liability to the possessor of the chattel if, but only if,
>
> (a) he dispossesses the other of the chattel, or
>
> (b) the chattel is impaired as to its condition, quality, or value, or
>
> (c) the possessor is deprived of the use of the chattel for a substantial time, or
>
> (d) bodily harm is caused to the possessor, or harm is caused to some person or thing in which the possessor has a legally protected interest.

Therefore, an interference resulting in physical dispossession is just one circumstance under which a defendant can be found liable. Defendants suggest that "[u]nless an alleged trespasser actually takes physical custody of the property or physically damages it, courts will not find the 'substantial interference' required to maintain a trespass to chattel claim." (Defendant's Memorandum at 13). To support this rather broad proposition, defendants cite only two cases which make any reference to the Restatement. In Glidden v. Szybiak, ... [63 A.2d 233 (N.H. 1949)], the court simply indicated that an action for trespass to chattels could not be maintained in the absence of some form of damage. The court held that where plaintiff did not contend that defendant's pulling on her pet dog's ears caused any injury, an action in tort could not be maintained. *Id.* 63 A.2d at 235. In contrast, plaintiff in the present action has alleged that it has suffered several types of injury as a result of defendants' conduct. In Koepnick v. Sears Roebuck & Co., ... [762 P.2d 609 (Ariz. 1988)] the court held that a two-minute search of an individual's truck did not amount to a "dispossession" of the truck as defined in Restatement § 221 or a deprivation of the use of the truck for a substantial time. It is clear from a reading of Restatement § 218 that an interference or intermeddling that does not fit the § 221 definition of "dispossession" can nonetheless result in defendants' liability for trespass. The *Koepnick* court did not discuss any of the other grounds for liability under Restatement § 218.

.... In the present case, any value CompuServe realizes from its computer equipment is wholly derived from the extent to which that equipment can serve its subscriber base. Michael Mangino, a software developer for CompuServe . . . , states by affidavit that handling the enormous volume of mass mailings that CompuServe receives places a tremendous burden on its equipment. . . . Defendants' more recent practice of evading CompuServe's filters by disguising the origin of their messages commandeers even more computer resources because CompuServe's computers are forced to store undeliverable e-mail messages and labor in vain to return the messages to an address that does not exist. . . . To the extent that defendants' multitudinous electronic mailings demand the disk space and drain the processing power of plaintiff's computer equipment, those resources are not available to serve CompuServe subscribers. Therefore, the value of that equipment to CompuServe is diminished even though it is not physically damaged by defendants' conduct.

Next, plaintiff asserts that it has suffered injury aside from the physical impact of defendants' messages on its equipment. Restatement § 218(d) also indicates that recovery may be had for a trespass that causes harm to something in which the possessor has a legally protected interest. Plaintiff asserts that defendants' messages are largely unwanted by its subscribers. . . . These inconveniences decrease the utility of CompuServe's e-mail service and are the foremost subject in recent complaints from CompuServe subscribers. . . . Defendants contend that CompuServe subscribers are provided with a simple procedure to remove themselves from the mailing list. However, the removal procedure must be performed by the e-mail recipient at his expense, and some CompuServe subscribers complain that the procedure is inadequate. . . .

Many subscribers have terminated their accounts specifically because of the unwanted receipt of bulk e-mail messages. . . . Defendants' intrusions into CompuServe's computer systems, insofar as they harm plaintiff's business reputation and goodwill with its customers, are actionable under Restatement § 218(d).

. . . . [D]efendants' persistent affirmative efforts to evade plaintiff's security measures have circumvented any protection those self-help measures might have provided. . . . However, . . . the implementation of technological means of self-help, to the extent that reasonable measures are effective, is particularly appropriate in this type of situation and should be exhausted before legal action is proper.

. . . .

Defendants' intentional use of plaintiff's proprietary computer equipment . . . after repeated demands that defendants cease . . . is an actionable trespass to plaintiff's chattel. . . .

Normally, a preliminary injunction is not appropriate where an ultimate award of monetary damages will suffice. . . . However, money damages are only adequate if they can be reasonably computed and collected. Plaintiff has demonstrated that defendants' intrusions into their computer systems harm plaintiff's business reputation and goodwill. This is the sort of injury that warrants the issuance of a preliminary injunction because the actual loss is impossible to compute. . . .

. . . . It is so ORDERED.

Notes

1. *See* Register.com, Inc. v. Verio, Inc., 356 F.3d 393, 404 (2d Cir. 2004) (affirming the grant of a preliminary injunction because the defendant's "use of search robots, consisting of software programs performing multiple automated successive queries, consumed a significant portion of the capacity of Register's computer systems," and was likely to constitute trespass to chattels); *but see* Intel Corp. v. Hamidi, 71 P.3d 296 (Cal. 2003) (holding that trespass to chattels does not encompass electronic communications that neither damage the recipient computer system nor impair its functioning; temporary use of some portion of computer processors or storage is not cognizable injury, nor is loss of productivity caused by employee's reading or trying to block unwanted messages).

2. ***Dispossession***. Section 218 of the Second Restatement now makes clear that damage will be inferred from any "dispossession." A plaintiff "may recover at least nominal damages for the loss of possession, even though it is of brief duration and he is not deprived of the use of the chattel for any substantial length of time." Restatement, Second, of Torts § 218 cmt. d. However:

> [A]n intermeddling with a chattel is not a dispossession unless the actor intends to exercise a dominion and control over it inconsistent with a possession in any person other than himself. Thus, a trivial removal of a chattel from one position to another with no intention to exercise further control over it or deprive the possessor of its use is not a dispossession.

Id. at § 221 cmt. b.

3. In Johnson v. Weedman, 5 Ill. 495 (1843), the defendant, a bailee, rode the plaintiff's horse fifteen miles, contrary to the terms of the bailment. In an action for conversion, in which the defendant was represented by Abraham Lincoln, the court held that there was no conversion and that the plaintiff was entitled only to nominal damages, as the unauthorized ride caused no injury to the horse.

Henson v. Reddin

Court of Appeals of Texas
358 S.W.3d 428 (Tex. App. 2012)

SUE WALKER, Justice.

....

The dispute between Henson and Reddin centered on a polyurethane machine used to spray truck bed liners.... The polyurethane machine was permanently mounted inside an enclosed gooseneck trailer that had "Discount Industrial Coating, Incorporated" emblazoned on it. The polyurethane machine had not been used for a while, so it had become clogged and was not in working order. Henson owned a one-half interest in Discount Industrial Coating, Inc.; Joseph Brophy owned the other one-half interest.

Henson decided that he wanted to sell his one-half interest in the company, and Reddin let Henson know that he was interested in purchasing the polyurethane machine if he could get it in working order. Reddin purchased parts and began working on the polyurethane machine in an attempt to get it in working order. After Reddin had purchased parts and had added them to the polyurethane machine, Henson moved the trailer in which the polyurethane machine was located. Henson did not return any parts to Reddin and did not disclose the location of the polyurethane machine.

.... The conversion claim was tried to ... the county court at law [which] signed a judgment for Reddin in the amount of $5,419.46....

... Henson argues that the evidence is legally and factually insufficient to establish that he converted any property belonging to Reddin; Henson argues that the evidence is legally and factually insufficient to establish that he knew at the time he removed the trailer that he was taking Reddin's property. Conversion is the unauthorized and wrongful assumption and exercise of dominion and control over the personal property of another to the exclusion of, or inconsistent with, the owner's rights.... Acting with good faith or innocence is not a defense to conversion....

The testimony at trial established that Reddin was attempting to get the polyurethane machine in working order, that Reddin had purchased parts for the machine, that Reddin had installed the parts on the machine, and that Henson thereafter moved the trailer in which the machine was mounted. Reddin testified that he had called Henson numerous times, attempting to retrieve the parts, but Henson did not answer; the one time that Henson answered, he refused Reddin's request. Viewing the evidence favorable to the trial court's findings, as we must, and disregarding the evidence to the contrary because a reasonable factfinder could do so based on a credibility determination, the evidence is legally sufficient to support the trial court's findings supporting each element of conversion of Reddin's property by Henson....

In considering the factual sufficiency of the evidence to support the trial court's findings, we consider Henson's testimony that is contrary to the findings. Henson testified that he did not know until after he moved the trailer that Reddin had parts on it. But even if Henson did not know about Reddin's parts until after the trailer was moved, his innocence is no defense to conversion.... Additionally, although the record contains conflicting testimony regarding Henson's refusal to return Reddin's parts to him — Henson claimed he offered to let Reddin call and come get the parts, while Reddin testified that Henson would not return his calls and refused to permit him to come get the parts — the trial court is the sole judge of the credibility of the witnesses and is to resolve any inconsistencies in their testimony.... Considering and weighing all of the evidence in the record ..., including that Henson's delay in authorizing the retrieval of the property that had the effect of destroying the parts, the credible evidence supporting the finding is not so weak, or so contrary to the overwhelming weight of all the evidence, that the finding should be set aside and a new trial ordered....

Generally, the measure of damages in a conversion case is the fair market value of the property converted at the time of the conversion, with legal interest.... Fair market value has been defined as the price that the property would bring when it is offered for sale by one who desires, but is not obliged to sell, and is bought by one who is under no necessity of buying it.... A property owner may testify about the market value of his property if his testimony shows that he is familiar with the market value and his opinion is based on that market value.... However, when converted property has no readily ascertainable fair market value, the measure of damages is the actual value of the property to the owner at the time of its loss.... In such circumstances, the purchase price is probative of actual value.... The original cost in the market and the manner and time and place of its use, the appearance before and after the alleged injury, and the relative usefulness and physical condition may be offered into evidence to establish conversion damages.... For example, the Beaumont court in ... [Wutke v. Yolton, 71 S.W.2d 549, 552 (Tex. Civ. App. 1934)] examined what type of evidence was admissible to determine actual value for secondhand furniture because no standard of market value existed.... The appellate court explained that the trial court

> did not err in receiving evidence as to what appellees paid for the furniture "several years before the date of the conversion." .... "When goods of this character are destroyed, a proper method of arriving at their value at the time of loss is to take into consideration the cost of the articles, the extent of their use, whether worn or out of date, their condition at the time, etc., and for them to determine what they were fairly worth. The cost alone would not be the correct criterion for the present value, but it would be difficult to estimate the value of such goods, except by reference to the former price in connection with wear, depreciation, change of style, and present condition."

....

Here, Reddin offered receipts for the parts into evidence and testified as to the purchase price of the parts that he had installed on the polyurethane machine. The receipts document that all of the parts were purchased within two to three weeks of the date they were installed on the polyurethane machine.... Reddin also testified that the parts were worthless after the conversion because they had been ruined by the resin crystallizing in the polyurethane machine. The evidence conclusively establishes that the new parts were installed on the polyurethane machine on a Friday and that Henson moved the trailer with the machine mounted in it either one or two days after the new parts were installed; when Reddin and Brophy returned to work on the machine on Monday, it was gone.

Considering the evidence favorable to the trial court's finding that Reddin purchased the parts for $4,561.52 and its finding that the value of the parts in Wise County, Texas, at the time was $4,561.52, legally sufficient evidence exists to support these findings....

... [W]e affirm the trial court's judgment.

Notes

1. ***Other Precedent.*** *See also* Russell v. American Real Estate Corp., 89 S.W.3d 204 (Tex. App. 2002) (in a case where a tenant's belongings were removed from a house, the defendant committed trespass to personal property with respect to items that were promptly returned upon request, and conversion with respect to items that were damaged or lost).

2. ***Demand for Return.*** Proof of a refused demand is not required if the demand would have been useless. Thus, there is no need to demand return from a thief. *See* State v. Seventh Regiment Fund, Inc., 774 N.E.2d 702 (N.Y. 2002).

3. ***Qualified Refusal.*** A person does not become a converter merely by making a qualified refusal to surrender a chattel under circumstances making immediate surrender unreasonable, as in the case of goods not readily accessible or a demand made after business has closed. *See* Restatement, Second, of Torts § 238 and cmts. b and c. In most cases, refusal to return goods before checking on the claimant's right to them is permissible. *See id.* at §§ 239 and 240.

4. ***Thieves, Defrauders, and Bona Fide Purchasers.*** A person who obtains property through theft or fraud is liable for conversion. So is one who later acquires the goods with notice of their illegitimate origin. *See* Morrow Shoe Mfg. Co. v. New England Shoe Co., 57 F. 685 (7th Cir. 1893) (auctioneer had notice of fraud).

Whether a subsequent good faith purchaser of improperly acquired goods is liable for conversion depends upon the manner in which the goods were first procured. A thief has no title to stolen property and can pass no rights to a subsequent party. Hence, a subsequent bona fide purchaser who pays full value nevertheless becomes a converter by exercising dominion over the goods. *See* Lovinger v. Hix Green Buick Co., 140 S.E.2d 83 (Ga. Ct. App. 1964); Restatement, Second, of Torts § 229 cmt. d.

A defrauder, in contrast, has "voidable" title to goods acquired by fraud. Although the victim of the fraud may equitably rescind the transaction and sue the defrauder for conversion, a bona fide purchase cuts off any equitable rights and precludes suit by the fraud victim against the good faith purchaser (but not against the person who committed the fraud). *See* Guckeen Farmers Elevator Co. v. South Soo Grain Co., 109 N.W.2d 728 (Neb. 1961); Restatement, Second, of Torts § 229 cmt. d.

These rules produce the anomalous result that some bona fide purchasers are liable for conversion and others are not. This disparity reflects the law's efforts to strike a workable balance between the need for consumers to have confidence in commercial transactions and the need of possessors for property protection. The differing treatment of bona fide purchasers can be justified on the ground that there is greater reason to protect possessors from losses by theft, to which they never consented, than from losses by fraud, where consent was given and there was some opportunity to scrutinize the facts.

Special rules apply to certain commercial dealings. For example, Uniform Commercial Code § 2-403(2) (Westlaw 2022) provides that "[a]ny entrusting of possession of goods to a merchant who deals in goods of that kind gives him power to transfer all rights of the entruster to a buyer in the ordinary course of business."

5. ***Finders***. "Under the common law, one who finds lost property cannot retain it against a claim by the property's true owner." Lira v. Greater Houston German Shepherd Dog Rescue, Inc., 488 S.W.3d 300, 303 (Tex. 2016). In *Lira*, a conversion action, the court reinstated an injunction ordering the return of a dog to the plaintiffs, noting that the defendant animal shelter cited "no common-law authority, nor can we find any, holding that dog owners' property rights are lost because their dog escapes and cannot be located for a few days." The owners, who kept searching for their dog had not abandoned their property and city ordinances did not divest them of their rights.

6. ***Bailees***. Detailed rules have evolved to protect bailees—persons temporarily holding goods belonging to others. The rules seek to avoid the inconvenience and delay of requiring bailees to inquire into the title of the items delivered to them. In general, at common law:

> (a) A bailee without notice that a chattel is lost or stolen is not liable for conversion merely by reason of receiving it. *See* Williams v. Roberts, 1 S.E.2d 587 (Ga. Ct. App. 1939).
>
> (b) A bailee who, without notice of other claims, redelivers a chattel to its bailor is not liable for conversion, even though the bailor is not the rightful possessor. *See* Thoms v. D.C. Andrews & Co., 54 F.2d 250 (2d Cir. 1931).
>
> (c) A bailee who redelivers a chattel to one entitled to immediate possession is not liable to the actual bailor for conversion. *See* Texas Diamond Int'l v. Tiffany & Co., 47 S.W.3d 589, 592 (Tex. App. 2001); Restatement, Second, of Torts § 234 cmt. d.

On the other hand:

> (d) A bailee with knowledge or reason to know that the bailor has no right to deliver the chattel becomes liable for conversion by receiving the goods. *See* Restatement, Second, of Torts § 230.
>
> (e) A bailee with notice of multiple claims to a chattel is under an absolute duty to redeliver the chattel to its true owner. *See* Edwards v. Max Thieme Chevrolet Co., 191 So. 569 (La. Ct. App. 1939). (The bailee's difficulty may be avoided by a relatively simple procedure whereby, pursuant to statute, the bailee deposits the goods in court and asks the court to resolve the dispute. *See* Cass v. Higenbotam, 3 N.E. 189, 192 (N.Y. 1885).)

Russell-Vaughn Ford, Inc. v. Rouse

Supreme Court of Alabama
206 So. 2d 371 (Ala. 1968)

SIMPSON, Justice.

[Appellee Rouse went to Russell-Vaughn Ford, Inc., to discuss trading his Falcon in on a new Ford. One of the salesmen asked Mr. Rouse for the keys to his Falcon. The keys were given to him and Mr. Rouse looked at new cars for a time and then proceeded with the negotiations. The salesman offered to trade a new Ford for the Falcon, plus $2,400; plaintiff declined to trade on this basis.]

.... Mr. Rouse asked for the return of the keys to the Falcon.... [B]oth salesmen ... said that they did not know where the keys were. Mr. Rouse then asked several people who appeared to be employees of Russell-Vaughn for the keys.... Several mechanics and salesmen were, according to plaintiff's testimony, sitting around on cars looking at him and laughing at him.

After a period of time the plaintiff called the police.... Shortly after the arrival of the policeman ..., the salesman Parker threw the keys to Mr. Rouse with the statement that he was a cry baby and that "they just wanted to see him cry a while."

.... The jury returned a general verdict in favor of the plaintiff in the amount of $5,000....

.... Initially it is argued that the facts of this case do not make out a case of conversion. It is argued that the conversion if at all, is a conversion of the keys to the automobile, not of the automobile itself.... We are not persuaded that the law of Alabama supports this proposition....

> ... [C]onversion may consist, not only in an appropriation of the property to one's own use, but in its destruction, *or in exercising dominion over it in exclusion or defiance of plaintiff's right....*

.... A remarkable admission ... was elicited by the plaintiff in examining one of the witnesses for the defense. It seems that according to [a] salesman for Russell-Vaughn Ford, Inc. it is a rather usual practice in the automobile business to "lose keys" to cars belonging to potential customers....

Further, appellants argue that there was no conversion since the plaintiff could have called his wife, at home, who had another set of keys and thereby gained the ability to move his automobile. We find nothing in our cases which would require the plaintiff to exhaust all possible means of gaining possession of a chattel which is withheld from him by the defendant, after demanding its return....

.... In Compton v. Sims, ... [96 So. 185 (Ala. 1923)] this court sustained a finding that there had been a conversion of cotton where the defendant refused to deliver to the plaintiff "warehouse tickets" which would have enabled him to gain possession of the cotton. The court spoke of the warehouse tickets as a symbol of the cotton and found that the retention of them amounted to a conversion of the cotton. So here, we think that the withholding from the plaintiff after demand of the keys to his automobile, without which he could not move it, amounted to a conversion of the automobile.

.... [The amount of the verdict was not excessive because an award of punitive damages was justified by the evidence.]

Affirmed.

Notes

1. ***Damages for Conversion.*** The rules governing damages in conversion cases are complex. *See* Restatement, Second, Torts §§ 911 and 927. In general:

a. ***Time and Place.*** In the usual case, the plaintiff is entitled to recover the market value of the chattel—what a willing buyer would pay a willing seller when neither is compelled to buy or to sell—at the time and place of the conversion. Successive converters may therefore be liable for different amounts. Where one person commits serial acts of conversion (*e.g.*, by stealing the chattel, refusing a demand to return it, and then destroying it), each conversion may give rise to a different amount of damages, and the plaintiff may elect to recover damages based on any one of the conversions, although damages for conversion may be recovered only once.

b. ***Unmarketable and Irreplaceable Items.*** Some items, such as a personal manuscript, an artificial eye, or a dog trained to obey only one master, are unmarketable, in the sense that they have little value to persons other than the owner. In these cases, damages are limited to replacement value, less an amount for depreciation.

If a chattel cannot be replaced, as in the case of a family portrait, the owner may recover an amount for its special value to the owner, as evidenced by its original cost and its condition at the time of the loss.

Traditionally, sentimental value has been disregarded in calculating damages. *See* MacGregor v. Watts, 5 N.Y.S.2d 525 (App. Div. 1938). However, some courts have endorsed a less restrictive rule. The defendant in Mieske v. Bartell Drug Co., 593 P.2d 1308 (Wash. 1979), negligently lost thirty-two rolls of movie film which contained pictures, taken over several decades, of plaintiff and his family. The court affirmed an award of $7,500, noting that "the [only] type of sentiment which is not compensable is that which relates to 'indulging in feeling to an unwarranted extent' or 'being affectedly or mawkishly emotional.'"

c. ***Commodities.*** In the case of commodities which fluctuate in value, such as stocks, bonds, other securities, and fungible goods such as grain, cotton, and oil, most courts agree that the plaintiff may recover the highest value of the commodity between the date of the conversion and a reasonable time for replacement. This rule prevents defendants from appropriating the speculative possibilities of increases in market values, while encouraging plaintiffs to mitigate damages by securing replacements.

d. ***Mental Distress.*** Damages for mental distress may be awarded if the defendant should have foreseen that psychic suffering would follow from the tort. In Fredeen v. Stride, 525 P.2d 166 (Or. 1974), a veterinarian advised the plaintiff, who could not afford expensive surgery for her injured dog, to have the dog put to sleep. Although plaintiff reluctantly agreed, the doctor failed to carry out the agreement and gave the dog to a third person. The plaintiff learned what had happened several months later. The court upheld an award of mental distress damages in a conversion action.

e. ***Punitive Damages.*** Punitive damages may be awarded in cases involving particularly outrageous conduct. *See* Bennett v. Reynolds, 315 S.W.3d 867 (Tex. 2010) (theft of cattle by a neighboring ranch).

2. ***Damages for Loss of a Pet.*** Most states limit recovery for the tortious death of a pet to the animal's market value, which is usually so low that it is not worthwhile for the owner to sue. Some writers have argued that damages should include an amount in compensation of the lost relationship between the owner and pet. This argument has been rejected by various courts. *See* Strickland v. Medlen, 397 S.W.3d 184 (Tex. 2013) (dog owners could not recover damages for loss of companionship); *but see* Plotnik v. Meihaus, 146 Cal. Rptr. 3d 585 (Cal. App. 2012) (permitting emotional distress damages based on intentional injury to a dog); Womack v. Von Rardon, 135 P.3d 542 (Wash. Ct. App. 2006) (allowing emotional distress damages where a cat was set on fire).

A few states have enacted statutes providing for civil liability for noneconomic damages relating to the death or injury of a pet. For example:

Tennessee Code Annotated § 44-17-403 (Westlaw 2022)

(a) If a person's pet is killed or sustains injuries which result in death caused by the unlawful and intentional, or negligent, act of another or the animal of another, the trier of fact may find the individual causing the death or the owner of the animal causing the death liable for up to five thousand dollars ($5,000) in noneconomic damages. . . .

(b) As used in this section, "pet" means any domesticated dog or cat normally maintained in or near the household of its owner.

(c) Limits for noneconomic damages set out in subsection (a) shall not apply to causes of action for intentional infliction of emotional distress or any other civil action other than the direct and sole loss of a pet.

(d) Noneconomic damages awarded pursuant to this section shall be limited to compensation for the loss of the reasonably expected society, companionship, love and affection of the pet.

(e) This section shall not . . . be construed to authorize any award of noneconomic damages in an action for professional negligence against a licensed veterinarian. . . .

Illinois Compiled Statutes Annotated § 70/16.3 (Westlaw 2022)

Any person who has a right of ownership in an animal that is subjected to an act of aggravated cruelty . . . or torture . . . in violation of this Act or in an animal that is injured or killed as a result of actions taken by a person who acts in bad faith . . . under . . . this Act may bring a civil action to recover the damages sustained by that owner. Damages may include, but are not limited to, the monetary value of the animal, veterinary expenses incurred on behalf of the animal, any other expenses incurred by the owner in rectifying the effects of the cruelty, pain, and suffering of the animal, and emotional distress suffered by the owner. In addition . . . , the owner is also entitled to punitive or exemplary damages of not less than $500 but not more than $25,000 for each act of abuse or neglect. . . . In addition, the court must award reasonable attorney's fees and costs. . . .

The remedies provided in this Section are in addition to any other remedies allowed by law.

In an action under this Section, the court may enter any injunctive orders reasonably necessary to protect animals from any further acts of abuse, neglect, or harassment by a defendant. . . .

See also Leith v. Frost, 899 N.E.2d 635 (Ill. App. Ct. 2008). The court recognized that under general tort principles, "when the cost of repairs exceeds the fair market value of the personal property, the value of the personal property becomes the ceiling on the amount of damages which can be recovered." Nevertheless, in a case where a neighbor's Siberian huskie attacked the plaintiff's dog, the court allowed recovery of $4,784 in compensatory damages. The court adopted the rule that "when an injured pet dog with no discernible market value is restored to its previous health, the measure of damages may include, but is not limited to, the reasonable and customary cost of necessary veterinary care and treatment."

3. ***Ethics in Law Practice: Treatment of Client Property.*** Lawyers often hold money or property for clients. For example, a client may advance funds to pay expenses of litigation (filing fees, expert witness costs, etc.) as they are incurred, or the lawyer may receive from a third person the proceeds of an executed court judgment or an amount paid in settlement of a claim. An attorney who appropriates client funds or property for personal use is subject not merely to a tort action (such as an action for conversion or fraud), but to professional discipline such as suspension from practice or disbarment.

The legal profession has adopted stringent rules for handling client funds and property. Rule 1.15 of the American Bar Association's Model Rules of Professional Conduct (Westlaw 2022) provides in part:

> (a) A lawyer shall hold property of clients or third persons that is in a lawyer's possession in connection with a representation separate from the lawyer's own property. Funds shall be kept in a separate account.... Other property shall be identified as such and appropriately safeguarded. Complete records of such account funds and other property shall be kept ... [for a period of years].
>
> ....
>
> (d) Upon receiving funds or other property in which a client or third person has an interest, a lawyer shall promptly notify the client or third person ... [and] promptly deliver to the client or third person any funds or other property that the client or third person is entitled to receive and ... render a full accounting regarding such property....

Similar duties are owed to prospective clients. *See* In re Spencer, 58 P.3d 228 (Or. 2002) (attorney suspended for 60 days for allowing documents entrusted by would-be client to be destroyed).

Commingling—the failure to segregate clients' property from the lawyer's—is a serious breach of ethical standards, even if the infraction is unintentional. Commingling not only creates an appearance of impropriety and subjects the client's property to jeopardy, it is often the first step toward conversion.

On appropriate facts, an attorney who refuses to deliver to a third party money to which that party is entitled may be sued for conversion. *See* Ellis v. City of Dallas, 111 S.W.3d 161 (Tex. App. 2003) (refusal to tender full payment of a lien); *but see* Vincent R. Johnson, *The Limited Duties of Lawyers to Protect the Funds and Property of Nonclients*, 8 St. Mary's J. Legal Mal. & Ethics 58 (2017).

4. ***Replevin.*** Someone whose property has been converted may wish to recover the chattel itself rather than receive the proceeds of the forced judicial sale which is the usual result of a conversion action. One alternative is to sue for replevin. An action for replevin allows the plaintiff to recover possession of the chattel *in specie*, and recoup incidental damages.

In Augillard v. Madura, 257 S.W.3d 494 (Tex. App. 2008), the defendant adopted a dog that had been rescued from New Orleans after Hurricane Katrina. The plaintiff tracked down the dog with the aid of a website (PawMatch.com) and proved that the dog was hers by DNA evidence gathered from the dog's old hairbrush. The appellate court held that the plaintiff was entitled to the return of the dog.

5. ***Art Theft.*** A number of replevin actions have arisen from the recent worldwide explosion in art theft. *See* Solomon R. Guggenheim Foundation v. Lubell, 569 N.E.2d 426 (N.Y. 1991) (Marc Chagall gouache); O'Keeffe v. Snyder, 416 A.2d 862 (N.J. 1980) (paintings by Georgia O'Keeffe). When artwork has been missing for many years and has passed through various hands, issues arise as to when the plaintiff's cause of action initially accrues and whether subsequent transfers are subject to a new statute of limitations.

In *O'Keeffe*, the court held that the plaintiff's cause of action accrues according to a "discovery rule":

> O'Keeffe's cause of action accrued when she first knew, or reasonably should have known through the exercise of due diligence, of the cause of action, including the identity of the possessor of the paintings.
>
> ... [U]nder the discovery rule, if an artist diligently seeks the recovery of a lost or stolen painting, but cannot find it or discover the identity of the possessor, the statute of limitations will not begin to run. The rule permits an artist who uses reasonable efforts to report, investigate, and recover a painting to preserve the rights of title and possession.

416 A.2d at 870–72. The court rejected the plaintiff's argument that each transfer of a chattel subsequent to the initial conversion was a separate act of conversion sufficient to start the statute of limitations running anew. Finding that the plaintiff's proposed rule would "tend to undermine the purpose of the statute in quieting titles and protecting against stale claims," the court said that the "majority and better view is to permit tacking, the accumulation of consecutive periods of possession by parties in privity with each other." *Id.* at 875. Under this view, the statute of limitations runs only once in cases of continuous dispossession, regardless of the number of acts of conversion. "The important point is not that there has been a substitution of possessors, but that there has been a continuous dispossession of the former owner." *Id.* at 874–75. *Accord* Restatement, Second, of Torts § 899 cmt. c.

Kremen v. Cohen

United States Court of Appeals for the Ninth Circuit
337 F.3d 1024 (9th Cir. 2003)

KOZINSKI, Circuit Judge.

....

"Sex on the Internet?" they all said. "*That'll* never make any money." But computer-geek-turned-entrepreneur Gary Kremen knew an opportunity when he saw it. The year was 1994; domain names were free for the asking.... With a quick e-mail to the domain name registrar Network Solutions, Kremen became the proud owner of sex.com. He registered the name to his business, Online Classifieds, and listed himself as the contact.

Con man Stephen Cohen, meanwhile, was doing time for impersonating a bankruptcy lawyer. He, too, saw the potential of the domain name.... Once out of prison, he sent Network Solutions what purported to be a letter he had received from Online Classifieds. It claimed the company had been "forced to dismiss Mr. Kremen," but "never got around to changing our administrative contact with the internet registration [sic] and now our Board of directors has decided to *abandon* the domain name sex.com." Why was this unusual letter being sent via Cohen rather than to Network Solutions directly? It explained:

> Because we do not have a direct connection to the internet, we request that you notify the internet registration on our behalf, to delete our domain name sex.com. Further, we have no objections to your use of the domain name sex.com and this letter shall serve as our authorization to the internet registration to transfer sex.com to your corporation.

Despite the letter's transparent claim that a company called "*Online* Classifieds" had no Internet connection, Network Solutions made no effort to contact Kremen. Instead, it accepted the letter at face value and transferred the domain name to Cohen. When Kremen contacted Network Solutions some time later, he was told it was too late to undo the transfer. Cohen went on to turn sex.com into a lucrative online porn empire.

.... [Kremen obtained a judgment against Cohen but was unable to collect it because Cohen "skipped the country, and his money is stashed in some offshore bank account."]

... Kremen seeks to hold someone else responsible for his losses. That someone is Network Solutions, the exclusive domain name registrar at the time of Cohen's antics. Kremen ... argues that Network Solutions was a "bailee" of his domain name and seeks to hold it liable for "conversion by bailee."

....

Kremen ... had an intangible property right in his domain name, and a jury could find that Network Solutions "wrongful[ly] dispos[ed] of" that right to his detriment by handing the domain name over to Cohen. ... The district court nevertheless rejected Kremen's conversion claim. It held that domain names, although a form of property, are intangibles not subject to conversion. This rationale derives from a distinction tort law once drew between tangible and intangible property: Conversion was originally a remedy for the wrongful taking of another's lost goods, so it applied only to tangible property. ... Virtually every jurisdiction, however, has discarded this rigid limitation to some degree. ... Many courts ignore or expressly reject it ..., including Astroworks, Inc. v. Astroexhibit, Inc., 257 F. Supp. 2d 609, 618 (S.D.N.Y. 2003) (holding that the plaintiff could maintain a claim for conversion of his website). ... Others reject it for some intangibles but not others. The Restatement, for example, recommends the following test:

> (1) Where there is conversion of a document in which intangible rights are merged, the damages include the value of such rights.
>
> (2) One who effectively prevents the exercise of intangible rights of the kind customarily *merged in a document* is subject to a liability similar to that for conversion, even though the document is not itself converted.

Restatement (Second) of Torts § 242 (1965) (emphasis added). An intangible is "merged" in a document when, "by the appropriate rule of law, the right to the immediate possession of a chattel and the power to acquire such possession is *represented by* [the] document," or when "an intangible obligation [is] *represented by*

[the] document, which is regarded as equivalent to the obligation." . . . .[13] The district court applied this test and found no evidence that Kremen's domain name was merged in a document.

The court assumed that California follows the Restatement on this issue. Our review, however, revealed that "there do not appear to be any California cases squarely addressing whether the 'merged with' requirement is a part of California law." . . . .

We conclude that California does not follow the Restatement's strict merger requirement. . . .

. . . [I]n Palm Springs-La Quinta Development Co. v. Kieberk Corp., 46 Cal. App.2d 234, 115 P.2d 548 (1941), the court of appeal allowed a conversion claim for intangible information in a customer list when some of the index cards on which the information was recorded were destroyed. The court allowed damages not just for the value of the cards, but for the value of the intangible information lost. . . . Section 242(1) of the Restatement, however, allows recovery for intangibles only if they are merged in the converted document. Customer information is not merged in a document in any meaningful sense. A Rolodex is not like a stock certificate that actually *represents* a property interest; it is only a means of recording information.

. . . .

California courts ignored the Restatement again in A & M Records, Inc. v. Heilman, 75 Cal. App.3d 554, 142 Cal. Rptr. 390 (1977), which applied the tort to a defendant who sold bootlegged copies of musical recordings. The court held broadly that "such misappropriation and sale of the intangible property of another without authority from the owner is conversion." . . . . It gave no hint that its holding depended on whether the owner's intellectual property rights were merged in some document. One might imagine physical things with which the intangible was associated — for example, the medium on which the song was recorded. But an intangible intellectual property right in a song is not merged in a phonograph record in the sense that the record *represents* the composer's intellectual property right. The record is not like a certificate of ownership; it is only a medium for one instantiation of the artistic work.

. . . .

In short, California does not follow the Restatement's strict requirement that some document must actually represent the owner's intangible property right. On the contrary, courts routinely apply the tort to intangibles without inquiring whether they are merged in a document and, while it's often possible to dream up *some* document the intangible is connected to in some fashion, it's seldom one that represents the owner's property interest. . . . [Endorsement of a] strict merger rule . . . is against

13. [Fn. 6:] The Restatement does note that conversion "has been applied by some courts in cases where the converted document is not in itself a symbol of the rights in question, but is merely essential to their protection and enforcement, as in the case of account books and receipts." *Id.* cmt. b.

the weight of authority. That rule cannot be squared with a jurisprudence that recognizes conversion of music recordings, radio shows, customer lists, regulatory filings, confidential information and even domain names.

Were it necessary to settle the issue once and for all, we would toe the line . . . and hold that conversion is "a remedy for the conversion of every species of personal property." . . . . But we need not do so to resolve this case. Assuming *arguendo* that California retains some vestigial merger requirement, it is clearly minimal, and at most requires only *some* connection to a document or tangible object — not representation of the owner's intangible interest in the strict Restatement sense.

Kremen's domain name falls easily within this class of property. He argues that the relevant document is the Domain Name System, or "DNS" — the distributed electronic database that associates domain names like sex.com with particular computers connected to the Internet. We agree that the DNS is a document (or perhaps more accurately a collection of documents). That it is stored in electronic form rather than on ink and paper is immaterial. *See, e.g., Thrifty-Tel,* 46 Cal. App.4th at 1565, 54 Cal. Rptr. 2d 468 (recognizing conversion of information recorded on floppy disk); *A & M Records,* 75 Cal. App.3d at 570, 142 Cal. Rptr. 390 (same for audio record); *Lone Ranger Television,* 740 F.2d at 725 (same for magnetic tape). It would be a curious jurisprudence that turned on the existence of a *paper* document rather than an electronic one. Torching a company's file room would then be conversion while hacking into its mainframe and deleting its data would not. That is not the law, at least not in California.

. . . .

Network Solutions also argues that the DNS is not a document because it is refreshed every twelve hours when updated domain name information is broadcast across the Internet. . . . A document doesn't cease being a document merely because it is often updated. . . . Whether a document is updated by inserting and deleting particular records or by replacing an old file with an entirely new one is a technical detail with no legal significance.

Kremen's domain name is protected by California conversion law, even on the grudging reading we have given it. Exposing Network Solutions to liability when it gives away a registrant's domain name on the basis of a forged letter is no different from holding a corporation liable when it gives away someone's shares under the same circumstances. . . . We have not "creat[ed] new tort duties" in reaching this result. . . . We have only applied settled principles of conversion law to what the parties and the district court all agree is a species of property.

The district court . . . was reluctant to apply the tort of conversion because of its strict liability nature. This concern rings somewhat hollow . . . because the district court effectively exempted Network Solutions from liability to Kremen altogether, whether or not it was negligent. Network Solutions made no effort to contact Kremen before giving away his domain name, despite receiving a facially suspect letter from a third party. A jury would be justified in finding it was unreasonably careless.

... [T]here is nothing unfair about holding a company responsible for giving away someone else's property even if it was not at fault.... Negligent or not, it was Network Solutions that gave away Kremen's property. Kremen never did anything. It would not be unfair to hold Network Solutions responsible and force *it* to try to recoup its losses by chasing down Cohen. This, at any rate, is the logic of the common law, and we do not lightly discard it.

The district court was worried that "the threat of litigation threatens to stifle the registration system by requiring further regulations by [Network Solutions] and potential increases in fees." .... Given that Network Solutions's "regulations" evidently allowed it to hand over a registrant's domain name on the basis of a facially suspect letter without even contacting him, "further regulations" don't seem like such a bad idea. And the prospect of higher fees presents no issue here that it doesn't in any other context. A bank could lower its ATM fees if it didn't have to pay security guards, but we doubt most depositors would think that was a good idea.

The district court thought there were "methods better suited to regulate the vagaries of domain names" and left it "to the legislature to fashion an appropriate statutory scheme." .... The legislature, of course, is always free (within constitutional bounds) to refashion the system that courts come up with. But that doesn't mean we should throw up our hands and let private relations degenerate into a free-for-all in the meantime. We apply the common law until the legislature tells us otherwise. And the common law does not stand idle while people give away the property of others.

.... The judgment of the district court is reversed on this count, and the case is remanded for further proceedings.

Notes

1. ***Merger in a Document.*** *See* Thyroff v. Nationwide Mut. Ins. Co., 864 N.E.2d 1272 (N.Y. 2007) (recognizing that some authorities still retain the "merger in a document" requirement, but holding that "the tort of conversion must keep pace with the contemporary realities of widespread computer use" and therefore applies to intangible electronic records that are stored on a computer); Thompson v. UBS Fin. Services, Inc., 115 A.3d 125, 132 (Md. 2015) (the mere failure of a company to inform the owners and beneficiaries of a second-to-die life insurance policy of loans taken out against the policy did not amount to conversion of intangible property).

2. ***Conversion of Funds.*** A person may convert funds by issuing unauthorized checks (*see* Martinez Management, Inc. v. Caston, 900 So. 2d 301 (La. Ct. App. 2005)), spending money (*see* Lopez v. Lopez, 271 S.W.3d 780 (Tex. App. 2008)), or wiring the proceeds of a real estate closing (*see* Trey Inman & Associates, P.C. v. Bank of America, N.A., 702 S.E.2d 711 (Ga. App. 2010)).

However, a claim for conversion of funds will only succeed if the plaintiff has a right to immediate possession of the funds. *See* Bailey v. Gallagher, 348 S.W.3d 322 (Tex. App. 2011). "[A] cause of action for conversion of money can be stated only where a defendant interferes with the plaintiff's possessory interest in a specific, identifiable sum"; "the simple failure to pay money owed does not constitute conversion." Voris v. Lampert, 446 P.3d 284, 291 (Cal. 2019). The money normally must consist of specific, segregated, or identifiable funds. In Roman v. Sage Title Group, LLC, 146 A.3d 479 (Md. Spec. App. 2016), the court wrote:

> [M]oney that is commingled with other funds "loses its specific identity[,]" and thus there can be no claim for conversion. . . .
>
> No Maryland appellate opinion, however, has dealt with a claim of conversion of money placed in an escrow account. . . . [S]everal jurisdictions have allowed conversion claims where the subject of conversion was money that by agreement of the parties was to be placed in escrow, even if the money was commingled with other funds or not placed in escrow at all. . . .
>
> . . . . Here, Roman's funds were placed into an escrow account at Sage Title. Roman identified $2,420,000 as the sum of three discrete payments by cashier's checks. . . . Roman admitted into evidence copies of these checks, as well as their corresponding notations on Sage Title's balance sheets. . . .
>
> . . . [W]e conclude that, although Roman's monies were placed with other funds in Sage Title's escrow account, the $2,420,000 deposited to that escrow account was sufficiently specific, segregated, and identifiable to support a claim for conversion. . . .

3. ***Absence of a Property Right.*** In Wieder v. Chemical Bank, 608 N.Y.S.2d 195 (App. Div. 1994), a former employee sued based on alleged removal of "writing samples" he had prepared during his three-year employment with the defendant. The action failed because "it is axiomatic that materials or products developed by an employee in the course of his or her employment, absent any agreement to the contrary, belong to his or her employer."

4. ***Photocopies.*** Consider FMC Corp. v. Capital Cities/ABC Inc., 915 F.2d 300 (7th Cir. 1990). During an evening news program, the defendant displayed documents (or copies thereof) relating the plaintiff's pricing policies and contract with the Defense Department. The documents were missing from the plaintiff's files. It was undisputed that the defendant was not directly responsible for the loss of the plaintiff's documents and that whatever it possessed had been provided by a third-party. In a suit for conversion, the court held that if an inspection revealed that the defendant had the original documents, it had to return them to the plaintiff "for it is axiomatic that property known to belong to another must be returned." More interestingly, the court held that the defendant could be liable for conversion if the documents it had were mere photocopies of the originals. According to the court, "[i]In such a case the copies become the functional equivalents of the originals." Does this make sense?

5. ***Conversion of Human Tissue.*** Moore v. Regents of the Univ. of Cal., 793 P.2d 479 (Cal. 1990), addressed the question whether the plaintiff stated a cause of action against his physician and other defendants for using rare cells removed from his body in potentially lucrative medical research without his permission. The court

held that the complaint stated a cause of action for breach of the physician's fiduciary disclosure obligations, which generally require a doctor to inform a patient of all information material to the patient's decision on a course of treatment. (*See* Chapter 5.) In rejecting the plaintiff's conversion claim, the court found that "To establish a conversion, [a] plaintiff must establish an actual interference with his ownership or right of possession...." It noted that Moore clearly did not expect to retain possession of his cells following their removal and that statutory law drastically limited any continuing interest of a patient in excised cells. Justice Panelli said:

> To be sure, the threat of liability for conversion might help to enforce patients' rights indirectly.... Unfortunately, to extend the conversion theory would utterly sacrifice the ... goal of protecting innocent parties.... [I]t would impose liability on all those into whose hands the cells come, whether or not the particular defendant participated in, or knew of, the inadequate disclosures that violated the patient's right to make an informed decision....
>
> The extension of conversion law into this area will hinder research by restricting access to the necessary raw materials. Thousands of human cell lines already exist in tissue repositories.... At present, human cell lines are routinely copied and distributed to other researchers for experimental purposes, usually free of charge. This exchange of scientific materials, which still is relatively free and efficient, will surely be compromised if each cell sample becomes the potential subject matter of a lawsuit....

Id. at 493–96.

Chapter 3

Defenses and Privileges

A. Consent

Total Bar to Liability. The plaintiff's consent to an otherwise-tortious act negates the wrongful element of the defendant's conduct and prevents the existence of a tort. This idea is captured in the well-known Latin maxim *volenti non fit injuria*: to one who is willing, no wrong is done. In the context of intentional torts, it is said that "[a]ll intended wrongs . . . have in common the element that they are inflicted without the consent of the victim." Fricke v. Owens-Corning Fiberglass Corp., 571 So. 2d 130, 132 (La. 1990).

Burden of Pleading and Proving. Consent is normally treated not as a defense or privilege for the defendant to plead and prove, but as an issue relevant to the plaintiff's prima facie case. Ordinarily, the burden of proving lack of consent is upon the plaintiff for each of the basic intentional torts, except for trespass to land.

Three Kinds of Consent. There are at least three kinds of consent, any one of which bars an action for an intentional tort: actual consent, apparent consent, and implied consent. Actual consent (sometimes called "consent in fact") exists if the plaintiff is in fact willing that the conduct (but not necessarily the consequences thereof) occur. Apparent consent is found whenever the plaintiff's conduct reasonably leads another to believe that the plaintiff has consented, even though the plaintiff did not actually consent. And implied consent is a legal fiction the courts indulge in the absence of consent (either actual or apparent) to justify desirable conduct which would otherwise be tortious. Not all courts use these terms precisely.

Relation to Assumption of Risk. The *volenti* principle also applies to tort actions not based on intentional conduct. In those cases, the principle is embodied in the doctrine of assumption of the risk, which is examined in Chapter 16.

1. Consent in Fact

Davies v. Butler

Supreme Court of Nevada
602 P.2d 605 (Nev. 1979)

MOWBRAY, Chief Justice.

. . . .

In their wrongful death action, the Davies claimed that . . . the respondents, the Sundowners, a voluntary unincorporated association, and nine of its individual members . . . caused to be administered to their son excessive and unreasonably dangerous amounts of alcohol, and that they subjected him to physical and mental abuse which resulted in his death. . . .

The club . . . is a social "drinking club" which sponsors various activities in conjunction with extra-curricular events at the University of Nevada, Reno.

. . . . On Thursday morning, October 9, 1975, Davies and four others were informed of their selection as initiates. From that time until Saturday night, initiates were directed to participate in morning, afternoon and evening activities, all of which were focused on their ability to consume alcoholic beverages. By Saturday evening, one of Davies' fellow initiates described himself as physically and mentally "exhausted."

On Saturday evening, . . . [at] midnight, . . . the initiates were taken outside to a parking lot and lined against a wall. There the "final ceremony" commenced. The five initiates, including Davies, were given and admonished to drink large quantities of alcohol, including 190 proof "Everclear," within a 20 to 30 minute period. After they had consumed the liquor, the initiates were instructed to climb into the open bed of a pickup truck. . . . [T]hey made two brief stops, then drove some 40 to 50 miles from Reno to a point near Pyramid Lake. There it was discovered that Davies had ceased breathing. . . . Davies eventually was taken to the nearest hospital, where he was pronounced dead. . . .

Testimony of witnesses regarding the treatment and condition of Davies during the "final ceremony" varied. Davies' sister and two of her friends, who observed the event from a car parked across the street, testified that they saw Davies struck in the stomach and on the head by either respondent Sallee or respondent Johnson. Two of these witnesses testified that they heard the decedent shout out "Stop" in protest.

Three other observers . . . testified that they saw Davies fall to the ground, where he was kicked and screamed at, and that they then saw him picked up and held against the wall, while a bottle was forced into his mouth. Two of these witnesses testified that Davies definitely appeared unable to stand on his own.

. . . .

The jury, by a six to three vote, returned a general verdict in favor of all defendants. . . . Appellants contend that reversal and a new trial are mandated by prejudicial errors in the instructions to the jury. . . .

The trial court instructed the jury, over appellants' objection, that "[a] person may expressly or by voluntarily participating in an activity consent to an act which would otherwise be a battery." In the context of this case, the giving of this instruction was reversible error.

.... The jury may well have deduced from this instruction that one who voluntarily participates in an activity ... assumes the risk of all negligent or intentional conduct by others....

... [I]n the context of this case, the instruction was so incomplete as to be misleading. "To be effective, consent must be (a) by one who has the capacity to consent ... and (b) to the particular conduct, or to substantially the same conduct." 4 Restatement (Second), Torts § 892A, at 364 (1979). As this court has held, consent is not effective as a defense to battery "where the beating is excessively disproportionate to the consent, given or implied, or where the party injured is exposed to loss of life or great bodily harm." .... Furthermore, capacity to consent requires the mental ability to appreciate the "nature, extent and probable consequences of the conduct consented to." Restatement, Torts, *supra*, comment b, at 365. As noted by Prosser, Law of Torts, § 18, at 102 (4th ed. 1971), "[i]f the plaintiff is known to be incapable of giving consent because of ... intoxication ... his failure to object, or even his active manifestation of consent will not protect the defendant."

In McCue v. Klein, ... [60 Tex. 168 (1883)], the widow of a man who had died as a result of drinking a toxic quantity of alcohol sued those who had furnished him the alcohol and induced him to drink it, on a wager. The court held, 60 Tex. at 169,

> [T]he maxim of *volenti non fit injuria* presupposes that the party is capable of giving consent to his own injury. If he is divested of the power of refusal by mental faculties, the damage cannot be excused on the ground of consent given. A consent given by a person in such condition is no consent at all,—more especially when his state of mind is well known to the party doing the injury....

We conclude that "in view of all the circumstances the instruction may have misled the jury, and it should not have been given." ....

... [W]e must reverse the order of the district court denying appellants' motion for a new trial and remand the case to the lower court for that purpose.

[The dissenting opinion of BATJER, J., is omitted.]

Notes

1. ***Fraternity Hazing.*** Most jurisdictions have outlawed hazing, usually by classifying the conduct as a criminal misdemeanor unless the acts would otherwise constitute a felony. *See, e.g.*, Conn. Gen. Stat. Ann. § 53-23a (Westlaw 2022) (defining hazing as "any action which recklessly or intentionally endangers the health or safety of a person for the purpose of initiation, admission into or affiliation with, or as a condition for continued membership in, a student organization"); Idaho Code

§ 18-917 (Westlaw 2022) (specifying examples of prohibited activities, such as compelled ingestion of any substance, sleep deprivation, and transportation and abandonment of a pledge).

Hazing may give rise to tort liability. *See* Ballou v. Sigma Nu Gen. Frat., 352 S.E.2d 488 (S.C. Ct. App. 1986) (national fraternity held liable for the death of a pledge following a "hell night" initiation); Haben v. Anderson, 597 N.E.2d 655 (Ill. App. Ct. 1992) (action stated against members of a university club that had a *de facto* drinking requirement).

2. ***Manifestation of Consent.*** Consent in fact may be manifested by words, by affirmative action, or by silence or inaction under circumstances showing that the silence or inaction gives consent. Actual consent bars an action even if it is not communicated to the defendant. *See* Restatement, Second, of Torts § 892, cmt. b. If, for example, the owner of a swimming pool tells a neighbor that anyone in the neighborhood can use the pool, another neighbor who uses the pool without knowing of this invitation has not committed a trespass; *id.*, illus. 1.

3. ***Capacity to Consent.*** Consent is ineffective if youth or mental deficiency precludes a person from appreciating the nature, extent, and probable consequences of the conduct allegedly consented to. *See* Restatement, Second, of Torts § 892A, cmt. b.

4. ***Scope of Consent.*** An action will be barred only if the invasion is within the scope of the plaintiff's consent. In Vitale v. Henchey, 24 S.W.3d 651 (Ky. 2000), a patient consented to surgery being performed by two doctors, but was operated on by a third. The court held that a suit for battery against the third doctor was not barred because that surgery was not within the scope of the consent. In addition, the fact that the first two doctors consented to the operation being performed by the third was irrelevant because consent must be given by one with capacity to consent. The first two doctors had no capacity to consent to surgery on the plaintiff.

In Carter v. Pain Ctr. of Arizona, P.C., 367 P.3d 68, 71 (Ariz. App. 2016), the court held that a plaintiff whose consent to pain treatment was conditioned upon receiving sedation could recover for battery by proving that the defendant doctor "administered the treatment 'in willful disregard of the conditional consent.'"

2. Apparent Consent

Apparent consent may arise from words or conduct. It may also arise from silence, if a reasonable person would voice objections. *Qui tacet consentire.*[1]

---

1. "Silence gives consent."

O'Brien v. Cunard S.S. Co.

Supreme Judicial Court of Massachusetts
28 N.E. 266 (Mass. 1891)

KNOWLTON, J.

This case presents two questions: *First*, whether there was any evidence to warrant the jury in finding that the defendant, by any of its servants or agents, committed an assault on the plaintiff; *secondly*, whether there was evidence on which the jury could have found that the defendant was guilty of negligence towards the plaintiff. To sustain the first count . . . the plaintiff relied on the fact that the surgeon who was employed by the defendant vaccinated her on ship-board, while she was on her passage from Queenstown to Boston. . . . In determining whether the act was lawful or unlawful, the surgeon's conduct must be considered in connection with the surrounding circumstances. If the plaintiff's behavior was such as to indicate consent on her part, he was justified in his act, whatever her unexpressed feelings may have been. In determining whether she consented, he could be guided only by her overt acts and the manifestations of her feelings. . . . It is undisputed that at Boston there are strict quarantine regulations in regard to the examination of emigrants, to see that they are protected from small-pox by vaccination, and that only those persons who hold a certificate from the medical officer of the steam-ship, stating that they are so protected, are permitted to land without detention in quarantine, or vaccination by the port physician. It appears that the defendant is accustomed to have its surgeons vaccinate all emigrants who desire it, and who are not protected by previous vaccination, and give them a certificate which is accepted at quarantine as evidence of their protection. Notices of the regulations at quarantine, and of the willingness of the ship's medical officer to vaccinate such as needed vaccination, were posted about the ship in various languages, and on the day when the operation was performed the surgeon had a right to presume that she and the other women who were vaccinated understood the importance and purpose of vaccination for those who bore no marks to show that they were protected. By the plaintiff's testimony, which, in this particular, is undisputed, it appears that about 200 women passengers were assembled below, and she understood from conversation with them that they were to be vaccinated; that she stood about 15 feet from the surgeon, and saw them form in a line, and pass in turn before him; that he "examined their arms, and, passing some of them by, proceeded to vaccinate those that had no mark;" that she did not hear him say anything to any of them; that upon being passed by they each received a card, and went on deck; that when her turn came she showed him her arm; he looked at it, and said there was no mark, and that she should be vaccinated; that she told him she had been vaccinated before, and it left no mark; "that he then said nothing; that he should vaccinate her again;" that she held up her arm to be vaccinated; that no one touched her; that she did not tell him she did not want to be vaccinated; and that she took the ticket which he gave her, certifying that he had vaccinated her, and used it at quarantine. . . . There was nothing in the conduct of the plaintiff to indicate to the surgeon that she did not wish to obtain a card which would save her from detention at quarantine, and to be vaccinated, if necessary, for that purpose. Viewing his conduct in the light of the surrounding circumstances, it was lawful; and there was no evidence tending to show that it was not....

[The court found the negligence claim to be without merit.].... Exceptions overruled.

Notes

1. ***Other Precedent.*** *See* Lesser v. Neosho County Comm. Coll., 741 F. Supp. 854, 865 (D. Kan. 1990) (a student-athlete's claim of battery, based on the military-style haircut he received as a member of a baseball team, was barred by consent).

2. ***Consent Based on Participation.*** *See* Smith v. Calvary Christian Church, 614 N.W.2d 590 (Mich. 2000) (holding that tort claims arising from public shaming were barred because, although the plaintiff had resigned his church membership, his subsequent active engagement and participation in the church manifested his consent to the church's disciplinary practices).

3. Implied Consent

In the absence of actual or apparent consent, special circumstances such as a medical emergency may make it desirable for a person to engage in conduct that would otherwise be tortious. In such instances, the law holds that consent is implied because the interests to be furthered by the invasion (*e.g.*, preservation of life or limb) are more important than those which will be sacrificed (*e.g.*, personal bodily integrity and freedom from unconsented contact). In such instances, there is no consent at all, actual or apparent, only a legal fiction called implied consent, which completely bars liability.

In Kozup v. Georgetown Univ., 851 F.2d 437 (D.C. Cir. 1988), an infant contracted AIDS as a result of a blood transfusion. The court recognized the medical emergency rule, but held that the trial court erred in granting summary judgment, for there was a material issue of fact as to whether an emergency in fact existed at the time the transfusion was administered.

The following case illustrates the rule relating to medical emergencies, although it rejects the rubric of "implied consent." (The *Miller* court seems to reserve that phrase for actual or apparent consent inferred from conduct.)

Miller v. HCA, Inc.

Supreme Court of Texas
118 S.W.3d 758 (Tex. 2003)

Justice ENOCH delivered the opinion of the Court.

The narrow question we must decide is whether Texas law recognizes a claim by parents for either battery or negligence because their premature infant, born alive but in distress at only twenty-three weeks of gestation, was provided resuscitative medical treatment by physicians at a hospital without parental consent. The court of appeals, with one justice dissenting, held that neither claim could be maintained....

.... First, there is no dispute ... that the Millers' premature infant could not be fully evaluated for medical treatment until birth. As a result, any decisions concerning treatment for the Millers' child would not be fully informed decisions until birth. Second, the evidence further established that once the infant was born, the physician attending the birth was faced with emergent circumstances—*i.e.*, the child might survive with treatment but would likely die if treatment was not provided before either parental consent or a court order overriding the withholding of such consent could be obtained.

... [A]pproximately four months before her due date, Karla Miller was admitted to ... (the "Hospital") in premature labor. An ultrasound revealed that Karla's fetus weighed about 629 grams or 1 1/4 pounds....

.... The physicians ... informed the Millers that if the infant was born alive, it would most probably suffer severe impairments, including cerebral palsy, brain hemorrhaging, blindness, lung disease, pulmonary infections, and mental retardation....

... Drs. Jacobs and Kelley asked the Millers to decide whether physicians should treat the infant upon birth.... At approximately noon that day, the Millers informed Drs. Jacob and Kelley that they wanted no heroic measures performed on the infant and they wanted nature to take its course.... Mark then left the Hospital to make funeral arrangements for the infant.

.... An afternoon of meetings involving Hospital administrators and physicians followed....

Moreover, the physicians at the meeting testified that they and Hospital administrators agreed only that a neonatologist would be present to evaluate the Millers' infant at birth and decide whether to resuscitate based on the infant's condition at that time....

Although Dr. Eduardo Otero, the neonatologist present in the delivery room when Sidney was born, did not attend that meeting, he confirmed that he needed to actually see Sidney before deciding what treatment, if any, would be appropriate....

Mark testified that, after the meeting, Hospital administrators asked him to sign a consent form allowing resuscitation according to the Hospital's plan, but he refused. Mark further testified that when he asked how he could prevent resuscitation,

Hospital administrators told him that he could do so by removing Karla from the Hospital, which was not a viable option given her condition. . . .

. . . [T]hat night, Karla delivered a premature female infant weighing 615 grams, which the Millers named Sidney. . . . [Sidney] was born alive.

Dr. Otero noted that Sidney had a heart beat. . . . He immediately "bagged" and "intubated" Sidney to oxygenate her blood; he then placed her on ventilation. . . .

. . . [A]t some point during the first few days after birth, Sidney suffered a brain hemorrhage. . . .

. . . . At the time of trial, Sidney was seven years old and could not walk, talk, feed herself, or sit up on her own. The evidence demonstrated that Sidney was legally blind, suffered from severe mental retardation, cerebral palsy, seizures, and spastic quadriparesis in her limbs. She could not be toilet-trained and required a shunt in her brain to drain fluids that accumulate there and needed care twenty-four hours a day. . . .

. . . . The jury found that the Hospital, without the consent of Karla or Mark Miller, performed resuscitative treatment on Sidney. . . . The jury concluded that HCA and the Hospital were grossly negligent and that the Hospital acted with malice. The jury also determined that Dr. Otero acted as the Hospital's agent in resuscitating Sidney and that HCA was responsible for the Hospital's conduct under alter ego and single business enterprise theories. The trial court rendered judgment . . . on the jury's verdict of $29,400,000 in actual damages for medical expenses, $17,503,066 in prejudgment interest, and $13,500,000 in exemplary damages.

. . . . As the United States Supreme Court has acknowledged, parents are presumed to be the appropriate decision-makers for their infants. . . .

The Texas Legislature has likewise recognized that parents are presumed to be appropriate decision-makers, giving parents the right to consent to their infant's medical care and surgical treatment. A logical corollary of that right . . . is that parents have the right not to consent to certain medical care for their infant, *i.e.*, parents have the right to refuse certain medical care.

. . . [T]he Supreme Court has also pointed out:

> [A]s long as parents choose from professionally accepted treatment options the choice is rarely reviewed in court and even less frequently supervened. . . .

. . . [T]he general rule in Texas is that a physician who provides treatment without consent commits a battery. But there are exceptions. For example, in Gravis v. Physicians & Surgeons Hospital [427 S.W.2d 310, 311 (Tex. 1968)], this Court acknowledged that "consent will be implied where the patient is unconscious or otherwise unable to give express consent and an immediate operation is necessary to preserve life or health."

In Moss v. Rishworth, [222 S.W. 225, 226–27 (Tex. Comm'n App. 1920, *judgm't approved*)], the court held that a physician commits a "legal wrong" by operating on a minor without parental consent when there is "an absolute necessity for a prompt operation, but not emergent in the sense that death would likely result immediately upon the failure to perform it." .... *Moss* ... implicitly acknowledges that a physician does not commit a legal wrong by operating on a minor without consent when the operation is performed under emergent circumstances — *i.e.,* when death is likely to result immediately upon the failure to perform it.

Moss guides us here. We hold that a physician, who is confronted with emergent circumstances and provides life-sustaining treatment to a minor child, is not liable for not first obtaining consent from the parents....

Providing treatment to a child under emergent circumstances does not imply consent to treatment despite actual notice of refusal to consent. Rather, it is an exception to the general rule that a physician commits a battery by providing medical treatment without consent. As such, the exception is narrowly circumscribed and arises only in emergent circumstances when there is no time to consult the parents or seek court intervention if the parents withhold consent before death is likely to result to the child....

... [T]he emergent circumstances exception acknowledges that the harm from failing to treat outweighs any harm threatened by the proposed treatment, because the harm from failing to provide life-sustaining treatment under emergent circumstances is death....

.... The jury found that the Hospital, through Dr. Otero, treated Sidney without the Millers' consent. The parties do not challenge that finding. Thus, we only address whether the Hospital was required to seek court intervention to overturn the lack of parental consent — which it undisputedly did not do — before Dr. Otero could treat Sidney without committing a battery.

The Millers ... contend that, as a matter of law, no emergency existed ... The Millers note ... "[a]nytime a group of doctors and a hospital administration ha[ve] the luxury of multiple meetings to change the original doctors' medical opinions ... there is no medical emergency."

... [T]he Millers' reasoning fails to recognize that, in this case, the evidence established that Sidney could only be properly evaluated when she was born. Any decision the Millers made before Sidney's birth concerning her treatment at or after her birth would necessarily be based on speculation. Therefore, we reject the Millers' argument that a decision could adequately be made pre-birth that denying all post-birth resuscitative treatment would be in Sidney's best interest. Such a decision could not control whether the circumstances facing Dr. Otero were emergent because it would not have been a fully informed one according to the evidence in this case.

... Sidney was born alive but in distress. At that time, Dr. Otero had to make a split-second decision on whether to provide life-sustaining treatment. While the Millers were both present in the delivery room, there was simply no time to obtain their consent to treatment or to institute legal proceedings to challenge their withholding of consent, had the Millers done so, without jeopardizing Sidney's life. . . .

. . . [W]e decline to impose liability on a physician solely for providing life-sustaining treatment under emergent circumstances to a new-born infant without . . . consent.

. . . . We affirm the court of appeals' judgment.

Justice O'NEILL and Justice SMITH did not participate in the decision.

Note

1. ***Implied Consent in Medical Emergencies***. In Barnett v. Bachrach, 34 A.2d 626, 628 (D.C. 1943), the court observed:

> . . . [I]n case of emergency a surgeon may lawfully perform, and it is his duty to perform, such operation as good surgery demands even when it means extending the operation further than was originally contemplated, and . . . for doing so he is neither to be held [liable] in damages, or denied recovery of his fee.
>
> . . . . The law does not insist that a surgeon shall perform every operation according to plans and specifications, approved in advance by the patient, and carefully tucked away in his office-safe for courtroom purposes.

4. Consent Given Because of a Mistake

DeMay v. Roberts

Supreme Court of Michigan
9 N.W. 146 (Mich. 1881)

MARSTON, C.J.

The declaration in this case . . . sets forth that the plaintiff was at a time and place named a poor married woman, and being confined in child-bed . . . employed in a professional capacity defendant De May who was a physician; that defendant visited the plaintiff as such, and against her desire and intending to deceive her wrongfully . . . introduced and caused to be present at the house and lying-in room of the plaintiff and while she was in the pains of parturition the defendant Scattergood, who intruded upon the privacy of the plaintiff, indecently, wrongfully and unlawfully laid hands upon and assaulted her, the said Scattergood, which was well known to defendant De May, being a young unmarried man, a stranger to the plaintiff and utterly ignorant of the practice of medicine, while the plaintiff believed that he was an assistant physician, a competent and proper person to be present and to aid her in her extremity.

. . . .

The evidence on the part of the plaintiff tended to prove the allegations of the declaration. On the part of the defendants evidence was given tending to prove that Scattergood very reluctantly accompanied Dr. De May at the urgent request of the latter; that the night was a dark and stormy one, the roads over which they had to travel in getting to the house of the plaintiff were so bad that a horse could not be rode or driven over them; that the doctor was sick and very much fatigued from overwork, and therefore asked the defendant Scattergood to accompany and assist him in carrying a lantern, umbrella and certain articles deemed necessary upon such occasions; that upon arriving at the house of the plaintiff the doctor knocked, and when the door was opened by the husband of the plaintiff, De May said to him, "that I had fetched a friend along to help carry my things;" he, plaintiff's husband, said all right, and seemed to be perfectly satisfied. They were bid to enter, treated kindly and no objection whatever made to the presence of defendant Scattergood. That while there Scattergood, at Dr. De May's request, took hold of plaintiff's hand and held her during a paroxysm of pain, and that both of the defendants in all respects throughout acted in a proper and becoming manner actuated by a sense of duty and kindness.

.... The plaintiff when examined as a witness was asked, what idea she entertained in reference to Scattergood's character and right to be in the house ... and answered that she thought he was a student or a physician. To this there could be no good legal objection. It was not only important to know the character in which Scattergood went there, but to learn what knowledge the plaintiff had upon that subject. It was not claimed that the plaintiff or her husband, who were strangers in that vicinity, had ever met Scattergood before this time or had any knowledge or information concerning him beyond what they obtained on that evening, and it was claimed by the defendant that both the plaintiff and her husband must have known, from certain ambiguous expressions used, that he was not a physician.

We are of [the] opinion that the plaintiff and her husband had a right to presume that a practicing physician would not, upon an occasion of that character, take with him and introduce into the house, a young man in no way, either by education or otherwise, connected with the medical profession; and that something more clear and certain as to his non-professional character would be required to put the plaintiff and her husband upon their guard, or remove such presumption, than the remark made by De May that he had brought a friend along to help carry his things....

.... To the plaintiff the occasion was a most sacred one and no one had a right to intrude unless invited or because of some real and pressing necessity which it is not pretended existed in this case. The plaintiff had a legal right to the privacy of her apartment at such a time, and the law secures to her this right by requiring others to observe it, and to abstain from its violation. The fact that at the time, she consented to the presence of Scattergood supposing him to be a physician, does not preclude her from maintaining an action and recovering substantial damages upon afterwards ascertaining his true character. In obtaining admission at such a time and under such circumstances without fully disclosing his true character, both parties were guilty of deceit, and the wrong thus done entitles the injured party to recover the damages afterwards sustained, from shame and mortification upon discovering the true character of the defendants.

. . . .

It follows therefore that the judgment must be affirmed with costs.

Notes

1. ***Types of Mistakes.*** In thinking about whether a mistake vitiates consent, it is useful to differentiate three kinds of cases. The categories are: (1) unilateral mistakes resulting from fraud by the defendant; (2) mutual mistakes made by both parties; and (3) mistakes resulting from the defendant's negligence.

2. ***Unilateral Mistakes Resulting from Fraud by the Defendant.*** Consent intentionally procured by fraud is invalid. Some authorities limit this rule to situations in which the misrepresentation relates to the "essence" of the transaction, holding that consent is vitiated only by deception bearing upon (1) the nature of the invasion, (2) the degree of harm reasonably to be expected, or (3) the existence of facts (perhaps relating to the relationship of the parties or the necessity of medical procedures) which make the interference harmful or offensive. This form of misrepresentation is called "fraud in the essence" or "fraud in the *factum*."

In contrast, "fraud in the inducement" is a misrepresentation that relates merely to a person's collateral reasons for agreement (as opposed to the nature of the invasion or the harm, if any, to be anticipated). Fraud in the inducement is insufficient to destroy consent.

If the defendant knowingly causes the plaintiff to unwittingly eat poisoned chocolate, the mistake is probably fraud in the essence, and the plaintiff can sue for battery. If the chocolate is not poisonous, but merely stale or inferior, the mistake may simply be fraud in the inducement, in which case the plaintiff's consent to eat the chocolate will bar an action for battery.

Although superficially appealing, the *factum*-inducement dichotomy breaks down in application and has little predictive value. It is often difficult or impossible to confidently differentiate between essential and collateral matters. For example, the Restatement, Second, of Torts sets forth two illustrations. The first says that a person who unknowingly accepts counterfeit money in exchange for submitting to intimate familiarities has no action for battery; the second allows a battery action to a person who unknowingly takes counterfeit money in exchange for agreeing to a blood transfusion. The distinction between these two situations—if it exists at all—is surely too elusive to provide useful guidance to the courts or the public.

Some modern scholarship rejects the traditional *factum*-inducement dichotomy and argues that any mistake sufficiently material to play a role in the plaintiff's decision-making process will invalidate consent if the defendant knows the plaintiff is making a mistake. Materiality simply means that the matter would be taken into account by a reasonable person making a decision, or is a matter the defendant knows is important to the plaintiff.

On the traditional view, see Restatement, Second, of Torts § 892B. Among the authorities rejecting the *factum*-inducement dichotomy is David A. Fischer, *Fraudulently Induced Consent to Intentional Torts*, 46 U. Cinn. L. Rev. 71 (1977). *See also* Fowler V. Harper, Fleming James, Jr., & Oscar S. Gray, Law of Torts § 3.10 (3d ed. 2006) ("Case law is thin . . . as to the proposed distinction [between collateral and non-collateral matters]"). Under both the traditional view and the modern view, consent is not destroyed unless the defendant knows the plaintiff is making a mistake.

3. ***Mutual Mistakes.*** A mutual mistake does not destroy consent. For example, in Marlow v. City of Sisters, 383 P.3d 908, 912–13 (Or. App. 2016), the plaintiffs granted a city permission to make certain street improvements near their property at a point in time when both they and the city believed that the city owned the land in question. When it was later determined that the plaintiffs owned the land, they sued for trespass. The court held that the action was barred by consent because the mistake was mutual (and therefore irrelevant). The city and the plaintiffs were both mistaken about the facts. The city did not take advantage of persons it knew were making a mistake.

4. ***Mistakes Negligently Caused by the Defendant.*** A defendant who negligently causes a plaintiff to make an ill-informed decision may be barred from asserting that consent precludes imposition of tort liability. In Mercado v. Mount Sinai Hosp. Med. Ctr., 889 N.E.2d 730 (Ill. App. Ct. 2008), the court wrote:

> Plaintiff alleged Dr. Cavens erred in diagnosing her pregnancy as an unviable and potentially dangerous ectopic pregnancy outside her uterus. Plaintiff agreed to terminate the ectopic pregnancy. . . . Plaintiff later learned the pregnancy was not ectopic but uterine, where it could have been viable.
>
> . . . .
>
> The statute at issue provides: "There shall be no cause of action against a physician or a medical institution for the wrongful death of a fetus caused by an abortion where the abortion was permitted by law and the *requisite consent* was lawfully given." . . . .
>
> . . . [W]e conclude that plaintiff could not have given the "requisite consent" for the termination of her uterine pregnancy. Plaintiff's consent was not "requisite" because she did not have the information necessary to understand "the nature of things." Plaintiff's agreement to terminate the pregnancy was not "consent" because she did not know her pregnancy was in her uterus. She agreed to the termination of an ectopic pregnancy. She received the termination of a uterine pregnancy. Without the requisite consent required by the statute, her wrongful death action on behalf of her fetus is not barred.

5. ***Problem 1: The Mistake About a Vasectomy.*** A man who had a sexual relationship with a woman eventually revealed to her that he had previously had a vasectomy. The woman suffered emotional distress and claimed that she had been misled into the relationship because the man knew she had little time left in which to become a biological mother, and she would not have become intimate with him had she known of the vasectomy. In a discussion about the future of their relationship, the woman had expressed her desire to have a family, and the man, who previously had four children, responded that a fortune teller had told him he would have six children, and that the plaintiff should not worry. The woman alleged that the man's failure to reveal that he had had a vasectomy was a fraud that vitiated her consent to sexual relations. In an action for battery, how should the court rule? Is the consent valid or unenforceable?

It may be helpful to think about this problem methodically: (1) Was the mistake unilateral or mutual? Mutual mistakes are irrelevant. (2) If the mistake was unilateral, did the defendant know that the plaintiff was making a mistake? If not, the mistake is irrelevant. (3) If the defendant knew the plaintiff was making a mistake, was the mistake sufficiently important to invalidate consent (that is, under the traditional view, was it essential, rather than collateral; under the modern view, was it material)? For one view, see Conley v. Romeri, 806 N.E.2d 933 (Mass. App. Ct. 2004), which arose from these facts.

6. ***Problem 2: Mistake About Improving Acting Skills.*** A distinguished acting teacher in his mid-sixties induced female students in their early twenties to engage in various sexual acts with him and with each other in his presence. The defendant told the students that the sexual activity would release their inhibitions and improve their acting skills. Should the consent of the students bar their actions for assault and battery? *See* Micari v. Mann, 481 N.Y.S.2d 967 (Sup. Ct. 1984). Follow the methodology set out above.

7. ***Problem 3: DeMay v. Roberts.*** Was the principal case properly decided according to either the traditional view or the modern view?

8. ***Consent and Duress.*** Consent is not effective if it is given under duress, such as the use or threat of force against one's person or property, or against the person or property of family members. *See* Restatement, Second, of Torts § 892B cmt. j; Trotter v. Okawa, 445 S.E.2d 121 (Va. 1994) (mentally ill patient's consent to sexual intercourse was vitiated by duress).

Courts have been reluctant to accept arguments that consent is vitiated by economic duress. For example, in Quinn v. Limited Express, Inc., 715 F. Supp. 127 (W.D. Pa. 1989), the court held that an employee's consent negated any action for assault and battery arising from her employer's use of a polygraph examination as a part of an investigation of missing funds. The court wrote:

> Our conclusion that plaintiff impliedly consented to the polygraph examination is supported by the absence of duress. Plaintiff testified that neither the examiner nor any representative from the company told her she had to take the polygraph test. Likewise, neither the examiner nor any company

> representative told her she had to sign the consent forms. . . . Plaintiff was never told she would be fired if she did not submit to the exam. We recognize that plaintiff "felt that if I did not submit to it that I would either be terminated or looked upon with disfavor and suspicion by my superiors." The plaintiff's perceptions of economic duress, however, are insufficient to negate plaintiff's conduct which manifested her implied consent.

9. ***Consent to a Criminal Act.*** There is a split of authority as to whether consent to a criminal act bars tort liability. The everyday case is that of two people who agree to "step outside and settle their differences": conduct which typically violates laws about assault (in the criminal sense) and disturbing the peace. Some courts say that the consent does not bar a tort action, on the theory that no person has the right to consent to what the law forbids. According to these authorities, when two persons engage in criminal conduct, there are really three parties, the third being the state, and neither of the individual actors has the right to speak for the state or waive its interests. Under this view, respect for the law demands that consent to a criminal act be held invalid.

The other position—which has been embraced by the Restatement—holds that "consent is effective to bar recovery in a tort action although the conduct consented to is a crime." Restatement, Second, of Torts § 829C(1). According to this view, the state's interests can be adequately advanced through criminal prosecutions (in which consent of the participants would not be a defense). *See* Hart v. Geysel, 294 P. 570 (Wash. 1930) (affirming the dismissal of a wrongful death action arising from the decedent's participation in an illegal prize fight).

10. ***Deterrence of Criminal Acts.*** Which rule better deters a breach of the peace: one which announces, "if you win the fight, you can still be held liable for damages" (the view holding consent to a criminal act invalid), or one which proclaims, "if you lose the fight, you may not seek a re-match in the courts" (the view holding consent to a criminal act valid)? Do criminals give any thought to tort liability when they engage in criminal acts?

11. ***Parties Not "In Pari Delicto."*** Consent to a criminal act will bar liability only if the parties were *in pari delicto.*[2] For example, the Restatement, Second, of Torts § 892C(2), provides that "if conduct is made criminal in order to protect a certain class of persons irrespective of their consent, the consent of members of that class to the conduct is not effective to bar a tort action." In Hudson v. Craft, 204 P.2d 1 (Cal. 1949), an 18-year-old participant in an illegal boxing match sued the promoter of the match for injuries he sustained. The court found that the boxing law, which required licensing and safety precautions, was intended to protect persons engaging in the activity from physical harm; the law was not intended to protect boxing promoters.

---

2. Parties stand "*in pari delicto*" when they are equally at fault. "The *in pari delicto* doctrine is based upon the premise that there is no recourse between wrongdoers." Patten v. Raddatz, 895 P.2d 633 (Mont. 1995) (a tort action arising from long-term relationship involving drug use and prostitution was barred).

Consequently, the plaintiff participant and the defendant promoter were not *in pari delicto*, and a suit against the promoter could be maintained, even though the plaintiff might have been criminally liable and would have been barred from suing another participant.

Statutes intended to protect a particular class of persons include those which forbid the sale of liquor to a person who is already intoxicated and forbid sexual intercourse with a child under sixteen, regardless of consent. *See* Restatement, Second, of Torts § 892C, illus. 7 & 8.

B. Defense of Self and Others

Silas v. Bowen

United States District Court for the District of South Carolina
277 F. Supp. 314 (D. S.C. 1967)

DONALD RUSSELL, District Judge.

[At defendant's parking lot, plaintiff engaged a mechanic to repair his car. The mechanic, though present at the lot, was not employed by the defendant. After receiving the car a week later, taking it for a drive, and discovering that the repairs were defective, plaintiff returned to the lot and heatedly demanded that the defendant immediately rectify the problem.]

. . . .

The testimony of the defendant and his two corroborating witnesses, one of whom, it is true, is his wife, seems [to be the] more credible. According to them, the plaintiff was drinking when he arrived at the parking lot; he was quite belligerent, was cursing, refused to depart when told to leave, approached the defendant in a threatening manner and grabbed him. When the difference in the size and age of the plaintiff and defendant is considered, the situation of the defendant was such as to strike fear and terror in the latter. The plaintiff was a young man, a professional athlete, robust, standing some six feet six inches, in perfect physical condition, weighing 225 to 230 pounds. The defendant, on the other hand, was of middle age, weighing about 135 pounds and standing five feet six inches. Facing a threat from the plaintiff, unable to induce him and his companions to leave his premises, already assaulted by the plaintiff, the defendant, under the emergency thus created and with reasonable cause to fear serious bodily harm from an individual so much more overpowering than he, fired his shotgun, not, I am convinced, with the intent of striking the plaintiff, but for the purpose of frightening him into desisting from his attack and into leaving his premises. Unfortunately, the shot, though directed downward towards the ground, struck the plaintiff in the foot. . . .

The commission of an assault and battery by the defendant on the plaintiff is conceded and defendant seeks exoneration on his affirmative plea of self-defense. . . .

.... While entry of the defendant's premises by the plaintiff was lawful, the defendant had a plain right to order the plaintiff and his companions to depart; and, when the plaintiff refused to withdraw voluntarily after such demand, to use reasonable force to eject them....

.... While this right to use reasonable force does not ordinarily encompass the use of a deadly weapon, such use will be authorized, by way of self-defense, if the conduct of the trespasser under all the circumstances is such as to produce in the mind of a person of reasonable prudence and courage an apprehension of an assault by such trespasser involving serious bodily harm....

.... In determining whether there was reasonable cause and justification for the use of a deadly weapon in such a situation, all the circumstances must be considered. Accordingly, it is generally stated that a defendant, in his own place of business, where he has a right to be, as the defendant was in this case, is not required to retreat in the face of a threatened assault in order to be able to plead self-defense.... Again, while it is well-settled that mere words, however "abusive, insulting, vexatious or threatening," will not in themselves justify the use of a deadly weapon, such words if "accompanied by an actual offer of physical violence" reasonably warranting fear of serious bodily harm, may be an integral part of a plea of self-defense against liability for an assault and battery.... Moreover, in determining whether there was reasonable cause for the apprehension of serious bodily harm, the difference in age, size, and relative physical strength of the parties to the controversy is a proper matter for consideration.... As the Court said in State v. Floyd (1859), 51 N.C. (6 Jones) 392, "One cannot be expected to encounter a lion as he would a lamb."

.... Of course, the defendant, in order to support his plea of self-defense must not have been at fault in provoking the difficulty..., but, by demanding that the plaintiff and his companions leave his parking lot, the defendant acted within his legal rights and can in no way be regarded as provoking the difficulty in this case....

This plea of self-defense, if sustained, is a bar to recovery in this action. One, who has acted in justifiable self-defense "can neither be punished criminally, nor held responsible for damages in a civil action."....

In my opinion, the defendant has made out his plea of self-defense under the facts and applicable law, as I have found and concluded. He acted in reasonable apprehension of serious bodily harm and to repel what he reasonably feared would be a serious and dangerous assault by a person of overpowering size.

Let judgment be entered for defendant....

Notes

1. ***Unlawful Provocation.*** The privilege of self-defense is not available to an aggressor: one who unlawfully provokes an attack. *See, e.g.*, Tripoli v. Gurry, 218 So. 2d 563 (La. 1969). Thus, if *A* strikes *B* without justification, and *B*, using reasonable force, returns the blow in self-defense, *A* is liable for any harm inflicted on *B* in the course of an effort to "defend" against *B*'s response.

The status of aggressor may shift as a confrontation escalates. For example, if *B*, the victim of the initial unlawful attack, responds by using *excessive* force, *B* is liable for those injuries caused by the unreasonableness of the force. *See* Ogden v. Claycomb, 52 Ill. 365, 366 (1869); Livesay v. Ambassador Operating Co., 92 S.W.2d 961, 963 (Mo. Ct. App. 1936). Moreover, it would be absurd for the law to conclude that *A*'s only recourse in the face of excessive force is to bring an action for damages. Rather, *A*, despite being the initial instigator, gains a limited right of self-defense. *See* Fraguglia v. Sala, 62 P.2d 783 (Cal. Ct. App. 1936). Though *A* will be responsible for the harm resulting from the initial attack on *B*, *A* will not be held liable for those damages proximately caused to *B* by a reasonable response to *B*'s use of excessive force. Each party may therefore be liable to the other for portions of the resulting damage.

Where self-defense is governed by statute, different rules may apply. *See* Rogers v. Peeler, 146 S.W.3d 765 (Tex. App. 2004) (holding that the privilege of self-defense was unavailable to a person unlawfully carrying a weapon).

2. ***Abandonment.*** An aggressor may regain a right of self-defense by communicating to the plaintiff an intent to cease the attack. *See* Jelly v. Dabney, 581 P.2d 622, 624 (Wyo. 1978). This may be difficult to do persuasively, especially if the attacker retains control of a weapon.

3. ***Differing Results.*** Because factual nuances unique to each case color the assessment of whether the force used in defense of self or defense of others was reasonable in amount, similar confrontations have given rise to divergent legal results. For example, in both McCullough v. McAnelly, 248 So. 2d 7 (La. Ct. App. 1971), and Lopez v. Surchia, 246 P.2d 111 (Cal. Ct. App. 1952), a father fired one or more shots in an attempt to aid his son, who was being attacked on the family's front lawn. The attacker, in each instance, suffered death or serious bodily injury. In *McCullough*, the force used was held to be reasonable; in *Lopez*, the privilege was denied on the ground that the response was excessive. A lawyer presenting a claim of self-defense or defense of others must carefully develop for the factfinder the circumstances of the particular case.

4. ***Mistake about the Need for Self-Defense.*** The defendant in Courvoisier v. Raymond, 47 P. 284 (Colo. 1896), was asleep in his bed when the building in which he lived was attacked by a mob, for reasons which do not appear in the opinion. The defendant got up, took his revolver, and attempted unsuccessfully to scare the mob away by firing into the air. Raymond, a police officer, emerged from the crowd and approached Courvoisier, who, perhaps believing that Raymond was one of the rioters, shot him. The trial court charged the jury that if it found from the evidence that Raymond was not assaulting Courvoisier, it should find Courvoisier liable for Raymond's injuries. This was held to be error: If Courvoisier reasonably, though mistakenly, believed that Raymond was attacking him, Courvoisier had a privilege to use force in self-defense. *See* Restatement, Second, of Torts § 63 cmt. h.

5. ***Retaliation.*** The privilege is one of defense, not retaliation. It does not allow a victim to "get even," but merely allows reasonable efforts to avoid the infliction of harm.

6. ***Mere Words.*** Mere words, unaccompanied by a hostile act, do not justify self-defense. *See* Penn v. Henderson, 146 P.2d 760, 765 (Or. 1944). However, abusive language is relevant to whether one reasonably believes there is an attack. *See* Pattershall v. Jenness, 485 A.2d 980, 985 (Me. 1984).

7. ***Common Law Duty to Retreat.*** Under common law principles, there is no duty to retreat rather than use *non-deadly* force. However, in some states, there is a duty to retreat rather than use *deadly* force in self-defense, but only if the defender could retreat with complete safety. (Deadly force is force likely to cause death or serious bodily injury.) Even in these states, the duty to retreat generally does not apply to one attacked at home or at work, unless that place was also the home or workplace of the assailant. The thought is that one's home or workplace is one's "castle." *See generally* Restatement, Second, of Torts § 65 & cmts. g–i (recognizing a duty to retreat and a "castle" exception).

8. ***Statutory Limitation of the Duty to Retreat.*** In 2005, Florida abrogated that state's duty to retreat. *See* Florida Stat. Ann. § 776.012 (Westlaw 2022) (providing in part that "a person is justified in the use of deadly force and does not have a duty to retreat if . . . [h]e or she reasonably believes that such force is necessary to prevent imminent death or great bodily harm to himself or herself or another or to prevent the imminent commission of a forcible felony"). As a result of lobbying by the National Rifle Association, other states have followed suit.

One recent article notes:

> Since 2005, there have been significant changes in how American self-defense law treats the situations and places where one is privileged to use deadly force in self-defense. Since that time, half of the states have enacted statutory provisions changing when, where, and how an actor may use deadly force in self-defense. These laws, commonly referred to as "castle laws," "stand-your-ground laws," or "shoot first, ask questions later laws" (depending on your political persuasion), have the common feature of strengthening legal protections for those who use deadly force in self-defense.

Wyatt Holliday, Comment, *"The Answer to Criminal Aggression is Retaliation": Stand-Your-Ground Laws and the Liberalization of Self-Defense*, 43 U. Tol. L. Rev. 407 (2012). In some states, the statutory language is intricate. For example, the Wisconsin law is replete with not only substantive provisions, but also presumptions and exceptions:

Wisconsin Statutes Annotated § 895.62 (Westlaw 2022)

Use of force in response to unlawful and forcible entry into a dwelling, motor vehicle, or place of business; civil liability immunity

> . . . .
>
> (2) Except as provided in sub. (4), an actor is immune from civil liability arising out of his or her use of force that is intended or likely to cause death or great bodily harm if the actor reasonably believed that the force

was necessary to prevent imminent death or bodily harm to himself or herself or to another person and either of the following applies:

(a) The person against whom the force was used was in the process of unlawfully and forcibly entering the actor's dwelling, motor vehicle, or place of business, the actor was on his or her property or present in the dwelling, motor vehicle, or place of business, and the actor knew or had reason to believe that an unlawful and forcible entry was occurring.

(b) The person against whom the force was used was in the actor's dwelling, motor vehicle, or place of business after unlawfully and forcibly entering it, the actor was present in the dwelling, motor vehicle, or place of business, and the actor knew or had reason to believe that the person had unlawfully and forcibly entered the dwelling, motor vehicle, or place of business.

(3) If sub. (2)(a) or (b) applies, the finder of fact may not consider whether the actor had an opportunity to flee or retreat before he or she used force and the actor is presumed to have reasonably believed that the force was necessary to prevent imminent death or bodily harm to himself or herself or to another person.

(4) The presumption described in sub. (3) does not apply if any of the following are true:

(a) The actor was engaged in a criminal activity or was using his or her dwelling, motor vehicle, or place of business to further a criminal activity at the time he or she used the force described in sub. (2).

(b) The person against whom the force was used was a public safety worker, as defined in § 941.375(1)(b), who entered or attempted to enter the actor's dwelling, motor vehicle, or place of business in the performance of his or her official duties. This paragraph applies only if at least one of the following applies:

1. The public safety worker identified himself or herself to the actor before the force described in sub. (2) was used by the actor.

2. The actor knew or reasonably should have known that the person entering or attempting to enter his or her dwelling, motor vehicle, or place of business was a public safety worker.

(5) In any civil action, if a court finds that a person is immune from civil liability under sub. (2), the court shall award the person reasonable attorney fees, costs, compensation for loss of income, and other costs of the litigation reasonably incurred by the person. . . .

There is sometimes a question as to whether statutory reforms, which are often part of a penal code, apply only to criminal cases and not to civil tort actions. However, certain states have left no doubt. As part of its penal code, Texas abrogated the duty to retreat. *See* Tex. Pen. Code § 9.32(c) (Westlaw 2022) (stating that "[a] person who has a right to be present at the location where the deadly force is used, who has not provoked the person against whom the deadly force is used, and who is not engaged in criminal activity at the time the deadly force is used is not required to retreat before using deadly force"). Then the Texas civil code was revised to provide for civil immunity if deadly force was justifiably used under the terms set forth in the penal code. *See* Tex. Civ. Prac. & Rem. Code § 83.001 (Westlaw 2022).

9. ***Battered-Woman Syndrome.*** Traditionally, self-defense may be invoked only if harm appears to be imminent. Despite that limitation, there have been efforts in criminal law to extend the defense to cases involving prolonged abuse of a spouse or significant other in which renewed harm is likely, though not imminent; cases in which, for example, wives who have been subjected to repeated beatings kill their husbands while they are sleeping. As yet, no reported tort case has recognized that expansion of the defense.

Drabek v. Sabley

Supreme Court of Wisconsin
142 N.W.2d 798 (Wis. 1966)

Action for damages for false imprisonment and assault and battery.

The jury found no false imprisonment and no assault and battery . . . [T]he court entered judgment dismissing the complaint. Plaintiff has appealed.

Plaintiff Thomas Drabek, 10 years old, lived with his parents on highway 67. . . . Tom and four other boys were across the highway from the Drabek home, throwing snowballs at passing cars. Defendant, Dr. Nanito Sabley, drove by, and his car was hit by a snowball, apparently thrown by one of the other boys. Dr. Sabley stopped his car and the boys ran. Dr. Sabley pursued Tom for about 100 yards, caught him, and, holding him by the arm, took him to the car and directed him to enter it. Dr. Sabley asked and was told Tom's name, but did not ask where he lived. Dr. Sabley, who had been driving north, turned his car around and drove into the village. He located a police officer, and turned Tom over to him. Tom told the officer the names of the other boys involved, and the officer took Tom to his home. Tom was with the defendant some 15 to 20 minutes.

. . . .

FAIRCHILD, Justice.

Interpreting the evidence, where in conflict, most favorably to the verdict, defendant effectively restrained Tom's physical liberty, and took him into the village for the purpose of having him tell the police officer the names of the other boys. Defendant held Tom by the arm both on the way to the car before driving into the village, and, at times, while they were in the village.

Thus there was false imprisonment unless the restraint was legally justified. Except for possible justification, the offensive holding of the arm was also a battery, albeit nominal.

Thomas E. Fairchild

. . . .

Defendant claims justification in that he witnessed acts that were dangerous to defendant and others and took reasonable steps to prevent further dangerous activities.

It is recognized that one may be privileged to interfere with the liberty of another, within limits, for the purpose of defending one's self, defending a third person, or preventing the commission of a crime. Dr. Sabley did not act in self defense, since he was no longer in danger. It is true that the boys momentarily terminated their offensive activity when he stopped his car, but it was reasonable to expect them to renew it. We perceive that throwing snowballs at moving cars creates a danger, as much because of the likelihood of startling the driver as of damage to the cars. Although it is a close question whether the threat to the safety of others was sufficiently immediate, after the boys had run away, it seems to us that Dr. Sabley, though not an officer, was privileged to take reasonable steps to prevent the resumption of the activity.

We conclude that Dr. Sabley's actions presented a jury question of reasonableness up to the time he put the boy in his car and drove away. Up to that time he had obtained the boy's name, and admonished him, according to the defendant's testimony, against carrying on the activity. The jury was entitled to believe that in holding the boy he used only such force as was reasonable for the purpose. Dr. Sabley may well have been justified in marching Tom across the road to his home and notifying his parents. We conclude, however, that it was unreasonable, as a matter of law, for Dr. Sabley to put 10-year-old Tom in his car a few yards from his home and drive him into the village for the purposes he did and under the circumstances of this case.

. . . .

Accordingly we conclude that the jury finding, in effect, that Dr. Sabley's conduct was reasonable exonerates him up to the time he put Tom in the car, but not afterward. The restraint of Tom's liberty continued, and after that point there was false imprisonment. Dr. Sabley admitted holding Tom while they looked for the officer, and this was a battery, though nominal.

It follows that there must be a determination of compensatory damages, though the record will not support a very substantial award, for the period of false imprisonment after the point just mentioned, and for the battery, consisting of the holding of the arm for a time after reaching the village. We think the first jury's findings that there was no false imprisonment and no assault and battery, imply a finding that there was no malice, and hence no punitory damages are recoverable. . . .

Judgment reversed, cause remanded for further proceedings.

[The dissenting opinion of Beilfuss, J., is omitted.]

Notes

1. *See also* Young v. Warren, 383 S.E.2d 381 (N.C. Ct. App. 1989). After breaking into his girlfriend's house, the plaintiff was ordered out by her father at gunpoint, then shot in the back. The facts failed to show that the father acted in "defense of family" for "at the time of the shooting . . . the plaintiff stood outside the house with his back to the defendant" and defendant's "daughter and children were inside the house, removed from any likely harm from plaintiff."

2. ***Range of Response***. In a given situation, more than one response may be reasonable, in which case the defender will not be faulted for not having selected the best course of action. As the court wrote in Wilson v. Dimitri, 138 So. 2d 618 (La. Ct. App. 1962):

> It was sufficient that he reasonably believed the danger to his brother's life to be imminent. . . . [I]mmunity from liability is not judicially withdrawn because some other reasonable man may have perceived the idea of disabling the assailant instead of shooting him. Detached reflection, or a pause for consideration, cannot be demanded under such trying circumstances which by their very nature require a split-second decision.

3. ***Mistaken Intervention***. Some (generally older) decisions discourage defense of others by holding that an intervenor steps into the shoes of the one being assisted; if that person has no right of self-defense, the intervenor's conduct is not privileged, regardless of what the intervenor believes. *See, e.g.*, Webb v. Snow, 132 P.2d 114, 120 (Utah 1942). Other jurisdictions encourage (or at least do not penalize) reasonable intervention efforts by holding that a reasonable mistake as to another's right of

self-defense does not destroy the privilege to defend the other. *See, e.g.*, Duplechain v. Turner, 444 So. 2d 1322 (La. Ct. App. 1984) (privilege barred recovery for the death of an off-duty officer who was shot and killed after being mistaken as the aggressor in a barroom fight).

C. Privileges Relating to Property

1. Defense of Property

In Oakley v. Dolan, 980 F.3d 279, 282 (2d Cir. 2020), the court noted that "a property owner has the right to use reasonable force to eject a trespasser from its premises." However, the court found that "When a plaintiff alleges that he was 'thrown to the ground' by actions that 'greatly exceeded the amount of force that was necessary' and 'clearly exceeded the bounds of reasonable behavior,' . . . the reasonable inference . . . is that he has been subjected to an unreasonable amount of force," and can state a claim for assault and battery. *Id.* at 283.

Katko v. Briney

Supreme Court of Iowa
183 N.W.2d 657 (Iowa 1971)

MOORE, Chief Justice.

The primary issue presented here is whether an owner may protect personal property in an unoccupied boarded-up farm house against trespassers and thieves by a spring gun capable of inflicting death or serious injury.

We are not here concerned with a man's right to protect his home and members of his family. Defendants' home was several miles from the scene of the incident. . . . Plaintiff's action is for damages resulting from serious injury caused by a shot from a 20-gauge spring shotgun set by defendants in a bedroom of an old farm house which had been uninhabited for several years. Plaintiff and his companion, Marvin McDonough, had broken and entered the house to find and steal old bottles and dated fruit jars which they considered antiques.

. . . . The jury returned a verdict for plaintiff and against defendants for $20,000 actual and $10,000 punitive damages.

. . . .

. . . . In 1957 defendant Bertha L. Briney inherited her parents' farm land. . . . Included was an 80-acre tract . . . where her grandparents and parents had lived. No one occupied the house thereafter. Her husband, Edward, attempted to care for the land. He kept no farm machinery thereon. The outbuildings became dilapidated.

For about 10 years, 1957 to 1967, there occurred a series of trespassing and housebreaking events with loss of some household items, the breaking of windows and "messing up of the property in general." . . . .

Defendants through the years boarded up the windows and doors in an attempt to stop the intrusions. They had posted "no trespass" signs on the land several years before 1967. The nearest one was 35 feet from the house.... [D]efendants set "a shotgun trap" in the north bedroom. After Mr. Briney cleaned and oiled his 20-gauge shotgun, the power of which he was well aware, defendants took it to the old house where they secured it to an iron bed with the barrel pointed at the bedroom door. It was rigged with wire from the doorknob to the gun's trigger so it would fire when the door was opened. Briney first pointed the gun so an intruder would be hit in the stomach but at Mrs. Briney's suggestion it was lowered to hit the legs. He admitted he did so "because I was mad and tired of being tormented" but "he did not intend to injure anyone." He gave no explanation of why he used a loaded shell and set it to hit a person already in the house. Tin was nailed over the bedroom window. The spring gun could not be seen from the outside. No warning of its presence was posted.

.... Prior to July 16, 1967 plaintiff and McDonough had been to the premises.... [T]hey made a second trip to the Briney property. They entered the old house by removing a board from a porch window which was without glass.... As ... [plaintiff] started to open the north bedroom door the shotgun went off striking him in the right leg above the ankle bone. Much of his leg, including part of the tibia, was blown away. Only by McDonough's assistance was plaintiff able to get out of the house and after crawling some distance was put in his vehicle and rushed to a doctor and then to a hospital....

.... Plaintiff testified he knew he had no right to break and enter the house with intent to steal.... He further testified he had entered a plea of guilty to larceny in the nighttime of property of less than $20 value from a private building....

.... The main thrust of defendants' defense ... is that "the law permits use of a spring gun in a dwelling or warehouse for the purpose of preventing the unlawful entry of a burglar or thief." They repeated this contention in their exceptions to the trial court's instructions....

.... In instruction 2 the court referred to the early case history of the use of spring guns and stated under the law their use was prohibited except to prevent the commission of felonies of violence and where human life is in danger. The instruction included a statement breaking and entering is not a felony of violence.

Instruction 5 stated: "You are hereby instructed that one may use reasonable force in the protection of his property, but such right is subject to the qualification that one may not use such means of force as will take human life or inflict great bodily injury. Such is the rule even though the injured party is a trespasser and is in violation of the law himself."

Instruction 6 stated: "An owner of premises is prohibited from willfully or intentionally injuring a trespasser by means of force that either takes life or inflicts great bodily injury; and therefore a person owning a premise is prohibited from setting out 'spring guns' and like dangerous devices which will likely take life or inflict great bodily injury, for the purpose of harming trespassers...."

Prosser on Torts, Third Edition, pages 116–118, states: "... [because] the law has always placed a higher value upon human safety than upon mere rights in property, it is the accepted rule that there is no privilege to use any force calculated to cause death or serious bodily injury to repel the threat to land or chattels, unless there is also such a threat to the defendant's personal safety as to justify a self-defense.... [S]pring guns and other man-killing devices are not justifiable against a mere trespasser, or even a petty thief...."

Restatement of Torts, section 85, page 180, states: "... A possessor of land cannot do indirectly and by a mechanical device that which, were he present, he could not do immediately and in person. Therefore, he cannot gain a privilege to install, for the purpose of protecting his land from intrusions harmless to the lives and limbs of the occupiers or users of it, a mechanical device whose only purpose is to inflict death or serious harm upon such as may intrude, by giving notice of his intention to inflict, by mechanical means and indirectly, harm which he could not, even after request, inflict directly were he present."

....

In Phelps v. Hamlett, 207 S.W. 425 (Tex. Civ. App. 1918), defendant rigged a bomb inside his outdoor theater so that if anyone came through the door the bomb would explode. The court reversed plaintiff's recovery because of an incorrect instruction but ... said: "While the law authorizes an owner to protect his property by such reasonable means as he may find to be necessary, yet considerations of humanity preclude him from setting out, even on his own property, traps and devices dangerous to the life and limb of those whose appearance and presence may be reasonably anticipated, even though they may be trespassers."

In United Zinc & Chemical Co. v. Britt, 258 U.S. 268, 275 [1922], the court states: "The liability for spring guns and mantraps arises from the fact that the defendant has ... expected the trespasser and prepared an injury that is no more justified than if he had held the gun and fired it."

....

Study and careful consideration of defendant's contentions on appeal reveal no reversible error.

Affirmed.

[The dissenting opinion of Justice Larson has been omitted.]

Notes

1. ***Mistake of Fact.*** With respect to defense of property, a mistake about the degree of force necessary does not destroy the common law privilege. However, a mistake in concluding that the intruder is not acting in the exercise of a superior privilege (such as to conduct a lawful search and seizure) does destroy the privilege, unless the mistake has been induced by the intruder (such as where police officers carrying

out a warrant fail to knock and announce their warrant). *See* Dan B. Dobbs, The Law of Torts 173 (2000).

2. ***Conduct Threatening Persons as Well as Property.*** Cases involving harm to property may also pose a risk of harm to persons, in which case the defendant's use of deadly force (i.e., self-defense or defense of others) may be permissible. *See* Graves v. Trudell, 765 N.Y.S.2d 104 (App. Div. 2003) (permitting a resident to use deadly force against an intruder).

The defendant in Bennett v. Dunn, 507 So. 2d 451 (Ala. 1987), was aroused from his sleep by an intruder who was attempting to steal his truck. According to the court, when the intruder failed to respond to barking dogs or the defendant's shouts and warning shots, the defendant did not act unreasonably in shooting the intruder. "[H]is actions taken to protect his family, himself, and his home were fully justified."

However, some courts are less willing to conclude that a risk to property also involves a risk to persons. *See* Goldfuss v. Davidson, 679 N.E.2d 1099 (Ohio 1997) (evidence did not warrant a jury instruction on self-defense in an action by a trespasser's estate claiming that a homeowner negligently shot and killed the trespasser, who was attempting to break into the homeowner's barn located at least 100 feet away from the house).

3. ***Defense against Animals.*** *See* Harrington v. Hall, 63 A. 875, 876 (Del. 1906). In an action for the killing of a foxhound, the court instructed the jury:

> A person may not maliciously injure or kill a dog for a mere trespass upon his premises, and the posting of notices against trespassing by dogs will not thereafter excuse or justify an unlawful killing of a dog found upon the premises. The remedy against such trespassing is, in a proper case, against the owner of the dog.
>
> .... [But] if the dog was upon the land of the defendant in the act of destroying his turkeys, the defendant was justified in killing him....

4. ***Statutory Expansion of the Right to Defend Property.*** A number of states have statutorily created a right to use deadly force to defend property. Consider the Texas law:

Texas Penal Code § 9.42 (Westlaw 2022)

Deadly Force to Protect Property

A person is justified in using deadly force against another to protect land or tangible, movable property:

(1) if he would be justified in using force against the other under Section 9.41 [dealing generally with "protection of one's own property"]; and

(2) when and to the degree he reasonably believes the deadly force is immediately necessary:

(A) to prevent the other's imminent commission of arson, burglary, robbery, aggravated robbery, theft during the nighttime, or criminal mischief during the nighttime; or

(B) to prevent the other who is fleeing immediately after committing burglary, robbery, aggravated robbery, or theft during the nighttime from escaping with the property; and

(3) he reasonably believes that:

(A) the land or property cannot be protected or recovered by any other means; or

(B) the use of force other than deadly force to protect or recover the land or property would expose the actor or another to a substantial risk of death or serious bodily injury.

Conduct consistent with these provisions in the Texas penal code may not serve as a basis for civil liability. *See* Tex. Civ. Prac. & Rem. Code § 83.001 (Westlaw 2022).

2. Recapture of Chattels

Efforts to recover personal property taken by fraud, force, or other tortious conduct may fall within the privilege to recapture chattels. A person suffering that kind of loss may use reasonable, non-deadly force to retake the goods, if the dispossession is discovered promptly and there is "fresh pursuit" of the wrongdoer. Any unreasonable delay in either discovery or pursuit destroys the privilege. And, to discourage persons from taking the law into their own hands over mere property interests, one exercising the privilege is liable for any mistake as to the facts which create the privilege—unless that mistake is knowingly induced by the plaintiff. *See generally* Restatement, Second, of Torts §§ 101–11. If the dispossessor resists the recapture efforts by using force against the person asserting the privilege, the privilege becomes one of self-defense, subject to the usual rules on that subject.

In Hodgeden v. Hubbard, 18 Vt. 504 (1846), plaintiff purchased a stove by making fraudulent representations as to his ability to pay and signing a promissory note. On the same day, soon after the sale, defendants discovered the fraud, chased the plaintiff, and took the stove from him during a scuffle in which, after the plaintiff drew a knife, the defendants allegedly "used violence and applied force to his person with great rudeness and outrage." In reversing a $1 judgment for the plaintiff, the court ruled that the plaintiff had no right to resist the defendants' efforts to regain the property, and "it was the right of the defendants to hold him by force, and, if they made use of no unnecessary violence, they were justified" in their actions.

Contrast *Hodgeden* with a case in which a buyer under a conditional sales contract merely defaults on payments. In that case, absent additional facts, there has been no dispossession by fraud, force, or other tortious conduct, and the seller has no right to retake the goods by force. In Roberts v. Speck, 14 P.2d 33 (Wash. 1932), a couple failed to make payments on their new car and the wife refused to get out of the vehicle when the seller came to reclaim it. Both the car and the wife were forcibly towed away. In a suit by the wife for damages resulting from wrongful arrest, the court reversed a judgment for the seller and granted a new trial, quoting an earlier decision:

> Because a party to a contract violates his contract, and refuses to do what he agreed to do, is no reason why the other party to the contract should compel the performance of the contract by force. The adoption of such a rule would lead to a breach of the peace.... The right to an enforcement of this part of the contract must ... be ... by due process of law, the same as any other contract.

3. Detention for Investigation

Dillard Department Stores, Inc. v. Silva

Supreme Court of Texas
148 S.W.3d 370 (Tex. 2004)

PER CURIAM.

....

Lyndon Silva went to a Dillard Department Store ... to exchange three shirts given to him as a gift. Silva attempted to exchange the shirts at the cosmetics/accessories counter, but was told to go to another department. Silva testified that on his way to exchange the shirts he was distracted by sale items and other merchandise in the store. Before exchanging his three shirts, Silva made three purchases.... While making these purchases and examining other merchandise, a Dillard sales associate reported him as a possible shoplifter to her supervisor who told her to call security. Kevin Rivera, an off-duty Houston police officer working security for Dillard, thereafter stopped Silva and asked to examine the contents of his bag. In the bag were the three items purchased by Silva that day with their receipts and the three shirts he had brought to exchange. There was no receipt in the bag for the three shirts although Silva maintained that he had one. He asked Rivera to go with him to his car to see if the receipt had fallen out there. Instead, Rivera accused him of theft, put him in handcuffs, and escorted him to an office where he was subsequently turned over to the Houston police. Silva was thereafter charged with misdemeanor theft but was ultimately acquitted of the criminal charge.

After that, Silva prosecuted the present suit against Dillard for false imprisonment.... The jury ... found Dillard liable.... The jury awarded Silva actual damages of $13,124.01 for mental anguish and for costs associated with his criminal prosecution. The jury also found that Dillard acted with malice, awarding $50,000 in exemplary damages. The court of appeals ... affirmed the award of actual and exemplary damages, finding evidence to support the jury's findings of false imprisonment and malice....

Dillard complains here that it did not falsely imprison Silva because it had the right to detain him under the shopkeeper's privilege. This privilege permits a shopkeeper to detain a person to investigate the ownership of property if the shopkeeper reasonably believes that the person has stolen or is attempting to steal store merchandise so long as the detention is in a reasonable manner and for a reasonable period of time. Tex. Civ. Prac. & Rem. Code §124.001. . . . Liability is not based on the customer's actual guilt or innocence, but rather on the reasonableness of the shopkeeper's actions under the circumstances. . . . The parties here disagree only about whether Silva was detained in a reasonable manner.

Silva testified that after he made his purchases, the Dillard security guard, Rivera, stopped him, accused him of theft, placed him on the floor, handcuffed him, emptied the contents of his bag on the floor, and questioned him while he lay handcuffed on the floor. Although Silva told Rivera that he had receipts for three of the shirts in his vehicle, Rivera declined to go look for them. Instead, Rivera escorted Silva in handcuffs up the escalator to an empty office. Silva testified to his embarrassment and humiliation at being led through the store in handcuffs. . . . Silva also testified that when the police arrived, Rivera placed him on the floor again with his knee on Silva's back to exchange handcuffs with the police. Although Dillard's witnesses contradicted much of Silva's testimony about his detainment, the jury obviously believed Silva. And when testimony is contradictory, credibility is for the fact finder to decide. . . . Because Silva's testimony is some evidence that Dillard did not detain Silva in a reasonable manner as the privilege requires, we agree with the court of appeals that there is evidence to support the jury's award of damages for false imprisonment.

. . . .

Because there is no clear and convincing evidence of malice in this case as the [punitive damages] statute requires, the court of appeals judgment is modified to delete the award of exemplary damages and, as modified, is affirmed.

Notes

1. ***Restatement Formulation***. The privilege to detain for investigation one suspected of theft is recognized by the Restatement, which provides:

> One who reasonably believes that another has tortiously taken a chattel upon his premises, or has failed to make due cash payment for a chattel purchased or services rendered there, is privileged, without arresting the other, to detain him on the premises for the time necessary for a reasonable investigation of the facts.

Restatement, Second, of Torts §120A. Elaborating on the reasons for the rule, the comment to §120A states:

> The privilege . . . is necessary for the protection of a shopkeeper against the dilemma in which he would otherwise find himself when he reasonably believes that a shoplifter has taken goods from his counter. If there were no such privilege, he must either permit the suspected person to walk out of the premises and disappear, or must arrest him, at the risk of liability for false arrest if the theft could not be proved.

2. ***Recapture of Chattels Contrasted***. Comment e to the Restatement, Second, of Torts §120A provides:

> The privilege stated in this Section differs from the privilege to use reasonable force for the recapture of chattels, in that it protects the actor who has made a reasonable mistake as to the wrongful taking.

Bonkowski v. Arlan's Dept. Store, 162 N.W.2d 347 (Mich. Ct. App. 1968), held that the privilege might apply even if the person detained had already left the defendant's store. In that case, a security officer called to the plaintiff to stop as she was walking to her car about 30 feet away in an adjacent parking lot. It seems clear that at some point the distance from the premises will be so great that the applicable privilege, if any, will be recapture of chattels rather than detention for investigation.

3. ***Historical Development.*** As explained in Alvarado v. City of Dodge City, 708 P.2d 174, 180–81 (Kan. 1985):

> [T]he merchant of days past, who owned a small shop and kept all of his goods stacked on shelves behind him or in a counter between him and his customers, may have been adequately protected by the common-law rule [on recapture of chattels], because there could be no doubt in his mind when someone was stealing from him. That situation changed, however, when modern methods of marketing goods came into existence. In modern department stores or supermarkets, where nearly all of the goods are on open shelves within reach of the customer, and where the shopper is expected to pick up and examine the goods before purchasing them, it is difficult for a merchant to be sure, even under apparently obvious circumstances, that a particular customer is pilfering from the shelves. Under these circumstances, the common-law rule did not work....

4. ***Reasonableness of Detention.*** The commentary to Section 120A of the Restatement, Second, of Torts observes:

> f. The privilege is one of detention ... for only the time necessary for a reasonable investigation. Investigation does not mean discovery of all of the facts, but only such inquiry as may reasonably be made under the circumstances, promptly and without undue detention. What is a reasonable time will depend upon all of the circumstances, including the nature of the misconduct suspected, the amount involved, the explanation or denial offered by the other, his willingness to cooperate, and the time required to consult readily available sources of information. Normally, such a reasonable time will be short. Fifteen minutes may be too long where all that is necessary is to ask a clerk whether the other has paid....
>
> g. The privilege is one of detention for investigation only and it does not extend to the coercion of payment, which is imprisonment for debt. Nor does it extend to the extortion of a confession of theft; and the actor is liable if he detains the other for that purpose....
>
> h. Reasonable force may be used to detain the suspected person; but, as in the case of recapture of chattels ..., the use of force intended or likely to cause serious bodily harm is never privileged for the sole purpose of

> detention to investigate, and it becomes privileged only where the resistance of the other makes it necessary for the actor to use such force in self-defense. In the ordinary case, the use of any force at all will not be privileged until the other has been requested to remain; and it is only where there is no time for such a request, or it would obviously be futile, that force is justified.

5. ***Resisting Detention.*** A shoplifter owes a duty to submit peaceably to lawful arrest or detention, and may be liable to a store employee who is injured while endeavoring to capture the shoplifter. *See* Smitherman v. McCafferty, 622 So. 2d 322 (Ala. 1993).

6. ***Nonmerchants.*** Although the common-law privilege to detain for purposes of investigation is frequently asserted by merchants, the privilege may be invoked by others. *See, e.g.*, Thornhill v. Wilson, 504 So. 2d 1205, 1208 (Miss. 1987) (detention of plaintiff for 15 minutes by police officers investigating frantic telephone calls regarding gunfire was not unreasonable).

7. ***Shoplifting Statutes.*** In a number of jurisdictions, the common-law privilege to detain a suspected shoplifter has been recognized, or expanded by, statute. *See* Jury v. Giant of Md., Inc., 491 S.E.2d 718 (Va. 1997) (holding that, in connection with the detention of a suspected shoplifter, a merchant has statutory immunity from civil liability based on a wide range of torts, but not in circumstances in which the tort is committed in a willful, wanton, or otherwise unreasonable or excessive manner).

Some statutes have extended the privilege to detain to persons other than merchants. *See, e.g.*, Cal. Penal Code § 490.5(f)(1) (Westlaw 2022) (persons employed by library facilities); Fla. Stat. Ann. § 812.015(3)(a) (Westlaw 2022) (law enforcement officer, merchant, farmer, or transit agency employee or agent); Tex. Civ. Prac. & Rem. Code Ann. § 124.001 (Westlaw 2022) (any "person who reasonably believes that another has stolen or is attempting to steal property").

8. ***Reference to Criminal Law Standards.*** Care must be exercised when attempting to shape tort principles by reference to criminal law provisions, which may serve different purposes. For example, in New Mexico, a person who willfully conceals merchandise among his or her belongings is presumed, *for purposes of criminal prosecution*, to have acted with a specific intent to shoplift. A *tort claim* for false imprisonment arose when a customer placed a can of hair mousse into her reusable, personal canvas bag to carry it to the front of the store to ask a clerk a question. The court found that the criminal-law presumption was irrelevant to the question of whether or not the merchant had a statutory privilege to detain the shopper for investigation. *See* Holguin v. Sally Beauty Supply Inc., 264 P.3d 732 (N.M. App. 2011).

D. Public Necessity and Private Necessity

Surocco v. Geary

Supreme Court of California
3 Cal. 69 (Cal. 1853)

MURRAY, Chief Justice, delivered the opinion of the Court.

. . . .

This was an action . . . to recover damages for blowing up and destroying the plaintiffs' house and property, during the fire of the 24th of December, 1849.

Geary, at that time Alcalde of San Francisco, justified, on the ground that he had the authority, by virtue of his office, to destroy said building, and also that it had been blown up by him to stop the progress of the conflagration then raging.

It was in proof, that the fire passed over and burned beyond the building of the plaintiffs, and that at the time said building was destroyed, they were engaged in removing their property, and could, had they not been prevented, have succeeded in removing more, if not all of their goods.

The cause was tried by the court sitting as a jury, and a verdict rendered for the plaintiffs, from which the defendant prosecutes this appeal. . . .

The only question for our consideration is, whether the person who tears down or destroys the house of another, in good faith, and under apparent necessity, during the time of a conflagration, for the purpose of saving the buildings adjacent, and stopping its progress, can be held personally liable in an action by the owner of the property destroyed.

This point has been so well settled in the courts of New York and New Jersey, that a reference to those authorities is all that is necessary to determine the present case.

The right to destroy property, to prevent the spread of a conflagration, has been traced to the highest law of necessity, and the natural rights of man, independent of society or civil government. "It is referred by moralists and jurists to the same great principle which justifies the exclusive appropriation of a plank in a shipwreck, though the life of another be sacrificed; with the throwing overboard goods in a tempest, for the safety of a vessel; with the trespassing upon the lands of another, to escape death by an enemy. . . ."

. . . . At . . . times, the individual rights of property give way to the higher laws of impending necessity.

A house on fire, or those in its immediate vicinity, which serve to communicate the flames, becomes a nuisance, which it is lawful to abate, and the private rights of the individual yield to the considerations of general convenience, and the interests of society. Were it otherwise, one stubborn person might involve a whole city in ruin, by refusing to allow the destruction of a building which would cut off the flames and check the progress of the fire, and that, too, when it was perfectly evident that his building must be consumed.

....

The counsel for the respondent has asked, who is to judge of the necessity of the destruction of property?

This must, in some instances, be a difficult matter to determine. The necessity of blowing up a house may not exist, or be as apparent to the owner, whose judgment is clouded by interest, and the hope of saving his property, as to others. In all such cases the conduct of the individual must be regulated by his own judgment as to the exigencies of the case. If a building should be torn down without apparent or actual necessity, the parties concerned would undoubtedly be liable in an action of trespass. But in every case the necessity must be clearly shown. It is true, many cases of hardship may grow out of this rule, and property may often in such cases be destroyed, without necessity, by irresponsible persons, but this difficulty would not be obviated by making the parties responsible in every case, whether the necessity existed or not.

....

In the absence of any legislation on the subject, we are compelled to fall back upon the rules of the common law.

The evidence in this case clearly establishes the fact, that the blowing up of the house was necessary, as it would have been consumed had it been left standing. The plaintiffs cannot recover for the value of the goods which they might have saved; they were as much subject to the necessities of the occasion as the house in which they were situate; and if in such cases a party was held liable, it would too frequently happen, that the delay caused by the removal of the goods would render the destruction of the house useless.

....

Judgment reversed.

Notes

1. ***Imminent Peril.*** In City of Rapid City v. Boland, 271 N.W.2d 60 (S.D. 1978), plaintiff's building was leveled during government clean-up efforts following a massive flood. The clean-up was intended to prevent the spread of disease. The court held that compensation for the building need not be paid if, at the time of the destruction, there was an imminent and impending peril to the public and it appeared to be necessary to destroy the property to prevent the spread of the peril. In remanding the case, the court quoted an 1848 decision:

> To fall within the privilege, there must be "[a] necessity, extreme, imperative, or overwhelming, [to] constitute such a justification, but mere expediency, or public good, or utility, will not answer."

See also Allen v. Camp, 70 So. 290 (Ala. 1915) (although it is permissible to kill a dog to fend off an attack, one who fails to do so cannot decapitate the animal days later to determine whether it was rabid).

2. ***Private Citizens.*** The privilege of public necessity is not confined to official representatives of the public and may be exercised by private citizens. *See* Restatement, Second, of Torts § 262 cmt. b.

3. ***Privilege No Greater than the Necessity.*** An actor seeking to avert a public disaster cannot cause greater harm than appears to be necessary. Thus, a firefighter needing to reach a conflagration cannot forcibly take the plaintiff's car, if the plaintiff is willing to drive the firefighter to the scene. Restatement, Second, of Torts § 262 illus. 3.

4. ***Problem: Dumped Jet Fuel.*** A jetliner making an emergency landing at a major American airport dumped fuel over a wide area of the city, including on an elementary school playground filled with children. Liability?

Wegner v. Milwaukee Mutual Insurance Co.

Supreme Court of Minnesota
479 N.W.2d 38 (Minn. 1991)

TOMLJANOVICH, Justice.

[The Minneapolis police department severely damaged a house owned by Harriet Wegner while attempting to apprehend an armed suspect who had fled into the house. In an attempt to expel the suspect, a "SWAT" team fired at least 25 rounds of chemical munitions and three "flash-bang" concussion grenades into the dwelling. Eventually the suspect was apprehended.]

.... Wegner sought compensation from the City of Minneapolis on trespass and constitutional "taking" theories. The district court granted the City's motion for summary judgment on the "taking" issue. The court of appeals affirmed, reasoning that although there was a "taking" within the meaning of the Minnesota Constitution, the "taking" was noncompensable under the doctrine of public necessity. We reverse.

....

Article I, section 13, of the Minnesota Constitution provides "Private property shall not be taken, destroyed or damaged for public use without just compensation, first paid or secured." ....

We hold that where an innocent third party's property is damaged by the police in the course of apprehending a suspect, that property is damaged within the meaning of the constitution.

....

We briefly address the application of the doctrine of public necessity to these facts. The Restatement (Second) of Torts § 196 describes the doctrine as follows:

> One is privileged to enter land in the possession of another if it is, or if the actor reasonably believes it to be, necessary for the purpose of averting an imminent public disaster.[3]

See McDonald v. City of Red Wing, 13 Minn. 38 (Gil. 25) (1868) (city excused from paying compensation under the doctrine of "public safety" where city officers destroyed building to prevent the spread of fire). Prosser, apparently somewhat troubled by the potential harsh outcomes of this doctrine, states:

> It would seem that the moral obligation upon the group affected to make compensation in such a case should be recognized by the law, but recovery usually has been denied.

Prosser and Keeton, The Law of Torts, § 24 (5th ed. 1984); *see also* Restatement (Second) of Torts § 196 comment h. Here, the police were attempting to apprehend a dangerous felon who had fired shots at pursuing officers. The capture of this individual most certainly was beneficial to the whole community. In such circumstances, an individual in Wegner's position should not be forced to bear the entire cost of a benefit conferred on the community as a whole.

. . . .

We are not inclined to allow the city to defend its actions on the grounds of public necessity under the facts of this case. *But see* Steele [v. City of Houston, 603 S.W.2d 786, 792 (Tex. 1980)].[4] We believe the better rule, in situations where an innocent third party's property is taken, damaged or destroyed by the police in the course of apprehending a suspect, is for the municipality to compensate the innocent party for the resulting damages. The policy considerations in this case center around the basic notions of fairness and justice. At its most basic level, the issue is whether it is fair to allocate the entire risk of loss to an innocent homeowner for the good of the public. We do not believe the imposition of such a burden on the innocent citizens of this state would square with the underlying principles of our system of justice. Therefore, the City must reimburse Wegner for the losses sustained.

---

3. [Fn. 6:] Prosser explains:

> Where the danger affects the entire community, or so many people that the public interest is involved, that interest serves as a complete justification to the defendant who acts to avert the peril to all. Thus, one who dynamites a house to stop the spread of a conflagration that threatens a town, or shoots a mad dog in the street, or burns clothing infected with smallpox germs, or in time of war, destroys property which should not be allowed to fall into the hands of the enemy, is not liable to the owner, so long as the emergency is great enough, and he has acted reasonably under the circumstances. This notion does not require the "champion of the public" to pay for the general salvation out of his own pocket. The number of persons who must be endangered in order to create a public necessity has not been determined by the courts.

Prosser and Keeton, The Law of Torts, § 24 (5th ed. 1984).

4. In *Steele*, the police set fire to the plaintiff's house in an effort to recapture escaped convicts who were hiding there. In remanding the case for a new trial on the issue of compensation, the court noted that the city could defend its actions by proof of a "great public necessity," but that evidence of "[m]ere convenience" would not justify uncompensated destruction. — Ed.

As a final note, we hold that the individual police officers, who were acting in the public interest, cannot be held personally liable. Instead, the citizens of the City should all bear the cost of the benefit conferred.

The judgments of the courts below are reversed and the cause remanded for trial on the issue of damages.

Affirmed in part, reversed in part and remanded.

Notes

1. ***Tort v. "Taking."*** Federal and state constitutions require just compensation if the government takes private property for public use. Courts are divided on whether property damage caused by the police should be treated as a tort or a "taking." *Compare* Simmons v. Loose, 13 A.3d 366 (N.J. Super. A.D. 2011) (holding the state police department was immune from liability in tort and that damages incurred incidental to execution of a search warrant were not compensable as a "taking"), *with* Customer Co. v. City of Sacramento, 41 Cal. Rptr. 2d 658, 670–73 (Cal. 1995) (in an action for damage to a convenience store caused by efforts to apprehend a suspect, the plaintiff could not recover under the theory of inverse condemnation, but could sue under provisions of the state tort claims act) *and* Sullivant v. City of Okla. City, 940 P.2d 220 (Okla. 1997) (potential tort, but no taking). The complexities of "takings" law are beyond the scope of a course on Torts, but *Wegner* makes clear that the doctrine of public necessity and its underlying policies may apply to such actions.

2. ***Public Necessity and Immunity.*** Governmental entities and persons acting on behalf of the government may be protected not only by the public-necessity privilege, but by governmental or official immunity. *See, e.g.*, Kelly v. Storey County Sheriff, 611 N.W.2d 475 (Iowa 2000) (holding, in an action by the owner of a residence to recover damages caused by a forcible entry to execute an arrest warrant, that the county, the sheriff, and sheriff's department employees were entitled to immunity because the officers had exercised "due care" within the terms of a state statute conferring immunity). Immunities are discussed in Chapter 18.

Vincent v. Lake Erie Transp. Co.

Supreme Court of Minnesota
124 N.W. 221 (Minn. 1910)

O'BRIEN, J.

The steamship Reynolds, owned by the defendant, was for the purpose of discharging her cargo on November 27, 1905, moored to plaintiff's dock in Duluth. While the unloading of the boat was taking place a storm from the northeast developed, which at about 10 o'clock p.m., when the unloading was completed, had so grown in violence that the wind was then moving at 50 miles per hour and continued to increase during the night. There is some evidence that one, and perhaps two, boats were able to enter the harbor that night, but it is plain that navigation was practically suspended. . . . After the discharge of the cargo the Reynolds signaled for a tug to tow her from the dock, but none could be obtained because of the severity of the storm. If the lines holding the ship to the dock had been cast off, she would doubtless have drifted away; but, instead, the lines were kept fast, and as soon as one parted or chafed it was replaced, sometimes with a larger one. The vessel lay upon the outside of the dock, her bow to the east, the wind and waves striking her starboard quarter with such force that she was constantly being lifted and thrown against the dock, resulting in its damage, as found by the jury, to the amount of $500.

.... One witness testified upon the trial that the vessel could have been warped into a slip, and that, if the attempt to bring the ship into the slip had failed, the worst that could have happened would be that the vessel would have been blown ashore upon a soft and muddy bank. The witness was not present in Duluth at the time of the storm, and, while he may have been right in his conclusions, those in charge of the dock and the vessel at the time of the storm were not required to use the highest human intelligence, nor were they required to resort to every possible experiment which could be suggested for the preservation of their property. Nothing more was demanded of them than ordinary prudence and care, and the record in this case fully sustains the contention of the appellant that, in holding the vessel fast to the dock, those in charge of her exercised good judgment and prudent seamanship.

....

The appellant contends ... that, because its conduct during the storm was rendered necessary by prudence and good seamanship under conditions over which it had no control, it cannot be held liable for any injury resulting to the property of others, and claims that the jury should have been so instructed....

.... If during the storm the Reynolds had entered the harbor, and while there had become disabled and been thrown against the plaintiffs' dock, the plaintiffs could not have recovered. Again, if while attempting to hold fast to the dock the lines had parted, without any negligence, and the vessel carried against some other boat or dock in the harbor, there would be no liability upon her owner. But here those in charge of the vessel deliberately and by their direct efforts held her in such a position that the damage to the dock resulted, and, having thus preserved the ship at the expense of the dock, it seems to us that her owners are responsible to the dock owners to the extent of the injury inflicted.

In Depue v. Flateau, 100 Minn. 299, 111 N.W. 1, 8 L.R.A. (N.S.) 485 [1907], this court held that where the plaintiff, while lawfully in the defendants' house, became so ill that he was incapable of traveling with safety, the defendants were responsible to him in damages for compelling him to leave the premises. If, however, the owner of the premises had furnished the traveler with proper accommodations and medical attendance, would he have been able to defeat an action brought against him for their reasonable worth?

....

Theologians hold that a starving man may, without moral guilt, take what is necessary to sustain life; but it could hardly be said that the obligation would not be upon such person to pay the value of the property so taken when he became able to do so. . . .

Let us imagine in this case that for the better mooring of the vessel those in charge of her had appropriated a valuable cable lying upon the dock. No matter how justifiable such appropriation might have been, it would not be claimed that, because of the overwhelming necessity of the situation, the owner of the cable could not recover its value.

This is not a case where life or property was menaced by any object or thing belonging to the plaintiff, the destruction of which became necessary to prevent the threatened disaster. Nor is it a case where, because of the act of God, or unavoidable accident, the infliction of the injury was beyond the control of the defendant, but is one where the defendant prudently and advisedly availed itself of the plaintiff's property for the purpose of preserving its own more valuable property, and the plaintiffs are entitled to compensation for the injury done.

Order affirmed.

[The dissenting opinion of LEWIS, J., is omitted.]

Notes

1. ***Avoiding Greater Harm***. The idea behind private necessity is that one may inflict some lesser harm in order to avoid greater harm. Conversely, one cannot inflict greater harm to avoid lesser harm. "Thus one whose chattel of small value is threatened with serious harm or even with complete destruction may not be privileged to destroy a far more valuable chattel of another in order to protect it." Restatement, Second, of Torts § 263, cmt. d.

2. ***Compensation in Cases of Private Necessity***. The privilege of private necessity is incomplete in the sense that one who acts to protect personal interests, or the interests of a third person, is liable to another whose interests are invaded by the act. However, the privilege is complete, and no compensation is owed, if the person whose interest is being protected is the owner of the property in question. For example, a defendant who uses the plaintiff's scarf as a tourniquet to stop the plaintiff's bleeding following an accident is not liable for the value of the scarf. Restatement, Second, of Torts § 263, cmt. e and illus. 1.

Ploof v. Putnam

Supreme Court of Vermont
71 A. 188 (Vt. 1908)

MUNSON, J.

It is alleged as the ground of recovery that on the 13th day of November, 1904, the defendant was the owner of a certain island in Lake Champlain, and of a certain dock attached thereto, . . . that the plaintiff was then possessed of and sailing upon said lake a certain loaded sloop, on which were the plaintiff and his wife and two minor children; that there then arose a sudden and violent tempest, whereby the sloop and the property and persons therein were placed in great danger of destruction; that, to save these from destruction or injury, the plaintiff was compelled to, and did, moor the sloop to defendant's dock; that the defendant, by his servant, unmoored the sloop, whereupon it was driven upon the shore by the tempest, without the plaintiff's fault; and that the sloop and its contents were thereby destroyed, and the plaintiff and his wife and children cast into the lake and upon the shore, receiving injuries. This claim is set forth in two counts—one in trespass, charging that the defendant by his servant with force and arms willfully and designedly unmoored the sloop; the other in case, alleging that it was the duty of the defendant by his servant to permit the plaintiff to moor his sloop to the dock, and to permit it to remain so moored during the continuance of the tempest, but that the defendant by his servant, in disregard of this duty, negligently, carelessly, and wrongfully unmoored the sloop. Both counts are demurred to generally.

There are many cases in the books which hold that necessity . . . will justify entries upon land and interferences with personal property that would otherwise have been trespasses. . . . A traveler on a highway who finds it obstructed from a sudden and temporary cause may pass upon the adjoining land without becoming a trespasser because of the necessity. . . . An entry upon land to save goods which are in danger of being lost or destroyed by water or fire is not a trespass. . . .

This doctrine of necessity applies with special force to the preservation of human life. One assaulted and in peril of his life may run through the close of another to escape from his assailant. 37 Hen. VII, pl. 26. One may sacrifice the personal property of another to save his life or the lives of his fellows. In Mouse's Case, 12 Co. 63, the defendant was sued for taking and carrying away the plaintiff's casket and its contents. It appeared that the ferryman of Gravesend took 47 passengers into his barge to pass to London, among whom were the plaintiff and defendant; and the barge being upon the water a great tempest happened, and a strong wind, so that the barge and all the passengers were in danger of being lost if certain ponderous things were not cast out, and the defendant thereupon cast out the plaintiff's casket. It was resolved that in case of necessity, to save the lives of the passengers, it was lawful for the defendant, being a passenger, to cast the plaintiff's casket out of the barge. . . .

It is clear that an entry upon the land of another may be justified by necessity, and that the declaration before us discloses a necessity for mooring the sloop. But the defendant questions the sufficiency of the counts because they do not negative the existence of natural objects to which the plaintiff could have moored with equal safety. The allegations are, in substance, that the stress of a sudden and violent tempest compelled the plaintiff to moor to defendant's dock to save his sloop and the people in it. The averment of necessity is complete, for it covers not only the necessity of mooring, but the necessity of mooring to the dock; and the details of the situation which created this necessity, whatever the legal requirements regarding them, are matters of proof, and need not be alleged. . . .

Judgment affirmed and cause remanded.

Notes

1. ***Other Precedent.*** A similar case is Rossi v. Del Duca, 181 N.E.2d 591 (Mass. 1962). There, an eight-year-old girl, frightened and chased by a dog, sought to make her escape by crossing private property. On that land, she was unexpectedly attacked by the landowner's two Great Danes. In an action against the property owner, the court held that the doctrine of private necessity saved the girl from liability for technical trespass and permitted her to recover for her injuries under a dog-bite statute that would have denied compensation if she was trespassing.

2. ***Overcoming Resistance to Privileged Entry.*** Assuming that Rossi's entry was privileged, would Rossi have been liable for harm to the dogs or for property damage reasonably inflicted in an attempt to escape or resist the attack? According to the Restatement, Second, of Torts:

> The important difference between the status of one who is a trespasser on land and one who is on the land pursuant to an incomplete privilege is that the latter is entitled to be on the land and therefore the possessor of the land is under a duty to permit him to come and remain there and hence is not privileged to resist his entry. Consequently, where the possessor of the land resists such a privileged entry, the actor's use of reasonable force to overcome such resistance to his entry or remaining on the land so long as the necessity continues is *completely* privileged. Therefore, he is not liable for harm so occasioned.

(§ 197 cmt. k; emphasis added.)

3. ***Emergencies of the Actor's Own Making.*** Even if the plaintiff in *Rossi* had provoked the incident by taunting the first dog, the result might have been the same, for the doctrine of private necessity is available even in an emergency of the actor's own making. Note, however, that a restriction may apply:

> [I]f the entry is [only] for the purpose of protecting the actor's land or chattels, such an entry would be reasonable only where the property sought to be saved is of considerably greater value than the amount of probable harm to the possessor's land or chattels likely to be done by saving the actor's property.

Restatement, Second, of Torts § 197 cmt. d (brackets added).

E. Unlawful Conduct

Barker v. Kallash

Court of Appeals of New York[5]
468 N.E.2d 39 (N.Y. 1984)

WACHTLER, Judge.

The question on this appeal is whether the 15-year-old plaintiff, who was injured while constructing a "pipe bomb," can maintain a tort action against the 9-year-old defendant who allegedly sold the firecrackers from which the plaintiff's companions extracted the gunpowder used to construct the bomb. The trial court granted summary judgment dismissing the cause of action against the defendant and his parents for alleged negligent supervision. The Appellate Division affirmed. . . .

The facts are in dispute; however . . . we must accept the plaintiff's version of the events, as the lower courts have done.

. . . [T]he plaintiff, George Barker, and two companions, Ayman and Anas Kallash, made a "pipe bomb" in the backyard of the Barker home in Brooklyn. At the time the plaintiff was nearly 15 years old and the Kallash brothers were 14 and 15, respectively. The bomb was made by filling a metal pipe, three or four inches long and one inch wide, with gunpowder.

The plaintiff concededly obtained the pipe from his father's home workshop where he also found the caps to seal it and a power drill he used to make a hole for the fuse. Although his father also used gunpowder to reload shotgun shells at home, the plaintiff contends that the gunpowder used in the bomb was supplied by the Kallash brothers who extracted it from firecrackers. He testified . . . that they had told him that the day before the incident they had purchased firecrackers from the defendant Daniel Melucci, Jr., who was not quite nine years old at the time. Indeed, the plaintiff testified that he had told the Kallash brothers where the firecrackers could be purchased. The injury occurred after the pipe had been capped at one end and the plaintiff, and one of the Kallash brothers, had poured the gunpowder into it. As the plaintiff was screwing the second cap on to the pipe it exploded, severely injuring his hands.

Plaintiff, through his father, brought an action against the Kallash brothers for their part in constructing the bomb, against Daniel Melucci, Jr., for allegedly selling the firecrackers to the Kallashes, and against Robert Judge, another infant, who allegedly sold the firecrackers to Melucci. In each instance the plaintiff also sued the infants' parents for negligent supervision.

. . . .

---

5. In New York, the highest state court is the Court of Appeals. Confusingly (at least to non-New Yorkers), the trial court is called the Supreme Court, and the intermediate appellate court is named the Supreme Court, Appellate Division.

At the outset a distinction must be drawn between lawful activities regulated by statute and activities which are entirely prohibited by law. In the first instance, it is familiar law that a violation of a statute governing the manner in which activities should be conducted, would merely constitute negligence or contributory negligence. . . . Such cases would today be resolved under the rule of comparative negligence. . . . However, when the plaintiff has engaged in activities prohibited, as opposed to merely regulated, by law, the courts will not entertain the suit if the plaintiff's conduct constituted a serious violation of the law and the injuries for which he seeks recovery were the direct result of that violation. In this latter instance recovery is denied, not because the plaintiff contributed to his injury, but because the public policy of this State generally denies judicial relief to those injured in the course of committing a serious criminal act (Reno v. D'Javid, 42 N.Y.2d 1040, 399 N.Y.S.2d 210, 369 N.E.2d 766 [1977]). In the *Reno* case a woman who submitted to an illegal abortion could not recover for alleged negligence on the part of the physician performing the operation. . . . The rule is based on "the paramount public policy imperative that the law, whatever its content at a given time or for however limited a period, be obeyed". . . . It extends the basic principle that one may not profit from his own wrong . . . to tort actions seeking compensation for injuries resulting from the plaintiff's own criminal activities of a serious nature.

The rule denying compensation to the serious offender would not apply in every instance where the plaintiff's injury occurs while he is engaged in illegal activity (*see* Restatement, Torts 2d, § 889, Comment b). Thus if the plaintiff in the example cited above had been injured in an automobile accident as a result of another's negligence, she would not be denied access to the courts merely because she was on the way to have the illegal operation performed (*see, e.g.*, Restatement, Torts 2d, § 889, Comment b, Illustration 3). A complaint should not be dismissed merely because the plaintiff's injuries were occasioned by a criminal act. . . . However, when the plaintiff's injury is a direct result of his knowing and intentional participation in a criminal act he cannot seek compensation for the loss, if the criminal act is judged to be so serious an offense as to warrant denial of recovery (Reno v. D'Javid, *supra*). Thus a burglar who breaks his leg while descending the cellar stairs, due to the failure of the owner to replace a missing step cannot recover compensation from his victims. . . .

The plaintiff urges that this rule should not apply to his case for a number of reasons. . . .

First, he contends that his acts were not so egregious and that the case in essence involves nothing more than "a claim arising out of injuries suffered by one of several youngsters playing with fireworks shortly before the Fourth of July." . . . In the case before us the plaintiff's conduct may not fairly be characterized as a minor dereliction. By his own admission his injuries did not result from the mere use of firecrackers, but from his efforts to incorporate the gunpowder extracted from the firecrackers into a pipe bomb. Constructing a bomb is a far more dangerous activity not only to the maker, but to the public at large, and is treated as a far more serious offense under the law. . . .

Secondly, the plaintiff claims dispensation from the general rule because of his age, not quite 15 at the time of the incident. He notes that at that age he could not be convicted of a criminal offense . . . and urges that he should be granted a similar exemption from the rule precluding tort recovery for injuries resulting from an otherwise serious criminal act. Although the plaintiff may not be held criminally responsible for his conduct, the fact remains that constructing a bomb is prohibited by law. . . .

The plaintiff was not a toddler. And building a bomb is not such an inherently innocuous activity that it can reasonably be presumed to be a legally permissible act by an average 15 year old. In fact, despite extensive pretrial proceedings below the plaintiff never claimed that he was ignorant of the fact that his conduct was wrongful or that he was unaware of the potential danger it posed to himself and other members of the public. . . .

Finally the plaintiff urges that the rule precluding such recovery was abrogated when the Legislature adopted CPLR 1411 which provides that the "culpable conduct" of a plaintiff "shall not bar recovery, but the amount of damages otherwise recoverable shall be diminished in the proportion which the culpable conduct attributable to the claimant or decedent bears to the culpable conduct which caused the damages." The plaintiff contends that the term "culpable conduct" includes illegal conduct, thus permitting a plaintiff who was injured while violating the law to recover from those who may have contributed to his injury. Since this statute went into effect on September 1, 1975 (L. 1975, ch. 69), prior to the injury sustained by the plaintiff in this case, he urges that it permits him to recover a proportionate share of his loss.

CPLR 1411 abolished the contributory negligence rule which had previously denied a plaintiff any recovery for a cognizable tort if it was shown that the plaintiff had in any way contributed to his own injury. . . . The history of these statutes shows that by referring to "culpable" conduct, rather than negligence, the Legislature intended to include tortious conduct generally, breaches of warranty and the like which had previously served to defeat otherwise cognizable causes of action for damages, or bar contribution among defendants. . . .

The lower courts properly held that CPLR 1411 has no application to the rule precluding a plaintiff from recovering for injuries sustained as a direct result of his own illegal conduct of a serious nature involving risk of physical harm. That rule is not based on the theory that a plaintiff, with an otherwise cognizable cause of action, cannot recover for an injury to which he has contributed. . . . It rests, instead, upon the public policy consideration that the courts should not lend assistance to one who seeks compensation under the law for injuries resulting from his own acts when they involve a substantial violation of the law. . . .

Accordingly, the order of the Appellate Division should be affirmed.

[JASEN, J., concurred in a separate opinion which has been omitted. SIMONS, J., dissented and voted to reverse in an opinion in which MEYER, J., concurred.]

Order affirmed, with costs.

Notes

1. ***Claims Related to Unlawful Conduct.*** Not long ago, American tort law clearly rejected an "outlaw" doctrine: a plaintiff engaged in tortious or criminal acts was not treated as an outlaw who could be injured with impunity. As this principle was expressed in Restatement, Second, of Torts § 889: "One is not barred from recovery for an interference with his legally protected interests merely because at the time of the interference he was committing a tort or a crime."

Various expressions in the Third Restatement appear to endorse a similar position. *See* Restatement, Third, of Torts: Liab. for Physical & Emotional Harm § 52 cmt. a (2012) ("tort law does not generally provide that bad persons forfeit their rights to personal security").

Nevertheless, many cases have denied relief to persons whose injuries were related to their unlawful conduct. *See* Price v. Purdue Pharma Co., 920 So. 2d 479 (Miss. 2006) ("'the wrongful conduct rule' . . . prevents a plaintiff from suing caregivers, pharmacies, and pharmaceutical companies and laboratories for addiction to a controlled substance which he obtained through his own fraud"); Fuentes v. Alecio, 2006 WL 3813780, *3 (S.D. Tex. 2006) (a claim based on the death of a person who perished while trying to enter the U.S. illegally was barred); Lord v. Fogcutter Bar, 813 P.2d 660 (Alaska 1991) (a drunken customer had no claim for damages against the bar that served him liquor in violation of a dramshop law); Chapman v. Superior Ct., 29 Cal. Rptr. 3d 852, 862 (Cal. Ct. App. 2005) (a legal malpractice action by a former public official who pleaded guilty to a crime was precluded); La Page v. Smith, 563 N.Y.S.2d 174 (App. Div. 1990) (an estate was barred from recovery for the death of an intoxicated driver during a high-speed race); Sharpe v. Turley, 191 S.W.3d 362, 369 (Tex. App. 2006) (a fraud action by a nonclient against an attorney was barred); Saks v. Sawtelle, Goode, Davidson & Troilo, 880 S.W.2d 466 (Tex. App. 1994) (public policy barred a legal malpractice action for damages suffered by clients who were convicted of knowingly committing bank fraud after they had allegedly received negligent advice relating to a loan transaction); Lee v. Nationwide Mut. Ins. Co., 497 S.E.2d 328 (Va. 1998) (a minor injured in an accident involving a stolen vehicle was barred from recovery against the driver).

In some cases, the plaintiff's (unsuccessful) argument is that the defendant should have prevented the plaintiff from committing the crime. *See* Burcina v. City of Ketchikan, 902 P.2d 817 (Alaska 1995) (patient who set fire to a mental health center and was convicted of arson did not have a cause of action against his psychiatrist or the facility); Turner v. Anderson, 704 So. 2d 748, 752 (Fla. Dist. Ct. App. 1998) (holding that a client could not sue the attorneys who allegedly advised him to commit perjury); Cole v. Taylor, 301 N.W.2d 766, 768 (Iowa 1981) (the plaintiff was barred from suing a psychiatrist for negligently failing to prevent her from committing a murder).

In some instances, the unlawful conduct defense is expressed in terms much less clear than those set forth in *Barker*. Courts sometimes say that recovery is barred by the doctrine of "unclean hands" or because the plaintiff and defendant are *in pari delicto. See* Vincent R. Johnson, *The Unlawful Conduct Defense in Legal Malpractice*, 77 UMKC L. Rev. 43 (2008) (surveying theories and arguing for careful articulation and limitation of the unlawful conduct defense).

2. ***Legislation Relating to Criminal Acts.*** In some states, versions of the unlawful conduct defense are embodied in statutory provisions. The statutes vary with respect to: (1) the nature of the unlawful conduct that triggers the rule; (2) the theories of recovery that are barred; (3) types of damages that may not be recovered; (4) how closely the unlawful conduct must be related to the injuries for which recovery is sought; and (5) whether there must have been a prior adjudication of criminal responsibility. Consider the following laws:

ALASKA STATUTES § 09.65.210 (Westlaw 2022)

A person who suffers personal injury or death . . . may not recover damages for the personal injury or death if the injury or death occurred while the person was

(1) engaged in the commission of a felony, the person has been convicted of the felony, including conviction based on a guilty plea or plea of nolo contendere, and the party defending against the claim proves by clear and convincing evidence that the felony substantially contributed to the personal injury or death;

(2) engaged in conduct that would constitute the commission of an unclassified felony, a class A felony, or a class B felony for which the person was not convicted and the party defending against the claim proves by clear and convincing evidence

(A) the felonious conduct; and

(B) that the felonious conduct substantially contributed to the personal injury or death;

. . . .

(4) operating a vehicle, aircraft, or watercraft while under the influence of intoxicating liquor or any controlled substance in violation of AS 28.35.030, was convicted, including conviction based on a guilty plea or plea of nolo contendere, and the party defending against the claim proves by clear and convincing evidence that the conduct substantially contributed to the personal injury or death; or

(5) engaged in conduct that would constitute a violation of AS 28.35.030 for which the person was not convicted if the party defending against the claim proves by clear and convincing evidence

(A) the violation of AS 28.35.030; and

(B) that the conduct substantially contributed to the personal injury or death.

California Civil Code § 3333.3 (Westlaw 2022)

In any action for damages based on negligence, a person may not recover any damages if the plaintiff's injuries were in any way proximately caused by the plaintiff's commission of any felony, or immediate flight therefrom, and the plaintiff has been duly convicted of that felony.

Ohio Revised Code Annotated § 2307.60 (Westlaw 2022)

. . . .

(B). . . . (2) Recovery on a claim for relief in a tort action is barred to any person . . . if . . . (a) [t]he person has been convicted of or has pleaded guilty to a felony, or to a misdemeanor that is an offense of violence, arising out of criminal conduct that was a proximate cause of the injury or loss for which relief is claimed in the action. . . .

(4) Divisions (B)(1) to (3) of this section does not apply to civil claims based upon alleged intentionally tortious conduct, alleged violations of the United States Constitution, or alleged violations of statutes of the United States pertaining to civil rights. . . .

Texas Civil Practice and Remedies Code §§ 86.002-93001 (Westlaw 2022)

§ 86.002. *Recovery of Damages for Injury to Convicted Person Prohibited*

(a) A claimant who has been convicted of a felony or misdemeanor may not recover damages for an injury sustained during the commission of the felony or misdemeanor if the injury would not have been sustained but for the commission of the felony or misdemeanor.

(b) Subsection (a) does not bar the claimant from recovering damages if the claimant shows that:

(1) the damages arose from an act entirely separate from any act intended to result in the:

(A) prevention of the commission of a felony or misdemeanor by the claimant; or

(B) apprehension of the claimant during or immediately after the commission of the felony or misdemeanor; and

(2) the damages did not arise from a premises defect or other circumstance that the claimant was exposed to as a result of the commission of the felony or misdemeanor.

§ 93.001. Assumption of the Risk: Affirmative Defense

(a) It is an affirmative defense to a civil action for damages for personal injury or death that the plaintiff, at the time the cause of action arose, was:

(1) committing a felony, for which the plaintiff has been finally convicted, that was the sole cause of the damages sustained by the plaintiff. . . .

In Sonoran Desert Investig., Inc. v. Miller, 141 P.3d 754 (Ariz. Ct. App. 2006), the court invalidated a statutory unlawful conduct defense on the ground that it violated a state constitutional provision requiring submission of issues of contributory negligence or assumption of the risk to a jury. However, in Caviglia v. Royal Tours of Am., 842 A.2d 125 (N.J. 2004), the court upheld a statutory bar against recovery of noneconomic damages by motorists who violated the law by failing to carry liability insurance.

3. ***Reconciling Statutory and Common Law Provisions***. Some states recognize both statutory and common law versions of the unlawful conduct defense. However, in Dugger v. Arredondo, 408 S.W.3d 825 (Tex. 2013), the Texas Supreme Court held that a common law unlawful acts doctrine was not available as an affirmative defense in personal injury and wrongful death cases because "[l]ike other common law assumption of the risk defenses, it was abrogated by *** [the state's adoption of a statutory] proportionate responsibility scheme." Clarifying that point, Justice Paul Green explained, "Unless the requirements of the affirmative defense in section 93.001[6] [a statutory unlawful conduct rule with a limited scope] are satisfied, a plaintiff's share of responsibility for his or her injuries should be compared against the defendant's."

4. ***General Justification***. Because the common law is continually adapted to new and changing circumstances, a defendant's conduct may be privileged under what might be called a doctrine of general justification even though it falls within none of the traditional categories of defenses and privileges. The rough contours of this concept were outlined in Sindle v. N.Y.C. Transit Auth., 307 N.E.2d 245 (N.Y. 1973). There, a school bus driver was charged with false imprisonment. He asserted that he was privileged to drive the children on the bus to the police station when some of them continued to engage in repeated acts of vandalism despite requests to desist. The court agreed: "[A] school bus driver, entrusted with the care of his student-passengers and the custody of public property, has the duty to take reasonable

---

6. [Editors' note:] Texas Civil Practice and Remedies Code § 93.001 (Westlaw 2022) provides:
§ 93.001. Assumption of the Risk: Affirmative Defense

(a) It is an affirmative defense to a civil action for damages for personal injury or death that the plaintiff, at the time the cause of action arose, was:

(1) committing a felony, for which the plaintiff has been finally convicted, that was the sole cause of the damages sustained by the plaintiff; or

(2) committing or attempting to commit suicide, and the plaintiff's conduct in committing or attempting to commit suicide was the sole cause of the damages sustained; provided, however, if the suicide or attempted suicide was caused in whole or in part by a failure on the part of any defendant to comply with an applicable legal standard, then such suicide or attempted suicide shall not be a defense.

(b) This section does not apply in any action brought by an employee, or the surviving beneficiaries of an employee, under the Workers' Compensation Law of Texas, or in an action against an insurer based on a contract of insurance, a statute, or common law.

(c) In an action to which this section applies, this section shall prevail over any other law.

measures for the safety and protection of both." The court held, in determining the existence of the privilege, that it was appropriate to take into account the need for the defendant to protect persons and property, the defendant's duty to aid in apprehending wrongdoers, the manner and place of the occurrence, and the feasibility of other alternative courses of action.

Chapter 4

Damages

A. In General

1. Introduction

Anderson v. Sears, Roebuck & Co.

United States District Court for the Eastern District of Louisiana
377 F. Supp. 136 (E.D. La. 1974)

CASSIBRY, District Judge:

... [T]he Britains' home was completely consumed by a fire which was ignited by a defective Sears' heater. Both Mildred Britain and her infant daughter, Helen Britain, were severely burned....

[At trial, a verdict was returned in favor of Helen Britain in the amount of $2 million].... The sole issue presently before the court is whether the damages awarded to Helen Britain were excessive.

....

The legal standard on which to gauge a jury verdict for remittitur purposes is the "maximum recovery rule." .... This rule directs the trial judge to determine whether the verdict of the jury exceeds the maximum amount which the jury could reasonably find and if it does, the trial judge may then reduce the verdict to the highest amount that the jury could properly have awarded. Functionally, the maximum recovery rule both preserves the constitutionally protected role of the jury as finder of facts and prevents the predilections of the judge from infecting the jury's determination. Thus, the court's task is to ascertain, by scrutinizing all of the evidence as to each element of damages, what amount would be the maximum the jury could have reasonably awarded. In this case there are five cardinal elements of damages: past physical and mental pain; future physical and mental pain; future medical expenses; loss of earning capacity; and permanent disability and disfigurement.

Past Physical and Mental Pain

The infant child Helen Britain, was almost burned to death in the tragic fire that swept her home. She was burned over forty per cent of her entire body; third degree burns cover eighty per cent of her scalp and second and third degree burns of the trunk and of her extremities account for the remainder. Helen Britain's immediate post-trauma treatment required hospitalization for twenty-eight days, during which time the child developed pneumonia, required numerous transfusions, suffered fever, vomiting, diarrhea, and infection, and underwent skin graft surgery, under general anesthesia, to her scalp, which was only partially successful. Keloid scarring caused webbing and ankylosis of the child's extremities and severely limited her motion. The child's fingers became adhered together; scarring bent the arm at the elbow in a burdensome, fixed position; and thick scarring on the thighs and on the side of and behind the knees impaired walking.

This child had to undergo subsequent hospitalizations. . . . The second major operation under general anesthesia was undertaken to graft new skin from the back and stomach to the remaining bare areas of the scalp. The third operation under general anesthesia was an attempt to relieve the deformity of her left hand caused by the webbing scars which bound down the fingers of that hand. A fourth operation under general anesthesia was performed to reduce scars which had grown back on the left hand again webbing the fingers. I cannot envisage the breadth and intensity of the pain experienced by Helen Britain throughout this ordeal.

The undisputed testimony reveals that one of the most tragic aspects of this case is that the horrible mental and emotional trauma caused to this child occurred at an age which medical experts maintain is crucial to a child's entire psyche and personality formation. Helen Britain's persistent emotional and mental disturbance is evidenced by bed wetting, nightmares, refusing to sleep alone, withdrawal, and speech impediments. Dr. Cyril Phillips, a psychiatrist, and Dr. Diamond both indicated that the child manifested to them, even at this early age, emotional illness and retarded mental growth.

The evidence reflects that an award of six hundred thousand dollars for this element of damages alone would not be unreasonable.

Future Physical and Mental Pain

There is clear evidence that the stretching, pulling, and breaking down of scars inherent in growth will continue to cause severe pain and a crippling limitation of motion in varying degrees to all of Helen Britain's upper and lower extremities. Very little can be done to improve the condition of the scalp which will never be able to breathe, sweat or grow hair. There will be risks, trauma and pain, both physical and mental, with each of the recommended twenty-seven future operations which will extend over most of the child's adult life, if she is in fact fortunate enough to be able to risk undergoing these recommended surgeries. Furthermore, Helen Britain must vigilantly guard against irritation, infection and further injury to the damaged and abnormal skin, scars and grafts because any injury, however slight, can generate cancer in these adynamic areas.

The inherent stresses and tensions of each new phase of life will severely tax this little girl's debilitated and delicate mental and emotional capacity. Throughout her future life expectancy of seventy-five years, it is reasonable to expect, that she will be deprived of a normal social life and that she will never find a husband and raise a family. On top of this, Helen Britain will always be subjected to rejection, stares and tactless inquiries from children and adults.

The court concludes that an award of seven hundred fifty thousand dollars for this element of damages alone would not be excessive.

Future Medical Expenses

A large award for future medical expenses is justified. The uncontradicted testimony was that Helen Britain would need the guidance, treatment and counseling of a team of doctors, including plastic surgeons, psychiatrists and sociologists, throughout her lifetime. Add to this the cost of twenty-seven recommended operations and the cost of private tutoring necessitated by the child's mental and emotional needs and the jury could justifiably award a figure of two hundred and fifty thousand dollars to cover these future expenses.

Loss of Earning Capacity

The evidence of Helen Britain's disabilities both physical, mental and emotional was such that this court holds that the jury could properly find that these disabilities would prevent her from earning a living for the rest of her life. Not only do the physical impairments to her extremities disable her but her emotional limitations require avoiding stress and the combined effect is the permanent incapacity to maintain serious employment.

The jury was provided with actuarial figures which accurately calculated both the deduction of interest to be earned and the addition of an inflationary buffer, on any award made for future loss of earning capacity. In view of these incontrovertible projections at trial, it was within the province of the jury to award as much as $330,000.00 for the loss of earning capacity.

Permanent Disability and Disfigurement

The award for this element of damage must evaluate in monetary terms the compensation due this plaintiff for the permanent physical, mental and emotional disabilities and disfigurements proved by the evidence adduced at trial. A narration treating Miss Britain's permanent disabilities and disfigurements would be lengthy and redundant; therefore, I resort to listing.

1. The complete permanent loss of 80% of the scalp caused by the destruction of sweat glands, hair follicles and tissue—all of which effects a grotesque disfigurement and freakish appearance.

2. The permanent loss of the normal use of the legs.

3. The permanent impairment of the left fingers and hand caused by recurring webbing and resulting in limited motion.

4. The permanent impairment of the right hand caused by scars and webbing of the fingers.

5. The permanent injury to the left elbow and left arm with ankylosis and resulting in a crippling deformity.

6. The permanent destruction of 40% of the normal skin. As a result of this a large portion of the body is covered by "pigskin." Pigskin resembles

the dry, cracked skin of an aged person and is highly susceptible to irritation from such ordinary things as temperature changes and washing.

7. Permanent scars over the majority of the body where skin donor sites were removed.

8. The permanent impairment of speech.

9. The loss of three years of formative and impressionable childhood.

10. Permanently reduced and impaired emotional capacity.

11. The permanent impairment of normal social, recreational and educational life.

12. The permanent imprint of her mother's hand on her stomach.

Considering each of the foregoing items, the court concludes that the jury had the prerogative of awarding up to one million, one hundred thousand dollars for this element of damages.

By totaling the estimated maximum recovery for each element of damages, the jury's actual award is placed in proper perspective. According to my calculations the maximum jury award supported by the evidence in this case could have been two million, nine hundred eighty thousand dollars. Obviously, the jury's two million dollar verdict is well within the periphery established by the maximum award test.

. . . .

The defendants' motions for a remittitur are denied.

Notes

1. ***Excessive Damages: Remittitur.*** Judges may not set aside damages awards merely because they would have reached a judgment different from that of the jury. However, a court may order a new trial if the jury's verdict is not supported by the evidence.

When a court finds an award of damages to be excessive, a common practice is to order a new trial (usually on the issue of damages only, but sometimes on both liability and damages) unless the plaintiff agrees to accept a smaller sum fixed by the court in place of the jury's award. This procedure is called "remittitur" because the plaintiff is being asked to "remit"—meaning cancel, give up, or refrain from exacting—part of the jury award. The cost in money and time of a new trial is typically so great that plaintiffs usually decide to take the lower sum, but they need not do so, and there are cases in which plaintiffs have gone through two or even three trials rather than accept a court's figure.

In some states, the standards or procedures for remittitur are set out by statute. *See, e.g.*, Fla. Stat. Ann. § 768.74 (Westlaw 2022); *see also* Tex. Rules App. Proc. §§ 46-1 to 46.5 (Westlaw 2022).

It is sometimes said that the standard for review is whether the jury's determination is "shocking to the judicial conscience" or grossly excessive. *Cf.* Carlson v.

Okerstrom, 675 N.W.2d 89 (Neb. 2004) (finding that an award of nearly a million dollars was not the "result of passion, prejudice, [or] mistake" where there was evidence of damage to a motorist's optic nerve). One kind of case in which judges tend to find damages excessive is that in which the jury awards a larger amount than the plaintiff's own witnesses' testimony supports.

Some states impose a lower standard for appellate review of mental distress damages. *See* Goady v. Utopia Home Care Agency, 759 N.Y.S.2d 183 (App. Div. 2003) (holding that a jury award of $200,000 for past pain and suffering, and $100,000 for future pain and suffering, to an infant upon whom a hot iron fell, deviated materially from what would be reasonable compensation, and a new trial on damages would be granted absent a stipulation reducing those damages to $125,000 and $25,000, respectively).

2. ***Inadequate Damages: Additur.*** A technique similar to remittitur, called "additur," allows a court to award the plaintiff a new trial on damages unless the defendant agrees to pay a larger amount than the jury awarded. As with remittitur, this can be done only if the award is against the weight of the evidence. *See* Cox v. Shelter Ins. Co., 34 So. 3d 398 (La. App. 2010) (finding that an award of $25,000 for serious back injuries was abusively low); Walsh v. Constantinopoulos, 2010 N.J. Super. Unpub. Lexis 1763 (App. Div. 2010) (finding an award of $100,000 for pain and suffering "grossly inadequate").

Additur is not permitted in some states, and in such instances the sole remedy for an award that is manifestly too small is a new trial. *See* Guckian v. Fowler, 453 S.W.2d 323 (Tex. App. 1970). A Supreme Court decision holds that federal courts cannot use additur because the practice violates the Seventh Amendment's right to a jury trial. *See* Dimick v. Schiedt, 293 U.S. 474 (1935). Remittitur is practiced in federal courts.

Whereas motions by losing parties for remittitur are common, motions by winning parties for additur are very rare. "To avoid contravention of the right to jury trial . . . , the trial court must obtain the consent of the party against whom the additur or remittitur is to be entered; if that party does not consent, the trial court must order a new trial." Borne v. Celadon Trucking Services, Inc., 532 S.W.3d 274, 309 (Tenn. 2017).

3. ***"Hedonic" Damages.*** Notably absent from the *Anderson* court's list of elements of tort damages is an award for the plaintiff's loss of ability to engage in enjoyable activities. Suppose, for example, that a minor injury to a plaintiff's arm causes permanent stiffness, which prevents the plaintiff from playing golf, which had been her favorite recreational activity. Some courts have approved awards of "hedonic" damages, to compensate for loss of some of life's pleasures. *See* McGee v. A C And S, Inc., 933 So. 2d 770 (La. 2006); Wesley B. Lambert, *The Price of Life: A Prediction of South Carolina's Approach to Expert Testimony on Hedonic Damages Using the Willingness-to-Pay Method*, 64 S.C. L. Rev. 1037, 1062 (2013) ("Of the states that recognize hedonic damages, many jurisdictions do not allow for the recovery of hedonic damages in a wrongful death suit").

The plaintiff in McDougald v. Garber, 536 N.E.2d 372 (N.Y. 1989), became permanently comatose as a result of brain injuries inflicted by the defendant's negligence. The New York Court of Appeals refused to allow any recovery for loss of enjoyment of life as a category separate from pain and suffering. It also held that, if the plaintiff's neurological functions were so impaired that she could feel nothing, she was not entitled to an award for pain and suffering. *McDougald* recognized, however, that the frustration of being unable to engage in one's favorite activities can be a component of a pain-and-suffering award if the plaintiff is conscious enough to suffer that kind of frustration. Other courts have ruled similarly.

4. ***Per Diem Arguments.*** To calculate damages for physical and mental pain and suffering, a majority of jurisdictions permit lawyers to make *per diem* arguments. Under this approach, counsel reduces the discomfort to small units of time, such as minutes, hours, or days; sets a value on each unit (*e.g.*, a penny a minute; a dollar an hour; ten dollars a day); and then argues that the jury should arrive at a total award by multiplying the unit value by the number of units of time that the discomfort may be expected to continue. Because a modest per unit figure may give rise to a very large long-term amount (*e.g.*, 10 cents per minute equals roughly $52,560 per year), some courts refuse to allow *per diem* arguments on the ground that they are inherently misleading. *See* John Campbell, Bernard Chao, & Christopher Robertson, *Time Is Money: An Empirical Assessment of Non-Economic Damages Arguments*, 95 Wash. U. L. Rev. 1, 33 (2017) (listing states that allow per diem calculations).

5. ***Pain and Suffering Awards in Similar Cases.*** In Jutzi-Johnson v. U.S., 263 F.3d 753 (7th Cir. 2001), a case involving a jail suicide, Judge Richard Posner wrote:

> Most courts . . . treat the determination of how much damages for pain and suffering to award as a standardless, unguided exercise of discretion by the trier of fact, reviewable for abuse of discretion pursuant to no standard to guide the reviewing court either. To minimize the arbitrary variance in awards bound to result from such a throw-up-the-hands approach, the trier of fact should, as is done routinely in England . . . , be informed of the amounts of pain and suffering damages awarded in similar cases. . . . And when the trier of fact is a judge, he should be required . . . to set forth in his opinion the damages awards that he considered comparable. We make such comparisons routinely in reviewing pain and suffering awards [citing cases from the First, Second, Fifth, and Seventh Circuits]. It would be a wise practice to follow at the trial level as well.
>
> . . . [B]oth parties have cited what they deem comparable cases. Only their notions of comparability are stunted. The plaintiff cites three cases in which damages for pain and suffering ranging from $600,000 to $1 million were awarded, but in each one the pain and suffering continued for hours, not minutes. The defendant confined its search for comparable cases to other prison suicide cases, implying that prisoners experience pain and suffering differently from other persons, so that it makes more sense to compare Johnson's pain and suffering to that of a prisoner who suffered a

> toothache than to that of a free person who was strangled, and concluding absurdly that any award for pain and suffering in this case that exceeded $5,000 would be excessive. The parties should have looked at awards in other cases involving asphyxiation, for example cases of drowning, which are numerous. . . . Had they done so, they would have come up with an award in the range of $15,000 to $150,000.

6. ***Review of Noneconomic Damages Awards in Defamation Cases.*** In Cantu v. Flanigan, 705 F. Supp. 2d 220 (E.D.N.Y. 2010), the court upheld an award of $150 million in noneconomic damages (*e.g.*, for harm to reputation and emotional distress) in a case involving defamation of a prominent business executive. The award far exceeded any previous award in a defamation case. The opinion emphasized that:

> [A] court . . . cannot simply catalogue the jury awards that have been acceptable in the past to determine whether the award under review is excessive. Indeed, "no two cases are exactly the same." . . . . New factual scenarios may arise that warrant larger awards than those approved in prior cases.

7. ***"Day-in-the-Life" Videos.*** An effective visual aid for dramatizing to the jury the hardships that an accident has imposed on the plaintiff is the "day-in-the-life" video. Such productions, which show a plaintiff's struggle with daily activities, such as dressing, bathing, eating, and therapy, are expensive and thus normally made only in cases involving serious injuries. Because a "day-in-the-life" video is prepared for admission into evidence, the defendant's attorney may have a right to be present during the filming, and the use of background music and other mechanisms for heightening drama will likely be precluded.

Another type of video production used in personal injury cases is the "video settlement documentary." It differs from a "day-in-the-life" video in that it is intended for viewing not by a jury, but by the opposing attorney and client. The content of a video settlement documentary is not constrained by rules of evidence. It may include footage showing the demonstrative evidence (*e.g.*, models of the accident site) and the expert witnesses the plaintiff will seek to present at trial. The purpose is to persuade the defendant to settle the case on generous terms. *See* Jeanmarie Whalen, *Illuminate Damages with a Video Settlement Brochure*, Trial (Apr. 2012), at 27.

8. ***Damages for "Loss of Consortium."*** "Consortium" means "[t]he benefits that one person, . . . [especially] a spouse, is entitled to receive from another, including companionship, cooperation, affection, aid, financial support, and (between spouses) sexual relations." Black's Law Dictionary (11th ed. 2019).

The common law of England allowed a husband whose wife was injured an action against the tortfeasor for "loss of consortium." A wife whose husband was injured had no comparable action. Today, in every state, the action is allowed to either spouse. *See* Fox v. Hayes, 600 F.3d 819, 845 (7th Cir. 2010) (affirming a $2.7 million loss of consortium award where the wrongful incarceration of her husband as a murder suspect "came at a crucial moment in their marriage" due to the death of the couple's daughter).

Damages in actions for loss of consortium include medical expenses paid by the plaintiff for the injured spouse, the costs of hiring someone to do the work an injured spouse can no longer do, and, in cases involving serious injuries, compensation for the loss of the companionship (sexual and otherwise) and affection of the plaintiff's spouse.

An action for loss of consortium usually must be tried together with the principal action. *Cf.* Desjarlais v. USAA Ins. Co., 824 A.2d 1272 (R.I. 2003) (wife and children's claims were barred due to failure to join). Furthermore, defenses — such as comparative negligence — that would affect recovery in the principal action will in most states have the same effect in an action for loss of consortium. Thus, if *D* negligently injures *H*, and if *H* was negligent as well, *H*'s negligence will eliminate or reduce not only his own award but also any award sought by *H*'s wife, *W*, for loss of consortium. A loss of consortium award ordinarily should not substantially exceed the award to the directly injured spouse. *See* Ashmore v. Hartford Hosp., 208 A.3d 256, 258 (Conn. 2019).

A jury is free to conclude, despite the testimony of the parties, that there was no loss of consortium with respect to household services and the like. In Dunn v. Bank-Tec South, 134 S.W.3d 315 (Tex. App. 2003), a jury found that a bank customer's injuries to his arm, which were caused when a mobile teller unit at a drive-in banking facility closed on it, were less than permanent, serious, and disabling, and that the customer's wife was not entitled to damages for loss of consortium. The appellate court concluded that the jury's determination was not manifestly unjust. The wife's testimony about her husband's inability to do yard work, about the reduction in the amount of time he spent helping her around the house, and about his increased isolation and decreased physical affection were inherently subjective in nature, and the wife was not a disinterested witness.

Persons other than the spouse of the victim may suffer when someone is injured: unmarried cohabitants, the victim's parents, and the victim's children or grandchildren come to mind.

Many jurisdictions allow the parents of an injured child to recover for financial losses (principally medical expenses). *But see* Hockema v. J.S., 832 N.E.2d 537 (Ind. App. 2005) (holding that parents could not recover for medical expenses they paid on behalf of an injured child because the child was more negligent than the defendant and the state followed a modified comparative fault system). In Rudnicki v. Bianco, 2021 WL 5875461 (Colo.), the court held that in tort cases involving an injured unemancipated minor child, either the child or the child's parents may recover the child's pre-majority medical expenses, but double recovery is not permitted.

In some states, legislation or case law allows a parent to recover for the loss of a child's companionship as well. *See* Gallimore v. Children's Hosp. Med. Ctr., 617 N.E.2d 1052 (Ohio 1993) (including loss of the child's services, companionship, comfort, love, and solace); *but see* Roberts v. Williamson, 111 S.W.3d 113, 117 (Tex.

2003) (rejecting claim for filial consortium and quoting precedent stating that "[a] lthough parents customarily *enjoy* the consortium of their children, in the ordinary course of events a parent does not *depend* on a child's companionship, love, support, guidance, and nurture in the same way and to the same degree that a husband depends on his wife, a wife depends on her husband, or a minor or disabled adult child depends on his or her parent").

At least one state has held that a grandparent standing in the place of a parent as caregiver and provider of affection may sue for loss of consortium. *See* Fernandez v. Walgreen Hastings Co., 968 P.2d 774 (N.M. 1998).

Some jurisdictions give the children of injured parents an action. *See Gallimore, supra* (including loss of parent's services, society, companionship, affection, comfort, guidance, and counsel). However, most states decline to do so. *See* Harrington v. Brooks Drugs, Inc., 808 A.2d 532, 534 (N.H. 2002) (indicating that "the overwhelming weight of authority . . . is against recognition of a cause of action for loss of parental consortium").

Some courts have permitted an award for loss of consortium in the case of siblings. *See, e.g.*, Sheahan v. Northeast Illinois Reg'l Commuter R.R. Corp., 496 N.E.2d 1179 (Ill. Ct. App. 1986).

Lozoya v. Sanchez, 66 P.3d 948 (N.M. 2003) (*infra*, p. 653), was the first unreversed case in the nation to recognize the right of an unmarried cohabitant standing in an "intimate familial relationship" to the injured party to sue for loss of consortium.

As an alternative to a claim for loss of consortium, those close to an accident victim may sometimes sue for the tort of negligent infliction of emotional distress, at least if they actually see the accident happen or were also placed in danger. *See* Chapter 11.

Meyer ex rel. Coplin v. Fluor Corporation

Supreme Court of Missouri, En Banc
220 S.W.3d 712 (Mo. 2007)

RICHARD B. TEITELMAN, Judge.

. . . [Defendants] are involved with the operation of the Doe Run lead smelter in Herculaneum. Each year, the smelter emits large quantities of lead into the local environment, allegedly resulting in higher levels of lead and other toxins than would otherwise be present. . . . There is no dispute that lead is toxic and that children are generally more susceptible to injury from lead poisoning than are adults. There is also no dispute that injuries from lead exposure are often latent injuries; that is, a diagnosable physical injury or illness is not immediately apparent and years may pass before symptoms are detected.

Plaintiff filed a petition asserting that she is a member of a class of children in and around Herculaneum who has been exposed to toxic emissions from the smelter. Plaintiff alleged negligence, strict liability, private nuisance, and trespass as theories of liability and sought compensatory damages to establish a medical monitoring program for class members. The purpose of the monitoring program would be to provide ongoing diagnostic testing to determine whether the exposure to lead and other toxins has caused or is in the process of causing an injury or illness. The proposed class consists of over 200 children....

The circuit court held a certification hearing and found that "individual issues will necessarily predominate over common issues in this case" and that the case could not be efficiently addressed on a class-wide basis. Accordingly, the court entered an order denying Plaintiff's motion for class certification.

On appeal, Plaintiff argues that the circuit court erred because its class action analysis assumed incorrectly that a present physical injury is a necessary element of a medical monitoring claim. Plaintiff asserts that the circuit court focused on individual proof issues that are primarily relevant to a personal injury action, not a medical monitoring claim....

.... The widely recognized tort law concepts premised upon a present physical injury are ill-equipped to deal with cases involving latent injury. To deal with this reality, tort law has evolved over the years to allow plaintiffs compensation for medical monitoring.[1].... The courts that have approved medical monitoring claims recognize that "significant economic harm may be inflicted on those exposed to toxic substances, notwithstanding the fact that the physical harm resulting from such exposure is often latent."....

... [I]n Elam v. Alcolac, Inc., 765 S.W.2d 42 (Mo. App. 1988), the court analyzed the admissibility of medical testimony in a toxic tort case and, in holding that the testimony was admissible, stated that:

> The evidence of significant, albeit unquantified, risk of cancer from the exposure to the toxic [chemicals], however, was competent to prove, as a separate element of damage, the need for medical surveillance of the immune system and other organs, and hence was admissible for that purpose.

The *Elam* court recognized that among the potential damages sustained by a plaintiff who is exposed to a toxin is the need for medical monitoring for the "early detection of serious disease from the chronic exposure" to toxins.... The court further reasoned that medical monitoring costs are recoverable because "compensation for necessary medical expenses reasonably certain to be incurred in the future rests on well-accepted legal principles."....These "well-accepted" principles of Missouri law provide that a plaintiff is entitled to recover for the prospective consequences of the defendant's tortious conduct if the injury is reasonably certain to occur.... Recognizing that a defendant's conduct has created the need for future medical

1. [Fn. 3:] *See, e.g.*,... [citing cases from the federal courts for the Third Circuit and the District of Colorado, and state courts in Arizona, California, Connecticut, Louisiana, Nevada, New Jersey, New York, Pennsylvania, Tennessee, Utah, and West Virginia].

monitoring does not create a new tort. It is simply a compensable item of damage when liability is established under traditional tort theories of recovery. . . .

Defendants assert that any recovery for medical monitoring is contingent upon the existence of a present physical injury. Although some courts have so concluded, a present physical injury requirement is inconsistent with the theory of recovery. . . . Just as an individual has a legally protected interest in avoiding physical injury, so too does an individual have an interest in avoiding expensive medical evaluations caused by the tortious conduct of others. "When a defendant invades this interest, the injury to which is neither speculative nor resistant to proof, it is elementary that the defendant should make the plaintiff whole by paying for the examinations." . . . . Even though a plaintiff may not have yet developed a diagnosable physical injury, it is not accurate to conclude that no compensable injury has been sustained. . . . The injury for which compensation is sought is not a present physical injury. Instead, medical monitoring damages compensate the plaintiff for the quantifiable costs of periodic medical examinations reasonably necessary for the early detection and treatment of latent injuries caused by the plaintiff's exposure to toxic substances. . . . A physical injury requirement is inconsistent with the reality of latent injury and with the fact that the purpose of medical monitoring is to facilitate the early diagnosis and treatment of latent injuries caused by exposure to toxins. . . .

These considerations have led a number of courts that have addressed this issue to conclude that recovering medical monitoring damages does not require a threshold showing of present physical injury. The general consensus that has emerged in these cases is that a plaintiff can obtain damages for medical monitoring upon a showing that "the plaintiff has a significantly increased risk of contracting a particular disease relative to what would be the case in the absence of exposure." . . . Once that has been proven, the plaintiff must then show that "medical monitoring is, to a reasonable degree of medical certainty, necessary in order to diagnose properly the warning signs of disease." . . . .

The circuit court misapplied the law by applying personal injury concepts to Plaintiff's medical monitoring claim and in holding that these individual personal injury issues were predominate over common issues. The judgment denying class certification is reversed, and the case is remanded.

WOLFF, C.J., STITH and WHITE, JJ., concur.

[The dissenting opinion of PRICE, J., in which RUSSELL, J., concurred, and the dissenting opinion of LIMBAUGH, J., have been omitted.]

Notes

1. ***Medical Monitoring.*** Contrary to the principal case, some courts reject medical monitoring, at least in specific contexts. *See* Lowe v. Philip Morris USA, Inc., 183 P.3d 181 (Or. 2008) (holding that a smoker was not entitled to medical monitoring damages based on accumulated exposure to cigarette smoke); Paz v. Brush

Engineered Materials, Inc., 949 So. 2d 1 (Miss. 2007) (holding that the state does not recognize medical monitoring claims in the absence of proof of physical injury).

2. ***Credit Monitoring in Cybersecurity Cases.*** Database possessors, such as universities and credit card issuers, hold computerized personal information about numerous individuals ("data subjects"), such as students, alumni, and credit card holders. When that information is hacked or otherwise subject to unauthorized access, data subjects are at risk of becoming victims of identity theft.

One way to guard the serious economic consequences that can flow from identity theft is to promptly detect unauthorized use of personal information. This can be done by subscribing to a service which monitors the three major credit reporting agencies daily and provides notice (sometimes on a daily basis) of changes in one's credit history, such as a new account or loan taken out in the individual's name. Such monitoring services cost only a few dollars per month, but they are not free. Nevertheless, the expenditure may be wise, particularly if one's data has been hacked, because it is extremely difficult to repair a ruined credit history.

Is unauthorized access to personal information (*e.g.*, social security numbers, names of family members, account identifiers) similar to toxic exposure? Should courts allow data subjects to recover credit monitoring damages from a database possessor who unreasonably failed to protect information from unauthorized access? *See* Vincent R. Johnson, *Cybersecurity, Identity Theft, and the Limits of Tort Liability*, 57 S.C. L. Rev. 255, 305–07 (2005) (arguing that tort law should endeavor to minimize the losses associated with identity theft by imposing liability for failure to protect data from unauthorized access and failure to promptly disclose evidence that a breach in security has occurred); *see also* Vincent R. Johnson, *Credit-Monitoring Damages in Cybersecurity Tort Litigation*, 19 Geo. Mason L. Rev. 113, 154–55 (2011), arguing that:

> In recent years, expenditures on credit monitoring have become common. Today, it is often the case that potential cybersecurity defendants voluntarily provide such services to affected data subjects; that courts approve settlements where compensation for credit monitoring is a large part of class-action recoveries; and that judicial and administrative sanctions order provision of credit monitoring or reimbursement for expenditures on such services. These developments, all of which are relatively new, cloak expenditures on credit monitoring with the indicia of legitimacy. . . .
>
> Expenditures on credit monitoring are a reasonable and necessary response to any serious breach of data security, and therefore, compensation for such amounts should normally be available. . . .

2. The Collateral-Source Rule

Helfend v. Southern California Rapid Transit District

Supreme Court of California, In Bank
465 P.2d 61 (Cal. 1970)

TOBRINER, Acting Chief Justice.

....

Plaintiff [who was injured in a bus-auto collision] filed a tort action against the Southern California Rapid Transit District, a public entity, and Mitchell, an employee of the transit district.... Defendant requested permission to show that about 80 percent of the plaintiff's hospital bill had been paid by plaintiff's Blue Cross insurance carrier and that some of his other medical expenses may have been paid by other insurance.... The court ruled that defendants should not be permitted to show that plaintiff had received medical coverage from any collateral source.

....

The Supreme Court of California has long adhered to the doctrine that if an injured party receives some compensation for his injuries from a source wholly independent of the tortfeasor, such payment should not be deducted from the damages which the plaintiff would otherwise collect from the tortfeasor....

Although the collateral source rule remains generally accepted in the United States, nevertheless many other jurisdictions have restricted or repealed it.... [C]ommentators have criticized the rule and called for its early demise....

The collateral source rule as applied here embodies the venerable concept that a person who has invested years of insurance premiums to assure his medical care should receive the benefits of his thrift. The tortfeasor should not garner the benefits of his victim's providence.

The collateral source rule expresses a policy judgment in favor of encouraging citizens to purchase and maintain insurance for personal injuries and for other eventualities. Courts consider insurance a form of investment, the benefits of which become payable without respect to any other possible source of funds. If we were to permit a tortfeasor to mitigate damages with payments from plaintiff's insurance, plaintiff would be in a position inferior to that of having bought no insurance, because his payment of premiums would have earned no benefit. Defendant should not be able to avoid payment of full compensation for the injury inflicted merely because the victim has had the foresight to provide himself with insurance.

Some commentators object that the above approach to the collateral source rule provides plaintiff with a "double recovery," rewards him for the injury, and defeats the principle that damages should compensate the victim but not punish the tortfeasor. We agree with Professor Fleming's observation, however, that "double recovery is justified only in the face of some exceptional, supervening reason, as in the case of accident or life insurance, where it is felt unjust that the tortfeasor should take advantage of the thrift and prescience of the victim in having paid the premiums." (Fleming, Introduction to the Law of Torts (1967) p. 131.). . . .

Furthermore, insurance policies increasingly provide for either subrogation or refund of benefits upon a tort recovery, and such refund is indeed called for in the present case. . . . Hence, the plaintiff receives no double recovery; the collateral source rule simply serves as a means of by-passing the antiquated doctrine of nonassignment of tortious actions and permits a proper transfer of risk from the plaintiff's insurer to the tortfeasor by way of the victim's tort recovery. The double shift from the tortfeasor to the victim and then from the victim to his insurance carrier can normally occur with little cost in that the insurance carrier is often intimately involved in the initial litigation and quite automatically receives its part of the tort settlement or verdict.

Even in cases in which the contract or the law precludes subrogation or refund of benefits, or in situations in which the collateral source waives such subrogation or refund, the rule performs entirely necessary functions in the computation of damages. For example, the cost of medical care often provides both attorneys and juries in tort cases with an important measure for assessing the plaintiff's general damages. . . . To permit the defendant to tell the jury that the plaintiff has been recompensed by a collateral source for his medical costs might irretrievably upset the complex, delicate, and somewhat indefinable calculations which result in the normal jury verdict. . . . We also note that generally the jury is not informed that plaintiff's attorney will receive a large portion of the plaintiff's recovery in contingent fees. . . . Hence, the plaintiff rarely actually receives full compensation for his injuries as computed by the jury. The collateral source rule partially serves to compensate for the attorney's share and does not actually render "double recovery" for the plaintiff. . . . In sum, the plaintiff's recovery for his medical expenses from both the tortfeasor and his medical insurance program . . . partially provides a somewhat closer approximation to full compensation for his injuries.[2]

If we consider the collateral source rule as applied here in the context of the entire American approach to the law of torts and damages, we find that the rule presently performs a number of legitimate and even indispensable functions. Without a thorough revolution in the American approach to torts and the consequent damages, the rule at least with respect to medical insurance benefits has become so integrated within our present system that its precipitous judicial nullification would work hardship. . . . The reforms which many academicians propose cannot easily be achieved through piecemeal common law development; the proposed

2. [Fn. 20:] Of course, only in cases in which the tort victim has received payments or services from a collateral source will he be able to mitigate attorney's fees by means of the collateral source rule. Thus the rule provides at best only an incomplete and haphazard solution to providing all tort victims with full compensation. Depriving some tort victims of the salutary protections of the collateral source rule will, short of a thorough reform of our tort system, only decrease the available compensation for injuries. . . .

changes, if desirable, would be more effectively accomplished through legislative reform. . . .

. . . . We therefore reaffirm our adherence to the collateral source rule in tort cases in which the plaintiff has been compensated by an independent collateral source — such as insurance, pension, continued wages, or disability payments — for which he had actually or constructively . . . paid or in cases in which the collateral source would be recompensed from the tort recovery through subrogation, refund of benefits, or some other arrangement. Hence, we conclude that in a case in which a tort victim has received partial compensation from medical insurance coverage entirely independent of the tortfeasor the trial court properly followed the collateral source rule. . . .

Defendants would have this court create a special form of sovereign immunity as a novel exception to the collateral source rule for tortfeasors who are public entities or public employees. . . . We see no justification for such special treatment. . . . The public entity or its insurance carrier is in at least as advantageous a position to spread the risk of loss as is the plaintiff's medical insurance carrier. To deprive Blue Cross of repayment for its expenditures on plaintiff's behalf merely because he was injured by a public entity rather than a private individual would constitute an unwarranted and arbitrary discrimination.

. . . .

The judgment is affirmed.

McCOMB, PETERS, MOSK, BURKE and SULLIVAN, JJ., concur.

Notes

1. ***Sources of Care or Compensation Unrelated to the Tortfeasor.*** *See* Hutchings v. Childress, 895 N.E.2d 520 (Ohio 2008) (allowing recovery of damages for the value of home health care services provided by an uninjured spouse and adopting the majority rule that "[t]he appropriate measure of damages . . . is the economic value of the care provided, not the value of the lost wages incurred in providing that care"). Care provided by a spouse who is a stockbroker is not necessarily more valuable than care provided by a spouse who is employed at minimum wage.

2. ***Amounts Previously Paid by Tortfeasors.*** The collateral-source rule does not apply to amounts paid to the plaintiff by the tortfeasor, or by one acting on that person's behalf (*e.g.*, by an insurance company), or by one who erroneously believes that he or she is subject to liability. *See* Restatement, Second, Torts § 920A. Thus, if a tortfeasor initially pays for part of plaintiff's medical expenses and then ceases such payments, the sums paid would fall outside of the collateral-source rule and their value would not be recoverable in a subsequent tort action.

3. ***Abrogation of the Collateral-Source Rule.*** The rule has been criticized and its existence in a given context cannot be taken for granted, particularly in medical malpractice actions. See Andrew Feeley, Kayla Horan, & David Schap, *Statutory*

Modification of the Collateral Source Rule, 23 J. Leg. Econ. 81, 90 (April 2017) (providing a state-by-state table and noting that "there has been a fair amount of change in the statutory modifications of the ordinary collateral source rule in little more than a decade from mid-2005 to mid-2016").

4. ***Medical Expenses "Paid or Incurred."*** If a medical care provider accepts as payment an amount less than what was billed, how much can the patient recover as damages from the person who caused the injuries that necessitated medical care? The amount billed or amount paid? In Haygood v. De Escabedo, 356 S.W.3d 390 (Tex. 2011), Justice Nathan Hecht wrote:

> Health care providers set charges they maintain are reasonable while agreeing to reimbursement at much lower rates determined by insurers to be reasonable, resulting in great disparities between amounts billed and payments accepted. Section 41.0105 of the Texas Civil Practice and Remedies Code . . . provides that "recovery of medical or health care expenses incurred is limited to the amount actually paid or incurred by or on behalf of the claimant." . . . [T]his statute limits recovery, and consequently the evidence at trial, to expenses that the provider has a legal right to be paid.

Specifically, the court held "that the common-law collateral source rule does not allow recovery as damages of medical expenses a health care provider is not entitled to charge." The court added:

> Of course, the collateral source rule continues to apply to . . . [medical expenses recoverable at trial], and the jury should not be told that they will be covered in whole or in part by insurance. Nor should the jury be told that a health care provider adjusted its charges because of insurance.

3. The Avoidable-Consequences Rule

Zimmerman v. Ausland

Supreme Court of Oregon, En Banc
513 P.2d 1167 (Or. 1973)

TONGUE, Justice.

This is an action for damages for personal injuries sustained in an automobile accident. Defendant admitted liability. The issue of damages was submitted to a jury, which returned a verdict of $7,500 in favor of plaintiff. Defendant appeals. We affirm.

Defendant contends that the trial court erred in submitting to the jury the issue whether plaintiff sustained a permanent injury, as alleged in her complaint. . . .

In support of that contention defendant says that . . . there was no evidence from which the jury could properly find that plaintiff's injuries were permanent; that in this case the evidence established that plaintiff's condition, involving an injury to her knee, "is curable by routine surgery"; that all injured persons have a duty to mitigate damages by submitting to surgery "where the risk is small and a favorable result reasonably probable"; and that this "precludes any instruction on permanency."

. . . .

Plaintiff testified . . . that as of the time of trial she still suffered swelling and pain in the knee after walking . . . and that as a substitute teacher she was no longer able to participate in physical education activities involving "physical games" or to play volleyball and tennis, as in the past.

Her doctor testified that plaintiff suffered from a torn semi-lunar cartilage in her knee; that "the probable future of this knee" was "one of gradual deterioration"; that her injury was "permanent"; and that it was "very probable" that she would "require a surgical procedure" to remove the torn cartilage. He also testified that after such an operation "the . . . [recovery] is fairly good" and that "the outlook for good recovery would be very optimistic."

In addition, plaintiff's doctor testified on cross-examination by defendant's attorney that he had not prescribed any "treatment" for plaintiff; that surgery is "not always" required in cases like this; . . . "it's pretty much a matter of how much it is bothering a patient."

Defendant's doctor, although disagreeing with the diagnosis that plaintiff suffered from a torn semi-lunar cartilage, testified that if she did have such an injury, as is "a very frequent injury seen in athletes," the torn cartilage should be "surgically exorcised," *i.e.*, "removed in total," and that after such an operation "the patient should recover completely" and be able "to return to all normal and usual activities."

. . . [T]he plaintiff in a personal injury case cannot claim damages for what would otherwise be a permanent injury if the permanency of the injury could have been avoided by submitting to treatment by a physician, including possible surgery, when a reasonable person would do so under the same circumstances. . . .

In considering whether plaintiff is required to mitigate her damages by submitting to surgery we must bear in mind that while plaintiff has the burden of proof that her injury is a permanent injury, defendant has the burden of proving that plaintiff unreasonably failed to mitigate her damages by submission to surgery. . . .

Ordinarily, of course, the questions whether an injury is permanent and whether a reasonable person under the same circumstances would submit to surgery are questions of fact for the jury, assuming that substantial evidence is offered. . . .

. . . [I]f under the circumstances, a reasonable person might well decline to undergo a surgical operation, a failure to do so imposes no disability against recovering full damages. . . .

The factors to be considered for this purpose ordinarily include the risk involved (i.e., the hazardous nature of the operation), the probability of success, and the expenditure of money or effort required. . . . Some courts also consider the pain involved as a factor. . . .

. . . [I]t has been held that there must be evidence relating to the extent of the risk involved in a particular type of surgical operation before a jury may properly consider the contention that a plaintiff acted unreasonably in declining to submit to a surgical operation. . . . The same must be true, *a fortiori*, when, as in this case, defendant contends that a court should hold as a matter of law that plaintiff unreasonably failed or refused to submit to a surgical operation. No such evidence was offered in this case.

Neither is there any evidence that plaintiff had been advised by any doctor that she should submit to a surgical operation on her knee and that she then failed or refused to do so. Indeed, both plaintiff's and defendant's doctors agreed that surgery was not indicated at the time of their examination. . . .

In numerous cases involving the question whether a plaintiff, to minimize damages, should have submitted to surgery or other treatment for the correction of conditions consequent upon a fractured or dislocated bone, it has been held, usually upon conflicting evidence as to the seriousness and effect of the treatment, that the jury should be permitted to decide whether the refusal of treatment was justified. . . .

Also, as stated by McCormick . . . , "[t]he courts . . . are cautious about insisting that due care requires submission to an operation."

. . . .

We hold [that the evidence was not] so clear and conclusive as to make it proper for the court to decide . . . [the questions at issue here] as a matter of law. . . .

. . . [W]e also hold that testimony was offered by plaintiff from which, if believed by the jury, it could properly find that plaintiff has suffered a permanent injury. . . . The verdict of the jury was supported by substantial evidence and the judgment of the trial court is affirmed.

Notes

1. ***Avoidable Consequences as Comparative Fault.*** In many states, unreasonable failure to mitigate damages is now treated as simply one form of comparative fault. *See* Section 1 of the Uniform Comparative Fault Act, quoted *infra* at pp. 876–77.

2. ***Religious Objections to Medical Treatment.*** Suppose that the plaintiff suffers injuries that would be minor if the plaintiff received prompt medical care, but which become serious when the plaintiff refuses, for religious reasons, to undergo treatment. Is this just one more case of the "eggshell skull" rule, which provides that you must take the plaintiff the way he or she is; you can't complain that you deserve a different plaintiff (*see* Chapter 7)? Or can the defendant insist that the jury be allowed to determine whether the plaintiff's failure to receive treatment was "reasonable"? Some courts skirt the issue by instructing the jury that the plaintiff must take "reasonable" steps to mitigate damages and that they may consider the plaintiff's beliefs as "a factor" in determining whether failure to obtain treatment was reasonable. *See* Williams v. Bright, 658 N.Y.S.2d 910 (App. Div. 1997), *infra* at p. 290.

3. ***Failure to Lose Weight.*** Tanberg v. Ackerman Inv. Co., 473 N.W.2d 193 (Iowa 1991), was an action brought by a motel guest who fell in a whirlpool bathtub and injured his back. The court held that the guest's failure to follow medical advice to attempt to lose weight to decrease back pain, and thereby mitigate damages, could be considered fault under the state's modified comparative fault statute. Because the jury found the plaintiff 70% at fault, recovery was denied. *Tanberg* was overruled on other grounds by Greenwood v. Mitchell, 621 N.W.2d 200 (Iowa 2001).

See also Morgan v. Scott, 291 S.W.3d 622, 641 (Ky. 2009) (noting that the defendant would "have been entitled to a failure to mitigate instruction relating to [the plaintiff's] failure to lose weight . . . after the accident if he had offered specific evidence showing that [the plaintiff's] continued . . . obesity had caused a worsening of her condition attributable to her failure to follow reasonable medical advice").

4. Pre-Judgment Interest

Suppose that an injured plaintiff would be entitled to an award of $100,000 if the trial were held immediately after the injury. In fact, of course, the trial will not occur for years. If the plaintiff receives a judgment for $100,000 five years after the injury, should the defendant have to pay five years' interest on the $100,000? The traditional answer was no, but the unfairness of this outcome has led a number of states to adopt legislation authorizing pre-judgment interest. Some courts have reached the same result by judicial decision.

A complicating factor is that some damages may not accrue until a date later than that of the injury. For instance, suppose that a jury awards the plaintiff $10,000 in lost wages for each of the five years the plaintiff has been out of work between the accident and the trial. In principle, the plaintiff should get approximately five years' worth of interest on the first year's wages, four years' worth on the second year's wages, and so on. Does the following statute do much to address this issue?

Texas Finance Code §§ 304.102 *et seq.* (Westlaw 2022)

§ 304.102.

A judgment in a wrongful death, personal injury, or property damage case earns prejudgment interest.

§ 304.103.

The prejudgment interest rate is equal to the postjudgment interest rate applicable at the time of judgment.

§ 304.104.

. . . [P]rejudgment interest accrues on the amount of a judgment during the period beginning on the earlier of the 180th day after the date the defendant receives written notice of a claim or the date the suit is filed and ending on the day preceding the date judgment is rendered. Prejudgment interest is computed as simple interest and does not compound.

§ 304.1045.

Prejudgment interest may not be assessed or recovered on an award of future damages.

§ 304.105.

(a) If judgment for a claimant is equal to or less than the amount of a settlement offer of the defendant, prejudgment interest does not accrue on the amount of the judgment during the period that the offer may be accepted.

(b) If judgment for a claimant is more than the amount of a settlement offer of the defendant, prejudgment interest does not accrue on the amount of the settlement offer during the period that the offer may be accepted.

§ 304.106.

To prevent the accrual of prejudgment interest under this subchapter, a settlement offer must be in writing and delivered to the claimant or the claimant's attorney or representative.

§ 304.107.

If a settlement offer does not provide for cash payment at the time of settlement, the amount of the settlement offer for the purpose of computing prejudgment interest is the cost or fair market value of the settlement offer at the time it is made.

Post-Judgment Interest. Statutes also provide for the award of post-judgment interest. *See, e.g.*, Ala. Code 1975 § 8-8-10 (Westlaw 2022) ("all other judgments [not based on a contract action] shall bear interest at the rate of 7.5 percent per annum").

B. Survival and Wrongful-Death Actions

Under the common law, the death of either party to most kinds of tort actions ended the action. Therefore, if *A* negligently injured *B*, *B's* claim against *A* would vanish if either *A* or *B* died. (This rule did not apply to contract claims, or to some claims involving rights in personal property, such as claims for conversion.) Furthermore, the common law gave no right of recovery to the survivors of someone whom the defendant had negligently or intentionally killed, so that if *A's* misconduct caused the death of *B*, *B's* penniless survivors had no claim against *A* for either their pecuniary losses or for the loss of *B's* companionship. Today, these rules have been changed by statute in every state.

Statutes which prevent a lawsuit from coming to an end when one of the parties dies are called "survival statutes"—they provide (sometimes with exceptions for particular kinds of cases, such as defamation) that an action survives the death of either party. Another kind of statute—the "wrongful-death statute"—creates a cause of action for the benefit of those left behind when the defendant has tortiously killed someone. In some states, a single statute both provides for the survival of actions when a party dies and creates a right of recovery for wrongful death.

Here are selected portions of New York's survival statute. The term "personal representative" means the person authorized to administer the decedent's estate; that is, the administrator or executor.

New York Estates, Powers & Trusts Law §§ 11-3.1–11-3.3 (Westlaw 2022)

§ 11-3.1 Actions

Any action, other than an action for injury to person or property, may be maintained by and against a personal representative in all cases and in such manner as such action might have been maintained by or against his decedent.

§ 11-3.2 Action for injury to person or property survives despite death of person in whose favor or against whom cause of action existed

(a) Action against personal representative for injury to person or property.

(1) No cause of action for injury to person or property is lost because of the death of the person liable for the injury. For any injury, the action may be brought or continued against the personal representative of the decedent, but punitive damages shall not be awarded nor penalties adjudged in any such action brought to recover damages for personal injury....

(2)....

(b) Action by personal representative for injury to person or property.

No cause of action for injury to person or property is lost because of the death of the person in whose favor the cause of action existed. For any injury an action may be brought or continued by the personal representative of the decedent.... No cause of action for damages caused by an injury to a third person is lost because of the death of the third person.

§ 11-3.3 Limitations upon recovery where injury causes death

(a) Where an injury causes the death of a person the damages recoverable for such injury are limited to those accruing before death and shall not include damages for or by reason of death, except that the reasonable funeral expenses of the decedent, paid by the estate or for the payment of which the estate is responsible, shall be recoverable in such action. The damages recovered become part of the estate of the deceased.

(b) Nothing contained herein shall affect the cause of action existing in favor of the next of kin under 5-4.1 [New York's wrongful-death statute, reproduced below—ed.], subject to the following:

(1) Such cause of action and the cause of action, under this section, in favor of the estate to recover damages may be prosecuted to judgment in a single action; a separate verdict, report or decision shall be rendered as to each cause of action.

(2) Where an action to recover damages for personal injury has been brought, and the injured person dies, as a result of the injury, before verdict, report or decision, his personal representative may enlarge the complaint in such action to include the cause of action for wrongful death under 5-4.1.

(3) Where an action to recover damages under this section and a separate action for wrongful death under 5-4.1 are pending against the same defendant, they may be consolidated on the motion of either party.

Here is an edited version of New York's wrongful-death statute. The term "distributee" means someone allowed by statute to share in the property of a decedent who leaves no will.

New York Estates, Powers & Trusts Law §§ 5-4.1–5-4.5 (Westlaw 2022)

§ 5-4.1 Action by personal representative for wrongful act, neglect or default causing death of decedent

1. The personal representative . . . of a decedent who is survived by distributees may maintain an action to recover damages for a wrongful act, neglect or default which caused the decedent's death against a person who would have been liable to the decedent by reason of such wrongful conduct if death had not ensued. Such an action must be commenced within two years after the decedent's death. When the distributees do not participate in the administration of the decedent's estate under a will appointing an executor who refuses to bring such action, the distributees are entitled to have an administrator appointed to prosecute the action for their benefit. . . .

§ 5-4.2 Trial and burden of proof of contributory negligence

On the trial of an action accruing before September first, nineteen hundred seventy-five to recover damages for causing death, the contributory negligence of the decedent shall be a defense, to be pleaded and proved by the defendant.

§ 5-4.3 Amount of recovery

(a) The damages awarded to the plaintiff may be such sum as the jury or, where issues of fact are tried without a jury, the court or referee deems to be fair and just compensation for the pecuniary injuries resulting from the decedent's death to the persons for whose benefit the action is brought. In every such action, in addition to any other lawful element of recoverable damages, the reasonable expenses of medical aid, nursing and attention incident to the injury causing death and the reasonable funeral expenses of the decedent paid by the distributees, or for the payment of which any distributee is responsible, shall also be proper elements of damage. . . .

(b) Where the death of the decedent occurs on or after September first, nineteen hundred eighty-two, in addition to damages and expenses recoverable under paragraph (a) above, punitive damages may be awarded if such damages would have been recoverable had the decedent survived.

(c)(i) In any action in which the wrongful conduct is medical malpractice or dental malpractice, evidence shall be admissible to establish the federal, state and local personal income taxes which the decedent would have been obligated by law to pay. . . .

§ 5-4.4 Distribution of damages recovered

(a) The damages, as prescribed by 5-4.3, whether recovered in an action or by settlement without an action, are exclusively for the benefit of the decedent's distributees and, when collected, shall be distributed to the persons entitled thereto under 4-1.1 and 5-4.5, subject to the following:

> (1) Such damages shall be distributed by the personal representative to the persons entitled thereto in proportion to the pecuniary injuries suffered by them such proportions to be determined after a hearing, on application of the personal representative or any distributee. . . .

(c) In the event that an action is brought, as authorized in this part, and there is no recovery or settlement, the reasonable expenses of such unsuccessful action, excluding counsel fees, shall be payable out of the assets of the decedent's estate.

§ 5-4.5 Non-marital children

For the purposes of this part, a non-marital child is the distributee of his father and paternal kindred and the father and paternal kindred of a non-marital child are that child's distributees to the extent permitted by 4-1.2.

Notes

1. To illustrate who can recover damages in wrongful-death and survivorship actions under the New York statutes reproduced above, suppose that *A*, a widow, dies as a result of *B's* tortious conduct. *A* leaves an adult child, *C*, and no other close relatives. *A's* will leaves half of her estate to *C* and the other half to her friend *D*. Suppose that litigation establishes that *A's* pre-death pain and suffering and medical expenses justify an award of $100,000 and that damages under the New York wrongful-death statute are $200,000. (Both figures are net of attorneys' fees.) Who gets how much?

The $100,000 awarded in the survivorship action will in this case be divided equally between *C* and *D*, because this action is brought on behalf of *A's* estate, and *C* and *D* are entitled by *A's* will to equal shares in that estate. Under the wrongful-death statute, the award of $200,000 goes to *C*. *C* is the only person who would have taken *A's* property under New York law if *A* had died without a will, and so *C* is the only "distributee." If *A* had been survived by more than one child, or by a child and a spouse, the calculation would have been more complex; *see* N.Y. EPTL § 5-4.4 (Westlaw 2022), above. The principle underlying these rules is that the survival statute preserves *A's* right to recover damages from *B*, so these damages become part of *A's* estate. The wrongful-death claim is a claim by *C* for an injury—generally loss of support and society—suffered by *C*, so the terms of *A's* will are irrelevant in deciding who gets the wrongful-death award.

2. *"Pre-Impact Damages" in Survival Actions.* If the decedent survives the accident for several weeks and suffers greatly during that period, damages in the survival action will include an award for the decedent's pain and suffering. But what if the decedent died immediately, as is common in cases involving plane crashes? Many courts allow juries to award substantial sums for the decedent's pre-impact terror, even though that terror may have lasted for only a few seconds, as when a plane crashes on takeoff or landing (the most common kinds of aviation accidents). The principal objection to awarding pre-impact damages is that they are speculative. In some aviation cases, testimony of passengers who survived the crash has been used to demonstrate the unpleasantness of experiencing the last seconds of the flight.

In Beynon v. Montgomery Cablevision L.P., 718 A.2d 1161 (Md. 1998), where a car skidded 71 feet prior to impact, the court affirmed a $1 million award for pre-impact fright, reduced to the statutory limit of $350,000. In *In re 91st Street Crane Collapse Litig.*, 62 N.Y.S.3d 11, 22 (App. Div. 2017), although "[w]itnesses described the look of sheer panic and fear" on the face of the operator of a falling crane, an award of $7.5 million for pre-impact terror was reduced to $2 million.

Gonzalez v. New York City Housing Authority

Court of Appeals of New York
572 N.E.2d 598 (N.Y. 1991)

KAYE, Judge.

Plaintiffs—the two grown grandchildren of a woman murdered in an apartment leased from defendant, New York City Housing Authority—were awarded damages for their grandmother's wrongful death, and for her conscious pain and suffering. Contesting neither liability nor the dollar amount of the award, defendant challenges the availability of wrongful death damages on the ground that plaintiffs have not established that they suffered any "pecuniary injuries" (EPTL 5-4.3[a]), and it challenges any award for conscious pain and suffering as lacking evidentiary basis....

Then 76 years old, decedent was murdered in March 1984 in her apartment.... She was discovered with her hands tied behind her back, a gag wrapped around her jaw and mouth, and her right foot tied to the leg of a bureau. An autopsy revealed fractures of her neck and eight ribs, bleeding where teeth had been knocked out, and bruises on the back of her head and hand. The cause of death was described in the autopsy report as "Asphyxia by gagging. Contusions of scalp, fractures of ribs and cervical spine." Her assailant was subsequently convicted of the murder, and of raping and robbing two other women in the building.

Decedent was survived by her daughter-in-law and two grandchildren: plaintiffs Marta Gonzalez, 21 years old at the time of the murder, and her brother Antonio Freire, then 19. Decedent had raised them both, because their father (her son) had died in 1965 and their mother (her daughter-in-law) was mentally ill; ... decedent had for many years been a "mother" to her grandchildren. At the time of the murder, however, both plaintiffs were financially independent and they no longer lived

Judith S. Kaye

with her. The granddaughter lived separately with her husband, and the grandson had a construction job and an apartment a few blocks away.

Although decedent had retired from her job as a house-keeper several years before the crime, she remained active. She prepared dinner every night for her daughter-in-law, who was unable to cook for herself. Marta Gonzalez went to her mother's house every day, and frequently had her meals with them. She testified that her grandmother had more patience with her mother than she did, and would help her cope with her mother's condition. Antonio Freire testified that he visited his grandmother every other day, and that she frequently prepared his meals as well.

The decedent also helped her granddaughter in other ways. The month before the crime, when her granddaughter was having marital problems, decedent permitted her to live with her for a week until she could return home. At the time of the murder, Marta Gonzalez was pregnant, and together she and her grandmother planned that the grandmother would care for the child while she returned to school.

After trial, a jury awarded plaintiffs $1,250,000 for wrongful death and $1,000,000 for conscious pain and suffering, which the trial court reduced to $100,000 and $350,000. Defendant appealed to the Appellate Division solely on the damages issues. That court unanimously affirmed....

Under the common law of England, it was not possible to maintain a damages action for wrongful death. This was the law in New York and other American jurisdictions as well.... "The result was that it was cheaper for the defendant to kill...

than to injure [the plaintiff], and that the most grievous of all injuries left the bereaved family of the victim, who frequently were destitute, without a remedy." (Prosser and Keeton, Torts § 127, at 945 [5th ed].)

That inequity was ameliorated in England in 1846 by passage of the Fatal Accidents Act [usually referred to as "Lord Campbell's Act"—Ed.], creating a remedy for wrongful death. New York was the first state to follow suit, and in 1847 adopted a statutory cause of action for wrongful death, now embodied in EPTL 5-4.1. . . .

The measure of damages obtainable in a wrongful death action "may be such sum as the jury or, where issues of fact are tried without a jury, the court or referee deems to be fair and just compensation for the pecuniary injuries resulting from the decedent's death to the persons for whose benefit the action is brought." . . . .

While other states now permit recovery for loss of society . . . , New York since its first wrongful death statute has steadfastly restricted recovery to "pecuniary injuries," or injuries measurable by money, and denied recovery for grief, loss of society, affection, conjugal fellowship and consortium. . . . Loss of support, voluntary assistance and possible inheritance, as well as medical and funeral expenses incidental to death, are injuries for which damages may be recovered. . . .

The "pecuniary injuries" caused by a wage earner's death may be calculated, in part, from factors relevant to the decedent's earning potential, such as present and future earnings, potential for advancement and probability of means to support heirs, as well as factors pertaining to the decedent's age, character and condition, and the circumstances of the distributees. . . . In the case of a decedent who was not a wage earner, "pecuniary injuries" may be calculated, in part, from the increased expenditures required to continue the services she provided, as well as the compensable losses of a personal nature, such as loss of guidance. . . .

. . . [W]e first conclude that plaintiffs' status as adult financially independent grandchildren does not, of itself, preclude their recovery.

. . . .

Nor is recovery barred solely because plaintiffs were self-supporting adults at the time of their grandmother's death. . . . Defendant points to Bumpurs v. New York City Hous. Auth., 139 A.D.2d 438, as support for its contention that adults cannot claim pecuniary injuries from loss of a parent's guidance. . . . However, the *Bumpurs* decision was properly distinguished by the Appellate Division in the present case: unlike the decedent here, the decedent in *Bumpurs* had provided no services to her adult children. . . .

Plaintiffs' status being no bar to recovery, the question then becomes whether the damages they have shown fall within the statutory confines of "pecuniary injuries."

Defendant urges that the only service decedent rendered to plaintiffs was the preparation of occasional meals outside their residences, which was not a compensable injury both because it was occasional and gratuitous and the plaintiffs therefore had no reason to rely on it, and because the service was not performed in their own households and plaintiffs therefore would not need to replace it.

As the record establishes, however, decedent contributed far more than "occasional meals," and her grandchildren relied upon her contributions. Decedent provided shelter for her granddaughter during a marital crisis, and helped both grandchildren cope with their mother's condition. The child care plan was more than occasional. Even the meals she furnished cannot accurately be called occasional—Marta Gonzalez testified that she ate dinner with her mother and grandmother every other day, while Antonio Freire testified that he visited his grandmother every other day and she frequently prepared his meals.

Nor is it significant that the decedent prepared meals in her daughter-in-law's home rather than in plaintiffs' homes. Wherever provided, the decedent's services would have to be replaced by plaintiffs. The same is equally true of her counseling, the shelter she provided for her granddaughter, and the meals she regularly prepared for both grandchildren.

Based upon this record, therefore, we conclude that plaintiffs presented evidence of "pecuniary injuries" they suffered by reason of their grandmother's wrongful death.

. . . .

Defendant's remaining argument is addressed to the award of damages for decedent's conscious pain and suffering. Defendant contends that there was no showing that it was more likely than not that she suffered any pain before she died, because two of the causes of death noted by the medical examiner—contusion of the scalp and fracture of the cervical spine—were equally consistent with a simultaneous loss of consciousness and death.

. . . [T]here was sufficient circumstantial evidence to support the conclusion that decedent was conscious when most of the injuries were inflicted. As the Appellate Division noted, if she had been unconscious at the outset of the assault there would have been no reason for the murderer to have bound and gagged her elaborately and injured her as he did. . . .

Order affirmed, with costs.

Notes

1. ***Compensation for the Death of Family Caretakers.*** Courts have approved widely disparate awards in cases involving the deaths of women primarily devoted to the care of their families, rather than employed outside the home. Why? *See* Martha Chamallas, *The Architecture of Bias: Deep Structures in Tort Law*, 146 U. Pa. L. Rev. 463 (1998) ("Most empirical studies indicate that women of all races and minority men continue to receive significantly lower damage awards than white men in personal injury and wrongful death suits").

2. ***Intra-Family Wrongful-Death Claims.*** *See* Tesar v. Anderson, 789 N.W.2d 351 (Wis. App. 2010) (holding that public policy did not preclude a prospective father's claim against the mother of a child that was stillborn as a result of the mother's negligent driving). Tort claims related to pre-natal injuries are discussed in Chapter 13.

Family members may suffer dramatically different losses as the result of a death in the family member. *See* Macke v. Patton, 591 S.W.3d 865, 867 (Mo. 2019) (affirming a judgment that apportioned 98 percent of the settlement to the decedent's father, 2 percent to the decedent's mother).

3. ***Wrongful-Death Damages Measured by Pecuniary Loss.*** The *Gonzalez* court, quoting Prosser, notes that it was cheaper under the common law for a defendant to kill someone than merely to inflict an injury. If the statute limits wrongful-death damages to "pecuniary" losses, that may still be the case, especially when the victim is a young child. In that case, it may be difficult or impossible to prove with reasonable certainty how much the child would have contributed to the parents if the child had lived, grown up, and earned money. *Cf.* Horner v. Sani-Top, Inc., 141 P.3d 1099 (Idaho 2006) (finding, in a case related to the death of a two-year-old, that the evidence was insufficient to support an award of economic damages to the child's parents for loss of financial support).

The calculation of "pecuniary" loss generally proceeds by determining the amount of support the decedent would have provided the plaintiffs but for the death; as a result, the defendant who kills a surgeon or a partner in a law firm is likely to face much more liability than the defendant who kills a low-income worker or an unemployed person. In some cases, even adult children can recover large amounts of compensation in the wrongful-death action. *See* Odom v. R.J. Reynolds Tobacco Co., 254 So. 3d 268, 273 (Fla. 2018) ($6,000,000 reduced to $4,500,000 based on the decedent's fault).

Some courts also allow a recovery for the loss of the inheritance the plaintiffs would have received had the decedent lived longer and saved more. *See* Yowell v. Piper Aircraft Corp., 703 S.W.2d 630 (Tex. 1986).

4. ***Wrongful-Death Damages for Loss of Companionship and Society.*** Most states now permit recovery in a wrongful-death action for the value of lost companionship, society, advice, and guidance. In some states, the issue is addressed by statute. Here is one example:

Massachusetts Annotated Laws Chapter 229 § 2 (Westlaw 2022)

> A person who . . . causes the death of a person under such circumstances that the deceased could have recovered damages for personal injuries if his death had not resulted . . . shall be liable in damages in the amount of:
>
> (1) the fair monetary value of the decedent to [the decedent's survivors], including but not limited to compensation for the loss of the reasonably expected net income, services, protection, care, assistance, society, companionship, comfort, guidance, counsel, and advice of the decedent to the persons entitled to the damages recovered;

(2) the reasonable funeral and burial expenses of the decedent;

(3) punitive damages in an amount of not less than five thousand dollars in such case as the decedent's death was caused by the malicious, willful, wanton or reckless conduct of the defendant or by the gross negligence of the defendant....

Some courts have interpreted statutes providing for recovery of "actual damages" as allowing recovery for "loss of the decedent's society" and for mental anguish; *e.g.* Sanchez v. Schindler, 651 S.W.2d 249 (Tex. 1983) (death of minor child).

Some states allow "recovery for the survivor's loss of companionship, society, advice and guidance ... on the theory that such elements have a pecuniary value." Dan B. Dobbs, The Law of Torts 812 (2000).

In Badall v. Durgapersad, 454 S.W.3d 626 (Tex. App. 2014), the court held that an award of $105,500 to a murder victim's wife for loss of companionship and society was not excessive, even though the wife had for most of the prior six years worked in another state and lived apart from the victim.

Some generous awards of damages survive judicial scrutiny. *See, e.g.*, Colella v. JMS Trucking Co. of Illinois, Inc., 932 N.E.2d 1163 (Ill. App. 2010) (affirming an award of $1 million for the decedent's pain and suffering, although he was conscious for only three or four minutes, because various fingers were severed and cuts to his abdomen exposed internal organs, and an award of $8 million for his family's loss of society, because the decedent had a 21.5-year life expectancy, an active family and social life, and his wife relied on his English skills).

5. ***Wrongful-Death Damages for Grief.*** *See* Andrew J. McClurg, *Dead Sorrow: A Story About Loss and a New Theory of Wrongful Death Damages*, 85 B.U. L. Rev. 1, 26 (2005), stating:

> [W]hile nearly all states allow society and companionship-type damages, only a minority of states allow recovery for grief or mental anguish. The wrongful death statutes of twelve states expressly provide for grief or mental anguish damages, while courts in eleven other states have interpreted their wrongful death statutes to allow such damages.

6. ***Wrongful Death and Profiting from One's Own Wrongdoing.*** Courts sometimes deny recovery on the grounds that otherwise the plaintiff would be permitted to profit from personal wrongdoing. However, in Bagley v. Bagley, 387 P.3d 1000, 1003 (Utah 2016), the court held that "a person acting in the capacity of sole heir and personal representative of an estate can sue him or herself as an individual for damages under the [Utah] wrongful death and survival action statutes," because under the plain language of the legislation the death was caused by the act "of another," that is, someone other than the decedent. The court candidly acknowledged that "[t]hrough this suit, Ms. Bagley [who allegedly negligently caused her husband's death hoped] to secure certain insurance money for herself as heir and to satisfy creditors of her common law husband's estate."

Economic Analysis
Damages, Deterrence, and Compensation: Valuing Lives and Safety Precautions

Alan Gunn

Two goals commonly assigned to the tort system are deterrence of dangerous activities and compensation of victims. The calculation of damages for wrongful death provides an opportunity to examine the extent to which these goals are inconsistent with each other, for the measure of damages which is desirable for deterrence differs from the measure appropriate for a compensation system.

As an example of the way in which deterrence and compensation support different measures of recovery, consider cases in which defendants tortiously cause the deaths of young children. If the only goal of tort law were compensation, the appropriate measure of damages in these cases might well be zero. The loss is devastating to the parents, but it is not a financial loss. It is, in fact, quite the opposite, as raising children is expensive in dollar-and-cents terms. Furthermore, this kind of loss cannot in any sense be "made up for" by awarding the parents money. Discussions of compensation often proceed by assuming that a large enough award of money can make the victim as well off as before the injury. When the loss in question is largely financial, as when the plaintiff's house or car is destroyed, this can make some sense. When the loss is the loss of a child, an award of cash will not help. It may even hurt, as when parents enriched by a tort recovery are reminded of their loss every time they spend their riches.

From a deterrence perspective, the death of a child becomes an example of a case in which damages should be very high. One should not lightly undertake an activity which has more than a remote chance of killing anyone — especially a child. Someone who might, in the absence of any serious risk of liability, undertake a fairly dangerous activity in the hope that it will work out for the best may be deterred by the prospect of having to pay a large sum if things go wrong.

A possible objection to using damages to deter accidental death is that people will take precautions anyway, out of simple morality. This is, of course, true; but less so for some people than for others. Consider, for instance, a suburban homeowner installing a swimming pool. Swimming pools are very dangerous to children, whose ingenuity in getting through latched gates far exceeds their caution around water. It is very plausible to think that some homeowners (not all, but encouraging care can be useful even if it doesn't *always* work) take extra care to keep their pools fenced and their gates locked because they know, or suspect, that they will be held liable if a drowning takes place. And the homeowner's insurance agent may insist on precautions that the homeowner is too careless or ignorant to come up with. Furthermore, if homeowners' liability insurers charge extra for policies on homes with pools, some homeowners may decide that a pool is not worth the extra expense. Charging the owners of pools large sums when drownings do occur creates a desirable incentive to take precautions, even if not all owners will respond sensibly to those incentives.

How can the appropriate amount of damages for purposes of deterrence be calculated? One way is by looking at the amount people are willing to spend to protect themselves against small risks of dying. For instance, economists have estimated the amounts that people are willing to spend for safety precautions like smoke detectors, automobile airbags, and other safety devices which can be purchased. In addition, economists have investigated the amount of higher pay received by those engaged in dangerous occupations, like firefighting, police work, and logging, as compared with the pay of those in comparable but safer work. The difference may be a measure of the value people place on safety in their own lives. If studies like this show that, on the average, people are willing to spend $2.00 (but not more) to guard against a one-in-a-million chance of premature death, potential defendants could be encouraged to take the appropriate level of safety precautions by being held liable for $2,000,000 whenever their activities actually do cause an accidental death.

Economists tend to summarize the results of studies like those described above by coming up with a figure for "the value of a life." If, for instance, people will typically spend $2.00 to eliminate a one-in-a-million chance of death, an economist might say that the "value of a life" is $2,000,000. This is a misleading way of putting it, as hardly anyone would agree to die immediately for a $2,000,000 payment. Furthermore, few people — including economists — would say that it is permissible to murder someone if the payoff is more than $2,000,000. The "value of a life" notion is best understood as a shorthand way of expressing the value of taking precautions against small risks of death. Current estimates of the "value of a life" are $7.5 million or more. Note that this figure is much higher than the recovery in most wrongful-death cases, especially in cases in which the decedent had a low income or left no dependents. Indeed, in the extreme case of a decedent with no family and no close friends, the appropriate amount of "compensation" is very close to zero, yet no one would argue that no precautions should be taken to save the life of such a person.

While this discussion has focused on damages for wrongful death, similar considerations apply in other areas of torts. Generally speaking, if deterrence is the main goal, the law would want much higher damages than if it were concerned only with compensation. Consider damages for "pain and suffering." Suppose that a woman has had a car door accidentally slammed on her hand, breaking a couple of her fingers. Unless she is a concert pianist or a surgeon, or otherwise makes a living with her hands, an award of her medical expenses is probably all the "compensation" she should receive. (Although the experience was and may still be painful, giving her money will not make the pain go away, so that "loss" is, like the loss of a child, inherently incapable of being compensated.) So "compensation" for this kind of injury might be only a few hundred dollars. From the point of view of deterrence, however, a much higher award might be appropriate — few persons would let someone slam a car door on their hands for even twice the medical bills that would be incurred.

Another example of the tension between deterrence and compensation is the collateral-source rule (*supra*, pp. 211–14). Someone whose lost wages or medical bills have been picked up by insurance needs no "compensation" to be made whole for those losses. But it may be almost as important to deter prospective defendants from injuring the insured as from injuring the uninsured. Therefore, the collateral-source rule makes excellent sense, from the point of view of deterrence, even though it may overcompensate some plaintiffs. (Note that if the *only* concern were with deterrence, it would not matter whether the victim even got the money; deterrence requires that the careless defendant be made to pay, but not that the payment go to the victim.)

Although "deterrence" considerations support much higher damages awards than "compensation" would justify, a system aimed at deterrence would typically allow recovery in many fewer cases than a system seeking compensation. For example, someone who falls ill from natural causes, or who is struck by lightning through no one's fault, needs "compensation" as badly as someone whose injuries have been occasioned by the negligence of another. Yet deterrence can operate only in those cases in which someone could have prevented the harm at reasonable cost. Therefore, some argue, the tort system cannot effectively pursue both deterrence and compensation at the same time. Compensation-oriented systems like workers' compensation and Social Security disability insurance typically allow many persons to recover fairly small amounts. Deterrence-oriented systems would award much more to fewer victims.

For a discussion of "valuing lives" more extensive than can be presented here, see Ted R. Miller, *Willingness to Pay Comes of Age: Will the Tort System Survive?*, 83 Nw. U. L. Rev. 876 (1989); *see also* Binyamin Appelbaum, *As U.S. Agencies Put More Value on a Life, Businesses Fret*, N.Y. TIMES, Feb. 16, 2011 (discussing three federal agencies that set the value of a life at between $6 million and $9.1 million for purposes of determining which regulations are cost-effective).

Problem: The Ford Pinto. In the early 1970s, Ford became concerned that the Pinto, an inexpensive compact car, was unsafe. Ford prepared a cost-benefit analysis, which showed that the cost of making certain proposed changes in the Pinto's design would outweigh the benefits. In measuring the "benefits" of saving a life, Ford used the figure of $200,000 for each life saved. Ford obtained this figure from the National Highway Traffic Safety Administration, which had based its calculations on the expected lifetime earnings of those who would die. Was this a sensible figure to use?

C. Damages for Loss of Earning Capacity

As discussed above, one element of tort damages for a disabled plaintiff is loss of earning capacity. Calculating an award for this kind of loss presents several serious problems. One complication involves discounting future earnings to their present value. An award to a young plaintiff who might have worked for another 50 years will include, among other things, compensation for the earnings the plaintiff would have received in year 50. To give the plaintiff the full amount of the year-50 salary today would seriously overcompensate the victim. To see why, suppose that plaintiff's salary for year 50 would have been $50,000. A plaintiff who received $50,000 today could invest the money and let it grow for 50 years. At an interest rate of 4% a year, compounded semi-annually, $50,000 will grow to $362,232. Therefore, an award of $50,000 today compensates for a loss of $362,232 fifty years from now, not for a loss of $50,000.

Reducing Future Wages to Present Value. By discounting future wages to present value, current awards can be made to correspond to some larger amount that would have been received in the future. The "present value" of an amount to be received in the future is the amount which, if invested today at a specified rate of interest, would grow to equal the future amount during the number of years in question. "Present value" calculations therefore depend upon the interest rate chosen and the time period in question — the higher the rate and the longer the time, the lower the present value of any particular future amount. The present value of $50,000 to be received in 50 years is $6,902 at an interest rate of 4% a year, compounded semiannually. At an interest rate of 6%, compounded semiannually, the present value of $50,000 to be received in 50 years is only $2,602. Note that a difference of only two percentage points changes the present value in this example by more than a factor of two.

Compulsory Periodic Payments. In Galayda v. Lake Hosp. Sys., Inc., 644 N.E.2d 298, 301 (Ohio 1994), a statute that required a trial court, upon the motion of a party, to order that any future damages award in excess of $200,000 be paid in a series of periodic payments (rather than in a lump sum) was held to be an impermissible abridgement of the right under the state constitution to trial by jury. *But see* Tex. Civ. Prac. & Rem. Code § 74.503(a) (Westlaw 2022) (providing that, "At the request of a defendant physician or health care provider or claimant, the court shall order that medical, health care, or custodial services awarded in a health care liability claim be paid in whole or in part in periodic payments rather than by a lump-sum payment"); *id.* at § 74.506(b) ("Periodic payments, other than future loss of earnings, terminate on the death of the recipient").

1. Earning History

O'Shea v. Riverway Towing Co.

United States Court of Appeals for the Seventh Circuit
677 F.2d 1194 (7th Cir. 1982)

POSNER, Circuit Judge.

[Margaret O'Shea, the plaintiff, was disabled in an accident caused by the defendant's negligence.]

.... Mrs. O'Shea's job as a cook paid her $40 a day, and since the custom was to work 30 days consecutively and then have the next 30 days off, this comes to $7200 a year although ... she never had earned that much in a single year. She testified that when the accident occurred she had been about to get another cook's job on a Mississippi towboat that would have paid her $60 a day ($10,800 a year). She also testified that she had been intending to work as a boat's cook until she was 70 — longer if she was able. . . .

Riverway argues . . . that it was wrong for the judge to award damages on the basis of a wage not validated, as it were, by at least a year's employment at that wage. Mrs. O'Shea had never worked full time, had never in fact earned more than $3600 in a full year, and in that year preceding the accident had earned only $900. But previous wages do not put a cap on an award of lost future wages. If a man who had never worked in his life graduated from law school, began working at a law firm at an annual salary of $35,000, and was killed the second day on the job, his lack of a past wage history would be irrelevant to computing his lost future wages. The present case is similar if less dramatic.

Mrs. O'Shea did not work at all until 1974, when her husband died. She then lived on her inheritance and worked at a variety of part-time jobs till January 1979, when she started working as a cook on the towboat. According to her testimony, which the trial judge believed, she was then working full time. It is immaterial that this was her first full-time job and that the accident occurred before she had held it for a full year. Her job history was typical of women who return to the labor force after their children are grown or, as in Mrs. O'Shea's case, after their husband dies, and these women are, like any tort victims, entitled to damages based on what they would have earned in the future rather than on what they may or may not have earned in the past.

. . . .

Judgment affirmed.

Notes

1. ***Loss of Earning Capacity.*** Note that O'Shea's damages were for the loss of her "earning capacity," which is not necessarily the same thing as her lost future earnings. Therefore, if O'Shea had still been a homemaker at the time she was injured, her damages would, in theory, have been based on the income she could have earned if she had worked, not the (zero) income she was actually earning. As a practical matter, an actual work history helps a lot in determining the amount a plaintiff would have been capable of earning but for an injury. Recall, however, that Helen Britain, who was a child at the time of her injuries, received a substantial award for loss of earning capacity (*supra*, p. 201).

2. ***The Earning Capacity of Athletes.*** In Felder v. Physiotherapy Assoc., 158 P.3d 877 (Ariz. App. 2007), the court found that a professional athlete had proved loss of future earning capacity with reasonable certainty. It wrote:

> There will always be uncertainty concerning the athlete's physical performance and success in competition. For damage to a sports career, the evidence reasonably available will generally be what was presented at trial in this case — qualified expert testimony concerning the athlete's prospects, statistics showing past performance, and comparative data concerning other

athletes.... Suffice it to say that the jury learned in detail about his batting averages, fielding performances, and injuries.... The jury also heard about the economics of baseball compensation, including how long a professional's career might be and what similar players were being paid.

.... No one can say with complete certainty whether Felder would, or would not, have been promoted to the major leagues or how long he might have played there. We can say, however, as the jury did, that his eye injury prevented him from having that chance.... [T]he amount of his damages for being deprived of that chance was for the jury to decide.

3. ***Diminished Earning Capacity and Undocumented Status.*** Defendants sometimes argue that damages for diminished earning capacity should be reduced or unavailable in the case of undocumented plaintiffs who are subject to deportation. In Escamilla v. Shiel Sexton Co., Inc., 73 N.E.3d 663, 669–70 (Ind. 2017), the court summarized the law as follows:

Most courts confronting the admissibility of a plaintiff's unauthorized immigration status apply... [a] balancing test in decreased earning capacity cases. They first determine whether immigration status is relevant, then—if it is—balance that relevance against the dangers of admitting the immigration status. This test has led several courts to exclude immigration status either because it is irrelevant or because the danger of unfair prejudice substantially outweighs its relevance.

.... Only New Hampshire has resolved the balance the other way, reasoning that while immigration status "may well be prejudicial," it is also "essential" to lost earning capacity claims.... [Rosa v. Partners in Progress, Inc., 868 A.2d 994, 1000 (N.H. 2005).]

A few other courts have skipped the balancing test altogether, apparently assuming the admissibility of a plaintiff's undocumented immigration status....

... [W]e conclude that even though unauthorized immigration status is relevant to decreased earning capacity claims, the dangers of confusion and unfair prejudice make it inadmissible unless the plaintiff is more likely than not to be deported.

4. ***Diminished Earning Capacity and Race or Ethnicity.*** In G.M.M. ex rel. Hernandez-Adams v. Kimpson, 116 F. Supp. 3d 126, 128–29 (E.D.N.Y. 2015), the court asked, "can statistics based on the ethnicity (in this case, "Hispanic") of a child be relied upon to find a reduced likelihood of his obtaining higher education, resulting in reduced damages in a tort case?" It answered:

The use of race-based statistics to obtain a reduced damage award—which is now extended to the use of ethnicity-based statistics, to calculate future economic loss—is unconstitutional.... It violates due process because it creates arbitrary and irrational state action, and equal protection, because it subjects the claimant to a "disadvantageous estimate" of damages "solely on the basis" of ethnic classification.

5. ***Inflation***. There is a split of authority as to whether the pressures of inflation should be taken into account in calculating damages awards. In order to be consistent, as noted in O'Shea v. Riverway Towing Co., 677 F.2d 1194 (7th Cir. 1982), inflation should either be taken into account both in projecting future lost earnings and in discounting those losses to present value, or inflation should be left out of both calculations altogether.

6. ***Restitution Versus Damages***. The difference between damages and restitution is the difference between loss and gain. Damages are measured by what the plaintiff lost; restitution is measured by what the defendant improperly gained. *See generally* Restatement (Third) of Restitution and Unjust Enrichment § 49 (2011).

Sometimes both damages and restitution are recoverable. Thus, under American law, a lawyer who commits malpractice can be sued to recover the compensation for harm the client suffered (damages) and for total or partial forfeiture of fees paid by the client (restitution to prevent unjust enrichment).

If a plaintiff is unable to prove damages, it may still be possible to sue for restitution if the defendant gained something. (Of course, some torts, like auto accidents, produce only losses, not gains.) For example, if repeated trespasses over the plaintiff's land saves the defendant substantial transportation expenditures that the defendant would have incurred to go around the land, but causes no harm to the land, the plaintiff can sue for restitution (what the defendant gained), rather than damages (what the plaintiff lost). The topic of restitution to prevent unjust enrichment is normally studied in law school courses on Remedies.

2. Taxation of Awards

Compensation for Personal Injuries Versus Other Kinds of Damages. Another problem in calculating damage awards for loss of earning capacity is how to treat income taxes. An award of compensatory damages in a case involving physical personal injuries is not taxable to the recipient. *See* 26 U.S.C. § 104 (Westlaw 2022) (stating that "gross income does not include . . . (2) the amount of any damages (other than punitive damages) received (whether by suit or agreement and whether as lump sums or as periodic payments) on account of personal physical injuries or physical sickness"). Punitive damages are income to the plaintiff who gets them, as are some compensatory damages in cases involving non-physical injuries, such as harm to reputation or emotional distress. *See* Murphy v. I.R.S., 493 F.3d 170 (D.C. Cir. 2007) (holding that damages awarded for loss of reputation and emotional distress in an administrative proceeding were taxable).

Anticipating Tax Consequences. "When preparing a settlement agreement, care should be taken to make clear that the settlement is for personal physical injuries sustained by the plaintiff, in order to substantiate a claim for exclusion. . . ." Erica

Dunmyer, *5 Things Every Plaintiffs Attorney Should Know About Tax Law*, Tex. Lawyer (Online) Aug. 19, 2010. Of course, such documentation will be challenged by the Internal Revenue Service if it does not correspond to the realities of the settlement.

Use of Structured Settlements to Minimize Taxes. The wages the plaintiff would have earned would have been taxable, and the interest or dividends the plaintiff earns by investing a lump-sum award will be taxable. However, if the case is settled, taxation of the earnings on the plaintiff's investment income can be avoided by arranging a "structured settlement." If, instead of paying the plaintiff a lump sum, the defendant (or, typically, the defendant's insurer) makes a series of payments, the full amount of the payments will be excludable from the plaintiff's income. So, instead of taking a lump sum payment of $100,000 and investing that amount to earn a $10,000 annual return (taxable), the plaintiff might agree to take $10,000 a year for 50 years, all tax-free. If there were no income tax, and if the appropriate interest rate is 10 percent, $100,000 now is worth more than $10,000 a year for 50 years. But the absence of any tax on payments under a structured settlement of $10,000 a year for 50 years could make that option more attractive to the plaintiff.

Ethics in Law Practice: Structured Settlements. Many companies specialize in offering structured settlements. A lawyer who recommends acceptance of a structured settlement to a client should make sure that the promised payments are guaranteed by a performance bond. Otherwise, if the promisor goes bankrupt, the lawyer may be liable for the lost payments (and lost tax advantages) in a legal malpractice action alleging that the lawyer failed to exercise reasonable care to prevent foreseeable harm. *See* Williams v. Lakin, 2007 WL 1170597 (N.D. Okla.) (malpractice claim stated).

Informing Juries About the Tax Treatment of Damages. Some courts are of the opinion that the jury should be informed of the rule of non-taxability of personal injury damages and told not to add to or subtract from the award because of that rule. *In re Air Crash Disaster Near Chicago on May 25, 1979*, 803 F.2d 304 (7th Cir. 1986), held that the failure to give such an instruction was an error which raised the possibility that the jury would inflate the award on the assumption that part of it would go to taxes. The court also found that evidence of the decedent's income tax status should have been admitted in the wrongful-death action pending before the court, because the state's wrongful-death statute measured damages by the amount the decedent would have contributed to the survivors; if the decedent had lived, he obviously could not have given the survivors money that would have been taken by taxes. For support, the court cited the Restatement, Second, of Torts § 914A cmt. b.

However, many states do not allow introduction in a wrongful-death action of evidence relating to the decedent's future tax status. For example, in Hoyal v. Pioneer Sand Co., Inc., 188 P.3d 716 (Colo. 2008), the court found that such evidence was inappropriate for purposes of calculating the survivor's net pecuniary loss because future tax rates are a matter of speculation and allowing such evidence would unduly complicate tort lawsuits. Every case would become a battle of tax experts opining on what legislators might do in the future and how the resulting rules might have applied to the decedent.

Some state statutes expressly address the issues of whether damages should be reduced because of tax considerations and what the jury should be told about taxation. For example:

Texas Civil Practice & Remedies Code § 18.091 (Westlaw 2022)

> (a) Notwithstanding any other law, if any claimant seeks recovery for loss of earnings, loss of earning capacity, loss of contributions of a pecuniary value, or loss of inheritance, evidence to prove the loss must be presented in the form of a net loss after reduction for income tax payments or unpaid tax liability pursuant to any federal income tax law.
>
> (b) If any claimant seeks recovery for loss of earnings, loss of earning capacity, loss of contributions of a pecuniary value, or loss of inheritance, the court shall instruct the jury as to whether any recovery for compensatory damages sought by the claimant is subject to federal or state income taxes.

D. Punitive Damages

As noted in Chapter 1, punitive damages (also called exemplary damages) are imposed in cases involving egregious conduct to punish or make an example of the defendant.

Type of Wrongdoing Required. Some states limit punitive damages awards to intentional or malicious acts. For example, Wisconsin requires proof that "the defendant acted maliciously toward the plaintiff or in an intentional disregard of the rights of the plaintiff." Wis. Stat. Ann. § 895.043(3) (Westlaw 2022).

Other states frame the standard more broadly. *See* S.C. Code 1976 § 15-32-520(D) (Westlaw 2022) ("wilful, wanton, or reckless conduct").

It is often difficult to demonstrate the type of egregious conduct that is a prerequisite to recovery of punitive damages. In Lompe v. Sunridge Partners, LLC, 818 F.3d 1041, 1057 (10th Cir. 2016), the court held that even if the evidence of Sunridge's minimal involvement in the operation of apartments, whose management was entrusted to another, could support a finding of negligence, it was "insufficient as a matter of law to establish the willful and wanton misconduct necessary to support an award of punitive damages in Wyoming" in a case involving injuries caused by carbon monoxide poisoning. As the court explained:

> Sunridge purchased the property for investment purposes and hired a reputable property manager [AMC] to take care of the day-to-day management of the apartments. . . .

> . . . [E]ven accepting that Sunridge was provided with the bids to replace certain furnaces, it had no reason to assume AMC would not respond appropriately to whatever circumstances had created the need to do so. Sunridge relied on AMC to manage the property competently and had prior experience suggesting that such trust was warranted.

See also Doe v. Isaacs, 579 S.E.2d 174 (Va. 2003) (holding, in a state requiring "willful recklessness" and not merely "gross negligence," that a motorist's behavior in rear-ending a vehicle and leaving the scene of an injury accident was not so "willful or wanton" as to show a conscious disregard for the rights of others, and therefore punitive damages could not be awarded); Diamond Shamrock Refining Co., L.P. v. Hall, 168 S.W.3d 164 (Tex. 2005) (holding that the plaintiff failed to prove gross negligence because the evidence did not show that the defendant knew of the risk of a gas compressor explosion and yet did not care).

In some states, a narrow definition of the predicate for punitive damages may produce unexpected results. In Komornik v. Sparks, 629 A.2d 721, 723–24 (Md. 1993), a driver whose blood alcohol was almost twice the level of *prima facie* intoxication caused an accident by depressing the clutch, rather than the brake, as he approached cars stopped at a traffic light. The court held that three prior instances of drunk driving did not warrant an award of punitive damages because what was needed was evidence of "evil motive, intent to injure, ill will, or fraud." The defendant's state of mind, the court found, was to the contrary of what was required, because his "intent was to avoid injury to those stopped ahead of him."

Is Additional Deterrence Needed? In Gyrc v. Dayton-Hudson Corp., 297 N.W.2d 727 (Minn. 1980), a four-year-old girl was severely burned when her pajamas burst into flames as she reached across an electric stove. The plaintiff's own expert witness conceded that no mills produced flame-retardant flannelette in commercial quantities when the pajamas in question were manufactured. Nevertheless, the court upheld a punitive-damages award against the manufacturer, based on its failure to use "flame-retardant processes which could [have been] applied to the fabric without adversely affecting its qualities enough to make it unsalable." The defendant contended that the $750,000 compensatory damage award and the resulting loss of sales and damage to reputation was an adequate deterrent. It also argued that since it no longer manufactured cotton flannelette and since the Flammable Fabrics Act subsequently imposed more stringent standards for children's sleepwear, no additional deterrent was needed. In response, the court stated:

> This argument ignores the fact that Riegel [the defendant] was shown to have acted in reckless disregard of the public for purely economic reasons in the past. A punitive damages award serves to deter Riegel from acting in a similar manner with respect to other products manufactured by it in the future. Furthermore, since the potential of compensatory damages awards and loss of sales and reputation did not serve to deter Riegel in the past, Riegel cannot now argue that these considerations act as an adequate deterrent.

Clear and Convincing Evidence. "A growing majority of states requires clear and convincing evidence before punitive damages can be considered." Rodriguez v. Suzuki Motor Corp., 936 S.W.2d 104 (Mo. 1996). In Colorado, a punitive damages award requires proof beyond a reasonable doubt. *See* Colo. Rev. Stat. Ann. §13-25-127(2) (Westlaw 2022).

Compensatory Damages Predicate? There is a split of authority as to whether an award of compensatory damages is a necessary predicate for punitive damages. Most states so hold, but others allow punitive damages to be tacked onto an award of nominal damages. Consider the Texas statute:

Texas Civil Practice & Remedies Code §41.004 (Westlaw 2022)

(a) Except as provided by Subsection (b), exemplary damages may be awarded only if damages other than nominal damages are awarded.

(b) Exemplary damages may not be awarded to a claimant who elects to have his recovery multiplied under another statute.

Factors Relevant to Amount of Punitive Damages. Some states offer juries little guidance with respect to setting the amount of punitive damages, other than to say that the purpose of punitive damages is to punish or make an example of the defendant. However, more detailed guidance is feasible, and probably desirable, as suggested by a model law.

Model Punitive Damages Act National Conference of Commissioners on Uniform State Laws (1996)

§7. Amount of Punitive Damages.

(a) If a defendant is found liable for punitive damages, a fair and reasonable amount of damages may be awarded.... The court shall instruct the jury in determining what constitutes a fair and reasonable amount of punitive damages to consider any evidence that has been admitted regarding the following factors:

(1) the nature of defendant's wrongful conduct and its effect on the claimant and others;

(2) the amount of compensatory damages;

(3) any fines, penalties, damages, or restitution paid or to be paid by the defendant arising from the wrongful conduct;

(4) the defendant's present and future financial condition and the effect of an award on each condition;

(5) any profit or gain, obtained by the defendant through the wrongful conduct, in excess of that likely to be divested by this and any other actions against the defendant for compensatory damages or restitution;

(6) any adverse effect of the award on innocent persons;

(7) any remedial measures taken or not taken by the defendant since the wrongful conduct;

(8) compliance or noncompliance with any applicable standard promulgated by a governmental or other generally recognized agency or organization whose function it is to establish standards; and

(9) any other aggravating or mitigating factors relevant to the amount of the award. . . .

This particular provision of the model act was crafted before the Supreme Court's landmark decision in State Farm v. Campbell, set forth below in the text.

Major State and Federal Law Obstacles to Recovery of Punitive Damages. In Nebraska, a constitutional provision precludes an award of punitive damages. *See* Distinctive Printing & Packaging Co. v. Cox, 443 N.W.2d 566, 574 (Neb. 1989).

In Washington state, a similar rule applies as a result of an early judicial decision. *See* Spokane Truck & Dray Co. v. Hoefer, 25 P. 1072 (Wash. 1891) (barring punitive damages).

In New Hampshire, punitive damages are not available, unless expressly provided for by statute. *See* N.H. Rev. Stat. Ann. § 507:16 (Westlaw 2022).

In Connecticut, punitive damages may not exceed litigation expenses less taxable costs. *See* Triangle Sheet Metal Works, Inc. v. Silver, 222 A.2d 220 (Conn. 1966).

The Federal Tort Claims Act does not permit the federal government to be held liable for punitive damages. *See* 28 U.S.C. §§ 1346(b), 2671, 2674 (Westlaw 2022).

A few states provide that the amount of punitive damages is to be determined by judges, not juries, either in all cases (*see* Kan. Stat. Ann § 60-3702 (Westlaw 2022)[3]) or at least in some suits (*see* Conn. Gen. Stat. Ann. § 52-240b (Westlaw 2022) (products liability)).

A number of states have enacted legislation barring punitive damages in certain suits against manufacturers of drugs or devices, if the product complied with federal or state regulations. *See, e.g.*, Tenn. Code Ann. T. C. A. § 29-28-104 (Westlaw 2022).

Perspective. Large punitive damages awards attract media attention — perhaps too much attention.

> Empirical studies of punitive damages in actual cases have found that juries award punitive damages relatively infrequently. Studies conducted by researchers at the RAND Corporation found that punitive damages are only awarded in 1–8% of civil cases. Other studies have found punitive damages to be awarded at similar rates. . . .
>
> . . . . Not only are punitive damages awarded infrequently, but they are typically not awarded in headline-grabbing amounts. . . . Median awards

3. Held to be an unconstitutional abridgement of the Seventh Amendment right to trial by jury in Capital Solutions, LLC v. Konica Minolta Business Solutions U.S.A., Inc., 695 F.Supp.2d 1149 (D. Kan. 2010).

> tend to be relatively low; several studies have found that the median award is approximately $50,000. . . .
>
> Mechanisms such as remittitur, appellate review, and settlement all contribute to the post-trial reduction of punitive awards, and judicial review of damage awards has become increasingly important. Studies . . . have found that awards were commonly reduced post-trial and that plaintiffs rarely received the amount awarded by the jury.

Jennifer K. Robbennolt, *Determining Punitive Damages: Empirical Insights and Implications for Reform*, 50 Buffalo L. Rev. 103, 161–65 (2002).

State Farm Mutual Automobile Insurance Co. v. Campbell

Supreme Court of the United States
538 U.S. 408 (2003)

Justice KENNEDY delivered the opinion of the Court.

. . . . The question is whether . . . an award of $145 million in punitive damages, where full compensatory damages are $1 million, is excessive and in violation of the Due Process Clause of the Fourteenth Amendment to the Constitution of the United States.

. . . .

In 1981, Curtis Campbell (Campbell) was driving with his wife. . . . He decided to pass six vans traveling ahead of them on a two-lane highway. Todd Ospital was driving a small car. . . . To avoid a head-on collision with Campbell, . . . Ospital swerved onto the shoulder, lost control of his automobile, and collided with a vehicle driven by Robert G. Slusher. Ospital was killed, and Slusher was rendered permanently disabled. . . .

. . . "[A] consensus was reached early on by the investigators and witnesses that Mr. Campbell's unsafe pass had indeed caused the crash." . . . . Campbell's insurance company, . . . (State Farm), nonetheless decided to contest liability and declined offers by Slusher and Ospital's estate (Ospital) to settle the claims for the policy limit of $50,000 ($25,000 per claimant). State Farm also ignored the advice of one of its own investigators and took the case to trial, assuring the Campbells that "their assets were safe, that they had no liability for the accident, that [State Farm] would represent their interests, and that they did not need to procure separate counsel." . . . . To the contrary, a jury determined that Campbell was 100 percent at fault, and a judgment was returned for $185,849, far more than the amount offered in settlement.

At first State Farm refused to cover the $135,849 in excess liability. Its counsel made this clear to the Campbells: "You may want to put for sale signs on your property to get things moving." . . . . Campbell obtained his own counsel to appeal the verdict. During the pendency of the appeal, in late 1984, Slusher, Ospital, and the Campbells reached an agreement whereby Slusher and Ospital agreed not to seek satisfaction of their claims against the Campbells. In exchange the Campbells agreed to pursue a bad faith action against State Farm.... Slusher and Ospital would receive 90 percent of any verdict against State Farm.

In 1989, the Utah Supreme Court denied Campbell's appeal in the wrongful death and tort actions.... State Farm then paid the entire judgment, including the amounts in excess of the policy limits. The Campbells nonetheless filed a complaint against State Farm alleging bad faith, fraud, and intentional infliction of emotional distress.... State Farm moved *in limine* to exclude evidence of alleged conduct that occurred in unrelated cases outside of Utah, but the trial court denied the motion. At State Farm's request the trial court bifurcated the trial into two phases conducted before different juries. In the first phase the jury determined that State Farm's decision not to settle was unreasonable because there was a substantial likelihood of an excess verdict.

Before the second phase of the action against State Farm we decided BMW of North America, Inc. v. Gore, 517 U.S. 559 ... (1996), and refused to sustain a $2 million punitive damages award which accompanied a verdict of only $4,000 in compensatory damages. Based on that decision, State Farm again moved for the exclusion of evidence of dissimilar out-of-state conduct.... The trial court denied State Farm's motion....

The second phase addressed State Farm's liability for fraud and intentional infliction of emotional distress, as well as compensatory and punitive damages. The Utah Supreme Court aptly characterized this phase of the trial:

> State Farm argued during phase II that its decision to take the case to trial was an 'honest mistake' that did not warrant punitive damages. In contrast, the Campbells introduced evidence that State Farm's decision to take the case to trial was a result of a national scheme to meet corporate fiscal goals by capping payouts on claims company wide. This scheme was referred to as State Farm's 'Performance, Planning and Review,' or PP & R, policy. To prove the existence of this scheme, the trial court allowed the Campbells to introduce extensive expert testimony regarding fraudulent practices by State Farm in its nation-wide operations....

Evidence pertaining to the PP & R policy concerned State Farm's business practices for over 20 years in numerous States. Most of these practices bore no relation to third-party automobile insurance claims, the type of claim underlying the Campbells' complaint against the company. The jury awarded the Campbells $2.6 million in compensatory damages and $145 million in punitive damages, which the trial court reduced to $1 million and $25 million respectively. Both parties appealed.

The Utah Supreme Court sought to apply the three guideposts we identified in *Gore,* ... and it reinstated the $145 million punitive damages award.... We granted certiorari....

While States possess discretion over the imposition of punitive damages, it is well established that there are procedural and substantive constitutional limitations on these awards.... The Due Process Clause of the Fourteenth Amendment prohibits the imposition of grossly excessive or arbitrary punishments on a tortfeasor.... The reason is that "[e]lementary notions of fairness enshrined in our constitutional jurisprudence dictate that a person receive fair notice not only of the conduct that will subject him to punishment, but also of the severity of the penalty that a State may impose." ....

Although these awards serve the same purposes as criminal penalties, defendants subjected to punitive damages in civil cases have not been accorded the protections applicable in a criminal proceeding.... Jury instructions typically leave the jury with wide discretion in choosing amounts, and the presentation of evidence of a defendant's net worth creates the potential that juries will use their verdicts to express biases against big businesses, particularly those without strong local presences....

... [I]n *Gore, supra,* we instructed courts reviewing punitive damages to consider three guideposts: (1) the degree of reprehensibility of the defendant's misconduct; (2) the disparity between the actual or potential harm suffered by the plaintiff and the punitive damages award; and (3) the difference between the punitive damages awarded by the jury and the civil penalties authorized or imposed in comparable cases.... We reiterated the importance of these three guideposts in *Cooper Industries* and mandated appellate courts to conduct *de novo* review of a trial court's application of them to the jury's award....

Under the principles outlined in BMW of North America, Inc. v. Gore, this case is neither close nor difficult. It was error to reinstate the jury's $145 million punitive damages award. We address each guidepost of *Gore* in some detail.

....

"[T]he most important indicium of the reasonableness of a punitive damages award is the degree of reprehensibility of the defendant's conduct." .... We have instructed courts to determine the reprehensibility of a defendant by considering whether: the harm caused was physical as opposed to economic; the tortious conduct evinced an indifference to or a reckless disregard of the health or safety of others; the target of the conduct had financial vulnerability; the conduct involved repeated actions or was an isolated incident; and the harm was the result of intentional malice, trickery, or deceit, or mere accident.... The existence of any one of these factors weighing in favor of a plaintiff may not be sufficient to sustain a punitive damages award; and the absence of all of them renders any award suspect. It should be presumed a plaintiff has been made whole for his injuries by compensatory damages, so punitive damages should only be awarded if the defendant's culpability, after having paid compensatory damages, is so reprehensible as to warrant the imposition of further sanctions to achieve punishment or deterrence....

... State Farm's handling of the claims against the Campbells merits no praise. The trial court found that State Farm's employees altered the company's records to make Campbell appear less culpable. State Farm disregarded the overwhelming likelihood of liability and the near-certain probability that, by taking the case to trial, a judgment in excess of the policy limits would be awarded. State Farm amplified the harm by at first assuring the Campbells their assets would be safe from any verdict and by later telling them, postjudgment, to put a for-sale sign on their house. While we do not suggest there was error in awarding punitive damages based upon State Farm's conduct toward the Campbells, a more modest punishment for this reprehensible conduct could have satisfied the State's legitimate objectives, and the Utah courts should have gone no further.

This case, instead, was used as a platform to expose, and punish, the perceived deficiencies of State Farm's operations throughout the country....

A State cannot punish a defendant for conduct that may have been lawful where it occurred.... Nor, as a general rule, does a State have a legitimate concern in imposing punitive damages to punish a defendant for unlawful acts committed outside of the State's jurisdiction....

Here, the Campbells do not dispute that much of the out-of-state conduct was lawful where it occurred.... Lawful out-of-state conduct may be probative when it demonstrates the deliberateness and culpability of the defendant's action in the State where it is tortious, but that conduct must have a nexus to the specific harm suffered by the plaintiff. A jury must be instructed, furthermore, that it may not use evidence of out-of-state conduct to punish a defendant for action that was lawful in the jurisdiction where it occurred.... A basic principle of federalism is that each State may make its own reasoned judgment about what conduct is permitted or proscribed within its borders, and each State alone can determine what measure of punishment, if any, to impose on a defendant who acts within its jurisdiction....

For a more fundamental reason, however, the Utah courts erred in relying upon this and other evidence: The courts awarded punitive damages to punish and deter conduct that bore no relation to the Campbells' harm. A defendant's dissimilar acts, independent from the acts upon which liability was premised, may not serve as the basis for punitive damages. A defendant should be punished for the conduct that harmed the plaintiff, not for being an unsavory individual or business. Due process does not permit courts, in the calculation of punitive damages, to adjudicate the merits of other parties' hypothetical claims against a defendant under the guise of the reprehensibility analysis, but we have no doubt the Utah Supreme Court did that here.... Punishment on these bases creates the possibility of multiple punitive damages awards for the same conduct; for in the usual case nonparties are not bound by the judgment some other plaintiff obtains....

...[T]he Utah Supreme Court's decision cannot be justified on the grounds that State Farm was a recidivist. Although "[o]ur holdings that a recidivist may be punished more severely than a first offender recognize that repeated misconduct is more reprehensible than an individual instance of malfeasance," ... in the context of civil actions courts must ensure the conduct in question replicates the prior transgressions....

The Campbells have identified scant evidence of repeated misconduct of the sort that injured them. Nor does our review of the Utah courts' decisions convince us that State Farm was only punished for its actions toward the Campbells. Although evidence of other acts need not be identical to have relevance in the calculation of punitive damages, the Utah court erred here because evidence pertaining to claims that had nothing to do with a third-party lawsuit was introduced at length.... The Campbells attempt to justify the courts' reliance upon this unrelated testimony on the theory that each dollar of profit made by underpaying a third-party claimant is the same as a dollar made by underpaying a first-party one.... [T]his argument is unconvincing. The reprehensibility guidepost does not permit courts to expand the scope of the case so that a defendant may be punished for any malfeasance, which in this case extended for a 20-year period. In this case, because the Campbells have shown no conduct by State Farm similar to that which harmed them, the conduct that harmed them is the only conduct relevant to the reprehensibility analysis.

....

Turning to the second *Gore* guidepost, we have been reluctant to identify concrete constitutional limits on the ratio between harm, or potential harm, to the plaintiff and the punitive damages award. *Gore, supra,* at 582... ("[W]e have consistently rejected the notion that the constitutional line is marked by a simple mathematical formula...").... We decline again to impose a bright-line ratio which a punitive damages award cannot exceed. Our jurisprudence and the principles it has now established demonstrate, however, that, in practice, few awards exceeding a single-digit ratio between punitive and compensatory damages, to a significant degree, will satisfy due process.... While these ratios are not binding, they are instructive. They demonstrate what should be obvious: Single-digit multipliers are more likely to comport with due process, while still achieving the State's goals of deterrence and retribution, than awards with ratios in range of 500 to 1, *id.,* at 582,... or, in this case, of 145 to 1.

Nonetheless, because there are no rigid benchmarks that a punitive damages award may not surpass, ratios greater than those we have previously upheld may comport with due process where "a particularly egregious act has resulted in only a small amount of economic damages.".... The converse is also true, however. When compensatory damages are substantial, then a lesser ratio, perhaps only equal to compensatory damages, can reach the outermost limit of the due process guarantee. The precise award in any case, of course, must be based upon the facts and circumstances of the defendant's conduct and the harm to the plaintiff.

In sum, courts must ensure that the measure of punishment is both reasonable and proportionate to the amount of harm to the plaintiff and to the general damages recovered. In the context of this case, we have no doubt that there is a presumption against an award that has a 145-to-1 ratio. The compensatory award in this case was substantial; the Campbells were awarded $1 million for a year and a half of emotional distress. This was complete compensation. The harm arose from a transaction in the economic realm, not from some physical assault or trauma; there were no physical injuries; and State Farm paid the excess verdict before the complaint was filed, so the Campbells suffered only minor economic injuries for the

18-month period in which State Farm refused to resolve the claim against them. The compensatory damages for the injury suffered here, moreover, likely were based on a component which was duplicated in the punitive award. Much of the distress was caused by the outrage and humiliation the Campbells suffered at the actions of their insurer; and it is a major role of punitive damages to condemn such conduct. Compensatory damages, however, already contain this punitive element....

The Utah Supreme Court sought to justify the massive award by pointing to ... the fact that State Farm's policies have affected numerous Utah consumers; the fact that State Farm will only be punished in one out of every 50,000 cases as a matter of statistical probability; and State Farm's enormous wealth....

... [T]he argument that State Farm will be punished in only the rare case, coupled with reference to its assets (which, of course, are what other insured parties in Utah and other States must rely upon for payment of claims) had little to do with the actual harm sustained by the Campbells. The wealth of a defendant cannot justify an otherwise unconstitutional punitive damages award....

The third guidepost in *Gore* is the disparity between the punitive damages award and the "civil penalties authorized or imposed in comparable cases." .... The existence of a criminal penalty does have bearing on the seriousness with which a State views the wrongful action. When used to determine the dollar amount of the award, however, the criminal penalty has less utility. Great care must be taken to avoid use of the civil process to assess criminal penalties that can be imposed only after the heightened protections of a criminal trial have been observed, including, of course, its higher standards of proof. Punitive damages are not a substitute for the criminal process, and the remote possibility of a criminal sanction does not automatically sustain a punitive damages award.

Here, we need not dwell long on this guidepost. The most relevant civil sanction under Utah state law for the wrong done to the Campbells appears to be a $10,000 fine for an act of fraud ..., an amount dwarfed by the $145 million punitive damages award. The Supreme Court of Utah speculated about the loss of State Farm's business license, the disgorgement of profits, and possible imprisonment, but here again its references were to the broad fraudulent scheme drawn from evidence of out-of-state and dissimilar conduct. This analysis was insufficient to justify the award.

....

An application of the *Gore* guideposts to the facts of this case, especially in light of the substantial compensatory damages awarded (a portion of which contained a punitive element), likely would justify a punitive damages award at or near the amount of compensatory damages. The punitive award of $145 million, therefore, was neither reasonable nor proportionate to the wrong committed, and it was an irrational and arbitrary deprivation of the property of the defendant. The proper calculation of punitive damages under the principles we have discussed should be resolved, in the first instance, by the Utah courts.

The judgment of the Utah Supreme Court is reversed, and the case is remanded for proceedings not inconsistent with this opinion.

[The dissenting opinions of Justices SCALIA, THOMAS, and GINSBURG are omitted.]

Notes

1. ***Other Supreme Court Precedent.*** In Motor Co., Ltd. v. Oberg, 512 U.S. 415 (1994), the court ruled that an amendment to the Oregon Constitution, prohibiting judicial review of the amount of punitive damages awarded by a jury "unless the court can affirmatively say there is no evidence to support the verdict," violated due process.

In BMW of North America, Inc. v. Gore, 517 U.S. 559 (1996), the court overturned a $2 million punitive damage award to a car purchaser who had not been told about the predelivery damage and repair of the vehicle he purchased. The jury had awarded $4,000 in compensatory damages.

An award of punitive damages may not be based, even in part, on a jury's desire to punish a defendant for harming nonparties. In Philip Morris USA v. Williams, 549 U.S. 346, 353–55 (2007), the jury made a large punitive damages award to the estate of a heavy smoker after the plaintiff made arguments about how many other smokers had been killed by the defendant's cigarettes. In remanding the case to the Oregon Supreme Court for further proceedings, Justice Stephen Breyer's opinion for the court explained:

> [T]he Constitution's Due Process Clause forbids a State to use a punitive damages award to punish a defendant for injury that it inflicts upon nonparties, . . . For one thing, the Due Process Clause prohibits a State from punishing an individual without first providing that individual with "an opportunity to present every available defense." . . . . Yet a defendant threatened with punishment for injuring a nonparty victim has no opportunity to defend against the charge, by showing, for example in a case such as this, that the other victim was not entitled to damages because he or she knew that smoking was dangerous or did not rely upon the defendant's statements to the contrary.
>
> For another, to permit punishment for injuring a nonparty victim would add a near standardless dimension to the punitive damages equation. How many such victims are there? How seriously were they injured? Under what circumstances did injury occur? The trial will not likely answer such questions as to nonparty victims. The jury will be left to speculate. . . .
>
> Respondent argues that she is free to show harm to other victims because it is relevant to a different part of the punitive damages constitutional equation, namely, reprehensibility. That is to say, harm to others shows more reprehensible conduct. Philip Morris, in turn, does not deny that a plaintiff may show harm to others in order to demonstrate reprehensibility. Nor

> do we. . . . Yet for the reasons given above, a jury may not go further than this and use a punitive damages verdict to punish a defendant directly on account of harms it is alleged to have visited on nonparties.
>
> Given . . . the risks of arbitrariness, the concern for adequate notice, and the risk that punitive damages awards can, in practice, impose one State's (or one jury's) policies (e.g., banning cigarettes) upon other States . . . it is particularly important that States avoid procedure that unnecessarily deprives juries of proper legal guidance. We therefore conclude that the Due Process Clause requires States to provide assurance that juries are not asking the wrong question, i.e., seeking, not simply to determine reprehensibility, but also to punish for harm caused strangers.

See also Exxon Shipping Co. v. Baker, 128 S. Ct. 2605 (U.S. 2008) (holding, in a case arising from an Alaskan oil spill, that under maritime law an award of punitive damages could not exceed the jury's award of $507.5 million in compensatory damages); Atlantic Sounding Co., Inc. v. Townsend, 557 U.S. 404 (2009) (holding that "[b]ecause punitive damages have long been an accepted remedy under general maritime law, . . . such damages for the willful and wanton disregard of the maintenance and cure obligation should remain available").

2. ***Evidence of Defendant's Financial Condition.*** It was once generally held that the defendant's wealth or poverty was relevant to the issue of punitive damages. The reason was that an amount which may be sufficient to punish or deter a poor person may not be sufficient to achieve a similar result with one who is rich. However, older precedent is now subject to re-examination in light of the Supreme Court's statement in *Campbell* that "[t]he wealth of a defendant cannot justify an otherwise unconstitutional punitive damages award."

3. ***"Substantial" Compensatory Awards and the 1-to-1. Ratio.*** In Bullock v. Philip Morris USA, Inc., 131 Cal. Rptr. 3d 382, 399–403 (Cal. App. 2011), the court expressly noted that the financial condition of the defendant was relevant to the constitutionality of a punitive damages award. Moreover, it approved a punitive award with a 16:1 ratio to compensatory damages, stating:

> Philip Morris argues that there is an emerging consensus that "six-figure damage awards are more than 'substantial' enough to trigger this 1:1 upper limit [mentioned in *Campbell*]." We cannot discern any emerging consensus in this regard relevant to the extremely reprehensible conduct at issue in this case. Moreover, we do not regard the amount of compensatory damages as a fixed upper limit where damages are "substantial."

See also Aleo v. SLB Toys USA, Inc., 995 N.E.2d 740, 757 (Mass. 2013) (approving an award of $18 million in punitive damages on top of $2,640,000 in compensatory damages, a ratio of roughly seven-to-one); Adeli v. Silverstar Automotive, Inc., 960 F.3d 452, 463 (8th Cir. 2020) (approving a 1:24.75 ratio in a case involving only $20,201 in compensatory damages).

4. ***Bifurcated and Trifurcated Trials.*** The introduction of evidence relating to how severely the defendant should be punished may prejudice the jury's assessment of the liability issue. Accordingly, many states hold that the better course is to divide the trial into separate stages dealing with compensatory damages liability, first, and punitive damages liability, second. This is called a bifurcated trial. *See, e.g.*, Cal. Civ. Code § 3295(d) (Westlaw 2022); N.J. Stat. Ann. § 2A:15-5.13 (Westlaw 2022); Tex. Civ. Prac. & Rem. Code § 41.009 (Westlaw 2022). *But see* Life Ins. Co. of Ga. v. Johnson, 701 So. 2d 524 (Ala. 1997) (bifurcation of trials on merits and punitive damages is not necessary to assure due process).

Some courts even employ a three-part process (a trifurcated trial) that addresses: first, whether the defendant should be liable for compensatory damages and, if so, in what amount; second, whether punitive damages should be imposed; and third, the amount of punitive damages.

5. ***Multiple Suits and Punitive Damages.*** When a product injures several consumers, or an airplane crash kills many victims, there is a risk that the defendant may be exposed to multiple awards of punitive damages in separate actions. However, the ruling in *Campbell*—restricting consideration of extra-jurisdictional evidence, barring consideration of hypothetical claims, and stating that the "precise award in any case . . . must be based upon the facts and circumstances of the defendant's conduct and the harm to the plaintiff"—would seem to go far toward reducing any risk of excessive punishment.

In attempting to grapple with the evidentiary questions relating to punitive damages in the mass tort context, one court wrote:

> . . . [E]vidence about the profitability of a defendant's misconduct and about any settlement amounts for punitive damages or prior punitive damages awards that the defendant has actually paid for the same course of conduct is admissible when the defendant offers it in mitigation of punitive damages. Such evidence is relevant because it better informs the fact finder about . . . the amount of punitive damages necessary to fairly punish a party and to deter the conduct in question. . . .
>
> Evidence that is not relevant, or is unduly prejudicial, and thus, not admissible to mitigate punitive damages, includes actual damage amounts paid by settlements or by judgments; the number of pending claims filed against a defendant for the same conduct; the number of anticipated claims for the same conduct; insurance coverage; unpaid punitive damages awards for the same course of conduct; and evidence of punitive damages that may be levied in the future. . . .
>
> . . . [O]nly prior paid awards and settlements for punitive damages should be considered by the fact finder. To hold otherwise risks unfair prejudice and jury confusion. . . . [M]any punitive damage awards are reduced after trial, reversed on appeal, or settled at a discount. . . .

Owens-Corning Fiberglas Corp. v. Malone, 972 S.W.2d 35, 40–42 (Tex. 1998).

6. ***Punitive Damages Caps.*** Some states have enacted limits on the amount of punitive damages. *See, e.g.*, Alaska Stat. § 09.17.020(f)–(h) (Westlaw 2022) (greater of three times compensatory damages or $500,000, except when action was motivated by financial gain, in which case punitive damages are limited to the greater of four times compensatory damages, four times aggregate amount of financial gain, or $7,000,000; different rules apply to unlawful employment practices); Colo. Rev. Stat. Ann. § 13-21-102 (Westlaw 2022) (award may not exceed actual damages or, if there are aggravating circumstances, three times actual damages); Conn. Gen. Stat. Ann. § 52-240b (Westlaw 2022) (twice the compensatory award in a products liability action); Kan. Stat. Ann. § 60-3701(1)(e)–(f) (Westlaw 2022) (no more than $5 million or the gross income of the defendant, whichever is less).

Suppose that a 85-year-old patient in a nursing home is seriously injured as a result of conscious neglect by the staff. Would an award of punitive damages be capped under the following statute?

Texas Civil Practice & Remedies Code § 41.008 (Westlaw 2022)

§ 41.008. Limitation on Amount of Recovery

. . . .

(b) Exemplary damages awarded against a defendant may not exceed an amount equal to the greater of:

(1) (A) two times the amount of economic damages; plus (B) an amount equal to any noneconomic damages found by the jury, not to exceed $750,000; or

(2) $200,000.

(c) This section does not apply to a cause of action against a defendant from whom a plaintiff seeks recovery of exemplary damages based on conduct described as a felony in the following sections of the Penal Code if, except for Sections 49.07 and 49.08, the conduct was committed knowingly or intentionally:

(1) Section 19.02 (murder);

(2) Section 19.03 (capital murder);

(3) Section 20.04 (aggravated kidnapping);

(4) Section 22.02 (aggravated assault);

(5) Section 22.011 (sexual assault);

(6) Section 22.021 (aggravated sexual assault);

(7) Section 22.04 (injury to a child, elderly individual, or disabled individual, but not if the conduct occurred while providing health care as defined by Section 74.001);

(8) Section 32.21 (forgery);

(9) Section 32.43 (commercial bribery);

(10) Section 32.45 (misapplication of fiduciary property or property of financial institution);

(11) Section 32.46 (securing execution of document by deception);

(12) Section 32.47 (fraudulent destruction, removal, or concealment of writing);

(13) Chapter 31 (theft) the punishment level for which is a felony of the third degree or higher;

(14) Section 49.07 (intoxication assault);

(15) Section 49.08 (intoxication manslaughter); or

(16) Section 21.02 (continuous sexual abuse of young child or children).

. . .

(f) This section does not apply to a cause of action for damages arising from the manufacture of methamphetamine. . . .

7. ***Insuring against Liability for Punitive Damages.*** There is a split of authority as to whether an insurance contract provision purporting to cover punitive damages is against public policy. In Price v. Hartford Accident and Indemnity Co., 502 P.2d 522 (Ariz. 1972), the court upheld the coverage. Turning aside arguments that the law should not allow irresponsible drivers to escape punishment and that permitting insurance would foist the burden of a punitive award onto the public at large, the court concluded that the insurance company was obliged to honor the clear language of the policy. Presumably, the company had been adequately compensated for taking the risk, and in any event the defendant and other drivers would be adequately deterred from misconduct by fear of criminal liability, increased insurance premiums, and the risk that a punitive damage award would exceed insurance coverage limits.

Unlike *Price*, some courts hold that insuring punitive damage awards would frustrate public policy. *See, e.g.*, Johnson & Johnson v. Aetna Cas. & Surety Co., 667 A.2d 1087 (N.J. 1995); Peterson v. Superior Court of Ventura Co., 642 P.2d 1305 (Cal. 1982); Hartford Accident and Indemnity Co. v. Village of Hempstead, 397 N.E.2d 737 (N.Y. 1979).

However, other courts are in accord with *Price*. *See* Westchester Fire Ins. Co. v. Admiral Ins. Co., 152 S.W.3d 172 (Tex. App. 2004) (holding, on specific facts, that coverage for punitive damages under a primary liability policy was not void as against public policy).

8. ***Vicarious Liability for Punitive Damages.*** Punitive damages may be imposed on an employer under a *respondeat superior* theory without violating due process. In Pacific Mutual Life Ins. Co. v. Haslip, 499 U.S. 1 (1991), the court wrote:

> Imposing exemplary damages on the corporation when its agent commits intentional fraud creates a strong incentive for vigilance by those in a position "to guard substantially against the evil to be prevented." . . . . If an insurer were liable for such damages only upon proof that it was at fault independently, it would have an incentive to minimize oversight of its agents. Imposing liability without independent fault deters fraud more than a less stringent rule. It therefore rationally advances the State's goal.

Some states have restricted vicarious liability for punitive damages by statute. For example:

Texas Civil Practice and Remedies Code § 41.005 (Westlaw 2022)

§ 41.005. Harm Resulting from Criminal Act

(a) In an action arising from harm resulting from an assault, theft, or other criminal act, a court may not award exemplary damages against a defendant because of the criminal act of another.

(b) The exemption provided by Subsection (a) does not apply if:

(1) the criminal act was committed by an employee of the defendant;

(2) the defendant is criminally responsible as a party to the criminal act . . . ;

(3) the criminal act occurred at a location where, at the time of the criminal act, the defendant was maintaining a common nuisance . . . and had not made reasonable attempts to abate the nuisance; or

(4) the criminal act resulted from the defendant's intentional or knowing violation of a statutory duty under Subchapter D, Chapter 92, Property Code, and the criminal act occurred after the statutory deadline for compliance with that duty.

(c) In an action arising out of a criminal act committed by an employee, the employer may be liable for punitive damages but only if:

(1) the principal authorized the doing and the manner of the act;

(2) the agent was unfit and the principal acted with malice in employing or retaining him;

(3) the agent was employed in a managerial capacity and was acting in the scope of employment; or

(4) the employer or a manager of the employer ratified or approved the act.

9. ***Punitive Damages Paid to the State***. Traditionally, the full amount of a punitive damages award has been paid to the prevailing party. This has changed in some jurisdictions that have enacted laws requiring a portion of each punitive damages award to be paid to the state, either to the general fund or to a special fund dealing, for example, with rehabilitation, medical assistance, or compensation of

criminal injuries. The state's share of punitive damages may be a fixed percentage (sometimes up to 75% or more) or an amount determined by the discretion of the judge. *See, e.g.*, Ga. Code Ann. § 51-12-5.1(e)(2) (Westlaw 2022) (in products liability actions, forfeiture of 75% less a proportionate part of the costs of litigation); 735 Ill. Comp. Stat. Ann. 5/2-1207 (Westlaw 2022) (discretionary amount); Iowa Code Ann. § 668A.1(2)(b) (Westlaw 2022) (forfeiture of at least 75%, unless the defendant's conduct was directed specifically at the claimant); Mo. Rev. Stat. § 537.675 (Westlaw 2022) (allowing the state to receive 50%); Or. Rev. Stat. § 31.735 (Westlaw 2022) (forfeiture of 70%).

In Pennsylvania, if punitive damages are awarded in a case involving violation of the Fine Arts Protection Act (which encompasses certain types of physical defacement, mutilation, alteration, or destruction of a work of fine art), "the court shall, in its discretion, select an organization or organizations engaged in charitable or educational activities involving the fine arts . . . to receive such damages." 73 Pa. Cons. Stat. § 2105(3) (Westlaw 2022).

Statutes forfeiting punitive damages to the state have been attacked as unconstitutional "takings" of private property or denials of equal protection — with mixed results. *Compare* Mack Trucks, Inc. v. Conkle, 436 S.E.2d 635 (Ga. 1993) (rejecting "takings" and equal protection challenges), *with* Kirk v. Denver Publishing Co., 818 P.2d 262, 273 (Colo. 1991) (finding the state statute unconstitutional). In general, the legislation has produced less money for state programs than might be expected, largely because most large punitive damages awards do not survive on appeal. In addition, most cases settle and, in such situations, there is no judicially approved award of punitive damages, which presumably makes punitive damages forfeiture laws in applicable.

10. ***Punitive Damages and Death of the Tortfeasor.*** It is not possible to punish a deceased tortfeasor. Should a claim for punitive damages survive the death of the wrongdoer? In Crabtree *ex rel.* Kemp v. Estate of Crabtree, 837 N.E.2d 135 (Ind. 2005), the court wrote:

> A minority of jurisdictions permit recovery of punitive damages after the tortfeasor's death. Although the decedent can be neither punished nor deterred, these courts have found punitive damages sufficiently justified by deterrence of others from engaging in similar conduct. . . . Some also note that punitive damages provide additional compensation to victims for remote losses, inconvenience, and attorney's fees. . . .
>
> We believe the majority view is persuasive and hold that Indiana law does not permit recovery of punitive damages from the estate of a deceased tortfeasor. The central purpose of punitive damages is to punish the wrongdoer and to deter him from future misconduct, not to reward the plaintiff and not to compensate the plaintiff. . . .

See also Whetstone v. Binner, 57 N.E.3d 1111, 1115 (Ohio 2016) (concluding that "in cases in which liability has been determined while the tortfeasor is alive, punitive damages are available to the plaintiff" because "[t]o hold otherwise would send a message that by delaying a damages hearing, a defendant or his or her estate might avoid the award of punitive damages").

11. ***Punitive Damages and Public Entities.*** An award of punitive damages may warrant careful scrutiny if the weight of the award will be borne by the public. *See* Payne v. Jones, 711 F.3d 85, 95 (2d Cir. 2013) (holding, in a case arising from abusive police conduct, that an award of $300,000 was excessive, and that the case would be remanded for a new trial on punitive damages unless the plaintiff agreed to accept $100,000, because "[w]hen . . . the wrongdoer is a public servant and receives indemnification for a court's award of damages, it is the taxpaying public that bears the brunt of an excessive award").

12. ***Punitive Damages in Alabama.*** A due process constitutional challenge to punitive damages in Alabama inevitably encounters special challenges. As the court explained in *In re Tylenol (Acetaminophen) Mktg., Sales Practices and Products Liab. Litig.*, 144 F. Supp. 3d 680, 684-87 (E.D. Pa. 2015):

> The Alabama wrongful death statute, Ala. Code. § 6–5–410(a)(1975), is like no other in the United States. "In Alabama, only punitive damages are available in wrongful death actions, and these damages may be awarded against a defendant based on its negligent conduct." . . . . The statute does not allow for compensatory damages or consideration of the decedent's losses. . . . The focus of a wrongful death claim under Alabama law is on the defendants' conduct. . . . The Alabama legislature and courts have made clear: the statute is intended to protect lives by imposing damages on tortfeasors causing death. . . . By making a wrongful death "expensive," Alabama seeks to deter similar tortious conduct. . . .
>
> "In calculating a damage award, an Alabama Wrongful Death Act jury is instructed to consider: (1) the finality of death, (2) the propriety of punishing the defendant, (3) whether the defendant could have prevented the victim's death, (4) how difficult it would have been for the defendant to have prevented the death, and (5) the public's interest in deterring others from engaging in conduct like the defendant's." . . . . "Because the policy of [Alabama] is to regard human life as being beyond measure in terms of dollars, the jury must disregard the decedent's wealth or lack of wealth, it must disregard the decedent's potential for accumulating great wealth or lack of potential to accumulate wealth; and it must disregard his or her talents and education, or lack of them, as well as his or her station in life." . . . .
>
> The statute and its punitive scheme date back to the late 1800s. . . . The United States Supreme Court first considered its constitutionality in 1927. . . . The main issue [in that case] was whether an employer could be vicariously liable under the statute. . . .
>
> Nonetheless, the Court found that imposing "punitive" damages for mere negligence was not per se unconstitutional:

> As interpreted by the state court, the aim of the present statute is to strike at the evil of the negligent destruction of human life by imposing liability, regardless of fault, upon those who are in some substantial measure in a position to prevent it. We cannot say that it is beyond the power of a Legislature . . . to attempt to preserve human life by making homicide expensive.
>
> . . . . The Court noted that "[t]he distinction between punitive and compensatory damages [was] a modern refinement." . . . . The Court ultimately upheld the statute to be constitutional, despite its unique nature. . . .
>
> The Alabama statute has remained virtually unchanged. The Alabama Legislature has declined to alter its unique character, even during tort reform efforts in the late 1980s and 1990s. The Alabama Supreme Court has continually upheld the statute as constitutional.

In *In re Tylenol*, the court held that an Alabama award of punitive damages was subject to review under the *Gore* guideposts. It found that just "[b]ecause an act is negligent does not mean it can't also be reprehensible." It further found that although the second Gore guidepost (ratio) could not be applied because the wrongful death statute does not provide for an award of compensatory damages, on the facts of the case, it could not "say that the absence of a ratio would necessarily render the entire evaluation under the 'guideposts' unconstitutional."

13. ***Ethics in Law Practice: Contingent Fees and Conflicts of Interest.*** On the plaintiff's side of the bar, tort litigation is usually handled on a contingent fee basis. If the client does not recover, the lawyer does not get paid. The contingency of the lawyer's fee creates a powerful incentive for the lawyer to work hard to win. One might think, therefore, that such a contractual arrangement does not create a conflict of interest; that the arrangement is a win-win situation. But the ethical analysis is not so simple.

An attorney employed under a contingent fee contract may be induced to pursue risky litigation strategies in search of a large contingent fee, even though a conservative course would be more consonant with the interests of the client. The attorney may also be tempted to settle a case quickly and with little expense in order to maintain a high volume of business, even though the specific client would be better served by more vigorous litigation. Despite these risks, ethics rules permit contingent fee contracts in all but a few areas (criminal representation and, in many jurisdictions, certain domestic relations matters). The dangers contingent fees pose to fair representation are generally thought to be outweighed by the fact that such agreements help to ensure that injured persons with colorable claims have access to the justice system, regardless of ability to pay.

Allocating a portion of a punitive damages award to the state may risk creating a conflict of interest between attorney and client, depending on how the arrangement is structured. If the attorney is permitted to receive a contingent fee out of the entire punitive damages award, and not simply the portion of the award eventually received by the client (*cf.* Life Ins. Co. of Ga. v. Johnson, 684 So. 2d 685, 699 (Ala. 1996), *overruled on remand*, 701 So. 2d 524 (Ala. 1997)), the interests of the lawyer and the client begin to differ. The attorney then has a stronger incentive than the client to pursue punitive damages. Another disadvantage for the client is that if a case goes to trial (for the purpose of securing a punitive award), the contingent fee contract may entitle the lawyer to a greater percentage as a fee (say, 35%, rather than 30%).

Aside from questions of forfeiture and diverging interests, it is worth remembering that, for tax reasons, a plaintiff may be better off if money received from a defendant is characterized as compensation, rather than punitive damages. The client has to pay federal income tax on receipt of punitive damages, but not on compensatory damages for physical personal injuries.

Problem: Overbilling Clients[4]

The Levoca Law Firm represents corporate clients in thirteen states. Roughly 20% of its business is located in State A, where Charles Canty, a client, is based. Canty, a solo practitioner, has been represented by the law firm for two years. Canty has sued The Levoca Law Firm for over-billing based on discrepancies in invoices submitted to and paid by Canty. Canty alleges that The Levoca Law Firm fraudulently induced him to pay for work that was never performed.

The evidence unearthed during discovery has revealed that Lance Lehman, a senior partner in The Levoca Law Firm, deliberately exaggerated the number of hours that he worked on Canty's legal matters. As a result of the over-billing, Canty paid The Levoca Law Firm at least $100,000 more than he should have paid for attorney's fees. The amounts enriched both The Levoca Law Firm generally and Lehman in particular, since his billable hours as a partner in the firm were overstated, thus affecting his share of the law firm's profits.

The discovery evidence also shows that Canty was not the only client over-billed by The Levoca Law Firm. In fact, as a result of massive fraudulent invoicing by Lehman, The Levoca Law Firm over-billed at least three dozen clients during a five-year period. About half of those clients are located in State A. The total amount of over-billing appears to be at least $5 million. In each instance, Lehman engaged in the same types of abusive billing conduct and the managing partners at The Levoca Law Firm failed to detect the unethical billing practices. This is the first case in which any of the over-billed clients has sued The Levoca Law Firm.

In State A, fraudulent conduct by a fiduciary, causing actual losses in excess of $1,000, is a Class C felony, punishable by a fine not exceeding $20,000 and/or no more than five years in jail.

If Canty seeks an award of punitive damages in his suit against The Levoca Law Firm, what substantive and procedural obstacles will he encounter, and what

4. This problem is borrowed from Vincent R. Johnson & Susan Saab Fortney, Legal Malpractice Law: Problems and Prevention 327-28 (West Academic Publishing, 3d ed. 2021).

factors are likely to be taken into account in determining the size of a punitive damages award?

E. Statutory Limits on Damage Recoveries and Related "Reform" Legislation

Every few years there is a new perceived "crisis" created by large verdicts, followed by a new wave of tort reform ostensibly intended to control the costs of liability insurance. In particular, limits on recoveries for "non-economic" damages (such as damages for pain and suffering) have been very common. *See, e.g.*, Alaska Stat. 09.17.010 (Westlaw 2022) (limiting non-economic damages to the greater of $400,000 or the injured person's life expectancy in years multiplied by $8,000, unless the plaintiff "suffers severe physical impairment or severe disfigurement," in which case non-economic damages are limited to the greater of one million dollars or the injured person's life expectancy multiplied by $25,000). A few statutes, particularly in the medical malpractice field, also limit total recoveries.

Caps on Noneconomic Damages. Plaintiffs have argued with some, but far from universal success, that statutory damage limits violate provisions in state or federal constitutions guaranteeing due process, equal protection, or other rights. Caps applicable only to non-economic damages have tended to survive constitutional scrutiny. *See, e.g.*, Simpkins v. Grace Brethren Church of Delaware, Ohio, 75 N.E.3d 122 (Ohio 2016) (reducing a jury's award of $3.5 million in noneconomic damages for a sexual assault victim to $350,000, pursuant to a cap, did not violate the victim's right to trial by jury, due process, or equal protection); *but see* Lebron v. Gottlieb Memorial Hosp., 930 N.E.2d 895 (Ill. 2010) (holding that certain caps on noneconomic damages in medical malpractice cases violated the separation of powers clause of the Illinois constitution); Rains v. Stayton Builders Mart, Inc., 410 P.3d 336 (Or. App. 2018) (holding that the application of a statutory cap to the non-economic damages claims of an injured worker and his wife violated the remedies clause of the state constitution).

Caps on Economic Damages. In contrast, damage caps which purport to limit both economic damages (*e.g.*, medical expenses) and non-economic damages (*e.g.*, pain and suffering) have tended to be held unconstitutional, often on the ground that they irrationally discriminate between victims on the basis of the severity of the injury and tend to have the greatest adverse effect on those most seriously injured.

Immunizing Tort Reform Legislation from Constitutional Attack. In 2003, the Texas legislature passed a law capping noneconomic damages in medical malpractice cases. Then, in an effort to immunize the caps from constitutional review, the legislature sent to the voters a constitutional amendment which, on the election ballot, asked them to vote for or against "The constitutional amendment concerning civil lawsuits against doctors and health care providers, and other actions, authorizing the legislature to determine limitations on non-economic damages."

The amendment, known as Proposition 12, was an example of direct citizen involvement in tort reform. Aggressive public relations campaigns were waged relating to the proposal, with proponents rallying voters to "Save Your Doctor," and opponents urging voters to "Save the Courts." The amendment to the Texas constitution passed with less than 51% of the vote in favor of the proposal. It reads:

TEXAS CONSTITUTION Article 3, Section 66 (Westlaw 2022)

(a) In this section "economic damages" means compensatory damages for any pecuniary loss or damage. The term does not include any loss or damage, however characterized, for past, present, and future physical pain and suffering, mental anguish and suffering, loss of consortium, loss of companionship and society, disfigurement, or physical impairment.

(b) Notwithstanding any other provision of this constitution, the legislature by statute may determine the limit of liability for all damages and losses, however characterized, other than economic damages, of a provider of medical or health care with respect to treatment, lack of treatment, or other claimed departure from an accepted standard of medical or health care or safety, however characterized, that is or is claimed to be a cause of . . . disease, injury, or death of a person. . . .

(c) Notwithstanding any other provision of this constitution, after January 1, 2005, the legislature by statute may determine the limit of liability for all damages and losses, however characterized, other than economic damages, in a claim or cause of action not covered by Subsection (b) of this section. This subsection applies . . . [to] any claim or cause of action based or sounding in tort, contract, or any other theory. . . .

. . . .

(e) A legislative exercise of authority under Subsection (c) of this section requires a three-fifths vote of all the members elected to each house and must include language citing this section.

Is it likely that voters reading the one sentence description of the amendment on Texas election ballots were adequately apprised of the scope of the amendment? Does this amendment merely mean that persons attacking damages caps passed by the state legislature in the future must base Equal Protection and Due Process challenges on the federal rather than Texas constitution? Is that a serious disadvantage? In the 1980s, the Texas Supreme Court relied upon the Texas Constitution's guarantee of "open courts" as a basis for striking down various tort reform legislation. There is no "open courts" clause in the federal Constitution.

Caps on Attorneys' Fees. Like certain other states, California has restricted the amount a lawyer can earn on a contingent-fee basis in a medical malpractice case. An attorney can recover 40% of the first $50,000, 33% of the next $50,000, 25 % of the next $100,000 and 10% of any amount over $200,000. This legislation has survived constitutional attack. *See Roa* v. Lodi Medical Group, Inc., 695 P.2d 164 (Cal.

1985); *see also* N.Y. Jud. Law § 474-a (Westlaw 2022) (setting forth a sliding scale of limitations on contingent fees in medical, dental and podiatric malpractice actions)

Many states have laws outside of the medical field limiting the size of the contingent fee a lawyer can charge for representing a client in a personal injury action. *See, e.g.*, Tex. Prob. Code Ann § 233 (Westlaw 2022) (fee for representing an estate ordinarily cannot exceed 33%).

Tort Reform and Public Opinion. In some parts of the country, the battle over "tort reform" is waged publicly. In Texas, for example, groups affiliated with Citizens Against Lawsuit Abuse, which is aligned with the insurance industry, erected billboards along major highways crying "Lawsuit Abuse . . . We All Pay, We All Lose." In some cities, it was almost impossible for a potential juror to reach the courthouse without reading these signs. The plaintiffs' bar has sometimes responded with its own billboards, ranging from the mildly amusing ("Prisons are for Common Criminals . . . Punitive Damages are for Corporate Criminals") to the more extreme ("Is 'Citizens Against Lawsuit Abuse' Racist?").

Tort Reform against Disfavored Classes. In the 1996 general election, California voters passed a referendum (Proposition 213) which by a 3–1 margin prohibited uninsured motorists and drunk drivers from collecting noneconomic damages arising from auto accidents, including pain and suffering, and prohibited fleeing felons from recovering any damages at all. *See* Cal. Civ. Code §§ 3333.3–3333.4 (Westlaw 2022); *see also* Quackenbush v. Superior Ct., 70 Cal. Rptr.2d 271 (Cal. Ct. App. 1998) (rejecting constitutional challenges).

Chapter 5

Negligence: Basic Principles

Unreasonable Conduct. Negligence is the largest and most important category of tort liability. Its flexible principles may be applied to virtually all types of conduct that give rise to accidental harm.

Unlike intentional tort liability, negligence is not directly concerned with the defendant's state of mind. Rather, it is concerned with the character of the defendant's conduct; the defendant's state of mind matters only because conduct is judged in the light of what the defendant knew, or reasonably should have known. Conduct that poses an *unreasonable* risk of harm to others is negligent. One's conduct need not be free of all risks of harm, only free of those risks which under the circumstances are unreasonable.

A. The Concept of Duty

Prosser's Four Elements. Dean William Prosser was of the view that there are four elements to a negligence cause of action: duty, breach, causation, and damage. Many courts have adopted this formulation, but the cases bear witness to the fact that Prosser's categories are less clear in application than in theory. Not surprisingly, a number of authorities have articulated the requirements somewhat differently. Some of those sources collapse the duty and breach elements into a more general inquiry which asks simply whether the defendant's conduct was "negligent," then separately address the issue of causation of damages.

Even from a Prosserian perspective, the concept of duty is an elusive one. As Prosser himself recognized in a frequently quoted passage:

> There is a duty if the court says there is a duty; the law, like the constitution, is what we make it. Duty is only a word with which we state our conclusion that there is or is not to be liability; it necessarily begs the essential question.... The word serves a useful purpose in directing attention to the obligation to be imposed upon the defendant, rather than the causal sequence of events; beyond that it serves none.

William L. Prosser, *Palsgraf Revisited*, 52 Mich. L. Rev. 1, 15 (1953).

From Limited Duty to General Duty. The modern law of negligence is of recent origin, having developed, for the most part, during the past 170 years. During the 19th century, a person was obliged to exercise care on behalf of others only in a relatively limited range of situations. Over the years, however, the ambit of potential liability has expanded. Thus, as a practical matter, it is useful to assume today that one owes a duty of reasonable care to those who may be harmed by one's actions if harm is foreseeable, unless the conduct falls within one of a few important limited-duty categories. The chief limited-duty rules — relating to such matters as failure to act, premises liability, negligent infliction of emotional distress, and alcohol-related injuries — are discussed in Chapters 9–12.

As to the general duty rule and its linkage to the concept of foreseeability, a useful perspective is presented by the majority opinion in Palsgraf v. Long Island R.R. Co., 162 N.E. 99 (N.Y. 1928). *Palsgraf* is recognized as the most famous (though not necessarily the most important) tort case of all time. It was decided by a group of highly esteemed jurists, who were described by Professor Irving Younger of Cornell University as "the greatest court that ever sat." Both the majority and the dissent in *Palsgraf* have been cited scores of times by courts throughout the country.

Palsgraf v. Long Island Railroad Co.

Court of Appeals of New York
162 N.E. 99 (N.Y. 1928)

CARDOZO, C.J.

Plaintiff was standing on a platform of defendant's railroad after buying a ticket to go to Rockaway Beach. A train stopped at the station, bound for another place. Two men ran forward to catch it. One of the men reached the platform of the car without mishap, though the train was already moving. The other man, carrying a package, jumped aboard the car, but seemed unsteady as if about to fall. A guard on the car, who had held the door open, reached forward to help him in, and another guard on the platform pushed him from behind. In this act, the package was dislodged, and fell upon the rails. It was a package of small size, about fifteen inches long, and was covered by a newspaper. In fact it contained fireworks, but there was nothing in its appearance to give notice of its contents. The fireworks when they fell exploded. The shock of the explosion threw down some scales at the other end of the platform many feet away. The scales struck the plaintiff, causing injuries for which she sues.

The conduct of the defendant's guard, if a wrong in its relation to the holder of the package, was not a wrong in its relation to the plaintiff, standing far away. Relatively to her it was not negligence at all. Nothing in the situation gave notice that the falling package had in it the potency of peril to persons thus removed. Negligence is not actionable unless it involves the invasion of a legally protected interest, the violation of a right. "Proof of negligence in the air, so to speak, will not do." Pollock, Torts (11th Ed.) p. 455. . . . If no hazard was apparent to the eye of ordinary vigilance, an act innocent and harmless, at least to outward seeming, with reference to her, did not take to itself the quality of a tort because it happened to be a wrong, though apparently not one involving the risk of bodily insecurity, with reference to someone else. "In every instance, before negligence can be predicated on a given act, back of the act

Benjamin N. Cardozo

must be sought and found a duty to the individual complaining, the observance of which would have averted or avoided the injury." .... "The ideas of negligence and duty are strictly correlative." .... The plaintiff sues in her own right for a wrong personal to her, and not as the vicarious beneficiary of a breach of duty to another.

A different conclusion will involve us, and swiftly too, in a maze of contradictions.... In this case, the rights that are said to have been violated, the interests said to have been invaded, are not even of the same order. The man was not injured in his person nor even put in danger. The purpose of the act, as well as its effect, was to make his person safe. If there was a wrong to him at all, which may very well be doubted[,] it was a wrong to a property interest only, the safety of his package. Out of this wrong to property, which threatened injury to nothing else, there has passed, we are told, to the plaintiff by derivation or succession a right of action for the invasion of an interest of another order, the right to bodily security. The diversity of interests emphasizes the futility of the effort to build the plaintiff's right upon the basis of a wrong to someone else....

.... What the plaintiff must show is "a wrong" to herself; *i.e.*, a violation of her own right, and not merely a wrong to someone else, nor conduct "wrongful" because unsocial, but not "a wrong" to anyone.... The risk reasonably to be perceived defines the duty to be obeyed and risk imports relation; it is risk to another or to others within the range of apprehension.... This does not mean, of course, that one who launches a destructive force is always relieved of liability, if the force, though known to be destructive, pursues an unexpected path. "It was not necessary that the defendant should have had notice of the particular method in which an accident would occur, if the possibility of an accident was clear to the ordinarily prudent eye." .... Some acts, such as shooting are so imminently dangerous to anyone who may come within reach of the missile however unexpectedly, as to impose a duty of prevision not far from that of an insurer.... The range of reasonable apprehension is at times a question for the court, and at times, if varying inferences are possible, a question for the jury. Here, by concession, there was nothing in the situation to suggest to the most cautious mind that the parcel wrapped in newspaper would spread wreckage through the station. If the guard had thrown it down knowingly and willfully, he would not have threatened the plaintiff's safety, so far as appearances could warn him. His conduct would not have involved, even then, an unreasonable probability of invasion of her bodily security. Liability can be no greater where the act is inadvertent.

Negligence, like risk, is thus a term of relation. Negligence in the abstract, apart from things related, is surely not a tort, if indeed it is understandable at all....

The law of causation, remote or proximate, is thus foreign to the case before us. The question of liability is always anterior to the question of the measure of the consequences that go with liability. If there is no tort to be redressed, there is no occasion to consider what damage might be recovered if there were a finding of a tort....

The judgment of the Appellate Division and that of the Trial Term should be reversed, and the complaint dismissed, with costs in all courts.

ANDREWS, J. (dissenting).

William S. Andrews

. . . . The result we shall reach depends upon our theory as to the nature of negligence. Is it a relative concept — the breach of some duty owing to a particular person or to particular persons? Or, where there is an act which unreasonably threatens the safety of others, is the doer liable for all its proximate consequences, even where they result in injury to one who would generally be thought to be outside the radius of danger? This is not a mere dispute as to words. We might not believe that to the average mind the dropping of the bundle would seem to involve the probability of harm to the plaintiff standing many feet away whatever might be the case as to the owner or to one so near as to be likely to be struck by its fall. If, however, we adopt the second hypothesis, we have to inquire only as to the relation between cause and effect. We deal in terms of proximate cause, not of negligence.

. . . .

But we are told that "there is no negligence unless there is in the particular case a legal duty to take care, and this duty must be one which is owed to the plaintiff himself and not merely to others." Salmond, Torts (6th Ed.) 24. This I think too narrow a conception. Where there is the unreasonable act, and some right that may be affected[,] there is negligence whether damage does or does not result. That is immaterial. Should we drive down Broadway at a reckless speed, we are negligent whether we strike an approaching car or miss it by an inch. The act itself is wrongful. It is a wrong not only to those who happen to be within the radius of danger, but to all who might have been there — a wrong to the public at large. Such is the language of the street. . . .

Due care is a duty imposed on each one of us to protect society from unnecessary danger, not to protect A, B, or C alone.

It may well be that there is no such thing as negligence in the abstract. "Proof of negligence in the air, so to speak, will not do." In an empty world negligence would not exist. It does involve a relationship between man and his fellows, but not merely a relationship between man and those whom he might reasonably expect his act would injure; rather, a relationship between him and those whom he does in fact injure. . . .

The proposition is this: Every one owes to the world at large the duty of refraining from those acts that may unreasonably threaten the safety of others. Such an act occurs. Not only is he wronged to whom harm might reasonably be expected to result, but he also who is in fact injured, even if he be outside what would generally be thought the danger zone. There needs be duty due to the one complaining, but this is not a duty to a particular individual because as to him harm might be expected. Harm to someone being the natural result of the act, not only that one alone, but all those in fact injured may complain. We have never, I think, held otherwise. . . . Unreasonable risk being taken, its consequences are not confined to those who might probably be hurt.

. . . . An overturned lantern may burn all Chicago. We may follow the fire from the shed to the last building. We rightly say the fire started by the lantern caused its destruction.

A cause, but not the proximate cause. What we do mean by the word "proximate" is that, because of convenience, of public policy, of a rough sense of justice, the law arbitrarily declines to trace a series of events beyond a certain point. This is not logic. It is practical politics....

Take the illustration given in an unpublished manuscript by a distinguished and helpful writer on the law of torts. A chauffeur negligently collides with another car which is filled with dynamite, although he could not know it. An explosion follows. A, walking on the sidewalk nearby, is killed. B, sitting in a window of a building opposite, is cut by flying glass. C, likewise sitting in a window a block away, is similarly injured. And a further illustration: A nursemaid, ten blocks away, startled by the noise, involuntarily drops a baby from her arms to the walk. We are told that C may not recover while A may. As to B it is a question for court or jury. We will agree that the baby might not. Because, we are again told, the chauffeur had no reason to believe his conduct involved any risk of injuring either C or the baby. As to them he was not negligent.

But the chauffeur, being negligent in risking the collision, his belief that the scope of the harm he might do would be limited is immaterial. His act unreasonably jeopardized the safety of anyone who might be affected by it. C's injury and that of the baby were directly traceable to the collision. Without that, the injury would not have happened. C had the right to sit in his office, secure from such dangers. The baby was entitled to use the sidewalk with reasonable safety.

The true theory is, it seems to me, that the injury to C, if in truth he is to be denied recovery, and the injury to the baby, is that their several injuries were not the proximate result of the negligence. And here not what the chauffeur had reason to believe would be the result of his conduct, but what the prudent would foresee, may have a bearing—may have some bearing, for the problem of proximate cause is not to be solved by any one consideration. It is all a question of expediency. There are no fixed rules to govern our judgment. There are simply matters of which we may take account.... There is in truth little to guide us other than common sense.

There are some hints that may help us. The proximate cause, involved as it may be with many other causes, must be, at the least, something without which the event would not happen. The court must ask itself whether there was a natural and continuous sequence between cause and effect. Was the one a substantial factor in producing the other? Was there a direct connection between them, without too many intervening causes? Is the effect of cause on result not too attenuated? Is the cause likely, in the usual judgment of mankind, to produce the result? Or, by the exercise of prudent foresight, could the result be foreseen? Is the result too remote from the cause, and here we consider remoteness in time and space.... Clearly we must so consider, for the greater the distance either in time or space, the more surely do other causes intervene to affect the result. When a lantern is overturned, the firing of a shed is a fairly direct consequence. Many things contribute to the spread of the conflagration—the force of the wind, the direction and width of streets, the character of intervening structures, other factors. We draw an uncertain and wavering line, but draw it we must as best we can.

Once again, it is all a question of fair judgment, always keeping in mind the fact that we endeavor to make a rule in each case that will be practical and in keeping with the general understanding of mankind.

.... We trace the consequences, not indefinitely, but to a certain point. And to aid us in fixing that point we ask what might ordinarily be expected to follow the fire or the explosion.

This last suggestion is the factor which must determine the case before us. The act upon which defendant's liability rests is knocking an apparently harmless package onto the platform. The act was negligent. For its proximate consequences the defendant is liable. If its contents were broken, to the owner; if it fell upon and crushed a passenger's foot, then to him; if it exploded and injured one in the immediate vicinity, to him also as to A in the illustration....

Under these circumstances I cannot say as a matter of law that the plaintiff's injuries were not the proximate result of the negligence....

The judgment appealed from should be affirmed, with costs.

POUND, LEHMAN and KELLOGG, JJ., concur with CARDOZO, C.J.

ANDREWS, J., dissents in opinion in which CRANE and O'BRIEN, JJ., concur.

Judgment reversed, etc.

Note

1. **Palsgraf *Today*.** The debate underlying the differing approaches of Cardozo and Andrews to the issue of negligence continues today. Courts and scholars still dispute, often in passionate terms, whether one owes a duty of care to the world in general (as Judge Andrews contended) or only to those foreseeably endangered (as Chief Judge Cardozo said). These questions were a focal point of discussions surrounding the Third Restatement. After vigorous debate, the American Law Institute voted to endorse a position that sides with Judge Andrews in dealing with the issue as one of causation, rather than duty, but which endorses Chief Judge Cardozo's result. Illustration 9 to § 29 of the Third Restatement describes a fact situation identical to that of *Palsgraf* and concludes that, as a matter of law, the harm to the victim was not within the scope of the defendant's liability for negligence. The commentary goes on to observe:

> Generally, application of the risk standard should avoid much of the need for consideration of unforeseeable plaintiffs.... In those cases in which the plaintiff was, because of time or geography, truly beyond being subject to harm of the type risked by the tortious conduct, but the plaintiff somehow suffers such harm, the defendant is not liable to that plaintiff for the harm.

Restatement, Third, of Torts: Liab. for Physical & Emotional Harm § 29 cmt. n (2010).

There is support in recent cases for Chief Judge Cardozo's "duty" approach. In Mellon Mortgage Co. v. Holder, 5 S.W.3d 654 (Tex. 1999), a woman was stopped by a police officer for an alleged traffic violation in the middle of the night. The officer took the woman's insurance and identification cards and told her to follow his squad car. The woman followed the officer for several blocks to a parking garage owned by Mellon. Once inside the garage, the officer sexually assaulted the woman in his squad car. The woman then sued Mellon for negligence, arguing that the company had provided inadequate security at the garage. After a detailed review of the opinions in *Palsgraf*, Justice Greg Abbott wrote:

> Certainly, Mellon expected that its employees would use the garage, often at times when it would be relatively vacant and thus more dangerous. It is not unreasonable to conclude that Mellon could foresee that an employee or some other person who frequents the garage could be the victim of a violent crime in the garage. To protect these garage users, Mellon provided armed security patrols weekdays from 5:45 a.m. to 11:30 p.m., in addition to random patrols by off-duty police officers during business hours. Holder [the injured woman], however, was not a member of this class nor any other that Mellon could have reasonably foreseen would be the victim of a criminal act in its garage.
>
> Unlike any foreseeable victim, Holder was pulled over in her car at 3:30 a.m. by a third party over whom Mellon had no control, and she was led from several blocks away to the actual crime scene. Not only did Mellon have no control over the criminal, Potter [the police officer], it had no knowledge of him nor any reason to know that he would pick the garage as the scene of his reprehensible crime. Moreover, Mellon had no knowledge of Holder nor any reason to believe that she, or a person similarly situated, could be subject to a crime on Mellon's property. It simply was not foreseeable, beyond a remote philosophic sense, that this tragic event would occur to Holder on Mellon's property. With relation to Mellon's allegedly wrongful act of not securing its garage at three in the morning, Holder was not so situated that injury to her might reasonably have been foreseen. She was, in short, beyond Mellon's reasonable apprehension.
>
> .... Holder's summary judgment evidence provides little more than "proof of negligence in the air." .... She provides no evidence of a foreseeable risk in relation to her.
>
> ....
>
> Accordingly, Mellon owed no legal duty to Holder. To the extent that Mellon's conduct may have created a risk of harm, it did not breach a duty to Holder because she was not so situated with relation to the wrongful act such that her injury might have been foreseen.

Similarly, in Demelus v. King Motor Co. of Fort Lauderdale, 24 So. 3d 759 (Fla. Dist. Ct. App. 2009), the court held that a car dealership from which a car was stolen by gang members did not create a foreseeable risk of third-party criminal conduct and therefore owed no duty to lessen the risks of harm to a motorist who was struck and injured by the stolen vehicle.

See also Satterfield v. Breeding Insulation Co., 266 S.W.3d 347 (Tenn. 2008) (holding that an employer owed a duty of care to protect an employee's child from exposure to asbestos fibers because it was foreseeable that the employee would wear contaminated clothes home from work, thereby repeatedly exposing the employee's daughter to asbestos fibers over an extended period of time); Kesner v. Super. Ct., 384 P.3d 283, 305 (Cal. 2016) (similar); Waters v. New York City Hous. Auth., 505 N.E.2d 922 (N.Y. 1987) (owner of an occupied building who had not kept the security system in good repair could not be held liable in tort to a crime victim solely because the building was used as a place to complete a crime that began on a public street; neither the victim nor the crime were connected with the owner's building and the victim was not within zone of foreseeable harm).

Wisconsin regularly follows Judge Andrews' approach. *See* Tesar v. Anderson, 789 N.W.2d 351, 356 (Wis. App. 2010) (holding that a woman had "a duty to the world at large to use ordinary care in operating her motor vehicle"). Georgia has taken precisely the opposite position. See Dept. of Labor v. McConnell, 828 S.E.2d 352, 358 (Ga. 2019) (rejecting "a general legal duty 'to all the world not to subject [others] to an unreasonable risk of harm'").

B. The Negligence Balancing Test

Since, as *Palsgraf* suggests, foreseeability of harm is a critical consideration in the negligence calculus, the question arises as to how foreseeable harm must be before liability will attach. The following cases explore this question and suggest that the answer lies in a balancing test.

Nussbaum v. Lacopo

Court of Appeals of New York
265 N.E.2d 762 (N.Y. 1970)

BURKE, Judge.

Plaintiff's home is situated on land abutting the thirteenth hole of the defendant country club. Between plaintiff's patio and the thirteenth fairway are approximately *20 to 30 feet of rough*, and located in that golfer's no man's land is a natural barrier of *45- to 60-foot-high trees*. Although plaintiff's real property line runs parallel to the thirteenth fairway, the direct and proper line of flight from the tee to the green was at a substantial angle . . . far to the right of the plaintiff's property line. . . .

On June 30, 1963, defendant Lacopo, a trespasser on the golf course, struck a ball from the thirteenth tee. *At that time the rough was dense and the trees were in full foliage*. The shot, a high, bad one, "hooked" and crossed over into the area of plaintiff's patio and there allegedly hit the plaintiff. Lacopo did not see plaintiff and did not shout the traditional golfer's warning: "Fore!"

....

Plaintiff, in his complaint, ... argued that defendant failed to give a timely warning. That duty, which extends to other players ..., did not extend to plaintiff. The duty is imposed to prevent accidents, and the relationship between the failure to warn and plaintiff's injuries is tenuous at best. It rests on the improbable assumption that plaintiff would have responded to it, even though no ball had ever struck his house. Living so close to a golf course, plaintiff would necessarily hear numerous warning shouts each day. As the warning would ordinarily be directed to other golfers, plaintiff could be expected to ignore them. We will not permit the submission of this case to the jury on the remote possibility that plaintiff could have recognized and acted upon any warning given by the golfer at this time.

... [A] warning is only required in favor of those who are "in such a position" that danger to them is reasonably anticipated.

The admission that this was a "bad shot" is not sufficient to warrant submission to a jury. Plaintiff made no effort to show that defendant failed to use due care in striking the ball. Pursuant to our rules of practice ..., plaintiff took an examination before trial of defendant. Not a single question was directed at the manner in which defendant swung. Moreover, two witnesses, who observed the shot, were available to plaintiff. Thus plaintiff could have shown, for example, that defendant aimed so inaccurately as to unreasonably increase the risk of harm.... [W]e will not permit an inference of negligence to be drawn merely from the fact that this shot "hooked" sharply.

... [E]ven the best professional golfers cannot avoid an occasional "hook" or "slice." ....

One last comment on the lack of foreseeability is necessary.... The mere fact that a person may have been careless in the performance of an act does not necessarily result in actionable negligence. It is only required that the care be commensurate with the risk and danger. The plaintiff failed to show that the act of this player as to him had possibilities of danger so many and apparent as to entitle him to be protected against the doing of it. His burden of proof required that the act testified to, which he asserts constituted negligence, was not merely possible, but probable. Here, only an extraordinarily misdirected shot attaining great height could possibly drop on plaintiff's property because of the height and density of the protective barrier. Against this kind of unlikely misfortune, the law does not confer protection. Looking back from the alleged injury to the event, we consider it highly exceptional that a player's conduct would have brought about harm.

.... Lack of due care is not demonstrated when the undisputed physical evidence proves that it could not have been reasonably anticipated that the harm complained of would result from the natural and probable consequences of the act claimed to be negligent.

. . . [T]he dismissal of the complaint as against both defendants at the close of the plaintiff's case is well founded.

Accordingly, the order of the Appellate Division should be affirmed.

[The dissenting opinion of BERGEN, J., in which BREITEL and GIBSON, J.J., concurred, has been omitted.]

Note

1. ***Improbable Occurrences.*** In Koch v. Southwestern Elec. Power Co., 544 F.3d 906 (8th Cir. 2008), the court wrote that "[i]t is not negligent . . . to 'fail . . . to anticipate events occurring only under unusual circumstances.'" The court held that the defendant was not liable to electrocuted workers, where a power line was twenty-five feet above a field and it was not shown that the defendant was aware that intact tents might be raised up in proximity to the power line.

In Rein v. Benchmark Const. Co., 865 So. 2d 1134 (Miss. 2004), a case where a nursing home patient died when fire ants invaded her room, the court affirmed a grant of summary judgment to a contractor (Benchmark), writing:

> Benchmark may have reasonably foreseen an insect infestation as a result of improper construction techniques and poor planning of the drainage system. However, Benchmark could not have reasonably foreseen that Mrs. Rein would be attacked and killed by fire ants two years after construction. . . .

See also Bain v. Gillespie, 357 N.W.2d 47, 49 (Iowa App. 1984) ("The law's standard is one of reasonable foresight, not prophetic vision"; because injury to novelty store owners' business interests was not a reasonably foreseeable result of a college basketball referee's call during a game, which eliminated the local team from the conference championship, the referee owed no duty to the store owners).

Gulf Refining Co. v. Williams

Supreme Court of Mississippi
185 So. 234 (Miss. 1938)

GRIFFITH, Justice.

Appellants are the distributors of petroleum products. . . . Shortly before the injury here complained of, appellants . . . sold and delivered to a planter in that vicinity a drum of gasoline for use in farm tractors. Appellee was the planter's employee and was engaged in operating a tractor. The drum of gasoline had been taken to the field, but no attempt had been made to use it, until, for the first time since its delivery, appellee undertook to remove the bunghole cap from the drum in order to replenish the fuel in the tractor, whereupon there was a sudden outburst of fire, caused, as the jury was justified in concluding . . . , by a spark which was produced by the condition of unrepair in the threads of the bung cap. . . .

Appellee was severely burned by the sudden fire, and recovered judgment. . . .

The chief argument of appellants is that the proof shows that an explosion or fire in drawing gasoline from a drum when, or on account of, taking off the bung cap is an unusual, extraordinary, and improbable occurrence, so much so that some of the witnesses say that no such happening had ever before been heard of by them; and that, therefore, appellant cannot be held liable as for a failure to anticipate the danger of any such improbable occurrence. . . .

The general language of the courts in stating the rule of the law of negligence in regard to the liability of the actor as to harmful results which are foreseeable is that he will be liable for all such harm as a reasonably prudent person would or should have anticipated as the natural and probable consequences of his act. . . .

This general language has led to the occasional misunderstanding as to what may be termed the degree of probability which is meant by these expressions, as used in the law of negligence; and it is sometimes supposed and argued that unless such a foreseeable consequence is one which is more likely to happen than not to happen there can be no liability. But these references to probability are in a different sense as compared with what is meant in the procedural law when there is under inquiry whether a certain event happened, or probably happened, in the past.

. . . .

When the inquiry is upon an issue whether a certain alleged fact existed or happened in the past, it is not sufficient to prove only or no more than a possibility, however substantial the possibility may be, so long as it is only a possibility. There the proof must establish the fact as a probability, using that word in its ordinary and common acceptation. . . . But when the inquiry is one of foreseeability, is as regards a thing that may happen in the future, and to which the law of negligence holds a party to anticipation as a measure of duty, that inquiry is not whether the thing is to be foreseen or anticipated as one which will probably happen, . . . but whether it is likely to happen, even though the likelihood may not be sufficient to amount to a comparative probability.

It is true . . . that remote possibilities are not within the rules of negligence as respects foreseeability. As said in Illinois Central Railroad Co. v. Bloodworth, [145 So. 333 (Miss. 1933)], these rules do not demand "that a person should prevision or anticipate an unusual, improbable, or extraordinary occurrence, though such happening is within the range of possibilities. . . ." On the other hand, in order to bring the rule of liability into operation, it is not necessary that the chances that a damage will result shall be greater than the chances that no damage will occur. The test as respects foreseeability is not the balance of probabilities, but the existence . . . of some real likelihood of some damage and the likelihood is of such appreciable weight and moment as to induce, or which reasonably should induce, action to avoid it on the part of a person of a reasonably prudent mind. . . .

The vendor of an inherently dangerous commodity, such as gasoline, is under duty to use cautious care to distribute the same in reasonably safe containers, the degree of care thereinabout to be commensurate with the danger, and the obligation of this duty is not dependent upon contractual relations, but extends to all who may lawfully use, or be in the vicinity of, the container. . . .

The drum, or gasoline container, involved herein was of standard material, construction and manufacture, and of the kind in general use; and had it been in reasonably good repair there would, of course, be no liability. But the proof is that the drum had been in use nine years; that the threads in the bung plug or bung cap were broken, bent and jagged; that this condition had been brought about by repeated hammering on the bung cap during the course of its use—a condition which had attracted the attention of one of appellants' employees before the container was sent out on this occasion. There is no adequate proof to show that appellee had equal knowledge or appreciation of the significance of this fact, or any knowledge which was sufficient to put the use at his risk as by the so-called assumption thereof, as contended for by appellants—leaving aside whether, if the facts were otherwise, there would be assumption of risk, rather than contributory negligence. . . . The proof is sufficient to show that a person of ordinary prudence, and mindful of the duty of cautious care with which appellants were charged, should have known of the condition aforesaid and should reasonably have anticipated, as a likelihood of weight and moment, that a sudden fire or explosion would be caused by the stated condition of unrepair; and hence appellants are liable for the injury to appellee which resulted.

. . . .

Affirmed.

Note

1. ***Other Precedent.*** *See also* Goodwin v. Yeakle's Sports Bar and Grill, Inc., 62 N.E.3d 384, 392 (Ind. 2016) ("[F]or purposes of determining whether an act is foreseeable in the context of duty we assess 'whether there is some probability or likelihood of harm that is serious enough to induce a reasonable person to take precautions to avoid it.'").

United States v. Carroll Towing Co.

United States Court of Appeals for the Second Circuit
159 F.2d 169 (2d Cir. 1947)

[After the defendant's servants negligently shifted its mooring lines, libellant's barge broke adrift, collided with another vessel, and sank. The trial court, pursuant to a comparative negligence rule in admiralty, reduced the amount of damages recoverable by the libellant, finding that it was negligent in not having a custodian on board who could have called for help and possibly have avoided the sinking once the damage from the collision became apparent. As to the propriety of this reduction in damages:]

L. HAND, Circuit Judge.

Learned Hand

... [T]here is no general rule to determine when the absence of a bargee or other attendant will make the owner of the barge liable for injuries to other vessels if she breaks away from her moorings. However, in any cases where he would be so liable for injuries to others, obviously he must reduce his damages proportionately, if the injury is to his own barge. It becomes apparent why there can be no such general rule, when we consider the grounds for such a liability. Since there are occasions when every vessel will break from her moorings, and since, if she does, she becomes a menace to those about her, the owner's duty, as in other similar situations, to provide against resulting injuries is a function of three variables: (1) The probability that she will break away; (2) the gravity of the resulting injury, if she does; (3) the burden of adequate precautions. Possibly it serves to bring this notion into relief to state it in algebraic terms: if the probability be called P; the injury, L; and the Burden, B; liability depends upon whether B is less than L multiplied by P: *i.e.*, whether $B < PL$. Applied to the situation at bar, the likelihood that a barge will break from her fasts and the damage she will do, vary with the place and time; for example, if a storm threatens, the danger is greater; so it is, if she is in a crowded harbor where moored barges are constantly being shifted about. On the other hand, the barge must not be the bargee's prison, even though he lives aboard; he must go ashore at times. We need not say whether, even in such crowded waters as New York Harbor a bargee must be aboard at night at all; it may be that the custom is otherwise. . . . We leave that question open; but we hold that it is not in all cases a sufficient answer to a bargee's absence without excuse, during working hours, that he has properly made fast his barge to a pier, when he leaves her. In the case at bar the bargee left at five o'clock in the afternoon of January 3rd, and the flotilla broke away at about two o'clock in the afternoon of the following day, twenty-one hours afterwards. The bargee had been away all the time, and we hold that his fabricated story was affirmative evidence that he had no excuse for his absence. At the *locus in quo*—especially during the short January days and in the full tide of war activity—barges were being constantly "drilled" in and out. Certainly it was not beyond reasonable expectation that, with the inevitable haste and bustle, the work might not be done with adequate care. In such circumstances we hold . . . that it was a fair requirement that the Conners Company should have a bargee aboard (unless he had some excuse for his absence), during the working hours of daylight.

. . . .

[The judgment was affirmed insofar as concerns the reduction in damages.]

Notes

1. ***Negligence as a Question of Fact.*** Whether a defendant (or plaintiff) was negligent is a question of fact. This means that if it is unclear whether someone acted negligently, the factfinder decides the matter. Although neither the trial judge (in a case tried to a jury) nor an appellate court can overrule a factfinder's determination about negligence, it may be so clear from the record that the factfinder's decision was wrong that a judge will rule that the party was, or was not, negligent "as a matter of law." The standard for making this kind of decision is whether reasonable persons can differ about whether someone was negligent. If they cannot—if, for instance, any reasonable factfinder would have to conclude from the evidence that the defendant was negligent—a finding of fact going the other way will be reversed.

To illustrate, consider Delao v. Carlson, 589 S.W.2d 525 (Texas Civ. App. 1979), a wrongful-death action against the driver of a car that had struck and killed the plaintiffs' son at night. Plaintiffs argued that the defendant had acted negligently by having his headlights on low beam at the time of the accident; reasonable care, they urged, required the use of high beams. The trial judge, acting as finder of fact in a non-jury proceeding, ruled that the defendant was not negligent. Holding that the question whether a reasonable driver would have used high beams at the time was one for the factfinder, the Court of Civil Appeals affirmed: not because it agreed on the merits with the factfinder's decision, but because questions of fact are for the factfinder, not for appellate courts. If by contrast, the defendant had been driving at night with no headlights, and if the factfinder had found this behavior not negligent, the appellate court would surely have reversed. Absent special circumstances, reasonable factfinders cannot find it reasonable to drive at night without headlights.

Because the question of negligence is for the factfinder, if reasonable persons can differ, it is a rare case in which a client can be assured in advance that a proposed course of conduct will not someday be found negligent if something goes wrong. Suppose, for instance, that the operator of a fast-food store asks a lawyer whether certain proposed measures to protect customers against crime will insulate the store from liability if a customer is injured or killed during a robbery. The lawyer considers the proposed measures and concludes that they are "reasonable." Should the lawyer advise the client that implementation of these measures will ensure that the client will not be liable? Certainly not. Although the lawyer considers those measures reasonable, a factfinder may disagree. Only if the lawyer can conclude that no reasonable person could find the proposed precautions inadequate—a standard very hard to satisfy—can the requested assurance be given.

See generally Restatement, Third, of Torts: Liab. for Physical & Emotional Harm § 8 (2010) (discussing the roles of judge and jury).

2. ***Other Formulations of the Test.*** The B < LP balancing test articulated by Judge Hand in *Carroll Towing* has been frequently quoted and widely influential. Nonetheless it is only one of many ways in which the negligence test may be articulated. *See* Restatement, Second, Torts § 291. Indeed, the negligence inquiry was defined in somewhat different terms by Judge Hand in Conway v. O'Brien, 111 F.2d 611, 612 (2d Cir. 1940):

> The degree of care demanded of a person by an occasion is the resultant of three factors: the likelihood that his conduct will injure others, taken with the seriousness of the injury if it happens, and balanced against the interest which he must sacrifice to avoid the risk.

There, he candidly recognized:

> All these [factors] are practically not susceptible of any quantitative estimate, and the second two are not so even theoretically. For this reason a solution always involves some preference, or choice between incommensurables, and it is consigned to a jury because their decision is thought most likely to accord with commonly accepted standards, real or fancied.

See also U.S. Fid. & Guar. Co. v. Jadranska Slobodna Plovidba, 683 F.2d 1022, 1026 (7th Cir. 1982) (observing that B, P, and L have never been precisely quantified in any lawsuit).

Negligence as an Economic Concept

Alan Gunn

The question whether someone has taken enough safety precautions can be thought of as raising issues of economics. Resources are scarce, so it would be wasteful either to devote too many of those resources to accident prevention or to devote too little to accident prevention. To take a simple example, injuries from automobile accidents could be reduced considerably if all drivers were prevented from exceeding fifteen miles an hour (perhaps by mandating that cars be designed so that they could not exceed that speed). Outlawing cars entirely would probably save thousands of lives each year. Yet these proposals are fantastic; the benefits people get—directly and indirectly—from driving are so great that few would be willing to give them up, even to save lives.

Allocation of Accident-Prevention Resources. Judge Learned Hand's "formula" in the *Carroll Towing* opinion has been widely used by economic analysts of the legal system as a starting point for defining "negligence" in economic terms. Judge Hand himself seems to have intended the formula only as a guide to the considerations which, in particular cases, should be taken into account in determining negligence. Even looked at in that way, the formula invites re-expression in economic terms. It suggests, for example, that if the chance of an accident is high, it makes more sense to devote resources to safety than if the chance of an accident is low, other things being equal. (For instance, a city planning to add one traffic light would be better advised to put it at an intersection where accidents have been common than at one at which accidents are rare.) And the formula teaches that, other things being equal, resources spent to prevent accidents that threaten serious injury are better spent than if they had gone to reduce minor scrapes; this is why the law insists that drivers keep to the right on two-way streets, while not bothering to make pedestrians on sidewalks stay in lanes. Being bumped by a pedestrian is likely to produce a much smaller "L" than being hit by a car. Furthermore, and perhaps less obviously, the formula indicates that some measures to reduce the costs of accidents are not worth taking, because the benefits of added safety would amount to less than the costs. Whenever a car is started there is an increased risk that someone will be injured, even if the car is driven very carefully (for instance, a pedestrian may faint and fall in front of the car). But it is not negligent to drive; the costs of not driving exceed the very small benefit in safety. These are economic arguments.

Marginal Utility. Strictly speaking, the Learned Hand formula must be expressed in marginal terms to give an economically accurate guide to how much in the way of safety precautions is enough. Suppose, for example, that one knows that spending an additional $1000 on safety would reduce losses from accidents by $1500. At first glance, it might seem that the actor should spend the $1000, and if the only choice is between spending $1000 and spending nothing, that is indeed the right answer. But suppose that spending $900 would reduce losses by $1300, and that each additional dollar spent on safety would reduce losses by only fifty cents. In that case, one should not spend more than $900; each additional dollar saves less than a dollar in losses. Would it be even better to spend *less* than $900? It depends. Ideally, one should decide how much to spend by asking whether an additional dollar will produce more than an additional dollar in safety benefits. As long as the answer is "yes," it is wise to spend the additional dollar.

Deliberate Decisions Versus Inadvertent Mistakes. In an article that has greatly clarified the place of negligence in the law of torts, Mark Grady has shown that approaching negligence questions by using the Learned Hand formula works much better in some kinds of cases than in others; Mark F. Grady, *Why Are People Negligent? Technology, Nondurable Precautions, and the Medical Malpractice Explosion*, 82 Nw. U. L. Rev. 293 (1988); *see also* Mark F. Grady, *Better Medicine Causes More Lawsuits, and New Administrative Courts Will Not Solve the Problem*, 86 Nw. U. L. Rev. 1068 (1992). In some cases — *Carroll Towing*, for example — someone actually made a decision that would affect safety. Whether that decision was "reasonable" determines whether the actor was negligent, and the Learned Hand formula can help to determine reasonableness. But in many negligence cases, the lapse in question consists not of a bad decision but rather of a momentary, inadvertent error, as when a normally careful driver fails to see a stop sign, or when a doctor accidentally overlooks a symptom. In cases like these, the Learned Hand formula does not help us determine whether the actor has been negligent. "Negligence" is in one sense obvious, as the actor has plainly made a mistake. As Grady points out, "negligence law does not forgive inadvertence, even reasonable amounts of it"; 82 Nw. U. L. Rev. at 295. Yet, according to the Learned Hand formula, the actor has not been "negligent" at all—no complex activity can be made error-free, and it is not "unreasonable" to drive, or to perform medical procedures, even if the actor knows that mistakes will occur.[1]

With respect to negligence of the "inadvertent lapse" variety, it may be more accurate to describe the law as imposing a sort of strict liability than to insist that liability is assigned according to "fault." Consider how the law of traffic accidents would differ in practice from the way it works now if, instead of saying that negligent drivers are liable for the harms they cause, the law said that drivers are strictly liable for abnormally dangerous driving (such as running stop signs, entering the wrong lane, failing to avoid pedestrians, and so on). One case in which it *would* make a difference is Cohen v. Petty, 65 F.2d 820 (D.C. Cir. 1933), *supra* at p. 23. Would holding the defendant in that case liable be any more unjust than holding someone with an excellent driving record liable for accidentally failing to notice a pedestrian stepping onto the road?

Negligence, Rationality, and the Limits of Law-and-Economics. One reason for examining Grady's distinction between the two very different kinds of conduct the law treats as "negligent" is that the distinction explains why a central prediction of the law-and-economics school fails to correspond to everyday observation. According to traditional law-and-economics analysis, negligence should be rare in a world in which those who are negligent must pay for their mistakes. If cost-justified (according to the Learned Hand formula) precautions are not taken and harm ensues, the actor will pay for the harm, which by definition makes it cheaper to take the precautions. Therefore, the argument goes, only those who are irrational will fail to take cost-justified precautions, and those people will soon be bankrupted by the tort system. In fact, everyday observation shows that negligence is rampant. The explanation may be that much of the "negligence" which one can observe on the highway, in the hospital, or in the opinions in this casebook, is negligence of the "inadvertent lapse" variety, which occurs not because people have made bad cost-benefit calculations, but because of inherent human limitations.[2] This kind of

1. If the actor knows that mistakes are very likely, engaging in the activity may be unreasonable, as when someone subject to seizures decides to drive a car.

2. This is not to say that "Learned Hand negligence" is never seen on the highway. Someone who decides to drive at 80 in a 35 mile per hour zone has probably made a conscious but unreasonable

negligence is not described by the Learned Hand formula, and is therefore beyond the scope of much traditional law-and-economics analysis. *See* Mark F. Grady, *Why Are People Negligent*, 82 Nw. U. L. Rev. at 294.

Chicago, B & Q. R.R. Co. v. Krayenbuhl

Supreme Court of Nebraska
91 N.W. 880 (Neb. 1902)

ALBERT, C.

This action was brought on behalf of Leo Krayenbuhl, . . . by his next friend, against the Chicago, Burlington & Quincy Railroad Company to recover for personal injuries received by the plaintiff while playing on a turntable belonging to the defendant.

. . . .

[Leo was four years old. The turntable was located between two branches of the defendant's line, 1600 feet from a passenger depot and 70 feet from the common footpath used by the general public and members of Leo's family. There was evidence that defendant's employees frequently disregarded the company's rules that the turntable was to be locked when not in use and that one of the staples on the turntable was so loose that it could be unfastened without difficulty. On the day of the accident, the turntable was found unlocked and unguarded, and when set in motion by Leo's playmates, severed his foot at thc ankle when it was caught between the rails. A verdict at trial was rendered in the child's favor.]

. . . . [W]here the owner of a dangerous premises knows, or has good reason to believe, that children so young as to be ignorant of the danger will resort to such premises[,] he is bound to take such precautions to keep them from such premises, or to protect them from injuries likely to result from the dangerous condition of the premises, while there, as a man of ordinary care and prudence, under like circumstances, would take. At first sight, it would seem that the principle, thus stated, is too broad, and that its application would impose unreasonable burdens on owners, and intolerable restrictions on the use and enjoyment of property. But it must be kept in mind that it requires nothing of the owner that a man of ordinary care and prudence would not do of his own volition, under like circumstances. . . .

It is true, as said in Loomis v. Terry, 17 Wend. 496, 31 Am. Dec. 306, "the business of life must go forward"; the means by which it is carried forward cannot be rendered absolutely safe. Ordinarily, it can be best carried forward by the unrestricted use of private property by the owner; therefore the law favors such use to the fullest extent consistent with the main purpose for which, from a social standpoint, such business is carried forward, namely, the public good. Hence, in order to determine

decision about how much to take in the way of safety precautions. This is a different kind of negligence from that of someone who overlooked a "school-crossing" sign and failed to slow down, but would have if the sign had been seen.

the extent to which such use may be enjoyed, its bearing on such main purpose must be taken into account, and a balance struck between its advantages and disadvantages. If, on the whole, such use defeats, rather than promotes, the main purpose, it should not be permitted.... [A] turntable is a dangerous contrivance, which facilitates railroading; the general benefits resulting from its use outweigh the occasional injuries inflicted by it; hence the public good demands its use. We may conceive of means by which it might be rendered absolutely safe, but such means would so interfere with its beneficial use that the danger to be anticipated would not justify their adoption; therefore the public good demands its use without them. But the danger incident to its use may be lessened by the use of a lock which would prevent children, attracted to it, from moving it; the interference with the proper use of the turntable occasioned by the use of such lock is so slight that it is outweighed by the danger to be anticipated from an omission to use it; therefore the public good, we think, demands the use of the lock....

Hence, in all cases of this kind in the determination of the question of negligence, regard must be had to the character and location of the premises, the purpose for which they are used, the probability of injury therefrom, the precautions necessary to prevent such injury, and the relations such precautions bear to the beneficial use of the premises. The nature of the precautions would depend on the particular facts in each case. In some cases a warning to the children or the parents might be sufficient; in others, more active measures might be required. But in every case they should be such as a man of ordinary care and prudence would observe under like circumstances....

[The judgment was reversed on other grounds and remanded for further proceedings.]

Notes

1. ***Utility of the Defendant's Conduct.*** How heavily the burden of taking precautions will weigh in the negligence calculus is often inextricably bound to an assessment of the goals the defendant seeks to advance. Stopping a car suddenly in traffic to avoid hitting a squirrel may be negligent, while an identical action taken to avoid hitting a child would not be. The Second Restatement said that the risk of harm from the act must be balanced against the "utility" of the actor's conduct. "Utility," in turn, depends upon the "social value" of the interest the actor is trying to advance, the chance that the action will in fact advance that interest, and other "factors." *See* Restatement, Second, of Torts §§ 291-293.

The Second Restatement's reference to the "social value" of the defendant's action must not be taken too broadly. A doctor driving to work in the morning must drive just as carefully as a slumlord on the way to evict widows and orphans, even though some would view the doctor's career as having more "social value" than the slumlord's. On the other hand, though, the driving of a doctor racing to the scene of a medical emergency would be evaluated quite differently than driving in other contexts.

In an effort to address the elusive role of "utility" in negligence analysis, the Third Restatement says:

> In those cases in which a plaintiff does allege negligence in the actor's decision to engage in an activity, the overall utility of the activity is a factor the court needs to consider. For more ordinary negligence claims, however, the utility of the activity is of minimal relevance, if any. Supplying electricity, for example, is of extraordinary value to the community. Even so, the transmission of electricity poses serious risks. If certain precautions can reduce those risks, it is the burden of those precautions, and not the value of the activity itself, that is of relevance in a negligence analysis.

Restatement, Third, of Torts: Liab. for Physical & Emotional Harm § 3 cmt. j (2010).

2. ***Alternatives.*** Whether a particular course of conduct is negligent may depend upon whether alternatives are available. In Adams v. Bullock, 125 N.E. 93 (N.Y. 1919), a young boy was shocked and burned when a long wire he was swinging struck an uninsulated power line above the defendant's trolley tracks. In concluding that the verdict for the plaintiff could not stand, Judge Cardozo wrote for the New York Court of Appeals:

> There is . . . a distinction not to be ignored between electric light and trolley wires. The distinction is that the former may be insulated. Chance of harm, though remote, may betoken negligence, if needless. Facility of protection may impose a duty to protect. With trolley wires, the case is different. Insulation is impossible. Guards here and there are of little value. To avert the possibility of this accident and others like it at one point or another on the route, the defendant must have abandoned the overhead system, and put the wires underground. Neither its power nor its duty to make the change is shown.

3. ***Advances in Technology.*** Because circumstances change and technology advances, conduct which at one point may have been considered reasonable may at another time be found to be unreasonable. In Davison v. Snohomish County, 270 P. 422 (Wash. 1928), plaintiffs sustained personal injuries and property damages when the car in which they were riding broke through allegedly insufficient guard rails on an elevated stretch of road. In reversing the jury's judgment in their favor, the court wrote:

> [M]unicipalities cannot be required to protect long stretches of roadway with railings or guards capable of preventing an automobile, moving at a rapid rate, from leaving the road. . . . "[To so hold] . . . would be to put a burden upon the public that it could not bear. . . ."

Forty years later the same court, in Bartlett v. Northern Pac. Ry. Co., 447 P.2d 735 (Wash. 1968), allowed a similar case to go to the jury. Noting that its earlier decision could no longer be regarded as authoritative on engineering issues and financial matters, the court held that the parties should have the opportunity to present evidence as to the "practicality (costwise and otherwise)" of installing guard rails to stop slow-moving vehicles.

C. The Reasonable-Person Standard

In General. The negligence formula, under which unreasonableness is determined by balancing the gravity and probability of harm against the burden of avoidance and the utility of the defendant's conduct, serves many purposes. It directs the attention of counsel to those factors which should be taken into account in evaluating a case or presenting an argument to the jury. It also guides trial and appellate court rulings on the evidence.

Phrasing the Test in Human Terms. Nevertheless, the law has frequently elected to articulate the same inquiry in anthropomorphic terms, asking simply whether the defendant acted as a reasonable, prudent person would have acted under the same or similar circumstances. For example, in Medlar v. Mohan, 409 S.E.2d 123 (Va. 1991), a negligence action arising from a collision at a very wet intersection, the court wrote that "the test is whether the driver used that degree of care which an ordinarily prudent person would have exercised, 'having regard to the duty of the driver to exercise increased caution in the face of the known and obvious dangerous condition' of the highway."

For purposes of jury instruction, the reasonable-person standard has a clear advantage over the negligence formula. In contrast to the abstract, almost cold and mathematical, nature of the latter, the reasonable-person standard invites lay jurors to address the matter of reasonableness in more familiar, human terms. To be sure, the issue is the same, regardless of which test is used. In either instance, the task is to determine whether the defendant's conduct posed an unacceptable risk of harm to the plaintiff. Presumably, the answer should be the same regardless of the test employed.

Four Ways of Establishing What a Reasonable Person Would Do. What a reasonable person would do may be established in any of four distinct ways.

(a) ***Factfinder Determination.*** First, the finder of fact, guided by applicable rules of law or appropriate instructions, focusing its attention on the circumstances of a single case, may determine on an *ad hoc* basis whether a particular defendant acted reasonably. Thus, the court or jury, within limits, defines the conduct of the reasonably prudent person. It is of course important for the factfinder to know what circumstances may be taken into account. For example, is the fact that the defendant is faced with an emergency, or is blind, aged, well-educated, or experienced relevant to the determination? These and similar questions are considered *infra* at pp. 280–330.

There are two difficulties with this facts-of-the-case approach to determining what is acceptable conduct. One is that by reason of being an after-the-fact determination, a prospective defendant is offered no advance warning of precisely what is expected. The other is that because such decisions are fact-specific and have no precedential force, juries can, and frequently do, arrive at inconsistent results in relatively similar cases. On the other hand, the flexibility of the case-by-case approach allows the decision maker to take into account numerous factual variables that might be ignored by a more rigid rule of law.

(b) ***Judge-Made Standards.*** The second way the standard of conduct of a reasonable person may be established is by judicial decision. *See* pp. 331–34, *infra*. Thus, when faced with a problem of a recurring nature, a court may state, as a matter of law, what conduct is required of a person confronted with those circumstances. The jury will be instructed that if it determines that the defendant failed to take the required steps, it must find that the defendant acted unreasonably and breached its duty of care to the plaintiff. The advance articulation of such a rule gives individuals clear notice of what conduct is expected and leads to consistency of results in similar cases. But as Justice Benjamin N. Cardozo wrote in Pokora v. Wabash Ry. Co., 292 U.S. 98 (1934), "[e]xtraordinary situations may not wisely or fairly be subjected to tests or regulations that are fitting for the commonplace." Thus, the use of this approach may be undesirable where the factors legitimately bearing upon the question of reasonableness are too numerous or variable to adequately be taken into account by a hard-and-fast rule.

(c) ***Legislatively Determined Standards.*** Third, sometimes the standard of conduct is defined by a legislative body through an appropriate enactment. *See* pp. 334–35, *infra*. Thus, where duly constituted representatives of the public expressly or implicitly declare that failure to take certain actions will give rise to civil liability, courts recognize such expressions as defining the applicable level of care. This approach not only lends itself to fair notice and uniformity of results, but allows the judiciary to express appropriate deference for the determinations of a co-equal branch of government.

(d) ***Judicially Declared Standards Based on Legislation.*** Finally, even if a legislative enactment does not expressly or implicitly establish a standard of care, a court, in the exercise of its inherent nomothetic powers, may define the standard of care with reference to that legislative enactment if the court finds that the legislation calls for appropriate behavior. *See* pp. 336–55, *infra*. Such a decision is in many respects similar to the second method of setting the standard of care, discussed above, since, in essence, the court is not required to adopt the standard, but is exercising its law-giving prerogative to do so. However, it differs from the second approach in that, among other things, it allows the court to draw upon the legislative history and vote underlying the enactment to support the reasonableness of its decision.

1. Jury Instructions on Reasonable Care

Formulation of Jury Instructions. If a jury is called upon to determine whether an actor was negligent in failing to exercise reasonable care, the judge will instruct the jury both about the applicable legal standards and which factors in the case may be taken into account. Thus, the instructions will cover both routine matters (such as the burden and standard of proof) and issues specifically raised by the evidence that are not part of every case (such as the fact that the actor was a child).

The jury instructions are normally drafted by the judge after the evidence in the case has been submitted, and read to the jury before the jury begins its deliberations. Some of the instructions will be drawn from pattern jury instructions books. See, for example, the Judicial Council of California Civil Jury Instructions (2022 ed.), which can be easily found on the web. Other instructions may be based on requests by the parties rooted in earlier judicial decisions. The instructions must correctly state the law of the jurisdiction. Otherwise, there will be grounds for appeal.

Challenges to Jury Instructions. An appeal arguing that the jury instructions were erroneous will almost inevitably fail if the relevant issue was not raised at the trial level. A party must assist the trial judge in correctly formulating the instructions by requesting a proper instruction on the relevant matter, or by objecting to an erroneous instruction. Otherwise, the alleged error is ordinarily not "preserved" for review on appeal. *See generally* Uriell v. Regents of University of California, 184 Cal. Rptr. 3d 79, 81–84 (Cal. App. 2015).

Relevant Factors. The following sections raise the issue of whether certain factors are relevant or irrelevant to the assessment of whether an actor exercised care. If a factor is relevant, it may also be necessary to consider whether the court should give a special instruction to the jury. In some situations, a factor is not merely relevant, but changes the standard of care, either by raising the standard of care or by absolving the actor of liability for negligence. The factors that will be discussed relate to: (a) good faith, (b) sudden emergency, (c) physical disabilities, (d) religious beliefs, (e) age, (f) mental deficiencies, (g) superior skills and knowledge, (h) professional credentials, and (i) race, gender, or ethnicity.

a. The Actor's Good Faith

Good Intentions Are Not Enough. An early case applying the reasonable person standard was Vaughan v. Menlove, 3 Bing. (N.C.) 467, 132 Eng. Rep. 490 (1837). There, the defendant constructed a hay rick in a location immediately adjacent to his neighbor's cottages. He was repeatedly warned by others that it might catch fire by spontaneous combustion, and thereby endanger the nearby buildings. Defendant replied that he would "chance it," and, predictably, the worst came to pass. In rejecting his argument that he should not be held liable for the destruction of the cottages if he had acted in good faith, "bona fide to the best of his judgment," Chief Justice Tindal wrote that to hold that liability for negligence was co-extensive with the judgment of each person would result in a standard "as variable as the length of the foot of each individual." "It is not enough that the defendant did the best he knew how." In other words, the reasonable person standard is intended to ensure some degree of predictability in the conduct of human affairs.

b. Sudden Emergencies

Bedor v. Johnson

Supreme Court of Colorado, En Banc
292 P.3d 924 (Colo. 2013)

Justice RICE delivered the Opinion of the Court.

. . . .

Bedor was driving eastbound outside of Telluride, Colorado . . . at about 7:00 a.m., when he the saw headlights of a westbound vehicle cross the center line. Bedor slowed down, but the westbound car, driven by Johnson, spun out of control and slid sideways into the front of Bedor's vehicle. Both Bedor and Johnson were injured in the accident. An investigation of the scene revealed that Johnson lost control of his vehicle when he hit an icy patch of snow on the road.

Bedor filed a negligence action against Johnson. The case proceeded to a jury trial. The investigating police officer testified that an ice patch regularly forms during the winter in the portion of the westbound lane in which Johnson was driving. Johnson acknowledged that he had previously experienced the ice patch in that area and "was aware of the possibility" that the ice might be present the morning of the accident. There was conflicting evidence at trial regarding whether Johnson was intoxicated, speeding, or both when he lost control and spun into Bedor's vehicle.

Johnson requested that the trial court instruct the jury on the sudden emergency doctrine. He argued that he did not cause the ice patch that led to the accident and that he acted reasonably in light of the sudden emergency the ice presented. Bedor's counsel objected, but the trial court overruled the objection and instructed the jury on the sudden emergency doctrine. The jury returned a verdict in Johnson's favor. It found that although Bedor indeed suffered injuries, damages, or losses on account of the accident, Johnson was not negligent. . . .

Bedor appealed the jury verdict to the court of appeals. He argued that the trial court abused its discretion when it instructed the jury on the sudden emergency doctrine and thereby prejudiced Bedor's case. The court of appeals affirmed the jury verdict. . . . It reasoned that the trial court properly issued the sudden emergency instruction because competent evidence at trial showed that Johnson was confronted with a sudden or unexpected occurrence — the ice patch — that was not of his own making. . . .

. . . . We now reverse the judgment of the court of appeals and abolish the sudden emergency doctrine. . . .

Although the pattern sudden emergency jury instruction given by the trial court correctly stated the law as it existed at the time of trial, see CJI–Civ. 4th 9:11, the trial court abused its discretion by instructing the jury on the sudden emergency doctrine because competent evidence did not support giving the instruction in this instance. *See* Young v. Clark, 814 P.2d 364, 366 (Colo. 1991).

CJI–Civ. 4th 9:11 states: "A person who, through no fault of his or her own, is placed in a sudden emergency, is not chargeable with negligence if the person exercises that degree of care that a reasonably careful person would have exercised under the same or similar circumstances."

The sudden emergency doctrine recognizes "that a person confronted with sudden or unexpected circumstances calling for immediate attention is not expected to exercise the judgment of one acting under normal conditions." . . . . A trial court has a duty to instruct the jury on sudden emergency if a party requests the instruction and competent evidence supports that request. . . . "Competent evidence" in this context is relevant evidence that a reasonable mind might accept as adequate to support the conclusion that there was a sudden emergency and that the party requesting the instruction did not cause the emergency. . . .

. . . [W]e recently determined in Kendrick [v. Pippin, 252 P.3d 1052 (Colo.2011)] that competent evidence did not support the trial court's decision to tender the instruction when the defendant put her car in four wheel drive in anticipation of wintery driving conditions. . . . Although the defendant took deliberate action to avoid a collision by applying her brakes and making an illegal right turn after hitting a slippery patch of road, we held that the trial court abused its discretion by giving the sudden emergency instruction because competent evidence did not show that the defendant was confronted with a "sudden or unexpected occurrence" when trial testimony showed that the defendant "anticipated that the roads and intersections would likely be icy that morning." . . . .

The evidence here showed that Johnson lost control of his vehicle upon encountering the snow patch. A loss of control does not constitute a deliberate response to a sudden emergency; rather, it indicates a complete lack of such a deliberate response. Thus, . . . the trial court should not have given the instruction in this instance. In addition, the evidence showed that Johnson was specifically aware of the possibility that snow and ice might be on the road in the vicinity of the snow patch because he drove that stretch of road on a regular basis. His awareness was therefore similar to the *Kendrick* defendant's cognizance of wintery driving conditions and thus did not merit a sudden emergency instruction.

Furthermore, additional, albeit inconclusive, evidence showed that Johnson may have been speeding and/or intoxicated when he lost control of his vehicle. This evidence tends to show that Johnson might have contributed to, if not caused, the alleged "sudden emergency" that led to the accident. That Johnson's pre-accident conduct may have caused or contributed to the emergency situation demonstrates that the trial court should not have instructed the jury on sudden emergency principles. In sum, the evidence presented does not competently or reasonably support the trial court's decision to tender the sudden emergency instruction in this case. The trial court therefore abused its discretion.

. . . . We accordingly reverse the judgment of the court of appeals and remand for a new trial.

Having decided the outcome of this case, we now address the question upon which we ordered supplemental briefing from the parties: whether a separate jury instruction concerning sudden emergencies should continue to be given in any negligence case. . . .

Today we join numerous other jurisdictions and abolish the sudden emergency doctrine because its minimal utility in Colorado's comparative negligence scheme is greatly outweighed by the instruction's danger of misleading the jury. . . .

The sudden emergency instruction has minimal utility for two reasons. First, the instruction is no longer necessary to serve the purpose for which it was originally enacted. . . . Courts developed the doctrine to "overcome the harsh effect of the former contributory negligence defense whereby a plaintiff's negligence acted as a complete bar to recovery." . . . . The General Assembly adopted the modern comparative negligence statute . . . for the same reason: to diminish the harshness of the total bar to a plaintiff's recovery that formerly resulted when the plaintiff's negligence contributed to his or her injuries. . . .

Second, the sudden emergency instruction does not enrich the body of negligence jury instructions. Instead, the sudden emergency instruction unnecessarily repeats the "reasonable care under the circumstances" standard articulated by two other pattern negligence instructions. . . .

. . . . The phrase "same or similar circumstances" in the general negligence and specific reasonable care instructions . . . sufficiently describes the standard of care and broadly encompasses all circumstances, including sudden emergencies. . . .

In addition to its minimal utility, the sudden emergency doctrine presents a serious risk of misleading the jury. . . .

First, the instruction is premised upon two key facts: (1) that there was a sudden emergency; and (2) that the emergency was not caused by the allegedly-negligent party. *See* CJI–Civ. 4th 9:11 ("A person who, through *no fault of his or her own*, is placed in a *sudden emergency*, is not chargeable with negligence if the person exercises that degree of care that a reasonably careful person would have exercised under the same or similar circumstances." (emphasis added)). The instruction does not, however, specifically charge the jury with determining whether or not the evidence establishes these two premises. . . . The jury could therefore interpret the instruction as an affirmative finding by the trial court that an emergency indeed existed, and that the allegedly-negligent party played no role in creating that emergency.

For example, in this case, the jury could have interpreted the sudden emergency instruction as a finding by the trial court that Johnson's actions leading up to the snow patch did not contribute to his loss of control, even though some evidence tended to show that Johnson may have been speeding or intoxicated. Such an interpretation would unfairly benefit the allegedly-negligent party — here, Johnson — because the jury would not have to consider whether that party's conduct caused the emergency, or even if the emergency actually occurred.

Second, even if the jury interpreted the instruction to require these two initial factual findings, the instruction does not define "sudden emergency." Therefore, the jury is left to its own devices to determine whether or not a "sudden emergency" occurred in each case. This lack of guidance can not only lead to inconsistent results among cases, but might also result in prejudice depending on how the jury defines the term.

In addition, the sudden emergency instruction can lead the jury to incorrectly apply a less stringent standard of care.... When given with the general negligence and reasonable care instructions, the separate sudden emergency instruction can imply to the jury that a sudden emergency gives rise to a different standard of care; otherwise there would be no need for a separate instruction....

Finally, the sudden emergency instruction can unduly focus the jury's attention on the allegedly-negligent party's actions during and after the emergency rather than on the totality of the circumstances....

.... Going forward, we abolish the sudden emergency doctrine because its potential to mislead the jury outweighs its minimal utility. [Reversed and remanded]

PATTERSON, C. J., and SUGG, BROOM and LEE, JJ., concur.

SMITH and ROBERTSON, P. JJ., and WALKER and COFER, JJ., dissent. [The dissenting opinions have been omitted.]

Notes

1. ***Sudden Emergency as a Relevant Factor.*** In contrast to *Bedor* and the cases it cites, many jurisdictions have not abolished jury instructions on the relevance of a sudden emergency. The California pattern jury instruction states:

> [Name of plaintiff/defendant] claims that [he/she] was not negligent because [he/she] acted with reasonable care in an emergency situation. [Name of plaintiff/defendant] was not negligent if [he/she] proves all of the following:
>
> 1. That there was a sudden and unexpected emergency situation in which someone was in actual or apparent danger of immediate injury;
>
> 2. That [name of plaintiff/defendant] did not cause the emergency; and
>
> 3. That [name of plaintiff/defendant] acted as a reasonably careful person would have acted in similar circumstances, even if it appears later that a different course of action would have been safer.

Judicial Council of California Civil Jury Instructions No. 452 (2022 ed.).

Evidence of an emergency does not change the standard of care. Instead, the emergency condition is merely one factor that is relevant in determining the reasonable character of the defendant's choice of action. Disagreements tend to focus not on the relevance of a sudden emergency, but on whether a separate instruction about this issue should be given to the jury. *See* Restatement, Third, of Torts: Liab. for Physical & Emotional Harm § 9 (2010).

2. ***Reasonable Errors of Judgment.*** If reasonable minds can differ as to the preferred course of action in an emergency, a defendant who makes a reasonable choice will not be held liable for having failed to select what an expert or jury might later decide was the best course. *See* De Gregorio v. Malloy, 52 A.2d 195, 197–98 (Pa. 1947) (a police officer's riding on the outside of a truck during an emergency was not contributorily negligent).

In upholding a judgment n.o.v. for the defendant-appellee in Murphy v. Neely, 179 A. 439 (Pa. 1935), a case arising out of the crash of a two-seater plane as it was flying about 250 feet above a prospective landing field, the court wrote:

> Appellee was bringing the ship around in a gentle bank to continue his examination of the field, when, three-quarters of the way around, in the turning movement, the nose dropped suddenly, and the ship fell almost vertically to the ground, injuring appellant. It was estimated that it was some five seconds from the time the fall began until the ship struck the ground. As the ship was falling, appellee cut the ignition switch in order to reduce the fire hazard when it crashed.
>
> ....
>
> The action of appellee in cutting off the ignition when confronted with an emergency not shown to have been brought about by tortious conduct upon his part was not unreasonable.... [T]he evidence is not sufficient to justify one in concluding that there is an accepted general opinion or practice with relation to the advisability of cutting off the ignition when a dive or spin begins as against maintaining ... speed and endeavoring to right the machine, so that the failure to do one or the other cannot be termed negligent and is nothing more than a permissible exercise of judgment.

3. ***Creators of Emergencies.*** An instruction on sudden emergency generally is not available where the crisis is of the defendant's own making. *See* Burns v. Martin, 589 So. 2d 147, 149 (Ala. 1991).

4. ***Competence, Beginners, and Emergencies.*** An actor's competence, or lack of it, may be the key fact in determining whether it was reasonable for the actor to attempt an activity. A law professor is not negligent simply because she lacks the skills of a surgeon, but if she attempts to take out a colleague's appendix with a paring knife, her lack of competence will be most relevant in the ensuing litigation.

Beginners need to attempt activities before they become good at them; were it otherwise, no one could attain competence. Nevertheless, the beginner's lack of skill may necessitate special precautions, so that it may be negligent to attempt one's first bicycle ride on a crowded street.

An emergency may well justify an attempt to do something despite incompetence. It may be better for an unskilled layperson to give a badly injured person first aid than to let the victim die. Restatement, Second, of Torts § 299 cmt. e.

5. ***Emergency Rooms.*** Good Samaritan statutes typically provide that volunteers who render aid at the scene of an accident are liable only for conduct more

blameworthy than ordinary negligence. *See* Chapters 8 and 9. Some "tort reform" legislation has extended the same protection to professionals in the emergency-room context.

Texas Civil Practice & Remedies Code § 74.153 (Westlaw 2022)

> In a suit . . . against a physician or health care provider for injury to or death of a patient arising out of the provision of emergency medical care in a hospital emergency department or obstetrical unit . . . , the claimant bringing the suit may prove that the treatment or lack of treatment by the physician or health care provider departed from accepted standards of medical care or health care only if the claimant shows by a preponderance of the evidence that the physician or health care provider, with wilful and wanton negligence, deviated from the degree of care and skill that is reasonably expected of an ordinarily prudent physician or health care provider in the same or similar circumstances.

In Gliemmo v. Cousineau, 694 S.E.2d 75, 77–79 (Ga. 2010), the court rejected constitutional challenges to a similar statute.

6. ***Ethics in Law Practice: Emergency Legal Work.*** In general, a lawyer must not undertake to provide legal services in a field in which the lawyer is not competent. However:

> In an emergency a lawyer may give advice or assistance in a matter in which the lawyer does not have the skill ordinarily required where referral to or consultation or association with another lawyer would be impractical. Even in an emergency, however, assistance should be limited to that reasonably necessary in the circumstances, for ill considered action under emergency conditions can jeopardize the client's interest.

Model Rules of Prof'l Conduct Rule 1.1 cmt. 3 (Westlaw 2022).

c. Physical Disabilities

Generally. Hill v. City of Glenwood, 100 N.W. 522 (Iowa 1904) addressed the question of whether a person's physical handicaps are relevant to the determination of whether that individual has acted reasonably. In *Hill*, a blind man had been injured in an accident on a public sidewalk. Regarding the issue of contributory negligence, the court said that a blind person need not exercise a higher degree of care than a sighted person, but merely the ordinary care that would be exercised by a person who is blind. In other words, the physical handicap was a relevant circumstance, but did not change the standard of care.

A similar approach is applied if, for example, a person is deaf, or unusually short, or lacks a sense of smell, or is ill. *See* Restatement, Third, of Torts: Liab. for Physical & Emotional Harm § 11(a) (2010) ("The conduct of an actor with a physical disability is negligent only if it does not conform to that of a reasonably careful person with the same disability"); Judicial Council of California Civil Jury Instructions No. 3429

(2022 ed.) ("A person with a physical disability is required to (know what/use the amount of care that) a reasonably careful person with the same physical disability would (know/use) in the same situation").

Intoxication. In Davies v. Butler, 602 P.2d 605 (Nev. 1979) (*see supra* p. 150), the plaintiff's decedent died after drinking a large quantity of alcohol during initiation into a social drinking club. In addressing a contributory negligence issue, Chief Justice Mowbray wrote:

> The court instructed the jury, over appellants' objection that "[i]ntoxication is no excuse for failure to act as a reasonably prudent person would act. A person who is intoxicated or under the influence of intoxicating liquor is held to the same standard of care as a sober person."
>
> While ordinarily the statement is an accurate summary of the law, the courts have refused to apply the basic rule strictly, at least as to the inebriate's duty to protect himself, if "when the liquor was furnished [plaintiff's decedent] was incapable of acting like a reasonable man." . . . .
>
> Where intoxication is involuntary, such as in the "highly unusual case in which one believes that he is drinking tea is plied with liquor, and so becomes disabled," the standard of conduct to which the actor must conform is that of a reasonable man under a like disability. . . . Where, however, the intoxication . . . results from deliberate drinking with knowledge of what is being consumed . . . , the policy of the law has refused to make any allowance for the resulting disability. . . .

Voluntary intoxication may be evidence of wrongdoing more serious than negligence. *See* Williams v. Crist, 484 N.E.2d 576 (Ind. 1985) (driving a motor vehicle while intoxicated is "wanton and wilful misconduct *per se*") (plurality opinion). *See also* Lasley v. Combined Transport, Inc., 261 P. 3d 1215, 1230 (Or. 2011) (holding that evidence of a driver's intoxication was relevant in determining comparative fault).

Illness. What if a person who is sick falls asleep at the wheel and has an accident after taking an over-the-counter medication bearing a label warning users that drowsiness may result and that they should not operate machinery? *See* Restatement, Third, of Torts: Liab. for Phys. & Emotional Harm § 11(b) (2010) ("The conduct of an actor during a period of sudden incapacitation or loss of consciousness resulting from physical illness is negligent only if the sudden incapacitation or loss of consciousness was reasonably foreseeable to the actor").

d. Religious Beliefs

Williams v. Bright

Supreme Court of New York, Appellate Division

658 N.Y.S.2d 910 (App. Div.), *appeal dismissed*, 686 N.E.2d 1368 (N.Y. 1997)

WALLACH, Justice.

Plaintiff Robbins was a passenger in an automobile driven by her 70-year-old father on an upstate highway. An eyewitness saw the car veer off the road at about 65 miles per hour and turn over.... There was circumstantial evidence that the driver ... had fallen asleep at the wheel. This was conduct that the jury found to be both negligent and a proximate cause of the accident. On this appeal, defendants, who include the lessors of the vehicle, do not seriously contest liability; the main issue is the trial court's treatment of plaintiff Robbins' alleged failure to mitigate damages due to her religious beliefs as a Jehovah's Witness....

... [A] party who claims to have suffered damage by the tort of another is bound "to use reasonable and proper efforts to make the damage as small as practicable," ... and if an injured party allows the damages to be unnecessarily enhanced, the incurred loss justly falls upon him....

Plaintiff Robbins suffered a severely damaged left hip, as well as a painful injury to her right knee. Her own expert testified that if these injuries were not alleviated by well-recognized and universally accepted surgical procedures, her prognosis was for a wheelchair-bound life.... Moreover, all the experts agreed that the surgical intervention available to this plaintiff ... offered her the prospect of a good recovery and a near normal life. However, Robbins, a devout Jehovah's Witness, presented proof ... that she was obliged to refuse these recommended surgeries because her church prohibits the blood transfusions they would necessarily entail.

... [T]he New York pattern jury instruction on the subject of damage mitigation refers to the actions of "a reasonably prudent person" (PJI 2:325) and measures the duty to mitigate in accordance with that standard.[3] Although the trial court acquainted the jury with the existence of that standard, it charged that in this case the standard to be applied was something very different (our emphasis added):

> You have to accept as a given that the dictates of her religion forbid blood transfusions.
>
> And so you have to determine ... whether she ... *acted reasonably as a Jehovah's Witness* in refusing surgery which would involve blood transfusions.

---

3. [Fn. 2:] "A person who has been injured is not permitted to recover for damages that could have been avoided by using means which a reasonably prudent person would have used to (cure the injury, alleviate the pain).... If you find that the plaintiff is entitled to recover in this action, then in deciding the nature and permanence of her injury and what damages she may recover for the injury, you must decide whether in refusing to have an operation the plaintiff acted as a reasonably prudent person would have acted under the circumstances."

> Was it reasonable for her, not what you would do or your friends or family, *was it reasonable for her given her beliefs*, without questioning the validity or the propriety of her beliefs?

In abandoning the "reasonably prudent person" test in favor of a "reasonable Jehovah's Witness" standard, over defendants' objection, the trial court perceived the issue as involving this plaintiff's fundamental right to the free exercise of her religion, protected by the First Amendment of the United States Constitution and article I (§ 3) of our State Constitution. The First Amendment prohibits any law "respecting an establishment of religion, or prohibiting the free exercise thereof." Essentially, the court held that if the jury were permitted to assess this plaintiff's refusal to accept additional surgery without total deference to her religious beliefs, it would unlawfully restrain "the free exercise" of her Jehovah's Witness faith and would thus be constitutionally prohibited. In effect, this plaintiff's religious beliefs were held, as a matter of law, to relieve her of any legal obligation to mitigate damages under the same standard required of all other persons similarly situated who do not share similar religious convictions.

.... Virtually all of the handful of jurisdictions to have considered the question have adopted the test of the reasonably prudent person instead of the formulation employed here....

In our view, the analysis of the trial court contained many flaws. The first error was in defining the fundamental issue as whether any jury verdict could be permitted to conflict with this plaintiff's "religious belief that it may be better to suffer present pain than to be barred from entering the Kingdom of Heaven".... [T]his is not the question that should have been presented; to put it in this manner inevitably skews the result.

No one suggests that the State, or, for that matter, anyone else, has the right to interfere with that religious belief. But the real issue here is whether the consequences of that belief must be fully paid for here on earth by someone other than the injured believer....

... [T]he State ... [has] a compelling interest in assuring that the proceedings before its civil tribunals are fair, and that any litigant is not improperly advantaged or disadvantaged by adherence to a particular set of religious principles. The State also has a compelling interest ... to extend equal protection of the law to every person....

.... The trial court's instruction to the jurors on mitigation directed them to pass upon the reasonableness of plaintiff Robbins' objection, on religious grounds, to a blood transfusion. The fallacy in this instruction was that the jury never received any evidence pertaining to the rationale of her religious convictions, nor how universally accepted they may have been by members of her faith.... The charge thus created a sham inquiry.... Let us recall, the jurors were told that they must ask themselves whether this plaintiff's refusal to accept a blood transfusion was reasonable, "given her beliefs, *without questioning the validity*" of those beliefs (emphasis added). Having thus removed from the jury's consideration any question as to the validity (that is to say, the reasonableness) of plaintiff Robbins' religious convictions, the court effectively directed a verdict on the issue.

Of course, the alternative — the receipt of "expert" testimony on this subject — presents an even worse prospect. Such evidence, if any conflict developed, would present a triable issue as to whether the conviction against transfusions was heretical — or orthodox — within the Jehovah's Witness faith.

The State may not endorse religion or any particular religious practice.... The trial court, in accepting the sincerity of plaintiff Robbins' beliefs as a given and asking the jury to consider the reasonableness of her actions only in the context of her own religion, effectively provided government endorsement to those beliefs....

... [W]e take note of an obvious problem with strict adherence to the pattern jury instruction that is provided as a general guide (*see*, n. 2, *supra*). We conclude that the unmodified application of that formulation would work an injustice in this case.... It seems apparent to us that a person in plaintiff Robbins' position must be permitted to present to the jury the basis for her refusal of medical treatment; otherwise, the jury would simply be left with the fact of her refusal, without any explanation at all. Once such evidence is (as it should be) received, the court is called upon to instruct the jurors as to how such evidence should affect their deliberations. Addressing this issue, we hold that the pattern jury instruction must be supplemented here with the following direction:

> In considering whether the plaintiff acted as a reasonably prudent person, you may consider the plaintiff's testimony that she is a believer in the Jehovah's Witness faith, and that as an adherent of that faith, she cannot accept any medical treatment which requires a blood transfusion. I charge you that such belief is a factor for you to consider, together with all the other evidence you have heard, in determining whether the plaintiff acted reasonably in caring for her injuries, keeping in mind, however, that the overriding test is whether the plaintiff acted as a reasonably prudent person, under all the circumstances confronting her.

.... [W]e reiterate that the court is not to permit the introduction of any "theological" proof, by way of either expert or lay testimony, as to the validity of religious doctrine, nor should the court issue any instructions whatsoever on that score.

....

Accordingly, the judgment ... should be reversed, on the law and the facts, without costs, and the matter remanded for new trial on damages alone.

[The dissenting opinion of ROSENBERGER, J., has been omitted.]

e. Age

Donovan v. Sutton

Supreme Court of Utah
2021 WL 4468421

Justice Petersen announced the opinion of the Court:

This case arose after a nine-year-old beginner skier collided with a woman on the "First Time" ski run in Park City. The woman sued the child and her parents, asserting claims for . . . negligence and negligent supervision. The district court granted summary judgment in favor of the child and her parents, and the court of appeals affirmed. . . .

. . . [W]e hold that the applicable standard of care is simply that a person has a duty to exercise reasonable care while skiing. . . . [U]nder the circumstances here, the child was not negligent, and her father did not negligently supervise her. . . .

. . . . Shortly before the resort closed for the day, the family took a final run on "First Time," "a green bunny hill for new skiers." Mr. Sutton's wife and youngest daughter skied to the bottom of the run, while Mr. Sutton remained with S.S., the couple's nine-year-old daughter. Mr. Sutton and S.S. (collectively, the Suttons) went down the run together, with Mr. Sutton skiing backwards so he could monitor S.S. They were moving slowly because S.S. was "fearful" and skiing cautiously, despite having had ski lessons the year before and "informal lessons" on the current trip.

S.S. was skiing in a "wedge," a common maneuver taught to beginner skiers to help them slow down, with the front tips of her skis together. She was traveling at approximately five miles per hour when she suddenly lost control and came out of the wedge. Although S.S. tried to "get back into" the wedge to slow down, she could not regain control and instead "just kind of straightened out." This caused her to accelerate past her father and collide with Stephanie Donovan. Ms. Donovan had stopped "just right of center" on the run to take a photograph of her husband and daughter. As Ms. Donovan was putting her camera away, she heard S.S. scream "look out!" But Ms. Donovan did not have time to react, and S.S. crashed into her from behind. Ms. Donovan suffered injuries to her arm and shoulder.

. . . .

At the close of discovery, the Suttons moved for summary judgment. In their motion, the Suttons relied on the court of appeals' decision in Ricci v. Schoultz, in which the court held that a skier owes "a duty to other skiers to ski reasonably and within control," but "an inadvertent fall on a ski slope, alone, does not constitute a breach of this duty." . . . . The Suttons argued that S.S. was skiing cautiously before she suddenly lost control and collided with Ms. Donovan, and she attempted to warn Ms. Donovan of the impending collision. The Suttons asserted that the collision was simply an accident that occurred absent any negligence on S.S.'s part. Further, recognizing that children in negligence actions are judged by a different standard of care than adults, the Suttons argued it was "not unreasonable for a 9-year-old beginner to be frightened, lose control, and fall, even under good ski conditions," and that S.S. was not "skiing unreasonably for her age or for the conditions."

. . . .

We have not previously articulated the standard of care for skiers. . . .

Here, the skier was a nine-year-old child. When a child is accused of negligence, the standard of care is measured by "that degree of care which ordinarily would be observed by children of the same age, intelligence and experience under similar circumstances." . . . .

. . . . There is no evidence in the record concerning S.S.'s intelligence, so we do not consider this factor. Otherwise, the record shows that S.S. was a beginner skier who had taken a professional ski lesson the year before and was being informally instructed by her father on a beginner ski run in normal conditions.

. . . .

We agree with the court of appeals that the undisputed facts here simply do not establish that S.S. breached her duty to ski with reasonable care. . . .

Ms. Donovan argues that she has demonstrated a breach of duty because, despite S.S.'s formal and informal ski lessons, "S.S. did not attempt to draw upon th[at] experience in a timely manner, even where the circumstances permitted her to do so." . . . . But these are merely conclusory assertions, not reasonable inferences. S.S. was skiing cautiously at a slow speed, under the supervision of her father on a beginner run, when she inadvertently lost control. Ms. Donovan has not identified any conduct by S.S. that departed from her duty to ski reasonably, other than the fact of her loss of control itself. This is insufficient.

[Ms. Donovan also failed to prove she had a viable claim for negligent supervision.]

We affirm.

Notes

1. ***Children's Standard.*** A child must normally exercise the degree of care that would be observed by children of similar "age, intelligence, and experience." Restatement, Third, of Torts: Liab. for Physical & Emotional Harm § 10(a) (2010). The children's standard has been applied to a wide range of activities. *See, e.g.*, Bauman v. Crawford, 704 P.2d 1181 (Wash. 1985) (bicycling); Farm Bureau Ins. Group

v. Phillips, 323 N.W.2d 477 (Mich. Ct. App. 1982) (building a fire); Purtle v. Shelton, 474 S.W.2d 123 (Ark. 1971) (hunting animals).

Some courts apply a non-adult standard only to children below 14 years of age. *See* Alpin v. Tew, 839 So. 2d 635 (Ala. 2002) (holding that a 14-year-old child who was injured by fireworks would be held to the general adult standard for contributory negligence).

2. ***Old Enough to Know Better.*** Under the children's standard, negligence is not simply a question of what the child "knows." In Plumley v. Birge, 124 Mass. 57 (1878), the court wrote:

> If the [trial] court had ruled that, if the plaintiff was old enough to know that striking the dog would be likely to incite him to bite, he could not recover, it would have been erroneous. This is not the true test. It entirely disregards the thoughtlessness and heedlessness natural to boyhood. The plaintiff may have been old enough to know, if he stopped to reflect, that striking a dog would be likely to provoke him to bite, and yet in striking him may have been acting as a boy of his age would ordinarily act under the same circumstances.

3. ***Activities Characteristically Undertaken by Adults and Distinctly Dangerous.*** The Restatement provides that a child will be held to an adult standard of care "when the child is engaging in a dangerous activity that is characteristically undertaken by adults." Restatement, Third, of Torts: Liab. for Physical & Emotional Harm § 10(c) (2010). "An activity is characteristically engaged in by adults if adults are the primary persons who ordinarily undertake the activity." *Id.* at cmt. f. In addition:

> Even if an activity is characteristically engaged in by adults, if it is not distinctly dangerous it is not covered by Subsection (c). For example, baking a meatloaf, although typically an adult activity, ordinarily is not distinctly dangerous. Accordingly, if a child by misusing a kitchen utensil is injured or injures another while assisting a parent in this activity, . . . a child standard applies to the evaluation of the child's conduct.

Id. According to the Restatement, "[h]andling firearms is best regarded as a dangerous adult activity." *Id.*

4. ***Inherently Dangerous Activities.*** Some courts have phrased the exception to the children's rule differently. In Robinson v. Lindsay, 598 P.2d 392 (Wash. 1979), a case arising from a snowmobile accident, the court refused to follow states that couched the exception in terms of children engaging in an activity which is "normally one for adults only." It found that it was preferable to state the exception in terms of whether the activity in which the child was engaged was "inherently dangerous." The court wrote:

> Such a rule protects the need of children to be children but at the same time discourages immature individuals from engaging in inherently dangerous

> activities. Children will still be free to enjoy traditional childhood activities without being held to an adult standard of care. . . .

The phrasing of the exception may be important. Riding a minibike, for example, may be considered "inherently dangerous," but it might not qualify as an activity "characteristically undertaken by adults" or "normally one for adults only."

See Goss v. Allen, 360 A.2d 388, 390 (N.J. 1976) ("We recognize that certain activities engaged in by minors are so potentially hazardous as to require that the minor be held to an adult standard of care. Driving a motor vehicle, operating a motor boat and hunting would ordinarily be so classified. However, as to the activities mentioned New Jersey law requires that the minor must be licensed and must first demonstrate the requisite degree of adult competence").

5. ***Presumed Incapacity Depending on the Age of the Child.*** According to the Restatement, a "considerable minority of jurisdictions" take a different approach to addressing the liability of children for negligence:

> Under that approach, for children above 14 there is a rebuttable presumption in favor of the child's capacity to commit negligence; for children between seven and 14, there is a rebuttable presumption against capacity; children under the age of seven are deemed incapable of committing negligence.

Restatement, Third, of Torts: Liab. for Physical & Emotional Harm § 10 cmt. b (2010). The Third Restatement rejects this minority approach but endorses a rule that "A child less than five years of age is incapable of negligence." *Id.* at § 10(b). Comment d explains:

> For very young children, moral judgments generally stem from instructions the children have received from their parents or from other external sources. . . . Moreover, pre-school-age children are commonly accompanied by their parents or other adults as they engage in activities inside and outside the home. These evaluations suggest focusing responsibility for the conduct of such children on parents or those other adults, under appropriate theories of negligent supervision. . . .

6. ***Old Age and Alzheimer's Disease.*** Old age, by itself, is not taken into account in determining whether an actor's conduct was negligent. Restatement, Third, of Torts: Liab. for Physical & Emotional Harm § 11 cmt. c (2010).

However, many cases involve Alzheimer's, a disease commonly associated with old age. When Alzheimer's patients escape liability for harm that they cause to their caregivers, it is usually not because they are held to a lower standard of care. Rather, the caregiver is deemed to have assumed the risks inherent in caring for potentially dangerous patients who are often unable to control their actions.

For example, in Gould v. American Family Mut. Ins. Co., 543 N.W.2d 282 (Wis. 1996), the court held that an Alzheimer's patient was not liable for injuries to her nurse because the plaintiff "was not an innocent member of the public unable to anticipate or safeguard against the harm," but rather "a caretaker specifically for dementia patients and knowingly encountered the dangers associated with such employment." The court concluded that "a person institutionalized . . . with a mental disability, and who does not have the capacity to control or appreciate his or her conduct cannot be liable for injuries caused to caretakers who are employed for financial compensation."

In Gregory v. Cott, 331 P.3d 179, 181 (Cal. 2014), California extended the rule that "Alzheimer's patients are not liable for injuries to caregivers in institutional settings" to "in-home caregivers who, like their institutional counterparts, are employed specifically to assist these disabled persons." The court noted that, "It is a settled principle that those hired to manage a hazardous condition may not sue their clients for injuries caused by the very risks they were retained to confront."

f. Mental Deficiencies

Generally, no allowance is made in the adult standard of care for any mental deficiency of a relatively minor nature. The actor is held to that level of intelligence and stability that would be employed by an ordinary, reasonable person. As Prosser vividly stated:

> The fact that the individual is a congenital fool, cursed with in-built bad judgment, or that in the particular instance the person "did not stop to think," or that the person is merely a stupid ox, or of an excitable temperament which causes him to lose his head and get "rattled," cannot be allowed to protect him from liability. Apart from the very obvious difficulties of proof as to what went on in the person's head, . . . [t]he harm to his neighbors is quite as great, and may be greater, than if the person had exhibited a modicum of brains. . . .

W. Page Keeton, et al., Prosser and Keeton on Torts 176–77 (5th ed. 1984).

As to more-severe mental problems, including those lumped together under the imprecise rubric of "insanity," the rule is largely the same: the actor is not relieved from liability for conduct that does not conform to the standard of the reasonable person under like circumstances. *See* Restatement, Third, of Torts: Liab. for Physical & Emotional Harm § 11(c) (2010) ("An actor's mental or emotional disability is not considered in determining whether conduct is negligent, unless the actor is a child").

As the following case and notes suggest, a few jurisdictions have created exceptions to the general rule that mental deficiency is irrelevant.

Breunig v. American Family Ins. Co.

Supreme Court of Wisconsin
173 N.W.2d 619 (Wis. 1970)

[Plaintiff was injured when his truck was struck by an automobile driven on the left side of the highway by Erma Veith. The action was brought against defendant insurance company under a Wisconsin law which permits a direct action against a liability insurer. The jury returned a verdict for plaintiff; defendant appealed.]

HALLOWS, Chief Justice.

There is no question that Erma Veith was subject at the time of the accident to an insane delusion which directly affected her ability to operate her car in an ordinarily prudent manner and caused the accident....

The psychiatrist testified Mrs. Veith told him she was driving on a road when she believed that God was taking ahold of the steering wheel and was directing her car. She saw the truck coming and stepped on the gas in order to become air-borne because she knew she could fly because Batman does it. To her surprise she was not air-borne before striking the truck, but after the impact she was flying.

....

The psychiatrist testified Erma Veith was suffering from "schizophrenic reaction, paranoid type, acute." He stated that [during the period immediately preceding the accident] ... she was not able to operate the vehicle with her conscious mind, and that she had no knowledge or forewarning that such illness or disability would likely occur.

....

The case was tried on the theory that some forms of insanity are a defense to and preclude liability ... [for] negligence.... We agree. Not all types of insanity vitiate responsibility for a negligent tort. The question of liability in every case must depend upon the kind and nature of the insanity. The effect of the mental illness or mental hallucination must be such as to affect the person's ability to understand and appreciate the duty which rests upon him to drive his car with ordinary care, or if the insanity does not affect such understanding and appreciation, it must affect his ability to control his car in an ordinarily prudent manner. And in addition, there must be an absence of notice or forewarning to the person that he may be suddenly subject to such a type of insanity or mental illness.

....

The policy basis of holding a permanently insane person liable for his tort is:

(1) Where one of two innocent persons must suffer a loss it should be borne by the one who occasioned it; (2) to induce those interested in the estate of the insane person (if he has one) to restrain and control him; and (3) the fear an insanity defense would lead to false claims of insanity to avoid liability....

We think the statement that insanity is no defense is too broad when it is applied to a negligence case where the driver is suddenly overcome without forewarning by a mental disability or disorder which incapacitates him from conforming his conduct to the standards of a reasonable man under like circumstances. These are rare cases indeed, but their rarity is no reason for overlooking their existence and the justification which is the basis of the whole doctrine of liability for negligence, *i.e.*, that it is unjust to hold a man responsible for his conduct which he is incapable of avoiding and which incapability was unknown to him prior to the accident.

.... All we hold is that a sudden mental incapacity equivalent in its effect to such physical causes as a sudden heart attack, epileptic seizure, stroke, or fainting should be treated alike and not under the general rule of insanity.

....

[Because evidence of past conduct permitted the jury to conclude that Mrs. Veith believed she had a special relationship to God and was the chosen one to survive at the end of the world, and that she could believe that God would take over the direction of her life to the extent of driving her car, the question as to whether she acted negligently was properly left to the jury.]

Judgment affirmed.

Notes

1. ***Other Forms of Inability to Control One's Actions.*** A few courts hold that if one is unable to *control* one's actions (as opposed to unable to *understand* the nature and consequences of one's actions), liability may not be imposed, even if the deficiency in ability to control results from a condition of long standing. In Padula v. New York, 398 N.E.2d 548 (N.Y. 1979), the court held that certified heroin addicts, who could not resist the temptation to get "high," could not be held to have been contributorily negligent for having ingested a dangerous concoction made from duplicating fluid (which contained a lethal form of alcohol) and a powdered breakfast drink called "Tang."

2. ***Mental Disability and Contributory Negligence.*** Traditionally, courts held that an actor's mental deficiency *could* be taken into account in determining whether the actor was contributorily negligent. Why? In the context of contributory negligence, the issue is not what degree of care an actor must exercise on behalf of others, but what degree of care a person must exercise for self-protection. Thus, the question is whether a negligent defendant should escape liability for a loss caused to a mentally deficient plaintiff who is incapable of guarding against such harm. However, the Restatement, Third, of Torts: Liab. for Physical & Emotional Harm § 11 cmt. e (2010) now provides that "the rule ... that an actor's mental disabilities shall be disregarded applies in the context of the actor's contributory negligence as well as the context of the actor's negligence."

3. ***Ethics in Law Practice: Clients with Diminished Capacity.*** Rule 1.14(a) of the Model Rules of Professional Conduct (Westlaw 2022) provides:

> When a client's capacity to make adequately considered decisions in connection with a representation is diminished, whether because of minority, mental impairment or for some other reason, the lawyer shall, as far as reasonably possible, maintain a normal client-lawyer relationship with the client.

The commentary to the Rule adds:

> The fact that a client suffers a disability does not diminish the lawyer's obligation to treat the client with attention and respect . . . particularly in maintaining communication.

g. Superior Skills or Knowledge

In General. Talent should not be wasted. It is therefore not surprising that the Restatement provides:

> If an actor has skills or knowledge that exceed those possessed by most others, these skills or knowledge are circumstances to be taken into account in determining whether the actor has behaved as a reasonably careful person.

Restatement, Third, of Torts: Liab. for Physical & Emotional Harm § 12 (2010).

Moreover, in a limited range of cases, certain "professionals," such as doctors, lawyers, architects, accountants, and engineers, are held to a higher standard of care because they possess special skills and knowledge. Thus, the Restatement, Second, of Torts provides:

> *§ 299A. Undertaking in Profession or Trade*
>
> Unless he represents that he has greater or less skill or knowledge, one who undertakes to render services in the practice of a profession or trade is required to exercise the skill and knowledge normally possessed by members of that profession or trade in good standing. . . .

Requiring professionals to measure up to the standard of customary practice in the profession provides an important measure of consumer protection. For example, when an unsophisticated client walks into a law office, not knowing what to expect in terms of professional treatment or even what questions to ask, the law assures the client that the lawyer comes with all of the "standard equipment." That includes knowledge of the law, legal research skills, diligent work habits, professional judgment, and ethical standards observed by ordinary members of the legal profession.

h. Professional Credentials: Legal Malpractice and Medical Malpractice

Professional Malpractice. Negligence by a professional is referred to as professional malpractice, although the term "malpractice" also typically encompasses other forms of liability including breach of fiduciary duty and intentionally tortious conduct. Malpractice actions determine not only whether an allegedly injured person will be compensated but how the profession will be practiced. Consider the case of lawyers. The rulings of courts on liability claims have an important impact on how much care lawyers exercise with respect to such matters as communicating information to clients, following clients' instructions, avoiding conflicts of interest, and safeguarding client information and property. The imposition of liability has great deterrent force, not only on lawyers who are held liable, but on other members of the profession who become aware of malpractice claims, settlements, and court rulings.

Malpractice principles have been applied to persons engaged in a wide range of callings, including, among others, pharmacists, nurses, dentists, pilots, engineers, social workers, and art experts. Any trade or profession with identifiable standards, or requiring specialized education, potentially falls within the scope of the malpractice principles.

The following cases consider some basic principles applicable to doctors and lawyers. For a detailed exploration of lawyer liability, see Vincent R. Johnson & Susan Saab Fortney, Legal Malpractice Law: Problems and Prevention (West Academic, 3d ed. 2021) and Vincent R. Johnson, Legal Malpractice Law in a Nutshell (West Academic, 3d ed. 2021).

Biomet Inc. v. Finnegan Henderson LLP

District of Columbia Court of Appeals
967 A.2d 662 (D.C. 2009)

WASHINGTON, Chief Judge:

. . . .

This case involves a legal malpractice claim brought by Biomet, a manufacturer of orthopedic devices, against Finnegan, a law firm, alleging that Finnegan failed to preserve a constitutional challenge to excessive punitive damages resulting in waiver of the issue. . . . In 1991, Dr. Raymond Tronzo brought a suit against Biomet in the United States District Court for the Southern District of Florida alleging that Biomet infringed and misused his patent and other confidential information. In 1996, following a jury verdict, the district court awarded $7,134,000 in compensatory damages and $20 million in punitive damages against Biomet for patent infringement, fraud, and violation of a confidential relationship. . . .

. . . . Finnegan handled Biomet's appeal to the Federal Circuit challenging the district court's ruling that the plaintiff had presented sufficient evidence to support a jury verdict of patent infringement. Finnegan did not appeal the punitive damage award as unconstitutional at that time because the ratio of punitive to compensatory damages after the initial trial was only 3:1, and the jury had found Biomet's conduct to be particularly reprehensible making such an argument extremely difficult. On appeal, Finnegan successfully obtained reversal of the patent infringement finding. . . .

Eric T. Washington

On remand from the Federal Circuit, the district court determined that Biomet was liable for only $520 in compensatory damages. Following the significant reduction in the compensatory damages, Finnegan moved for a reduction of the $20 million punitive damage award in light of the Supreme Court's ruling in BMW of North America, Inc. v. Gore, 517 U.S. 559 (1996), which held that excessive punitive damages can violate constitutional due process. The district court agreed that the new 38,000:1 ratio of punitive to compensatory damages was unconstitutionally excessive and reduced the punitive damages to $52,000. On appeal . . . , the Federal Circuit held that because punitive damages were not challenged in the initial appeal, Biomet had waived its right to seek relief from the punitive damage award. . . . Therefore, the Federal Circuit reinstated the $20 million punitive damage award.

. . . [T]o prevail on a claim of legal malpractice, a plaintiff must establish the applicable standard of care, a breach of that standard, and a causal relationship between the violation and the harm complained of. . . . Here, there is no dispute, that, with regard to the initial appeal to the Federal Circuit, Finnegan was the attorney of record, Finnegan and Biomet had an attorney-client relationship, and Finnegan owed a duty to Biomet based on that relationship. Specifically, Finnegan owed Biomet a duty to work in Biomet's interests using a reasonable degree of knowledge, care, and skill. *See* Morrison v. MacNamara, 407 A.2d 555, 561 (D.C. 1979) ("[A] lawyer must exercise that degree of reasonable care and skill expected of lawyers acting under similar circumstances."). . . . The issue before us is whether Finnegan could be found to have breached its duty of care to Biomet by failing to include a constitutional challenge to punitive damages in its initial appeal to the Federal Circuit.

Below, the trial court found that Finnegan's decision not to challenge the punitive damage award as constitutionally excessive in the initial appeal was a protected exercise of legal judgment and not a basis for legal malpractice. . . .

It has long been recognized that an attorney is not liable for mistakes made in the honest exercise of professional judgment. *See* National Sav. Bank v. Ward, 100 U.S. 195, 198 (1880) ("[I]t must not be understood that an attorney is liable for every mistake that may occur in practice, or that he may be held responsible to his client for every error of judgment in the conduct of his client's cause."). In *Ward,* the Supreme Court recognized that, where an attorney makes an error in judgment, "the rule is that if he acts with a proper degree of skill, and with reasonable care and to the best of his knowledge, he will not be held responsible." . . . .

Essentially, the judgmental immunity doctrine provides that an informed professional judgment made with reasonable care and skill cannot be the basis of a legal malpractice claim. Central to the doctrine is the understanding that an attorney's judgmental immunity and an attorney's obligation to exercise reasonable care coexist such that an attorney's non-liability for strategic decisions "is conditioned upon the attorney acting in good faith and upon an informed judgment after undertaking reasonable research of the relevant legal principles and facts of the given case." . . . "To hold that an attorney may not be held liable for the choice of trial tactics and the conduct of a case based on professional judgment is not to say, that an attorney may not be held liable for any of his actions in relation to a trial. . . ."

In order to find that the trial court properly granted summary judgment for Finnegan based on judgmental immunity, we must be satisfied that (1) the alleged error is one of professional judgment, and (2) the attorney exercised reasonable care in making his or her judgment. . . . Neither party disputes the fact that Finnegan's decision about how to structure the initial appeal was an exercise of professional judgment. . . . Indeed, the evidence in the record shows that Finnegan originally included a challenge to punitive damages in early drafts of its proposed appellate brief to the Federal Circuit before removing that section in its later drafts. Clearly, the process of structuring an appellate brief and deciding which arguments are best raised is a strategic, litigation decision and an exercise of professional judgment. *See* Smith v. Murray, 477 U.S. 527, 536 (1986) ("Th[e] process of winnowing out weaker arguments on appeal and focusing on those more likely to prevail, far from being evidence of incompetence, is the hallmark of effective appellate advocacy."). . . .

Because Finnegan's decision not to challenge the punitive damage award as unconstitutional in the initial appeal was an exercise of professional judgment, we now must determine whether that professional judgment was reasonable at the time it was made, not whether a different strategy may have resulted in a more favorable judgment. Biomet argues that Finnegan, as seasoned appellate counsel, should have known that a failure to challenge the punitive damage award in the initial appeal to the Federal Circuit risked waiver of the constitutional issue on remand, and for that reason, Finnegan's decision was unreasonable. In response, Finnegan asserts that because it was aware of the Supreme Court's ruling in *BMW*, it intentionally chose not to seek a reduction of the punitive damage award during its initial appeal for two reasons: (1) because there was really no basis for initially appealing the punitive damage award given the relatively low ratio of punitive to compensatory damages, and (2) to raise it as part of the initial appeal required Finnegan to reargue evidence of Biomet's reprehensible conduct that was presented at trial; an argument that would have diluted its stronger argument regarding the lack of evidence supporting the patent infringement finding.

More importantly, Finnegan also asserts that it did not believe that a constitutional challenge alleging excessive punitive damages was viable prior to the reduction in compensatory damages on remand. . . . Specifically, Finnegan argues that it was a reasonable exercise of professional judgment to conclude that the constitutional challenge to the excessiveness of the punitive damage award would not have been waived by failing to raise it in the initial appeal because the constitutional problem only came into being once the compensatory damages were reduced on remand and the new ratio became unconstitutionally excessive.[4]. . . . Finnegan maintains that, despite the Federal Circuit's contrary opinion, its judgment was reasonable at the time it was made because, prior to the Federal Circuit's ruling, the law was unsettled and reasonable attorneys could disagree as to whether the constitutional challenge was waived if not raised in the initial appeal.

. . . [We have previously] recognized that "[a]n attorney is not liable for an error of judgment regarding an unsettled proposition of law" and that if "reasonable attorneys could differ with respect to the legal issues presented, the second-guessing after the fact of . . . professional judgment [i]s not a sufficient foundation for a legal malpractice claim." . . . . That the existence of unsettled law relieves an attorney of malpractice liability is based on the understanding that an attorney is not expected, much less required, to accurately predict developments in the law. The law is not static, it ever-evolves and changes, and so "[b]ecause of those concerns, the rule that an attorney is not liable for an error of judgment on an unsettled proposition of law is universally recognized." . . . .

. . . . [B]ecause the existence of unsettled law immunizes an attorney's informed, albeit erroneous, judgment, the fact that the Federal Circuit found the issue waived is not in itself dispositive of the reasonableness of Finnegan's actions. . . . Whether Finnegan's strategy of challenging only liability in the initial appeal was reasonable requires consideration of the state of the law regarding constitutional challenges to excessive punitive damages at the time of the appeal.

4. [Fn. 1:] Finnegan relies on cases in the vein of Texas v. United States, 523 U.S. 296, 300 (1998) ("A claim is not ripe for adjudication if it rests upon 'contingent future events that may not occur as anticipated,' or indeed may not occur at all."). . . .

The Supreme Court's decision in *BMW, supra,* 517 U.S. at 581, the first case where the Court found punitive damages to be unconstitutionally excessive, was issued a year before Finnegan filed the initial appeal on behalf of Biomet. As the Court's latest word on the issue of unconstitutionally excessive punitive damages, the *BMW* opinion provided litigants the best guidance on the criteria used to evaluate the excessiveness of punitive damage awards.... [A] fair reading of *BMW* suggests that while a high ratio of punitive to compensatory damages could be unconstitutionally excessive, a low ratio would not be, and that, a ratio of 10:1 punitive to compensatory damages is not excessive....

.... We agree with the trial court that, prior to the Federal Circuit's ruling, whether the constitutionality of the punitive damage award could be raised for the first time following a reduction in compensatory damages occasioned by a favorable appeal was a debatable point of unsettled law....

Because there was a substantial question, as to whether a constitutional challenge to punitive damages had to be raised during an initial appeal when the punitive damage award at that time was not unconstitutionally excessive when compared with the compensatory damage award, and because there was no clear precedent one way or the other prior to the Federal Circuit's opinion in the underlying case, and thus, reasonable attorneys could disagree, we are satisfied that, as a matter of law, there was no legal malpractice in this case.

....

Affirmed.

Notes

1. ***The Duties Owed by Lawyers.*** A negligence action against a lawyer revolves around the same issues as any other negligence action: duty, breach, causation, damages, and affirmative defenses.

(a) ***Duties to Clients.*** An attorney owes a duty of care to anyone who becomes a client, even if the relationship is created informally. For example, suppose that during a social event an attorney promises a teacher to "check into" a legal question they have discussed. If the teacher reasonably relies on that promise and the statute of limitations expires before the attorney acts, the attorney may be liable even though no lawyer-client relationship was formally consummated. *See* Restatement, Third, of the Law Governing Lawyers § 14 (2000).

(b) ***Duties to Prospective Clients.*** Lawyers owe some duties to prospective clients, such as the duty to keep those persons' information confidential. *See* Restatement, Third, of the Law Governing Lawyers § 15 (2000).

(c) ***Duties to Nonclients.*** A duty of care may extend to intended third-party beneficiaries of the attorney-client relationship, such as those who would benefit under a will or trust drafted by the attorney. *See* Lucas v. Hamm, 364 P.2d 685 (Cal. 1961). In Meighan v. Shore, 40 Cal. Rptr. 2d 744 (Ct. App. 1995), a lawyer representing a client in a medical malpractice action was negligent in failing to inform the client's wife that she might have a derivative claim for loss of consortium.

A duty may also extend to persons who foreseeably rely on documents provided by an attorney, such as opinion letters about the lawfulness or tax consequences of a transaction. *See* Petrillo v. Bachenberg, 655 A.2d 1354, 1359 (N.J. 1995).

Some states follow a "strict privity" approach that greatly limits duties to nonclients. *See* Barcelo v. Elliott, 923 S.W.2d 575 (Tex. 1996) (no liability to trust beneficiaries); Taco Bell Corp. v. Cracken, 939 F. Supp. 528 (N.D. Tex. 1996) (litigant had no right to recover from other parties' attorneys).

(d) ***Duties to Other Attorneys.*** Sometimes a lawyer owes a duty to another attorney. *See* Parker & Wobber v. Miles & Stockbridge, P.C., 756 A.2d 526 (Md. 2000) (permitting contribution and indemnity claims related to an allegedly negligent settlement by successor counsel). However, there is authority to the contrary.

(e) ***Scope of Representation.*** An attorney's duties to a client generally extend no further than the scope of the representation. *See* Lerner v. Laufer, 819 A.2d 471 (N.J. 2003) (an attorney hired to look over a settlement agreement hammered out by the client was not required to launch a full-blown investigation into whether she could lay claim to more of the marital estate).

2. ***Breach of the Legal Malpractice Standard of Care.***

(a) ***Errors of Judgment.*** There is no rule that insulates a lawyer from liability for a "mere error of judgment." Rather, a lawyer must always act reasonably when charting a course, recommending actions, or choosing among alternatives.

(b) ***No Good Faith Exception.*** The issue is whether a lawyer acted reasonably, not whether a lawyer acted in good faith. According to Cosgrove v. Grimes, 774 S.W.2d 662, 664–65 (Tex. 1989):

> There is no subjective good faith excuse for attorney negligence. A lawyer . . . is held to the standard of care which would be exercised by a reasonably prudent attorney. . . .
>
> If an attorney makes a decision which a reasonably prudent attorney *could* make in the same or similar circumstance, it is not an act of negligence even if the result is undesirable. . . .

Conversely, if a lawyer does what no reasonably prudent lawyer could do, or fails to do what every reasonably prudent lawyer must do, the lawyer is subject to negligence liability for malpractice.

(c) ***Debatable Questions and Novel Theories.*** Although there is no duty to predict the ultimate resolution of unsettled legal questions, an attorney is obliged "to undertake reasonable research in an effort to ascertain relevant legal principles and to make an informed decision as to a course of conduct based upon an intelligent assessment of the problem." Smith v. Lewis, 530 P.2d 589 (Cal. 1975) (imposing liability on an attorney who, as a result of ignorance, failed to claim that his client had a community property interest in her husband's vested retirement benefits, even though that right was uncertain and there might have been reasons for forgoing the claim; "there is nothing strategic or tactical about ignorance").

However, there are limits to how far this duty extends. In Darby & Darby, P.C. v. VSI Int'l, Inc., 739 N.E.2d 744 (N.Y. 2000), a particular theory of insurance coverage had been rejected in Florida and New York, the two states "most relevant" to the dispute, and accepted by "only a handful of courts, particularly in California." The court wrote:

> [A]ttorneys should familiarize themselves with current legal developments so that they can make informed judgments and effectively counsel their clients.... However, ... [the attorneys] in this case should not be held liable for failing to advise defendants about a novel and questionable theory pertaining to their insurance coverage.... Because plaintiff acted in a manner that was reasonable and consistent with the law as it existed at the time of representation, it had no duty to inform defendants about possible "advertising liability" insurance coverage for their patent infringement litigation expenses.

(d) ***Liability for Inadequate Settlements.*** There is a split of authority as to whether an attorney is liable for negligence resulting in the client's acceptance of an inadequate settlement. Some courts hold that to permit such actions would "create chaos" in the civil litigation system, for lawyers "would be reluctant to settle a case for fear some enterprising attorney representing a disgruntled client will find a way to sue them for something that 'could have been done, but was not'." Muhammad v. Strassburger, *et al.*, 587 A.2d 1346, 1349 (Pa. 1991) (permitting only actions based on fraudulent inducement of inadequate settlements).

Other courts, recognizing that litigants rely heavily on professional advice when deciding to accept or reject offers of settlement, insist that lawyers advise clients with respect to settlements with the same skill, knowledge, and diligence with which they must pursue other legal tasks. *See* Ziegelheim v. Apollo, 607 A.2d 1298 (N.J. 1992).

(e) ***Duty to Recommend a Specialist.*** Like other professionals, a lawyer must refer a client to a specialist if, under the circumstances, a reasonably careful lawyer would do so. *See, e.g.*, Horne v. Peckham, 158 Cal. Rptr. 714, 724 (Ct. App. 1979) (general practitioner had a duty to refer a client seeking an irrevocable trust tax shelter to a tax law specialist). Of course, care must be exercised in making referrals.

3. ***Proof of Causation of Damages in Legal Malpractice Cases.*** In a legal malpractice action based on negligence, the plaintiff must prove that the defendant's breach of the applicable standard of care resulted in damage.

What this means as to errors in litigation is reasonably clear. If an attorney has failed to take appropriate action within the statute of limitations, the plaintiff ordinarily must establish not only that the deadline was missed, but that had the statute not run the plaintiff would have prevailed in the underlying action. Consequently, the plaintiff is faced with a heavy burden of proof. As to litigation errors, it is often said there must be a "trial within a trial." *See* Environmental Network Corp. v. Goodman Weiss Miller, L.L.P., 893 N.E.2d 173, 175 (Ohio 2008) (holding that "when a plaintiff premises a legal-malpractice claim on the theory that he would have received a better outcome if his attorney had tried the underlying matter to conclusion rather than settled it, the plaintiff must establish that he would have prevailed in the underlying matter and that the outcome would have been better than the outcome provided by the settlement").

Transactional errors entail a somewhat different approach to proof of causation of damage because a lawsuit was not planned. Thus, in Viner v. Sweet, 70 P.3d 1046 (Cal. 2003), a case involving legal work relating to the sale of a business, the defendant argued, and the court agreed, that the plaintiffs were required to show that but for the defendant's negligence "(1) they would have had a more advantageous agreement (the 'better deal' scenario), or (2) they would not have entered into the transaction . . . and therefore would have been better off (the 'no deal' scenario)."

See also Thabault v. Chait, 541 F.3d 512 (3d Cir. 2008) (affirming an auditing malpractice judgment of $119 million in compensatory damages, plus $63 million in prejudgment interest, because the receiver for an insolvent company proved that the company wrote insurance that "produced claims that cost more than the premiums," which would never have been written but for the negligent audit).

It is important to remember that many disputes are resolved by settlement, rather than by litigation, and a settlement may be based on considerations other than the strict legal merits. In Estate of Campbell v. Chaney, 485 N.W.2d 421 (Wis. Ct. App. 1992), the attorneys were allegedly negligent in drafting a prenuptial agreement. As a result, the deceased client's estate was subjected to a claim by the decedent's widow, which it eventually settled. In the ensuing malpractice action, the court held that the estate was not required to prove that the agreement would have been held unenforceable if its validity had been litigated. Rather, the estate could recover if it showed that the negligence caused a weakness in the agreement, that the weakness of the agreement caused the litigation, and that the decision to settle the claim was caused by the weakness in the agreement, rather than by other facts establishing that the widow had a strong claim.

See also Vahila v. Hall, 674 N.E.2d 1164, 1169–70 (Ohio 1997), a case involving legal representation in various civil, criminal, and administrative proceedings, where the court noted that a "strict 'but for' test" for causation tends to over-protect errant attorneys and require the introduction of "remote and speculative" evidence. While acknowledging that "the requirement of causation often dictates that the merits of the malpractice action depend upon the merits of the underlying case," *Vahila* refused to "endorse a blanket proposition that requires a plaintiff to prove, in every instance, that he or she would have been successful in the underlying matter."

4. ***Damages for Legal Malpractice.*** Damages in legal malpractice actions normally include only economic losses suffered by clients. Emotional distress damages

are rarely recoverable, and legal malpractice typically does not result in personal injuries, death, or damage to property.

(a) ***Punitive Damages for Malpractice.*** If the facts are egregious and therefore establish more than mere negligence (*i.e.*, intentional wrongdoing or recklessness), punitive damages based on the attorney's misconduct normally may be recovered in a malpractice action.

(b) ***Liability for "Lost" Punitive Damages.*** May an attorney be held liable for "lost punitive damages" — punitive damages that might have been recovered from a third person but for the lawyer's malpractice? In Ferguson v. Lieff, Cabraser, Heimann & Bernstein, 135 Cal. Rptr. 2d 46 (Cal. 2003), the court refused to recognize this element of malpractice damages, stating:

> Making a negligent attorney liable for lost punitive damages would not serve a societal interest, because the attorney did not commit and had no control over the intentional misconduct justifying the punitive damages award.

The court added that permitting recovery of lost punitive damages would also violate the public policy against speculative damages, necessitate an excessively complex standard of proof, and exact a significant social cost in terms of the cost and availability of malpractice insurance.

5. ***Affirmative Defenses and Obstacles to Legal Malpractice Liability.*** In an action for professional negligence, contributory negligence by the plaintiff is a defense under the applicable common law, comparative negligence, or comparative fault regime. For example, if a client fails to provide necessary information to a lawyer or neglects to take steps that the lawyer recommends, those actions may be a form of carelessness by the plaintiff that reduces or precludes recovery.

Other defenses that may be raised in a legal malpractice action:

(a) ***Failure to Appeal.*** Errors in litigation are sometimes corrected on appeal. Can an attorney argue that a plaintiff failed to mitigate damages by not pursuing an appeal prior to suing for malpractice? In Hewitt v. Allen, 43 P.3d 345, 348–49 (Nev. 2002), the court wrote:

> If an appeal would be a futile gesture, that is, the appeal would most likely be denied, then litigants should be able to forgo an appeal, or dismiss a pending appeal, without abandoning their legal malpractice actions. . . .
>
> . . . [B]ecause the issue is raised in the context of an affirmative defense, the attorney defendant has the burden of proof to establish that an appeal would have been successful. Finally, whether an appeal is likely to succeed is a question of law to be determined by the trial court.

(b) ***Fee Offsets.*** If an attorney working on a contingent fee basis negligently causes loss of the claim, should the aggrieved client receive the full value of the claim or the net value of the claim minus the contingent fee that would have been paid to the attorney? Although there is authority to the contrary, many courts refuse to make any reduction. *See* Foster v. Duggin, 695 S.W.2d 526 (Tenn. 1985) ("deduction of . . . [the malpracticing attorney's anticipated] fee would not fully compensate the client who has incurred additional legal fees in pursuing the malpractice action").

(c) ***Collectibility.*** Most courts also hold that a malpractice plaintiff must prove that the judgment which would have been won, but for the negligence of the defendant, would have been collectible. *See, e.g.*, Lavigne v. Chase, 50 P.3d 306 (Wash. Ct. App. 2002). Other courts treat uncollectibility as a matter that must be pleaded and proved by the defendant as an affirmative defense. *See* Kituskie v. Corbman, 714 A.2d 1027 (Pa. 1998) (expressly rejecting the majority rule).

(d) ***Exoneration or Innocence.*** Courts generally require a former criminal defendant to prove exoneration or innocence of the crime charged, as an element of a malpractice claim alleging that counsel was negligent in conducting the defense. In part, the rule is intended to prevent guilty parties from "profiting" from their wrongdoing. *See* Peeler v. Hughes & Luce, 909 S.W.2d 494 (Tex. 1995); Hicks v. Nunnery, 643 N.W.2d 809 (Wis. 2002). An exoneration or innocence requirement is one way in which the unlawful conduct defense (discussed in Chapter 3) manifests itself in legal malpractice actions. *See* Vincent R. Johnson, *The Unlawful Conduct Defense in Legal Malpractice*, 77 UMKC L. Rev. 43 (2008).

Russo v. Griffin

Supreme Court of Vermont
510 A.2d 436 (Vt. 1986)

HILL, Justice.

This is a legal malpractice action. The trial court found for defendants. . . . We reverse.

. . . . In 1975, Mr. Russo . . . [turned over his Rutland, Vermont, paving business] to his two sons, . . . [Tony and Frank].

In early 1978, Frank entertained thoughts of purchasing a laundromat . . . , and he entered into discussions with his brother concerning the sale of his interest in the corporation. . . . [The negotiations culminated in a meeting in the office of Mr. Griffin, a Rutland attorney who in the past had done work for the corporation. Documents were prepared selling Frank's interest in the corporation to Tony.]

. . . .

At no time during the meeting did defendant Griffin inform the corporation or Tony Russo, the sole remaining shareholder, of the desirability of obtaining a covenant not to compete or explain the implications thereof. Three months after the stock transfer, Frank went back into the paving business in Rutland in direct competition with the plaintiff corporation. A properly drafted noncompetition covenant would have prevented this from occurring.

At trial, plaintiff introduced two expert witnesses, both well-respected practicing attorneys from the Burlington area, who testified that defendant Griffin's failure to advise the corporation to exact a covenant not to compete deviated from the standard of care required of attorneys practicing in Vermont at that time. Defendants introduced two similarly qualified Rutland attorneys who testified that defendant Griffin's conduct comported with the standard of care then expected of Rutland attorneys.

The question for determination was clearly whether defendant Griffin's conduct violated the attorney standard of care as it existed at the time of the alleged breach. . . . The [trial] court ultimately chose to accept the testimony of defendants', rather than plaintiff's, expert witnesses on the premise that "those attorneys whose practice primarily was conducted in the Rutland area prior to and during 1978 are more familiar with the standard of care then required of lawyers."

. . . . The court concluded:

> The *standard of care in the Rutland area* in 1978 required of an attorney did not require him to suggest or recommend to a purchasing client that a noncompete agreement be obtained from a seller who is a relative and who has been a business associate for several years, the transaction not being one at arms length. (Emphasis added).

In Hughes v. Klein, 139 Vt. 232, 233, 427 A.2d 353, 354 (1981), this Court held that the standard of care within the legal profession required lawyers to exercise "the customary skill and knowledge which normally prevails at the time and place." We are now asked to reexamine the underlying rationale and continued vitality of the so-called locality rule.

The locality rule . . . was first applied to the medical profession approximately a century ago when there existed a great disparity between standards of practice in large urban centers and remote rural areas. . . . "The rule was unquestionably developed to protect the rural and small town practitioner, who was presumed to be less adequately informed and equipped than his big city brother." . . . .

The shortcomings of the locality rule are well recognized. It immunizes persons who are sole practitioners in their community from malpractice liability and it promotes a "conspiracy of silence" in the plaintiffs' locality which, in many cases, effectively precludes plaintiffs from retaining qualified experts to testify on their behalf. . . . Recent developments in technology and the trend toward standardization have further undermined support for the rule. . . .

According to defendants, the reasoning of the courts which have rejected the locality rule in medical malpractice decisions is inapposite to legal malpractice. We disagree.

> The ability of the practitioner and the minimum knowledge required should not vary with geography. The rural practitioner should not be less careful, less able or less skillful than the urban attorney. The fact that a lower degree of care or less able practice may be prevalent in a particular local community should not dictate the standard of care.

Mallen & Levit, Legal Malpractice § 254, at 334 (2d ed. 1981). Defendants correctly note that "knowledge of local practices, rules, or customs may be determinative of, and essential to, the exercise of adequate care and skill." *Id.* To argue this fact in support of continued application of the locality rule, however, is to confuse "the *degree* of 'skill and knowledge' and the relevance of local factors which constitute the *knowledge* required by the standard of care." *Id.* at 337. Although attorneys throughout this state may be required to familiarize themselves with local practices, rules or customs peculiar to their area, the crucial inquiry for malpractice purposes turns not on the substance of the underlying practice, rule, or custom but on whether a reasonable and prudent attorney can be expected to know of its existence and practical applications.

In selecting a territorial limitation on the standard of care, we believe that the most logical is that of the state. *See* Mallen & Levit, *supra*, at 336; *see also* Restatement, Second, of Torts § 299A Comment g (1965) (allowance for variations in type of community or degree of skill and knowledge possessed by practitioners therein has seldom been made in legal profession as such variations either do not exist or are not worthy of recognition). In Vermont, the rules governing the practice of law do not vary from community to community but are the same throughout the state. Moreover, in order to practice law in Vermont attorneys must successfully complete the requirements for admission established by this Court and administered by the Vermont Board of Bar Examiners.

.... Accordingly, we hold that the appropriate standard of care to which a lawyer is held in the performance of professional services is "that degree of care, skill, diligence and knowledge commonly possessed and exercised by a reasonable, careful and prudent lawyer in the practice of law in this jurisdiction." ....

Unlike the medical profession, the legal profession has not yet established a certification and licensing process which is national in scope. Mallen, *supra*, § 254, at 337. Nevertheless, "[w]hen certain recognized specialties are involved a national standard may be appropriate." *Id.* These "national law" specialties might include federal taxation law, securities law, patent law, and bankruptcy law where the need for uniformity is clearly apparent. *Id.* at 338. Regardless of whether a state or national standard is applied, however, our holding points out the need to advise clients as to the limits of one's professional capabilities and to refer them to specialists in appropriate cases.

In this case ..., the trial court erroneously applied the locality rule in defining the applicable standard of care.... Accordingly, the decision of the superior court is reversed and the cause is remanded for a new trial.

....

HAYES, Justice, concurring in part and dissenting in part.

I agree with the majority that the correct standard to which an attorney should be held in the performance of professional services is *not* the standard of his or her locality. If there are only two lawyers in a small town, and both are incompetent, they cannot set a standard of inferiority for a third who comes to town.

I disagree with the Court's holding that the applicable standard of care should be a *state* standard. Doctors in Vermont are required to adhere to standards based upon the medical profession generally. Lawyers should be subject to a similar standard....

.... The law schools of today are truly national in legal training. Vermont and almost all other states give a multistate bar examination. Much of our continuing legal education is national in scope....

I would require that the standard of care for Vermont lawyers be based upon the legal profession generally, and I would reject a state or local standard.

Notes

1. ***The Locality Rule.*** The locality rule receives greater recognition in medical malpractice actions than in suits against lawyers, but even in that context it is waning. *See* Vergara by Vergara v. Doan, 593 N.E.2d 185 (Ind. 1992) (abandoning the "same or similar" locality rule and holding that a physician must exercise that degree of care, skill, and proficiency exercised by reasonably careful, skillful, and prudent practitioners under the same or similar circumstances considering the locality, advances in the profession, availability of facilities, and whether the doctor is a specialist or general practitioner).

2. ***Educational Malpractice.*** Courts have typically refused to recognize educational malpractice as a cause of action. Although the reasoning differs according to the nature of the claim, the decisions are often based on beliefs that the court system should not interfere in school administrative practices, that imposing negligence liability would subject schools to numerous burdensome claims, that judges and juries should not second-guess teachers on debatable pedagogical questions, and that whether a student develops reading, writing, and other skills is influenced by many factors beyond the classroom, making it impossible in many cases to establish causation of harm.

Illustratively, courts have denied relief for alleged negligence in allowing a functionally illiterate student to graduate from high school (Donohue v. Copiague Union Free Sch. Dist., 391 N.E.2d 1352 (N.Y. 1979)); misevaluating and misplacement of a learning-disabled student (Hunter v. Board of Educ., 439 A.2d 582 (Md. 1982)); failing to provide remedial education (Meyers v. Medford Lakes Bd. of Educ., 489 A.2d 1240 (N.J. Super. Ct. App. Div. 1985)); failing to retest a child classified as mentally retarded (Hoffman v. Board of Educ., 400 N.E.2d 317 (N.Y. 1979)); and enrolling student athletes into "hundreds of sham courses" (Arnold v. U. of N. Carolina at Chapel Hill, 798 S.E.2d 442, 443 (N.C. App. 2017)).

In Krebs v. Charlotte Sch. of L., LLC, 2017 WL 3880667, at *5 (W.D.N.C.), the court found claims about alleged misrepresentations by a law school related to its ABA accreditation were an "impermissible attempt to allege a cause of action for educational malpractice," which North Carolina courts have repeatedly rejected.

3. ***Ethics in Law Practice: Non-Competition Agreements Among Attorneys.*** Courts will normally enforce a non-competition agreement of the type at issue in *Russo*, provided it is reasonable in terms of time and place. However, different standards apply to the legal profession, and between attorneys non-competition agreements will often be held invalid on ethical grounds.

> The reasons underlying the ethical rule are twofold. On the one hand, it protects the public from having only a restricted pool of attorneys from which to select counsel. On the other, the rule protects attorneys, particularly young practitioners, from bargaining away an important aspect of their right to open offices of their own upon leaving a firm or other employer. These considerations dictate that ordinary commercial standards not be used to evaluate the reasonableness of lawyer restrictive covenants.

Vincent R. Johnson, *Solicitation of Law Firm Clients by Departing Partners and Associates: Tort, Fiduciary, and Disciplinary Liability*, 50 U. Pitt. L. Rev. 1, 111-14 (1988).

Boyce v. Brown

Supreme Court of Arizona
77 P.2d 455 (Ariz. 1938)

LOCKWOOD, Judge.

Berlie B. Boyce and Nannie E. Boyce, his wife, . . . brought suit against Edgar H. Brown, . . . to recover damages for alleged malpractice by the defendant upon the person of Nannie E. Boyce. . . . [A]t the close of the evidence for plaintiffs, the court granted a motion for an instructed verdict in favor of the defendant, on the ground that there was no competent testimony that he was guilty of any acts . . . sufficient, as a matter of law, to charge him with malpractice. Judgment was rendered on the verdict. . . .

. . . . The sole question for our consideration . . . is whether, taking the evidence as strongly as is reasonably possible in support of plaintiffs' theory of the case, as we must do when the court instructs a verdict in favor of defendant, there was sufficient evidence to sustain a judgment in favor of plaintiffs.

. . . . About September 1, 1927, plaintiffs engaged the services of defendant . . . to reduce a fracture of Mrs. Boyce's ankle. This was done by means of an operation which consisted, in substance, of making an incision at the point of fracture, bringing the broken fragments of bone into apposition, and permanently fixing them in place by means of a metal screw placed in the bone. Defendant continued to attend Mrs. Boyce for three or four weeks following such operation until a complete union of the bone had been established, when his services terminated. There is no serious contention in the record that defendant did not follow the approved medical standard in the treatment of the fractured bone up to this time. No further professional relations existed between the parties until seven years later, in November, 1934, when Mrs. Boyce again consulted him, complaining that her ankle was giving her considerable pain. He examined the ankle, wrapped it with adhesive tape, and then filed the edge of an arch support, which he had made for her seven years before, and which, from use, had grown so thin that the edge was sharp. About a week later he removed the bandage. Her ankle, however, did not improve after this treatment, but continued to grow more painful until January, 1936. . . . At this last-mentioned time she returned to defendant, who again examined the ankle. A few days later she went to visit Dr. Kent of Mesa, who, on hearing the history of the case, and noticing some discoloration and swelling, caused an X-ray of the ankle to be made. This X-ray showed that there had been some necrosis of the bone around the screw. Dr. Kent operated upon Mrs. Boyce, removing the screw, and she made an uneventful recovery, the ankle becoming practically normal.

There are certain general rules of law governing actions of malpractice, which are almost universally accepted by the courts, and which are applicable to the present situation. We state them as follows: (1) One licensed to practice medicine is presumed to possess the degree of skill and learning which is possessed by the average member of the medical profession in good standing in the community in which he practices, and to apply that skill and learning, with ordinary and reasonable care, to cases which come to him for treatment. If he does not . . . , he is guilty of malpractice. . . . (2) Before a physician or surgeon can be held liable as for malpractice, he must have done something in his treatment of his patient which the recognized standard of good medical practice in the community in which he is practicing forbids in such cases, or he must have neglected to do something which such standard requires. . . . (3) . . . [T]he standard of medical practice in the community must be shown by affirmative evidence, and, unless there is evidence of such a standard, a jury may not be permitted to speculate as to what the required standard is, or whether the defendant has departed therefrom. . . . (4) Negligence on the part of a physician or surgeon in the treatment of a case is never presumed, but must be affirmatively proven, and no presumption of negligence nor want of skill arises from the mere fact that a treatment was unsuccessful, failed to bring the best results, or that the patient died. . . . (5) The accepted rule is that negligence on the part of a physician or surgeon, by reason of his departure from the proper standard of practice, must be established by expert medical testimony, unless the negligence is so grossly apparent that a layman would have no difficulty in recognizing it. . . . (6) The testimony of other physicians that they would have followed a different course of treatment than that followed by the defendant is not sufficient to establish malpractice unless it also appears that the course of treatment followed deviated from one of the methods of treatment approved by the standard in that community. . . .

With these principles of the law . . . as a guide, let us consider the record. . . . Two questions present themselves to us: (a) What was the treatment which defendant gave Mrs. Boyce in November, 1934? and (b) What was the medical standard which he was required to conform to, under all the circumstances, in giving her treatment at that time? . . . . The evidence does not show that she ever came back to defendant for further treatment in November, 1934, or, indeed, until January, 1936.... The only testimony we have which, in any manner, bears upon medical standards or the proper treatment of Mrs. Boyce in November, 1934, is that of Dr. Kent, who performed the operation on the ankle in January, 1936, and of defendant. The latter testified that he did what was required by Mrs. Boyce's condition as it existed then.... [Dr. Kent] was asked as to how long prior to that time the screw should have been removed, and stated that he could not answer; that, if the ankle was in the same condition as it was when he operated, he would say that the screw should have been removed, but that it was impossible for him to testify as to when the condition justifying removal arose. He was questioned more fully and answered substantially that his first conclusion, if he had been in the position of defendant, when Mrs. Boyce called on the latter in November, 1934, would have been that arthritis in the ankle joint was causing the pain, but that he would not have been fully satisfied without having an X-ray made of the ankle.... Nowhere, however, did Dr. Kent testify as to what was the proper standard of medical care required at the time defendant treated Mrs. Boyce in 1934, or as to whether, in his opinion, the treatment given deviated from that standard. The nearest he came to such testimony was the statement that he personally would have had an X-ray taken, but he did not say the failure to do so was a deviation from the proper standard of treatment.

Counsel for plaintiffs, in their oral argument, apparently realized the weakness of their evidence on the vital point of what the proper medical standard required in 1934, and based their claim of negligence almost entirely upon the failure of defendant to take an X-ray of Mrs. Boyce's ankle at that time. They urge that this comes within the exception to the general rule, in that a failure to do so is such obvious negligence that even a layman knows it to be a departure from the proper standard. We think this contention cannot be sustained. It is true that most laymen know that the X-ray usually offers the best method of diagnosing physical changes of the interior organs of the body, and particularly of the skeleton, short of an actual opening of the body for ocular examination, but laymen cannot say that in all cases where there is some trouble with the internal organs that it is a departure from standard medical practice to fail to take an X-ray. Such things are costly and do not always give a satisfactory diagnosis, or even as good a one as other types of examination may give. In many cases the taking of an X-ray might be of no value and put the patient to unnecessary expense, and, in view of the testimony in the present case as to the arthritis which Mrs. Boyce had, and which Dr. Kent testified would have been his first thought as to the cause of Mrs. Boyce's pain in 1934, we think it is going too far to say that the failure to take an X-ray of Mrs. Boyce's ankle at that time was so far a departure from ordinary medical standards that even laymen would know it to be gross negligence. Since, therefore, there was insufficient evidence in the record to show that defendant was guilty of malpractice, under the rules of law above set forth, the court properly instructed a verdict in favor of the defendant.

The judgment of the superior court is affirmed.

Notes

1. ***Jury Instructions.*** Parts 1, 2, 3, and 6 of the charge in *Boyce* may be subject to objection. *See* Russo v. Griffin, 510 A.2d 436 (Vt. 1986), *supra* at p. 310.

2. ***"Average" Professional?*** Part 1 of the charge refers to the "average" member of the profession. Consider the following:

> Not only would this ["average" standard] put a jury in a predicament as to how to arrive at an "average" but it seems to us that requiring the skill of the "average qualified practitioner" automatically makes approximately one-half of the doctors guilty of malpractice. The question is not one of the "average" or "medium" skill, but of the minimum skill.

Gambill v. Stroud, 531 S.W.2d 945, 950 (Ark. 1976).

3. ***Physician Liability to Third Parties.*** In some states, duties to third parties may be imposed on physicians. *See* Tenuto v. Lederle Labs., 687 N.E.2d 1300 (N.Y. 1997) (duty to warn parents of risks to their health resulting from vaccination of their child); DiMarco v. Lynch Homes-Chester County, Inc., 583 A.2d 422 (Pa. 1990) (claim stated by a third person against a doctor who negligently advised a patient with a communicable disease).

But see Schmidt v. Mahoney, 659 N.W.2d 552 (Iowa 2003) (a physician who allegedly advised a seizure patient that she could safely operate a car owed no duty to a third party who was seriously injured when the patient suffered a seizure); Althaus v. Cohen, 756 A.2d 1166 (Pa. 2000) (the special nature of the relationship between a therapist and child patient in a sexual abuse case precluded recognition of a duty to the parents).

4. ***Proving the Standard of Care in Malpractice Actions.***

(a) ***Matters of Common Knowledge.*** Expert testimony is not necessary in a malpractice action if the conduct required of a professional is a matter of common knowledge. Some courts hold that a surgeon is negligent as a matter of law if a foreign object, such as a sponge, is left in a patient following an operation. *See* Rudeck v. Wright, 709 P.2d 621 (Mont. 1985).

See also Schneider v. Haws, 118 S.W.3d 886 (Tex. App. 2003) (whether the failure to provide a patient with an escort or mechanism capable of safely returning her to the waiting room caused her to strike her head was a matter within the range of general experience and common sense, and therefore no expert testimony was needed); Sherbert v. Alcan Alum. Corp., 66 F.3d 965 (8th Cir. 1995) (expert testimony was not required to establish a breach of the standard of care applicable to a forklift operator because "[o]ne does not have to be a physicist to understand that tilting a 6,000 pound pile of slippery material, precariously balanced on the end of a forklift, involves the risk that some of the material will fall").

Many courts have narrowly interpreted the common-knowledge exception. *See, e.g.*, Gudin v. 6108 Hudson Ave., LLC, 2017 WL 4640058, at *3 (N.J. Super. App. Div.)

("[P]laintiff's belated and facially disingenuous attempt to jettison the requirement of expert testimony on the day of trial and rely instead on the common knowledge doctrine does not warrant discussion"); Osborn v. Irwin Mem. Blood Bank, 7 Cal. Rptr. 2d 101 (Ct. App. 1992) (the steps that should have been taken to safeguard the blood supply from AIDS in 1983 were not a matter of "common knowledge").

Other courts have been more generous. In Vasquez v. Macri, 2012 WL 4856024 (N.J. Super. A.D.), the court acknowledged that "as a general proposition, the nature and scope of an attorney's professional responsibilities to a client in a real estate closing may be outside the ken and experience of the average lay juror." Presumably, the typical juror would not know whether the validity of a transaction depended upon producing a certificate of occupancy (CO) or a certificate of continued occupancy (CCO). However, the court held that the plaintiff did not need to produce expert testimony about the standard of care because:

> Macri [the defendant lawyer] conceded that: (1) the Borough requires a CCO upon the transfer of title; (2) as attorney for the buyer, he was responsible for ensuring that plaintiff obtained clear title to the property; and (3) he mistakenly believed the seller's agent obtained and delivered to him a CCO at the time of closing.

Expert testimony is often required in tort actions against professionals other than doctors or lawyers. *See* Sage Title Group, LLC v. Roman, 166 A.3d 1026, 1043 (Md. 2017) (expert testimony was necessary to establish a title company's duties to a lender).

(b) ***Qualifying as an Expert Witness.*** Courts perform an important gatekeeping function in deciding who is qualified to testify as an expert. On the one hand, they must keep "junk science" out of the courtroom; on the other hand, the criteria for experts cannot be so demanding that litigants with potentially valid claims will not be able to meet them. Legislative encroachments on the gatekeeping function are sometimes resented by the judiciary. In Broussard v. St. Edward Mercy Health System, Inc., 2012 WL 149761 (Ark.), the court held that a statute which provided that expert testimony may only be given by "medical care providers of the same specialty as the defendant" violated the separation-of-powers doctrine.

(c) ***Expert Reliance on Disciplinary Rules.*** In legal malpractice actions, expert witnesses routinely rely on the ethics rules relating to lawyer discipline as evidence of the standard of care, even though those enactments typically provide that a violation does not automatically create a civil cause of action. The experts consider those provisions in preparing their opinions, and they often refer to them on the witness stand. In some states, attorneys litigating malpractice suits may prepare demonstrative evidence, for use as part of the expert's testimony or perhaps in closing argument, showing in enlarged font the text of relevant disciplinary rules. This can be powerful evidence of what type of conduct is required of a lawyer, for disciplinary rules often speak in sharply mandatory terms, using words like "shall" and "shall not." It can be persuasive evidence in a case involving alleged mishandling of client trust funds to be able to point to a large exhibit quoting a disciplinary rule saying, for example, that "Upon receiving funds . . . a lawyer *shall* promptly notify the client. . . . *shall* promptly deliver [the funds] to the client . . . and . . . *shall* promptly render a full accounting. . . ." *See* Model Rules of Prof'l Conduct Rule 1.15 (Westlaw 2022) (emphasis added). *See generally* Douglas R. Richmond, *Why Legal Ethics Rules Are Relevant to Lawyer Liability*, 38 St. Mary's L.J. 929, 947 (2007).

(d) ***Expert Witness Malpractice?*** Can an expert witness be sued for malpractice? In-court statements of an expert witness are protected by absolute immunity. *See* McGregor v. Rutberg, 478 F.3d 790, 791–92 (7th Cir. 2007).

Whether that immunity extends to the expert's pre-trial preparations—such as conducting tests or reviewing documents—is a matter of dispute. *See* Douglas R. Richmond, *The Emerging Theory of Expert Witness Malpractice*, 22 Cap. U. L. Rev. 693, 695-708 (1992). Richmond argues that expert witness liability "should mirror the scheme of the potential liability to which trial lawyers are subject."

> There is no question that an attorney's defamatory statement during a judicial proceeding is shielded from subsequent attack under the doctrine of immunity. However, the same attorney remains liable to his or her own client for any acts of malpractice that occur in that very forum.

See also LLMD of Mich., Inc. v. Jackson-Cross Co., 740 A.2d 186 (Pa. 1999) (holding that immunity did not bar a malpractice action based on an expert's allegedly negligent performance of mathematical calculations required to determine lost profits).

5. ***Ethics in Law Practice: Intimidating Experts.*** In Ky. Bar Assn. v. Mussler, 19 S.W.3d 87 (Ky. 2000), an attorney was publicly reprimanded for telling the opposing side's expert, during a deposition, that his client was filing suit against the expert based on the way in which the expert had conducted a medical examination of the client.

6. ***Hospital Liability.*** Originally, hospitals were free from tort liability under the doctrine of charitable immunity. Since abrogation of that doctrine (*see* Chapter 18), at least three theories have been used to hold hospitals liable for the negligence of a physician. First, *respondeat superior* liability may be imposed if the doctor is employed by the hospital and the negligence occurs within the scope of the doctor's employment. Second, even if a doctor is an independent contractor, many courts hold there is an "ostensible agency" (*see* Chapter 14), if the patient reasonably believes, based on the conduct of the hospital, that the physician is its employee. Finally, an increasing number of courts have endorsed the theory of "corporate negligence," under which a hospital may be held liable for failure to review a doctor's treatment of patients or require consultation. *See* Thompson v. Nason Hosp., 591 A.2d 703 (Pa. 1991).

7. ***Standard of Care for Medical Entities.*** In some suits against an entity, such as a hospital or blood bank, it makes sense to frame the standard of care in terms of what would be done by other similar institutions. *See* Osborn v. Irwin Mem. Blood Bank,

7 Cal. Rptr. 2d 101 (Ct. App. 1992) ("'that reasonable degree of skill, knowledge, and care ordinarily possessed and exercised' by other blood banks").

8. ***Federal Preemption of Health Care Claims.*** Many state law claims related to health care under employee benefit plans are preempted by federal law. *See* Aetna Health, Inc. v. Davila, 542 U.S. 200 (2004). Preemption is discussed in Chapter 15.

9. ***Professional-Layperson Sexual Relations.*** According to one article, "[s]exual misconduct is the leading cause of action against psychologists." The malpractice theory is that "the patient has given the therapist enormous power by revealing intimate details . . . , and the therapist has a duty not to abuse that power [by becoming sexually involved with the patient]." Julie Gannon Shoop, *Dangerous Liaisons: Patients Sue Therapists for Sexual Abuse*, Trial, Oct. 1992, at 12–13.

10. ***Statutes Relating to Malpractice.*** As noted in Chapter 4, numerous tort-reform statutes have modified the rules applicable to medical malpractice actions. For example, a statute in Texas (Tex. Civ. Prac. & Rem. Code § 74.301 *et seq.* (Westlaw 2022)) limits non-economic damages for a "health care liability claim" to $250,000 for each claimant. The law also imposes strict requirements with respect to expert witnesses and their reports (§ 74.351). Another provision caps damages in medical malpractice cases resulting in death (§ 74.303).

11. ***Affidavits of Merit.*** Some states require a malpractice plaintiff to file a certificate of merit at the start of the litigation. *See, e.g.*, N.J. Stat. Ann. 2a:53A-27 (Westlaw 2022) (requiring the filing of an expert "affidavit of merit" within 60 days of the defendant's answer in all professional malpractice actions against a "licensed person in his profession or occupation").

Scott v. Bradford

Supreme Court of Oklahoma
606 P.2d 554 (Okla. 1979)

DOOLIN, Justice.

This appeal is taken by plaintiffs . . . from a judgment in favor of defendant rendered on a jury verdict in a medical malpractice action.

Mrs. Scott's physician advised her she had several fibroid tumors on her uterus. He referred her to defendant surgeon. Defendant admitted her to the hospital where she signed a routine consent form prior to defendant's performing a hysterectomy. After surgery, Mrs. Scott experienced problems with incontinence. She visited another physician . . . This physician referred her to an urologist who, after three surgeries, succeeded in correcting her problems.

Mrs. Scott, joined by her husband, filed the present action alleging medical malpractice, claiming defendant failed to advise her of the risks involved or of available alternatives to surgery. She further maintained had she been properly informed she would have refused the surgery.

. . . .

The issue involved is whether Oklahoma adheres to the doctrine of informed consent as the basis of an action for medical malpractice, and if so did the present instructions adequately advise the jury of defendant's duty.

Anglo-American law starts with the premise of thoroughgoing self-determination, each man considered to be his own master. This law does not permit a physician to substitute his judgment for that of the patient by any form of artifice. The doctrine of informed consent arises out of this premise.

Consent to medical treatment, to be effective, should stem from an understanding decision based on adequate information about the treatment, the available alternatives, and the collateral risks. This requirement, labeled "informed consent," is, legally speaking, as essential as a physician's care and skill in the *performance* of the therapy. The doctrine imposes a duty on a physician or surgeon to inform a patient of his options and their attendant risks. If a physician breaches this duty, patient's consent is defective, and physician is responsible for the consequences.

If treatment is completely unauthorized and performed without any consent at all, there has been a battery. However, if the physician obtains a patient's consent but has breached his duty to inform, the patient has a cause of action sounding in negligence for failure to inform the patient of his options, regardless of the due care exercised at treatment, assuming there is injury.

... [E]arlier decisions seemed to perpetuate medical paternalism by giving the profession sweeping authority to decide unilaterally what is in the patient's best interests....

More recently, in perhaps one of the most influential informed consent decisions, Canterbury v. Spence, 464 F.2d 772 (D.C. Cir. 1972), ... the doctrine [of informed consent] received perdurable impetus. Judge Robinson ... emphasized the fundamental concept in American jurisprudence that every human being of adult years and sound mind has a right to determine what shall be done with his own body. True consent to what happens to one's self is the informed exercise of a choice. This entails an opportunity to evaluate knowledgeably the options available and the risks attendant upon each. It is the prerogative of every patient to chart his own course and determine which direction he will take.

The decision in *Canterbury* recognized the tendency of some jurisdictions to turn this duty on whether it is the custom of physicians practicing in the community to make the particular disclosure to the patient. That court rejected this standard and held the standard measuring performance of the duty of disclosure is conduct which is reasonable under the circumstances: "[We cannot] ignore the fact that to bind disclosure obligations to medical usage is to arrogate the decision on revelation to the physician alone." We agree. A patient's right to make up his mind whether to undergo treatment should not be delegated to the local medical group. What is reasonable disclosure in one instance may not be reasonable in another. We decline to adopt a standard based on the professional standard. We ... hold the scope of a physician's communications must be measured by his patient's need to know enough to enable him to make an intelligent choice. In other words, full disclosure of all *material risks* incident to treatment must be made. There is no bright line separating the material from the immaterial; it is a question of fact. A risk is material if it would be likely to affect patient's decision. When non-disclosure of a particular risk is open to debate, the issue is for the finder of facts.

This duty to disclose is the first element of the cause of action in negligence based on lack of informed consent. However, there are exceptions. . . . There is no need to disclose risks that either ought to be known by everyone or are already known to the patient. Further, the primary duty of a physician is to do what is best for his patient and where full disclosure would be detrimental to a patient's total care and best interests a physician may withhold such disclosure, for example, where disclosure would alarm an emotionally upset or apprehensive patient. Certainly too, where there is an emergency and the patient is in no condition to determine for himself whether treatment should be administered, the privilege may be invoked.

The patient has the burden of going forward with evidence tending to establish *prima facie* the essential elements of the cause of action. The burden of proving an exception to his duty and thus a privilege not to disclose, rests upon the physician as an affirmative defense.

The cause of action, based on lack of informed consent, . . . requires that plaintiff patient would have chosen no treatment or a different course of treatment had the alternatives and material risks of each been made known to him. If the patient would have elected to proceed with treatment had he been duly informed of its risks, then the element of causation is missing. In other words, a causal connection exists between physician's breach of the duty to disclose and patient's injury when and only when disclosure of material risks incidental to treatment would have resulted in a decision against it. A patient obviously has no complaint if he would have submitted to the treatment if the physician had complied with his duty and informed him of the risks. This fact decision raises the difficult question of the correct standard on which to instruct the jury.

The court in Canterbury v. Spence, *supra*, . . . permits liability only if non-disclosure would have affected the decision of a fictitious "reasonable patient," even though actual patient testifies he would have elected to forego therapy had he been fully informed.

. . . .

Although the *Canterbury* rule is probably that of the majority, its "reasonable man" approach has been criticized . . . as backtracking on its own theory of self-determination. The *Canterbury* view certainly severely limits the protection granted an injured patient. To the extent the plaintiff, given an adequate disclosure, would have declined the proposed treatment, and a reasonable person in similar circumstances would have consented, a patient's right of self-determination is *irrevocably lost.* This basic right to know and decide is the reason for the full-disclosure rule.

Accordingly, we decline to jeopardize this right by the imposition of the "reasonable man" standard.

If a plaintiff testifies he would have continued with the proposed treatment had he been adequately informed, the trial is over under either the subjective or objective approach. If he testifies he would not, then the causation problem must be resolved by examining the credibility of plaintiff's testimony. The jury must be instructed that it must find plaintiff would have refused the treatment if he is to prevail.

Although it might be said this approach places a physician at the mercy of a patient's hindsight, a careful practitioner can always protect himself by insuring that he has adequately informed each patient he treats. If he does not breach this duty, a causation problem will not arise.

The final element of this cause of action is that of injury. The risk must actually materialize and plaintiff must have been injured as a result of submitting to the treatment. Absent occurrence of the undisclosed risk, a physician's failure to reveal its possibility is not actionable.

. . . .

Because we are imposing a new duty on physicians, we hereby make this opinion prospective only, affecting those causes of action arising after the date this opinion is promulgated.

. . . . The instructions objected to did instruct that defendant should have disclosed material risks of the hysterectomy and feasibility of alternatives. Instructions are sufficient when considered as a whole they present the law applicable to the issues. . . . We find no basis for reversal.

Affirmed.

[The opinion of Justice BARNES, concurring in part and dissenting in part, has been omitted.]

Notes

*1. **Subjective Test, Objective Test, and Combined Test.*** Pennsylvania appears to employ a subjective test that is somewhat different from the subjective test in *Scott. See* Fitzpatrick v. Natter, 961 A.2d 1229, 1237 (Pa. 2008) (stating that a patient bringing a claim based on lack of informed consent must prove that the undisclosed "information would have factored substantially into her decision-making process. . . . The patient need not show that she would have chosen differently had she possessed the missing information, but only that the missing information would have been a substantial factor in this decision").

Most cases reject a subjective test for causation in informed consent cases. *See* Ashe v. Radiation Oncology Assoc., 9 S.W.3d 119 (Tenn. 2000) (endorsing the majority objective standard, which requires the jury to find that a reasonable person would have made a different decision).

"Several states have explicitly held that both subjective and objective tests must be met, so that the plaintiff will fail if she would have accepted the medical procedure even when fully informed, and she will also fail if she would have rejected it but a reasonable person would not have." Dan B. Dobbs, Paul T. Hayden, & Ellen M. Bublick, Hornbook on Torts 522 (2d ed. 2016).

2. ***Informed Consent and Infertility.*** In Brodsky v. Osunkwo, 2012 WL 1161598 (N.J. Super. A.D.), the court reinstated an informed-consent negligence claim against a doctor who failed to tell a sixteen-year-old male leukemia patient that chemotherapy would cause infertility and that he could have banked his sperm before submitting to the treatment.

3. ***Disclosure of Physician's Interests and Experience.*** Moore v. Regents of the Univ. of Cal., 793 P.2d 479 (Cal. 1990), extended the informed-consent doctrine to require disclosure of the physician's economic or research interests in the proposed medical procedure. *See also* Howard v. Univ. of Med., 800 A.2d 73 (N.J. 2002) ("[A] serious misrepresentation concerning the quality or extent of a physician's professional experience . . . can be material to the grant of intelligent and informed consent").

4. ***Informed-Consent Statutes.*** In some states, the common-law doctrine of informed consent in medicine has been augmented or replaced by statutory developments. For example, Texas has adopted detailed legislation (Tex. Civ. Prac. & Rem. Code § 74.101 *et seq.* (Westlaw 2022)) which creates a state Medical Disclosure Panel "to determine which risks and hazards related to medical care and surgical procedures must be disclosed by health care providers or physicians." *Id.* at § 74.102(a).

A New York statute provides:

New York Public Health Law § 2805-d (Westlaw 2022)
Limitation of medical, dental or podiatric malpractice action based on lack of informed consent

1. Lack of informed consent means the failure of the person providing the professional treatment or diagnosis to disclose to the patient such alternatives thereto and the reasonably foreseeable risks and benefits involved as a reasonable medical, dental or podiatric practitioner under similar circumstances would have disclosed, in a manner permitting the patient to make a knowledgeable evaluation.

2. The right of action to recover for medical, dental or podiatric malpractice based on a lack of informed consent is limited to those cases involving either (a) non-emergency treatment, procedure or surgery, or (b) a diagnostic procedure which involved invasion or disruption of the integrity of the body.

3. For a cause of action therefor it must also be established that a reasonably prudent person in the patient's position would not have undergone the treatment or diagnosis if he had been fully informed and that the lack of

informed consent is a proximate cause of the injury or condition for which recovery is sought.

4. It shall be a defense to any action for medical, dental or podiatric malpractice based upon an alleged failure to obtain such an informed consent that:

(a) the risk not disclosed is too commonly known to warrant disclosure; or

(b) the patient assured the medical, dental or podiatric practitioner he would undergo the treatment, procedure or diagnosis regardless of the risk involved, or the patient assured the medical, dental or podiatric practitioner that he did not want to be informed of the matters to which he would be entitled to be informed; or

(c) consent by or on behalf of the patient was not reasonably possible; or

(d) the medical, dental or podiatric practitioner, after considering all of the attendant facts and circumstances, used reasonable discretion as to the manner and extent to which such alternatives or risks were disclosed to the patient because he reasonably believed that the manner and extent of such disclosure could reasonably be expected to adversely and substantially affect the patient's condition.

5. ***Contributory Negligence in Informed-Consent Cases.*** In Brown v. Dibbell, 595 N.W.2d 358 (Wis. 1999), the court held that a patient's contributory negligence could be a defense in an action under the state medical informed-consent statute. The court wrote:

> A patient is usually the primary source of information about the patient's material personal, family and medical histories. If a doctor is to provide a patient with the information required by Wis. Stat. § 448.30, it is imperative that in response to a doctor's material questions a patient provide information that is as complete and accurate as possible under the circumstances. . . .

6. ***Informed Consent in Legal Malpractice.*** Informed consent principles apply as readily in law as in medicine. *See* Vincent R. Johnson, *The Informed Consent Doctrine in Legal Malpractice Law*, 11 St. Mary's J. Legal Mal. & Ethics 362 (2021):

> The doctrine of informed consent is now deeply embedded into the law of legal ethics. In legal malpractice litigation, the doctrine holds that a lawyer has a duty to disclose to a client material information about the risks and alternatives associated with a course of action. A lawyer who fails to make such required disclosures and fails to obtain informed consent is negligent, regardless of whether the lawyer otherwise exercises care in representing a client. If such negligent nondisclosures cause damages, the lawyer can be held accountable for the client's losses.

Id.

7. ***Comparative Law Perspective: Informed Consent in China.*** Yuan v. Yunnan Province No.1 People's Hospital was a medical malpractice case that arose in 2003 when Yuan Tian, a local radio station host, checked into a hospital for a voice treatment. Without written consent, the doctor performed surgery on her. After the surgery, Yuan's voice problems worsened, and she lost her job. Yuan sued the hospital to recover compensation for medical expenses, pain and suffering, lost wages, emotional distress, and attorney's fees. Yuan claimed that the hospital failed to obtain her consent and failed to fully inform her of the treatment risks and alternatives.

According to Chinese tort law, a doctor must explain the diagnosis, treatment, medical procedures, and risks associated with proposed treatment to the patient or to the patient's close family members. The doctor is also required to answer questions the patient has. The doctor must respect the patient's right to know about the treatment and right to decide whether to accept treatment. Prior to performing a surgery, the doctor must obtain written consent.

In *Yuan*, the doctor failed to obtain informed consent. The trial court's modest award of damages to the plaintiff was affirmed on appeal.

In contrast to Scott v. Bradford, *supra*, the Chinese court did not analyze whether the patient would have chosen the surgery had she known the risks. The reason for that omission is that Chinese tort law does not specifically address how causation issues should be handled at trial. Not surprisingly, Chinese judges often avoid any detailed discussion of causation in their judicial opinions. In addition, China does not have a common law system, so cases are not sources of binding legal principles applicable to later disputes. In writing opinions, judges have no discretion to cite previously decided cases to assist their analysis. Instead, their job is to focus on the relevant codified legal principles.

If a legal system does not have clear rules governing issues of causation, who benefits? Is it easier for plaintiffs to recover damages, or for defendants to avoid liability? Can a tort system operate fairly in the absence of such rules?

8. ***Ethics in Law Practice: Client Decisionmaking.*** Comment 1 to Rule 1.2 of the Model Rules of Professional Conduct (Westlaw 2022) states:

> [T]he client [has] the ultimate authority to determine the purposes to be served by legal representation, within the limits imposed by law and the lawyer's professional obligations.... With respect to the means by which the client's objectives are to be pursued, the lawyer shall consult with the client... and may take such action as is impliedly authorized to carry out the representation.

9. ***Breach of Confidentiality.*** The unauthorized disclosure of nonpublic information relating to a patient or client may be actionable under a variety of theories, including invasion of privacy, breach of contract, or breach of fiduciary duty. Some states simply recognize an independent common-law tort action for breach of confidence in the physician-patient setting. *See* Biddle v. Warren Gen. Hosp., 715 N.E.2d 518 (Ohio 1999).

i. Race, Gender, and Ethnicity

In tort law, the same standard of care applies to both men and women. However, recent years have seen the emergence of an important school of jurisprudence often described as "Law and Feminism." To simplify a complex subject greatly, feminists are somewhat divided in their approach to such matters as the place of women as participants in the legal system. Years ago, when stereotypes were somewhat more prevalent than today, feminists emphasized similarities between men and women, in opposition, for example, to those who thought that women were not "tough enough" to be lawyers. Today, some feminist scholars tend to focus upon differences between the ways in which men and women look at the world, in the hope that feminist views will reveal ways in which "male thinking" has (mis)shaped the law.

In *A Lawyer's Primer on Feminist Theory and Tort*, 38 J. Legal Educ. 3 (1988), Professor Leslie Bender argues that negligence law is permeated by traditional male values and perspectives:

> Our legal system . . . is a system that resolves problems through male inquiries formulated from distanced, abstract, and acontextual vantage points, while feminism emphasizes relationships, context, and factual particulars for resolving human problems.

Turning to the reasonable person standard, Professor Bender writes:

> It was originally believed that the "reasonable man" standard was gender neutral. "Man" was used in the generic sense to mean person or human being. But man is not generic except to other men. Would men regard a "prudent woman" standard as an appropriate measure of their due care? As our social sensitivity to sexism developed, our legal institutions did the "gentlemanly" thing and substituted the neutral word "person" for "man." . . . . The language of tort law was neutered, made "politically correct," and sensitized. Although tort law protected itself from allegations of sexism, it did not change its content and character.
>
> . . . . When the standard was written into judicial opinions, treatises, and casebooks, it was written about and by men. . . . When the authors of such works said "reasonable man," they meant "male," "man" in a gendered sense. . . . When . . . [the term] was converted to "reasonable person," it still meant "person who is reasonable by my standards" almost exclusively from the perspective of a male judge, lawyer, or law professor, or even a female lawyer trained to be "the same as" a male lawyer.
>
> Changing the word without changing the underlying model does not work. . . .
>
> . . . . If we are wedded to the idea of an objective measure, would it not be better to measure the conduct of a tortfeasor by the care that would be taken by a "neighbor" or "social acquaintance" or "responsible person with conscious care and concern for another's safety"?

> Perhaps we have gone astray in tort-law analysis because we use "reason" and caution as our standard of care, rather than focusing on care and concern. . . .
>
> . . . . Tort law should begin with a premise of responsibility rather than rights, or interconnectedness rather than separation, and a priority of safety rather than profit or efficiency. The masculine voice of rights, autonomy, and abstraction has led to a standard that protects efficiency and profit; the feminine voice can design a tort system that encourages behavior that is caring about others' safety and responsive to others' needs or hurts, and that attends to human contexts and consequences.[5]

Other feminists have questioned Bender's assumption that negligence standards and cases are always based on a "male" perspective. Professor Margo Schlanger has examined three categories of nineteenth and early twentieth century cases, those involving injuries to women who were car and wagon passengers, those involving injuries to female wagon drivers, and those involving injuries to women getting on and off trains. She writes that:

> [r]eported decisions in these categories evince common understandings of gender differences courts considered relevant: that wives had less authority than husbands, that women were less competent in the public sphere of transportation than men, and that women were less physically agile than men. . . . The results of . . . [the] interplay [between those understandings and tort doctrine] were as complex as gender differences and tort law themselves . . . [O]ne solid conclusion to be drawn from all three categories is that, as might be expected given the existence of female accident victims and the importance of gender to social ordering, the accusation of erasure of gender difference is incorrect. Far from naively erasing gender by subsuming women into the male category of "reasonable men" or a purportedly neutral, but no less male category of "reasonable persons," courts actually treated gender as an important factor in assessing appropriate standards of care. Neither do the cases support a charge of invariable refusal to take account of women's experience, or of consistent deprecation of women's capabilities. Each of the three categories of opinions serves as a case study of tort law's intricate interaction with gender difference, illuminating the diversity of possible and actual legal approaches to thinking about women's agency, authority, and capabilities. Together, in rhetoric, analysis, and result, they present a world frequently, although not uniformly, friendly to women and their needs.

Margo Schlanger, *Injured Women Before Common Law Courts, 1860–1930*, 21 Harv. Women's L.J. 79 (1998).

---

5. Reprinted with permission.

Even if the historical background of the reasonable person standard is more complicated than Bender suggests, do Bender's observations shed interesting light on tort law? How would tort law be different if it began with a premise of responsibility, care, and connectedness? For example, would loss of consortium compensation be broader or narrower than it is?

As the following case indicates, there is some support for the idea that the circumstances of the actor might change the standard of care.

John Doe BF v. Diocese of Gallup

Supreme Court of the Navajo Nation
No. SC-CV-06-10 (Nav. Sup. Ct. Sept. 9, 2011)

Before YAZZI, C.J., and SHIRLEY and PLATERO, JJ.

. . . .

Appellant alleged that as a 14–15 year old child, he had been sexually molested by Cichanowicz "on the Navajo reservation" after being given alcohol by Cichanowicz, who was then his priest.... Appellant alleged that Cichanowicz threatened him with exposure if he told anyone about the abuse. Appellant asserts that the Diocese, Baptist Order and Guadalupe Order aided and encouraged Cichanowicz in the abuse by transferring him when he was caught sexually abusing children, continuing to assign him to parishes with unsupervised access to children, failing to report his wrongful conduct to authorities and the public, and in having no system in place to supervise priests, such as Cichanowicz, to ensure that no minors were abused in their care.

Appellant did not file his complaint until more than twenty years had passed after the alleged abuse occurred. Explaining the delay, Appellant claimed that until May 2007, he did not discover that he had been injured by the abuse, the injuries did not manifest themselves in a psychological and objective manner and were not ascertainable to him, and due to the nature of the injuries, it was not possible for him to connect the symptoms and injuries to the acts of abuse before then....

7 N.N.C. § 602(A)(4) provides:

> No cause of action accrues for personal injury or wrongful death until the party having the right to sue has discovered the nature of the injury, the cause of the injury, and the identity of the party whose action or inaction caused the injury, or until, in the exercise of reasonable diligence, in light of available knowledge and resources, the party should have discovered these facts, whichever is earlier. This Subsection applies to and revives all injured parties' claims, regardless of whether the claim may have been barred in the absence of this Subsection.

Appellant submitted a sworn affidavit and articles on childhood sex abuse in support of his assertion that he was unable to discover that the abuse was the cause of his injury, nor the nature of his injury, for over twenty years. The district court gave little weight to this evidence and concluded that Appellant's mere assertion of delayed insight or delayed discovery was not enough to permit the late filing of his complaint under the conditions set forth in Section 602(A)(4). . . .

Our courts have not previously been asked to interpret the meaning of 7 N.N.C. § 6702(A)(4)'s requirement for "the exercise of reasonable diligence, in light of available knowledge and resources" in relation to a childhood sex abuse case. The legislative history of Section 602(A)(4) shows that it was enacted in order to give uranium radiation victims extra time for their injuries to manifest before filing a personal injury claim. . . . Widespread child sex abuse by priests was not yet well-known. No Navajo Nation law specifically addresses child sex abuse victimization as a civil proceeding.

. . . . Appellant's submitted materials include journal articles on the severity of child sex abuse in Indian Country. . . . The articles suggest that Native American boys, as a "relatively powerless minority" may be expected to have acute effects of withdrawal and loss of contact with community when exposed to such abuse, where healing is traditionally achieved through social integration. . . . [I]t is the right of children to be free of abuse. The vital status of tribal children is further recognized under federal law at 25 U.S.C. § 1901(3) (ICWA). . . .

Tracing psychological and mental injuries over many years primarily to this abuse and not to other causes will not be a simple task. However, we hold that this is a factual issue suitable for a jury to consider at trial, not weighed by a judge in a preliminary motion. Our courts have a duty, in *parens patriae*, to ensure allegations of harm to our children are fully heard and not dismissed on mere technicalities.

Appellant asks that the Court use the "Objective person in Plaintiff's position" standard, taking into account a person's upbringing, culture and circumstances after having been subjected to the abuse. This Court agrees that such a standard is applicable on the Navajo Nation. Under this standard in this case, "reasonable diligence" in 7 N.N.C. § 602(A)(4) must be applied to a Navajo person, not a faceless individual whose "reasonable diligence" is measured by an objective standard applied by the dominant culture. . . . We do not blindly accept what the phrases have been taken to mean by other societies. To determine what is reasonable for a member of the Navajo Nation, it is entirely appropriate to consider factors such as historical trauma and the deference expected of a people by authority figures of a colonizing culture. Citing Martinez-Sandoval v Kirsch, 118 N.M. 616, 618–20 (N.M. Ct. App. 1994), Appellant further asks that the standard of the "reasonable person who has been subjected to the conduct" whose judgment is "altered in some way" be adopted in assessing whether a reasonable person could have discovered the cause or nature of an injury sooner. The Court finds this standard applicable, given the language of 7 N.N.C. § 602(A)(4) pertaining to "available knowledge and resources."

. . . .

The District Court's Order to Dismiss is Vacated. This matter is hereby remanded for further proceedings consistent with this opinion.

2. Judge-Made Standards

As noted earlier, one of the disadvantages of allowing the finder of fact to determine on a case-by-case basis whether a particular defendant exercised reasonable care is that similar cases may give rise to different results. Disparities may arise solely because of differences in the temperaments of juries, or the skills of counsel, or the attractiveness of the parties in the eyes of the jurors. Another disadvantage is that a prospective defendant is given no clear notice of what conduct is expected. In addition, when the same fact patterns recur, judicial resources may be wasted in hearing and resolving largely identical suits.

A possible approach to the reasonable care question is for a court, in the context of a given case, to attempt to articulate definite rules of conduct on issues of continuing importance. That is, in abstract terms, a court could rule that "In situation X, it is negligent as a matter of law for a person not to do Y." Theoretically, this rule would then be followed in subsequent cases involving situation X, thereby eliminating the problem of inconsistent results. The existence of the rule would give potential defendants notice of what type of care is expected. It would also encourage out-of-court settlements, because the outcome of litigation under the rule would be more predictable.

Settling Matters "Once and for All." The difficulty with this approach is that even apparently similar disputes frequently involve important details which call for a result contrary to the general rule. For example, early in the twentieth century, accidents were common in which cars had been struck by trains after proceeding across railroad tracks where vision was obstructed. Attempting to resolve the matter "once and for all," Justice Oliver Wendell Holmes, in B & O R. Co. v. Goodman, 275 U.S. 66 (1927), wrote: "if a driver cannot be sure otherwise whether a train is dangerously near he must stop and get out of his vehicle . . . and look." The rule seemed sensible, but in practice it proved unrealistic. Road conditions vary greatly from one place to another, and it is impossible to say with certainty that it is always less dangerous to get out of one's car and reconnoiter than to proceed ahead with caution. The Court's effective repudiation of the *Goodman* rule in Pokora v. Wabash Ry. Co., 292 U.S. 98 (1934), just seven years after its adoption, stands as a lesson that courts should be cautious in articulating inflexible rules to govern varying and complex occurrences.

Duty to Wear a Seat Belt. Suppose the issue is whether the failure of the driver of a car to wear a seat belt was negligent. This may be a matter on which reasonable persons could differ; if so, it seems to fit the model of a factual question. But does it make any sense to try this question again and again, with some factfinders determining that the conduct was negligent and others finding it not negligent? The Third Restatement takes the position that this particular issue should be dealt with as a question of law:

> Occasionally . . . the need for providing a clear and stable answer to the question of negligence is so overwhelming as to justify a court in withdrawing the negligence evaluation from the jury. In highway-accident cases, for

> example, the question recurrently arises whether it is contributory negligence not to wear an available seat belt. Granted, the advantages to wearing a seat belt vary to some extent from case to case.... Still, the benefits of having the contributory-negligence question settled in advance are of such force as to make it acceptable for a state's highest court to reach a final, general decision as to whether not wearing seat belts is or is not contributory negligence.

Restatement, Third, of Torts: Liab. for Physical & Emotional Harm § 8 cmt. c (2010).

One well-known example of judicial declaration of the standard of care is Helling v. Carey.

Helling v. Carey

Supreme Court of Washington
519 P.2d 981 (Wash. 1974)

HUNTER, Associate Justice.

This case arises from a malpractice action instituted by the plaintiff..., Barbara Helling.

The plaintiff suffers from primary open angle glaucoma... [,] a condition of the eye in which there is an interference in the ease with which the nourishing fluids can flow out of the eye. Such a condition results in pressure gradually rising above the normal level to such an extent that damage is produced to the optic nerve and its fibers with resultant loss in vision. The first loss usually occurs in the periphery of the field of vision. The disease usually has few symptoms and, in the absence of a pressure test, is often undetected until the damage has become extensive and irreversible.

The defendants..., Dr. Thomas F. Carey and Dr. Robert C. Laughlin, are partners who practice the medical specialty of ophthalmology. Ophthalmology involves the diagnosis and treatment of defects and diseases of the eye.

The plaintiff first consulted the defendants for myopia, nearsightedness, in 1959. At that time she was fitted with contact lenses. She next consulted the defendants in September, 1963, concerning irritation caused by the contact lenses. Additional consultations occurred in October, 1963; February, 1967; September, 1967; May, 1968; July, 1968; August, 1968; September, 1968; and October, 1968. Until the October 1968 consultation, the defendants considered the plaintiff's visual problems to be related solely to complications associated with her contact lenses. On that occasion,... Dr. Carey, tested the plaintiff's eye pressure and field of vision for the first time. This test indicated that the plaintiff had glaucoma. The plaintiff, who was then 32 years of age, had essentially lost her peripheral vision and her central vision was reduced to approximately 5 degrees vertical by 10 degrees horizontal....

After consulting other physicians, the plaintiff filed a complaint against the defendants alleging... that she sustained severe and permanent damage to her eyes as a proximate result of the defendants' negligence.... [T]he testimony of the medical experts for both the plaintiff and the defendants established that the standards of the profession for that specialty in the same or similar circumstances do not require routine pressure tests for glaucoma upon patients under 40 years of age. The reason ... is that the disease rarely occurs in this age group. Testimony indicated, however, that the standards of the profession do require pressure tests if the patient's complaints and symptoms reveal to the physician that glaucoma should be suspected.

The trial court entered judgment for the defendants following a defense verdict. The plaintiff thereupon appealed to the Court of Appeals, which affirmed....

We find this to be a unique case. The testimony of the medical experts is undisputed concerning the standards of the profession for the specialty of ophthalmology.... The issue is whether the defendants' compliance with the standard of the profession of ophthalmology, which does not require the giving of a routine pressure test to persons under 40 years of age, should insulate them from liability....

The incidence of glaucoma in one out of 25,000 persons under the age of 40 may appear quite minimal. However, that one person, the plaintiff in this instance, is entitled to the same protection, as afforded persons over 40, essential for timely detection of the evidence of glaucoma where it can be arrested to avoid the grave and devastating result of this disease. The test is a simple pressure test, relatively inexpensive. There is no judgment factor involved, and there is no doubt that by giving the test the evidence of glaucoma can be detected. The giving of the test is harmless if the physical condition of the eye permits. The testimony indicates that although the condition of the plaintiff's eyes might have at times prevented the defendants from administering the pressure test, there is an absence of evidence in the record that the test could not have been timely given.

... [R]easonable prudence required the timely giving of the pressure test to this plaintiff. The precaution of giving this test to detect the incidence of glaucoma to patients under 40 years of age is so imperative that irrespective of its disregard by the standards of the ophthalmology profession, it is the duty of the courts to say what is required to protect patients under 40 from the damaging results of glaucoma.

We therefore hold, as a matter of law, that the reasonable standard that should have been followed under the undisputed facts of this case was the timely giving of this simple, harmless pressure test to this plaintiff and that, in failing to do so, the defendants were negligent, which proximately resulted in the blindness sustained by the plaintiff for which the defendants are liable.

....

The judgment of the trial court and the decision of the Court of Appeals is reversed, and the case is remanded for a new trial on the issue of damages only.

[The concurring opinion of UTTER, Associate Justice, has been omitted.]

Notes

1. ***Overruling Controversial Decisions***. The decision in *Helling* was promptly followed by legislative action. Section 4.24.290 of the Washington Revised Code now

provides that in order to prevail in a medical malpractice action, other than an action based on failure to obtain informed patient consent, a plaintiff must:

> prove by a preponderance of the evidence that the defendant or defendants failed to exercise that degree of skill, care, and learning possessed at that time by other persons in the same profession....

This statute seems to have been intended to overrule Helling v. Carey. However, in Gates v. Jenson, 595 P.2d 919, 924 (Wash. 1979), a subsequent case involving glaucoma testing, the court reaffirmed the *Helling* view that reasonable prudence may sometimes still require a higher standard of care than is followed by other professionals. The court reasoned that the quoted statute did not abrogate *Helling*. In recent years, some legislatures overruling judge-made law have cited the specific decisions meant to be overruled, to reduce the danger of misinterpretation.

2. ***Lightning***. In Maussner v. Atlantic City Country Club, 691 A.2d 826 (N.J. Super Ct. App. Div. 1997), the court wrote:

> All golf courses have a duty to post a sign that details what, if any, safety procedures are being utilized by the golf course to protect its patrons from lightning. If a particular golf course uses no safety precautions, its sign must inform golfers that they play at their own risk and that no safety procedures are being utilized to protect golfers from lightning strikes.

3. ***Lead Paint***. In Antwaun A. v. Heritage Mut. Ins. Co., 596 N.W.2d 456 (Wis. 1999), the court held that, as a matter of common law, a duty to test for lead paint arises whenever the landlord of a residential property constructed before 1978 either knows or should know that there is peeling or chipping paint on the rental property. The court noted that in 1978 the Consumer Products Safety Commission banned the use of lead paint on residential properties.

3. Standards Created by Statute

Statutes Expressly Creating a Civil Cause of Action. Some statutes expressly provide that a violation gives rise to a tort action for damages. There are at least three subcategories:

First, many of these statutes clearly state what must be done to avoid liability when engaging in an activity. For example, in Norton v. Wilbur Waggoner Equip. Rental, 394 N.E.2d 403 (Ill. 1979), the statute at issue required any person having charge of the erection of a building to "provide planking or scaffolding" for workers to stand on. It further provided:

> For any injury to person ... occasioned by wilful violations of this act ... a right of action shall accrue to the party injured, for any direct damages sustained thereby.

There was no question in *Norton* that scaffolding had not been provided — the standard of care had been violated — and that injuries had been sustained by the plaintiff.

The court devoted its attention to the question of who was the person "in charge," within the language of the statute.

Second, some statutes prohibit or discourage certain activities by raising a threat of liability. For example, Minn. Stat. § 617.245(2) (Westlaw 2022) provides:

> A cause of action exists for injury caused by the use of a minor in a sexual performance. The cause of action exists against a person who promotes, employs, uses, or permits a minor to engage . . . in posing or modeling alone or with others in a sexual performance, if the person knows or has reason to know that the conduct intended is a sexual performance.
>
> A person found liable for injuries under this section is liable to the minor for damages. . . .

Third, some statutes refer to the common law duty of reasonable care and make it clear it applies in a particular context and that an injured person can sue for damages. For example, in Scott v. Minneapolis Pub. Sch., Spec. Dist. No. 1, 2006 WL 997721 (Minn. App. 2006), the state Government Data Practices Act required school districts to "establish appropriate security safeguards for all records containing data on individuals" and expressly provided for civil remedies "stating that a responsible authority who violates any provision of the act is liable to a person 'who suffers any damage' as a result of the violation." The court held that the defendant school district was liable to a child where education records were improperly disposed of and came into the possession of other children who ridiculed the plaintiff as "dumb" and "retarded."

Whenever a legislative enactment expressly creates a tort cause of action, the court's deliberations will normally be confined to questions of the enactment's applicability to the facts at hand and its constitutionality.

Sexual Abuse Statutes. In Marquay v. Eno, 662 A.2d 272 (N.H. 1995), the court held that a statute requiring any person having reason to suspect that a child has been abused or neglected to report the abuse to the state did not create a private cause of action in favor of abused former students against school employees who allegedly violated the statute's reporting requirement since neither the statute nor the legislative history directly revealed any such legislative intent.

However, some states have sexual abuse statutes that expressly recognize a cause of action against the abuser. For example, the New Jersey law expressly provides:

> b. In any civil action for injury or illness based on sexual abuse, the cause of action shall accrue at the time of reasonable discovery of the injury and its causal relationship to the act of sexual abuse. . . .
>
> h. A plaintiff who prevails in a civil action pursuant to this act shall be awarded damages in the amount of $10,000, plus reasonable attorney's fees, or actual damages, whichever is greater. . . .

N.J. Stat. Ann. § 2A:61B-1 (Westlaw 2022).

4. Standards Adopted by Courts Based on Legislation

Many statutes impose standards of care, but do not expressly make those standards applicable to tort cases. For example, laws establishing speed limits typically provide only for criminal or administrative sanctions, such as a fine payable to the state or suspension of a driver's license. In dealing with this kind of legislative enactment, a court may adopt the statute as stating the standard for civil suits. The essential inquiry is whether the statute was intended to protect this class of persons from the type of harm that occurred.

Some states have enacted statutes which state these requirements. In other jurisdictions, the relevant factors are set down in common law principles.

In Hickey v. Gen. Electric Co., 539 S.W.3d 19 (Ky. 2018), an employee stated a tort action against his former employer pursuant to Kentucky's negligence per se statute by alleging that the employer falsely told the Division of Unemployment Insurance that the employee had voluntarily quit. That type of assertion violated the State's criminal prohibition against making false statements during unemployment proceedings. The plaintiff was permitted to sue in tort to recover damages because he was a member of the class the penal statute was intended to protect (namely, employees) and the harm was the type the penal statute was intended to prevent (loss of employment benefits).

a. In General

Gipson v. Kasey

Supreme Court of Arizona
150 P.3d 228 (Ariz. 2007)

BALES, Justice.

. . . .

. . . . Kasey attended an employee holiday party hosted by the restaurant where he worked. Also present were his co-worker, Nathan Followill, and Followill's girlfriend, Sandy Watters. The restaurant provided beer for the guests. Kasey brought whiskey to the party and he gave shots to others present, including Followill, who was twenty-one years old. Kasey also brought pain pills containing oxycodone, a narcotic drug, which he had been prescribed for back pain. On prior occasions, Kasey had given pain pills to other co-workers for their recreational use.

During the party, Watters asked Kasey for one of his pain pills. Kasey gave Watters eight pills. . . . Although Kasey knew that combining the pills with alcohol or taking more than the prescribed dosage could have dangerous side effects, including death, he did not tell Watters this information.

When Kasey gave the pills to Watters, he knew that she was dating Followill. Kasey also knew that Followill was interested in taking prescription drugs for recreational purposes because Followill had on prior occasions asked Kasey for some of his pills, but Kasey had refused because he thought Followill was "too stupid and immature to take drugs like that."

Shortly after she obtained the pills from Kasey, Watters told Followill she had them, and Followill took the pills from her. As the night progressed, Followill became increasingly intoxicated. Around 1:00 a.m., Watters and Followill left the party. The next morning, Watters awoke to find that Followill had died in his sleep. The cause of death was the combined toxicity of alcohol and oxycodone.

Gipson, Followill's mother, filed a wrongful death action against Kasey. The superior court granted summary judgment for Kasey, finding that he owed Followill no duty of care....

The court of appeals reversed....

.... Whether the defendant owes the plaintiff a duty of care is a threshold issue; absent some duty, an action for negligence cannot be maintained....

It is well settled that "[t]he existence of a statute criminalizing conduct is one aspect of Arizona law supporting the recognition of [a] duty." .... Not all criminal statutes, however, create duties in tort. A criminal statute will "establish a tort duty [only] if the statute is 'designed to protect the class of persons, in which the plaintiff is included, against the risk of the type of harm which has in fact occurred' as a result of its violation...."

....

Several Arizona statutes prohibit the distribution of prescription drugs to persons lacking a valid prescription.... As the court of appeals recognized, "[t]hese statutes are designed to avoid injury or death to people who have not been prescribed prescription drugs, who may have no medical need for them and may in fact be endangered by them, and who have not been properly instructed on their usage, potency, and possible dangers." .... Because Followill is within the class of persons to be protected by the statute and the harm that occurred here is the risk that the statute sought to protect against, these statutes create a tort duty.

Kasey argues that because the legislature did not create a civil duty for a violation of these criminal statutes, a duty does not exist. But this notion was rejected in ... [an earlier case]: "[A] duty of care and the attendant standard of conduct may be found in a statute silent on the issue of civil liability." ....

Kasey also contends that because Arizona law does not impose a duty on social hosts who serve alcohol to adults, there should similarly be no duty here. We disagree.... [T]he legislature specifically exempted social hosts from liability for harm caused by a consumer of legal drinking age. No similar statute exempts those who improperly give their prescription drugs to others....

Kasey argues that this Court should adopt a no-duty rule precluding recovery on the grounds that a person who voluntarily becomes intoxicated and thereby sustains an injury should not be able to recover from the person supplying the intoxicants. We reject this reasoning. Followill's own actions may reduce recovery under comparative fault principles or preclude recovery if deemed a superseding cause of the harm, but those are determinations to be made by the factfinder....

We hold that Kasey did owe a duty of care based on Arizona's statutes prohibiting the distribution of prescription drugs to persons not covered by the prescription. Accordingly, we vacate ... and remand ... for further proceedings....

[The concurring opinion of HURWITZ, J., has been omitted.]

Notes

1. ***Wrong Class of Persons.*** In Barnett v. Ludwig and Company, 960 N.E.2d 722 (Ill. App. 2011), the court held that a 17-year-old guest who drowned in an apartment complex swimming pool was not within the class of persons intended to be protected by a statute requiring lifeguards "at all pools ... when persons under the age of 16 are allowed in the pool."

In Smrtka v. Boote, 2017 WL 1235471 (Ohio App.), a patient of a chiropractor was bitten in the doctor's waiting room by a dog who was also a patient of the doctor. The injured patient (Smrtka) argued that the doctor was negligent *per se* because a state statute prohibited veterinary practice without a license. The court rejected that argument, finding that statute was not intended to protect patients (like Smrtka), but simply imposed duties owed to the veterinary licensing board.

Safety statutes are often interpreted as not intended to protect professional rescuers from harm. *See* Entwistle v. Draves, 490 A.2d 313 (N.J. Super. Ct. App. Div. 1985) (statute prohibiting tavern brawls and other disorderly conduct was intended to protect the general public, not police officers called upon to restore order).

2. ***Wrong Type of Harm.*** In Pelkey v. Brennan, 209 N.Y.S.2d 691 (App. Div. 1961), a 13-year-old girl was injured while roller skating. In an action against the rink, the court held that the statute, which prohibited the rink from allowing children under the age of 16 to frequent the establishment after 7:00 p.m. unaccompanied by an adult, did not set the applicable standard of care. The statute was intended not to prevent physical injuries, but to protect the moral well-being and study habits of children.

See also de Villers v. County of San Diego, 67 Cal. Rptr. 3d 253 (Ct. App. 2007) (holding that a regulation to prevent the theft of drugs was not intended to protect the public from the danger that stolen drugs would be used to commit premeditated murder); Remsburg v. Montgomery, 831 A.2d 18 (Md. 2003) (holding that a statute regulating hunting on privately owned land was intended to prevent harm to property, not accidental shooting of a person).

3. ***Alternative to Negligence Per Se.*** Even if a statute does not set the standard of care on the ground that it was intended to protect a different class of persons or prevent a different type of harm, negligence may be established under the reasonable-person standard applied to the facts of the case. For example, in De Gregorio v. Malloy, 52 A.2d 195 (Pa. 1947), a police officer escorting an emergency vehicle through heavy traffic was injured while riding on its running board. The court held that the

plaintiff's violation of legislation prohibiting persons from hanging onto or riding on the outside of vehicles did not establish contributory negligence because the statute, entitled "Tampering with vehicles," was intended to prevent injuries to *trespassing persons*. The court nevertheless held that the jury could determine, based on its assessment of the facts, that the plaintiff acted unreasonably and was contributorily negligent.

In some instances, it is appropriate for a jury to take into account the fact that the conduct of an actor ran afoul of a statute that did not set the standard of care. *See* Restatement (Third) of Torts: Liab. for Physical and Emotional Harm § 14 cmt. j (2010) (discussing inapplicable statutes).

4. ***Assessing Legislative Intent.*** In interpreting legislation, a court will look to the language of the statute, including its title, and to the legislative history of the act, including statements by the bill's sponsor, committee findings, and the like. A court often enjoys considerable discretion in making this assessment, and reasonable minds may differ.

For example, in Ney v. Yellow Cab Co., 117 N.E.2d 74 (Ill. 1954), the plaintiff was struck by the defendant's taxi while it was being driven by a thief who had stolen it. Contrary to statute, the cab had been left unattended, with the key in the ignition and the motor running. Upon considering the legislation, the majority concluded that the key-removal provision was intended to protect the public from harm to persons or property, and that there was no reason to think that the legislature had intended to distinguish between harm precipitated by the intervention of a criminal actor and other causes of harm. Taking precisely the opposite view, the dissenter concluded that because there was no direct indication that the legislature had considered the issue of harm occasioned by theft, as opposed to harm caused by negligent or inadvertent operation of a vehicle in which a key had been left, the statute was not intended to prevent the type of accident which had occurred.

Stachniewicz v. Mar-Cam Corp.

Supreme Court of Oregon
488 P.2d 436 (Or. 1971)

HOLMAN, Justice.

The patron of a drinking establishment seeks to recover against the operator for personal injuries allegedly inflicted by other customers during a barroom brawl. The jury returned a verdict for defendant. Plaintiff appealed.

From the evidence introduced, the jury could find as follows:

A fight erupted in a bar between a group of persons of American Indian ancestry, who were sitting in a booth, and other customers who were at an adjacent table with plaintiff. One of plaintiff's friends had refused to allow a patron from the booth to dance with the friend's wife because the stranger was intoxicated. Thereafter, such threats as, "Hey, Whitey, how big are you?" were shouted from the booth at plaintiff and his companion. One of the persons at the table, after complaining to the bartender, was warned by him, "Don't start trouble with those guys." Soon thereafter, those individuals who had been sitting in the booth approached the table and one of them knocked down a person who was talking to a member of plaintiff's party. With that, the brawl commenced.

After a short melee, someone shouted "Fuzz!" and those persons who had been sitting in the booth ran out a door and into the parking lot, with one of plaintiff's friends in hot pursuit. Upon reaching the door, the friend discovered plaintiff lying just outside with his feet wedging the door open.

Plaintiff suffered retrograde amnesia and could remember nothing of the events....

The customers in the booth had been drinking in defendant's place of business for approximately two and one-half hours before the affray commenced.

The principal issue is whether ... violations of ORS 471.410(3) and of Oregon Liquor Control Regulation No. 10-065(2) constitute negligence as a matter of law. The portion of the statute relied on by plaintiff reads as follows:

> (3) No person shall give or otherwise make available any alcoholic liquor to a person visibly intoxicated....

The portion of the regulation to which plaintiff points provides:

> (2) No licensee shall permit or suffer any loud, noisy, disorderly or boisterous conduct, or any profane or abusive language, in or upon his licensed premises, or permit any visibly intoxicated person to enter or remain upon his licensed premises.

The trial court held that a violation of either the statute or the regulation did not constitute negligence *per se*....

A violation of a statute or regulation constitutes negligence as a matter of law when the violation results in injury to a member of the class of persons intended to be protected by the legislation and when the harm is of the kind which the statute or regulation was enacted to prevent.... The reason behind the rule is that when a legislative body has generalized a standard from the experience of the community and prohibits conduct that is likely to cause harm, the court accepts the formulation....

However, in addition, it is proper for the court to examine preliminarily the appropriateness of the standard as a measure of care for civil litigation under the circumstances presented.... The statute in question prevents making available alcohol to a person who is *already visibly intoxicated*. This makes the standard particularly inappropriate for the awarding of civil damages because of the extreme difficulty, if not impossibility, of determining whether a third party's injuries would have been caused, in any event, by the already inebriated person. Unless we are prepared to say that an alcoholic drink given after visible intoxication is the cause of a third party's injuries as a matter of law, a concept not advanced by anyone, the standard would be one almost impossible of application by a factfinder in most circumstances.

....

The regulation promulgated by the commission is an altogether different matter. The regulation required certain conduct of licensees in the operation of bars....

An examination of the regulation discloses that it concerns matters having a direct relation to the creation of physical disturbances in bars which would, in turn, create a likelihood of injury to customers. A common feature of our western past, now preserved in story and reproduced on the screen hundreds of times, was the carnage of the barroom brawl. No citation of authority is needed to establish that the "abuses associated with saloons," which the Liquor Control Act seeks to prevent, included permitting on the premises profane, abusive conduct and drunken clientele (now prohibited by the regulation) which results in serious personal injuries to customers in breach of the bar owner's duty to protect his patrons from harm. We find it reasonable to assume that the commission, in promulgating the regulation, intended to prevent these abuses, and that they had in mind the safety of patrons of bars as well as the general peace and quietude of the community....

.... We believe it would be fair for the jury to infer, in the circumstances set forth in the statement of the facts, that plaintiff was injured by one of the persons in the booth who had created the disturbance and that the injuries would not have occurred except for defendant's violation of the commission's regulation, as alleged.

The judgment of the trial court is reversed and the case is remanded for a new trial.

Notes

1. ***Exclusive Penalties.*** A court may not adopt a statute as setting the civil standard of care if the legislature intended that the specified penalty would be the exclusive sanction for an infraction, or if there is other evidence that the legislature intended to bar use of the statutory standard in tort cases. Some statutes expressly state that evidence of a violation of their provisions shall not be admissible in a civil action. *See, e.g.*, Tex. Health & Safety Code § 242.017 (Westlaw 2022) (nursing home law).

2. ***Private Rights of Action Under Federal Law.*** It is often difficult to argue successfully that federal laws create implied causes of action for harm caused by breaches of their terms. *See In re Matthys*, 2010 WL 2176086 (Bkrtcy. S.D. Ind.) (no implied right of action under a law requiring creditors to redact social security numbers from documents filed with a bankruptcy court).

3. ***Laws That Invite Reliance.*** Occasionally one finds the opposite of an exclusive penalty: a legislative enactment that invites judicial reliance. One such provision can be found in the City of San Antonio (Texas) Code of Ethics. When the code was drafted, reformers were faced with a dilemma concerning enforcement mechanisms. Cities, even large cities, have limited powers. They cannot create new tort causes of action. However, to create the possibility that the code's conflict of interest and other rules could be backed up by the imposition of civil liability, the drafters included this language in the section on sanctions (sec. 2-87(f)(2)):

> This code of ethics has been enacted . . . to protect the City and any other person from any losses or increased costs incurred by the City or other person as a result of the violation of these provisions. It is the intent of the City that this ethics code can and should be recognized by a court as a proper basis for a civil cause of action for damages or injunctive relief based upon a violation of its provisions, and that such forms of redress should be available in addition to any other penalty or remedy contained in this code of ethics . . . or any other law.

Suppose that a business bidding on a city contract violates the ethics rules and there needs to be a new round of proposals. Under this language, the city and the bidders may then be able to sue the violator to recover the costs incurred in conducting or participating in the new bidding process.

4. ***Vague Legislation.*** A court may decline to embrace as setting the standard of care a legislative enactment that lacks specificity. In Heath v. La Mariana Apts., 180 P.3d 664 (N.M. 2008), a child fell through a balcony guardrail and sustained serious injuries. The railing complied with the building code that was in effect when the apartments were built (allowing nine-inch spacing), but not with more recent building codes (which reduced permissible spacing to four inches). Applicable provisions said that retrofitting an existing building to bring it into compliance with the current code was not required unless existing conditions were "dangerous to human life." The court affirmed a judgment against the tenant on its negligence *per se* claim, stating:

> In the absence of something more specific in terms of a required course of conduct for property owners, the term "dangerous to life" is too broad and lacks the requisite focus to form the basis for a negligence *per se* instruction. Put another way, the statutory term adds little if anything to the common law standard of ordinary care because, if property owners have to exercise ordinary care, then obviously they have to respond to a life-threatening condition.

5. ***Judicial Restraint.*** In Bruegger v. Faribault County Sheriff's Dept., 497 N.W.2d 260 (Minn. 1993), the court held that a violation of the Crime Victims Reparations Act (CVRA) did not create a private cause of action against the law enforcement agencies which failed to inform the plaintiffs of their right to seek reparations. It wrote:

> Principles of judicial restraint preclude us from creating a new statutory cause of action that does not exist at common law where the legislature has not either by the statute's express terms or by implication provided for civil tort liability.

6. ***Statutes Duplicating the Common Law.*** According to Restatement, Third, of Torts: Liab. for Physical & Emotional Harm § 14 cmt. e (2010):

> Many statutes impose obligations on actors that largely correspond to or codify obligations imposed by negligence law. . . . Thus, a statute might

> require motorists to drive their vehicles at a "reasonable and prudent" speed, or might prohibit driving the vehicle "carelessly." To find that an actor has violated such a statute, the jury would also need to find that the actor has behaved negligently. In such situations, the doctrine of negligence *per se* is largely superfluous in ascertaining the actor's liability.

See County of Dallas v. Poston, 104 S.W.3d 719 (Tex. App. 2003) (holding that the statutory duty of the operator of a motor vehicle about to enter or cross a highway to yield the right-of-way to an approaching vehicle is not absolute and therefore not a proper basis for a finding of contributory negligence as a matter of law).

7. ***Licensing Statutes.*** In some instances, proof that the defendant's conduct violated a statute adds little to the plaintiff's case for negligence. In Brown v. Shyne, 151 N.E. 197 (N.Y. 1926), the plaintiff became paralyzed after receiving chiropractic treatments from the defendant. In her negligence action, the plaintiff sought to rely on the fact that the chiropractor had never been licensed, as required by statute. The court held that the licensing law was intended to protect the public only against unskilled and unlearned practitioners, not to impose strict liability upon those who exercise skill and care merely by reason of the fact that they lack a license. Thus, since the plaintiff would have had to show lack of skill and care in order to bring the injury within the category of harm the legislation had sought to prevent, negligence would already be established without regard to the violation of the statute. The court held that it was error to instruct the jury that negligence might be inferred from the defendant's lack of a license. Legislatures are, of course, free to differ with courts. N.Y. C.P.L.R. § 4504(d) (Westlaw 2022) now provides that the absence of a license to practice medicine shall be "*prima facie* evidence" of negligence in a medical-malpractice action. *See generally* Restatement, Third, of Torts: Liab. for Physical & Emotional Harm § 14 cmt. h (2010).

8. ***Revenue-Raising Statutes.*** Many licensing statutes are intended to raise revenue, rather than promote safety, and are therefore not appropriate predicates for establishing negligence. *See* Inland Steel v. Pequignot, 608 N.E.2d 1378 (Ind. Ct. App. 1993).

9. ***Disagreements About What a Statute Requires.*** Questions sometimes arise as to the extent of the duties imposed by a statute. For example, in Miglino v. Bally Total Fitness of Greater N.Y., 937 N.Y.S.2d 63 (App. Div. 2011), the intermediate New York court took the sensible position that a statute requiring gyms to have automated external defibrillators (AEDs) available, and to have personnel on duty trained in their use, also imposed on the gym a duty to use the AED in the case of an emergency. However, the highest court of New York did not agree that the statute required a gym to use its AED. 20 N.Y.3d 342 (N.Y. 2013). Therefore, the defendant's motion to dismiss a negligence per se claim arising from the death of a gym member was improperly dismissed.

b. Unexcused Violations of Statute

Martin v. Herzog

Court of Appeals of New York
126 N.E. 814 (N.Y. 1920)

CARDOZO, J.

The action is one to recover damages for injuries resulting in death. Plaintiff and her husband, while driving toward Tarrytown in a buggy on the night of August 21, 1915, were struck by the defendant's automobile coming in the opposite direction. They were thrown to the ground, and the man was killed. At the point of the collision the highway makes a curve.... Negligence is charged against the defendant, the driver of the car, in that he did not keep to the right of the center of the highway.... Negligence is charged against the plaintiff's intestate, the driver of the wagon in that he was traveling without lights. Highway Law, § 329a, as amended by Laws 1915, c. 367.... The jury found ... [defendant] delinquent and his victim blameless....

We agree with the Appellate Division that the charge to the jury was erroneous and misleading.... In the body of the charge the trial judge said that the jury could consider the absence of light "in determining whether the plaintiff's intestate was guilty of contributory negligence in failing to have a light upon the buggy as provided by law. I do not mean to say that the absence of light necessarily makes him negligent, but it is a fact for your consideration." The defendant requested a ruling that the absence of a light on the plaintiff's vehicle was "*prima facie* evidence of contributory negligence." This request was refused, and the jury were again instructed that they might consider the absence of lights as some evidence of negligence, but that it was not conclusive evidence. The plaintiff then requested a charge that "the fact that the plaintiff's intestate was driving without a light is not negligence in itself," and to this the court acceded....

We think the unexcused omission of the statutory signals is more than some evidence of negligence. It *is* negligence in itself. Lights are intended for the guidance and protection of other travelers on the highway. Highway Law, § 329a. By the very terms of the hypothesis, to omit, willfully or heedlessly, the safeguards prescribed by law for the benefit of another that he may be preserved in life or limb, is to fall short of the standard of diligence to which those who live in organized society are under a duty to conform....

.... A rule less rigid has been applied where the one who complains of the omission is not a member of the class for whose protection the safeguard is designed.... Some relaxation there has also been where the safeguard is prescribed by local ordinance, and not by statute.... Courts have been reluctant to hold that the police regulations of boards and councils and other subordinate officials create rights of action beyond the specific penalties imposed. This has led them to say that the violation of a statute is negligence, and the violation of a like ordinance is only evidence of negligence. An ordinance, however, like a statute, is a law within its sphere of operation, and so the distinction has not escaped criticism. . . .

. . . . [Here, the jurors] were allowed to "consider the default as lightly or gravely" as they would . . . Jurors have no dispensing power, by which they may relax the duty that one traveler on the highway owes under the statute to another. It is error to tell them that they have. The omission of these lights was a wrong, and, being wholly unexcused, was also a negligent wrong. No license should have been conceded to the triers of the facts to find it anything else.

We must be on our guard, however, against confusing the question of negligence with that of the causal connection between the negligence and the injury. . . .

We think, however, that evidence of a collision occurring more than an hour after sundown between a car and an unseen buggy, proceeding without lights, is evidence from which a causal connection may be inferred between the collision and the lack of signals. . . .

There may, indeed, be times when the lights on a highway are so many and so bright that lights on a wagon are superfluous. If that is so, it is for the offender to go forward with the evidence, and prove the illumination as a kind of substituted performance. The plaintiff asserts that she did so here. She says that the scene of the accident was illumined by moonlight, by an electric lamp, and by the lights of the approaching car. Her position is that, if the defendant did not see the buggy thus illumined, a jury might reasonably infer that he would not have seen it anyhow. We may doubt whether there is any evidence of illumination sufficient to sustain the jury in drawing such an inference; but the decision of the case does not make it necessary to resolve the doubt, and so we leave it open. . . .

The order of the Appellate Division should be affirmed, and judgment absolute directed on the stipulation in favor of the defendant, with costs in all courts.

[The dissenting opinion of HOGAN, J., addressed chiefly to the issue of causation, is omitted.]

Notes

1. ***Procedural Effect of Unexcused Violations of Statute.*** There are three views as to the procedural effect of evidence establishing an unexcused violation of a standard-setting statute: negligence *per se*; *prima facie* negligence; and some evidence of negligence.

(a) ***Negligence Per Se.*** Some states hold that an unexcused violation of statute is negligence *per se* (negligence "in itself"). The unexcused violation conclusively establishes that the defendant breached a duty of reasonable care to the plaintiff; the only issues remaining for the jury are causation, defenses, and damages. *See generally* Restatement, Third, of Torts: Liab. for Physical & Emotional Harm § 14 (2010) (discussing negligence *per se*); *see also* Jones v. Southwestern Newspapers Corp.,

694 S.W.2d 455 (Tex. App. 1985) (driving on the left side of the road to deliver newspapers is negligence *per se*).

(b) ***Prima Facie Negligence***. Other states hold that proof of a violation of a standard-setting statute is *prima facie* negligence. The evidence of the violation raises a presumption of negligence, and if the presumption is not rebutted by proof of an excuse or evidence of reasonable care, a breach of duty is established, in which case, again, the only issues remaining for the jury are causation, defenses, and damages.

(c) ***Some Evidence of Negligence***. A few states take the position that proof of a violation of a standard-setting statute is only some evidence of negligence which the jury can either accept or reject. Thus, even after the violation is established, the jury must still decide the question of breach of duty, as well as issues related to causation, defenses, and damages.

Courts endorsing the negligence *per se* or *prima facie* negligence rules sometimes treat violation of a legislative enactment emanating from an inferior tribunal (for example, an ordinance passed by a city council) as merely some evidence of negligence.

According to *Martin*, which rule is followed in New York? Is the same view followed in Michigan? *See* Zeni v. Anderson, 243 N.W.2d 270 (Mich. 1976), *infra* at p. 348.

c. Excused Violations of Statute

Ranard v. O'Neil

Supreme Court of Montana
531 P.2d 1000 (Mont. 1975)

HASWELL, Justice.

. . . [P]laintiff was struck and injured by an automobile driven by defendant. The incident occurred on a Helena city street at approximately 9:00 p.m. The street was snow packed and icy; it was illuminated by street lights.

Plaintiff, whose eighth birthday was on the day following the accident, was on his way home from a boxing lesson. His instructor had driven plaintiff and his brother to the street in front of their home, double-parking across from their home. The brother, who was a year older than plaintiff, ran across the street, followed almost immediately by the younger boy.

As plaintiff reached the middle of the street, he saw defendant's headlights, stopped, and then ran in an attempt to avoid being struck. Defendant, upon seeing the boy, applied her brakes but was unable to avoid hitting him. . . .

Plaintiff, in a deposition taken some eight and one-half months after the accident, admitted that he had not looked before he ran into the path of defendant's vehicle. Although he admitted that he knew he should check for traffic, he said that he had just forgotten.

. . . .

Following discovery, the district court granted defendant's motion for summary judgment, on the ground . . . [that plaintiff was contributorily negligent].

. . . [D]efendant asserts that plaintiff violated Montana statutes regulating the conduct of pedestrians, and therefore he was contributorily negligent, as a matter of law. Her argument is that section 32-2178, R.C.M. 1947, sets the standard for determining the care which must be exercised by *any* pedestrian. That section provides, in pertinent part:

> (a) Every pedestrian crossing a roadway at any point other than within a marked crosswalk or within an unmarked crosswalk at an intersection shall yield the right of way to all vehicles upon the roadway.

That statute makes no express exceptions for anyone, and certainly not for children. Pedestrians are defined as "any person afoot" and persons include "every natural person." . . . .

Authorities recognize the inconsistency inherent in a standard which imposes adult guidelines on children who violate statutes, but applies a lesser-than-adult standard to a child's conduct outside statutory regulation. *See* Prosser, Law of Torts, 4th ed. § 36, n.13.

2 Restatement of Torts 2d, § 288A, p. 32 uses this language:

> (1) An excused violation of a legislative enactment or an administrative regulation is not negligence.
>
> (2) Unless the enactment or regulation is construed not to permit such excuse, its violation is excused when
>
> (a) the violation is reasonable because of the actor's incapacity.

This illustrative comment in § 288A is particularly pertinent here:

> 2. A statute provides that pedestrians shall not step into the street without looking in both directions for approaching traffic. A, a boy eight years of age, dashes into the street without looking, in pursuit of a ball. A's violation of the statute may be found not to be negligence if his conduct was reasonable for a child of similar age, intelligence, and experience.

The statutory violation may thus be excused if the plaintiff lacked the capacity for compliance.

The summary judgment for defendant is vacated. The case is remanded to the district court for further proceedings.

Zeni v. Anderson

Supreme Court of Michigan
243 N.W.2d 270 (Mich. 1976)

WILLIAMS, Justice.

. . . .

The accident which precipitated this action occurred one snowy morning, March 7, 1969, when the temperature was 11 degrees F, the sky was clear and the average snow depth was 21 inches. Plaintiff Eleanor Zeni, then a 56-year-old registered nurse, was walking to her work at the Northern Michigan University Health Center in Marquette. Instead of using the snow-covered sidewalk, which in any event would have required her to walk across the street twice to get to her job, she traveled along a well-used pedestrian snowpath, with her back to oncoming traffic.

Defendant Karen Anderson, a college student, was driving within the speed limit in a steady stream of traffic on the same street. Ms. Anderson testified that she had turned on the defroster in the car and her passenger said she had scraped the windshield. An eyewitness whose deposition was read at trial, however, testified that defendant's windshield was clouded and he doubted that the occupants could see out. He also testified that the car was traveling too close to the curb and that he could tell plaintiff was going to be hit.

. . . .

Ms. Zeni's injuries were serious. . . . She has retrograde amnesia and therefore, because she does not remember anything from the time she began walking that morning until sometime after the impact, there is no way to determine whether she knew defendant was behind her. . . .

Testimony at trial indicated that it was common for nurses to use the roadway to reach the Health Center, and a security officer testified that in the wintertime it was safer to walk there than on the one sidewalk. Apparently, several days before the accident, Ms. Zeni had indeed fallen on the sidewalk. Although she was not hurt when she fell, the Director of University Security was hospitalized when he fell on the walk.

Defendant, however, maintained plaintiff's failure to use that sidewalk constituted contributory negligence because, she said, it violated M.C.L.A. § 257.655; M.S.A. § 9.2355, which requires:

> Where sidewalks are provided, it shall be unlawful for pedestrians to walk upon the main traveled portion of the highway. Where sidewalks are not provided, pedestrians shall, when practicable, walk on the left side of the highway facing traffic which passes nearest.

. . . . [Although the trial court instructed the jury on this point, the jury found against the defendant. The intermediate appellate court reversed and remanded on other grounds. The Supreme Court granted leave to appeal.]

In a growing number of states, the rule concerning the proper role of a penal statute in a civil action for damages is that violation of the statute which has been found to apply to a particular set of facts establishes only a *prima facie* case of negligence, a presumption which may be rebutted by a showing on the part of the party violating the statute of an adequate excuse under the facts and circumstances of the case. The excuses may not necessarily be applicable in a criminal action, since, in the absence of legislatively-mandated civil penalties, acceptance of the criminal statute itself as a standard of care in a civil action is purely discretionary. . . .

Michigan cases . . . have almost consistently adopted a rebuttable presumption approach, even though the language of the statute is not written in terms of a presumption.

. . . [One] attraction of this approach is that it is fair. "If there is sufficient excuse or justification, there is ordinarily no violation of a statute and the statutory standard is inapplicable." . . . . It would be unreasonable to adhere to an automatic rule of negligence "where observance would subject a person to danger which might be avoided by disregard of the general rule." . . . .

The approach is logical. Liability without fault is not truly negligence, and in the absence of a clear legislative mandate to so extend liability, the courts should be hesitant to do so on their own. Because these are, after all, criminal statutes, a court is limited in how far it may go in plucking a statute from its criminal milieu and inserting it into the civil arena. The rule of rebuttable presumption has arisen in part in response to this concern, and in part because of the reluctance to go to the other extreme and in effect, discard or disregard the legislative standard.

. . . .

We have not . . . chosen to join that small minority which has decreed that violation of a statute is only evidence of negligence. In view of the fairness and ease with which the rebuttable presumption standard has been and can be administered, we believe the litigants are thereby well served and the Legislature is given appropriate respect.

. . . .

An accurate statement of our law is that when a court adopts a penal statute as the standard of care in an action for negligence, violation of that statute establishes a *prima facie* case of negligence, with the determination to be made by the finder of fact whether the party accused of violating the statute has established a legally sufficient excuse. If the finder of fact determines such an excuse exists, the appropriate standard of care then becomes that established by the common law. Such excuses shall include, but shall not be limited to, those suggested by the Second Restatement of Torts, § 288A, and shall be determined by the circumstances of each case.

In the case at bar, moreover, the statute itself provides a guideline for the jury, for a violation will not occur when it is impracticable to use the sidewalk or to walk on the left side of a highway. This is ordinarily a question for the finder of fact, . . . and thus the statute itself provides not only a legislative standard of care which may be accepted by the court, but a legislatively mandated excuse as well.

. . . [W]e find the jury was adequately instructed as to the effect of the violation of this particular statute on plaintiff's case. . . .

. . . . The Court of Appeals is reversed and the trial court is affirmed. Costs to plaintiff.

[The dissenting opinions of LINDEMER and COLEMAN, JJ., have been omitted.]

Notes

1. ***Excuses Under the Third Restatement.*** Restatement (Third) of Torts: Liab. for Physical & Emotional Harm § 15 (2010) provides:

> An actor's violation of a statute is excused and not negligent if:
>
> (a) the violation is reasonable in light of the actor's childhood, physical disability, or physical incapacitation;
>
> (b) the actor exercises reasonable care in attempting to comply with the statute;
>
> (c) the actor neither knows nor should know of the factual circumstances that render the statute applicable;
>
> (d) the actor's violation of the statute is due to the confusing way in which the requirements of the statute are presented to the public; or
>
> (e) the actor's compliance with the statute would involve a greater risk of physical harm to that person or to others than noncompliance.

In addition, "there may be further excuses worthy of recognition." *Id.* at cmt. g.

2. ***Carefully Violating a Statute.*** Presumably, there is an important difference between making reasonable efforts *to comply with a statute* (§ 15(b), *supra*) and *carefully violating a statute.* Suppose that a defendant is innocently delayed in traffic, then, while racing in excess of the speed limit to get to a wedding on time, is involved in an accident. The fact that the driver was really "focused," and trying to be extremely careful while speeding, is probably no excuse in a negligence *per se* state. If the jurisdiction adheres to a *prima facie* negligence view, which holds that a statutory violation raises a rebuttable presumption of negligence, could the carefulness of the driver be held to overcome the presumption of lack of care arising from the statutory infraction?

3. ***Matters Not Amounting to an Excuse.*** *See* Restatement, Third, of Torts: Liab. for Physical & Emotional Harm § 15 cmt. a (2010):

> [I]t is useful to set forth circumstances that do not count as an excuse. The violation of a statute is not excused by the fact that the person sincerely or reasonably believes that the requirement set by the statute is excessive or unwise; nor is it an excuse if the person is unaware or ignorant of the

statutory requirement; nor is it an excuse if there is a custom to depart from the statutory requirement.

d. Compliance with Statute

Montgomery v. Royal Motel

Supreme Court of Nevada
645 P.2d 968 (Nev. 1982)[6]

MANOUKIAN, Justice.

On January 10, 1978, appellants Helen and Kenneth Montgomery rented a room at respondent Royal Motel, a fourteen unit building in Las Vegas. On February 1, the Montgomerys had just returned to their motel room when they were assaulted and robbed by an unknown assailant. The door to their room was not self-locking, but was equipped with an operable deadbolt latch. The door was not locked when the assault occurred, although the Montgomerys customarily locked the door immediately upon entry.

The trial court granted respondent's motion for summary judgment upon respondent's presentation of evidence of a Las Vegas municipal ordinance, 4-10-2, "Housing Security Standards," which the trial court found set the applicable standard of conduct for the motel proprietors. The ordinance requires deadbolt locks, but not self-locking doors at units such as those at respondent's motel.

The main issue confronting us is whether the trial court erred in its determination that, as a matter of law, respondent motel met the required standard of conduct in protecting its guests from criminal acts of third parties by complying with the ordinance.

The ordinance . . . applies to motels with individual entrances such as the Royal. Appellants contend, however, that the ordinance establishes only a minimum standard of conduct and that reasonably prudent conduct might require additional precautions under the circumstances (i.e., a self-locking door), raising a question of fact for the jury.

. . . .

We recognize that the standard of conduct defined by a legislative enactment is usually a minimum standard and that special circumstances may support a finding of negligence, despite compliance, if a reasonable person would have taken additional precautions. . . . But when the facts pose a "normal" situation, within that contemplated by the enactment, "it may be found, and can be ruled as a matter of law, that the actor has done his full duty by complying with the statute. . . ." Prosser on Torts, § 36 (4th ed. 1971). . . .

---

6. Subsequent to publication, this opinion was withdrawn. Before the case was reargued, the appeal was dismissed pursuant to a stipulation of the parties. The withdrawn opinion appears to state good law. — Ed.

In the affidavits in opposition to the motion for summary judgment, the Montgomerys failed to present facts which would indicate that the case posed special circumstances requiring affirmative action beyond the requirements of the ordinance. So far as appears, the proprietor had no reason to suspect that an attacker was near the premises, there was no showing of a history of prior similar incidents, nor were the Montgomerys deceived by the door's appearance. . . .

We affirm the judgment below.

Notes

1. ***Other Precedent.*** *Compare Montgomery with* Medlar v. Mohan, 409 S.E.2d 123 (Va. 1991). There, in a case arising from an intersection collision, the plaintiff argued that the trial court erred in submitting the issue of her contributory negligence to the jury because "she was traveling no faster than the speed limit . . . [and] had a green light." Answering this contention, the court wrote:

> "[A] green light is [not] an unqualified command to a motorist to move in the direction indicated under any and all circumstances. It is only a command to do so in the exercise of reasonable care. . . ." . . . . "The mere fact that one vehicle has the right of way over another at a street intersection does not relieve the driver thus favored from the duty of keeping a reasonable lookout and otherwise exercising ordinary care to avoid a collision." . . . .

2. ***Regulatory Agency Approval and Compliance with Agency-Prescribed Standards.*** Closely related to compliance with statute is the question whether following the standards of a regulatory agency should insulate the defendant from liability for negligence. Many writers have argued that such standards should control. However, there are good reasons to think that standards promulgated by regulatory agencies may be seriously defective.

> [One author] . . . proposes barring recovery in tort where a product which causes harm has been placed on the market with regulatory agency approval or where an allegedly defective warning conforms to agency-prescribed standards. Aside from the fact that to so hold would remove important incentives for manufacturers to improve many products, this plan for short-circuiting the ordinary channels of judicial review is subject to criticism on at least four grounds. . . .
>
> First, regulatory agencies — such as those which license or regulate new drugs, medical devices, aircraft, nuclear power, and a wide range of consumer products — all operate on limited budgets. . . . [T]hey are frequently underfunded and lack the personnel and other resources that are needed to set standards effectively or to evaluate thoroughly the applications and products which they are called upon to review. These budgetary limitations, coupled with often "staggering workloads," counsel caution . . . in according conclusive status to agency determinations. . . . An affirmative decision by an agency to permit the use or sale of a product may more accurately

reflect a scarcity of regulatory resources than a thoroughly considered judgment that a product is harmless or that it would be unfair to hold the purveyor liable for resulting injuries. Similarly, an agency's lack of dispatch in revoking previously conferred approval for marketing of a product may be more a function of budgetary constraints than of doubt as to the validity of new evidence tending to demonstrate the unsoundness of a prior decision.

. . . .

In contrast to the dearth of resources available to regulatory bodies, personal injury attorneys representing injured individuals often enjoy both the contingent-fee incentive and the financial wherewithal necessary to promote a full exploration of questions relating to product safety through litigation. Potential liability provides regulated firms with good reason to vigorously defend their practices, thus ensuring a sharp, adversarial presentation of relevant arguments in court. To slam the courthouse door preemptively on all cases where regulatory approval has been obtained would in many instances preclude a proper resolution of important issues never before fully considered.

This is not to suggest that regulatory agencies play an unimportant role in the advancement of public safety or that courts should freely disregard their findings. Indeed, regulatory determinations may make substantial contributions to product quality control, and at least where the process is adequately funded and working well, agency findings are entitled to some degree of deference. Nevertheless, the competence of regulatory agencies is sufficiently variable, and budgetary limitations are frequently so severe, that there is good reason for not according regulatory agency approval or compliance with agency-prescribed warnings the status of an irrebuttable defense to tort liability.

. . . .

Second, unlike courts, regulatory agencies frequently are the object of direct and indirect lobbying by special interests which may affect not only the nature of applicable standards, but the extent of their enforcement. The representatives of commercial enterprises, in many instances, endeavor to persuade agency decision-makers of the merits of a position through advocacy that is neither objective nor balanced in its presentation of the relevant facts. The risk of distortion of the decision-making process is serious because managers in regulated industries often have close working relationships with regulatory officials. In contrast, the interests of the victims of product defects may go largely unchampioned by persons outside of the regulatory agency, since public interest lobbies "rarely have the legal staffs or war chests of a well-heeled business lobby."

The risk that agency determinations may unfairly favor the interests of the companies seeking regulatory approval are all the more ominous in

> view of the revolving door between government work and the private sector, which tempts agency employees to render decisions which may enhance their own employment chances with the same regulated firms they are charged with overseeing.
>
> ....
>
> Third, administrative agencies, far more than courts, are subject to political pressures. When a new Administration comes into power at the federal level, its political agenda has an impact on the entire range of agency actions, from enforcement of pollution laws, to approval of vaccines and food additives, to disposal of toxic chemicals. The chances of an abrupt, and perhaps ill-considered, change in administrative course with respect to product safety are not insubstantial—and this despite the fact that many would argue that rights of individuals to compensation for injuries should depend on principles more lasting than the results of the latest election....
>
> Finally, [a] ... proposal that the duty of a potential defendant to warn consumers of product dangers should extend no further than compliance with agency-prescribed warnings is ill-conceived on at least two accounts. First, as courts have frequently recognized, "The warnings required by such agencies may be only minimal in nature." Where that is the case, and the manufacturer or supplier has reason to know of greater dangers not included in the prescribed warning, the only sound course for minimizing accidents and preventing the wasting of human and material resources is to require disclosure of the added dangers to otherwise unknowing consumers....
>
> Second, even where an agency-prescribed warning is adequate to insure disclosure of all dangers which would ordinarily be encountered, the warning may be eroded or even nullified by the over-promotion of the product through a vigorous sales program that may persuade the user to disregard warnings. Again, the better course is to evaluate the adequacy of a warning in light of the surrounding circumstances—with due deference paid to the extent of the disclosures required by regulatory agencies.

Vincent R. Johnson, *Liberating Progress and the Free Market From the Specter of Tort Liability*, 83 Nw. U. L. Rev. 1027, 1048-54 (1989). *See* United Blood Servs. v. Quintana, 827 P.2d 509 (Colo. 1992) (a blood bank's compliance with FDA recommendations and national guidelines was some evidence of care to prevent the spread of AIDS, but not conclusive on that issue).

e. Defenses to Liability Based on Statute

Ordinarily, the plaintiff's conduct may be raised as a defense (i.e., contributory negligence, comparative negligence, or comparative fault) even though the defendant's liability is based on statute. However, there are at least two exceptions to the rule. The first is where the statute was intended to protect a vulnerable class of persons, and the second is where the legislature intended the violator of the statute to bear full liability.

Statutes Intended to Protect Class Members from Inability to Protect Themselves. *See* Zerby v. Warren, 210 N.W.2d 58 (Minn. 1973) (a retailer who sold glue to a minor in violation of a statute was absolutely liable for the death of another minor who intentionally sniffed the glue; assumption of risk and comparative negligence were no defense); *but see* District of Columbia v. Brown, 589 A.2d 384 (D.C. 1991) (elevator safety law was not intended to protect persons from their own negligence, and therefore recovery was barred for the death of a 19-year-old, 320-pound former football player who was contributorily negligent as a matter of law when he drove his shoulder against an elevator door in a public housing project and fell into the shaft).

In actions based on violations of worker-protection statutes, such as those requiring adequate worksite lighting or safety devices, the defenses of contributory negligence and assumption of the risk are typically not available. *See, e.g.*, Ferris v. Benbow Chem. Packaging, Inc., 905 N.Y.S.2d 394 (N.Y. App. Div. 2010) ("[W]hether plaintiff was negligent in using the A-frame ladder in the closed position is irrelevant inasmuch as 'contributory negligence will not exonerate a defendant who has violated' a scaffolding law").

Comment c to Restatement, Second, of Torts § 288A points out that some statutes have been interpreted as admitting of no excuses for violations, even when applied in tort cases. An example is a statute prohibiting the employment of children under a certain age in occupations involving dangerous machinery.

Statutes Intended to Impose Full Liability on the Violator. In Seim v. Garavalia, 306 N.W.2d 806 (Minn. 1981), a young girl was bitten by a neighbor's dog. The court held that any contributory fault on the part of the girl was irrelevant to the case, even though the state had adopted a comparative-fault statute, for the dog-bite statute was intended to impose absolute liability on the owner of the animal. This statute was not intended to protect a vulnerable class of persons because it protected all persons bitten by dogs, not just, for example, young children who might be unable to protect themselves. Nevertheless, based upon its review of the language of the statute and the legislative history, the court found a clear intent on the part of the legislature to place the entire loss on the owner of the dog, presumably for purposes of deterrence. Therefore, no defense based on the plaintiff's conduct could be asserted.

D. Special Standards of Care

Gradations of Negligence: Slight, Ordinary, and Gross. In general, courts have eschewed gradations in the negligence standard, for while such distinctions are theoretically possible, they often prove impractical in application. The question of whether a party's negligence is slight, ordinary, or gross can be highly fact-specific, time-consuming, and subject to dispute on appeal. To avoid devoting disproportionate judicial resources to inquiries which have no precedential value, courts tend to distinguish negligence only from such other broad categories of tort liability as intentional harm, recklessness, and strict-liability conduct. As one court commented:

> We think the abstract concept of reasonable care is in itself quite difficult enough to grapple with and apply in our law without our courts gratuitously conferring honorary degrees upon it. There is only *one* degree of care in the law, and that is the standard of care which may reasonably be required or expected under all the circumstances of a given situation. . . .

Spence v. Three Rivers Bldrs. & Masonry Supply, 90 N.W.2d 873, 878 (Mich. 1958). However, legislatures have shown a greater propensity to subdivide the negligence category or invent terms having no established meaning in the common law of torts (see the reference to "heedlessness" in the statute discussed in Whitworth v. Bynum, 699 S.W.2d 194 (Tex. 1985)).

Common Carriers and Bailees. It is sometimes said that a common carrier will be held liable for slight negligence, and that a gratuitous bailee will be liable only for gross negligence. *See* Andrews v. United Airlines, Inc., 24 F.3d 39, 40–41 (9th Cir. 1994) (because a common carrier owes "both a duty of utmost care and the vigilance of a very cautious person towards [its] passengers," there was a genuine issue of material fact as to whether the airline had done "everything technology permits and prudence dictates" to protect passengers from harm caused by baggage falling from overhead compartments). *But see* Bethel v. N.Y. City Transit Auth., 703 N.E.2d 1214 (N.Y. 1998) (holding that "the rule of a common carrier's duty of extraordinary care is no longer viable").

Automobile Guest Statutes. Legislatures have sometimes immunized classes of defendants from suits based on ordinary negligence, imposing liability only for aggravated levels of misconduct. For example, persistent lobbying by insurance companies led to the passage of automobile guest statutes in more than half of the states between 1920 and 1970. While they differed in their language, these statutes generally provided that the owner or operator of a car was liable to a non-paying passenger only for aggravated misconduct that in some way exceeded ordinary negligence. Eventually such laws came under attack, and they were held unconstitutional or legislatively repealed. As suggested in Whitworth v. Bynum, 699 S.W.2d 194 (Tex. 1985), courts frequently found that neither of the two justifications traditionally offered to support such statutes—(1) protection of hospitality and (2) prevention of collusive lawsuits—constituted a rational basis for differential treatment. Regarding hospitality, courts tended to say that there was no valid reason to distinguish between automobile guests and other types of guests, and that exposure to liability for ordinary negligence would not deter hospitality because automobile insurance is widely available, often compulsory, and would spread a loss so that it would not fall heavily on the driver or owner. As to preventing collusive claims against insurance companies, courts generally held that guest statutes were over-inclusive and irrational because they barred not only the few fraudulent claims but the great majority of valid ones as well.

Obsolete Statutes. The cases invalidating automobile guest statutes may be best understood as judicial attempts to grapple with apparently obsolete statutes that restricted tort liability in the face of a strong trend favoring compensation of accident victims and spreading of losses. According to conventional wisdom, a court faced with an out-of-date statute has essentially no options other than to apply it as written, hold it unconstitutional, or attempt to force, sometimes disingenuously, a more functional interpretation. However, there is some support (at least in academic circles) for the view that other avenues of judicial action may be available. *See* Guido Calabresi, A Common Law for the Age of Statutes (1982). For example, if a court thinks that a statute no longer fits the legal landscape and in all likelihood would not be repassed, it may be better to act in a manner that will facilitate, rather than preclude, legislative reconsideration. Thus, rather than holding an automobile guest statute to be unconstitutional, a court might consider attempting to break the legislative inertia on the subject by, for example, (1) applying the law to the instant case, but criticizing it on policy grounds; (2) applying the law to the instant case, but raising doubts whether it will survive constitutional scrutiny in future cases; or perhaps even (3) declining to enforce the law unless it is repassed by the legislature. (The last option is a radical alternative; the first two alternatives are not and have plenty of precedent.) In each instance, the idea would be for the court to exercise its common-law expertise in determining when a rule is outdated and to then act in a way which best facilitates reconsideration and perhaps revision of the obsolete rule. Whether courts should exercise such powers is a subject of much debate.

Chapter 6

Proving Negligence

"The burden of proving negligence is on the party alleging it, and merely establishing that an accident happened does not prove it." Macfie v. Kaminski, 364 N.W.2d 31 (Neb. 1985) (the skidding of a car without more does not prove negligence).

A. Evidence of Custom

The T.J. Hooper

United States Court of Appeals for the Second Circuit
60 F.2d 737 (2d Cir. 1932)

L. HAND, Circuit Judge.

The barges No. 17 and No. 30, belonging to the Northern Barge Company, had lifted cargoes of coal at Norfolk, Virginia, for New York in March, 1928. They were towed by two tugs of the petitioner, the 'Montrose' and the 'Hooper,' and were lost off the Jersey Coast on March tenth, in an easterly gale. The cargo owners sued the barges under the contracts of carriage; the owner of the barges sued the tugs under the towing contract, both for its own loss and as bailee of the cargoes.... [T]he judge found that all the vessels were unseaworthy; the tugs, because they did not carry radio receiving sets by which they could have seasonably got warnings of a change in the weather which should have caused them to seek shelter in the Delaware Breakwater en route. He therefore entered an interlocutory decree holding each tug and barge jointly liable to each cargo owner, and each tug for half damages for the loss of its barge. The petitioner appealed, and the barge owner appealed and filed assignments of error.

....

The weather bureau at Arlington broadcasts two predictions daily, at ten in the morning and ten in the evening. Apparently there are other reports floating about, which come at uncertain hours but which can also be picked up. The Arlington report of the morning read as follows: "Moderate north, shifting to east and southeast winds, increasing Friday, fair weather to-night." The substance of this, apparently from another source, reached a tow bound north to New York about noon, and, coupled with a falling glass, decided the master to put in to the Delaware Breakwater in the afternoon. The glass had not indeed fallen much and perhaps the tug was over cautious; nevertheless, although the appearances were all fair, he thought discretion the better part of valor. Three other tows followed him, the masters of two of which testified. Their decision was in part determined by example; but they too had received the Arlington report or its equivalent, and though it is doubtful whether alone it would have turned the scale, it is plain that it left them in an indecision which needed little to be resolved on the side of prudence; they preferred to take no chances, and chances they believed there were. . . .

Moreover, the "Montrose" and the "Hooper" would have had the benefit of the evening report from Arlington had they had proper receiving sets. This predicted worse weather. . . . The master of the "Montrose" himself, when asked what he would have done had he received a substantially similar report, said that he would certainly have put in. . . . Taking the situation as a whole, it seems to us that these masters would have taken undue chances, had they got the broadcasts.

They did not, because their private radio receiving sets, which were on board, were not in working order. These belonged to them personally, and were partly a toy, partly a part of the equipment, but neither furnished by the owner, nor supervised by it. It is not fair to say that there was a general custom among coastwise carriers so to equip their tugs. One line alone did it; as for the rest, they relied upon their crews, so far as they can be said to have relied at all. An adequate receiving set suitable for a coastwise tug can now be got at small cost and is reasonably reliable if kept up; obviously it is a source of great protection to their tows. Twice every day they can receive these predictions, based upon the widest possible information, available to every vessel within two or three hundred miles and more. Such a set is the ears of the tug to catch the spoken word, just as the master's binoculars are her eyes to see a storm signal ashore. Whatever may be said as to other vessels, tugs towing heavy coal laden barges, strung out for half a mile, have little power to manoeuvre, and do not, as this case proves, expose themselves to weather which would not turn back stauncher craft. They can have at hand protection against dangers of which they can learn in no other way.

Is it then a final answer that the business had not yet generally adopted receiving sets? There are, no doubt, cases where courts seem to make the general practice of the calling the standard of proper diligence; we have indeed given some currency to the notion ourselves. . . . Indeed in most cases reasonable prudence is in fact common prudence; but strictly it is never its measure; a whole calling may have unduly lagged in the adoption of new and available devices. It never may set its own tests, however persuasive be its usages. Courts must in the end say what is required; there are precautions so imperative that even their universal disregard will not excuse their omission. . . . But here there was no custom at all as to receiving sets; some had them, some did not; the most that can be urged is that they had not yet become general. Certainly in such a case we need not pause; when some have thought a device necessary, at least we may say that they were right, and the others too slack. . . . We hold the tugs [negligent] therefore because had they been properly equipped, they would have got the Arlington reports. The injury was a direct consequence of this unseaworthiness.

Decree affirmed.

Note

1. ***What Was the Custom in* The T.J. Hooper?** Judge Hand was wrong in thinking that there was no generally followed custom with regard to receivers: nearly all tugs carried them. One reason why the trial judge in *The T.J. Hooper* ruled that the T.J. Hooper and the Montrose were unseaworthy was that 90 percent of coastwise tugs carried radio receivers; 53 F.2d 107 (S.D. N.Y. 1931). Judge Hand may have been misled by the fact that many of the receivers belonged to the captains of the tugs, rather than to the tugs' owners. To say that there was no custom of having receivers because the captains, rather than the owners, often provided the radios makes no more sense than to say that it is customary for automobile repairs to be done without wrenches on the ground that mechanics, rather than the garages which employ them, usually provide hand tools.

Low v. Park Price Co.

Supreme Court of Idaho
503 P.2d 291 (Idaho 1972)

DONALDSON, Justice.

The defendant-respondent, Highway Motor Company, dba Park Price Motors, operates an automobile repair garage in Pocatello, Idaho. On December 2, 1969, Cal Dale Low, the son of plaintiff-appellant Dale K. Low, brought the latter's car to the respondent's garage for repairs. In order to make these repairs, it was necessary to remove the engine from the appellant's car. Having removed the engine, the respondent stored the car in an unfenced area between the garage and an adjacent street. While the vehicle was stored in this location, its transmission disappeared. On or about December 18, the respondent told the appellant that the transmission had been stolen. Exactly when and by whom the transmission was removed are facts which remain unknown.

The respondent disclaimed any obligation to compensate the appellant for the loss of his transmission. The appellant then commenced this action for conversion and, in the alternative, for negligence. The parties stipulated that the lost transmission had a reasonable market value of five hundred dollars.... [T]he respondent admitted its status as "bailee" of the appellant's automobile. After a nonjury trial, the district court entered judgment in favor of the respondent garage owner and denied the appellant car owner's motion for a new trial. This appeal followed.

.... As a bailee for hire, a repair garage operator is required to exercise ordinary or reasonable care to protect vehicles entrusted to his custody for repairs or servicing....

.... While courts are ordinarily reluctant to impose upon defendants the duty of proving the non-existence of negligence, an exception is justified in bailment cases....

In its defense at trial, the respondent-bailee introduced testimony as to the currently prevailing custom and usage regularly observed by other service garages in the area.... As a general rule, the customs of the community, or of others under like circumstances, are factors to be taken into account in determining whether conduct is negligent. Restatement (Second) of Torts § 295A (1965). We do not think this is one of the extreme cases where it may be said that the defendant's practices, or those customarily adhered to by others similarly situated, are negligent as a matter of law. Therefore, the evidence of custom was properly admitted in this case. But the appellant further contends that the trial court erroneously reasoned that simply *because* the respondent had adhered to the customary practices among garage owners in the area, the respondent was, for that reason — and for that reason only — not negligent. "In determining whether conduct is negligent, the customs of the community, or of others under like circumstances, are factors to be taken into account, *but are not controlling where a reasonable man would not follow them.*" *Id.* (emphasis added). In other words, "custom or usage does not determine ordinary care, but the standard is what a reasonably prudent man under like circumstances would do." .... Or, as Justice Holmes succinctly stated the rule: "What usually is done may be evidence of what ought to be done, but what ought to be done is fixed by a standard of reasonable prudence, whether it usually is complied with or not." .... A good summary of the law is contained in comments b and c to § 295A of the Restatement (Second) of Torts (1965):

> b. *Relevance of Custom.* Any such custom of the community in general, or of other persons under like circumstances, is always a factor to be taken into account in determining whether the actor has been negligent. Evidence of the custom is admissible, and is relevant, as indicating a composite judgment as to the risks of the situation and the precautions required to meet them, as well as the feasibility of such precautions, the difficulty of any change in accepted methods, the actor's opportunity to learn what is called for, and the justifiable expectation of others that he will do what is usual, as well as the justifiable expectation of the actor that others will do the same. If the actor does what others do under like circumstances, there is at least a possible inference that he is conforming to the community standard of reasonable conduct; and if he does not do what others do, there is a possible inference that he is not so conforming. In particular instances, where there is nothing in the situation or in common experience to lead to the contrary conclusion, this inference may be so strong as to call for a directed verdict, one way or the other, on the issue of negligence. Thus, even in the absence of any applicable traffic statute, one who drives on the right side of a private way is under ordinary circumstances clearly not negligent in doing so, and one who drives on the left side is under ordinary circumstances clearly negligent.

On the same basis, evidence of the past practices of the parties to the action in dealing with each other is admissible, and relevant, as indicating an understood standard of conduct, or the reasonable expectation of each party as to what the other will do.

c. *When Custom [Is] Not Controlling*. . . . Customs which are entirely reasonable under the ordinary circumstances which give rise to them may become quite unreasonable in the light of a single fact in the particular case. It may be negligence to drive on the right side of the road, and it may not be negligence to drive on the left side when the right side is blocked by a dangerous ditch. Beyond this, customs and usages themselves are many and various. Some of them are the result of careful thought and decision, while others arise from the kind of inadvertence, neglect, or deliberate disregard of a known risk which is associated with negligence. No group of individuals and no industry or trade can be permitted, by adopting careless and slipshod methods to save time, effort, or money, to set its own uncontrolled standard at the expense of the rest of the community. If the only test is to be what has always been done, no one will ever have any great incentive to make any progress in the direction of safety. It follows, therefore, that whenever the particular circumstances, the risk, or other elements in the case are such that a reasonable man would not conform to the custom, the actor may be found negligent in conforming to it; and whenever a reasonable man would depart from the custom, the actor may be found not to be negligent in so departing. . . .

. . . [W]e note that since the respondent has shown that it has done what others do under like circumstances, there is at least an inference that it is conforming to the community's idea of reasonable behavior. . . . Where there is nothing in the evidence or in common experience to lead to a contrary conclusion, the inference arising from conformity to custom may be so strong that the issue of negligence may be determined as a matter of law. . . . We conclude that this is such a case. . . . [E]ven though the burden of persuasion is on the respondent-bailee, in this case the bailee proved, by a preponderance of the evidence, its freedom from negligence.

. . . .

Judgment affirmed. Costs to respondent.

Notes

1. ***Third Restatement.*** *See generally* Restatement, Third, of Torts: Liab. for Physical and Emotional Harm § 13 (2010) (discussing custom).

2. ***Social Customs.*** *See* Bouton v. Allstate Ins. Co., 491 So. 2d 56, 58 (La. Ct. App. 1986) (in finding that trick-or-treaters were not negligent in frightening a homeowner, the court noted that "society encourages children to transform themselves into witches, demons, and ghosts, and play a game threatening neighbors into giving them candy").

3. ***Industry Customs and Practices.*** In Ray v. American Natl. Red Cross, 696 A.2d 399, 407 (D.C. 1997), a suit involving HIV-contaminated blood, the court held that an instruction which "focused the jury's attention almost exclusively on the evidence concerning industry practice" and, at least initially, defined "the standard of care in terms of industry custom and practice" was erroneous. The standard was "what [a] reasonable and prudent blood bank[ ] would do under the same or similar circumstances."

Nevertheless, conformance with or departure from industry customs may be important. For example, suppose that law schools operating study abroad programs in western Europe customarily do not staff their foreign program offices on weekends because students and faculty normally travel to other cities. Absent unusual facts requiring special precautions, it will be hard to argue that a law school was negligent in not having its staff work weekends to be available to address student emergencies. Conversely, if undergraduate study abroad programs customarily provide chaperoned transportation for students traveling between the United States and a certain foreign location, it will be easier to argue that a program that fails to do so has fallen below the standard of care.

The rule relating to custom means that it is important for colleges and universities operating study abroad programs to be aware of, and act consistently with, the current "state of the art" in administering foreign programs. Moreover, if customary practices have been reduced to writing (*e.g.*, as part of the standards that guide the accreditation of programs operating in foreign locations), it is important for those practices to be observed, unless there is good reason for variation. For example, the American Bar Association requires a law school study abroad program to provide students with the U.S. State Department's country-specific information for the country in which a program will be conducted. That bulletin discloses in detail dangers which travelers are likely to encounter in the country. A law school that fails to provide students with this information may not only lose accreditation of its program, but may be open to a negligence claim by a student who is injured by one of the dangers that was not disclosed. *See* Vincent R. Johnson, *Americans Abroad: International Education Programs and Tort Liability*, 32 J.C.U.L. 309 (2006).

B. Circumstantial Evidence

There are two chief categories of evidence, direct and circumstantial. Evidence falling within either category may be used to prove the defendant's negligence and other issues in a tort action.

Direct evidence is evidence which tends directly to support a finding of a fact at issue, such as eyewitness testimony that the defendant's vehicle was traveling in the wrong lane. Circumstantial evidence, in contrast, is evidence not of a disputed fact, but of one or more other facts from which the existence or non-existence of the fact in issue may reasonably be inferred. For example, evidence of skid marks may be used to prove circumstantially that the defendant's car was traveling faster than the speed limit.

The strength of either type of evidence will vary according to the particular facts, including the credibility of the witnesses providing the evidence and the presence or absence of corroborating facts. It is a serious mistake to think that direct evidence is always more persuasive than circumstantial evidence, for while eyewitness testimony from a credible source is valuable evidence, it often pales in comparison to such circumstantial evidence as footprints, fingerprints, or traces of blood. Eyewitness testimony that the defendant chopped off the plaintiff's foot is worthless if the plaintiff shows up in court with two perfectly functioning feet.

1. Constructive Notice

Goddard v. Boston & M.R. Co.

Supreme Judicial Court of Massachusetts
60 N.E. 486 (Mass. 1901)

Action by Wilfred H. Goddard against the Boston & Maine Railroad Company for personal injuries received by falling upon a banana skin lying upon the platform at defendant's station at Boston. The evidence showed that plaintiff was a passenger who had just arrived, and was about the length of the car from where he alighted when he slipped and fell. There was evidence that there were many passengers on the platform. Verdict directed for defendant, and plaintiff excepts. . . .

HOLMES, C.J.

The banana skin upon which the plaintiff stepped and which caused him to slip may have been dropped within a minute by one of the persons who was leaving the train. It is unnecessary to go further to decide the case.

Exceptions overruled.

Note

1. ***Length of Time the Dangerous Condition Existed.*** *See* Kennedy v. Wal-Mart Stores, 733 So. 2d 1188 (La. 1999) (holding that a customer who produced evidence that a large puddle of water was in an area within view of the customer service podium, and that it was raining on the evening in question, failed to prove constructive notice because there was "absolutely no evidence as to the length of time the puddle was on the floor").

See Threlkeld v. Total Petroleum, Inc., 211 F.3d 887 (5th Cir. 2000) ("if a plaintiff cannot prove facts to establish that it is more likely than not that the dangerous condition existed long enough that a proprietor should have known of its presence, there is simply no basis for recovery").

Anjou v. Boston Elevated Ry. Co.

Supreme Judicial Court of Massachusetts
94 N.E. 386 (Mass. 1911)

Action by Helen G. Anjou against the Boston Elevated Railway Company. Verdict was directed for defendant. . . .

RUGG, J.

The plaintiff arrived on one of defendant's cars on the upper level of the Dudley Street terminal; other passengers arrived on same car, but it does not appear how many. She waited until the crowd had left the platform, when she inquired of one of defendant's uniformed [employees] the direction to another car. He walked along a narrow platform, and she, following a few feet behind him toward the stairway he had indicated, was injured by slipping upon a banana peel. It was described by several who examined it in these terms: It "felt dry, gritty, as if there were dirt upon it," as if "trampled over a good deal," as "flattened down, and black in color," "every bit of it was black, there wasn't a particle of yellow," and as "black, flattened out and gritty." It was one of the duties of [employees] of the defendant, of whom there was one at this station all the time, to observe and remove whatever was upon the platform to interfere with the safety of travelers. . . .

The inference might have been drawn from the appearance and condition of the banana peel that it had been upon the platform a considerable period of time, in such position that it would have been seen and removed by the [employees] of the defendant if they had been reasonably careful in performing their duty. Therefore there is something on which to base a conclusion that it was not dropped a moment before by a passenger, and Goddard v. Boston & Maine R.R., 179 Mass. 52, 60 N.E. 486 . . . [is] plainly distinguishable. The obligation rested upon the defendant to keep its station reasonably safe for its passengers. It might have been found that the platform was suffered to remain in such condition as to be a menace to those rightfully walking upon it. Hence there was evidence of negligence on the part of the defendant, which should have been submitted to the jury. . . .

Judgment for the plaintiff for $1,250 with costs.

Notes

1. ***Discoloration.*** Courts may differ as to what inferences may be drawn from relatively similar sets of facts, and minor differences in factual detail may precipitate different results. In Joye v. Great Atl. and Pac. Tea Co., 405 F.2d 464 (4th Cir. 1968), the plaintiff slipped on a banana which was "brown in color, having dirt and sand on it." Noting that "[t]here was dirt on the floor near the banana, and that the banana was sticky around the edges," the court held that the evidence was insufficient to present a jury issue as to constructive notice. "[T]he jury could not tell whether the banana had been on defendant's floor for 30 seconds or 3 days." In contrast, in J.C. Penney Co., Inc. v. Chavez, 618 S.W.2d 399, 401 (Tex. Civ. App. 1981), the court upheld a judgment in a slip-and-fall case where the evidence established that

the banana on which the plaintiff slipped was "discolored, 'gooey' and 'black with yellow stripes.'" In *Chavez*, a bystander testified that "the banana peel looked like it was several hours old."

In Habershaw v. Michaels Stores, Inc., 42 A.3d 1273, 1277 (R.I. 2012), "[t]he plaintiff did not testify that her fall was occasioned by any foreign substance on the floor, or that polish or wax had been negligently applied to the floor by defendant." The court held that the plaintiff's mere allegation that the floor was shiny, without more, was not "competent evidence" of defendant's negligence.

2. ***Proximity and Opportunity to Discover.*** How can you prove constructive notice of a clear liquid, such as water, which does not discolor with age? Some courts hold that proximity to the site of the danger is a basis for concluding that the danger should have been discovered and remedied. For example, in Thoma v. Cracker Barrel Old Country Store, 649 So. 2d 277, 278–79 (Fla. Dist. Ct. App. 1995), the court reversed a grant of summary judgment for the defendant, observing:

> The area of the fall was in clear view of Cracker Barrel employees, since they traversed it regularly on their way in and out of the kitchen. If a jury were to believe Thoma's description of the liquid as covering an area 1 foot by 2 feet, it might also be convinced that Cracker Barrel employees, in the exercise of due diligence, should have noticed the liquid before the accident. . . .

However, other courts hold that:

> An employee's proximity to a hazard, with no evidence indicating how long the hazard was there, merely indicates that it was *possible* for the premises owner to discover the condition, not that the premises owner reasonably *should* have discovered it. . . .

Wal-Mart Stores, Inc. v. Reece, 81 S.W.3d 812 (Tex. 2002).

3. ***Absence of Inspection.*** The absence of an inspection is sometimes relevant to the issue of constructive notice. In Ortega v. K-Mart Corp., 114 Cal Rptr. 2d 470 (Cal. 2001), the court held that evidence that a supermarket operator had not inspected the aisle where a patron slipped on a puddle of milk for at least 15 to 30 minutes, and that the milk could have been on the floor for as long as two hours, permitted an inference that the dangerous condition had existed long enough for it to be discovered by the owner. The court noted, quoting an earlier case:

> "A person operating a grocery and vegetable store in the exercise of ordinary care must exercise a more vigilant outlook than the operator of some other types of business where the danger of things falling to the floor is not so obvious."

4. ***Prior Occurrence.*** A jury sometimes may infer constructive notice of a dangerous condition from evidence of similar dangers on previous occasions. In Beach Bait & Tackle v. Bull, 82 S.W.3d 663 (Tex. App. 2002), the court held that because there was evidence that water seeping under a wall had previously caused water to be present at the location where the plaintiff fell, the jury could conclude that

the defendant knew that there would be water on the floor in that location after it rained. *See also* Nicholson v. St. Anne Lanes, Inc., 483 N.E.2d 291 (Ill. App. Ct. 1985) (a bartender previously observed soap on the restroom floor and knew that the small bars of soap used by the defendant could create a potentially dangerous condition).

2. Mode of Operation

Sheehan v. Roche Brothers Supermarkets, Inc.

Supreme Judicial Court of Massachusetts
863 N.E.2d 1276 (Mass. 2007)

IRELAND, J.

After the plaintiff slipped and fell on a grape in a grocery store owned by the defendant . . . , he filed a complaint seeking damages . . . for negligence. A Superior Court judge . . . applied the "traditional approach" to premises liability and ruled that the plaintiff could not establish that the defendant had actual or constructive knowledge of the condition that caused the plaintiff to slip and fall. . . . On [direct] appeal, the plaintiff . . . urges this court to follow a more modern trend and adopt a "mode of operation" approach to determine premises liability. . . .

After falling, the plaintiff observed the area where he fell and spotted the pulp of a grape on the floor. The store manager . . . testified in a deposition that he also observed the area and noticed a small piece of grape and a small amount of clear liquid next to it. In this particular . . . grocery store, all grapes were packaged in individually sealed bags, easily opened by the hand, and placed in a wicker basket. The grapes were located on a tiered display table, surrounded by mats, in the produce department.

. . . . [T]he judge . . . stated that there was no evidence pertaining to when the grape fell, and the grape's appearance was not indicative that it had been lying on the floor long enough for the defendant to be put on notice of the potential hazard it posed. . . .

1. *The Restatement and traditional premises liability approach. . . .*

Under the traditional approach to premises liability, the plaintiff is required to prove a grocery store caused a substance, matter, or item to be on the floor; the store operator had actual knowledge of its presence; or the substance, matter, or item had been on the floor so long that the store operator should have been aware of the condition. . . .

Historically, Massachusetts has also followed the traditional approach governing premises liability. . . . In determining whether an owner has actual or constructive notice in slip and fall cases involving vegetable or fruit matter, an emphasis has been placed on the physical characteristics of the substance to determine how long it had been left on the floor. . . .

2. *Modern trends in premises liability.* Other jurisdictions have modified premises liability laws.... The modification of the traditional premises liability approach is, in large part, based on the change in grocery stores from individualized clerk-assisted to self-service operations and focuses on the reasonable foreseeability of a patron's carelessness in the circumstances, instead of on constructive or actual notice.... In a self-service grocery store, merchandise is easily accessible to customers, which results in foreseeable spillage and breakage that customers may encounter while shopping, thus requiring store owners to use a degree of care commensurate with the risks involved....

Although these jurisdictions have modified the plaintiff's burden of proof in slip and fall cases, they differ as to the extent of their modification of the traditional approach. There appear to be at least two other premises liability approaches, i.e., "mode of operation" and "burden shifting."....

a. *Mode of operation approach.* One variation to the traditional premises liability approach is called the mode of operation approach. This approach focuses on "the nature of the defendant's business [that] gives rise to a substantial risk of injury to customers from slip and fall accidents.".... Courts adopting this approach have concluded that where an owner's chosen mode of operation makes it reasonably foreseeable that a dangerous condition will occur, a store owner could be held liable for injuries to an invitee if the plaintiff proves that the store owner failed to take all reasonable precautions necessary to protect invitees from these foreseeable dangerous conditions....

Under the mode of operation approach, the plaintiff's burden to prove notice is not eliminated.... [T]he plaintiff... is still required to prove that the defendant failed to take reasonable measures commensurate with the risks involved... to prevent injury to invitees and "bears the burden of persuading the jury that the defendant acted unreasonably."....

b. *Burden-shifting approach.* Under... the burden-shifting approach, several jurisdictions have eliminated the plaintiff's traditional burden of establishing actual or constructive notice of the condition that caused their particular injury. Instead, when a plaintiff proves that an injury occurred resulting from a premise hazard or a transitory foreign substance in a self-service store, a rebuttable presumption of negligence arises. The burden then shifts to the defendant "to show by the greater weight of evidence that it exercised reasonable care in the maintenance of the premises under the circumstances."....

3. *Adoption of mode of operation approach....*

Of the two modern approaches... the mode of operation approach is in our view the more preferable, and we now adopt it....

Adopting this new approach... removes the burden on the victim of a slip and fall to prove that the owner or the owner's employees had actual or constructive notice of the dangerous condition or to prove the exact failure that caused the accident....

Under the mode of operation approach, a "plaintiff's proof of a particular mode-of-operation simply substitutes for the traditional elements of a *prima facie* case—the existence of a dangerous condition and notice of a dangerous condition." . . . . A plaintiff would still be required to present evidence supporting his or her case and to bear the burden of persuading the trier of fact that the defendant acted unreasonably in the circumstances. . . .

. . . . [T]he trier of fact must determine whether the owner could reasonably foresee or anticipate that a foreseeable risk stemming from the owner's mode of operation could occur and whether the owner exercised reasonable care in maintaining the premise in a safe condition commensurate with these foreseeable risks.

. . . . We vacate the judge's decision granting summary judgment . . . and remand the case to the Superior Court for further proceedings consistent with this opinion.

Note

1. ***Foreseeability of Danger Based on Mode of Operation.*** In Jasko v. Woolworth Co., 494 P.2d 839 (Colo. 1972), where the plaintiff was injured after slipping on a piece of pizza, the court explained:

> The practice of extensive selling of slices of pizza on waxed paper to customers who consume it while standing creates the reasonable probability that food will drop to the floor. Food on a terrazzo floor will create a dangerous condition. In such a situation, notice to the proprietor of the specific item on the floor need not be shown.
>
> The basic notice requirement springs from the thought that a dangerous condition, when it occurs, is somewhat out of the ordinary. . . . However, when the operating methods of a proprietor are such that dangerous conditions are continuous or easily foreseeable, the logical basis for the notice requirement dissolves. . . .

But see also Wal-Mart Stores, Inc. v. Diaz, 109 S.W.3d 584 (Tex. App. 2003) (a store's policy of allowing customers to carry drinks in the store did not alone establish negligence).

C. *Res Ipsa Loquitur*

Definitions and Examples. The Latin phrase *res ipsa loquitur* means "the thing speaks for itself." In tort law, *res ipsa loquitur* evidence is one form of circumstantial evidence which may satisfy the plaintiff's burden of proof on the issues of breach of duty and causation.

Under the *res ipsa loquitur* doctrine, facts establishing the special nature of the accident and the defendant's relationship to it may justify a jury's decision that the defendant more likely than not was negligent. Although authorities vary in articulating the requirements of the doctrine, all agree that the event giving rise to the harm must be of the type which does not ordinarily occur in the absence of negligence. In addition, there must be other facts which make it fair to conclude that the defendant was a legal cause of the event giving rise to the injuries.

1. Probably the Result of Negligence

There is reason to think that negligence was more likely than not the cause of the accident if:

- an automatic door or elevator door malfunctions and strikes a person using the door (McDaid v. Aztec W. Condo. Assn., 189 A.3d 321, 331 (N.J. 2018));
- an elevator mis-levels three inches below the floor (Gutierrez v. Broad Fin. Ctr., LLC, 924 N.Y.S.2d 333, 334 (App. Div. 2011));
- grease catches fire (Clinkscales v. Nelson Securities, Inc., 697 N.W.2d 836, 848 (Iowa 2005));
- a car falls off a jack (Cramer v. Mengerhausen, 550 P.2d 740, 743 (Or. 1976)); or leaves the highway without apparent reason (Merchants Fast Motor Lines v. State, 917 S.W.2d 518 (Tex. App. 1996)); or detaches from a tow truck (Imig v. Beck, 503 N.E.2d 324 (Ill. 1986));
- a riding mower turns over (Conaway v. Roberts, 725 S.W.2d 377 (Tex. App. 1987));
- a patient suffers a broken toe during a hemorrhoidectomy (Martin v. Petta, 694 S.W.2d 233 (Tex. App. 1985)); or falls out of bed despite restraining devices (Keyes v. Tallahassee Mem. Reg. Med. Ctr., 579 So. 2d 201 (Fla. Dist. Ct. App. 1991));
- an atomic simulator unexpectedly explodes (Jenkins v. Whittaker Corp., 785 F.2d 720 (9th Cir. 1986)); or
- a light fixture falls from the ceiling (Anderson v. Serv. Merch., 485 N.W.2d 170 (Neb. 1992)).

Accidents That are No One's Fault. The mere fact that harm was caused by an "accident" is not sufficient to make out a *res ipsa loquitur* case. As Prosser explained:

> [There are many] accidents which, as a matter of common knowledge, occur frequently enough without anyone's fault. A tumble downstairs, . . . an ordinary slip and fall, . . . a fire of unknown origin, will not in themselves justify the conclusion that negligence is the most likely explanation; and to such events *res ipsa loquitur* does not apply.

W. Page Keeton *et al.*, Prosser and Keeton on Torts 246 (4th ed. 1984).

Similarly, in Lamprecht v. Schluntz, 870 N.W.2d 646, 656–57 (Neb. App. 2015), the court stated, based on its review of caselaw:

> [I]t is clear that unexplained fires can occur during harvesting and farming operations, on or around trucks or other equipment used in farming

> operations.... Courts are reluctant to draw an inference of negligence from the starting of fires because fires are frequent occurrences and, in many cases, resulted without negligence on the part of anyone....
>
> We note that there are cases where *res ipsa loquitur* has been applied to vehicles alleged to have started a fire. In one case, for example, a truck backed into a barn filled with hay and allegedly caused a fire from its hot exhaust gas and sparks; the court found that fires do not ordinarily occur during the loading or unloading of bales of hay in a barn absent someone's negligence....
>
> [However, in] ... Nebraska, as a general rule, the mere occurrence of a fire, with resultant damage, does not raise a presumption of negligence, unless the circumstances under which a fire occurs justify the application of *res ipsa loquitur*.... In the instant case, the only evidence presented with respect to the fire's cause was that Brent saw a "flash" underneath the tractor and that he found a "burnt wire" under the tractor. Kresser testified that a field fire can start when a bearing goes out or gets hot or that an exhaust pipe can start a fire, and Brent thought the fire could have been caused by an electrical short on the tractor. However, none of those explanations are ones which are more likely than not explained by negligence; and the mere fact that a fire started under Brent's tractor does not lead to an inference that there was negligence. Even though a fire in a wheatfield may not ordinarily happen, such an occurrence is not so unusual as to justify an inference of negligence based upon an alleged lack of due care by the owner and/or operator of a tractor or other equipment being used to harvest the wheat.... Moreover, we bear in mind that the doctrine of *res ipsa loquitur* is of limited and restricted scope and should ordinarily be applied sparingly....

Nevertheless, some courts are reluctant to accept a defendant's argument that an accident "just happened" and was not caused by lack of due care. In Clark v. Darden Rest., Inc., 2013 WL 104052 (D.N.J. 2013), the court wrote:

> Defendants have admitted that at one of their restaurants, their employee, Stephen Harrison, was carrying a plate of food to Plaintiff's table, and that plate slipped from Harrison's hand, fell to the table, and broke.... Approximately ten minutes following the incident, Harrison testified that he returned to Plaintiff's table and noticed that "there was some indication that something had become lodged in [Plaintiff's] eye."....
>
> ... [I]t is axiomatic that a server in a restaurant has a duty not to drop a plate onto the table in front of patrons, particularly a breakable plate....
>
> ... Defendants argue that Harrison did not violate any standard of care by dropping the plate because it was merely accidental, and thus the doctrine of *res ipsa loquitur* is inapplicable to this case. Defendants' argument is circular and unavailing; the very crux of this case is whether Harrison's "accident" was the result of negligence....

> "Whether an occurrence ordinarily bespeaks negligence is based on the probabilities in favor of negligence." ... [Harrison] testified that he had only dropped objects less than ten times in his five years of experience as a server—and he had never dropped a plate on a table or ever seen another server drop something on a patron's table.... Simply put, Harrison's testimony demonstrates that it is significantly more probable than not that the plate fell from his hands due to some failure to exercise due care on his part or the part of the Defendants.... I conclude that Plaintiff is entitled to an inference of negligence under the doctrine of *res ipsa loquitur*, which Defendants have not rebutted, and thus I conclude that Harrison and Defendants breached the duty of care owed to Plaintiff when Harrison dropped the plate onto Plaintiff's table....

The Role of Expert Testimony. Expert testimony is frequently used to assist the jury in determining whether harm was more likely than not caused by negligence. *See* States v. Lourdes Hosp., 792 N.E.2d 151 (N.Y. 2003) (involving alleged negligence by an anesthesiologist in positioning a patient's arm during surgery). However, expert testimony is not always necessary. In Pritchard v. Stanley Access Technologies, LLC, 2011 WL 309662, *4 (D. Mass. 2011), the court explained:

> An automatic door may be a highly sophisticated piece of machinery, but it *probably* does not close on an innocent patron causing injury unless the premises' owner negligently maintained it. That conclusion can be reached based on common knowledge without resort to expert testimony. A jury does not need an expert to tell it what it already knows.

Common Sense and Necessity. In one sense, the *res ipsa loquitur* doctrine is nothing more than common sense. It recognizes that it is appropriate to draw conclusions from circumstantial evidence.

In a different sense, *res ipsa loquitur* is a rule of necessity, for without it the plaintiff would often be unable to establish the defendant's negligence. Some courts hold that the doctrine is not available to a plaintiff who has access to conventional kinds of evidence of what went wrong.

Res ipsa loquitur is inapplicable if a plaintiff offers expert testimony that purports to furnish a complete explanation of the specific cause of an accident. *See* Dover Elevator Co. v. Swann, 638 A.2d 762 (Md. 1994) (the doctrine could not be used in a case involving an elevator's misleveling because the plaintiff's expert fully explained that the contacts were "burned," which caused the elevator to either "overshoot" or "stall" in the leveling zone).

2. Facts Pointing to the Defendant

a. Control

Mobil Chemical Co. v. Bell

Supreme Court of Texas
517 S.W.2d 245 (Tex. 1974)

McGEE, Justice.

This is a common law damage suit for personal injuries sustained by Edward L. Bell and J. A. Hurley, employees of an independent contractor constructing a large chemical plant for Mobil Chemical Company, when acetic acid escaped from a portion of the plant already completed and turned over to Mobil. A jury failed to find that Mobil was guilty of specific acts of negligence but answered *res ipsa loquitur* issues favorably to the plaintiffs. Based on these findings, judgment was entered that each plaintiff recover $12,000 from Mobil. The court of civil appeals has held ... that the *res ipsa* theory was improperly submitted to the jury and has reversed and remanded for a new trial. ...

As in any *res ipsa* case, the particular facts surrounding the event are extremely important. This case involves a plant being constructed to manufacture terephthalic acid [TPA]. ... [As part of the manufacturing process, a liquid compound was pumped into a mechanism called "Unit A" and was subjected to great pressure. To avoid clogging in a "relief valve," the unit incorporated two "rupture disks." If a disk ruptured, a positive reading was to register on a pressure gauge to inform the operator to take the appropriate steps. The pressure gauge was connected to the main assembly by a pipe incorporating a fitting called "Valve A."]

....

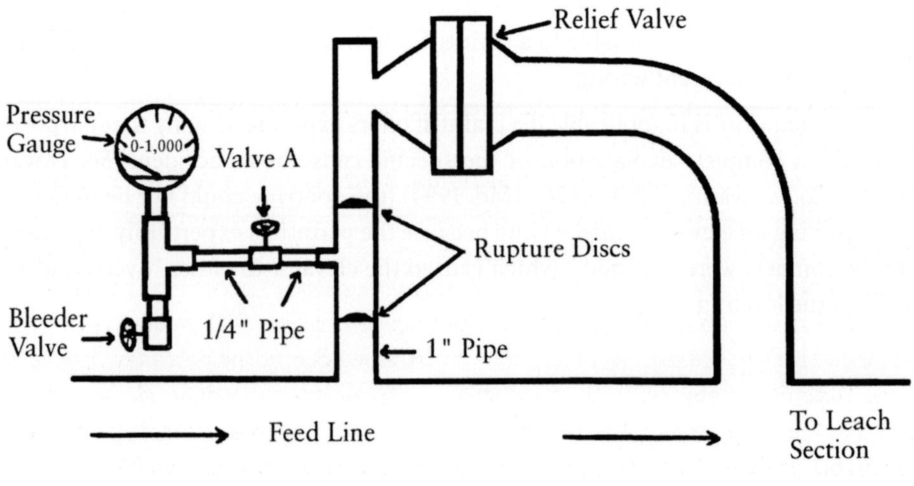

Diagram of Unit A.

Shortly after noon on April 4, 1966 a pressure surge caused the pressure in the feed line to exceed 850 p.s.i. At this time the pressure relief mechanism worked perfectly—the discs ruptured, the relief valve relieved the pressure, and the pressure gauge indicated that the discs were ruptured. Mobil maintenance personnel then replaced the discs, bled the acetic acid out of the relief mechanism, and continued the commissioning process. Just before 5:00 P.M., April 5, 1966 the feed line was again overpressured. This time, however, the pressure relief mechanism failed and acetic acid under high pressure spurted . . . into the atmosphere, creating both a danger to personnel and a fire hazard. As soon as he realized where the leak was, Jerry Griffith, Mobil's process superintendent, put on protective equipment, crawled out on the feed line and stopped the leak by closing Valve A.

Plaintiffs Bell and Hurley were employees of C.F. Braun and were working on Unit B of the plant at a point some 70 feet from the rupture. Both were exposed to strong acetic acid vapor and suffered respiratory damage for which they seek recovery. They alleged specific acts of negligence in failing to either have the pressure gauge in place or close Valve A and in the alternative pleaded *res ipsa loquitur.* The jury failed to find that the specific acts of negligence were committed and these findings have not been attacked on appeal. The jury did find, however, that Mobil failed to use ordinary care in maintaining the plant and that such failure was a proximate cause of the incident in question. . . .

. . . [I]t is helpful to focus on exactly what is encompassed within the doctrine of *res ipsa loquitur.* The phrase, meaning "the thing speaks for itself," was used by Pollock, C.B., in discussing a barrel of flour which fell from the defendant's window, Byrne v. Boadle, 2 H. & C. 722, 159 Eng. Rep. 299 (Ex. 1863), and has come to signify that in certain limited types of cases the circumstances surrounding an accident constitute sufficient circumstantial evidence of the defendant's negligence to support such a fact finding. . . . These cases are those in which the circumstances surrounding the event are such that the mere occurrence of the accident supports reasonable inferences that there was negligence involved and that the defendant was the negligent party. . . .

The *res ipsa* doctrine is applicable when two factors are present: (1) the character of the accident is such that it would not ordinarily occur in the absence of negligence; and (2) the instrumentality causing the injury is shown to have been under the management and control of the defendant. . . . The first factor is necessary to support the inference of negligence and the second factor is necessary to support the inference that the defendant was the negligent party. . . . As such the "control" requirement is not a rigid rule that the instrumentality must have always been in the defendant's possession or even that it must have been in the defendant's control at the time of the injury. . . . It is sufficient if the defendant was in control at the time that the negligence inferable from the first factor probably occurred, so that the reasonable probabilities point to the defendant and support a reasonable inference that he was the negligent party. . . . The possibility of other causes does not have to be completely eliminated, but their likelihood must be so reduced that the jury can reasonably find by a preponderance of the evidence that the negligence, if any, lies at the defendant's door. . . .

In Texas it is well settled that *res ipsa loquitur* is simply a rule of evidence whereby negligence may be inferred upon proof of the factors stated above. . . . Texas courts have quoted with approval the following language of the U.S. Supreme Court in Sweeney v. Erving, 228 U.S. 233, 240 (1913):

> In our opinion, *res ipsa loquitur* means that the facts of the occurrence warrant the inference of negligence, not that they compel such an inference; that they furnish circumstantial evidence of negligence when direct evidence of it may be lacking, but it is evidence to be weighed, not necessarily to be accepted as sufficient; that they call for explanation or rebuttal, not necessarily that they require it; that they make a case to be decided by the jury. . . . When all the evidence is in, the question for the jury is whether the preponderance is with the plaintiff.

. . . [T]he effect of successfully invoking the *res ipsa* doctrine is that the plaintiff can survive no-evidence procedural challenges—he has produced some evidence of the defendant's negligence. He is in the same position as any other plaintiff who has made out a case for the jury. . . . [I]t is the rare *res ipsa* case where the defendant is in danger of a directed verdict if he chooses not to explain the accident. . . . This is because the inferences to be drawn from the circumstances of the accident are within the province of the jury, not the court. Only in extraordinary circumstances does the mere occurrence of the accident so strongly compel a conclusion that the defendant was negligent that the jury could not reasonably find otherwise. . . . Of course, in any case the defendant may, if he chooses, produce evidence to lessen the impact of the plaintiff's circumstantial evidence. . . .

In order to rely on the *res ipsa* doctrine, the plaintiff must produce evidence from which the jury can conclude, by a preponderance of the evidence, that both the "type of accident" and "control" factors are present. This is not so much a rule of law as it is a rule of logic—unless these factors are present, the jury cannot reasonably infer from the circumstances of the accident that the defendant was negligent. In a great many cases the plaintiff can rely upon a general knowledge to prove the accident in question is the type of accident which does not ordinarily happen in the absence of negligence. . . . However, expert testimony on this factor is clearly admissible and may be necessary to the plaintiff's case. . . .

. . . . Both lower courts have held that the facts of this case raise the *res ipsa* doctrine. We agree. The facts show that the entire plant was designed as a closed system so that acid vapors would not be released into the atmosphere. The relief mechanism was included to prevent the same sort of occurrence as happened here. It is true that this was a new plant just being started up. However, we are not dealing with a minor leak of the type that can hardly be avoided with new equipment, but a violent rupture spewing acid 30 feet into the air. It seems reasonable to infer that due care could have prevented the accident. And since Mobil had accepted the Unit only after extensive tests, had been in control of the equipment for at least two weeks, and had been performing additional tests and maintenance, it is reasonable to infer that if negligence was involved, Mobil was the negligent party. From the circumstances of the accident, a jury could reasonably decide that Mobil's negligence probably caused the accident and the resulting injuries. We conclude that Plaintiffs Bell and Hurley made out a *res ipsa* case....

The [defendant's second argument is] that Mobil's rebutting evidence completely negated the plaintiff's *res ipsa* case and made it unreasonable to infer that Mobil's negligence caused the accident. Mobil's evidence consisted primarily of testimony by Marvin Fannin, a chemical engineer with Mobil, who saw the equipment after the accident. He testified that the quarter inch pipe broke between Valve A and the pressure gauge, which caused the acid to spew out horizontally. He theorized that the pipe might have broken because (1) it was defectively manufactured, (2) the metal crystallized when threads were cut improperly, or (3) the metal crystallized when the pipe was overly tightened upon installation. He explained that the pipe could have been further weakened by operational vibrations until it was so weak that it broke under the sudden pressure.

While the jury was certainly entitled to believe this explanation, it was not compelled to.... [T]he jury could still reasonably infer from the circumstances of the accident that the accident was probably caused by Mobil's negligence. Therefore, we hold that the trial court did not err in submitting the *res ipsa* issues to the jury....

Since ... this case will be [re-tried] ... we think it appropriate to further express our views ... with respect to cases, such as this one, tried on alternate theories of specific negligence and *res ipsa loquitur.*

First, it should be noted that a plaintiff does not necessarily lose the right to rely on the *res ipsa* doctrine by pleading specific acts of negligence. "The purpose of pleading is to apprize opposing parties of the exact grounds of complaint against them, so that they may prepare to meet the issues thus made." .... If a plaintiff pleads specific acts of negligence only, his proof is limited to those specific acts but may consist of circumstantial evidence, including the circumstances of the accident if the inferences reasonably arising from such circumstances are relevant to the specific acts alleged. However, if the plaintiff's pleading gives fair notice that he is not relying solely on specific acts but instead intends to also rely on any other negligent acts reasonably inferable from the circumstances of the accident, his proof is not limited to the specific acts alleged....

Likewise, proof of specific acts of negligence does not necessarily make the *res ipsa* doctrine inapplicable since proof of specific acts is not necessarily inconsistent with inferences of other facts. Of course, if the evidence, whether introduced by the plaintiff or the defendant, conclusively establishes the facts surrounding the accident, then there is no room for inferences and the *res ipsa* doctrine is not applicable.... But where the evidence is inconclusive, the plaintiff is still entitled to rely on any inferences that are consistent with the evidence....

A final question to be considered is whether the trial court should give an instruction about *res ipsa loquitur* in an appropriate case....

.... In some cases the inferences arising from the circumstances of the accident are so apparent that no special instruction is necessary. In other cases it is sufficient to give the jury a circumstantial evidence instruction to instruct them that acts of negligence can be proved both by direct evidence and by inferences from other facts proved. Finally, there are some cases in which it is helpful to give the jury a more specialized *res ipsa* instruction to the effect that if they find the two required factors, they are entitled, but not compelled, to infer that the defendant was negligent.

... [W]e believe that if the same evidence is presented at retrial of the instant case... [a]mong the definitions in the forepart of the charge, the trial court may include an explanation of *res ipsa loquitur* similar to the following:

> You are instructed that you may infer negligence by a party but are not compelled to do so, if you find that the character of the accident is such that it would ordinarily not happen in the absence of negligence and if you find that the instrumentality causing the accident was under the management and control of the party at the time of the negligence, if any, causing the accident probably occurred.

This general instruction may require variations under the particular circumstances of individual cases.

....

[The concurring opinion of DANIEL, J., is omitted.]

Notes

1. ***Exclusive Control***. The key question is who was in control at the time the negligence more likely than not occurred. In Wright v. Carter, 622 N.E.2d 170 (Ind. 1993), the fact that a piece of wire that a radiologist had inserted into the patient's breast prior to surgery to aid a surgeon remained in her body after surgery raised an inference of negligence against the surgeon and hospital, but not against the radiologist. Before the end of the operation, the radiologist had finished his work and departed, and the patient was under the exclusive control of the surgeon when the fragment was left behind.

In some instances, the evidence is too weak to permit an inference that the defendant was the responsible person. For example, in Kmart Corp. v. Bassett, 769 So. 2d 282 (Ala. 2000), the court said that *res ipsa loquitur* could not be used to impose liability on a business owner for harm caused by a malfunctioning automatic door because the malfunction could have occurred because the doors were defective or because the company that serviced the doors had been negligent, and expert testimony was insufficient to show that automatic doors do not malfunction unless a premises owner fails to use reasonable care to keep them in safe condition.

In deciding whether the defendant had exclusive control at the time of the negligence, it is important to consider other possible causes of the harm. In Gonzalez v. Otis Elevator Co., 2012 WL 993476 (S.D.N.Y. 2012), the plaintiffs were injured when a hospital elevator fell. In a suit against the elevator repair company, the defendant argued that the accident happened because the plaintiffs were "horsing around." Finding no evidence of such conduct, the court concluded that the *res ipsa loquitur* doctrine was applicable:

> For twenty years, Otis provided all maintenance and repair services on the hospital's elevator.... Additionally, Otis maintained a resident mechanic at the hospital from 8:00 a.m. to 4:30 p.m. Monday through Friday.... It is clear from the facts that Otis provided all maintenance to the elevator. Such an undertaking renders the elevator at issue in Otis's exclusive control of its maintenance, sufficient to meet the ... [elements] of the doctrine, "although it obviously was not in exclusive continuous control of the possession and operation of the elevator."

In some cases, even a loosely interpreted "exclusive control" requirement may preclude recovery. For example, in Dermatossian v. New York City Transit Auth., 492 N.E.2d 1200 (N.Y. 1986), a passenger on a city bus brought suit to recover for injuries allegedly sustained when he stood up and struck his head on a grab handle which projected straight down from the ceiling, instead of at the customary angle of about 45 degrees. The court, while recognizing that the exclusive control requirement should not be "literally" applied as a "fixed, mechanical or rigid rule," held that a *res ipsa loquitur* case was not made out, for the "grab handle was continuously available for use by defendant's passengers" and the "proof did not exclude the chance" that the handle had been damaged by one of the passengers. Thus, as in many cases, the question was really whether the defendant, more likely than not, had control at the time the negligence probably occurred. The facts could not establish that probability.

Pearson v. BP Products N.A., Inc., 449 Fed. Appx. 389, 392 (5th Cir. 2011), involved claims that arose from events at an industrial facility. The court wrote:

> Here, there was a report of a noxious gas that the Appellees claimed caused their injuries. [However, no] ... monitors or detectors registered any harmful gas release.... None of the Appellants' experts could identify where the odor came from or whether if it was even from BP's property. The Appellees have shown neither that the character of the accident is one that would not usually occur absent negligence nor that the injury-causing instrumentality was in BP's control.... In such circumstances, the district court should not have instructed the jury on *res ipsa loquitur.*

2. ***Rebuttal Evidence.*** As *Bell* suggests, the defendant's introduction of evidence of due care does not ordinarily preclude the plaintiff from successfully invoking *res*

ipsa loquitur. In Cox v. Nw. Airlines, 379 F.2d 893 (7th Cir. 1967), plaintiff's husband was killed when the plane on which he was a passenger went down over the ocean.

> The evidence of due care to which appellant allude[d] concern[ed] its maintenance records and procedures with respect to the aircraft involved; the qualified and certified status, and the competence, of the operating personnel of the aircraft and of the dispatcher; the safety training received by the crew; and the evidence that the flight was properly dispatched and the weather normal.

In affirming a finding of liability, the court held that the doctrine of *res ipsa loquitur* was correctly applied to the case.

3. ***Specific Evidence of Negligence.*** As *Bell* indicates, it is important to consider the relationship between the *res ipsa loquitur* doctrine and specific evidence of negligence. In Conner v. Menard, Inc., 705 N.W.2d 318 (Iowa 2005), the court noted that its decisions had become "very circumspect" in their application of *res ipsa loquitur* and wrote:

> The evidence presented at trial was undisputed. The plaintiff's husband, who witnessed the incident, testified that a Menard employee tried to pull insulation from the bottom of the pile. When this did not work, the employee (and possibly two employees) climbed up the side of a divider fifteen-to eighteen-feet tall. The husband testified that a bundle of insulation fell on the plaintiff, and in fact, he believed several fell. At least one employee was at the top of the pile at the time the insulation fell. . . .
>
> This evidence was accessible to the plaintiff and was "so strong and extensive as to leave nothing for inference." . . . .
>
> . . . . Under our general rule . . . direct evidence of the essential elements of the claim precludes the *res ipsa* inference.

b. Greater Access to Information

Mahowald v. Minnesota Gas Co.

Supreme Court of Minnesota
344 N.W.2d 856 (Minn. 1984) (en banc)

KELLEY, Justice.

On the morning of February 26, 1977, the home of Alice and Michael Kannegieter exploded. . . . Investigation revealed that a natural gas main pipe located in the right-of-way in front of the Kannegieter residence had fractured, causing natural gas to leak into the home.

. . . .

In November 1970, Minnesota Gas Company (Minnegasco) installed a gas main in the right-of-way. . . . The main was installed at a depth of 42 inches, exceeding the depth required by federal regulations and company policy. . . . There is no evidence in the record that the line was improperly installed.

Pursuant to Minnegasco's ownership and obligation to maintain its gas lines, periodic leak checks were performed on the line in compliance with federal requirements. No leaks in the gas line were ever detected prior to the 1977 explosion.

No further construction occurred in the area of the gas line until 1974 when Barbarossa and Sons was hired by the City of Prior Lake to install water and sewer lines in . . . the development in which the Kannegieter residence was to be located. On April 30, 1974, Barbarossa struck and severed a gas main with a backhoe. The strike was reported to and repaired by Minnegasco.

On May 15, 1974, Barbarossa again struck a gas main. The pipe was scraped and bent a distance of approximately 16 feet from where the explosion-causing fracture eventually occurred. Minnegasco was notified of the hit and sent a repairman to the site. Because the pipe itself was not physically damaged, the pipe was wrapped with special tape, sealed, and reburied.

. . . .

In addition . . . other entities apparently engaged in excavating or other digging activities in the street. These entities were not named as defendants and . . . include telephone, electric, and landscaping companies.

Alice and Michael Kannegieter and their two children moved into their newly built home . . . in September 1976. On Saturday morning, February 26, 1977, Alice went to the garage to start the family car, while Michael gathered the children in the family room. Alice placed her key into the car's ignition. The house exploded causing its total destruction.

. . . [T]he case was submitted to the jury under a theory of negligence only. The jury found both . . . [Barbarossa and Minnegasco] not negligent and set damages at $110,850.

. . . . Appellants, in the alternative, urge us to hold that the trial court erred in refusing to submit a *res ipsa loquitur* instruction. Moreover, they contend the doctrine should apply to both the utility and Barbarossa. . . .

The burden of proving that a natural gas company was negligent in the operation of its gas distribution system is indeed onerous. That is true, in part at least, because the gas company does not have complete exclusive control over its distribution lines located on public right-of-ways. Activities, of which the gas company frequently has no notice, are normally taking place on streets over which the company has no meaningful control. Here, for example, the city laid water and sewer lines in proximity to the gas lines; contractors tapped those mains to make service connections; either the city or the developer reduced the street grade after installation of the gas mains; and the city contracted for street servicing. . . .

In declining to submit a *res ipsa loquitur* instruction in this case, the trial court felt that one element necessary before that rule is applicable was missing—to wit, exclusive control. . . .[1]

. . . . In ordinary parlance, "exclusive control" connotes that no other person or entity had any control over the instrumentality which caused the damage. If viewed in that light, Minnegasco did not have "exclusive control" during the 7 years preceding the explosion. Nevertheless, some jurisdictions, including Minnesota, in natural gas explosion cases have found such "exclusive control" where the gas distributor has the non-delegable responsibility to maintain and inspect its mains in the public streets at all times. As pointed out by Professor Prosser, a rigid adherence to the literal meaning of "exclusive control" could be pernicious and misleading unless control is seen as a flexible term. W. Prosser, Law of Torts § 39, at 218-21 (4th ed. 1971). Really what we are considering in a determination of whether *res ipsa loquitur* applies is the shifting of the burden of proof to someone who is responsible for the instrumentality that caused the damage. In a gas explosion case such as here, the gas distributor is responsible for the reasonable inspection and maintenance of its lines. It is this responsibility for its gas line that constitutes the type of control that establishes this element allowing the application of *res ipsa loquitur*. . . . In somewhat similar contexts, other courts have shifted the burden of proof where the plaintiff was blameless but the instrumentality causing the harm could not be readily identified or was not exclusively in control of a charged defendant, although the person charged was responsible to see the instrumentality was not negligently used so as to cause harm to others. *See, e.g.*, Summers v. Tice, 33 Cal. 2d 80, 199 P.2d 1 (1948) [*infra* at p. 420]. Likewise, a bailee has the burden of proving that personal property damaged while entrusted to him was not caused by his fault whether or not, at the time of the damage, the bailee was in actual physical control. . . .

In the ordinary course of events, natural gas does not escape from gas mains in public streets so as to cause explosion. When it does so escape and does result in an explosion, an inference of fault on the part of the gas distribution company is justifiable. Even though the gas company may be faultless, in view of its superior knowledge of the gas distribution system, its access and opportunity to identify persons acting in the vicinity of the gas mains, its inspection and control over the mains, and its responsibility for the safety of the persons and property in the community, the gas company should have the obligation to show it was not negligent or to establish who was. . . . As between the gas company and the person who sustains injury to person or property, the gas company is by far in a better position to make that showing. In essence, this is the rationale of *res ipsa loquitur*: to allow a plaintiff

1. [Fn. 4:] We note the *res ipsa loquitur* issue raised in appellants' brief differs from the issue presented to the trial court and in their prehearing conference statements to this court. In those documents, the appellants sought only a *res ipsa loquitur* instruction as to Minnegasco. On appeal we address only issues presented to the trial court. . . .

to get to the jury by allowing the jury, in an appropriate case, to draw an inference of negligence on the part of the gas company.

.... Had the plaintiffs had the advantage of the *res ipsa loquitur* instruction, the jury could have concluded that plaintiffs had met their burden of proof. Therefore, we reverse and remand for a new trial against Minnegasco only.

Reversed and remanded.

[The dissenting opinion of Justice TODD is omitted.]

c. Res Ipsa, *the Plaintiff's Own Conduct, and Other Possible Causes*

It was once said that, for *res ipsa loquitur* to apply, the plaintiff had to prove that the negligence which caused the injury was not attributable to the plaintiff. This meant that *res ipsa loquitur* was inapplicable in any case involving contributory negligence. The advent of comparative negligence and comparative fault necessitated modification of the old rule, for under comparative principles fault on the part of the plaintiff no longer always requires a denial of recovery. In a typical decision, Montgomery Elevator Co. v. Gordon, 619 P.2d 66 (Colo. 1980), the court held that under comparative negligence a *res ipsa loquitur* plaintiff is required to show only that the "defendant's inferred negligence was, more probably than not, *a cause* [not *the cause*] of the injury, ... even though plaintiff's negligent acts or omissions may also have contributed to the injury."

Nevertheless, the plaintiff's own conduct can still be an obstacle to reliance on *res ipsa loquitur*. For example, in Lawson v. Mitsubishi Motor Sales of Am., Inc., 938 So. 2d 35 (La. 2006), a driver was injured when an airbag deployed after the driver sounded the car's horn. An important theory in the case was that a "clock spring" had been misaligned, causing the accident. In ruling for the defendant, the Louisiana Supreme Court wrote:

> Had the Plaintiffs' experts not tampered with the positioning of the clock spring, direct evidence would have been available to prove or disprove the Plaintiffs' theory of misalignment. We do not believe that the Plaintiffs should be able to take advantage of the doctrine of *res ipsa loquitur*, since direct evidence of a possible misalignment was available prior to Plaintiffs' disassembly of the supplemental restraint system.

Calculating Comparative Negligence in a Res Ipsa Case. If a *res ipsa loquitur* argument is allowed in a comparative negligence or comparative fault state in a suit where the plaintiff is not blameless, how is the jury to compare the negligence of the defendant with that of the plaintiff in order to reduce damages to an appropriate level? The jury, by definition, is unaware in a *res ipsa loquitur* case of precisely what the defendant did wrong. The court in *Montgomery Elevator Co.* was not seriously troubled by the issue:

> [T]he jury will know the general nature of the breach of duty committed by the defendant, such as the general failure to keep an elevator in good

> working condition. Since the process of comparison of negligence lacks scientific precision, the ruling should not result in an additional undue burden on the jury.

The theory appears to be that a rough allocation of damages is better than no allocation at all.

d. Procedural Effect

Three Views: What is the value of having a *res ipsa loquitur* case? The procedural effect varies from jurisdiction to jurisdiction. In general, there are three views:

(1) In most jurisdictions, establishing the elements of *res ipsa loquitur* creates a permissible inference of negligence (meaning, here, breach of duty and causation). The evidence allows the plaintiff's case to survive a no-evidence challenge and get to the jury, but the jury may still find as a fact that the defendant was not negligent. *See* Restatement, Third, of Torts: Liab. for Physical and Emotional Harm § 17 (2010) (endorsing the permissible-inference view).

(2) In some states, *res ipsa loquitur* evidence creates a presumption of negligence which shifts the burden of going forward with evidence to the defendant. Unless the defendant introduces some evidence that tends to rebut the presumption, the plaintiff is entitled to judgment on the issue of negligence. However, if the defendant introduces competing evidence, the plaintiff still bears the burden of persuasion.

(3) In the rare jurisdiction, *res ipsa loquitur* evidence creates a presumption of negligence which shifts to the defendant both the burden of going forward with evidence and the burden of persuasion. Unless the defendant proves by a preponderance of the evidence that the defendant was not negligent, the defendant will be held liable.

Some opinions—particularly older ones—are notoriously careless in how they use the terms "inference" and "presumption." In reading any *res ipsa loquitur* case, it is useful to ask to which of the three views does the jurisdiction subscribe?

Motions for Summary Judgment. The application of the principles governing the procedural effect of a *res ipsa loquitur* showing takes place against the backdrop of ordinary rules of civil procedure which require a defendant to raise a material issue of fact to survive a motion by the plaintiff for summary judgment. In Mangual v. Berezinsky, 53 A.3d 664 (N.J. Super. Ct. App. Div. 2012), the driver of a car failed to provide any explanation for why the vehicle went out of control and "slammed" into the plaintiffs who were standing on the shoulder of the road beside their disabled car in good weather, during the middle of the day, when there was "no traffic." The driver simply denied being negligent. The court held that the injured plaintiffs were entitled to summary judgment because no rational, fair-minded jury could conclude anything other than that the driver negligently lost control of his car. Thus, while the doctrine of *res ipsa loquitur* typically allows a plaintiff to get to a jury, such a case does not have to go to a jury if there is no disputed question of material fact.

D. Multiple Defendants

Ybarra v. Spangard

Supreme Court of California
154 P.2d 687 (Cal. 1944)

GIBSON, Chief Justice.

This is an action for damages for personal injuries alleged to have been inflicted on plaintiff by defendants during the course of a surgical operation. The trial court entered judgment of nonsuit as to all defendants and plaintiff appealed.

On October 28, 1939, plaintiff consulted defendant Dr. Tilley, who diagnosed his ailment as appendicitis, and made arrangements for an appendectomy to be performed by defendant Dr. Spangard at a hospital owned and managed by defendant Dr. Swift. Plaintiff entered the hospital, was given a hypodermic injection, slept, and later was awakened by Drs. Tilley and Spangard and wheeled into the operating room by a nurse whom he believed to be defendant Gisler, an employee of Dr. Swift. Defendant Dr. Reser, the anesthetist, also an employee of Dr. Swift, adjusted plaintiff for operation, pulling his body to the head of the operating table.... Dr. Reser then administered the anesthetic and plaintiff lost consciousness. When he awoke early the following morning he was in his hospital room attended by defendant Thompson, the special nurse, and another nurse who was not made a defendant.

Plaintiff testified that prior to the operation he had never had any pain in, or injury to, his right arm or shoulder, but that when he awakened he felt a sharp pain about half way between the neck and the point of the right shoulder.... The pain did not cease ... and after his release from the hospital ... [he] developed paralysis and atrophy of the muscles around the shoulder....

[Two doctors testified for the plaintiff that the injury was of a traumatic origin.] ....

Plaintiff's theory is that the foregoing evidence presents a proper case for the application of the doctrine of *res ipsa loquitur*, and that the inference of negligence arising therefrom makes the granting of a nonsuit improper. Defendants' ... main defense may be briefly stated in two propositions: (1) that where there are several defendants, and there is a division of responsibility in the use of an instrumentality causing the injury, and the injury might have resulted from the separate act of either one of two or more persons, the rule of *res ipsa loquitur* cannot be invoked against any one of them; and (2) that where there are several instrumentalities, and no showing is made as to which caused the injury or as to the particular defendant in control of it, the doctrine cannot apply. We are satisfied . . . that these objections are not well taken. . . .

The present case is of a type which comes within the reason and spirit of the doctrine more fully perhaps than any other. The passenger sitting awake in a railroad car at the time of a collision, the pedestrian walking along the street and struck by a falling object or the debris of an explosion, are surely not more entitled to an explanation than the unconscious patient on the operating table. . . . Without the aid of the doctrine a patient who received permanent injuries of a serious character, obviously the result of someone's negligence, would be entirely unable to recover unless the doctors and nurses in attendance voluntarily chose to disclose the identity of the negligent person and the facts establishing liability. . . . If this were the state of the law of negligence, the courts, to avoid gross injustice, would be forced to invoke the principles of absolute liability, irrespective of negligence, in actions by persons suffering injuries during the course of treatment under anesthesia. But we think this juncture has not yet been reached, and that the doctrine of *res ipsa loquitur* is properly applicable to the case before us.

The condition that the injury must not have been due to the plaintiff's voluntary action is of course fully satisfied under the evidence produced herein; and the same is true of the condition that the accident must be one which ordinarily does not occur unless someone was negligent. . . .

The argument of defendants is simply that plaintiff has not shown an injury caused by an instrumentality under a defendant's control, because he has not shown which of the several instrumentalities that he came in contact with while in the hospital caused by the injury; and he has not shown that any one defendant or his servants had exclusive control over any particular instrumentality. Defendants assert that some of them were not the employees of other defendants, that some did not stand in any permanent relationship from which liability in tort would follow, and the different functions performed by each, they could not all be liable for the wrong, if any.

We have no doubt that in a modern hospital a patient is quite likely to come under the care of a number of persons in different types of contractual and other relationships with each other. For example, in the present case it appears that Drs. [Swift], Spangard and Tilley were physicians or surgeons commonly placed in the legal category of independent contractors; and Dr. Reser, the anesthetist, and defendant Thompson, the special nurse, were employees of Dr. Swift and not of the other doctors. But we do not believe that either the number or relationship of the defendants alone determines whether the doctrine of *res ipsa loquitur* applies. Every defendant in whose custody the plaintiff was placed for any period was bound to exercise ordinary care to see that no unnecessary harm came to him and each would be liable for failure in this regard. Any defendant who negligently injured him, and any defendant charged with his care who so neglected him as to allow injury to occur, would be liable. The defendant employers would be liable for the neglect of their employees;

and the doctor in charge of the operation would be liable for the negligence of those who became his temporary servants for the purpose of assisting in the operation.

. . . .

It may appear at the trial, that, consistent with the principles outlined above, one or more defendants will be found liable and others absolved, but this should not preclude the application of the rule of *res ipsa loquitur.* The control at one time or another, of one or more of the various agencies or instrumentalities which might have harmed the plaintiff, was in the hands of every defendant or of his employees or temporary servants. This, we think, places upon them the burden of initial explanation. Plaintiff was rendered unconscious for the purpose of undergoing surgical treatment by the defendants; it is manifestly unreasonable for them to insist that he identify any one of them as the person who did the alleged negligent act.

. . . [I]f we accept the contention of defendants herein, there will rarely be any compensation for patients injured while unconscious. A hospital today conducts a highly integrated system of activities, with many persons contributing their efforts. . . . The number of those in whose care the patient is placed is not a good reason for denying him all reasonable opportunity to recover for negligent harm. It is rather a good reason for re-examination of the statement of legal theories which supposedly compel such a shocking result.

We do not at this time undertake to state the extent to which the reasoning of this case may be applied to other situations in which the doctrine of *res ipsa loquitur* is invoked. We merely hold that where a plaintiff receives unusual injuries while unconscious and in the course of medical treatment, all those defendants who had any control over his body or the instrumentalities which might have caused the injuries may properly be called upon to meet the inference of negligence by giving an explanation of their conduct.

The judgment is reversed.

Notes

1. ***The Subsequent Trial.*** At a second trial, each defendant (except the owner of the hospital) gave evidence and denied seeing anything which could have produced the injury to plaintiff's arm and shoulder. The trial court found that this did not outweigh the inference of negligence raised by the doctrine of *res ipsa loquitur,* and found against all defendants. The judgment was affirmed, 208 P.2d 445 (Cal. Ct. App. 1949).

2. ***Joint Control or Shared Responsibility.*** *Ybarra* is the seminal decision on whether *res ipsa loquitur* may be invoked against multiple defendants, and has often been cited. It is generally agreed that the doctrine cannot be applied to multiple defendants unless they exercised joint control over, or had joint responsibility for, the dangerous instrumentality or conduct. *See* Restatement, Third, of Torts: Liab. for Physical and Emotional Harm § 17 cmt. f (2010).

3. ***Medical Contexts.*** Many cases have involved operating-room injuries. *See* Antoniato v. Long Island Jewish Med. Ctr., 871 N.Y.S.2d 659 (App. Div. 2009) (finding sufficient evidence that the operating room, surgical instruments, and the surgical procedure itself were under the defendants' joint and exclusive control).

In Backus v Kaleida Health, 937 N.Y.S.2d 773 (App. Div. 2012), the court found the doctrine applicable to claims against two doctors involved in a kidney transplant because "[t]here was evidence . . . that both plaintiff's positioning, which Dr. Beasley primarily controlled, and the length of the surgery, for which Dr. Laftavi was at least partly responsible, contributed to plaintiff's injuries."

4. ***Nonmedical Contexts.*** *Res ipsa loquitur* has been found applicable to multiple defendants in cases where joint control or shared responsibility related to:

- a construction site used by subcontractors (*see* Jackson v. H.H. Robertson Co., Inc., 574 P.2d 822 (Ariz. 1978));
- a hallway accessed by a landlord and tenant (*see* Barb v. Farmers Ins. Exch., 281 S.W.2d 297 (Mo. 1955));
- scaffolding supplied or assembled by the defendants (*see* Meny v. Carlson, 77 A.2d 245 (N.J. 1950));
- a barricade that collapsed (*see* Schroeder v. City & County Savings Bank, Albany, 57 N.E.2d 57 (N.Y. 1944)); or
- an elevator that plummeted (*see* Bond v. Otis Elevator Co., 388 S.W.2d 681 (Tex. 1965)).

Of course, even if evidence is insufficient to establish joint control on the part of multiple defendants, it may show that one of the defendants had exclusive control and therefore is subject to *res ipsa loquitur. See* Anderson v. Serv. Merch. Co., Inc., 485 N.W.2d 170 (Neb. 1992) (holding, in an action by a customer who was struck by a falling light fixture, that a lighting contractor did not have sufficient control over store's lighting system to permit application of *res ipsa loquitur*, but that store operator was in "exclusive control" of the store premises and therefore subject to the doctrine).

5. ***Not Applied to Unrelated Persons.*** The ruling in *Ybarra* appears to be grounded in part on the fact that the defendants all stood in an integrated relationship as professional colleagues and all had some responsibility for the plaintiff's safety. In cases in which the defendants are strangers to one another—as when a pedestrian injured in a collision sues the drivers of two cars independently involved in the crash—invocation of the doctrine has generally not been allowed, even if it is clear that at least one of the defendants must have been negligent. *See* Dean v. Young, 636 N.E.2d 745, 747 (Ill. Ct. App. 1994).

6. ***Tort Reform and Res Ipsa Loquitur.*** Some states have limited the use of *res ipsa loquitur* in certain types of cases, such as those involving medical malpractice. *See, e.g.*, Tex. Civ. Prac. & Rem. Code § 74.201(Westlaw 2022) (restricting the doctrine in health care liability claims to those types of cases in which it had been applied prior to August 29, 1977).

E. Disposing of Unfavorable Evidence

The best evidence that a defendant has acted negligently may be contained in the defendant's files, or may consist of the condition of a vehicle or other piece of property belonging to the defendant. In these cases, the defendant has every incentive to destroy or alter the evidence. Altering the evidence for the purpose of misleading a factfinder is plainly fraudulent, and may well subject the defendant to criminal and civil sanctions. Destroying evidence is a more-complex matter: the law cannot require every person who might possibly be sued for negligence to keep forever all documents or objects that a plaintiff might someday find useful.

One possible response to the problem of evidence retention in tort cases is to create another tort—the tort of "spoliation of evidence."

Trevino v. Ortega

Texas Supreme Court
969 S.W.2d 950 (Tex. 1998)

ENOCH, Justice, delivered the opinion of the Court . . . :

The issue in this case is whether this Court should recognize an independent cause of action for intentional or negligent spoliation of evidence by parties to litigation.[2] . . . .

In 1988, Genaro Ortega, individually and as next friend of his daughter, Linda Ortega, sued Drs. Michael Aleman and Jorge Trevino and McAllen Maternity Clinic for medical malpractice. Ortega alleged that the defendants were negligent in providing care and treatment during Linda's birth in 1974.[3] Discovering that Linda's medical records from the birth had been destroyed, Ortega then sued Dr. Trevino in a separate suit for intentionally, recklessly, or negligently destroying Linda Ortega's medical records from the birth.

. . . . Here, Ortega claims that Trevino had a duty to preserve Linda's medical records and that destroying the records materially interferes with Ortega's ability to prepare his medical malpractice suit. Ortega explains that Aleman, the attending physician, testified that he has no specific recollection of the delivery and, therefore, the missing medical records are the only way to determine the procedures used to deliver Linda. Because the medical records are missing, Ortega's expert cannot render an opinion about Aleman's, the Clinic's, or Trevino's negligence.

. . . . The court of appeals reversed the trial court's dismissal order and held that Texas recognizes an independent cause of action for evidence spoliation. . . .

This Court treads cautiously when deciding whether to recognize a new tort. . . . While the law must adjust to meet society's changing needs, we must balance that

2. [Fn. 1:] Whether we recognize a cause of action for spoliation of evidence by persons who are not parties to the underlying lawsuit is not before the Court, and therefore we do not consider it.

3. [Fn. 2:] At the time of submission, this case was still pending in district court.

adjustment against boundless claims in an already crowded judicial system. We are especially averse to creating a tort that would only lead to duplicative litigation, encouraging inefficient relitigation of issues better handled within the context of the core cause of action. . . . A number of jurisdictions that have considered the issue have been hesitant to recognize an independent tort for evidence spoliation for a variety of different reasons. . . .[4]

Evidence spoliation is not a new concept. For years courts have struggled with the problem and devised possible solutions. Probably the earliest and most enduring solution was the spoliation inference or *omnia praesumuntur contra spoliatorem*: all things are presumed against a wrongdoer. . . . In other words, within the context of the original lawsuit, the factfinder deduces guilt from the destruction of presumably incriminating evidence.

This traditional response to the problem of evidence spoliation properly frames the alleged wrong as an evidentiary concept, not a separate cause of action. Spoliation causes no injury independent from the cause of action in which it arises. . . .

Even those courts that have recognized an evidence spoliation tort note that damages are speculative. . . . The reason that the damages inquiry is difficult is because evidence spoliation tips the balance in a lawsuit; it does not create damages amenable to monetary compensation.

Our refusal to recognize spoliation as an independent tort is buttressed by an analogous line of cases refusing to recognize a separate cause of action for perjury or embracery.[5] Like evidence spoliation, civil perjury and civil embracery involve improper conduct by a party or a witness within the context of an underlying lawsuit. A number of courts considering the issue have refused to allow the wronged party to bring a separate cause of action for either perjury or embracery. . . . These decisions rely on public policy concerns such as ensuring the finality of judgments, avoiding duplicative litigation, and recognizing the difficulty in calculating damages. . . . Similarly, recognizing a cause of action for evidence spoliation would create an impermissible layering of liability and would allow a plaintiff to collaterally attack an unfavorable judgment with a different factfinder at a later time, in direct opposition to the sound policy of ensuring the finality of judgments.

. . . [W]hen spoliation occurs, there must be adequate measures to ensure that it does not improperly impair a litigant's rights. . . . It is simpler, more practical, and more logical to rectify any improper conduct within the context of the lawsuit in which it is relevant. . . . Trial judges have broad discretion to take measures ranging

4. [Fn. 3:] Courts in more than twenty states have considered the issue, but . . . [few] have recognized a cause of action for negligent or intentional spoliation. *See* Hazen v. Municipality of Anchorage, 718 P.2d 456, 463 (Alaska 1986) (intentional); . . . Callahan v. Stanley Works, . . . [703 A.2d 1014, 1017–19 (N.J. Super. L. 1997)] (negligent); . . . Smith v. Howard Johnson Co., . . . [615 N.E.2d 1037 (Ohio 1993)] (intentional).

5. [Fn. 4:] Embracery is "[t]he crime of attempting to influence a jury corruptly to one side or the other." Black's Law Dictionary 522 (6th ed. 1990).

from a jury instruction on the spoliation presumption to, in the most egregious case, death penalty sanctions.... As with any discovery abuse or evidentiary issue, there is no one remedy that is appropriate for every incidence of spoliation; the trial court must respond appropriately based upon the particular facts of each individual case.

Ortega also argues that the failure to maintain Linda's medical records violated a statutory duty to maintain such records as required by section 241.103(b) of the Texas Health and Safety Code. Assuming without deciding that such a duty exists and that there was a breach of that duty, it does not necessarily follow that an independent cause of action arises. Nor does a cause of action necessarily arise from a party's obligation to comply with the rules of discovery.... [O]bligations not to destroy evidence arise in the context of particular lawsuits; consequently, spoliation is best remedied within the lawsuit itself, not as a separate tort.

We reverse the court of appeals' judgment and render judgment that Ortega take nothing.

BAKER, Justice, concurring.

.... [C]ourts have been hesitant to apply remedies for spoliation.... Accordingly, I believe it appropriate to review what remedies are available ... and when the remedies should be applied.

....

When a party believes that another party has improperly destroyed evidence, it may either move for sanctions or request a spoliation presumption instruction....

Upon a spoliation complaint, the threshold question should be whether the alleged spoliator was under any obligation to preserve evidence. A party may have a statutory, regulatory, or ethical duty to preserve evidence....

Other jurisdictions have held that there is also a common law duty to preserve evidence....

.... While there is no question that a party's duty to preserve relevant evidence arises during pending litigation, courts have been less clear about whether a duty exists prelitigation.... A party should not be able to subvert the discovery process and the fair administration of justice simply by destroying evidence before a claim is actually filed....

.... Courts that have imposed a prelitigation duty to preserve evidence have held that once a party is on "notice" of potential litigation a duty to preserve evidence exists.... Most courts have not elaborated on the concept of notice. But, a few courts have determined that a party is on notice of potential litigation when the litigation is reasonably foreseeable....

... [I]n spoliation cases a party should be found to be on notice of potential litigation when, after viewing the totality of the circumstances, the party either actually anticipated litigation or a reasonable person in the party's position would have anticipated litigation....

.... A party that is on notice of either potential or pending litigation has an obligation to preserve evidence that is relevant to the litigation. "While a litigant is under no duty to keep or retain every document in its possession ... it is under a duty to preserve what it knows, or reasonably should know, is relevant in the action, is reasonably calculated to lead to the discovery of admissible evidence, is reasonably likely to be requested during discovery, [or] is the subject of a pending discovery sanction." ....

If the trial court finds that a party has a duty to preserve evidence, it should then decide whether the party breached its duty. Parties need not take extraordinary measures to preserve evidence; however, a party should exercise reasonable care in preserving evidence....

Some courts have allowed sanctions or the presumption only for intentional or bad faith spoliation....

Because parties have a duty to reasonably preserve evidence, it is only logical that they should be held accountable for either negligent or intentional spoliation....

A spoliator can defend against an assertion of negligent or intentional destruction by providing other explanations for the destruction. For example, if the destruction of the evidence was beyond the spoliator's control or done in the ordinary course of business, the court may find that the spoliator did not violate a duty to preserve evidence. Importantly though, when a party's duty to preserve evidence arises before the destruction or when a policy is at odds with a duty to maintain records, the policy will not excuse the obligation to preserve evidence....

Though a party may have improperly spoliated evidence, the nonspoliating party may not be entitled to a remedy.... A party is entitled to a remedy only when evidence spoliation hinders its ability to present its case or defense....

Courts should look to a variety of factors in deciding whether destroying evidence has prejudiced a party. Most importantly, courts should consider the destroyed evidence's relevancy....

Additionally, courts should consider whether the destroyed evidence was cumulative of other competent evidence ... and whether the destroyed evidence supports key issues in the case....

Once a court finds that evidence has been improperly spoliated and that the nonspoliating party was prejudiced by the spoliation, the court should decide what sanction to apply....

.... Important factors for the trial court to weigh include the degree of the spoliator's culpability and the prejudice the nonspoliator suffers....

The most severe sanction for evidence spoliation is to dismiss the action or render a default judgment.... [C]ourts have found that a dismissal or default judgment is justified when a party destroys evidence with the intent to subvert discovery.... Thus, courts can dismiss an action or render a default judgment when the spoliator's conduct was egregious, the prejudice to the nonspoliating party was great, and imposing a lesser sanction would be ineffective to cure the prejudice....

Another effective sanction is excluding evidence or testimony. Courts generally use this sanction when the spoliating party is attempting to admit testimony or evidence adduced from the destroyed evidence.... Understandably, it will be extremely difficult for the nonspoliating party to defend against the spoliating party's allegations without being able to inspect the evidence. Thus, in some instances, it is proper for courts to exclude the spoliating party's evidence.

In addition to sanctions,... trial courts may submit a spoliation presumption instruction....

Depending on the severity of prejudice resulting from the particular evidence destroyed, the trial court can submit one of two types of presumptions.... The first and more severe presumption is a rebuttable presumption. This is primarily used when the nonspoliating party cannot prove its *prima facie* case without the destroyed evidence.... The trial court should begin by instructing the jury that the spoliating party has either negligently or intentionally destroyed evidence and, therefore, the jury should presume that the destroyed evidence was unfavorable to the spoliating party on the particular fact or issue the destroyed evidence might have supported. Next, the court should instruct the jury that the spoliating party bears the burden to disprove the presumed fact or issue.... This means that when the spoliating party offers evidence rebutting the presumed fact or issue, the presumption does not automatically disappear. It is not overcome until the fact finder believes that the presumed fact has been overcome by whatever degree of persuasion the substantive law of the case requires....

... [B]y shifting the burden of proof, the presumption will support the nonspoliating party's assertions and is some evidence of the particular issue or issues that the destroyed evidence might have supported. The rebuttable presumption will enable the nonspoliating party to survive summary judgment....

The second type of presumption is less severe. It is merely an adverse presumption that the evidence would have been unfavorable to the spoliating party.... The presumption itself has probative value and may be sufficient to support the nonspoliating party's assertions.... However, it does not relieve the nonspoliating party of the burden to prove each element of its case.... Therefore, it is simply another factor used by the factfinder in weighing the evidence.

... Ortega can move for sanctions or request a spoliation presumption in the underlying malpractice action. If he shows that Dr. Trevino had a duty to preserve evidence, Dr. Trevino violated that duty, and the destruction prejudiced Ortega's ability to bring suit, the trial court can remedy the spoliation.

Notes

1. ***Other Precedent.*** *See* Coastal Bridge Co., L.L.C. v. Heatec, Inc., 833 Fed. Appx. 565, 573 (5th Cir. 2020) ("A plaintiff alleging spoliation must establish that the

defendant *intentionally* destroyed the evidence for the purpose of depriving opposing parties of its use"), *but see* Brookshire Bros., Ltd. v. Aldridge, 438 S.W.3d 9, 25 (Tex. 2014) ("On rare occasions, a situation may arise in which a party's negligent breach of its duty to reasonably preserve evidence irreparably prevents the nonspoliating party from having any meaningful opportunity to present a claim or defense").

2. ***Independent Actions for Spoliation.*** Whether an independent action for spoliation will be recognized sometimes depends on the position and culpability of the defendant. *See* Hannah v. Heeter, 584 S.E.2d 560 (W. Va. 2003) (holding that intentional spoliation is actionable as a stand-alone tort regardless of whether the spoliator is a party or third party, but that negligent spoliation is independently actionable only against a third party with a special duty to preserve evidence); Rizzuto v. Davidson Ladders, Inc., 905 A.2d 1165 (Conn. 2006) (allowing an independent action against a first-party spoliator); *but see* Pyeritz v. Com., 32 A.3d 687, 695 (Pa. 2011) (no cause of action for negligent spoliation).

3. ***Sanctions Rather Than Independent Actions.*** Many decisions have found that spoliation is better addressed through sanctions than by allowing a separate cause of action. *See, e.g.*, Martino v. Wal-Mart Stores, Inc., 908 So. 2d 342 (Fla. 2005) (holding that first-party spoliation involving a store's failure to preserve a videotape and shopping cart could be adequately remedied through a presumption and sanctions).

4. ***Examples of Sanctions.*** *See* Gutman v. Klein, 2008 WL 5084182 (E.D.N.Y. 2008) (default judgment); Allstate Ins. Co. v. Sunbeam Corp., 53 F.3d 804 (7th Cir. 1995) (dismissal of subrogation claim).

5. ***Spoliation by Third Parties.*** Boyd v. Travelers Ins. Co., 652 N.E.2d 267 (Ill. 1995), addressed whether a person who is not a party may be held liable for spoliation of evidence. There, after an employee was injured when a heater exploded, the employer's workers' compensation insurer took possession of the damaged heater and lost it. The employee sued the insurer, alleging that its negligence impaired his ability to bring a products liability action against the manufacturer of the heater. The court held that an action for negligent spoliation was available under existing negligence principles without creating a new tort and that the employee should be allowed to try that claim concurrently with the claim against the manufacturer.

> A single trier of fact would be in the best position to resolve all the claims fairly and consistently. If a plaintiff loses the underlying suit, only the trier of fact who heard the case would know the real reason why....

In contrast, Smith v. Atkinson, 771 So. 2d 429 (Ala. 2000), agreed that an action for spoliation by a third party could be stated under ordinary negligence principles, but endorsed a very different approach. The court stated that the third-party spoliation claim did not need to be joined with the underlying claim and that the plaintiff did not even need to "file an action pursuing the underlying cause of action and be denied recovery," provided the plaintiff could show that the lost or destroyed evidence was so important that its absence would have kept the plaintiff's underlying claim from surviving a motion for summary judgment.

Some courts have refused to permit actions for third-party spoliation, occasionally focusing on the issue of duty. *See* MetLife Auto & Home v. Joe Basil Chevrolet, Inc., 807 N.E.2d 865 (N.Y. 2004) (holding that a vehicle insurer had no duty to a home insurer to preserve a vehicle, because even though the home insurer made a verbal request, "it never placed that request in writing or volunteered to cover the costs associated with preservation" and there was "no duty, court order, contract or special relationship"); Fletcher v. Dorchester Mut. Ins. Co., 773 N.E.2d 420 (Mass. 2002) (holding that in the absence of an agreement or a subpoena *duces tecum*, a non-party ordinarily does not have a duty to preserve evidence "merely because that item may be of use to others in pending or anticipated litigation").

States rejecting a cause of action for third-party spoliation are sometimes fearful of problems relating to the difficulty of proving causation. *See* Ortega v. City of New York, 876 N.E.2d 1189 (N.Y. 2007) ("there is no way of ascertaining to what extent the proof would have benefitted either the plaintiff or defendant in the underlying lawsuit"); Dowdle Butane Gas Co. v. Moore, 831 So. 2d 1124 (Miss. 2002) (refusing to recognize an independent action for either first-party or third-party intentional spoliation because "the costs to defendants and courts would be enormous," particularly relating to the risks of erroneous determinations of liability and the extraordinary measures that would be taken to avoid those risks).

6. ***Belated Evidence of Spoliation.*** In Davis v. Wal-Mart Stores, Inc., 756 N.E.2d 657 (Ohio 2001), the court held that claims for spoliation of evidence may be brought after the primary action has been concluded only when evidence of spoliation is not discovered until after the termination of the primary action.

7. ***Ethics in Law Practice: Destruction of Evidence.*** A lawyer may be reprimanded, suspended, or disbarred for destroying evidence. Rule 3.4 of the Model Rules of Professional Conduct (Westlaw 2022) states:

> A lawyer shall not:
>
> (a) unlawfully obstruct another party's access to evidence or unlawfully alter, destroy or conceal a document or other material having potential evidentiary value. A lawyer shall not counsel or assist another person to do any such act; [or]
>
> (b) falsify evidence, counsel or assist a witness to testify falsely, or offer an inducement to a witness that is prohibited by law. . . .

Presumably, the word "unlawfully," as used in subparagraph (a), includes any conduct that violates federal or state criminal laws or tort standards governing alteration, destruction, or concealment of evidence.

In addition to discipline and other sanctions, attorneys are subject to tort liability based on spoliation. If the attorney's failure to preserve evidence harms the client, the lawyer may be sued for malpractice.

Chapter 7

Factual Causation

A. An Overview of Causation

Williams v. Steves Industries, Inc.

Supreme Court of Texas
699 S.W.2d 570 (Tex. 1985)

ROBERT M. CAMPBELL, Justice.

....

On July 30, 1981, Mrs. Williams was driving her car on a four-lane segment of Interstate 35 in Austin. Her two children were riding in the back seat. The car ran out of gas and stalled in one of the center lanes. Mrs. Williams restarted the car but continued only a short distance before it stalled again. There was testimony the car was hidden from the view of approaching traffic by shadows of an overpass. Robinson, who was driving an eight-ton equipment repair truck owned by Steves Industries, hit Mrs. Williams' car from behind. Mrs. Williams and her children were injured and the children died from those injuries. [Mrs. Williams and her husband sought to recover from Steves Industries for personal injuries and wrongful death based on a theory of negligent entrustment. As to the issue of comparative negligence:]

.... Renee Williams traveled only five miles from her home when her car stalled. After the accident, a fireman at the scene checked the gas tank for a possible fire hazard, but found no gasoline. A wrecker service employee drained the tank through a hole in the gas tank and less than a cupful of gasoline ran out of the tank....

The jury found Renee Williams negligent for failing to have enough gasoline in her car to make the trip, and found her negligence to be a proximate cause of the accident. The jury also found that her negligence contributed twenty-five percent to the collision. Renee Williams does not attack the negligence finding but contends that as a matter of law her negligence was not a proximate cause of the accident. The two elements of proximate cause are cause in fact and foreseeability.... We will consider each element separately.

The first issue, therefore, is whether there is some evidence that Mrs. Williams' negligence was a cause in fact of the accident. If a negligent act or omission is a substantial factor in bringing about the injury and without which no harm would have occurred, the act or omission is a cause in fact of the injury.... Had Mrs. Williams had enough gasoline in her car to make her trip, her car would not have stalled in the middle of Interstate 35. A jury could infer that had the car not stalled in the middle of the highway, Robinson would not have collided with it. Thus, we find some evidence that Mrs. Williams' negligence was a cause in fact of the accident.

.... "Foreseeability means that the actor, as a person of ordinary intelligence, should have anticipated the dangers that his negligent act created." .... Furthermore, the actor need only anticipate an injury of the same general character as the actual injury:

> [I]t is not required that the particular accident complained of should have been foreseen. All that is required is "that the injury be of such a general character as might reasonably have been anticipated; and that the injured party should be so situated with relation to the wrongful act that injury to him or to one similarly situated might reasonably have been foreseen." ....

Carey v. Pure Distributing Corp., 133 Tex. 31, 124 S.W.2d 847, 849 (1939)....

On the day of the accident Mrs. Williams knew the route she was taking; therefore, she knew that she would be traveling on a high traffic section of an interstate highway. The jury found that she knew or should have known that she did not have enough gas to make the trip. The jury could reasonably conclude that a person of ordinary intelligence would anticipate that if his car ran out of gas it might stall on the highway and that a stalled car on a highly traveled section of an interstate highway would create a danger of another vehicle colliding with it. Thus, there is some evidence of foreseeability.

We affirm the judgment of the court of appeals.

[The dissenting opinion of Justice RAY, relating to punitive damages, is omitted.]

Notes

1. ***Burden of Proof.*** In nearly every tort action—whether based on intentional wrongdoing, failure to exercise care, or strict liability—the plaintiff must prove causation.

2. ***Two-Step Inquiry.*** As *Williams* indicates, the issue of causation involves a two-step inquiry. The first step asks whether in fact there was a connection between the allegedly tortious conduct and the plaintiff's injury. One way (but not the only way) to meet this requirement is to show that "but for" the defendant's conduct the harm would not have occurred.

The second step in the causation analysis concerns the fairness of imposing liability for harm in fact caused by the defendant. That is, notwithstanding the fact that the defendant played a substantial role in the plaintiff's injury, it may be unfair to impose liability. This determination is sometimes framed in terms of foreseeability, on the belief that it is fair to hold a defendant responsible for those consequences of conduct which could have been foreseen, and unfair to impose liability for results which could not have been anticipated. While foreseeability plays a large role in the second step of the causation analysis, Chapter 8 will show that other considerations may also be important.

The terms "cause in fact" or "factual causation" are often used to refer to the first step in the causation analysis, and "proximate causation" often denotes the second step. This book follows that terminology. Chapter 7 deals with factual causation. The difficult subject of proximate causation is considered in Chapter 8. Note, however, that some authorities, such as *Williams*, use "proximate causation" to describe the overall two-step inquiry.

3. ***"Cause in Fact" and "Proximate Cause."*** In everyday speech, "cause" is used to indicate responsibility. If *A* drives too fast, slides off the road, and strikes *B*, most observers would say that *A*'s conduct "caused" the accident, and that the conduct of *B*, who was walking along minding her own business, did not cause the accident. This way of discussing the problem is not suitable for legal analysis. The problem is that it is too conclusory: on the facts given, it may well make sense to hold *A* liable for *B*'s injuries, but lawyers and judges must be able to say specifically what it was about *A*'s conduct—and *B*'s—that requires *A* to pay. Simply saying "*A* caused the accident" will not do, because to say that is to state the conclusion that *A* should be responsible, not to justify it. Most cases like the one described here will indeed be cases in which *A* is liable to *B*, because in most cases like this *A* was negligent. But if *A*'s speeding resulted from a sudden and unforeseeable seizure, *A* will not be liable.

As a simple illustration of the role of "but-for causation" or "cause in fact" in the law of negligence, suppose that the plaintiff is struck by a speeding hit-and-run driver and that the plaintiff sues the defendant. If the factfinder determines that the defendant was not the driver who struck the plaintiff, the case is over—even if the defendant was negligent. (Suppose, for instance, that the evidence shows that the defendant was speeding on a street ten miles from the scene of the accident.) Many tort cases turn primarily on issues like this: was it the defendant whose car hit the plaintiff; was it the defendant who made the defective product that injured the plaintiff; was it the defendant who set off the explosion that knocked down the plaintiff's barn?

Every accident has countless "causes" in the but-for sense, and so "but-for causation" can never be, in itself, the sole reason for holding a defendant liable. Suppose, for example, that the plaintiff, while walking to church one morning, is run down by a drunken driver. The driver's conduct is obviously a "but-for cause" of the accident. But so is the *plaintiff's* conduct—but for the plaintiff's decision to go to church that morning, the accident would not have happened. Similarly, if the person from whom the defendant bought the car had not sold the car to the defendant the accident would not have happened, so that person's conduct is a "but-for cause" of the accident. So is the church's decision to have a service that morning, or to have it at ten rather than at ten thirty, for if the service had not been held, or had been held at a different time, the plaintiff would not have been in position to be struck by the defendant's car. Causation, in the but-for sense, is normally required if the defendant is to be liable. But causation in the but-for sense is *never* enough, by itself, to establish liability. "Only those causes attributable to tortious conduct are legally relevant in determining liability and apportioning liability for the plaintiff's harm." Restatement, Third, of Torts: Liab. for Physical and Emotional Harm § 28 cmt. c (2010).

B. The Traditional Rules of Factual Causation

1. *Sine Qua Non*: The But-For Test

Reynolds v. Texas and Pacific Railway Co.

Supreme Court of Louisiana
37 La. Ann. 694 (1885)

FENNER, J.

The plaintiff and his wife claim damages of the defendant company for injuries suffered by the wife and caused by the alleged negligence of the company.

....

The mode of getting from the depot to the [railroad] cars was as follows: passengers went down a stairway of several steps, which ran parallel to the track and led to a lower platform....

.... Although both the east and west-bound trains customarily stopped at this station in the night-time, no stationary lights were provided for the depot platform or the steps. There was no moon on this night.... The lights in the rooms of the station could have shed no light on the bottom of the steps.... After an attentive study of the evidence, we clearly concur in the conclusion of the district judge that there was no sufficient light....

The train was behind time. Several witnesses testify that passengers were warned to "hurry up." Mrs. Reynolds, a corpulent woman, weighing two hundred and fifty pounds, emerging from the bright light of the sitting-room, which naturally exaggerated the outside darkness, and hastening down these unlighted steps, made a misstep in some way and was precipitated beyond the narrow platform in front and down the slope beyond, incurring the serious injuries complained of.

Upon what grounds does the company claim exemption from liability?

....

2nd. It contends that, even conceding the negligence of the company in the above respect, it does not follow that the accident to plaintiff was necessarily caused thereby, but that she might well have made the misstep and fallen even had it been broad daylight. We concede that this is possible, and recognize the distinction between *post hoc* and *propter hoc*. But where the negligence of the defendant greatly multiplies the chances of accident to the plaintiff, and is of a character naturally leading to its occurrence, the mere possibility that it might have happened without the negligence is not sufficient to break the chain of cause and effect between the negligence and the injury.... The whole tendency of the evidence connects the accident with the negligence.

....

Judgment affirmed.

Notes

1. ***Jury Question.*** Normally, it is a question of fact for the jury to determine, based on common experience, whether a particular course of conduct multiplied the chances of injury and justifies a finding of factual causation. *See* Rost v. Ford Motor Co., 151 A.3d 1032, 1052 (Pa. 2016) (concluding it was for the fact finder to decide whether exposure to asbestos caused mesothelioma).

However, if the matter is beyond the ken of the ordinary juror, expert testimony is needed to guide the finder of fact. *See* Dodge-Farrar v. American Cleaning Services Co., Inc., 54 P.3d 954 (Idaho Ct. App. 2002) (holding that the causal relationship between an employee's slip and fall and immediate symptoms in the ankle, knee, and back (such as pain, swelling, and the inability to sit, stand, or walk without assistance) was within the usual and ordinary experience of the average person, but that expert testimony was necessary to establish that the fall caused a permanent ankle deformity).

Expert testimony is normally necessary in cases involving medicine and other sciences. *See, e.g.*, Money v. Manville Corp. Asbestos Disease Comp. Trust Fund, 596 A.2d 1372 (Del. 1991) (the fact that plaintiffs had been exposed to defendants' products containing asbestos and suffered from an asbestos-related disease did not permit the jury to infer causation without expert testimony).

2. ***Causation Based on Circumstantial Evidence.*** Circumstantial evidence may be sufficient to establish factual causation. *See* Havner v. E-Z Mart Stores, Inc., 825 S.W.2d 456 (Tex. 1992) (a jury's finding that a convenience store's negligently deficient security system was a cause in fact of an employee's abduction and murder by an unknown assailant was supported by circumstantial evidence that negated the possibility that the employee voluntarily left the store, and by a police investigation that produced no evidence indicating that the employee had been murdered by an acquaintance); McCarley v. West Quality Food Serv., 960 S.W.2d 585, 587 (Tenn. 1998) (where the plaintiff consumed both bacon and chicken, either of which could have contained the bacteria that made the plaintiff ill, the plaintiff's testimony that the chicken "looked strange, and 'didn't taste right,'" supported an inference that the chicken was the source of the bacteria that caused the harm).

3. ***Causation Based on Breach of Statute.*** The breach of a statutory duty may give rise to an inference that an injury was caused by the violation. *See, e.g.*, Lucas v. Hesperia Golf & Country Club, 63 Cal. Rptr. 189, 196 (Ct. App. 1967) (failure to have a lifeguard on duty at a swimming pool).

Sometimes statutes shift the burden of proof on causation. Discussing the National Vaccine Injury Compensation Program in Bruesewitz v. Wyeth LLC, 131 S. Ct. 1068 (2011), Justice Antonin Scalia wrote:

> The Act establishes a no-fault compensation program "designed to work faster and with greater ease than the civil tort system."
>
> Fast, informal adjudication is made possible by the Act's Vaccine Injury Table, which lists the vaccines covered under the Act; describes each

vaccine's compensable, adverse side effects; and indicates how soon after vaccination those side effects should first manifest themselves. Claimants who show that a listed injury first manifested itself at the appropriate time are *prima facie* entitled to compensation. No showing of causation is necessary; the Secretary bears the burden of disproving causation. A claimant may also recover for unlisted side effects, and for listed side effects that occur at times other than those specified in the Table, but for those the claimant must prove causation. . . .

Kramer Service, Inc. v. Wilkins

Supreme Court of Mississippi
186 So. 625 (Miss. 1939)

GRIFFITH, Justice.

Appellant was and is the owner and operator of a large hotel. About 5:30 o'clock P.M. on January 15, 1935, one Clockey registered as a guest and was given a room, to which he was conducted by a bellboy. . . .

Soon after entering the room, Clockey discovered that . . . the transom [could not be] lowered so as to give ventilation. The reason . . . was that there was a break in the glass thereof. . . .

About two hours later appellee came to Clockey's room in response to . . . [a] telephone message, and when the business conference was concluded appellee was in the act of leaving the room. When he opened the door, . . . the broken piece of the transom fell striking appellee upon the head. Three wounds were thus made upon appellee's head, one of which was a jagged abrasion on the temple.

. . . . There is . . . competent evidence to the effect that the condition of unrepair . . . had existed for a sufficient length of time to charge appellant with responsible notice thereof, and that the condition was such that a reasonably prudent and careful operator should have foreseen the fall of the broken glass and an injury thereby as a likelihood of appreciable weight and moment. . . . There is no reversible error in the record on the issue of liability. . . .

But there is plain and serious error in the matter of the amount of the damages. The wound on the temple did not heal, and some months after the injury appellee was advised by his local physician to visit a specialist in skin diseases, which he did . . . about two years after the injury, and it was then found that at the point where the injury occurred to appellee's temple, a skin cancer had developed, of which a cure had not been fully effected at the time of the trial. . . .

Appellee sued for a large sum in damages, . . . contending that the cancer resulted from the stated injury; and the jury evidently accepted that contention, since there was an award by the verdict in the sum of twenty thousand dollars. Appellant requested an instruction to the effect that the cancer or any prolongation of the trouble on account thereof should not be taken into consideration by the jury, but this instruction was refused.

Two physicians or medical experts, and only two, were introduced as witnesses.... One testified that it was possible that a trauma such as appellee suffered upon his temple, could or would cause a skin cancer at the point of injury, but that the chances that such a result would ensue from such a cause would be only one out of one hundred cases. The other testified that there is no causal connection whatsoever between trauma and cancer, and went on to illustrate that if there were such a connection nearly every person of mature age would be suffering with cancer....

It seems therefore hardly to be debatable but that appellant was entitled to the requested instruction as regards the cancer; and since, except as to that element, the verdict could not have been large, the verdict and judgment must be reversed on the issue of the amount of the damages.

There is one heresy in the judicial forum which appears to be Hydra-headed, and although cut off again and again, has the characteristic of an endless renewal. That heresy is that proof that a past event possibly happened, or that a certain result was possibly caused by a past event, is sufficient in probative force to take the question to a jury. Such was never the law in this state, and we are in accord with almost all of the other common-law states. Nearly a half century ago, ... Chief Justice Campbell said in Railroad v. Cathey, 70 Miss. 332, 337, 12 So. 253: "It is not enough that negligence of the employer and injury to the employee coexisted, but the injury must have been caused by the negligence.... '*Post hoc ergo propter hoc*' is not sound as evidence or argument. Nor is it sufficient for a plaintiff seeking recovery for alleged negligence by an employer towards an employee to show a possibility that the injury complained of was caused by negligence. Possibilities will not sustain a verdict. It must have a better foundation."

....

Taking the medical testimony in this case in the strongest light in which it could be reasonably interpreted in behalf of the plaintiff, this testimony is that as a possibility a skin cancer could be caused by an injury such as here happened, but as a probability the physicians were in agreement that there was or is no such a probability.

... [A]fter long and anxious years of research the exact cause of cancer remains unknown.... If, then, the cause be unknown to all those who have devoted their lives to a study of the subject, it is wholly beyond the range of the common experience and observation of judges and jurors, and in such a case medical testimony when undisputed, as here, must be accepted ...; otherwise the jury would be allowed to resort to and act upon nothing else than the proposition *post hoc ergo propter hoc*, which, as already mentioned, this Court has long ago rejected as unsound....

Affirmed as to liability; reversed and remanded on the issue of the amount of the damages.

Notes

1. ***Mere Possibility Does Not Prove Factual Causation.*** In Turpin v. Merrell Dow Pharmaceuticals, Inc., 959 F.2d 1349 (6th Cir. 1992), studies demonstrated only a

possibility, not a probability, that the drug Bendectin caused birth defects in human babies.

2. ***Multiple But-For Causes.*** An accident may, indeed *must,* have more than one but-for cause, and so more than one defendant may be liable for an injury. In a case in which one defendant was negligent in leaving his truck parked in the road, and the other defendant was negligent in failing to take evasive measures to avoid hitting it, both actions were factual causes of the injuries sustained by a passenger in the second vehicle. But for the negligence of each defendant, the accident would not have occurred. Hill v. Edmonds, 270 N.Y.S.2d 1020 (App. Div. 1966).

Saelzler v. Advanced Group 400

California Supreme Court
23 P.3d 1143 (Cal. 2001)

CHIN, J.

... [P]laintiff Marianne Saelzler was an employee of Federal Express. Defendants were owners of the Sherwood Apartments, a 28-building, 300-unit apartment complex located on a several-acre site in Bellflower. Plaintiff came to the complex in midafternoon to deliver a package to a resident. As she entered through one of the many gated entrances to the premises, she saw two young men loitering outside a security gate that had been propped open. While walking across the grounds she saw another young man already on the premises.

Plaintiff's attempt to deliver the package proved unsuccessful because the resident was not at home. When plaintiff returned down a walk path with the package in hand, the three men confronted her.... Then the three of them beat her and attempted to rape her, inflicting serious injuries. After assaulting plaintiff, her assailants fled and were never apprehended.

Plaintiff's complaint alleged that defendants, knowing that dangerous persons frequented their premises, nonetheless failed to maintain the premises in a safe condition, failed to provide adequate security, and failed to warn others of the unsafe conditions. Defendants moved for summary judgment on the basis that plaintiff was unable to establish any substantial causal link between defendants' omissions and plaintiff's injury. Plaintiff offered no evidence showing the identity of her assailants, whether they were gang members, whether they trespassed on defendants' property to assault her, or whether they were tenants of the building who were permitted to pass through the security gates. Similarly, plaintiff submitted no evidence showing that the propped-open security gate was actually broken or otherwise not functioning properly, or whether her assailants entered through the gate or themselves broke it and entered....

As the trial court found, plaintiff presented evidence that defendants knew of frequent recurring criminal activity on the premises of their 28 building apartment complex. The community of Bellflower was itself a high-crime area, with considerable juvenile gang activity occurring both on and off defendants' premises....

Defendants' security manager acknowledged that during the year preceding the assault on plaintiff, several nighttime assaults, and actual or attempted rapes, occurred on the premises....

Plaintiff observes that police officers advised both defendants' apartment manager and the head of the security firm they employed that they should hire *daytime* as well as nighttime security patrols. Plaintiff filed a lengthy declaration from a security expert, Robert Feliciano.... His qualifications included service as Director of Police and Safety for the Housing Authority of Los Angeles County, as well as advanced education in public safety and several years in law enforcement. At the time he made his declaration, he was a full-time instructor in criminal justice and police science at a community college. Feliciano expressed the opinion "that this attack... would not have occurred had there been daytime security and a more concerted effort to keep the gates repaired and closed...."

The trial court granted summary judgment for defendants, finding plaintiff had failed to show defendants' breach of duty to safeguard her was a proximate cause of her assault....

A majority of the Court of Appeal reversed, concluding that plaintiff's showing was sufficient to raise a triable causation issue for the jury. In summary, the majority held, relying primarily on commonsense and ordinary experience, that defendants' "complete absence of required security measures" by itself reasonably could be deemed a contributing cause of any criminal activity in the area.

The Court of Appeal majority also held that defendants' failure to provide additional security justified shifting the burden of proof to defendants, for purposes of their summary judgment motion, to conclusively establish the absence of a causal relation between their breach of duty and the assault on plaintiff by showing this particular assault would have occurred even if reasonable security measures had been taken....

Finally, according to the Court of Appeal majority, the testimony of plaintiff's expert, opining that the assault on plaintiff would not have occurred but for the lack of daytime security measures, was "both admissible and credible" on the causation issue.

....

Plaintiff admits she cannot prove the identity or background of her assailants. They might have been unauthorized trespassers, but they also could have been tenants of defendants' apartment complex, who were authorized and empowered to enter the locked security gates and remain on the premises. The primary reason for having functioning security gates and guards stationed at every entrance would be to exclude *unauthorized* persons and trespassers from entering. But plaintiff has not shown that her assailants were indeed unauthorized to enter. Given the substantial number of incidents and disturbances involving defendants' own tenants, and defendants' manager's statement that a juvenile gang was "headquartered" in one of the buildings, the assault on plaintiff could well have been made by tenants having authority to enter and remain on the premises. That being so, and despite the speculative opinion of plaintiff's expert, she cannot show that defendants' failure to provide increased daytime security at each entrance gate or functioning locked gates was a substantial factor in causing her injuries. . . . Put another way, she is unable to prove it was "more probable than not" that additional security precautions would have prevented the attack. . . .

Plaintiff also argues in favor of the Court of Appeal majority's practical approach to the causation issue. . . . [T]he majority held that common sense and common experience should lead us to conclude that a defendant's "complete absence of required security measures" is necessarily a "contributing cause of most crimes occurring on that property." Defendants observe, of course, that the evidence fails to show any such complete absence of security, as defendants provided, among other things, nighttime roving security patrols and regular daytime inspections to repair broken gates.

More fundamentally, we hesitate to adopt a rule of common sense that seemingly would prevent summary judgment on the causation issue *in every case* in which the defendant failed to adopt increased security measures of some kind. . . .

. . . [T]o demonstrate actual or legal causation, the plaintiff must show that the defendant's act or omission was a "substantial factor" in bringing about the injury. . . . In other words, plaintiff must show some substantial link or nexus between omission and injury. Under the Court of Appeal's "common sense" rule, the defendants' omission itself would constitute the missing link.

. . . [I]n a given case, direct or circumstantial evidence may show the assailant took advantage of the defendant's lapse (such as a failure to keep a security gate in repair) in the course of committing his attack, and that the omission was a substantial factor in causing the injury. Eyewitnesses, security cameras, even fingerprints or recent signs of break-in or unauthorized entry, may show what likely transpired at the scene. In the present case no such evidence was presented. . . .

Plaintiff also urges us to adopt the Court of Appeal's novel approach of shifting the proof burden on the causation issue to defendants. . . .

We think such a drastic shifting of the proof burden is unjustified by either the evidence in this case or prior statutory and case law. First, and contrary to the Court of Appeal's hyperbole, the evidence discloses no flagrant failure in this case. As we have seen, most of the assaults and similar incidents of crime plaintiff has cited occurred during the night, and the record indicates defendants did provide extensive nighttime security. Moreover, plaintiff's own evidence showed that defendants at least attempted to keep all security gates in working order, performing regular inspections and repairs.

But again, even assuming a triable issue existed regarding the extent or reasonableness of defendants' security efforts, even a flagrant failure to provide such measures would not justify shifting to defendants the burden of conclusively proving the absence of causation. No matter how inexcusable a defendant's act or omission might appear, the plaintiff must nonetheless show the act or omission caused, or substantially contributed to, her injury. Otherwise, defendants might be held liable for conduct which actually caused no harm, contrary to the recognized policy against making landowners the *insurer* of the absolute safety of anyone entering their premises. . . .

. . . . The evidence at hand, however, merely shows the speculative possibility that additional daytime security guards and/or functioning security gates might have prevented the assault. Plaintiff's evidence is no less speculative because she offered a security expert's testimony. Because he was equally unaware of the assailants' identities, his opinion regarding causation is simply too tenuous to create a triable issue whether the absence of security guards or functioning gates was a substantial factor in plaintiff's assault.

The judgment of the Court of Appeal is reversed with directions to affirm the award of summary judgment in defendants' favor.

GEORGE, C.J., BAXTER, J., and BROWN, J., concur.

[The dissenting opinion of KENNARD, J., in which WERDEGAR, J., concurred, and dissenting opinion of WERDEGAR, J., in which MOSK, J., and KENNARD, J., concurred, are omitted.]

Notes

1. ***No Speculation***. "[S]ome suspicion linked to other suspicion produces only more suspicion, which is not the same as some evidence" and "an inference stacked only on other inferences is not legally sufficient evidence." Marathon Corp. v. Pitzner, 106 S.W.3d 724, 728 (Tex. 2003).

Pitzner was a suit to recover for catastrophic injuries sustained by an electrician who did not remember what happened when he fell from a roof while working on air conditioning equipment that violated various building and mechanical codes. There was a screwdriver with a burnt tip on the ground near the body of the electrician, and an expert testified the most likely scenario was that the electrician must have come into contact with the high voltage wire on the defectively installed equipment and was shocked, causing him to tumble backwards over the edge of the roof. However, there was also evidence that electricians often carry with them screwdrivers with burnt tips to use when they need to short a circuit. A ladder that was used by the electrician to access the roof was missing. Also, the plaintiff had suffered various injuries to his head, which could have been caused by the fall or may have resulted from a struggle with an attacker (which is what the paramedic and physician, but not the police, thought). The court concluded that there was no evidence that made one scenario more likely than another, and that the expert's opinion was mere speculation. The court reversed a judgment of almost $8 million dollars and ordered that the plaintiff take nothing for his "devastating" injuries.

See Vaillancourt v. Latifi, 840 A.2d 1209 (Conn. App. 2004) (no liability based on an umpire's alleged failure to warn softball players that a runner coming into home base must slide because the "[h]ighly competitive members of athletic teams often take chances and risks that cause them to forget or to ignore the rules of the game," and thus the injury might have happened anyway); Southwest Key Program, Inc. v. Gil-Perez, 81 S.W.3d 269 (Tex. 2002) (no liability for an allegedly negligent failure to provide protective equipment to a boy participating in an amateur football game because plaintiff's expert said only that it was a matter of "speculation" whether those precautions would have prevented the knee injury).

See also Jea v. Cho, 183 S.W.3d 466 (Tex. App. 2005) (finding that although certain precautions (*i.e.*, providing a key to lock the front door from the inside, installing adequate exterior lighting, and supplying a second employee to assist when cash was counted at closing time) "might have theoretically made the store somewhat more difficult to rob," the plaintiff employee who was shot during a closing-time robbery failed to establish a reasonable probability "that this particular robbery or shooting would have been deterred or thwarted").

2. ***Causation in Toxic-Tort Cases.*** Tort cases involving exposure to toxic substances raise difficult issues relating to proof of factual causation, including whether a substance is generally capable of causing a particular disease and, if so, whether the exposure to the substance caused the plaintiff in particular to contract the disease. In adjudicating toxic-tort cases, some courts have been inclined to place heavy reliance on scientific evidence developed in group (epidemiological) studies.

Proof of causation in toxic-exposure cases is beyond the scope of a basic course in torts. However, this subject is extensively addressed in Restatement, Third, of Torts: Liab. for Physical and Emotional Harm § 28 cmt. c (2010). The Restatement warns that:

> Courts . . . should be cautious about adopting specific "scientific" principles, taken out of context, to formulate bright-line legal rules or conclude that reasonable minds cannot differ about factual causation.

It notes that:

> [M]ost courts have appropriately declined to impose a threshold requirement that a plaintiff always must prove causation with epidemiologic evidence. . . .

The Restatement opines that for a number of reasons:

> [A]ny judicial requirement that plaintiffs must show a threshold increase in risk or a doubling in incidence in a group study in order to satisfy the burden of proof of specific causation is usually inappropriate. . . .

Comment c was developed by the American Law Institute in consultation with the National Academy of Sciences and prominent epidemiologists.

In Green v. Alpharma, Inc., 373 Ark. 378 (2008), the court held that genuine issues of material fact precluded summary judgment on a claim that poultry producers caused a child to contract leukemia. The court held the plaintiffs were required to prove that "(1) . . . [the child] Green was exposed to the arsenic-laced chicken litter spread by the poultry producers, (2) with sufficient frequency and regularity, (3) in proximity to where he . . . lived and went to school . . . , [and] (4) such that it is probable that the exposure to the arsenic-laced chicken litter caused . . . [the child's] injuries."

2. Independently Sufficient Causes and Related Problems

If several senators simultaneously stab Caesar on the steps of the Senate, none of them is a but-for cause of Caesar's death. Should each of the assailants escape liability? Not surprisingly, the answer is no.

> The "but for" rule serves to explain the vast majority of cases wherein a causation instruction is required. However, there is one type of situation in which it fails. If two or more causes concur to bring about an event, and any one of them, operating alone, would have been sufficient to cause the identical result, some other test is needed. In such cases it is quite clear that each cause has in fact played so important a part in producing the result that responsibility should be imposed upon it; and it is equally clear that neither can be absolved from that responsibility upon the ground that the identical harm would have occurred without it, or there would be no liability at all.

Rudeck v. Wright, 709 P.2d 621, 628 (Mont. 1985).

Anderson v. Minneapolis, St. P. & S.S.M. Ry. Co.

Supreme Court of Minnesota
179 N.W. 45 (Minn. 1920)

[Plaintiff's property was destroyed by fire. The destruction was caused by either (a) a bog fire which resulted from the negligence of the defendant, (b) a fire of independent and uncertain origin which was sweeping through the Northeastern part of the state, or (c) a fire which resulted from the combining of the fire caused by the defendant with the fire of independent origin.]

LEES, C.

. . . . Plaintiff had a verdict. The appeal is from an order denying a motion in the alternative for judgment notwithstanding the verdict or for a new trial.

[The defendant contends that the following jury instruction was error:]

> If the plaintiff was burned out by some fire other than the bog fire, which other fire was not set by one of the defendant's engines, then, of course, defendant is not liable. . . .
>
> If you find that other fires not set by one of defendant's engines mingled with one that was set by one of the defendant's engines, there may be difficulty in determining whether you should find that the fire set by the engine was a material or substantial element in causing plaintiff's damage. If it was, the defendant is liable; otherwise, it is not. . . .

> If you find that the bog fire was set by the defendant's engine, and that some greater fire swept over it before it reached the plaintiff's land, then it will be for you to determine whether the bog fire . . . was a material or substantial factor in causing plaintiff's damage. If it was, the defendant is liable. If it was not, defendant is not liable. . . .

The following proposition is stated in defendant's brief and relied on for reversal:

> If plaintiff's property was damaged by a number of fires combining, one being the fire pleaded, and the others being of no responsible origin, but of such sufficient or superior force that they would have produced the damage to plaintiff's property regardless of the fire pleaded, then defendant was not liable.

This proposition is based on Cook v. Minneapolis, St. P. & S.S.M. Ry. Co., 98 Wis. 624, 74 N.W. 561. . . . If the *Cook* case merely decides that one who negligently sets a fire is not liable if another's property is damaged, unless it is made to appear that the fire was a material element in the destruction of the property, there can be no question about the soundness of the decision. But if it decides that if such fire combines with another of no responsible origin, and after the union of the two fires they destroy the property, and either fire independently of the other would have destroyed it, then, irrespective of whether the first fire was or was not a material factor in the destruction of the property, there is no liability, we are not prepared to adopt the doctrine as the law of this state. . . .

We find no error requiring a reversal, and hence the order appealed from is affirmed.

Notes

1. ***The "Two Fires" Cases and But-For Causation.*** In cases in which two fires merge and the combined fire destroys the plaintiff's property, the negligent conduct of the person who started one of the fires may or may not be a cause of the harm in a but-for sense. Consider the following hypothetical cases:

> Case (1): Denise negligently starts a small fire in the woods. If this had been the only fire at that time, the fire department could easily have handled it and the plaintiff's property would not have been destroyed. However, the fire set by Denise merges with a much larger fire. The larger fire could not have been stopped by the fire department. The merged fire burns the plaintiff's house to the ground. Denise's negligence is not a but-for cause of the loss of the plaintiff's house, and she will not be liable for the loss. If the other fire was negligently set, that negligence is a but-for cause of the loss.
>
> Case (2): Darryl negligently sets a small fire, which merges with one negligently set by Donald. The fire department could have handled either fire alone, but the combined fire is too much for the department's resources, and the plaintiff's house burns. Darryl's negligence is a but-for cause of the damage, as "but for" that negligence the house would not have burned, so

Darryl is liable. For the same reason, Donald's negligence is a but-for cause of the damage, so Donald is also liable.

Case (3): Donna and David, acting independently, negligently set large fires. Each fire, by itself, is too much for the fire department; they merge, and the merged fire destroys the plaintiff's house. In this case, neither the negligence of Donna nor that of David is a but-for cause of the harm. If, for example, Donna had not set a fire, the plaintiff's house would have burned, so Donna's negligence is not a *sine qua non*. Similar reasoning shows that David's negligence was not a but-for cause of the harm. Nevertheless, both Donna and David are liable for the harm: this is like a case in which two persons, acting independently but at the same time, shoot the plaintiff in the head. This situation is often described as involving "independently sufficient causes."

2. ***The "Substantial Factor" Test for Causation.*** There is no doubt that both negligent defendants are liable to the plaintiff in cases of independently sufficient causes, despite the absence of but-for causation. There has, however, been controversy as to how juries in these cases should be instructed. One possibility is simply to tell the jury that both defendants are liable if the jury finds that each defendant's negligence was an independently sufficient cause of the harm. Another is to instruct the jury that it may find the defendant liable if the defendant's negligence was a "substantial factor" in producing the harm.

In Mitchell v. Gonzales, 819 P.2d 872 (Cal. 1991), a pattern jury instruction asking whether the injury would not have occurred but for the defendant's conduct was discontinued in favor of one asking whether the defendant's conduct was a substantial factor in bringing about the harm. However, in Viner v. Sweet, 70 P.3d 1046 (Cal. 2003), the same court made clear:

> In so holding, *Mitchell* did not abandon or repudiate the requirement that the plaintiff must prove that, *but for* the alleged negligence, the harm would not have happened. On the contrary, *Mitchell* stated that jury instructions on causation in negligence cases should use the "substantial factor" test articulated in the Restatement Second of Torts (Restatement), and *Mitchell* recognized that "the 'substantial factor' test subsumes the 'but for' test." ....
>
> The text of Restatement section 432 demonstrates how the "substantial factor" test subsumes the traditional "but for" test of causation. Subsection (1) of section 432 provides: "Except as stated in Subsection (2), the actor's negligent conduct is *not a substantial factor* in bringing about harm to another *if the harm would have been sustained even if the actor had not been negligent.*" .... Subsection (2) states that if "two forces are actively operating ... and each of itself is sufficient to bring about harm to another, the actor's negligence may be found to be a substantial factor in bringing it about."

The *Viner* court held that because the transactional legal malpractice action before it did not involve concurrent independent causes, the plaintiffs had to satisfy the but-for test and show that it was more likely than not that they would have obtained a more favorable result absent the malpractice. *See also* Callahan v. Cardinal Glennon Hosp., 863 S.W.2d 852, 860 (Mo. 1993) (en banc) (but-for test applies to all cases except those involving two independently sufficient torts); Williams v. Steves Indus., Inc., 699 S.W.2d 570 (Tex. 1985) (test is whether the negligence was "a *substantial factor* in bringing about the injury and *without which no harm would have occurred*"; emphasis added). The Third Restatement rejects the "substantial factor" approach on the ground that it "has not . . . withstood the test of time, as it has proved confusing and been misused." Restatement, Third, of Torts: Liab. for Physical and Emotional Harm § 26 cmt. j (2010).

See Doull v. Foster, 163 N.E.3d 976, 990–91 (Mass. 2021) ("[W]e conclude that a but-for standard, rather than a substantial factor standard, is the appropriate standard for factual causation in negligence cases involving multiple alleged causes of the harm. . . . [I]n the rare cases presenting the problem of multiple sufficient causes, the jury should receive additional instructions on factual causation. . . . [T]he jury should be instructed, 'A defendant whose tortious act was fully capable of causing the plaintiff's harm should not escape liability merely because of the happenstance of another sufficient cause'").

A small, but significant, number of cases continue to apply a "substantial factor" test when addressing issues of factual causation. *See* Wager v. Moore, 220 A.3d 48, 58 (Conn. App. 2019) ("To prove contributory negligence, the defendant must prove that the plaintiff's negligence was a proximate cause of or a substantial factor in the resulting harm"); Garcia v. Windley, 164 P.3d 819 (Idaho 2007) (holding that "the 'but for' test may be employed when there is a single possible cause of the injury; however, the 'substantial factor' test must be employed when there are multiple possible causes of injury"); Estate of Re v. Kornstein Veisz & Wexler, 958 F. Supp. 907 (S.D.N.Y. 1997) (holding that the "substantial factor" test, rather than the more demanding but-for rule, applies to a tort claim against an attorney for breach of fiduciary duty). Some cases imply that even if the defendant's conduct did not make an indispensable contribution to the plaintiff's harm (*i.e.*, does not satisfy the but-for rule), and was not independently sufficient to cause that harm (*i.e.*, does come within the Restatement exception to the but-for rule), the conduct might nevertheless still be "substantial" and therefore a factual cause of the plaintiff's harm. Thus, the question is whether factual causation encompasses three subcategories ((1) indispensable causes, (2) independently sufficient causes, and (3) "otherwise substantial" causes) or just the first two of those subcategories (as discussed in the Third Restatement). The tripartite scenario makes it easier to account for liability in some cases. If Caesar is simultaneously stabbed by many Senators, it may be difficult to say that the wound inflicted by each Senator would have been independently sufficient to cause Caesar's death, and easier to conclude that each stabbing was a substantial factor that should not be overlooked in the imposition of liability. Likewise in a case involving multiple fires, it may be hard to conclude that each fire was independently sufficient to cause the harm suffered by the plaintiff, and yet possible to say that a particular tortfeasor's contribution was sufficiently substantial to warrant an adverse judgment. Nevertheless, it is important to remember that the *Restatement*, and the law of most states recognizes only two ways to establish factual causation: the but-for rule and the independently-sufficient rule.

3. ***Concurrence with Destructive Natural Forces.*** In addition to cases of independently sufficient tortious causes, a case in which some courts may find a "substantial factor" instruction appropriate is this:

> Case (4): Doris negligently sets a large fire. This fire alone would be enough to overwhelm the fire department and destroy the plaintiff's house. The fire merges with another large fire, which was set by a lightning strike, without fault on anyone's part.

This is a difficult case. As in Case (3), above, Doris's negligence was not a but-for cause of the fire. Unlike Case (3), holding that Doris is not liable would not entail leaving a loss caused by the actions of two negligent people on the innocent plaintiff. (In Case (3), if the defendants were held not liable, the plaintiff would be worse off than if one defendant had stayed home that day instead of cooking hot dogs in the woods. In this case, the plaintiff would not have been worse off if Doris had stayed home.) Would the *Anderson* court approve of a "substantial factor" charge in this case? If the facts (in a "what happened" sense) are known, should juries be allowed to hold some defendants liable and to exonerate others, or should the law provide an answer? The *Cook* decision, cited in *Anderson*, holds that the defendant is not liable in a case like this.

Section 27 of the Restatement, Third, of Torts: Liab. for Physical and Emotional Harm (2010) deals with the independently sufficient cause problem by saying:

> If multiple acts exist, each of which under § 26 alone would have been a factual cause of the physical harm at the same time in the absence of the other act(s), each act is regarded as a factual cause of the harm.

Under the Restatement's approach as applied to the two-major-fires case, it does not matter whether the fire not set by the defendant is of tortious or natural origins.

4. ***Joint and Several Liability.*** In cases in which more than one defendant is liable for the destruction of the plaintiff's house, the plaintiff does not get a double recovery. In some states, the defendants will be jointly and severally liable, which means that the plaintiff can collect from either, or partly from both, but is not entitled to more than the total loss. If one defendant pays more than an appropriate share of the damages, that defendant may be entitled to recover the excess from the other tortfeasor. In other states, joint and several liability has been abolished, at least in some circumstances, and each tortfeasor will be liable only for a portion of the total harm. These matters are examined in Chapter 17.

3. The "Loss of a Chance" Rule

Matsuyama v. Birnbaum

Supreme Judicial Court of Massachusetts
890 N.E.2d 819 (Mass. 2008)

MARSHALL, C.J.

We are asked to determine whether Massachusetts law permits recovery for a "loss of chance" in a medical malpractice wrongful death action, where a jury found that the defendant physician's negligence deprived the plaintiff's decedent of a less than even chance of surviving cancer. We answer in the affirmative.[1] ... [T]he loss of chance doctrine views a person's prospects for surviving a serious medical condition as something of value, even if the possibility of recovery was less than even prior to the physician's tortious conduct....

[The] ... jury found the defendant physician negligent in misdiagnosing the condition of the decedent over a period of approximately three years. They found as well that the physician's negligence was a "substantial contributing factor" to the decedent's death. They awarded $160,000 to the decedent's estate for the pain and suffering caused by the physician's negligence, and $328,125 to the decedent's widow and son for the decedent's loss of chance. The defendants appealed....

... [A] substantial and growing majority of the States that have considered the question have indorsed the loss of chance doctrine, in one form or another, in medical malpractice actions.[2] ....

.... The doctrine originated in dissatisfaction with the prevailing "all or nothing" rule of tort recovery. *See generally* [Joseph H.] King, Jr., *Causation, Valuation, and Chance in Personal Injury Torts Involving Preexisting Conditions and Future Consequences*, 90 Yale L.J. 1353, 1365–1366 (1981). Under the all or nothing rule, a plaintiff may recover damages only by showing that the defendant's negligence more likely than not caused the ultimate outcome, in this case the patient's death; if the plaintiff meets this burden, the plaintiff then recovers 100% of her damages. Thus, if a patient had a 51% chance of survival, and the negligent misdiagnosis or treatment caused that chance to drop to zero, the estate is awarded *full* wrongful death damages. On the other hand, if a patient had a 49% chance of survival, and the negligent misdiagnosis or treatment caused that chance to drop to zero, the plaintiff receives nothing. So long as the patient's chance of survival before the physician's negligence was less

---

1. [Fn. 3:] The loss of chance doctrine is also known as the "lost opportunity" doctrine. *See* Restatement (Third) of Torts: Liability for Physical Harm § 26 comment n (Proposed Final Draft No. 1, 2005) (Draft Restatement)....

2. [Fn. 23:] The highest courts of at least twenty States and the District of Columbia have adopted the loss of chance doctrine....

Ten States' high courts have, in contrast, refused to adopt the loss of chance doctrine....

Other States' high courts have not addressed the issue or have explicitly left the question open....

Margaret H. Marshall

than even, it is logically impossible for her to show that the physician's negligence was the but-for cause of her death, so she can recover nothing. . . .

. . . . The all or nothing rule "fails to deter" medical negligence because it immunizes "whole areas of medical practice from liability." . . . .

As the Supreme Court of Wyoming recently stated:

> . . . . Much treatment of diseases is aimed at extending life for brief periods and improving its quality rather than curing the underlying disease. Much of the American health care dollar is spent on such treatments, aimed at improving the odds. In the words of the Delaware Supreme Court, "[i]t is unjust not to remedy such a loss." . . . . As Judge Posner wrote in DePass v. United States, "A tortfeasor should not get off scot free because instead of killing his victim outright he inflicts an injury that is likely though not certain to shorten the victim's life."

. . . . The defendants argue that the loss of chance doctrine "lowers the threshold of proof of causation" by diluting the preponderance of the evidence standard that "has been the bedrock of the Massachusetts civil justice system." We reject this. . . . [I]n a case involving loss of chance, as in any other negligence context, a plaintiff must establish by a preponderance of the evidence that the defendant caused his injury.

However, "injury" need not mean a patient's death. Although there are few certainties in medicine or in life, progress in medical science now makes it possible, at least with regard to certain medical conditions, to estimate a patient's probability of survival to a reasonable degree of medical certainty. . . . When a physician's negligence diminishes or destroys a patient's chance of survival, the patient has suffered real injury. The patient has lost something of great value: a chance to survive, to be cured, or otherwise to achieve a more favorable medical outcome. . . . Thus we recognize loss of chance not as a theory of causation, but as a theory of injury. . . .

. . . . In order to prove loss of chance, a plaintiff must prove by a preponderance of the evidence that the physician's negligence caused the plaintiff's likelihood of achieving a more favorable outcome to be diminished. . . .

We reject the defendants' contention that a statistical likelihood of survival is a "mere possibility" and therefore "speculative." The magnitude of a probability is distinct from the degree of confidence with which it can be estimated. A statistical survival rate cannot conclusively determine whether a particular patient will survive a medical condition. But survival rates are not random guesses. They are estimates based on data obtained and analyzed scientifically and accepted by the relevant medical community as part of the repertoire of diagnosis and treatment. . . .

The defendants also point out that "[t]he cause, treatment, cure and survivability related to cancer is tremendously uncertain and complex," and argue that loss of chance is "rife with practical complexities and problems." Such difficulties are not confined to loss of chance claims. A wide range of medical malpractice cases, as well as numerous other tort actions, are complex and involve actuarial or other probabilistic estimates. Wrongful death claims, for example, often require, as part of the damages calculation, an estimate of how long the decedent might have lived absent the defendant's conduct. The calculation of damages in a claim for lost business opportunities may be similarly complex. . . .

The key is the reliability of the evidence available to the fact finder. . . . Reliable modern techniques of gathering and analyzing medical data have made it possible for fact finders to determine based on expert testimony . . . whether a negligent failure to diagnose a disease injured a patient by preventing the disease from being treated at an earlier stage, when prospects were more favorable. . . .

. . . . We emphasize that our decision today is limited to loss of chance in medical malpractice actions. Such cases are particularly well suited to application of the loss of chance doctrine. . . . [R]eliable expert evidence establishing loss of chance is more likely to be available in a medical malpractice case than in some other domains of tort law. . . .

. . . [A] challenging issue is how to calculate the monetary value for the lost chance. Courts adopting the loss of chance doctrine have arrived at different methods for calculating such damages. . . . The most widely adopted of these methods of valuation is the "proportional damages" approach. . . . Under the proportional damages approach, loss of chance damages are measured as "the percentage probability by which the defendant's tortious conduct diminished the likelihood of achieving some more favorable outcome." . . . The formula aims to ensure that a defendant is liable in damages only for the monetary value of the *portion* of the decedent's prospects that the defendant's negligence destroyed. . . .

Deriving the damages for which the physician is liable will require the fact finder to undertake the following calculations:[3]

(1) The fact finder must first calculate the total amount of damages allowable for the death under the wrongful death statute . . . , or, in the case of medical malpractice not resulting in death, the full amount of damages allowable for the injury. This is the amount to which the decedent would be entitled if the case were *not* a loss of chance case: the full amount of compensation for the decedent's death or injury.

(2) The fact finder must next calculate the patient's chance of survival or cure immediately preceding ("but for") the medical malpractice.

(3) The fact finder must then calculate the chance of survival or cure that the patient had as a result of the medical malpractice.

(4) The fact finder must then subtract the amount derived in step 3 from the amount derived in step 2.

(5) The fact finder must then multiply the amount determined in step 1 by the percentage calculated in step 4 to derive the proportional damages award for loss of chance.

To illustrate, suppose in a wrongful death case that a jury found, based on expert testimony and the facts of the case, that full wrongful death damages would be $600,000 (step 1), that the patient had a 45% chance of survival prior to the medical malpractice (step 2), and that the physician's tortious acts reduced the chances of survival to 15% (step 3). The patient's chances of survival were reduced 30% (*i.e.*, 45% minus 15%) due to the physician's malpractice (step 4), and the patient's loss of chance damages would be $600,000 multiplied by 30%, for a total of $180,000 (step 5). . . .

. . . . Expert testimony is required to ascertain what measure of a more favorable outcome is medically appropriate (for example, five-year survival as in this case), to determine what statistical rates of survival apply in what circumstances. . . .

---

3. [Fn. 41:] . . . . We pause to clarify the issue of damages for *pain and suffering*, of which there are potentially two kinds. First, a jury could find, on appropriate evidence, that a physician's negligence caused pain and suffering quite apart from the loss of chance. Compensatory damages for this type of pain and suffering should be awarded in the same manner as in any malpractice case. . . .

Second, a jury could find, on appropriate evidence, that the ultimate injury — in this case, dying of gastric cancer — involved pain and suffering. This second category of pain and suffering would more likely than not have occurred even absent the physician's negligent conduct. Thus, the physician may only be held liable for this pain and suffering to the extent that his negligent conduct diminished the decedent's likelihood of avoiding this outcome. Thus, this second category of pain and suffering is properly subject to the proportional damages calculation set out here. . . .

The defendants protest that such reliance on experts is likely to result in "imprecise" and "skewed" evidence on which to base a damages award.... [W]e disavow the defendants' claim that reliance on statistical evidence is "generally disfavored in the law." ... [P]robabilistic evidence, in the form of actuarial tables, assumptions about present value and future interest rates, statistical measures of future harm, and the like, is the stock-in-trade of tort valuation....

The defendants claim that the evidence was insufficient to show that, as the judge instructed the jury, "an act or omission of Birnbaum was a substantially contributing factor to the death of Mr. Matsuyama." The "substantial contributing factor" test is useful in cases in which damage has multiple causes, including but not limited to cases with multiple tortfeasors in which it may be impossible to say for certain that any *individual* defendant's conduct was a but-for cause of the harm, even though it can be shown that the defendants, in the aggregate, caused the harm..... The proper test in a loss of chance case concerning the conduct of a single defendant is whether that conduct was the but-for cause of the loss of chance.

....

Judgment affirmed.

Notes

1. ***Other Precedent.*** In a companion case to *Matsuyama*, the court held that loss of a chance damages are recoverable where a physician's negligence reduces a patient's chances of survival from a better than even chance of survival to one less than even, and that if the patient dies the damages are calculated in accordance with the five-step method for computing proportional damages set forth in *Matsuyama*. *See* Renzi v. Paredes, 890 N.E.2d 806 (Mass. 2008).

2. ***Damages for "Loss of a Chance."*** As to valuing the lost chance, compare the approach discussed in *Matsuyama* with Smith v. State Dept. of Health & Hosp., 676 So. 2d 543 (La. 1996) (the factfinder should make a subjective determination of the value of the lost chance without going through the illusory exercise of setting a value for a wrongful death or survival claim and then reducing that amount by some percentage).

3. ***Legal Malpractice and Other Contexts.*** Recall that in cases involving *legal* malpractice the victim must establish that the malpractice caused a loss (*see* Chapter 5). Is a loss-of-a-chance rule any less desirable for legal malpractice cases than for medical malpractice cases? What if the lawyer's negligence causes a client to lose an opportunity to settle on favorable terms a case that could not be won? Without using the term "loss of a chance," the Supreme Court of Ohio held that, in order to succeed in a malpractice action, the plaintiffs were not required to show that they would have prevailed in certain civil, criminal, and administrative proceedings absent negligence of their attorneys. The court wrote:

> [W]e reject any finding that the element of causation in the context of a legal malpractice action can be replaced ... with a rule of thumb requiring that

> a plaintiff... prove in every instance that he or she would have been successful in the underlying matter(s) giving rise to the complaint.... A strict "but for" test... ignores settlement opportunities lost due to the attorney's negligence.

Vahila v. Hall, 674 N.E.2d 1164, 1168–69 (Ohio 1997).

The Restatement, noting that loss-of-a-chance has been "almost universally limited" to cases of medical malpractice and that the doctrine's expansion into other areas would be a reform "of potentially enormous scope," takes no position on the issue of expansion. Restatement, Third, of Torts: Liab. for Physical and Emotional Harm § 26 cmt. n (2010).

See also Hardy v. Southwestern Bell Telephone Co., 910 P.2d 1024 (Okla. 1996) (refusing to extend the loss-of-a-chance doctrine to ordinary negligence cases, such as where negligence causes a 911 emergency system to fail and prevents aid from being summoned for a heart attack victim, because the trier of fact would "have no more than mere conjecture as to what damages plaintiff suffered by reason of defendant's action").

"Loss of a Chance" and Deterrence

Alan Gunn

Compare two rules: (1) negligent defendants must pay full damages to victims who would have had a better than 50-percent chance of survival, but for the negligence, and (2) in all cases, negligent defendants pay according to the chance the plaintiff has lost, so that a plaintiff whose lost chance of survival was 70 percent gets a 70-percent recovery, and so on. On an overall basis, the amount a defendant should expect to pay under either of these rules should be roughly the same. Indeed, even on an *individual* basis, payments under either rule should be similar, as most cases are settled, not tried, and the greater the plaintiff's chances of convincing a jury that the chance of survival was high, the greater the settlement value of the plaintiff's case, under either rule.

If, however, the loss-of-a-chance rule comes into play only for plaintiffs whose chance was 50 percent or less, with other plaintiffs getting full recovery, the loss-of-a-chance rule will increase the amount defendants will pay, and in theory this will over-deter them. Similarly, if plaintiffs with less than a 50 percent chance of survival recover nothing, and other plaintiffs recover only the chance they have lost, the rules will produce under-deterrence.

The use of the loss-of-a-chance doctrine is a recent development. In other contexts, however, the victim's chance of survival has long been taken into account. For example, the damages assessed in a wrongful-death case in which the defendant's wrongdoing plainly caused the death are, in a sense, damages for the decedent's "loss of a chance of survival." The decedent's life expectancy — which fixes the number of years which the decedent would have had a 50-50 chance of living — is routinely used to calculate wrongful-death damages. For a dramatic instance of taking the victim's chance of survival into account, see Dillon v. Twin State Gas & Elec. Co., 163 A. 111 (N.H. 1932) (damages for death by electrocution were reduced to reflect the pre-existing fact that at the time the decedent touched the defendant's wires he had lost his balance and begun to fall from a bridge, and the fall would certainly have killed him). *See also* McCahill v. New York Transp. Co., 94 N.E. 616 (N.Y. 1911) (*infra*, p. 468) (damages reduced to reflect the fact that premature death might have otherwise resulted from the decedent's preexisting alcoholism).

C. Modifications of the Traditional Approach

1. Multiple Fault and Alternative Liability

Summers v. Tice

Supreme Court of California
199 P.2d 1 (Cal. 1948)

CARTER, Justice.

... [P]laintiff and the two defendants were hunting quail on the open range. Each of the defendants was armed with a 12 gauge shotgun loaded with shells containing 7H size shot. Prior to going hunting plaintiff discussed the hunting procedure with defendants, indicating that they were to exercise care when shooting and to "keep in line." ....

.... There is evidence that both defendants, at about the same time or one immediately after the other, shot at a quail and in so doing shot toward plaintiff who was uphill from them, and that they knew his location. That is sufficient [evidence] from which the trial court could conclude that they acted with respect to plaintiff other than as persons of ordinary prudence. ...

The problem presented in this case is whether the judgment against both defendants may stand. It is argued by defendants that ... there is not sufficient [evidence] to show which defendant was guilty of the negligence which caused the injuries—the shooting by Tice or that by Simonson. ...

... [I]t is clear that the court ... determined that the negligence of both defendants was the legal cause of the injury—or that both were responsible. Implicit in such finding is the assumption that the court was unable to ascertain whether the shots were from the gun of one defendant or the other or one shot from each of them. The one shot that entered plaintiff's eye was the major factor in assessing damages and that shot could not have come from the gun of both defendants. It was from one or the other only.

It has been held that where a group of persons are on a hunting party, or otherwise engaged in the use of firearms, and two of them are negligent in firing in the direction of a third person who is injured thereby, both of those so firing are liable for the injury suffered by the third person, although the negligence of only one of them could have caused the injury.... The same rule has been applied in criminal cases ... and both drivers have been held liable for the negligence of one where they engaged in a racing contest causing an injury to a third person.... These cases speak of the action of defendants as being in concert as the ground of decision, yet it would seem they are straining that concept....

".... The real reason for the rule that each joint tortfeasor is responsible for the whole damage is the practical unfairness of denying the injured person redress simply because he cannot prove how much damage each did, when it is certain that between them they did all; let them be the ones to apportion it among themselves. Since, then, the difficulty of proof is the reason, the rule should apply whenever the harm has plural causes, and not merely when they acted in conscious concert...." (Wigmore, Select Cases on the Law of Torts, § 153)....

When we consider the relative position of the parties and the results that would flow if plaintiff was required to pin the injury on one of the defendants only, a requirement that the burden of proof on that subject be shifted to defendants becomes manifest. They are both wrongdoers — both negligent toward plaintiff. They brought about a situation where the negligence of one of them injured the plaintiff, hence it should rest with them each to absolve himself if he can. The injured party has been placed by defendants in the unfair position of pointing to which defendant caused the harm. If one can escape the other may also and plaintiff is remediless. Ordinarily defendants are in a far better position to offer evidence to determine which one caused the injury.... In a quite analogous situation this Court held that a patient injured while unconscious on an operating table in a hospital could hold all or any of the persons who had any connection with the operation even though he could not select the particular acts by the particular person which led to his disability. Ybarra v. Spangard, 154 P.2d 687 (Cal. 1944). There the Court was considering whether the patient could avail himself of *res ipsa loquitur*, rather than where the burden of proof lay, yet the effect of the decision is that plaintiff has made out a case when he has produced evidence which gives rise to an inference of negligence which was the proximate cause of the injury.... Similarly in the instant case plaintiff is not able to establish which of defendants caused his injury.

....

The judgment is affirmed.

Notes

1. ***Alternative Liability.*** The rule of "multiple fault and alternative liability" set forth in *Summers* has been embodied in Restatement, Third, of Torts: Liab. for Physical and Emotional Harm § 28(b) (2010):

> When the plaintiff sues all of multiple actors and proves that each engaged in tortious conduct that exposed the plaintiff to a risk of physical harm and that the tortious conduct of one or more of them caused the plaintiff's harm

> but the plaintiff cannot reasonably be expected to prove which actor caused the harm, the burden of proof, including both production and persuasion, on factual causation is shifted to the defendants.

Section 28 provides for liability even in cases in which more than two defendants have acted negligently. It requires, however, that all negligent defendants be joined, at least if all of them are subject to the court's jurisdiction and not immune from liability. The joinder requirement is based on a concern that the party actually responsible could escape liability if fewer than all the persons who acted tortiously are made defendants.

Discussing *Summers*, the New York Court of Appeals said:

> The central rationale for shifting the burden of proof in such a situation is that without this device both defendants will be silent, and plaintiff will not recover; with alternative liability, however, defendants will be forced to speak, and reveal the culpable party, or else be held jointly and severally liable themselves. Consequently, use of the alternative liability doctrine generally requires that the defendants have better access to information than does the plaintiff, and that all possible tortfeasors be before the court.... It is also recognized that alternative liability rests on the notion that where there is a small number of possible wrongdoers, all of whom breached a duty to the plaintiff, the likelihood that any one of them injured the plaintiff is relatively high, so that forcing them to exonerate themselves, or be held liable, is not unfair....

Hymowitz v. Eli Lilly & Co., 539 N.E.2d 1069, 1074 (N.Y. 1989) (*see infra* p. 431).

Although *Summers* has been widely cited with approval, at least one court has declined to follow it on nearly identical facts. *See* Leuer v. Johnson, 450 N.W.2d 363 (Minn. Ct. App. 1990).

2. ***Requirement of Multiple Fault.*** The alternative liability rationale is applicable only where all of the defendants are shown to have acted tortiously. Therefore, the rule does not apply to shift the burden of proof, if a pedestrian injured by a falling object sues all of the occupants of the dozens of hotel rooms from which the object might have fallen. *See* Restatement, Third, of Torts: Liab. for Physical and Emotional Harm §28 illus. 6 (2010); *see also* Garcia v. Joseph Vince Co., 148 Cal. Rptr. 843, 846–47 (Ct. App. 1978) (finding that the alternative liability theory was inapplicable in a suit against two saber manufacturers, where the plaintiff was unable to identify which of the two had produced the defective weapon that injured him because it had been commingled with other sabers after the accident).

2. Market-Share Liability and Enterprise Liability

Sindell v. Abbott Laboratories

Supreme Court of California
163 Cal. Rptr. 132 (Cal. 1980)

MOSK, Justice.

....

Plaintiff Judith Sindell brought an action against eleven drug companies and Does 1 through 100, on behalf of herself and other women similarly situated. The complaint alleges as follows:

Between 1941 and 1971, defendants were engaged in the business of manufacturing, promoting, and marketing diethylstilbestrol (DES), ... a synthetic compound of the female hormone estrogen. The drug was administered to plaintiff's mother ... for the purpose of preventing miscarriage. In 1947, the Food and Drug Administration authorized the marketing of DES as a miscarriage preventative, but only on an experimental basis....

DES may cause cancerous vaginal and cervical growths in the daughters exposed to it before birth.... The form of cancer from which these daughters suffer ... manifests itself after a minimum latent period of 10 or 12 years. It is a fast-spreading and deadly disease....

In 1971, the Food and Drug Administration ordered defendants to cease marketing and promoting DES..., and to warn physicians and the public that the drug should not be used by pregnant women because of the danger to their unborn children.

During the period defendants marketed DES, they knew or should have known that ... there was a grave danger after varying periods of latency it would cause cancerous and precancerous growths in the daughters of the mothers who took it, and that it was ineffective to prevent miscarriage. Nevertheless, defendants continued to advertise and market the drug.... They failed to test DES for efficacy and safety; the tests performed by others, upon which they relied, indicated that it was not safe or effective....

The first cause of action alleges that defendants were jointly and individually negligent....

Defendants demurred to the complaint.... [T]he trial court sustained the demurrers of these defendants without leave to amend on the ground that plaintiff did not and stated she could not identify which defendant had manufactured the drug responsible for her injuries. Thereupon, the court dismissed the action. This appeal involves only five of [the] ... defendants named in the complaint.

... [A]s a general rule, the imposition of liability depends upon a showing by the plaintiff that his or her injuries were caused by the act of the defendant or by an instrumentality under the defendant's control....

There are, however, exceptions to this rule.... The first of these theories, classically illustrated by Summers v. Tice, 199 P.2d 1 (Cal. 1948), places the burden of proof of causation upon tortious defendants in certain circumstances. The second basis of liability emerging from the complaint is that defendants acted in concert to cause injury to plaintiff. There is a third and novel approach to the problem, sometimes called the theory of "enterprise liability," but which we prefer to designate by the more accurate term of "industry-wide" liability, which might obviate the necessity for identifying the manufacturer of the injury-causing drug. We shall conclude that these doctrines, as previously interpreted, may not be applied to hold defendants liable under the allegations of this complaint. However, we shall propose and adopt a fourth basis for permitting the action to be tried, grounded upon an extension of the *Summers* doctrine.

....

Defendants assert that... [the principles of Summers v. Tice, 199 P.2d 1 (Cal. 1948), *supra* at p. 420, and Ybarra v. Spangard, 154 P.2d 687 (Cal. 1944), *supra* at p. 385] are inapplicable here. First, they insist that a predicate to shifting the burden of proof under *Summers-Ybarra* is that the defendants must have greater access to information regarding the cause of the injuries than the plaintiff, whereas in the present case the reverse appears.

....

In *Summers*, the circumstances of the accident themselves precluded an explanation of its cause. To be sure, *Summers* states that defendants are "[o]rdinarily... in a far better position to offer evidence to determine which one caused the injury" than a plaintiff..., but the decision does not determine that this "ordinary" situation was present. Neither the facts nor the language of the opinion indicate that the two defendants, simultaneously shooting in the same direction, were in a better position than the plaintiff to ascertain whose shot caused the injury.... Nevertheless, burden of proof was shifted to the defendants.

Here, as in *Summers*, the circumstances of the injury appear to render identification of the manufacturer of the drug ingested by plaintiff's mother impossible by either plaintiff or defendants, and it cannot reasonably be said that one is in a better position than the other to make the identification....

It is important to observe, however, that while defendants do not have means superior to plaintiff to identify the maker of the precise drug taken by her mother, they may in some instances be able to prove that they did not manufacture the injury-causing substance. In the present case, for example, one of the original defendants was dismissed from the action upon proof that it did not manufacture DES until after plaintiff was born.

... [T]he fact defendants do not have greater access to information which might establish the identity of the manufacturer of the DES which injured plaintiff does not per se prevent application of the *Summers* rule.

Nevertheless, . . . [t]here is an important difference between the situation involved in *Summers* and the present case. There, all the parties who were or could have been responsible for the harm to the plaintiff were joined as defendants. Here, by contrast, there are approximately 200 drug companies which made DES, any of which might have manufactured the injury-producing drug.

Defendants maintain that, while in *Summers* there was a 50 percent chance that one of the two defendants was responsible for the plaintiff's injuries, here since any one of 200 companies which manufactured DES might have made the product which harmed plaintiff, there is no rational basis upon which to infer that any defendant in this action caused plaintiff's injuries, nor even a reasonable possibility that they were responsible.

. . . [D]efendants appear to be correct that the rule, as previously applied, cannot relieve plaintiff of the burden of proving the identity of the manufacturer which made the drug causing her injuries.

[The court next held that there was no concert of action among the defendants within the meaning of that doctrine. *See infra* pp. 439–50, discussing concerted action.]

. . . .

A third theory upon which plaintiff relies is the concept of industry-wide liability, or according to the terminology of the parties, "enterprise liability." This theory was suggested in Hall v. E. I. Du Pont de Nemours & Co., Inc., 345 F. Supp. 353 (E.D.N.Y. 1972). In that case, plaintiffs were 13 children injured by the explosion of blasting caps in 12 separate incidents which occurred in 10 different states between 1955 and 1959. The defendants were six blasting cap manufacturers, comprising virtually the entire blasting cap industry in the United States, and their trade association. There were, however, a number of Canadian blasting cap manufacturers which could have supplied the caps. The gravamen of the complaint was that the practice of the industry of omitting a warning on individual blasting caps and of failing to take other safety measures created an unreasonable risk of harm, resulting in the plaintiffs' injuries. The complaint did not identify a particular manufacturer of a cap which caused a particular injury.

The court reasoned as follows: there was evidence that defendants, acting independently, had adhered to an industry-wide standard with regard to the safety features of blasting caps, that they had in effect delegated some functions of safety investigation and design, such as labeling, to their trade association, and that there was industry-wide cooperation in the manufacture and design of blasting caps. In these circumstances, the evidence supported a conclusion that all the defendants jointly controlled the risk. Thus, if plaintiffs could establish by a preponderance of the evidence that the caps were manufactured by one of the defendants, the burden of proof as to causation would shift to all the defendants. The court noted that this theory of liability applied to industries composed of a small number of units, and that what would be fair and reasonable with regard to an industry of five or ten producers might be manifestly unreasonable if applied to a decentralized industry composed of countless small producers.

. . . .

We decline to apply this theory in the present case. At least 200 manufacturers produced DES; *Hall* . . . cautioned against application of the doctrine espoused therein to a large number of producers. . . . Moreover, in *Hall*, the conclusion that the defendants jointly controlled the risk was based upon allegations that they had delegated some functions relating to safety to a trade association. There are no such allegations here. . . .

If we were confined to the theories of *Summers* and *Hall*, we would be constrained to hold that the judgment must be sustained. Should we require that plaintiff identify the manufacturer which supplied the DES used by her mother or that all DES manufacturers be joined in the action, she would effectively be precluded from any recovery. As defendants candidly admit, there is little likelihood that all the manufacturers who made DES at the time in question are still in business or that they are subject to the jurisdiction of the California courts. There are, however, forceful arguments in favor of holding that plaintiff has a cause of action.

In our contemporary complex industrialized society, advances in science and technology create fungible goods which may harm consumers and which cannot be traced to any specific producer. The response of the courts can be either to adhere rigidly to prior doctrine, . . . or to fashion remedies to meet these changing needs. . . .

The most persuasive reason for finding plaintiff states a cause of action is that advanced in *Summers*: as between an innocent plaintiff and negligent defendants, the latter should bear the cost of the injury. Here, as in *Summers*, plaintiff is not at fault in failing to provide evidence of causation, and although the absence of such evidence is not attributable to the defendants either, their conduct in marketing a drug the effects of which are delayed for many years played a significant role in creating the unavailability of proof.

From a broader policy standpoint, defendants are better able to bear the cost of injury resulting from the manufacture of a defective product. As was said by Justice Traynor in Escola [v. Coca Cola Bottling Co., 150 P.2d 436 (1944)], "[t]he cost of an injury and the loss of time or health may be an overwhelming misfortune to the person injured, and a needless one, for the risk of injury can be insured by the manufacturer and distributed among the public as a cost of doing business." (24 Cal.2d p. 462, 150 P.2d p. 441; *see also* Rest. 2d Torts, § 402A, com. c, pp. 349–350.) The manufacturer is in the best position to discover and guard against defects in its products and to warn of harmful effects; thus, holding it liable for defects and failure to warn of harmful effects will provide an incentive to product safety. . . . These considerations are particularly significant where medication is involved, for the consumer is virtually helpless to protect himself from serious, sometimes permanent, sometimes fatal, injuries caused by deleterious drugs.

Where, as here, all defendants produced a drug from an identical formula and the manufacturer of the DES which caused plaintiff's injuries cannot be identified through no fault of plaintiff, a modification of the rule of *Summers* is warranted. . . .

. . . [W]e hold it to be reasonable in the present context to measure the likelihood that any of the defendants supplied the product which allegedly injured plaintiff by the percentage which the DES sold by each of them for the purpose of preventing miscarriage bears to the entire production of the drug sold by all for that purpose. Plaintiff asserts in her briefs that Eli Lilly and Company and 5 or 6 other companies produced 90 percent of the DES marketed. If at trial this is established to be the fact, then there is a corresponding likelihood that this comparative handful of producers manufactured the DES which caused plaintiff's injuries, and only a 10 percent likelihood that the offending producer would escape liability.

If plaintiff joins in the action the manufacturers of a substantial share of the DES which her mother might have taken, the injustice of shifting the burden of proof to defendants to demonstrate that they could not have made the substance which injured plaintiff is significantly diminished. . . .

The presence in the action of a substantial share of the appropriate market also provides a ready means to apportion damages among the defendants. Each defendant will be held liable for the proportion of the judgment represented by its share of that market unless it demonstrates that it could not have made the product which caused plaintiff's injuries. In the present case, as we have seen, one DES manufacturer was dismissed from the action upon filing a declaration that it had not manufactured DES until after plaintiff was born. Once plaintiff has met her burden of joining the required defendants, they in turn may cross-complaint against other DES manufacturers, not joined in the action, which they can allege might have supplied the injury-causing product.

Under this approach, each manufacturer's liability would approximate its responsibility for the injuries caused by its own products. Some minor discrepancy in the correlation between market share and liability is inevitable; therefore, a defendant may be held liable for a somewhat different percentage of the damage than its share of the appropriate market would justify. It is probably impossible, with the passage of time, to determine market share with mathematical exactitude. But just as a jury cannot be expected to determine the precise relationship between fault and liability in applying the doctrine of comparative fault . . . or partial indemnity, the difficulty of apportioning damages among the defendant producers in exact relation to their market share does not seriously militate against the rule we adopt. . . .

The judgments are reversed.

BIRD, C. J., and NEWMAN and WHITE, JJ., concur.

RICHARDSON, Justice, dissenting.

. . . [T]he majority adopts a wholly new theory which contains these ingredients: The plaintiffs were not alive at the time of the commission of the tortious acts.

They sue a generation later. They are permitted to receive substantial damages from multiple defendants without any proof that any defendant caused or even probably caused plaintiff's injuries. Although the majority purports to change only the required burden of proof by shifting it from plaintiffs to defendants, the effect of its holding is to guarantee that plaintiffs will prevail on the causation issue because defendants are no more capable of disproving factual causation than plaintiffs are of proving it. "Market share" liability thus represents a new high water mark in tort law. The ramifications seem almost limitless. . . .

. . . . Notably lacking from the majority's expression of its new rule, unfortunately, is any definition or guidance as to what should constitute a "substantial" share of the relevant market. . . . [T]he answer, presumably, is anyone's guess.

Much more significant, however, is the consequence of this unprecedented extension of liability. . . . In other words, a particular defendant may be held proportionately liable *even though mathematically it is much more likely than not that it played no role whatever in causing plaintiff's injuries*. . . .

[I]t is readily apparent that "market share" liability will fall unevenly and disproportionately upon those manufacturers who are amenable to suit in California. . . .

The majority attempts to justify its new liability on the ground that defendants herein are "better able to bear the cost of injury resulting from the manufacture of a defective product." . . . . This "deep pocket" theory of liability, fastening liability on defendants presumably because they are rich, has understandable popular appeal and might be tolerable in a case disclosing substantially stronger evidence of causation than herein appears. But as a general proposition, a defendant's wealth is an unreliable indicator of fault, and should play no part, at least consciously, in the legal analysis of the problem. In the absence of proof that a particular defendant caused or at least probably caused plaintiff's injuries, a defendant's ability to bear the cost thereof is no more pertinent to the underlying issue of liability than its "substantial" share of the relevant market. A system priding itself on "*equal* justice under law" does not flower when the *liability* as well as the *damage* aspect of a tort action is determined by a defendant's wealth. . . .

Given the grave and sweeping economic, social, and medical effects of "market share" liability, the policy decision to introduce and define it should rest not with us, but with the Legislature which is currently considering not only major statutory reform of California product liability law in general, but the DES problem in particular. . . .

I would affirm the judgments of dismissal.

CLARK and MANUEL, JJ., concur.

. . . .

Notes

1. ***Absence of Evidence Attributable to Defendant.*** If the absence of evidence of causation is the direct and foreseeable result of the defendant's negligence, the

burden of proof on the issue of causation may shift to the defendant. Haft v. Lone Palm Hotel, 478 P.2d 465 (Cal. 1970), was an action for damages by the survivors of a father and son who had drowned in the defendant's swimming pool. State statutes required motels either (1) to have a lifeguard on duty, or (2) to post a sign saying that no lifeguard was on duty. The defendant did neither, and so plainly was negligent. But did the defendant's negligence "cause" the drownings? As the victims were the only users of the pool, it must have been obvious to them that there was no lifeguard, so a "no lifeguard" sign would surely not have helped. But if the defendant had complied with the statutes by hiring a lifeguard, the decedents probably would not have drowned. The court ruled that the defendant's negligence (in the form of having no lifeguard) prevented there being anyone to witness the drownings and report how they had occurred, so that the burden of proving that the defendant's statutory violations did not cause the drownings was on the defendant.

If the statute in question had simply required that all pools have a lifeguard, *Haft* would have been a fairly routine case. The court's opinion passed lightly over the difficulties raised by the fact that the defendant could have complied with the statute by posting a sign and repeatedly described the negligence in question as failure to have a lifeguard.

In *Sindell*, the court expressly declined to follow *Haft* on the ground that while plaintiff "alleged that . . . [defendants] produced a defective product with delayed effects and without adequate warnings, the difficulty or impossibility of identification result[ed] primarily from the passage of time rather than from their allegedly negligent acts of failing to provide adequate warnings."

2. ***Required Percentage for Market-Share Liability.*** In a case subsequent to *Sindell* against a single manufacturer of DES, the California Supreme Court held that the manufacturer's 10 percent share of the national market was an insufficient predicate for shifting the burden of proof on the issue of causation from the injured party to the manufacturer. Murphy v. E. R. Squibb & Sons, Inc., 710 P.2d 247 (Cal. 1985). The court did not say what percentage would have been sufficient, although it did note that "a major reason why shifting the burden of proof . . . was warranted in *Summers* was that . . . there was a 50 percent chance that one of the defendants was responsible for the injury."

3. ***Asbestos, Lead-Based Paint, Tobacco, and Breast Implants.*** Attempts to invoke market-share liability usually involve mass-marketed products.

A number of cases have held that market-share liability is inappropriate for asbestos litigation. Some courts have based their decision on the fact that asbestos, unlike DES, is not a fungible product. Marshall v. Celotex Corp., 660 F. Supp. 772 (E.D. Mich. 1987). Matter of New York State Silicone Breast Implant Litigation, 631 N.Y.S.2d 491 (Sup. Ct. 1995), *aff'd without op.*, 650 N.Y.S.2d 558 (App. Div. 1996), reached a similar conclusion in a case involving silicone breast implants.

In Gaulding v. Celotex Corp., 772 S.W.2d 66 (Tex. 1989), the asbestos which allegedly caused the decedent's death was contained in a home-made vanity cabinet. In rejecting the claim based on market-share liability against the five asbestos manufacturers who allegedly "dominated the market," the court wrote:

> It is undisputed that the asbestos board to which Gaulding was exposed was purchased at a salvage yard. There is no way to know whether this product was initially sold in Texas or whether it was placed into the stream of commerce someplace far away.... [T]he practical impossibility of determining where or when the product was marketed makes insurmountable the problem of identifying the defendants' relevant market shares. We conclude that no variation of market share liability could be applied rationally and fairly on the facts of this case....

Similarly, in Santiago v. Sherwin Williams Co., 3 F.3d 546 (1st Cir. 1993), the court held that a plaintiff who was allegedly exposed to lead paint when she was a child could not recover from paint manufacturers under market-share liability because the plaintiff was unable to pinpoint with any degree of precision when the injury-causing paint was applied. *See also* Skipworth v. Lead Indus. Ass'n, Inc., 690 A.2d 169 (Pa. 1997) (rejecting market-share and alternative liability in a suit against entities that manufactured lead paint over a 100-year period); Brenner v. American Cyanamid Co., 699 N.Y.S.2d 848 (App. Div. 1999) (similar).

A small number of non-DES cases have endorsed market-share liability. *See* Ray v. Cutter Labs., 754 F. Supp. 193 (M.D. Fla. 1991) (negligence actions for AIDS infections resulting from contaminated blood products); Smith v. Cutter Biological, Inc., 823 P.2d 717, 728 (Haw. 1991) (blood-factor products). *See generally* Gibson v. American Cyanamid Co., 719 F. Supp. 2d 1031, 1036 n.7 (E.D. Wis. 2010) (collecting cases accepting and rejecting market-share liability).

4. ***Enterprise Liability.*** In refusing to embrace enterprise liability, the Texas Supreme Court said in Gaulding v. Celotex Corp., 772 S.W.2d 66 (Tex. 1989):

> Enterprise liability as embodied in *Hall* has been rejected by virtually all other jurisdictions that have considered this concept.... The prominent reason for declining recovery under this theory is its limited application to cases which involve only a small number of manufacturers in a highly centralized industry....

See also Hurt v. Philadelphia Housing Auth., 806 F. Supp. 515 (E.D. Pa. 1992) (rejecting enterprise liability in a suit against a relatively small number of manufacturers of lead-based paints, because plaintiffs failed to allege the delegation of safety responsibility to a trade association).

Hymowitz v. Eli Lilly and Co.

Court of Appeals of New York
539 N.E.2d 1069 (N.Y. 1989)

WACHTLER, C.J.

Plaintiffs in these appeals allege that they were injured by the drug diethylstilbestrol (DES) ingested by their mothers during pregnancy. They seek relief against defendant DES manufacturers. While not class actions, these cases are representative of nearly 500 similar actions pending in the courts in this State; the rules articulated by the Court here, therefore, must do justice and be administratively feasible in the context of this mass litigation. With this in mind, we now . . . adopt a market share theory, using a national market, for determining liability and apportioning damages in DES cases in which identification of the manufacturer of the drug that injured the plaintiff is impossible. . . . We also hold that the Legislature's revival for one year of actions for injuries caused by DES that were previously barred by the statute of limitations . . . is constitutional under the State and Federal Constitutions.

. . . [E]xtant common law doctrines, unmodified, provide no relief for the DES plaintiff unable to identify the manufacturer of the drug that injured her. . . . Some courts, upon reaching this conclusion, have declined to find any judicial remedy for the DES plaintiffs who cannot identify the particular manufacturer of the DES ingested by their mothers (*see*, Zafft v. Lilly & Co., . . . [676 S.W.2d 241 (Mo. 1984) (en banc)]; Mulcahy v. Lilly & Co., . . . [386 N.W.2d 67 (Iowa 1986) (stating that any change in the law to allow for recovery in non-identification DES cases should come from the legislature)]). Other courts, however, have found that some modification of existing doctrine is appropriate to allow for relief for those injured by DES of unknown manufacture (*e.g.*, Sindell v. Abbott Labs., . . . [607 P.2d 924 (Cal. 1980)]; Collins v. Lilly & Co., . . . [342 N.W.2d 37 (Wis. 1984)]; Martin v. Abbott Labs., . . . [689 P.2d 368 (Wash. 1984)]).

. . . .

Indeed, it would be inconsistent with the reasonable expectations of a modern society to say to these plaintiffs that because of the insidious nature of an injury that long remains dormant, and because so many manufacturers, each behind a curtain, contributed to the devastation, the cost of injury should be borne by the innocent and not the wrongdoers. This is particularly so where the legislature consciously created these expectations by reviving hundreds of DES cases. Consequently, the ever-evolving dictates of justice and fairness, which are the heart of our common-law system, require formation of a remedy for injuries caused by DES. . . .

We stress, however, that the DES situation is a singular case, with manufacturers acting in a parallel manner to produce an identical, generically marketed product, which causes injury many years later, and which has evoked a legislative response reviving previously barred actions. Given this unusual scenario, it is more appropriate that the loss be borne by those that produced the drug for use during pregnancy, rather than by those who were injured by the use, even where the precise manufacturer of the drug cannot be identified in a particular action. We turn then to the question of how to fairly and equitably apportion the loss occasioned by DES, in a case where the exact manufacturer of the drug that caused the injury is unknown.

. . . .

The past decade of DES litigation has produced a number of alternative approaches to resolve this question. Thus, in a sense, we are now in an enviable position; the efforts of other courts have provided examples for contending with this difficult issue, and enough time has passed so that the actual administration and real effects of these solutions now can be observed. With these useful guides in hand, a path may be struck for our own conclusion.

. . . .

A . . . basis for liability, tailored . . . closely to the varying culpableness of individual DES producers, is the market share concept. First judicially articulated by the California Supreme Court in Sindell v. Abbott Labs. (*supra*), variations upon this theme have been adopted by other courts (*see*, Collins v. Lilly & Co., *supra*; Martin v. Abbott Labs., *supra*). In Sindell v. Abbott Labs. (*supra*), the Court synthesized the market share concept by modifying the Summers v. Tice (*supra*) alternative liability rationale in two ways. It first loosened the requirement that all possible wrongdoers be before the court, and instead made a "substantial share" sufficient. The court then held that each defendant who could not prove that it did not actually injure plaintiff would be liable according to that manufacturer's market share. The court's central justification for adopting this approach was its belief that limiting a defendant's liability to its market share will result, over the run of cases, in liability on the part of a defendant roughly equal to the injuries the defendant actually caused. . . .

In the recent case of Brown v. Superior Court (44 Cal. 3d 1049), the California Supreme Court resolved some apparent ambiguity in Sindell v. Abbott Labs., and held that a manufacturer's liability is several only, and, in cases in which all manufacturers in the market are not joined for any reason, liability will still be limited to market share, resulting in a less than 100% recovery for a plaintiff. Finally, it is noteworthy that determining market shares under Sindell v. Abbott Labs. proved difficult and engendered years of litigation. After attempts at using smaller geographical units, it was eventually determined that the national market provided the most feasible and fair solution, and this national market information was compiled. . . .

Four years after Sindell v. Abbott Labs., the Wisconsin Supreme Court followed with Collins v. Lilly & Co. (116 Wis. 2d 166). Deciding the identification issue without the benefit of the extensive California litigation over market shares, the Wisconsin court held that it was prevented from following *Sindell* due to "the practical difficulty of defining and proving market share" (*id.* at 189). Instead of focusing on tying liability closely to the odds of actual causation, as the *Sindell* court attempted, the *Collins* court took a broader perspective, and held that each defendant is liable in proportion to the amount of risk it created that the plaintiff would be injured by

DES. Under the *Collins* structure, the "risk" each defendant is liable for is a question of fact in each case, with market shares being relevant to this determination.... Defendants are allowed, however, to exculpate themselves by showing that their product could not have caused the injury to the particular plaintiff....

The Washington Supreme Court... took yet another approach (*see*, Martin v. Abbott Labs., 102 Wash. 2d 581). The *Martin* court first rejected the *Sindell* market share theory due to the belief (which later proved to be erroneous in Brown v. Superior Court [*supra*]) that California's approach distorted liability by inflating market shares to ensure plaintiffs of full recovery.... The *Martin* court instead adopted what it termed "market share alternative liability," justified, it concluded, because "[e]ach defendant contributed to the *risk* of injury to the public, and consequently, the risk to individual plaintiffs"....

Under the Washington scheme, defendants are first allowed to exculpate themselves by proving by the preponderance of the evidence that they were not the manufacturer of the DES that injured plaintiff. Unexculpated defendants are presumed to have equal market shares, totaling 100%. Each defendant then has the opportunity to rebut this presumption by showing that its actual market share was less than presumed. If any defendants succeed in rebutting this presumption, the liability shares of the remaining defendants who could not prove their actual market share are inflated, so that the plaintiff received a 100% recovery.... The market shares of defendants is a question of fact in each case, and the relevant market can be a particular pharmacy, or county, or state, or even the country, depending upon the circumstances the case presents....

Turning to... New York, we heed both the lessons learned through experience in other jurisdictions and the realities of the mass litigation of DES claims in this State. Balancing these considerations, we are led to the conclusion that a market share theory, based upon a national market, provides the best solution. As California discovered, the reliable determination of any market smaller than the national one likely is not practicable. Moreover, even if it were possible, of the hundreds of cases in the New York courts, without a doubt there are many in which the DES that allegedly caused injury was ingested in another State. Among the thorny issues this could present, perhaps the most daunting is the spectre that the particular case could require the establishment of a separate market share matrix. We feel that this is an unfair, and perhaps impossible burden to routinely place upon the litigants in individual cases.

Nor do we believe that the Wisconsin approach of assessing the "risk" each defendant caused a particular plaintiff, to be litigated anew as a question of fact in each case, is the best solution for this State. Applied on a limited scale this theory may be feasible, and certainly is the most refined approach by allowing a more thorough consideration of how each defendant's actions threatened the plaintiff. We are wary, however, of setting loose, for application in the hundreds of cases pending in this State, a theory which requires the factfinder's individualized and open-ended assessment of the relative liabilities of scores of defendants in every case. Instead, it is our perception that the injustices arising from delayed recoveries and inconsistent results which this theory may produce in this State outweigh arguments calling for its adoption.

Consequently, for essentially practical reasons, we adopt a market share theory using a national market. We are aware that the adoption of a national market will likely result in a disproportion between the liability of individual manufacturers and the actual injuries each manufacturer caused in this State. Thus our market share theory cannot be founded upon the belief that, over the run of cases, liability will approximate causation in this State.... Nor does the use of a national market provide a reasonable link between liability and the risk created by a defendant to a particular plaintiff.... Instead, we choose to apportion liability so as to correspond to the overall culpability of each defendant, measured by the amount of risk of injury each defendant created to the public at large. Use of a national market is a fair method, we believe, of apportioning defendants' liabilities according to their total culpability in marketing DES for use during pregnancy. Under the circumstances, this is an equitable way to provide plaintiffs with the relief they deserve, while also rationally distributing the responsibility for plaintiffs' injuries among defendants.

To be sure, a defendant cannot be held liable if it did not participate in the marketing of DES for pregnancy use; if a DES producer satisfies its burden of proof of showing that it was not a member of the market of DES sold for pregnancy use, disallowing exculpation would be unfair and unjust. Nevertheless, because liability here is based on the overall risk produced, and not causation in a single case, there should be no exculpation of a defendant who, although a member of the market producing DES for pregnancy use, appears not to have caused a particular plaintiff's injury. It is merely a windfall for a producer to escape liability solely because it manufactured a more identifiable pill, or sold only to certain drugstores. These fortuities in no way diminish the culpability of a defendant for marketing the product, which is the basis of liability here.

Finally, we hold that the liability of DES producers is several only, and should not be inflated when all participants in the market are not before the court in a particular case. We understand that, as a practical matter, this will prevent some plaintiffs from recovering 100% of their damages. However, we eschewed exculpation to prevent the fortuitous avoidance of liability, and thus, equitably, we decline to unleash the same forces to increase a defendant's liability beyond its fair share of responsibility.

....

The constitutionality of the revival statute remains to be considered (*see*, L. 1986, ch. 682, § 4). This section revives, for the period of one year, actions for damages caused by the latent effects of DES, tungsten-carbide, asbestos, chlordane, and polyvinylchloride. Defendants argue that the revival of barred DES claims was unconstitutional as a denial of both due process and equal protection, under the State and Federal Constitutions (*see* N.Y. Const. art. 1, §§ 6, 11; U.S. Const., 14th Amend., § 1)....

The Federal Due Process Clause provides very little barrier to a State Legislature's revival of time-barred actions (*see*, Chase Securities Corp. v. Donaldson, 325 U.S. 304). In *Chase*, the United States Supreme Court upheld the revival of a time-barred action, stating that Statutes of Limitation "represent a public policy about the privilege to litigate . . . the history of pleas shows them to be good only by legislative grace and to be subject to a relatively large degree of legislative control". . . . [The court then found that doctrinal limitations imposed by state law did not bar revival of DES claims.]

. . . .

Defendants also argue that the revival statute violates equal protection, because the Legislature designated only five substances for revival, including DES, while instituting a prospective only discovery rule for other substances. Defendants claim that this categorization is without sufficient basis, and that it is the result of a "political compromise." But most, if not all legislation is the product of some compromise, so that this objection surely is no basis for finding the revival statute unconstitutional. Instead, here we must proceed on the presumption that the law is constitutional, and will hold otherwise only if it is established that the distinction drawn has no reasonable basis. . . .

As it pertains to DES, surely the revival statute has a rational basis, and the Legislature acted within its broad range of discretion in enacting the law. The number of DES-caused injuries was relatively well known by the Legislature, which allowed for the ramifications of revival of DES claims, such as the effect on insurance interests, and the other costs, to be reasonably predicted. . . . Furthermore, it was also well known . . . that DES victims were prejudiced under current law. This, we believe, is enough of a basis for the Legislature to revive DES claims now, and wait as to other substances until it is felt that these substances present a problem suitable for resolution. The Legislature does not violate equal protection by providing a rationale piecemeal remedy for what may be a larger problem. . . .

Accordingly, in each case the order of the Appellate Division should be affirmed, with costs, and the certified question answered in the affirmative.

[The opinion of MOLLEN, J., concurring in part and dissenting in part, has been omitted.]

[ALEXANDER, TITONE, and HANCOCK, JJ., concurred with WACHTLER, C.J. MOLLEN, J., concurred and dissented. SIMONS, KAYE, and BELLACOSA, JJ., took no part.]

Notes

1. ***Factors Relevant to Market-Share Liability.*** Comment c to § 15 of the Restatement, Third, of Torts: Products Liability (1998), says with respect to market-share liability:

> In deciding whether to adopt a rule of proportional liability, courts have considered the following factors: (1) the generic nature of the product; (2) the

> long latency period of the injury; (3) the inability of plaintiffs to discover the identity of the defendant even after exhaustive discovery; (4) the clarity of the causal connection between the defective product and the injury suffered by plaintiffs; (5) the absence of medical or environmental factors that could have caused or materially contributed to the injury; and (6) the availability of sufficient "market share" data to support a rational apportionment of liability. . . .

2. ***The Commingled Product Theory of Causation.*** Courts continue to grapple with causation problems related to the mass marketing of products. *See In re Methyl Tertiary Butyl Ether (MTBE) Products Liab. Litig.*, 591 F. Supp. 2d 259 (S.D.N.Y. 2008). In that case, county water suppliers could not prove which manufacturers of gasoline containing MTBE were responsible for the contamination of wells. Finding it significant that the manufacturers commingled their gasoline in pipelines or shipments to New York harbor, the court employed a novel causation theory under which the manufacturers could be liable unless they were able to prove that their MTBE was not at the relevant place at the relevant time. The court said that in a sense, "the commingled product theory is closer to traditional causation than market share liability."

3. ***Collective Justice and Mass Torts.*** In tort law, the prevailing paradigm for accident compensation is a highly individualized process. An injured party is entitled to a "day in court" during which the story of the accident will be told, including the many details of the exact injuries sustained. So, too, the defendant has a right to have the factfinder focus specifically on its conduct. Liability may not be imposed unless there is evidence establishing *this* defendant's responsibility to *this* particular plaintiff, and, even then, the amount of damages will be tailored to the facts of the case. When viewed against that paradigm, cases like *Sindell* and *Hymowitz* are startling departures from the usual rules of the game. However, accident compensation is often less individualized or fact specific than the paradigm might suggest. Such pervasive features of accident law as workers' compensation, class action procedures, and statutory capping of damages all depart, to a greater or lesser extent, from any highly individualized models of litigation or compensation. These examples of what might be loosely termed "collective justice" suggest that sometimes the public interest favors the goal of achieving "rough" justice on a system-wide basis over according particularized treatment to individual cases.

"Mass torts" are events, products, or practices that give rise to large numbers of claims, such as hotel fires, industrial accidents, collapsing buildings, and defective consumer goods. The 1995 bombing of the federal building in Oklahoma City, and the September 11, 2001, attacks on the World Trade Center quickly come to mind.

An emerging body of literature explores the question whether these cases differ qualitatively, as well as quantitatively, from traditional tort litigation, and, if so, how the law should respond to such demands. *See* Linda Mullenix, Mass Tort Litigation: Cases and Materials (2d ed. 2008); Glen O. Robinson & Kenneth S. Abraham, *Collective Justice in Tort Law*, 78 Va. L. Rev. 1481 (1993); Jack B. Weinstein, *Preliminary*

Reflections on Law's Reaction to Disaster, 11 Colum. J. Envtl. L. 1 (1986); Kenneth S. Abraham, *Individual Action and Collective Responsibility: The Dilemma of Mass Tort Reform*, 73 Va. L. Rev. 845 (1987); David Rosenberg, *Class Actions for Mass Torts: Doing Individual Justice by Collective Means*, 62 Ind. L.J. 561 (1987).

Viewed as part of the law's interest in achieving collective justice, cases like *Sindell* and *Hymowitz* are less surprising than they may seem at first glance.

4. ***The September 11th Victim Compensation Fund of 2001.*** In the wake of the September 11, 2001, attacks on the World Trade Center and the Pentagon, and the related air crash in Pennsylvania, Congress established a Victim's Compensation Fund. The legislation allowed victims or their survivors to make a claim for compensation from the Fund, but required claimants to waive their right to sue the airlines. Persons who did not make a compensation claim could sue, but airline liability for all claims was restricted to the amount of the airlines' liability insurance, estimated at $1.5 billion, for each of the four flights. *See* Patrick J. Keating, Kevin R. Sutherland, Gerald V. Cleary III, and Timothy J. Walsh, *Recent Developments in Aviation and Space Law*, 38 Tort Trial & Ins. Prac. L.J. 205 (2003). According to one assessment:

> [T]he September 11th Victim Compensation Fund . . . worked remarkably well. A no fault, administrative remedy provided over $7 billion in assistance to victims and families, without resort to the time-consuming, expensive process inherent in the tort system.

Robert M. Ackerman, *Mitigating Disaster: A Communitarian Response*, 9 Cardozo J. Conflict Resol. 283, 293 (2008).

Interestingly, in establishing the Fund, Congress gave the Special Master largely unfettered discretion as to how to structure the program, but expressly rejected the concept of equal awards (say, $2 million to the family of each victim) and required "different awards based on individual economic circumstances." Kenneth R. Feinberg, What is Life Worth?: The Unprecedented Effort to Compensate the Victims of 9/11 (2005), at 25.

5. ***Problem: Statistical Evidence and the Case of the Blue Bus.*** Consider the following hypothetical from Laurence H. Tribe, *Trial by Mathematics: Precision and Ritual in the Legal Process*, 84 Harv. L. Rev. 1329, 1340–41 (1971):

> Mrs. Smith was driving on a public street and was forced off the road by a negligently driven bus. She is able to testify that the bus was blue, but is unable to describe the bus to any greater extent. Blue Bus Co. owns and operates 80% of the blue buses operating in the town. Mrs. Smith files a negligence action against Blue Bus Co. alleging the foregoing. Does she recover?

See the analysis in Stephen A. Spitz, *From Res Ipsa Loquitur to Diethylstilbestrol: The Unidentified Tortfeasor in California*, 65 Ind. L.J. 591, 629–36 (1990).

6. ***Comparative Law Perspective: Falling Objects in China.*** Modern Chinese cities have "forests" of buildings rising thirty or more stories, and millions of persons

live in the sky. Who should bear the loss when a person is harmed by a falling object, and what kind of rules minimize the likelihood of such accidents? These are important issues in China.

In Wen v. Owner, Mr. Hao was chatting with his neighbor outside a residential building in which twenty-two families lived. An ashtray suddenly fell from the building and fractured Hao's skull. Hao became mentally disabled and lost his ability to speak. Unable to find who threw the ashtray, Hao sued the twenty-two families in the building. Except for two families that proved that they were not in the building at the time of the accident, the remaining twenty families failed to prove that they did not cause the ashtray to fall. The court held that the twenty families were responsible in equal shares for Hao's injuries.

Would the result be the same in the United States? Is this a case where *res ipsa loquitur*, alternative liability, enterprise liability, or market share liability applies? Is it fair to shift the burden of proof to the defendant families or to impose strict liability?

Today, Article 87 of the Chinese Tort Liability (Lawinfochina 2018) provides:

> Where any object thrown out of a building or falling down from a building causes any harm to another person and it is hard to determine the specific tortfeasor, all the users of the building who possibly commit[ted] the tort[,] except those who can prove that they are not the tortfeasor[,] shall make indemnity.

7. ***Ethics in Law Practice: Expenses of Suit and Frivolous Litigation.*** The lawyer for a plaintiff harmed by a product manufactured by an unknown producer faces practical and ethical barriers, as well as doctrinal obstacles, to suing every manufacturer in an effort to shift the burden of proof on causation. To begin with, lawsuits are expensive. Typically, the more parties there are, the greater the expenses. In personal-injury litigation, such essential disbursements as medical examination fees, filing costs, expert witness fees, and deposition transcripts are often advanced by the plaintiff's attorney on a contingent basis. This arrangement is ethically permissible in most states (*see* Model Rules of Professional Conduct Rule 1.8(e)(1) (Westlaw 2022)), and it is usually a matter of necessity, for few victims have the cash that it takes to litigate a claim.[4]

If the suit is unsuccessful, the amounts contingently advanced by the attorney are never recovered, and if the legal work was on a contingent fee basis, the attorney is paid nothing for time spent on the suit. In routine cases, expenses can easily amount

4. A case in point is Helen Palsgraf, the unsuccessful plaintiff in the most famous tort case of all time, Palsgraf v. Long Island R.R. Co., 162 N.E. 99 (N.Y. 1928). Palsgraf was a Brooklyn janitor. Her annual salary was $416. At the time of trial, an outstanding bill for $70 in medical care was three years past due. Not counting attorneys' fees and expert witness fees, the cost of litigating her case through three courts was at least $350. "It is improbable to the point of implausibility" that Helen Palsgraf had cash on hand to finance her case. John T. Noonan, Persons and Masks of the Law 125, 144 (1976).

to a thousand dollars or more. In mass tort litigation, out-of-pocket expenses can run into the hundreds of thousands or millions of dollars, and the resulting temptation for the attorney to litigate the case in a way which ensures the recovery of those advances may create serious conflicts of interest between client and attorney. *See* Vincent R. Johnson, *Ethical Limitations on Creative Financing of Mass Tort Class Actions*, 54 Brook. L. Rev. 539 (1988) (discussing the novel and ethically impermissible arrangement used to fund the Agent Orange litigation, then the largest mass tort claim in history).

D. Liability Based on Concerted Action

Herman v. Wesgate

Supreme Court of New York, Appellate Division
464 N.Y.S.2d 315 (App. Div. 1983)

MEMORANDUM:

Plaintiff was injured while a guest at a stag party to celebrate the impending marriage of defendant Thomas Hauck. The party was held on board a barge owned by defendants Donald Wesgate and Thomas Rouse. Following a three-hour cruise, the barge was anchored near the shoreline of Irondequoit Bay. The depth of the water off the bow of the barge was approximately two feet. Several guests began "skinny dipping" and, within a brief period of time, some in the party began to throw others still clothed off the bow into the water. Two or more individuals escorted plaintiff to the bow of the barge where, unwillingly, he went overboard. Trauma to his head or neck resulted in injury to his spinal cord.

. . . .

It was improper to grant the motions [for summary judgment, etc.] of defendants John Hauck and James Hauck. Plaintiff's complaint alleges concerted action by all of the defendants.

"Concerted action liability rests upon the principle that '[a]ll those who, in pursuance of a common plan or design to commit a tortious act, actively take part in it, or further it by cooperation or request, or who lend aid or encouragement to the wrongdoer, or ratify and adopt his acts done for their benefit, are equally liable with him' (Prosser, Torts [4th ed.], § 46, at p. 292; *see also*, Restatement, Torts 2d, § 876). An injured plaintiff may pursue any one joint tort-feasor on a concerted action theory.... Such tort-feasor may, in turn, seek contribution from others who acted in concert with him...." ....

Here, the conduct of the defendants alleged to be dangerous and tortious is the pushing or throwing of guests, against their will, from the barge into the water. Liability of an individual defendant will not depend upon whether he actually propelled plaintiff into the water; participation in the concerted activity is equivalent to participation in the accident resulting in the injury....

Whether codefendants acted in concert is generally a question for the jury.... The complaint states a cause of action against each of the defendants and the record presents questions of fact as to whether defendants John Hauck and James Hauck acted in concert with the other defendants. Thus summary judgment should not have been granted....

Order unanimously modified and as modified affirmed with costs.

Kubert v. Best

Superior Court of New Jersey, Appellate Division
75 A.3d 1214 (N.J. Super. App. Div. 2013)

ASHRAFI, J.A.D.

Plaintiffs Linda and David Kubert were grievously injured by an eighteen-year-old driver who was texting while driving and crossed the center-line of the road. Their claims for compensation from the young driver have been settled and are no longer part of this lawsuit. Plaintiffs appeal the trial court's dismissal of their claims against the driver's seventeen-year-old friend who was texting the driver much of the day and sent a text message to him immediately before the accident.

New Jersey prohibits texting while driving. A statute under our motor vehicle laws makes it illegal to use a cell phone that is not "hands-free" while driving, except in certain specifically-described emergency situations.... An offender is subject to a fine of $100....

The issue before us is not directly addressed by these statutes.... We must determine as a matter of civil common law whether one who is texting from a location remote from the driver of a motor vehicle can be liable to persons injured because the driver was distracted by the text....

The Kuberts' claims against defendant Shannon Colonna, the teenage sender of the texts, were never heard by a jury. Since this appeal comes to us from summary judgment in favor of Colonna, we view all the evidence and reasonable inferences that can be drawn from the evidence favorably to plaintiffs, the Kuberts....

.... Best and Colonna were seeing each other socially but not exclusively; they were not boyfriend and girlfriend. Nevertheless, they texted each other many times each day. Best's cell phone record showed that he and Colonna texted each other sixty-two times on the day of the accident....

.... In her deposition, Colonna acknowledged that it was her habit also to text more than 100 times per day. She said: "I'm a young teenager. That's what we do." She also testified that she generally did not pay attention to whether the recipient of her texts was driving a car at the time or not....

The accident occurred about four or five minutes after Best began driving home from the YMCA....

.... It appears ... that Best collided with the Kuberts' motorcycle immediately after sending a text at 5:48:58. It can be inferred that he sent that text in response to Colonna's text to him that he received twenty-five seconds earlier....

Missing from the evidence is the content of the text messages....

... [Colonna] moved for summary judgment. Her attorney argued to the trial court that Colonna had no liability for the accident because she was not present at the scene, had no legal duty to avoid sending a text to Best when he was driving, and further, that she did not know he was driving. The trial judge ... conducted independent research on the law, and ultimately concluded that Colonna did not have a legal duty to avoid sending a text message to Best, even if she knew he was driving. The judge dismissed plaintiffs' claims against Colonna.

... [P]laintiffs argue that a duty of care should be imposed upon Colonna because she aided and abetted Best's violation of the law when he used his cell phone while driving.... Under section 876 of the Restatement, an individual is liable if he or she knows that another person's "conduct constitutes a breach of duty and gives substantial assistance or encouragement to the other."

To illustrate this concept, the Restatement provides the following hypothetical example:

> A and B participate in a riot in which B, although throwing no rocks himself, encourages A to throw rocks. One of the rocks strikes C, a bystander. B is subject to liability to C.

.... The example illustrates that one does not actually have to be the person who threw a rock to be liable for injury caused by the rock....

In this case, plaintiffs assert that Colonna and Best were acting in concert in exchanging text messages. Although Colonna was at a remote location from the site of the accident, plaintiffs say she was "electronically present" in Best's pick-up truck immediately before the accident and she aided and abetted his unlawful use of his cell phone.

In Champion ex rel. Ezzo v. Dunfee, ... [939 A.2d 825 (N.J. Super. Ct. App. Div. 2008)], we analyzed Restatement § 876 in a context where the defendant was actually present at the site of the accident. In *Champion*, the injured plaintiff was a backseat passenger in a car driven by a friend who had been drinking. The driver's girlfriend was also a passenger in the car, sitting in the front seat. The car approached speeds of 100 miles per hour as the driver tried to prove the performance capabilities of his car. The car hit a bump and crashed, severely injuring the backseat passenger.... He sued the driver, and subsequently, added the driver's girlfriend as a defendant in his lawsuit on a theory that she had a duty to prevent her boyfriend from driving because she knew he had been drinking....

.... We reviewed common law precedents from other jurisdictions where passengers in a car had encouraged the driver to consume alcohol or drugs or otherwise to drive dangerously, and we compared those precedents to others where the passengers were present but neither encouraged nor prevented the negligent conduct of the driver.... We concluded in *Champion* that the law permits recovery against a passenger under two conditions. One is a "special relationship" that gave the passenger control over the driver's conduct, such as an employer-employee or parent-child relationship.... The second is "that the defendant passenger actively encouraged the driver to commit" the negligent act.... Mere failure to prevent wrongful conduct by another is ordinarily not sufficient to impose liability.... In *Champion*, the girlfriend could not be held liable merely for failing to prevent her boyfriend's negligent driving....

In this case, Colonna did not have a special relationship with Best by which she could control his conduct. Nor is there evidence that she actively encouraged him to text her while he was driving. Colonna sent two texts to Best in the afternoon of September 21, 2009, one about two hours and the second about twenty-five seconds before the accident.... Even if a reasonable inference can be drawn that she sent messages requiring responses, the act of sending such messages, by itself, is not active encouragement that the recipient read the text and respond immediately, that is, while driving and in violation of the law.

Another case decided by this court, Podias v. Mairs, ... [926 A.2d 859 (N.J. Super. Ct. App. Div. 2007)], also provides some guidance.... In *Podias*, we reviewed claims against two passengers who were present when an eighteen-year-old driver who had been drinking struck and injured a motorcyclist at 2:00 a.m. on the Garden State Parkway.... Rather than calling for medical aid for the unconscious motorcyclist, the passengers discussed how to prevent detection of their own involvement in the incident. They had cell phones, but they did not call the police, and they also told the driver not to call the police and not to get them involved.... The driver and passengers all fled the scene of the accident. The motorcyclist was killed by another driver who did not see him lying injured in the roadway....

We reviewed Restatement § 876 and held that the passengers could be found liable for giving "substantial assistance" to the driver in failing to fulfill his legal duty to remain at the scene of the accident and to notify the police.... We found "an aiding and abetting theory" to be viable because the passengers had taken "affirmative steps in the immediate aftermath [of the accident] to conceal their involvement" and to encourage the driver's violation of the law....

Unlike the facts of *Podias*, the evidence in this case is not sufficient for a jury to conclude that Colonna took affirmative steps and gave substantial assistance to Best in violating the law. Plaintiffs produced no evidence tending to show that Colonna urged Best to read and respond to her text while he was driving.

The evidence available to plaintiffs is not sufficient to prove Colonna's liability to the Kuberts on the basis of aiding and abetting Best's negligent driving while using a cell phone.

.... Plaintiffs argue alternatively that Colonna independently had a duty not to send texts to a person who she knew was driving a vehicle....

[After a discussion of relevant precedent, the court wrote:] It is foreseeable that a driver who is actually distracted by a text message might cause an accident and serious injuries or death, but it is not generally foreseeable that every recipient of a text message who is driving will neglect his obligation to obey the law and will be distracted by the text. Like a call to voicemail or an answering machine, the sending of a text message by itself does not demand that the recipient take any action. The sender should be able to assume that the recipient will read a text message only when it is safe and legal to do so, that is, when not operating a vehicle....

... [W]e do not hold that someone who texts to a person driving is liable for that person's negligent actions; the driver bears responsibility for obeying the law and maintaining safe control of the vehicle. We hold that, when a texter knows or has special reason to know that the intended recipient is driving and is likely to read the text message while driving, the texter has ... [an independent] duty to users of the public roads to refrain from sending the driver a text at that time.

.... No testimony established that ... [Colonna] was aware Best would violate the law and read her text as he was driving, or that he would respond immediately. The evidence of multiple texting at other times when Best was not driving did not prove that Colonna breached the limited duty we have described.

....

Affirmed.

[The concurring opinion of Espinosa, J., is omitted.]

Lussier v. Bessette

Supreme Court of Vermont
16 A.3d 580 (Vt. 2010)

REIBER, C.J.

....

... [D]efendants Rene Lussier, Anthony Bessette, and Adam Reed were hunting with their friend Collin Viens, who is not a party to this lawsuit. During the hunt, Mr. Viens accidentally shot and killed Rejean Lussier, who was seated in the cab of a tractor in one of his fields. Mr. Viens was convicted of involuntary manslaughter....

On the day of the shooting, the hunting party was engaged in a practice known as "pushing" or "driving," in which several hunters (called "pushers") walk through an area in a line to force game toward one or more "sitters." On the occasion in question, defendants were the pushers, and Mr. Viens was the sitter....

Apparently, while waiting in the field, Mr. Viens had shouldered his rifle, released the safety, and with his finger on the trigger, scanned his surroundings through the scope of the rifle. It is unclear whether Mr. Viens shot at the tractor in an intentional act of vandalism, or if the shot was an unfortunately timed misfire of his weapon. What is clear, is that Mr. Viens saw the tractor through his scope immediately prior to his rifle discharging, killing Mr. Lussier. At the time of the shooting, Mr. Viens was standing approximately 240 yards from Mr. Lussier and had a clear view of the tractor. Mr. Viens's handling of his rifle in the manner described violated several basic rules of hunting. Although Mr. Viens had no hunting license at the time of the shooting, it does not appear that defendants were aware of this fact.... Defendants knew that Mr. Viens was a relatively novice hunter; however, they also knew he had hunted on prior occasions.

.... The trial court ... concluded in order to be liable under a concerted action theory, defendants needed to have some knowledge that they were encouraging specific, tortious conduct.

Although there is little precedent, the trial court's analysis seems to track the Restatement (Second) of Torts, and those few cases which have addressed the issue of concerted action liability. As adopted by this Court, the Restatement sets out three alternative tests:

> A person is subject to liability for harm resulting to a third person from the tortious conduct of another if the person: (1) commits a tortious act as part of a common design with the other; (2) gives substantial assistance to the other knowing that the other's conduct is a breach of duty; or (3) gives substantial assistance to the other to accomplish a tortious result while also acting in a manner that is a breach of duty to the third person.

.... In determining whether a tortious act has been done as part of a common design with another tortfeasor under the first prong of the Restatement, it appears that at least some level of knowledge or awareness of the pertinent attendant circumstances is required. In Kuhn v. Bader, 89 Ohio App. 203, 101 N.E.2d 322, 329–30 (1951), the defendants were taking turns shooting an extremely high-powered rifle at a pile of gravel. One of the shots ricocheted and struck the plaintiff in the head while he was unloading hay on a nearby farm, causing him serious injury. The court took judicial notice "that bullets fired into gravel have a tendency to ricochet" and held that "shooting of this rifle upon plaintiff's premises, *under the circumstances and surroundings shown by the evidence,* constituted a tortious act on the part of both defendants for which they are jointly and severally liable." .... The defendants were engaged in identical tortious conduct and all knew the attendant circumstances—that an inadequate gravel backstop was being used with a high-powered gun—yet all chose to engage in and encourage conduct, which under the circumstances, created a foreseeable risk of harm....

The Restatement itself offers several illustrations which demonstrate at least a minimal knowledge requirement must be met before liability can be imposed on a common design theory. One illustration involves two drivers, A and B, drag racing on a public highway. Restatement (Second) of Torts § 876 cmt. a illus. 2. During the race, A collides with a third vehicle. *Id.* According to the Restatement, B would be liable under a concerted action theory in this instance. *Id.* B's actions are concerted with A's because B knows his own actions are dangerous, he knows A's actions are dangerous, and he knows that by continuing the race he is actively encouraging A to race.... But if A had told B the road was closed for their drag race, their actions could not be concerted and B would not be liable, because the harm would not have been foreseeable under the conditions known to B....

Here though, defendants did not have the requisite knowledge of the circumstances attending Mr. Viens's conduct such that their actions should be considered part of a common design. Neither party disputes that Mr. Viens was at least ten minutes ahead of the defendants. Although some in the party were familiar with the general area, defendants had no direct knowledge of Mr. Viens's location, his surroundings, or the location of the tractor at the time of the shooting because no one had walked the area that day. Mr. Viens had never been admonished for reckless hunting practices, none of the defendants knew he had no hunting license, and all knew he had passed his hunters' safety course. At the time of the shooting, defendants did not know that Mr. Viens had disengaged the safety and pointed his gun at a tractor, with his finger on the trigger, or even that Mr. Viens was aiming in an unsafe direction. Defendants thus lacked the requisite knowledge to have been engaged in a common design with Mr. Viens at the time of the shooting.

The second prong of the Restatement imposes concerted action liability when a party "knows that [another tortfeasor's] conduct constitutes a breach of duty *and* gives substantial assistance or encouragement to the other" tortfeasor. Restatement (Second) of Torts § 876(b) (emphasis added). As discussed above, defendants had no knowledge, nor any reason to suspect, that Mr. Viens was engaging in flagrant hunting violations in breach of his duty to Mr. Lussier. Because defendants did not know that Mr. Viens was engaged in conduct constituting a breach of his duty to Mr. Lussier, they cannot be found guilty of concerted action liability under this prong.

The final prong of Restatement § 876 imposes concerted action liability where a party "gives substantial assistance to the [tortfeasor] in accomplishing a tortious result *and* his own conduct, separately considered, constitutes a breach of duty to the third person." Restatement (Second) of Torts § 876(c) (emphasis added).... There was nothing in defendants' hunting plan—walking through the woods to flush a deer—that would have Mr. Viens's hunting violations as its natural and probable result. Neither were defendants' actions a breach of some separate duty owed to Mr. Lussier. It is not the duty of those in a hunting party to supervise other members.... Because defendants breached no separate duty to Mr. Lussier and because their actions did not proximately cause his death, they are not liable under this final prong.

Whatever the outcome of the above analyses, the Restatement cautions: "although a person who encourages another to commit a tortious act may be responsible for other acts by the other, ordinarily he is not liable for other acts that, although done in connection with the intended tortious act, were not foreseeable by him." Restatement (Second) of Torts § 876 cmt. d....

.... The defendants may have created the risk that someone would be shot when Mr. Viens attempted to shoot a deer in accordance with the group's hunting plan, but, Mr. Viens was not acting pursuant to the plan when he looked through his scope at the tractor in boredom or poor judgment....

Affirmed.

Notes

1. ***Aiding-and-Abetting.*** Some form of liability for concerted action is imposed in all jurisdictions. The two prominent categories of concerted action liability are (1) aiding-and-abetting (concerted action based on substantial assistance) and (2) civil conspiracy (concerted action by agreement). A single course of conduct may constitute both aiding-and-abetting and civil conspiracy, but the theories are distinguishable.

An example of aiding-and-abetting is Price v. Halstead, 355 S.E.2d 380 (W. Va. 1987) (holding that an allegation that passengers directly participated and encouraged a driver to continue to drink and smoke marijuana when he was already visibly intoxicated stated a cause of action).

A "person who bribes an agent of a principal has 'aided and abetted' the agent in the breach of the agent's fiduciary duty of loyalty to the principal." *See* Franklin Med. Assoc. v. Newark Pub. Schools, 828 A.2d 966, 975–76 (N.J. Super. Ct. App. Div. 2003). (Breach of fiduciary duty is a tort; see Chapter 11.)

See also Montgomery v. Devoid, 915 A.2d 270 (Vt. 2006) (finding that there was a question of fact as to whether a father should be liable for funds and other things stolen by his son because there was evidence that the father had stored vehicles purchased with the stolen money and had removed several of the most valuable stolen items from his son's apartment, at his son's request, shortly before the police executed a search warrant); Hellums v. Raber, 853 N.E.2d 143 (Ind. App. 2006) (finding, in a case involving a hunting accident in which Hellums was shot, that a genuine issue of material fact existed "as to whether the conduct of Alan was negligent and whether rapidly firing four rounds from his shotgun in the direction of Hellums's party prompted or substantially encouraged Ernest to discharge his weapon in the same direction").

2. ***Civil Conspiracy.*** An example of civil conspiracy is Charles v. Florida Foreclosure Placement Center, LLC, 988 So. 2d 1157 (Fla. App. 2008). The court found that a homeowner had adequately alleged that a foreclosure assistance company, title company, and mortgage broker and its principal had conspired to defraud her out of the equity in her home.

Civil conspiracy requires intent to accomplish an unlawful purpose or to accomplish a lawful purpose by unlawful means. Merely proving that there was joint intent to engage in conduct that resulted in injury is not sufficient to establish a cause of action. In Juhl v. Airington, 936 S.W.2d 640 (Tex. 1996), the court held that allegations by a police officer that he had suffered injuries while he was attempting to physically remove anti-abortion demonstrators who had blocked access to a health clinic were insufficient to state a claim for civil conspiracy against other demonstrators because the officer's pleadings alleged only that the other demonstrators had been negligent.

See also Brown v. Birman Managed Care, Inc., 42 S.W.3d 62 (Tenn. 2001) (holding that if a former husband's employers conspired with him to intentionally reduce his income so that he could avoid paying the full amount of child support, they could be liable to his former wife for fraud, even though the fraudulent representations on which the former wife relied were made only by the former husband); Pedroza v. Lomas Auto Mall, Inc., 600 F. Supp. 2d 1162 (D. N.M. 2009) (finding that, in light of a cover-up, there was sufficient evidence to support a claim that an insurer was part of a civil conspiracy with the auctioneer and a purchaser of a vehicle).

3. ***Conscious Parallel Activity.*** Bichler v. Eli Lilly & Co., 436 N.E.2d 182 (N.Y. 1982), was an action by a DES daughter against a single manufacturer of the drug based on a concerted-action theory. The suit alleged that even if the defendant did not produce the dosages of the drug consumed by the plaintiff's mother, it was liable for the plaintiff's injuries because it had acted in concert with the manufacturer who did. In seeking government approval to market DES, all manufacturers had relied upon the same negligently performed studies and had requested permission to make the same strength tablet. The jury was instructed based on a theory of concerted action which substituted proof of conscious parallel activity by the manufacturers for the usual common-law requirement of an actual agreement between actors to act tortiously. Because the defendant did not object to the instruction, the modified-concerted-action theory became the law of the case, and liability was imposed.

In Hymowitz v. Eli Lilly & Co., 539 N.E.2d 1069, 1076 (N.Y. 1989) (*supra* p. 431), the court repudiated the conscious-parallel-activity theory of concerted action liability, writing:

> Parallel behavior . . . is a common occurrence in industry generally. We believe, therefore, that inferring agreement from the fact of parallel activity alone improperly expands the concept of concerted action beyond a rational or fair limit; among other things, it potentially renders small manufacturers, in the case of DES and in countless other industries, jointly liable for all damages stemming from the defective products of an entire industry. . . .

4. ***Concerted Action and the First Amendment.*** May civil liability be imposed merely because an individual belonged to or supported a group, some members of which committed tortious acts? Probably not.

In Chavers v. Gatke Corp., 132 Cal. Rptr. 2d 198 (Ct. App. 2003), a former automobile and truck mechanic and his spouse sought to hold a manufacturer of friction brake products liable on concerted-action theories based on allegations that the manufacturer participated in a conspiracy with other manufacturers to conceal a study that reported the harmful effects of products containing asbestos. The court rejected the plaintiffs' arguments, writing:

> "[t]o impose liability without a finding that the [defendant] authorized—either actually or apparently—or ratified unlawful conduct would impermissibly burden the rights of political association that are protected by the First Amendment." .... It is necessary ... to show that "'the group itself possessed unlawful goals and that the individual held a specific intent to further those illegal aims.'"....
>
> We are skeptical that the record here satisfies such an exacting constitutional standard, requiring as it would evidence that Gatke, a minor player contributing about $250 a year to the Saranac Laboratory research investigations, possessed the specific intent to promote the sale of asbestos products made by its competitors. The testimony that was produced at trial tended to show that Gatke sought access to the Saranac Laboratory report in order to assist its defense of workers compensation claims filed against it in Massachusetts.... [R]equiring a manufacturer "to stand trial for civil conspiracy and concert of action predicated solely on its exercise of its First Amendment freedoms could generally chill the exercise of the freedom of association by those who wish to contribute to, attend the meetings of, and otherwise associate with trade groups and other organizations that engage in public advocacy and debate."

In Boim v. Quranic Literacy Institute, 291 F.3d 1000 (7th Cir. 2002), the decedent was killed by members of a militant Palestinian organization while waiting at a bus stop in Israel's West Bank. His parents sued two U.S.-based non-profit organizations for tort damages. The court held that the First Amendment right of free association did not prohibit imposition of civil liability against organizations under a federal statute providing a civil cause of action for those injured by an act of international terrorism for directing funds to terrorist groups for the purpose of funding terrorist activities. However, an aiding-and-abetting claim, the court said, would require proof that the organizations knew about the terrorist group's illegal operations and provided aid to the terrorist group with the intent to facilitate those illegal activities.

5. ***Joint Enterprise Doctrine.*** One form of concerted action is the "joint enterprise" (sometimes called "joint venture"), a form of liability which rests on agency principles:

> A "joint enterprise" is in the nature of a partnership, but is a broader and more inclusive term. In a partnership, there is a more or less permanent business arrangement, creating a mutual agency between the partners for the purpose of carrying on some general business dealings, so that the acts of one are to be charged against the others. A joint enterprise includes a partnership, but it also includes less formal arrangements for cooperation, for a more limited period of time and a more limited purpose. It includes an undertaking to carry out a small number of activities or objectives, or even a single one, entered into by members of the group under such circumstances that all have a voice in directing the conduct of the enterprise. The law then considers that each is the agent or servant of the others, and that

> the act of any one within the scope of the enterprise is to be charged vicariously against the rest. While it is by no means impossible that the principle may be applied to other activities, the very great majority of the decisions applying it have involved the use of motor vehicles.

Buteas v. Raritan Lodge No. 61 F. & A.M., 591 A.2d 623 (N.J. Super. Ct. App. Div. 1991) (quoting Restatement, Second, of Torts § 491).

It is often said that there are four elements to proving a joint enterprise: (1) an agreement among the members of a group; (2) to carry out a common purpose; (3) under circumstances where the members share a community of pecuniary interest; and (4) have an equal right to a voice in the direction and control of the enterprise.

See Texas Dep't of Transp. v. Able, 35 S.W.3d 608 (Tex. 2000) (governmental entity held liable under joint enterprise doctrine for negligence in the operation and maintenance of a public transportation system).

Some cases reject the Restatement's suggestion that the community of interest necessary for a joint enterprise must be of a business or pecuniary nature. *See* Pittman v. Frazer, 129 F.3d 983 (8th Cir. 1997) (a finding of contributory negligence based on joint enterprise by a couple was upheld where a car belonging to a woman's parents was driven by her lover directly into the path of a train while the couple was returning from a secluded area on private property).

Other cases strictly apply the "community of pecuniary interest" requirement, which makes it difficult to establish a joint enterprise. For example, in St. Joseph Hosp. v. Wolff, 94 S.W.3d 513 (Tex. 2002), the court held that a common business or pecuniary interest is not sufficient to establish a joint enterprise. Rather, to establish a "community of pecuniary interest" there must be a monetary interest common among the members of the group that is "shared without special or distinguishing characteristics." The court ruled that a joint enterprise did not exist between a teaching hospital that sponsored a medical residency program and a foundation that employed and was training a surgical resident when he negligently treated a patient. The evidence showed that the parties did not share any income from the residency program's operations at the hospital, as the foundation billed for the residents' services and kept all the revenue.

However, in Am. Fam. Mut. Ins. Co. v. AN/CF Acq. Corp., 361 P.3d 1098, 1102–03 (Colo. App. 2015), the court held that there was a joint venture between a car dealer and a prospective car purchaser that made the dealer liable to damages caused during a test drive, even though the dealer and purchaser had differing financial interests. As the court explained:

> ... Go Courtesy Ford and Hart shared a common purpose in conducting the test drive itself.... [T]he purpose of the test drive was to determine whether a particular car would be the subject of a transaction, and both Go Courtesy Ford and Hart had "an interest in the [car's] satisfactory performance throughout the test." .... Indeed, the Go Courtesy Ford salesman

who accompanied Hart on the test drive testified in his deposition that he and Hart had already negotiated and agreed on a price.

... [In addition,] Go Courtesy Ford had a right to control the operation of the car because it owned the car and its salesman accompanied Hart as a passenger....

6. ***Ethics in Law Practice: Assisting Unlawful Conduct.*** "A lawyer shall not counsel a client to engage, or assist a client, in conduct that the lawyer knows is criminal or fraudulent...." Model Rules of Prof. Conduct Rule 1.2(d) (Westlaw 2022). Such conduct may give rise to civil liability, as well as discipline. *See* Morganroth & Morganroth v. Norris, McLaughlin & Marcus, 331 F.3d 406 (3d Cir. 2003) ("when a complaint alleges that an attorney has knowingly and intentionally participated in a client's unlawful conduct to hinder, delay, and/or fraudulently obstruct the enforcement of a judgment of a court, the plaintiff has stated a claim ... for creditor fraud against the attorney").

E. Incitement

As Herman v. Wesgate, 464 N.Y.S.2d 315 (App. Div. 1983), *supra* at p. 439, pointed out, citing Prosser, those who "lend aid or encouragement to the wrongdoer," are liable for the harm the wrongdoer does. As applied to someone who urges the defendant to punch the plaintiff in the mouth, this notion is not at all troublesome. Nevertheless, liability for "incitement" is a concept that, if not carefully limited, may clash with principles of free speech and free press. Suppose, for example, that a newspaper denounces "greedy slumlords," giving examples of wealthy tenement owners whose tenants live in wretched conditions, and an irate reader beats a landlord senseless. One doubts that the newspaper would, or should, be liable. It is well known that dramatic crimes often lead to the commission of similar, "copycat" crimes, yet it has never been thought that those who report the original crimes are liable to the victims of the later ones.

Relevant Variables. In thinking about whether a person who has said something, orally or in writing, should be held liable for harm caused to another because of that statement, it is useful to focus on three variables. First, the defendant's level of culpability. Presumably, a mere lack of care (negligence) will be less likely than conscious indifference to a known risk of harm (recklessness), or knowing advocacy of a harmful result (intentionally tortious conduct) to give rise to liability. Second, it is important to consider whether the defendant's statement is protected under the First Amendment. If so, it may be difficult or impossible to impose liability. Indeed, in Brandenburg v. Ohio, 395 U.S. 444 (1969), the Supreme Court held that the First Amendment right to freedom of speech includes the right to advocate lawlessness, at least in the abstract. Finally, foreseeability plays a role. Liability ordinarily will not be imposed for harm that is unforeseeable, or for harm which, although foreseeable, is too attenuated in time or space for it to be fair to hold the defendant responsible.

Culpability. A leading case imposing liability for incitement is Weirum v. RKO General, Inc., 539 P.2d 36 (Cal. 1975), holding the owner of a radio station liable for the death of a motorist who was killed when a car driven by a teenager forced her off the road. The teenager was trying to win a $25 cash prize by being the first to locate one of the station's disc jockeys, "The Real Don Steele," who was driving from place to place in the Los Angeles area. The station broadcast information about Steele's location and destination and urged its listeners to try to find him. Holding that the record justified the jury in finding that the station's contest created a foreseeably "grave danger" to those on the roads, as bored teenagers would likely drive unsafely in an attempt to win the prize, the court upheld a verdict finding the station negligent. The defendant argued that this holding would make anyone who advertised limited quantities of desirable items liable for the negligence of others, as when a sports fan is injured while rushing to purchase a ticket to the big game. In response, the court observed:

> The giveaway contest was no commonplace invitation to an attraction available on a limited basis. It was a competitive scramble in which the thrill of the chase to be the one and only victor was intensified by the live broadcast which accompanied the pursuit.

Weirum is in many respects a high watermark in the law of incitement. The defendant was held liable for mere negligence based on oral statements that caused an unknown driver to act in a way that caused harm to an unknown person in a manner that was only loosely foreseeable.

Braun v. Soldier of Fortune Magazine, 968 F.2d 1110 (11th Cir. 1992), and Rice v. Paladin Enterprises, Inc., 128 F.3d 233 (4th Cir. 1997), involved more egregious facts, and it is easier to see why liability was imposed. In *Braun*, the defendant published an advertisement offering services as a "gun-for-hire," with "all jobs considered." The court held that the survivors of the victim who was murdered by the person who placed the ad stated a valid claim against the magazine.

In *Rice*, suit was brought by the survivors of three people murdered by a hit man hired by the father of one of the victims, who wanted his son killed so that he would get the money the son had received in a personal-injury settlement. The hit man had learned his trade by reading "Hit Man," a book published by the defendant, which gave very detailed instructions on how to murder people in a variety of ways and which glorified the career of being a professional killer (one's first murder, according to the book, would "verify your manhood"). In a stipulation of facts which the court termed "extraordinary," the defendant acknowledged that it had intended, in publishing the book, "to provide assistance to murderers and would-be murderers which would be used by them 'upon receipt,' and that it in fact assisted Perry [the man who had killed the victims] in particular in the commission of the murders."

Freedom of Speech. The *Weirum* court, *supra*, failed to see any constitutional obstacle to the imposition of liability in the case involving the contest to find the disc jockey. The court wrote simply:

> Defendant's contention that the giveaway contest must be afforded the deference due society's interest in the First Amendment is clearly without merit. The issue here is civil accountability for the foreseeable results of a broadcast which created an undue risk of harm to decedent. The First Amendment does not sanction the infliction of physical injury merely because achieved by word, rather than act.

Other courts have been more troubled about First Amendment concerns.

For example, in Herceg v. Hustler Magazine, Inc., 814 F.2d 1017 (5th Cir. 1987), the defendant published an article, called *Orgasm of Death*, describing the practice of autoerotic asphyxia and warning that the reader should not attempt the practice (which was said to be described for "educational reasons"). The parents of a fourteen-year-old, who read the article, tried the technique, and died, failed to state a cause of action against the magazine.

> If the shield of the first amendment can be eliminated by proving after publication that an article discussing a dangerous idea negligently helped bring about a real injury simply because the idea can be identified as "bad," all free speech becomes threatened. An article discussing the nature and danger of "crack" usage—or of hang gliding—might lead to liability just as easily.... Mere negligence ... cannot form the basis of liability under the incitement doctrine....

The court held that for liability to arise, the plaintiffs had to establish that the publication went beyond mere advocacy and amounted to incitement, and that the incitement was directed toward producing imminent action. The court found that under no fair reading could the article be seen as advocacy, let alone incitement, for it repeatedly warned the reader against engaging in the practice it described.

The *Rice* court, in holding that the claim had been stated against the publisher of "Hit Man," also implicitly recognized that the constitution imposes a high barrier to recovery. It cited cases holding that the First Amendment does not protect speech that is criminal aiding and abetting, "at least where, as here, the defendant has the specific purpose of assisting and encouraging commission of such conduct and the alleged assistance and encouragement takes a form other than abstract advocacy."

Because the facts of *Rice* were so extreme, it is hard to know how willing the court might have been to impose liability for aiding and abetting on less outrageous facts. For example, one can find publications, aimed at paintball enthusiasts, giving detailed instructions on how to make a silencer for a paintball gun. Such a silencer can be used as easily on a real gun as on a paintball gun, as those who publish this information know. If someone considering murder obtains these instructions, follows them, and uses a silenced gun to commit a murder, would the First Amendment protect the publisher?

In many cases, the First Amendment has been found to bar recovery against persons who made statements that led to harmful results. *See* Sanders v. Acclaim

Entertainment, Inc., 188 F. Supp. 2d 1264 (D. Col. 2002) (violent movie and video games that allegedly led to the shooting at Columbine high school were not directed to inciting or producing imminent lawless action and thus were protected by the First Amendment); Walt Disney Prods., Inc. v. Shannon, 276 S.E.2d 580 (Ga. 1981) (holding that the First Amendment barred an action against the creators of a children's television program for injuries sustained when a child sought to reproduce a sound effect demonstrated on the program by rotating a BB inside an inflated balloon).

Unforeseeability of the Injurer, the Conduct, or the Victim. Courts generally have been unwilling to impose liability on an aiding and abetting theory against sellers of goods or media defendants in cases involving harm to unknown persons. For example:

- James v. Meow Media, Inc., 300 F.3d 683 (6th Cir. 2002). Companies that produced or maintained video games, movies, and Internet websites which allegedly desensitized a student to violence, causing him to shoot and kill three classmates, did not owe a duty of care to the classmates under a theory that their games, movies, and Internet sites gave the student "psychological tools" to commit such murders. Even if the ideas and images conveyed by such products could be deemed to be tools for the student's criminal acts, the companies did not know that the student existed and were not aware of his particular idiosyncrasies that made their products particularly dangerous in his hands.
- Waller v. Osbourne, 763 F. Supp. 1144 (M.D. Ga. 1991), *aff'd without op.* 958 F.2d 1084 (11th Cir. 1992). The creators of a song which allegedly contained subliminal messages did not engage in culpable incitement to commit suicide. There was no evidence that the music was directed toward any particular person or group, or likely to cause imminent acts of suicide, and therefore the First Amendment barred claims for negligence, nuisance, fraud, and invasion of privacy.
- Winter v. G.P. Putnam's Sons, 938 F.2d 1033 (9th Cir. 1991). The publisher of a mushroom encyclopedia was not liable to plaintiffs who relied on the book's erroneous advice while gathering wild mushrooms and became critically ill, requiring liver transplants.
- Sakon v. PepsiCo Inc., 553 So. 2d 163 (Fla. 1989). A soft-drink manufacturer breached no duty by broadcasting a commercial portraying youths engaged in a sporting activity which could be dangerous if not done by skilled persons under proper conditions. The accident, which occurred when a 14-year-old boy attempted the same stunt (lake jumping on a bicycle) and broke his neck, was not a foreseeable consequence of the advertising.

However, where the publication of material has posed a risk of harm specifically to the plaintiff, a number of courts have imposed liability. For example:

- S & W Seafoods v. Jacor Broadcasting, 390 S.E.2d 228 (Ga. Ct. App. 1989). A restaurant manager stated a claim for intentional infliction of mental distress against a radio station on which a talk show host urged listeners to confront the manager with rude gestures and spit on him.

- Hyde v. City of Columbia, 637 S.W.2d 251 (Mo. Ct. App. 1982). A newspaper could be held liable for negligent publication of a crime victim's name and address while her abductor was still at large. *But see* Orozco v. Dallas Morning News, Inc., 975 S.W.2d 392 (Tex. App. 1998) (newspaper had no duty to refrain from publishing the street name and block number of a criminal suspect's address and thus could not be held liable on a negligence theory for the retaliatory shooting of the suspect's family members on the day of the publication of the article; the likelihood of injury was outweighed by the social utility of crime reporting).
- Times Mirror Co. v. Superior Court (Doe), 244 Cal. Rptr. 556 (Ct. App. 1988). The defendant published the name of the witness to a murder, with the almost-inevitable result.

Statutory Civil Remedies for Incitement. Some statutes create a civil cause of action for damages resulting from incitement of injurious conduct.

California Government Code § 6218 (Westlaw 2022)

§ 6218. Prohibition on soliciting, selling, trading, or posting on Internet private information of those involved with reproductive health services; remedies for violation; exceptions

(a)(1) No person, business, or association shall knowingly publicly post or publicly display on the Internet the home address, home telephone number, or image of any provider, employee, volunteer, or patient of a reproductive health services facility or other individuals residing at the same home address with the intent to do either of the following:

(A) Incite a third person to cause imminent great bodily harm to the person identified in the posting or display, or to a coresident of that person, where the third person is likely to commit this harm.

(B) Threaten the person identified in the posting or display, or a coresident of that person, in a manner that places the person identified or the coresident in objectively reasonable fear for his or her personal safety.

(2) A provider, employee, volunteer, or patient of a reproductive health services facility whose home address, home telephone number, or image is made public as a result of a violation of paragraph (1) may do either or both of the following:

(A) Bring an action seeking injunctive or declarative relief in any court of competent jurisdiction. If a jury or court finds that a violation has occurred, it may grant injunctive or declarative relief and shall award the successful plaintiff court costs and reasonable attorney's fees.

(B) Bring an action for money damages in any court of competent jurisdiction. In addition to any other legal rights or remedies, if a jury or court finds that a violation has occurred, it shall award damages to that individual in an amount up to a maximum of three times the actual damages, but in no case less than four thousand dollars ($4,000).

. . . .

(c)(1) No person, business, or association shall solicit, sell, or trade on the Internet the home address, home telephone number, or image of a provider, employee, volunteer, or patient of a reproductive health services facility with the intent to do either of the following:

(A) Incite a third person to cause imminent great bodily harm to the person identified in the posting or display, or to a coresident of that person, where the third person is likely to commit this harm.

(B) Threaten the person identified in the posting or display, or a coresident of that person, in a manner that places the person identified or the coresident in objectively reasonable fear for his or her personal safety.

(2) A provider, employee, volunteer, or patient of a reproductive health services facility whose home address, home telephone number, or image is solicited, sold, or traded in violation of paragraph (1) may bring an action in any court of competent jurisdiction. In addition to any other legal rights and remedies, if a jury or court finds that a violation has occurred, it shall award damages to that individual in an amount up to a maximum of three times the actual damages, but in no case less than four thousand dollars ($4,000).

Chapter 8

Proximate Causation

A. Introduction

A Question of Policy. Even if the defendant's conduct was unreasonable and was a factual cause of the plaintiff's harm, it may be undesirable to impose liability. Consider, for example, a case in which the defendant has negligently injured the plaintiff, inflicting minor harm. While taking a bus to the doctor's office for treatment of those injuries, the plaintiff then suffers additional injuries in a collision between the bus and a truck. Although the defendant's negligence was a factual cause of the injuries the plaintiff sustained in the bus accident — "but for" the defendant's negligence, the plaintiff would not have been on the bus and so would not have been hurt when the bus hit the truck — it is inconceivable that the defendant would be held liable for those injuries. Holding the defendant liable for all harm that results, in a "but for" sense, from negligence or other wrongdoing could lead to liability wildly disproportionate to fault. Moreover, intervening events may make it unjust to hold the defendant, as opposed to someone else, responsible for subsequent consequences. In the posited case, any court would say that the defendant's negligence was not the "proximate cause" of the injuries sustained on the bus.

The use of the term "proximate cause" to draw judicial lines beyond which liability will not extend can be seen as an instrument of fairness and policy. Some scholars have suggested that the process has nothing at all to do with "cause." On the other hand, the cases in which proximate cause is lacking are always cases in which the defendant is relieved of liability because of something about the way in which the defendant's conduct caused the injury. The language of causation therefore is suitable for use in discussing this matter.

Terminology. Some authorities have used the term "proximate cause" to denote the overall two-step inquiry into both factual connection and the fairness of imposing liability. *See, e.g.*, Williams v. Steves Indus., Inc., 699 S.W.2d 570 (Tex. 1985). Others, in an attempt to distinguish the policy determination of whether liability should attach from the "factual causation" inquiry into whether there is an actual cause and effect relationship, have avoided the use of the term "proximate causation" altogether. For example, the Restatement, Second, of Torts speaks simply in terms of whether "there is . . . [a] rule of law relieving the actor from liability." (§ 431.) The Third Restatement rejects the term "proximate cause" as "an especially poor one to describe the idea to which it is connected." Restatement, Third, of Torts: Liab. for Physical & Emotional Harm Ch. 6 spec. note (2010). In place of "proximate cause," the new Restatement speaks of rules concerning the "scope of liability" for tortious conduct. Some cases also eschew the use of the term "proximate cause." Nevertheless, this chapter—which is concerned with the fairness of assessing liability, rather than merely with factual connection—is entitled "proximate causation." That choice is a concession to reality. Most lawyers in practice, not to mention judicial decisions, use the term "proximate cause" to refer to the rules and concepts discussed in this chapter.

"Proximate" Not "Proximity." Proximate causation frequently has little to do with "proximity" in the ordinary sense of the word. Only in the rarest of instances has the law sought to define the scope of liability based solely on physical distance. The classic example of such an approach is the "New York Fire Rule." Originally, the rule held that one who negligently starts a fire is liable for the destruction of the first building it reaches, not the second or any other. Ryan v. New York Cent. R.R. Co., 35 N.Y. 210 (1866). Mindful of the fact that the first building may be on the defendant's own land, the rule was later modified to allow recovery by the first other landowner to whose property the fire spread. *See* Webb v. Rome, W. & O. R. Co., 49 N.Y. 420 (1872); Homac Corp. v. Sun Oil Co., 180 N.E. 172 (N.Y. 1932). Other jurisdictions have rejected the rule, which is not surprising because propinquity is only one of the many considerations which may bear on the question of whether it makes sense to limit liability.

"Sole Proximate Cause." There can be more than one proximate cause of harm. However, defense attorneys often argue that something other than their clients' conduct was the "sole proximate cause" of the plaintiff's loss and that therefore their clients should not be held liable. There is nothing wrong with this strategy for avoiding liability, except when it leads a court or jury to believe erroneously that as a matter of law (rather than a matter of fact) there can be only one proximate cause of harm. In most states, "[t]here is no requirement that a . . . proximate cause . . . be the sole cause, the last act, or the one nearest to the injury." McClenahan v. Cooley, 806 S.W.2d 767, 775 (Tenn. 1991). However, the concept of "sole proximate cause" sometimes appears in statutes. *See* First Assembly of God v. Texas Utilities Elec. Co., 52 S.W.3d 482, 489 (Tex. App. 2001) (indicating that, under a state statutory tariff, a utility was not liable for a church fire unless the utility's negligence was the "sole proximate cause" of the harm).

The Restatement says the term "sole proximate cause" is confusing and should be avoided. *See* Restatement, Third, of Torts: Liab. for Physical and Emotional Harm § 34 cmt. f (2010). Some courts are reluctant to accept a "sole proximate cause" argument. *See, e.g.*, Soto v. New York City Transit Auth., 846 N.E.2d 1211 (N.Y. 2006) (refusing to hold that a teenager's reckless conduct in entering a catwalk abutting a subway track after consuming alcohol was the sole proximate cause of injuries sustained when he was struck by a subway train).

Different Ways of Talking About Fairness. There are different ways of talking about the fairness of imposing liability—and thus different ways of phrasing the proximate causation inquiry. Some say that it is fair to hold a defendant liable for harm that directly results from tortious conduct, and unfair to impose liability for harm that is indirect, attenuated, remote, or the product of intervening forces. This perspective on proximate causation is discussed in Part B, which deals with "direct causation." Others say that foreseeability, not directness, is the key consideration in proximate causation inquiries, and that it is fair to hold a tortfeasor liable for harm that was foreseeable, but unfair to hold a defendant liable for unforeseeable consequences. The foreseeability view of proximate causation is discussed in Part C. Some say that the relevant question is whether the injurious result falls within the scope of the risks that made the defendant's conduct tortious. If so, it is fair to impose liability; but if not, liability should not be imposed. In some cases, determining whether a result was within the scope of the risks created by the defendant's conduct requires an assessment of whether the negligence had "run its course," or whether things were "back to normal," at the time the injury occurred. The "result within the risk" view of proximate causation is discussed in Part D. Finally, some say that it is fair to impose liability for results that are "normal" or "ordinary" rather than "bizarre" or "extraordinary." These views are discussed in Part E, which deals with the proximate causation subtopic of "intervening" and "superseding" causes.

None of these four ways of talking about proximate causation — directness, foreseeability, risk, or normality — is inevitably preferable to the others. Each makes sense in certain contexts. On a given set of facts, it may be wise (and indeed necessary under State precedent) to employ one of these rubrics, but on other occasions it may be preferable (and possible) to discuss in different terms whether the defendant should be held liable. Fortunately, the law on proximate causation is so richly complex that it allows advocates leeway in selecting the language with which to argue the question as to whether it is fair to hold a defendant liable for harm to a plaintiff.

Andrews' Dissent. It is important to remember that the dissenter in Palsgraf v. Long Island Railroad Co, 162 N.E. 99 (N.Y. 1928) (*supra* p. 260), may have been right that all of the considerations mentioned above must be taken into account in determining whether conduct is a proximate cause of harm. Judge William S. Andrews wrote:

> The court must ask itself whether there was a natural and continuous sequence between cause and effect. Was the one a substantial factor in producing the other? Was there a direct connection between them, without too many intervening causes? Is the effect of cause on result not too attenuated? Is the cause likely, in the usual judgment of mankind, to produce the result? Or, by the exercise of prudent foresight, could the result be foreseen? Is the result too remote from the cause, and here we consider remoteness in time and space.... Clearly ... the greater the distance either in time or space, the more surely do other causes intervene to affect the result.... We draw an uncertain and wavering line, but draw it we must as best we can.

162 N.E. at 104.

B. Direct Causation

Under the "direct causation" approach to proximate causation, liability is assessed whenever there is a direct connection between the negligence of the defendant and the injury to the plaintiff. Thus, unless the thread of causation between the negligent act and the resulting harm is broken by the intervention of some new cause, liability attaches, no matter how bizarre or unexpected the harm might seem to the negligent actor. The famous *Polemis* decision, studied by generations of torts students, subscribed to this view. *See In Re Arbitration Between Polemis and Furness, Withy & Co., Ltd.*, 3 K.B. 560 (Court of Appeal 1921).

In *Polemis*, a ship hand negligently knocked a plank into the hold of a ship which was carrying benzine and petrol in cases. It might have been expected that the falling of the plank would have dented the ship or crushed part of its contents, or have struck a person walking below, causing damage within a relatively limited sphere. Instead, the plank unexpectedly struck a spark, which in turn ignited petroleum vapor that had collected in the hold, and the resulting fire completely destroyed the vessel. Although the arbitrators found that "the spark could not reasonably have been anticipated from the falling of the board," Bankes, L.J., wrote that "given the damage as a direct result of . . . [the] negligence, the anticipations of the person whose negligent act has produced the damage appear . . . to be irrelevant." More pointedly, Scrutton, L.J., said:

> To determine whether an act is negligent, it is relevant to determine whether any reasonable person would foresee that the act would cause damage; if he would not, the act is not negligent. But if the act would or might probably cause damage, the fact that the damage it in fact causes is not the exact kind of damage one would expect is immaterial, so long as the damage is in fact directly traceable to the negligent act, and not due to the operation of independent causes having no connection with the negligent act, except that they could not avoid its result. Once the act is negligent, the fact that its exact operation was not foreseen is immaterial.

Liability was imposed for the loss of the ship.

The direct-causation approach has influenced American jurisprudence, particularly in cases concerning liability for harm caused by intentional conduct. Intentional tortfeasors are often held liable for unforeseeable harm. *See* Restatement, Third, of Torts: Liab. for Physical and Emotional Harm § 33(a) (2010) ("even if it was unlikely to occur").

Natural and Continuous Sequence. Indeed, even in cases not involving intentional torts, courts often state the test for proximate causation in terms that sound very much like a direct-causation inquiry. For example, in Cleveland v. Rotman, 297 F.3d 569, 573 (7th Cir. 2002), the court wrote:

> A proximate cause is one that produces an injury through a natural and continuous sequence of events unbroken by any effective intervening cause.

The Remoteness Doctrine. In recent years, a remoteness doctrine has begun to take shape in American tort law. The doctrine's ultimate contours and importance have yet to be determined, but it seems to be closely linked to concerns about whether, in a particular case, an injury is a sufficiently direct result of tortious conduct to warrant the imposition of liability.

One example of the remoteness doctrine is Owens Corning v. R.J. Reynolds Tobacco Co., 868 So. 2d 331 (Miss. 2004). In that case, Owens Corning, a producer of asbestos materials, which had settled tort claims with individuals, sued tobacco companies seeking reimbursement for its losses on a variety of grounds. The trial court entered summary judgment in favor of the tobacco companies based on the "remoteness doctrine." In affirming the judgment, the Supreme Court of Mississippi wrote:

> Owens Corning argues that Tobacco Defendants knowingly and intentionally engaged in fraudulent and tortious conduct designed to defraud the public . . . about the health risks of smoking and the true cause of lung disease. Owens Corning contends that a primary intended consequence of Tobacco Defendants' conduct was to cause Owens Corning to pay billions of dollars to litigate and resolve lawsuits by persons with lung injuries, caused at least in part, by smoking. Further, Owens Corning argues that by effectively shifting liability for smoking related disease to it, Tobacco Defendants have been unjustly enriched at Owens Corning's expense.
>
> . . . .
>
> Nine federal courts of appeals and several state appellate courts have weighed this issue and have rejected claims similar to Owens Corning's. The plaintiffs in these cases have included insurance companies, public hospitals, unions, health benefit funds, and other health care providers who sued tobacco companies to recover money expended to provide medical treatment to their plan participants for tobacco-related illnesses. In all of these cases, regardless of the theory of liability, the courts have determined that injuries to these provider plaintiffs were either too remote to be compensable or were not proximately caused by the defendant's conduct. . . .
>
> . . . . Despite Owens Corning's characterization that its claims are direct, we conclude that the claims hinge on the payment of damage awards to thousands of smoking asbestos claimants and are thus indirect.

Passage of Time and the "Test of Temporal Duration." An injury may be "remote" in time or space. At some point so much time has passed, and so many developments have occurred, that it becomes unfair to impose liability. In Cleveland v. Rotman, 297 F.3d 569, 574 (7th Cir. 2002), a widow argued that bad tax advice had caused her husband to commit suicide. Rejecting the negligence claim, the court wrote:

> Even assuming that Rotman's allegedly erroneous advice precipitated the audit, Cleveland was aware of the impending audit for almost a year before taking his life. Given the significant time lapse between the allegedly triggering event and Cleveland's suicide, as well as Cleveland's history of

> depression which had its origins in events that preceded his relationship with Rotman—including the loss of his legal practice, his disbarment, the confiscation of his assets and income, and his mounting debt—Cleveland's suicide did not follow Rotman's advice through a natural and continuous sequence of events unbroken by any effective intervening cause.

A similar situation was presented in Williams v. State, 969 N.E.2d 197 (N.Y. 2012), where a woman was injured by a man who had escaped from a state psychiatric center two years earlier. The center had allegedly been negligent in allowing the man to escape and in classifying the matter in a way that it did not need to be reported to the police. In holding that the state was entitled to dismissal of the claim against it, the court explained:

> The causal connection ... is simply too attenuated and speculative to support liability.... Proximate cause analysis incorporates a "test of temporal duration," which asks if "the occurrence of the injury [was] tied to the claimed negligent act or omission within a reasonable lapse of time".... Here, the lapse of time was not reasonable....

In Allways Auto Group, Ltd. v. Walters, 530 S.W.3d 147 (Tex. 2017), a motorist who was injured in a collision with an intoxicated oncoming driver brought an action for negligent entrustment against the automobile dealership that had lent the oncoming driver a pickup truck while oncoming driver's own vehicle was being repaired. In reversing a judgment for the plaintiff, the Texas Supreme Court wrote:

> If Heyden were visibly intoxicated when he got the loaner, Allways could reasonably have anticipated he might have a wreck before he sobered up. But Allways could not have foreseen that Heyden would get drunk eighteen days later (after repairs were delayed and he lost his job) and drive his vehicle into Walters' vehicle.
>
> .... Even if Heyden were visibly intoxicated when he obtained the loaner, driving into Walters eighteen days later was not a natural and probable result of that intoxication.

Id. at 148–49.

C. Foreseeability

Many lawyers regard "proximate causation" as synonymous with "foreseeability." This overstates the importance of foreseeability, but offers an indication of how significant this factor is in proximate causation analysis.

("Wagon Mound No. 1") Overseas Tankship (U.K.) Ltd. v. Morts Dock & Engineering Co., Ltd.

Privy Council
[1961] A.C. 388

[The freighter Wagon Mound, owned by the defendants, carelessly discharged a large quantity of furnace oil into Sydney Harbor. The oil was carried by wind and tide to plaintiffs' wharf (Morts Dock), about 600 feet away, where workmen were using welding equipment. Some cotton waste or a rag on a piece of floating debris beneath the wharf was set on fire by falling molten metal. The oil then caught fire, and the conflagration seriously damaged the wharf. The trial judge specifically found that the defendant's employees did not know, and could not have been expected to know, that the furnace oil was capable of being set on fire when spread on water. A judgment was rendered for the plaintiffs on the ground that the damage to the wharf was the direct result of the negligent escape of the oil. The Supreme Court of New South Wales affirmed. The case was appealed to the Privy Council.]

The judgment of their Lordships was delivered by VISCOUNT SIMONDS. . . .

. . . . The trial judge held that apart from damage by fire the [plaintiffs] had suffered some damage from the spillage of oil in that it had got upon their slipways and congealed upon them and interfered with their use of the slips. He said:

> The evidence of this damage is slight and no claim for compensation is made in respect of it. Nevertheless it does establish some damage, which may be insignificant in comparison with the magnitude of the damage by fire, but which nevertheless is damage which, beyond question, was a direct result of the escape of the oil.

It is upon this footing that their Lordships will consider the question whether the [defendants] are liable for the fire damage. . . .

. . . [T]he authority of *Polemis* has been severely shaken though lip-service has from time to time been paid to it. In their Lordships' opinion it should no longer be regarded as good law. It is not probable that many cases will for that reason have a different result, though it is hoped that the law will be thereby simplified, and that in some cases at least palpable injustice will be avoided. For it does not seem consonant with current ideas of justice or morality that for an act of negligence, however slight or venial, which results in some trivial foreseeable damage the actor should be liable for all consequences however unforeseeable and however grave, so long as they can be said to be "direct." It is a principle of civil liability, subject only to qualifications which have no present relevance, that a man must be considered to be responsible for the probable consequences of his act. To demand more of him is too harsh a rule, to demand less is to ignore that civilized order requires the observance of a minimum standard of behavior.

. . . [I]f it is asked why a man should be responsible for the natural or necessary or probable consequences of his act . . . the answer is that . . . he ought to have foreseen them. Thus it is that ... in different judgments in the same case and sometimes in a single judgment liability for a consequence has been imposed on the ground that it was reasonably foreseeable or alternatively on the ground that it was natural or necessary or probable. The two grounds have been treated as coterminous, and so they largely are. But, where they are not, the question arises to which the wrong answer was given in *Polemis*. For, if some limitation must be imposed upon the consequences for which the negligent actor is to be held responsible — and all are agreed that some limitation there must be — why should that test (reasonable foreseeability) be rejected which, since he is judged by what the reasonable man ought to foresee, corresponds with the common conscience of mankind, and a test (the "direct" consequence) be substituted which leads to nowhere but the never ending and insoluble problems of causation....

... [T]here can be no liability until the damage has been done. It is not the act but the consequences on which tortious liability is founded. Just as ... there is no such thing as negligence in the air, so there is no such thing as liability in the air. Suppose an action brought by A for damage caused by the carelessness (a neutral word) of B, for example a fire caused by the careless spillage of oil.... It is vain to isolate the liability from its content and to say that B is or is not liable and then to ask for what damage he is liable. For his liability is in respect of that damage and no other. If, as admittedly it is, B's liability (culpability) depends on the reasonable foreseeability of the consequent damage, how is that to be determined except by the foreseeability of the damage which in fact happened — the damage in suit?....

.... Their Lordships have already observed that to hold B liable for consequences however unforeseeable of a careless act, if, but only if, he is at the same time liable for some other damage however trivial, appears to be neither logical nor just. This becomes more clear if it is supposed that similar unforeseeable damage is suffered by A and C but other foreseeable damage, for which B is liable, by A only. A system of law which would hold B liable to A but not to C for the similar damage suffered by each of them could not easily be defended. Fortunately, the attempt is not necessary. For the same fallacy is at the root of the proposition. It is irrelevant to the question whether B is liable for unforeseeable damage that he is liable for foreseeable damage, as irrelevant as would the fact that he had trespassed on Whiteacre be to the question whether he had trespassed on Blackacre. Again suppose a claim by A for damage by fire by the careless act of B. Of what relevance is it to that claim that he has another claim arising out of the same careless act? It would surely not prejudice his claim if that other claim failed: it cannot assist it if it succeeds. Each of them rests on its own bottom and will fall if it can be established that the damage could not reasonably be foreseen.

.... As Denning, L.J. said in King v. Phillips, [1953] 1 Q.B. 429 at p. 441, "there can be no doubt since Bourhill v. Young that the test of *liability for shock* is foreseeability of *injury by shock*." Their Lordships substitute the word "fire" for "shock" and endorse this statement of the law.

....

Their Lordships humbly advise Her Majesty that this appeal should be allowed, and the [plaintiffs'] action so far as it related to damage caused by the negligence of the [defendants] be dismissed with costs.... [A nuisance claim was remitted.]

Notes

1. ***Foreseeability of What?*** Although foreseeability is a major consideration in determining whether the defendant's lapse is the proximate cause of the plaintiff's injury, the concept cannot be used mechanically. Indeed, were the plaintiff required to prove that one standing in the position of the defendant would reasonably have foreseen in precise detail the sequence of events and the extent of harm to be sustained, liability would be denied in a great many cases in which the defendant's conduct is blameworthy. The specific contours of any accident—whether the plaintiff landed on his head, or twisted her right ankle, for instance—are almost always unforeseeable in some sense.

What the law requires is not that the defendant could have foreseen, precisely, everything that happened, but simply that the plaintiff fall, at least generally, within the class of persons endangered by the defendant's conduct (*see* Palsgraf v. Long Island R.R. Co., 162 N.E. 99 (N.Y. 1928), *supra* at p. 260) and that the broad outlines of the harm be foreseeable, though not the specific details or the manner of the occurrence (*see* Merhi v. Becker, 325 A.2d 270 (Conn. 1973), *infra* at p. 471). Foresight of a remote possibility of harm may be sufficient not only to trigger a duty of care (*see* Gulf Refining Co. v. Williams, 185 So. 234 (Miss. 1938), *supra* at p. 269), but also to establish proximate causation, if the gravity of the threatened harm is great and the cost of adequate precautions is minimal (*see Wagon Mound No. 2*, 1 A.C. 617 (1967), *infra* at p. 466). The full extent of the resulting harm need not be foreseen if the damage that ensues, though other and greater than expected, is of the same general sort which is anticipated and demands precautions (*see Kinsman No. 1*, 338 F.2d 708 (2d Cir. 1964), *infra* at p. 473).

2. ***Proximate Causation as a Jury Question.*** The issue of proximate causation is normally for the jury. Thus, in Marshall v. Nugent, 222 F.2d 604 (1st Cir. 1955), the court wrote:

> When an issue of proximate cause arises in a borderline case, as not infrequently happens, we leave it to the jury with appropriate instructions. We do this because it is deemed wise to obtain the judgment of the jury, reflecting as it does the earthy viewpoint of the common man—the prevalent sense of the community—as to whether the causal relation between the negligent act and the plaintiff's harm which in fact was a consequence of the tortious act is sufficiently close to make it just and expedient to hold the defendant answerable in damages....

3. ***Proximate Causation as a Question of Law.*** A court will decide the issue of proximate causation as a matter of law if reasonable minds cannot differ. Thus, in Shideler v. Habiger, 243 P.2d 211, 215 (Kan. 1952), the court wrote:

> [I]t may be said as a matter of law that the allegations of the petition that the driver of an automobile who violates the traffic laws and collides with another vehicle which veers into an electric light pole and breaks it off so that it falls with the wires it carries, and the stress of those wires causes another pole to break off below the ground and an employee of the light company [the alleged rescuer] climbs the latter pole and is injured by its fall, discloses a series of facts which would occur so infrequently that the injury to the person of the climber of the pole may not be said to be the natural and probable result of the negligence of the driver.

Because proximate cause is a very difficult concept, hard to explain to a jury in a brief charge, the doctrine's practical importance may lie more in the courts' ability to override a verdict on proximate-cause grounds than in its effect on the outcomes of jury deliberations.

("Wagon Mound No. 2") Overseas Tankship (U.K.) Ltd. v. Miller Steamship Co.

Privy Council 1966
[1967] 1 A.C. 617

[The fire which consumed Morts Dock in Wagon Mound No. 1 also destroyed two ships moored at the dock. The owners of those vessels commenced this action, based on nuisance and negligence, against the owners of the Wagon Mound. The trial court, Walsh, J., found as follows:

> (1) Reasonable people in the position of the officers of the Wagon Mound would regard the furnace oil as very difficult to ignite upon water. (2) Their personal experience would probably have been that this had very rarely happened. (3) If they had given attention to the risk of fire from the spillage, they would have regarded it as a possibility, but one which could become an actuality only in very exceptional circumstances. (4) They would have considered the chances of the required exceptional circumstances happening whilst the oil remained spread on the harbor waters as being remote. (5) I find that the occurrence of damage to the plaintiff's property as a result of the spillage not reasonably foreseeable by those for whose acts the defendant would be responsible. (6) I find that the spillage of oil was brought about by the careless conduct of persons for whose acts the defendant would be responsible.... (8) Having regard to those findings, and because of finding (5), I hold that the claim of each of the plaintiffs, framed in negligence, fails.

A judgment for the defendants was affirmed by the Supreme Court of New South Wales. The plaintiffs appealed to the Privy Council.]

The judgment of the Board was delivered by LORD REID.

....

It is ... necessary to turn to the respondents' submission that the trial judge was wrong in holding that damage from fire was not reasonably foreseeable. In *The*

Wagon Mound (No. 1), the finding upon which the Board proceeded was that of the trial judge: "The defendant did not know and could not reasonably be expected to have known that [the oil] was capable of being set afire when spread on water." In the present case the evidence led was substantially different from the evidence led in *The Wagon Mound (No. 1)* and the findings of Walsh, J. are significantly different. This is not due to there having been any failure by the plaintiff in *The Wagon Mound (No. 1)* in preparing and presenting their case. The plaintiffs there were no doubt embarrassed by a difficulty which does not affect the present plaintiffs. The outbreak of the fire was consequent on the act of the manager of the plaintiffs in *The Wagon Mound (No. 1)* in resuming oxy-acetylene welding and cutting while the wharf was surrounded by this oil. So if the plaintiffs in the former case had set out to prove that it was foreseeable by the engineers of the Wagon Mound that this oil could be set alight, they might have had difficulty in parrying the reply that this also must have been foreseeable by their manager. There would have been contributory negligence and at that time contributory negligence was a complete defense in New South Wales.

. . . .

In *The Wagon Mound (No. 1)* the Board were not concerned with degrees of foreseeability because the finding was that the fire was not foreseeable at all. . . . But here the findings show that some risk of fire would have been present to the mind of a reasonable man in the shoes of the ship's chief engineer. . . .

. . . [I]t does not follow that, no matter what the circumstances may be, it is justifiable to neglect a risk of such a small magnitude. A reasonable man would only neglect such a risk if he had some valid reason for doing so, e.g., that it would involve considerable expense to eliminate the risk. He would weigh the risk against the difficulty of eliminating it.

. . . .

In the present case there was no justification whatever for discharging the oil into Sydney Harbor. Not only was it an offence to do so, but it involved considerable loss financially. If the ship's engineer had thought about the matter, there could have been no question of balancing the advantages and disadvantages. From every point of view it was both his duty and his interest to stop the discharge immediately.

It follows that in their Lordships' view the only question is whether a reasonable man having the knowledge and experience to be expected of the chief engineer of the Wagon Mound would have known that there was a real risk of the oil on the water catching fire in some way: if it did, serious damage to ships or other property was not only foreseeable but very likely. . . .

. . . . The findings show that he ought to have known that it is possible to ignite this kind of oil on water, and that the ship's engineer probably ought to have known that this had in fact happened before. The most that can be said to justify inaction is that he would have known that this could only happen in very exceptional circumstances. But this does not mean that a reasonable man would dismiss such a risk from his mind and do nothing when it was so easy to prevent it. If it is clear that the reasonable man would have realized or foreseen and prevented the risk, then it must follow that the appellant is liable in damages. . . .

[The appeal of the ship owners was allowed.]

1. The "Eggshell Skull" Doctrine

With regard to personal injuries, the defendant takes the plaintiff "as is" and need not foresee the full extent of the resulting injuries in order to be held liable. For example, in McCahill v. New York Transp. Co. 94 N.E. 616 (N.Y. 1911), the defendant's taxi negligently struck the plaintiff's intestate. Two days later the man died of delirium tremens, which could not have resulted had he not been an alcoholic. The court held the defendant responsible for the death, finding that the negligent act had directly set into motion the sequence of events which caused the death. The possibility that the intestate might have died later from delirium tremens because he was an alcoholic was not a defense but could be taken into consideration in determining damages.

Simeonidis v. Mashantucket Pequot Gaming Enterprise

Mashantucket Pequot Tribal Court
2013 Mashantucket Trib. LEXIS 8

This case stems from an incident at Foxwoods Resort and Casino . . . , which is operated by the Defendant. . . . The Plaintiff, Joanne Simeonidis, alleges that on July 23, 2010, she sustained an injury to her back due to a loose chair at one of the slot machines, which suddenly shifted and gave way, causing her to twist her torso. At trial, the Defendant conceded liability. . . .

. . . . Prior to the incident at Foxwoods, the Plaintiff was treating for back pain at Orthopedic & Sports Medicine. . . . About two weeks before the incident at Foxwoods, on July 12, 2010, the Plaintiff underwent an MRI. . . . . Three days before the incident, on July 20, 2010, the Plaintiff was seen by Dr. Mark Wilchinsky, who reviewed the Plaintiff's July 12 MRI and noted: "At this point her MRI scan is impressive but her pain has markedly improved, therefore, I have recommended that she continue doing exercises. . . ." . . .

. . . . The primary issue . . . is whether subsequent medical costs related to treatment of the Plaintiff's back should be included in an award of damages.

. . . .

This case illustrates the delicate interplay between causation, the "eggshell plaintiff" rule, and proof of damages. . . . Once liability is established, the Gaming Enterprise must take the Plaintiff as it finds her. . . . This is commonly referred to as the "eggshell plaintiff" rule.

The eggshell plaintiff rule was recently summarized by the Connecticut Appellate Court in Rua v. Kirby, 125 Conn. App. 514, 8 A.3d 1123 (2010).

> The eggshell plaintiff doctrine states that [w]here a tort is committed, and injury may reasonably be anticipated, the wrongdoer is liable for the proximate results of that injury, although the consequences are more serious than they would have been, had the injured person been in perfect health.... The eggshell plaintiff doctrine ... makes the defendant responsible for all damages that the defendant legally caused even if the plaintiff was more susceptible to injury because of a pre-existing condition or injury. Under this doctrine, the eggshell plaintiff still has to prove the nature and probable duration of the injuries sustained.

.... "[G]enerally, a plaintiff with a pre-existing condition who is subsequently injured is entitled to full recovery. A plaintiff who suffers from a pre-existing disability that is made worse by an injury, however, can recover only to the extent of the aggravation of the injury." ....

On October 11, 2010, the Plaintiff returned to Dr. Wilchinsky for a follow up appointment. The Plaintiff reported that ... she was still experiencing pain in her leg and left buttock. Dr. Wilchinsky ordered an orthopedic consult with Dr. Gerald Girasole and explained to the Plaintiff that "the only way to definitively address [her] complaints are by a surgical means....

On October 25, 2010, the Plaintiff consulted with Dr. Girasole, who discussed the possibility of spinal fusion. On February 3, 2011, the Plaintiff underwent the fusion surgery and engaged in post-operative physical therapy....

... [T] he parties submitted the videotaped depositions of two experts. The Plaintiff's expert, Dr. Girasole, is an orthopaedic spine surgeon and performed the Plaintiff's spinal fusion. The Defendant's expert, Dr. Elcon Levinson, is a board certified radiologist, who specializes in interpreting MRI exams. The fundamental difference between the two expert opinions is whether a cyst in the Plaintiff's back existed at the time of the incident at Foxwoods. The Plaintiff's expert opined that the cyst formed subsequently.... The Defendant's expert opined that the cyst was present on the July 12 MRI....

Of particular significance is Dr. Girasole's testimony in response to Plaintiff's counsel's inquiry as to whether the Plaintiff would have had to undergo the spinal fusion had she not been injured at Foxwoods. Dr. Girasole testified that he could not say definitively that the Plaintiff would not have needed the surgery if the incident had not occurred.... Dr. Girasole opined that the injury expedited the need for surgery, but could not state with a reasonable degree of medical certainty that the Plaintiff needed the surgery based on the incident at Foxwoods.

....

The objective facts show that prior to the incident the Plaintiff was told that she had a back problem, but that she had successfully completed her physical therapy regime and that she could simply continue to do exercises at home. After the incident at Foxwoods, the Plaintiff needed to return to physical therapy and receive an epidural injection and a facet joint injection. The evidence shows that the Plaintiff's pre-existing disability was aggravated by the injury at Foxwoods; the Plaintiff is entitled to recover the reasonable value of the physical therapy and injections that directly followed.

The Court must draw the line, however, at inclusion of the costs of the spinal fusion surgery and subsequent care. There has been no evidence presented that shows, based on a reasonable degree of medical certainty, that the need for the spinal fusion was due to the aggravation of the Plaintiff's disability.... The Plaintiff is entitled to actual damages in the amount of the reasonable value of her medical care up to the time of her spinal fusion surgery, but not including the surgery itself or subsequent care.

.... [The court awarded $39,988.85 in damages.]

Notes

1. ***The "Eggshell Skull" Doctrine.*** The "eggshell skull" rule — which refers to a person with an eggshell skull who suffers greater than normal injuries from a blow to the head — is uniformly endorsed. It holds that once a plaintiff suffers any foreseeable physical injury, even a trivial one, the defendant is liable for all physical consequences, even unforeseeable injuries, so long as they do not stem from preexisting or subsequent superseding causes. *See, infra,* pp. 489–508 (discussing superseding causes); *cf.* Juisti v. Hyatt Hotel Corp., 94 F.3d 169, 171 (4th Cir. 1996). In reinstating an action by a hotel guest who suffered a collapsed lung while fleeing a building when a fire alarm went off, the *Juisti* court wrote:

> The question of proximate cause ... is not whether the hotel's negligence in setting off the alarm could reasonably be expected to cause the plaintiff's specific injury, but whether such negligence could reasonably be expected to cause the plaintiff any injury.

2. ***Aggravation of Pre-Existing Conditions.*** As the principal case illustrates, an accident which produces physical injury by precipitating the development of a latent condition or by aggravating a pre-existing condition may be a proximate cause of the injury. The defendant must take the plaintiff "as is." *See* Restatement, Third, of Torts: Liab. for Physical and Emotional Harm § 31 (2010).

Economic Analysis
"Eggshell Skulls" and Proximate Cause

Alan Gunn

At first glance, the doctrine of the *McCahill* case (*see, supra*, p. 468) seems inconsistent with standard proximate-cause doctrine, for the defendant is held liable, under *McCahill,* even for results that could not easily have been foreseen. Yet both doctrines are similar in one respect: They tend to make the amount of damages actually paid by negligent defendants (as a whole) approximately equal to the amount of harm done by those defendants. Without a doctrine like that of *McCahill,* potential injurers would be seriously underdeterred. To illustrate, suppose that the average amount of harm done to the victims of a particular kind of accident is $100,000. This is the average of the harms done to individual victims, which may range from a low of $1.00 (for a handful of very resilient victims) to a high of $1,000,000 (for the rare victim with an "eggshell skull"). Proper deterrence requires that a potential injurer's expected liability be $100,000. If there were no "eggshell skull" doctrine, so that those injurers whose victims suffered $1,000,000 in damages had to pay only the expected damages of $100,000 or so, the average damage payment would be less than the average harm of $100,000. In a sense, holding injurers liable for all of the harm suffered by unusually sensitive victims makes up for the benefits that some injurers get when their victims turn out to be unusually hardy.

Although the eggshell-skull doctrine can lead to liability for harms not easily foreseeable, it seems consistent with a result-within-the-risk analysis. One of the reasons for taking precautions against striking pedestrians with a car is surely that some pedestrians may be unusually fragile. Even a very unlikely result may be "within the risk" created by dangerous behavior.

2. Manner of Occurrence and Kind and Extent of Harm

Merhi v. Becker

Supreme Court of Connecticut
325 A.2d 270 (Conn. 1973)

BOGDANSKI, Associate Justice.

The plaintiff, Ronald Merhi, brought this action in four counts to recover damages for personal injuries.... From a verdict and judgment rendered against it, Local 1010 has appealed to this court....

Local 1010 contends (1) that the jury could not reasonably have found that the defendant was negligent in discharging its duty of care toward those attending the picnic and (2) that even if the jury found the defendant negligent, it could not reasonably have found that its negligence was the proximate cause of the plaintiff's injuries.

There was evidence from which the jury could find the following facts: On July 21, 1962, the plaintiff, a member of Local 1010, attended an outdoor picnic planned and sponsored by the defendant Local 1010 for the benefit of its union members and their guests.... [A]pproximately 500 people attended.

The committee designated by the union to be in charge of the picnic decided to have three or four policemen on duty at the grounds and a member of the committee was paid by the union to hire the policemen. In fact, however, only one person was assigned to police the grounds and he was not a regular member of any police force, normally worked in a shop, and was sixty years of age. On the morning of the picnic, the chairman of the committee determined that more police protection was needed. No additional police, however, were obtained.

The admission price entitled the patrons to all the food and beer they desired. Some of the union members brought their own liquor. The tenor of the picnic became noisy and inharmonious. Many men and women went swimming in the pool with their clothes on. Richard Becker testified that during the day he had more than five beers and "it could have been more than a thousand." Everyone had been drinking quite a bit. Becker was involved in two fights during the picnic, one with John Keiper, a member of the committee sponsoring the picnic. . . .

Becker was not arrested, evicted or escorted from the grounds after his physical involvement with Keiper. About a half-hour later Becker went to his car which was parked in the picnic area, drove the car into the area of the picnickers, aimed and steered it in the direction of Keiper, but struck and injured the plaintiff instead.

. . . . On the evidence, the jury could properly find that the defendant Local 1010 had failed to perform its duty to provide adequate police protection or otherwise to control the activities of its beer drinking guests, especially after the earlier outbreak of fisticuffs.

. . . . The defendant Local 1010, nevertheless, further contends that even if the jury did find it was negligent, it could not have found its negligence was the cause of the plaintiff's injuries because no person in the defendant's position, knowing what it knew or should have known, could have anticipated that the harm of the nature suffered by the plaintiff was likely to result.

"If the . . . [defendant's] conduct is a substantial factor in bringing about harm to another, the fact that the . . . [defendant] neither foresaw nor should have foreseen the extent of the harm or the manner in which it occurred does not prevent him from being liable." Restatement (Second), of Torts § 435(1). Neither foreseeability of the extent nor the manner of the injury constitutes the criteria for deciding questions of proximate cause. The test is whether the harm which occurred was of the same general nature as the foreseeable risk created by the defendant's negligence. . . . Here, the jury could have found that the events at the picnic fulfilled the test for proximate cause; that the inadequate policing of a large crowd served alcoholic beverages all day created the foreseeable risk that boisterous and angry occurrences might result in injury to bystanders, and that this risk became more obvious once the brawls involving Becker occurred. Consequently, no matter how one characterizes the exact nature of Becker's action in harming the plaintiff, the jury could reasonably have found that it constituted an instance of the general kind of harm that the defendant's negligence would cause, i.e., harm to patrons from inadequately deterred raucous, violent conduct.

. . . .

We conclude therefore, that the verdict of the jury is clearly supported by the evidence and the law and that the court properly denied the motion to set aside the verdict.

There is no error.

In this opinion the other judges concurred.

Note

1. ***General Nature, Not Precise Manner.*** The weight of authority agrees with the principal case that an unforeseeable difference in manner of occurrence will not preclude a finding of proximate causation if the harmful result was foreseeable. For example, in Davis v. Christian Brotherhood Homes of Jackson, Mississippi, Inc., 957 So. 2d 390, 404–05 (Miss. Ct. App. 2007), the court wrote:

> Christian Brotherhood repeatedly asserts that it could not have foreseen that two accomplices to a burglary would get into an argument over that burglary in the back seat of a car and one end up shooting the other. We are not persuaded by this argument. "Foreseeability does not require that a person anticipate the precise manner in which injury will occur once he has created a dangerous situation through his negligence." . . . . Rather, "what is required to be foreseeable is the general nature of the event or harm, not its precise manner or occurrence." . . . . In light of the nature, amount, and frequency of the crimes against persons reported at and in the vicinity of CBA, we find that a reasonable jury could conclude that an individual being shot and killed on the premises of CBA was foreseeable.

("Kinsman No. 1") Petition of Kinsman Transit Co.

United States Court of Appeals for the Second Circuit
338 F.2d 708 (2d Cir. 1964)

[The Buffalo River flows through Buffalo from east to west, with many bends and turns, until it empties into Lake Erie. About a mile from the mouth, the City of Buffalo maintains a bridge at Michigan Avenue. The Shiras, owned by Kinsman Transit Co., was improperly moored at a dock operated by the Continental Grain Company, about three miles upstream from the Michigan Avenue Bridge. The river, which was about 200 feet wide, moved rapidly and was full of floating ice. Because the Shiras, which was more than 400 feet in length, extended considerably beyond the length of the dock near a turn in the river, ice and debris accumulated between the ship and the dock. As a result of the pressure, the mooring lines began to part, and a "deadman," to which a mooring cable was attached, pulled out of the ground, the judge finding that it had not been properly constructed or inspected. Careening downstream, the Shiras struck another ship, the Tewksbury, which had been properly moored. The Tewksbury broke loose, and the two ships continued to move with the current. Several frantic telephone calls were made to have the bridge raised. However, because one crew had left early, and another was late arriving on duty, the bridge was just beginning to be raised when the ships crashed into its center. Ice jammed behind the wreckage which fell into the river; the river backed up; and property along the banks was flooded as far upstream as the Continental dock. On the claims for the property damage, the trial court held that Kinsman, Continental, and the City of Buffalo were liable for negligence. All three appealed.]

FRIENDLY, Circuit Judge.

. . . [A] ship insecurely moored in a fast flowing river is a known danger not only to herself but to the owners of all other ships and structures down-river and to persons upon them. No one would dream of saying that a shipowner who "knowingly and wilfully" failed to secure his ship at a pier on such a river "would not have threatened" persons and owners of property downstream in some manner. The shipowner and the wharfinger in this case having thus owed a duty of care to all within the reach of the ship's known destructive power, the impossibility of advance identification of the particular person who would be hurt is without legal consequence. . . . Similarly the foreseeable consequences of the City's failure to raise the bridge were not limited to the Shiras and the Tewksbury. Collision plainly created a danger that the bridge towers might fall onto adjoining property, and the crash of two uncontrolled lake vessels, one 425 feet and the other 525 feet long, into a bridge, over a swift ice-ridden stream, with a channel only 177 feet wide, could well result in a partial damming that would flood property upstream. . . .

. . . [A]ll the claimants here met the *Palsgraf* requirement of being persons to whom the actors owed a "duty of care". . . . But this does not dispose of the alternative argument that the manner in which several of the claimants were harmed particularly by flood damage was unforeseeable. . . .

So far as concerns the City, the argument lacks factual support. Although the obvious risks from not raising the bridge were damage to itself and to the vessels, the danger of a fall of the bridge and of flooding would not have been unforeseeable under the circumstances to anyone who gave them thought. And the same can be said as to the failure of Kinsman's shipkeeper to ready the anchors after the danger had become apparent. The exhibits indicate that the width of the channel between the Concrete Elevator and the bridge is at most points less than two hundred fifty feet. If the Shiras caught upon a dock or vessel moored along the shore, the current might well swing her bow across the channel so as to block the ice floes, as indeed could easily have occurred at the Standard Elevator dock where the stern of the Shiras struck the Tewksbury's bow. At this point the channel scarcely exceeds two hundred feet, and this was further narrowed by the presence of the Druckenmiller moored on the opposite bank. Had the Tewksbury's mooring held, it is thus by no means unlikely that these three ships would have dammed the river. Nor was it unforeseeable that the drawbridge would not be raised since, apart from any other reason, there was no assurance of timely warning. What may have been less foreseeable was that the Shiras would get that far down the river, but this is somewhat negated both by the known speed of the current when freshets developed and by the evidence that, on learning of the Shiras' departure, Continental's employees and those they informed foresaw precisely that.

Continental's position on the facts is stronger. It was indeed foreseeable that the improper construction and lack of inspection of the "deadman" might cause a ship to break loose and damage persons and property on or near the river — that was what made Continental's conduct negligent. With the aid of hindsight one can also say that a prudent man, carefully pondering the problem, would have realized that the danger of this would be greatest under such water conditions as developed during the night of January 21, 1959, and that if a vessel should break loose under those circumstances, events might transpire as they did. But such *post hoc* step by step analysis would render "foreseeable" almost anything that has in fact occurred; if the argument relied upon has legal validity, it ought not to be circumvented by characterizing as foreseeable what almost no one would in fact have foreseen at the time.

The effect of unforeseeability of damage upon liability for negligence has recently been considered by the Judicial Committee of the Privy Council, Overseas Tankship (U.K.) Ltd. v. Morts Dock & Engineering Co. (*The Wagon Mound [No. 1]*). The Committee there disapproved the proposition, thought to be supported by *Re Polemis and Furness, Withy & Co. Ltd.*, [1921] 3 K.B. 560 (C.A.) "that unforeseeability is irrelevant if damage is 'direct.'" We have no difficulty with the result of *The Wagon Mound*, in view of the finding that the appellant had no reason to believe that the floating furnace oil would burn.... On that view the decision simply applies the principle which excludes liability where the injury sprang from a hazard different from that which was improperly risked.... Although some language in the judgment goes beyond this, we would find it difficult to understand why one who had failed to use the care required to protect others in the light of expectable forces should be exonerated when the very risks that rendered his conduct negligent produced other and more serious consequences to such persons than were fairly foreseeable when he fell short of what the law demanded. Foreseeability of danger is necessary to render conduct negligent; where as here the damage was caused by just those forces whose existence required the exercise of greater care than was taken—the current, the ice, and the physical mass of the Shiras, the incurring of consequences other and greater than foreseen does not make the conduct less culpable or provide a reasoned basis for insulation.... The oft encountered argument that failure to limit liability to foreseeable consequences may subject the defendant to a loss wholly out of proportion to his fault seems scarcely consistent with the universally accepted rule that the defendant takes the plaintiff as he finds him and will be responsible for the full extent of the injury even though a latent susceptibility of the plaintiff renders this far more serious than could reasonably have been anticipated....

The weight of authority in this country rejects the limitation of damages to consequences foreseeable at the time of the negligent conduct when the consequences are "direct," and the damage, although other and greater than expectable, is of the same general sort that was risked.... Other American courts, purporting to apply a test of foreseeability to damages, extend that concept to such unforeseen lengths as to raise serious doubt whether the concept is meaningful....

We see no reason why an actor engaging in conduct which entails a large risk of small damage and a small risk of other and greater damage, of the same general sort, from the same forces, and to the same class of persons, should be relieved of responsibility for the latter simply because the chance of its occurrence, if viewed alone, may not have been large enough to require the exercise of care. By hypothesis the risk of the lesser harm was sufficient to render his disregard of it actionable; the existence of a less likely additional risk that the very forces against whose action he was required to guard would produce other and greater damage than could have been reasonably anticipated should inculpate him further rather than limit his liability. This does not mean that the careless actor will always be held for all damages for which the forces that he risked were a cause in fact. Somewhere a point will be reached when courts will agree that the link has become too tenuous — that what is claimed to be consequence is only fortuity. Thus, if the destruction of the Michigan Avenue Bridge had delayed the arrival of a doctor, with consequent loss of a patient's life, few judges would impose liability on any of the parties here, although the agreement in result might not be paralleled by similar unanimity in reasoning; perhaps in the long run one returns to Judge Andrews' statement in *Palsgraf*, 248 N.Y. at 354–355, 162 N.E. at 104 (dissenting opinion). "It is all a question of expediency, . . . of fair judgment, always keeping in mind the fact that we endeavor to make a rule in each case that will be practical and in keeping with the general understanding of mankind." It would be pleasant if greater certainty were possible . . . , but the many efforts that have been made at defining the *locus* of the "uncertain and wavering line," 248 N.Y. at 354, 162 N.E. 99, are not very promising; what courts do in such cases makes better sense than what they, or others, say. Where the line will be drawn will vary from age to age; as society has come to rely increasingly on insurance and other methods of loss-sharing, the point may lie further off than a century ago. Here it is surely more equitable that the losses from the operators' negligent failure to raise the Michigan Avenue Bridge should be ratably borne by Buffalo's taxpayers than left with the innocent victims of the flooding; yet the mind is also repelled by a solution that would impose liability solely on the City and exonerate the persons whose negligent acts of commission and omission were the precipitating force of the collision with the bridge and its sequelae. We go only so far as to hold that where, as here, the damages resulted from the same physical forces whose existence required the exercise of greater care than was displayed and were of the same general sort that was expectable, unforeseeability of the exact developments and of the extent of the loss will not limit liability. Other fact situations can be dealt with when they arise.

[Affirmed as to liability, but modified as to damages.]

[The opinion of MOORE, J., concurring and dissenting, has been omitted.]

Note

1. ***Third Restatement.*** *See* Restatement, Third, of Torts: Liab. for Physical and Emotional Harm § 29 cmt. p (2010) ("If the type of harm that occurs is within the scope of the risk, the defendant is liable for all such harm caused, regardless of its extent").

("Kinsman No. 2") Petition of Kinsman Transit Co.

United States Court of Appeals for the Second Circuit
388 F.2d 821 (2d Cir. 1968)

[The background facts are the same as in *Kinsman No. 1*, 338 F.2d 708 (2d Cir. 1964), *supra* at p. 473. The action was commenced by the owners of wheat stored aboard a ship berthed in the Buffalo harbor below the bridge, for transportation expenses incurred because the ship could not be moved to the shipper's grain elevators located above the bridge, and for storage costs and the purchase of replacement wheat.]

IRVING R. KAUFMAN, Circuit Judge.

... [We] conclude that recovery was properly denied on the facts of this case because the injuries to [the shippers] were too "remote" or "indirect" a consequence of defendants' negligence.

Numerous principles have been suggested to determine the point at which a defendant should no longer be held legally responsible for damages caused "in fact" by his negligence.... Such limiting principles must exist in any system of jurisprudence, for cause and effect succeed one another with the same certainty that night follows day and the consequences of the simplest act may be traced over an ever-widening canvas with the passage of time. In Anglo-American law, as Edgerton has noted, "except only the defendant's intention to produce a given result, no other consideration so affects our feeling that it is or is not just to hold him for the result so much as its foreseeability." ....

When the instant case was last here, we held—although without discussion of the [claims of these shippers]—that it was a foreseeable consequence of the negligence of the city of Buffalo and Kinsman Transit Company that the river would be dammed. It would seem to follow from this that it was foreseeable that transportation on the river would be disrupted and that some would incur expenses because of the need to find alternative routes of transportation or substitutes for goods delayed by the disaster....

On the previous appeal we stated aptly: "somewhere a point will be reached when courts will agree that the result has become too tenuous—that what is claimed to be consequence is only fortuity." .... We believe that this point has been reached with [these] claims.... The instant claims occurred only because the downed bridge made it impossible to move traffic along the river. Under all the circumstances of this case, we hold that the connection between the defendants' negligence and the claimants' damages is too tenuous and remote to permit recovery....

In the final analysis the circumlocution whether posed in terms of "foreseeability," "duty," "proximate cause," "remoteness," etc. seems unavoidable.... We return to Judge Andrews' frequently quoted statement in Palsgraf v. Long Island R.R.: "It is all a question of expediency ... of fair judgment, always keeping in mind the fact that we endeavor to make a rule in each case that will be practical and in keeping with the general understanding of mankind."

Affirmed.

Notes

1. ***Liability for Purely Economic Loss.*** One possible reading of *Kinsman No. 2* is to focus on the nature of the harm, namely purely economic harm rather than property damage or personal injury. In general, in American tort law, there is no liability for negligent interference with economic interests. *See* Restatement, Second, of Torts §766C. However, there are many exceptions to this rule, such as where the negligence relates to legal or accounting malpractice, misrepresentation, failure to settle an insurance claim within policy limits, spoliation of evidence, or breach of fiduciary duty. *See* Chapter 15 (discussing the "economic loss rule"). Thus, one might argue that *Kinsman No. 2* denied recovery not because the losses were too "tenuous" or "remote," but because, unlike in *Kinsman No. 1*, they involved purely economic losses (i.e., increased costs for transportation), rather than personal injuries or property damages.

2. ***No-Duty Versus No-Proximate Causation.*** A determination that liability should not attach may be expressed by stating that the defendant is under "no duty" to exercise care on behalf of the plaintiff or that the defendant's conduct, even if negligent, is not a "proximate cause" of the plaintiff's injuries. The difference may be important. The question of duty is always one for the court, and its decision on that issue carries with it precedential force and governs subsequent cases. The issue of proximate causation, in contrast, is normally a factual question for the jury, and carries no precedential weight.

D. Result within the Risk

1. In General

The principle of foreseeability has played a major role in proximate causation analysis. However, it cannot be the whole story, as there are some cases in which the defendant plainly should not be liable even for some foreseeable harms. Consider an example from the Restatement in which the defendant negligently leaves a loaded pistol lying on a table, where it is found by a child. If the child shoots someone, the defendant will be liable: the risk that the child will shoot someone is just what makes the defendant's conduct negligent. But suppose the child shoots nobody, but accidentally drops the pistol on a playmate's toe: should the defendant be liable for that injury? If "foreseeability" is the test, the answer must be "yes," as this kind of accident is just as foreseeable as a shooting. Yet the risk of injury from having the pistol dropped on a toe is not one of the risks that makes the defendant's conduct negligent (assuming that it would not have been negligent to leave a heavy but non-lethal object, such as a toy gun, where a child could find it). Therefore, there should be no liability. *See* Restatement, Second, Torts, § 281, illus. 3.

What unforeseeable consequences (like the fire in *Wagon Mound No. 1*) and the foreseeable consequences that are not proximately caused by the defendant's negligence (like the pistol's being dropped on a toe) have in common is this: neither consequence resulted from one of the risks that made the defendant's conduct negligent. An approach to proximate cause that asks whether those risks that made the defendant's behavior negligent included the risk that led to the plaintiff's injuries explains many proximate-cause cases better than simply asking whether the result was "foreseeable."

For example, in Di Ponzio v. Riordan, 679 N.E.2d 616 (N.Y. 1997), the defendant operator of a filling station was allegedly negligent in failing to train its employees, who violated a company rule requiring that customers be warned to turn off their engines before fueling their vehicles. The plaintiff was injured when he was struck by a vehicle that slipped out of the park gear and began to roll backward while it was being filled with gas while the engine was running. When a vehicle's engine is left running in an area where gasoline is being pumped, there is a natural and foreseeable risk of fire or explosion because of the highly flammable properties of the fuel. Because the type of accident that injured the plaintiff was not among the hazards that are naturally associated with leaving a car engine running during the operation of a gas pump, the alleged misconduct of the defendant's employees did not give rise to liability. Consequently, it is fair to say that, for purposes of proximate causation, a difference in manner of occurrence is irrelevant only if the result was within the risks that made the defendant's conduct negligent.

Thompson v. Kaczinski

Supreme Court of Iowa 774 N.W.2d 829 (Iowa 2009)

HECHT, Justice.

A motorist lost control of his car on a rural gravel road and crashed upon encountering a trampoline that had been displaced by the wind from an adjoining yard to the surface of the road. He and his spouse sued the owners of the trampoline. The district court granted summary judgment, concluding the defendants owed no duty to the motorist under the circumstances and the personal injuries resulting from the crash were not proximately caused by the defendants' alleged negligence....

James Kaczinski and Michelle Lockwood resided in rural Madison County... During the late summer..., they disassembled a trampoline and placed its component parts on their yard approximately thirty-eight feet from the road. Intending to dispose of them at a later time, Kaczinski and Lockwood did not secure the parts in place. A few weeks later... a severe thunderstorm moved through the Earlham area. Wind gusts from the storm displaced the top of the trampoline from the yard to the surface of the road.

Later that morning, while driving from one church to another where he served as a pastor, Charles Thompson approached the defendants' property. When he swerved to avoid the obstruction on the road, Thompson lost control of his vehicle. His car entered the ditch and rolled several times. Kaczinski and Lockwood were awakened by Thompson's screams at about 9:40 a.m., shortly after the accident. When they went outside to investigate, they discovered the top of their trampoline lying on the roadway....

Thompson and his wife filed suit, alleging Kaczinski and Lockwood breached statutory and common law duties by negligently allowing the trampoline to obstruct the roadway.... The district court granted the ... [defendants' motion for summary judgment], concluding Kaczinski and Lockwood breached no duty and the damages claimed by the plaintiffs were not proximately caused by the defendants' negligence. The Thompsons appealed. We transferred the case to the court of appeals, which affirmed the district court's ruling....

.... We conclude the district court erred in determining Kaczinski and Lockwood owed no common law duty under the circumstances presented here.

.... Although the memorandum filed by Kaczinski and Lockwood in support of their motion for summary judgment raised only the questions of whether a duty was owed and whether a duty was breached, the district court concluded the plaintiffs' claims must fail for the further reason that they did not establish a causal connection between their claimed injuries and damages and the acts and omissions of Kaczinski and Lockwood. Again relying on its determination that the risk of the trampoline's displacement from the yard to the roadway was not foreseeable, the court resolved the causation issue against the Thompsons as a matter of law.

We have held causation has two components: cause in fact and legal cause.... The latter component requires a policy determination of whether "the policy of the law must require the defendant to be legally responsible for the injury." ....

We have previously applied the test articulated in the Restatement (Second) of Torts when determining if a defendant's conduct is a legal or proximate cause of the plaintiff's damages. This test holds "[t]he actor's negligent conduct is a legal cause of harm to another if (a) his conduct is a substantial factor in bringing about the harm, and (b) there is no rule of law relieving the actor from liability." Restatement (Second) of Torts § 431, at 428 (1965).... In deciding whether conduct is a substantial factor in bringing about the harm, we have considered the "proximity between the breach and the injury based largely on the concept of foreseeability." ....

The formulation of legal or proximate cause outlined above has been the source of significant uncertainty and confusion.... Although we have previously noted our uneven approach to proximate cause questions and acknowledged the criticism of the doctrine, we have not yet had the opportunity to clarify this area of law.... We do now.

... [I]n an attempt to eliminate unnecessary confusion caused by the traditional vernacular, the drafters of the Third Restatement refer to the concept of proximate cause as "scope of liability."

....

Most importantly, the drafters of the Restatement (Third) have clarified the essential role of policy considerations in the determination of the scope of liability. "An actor's liability is limited to those physical harms that result from the risks that made the actor's conduct tortious." *Id.* § 29, at 575. This principle, referred to as the "risk standard," is intended to prevent the unjustified imposition of liability by "confining liability's scope to the reasons for holding the actor liable in the first place." .... As an example of the standard's application, the drafters provide an illustration of a hunter returning from the field and handing his loaded shotgun to a child as he enters the house.... The child drops the gun (an object assumed for the purposes of the illustration to be neither too heavy nor unwieldy for a child of that age and size to handle) which lands on her foot and breaks her toe.... Applying the risk standard described above, the hunter would not be liable for the broken toe because the risk that made his action negligent was the risk that the child would shoot someone, not that she would drop the gun and sustain an injury to her foot....

The scope-of-liability issue is fact-intensive as it requires consideration of the risks that made the actor's conduct tortious and a determination of whether the harm at issue is a result of any of those risks.... When, as in this case, the court considers in advance of trial whether

the plaintiff's harm is beyond the scope of liability as a matter of law, courts must initially consider all of the range of harms risked by the defendant's conduct that the jury could find as the basis for determining [the defendant's] conduct tortious. Then, the court can compare the plaintiff's harm with the range of harms risked by the defendant to determine whether a reasonable jury might find the former among the latter.

....

The drafters advance several advantages of limiting liability in this way. First, the application of the risk standard is comparatively simple.... The standard "appeals to intuitive notions of fairness and proportionality by limiting liability to harms that result from risks created by the actor's wrongful conduct, but for no others." .... It also is flexible enough to "accommodate fairness concerns raised by the specific facts of a case." ....

Foreseeability has previously played an important role in our proximate cause determinations.... When, as in this case, we have been called upon to consider the role of an intervening or superseding cause, the question of the foreseeability of the superseding force has been critical....

The drafters of the Restatement (Third) explain that foreseeability is still relevant in scope-of-liability determinations. "In a negligence action, prior incidents or other facts evidencing risks may make certain risks foreseeable that otherwise were not, thereby changing the scope-of-liability analysis." .... In fact, they acknowledge the similarity between the risk standard they articulate and the foreseeability tests applied by most jurisdictions in making causation determinations in negligence cases.

Properly understood, both the risk standard and a foreseeability test exclude liability for harms that were sufficiently unforeseeable at the time of the actor's tortious conduct that they were not among the risks—potential harms—that made the actor negligent.... [W]hen scope of liability arises in a negligence case, the risks that make an actor negligent are limited to foreseeable ones, and the factfinder must determine whether the type of harm that occurred is among those reasonably foreseeable potential harms that made the actor's conduct negligent.

.... Although the risk standard and the foreseeability test are comparable in negligence actions, the drafters favor the risk standard because it "provides greater clarity, facilitates clearer analysis in a given case, and better reveals the reason for its existence." .... They explain that a foreseeability test "risks being misunderstood because of uncertainty about what must be foreseen, by whom, and at what time." ....

We find the drafters' clarification of scope of liability sound and are persuaded by their explanation of the advantages of applying the risk standard as articulated in the Restatement (Third), and, accordingly, adopt it.

Our next task, then, is to consider whether the district court erred in concluding the harm suffered by the Thompsons was, a matter of law, outside the scope of the risk of Kaczinski and Lockwood's conduct. We conclude the question of whether a serious injury to a motorist was within the range of harms risked by disassembling the trampoline and leaving it untethered for a few weeks on the yard less than forty feet from the road is not so clear in this case as to justify the district court's resolution of the issue as a matter of law at the summary judgment stage. A reasonable fact finder could determine Kaczinski and Lockwood should have known high winds occasionally occur in Iowa in September and a strong gust of wind could displace the unsecured trampoline parts the short distance from the yard to the roadway and endanger motorists. Although they were in their home for several hours after the storm passed and approximately two-and-a-half hours after daybreak, Kaczinski and Lockwood did not discover their property on the nearby roadway, remove it, or warn approaching motorists of it. On this record, viewed in the light most favorable to the Thompsons, we conclude a reasonable fact finder could find the harm suffered by the Thompsons resulted from the risks that made the defendants' conduct negligent. Accordingly, the district court erred in deciding the scope-of-liability question as a matter of law in this case.

.... Accordingly, we reverse the district court's dismissal of this claim and remand this case for trial.

[The concurring opinion of CADY, J., is omitted.]

Notes

1. ***"Result within the Risk" and the Third Restatement.*** The Third Restatement wholeheartedly adopts the result-within-the-risk approach to proximate causation (which the Restatement insists on calling "scope of liability"):

> § 29. Limitations on Liability for Tortious Conduct
>
> An actor's liability is limited to those harms that result from the risks that made the actor's conduct tortious.
>
> § 30. Risk of Harm Not Generally Increased by Tortious Conduct
>
> An actor is not liable for harm when the tortious aspect of the actor's conduct was of a type that does not generally increase the risk of that harm.

Restatement, Third, of Torts: Liab. for Physical and Emotional Harm (2010).

2. ***"Result within the Risk" and Statutory Violations.*** One kind of case in which the result-within-the-risk analysis is routinely applied is that in which the defendant's conduct violates a statute that has a particular purpose. Suppose, for instance, that the defendant has parked illegally in front of a fire hydrant. If the plaintiff's building catches fire and burns to the ground because the defendant's car keeps the fire department from getting to the hydrant, the defendant should be held liable. But if a skateboarder trips and hits her head on the car—an accident that would not have happened if the car had not been in that particular place—the defendant's negligence would not be a proximate cause of the harm: it is illegal to park in front of hydrants because this increases the risks of fire, not because a skateboarder may fall against a car in that particular spot.

Consider again the problem of the defendant whose conduct is perfectly proper, except that he is engaging in an activity requiring a license, which the defendant does not have. Suppose that an unlicensed driver, who is in fact driving very carefully, runs over a pedestrian who has fainted and fallen in front of her car. It is quite clear that the defendant is not liable for the pedestrian's injuries, even though the defendant's actions violated a law that was enacted as a safety measure. One way to analyze this problem is to say that the statute, although a "safety statute" in a sense, is not a statute that prescribes a standard of care: the defendant was observing all of the standards of care required of drivers (paying attention to traffic, staying in her lane, not speeding, and so on). Her actions were therefore not negligent, because they created no excessive risk of harm, even though they were illegal. Another way to explain the result is to invoke proximate cause. The reason for licensing statutes is to keep incompetent drivers off the road. If a particular driver, though involved in an accident, was driving competently, the harm in question was not the kind of harm the licensing statute was adopted to prevent.

3. ***Negligent Medical Treatment.*** A common situation involves a plaintiff who is tortiously injured, and whose injuries are aggravated by the negligence of the plaintiff's physician. It is generally agreed that the defendant is liable for all of the harm, including that attributable to the negligent treatment. As the Indiana Court

of Appeals put it in Whitaker v. Kruse, 495 N.E.2d 223 (Ind. Ct. App. 1986), "[s]ince he put the injured person in the position of needing medical services, the tortfeasor is responsible for any additional injury resulting from the medical treatment."

If medical misconduct is so extraordinary that it can no longer be thought of as a risk inherent in the necessity of submitting to medical treatment, the antecedent tortfeasor will not be liable for the aggravation of the plaintiff's injuries. *See* Restatement, Third, of Torts: Liab. for Physical & Emotional Harm § 35 cmt. c (2010) ("The actor is not subject to liability for enhanced harm caused by extraordinary or unusual acts that create risks of harm different from those normally created by efforts to render aid"). The line is drawn somewhere between ordinary negligence on the one hand and intentionally inflicted injury on the other, but beyond that generalization, its precise location is unclear. *See* W. Page Keeton *et al.*, Prosser and Keeton on Torts 309–10 (5th ed. 1984).

Suppose that, instead of suffering additional injuries because of negligent medical treatment, the victim of negligence is injured while driving to the doctor's office for treatment. This case, as we have seen, is a classic example of an injury that would not be regarded as proximately caused by the original tortfeasor's conduct. The difference cannot be that medical malpractice is more easily "foreseeable" than a traffic accident: traffic accidents are everyday occurrences. A result-within-the-risk analysis makes sense of these results. One of the risks created by negligent driving is the risk that whatever injuries others sustain will be aggravated by improper care, so that kind of harm is "within the risk." On the other hand, while it is certainly foreseeable that a victim of negligence may be injured while driving to see a doctor, that further risk is no greater than the risks of driving the plaintiff would have encountered anyway. It would therefore seem odd to say that one of the reasons why it is negligent to drive carelessly is that this may lead to further injuries while the plaintiff is driving to the doctor's office. (Contrast a case in which the victim's injuries are very serious, so the ambulance taking the victim to the hospital drives at 90 miles an hour and, because of its high speed, crashes.)

4. ***Negligence That Has "Run Its Course."*** In some cases, courts have focused upon whether the risks created by the tortfeasor had "run their course" or "come to rest" before the plaintiff was injured. This is another way of talking about whether the result fell outside of the risks that made the actor's conduct tortious.

Compare Union Pump Co. v. Allbritton, 898 S.W.2d 773 (Tex. 1995)[1] (injuries were not proximately caused by the manufacturer of a pump which caught fire because at the time the plaintiff, who was still in firefighting gear, fell off a wet pipe rack, the fire had been extinguished and the forces generated by the fire had "come to rest"), *with* Henry v. Houston Lighting & Power Co., 934 S.W.2d 748 (Tex. App. 1996) (injury to a rescuer was proximately caused by negligent damage to a

1. *Abrogated on other grounds by* Ford Motor Co. v. Ledesma, 242 S.W.3d 32 (Tex. 2007).

pipe because the dangerous gas leak had not been repaired when the plaintiff was injured while fleeing the scene when another worker yelled "fire").

In Marshall v. Nugent, 222 F.2d 604 (1st Cir. 1955), the plaintiff Marshall had been a passenger in a car belonging to Harriman, which was forced off the road by the negligent driving of defendant Socony's employee, Prince. While the others attempted to return the car to the road, plaintiff walked to the crest of the hill to warn oncoming traffic, and in the process was struck by a third vehicle driven by Nugent, which skidded out of control on the snow-covered pavement. In affirming a judgment against Socony, Chief Judge Magruder wrote:

> Plaintiff Marshall was a passenger in the oncoming Chevrolet car, and thus was one of the persons whose bodily safety was primarily endangered by the negligence of Prince.... Though this particular act of negligence was over and done with when the truck pulled up alongside of the stalled Chevrolet without having actually collided with it, still the consequences of such past negligence were in the bosom of time, as yet unrevealed.
>
> If the Chevrolet had been pulled back onto the highway, and Harriman and Marshall, having got in it again, had resumed their journey and had had a collision with another car five miles down the road, in which Marshall suffered bodily injuries, ... the courts would no doubt conclude, "as a matter of law," that Prince's earlier negligence in cutting the corner was not the "proximate cause" of this later injury received by the plaintiff. That would be because the extra risks to which such negligence by Prince had subjected the passengers in the Chevrolet car were obviously entirely over; the situation had been stabilized and become normal, and, so far as one could foresee, whatever subsequent risks the Chevrolet might have to encounter in its resumed journey were simply the inseparable risks, no more and no less, that were incident to the Chevrolet's being out on the highway at all. But in the case at bar, the circumstances under which Marshall received the personal injuries complained of presented no such clear-cut situation.
>
> ... [T]he extra risks created by Prince's negligence were not all over at the moment the primary risk of collision between the truck and the Chevrolet was successfully surmounted.... It is true, the Chevrolet car was not owned by the plaintiff Marshall, and no doubt, without violating any legal duty to Harriman, Marshall could have crawled up onto the snowbank at the side of the road out of harm's way and awaited there, passive and inert, until his journey was resumed. But the plaintiff, who as a passenger in the Chevrolet car had already been subjected to a collision risk by the negligent operation of the Socony truck, could reasonably be expected to get out onto the highway and lend a hand to his host in getting the Chevrolet started again.... The injury Marshall received by being struck by the Nugent car was not remote, either in time or place, from the negligent conduct of defendant Socony's servant, and it occurred while the traffic mix-up occasioned

> by defendant's negligence was still persisting, not after the traffic flow had become normal again. In the circumstances presented we conclude that the district court committed no error in leaving the issue of proximate cause to the jury for determination.

5. ***Problem: Negligent Entrustment.*** Pete has a tendency to drink heavily, as his friend Dave well knows. Pete borrows Dave's car so that, as he tells Dave, he can "go to the tavern tonight and get plowed with the guys." If Pete should get drunk and, as a result, injure a pedestrian while driving home, Dave would be liable for the pedestrian's injuries. If, on the way to the tavern, while sober, Pete drives negligently and injures Paula, is Dave liable to Paula? It is, of course, quite foreseeable that someone to whom a car has been lent may drive carelessly even when sober: nearly everybody drives carelessly some of the time. (Assume that the state in question does not have an "owner liability" law. These laws make the owners of motor vehicles liable for the negligent driving of anyone using their cars with permission. *See* Chapter 14.)

6. ***Results Outside of the Risk.*** In Barr v. Jacobson, 795 So. 2d 1244 (La. Ct. App. 2001), a child was injured when she stepped in a hole in the ground after an auto accident. In finding that the driver's alleged breach of duty was not a legal cause of the injuries from the misstep, the court wrote:

> [T]he duty of reasonable care in the operation of motor vehicles was not designed to protect automobile passengers involved in an accident from all conceivable harms. We find that the danger of stepping into holes located off of the roadway while embarking on a second trip to observe other vehicles or persons involved, out of curiosity or personal interest, six or seven minutes after the accident, is simply not within the scope of this duty.

2. Policy and Proximate Cause

One way to look at the "proximate cause" restriction on plaintiffs' recoveries is to see it as denying recovery when the defendant's negligence was not the sort of misconduct that tends to lead to the kind of harm that resulted. For example, suppose that a tree falls on a speeding car, injuring a passenger.[2] The driver's speeding is negligent because it creates an excessive risk that the car may slide off the road on a sharp corner, or that the driver may not be able to stop in time if vehicles ahead slow down or change lanes. The reason for calling the driver's conduct negligent has nothing to do with threats from falling trees. Indeed, speeding may reduce the danger of being hurt by falling trees: the faster one drives, the less time one spends on the road and under the trees. Therefore, although the excessive speed was a "but for" cause of the accident—the speed happened to put the car in position to be hit by the tree—it was not a proximate cause of the accident.

---

2. This example is adapted from one in Prosser and Keeton on Torts, § 41 (5th ed. 1984), which in turn comes from Berry v. Sugar Notch Borough, 43 A. 240 (Pa. 1899), in which the vehicle was a trolley.

Economic Analysis
Avoiding Over-Deterrence

Alan Gunn

Looking at tort law from the point of view of deterrence, the examples above show that a proximate-cause rule is essential to prevent the law from over-deterring conduct that can cause injuries. Consider, for instance, the question of how much the law should deter drivers from exceeding the speed limit by five miles an hour on uncrowded interstate highways. The answer is: a bit, but not very much. Speed saves time and money, though it causes some harm. If the law makes those who exceed the speed limit liable for all of the additional accidents that can be expected to result from this small increase in speed, it gives those drivers just the right incentive. Those for whom getting to their destination quickly is very important will accept the risk; those for whom it isn't will not. But now suppose that these drivers are liable not only for the harms done in accidents predictably caused by their excessive speed, but also for any accident in which they were involved while speeding—even if the only contribution of speed to the accident was that it happened to put the car in the place where the accident occurred, as in the falling-tree hypothetical. Now, drivers will (in theory) know that if they exceed the speed limit, even by a very small amount, they will be liable for any accident that happens. This imposes a burden quite disproportionate to the harm one would foresee from the conduct, and so would have too great a deterrent effect.

The argument above can be restated in a more general way. Proper deterrence requires making those who contemplate dangerous conduct liable for all of the increased harm that occurs whenever that dangerous conduct is undertaken. Making actors liable for more than that over-deters. Without a doctrine of proximate cause to limit liability, the prospective penalty for any conduct that a factfinder might find negligent would be far in excess of the additional harm one can foresee as resulting from the conduct.

As another illustration of both proximate cause and of the economic rationale for the doctrine, consider a case in which *A* is driving her friend *B* to the airport. They are somewhat late for the flight, so *A* speeds. The law should deter *A* somewhat from doing this, as *A*'s speeding creates a danger for other users of the highway. But if the highway is empty, the road is dry, the weather is clear, and it is important for *B* to make her plane, speeding may be the economically sensible thing to do. If *A* knows that she will be liable for any accident of the sort the rule against speeding is designed to prevent, she is in a position to make an intelligent choice. But suppose there were no doctrine of proximate cause. Now, *A*'s speeding would make her liable for all of the consequences of *B*'s catching her plane on time, so that, for example,

(1) If *B*'s plane crashes, *A* would be liable for *B*'s injuries ("but for" *A*'s speeding, *B* would have missed the plane and so would not have been hurt).

(2) If *B*, driving a rental car in the city to which she flew, ran over a pedestrian, *A* would be liable for the pedestrian's injuries ("but for" *A*'s speeding,

B would have missed the plane and would not have been driving her rental car the next day).

If anyone who speeds could be held liable for every harm that could be traced to the speeding in a "but for" sense, potential liability for speeding would greatly exceed the harm that the speeding could be expected to cause.

Cases involving defendants who are vicariously liable, such as employers, illustrate the need for limiting liability. In Edwards v. Honeywell, Inc., 50 F.3d 484, 490 (7th Cir. 1995), holding that a fire-alarm service's negligence did not breach a duty to a firefighter who died fighting a fire, Judge Posner observed:

> [T]he arguments in favor of the . . . limitation are twofold. The first arises from the fact that a corporation or other enterprise does not have complete control over its employees, yet it is strictly liable under the principle of *respondeat superior* for the consequences of their negligent acts committed in the scope of their employment. It is not enough to say to the enterprise be careful and you have nothing to fear. The carelessness of its employees may result in the imposition of a crushing liability upon it. In order to know how many resources (in screening new hires and in supervising and disciplining workers after they are hired) to invest in preventing its employees from being careless, the employer must have some idea, some foresight, of the harms the employees are likely to inflict. . . .
>
> The second argument . . . is that the defendant may not be in the best position to prevent a particular class of accidents, and placing liability on it may merely dilute the incentives of other defendants. . . .

For an economic analysis of proximate cause much more complete and rigorous than that presented here, see Steven Shavell, *An Analysis of Causation and the Scope of Liability in the Law of Torts*, IX J. Legal Stud. 463 (1980).

Fairness. While the above analysis focused on deterrence, and so was an "economic" explanation of proximate cause, much the same sort of analysis can be made in terms of "fairness." A common-sense notion of justice is that the penalty for wrongful behavior should not be disproportionate to the seriousness of the misbehavior. Without a doctrine of proximate cause, the most trivial lapses could subject an actor (and sometimes the actor's employer) to massive liability, just because the lapse happened to contribute, in an unforeseeable and minor way, to a serious accident (as by putting the actor on a particular road at a particular time). A law of torts without proximate cause would often impose liability wildly disproportionate to the seriousness of an actor's wrongdoing. Here, as in so many other areas, an analysis of a problem in economic terms ("deterrence") can be restated in terms of everyday notions of fairness. Proximate cause was developed by courts quite ignorant of and mostly indifferent to economics. That it serves an important economic goal illustrates that ordinary notions of justice often tend to promote efficiency as well.

E. Intervening and Superseding Causes

An intervening force (sometimes called intervening cause or intervening act) is a force which comes into play after the tortious conduct of the defendant, and which participates along with the defendant's conduct in causing injury to the plaintiff.

A superseding cause is the type of intervening force which breaks the "chain" of proximate causation between the defendant's negligence and the plaintiff's harm and thus absolves the defendant of legal responsibility. Not all intervening forces qualify as superseding causes.

1. Foreseeable End Results

Derdiarian v. Felix Contracting Corp.

Court of Appeals of New York
414 N.E.2d 666 (N.Y. 1981)

[Felix Contracting Corporation had excavated a work site in the street while installing an underground gas main. Plaintiff Derdiarian, an employee of a subcontractor, was injured while sealing a gas main at the site, and sued Felix.]

COOKE, Chief Judge.

....

On the afternoon of November 21, 1973, defendant James Dickens suffered an epileptic seizure and lost consciousness, allowing his vehicle to careen into the work site and strike plaintiff with such force as to throw him into the air. When plaintiff landed, he was splattered over his face, head and body with 400 degree boiling hot liquid enamel from a kettle struck by the automobile. The enamel was used in connection with sealing the gas main. Although plaintiff's body ignited into a fire ball, he miraculously survived the incident.

At trial, plaintiff's theory was that defendant Felix had negligently failed to take adequate measures to insure the safety of workers on the excavation site....

To support his claim of an unsafe work site, plaintiff called as a witness Lawrence Lawton, an expert in traffic safety. According to Lawton, the usual and accepted method of safeguarding the workers is to erect a barrier around the excavation. Such a barrier, consisting of a truck, a piece of heavy equipment or a pile of dirt, would keep a car out of the excavation and protect workers from oncoming traffic. The expert testified that the barrier should cover the entire width of the excavation. He also stated that there should have been two flagmen present, rather than one, and that warning signs should have been posted advising motorists that there was only one lane of traffic and that there was a flagman ahead.

.... Felix now argues that plaintiff was injured in a freakish accident, brought about solely by defendant Dickens' negligence, and therefore there was no causal link, as a matter of law, between Felix' breach of duty and plaintiff's injuries.

The concept of proximate cause, or more appropriately legal cause, has proven to be an elusive one.... This is, in part, because the concept stems from policy considerations that serve to place manageable limits upon the liability that flows from negligent conduct....

Where the acts of a third person intervene between the defendant's conduct and the plaintiff's injury, the causal connection is not automatically severed.... [L]iability turns upon whether the intervening act is a normal or foreseeable consequence of the situation created by the defendant's negligence.... If the intervening act is extraordinary under the circumstances, not foreseeable in the normal course of events, or independent of or far removed from the defendant's conduct, it may well be a superseding act which breaks the causal nexus.... [T]hese issues generally are for the fact finder to resolve.

... [W]e cannot say as a matter of law that defendant Dickens' negligence was a superseding cause.... From the evidence in the record, the jury could have found that Felix negligently failed to safeguard the excavation site. A prime hazard associated with such dereliction is the possibility that a driver will negligently enter the work site and cause injury to a worker. That the driver was negligent, or even reckless, does not insulate Felix from liability.... Nor is it decisive that the driver lost control of the vehicle through a negligent failure to take medication, rather than a driving mistake.... The precise manner of the event need not be anticipated. The finder of fact could have concluded that the foreseeable, normal and natural result of the risk created by Felix was the injury of a worker by a car entering the improperly protected work area. An intervening act may not serve as a superseding cause, and relieve an actor of responsibility, where the risk of the intervening act occurring is the very same risk which renders the actor negligent.

.... Serious injury, or even death, was a foreseeable consequence of a vehicle crashing through the work area. The injury could have occurred in numerous ways, ranging from a worker being directly struck by the car to the car hitting an object that injures the worker.... That defendant could not anticipate the precise manner of the accident or the exact extent of injuries, however, does not preclude liability as a matter of law where the general risk and character of injuries are foreseeable.

... [T]he order of the Appellate Division should be affirmed, with costs.

Notes

1. ***End Results Within the Risk.*** *Derdiarian*, like many other cases, can be read to stand for the proposition that if the end result is foreseeable, lack of foreseeability of the precise contours of the intervening force is irrelevant, and does not preclude a finding of proximate causation. This is consistent with cases holding that liability does not hinge upon foresight of the exact manner in which harm occurs. *See* Merhi v. Becker, *supra* at p. 471.

Is *Derdarian* also consistent with the "result within the risk" approach to proximate cause? What risks make it negligent to fail to erect a barrier around an excavation? Suppose that Derdiarian had been hurt not by a car that went out of control but by a stray bullet fired by a police officer at a fleeing suspect. If a barrier would have kept this shot from hitting Derdiarian, would Felix be liable?

2. ***Problem: The Loose Lid.*** Suppose an automobile lessor supplies a car with a defective latch on the trunk lid. While the car is in motion, the lid springs open. The lessee, upon stopping to make repairs, is injured by the negligent driving of a third person. Is the lessor liable for the injuries?

2. Intervening Acts

Foreseeable Intervening Acts Not Superseding. In Kimble v. Mackintosh Hemphill Co., 59 A.2d 68 (Pa. 1948), a negligently maintained foundry roof was blown off during a high wind, striking and killing the plaintiff's husband. There was conflicting evidence as to the speed of the wind on the date of the accident and on previous occasions in that locality. While a force of nature (sometimes called an Act of God, Act of Providence, or *Vis Major*) which no prudent person would reasonably anticipate will ordinarily serve to cut off liability, the jury could have found that the strength of the wind that caused the harm was foreseeable. That being true, the defendant's conduct was negligent precisely because of the risk that such a wind would produce injury. Consequently, the defendant should not be relieved of liability merely because the risk came to fruition. The wind was not a superseding cause.

Similarly, in Chapman v. Milford Towing & Service, Inc., 2012 WL 3871868 (6th Cir. 2012), it was foreseeable that the driver of a tractor-trailer being towed might be in the cab, and therefore might be in danger, at the time the tow truck started to move the rig. Consequently, the tractor-trailer driver's lack of care in exiting the cab when the towing commenced was not a superseding cause that absolved the tow truck operator and his employer from liability for negligent failure to take precautions.

Two Exceptions. There are two exceptions to the general rule that an intervening cause does not preclude a finding of proximate causation if either the new force or the end result is foreseeable. First, liability is superseded even if the intervening force is foreseeable, if the defendant's conduct in no way increases the risk of harm by the intervening force. Thus, a driver who negligently causes a traffic accident, which blocks the highway during an electrical storm, will not be liable to another whose car is struck by lightning while waiting for the road to be cleared, unless there is some basis for saying that the driver's conduct increased the likelihood that lightning would strike—which probably is not the case. This rule is consistent with the requirement in factual causation that the defendant's conduct must multiply the chances of harm to the plaintiff. (*See* Chapter 7.) Second, even if the ultimate harm is foreseeable, liability for antecedent tortious conduct is superseded by the intervention of unforeseeable criminal or intentionally tortious conduct.

Note

1. ***"Normal" Developments.*** In the context of intervening cause, the requirement of foreseeability often means nothing more than that the intervening force was a "normal" consequence of the defendant's conduct—"normal" not in the sense that it was usual or customary, but in the sense that it was not bizarre or extraordinary. *See* Restatement, Second, of Torts § 443 and Comment b.

Johnson v. Jacobs

Court of Appeals of Indiana
970 N.E.2d 666 (Ind. Ct. App. 2011)

BAKER, Judge.

Eric Johnson and his estranged wife, Beth, were in the midst of a divorce. Eric was taking flight lessons and in March 2007, he took Emily, their eight-year-old daughter, on a solo airplane flight in Lawrence County.... Eric crashed the plane into Vivian Pace's house, killing himself and Emily. Pace is Beth's mother....

Beth sued the Lawrence County ... [Aviation Board], Eric's Flight Instructor, Tony Newbold, and the Lawrence County Commissioners (collectively, the appellees) seeking damages for Emily's wrongful death. Summary judgment was entered for all defendants....

As part of an agreement that permitted Eric to take Emily on that vacation, Eric was supposed to take Emily to school on March 5, 2007....

Rather than taking Emily to school, Eric went to Grissom Airport at approximately 8:45 a.m. and retrieved from Lance Jacobs, an airport employee, some keys for one of the airplanes. Eric arrived at the airport building alone, and Jacobs recognized Eric from a photograph on the wall, demonstrating that Eric was Newbold's student. Jacobs knew that it was routine policy for student pilots to retrieve the keys to the hangar, pull out the airplane, and wait for the instructor to join them.

.... At approximately 9:00 a.m., Eric took off in a Cessna Airplane with Emily as his passenger....

.... Approximately one hour and fifteen minutes into the flight, Beth answered Eric's third telephone call. Eric was angry and yelling and cursing during the conversation with Beth....

.... At approximately 10:35 a.m., Ryan Patterson ... saw the plane that Eric was flying. Although Patterson thought that the plane was going to land on one of the runways, it had the wind at its tail, which was contrary to the protocol for landing planes at Grissom. Patterson also noted that the Cessna's landing flaps were not down. Patterson then saw the Cessna fly at a 45 degree angle toward the ground and believed that the Cessna had crashed.

... Greg Rollins—a private pilot with nearly 250 hours of flight experience—was also watching from his driveway.... Rollins noticed that the plane's flaps were not in the correct landing position. Rollins then heard the Cessna's engine throttle increase approximately 500 feet past his house. Rollins observed the Cessna bank "hard left and nose down." .... Although Rollins lost sight of the aircraft, he heard the impact.... The NTSC investigated the crash and issued a report that suicide was the probable cause of the crash.

... Johnson filed an action for wrongful death against the Aviation Board, and several of its members, and the Lawrence County Commissioners. The Complaint alleged that the appellees were liable for Emily's death because ... [the defendants knew or should have known that Eric Johnson was a student pilot, that as a student pilot he was not qualified and was not certified to start, to taxi, or to control an aircraft without a certified flight instructor being aboard at all times, and that he was not qualified and not certified to take a passenger on board while he was piloting an airplane].

... [T]he trial court concluded that Johnson's conduct was a superseding intervening cause that broke the chain of causation.

....

Beth argues that the trial court erred in granting the appellees' motions for summary judgment because the trial court erroneously concluded that Eric committed suicide and murdered Emily. Instead, Beth argues that there is a genuine issue of material fact because the designated evidence also supports the reasonable inference that the "aircraft crash that killed Emily ... and her father was simply a tragic accident." ....

[The court reviewed the evidence and concluded] ... that Eric's intentional criminal actions triggered the intervening, superseding cause doctrine and broke the causal chain between the Aviation Board's alleged negligence and Emily's death....

... Beth argues that even if Eric's acts were intentional, the trial court improperly granted summary judgment ... because it should have been found that Eric's intentional misuse of the airplane was a foreseeable consequence of Grissom's nonexistent security procedures. More particularly, Beth maintains that it was foreseeable that an unauthorized individual could have taken the airplane and flown off in it. Beth asserts that had proper security measures been in place at Grissom and had the airplane been secured, the tragedy could have been prevented. In general, reasonably foreseeable intervening acts do not break the chain of causation, and the original wrongful act can still be deemed the proximate cause of the injury....

In support of her foreseeability claim, Beth relies on Estate of Heck ex rel. Heck v. Stoffer, 786 N.E.2d 265 (Ind. 2003).[3] In *Heck*, a police officer was murdered by the

---

3. Editors' Note: In Goodwin v. Yeakle's Sports Bar and Grill, Inc., 62 N.E.3d 384, 392 (Ind. 2016), the Supreme Court of Indiana disapproved of *Estate of Heck*, stating:

> [B]ecause almost any outcome is possible and can be foreseen, the mere fact that a particular outcome is "sufficiently likely" is not enough to give rise to a duty. Instead, for purposes of determining whether an act is foreseeable in the context of duty we assess

fugitive felon son of the defendant parents. The son used his parents' loaded firearm that he had taken without their permission or knowledge. . . . The decedent police officer's estate brought a negligence claim against the parents. Discovery revealed that the son, over a nine-year period, was charged or convicted of three instances of resisting law enforcement, two instances of battery, burglary, theft, drug possession, multiple counts of forgery and check deception, escape, non-support and contempt. Moreover, the son had stolen from his parents on numerous occasions, but they still permitted him to keep a key to their house.

Just before the shooting, the father told the police that he knew his son was consumed by a desperate frame of mind because the son knew that the police were looking for him, but the son did not want to be captured. Moreover, the father testified that his son had a "death wish." . . . . Despite all of this, the parents stored their gun between the cushions of a chair in their bedroom, where their son could easily find it. . . .

The parents moved for summary judgment, based on: 1) lack of duty to the deceased police officer; and 2) no proximate cause based on the superseding criminal act of their son. The trial court granted summary judgment and we affirmed. . . .

Our Supreme Court granted transfer and reversed on both grounds. First, it was determined that a gun owner does owe a duty of care to the public generally and under the facts at issue. Thus, a jury question existed as to whether or not the parents breached their duty of care through their method of storing the firearm. . . .

Second, it was determined that because the officer's murder was a natural probable and foreseeable consequence of the defendants' act of leaving a loaded firearm in a location that was accessible to their son — a desperate fugitive from justice — the son's criminal act did not constitute a superseding cause. . . .

The "foreseeability" issue here, of course, concerns Emily's death. More specifically, the question is whether the appellees should have foreseen that Eric would permit Emily to board as his passenger when he knew that he was not yet authorized to carry a passenger, take off from the airport, and intentionally crash into his mother-in-law's residence.

As noted above, Eric was not some unknown, unauthorized person who gained access to the airplane in question on the date of the incident. To the contrary, Eric was known to those who were operating the airport, including Jacobs, the airport employee, who gave the airplane's keys to Eric on the date of the incident because he had a scheduled flying lesson on the airport calendar. Jacobs did not think that Eric was acting strangely when he saw him at the airport that day, and there was nothing out of the ordinary about a student pilot obtaining the keys to an airplane and taxiing it out to the runway before a scheduled flying lesson. . . . None of the employees

---

"whether there is some probability or likelihood of harm that is serious enough to induce a reasonable person to take precautions to avoid it."

saw Emily on the day of the flight and Eric gave no indication to anyone that he was taking a passenger with him. . . .

In short, unlike the circumstances in *Heck*, nothing in the record suggests that the appellees should have foreseen that Eric would use the rented airplane to commit murder and suicide. Put another way, the designated evidence fails to establish that Eric's murder of Emily by intentionally crashing the airplane was a natural, probable, and foreseeable consequence of the appellees' purported violation of a duty to properly secure the airplane.

. . . .

The judgment of the trial court is affirmed.

Notes

1. ***Unforeseeable Criminal or Intentionally Tortious Acts.*** *Unforeseeable* criminal or intentionally tortious conduct precludes a finding of proximate causation, even though the plaintiff's injuries are of a type that were, or could have been, anticipated. According to Comment c to § 442B of the Restatement, Second, of Torts:

> The reason usually given by the courts is that in such a case the third person has deliberately assumed control of the situation, and all responsibility for the consequences of his act is shifted to him.

From a different perspective, one might say that intentionally tortious or criminal conduct so differs in degree, if not in kind, from other types of intervening forces that it is unfair to hold the original actor responsible. Without this exception to the general rule, there would be a very substantial risk of imposing liability disproportionate to fault. *See generally* Restatement, Third, of Torts: Liab. for Physical and Emotional Harm § 34 cmt. e (2010) (discussing unforeseeable, unusual, or highly culpable intervening acts).

In Gaines-Tabb v. ICI Explosive USA, Inc., 160 F.3d 613 (10th Cir. 1998), victims of a terrorist bombing brought a class action against the manufacturer of ammonium nitrate that was sold as fertilizer and was allegedly used to construct a bomb that destroyed a federal building in Oklahoma City. The court found that the terrorist's act was a superseding cause precluding negligence liability on the part of the manufacturer.

See also Roach v. Dental Arts Lab., Inc., 79 S.W.3d 265 (Tex. App. 2002) (borrower's act of loaning out a borrowed car in exchange for crack cocaine was unforeseeable and therefore a superseding cause precluding a claim against the owner of the car on a negligent entrustment theory); Spears v. Coffee, 153 S.W.3d 103 (Tex. App. 2004) (holding that a violent attack by one minor house guest on another was so unforeseeable that the owners of the house could not be liable for allegedly negligent failure to protect the injured guest from harm).

2. ***Foreseeable Criminal or Intentionally Tortious Acts.*** A *foreseeable* criminal or intentionally tortious intervening act ordinarily does not preclude a finding

of proximate causation. *See* Herrera v. Quality Pontiac, 73 P.3d 181 (N.M. 2003) (a jury could find that harm was proximately caused where "[d]efendant, leaving the car unlocked, unattended, and with the key in the ignition, could have reasonably foreseen ... intervening theft of the vehicle ... and negligent operation of it"); Haselhorst v. State, 485 N.W.2d 180 (Neb. 1992) (criminal acts of sexual abuse by a foster child were not a superseding cause because the likelihood of that behavior was what made the defendant's conduct negligent).

In Nixon v. Mr. Property Mgmt. Co., Inc., 690 S.W.2d 546 (Tex. 1985), a young girl was abducted, taken across the street into an abandoned, dilapidated apartment complex, and raped. In an action against the complex, based on its negligent failure to comply with a city ordinance regarding maintenance of buildings, the court held that the criminal acts of the abductor did not prevent a finding of proximate causation. During the prior two years, 34 crimes had been committed in the apartments. Although there had been no rapes, there had been crimes involving violent harm to persons, and thus it was foreseeable that another crime of violence might occur. It was important to the *Nixon* court that there was evidence that the abductor proceeded directly to the vacant building. If the building had been used as a place for the crime only as a last resort after other plans had failed, the case might have turned out differently, for it would have been difficult to establish that the dilapidation of the vacant building (*i.e.*, the alleged negligence of the defendant) substantially increased the chance that someone would be raped.

In Carsanaro v. Colvin, 716 S.E.2d 40 (N.C. App. 2011), a husband sued his wife's paramour for negligent infliction of a sexually transmitted disease. In refusing to dismiss the claim, the court wrote:

> Defendant [paramour] contends that since plaintiff [husband] was actually infected with herpes by Mrs. Carsanaro [wife], it was she, and not defendant, who was the proximate cause of plaintiff's injury....
>
> Where a second actor has become aware of the existence of a potential danger created by the negligence of an original tortfeasor, and thereafter, by an independent act of negligence, brings about an accident, the first tortfeasor is relieved of liability, because the condition created by him was merely a circumstance of the accident and not its proximate cause....
>
> In the instant case, Mrs. Carsanaro would only become an intervening cause of plaintiff's herpes infection if she knew or had reason to know that she herself was infected with herpes when she engaged in sexual intercourse with plaintiff.... Plaintiff's complaint is silent as to when Mrs. Carsanaro discovered that defendant had infected her with herpes; therefore, dismissal on this basis ... is not appropriate....

3. ***Efforts to Escape Injury.*** A tortfeasor may be liable for injuries sustained by another in an effort to escape threatened harm, if such measures are based on a well-grounded belief that harm will otherwise occur. *See* Palmer v. Warren St. Ry. Co.,

56 A. 49 (Pa. 1903) (leap from path of vehicle); Lehner v. Pittsburgh Rys. Co., 72 A. 525 (Pa. 1909) (jump from careening street car).

4. ***Conditions Versus Causes.*** Courts have sometimes endeavored to draw a distinction between actionable "causes" and nonactionable "conditions." For example, in Lear Siegler, Inc. v. Perez, 819 S.W.2d 470, 472 (Tex. 1991), the court held that legal cause is not established if the defendant's conduct or product does no more than furnish the condition that makes the plaintiff's injury possible. *See* Bonham v. Texas Dept. of Crim. Justice, 101 S.W.3d 153 (Tex. App. 2003) (holding that a correctional facility's layout was not a proximate cause of a guard's sexual assault of an inmate because "it was, at most, a condition that made the guard's intervening intentional act possible"); *but see* Homeland Express L.L.C., v. Seale, 2012 WL 5354016 (Tex. App.) (holding that where there was evidence that the defendant's tractor trailer was not pulled completely within the shoulder of the highway, and as a result protruded into the right-hand lane, and that the driver failed to place reflective warning devices behind the rig, the defendant's negligence was a substantial cause, not merely a condition, of the resulting accident). The condition-versus-cause distinction has been rejected by most courts.

3. Special Applications of the Rules on Intervening and Superseding Causes

a. Rescuers

The rules governing intervening and superseding causes find frequent application in cases involving rescuers. To deal with these cases, a special body of rules—the "rescue doctrine"—has emerged.

Altamuro v. Milner Hotel, Inc.

United States District Court for the Eastern District of Pennsylvania
540 F. Supp. 870 (E.D. Pa. 1982)

McGLYNN, District Judge.

This is a diversity case brought by Doris E. Altamuro, administratrix of the estate of her husband, Joseph S. Altamuro, against the defendant, Milner Hotel, Inc. ("Hotel"), for damages for the death of her husband resulting from the inhalation of fumes and carbon monoxide while attempting to rescue residents of the Hotel during a three-alarm fire....

Plaintiff's case against the defendant, Milner Hotel, is based principally on the "rescue doctrine"....

Perhaps the most quoted articulation of this doctrine was that by then New York Court of Appeals [Judge] Cardozo:

> Danger invites rescue. The cry of distress is the summons to relief. The law does not ignore these reactions of the mind in tracing conduct to its

> consequences. It recognizes them as normal. It places their effects within the range of the natural and probable. The wrong that imperils life is a wrong to the imperiled victim; it is a wrong also to his rescuer. The state that leaves an opening in a bridge is liable to the child that falls into the stream, but liable also to the parent who plunges to its aid. . . . The risk of rescue, if only it not be wanton, is born of the occasion. The emergency begets the man. The wrongdoer may not have foreseen the coming of the deliverer. He is accountable as if he had. . . .

Wagner v. International Railway Co., 232 N.Y. 176, 180, 133 N.E. 437, 438 (1921). Twenty-one years earlier, the Pennsylvania Supreme Court stated:

> A rescuer—one who, from the most unselfish motives, prompted by the noblest impulses that can impel man to deeds of heroism, faces deadly peril—ought not to hear from the law words of condemnation of his bravery, because he rushed into danger, to snatch from it the life of a fellow creature imperiled by the negligence of another; but he should rather listen to words of approval, unless regretfully withheld on account of the unmistakable evidence of his rashness and imprudence.
>
> . . . . The law has so high a regard for human life, that it will not impute negligence to an effort to preserve it, unless made under such circumstances as to constitute rashness in the judgment of prudent persons. . . . One who imperils his own life for the sake of rescuing another from imminent danger is not chargeable, as a matter of law, with contributory negligence; and, if the life of the rescued person was endangered by the defendant's negligence, the rescuer may recover for the injuries which he suffered from the defendant in consequence of his intervention.

Corbin v. City of Philadelphia, 195 Pa. 461, 468–472, 45 A. 1070, 1072–1074 (1900). . . . In applying the rescue doctrine, I must first determine the negligence *vel non* of the Milner Hotel.

. . . .

Here, the fire at The Milner Hotel . . . originated in the defective television set in Room 706. The defective condition of the television was known to the Hotel through its employee, Jennings, who nevertheless left the set plugged in, unattended and with the power switch in the "on" position. . . . [G]iven the substantial risk of fire . . . , Jennings' conduct clearly amounted to negligence and his negligence was a substantial factor in placing the lives of the Hotel guests in peril. . . . Of course, Jennings' negligence is imputed to his employer under the doctrine of *respondeat superior*. . . .

That a fire in a ten-story hotel presents an imminent danger to the residents cannot be gainsaid. . . .

Defendant Hotel argues that since Altamuro's death occurred after the firemen ordered all civilians out of the Hotel and because it can be inferred from the evidence that the deceased heard the command by his conduct in immediately leaving the Hotel, then his final rescue effort was so unreasonable as to preclude recovery by his administratrix. The test . . . is whether the rescuer "acted with due regard for his own safety, or so rashly and imprudently" as to bar recovery. . . . "[W]here another is in great and imminent danger, he who attempts a rescue may be warranted, by surrounding circumstances, in exposing his limbs or life to a very high degree of danger. In such a case, he should not be charged with the consequences of errors of judgments resulting from the excitement and confusion of the moment". . . . Thus the standard of care for a rescuer is not to act rashly or imprudently.

In any event, Pennsylvania has abolished the defense of contributory negligence and has replaced it with comparative negligence. . . . [T]he instant case clearly falls within the literal language of Act, which states that the Act is to be applied to "*all actions* brought to recover damages for negligence resulting in death or injury to person or property. . . ." . . . . Courts in other jurisdictions have applied their comparative negligence schemes in similar circumstances, holding that if "the trier of fact finds that the rescue is unreasonable or unreasonably carried out the factfinder should then make a comparison of negligence between the rescuer and the one whose negligence created the situation to which the rescue was a response." . . . . While I believe Pennsylvania courts would reach a similar result, it is not necessary for me to decide the issue because I find that Altamuro did not act rashly, imprudently or so unreasonably as to constitute negligence on his part under the rescue doctrine.

There is no dispute that during the initial phase of the fire, Altamuro busied himself warning guests at the Hotel of the fire, and later he assisted Officer Markowski in helping people out of the building. The last time Altamuro was seen alive was when he left the Hotel after the firemen ordered all civilians out of the building. There was no evidence as to how Altamuro got back into the building. What prompted his return can only be surmised but, having been successful in two prior missions to the upper floors of the Hotel, I am not convinced that it was unreasonable for him to conclude that he could successfully complete another mission without unduly imperiling his own safety even though he disobeyed the order of the firemen by returning to the building.

. . . . Plaintiff is entitled to judgment in her favor and against defendant The Milner Hotel, Inc. in the amount of $396,373.

. . . .

Notes

1. ***Policy Basis of the Rescue Doctrine.*** The law encourages persons to render aid in emergencies. It does this by modifying the usual tort rules so that a rescuer will be less readily held liable for mistakes and more readily able to recover for injuries sustained in the rescue efforts.

2. ***Scope of the Rescue Doctrine.*** Although rescue cases typically involve three different actors — the person who creates the peril, the endangered victim, and the

rescuer—the doctrine sometimes applies to situations where the victim has been endangered by personal lack of care. *See* Provenzo v. Sam, 244 N.E.2d 26 (N.Y. 1968) (an intoxicated motorist was held liable to a rescuer who was struck by a passing car); *but see* Struempler v. Estate of Kloepping, 626 N.W.2d 564 (Neb. 2001) (refusing to apply the rescue doctrine to a two-party case where a neighbor injured her back while helping an elderly invalid who had fallen from his wheelchair).

3. ***Five Distinct Issues.*** The rescue doctrine is a matrix of rules which encompasses at least five distinct issues:

(a) ***Superseding Cause.*** Normal rescue efforts, even if negligent, do not break the chain of proximate causation. The initial tortfeasor is liable to the victim for injuries arising from the rescuer's normal rescue efforts. *See* Restatement, Third, of Torts: Liab. for Physical & Emotional Harm § 35 (2010). In contrast, abnormal rescue efforts which are so extraordinary as to be no longer a part of the risks inherent in the original wrongdoing are sufficient to constitute a superseding cause.

(b) ***Rescuer's Liability to the Victim and Good Samaritan Laws.*** A rescuer whose careless intervention injures the person in peril may be liable for that harm. However, the emergency nature of the circumstances will be taken into account in determining whether the rescuer was in fact negligent.

Some Good Samaritan statutes limit the liability of rescuers to cases of aggravated misconduct. *See, e.g.*, Alaska Stat. § 09.65.090(a) and (d) (Westlaw 2022) (permitting liability for gross negligence, recklessness, or intentional misconduct). The Texas statute, which has parallels in other states, provides:

Texas Civil Practice & Remedies Code § 74.151 (Westlaw 2022)

> (a) A person who in good faith administers emergency care is not liable in civil damages for an act performed during the emergency unless the act is wilfully or wantonly negligent. . . .
>
> (b) This section does not apply to care administered: . . . (2) by a person who was at the scene of the emergency because he or a person he represents as an agent was soliciting business or seeking to perform a service for remuneration. . . .
>
> (e) This section does not apply to a person whose negligent act or omission was a producing cause of the emergency for which care is being administered.

Other statutes go even further and provide that immunity extends to any acts undertaken simply in good faith. *See* Wis. Stat. Ann. § 895.48(1) (Westlaw 2022) (stating that "[a]ny person who renders emergency care at the scene of any emergency or accident in good faith shall be immune from civil liability for his or her acts or omissions in rendering such emergency care. This immunity does not extend when employees trained in health care or health care professionals render emergency care for compensation . . .").

Good Samaritan statutes are sometimes narrowly construed. *See* Mueller v. McMillan Warner Ins. Co., 704 N.W.2d 613 (Wis. App. 2005) ("[s]uggesting that a bloody and vomiting woman lie in a bed rather than on a floor, covering her with a quilt, leaving her alone in a dark room for six or more hours, and periodically asking if she felt all right does not . . . constitute emergency care").

In Van Horn v. Watson, 197 P.3d 164 (Cal. 2008), the court held that the term "emergency care" meant emergency *medical* care, and that a statute did not bar a claim for injuries that an accident victim sustained while being removed from her vehicle. Thereafter, "the Legislature amended the relevant statute to state explicitly that 'No person who in good faith, and not for compensation, renders emergency medical *or nonmedical care* at the scene of an emergency shall be liable for any civil damages resulting from any act or omission.'" Verdugo v. Target Corp., 327 P.3d 774, 783 (Cal. 2014) (emphasis added).

(c) ***Injuries Sustained by Rescuers as a Result of Rescue Efforts.*** As *Altamuro* indicates, one who places another in danger may also be held liable for injuries sustained by a rescuer. Thus, the duty of care owed by the tortfeasor to the victim extends to potential rescuers, and the policies underlying this rule normally cannot be frustrated by claims of lack of proximate causation. *See* Restatement, Third, of Torts: Liab. for Physical and Emotional Harm § 32 (2010); Leaders v. Dreher, 169 N.W.2d 570 (Iowa 1969) (injuries which plaintiff sustained while chasing defendant's sow off plaintiff's land were proximately caused).

(d) ***Defenses Based on the Rescuer's Conduct.*** *Altamuro* held that "the standard of care for a rescuer is not to act rashly or imprudently." As these imprecise terms suggest, there is uncertainty about when an injured rescuer's failure to exercise care will preclude or reduce recovery of damages by the rescuer. There appear to be three different approaches.

(1) Some courts hold that a rescuer who acts "rashly" or "recklessly" will be barred from reliance on the rescue doctrine. For example, in Zivojinovich v. Barner, 525 F.3d 1059, 1070 (11th Cir. 2008), the court wrote:

> Alex's effort to rescue his son consisted of trying to push past Deputy Stanford and cover Justin's body with his own. That happened after Deputy Knott had pointed a taser gun at Alex and told him not to interfere. Attempting to get between a law enforcement officer and an apparently noncompliant suspect is both reckless and rash. Alex's actions unreasonably escalated an already volatile situation, increasing the risk to everyone and making his rescue attempt counterproductive. We conclude that Alex cannot invoke the rescue doctrine. Without it he cannot make out a claim against [the defendant hotel and its employee who allegedly acted negligently in calling the police to have Justin removed from the premises.]

(2) Other courts hold that the rule about "rash" and "reckless conduct" means that rescuers are less likely to be found comparatively negligent. *See* Ouellette v.

Carde, 612 A.2d 687 (R.I. 1992) (holding that comparative principles apply only if the rescuer's actions were "rash and reckless").

(3) Other states essentially disregard references to "rash" and "reckless" as linguistic relics of an earlier pre-comparative era, and simply assess whether the rescuer was comparatively at fault by considering the nature of the emergency to which the rescuer was responding. *See* Rosell v. Cent. W. Motor Stages, Inc., 89 S.W.3d 643 (Tex. App. 2002) (finding that the jury was correctly instructed on emergency and that it was proper for the court to refuse to instruct the jury that the conduct of a rescuer is not negligent unless the rescuer acts rashly or recklessly); *see also* Tirpak v. Hutsell, 2008 WL 612227 (N.J. Super. Ct. A.D. 2008) (indicating that a "rescuer generally cannot be deemed negligent as the result of coming to the aid of the victim" and that "recovery is discounted only if the jury determines that he acted unreasonably during his rescue effort").

(e) ***Injuries to Rescuers Arising from Another's Negligence during the Rescue.*** Injuries to a rescuer may result from the negligent conduct of another that occurs after the rescue has begun. For example, a rescuer standing in the road to warn oncoming motorists of a fallen tree may be struck by a negligently driven car. In these actions, the rescue doctrine may be relevant if the doctrine is seen as enlarging the scope of actions which a rescuer may take without being barred from recovery by allegedly unreasonable conduct. *But see* Hutton v. Logan, 566 S.E.2d 782 (N.C. Ct. App. 2002) (holding that the rescue doctrine has no applicability to a third-party defendant who had nothing to do with the original peril).

4. ***Three Requirements of the Rescue Doctrine.*** For the rescue doctrine to apply, there must be (1) a risk of imminent peril to the person or (perhaps) property of another and (2) an act of intervention in response to the peril. In addition, if the action is against the creator of the peril, the plaintiff must (3) establish that the peril resulted from the creator's tortious conduct.

5. ***Apparent Imminent Peril.*** The standard for determining the imminence of the peril is an objective one. Peril need only be apparent, not actual. Thus, the Court of Appeals of New York has said:

> [T]o have been a reasonable course of conduct at the time, it is of no import that the danger was not as real as it appeared. . . . It is conceded that something more than a mere suspicion of danger to the life of another is requisite before the doctrine should be implemented.

Provenzo v. Sam, 244 N.E.2d 26 (N.Y. 1968).

The objective of the rescue doctrine is to dispel the would-be rescuer's doubts and tip the scales in favor of intervention when there is a need for prompt action. However, if harm is not imminent, the reason for the rule ceases, and the benefits of the doctrine will not be available. *See* Trapp v. Vess, 847 So. 2d 304 (Ala. 2002) (a passing motorist who helped to pull a car out of the ditch could not recover for his own injuries under the rescue doctrine because there was no imminent peril); Stevenson

v. Delahaye, 310 So. 2d 651 (La. Ct. App. 1975) (man injured while consoling accident victims after flares had been set and a crowd had gathered).

6. ***Intervention Versus Investigation.*** In Barnes v. Geiger, 446 N.E.2d 78 (Mass. App. Ct. 1983), the court held that the rescue doctrine does not extend to those who are injured while running to the scene of an accident to see what happened. The court wrote:

> Danger invites rescue; accidents invite onlookers. It is not reasonable that the rescue doctrine be extended to all who run to the scene of a calamity to see what happened and on the chance that they might be able to do some good.

In Lambert v. Parrish, 492 N.E.2d 289, 291 (Ind. 1986), the rescue doctrine was held inapplicable to the claim of a husband who, after being told that his wife had been injured a block away, slipped on a patch of ice and sustained back injuries while running to the crash site. The court said:

> [A] rescuer must in fact attempt to rescue someone.... [Husband's] only attempt was to reach the scene of the accident. He exerted no physical activity to facilitate the rescue of his wife from the consequences of the allegedly tortious act.

Until the would-be rescuer does something to distinguish himself from a curiosity-seeker, it is largely a matter of speculation whether assistance will be forthcoming. However, if there is good reason to believe that aid would have been given if the rescuer had reached the victim, the rescue doctrine should apply. Would it make sense to consider such factors as the "rescuer's" relationship to the victim, proximity to the peril, and contemporaneous observation of the developing crisis?

7. ***Peril Created by Tortious Conduct.*** A person will be held liable to a rescuer only if that person has engaged in tortious conduct. *See* Allen v. Albright, 43 S.W.3d 643 (Tex. App. 2001) (holding that a woman whose house was fire bombed was not liable to a rescuer even if the woman's decision to remain in a burning house and run from her rescuers contributed to the rescuer's injury).

8. ***Responding to a Peril of One's Own Making.*** Years ago, it was universally held that the benefits of the rescue doctrine could not be invoked by one whose negligence contributed to the creation of the peril. *See, e.g.*, Nelson v. Pendleton, 198 S.E.2d 593 (Va. 1973) (babysitter failed to secure door to basement stairs and later fell while trying to rescue a small child who had started down the steps). There is now precedent indicating that the rescuer's contribution to the creation of the peril will not necessarily bar reliance on the rescue doctrine, but will be taken into account in determining whether compensation is available under comparative principles. *See* Zimny v. Cooper-Jarrett, Inc., 513 A.2d 1235 (Conn. App. Ct. 1986).

9. ***Professional Rescuers.*** Ordinarily, the rescue doctrine does not apply to firefighters and other professional rescuers because they have a duty to rescue. See the discussion of the "firefighter's rule" in Chapter 16.

10. ***Problem: Triple Trouble.*** Years ago, a grocery store tabloid carried an article which read as follows:

> The 18th hole meant triple trouble for golfer Mike Megala. As he walked toward the tee at Seven Springs Golf Course in Pittsburgh, Pennsylvania, he was beaned by a stray ball.
>
> Then an ambulance taking him to nearby McKeesport Hospital was hit by a car.
>
> The car driver and two attendants were injured, so they joined Megala . . . in a second ambulance, but a few miles down the road, it was hit by another car.
>
> In all, seven people required medical treatment.

Is the golfer who hit the errant shot liable? To whom? For what?

b. Victim Suicide

Involuntary Suicide. The most dramatic example of an intervening act by the victim of tortious conduct is suicide. The early American common law dealt with such matters sternly, perhaps because of the puritanical sense of self-determination and rugged individualism that contributed to the shaping of many areas of the law. If the victim retained any capacity to know what he or she was doing, recovery for the death was denied. As explained in McGuire v. Almy, 8 N.E.2d 760, 762 (Mass. 1937):

> [T]he rule was laid down that where an accident causes insanity, and while insane the victim takes his own life, the causal connection between the accident and the death is broken by the voluntary act of the insane person, if he entertains the purpose of causing his death and understands the physical effect of his acts, *even though his mind is so far impaired that he can no longer form sound judgments or weigh the reasons which should induce him to refrain from the act*; but the causal connection is not broken if the act results from uncontrollable impulse, delirium or frenzy without conscious volition.

(Emphasis added.) Cases still hold that "suicide properly constitutes an independent intervening cause in most wrongful death actions" and bars recovery. MacDermid v. Discover Financial Services, 488 F.3d 721 (6th Cir. 2007) (denying recovery where a woman harassed by debt collectors committed suicide). Nevertheless, "employing superseding cause to bar a plaintiff's recovery based on the plaintiff's conduct is difficult to reconcile with modern notions of comparative responsibility." Restatement, Third, of Torts: Liab. for Physical & Emotional Harm § 34 cmt. c (2010).

Texas has a statutory provision dealing with suicide.

TEXAS CIVIL PRACTICE AND REMEDIES CODE (Westlaw 2022)

§ 93.001. *Assumption of the Risk: Affirmative Defense*

(a) It is an affirmative defense to a civil action for damages for personal injury or death that the plaintiff, at the time the cause of action arose, was:

. . . .

(2) committing or attempting to commit suicide, and the plaintiff's conduct in committing or attempting to commit suicide was the sole cause of the damages sustained; provided, however, if the suicide or attempted suicide was caused in whole or in part by a failure on the part of any defendant to comply with an applicable legal standard, then such suicide or attempted suicide shall not be a defense.

. . . .

(c) In an action to which this section applies, this section shall prevail over any other law.

Irresistible Suicide. Some decisions take a less-stringent position. They hold that even if the victim was conscious, life may have been made so physically and mentally painful that the victim may have been deprived of any real choice in the matter. These courts recognize that beyond a certain point it is unrealistic to expect the ordinary person to be heroic. One jurisdiction has articulated its position in terms of a type of irresistible-impulse test. In Fuller v. Preis, 322 N.E.2d 263 (N.Y. 1974), head injuries suffered as a result of the defendant's negligence caused the decedent to become constantly depressed, physically unsteady, unable to continue his practice of surgery, and subject to epileptic seizures that became progressively more frequent and severe. The court held that although suicide notes demonstrated that the decedent, who took his own life, "obviously knew what he was doing and intended to do what he did," the pivotal issue was whether, because of mental derangement, he was "incapable of resisting the impulse to destroy himself." Finding that there was evidence to support a determination of irresistible impulse, the court affirmed the judgment for the decedent's estate.

Unforeseeable Suicide. If the risk of suicide is unforeseeable, it will almost certainly prevent a finding that the death was proximately caused by the negligence of another. *See* Johnstone v. City of Albuquerque, 145 P.3d 76 (N.M. App. 2006) (finding that a teenager's act of committing suicide was an independent intervening cause which relieved her stepfather of any liability for alleged negligence in not safeguarding a gun); Perez v. Lopez, 74 S.W.3d 60 (Tex. App. 2002) (child did not do or say anything that would have led locksmiths to believe that the child was suicidal when they removed a trigger lock on a rifle and returned the rifle to the child).

Suicide and the Special Relationship Exception. In City of Richmond Hill v. Maia, 301 Ga. 257 (Ga. 2017), the court explained that the general rule that suicide breaks the causal connection between an alleged negligent act and the resulting death is subject to a special relationship exception. The exception may arise in cases involving a doctor-patient or hospital-patient relationship, or between a police officer or jailer and a detainee or prisoner, because a duty to protect arises under such circumstances. These types of special relationships are discussed in Chapter 9. *But see* Providence Health Center v. Dowell, 262 S.W.3d 324 (Tex. 2008) (holding that the allegedly negligent discharge of a patient who had attempted suicide was not a proximate cause of the patient's death by suicide 33 hours later).

Attorneys and Suicide by Clients. In McPeake v. William T. Cannon, Esq., P.C., 553 A.2d 439 (Pa. Super. Ct. 1989), an attorney was allegedly negligent in representing a client who was charged with burglary, rape, indecent assault, and corrupting the morals of a minor. When a guilty verdict was returned at the trial, the client jumped from the fifth floor of the courthouse. The suicide was foreseeable because the client had threatened to kill himself if he was found guilty, but the attorney was not held liable for the death. The court reasoned that an attorney is not required to protect a client against suicidal tendencies because lawyers have no ability to identify or treat that kind of problem. Moreover, to impose a risk of liability would discourage attorneys from representing "a sizeable number of depressed or unstable criminal defendants," and would therefore defeat the important goal of making legal counsel available to those who need it.

Suicide in Jail. Is it foreseeable that a prison inmate will commit suicide? Empirical evidence shows that suicide among inmates is many times more likely than among the general population, particularly during the early days of confinement. However, courts sometimes go to great lengths to hold that prisons are not liable for suicides committed by prisoners. *See* Jutzi-Johnson v. United States, 263 F.3d 753 (7th Cir. 2001).

Encouraged or Provoked Suicide. The wisdom of some decisions relating to suicide is open to question. In Doe v. Doe, 67 N.E.3d 520, 525 (Ill. App. 2016), the court stood by the general rule that there is no liability for another's deliberate suicide, even though a minor male defendant had allegedly encouraged a minor social media user to take her own life. In City of Richmond Hill v. Maia, 800 S.E.2d 573, 576-79 (Ga. 2017):

> Appellee's daughter, Sydney Sanders, attempted suicide by cutting herself in the neck, chest, and abdomen, and she was subsequently taken to the hospital for medical treatment. Officers with the Richmond Hill Police Department . . . , including Officer Douglas Sahlberg, responded to the hospital to investigate, and Sanders's injuries were photographed by the officers. Later that month, Sahlberg accessed those photographs on his work computer and showed them to his daughter, K.S., who was a classmate of Sanders; shortly thereafter, K.S. was seen using her cell phone to show the images to other classmates, and Sanders was distraught and mortified to discover that the photographs had been shared.

Sanders later committed suicide. In a subsequent unsuccessful tort action against the city, the court wrote:

> At the time of the alleged negligent conduct [namely, disclosing the photographs] and at the time of the subsequent suicide, Sahlberg had no ability to supervise Sanders, to make decisions about her healthcare, or to exercise custody or control over her. . . . As such, the special-relationship exception does not apply here. Likewise, neither Sanders's continued distress regarding the disclosure of the photos nor her subsequent "rampage"

> wherein she ranted to her softball coach about the various stressors in her life, is sufficient to evidence that Sanders killed herself during a rage or frenzy, or in response to an uncontrollable impulse..... In fact, the record indicates that Sanders's final conversation with her mother was calm and rational. Accordingly, this exception does not apply.

Intentional Torts, Sexual Assault, and Victim Suicide. In Rondini v. Bunn, 2021 WL 1939171, at *4 (Ala.), the Supreme Court of Alabama held that "[w]hen a person commits suicide after an alleged sexual assault, that act does not as a matter of law break the chain of causation so as to absolve the alleged assailant of liability." As the court explained:

> We have previously recognized that intentional-tort claims are different from negligence (or wantonness) claims because, in intentional-tort cases, the tortfeasor specifically intended to cause injury to the victim.... And traditional negligence concepts like foreseeability and proximate cause, which form the backbone of the negligence analysis ... have a more limited application in intentional-tort cases.... *See* ... W. Page Keeton *et al.*, Prosser and Keeton on the Law of Torts § 9 at 40 (5th ed. 1984) (explaining that in most cases involving intentional torts "[t]he defendant's liability for the resulting harm extends ... to consequences which the defendant did not intend, and could not reasonably have foreseen, upon the obvious basis that it is better for unexpected losses to fall upon the intentional wrongdoer than upon the innocent victim" (footnote omitted)).
>
> Alabama law is not unique in this respect....
>
> We ... now hold that a wrongful-death action may be pursued against a defendant when there is substantial evidence both that the defendant sexually assaulted the decedent and that the assault was a cause in fact of the decedent's later suicide. In such cases, it is unnecessary to analyze whether the decedent's suicide was a foreseeable consequence of the sexual assault; liability may attach without regard to whether the defendant intended or could have reasonably foreseen that result....
>
> It is unnecessary for us to define today the universe of intentional torts that might appropriately give rise to a wrongful-death action based on a suicide.... Whether other intentional torts stemming from a defendant's extreme and outrageous conduct that causes severe emotional distress to the victim might also support a wrongful-death action after a suicide is a question for another day.

4. Relationship to Comparative Principles

Like many now-abrogated common-law principles — for example, the 100% bar of contributory negligence, the 100% bar of implied assumption of the risk, and the total exception to contributory negligence called "last clear chance" (*see* Chapter 16) — the rule on superseding causation is an all-or-nothing determination, which, if satisfied, totally overlooks the negligence of one of the parties to an accident. The question arises as to whether the adoption of comparative principles requires the abandonment of the superseding causation rules. "[T]he need for aggressive use of superseding cause to absolve a tortfeasor from liability has subsided in light of the modification of joint and several liability [see Chapter 17] and of the trend [in a minority of states] toward permitting comparative responsibility to be apportioned among negligent and intentional tortfeasors." Restatement, Third, of Torts: Liab. for Physical and Emotional Harm § 34 cmt. c (2010).

Superseding Causation Survives. In Exxon v. Sofec, Inc., 517 U.S. 830 (1996), the Supreme Court held that the proximate causation requirement, and related superseding-cause doctrine, are applicable in admiralty, notwithstanding the Court's adoption of the comparative-fault principle. Similarly, in Control Techniques, Inc. v. Johnson, 762 N.E.2d 104 (Ind. 2002), the court found that the adoption of comparative fault did not abolish the doctrine of superseding causation.

Superseding Causation Abrogated. In Barry v. Quality Products, Inc., 820 A.2d 258 (Conn. 2003), the court unanimously abandoned the superseding cause doctrine—in a limited range of cases:

> [T]he doctrine of superseding cause no longer serves a useful purpose in our jurisprudence when a defendant claims that a subsequent negligent act by a third party cuts off its own liability for the plaintiff's injuries. . . . [B]ecause our statutes allow for apportionment among negligent defendants . . . and because Connecticut is a comparative negligence jurisdiction . . . the simpler and less confusing approach to cases . . . where the jury must determine which, among many, causes contributed to the plaintiffs' injury, is to couch the analysis in proximate cause rather than allowing the defendants to raise a defense of superseding cause.
>
> . . . [I]t is inconsistent to conclude simultaneously that all negligent parties should pay in proportion to their fault, as § 52-572h requires, but that one negligent party does not have to pay its share because its negligence was somehow "superseded" by a subsequent negligent act. . . .

The *Barry* decision is limited in scope. The court noted that:

> Our conclusion does not necessarily affect those cases where the defendant claims that an unforeseeable intentional tort, force of nature, or criminal event supersedes its tortious conduct.

F. Shifting Responsibility

One way to talk about proximate causation is to say that the defendant's conduct is not a proximate cause because the duty to prevent harm, from a certain point forward, shifted from the defendant to some other person.

Relevant Factors. Among the many factors relevant to the issue of whether there has been a shift of responsibility from the defendant to a third person are:

- the existence of a contract between the defendant and the third person purporting to define their obligations;
- the magnitude of the threatened harm;
- the character and position of the third person and that person's ability to take remedial action;
- the likelihood that the third person will act to prevent that harm, including such considerations as expense, inconvenience, and exposure to, or immunity from, legal liability;
- the third person's relationship to the plaintiff; and
- the lapse of time.

See generally Restatement, Second, of Torts § 452 and comments.

General Rule: Omissions by Another are Not a Superseding Cause. A third party's omission is not ordinarily viewed as a superseding cause. *See* Restatement, Second, of Torts § 452. Thus, *X*'s failure to stop and render aid to an auto accident victim will not limit a negligent hit-and-run driver's liability to the victim. This is true even if *X* could have acted without personal risk or inconvenience, and even if *X*'s conduct violates a statutory duty to stop and render aid. *Id.*, illus. 4.

See Osborne v. U.S., 166 F. Supp. 2d 479 (S.D. W. Va. 2001) (the failure of an auto parts store employee to notify authorities of a driver's impaired condition and of a police officer to arrest the driver were not intervening causes that absolved a physician of liability relating to negligent prescription of addictive medications); NKC Hosps., Inc. v. Anthony, 849 S.W.2d 564 (Ky. Ct. App. 1993) (the negligence of a primary care physician in failing to diagnose a ruptured appendix after a patient was readmitted to the hospital was not a superseding cause relieving the hospital from liability for its negligence in connection with the patient's prior admission and discharge); Nat'l Health Labs. v. Ahmadi, 596 A.2d 555 (D.C. 1991) (negligent failure to discover a medical test error was not necessarily unforeseeable or extraordinary, and therefore it was not a superseding cause as a matter of law).

In limited circumstances, however, the burden of preventing harm to the plaintiff may "shift" from an antecedent tortfeasor to a third person. In these cases, the third person's failure to prevent the harm is a superseding cause which relieves the original tortfeasor of liability for any harm incurred subsequent to the shifting of the responsibility.

Goar v. Village of Stephen

Supreme Court of Minnesota
196 N.W. 171 (Minn. 1923)

STONE, J.

Action for personal injuries caused by electrical burns, wherein plaintiff had a verdict against both defendants, the Village of Stephen, a municipal corporation, and Minnesota Electric Distributing Company. . . .

Each defendant moved separately in the alternative for judgment notwithstanding the verdict or a new trial. The motions were denied upon condition that plaintiff consent to a reduction of the $12,500 verdict to $8,500. She so consented but both defendants have appealed.

While in her own home in Stephen, plaintiff was injured on August 10, 1922, by a high voltage current, for the escape of which, from its proper conductors into the Goar dwelling, one or both of the defendants is responsible. For convenience, we refer to the parties as plaintiff, the Village and the Company.

[The Company, as an independent contractor, undertook to reconstruct an electricity distribution system for the Village. The contract provided in part: "The contractor shall guarantee all apparatus and appliances . . . to be free from defects of any kind for a period of one year from date of acceptance, and shall make all repairs . . . free of charge." As part of the reconstruction, the company installed a transformer pole, with a complicated arrangement of wires, near plaintiff's home. Two of the wires were negligently placed too close together and, as a result of "the more or less constant but sometimes none too gentle breezes that play over the Red River Valley," the wires eventually wore through. Approximately seventeen and one-half months after completion of the reconstruction by the company, and the acceptance of the work by the Village, a 2,300 volt current was sent into the Goar residence, severely injuring the plaintiff. On appeal, the Minnesota Supreme Court found the evidence of the village's negligent failure to inspect and maintain adequate to support liability.]

. . . .

It does not follow, however, that the Company is liable, even though it was negligent in the manner indicated. That initial negligence was followed by the serious and wrongful inaction of the Village. Before the verdict against the Company can be sustained, we must resolve against it the question as to whether the negligence of the Village was a new agency severing causal connection between the Company's negligence and plaintiff's hurt; or whether, on the other hand, such negligence simply concurred with that of the Company so as to charge both defendants.

. . . .

In such a case, the contractor has a right to rely upon the owner's assuming, immediately upon his acceptance of the work, the duty of inspection and maintenance, which confessedly was not performed here. If it had been, the plaintiff would not have been injured for the fact that the original clearance was lessening and growing dangerous would have been discovered before the insulation was worn through. It took a year and a half of neglect, and the consequent freedom of the elements to work their will, before any injury resulted.

Not only was the Village in exclusive control, and, in consequence, the only agency upon which rested the burden of inspection and maintenance, but the Company was deprived, upon its delivery of the plant to the Village, of the opportunity and means of protecting the property from deterioration, and itself from resulting liability.

While the law of contract does not help us, the presence in the case of the contract is a fact to which proper reference may be made, and which may be given its appropriate place with the other facts. One of the facts established by the contract is that the Village, by the guaranty clause, assumed the duty, as between the two, of notifying the Company of any defect in the plant which it could be required to make good. As between the defendants, then, the Company has a much better standing than the Village. They could, by contract, adjust their reciprocal duties to suit themselves. The duty so allocated to the Village was not performed. As against the Company, it has no complaint, because, it must be assumed, had the decreasing clearance between the two wires been called to the Company's attention, the condition would have been rectified.

How serious and long continued must such obvious neglect be in order to become an independent cause of injury? Is there no limit of time beyond which a contractor will cease to be liable, with the owner, for an injury which could not have happened but for the negligence of the latter?

If the Company is liable in this case, there is no rule of law which would prevent the same result were the accident to occur ten years later. . . .

Our examination of the problem and the authorities . . . leads us to the conclusion, and we so hold, as a matter of law, that, under the circumstances of this case, the negligence of the Village was an independent producing agency of such character, that it broke the causal connection between the negligence of the Company and plaintiff's injury, and thereby became the proximate cause of the latter.

. . . [W]here there has been such a lapse of time as we have here, and there is a duty, clear and affirmative, on the part of the purchaser, to inspect and maintain as against that sure deterioration which is bound to follow from ordinary use, and a complete failure of the performance of duty, but for which the accident could not have happened, such failure becomes the proximate and not merely a concurring cause.

. . . .

On the appeal of the Village there must be an affirmance, and on that of the Company, a reversal. . . .

So ordered.

Notes

1. ***Responsibility Shifted.*** *See* Kent v. Commonwealth, 771 N.E.2d 770 (Mass. 2002) (holding that a board's decision to parole an inmate pursuant to an INS deportation warrant shifted the duty to prevent harm to the INS, which could lawfully be relied on to safely perform the responsibilities it had assumed); Braun v. New Hope Twp., 646 N.W.2d 737 (S.D. 2002) (holding that the lapse of time, the independent statutory duty of a township to erect guards and maintain appropriate signs warning of washouts, and the affirmative performance of that duty in an allegedly negligent manner were superseding causes that relieved farmers of their liability for breaking the warning sign, and thus liability for a motorist's injuries shifted to the township).

2. ***Ethics in Law Practice: Successor Counsel and Shifting Responsibility.*** If one attorney is discharged or withdraws and another attorney is engaged to represent a client, the duty to exercise care to protect the client shifts to the successor counsel. The substitution of counsel may also relieve the first lawyer of liability for earlier negligence *if* the second lawyer has the opportunity to protect the client's interests. *See* Ramcharan v. Pariser, 799 N.Y.S.2d 564 (App. Div. 2005) (holding that because successor counsel had sufficient time to comply with a demand to resume prosecution before a 90-day period expired, predecessor counsel could not be held liable for any damages to the client resulting from their failure to do so).

However, in some cases, the negligence of the first lawyer may still pose a continuing risk of harm, even though a second lawyer has been hired. That may be true if, because of the shortness of time, the second lawyer has no real opportunity to file suit before the statute of limitations lapses. In that case, fairness may require the law to hold that mere engagement of a second attorney does not cut off the first lawyer's liability.

Moreover, the mere possibility that someone else could have averted threatened harm is generally insufficient to relieve an antecedent tortfeasor of liability. In Lopez v. Clifford Law Offices, P.C., 841 N.E.2d 465 (Ill. Ct. App. 2005), the court held that the "client's" meeting with the second attorney who declined to take the case was not a superseding cause as a matter of law, and that a jury should decide, as a matter of fact, whether the negligence of the initial attorney, who misstated the statute of limitations in his withdrawal letter, was a proximate cause of the untimely filing of the suit.

Bailey v. Lewis Farm, Inc.

Supreme Court of Oregon
171 P.3d 336 (Or. 2007)

KISTLER, J.

The axle failed on a used tractor-trailer that May Trucking Company (defendant) had sold to another entity [Lewis Farm, Inc.] approximately a year earlier. As a result . . . , the tractor-trailer's wheels came off, bounced across the road, and hit plaintiff's vehicle in the oncoming lane of traffic, resulting in substantial injuries to plaintiff. Plaintiff sued, alleging that defendant's negligent maintenance of the axle during the time that it had owned the tractor-trailer was a substantial cause of the axle's failure. Defendant moved to dismiss plaintiff's complaint against it, reasoning that its sale of the tractor-trailer approximately a year before the accident occurred excused it from any responsibility for negligently maintaining the axle. The trial court agreed with defendant's position, dismissed plaintiff's negligence claim. . . . The Court of Appeals affirmed. . . .

. . . . The complaint alleges that defendant bought a 1993 Kenworth tractor-trailer when it was "new or nearly new." Defendant sold the tractor-trailer in November 1999, after driving it approximately 500,000 miles. . . .

The complaint alleges that defendant was negligent in failing to follow the . . . [manufacturer's recommended maintenance schedule] regarding the rear axle assembly and bearings. The complaint also alleges that defendant was negligent "in that any maintenance to the rear axle shaft and/or drive axle [that defendant performed while it owned the tractor-trailer and that, as a result, the truck was not] . . . safe to operate."

. . . . According to the complaint, defendant's negligent maintenance of the axle "was a substantial contributing cause of the failure of the rear axle" and the resulting injuries to plaintiff.

Plaintiff brought this action against defendant, Lewis Farm, and Paccar, Inc., which had manufactured the Kenworth tractor-trailer. Plaintiff's claims against Lewis Farm and Paccar have been resolved, and only his negligence claim against defendant remains. . . .

Because this case arises on defendant's motion to dismiss, we assume, as the complaint alleges, that defendant negligently maintained the axle that later failed. We also assume . . . that defendant's negligent maintenance of the axle "was a substantial contributing cause of the failure of the rear axle . . . and of plaintiff's damages." In light of those allegations, if defendant had continued to own and operate the tractor-trailer at the time of the accident, there can be little dispute that plaintiff's complaint would state a claim for negligence against defendant. . . .

. . . . According to the allegations before us, the only factual basis that defendant can invoke for saying that it is not responsible for the consequences of its negligence is that it sold the tractor-trailer approximately a year before the axle failed. . . .

Defendant reasons that it owed no duty to plaintiff because a federal regulation and an analogous state statute imposed an obligation on Lewis Farm, the owner of the tractor-trailer at the time of the accident, to maintain it in a safe condition....

The federal regulation on which defendant relies provides, in part, that "[e]very motor carrier shall systematically inspect, repair, and maintain ... all motor vehicles subject to its control." .... Even if we assume that Lewis Farm is a motor carrier within the meaning of the regulation, the terms of that regulation imposed an obligation on Lewis Farm to maintain the tractor-trailer. They do not excuse a prior owner, such as defendant, from the consequences of its negligence during the time it owned the motor vehicle. If anything, the regulation cuts against defendant's argument; it implies that defendant had a duty to maintain the vehicle in a safe condition during the time it owned it.

... [T]he state statute on which defendant relies ... poses the same problem for defendant's argument. That statute makes it a traffic offense for the owner of a vehicle to "caus[e] or knowingly permi[t] the vehicle to be driven or moved on any highway when the vehicle is in such unsafe condition as to endanger any person." Nothing in the terms of that statute purports to excuse a prior owner from the consequences of its negligence. Rather, the statute establishes only that the current owner of a vehicle must ensure that a vehicle is safe to operate....

Defendant's "no duty" argument may rest on an alternative proposition ... that, if Lewis Farm had a statutory or regulatory duty to inspect, repair, and maintain the tractor-trailer, then, as a matter of general negligence law, the existence of that duty relieved defendant of the consequences of its earlier negligence. To the extent that defendant's "no duty" argument rests on that proposition, it is at odds with this court's decision in Hills v. McGillvrey, 240 Or. 476, 402 P.2d 722 (1965), as well as general principles of tort law.

In *Hills,* an automobile parts store negligently supplied the wrong wheel bearing to a mechanic, who negligently failed to realize that fact and installed it in a customer's car.... As a result of installing the wrong wheel bearing, the brakes failed, causing the customer to lose control of her car and kill another person.... The deceased person's estate brought a negligence action against both the automobile parts store that supplied the wrong part and the mechanic who failed to recognize that fact.... In response to the estate's claim, the parts store contended that "it was the duty of the mechanic to install the part with due care, and that if [the mechanic] had exercised due care he would have discovered that he had been given the wrong part and presumably would not have installed it." .... The automobile parts store argued that, as a matter of law, the mechanic's duty to install the correct part excused the parts store from the consequences of its negligence in supplying the wrong part....

This court held otherwise. It explained that,

> [i]f it was reasonably foreseeable that some harm to the traveling public could result from the installation of the wrong part on an automobile, and if it was reasonably foreseeable that the mechanic might negligently install

> on an automobile a part supplied him for such a purpose, then it would follow that there was a duty on the part of the suppliers not to supply the mechanic the wrong part.

....

The automobile parts store's argument in *Hills* is difficult to distinguish from the argument that defendant advances in this case. If the mechanic's breach of his duty in *Hills* did not excuse the parts store from the foreseeable consequences of its prior negligence, then it is difficult to see how Lewis Farm's duty to maintain the tractor-trailer axle relieved defendant of liability for the foreseeable consequences of its prior negligence. Not only could a reasonable juror find that it was foreseeable that Lewis Farm would be as deficient in maintaining the axle as defendant allegedly had been, but the claim for relief against defendant did not even allege that Lewis Farm had been deficient in maintaining the axle during the time it owned the truck.

The holding in *Hills* is consistent with the general rule that "the failure of a third person to act to prevent harm to another threatened by the actor's negligent conduct" does not excuse the actor from responsibility for his or her own negligence. *See* Restatement (Second) of Torts § 452(1) (1965) (stating general rule); Fowler V. Harper, Fleming James, Jr., and Oscar S. Gray, 4 Harper, James and Gray on Torts § 20.5, 201–02 and n. 47 (3d ed. 2007).... We note that some courts have recognized that there are "exceptional cases" where the responsibility has been shifted to another party, by express agreement or otherwise, such that "the original actor is relieved of liability for the result which follows from the operation of his own negligence."....

In the context of the sale of used vehicles, some courts have looked to a combination of factors, such as the terms of the sale, whether the original owner sold the used vehicle to a dealer, which may be expected to inspect the vehicle before reselling it, and whether the defect resulting from the original owner's negligence was patent, in deciding whether to hold, as a matter of law, that the original owner was excused from the consequences of its prior negligence....

We need not decide ... whether those factors, or some combination of them, would be sufficient to permit a court to say, as a matter of law, that defendant is completely excused from the consequences of its prior negligence. The limited allegations before us do not disclose whether any of the facts that were critical to those other decisions are present in this case. Rather, defendant moved to dismiss plaintiff's claim for relief against it, and the only allegation in that claim on which defendant can base its defense is that Lewis Farm owned the tractor-trailer approximately a year before the accident occurred. Under this court's decisions, that allegation is not sufficient for a court to say, as a matter of law, that defendant is not responsible for the consequences of its negligence.

... The judgment of the circuit court is reversed, and the case is remanded ... for further proceedings.

[The concurring opinion of BALMER, J., has been omitted.]

Notes

1. ***Product Recalls and Doing Everything Possible to Prevent Harm.*** In Balido v. Improved Mach., Inc., 105 Cal. Rptr. 890 (App. Ct. 1973), several years after a machine was built and sold, the manufacturer discovered that the machine was defective and notified the present, second-hand owner of its willingness to remedy the problem at a cost of five hundred dollars. The company owning the machine did not accept the offer, and subsequently the defective condition caused the hand of one of its employees to be crushed. Regarding the liability of the manufacturer to the employee, the court held that neither the passage of time itself, nor notification to the present owner of the defect, required a finding of superseding cause as a matter of law. Rather, it was an issue of fact for the jury to determine whether the manufacturer had taken all reasonable steps to correct the defect. The court wrote:

> A manufacturer who has taken all reasonable steps to correct its error may succeed in absolving itself from future liability. An example ... is found in the leading case of Ford Motor Co. v. Wagoner, 192 S.W.2d 840, 842 (Tenn. 1946), where an automobile manufacturer discovered a defect in a hood catch and distributed an auxiliary catch to its dealers with instructions to install the catch on defective automobiles at no cost. The owner of an automobile with the defective catch refused to have the auxiliary catch installed, and a subsequent owner of the vehicle was injured in an accident caused by the defect. The court held that the original owner's refusal to accept free repair of the defect amounted to an independent superseding cause of the accident that cut off the manufacturer's liability.... Similarly in Rekab, Inc. v. Frank Hrubetz & Company, 274 A.2d 107 (Md. 1971), the court found that a manufacturer of Ferris wheels did all that was reasonably possible to correct a deficiency in the design of one of his products when he notified the customer of the deficiency, shipped free replacement parts, and offered free installation of the new parts.

See also Springmeyer v. Ford Motor Co., 71 Cal. Rptr. 2d 190 (Cal. Ct. App. 1998) (whether a prior owner's failure to replace a fan blade in response to a recall was a superseding cause of an accident was a question for the jury).

2. ***Foreseeability of an Omission.*** In addressing the subject of proximate causation, some decisions place great weight on whether a subsequent omission was foreseeable. For example, in Gracyalny v. Westinghouse Elec. Corp., 723 F.2d 1311, 1323 (7th Cir. 1983), the court wrote:

> [W]here a plaintiff is injured by a manufacturer's product, the intervening negligence of the plaintiff's employer [the purchaser] does not insulate the manufacturer from liability unless the employer's acts or omissions are unforeseeable.

Because there was evidence that the employer was confused about which circuit breaker remedial parts were to be installed, the foreseeability of the lapse was a question of fact rendering summary judgment inappropriate.

3. ***Shifting Responsibility and Premises Liability.*** A possessor of land who creates a risk on the property does not automatically escape liability for harm caused by the risk by transferring property to another. *See* Restatement, Third, of Torts: Liab. for Physical & Emotional Harm § 51 cmt. t & illus. 10–11 (2012).

Chapter 9

Limited Duty: Failure to Act

In many negligence cases, the element of "duty" poses no problem. Under the rule of Palsgraf v. Long Island Railroad Co., 162 N.E. 99 (N.Y. 1928) (*see* Chapter 5), if there is a "risk reasonably to be perceived," there is a "duty to be obeyed." Thus, in the usual case, a person conducting an activity plainly has a duty to use reasonable care to prevent it from causing foreseeable harm.

However, in a few areas, the law takes a different approach. As discussed in this chapter, the law of torts does not, in general, require someone to protect others against injuries inflicted by third parties, or to aid them when they are in need. For example, one may spend the evenings at home, without risk of legal liability, even though there is a dangerous intersection nearby, and even though one might be able to prevent harm by going to that intersection and helping pedestrians cross the street. Furthermore, the common law traditionally said that possessors of land owe trespassers and even social guests only limited duties of care; this subject will be explored in Chapter 10. Finally, a variety of cases present serious problems of allocating responsibility, of distinguishing meritorious claims from fraudulent ones, or of determining appropriate measures of recovery even if a wrong has plainly been done. One response to those problems is to adopt rules to the effect that defendants are not liable for certain kinds of harms they have negligently caused. These rules are sometimes (but not always) called "limited duty" or "no-duty" rules. Chapters 11, 12, and 13 will examine three of these situations: negligent infliction of emotional distress, negligence involving alcohol-related injuries, and negligence relating to conception, pregnancy, birth, and adoption.

A. The Traditional Rule of No Liability for Nonfeasance

In general, there is no duty to render assistance to another who is in peril, no matter how easily aid might be furnished, and regardless of whether the failure to act is inadvertent or intentional. This was the law a hundred years ago, and, in the absence of an exception, it is still the rule today. *See* Restatement, Third, of Torts: Liab. for Phys. & Emotional Harm § 37 (2012).

Johnson v. Minnesota

Supreme Court of Minnesota
553 N.W.2d 40 (Minn. 1996)

ANDERSON, Justice.

.... At approximately 12:00 p.m. on Independence Day . . . , Scott Edward Stewart was released from Minnesota's maximum security prison in St. Cloud and told to report to 180 Degrees, a halfway house located in Minneapolis. . . . Stewart's parole agreement stated that he was to report directly to 180 Degrees and to telephone his supervising agent within 24 hours of his release. Stewart did neither; instead, he engaged in an eight-day crime spree.

During this crime spree, Stewart abducted [Melissa] Johnson at gunpoint . . . [on] July 9. He forced Johnson into his car and drove her to the outskirts of the city, where he raped [and murdered her]. . . .

[Johnson's family sued the state, the county, and the halfway house. The district court granted the defendants' motions to dismiss, and the court of appeals reversed in relevant part. The opinion of the court of appeals stated that "Agents at the St. Cloud facility did not contact 180 Degrees on July 5 to find out whether Stewart had arrived. Nor did 180 Degrees contact the corrections facility to find out why Stewart had not arrived." . . . .]

The state and the county, along with 180 Degrees, . . . argue that they had no duty to control Stewart and determine his whereabouts when Stewart failed to arrive at 180 Degrees or to telephone Lamb [Stewart's supervising agent] as instructed . . . Because the state and county are protected by statutory immunity and their agents by official immunity, we need not reach the issue of whether they had a duty to control Stewart or to immediately issue a warrant. . . .

The fact that an actor realizes or should realize that action on his part is necessary for another's aid or protection does not of itself impose upon the actor a duty to take such action. Restatement (Second) of Torts § 314 (1965) (Restatement). Under fundamental principles of tort law,

> There is no duty so to control the conduct of a third person as to prevent him from causing physical harm to another unless
>
> (a) a special relation exists between the actor and the third person which imposes a *duty* upon the actor *to control* the third person's conduct, or
>
> (b) (b) a special relation exists between the actor and the other which gives to the other a right to protection.

Restatement § 315 (emphasis added). . . . [S]uch "special relationships exist between parents and children, masters and servants, possessors of land and licensees, common carriers and their customers, or people who have *custody* of a person with dangerous propensities.". . . .

Restatement § 319 also states:

> One who *takes charge* of a third person whom he knows or should know to be likely to cause bodily harm to others if not controlled is under a duty to exercise reasonable care to control the third person to prevent him from doing such harm.

(Emphasis added.)

180 Degrees argues that it had no legal "duty to control" Stewart under Restatement § 315, that it did not have "custody" of Stewart . . . , and that it did not "take charge" of him pursuant to Restatement § 319. . . .

We find no basis in the case law nor in this court's treatment of relevant provisions of the Restatement to impose a legal duty on 180 Degrees under the facts and circumstances of this case. . . . 180 Degrees neither had custody of Stewart nor had entered into a special relationship with him due to his failure to arrive at the halfway house. . . . 180 Degrees had no "ability to control" Stewart due to his failure to arrive at the halfway house. . . . Stewart's release from prison without supervision was an initial and virtually irremediable relinquishing of control such that 180 Degrees cannot be held to have a legal duty to "reassert" control over him. We reverse the court of appeals and hold that, under the facts and circumstances of this case, 180 Degrees had no legal duty to control Stewart.

. . . .

Reversed.

Notes

1. ***General Rule: No Duty to Act.*** The rule that there is no duty to act, no matter how easily one might do so, is widely applied. *See:*

- Estate of Campagna v. Pleasant Point Properties, LLC, 234 A.3d 348, 365 (N.J. Super. App. Div. 2020) (a rooming house owner did not have a duty at common law to conduct a criminal background check of other residents before accepting the decedent's rental application);
- Martinez v. Govt. Employees Ins. Co., 473 P.3d 316, 322 (Alaska 2020) (a tortfeasor's insurer owed no duty, independent of the duty it owed to the tortfeasor, with respect to the cleanup of property that was damaged when the tortfeasor crashed his vehicle into a cabin);
- Kassis v. Lease and Rental Management Corp., 950 N.E.2d 451 (Mass. App. Ct. 2011) (the long-term lessor of a vehicle owed no duty of care to a pedestrian who was injured as a result of a mechanical defect that arose after the lease began);
- Muela v. Gomez, 343 S.W.3d 491 (Tex. App. 2011) (a homeowner's son had no duty to restrain or prevent an attack by a pit bull, absent evidence that he owned or had possession of the dog);

- Iseberg v. Gross, 879 N.E.2d 278 (Ill. 2007) (the defendants had no duty to warn their former business partner, who was later shot at his home, that a disappointed former investor had made threats against him);
- Remsburg v. Montgomery, 831 A.2d 18 (Md. 2003) (a hunting party leader had no duty to protect a property owner from his adult son, a hunting party member, who accidentally shot and injured the property owner);
- Murillo v. Seymour Ambulance Assn., 823 A.2d 1202 (Conn. 2003) (a hospital had no duty to prevent the plaintiff from fainting and breaking her jaw when she said she was about to pass out while watching a needle being inserted into her sister's arm);
- Entex v. Gonzalez, 94 S.W.3d 1 (Tex. App. 2002) (a utility had no duty to inspect a customer's wiring or appliances before supplying natural gas);
- A.H. Belo Corp. v. Corcoran, 52 S.W.3d 375 (Tex. App. 2001) (a television station and reporter who interviewed a mother and her abducted child in a secret location owed no duty to the father to reveal the location of the child);
- San Benito Bank & Trust Co. v. Landair Travels, 31 S.W.3d 312 (Tex. App. 2000) (an employer, the victim of embezzlement by an employee, owed no duty to warn the employee's next employer about the crime or report it to authorities);
- Bishop v. City of Chicago, 257 N.E.2d 152 (Ill. App. Ct. 1970) (an airport operator had no duty to dispatch rescuers to aid survivors of a plane which crashed into water short of the runway).

The Second Restatement illustrates the rule with this example:

> *A* sees *B*, a blind man, about to step into the street in front of an approaching automobile. *A* could prevent *B* from so doing by a word or touch without delaying his own progress. *A* does not do so, and *B* is run over and hurt. *A* is under no duty to prevent *B* from stepping into the street, and is not liable to *B*.

Restatement, Second of Torts, § 314 illus. 1.

2. ***Policy.*** Many writers have suggested that someone who could *easily* prevent serious harm at little cost should be liable for failure to do so, so that *A*, in the Restatement's example, would be liable to *B*. But few writers have proposed that every pedestrian hit by a car should be able to recover from anyone who might "reasonably" have foreseen and prevented the accident.

Complete abrogation of the no-duty rule would often subject dozens, or even hundreds, of persons near an accident to the risk of a lawsuit. It is worth remembering that "reasonableness" is much easier to assume in hypothetical cases than to determine in the real world.

3. ***Misfeasance and Nonfeasance.*** There is no liability for "nonfeasance," absent special circumstances. In contrast, "misfeasance" readily gives rise to liability. *See* U.S. v. Stevens, 994 So. 2d 1062 (Fla. 2008) (holding that a research facility's

ownership and handling of biohazards were affirmative acts giving rise to a duty to protect others from harm arising out of that activity); Wal-Mart Stores E., L.P. v. Ankrom, 854 S.E.2d 257, 268-69 (W. Va. 2020) (holding that store employees exposed a customer to a foreseeable risk of harm by trying to apprehend a shoplifter and that the store therefore had a duty to protect the customer from the shoplifter's criminal conduct).

The distinction between "misfeasance" (such as carelessly driving a car) and "nonfeasance" (such as failing to avoid hitting a child in the street) is sometimes elusive. Fortunately, recognizing and applying the distinction seldom presents serious problems. For instance, suppose that *A*, driving along with the car's cruise control set at 45 miles an hour, does nothing upon seeing *B* asleep in the road ahead and runs over *B*. An argument that *B* should not recover because *A*'s negligence consisted entirely of the "nonfeasances" of failing to step on the brakes and failing to turn the steering wheel would be ludicrous, though ingenious. *See* Restatement, Third, of Torts: Liab. for Phys. & Emotional Harm § 37 cmt. c (2012) (the relevant question is "whether the actor's *entire conduct* created a risk of physical harm"; emphasis added).

Some cases do present difficult issues, however. For example, suppose that the operator of a parking garage knows that drivers sometimes speed out of the garage after paying, endangering pedestrians. The operator could reduce this danger inexpensively by installing a barrier, like those at railroad crossings, to force drivers to stop at the edge of the sidewalk. If it does nothing, and a pedestrian is hurt, has the operator (1) designed and operated a dangerous parking facility (misfeasance) or (2) failed to protect pedestrians against dangerous drivers (nonfeasance)? For one answer, see Pulka v. Edelman, 358 N.E.2d 1019 (N.Y. 1976), holding that the garage had no duty to protect pedestrians against this kind of harm.

Satterfield v. Breeding Insulation Co., 266 S.W.3d 347 (Tenn. 2008), contains an extensive discussion of misfeasance and nonfeasance. In that case, an employee's daughter died of mesothelioma caused by asbestos fibers carried on contaminated clothing the employee wore home from work over a period of years. The court wrote:

> Even though Alcoa was aware of the dangerous amounts of asbestos on its employees' clothes, Alcoa did not inform its employees that the materials that they were handling contained asbestos or of the risks posed by asbestos fibers to the employees or to others. The danger was compounded even further because Alcoa dissuaded its employees from using on-site bathhouse facilities, and it failed to provide coveralls or to wash its employees' work clothes at the factory. . . .
>
> . . . . Alcoa engaged in misfeasance that set in motion a risk of harm to Ms. Satterfield. Because Ms. Satterfield's complaint rests on the basic tort claim of misfeasance, it is not necessary to analyze in detail whether Alcoa also had duties arising from special relationships with third parties.

The court held that the defendant employer owed a duty of care to the employee's deceased daughter that would support a negligence action.

B. Qualifications and Exceptions

1. Duties Based on the Defendant's Relationship to the Victim or the Injurer

A key fact in most of the no-duty cases described above is that the victim, the defendant, and the person who caused the harm were strangers. The law has long held that some persons have duties either to protect certain others from being harmed or to prevent persons in their custody from causing harm. The captain of a ship cannot sail on, ignoring the cries of a passenger who, through no fault of the captain's, has fallen overboard. A father who knows that his child likes to stab smaller children cannot sit idly by while the child invites a playmate to come in and see some hunting knives. This section looks at cases in which the no-duty rule may be overridden because of the defendant's relationship with the victim or with the person who caused the harm. *See generally* Restatement, Third, of Torts: Liab. for Physical & Emotional Harm §§ 40 & 41 (2012).

De Vera v. Long Beach Public Transportation Co.

Court of Appeal of California
225 Cal. Rptr. 789 (Ct. App. 1986)

DANIELSON, Associate Justice.

Defendant . . . appeals from a judgment awarding plaintiff Federico De Vera $17,500 as damages for injuries he sustained when another motor vehicle ran into the rear end of defendant's bus. The fundamental question presented by defendant's appeal is whether a common carrier owes a duty to its passengers to investigate an accident caused by a third party for the purpose of facilitating a claim by the passenger against the third party tortfeasor. . . .

. . . .

Plaintiff sustained injuries when a bus owned and operated by defendant was rear-ended by a vehicle owned and operated by a third party. He filed a complaint alleging . . . that defendant, through its employees, "negligently lost or failed to obtain the identity of the motor vehicle and its driver . . . [involved in the collision," and that as] a proximate result . . . plaintiff has been deprived of pursuing a claim against the driver of the other motor vehicle and other related parties. . . .

. . . . The carrier's duty is described in Civil Code § 2100, which provides: "A carrier of persons for reward must use the utmost care and diligence for their safe carriage, must provide everything necessary for that purpose, and must exercise to that end a reasonable degree of skill." . . . .

. . . . We find no case, and plaintiff cites none, in which a carrier's duty has been held to extend beyond the duty to protect its passengers from physical harm and to see that they are cared for if injured. According to the Restatement, "A common carrier is under a duty to its passengers to take reasonable action . . . (a) to protect them against unreasonable risk of physical harm, and . . . (b) to give them first aid after it knows or has reason to know that they are ill or injured, and to care for them until they can be cared for by others." (Rest. 2d Torts, § 314A.). . . .

In the case at bench, we are asked to recognize an expanded duty on the part of the carrier to assist its passengers in pursuing civil litigation against third parties who cause them harm. The term "duty" is "only an expression of the sum total of those considerations of policy which lead the law to say that the particular plaintiff is entitled to protection.". . . . The existence of "duty" is a question of law. . . .

. . . . [In considering the existence of duty in a given case several factors require consideration including the foreseeability of harm to the plaintiff, the degree of certainty that the plaintiff suffered injury, the closeness of the connection between the defendant's conduct and the injury suffered, the moral blame attached to the defendant's conduct, the policy of preventing future harm, the extent of the burden to the defendant and consequences to the community of imposing a duty to exercise care with resulting liability for breach, and the availability, costs, and prevalence of insurance for the risk involved. When public agencies are involved, additional elements include the extent of the agency's powers, the role imposed upon it by law and the limitations imposed upon it by budget.]

When we apply the relevant considerations of policy we find that they militate strongly in favor of a finding of duty. A carrier can readily foresee the possibility of harm to its passengers by reason of its failure to collect and preserve information concerning a motorist involved in an accident with the carrier's vehicle, in that the passengers could be foreclosed, as was plaintiff, from recovery against such a motorist for any injuries they sustained in the accident. The duty to collect and preserve accident-related information imposes no undue burden upon a carrier, which would presumably, as did defendant, have a procedure in place for the reporting of accidents by its drivers, if only for its own benefit.

Conversely, absent such a duty on the part of the carrier, each passenger would be obliged to alight from the carrier's vehicle and seek the requisite information for himself or herself. Such a practice would be unwieldy, unduly time-consuming, and possibly even dangerous. It would also require the cooperation of the carrier's driver in waiting for passengers to collect the information, a process that could seriously interfere with the carrier's schedule.

We hold that, following an accident between its vehicle and that of another, a common carrier has a duty to collect and preserve information concerning the other vehicle and its driver for use by the carrier's passengers in future civil litigation.

. . . .

The judgment and order are affirmed.

Notes

1. ***Possessors of Land.*** A duty of care has frequently been found to exist where the plaintiff was rightfully on the defendant's land at the time the need for assistance arose. *See* Chapter 10.

However, there are limits to what an invitor must do on behalf of an invitee. *See* L.A. Fitness Intern., LLC v. Mayer, 980 So. 2d 550 (Fla. Dist. Ct. App. 2008) (the duty to render "first aid" did not impose a duty to perform skilled treatment, such as CPR); Atcovitz v. Gulph Mills Tennis Club, Inc., 812 A.2d 1218 (Pa. 2002) (a tennis club did not owe a duty to acquire and maintain an automated external defibrillator on its premises for emergency use); Lee v. GNLV Corp., 22 P.3d 209 (Nev. 2001) (a restaurant had a duty to aid a choking patron, but no duty to administer the Heimlich maneuver).

"[I]n the absence of any contrary authority," a Pennsylvania court held that "a business satisfies its duty to aid a business invitee [being assaulted by a third party] by calling 911 . . ." Reason v. Kathryn's Korner Thrift Shop, 169 A.3d 96, 105–06 (Pa. Super. 2017).

2. ***Lessors.*** A landlord has a duty to protect tenants against foreseeable attacks by third persons in areas under the landlord's control. For example, in Kline v. 1500 Massachusetts Ave. Apartment Corp., 439 F.2d 477 (D.C. Cir. 1970), a landlord had notice that an increasing number of assaults, larcenies, and robberies were being perpetrated on tenants in the common areas of a large apartment building. In holding the landlord responsible for a subsequent attack on the plaintiff, the court said that while a landlord is by no means an insurer of the safety of its tenants, there was a duty to take such precautions as are within the landlord's power and capacity. The court emphasized that the landlord was the only party in a position to take measures to secure the common areas.

3. ***Data Possessors.*** Consider database possessors, such as banks, credit card companies, and educational institutions, all of whom maintain huge databases of information about data subjects, such as customers, students, and alumni.

> Individual data subjects are in a poor position to protect database information from intruders. The database possessor, in contrast, is the only one with the ability to mitigate the risk that intruders may cause harm. As in *Kline* [*supra*], the database possessor can spread the cost of providing database security to a broader class of data subjects, at least in cases where there is a customer relationship between the plaintiff and defendant. *Kline* . . . suggests that . . . database possessors should owe data subjects a duty to exercise reasonable care to protect data from intruders.

Vincent R. Johnson, *Cybersecurity, Identity Theft, and the Limits of Tort Liability*, 57 S.C. L. Rev. 255, 274 (2005).

Munn v. The Hotchkiss School

Supreme Court of Connecticut
165 A.3d 1167 (Conn. 2017)

ROGERS, C. J.

The issues in this case, which comes to us on certification from the . . . Second Circuit . . . , are: (1) Does Connecticut public policy support imposing a duty on a school to warn about or protect against the risk of a serious insect-borne disease when it organizes a trip abroad? (2) If so, does a damages award of approximately $41.5 million, $31.5 million of which are noneconomic damages, warrant a remittitur? . . . .

. . . . The defendant, The Hotchkiss School, is a private boarding school. . . . [T]he plaintiff, Cara L. Munn, was a student there. In . . . 2007, the plaintiff, who recently had turned fifteen years old and completed her freshman year, joined other students and faculty of the school on an educational trip to China. In July, she contracted tick-borne encephalitis, a viral infectious disease that attacks the central nervous system, as a result of being bitten by an infected tick during a hike on Mount Panshan, which is located in a forested area approximately sixty miles from Tianjin, . . . in northeastern China. . . . [T]he plaintiff suffered permanent brain damage. . . .

. . . . The jury returned a verdict in the plaintiff's favor. . . .

. . . . The defendant appealed from the District Court's judgment to the Second Circuit. . . .

. . . . Jean Yu, . . . the leader of the trip, and David Thompson, the director of the defendant's international programs, provided the students who would be traveling to China with information about the trip. A list of places that the students would be visiting included "Mount Pan". . . .

The students and parents also received some written medical advice for the trip in an e-mail including a hyperlink to a United States Centers for Disease Control and Prevention (CDC) website that erroneously directed users to the page addressing Central America, rather than the one addressing China. The same document . . . indicated that the defendant's infirmary could serve as a travel clinic, although the infirmary was not qualified to provide travel related medical advice. Finally, a packing list provided to the students going on the China trip included "[b]ug spray or lotion (or bug spray wipes)," but that item was listed only under the heading "Miscellaneous Items," along with other, seemingly optional things like "[t]ravel umbrella" and "[m]usical instrument." None of the foregoing documents provided any warning about insect-borne illnesses. . . .

Prior to the trip, Thompson viewed the page on the CDC website directed at travelers to China. . . . [T]he page stated that "[tick borne] encephalitis occurs in forested regions in northeastern China. . . . Protecting yourself against insect bites . . . will help to prevent these diseases." A section that followed . . . instructed travelers to use insect repellent containing the chemical compound DEET and to wear long sleeves and long pants when outdoors. At trial, Thompson admitted seeing this information at the time of the trip, and . . . he subsequently agreed that Tianjin is in northeastern China. . . . No one on behalf of the defendant, including Thompson, warned students or their parents about the presence of tick-borne encephalitis in forested regions of northeastern China or the need to protect against it.

. . . . No one warned the students to wear clothing that would protect them against insect bites or to apply insect repellent. . . . The group ascended Mount Panshan together on a paved pathway, dressed in shorts and T-shirts or tank tops, but split up for the descent. . . . The plaintiff and two or three other students, however, were permitted to walk down the mountain by themselves. On the way down, the plaintiff and her cohorts . . . became lost . . . [and] received many insect bites. . . . Ten days later, she began to experience the first symptoms of tick-borne encephalitis.

As to the rationale for imposing an affirmative duty to protect in this context, "[t]he relationship between a school and its students parallels aspects of several other special relationships — it is a custodian of students, it is a land possessor who opens [its] premises to a significant public population, and it acts partially in the place of parents." . . . .

"[T]he scope of the duty imposed by the student-school relationship is not limitless. . . . [T]he duty is . . . is bounded by geography and time, encompassing risks such as those that occur while the student is at school or otherwise under the school's control." . . . [C]ourts have found the duty applicable in such settings as school bus rides; . . . athletic events; . . . field trips; . . . off campus picnics; . . . off campus "[w]orkday" activities; . . . but not applicable to off campus occurrences that are unconnected with any school programming. *See, e.g.*, . . . [cases finding "no duty to supervise college students' [who] independently organized [an] excursion to Mount Everest during [a] study abroad trip to China," "no duty to prevent [an] after school fight that occurred on [a] public sidewalk outside of [the] school gates" and "no duty to prevent harm once [a] student disembarked [from a] school bus safely at [a] scheduled destination"].

The potential harms to be protected against vary widely. They have included physical and sexual assaults by strangers, other students or school employees; . . . student suicide; . . . accidents caused by students' drunk driving; . . . physical hazards [such as a partially disassembled fence, an inadequately supervised golf cart, a trash burner, an open fireplace, and a hydraulic wood splitter] . . . ; and aggravation of injuries suffered in a spontaneous medical emergency during a soccer game. . . .

. . . . "While [a] school is not an insurer of the safety of its students, it is obligated to exercise such care over students in its charge that a parent of ordinary prudence would exercise under comparable circumstances. . . ." . . . .

. . . . The question we must consider, then, is whether there is something unique and/or compelling about foreseeable insect-borne diseases that should excuse schools that are organizing educational trips abroad from exercising reasonable care to minimize the possibility that the minors entrusted to their custody will contract such diseases. . . .

. . . . School personnel who are organizing an educational trip abroad typically will have superior knowledge of travel planning in general, and the trip itinerary in particular, and . . . have a general responsibility to protect the minors in their charge while they are away from the custody of their parents. Given the potential dangers posed by serious insect-borne diseases, the existence of methods by which to avoid such diseases and the availability of useful information about them, trip participants naturally would expect the organizer of the trip to pass along appropriate warnings and to use ordinary care to minimize the disease risks posed by the insects in the particular areas to be visited. . . .

In sum, we conclude that the public policy of Connecticut does not preclude imposing a duty on a school to warn about or to protect against the risk of a serious insect-borne disease when organizing a trip abroad. . . .

We turn to the second certified question. . . . We conclude that the award, although sizeable, fell within the necessarily uncertain limits of just damages. . . .

In this opinion the other justices concurred. [The concurring opinion of McDonald, J., has been omitted.]

Notes

1. ***Educational Institutions.*** *See* James v. Jackson, 898 So. 2d 596 (La. App. 2005) (a high school breached its duty of care to a 327-pound student who was allowed to participate in a basketball game in a poorly ventilated gym); Marquay v. Eno, 662 A.2d 272 (N.H. 1995) (school employees who have supervisory responsibility over students, and who know or should know of sexual abuse of a student, are subject to liability if their level of supervision is unreasonable); Mirand v. City of N.Y., 637 N.E.2d 263 (N.Y. 1994) (a school was liable for failing to take adequate measures in light of a death threat by one student against another).

Failure to protect students from bullying may give rise to liability. *See* Miranda Leitsinger, $4.2 Million Settlement for Student Paralyzed by Bully, NBC News, Apr. 19, 2012.

In Stanton v. Univ. of Maine, 773 A.2d 1045 (Me. 2001), the court held that a university owed a duty to a 17-year-old student-athlete, as a business invitee attending a pre-season soccer program, to advise the student of steps she could take to improve her personal safety. The student was sexually assaulted by a companion she had admitted to her dormitory. *See also* R.I. Gen. Laws 1956, § 16-85-1 *et seq.* (Westlaw 2022) (requiring schools to provide dating violence education and training, but not creating a civil cause of action for breach of those duties); Tex. Educ. Code § 37.0831 (Westlaw 2022) (requiring school districts to implement dating violence policies).

At the post-secondary level, the duties to students are sometimes limited because the students can be expected to exercise care on their own behalf. For example:

> There is generally no duty to warn college or university students of known or obvious dangers, such as a pothole in a parking lot, snow or ice on exterior steps, discovered water in a hallway, or the risk of falling from a high bluff. This is because it is reasonable to expect persons who have reached maturity to guard against risks that are already known or obvious.... A student who engages in rock climbing while participating in an educational program need not be told of the risk of falling, since "[f]alling, whether because of one's own slip, a co-climber's stumble, or an anchor system giving way, is the very risk inherent in the sport of mountain climbing and cannot be completely eliminated without destroying the sport itself."

Vincent R. Johnson, *Americans Abroad: International Education Programs and Tort Liability*, 32 J.C.U.L. 309, 341 (2006) (citations omitted).

The duties of a school may be found not to extend beyond official hours. In Young v. Salt Lake City Sch. Dist., 52 P.3d 1230 (Utah 2002), the court held that because a school district did not have custody of an elementary school student at the time he was injured when he was struck by a vehicle while riding his bicycle to a mandatory parent-teacher-student conference after school had adjourned, the district had no duty to inform him of dangerous conditions or provide a crossing guard or warning light.

In Kleinknecht v. Gettysburg College, 989 F.2d 1360 (3d Cir. 1993), a lacrosse player suffered a cardiac arrest during practice and died. The court held that a college has a duty to be reasonably prepared to handle medical emergencies arising from intercollegiate contact sports.

2. ***Wardens and Prisoners.*** A warden is obliged to exercise reasonable care to prevent harm to a prisoner. An unusual application of this rule may be found in State v. Tidwell, 735 S.W.2d 629 (Tex. App. 1987). Plaintiff was arrested by two game wardens for hunting squirrels out of season. On the way back to town, the wardens saw a large rattlesnake on the road, and plaintiff, who was intoxicated, told the officers: "Hell, turn around, I'll catch that snake.... I have caught snakes all my life." The wardens turned the car around and parked within twenty feet of the snake. Plaintiff jumped out, caught the snake, was bitten, and spent two weeks in intensive care. The court upheld a judgment against the wardens and the state, which the jury had reduced by 40% to make allowance for the plaintiff's own comparative negligence.

But see Oddo v. Queens Village Comm. for Mental Health, 71 N.E.3d 946, 947 (N.Y. 2017) (holding that a treatment facility, which functioned as an alternative to incarceration, was not liable for an attack perpetrated by a former resident soon after being discharged; the facility "lacked control over him at the time of the incident,... and owed no duty of care to plaintiff").

3. ***Family Members.*** One would expect that a duty to act will be imposed on close family members. However, there is little precedent, in part because of once-strong, but now diminished, intra-family immunities (*see* Chapter 18). The Restatement, Third, of Torts does not recognize the parent-minor child relationship as an

exception to the basic no-duty-to-protect rule, due to the paucity of judicial rulings on the subject.

> [However, the] dearth of reported cases on the question of parental civil liability should not obscure the fact that there is support for the principle that parents have a duty to protect minor children. Commentators frequently recognize the parent-child relationship as imposing an affirmative duty of care. Dicta in cases state that the duty exists, and occasional decisions have relied upon the principle to resolve disputes. For example, in Laser v. Wilson, [473 A.2d 523, 529 (Md. 1982)] the high court of Maryland found that the parents of a two-year-old child, and not their hosts, who had invited the parents and their child to a family gathering, had the duty to protect the child from the obvious danger of an open stairwell. In a Texas case [reported in the Dallas Morning News], a trial court entered a tort verdict against a mother who had failed to protect her daughters from abuse by their father. In another passive-parent case [reported in the ABA Journal], in Minnesota, "the mother of a 21-year-old woman who was molested by her father as a child [was] found jointly liable for part of a $2.4 million jury award against him."
>
> There is good reason for courts to hold that parents have an affirmative duty under tort law to protect their minor children from serious physical harm. Quite simply, it is morally reprehensible for parents knowingly to allow their minor child to drown, to be sexually abused or to suffer from lack of medical attention.... [O]ther good arguments can also be made in favor of imposing a tort duty on parents based on well-recognized public policies relating to deterrence, minimal burden, and community consequences....

Vincent R. Johnson & Claire G. Hargrove, *The Tort Duty of Parents to Protect Minor Children*, 51 Villanova L. Rev. 311, 317–19 (2006).

See also Lundman v. McKown, 530 N.W.2d 807 (Minn. App. 1995) (stepfather owed a duty of care to a child whose afflictions were treated by "spiritual means"); Cain v. Cain, 870 S.W.2d 676 (Tex. Ct. App. 1994) (duty to prevent son-in-law from raping niece, both of whom lived in defendant's house).

4. ***Social Companions.*** In Farwell v. Keaton, 240 N.W.2d 217, 222 (Mich. 1976), the court imposed a duty on a 16-year-old to seek medical attention for a friend, with whom he had been out drinking, who had been injured in a fight with other boys. *But see* Filiberto v. Herk's Tavern, Inc., 830 N.Y.S.2d 813 (App. Div. 2007) (holding that an off-duty bartender had no duty to prevent a highly intoxicated friend from ordering a roast beef sandwich which required extensive chewing, and on which the friend choked to death).

5. ***Churches.*** Sex-related cases involving allegations that a church acted negligently often turn on issues relating to the foreseeability of the abuse and opportunity to control the abuser. In Willams v. Pentecostal Church Int'l, 115 S.W.3d 612 (Tex. App. 2003), the court held that a district church organization owed no duty

to prevent a local church leader from sexually abusing children within the local church. Although church officials had general knowledge about the risk of sexual abuse of minors in church programs, and had instituted preventive measures at its youth camps, the particular church leader's alleged conduct was not foreseeable to the district organization, which had no right to control the leader's activities.

In some instances, the injury has too little to do with the church to support an action for negligence. *See* Napieralski v. Unity Church, 802 A.2d 391 (Me. 2002) ("Napieralski does not allege that Reverend Williamson was engaged in the Church's business, that she was attending any type of religious event with him, or that her presence at his home pertained to church-related matters"). However, in other cases liability has been imposed. *See* Doe v. Oregon Conference of Seventh-Day Adventists, 111 P.3d 791 (Or. App. 2005) (by failing to require a pastor to supervise his son, a church created a foreseeable risk that the son would molest the daughter of a parishioner).

In A.H. by Next Friends C.H. v. Church of God in Christ, Inc., 831 S.E.2d 460, 473 (Va. 2019), a claim for negligence was stated based upon a special-relationship duty of the church defendants to protect a minor from sexual abuse by their alleged employee and agent, while the minor was in their custody.

6. ***Care Facilities.*** In Texas Home Mgt., Inc. v. Peavy, 89 S.W.3d 30 (Tex. 2002), the survivors of a victim who was shot and killed by a patient on family leave from his court-mandated residence at an intermediate care facility for people with intellectual disabilities sued the facility's management company. The court held that the company had sufficient control over the patient to create a special relationship imposing a duty on the company to use reasonable care in determining whether the patient should be allowed to continue unsupervised home visits.

7. ***Adults Who Agree to Supervise Children.*** An adult who agrees to supervise and care for a minor child has a duty to exercise reasonable care. *See* Kellermann v. McDonough, 684 S.E.2d 786 (Va. 2009) (involving a fatal injury to a 14-year-old girl riding in a car with a 17-year-old driver with a reputation for reckless behavior).

8. ***Employers.*** An employer has a common-law duty to provide employees with a reasonably safe workplace. *See* Widera v. Ettco Wire and Cable Corp., 611 N.Y.S.2d 569 (App. Div. 1994).

In some circumstances, employers have a duty to protect their employees from foreseeable criminal attacks. *See* Dupont v. Aavid Thermal Tech., Inc., 798 A.2d 587 (N.H. 2002) (stating a claim because there were allegations that the supervisors of the plaintiff, who was shot to death in the parking lot by a co-worker, saw the co-worker become increasingly agitated, then escorted the plaintiff and the co-worker outside, without warning the plaintiff that the co-worker was armed or calling the police).

9. ***Threats Posed by One's Minor Children.*** Even though the Third Restatement does not recognize a parental duty to protect dependent children from harm by third persons, it does recognize a parental duty to protect third persons from harm

by dependent children. *See* Restatement, Third, of Torts: Liab. for Physical & Emotional Harm § 41(b)(1) (2012). Liability generally requires knowledge of a specific dangerous propensity of the child.

In Linder v. Bidner, 270 N.Y.S.2d 427 (Sup. Ct. 1966), the defendants' son, an 18-year-old, had assaulted and injured the plaintiff, a young child. The court refused to dismiss the complaint against the parents, since it alleged that they had knowledge of their son's propensity for mistreating younger children and that they had failed to act to control their child. *But see* Childers v. A.S., 909 S.W.2d 282 (Tex. App. 1995) (mother of a minor child, of whose prior sexual activities the mother was aware, owed no duty to the child's friend or the friend's parents to prevent the minor child from harming the friend by inappropriate sexual contacts).

Sometimes an institution stands in the place of parents (*in loco parentis*). Nova Univ. v. Wagner, 491 So. 2d 1116 (Fla. 1986), held that a university which operated a residential center for children with behavioral problems was liable when two residents of the center ran away and, several days later, killed one child and injured another.

What about the obligations of divorced or separated parents? In K.H. v. J.R., 826 A.2d 863 (Pa. 2003), the court held that parents of a minor child who was injured when another minor child shot him in the abdomen with a BB gun could not recover against the shooter's father for negligent supervision. Although the father had legal custody and shared physical custody of the shooter, had purchased the BB gun, and had agreed to allow the shooter to take it to his mother's home, the shooter was in the mother's custody at the time of the shooting.

10. ***Threats Posed by One's Adult Children.*** How should adult children be treated? *Compare* Silberstein v. Cordie, 474 N.W.2d 850 (Minn. Ct. App. 1991) (an action was stated against parents for allegedly failing to control their schizophrenic 27-year-old son who lived with them at the time he committed a murder), *with* Newsom v. B.B., 306 S.W.3d 910 (Tex. App. 2010) (a rancher who had no control or right of control over his adult son owed no duty to prevent injuries to boys resulting from foreseeable sexual assaults), *and* Grover v. Stechel, 45 P.3d 80 (N.M. Ct. App. 2002) (a mother's payment of her adult son's living expenses at the time of the son's assault on the victim did not impose a legal duty on the mother to control her adult son, who was using drugs).

11. ***Threats Posed by One's Spouse.*** There is authority that a woman who has actual knowledge or "special reason to know" that her husband is engaging in sexually abusive behavior against a particular person has a duty of care to take reasonable steps to prevent or warn of the harm. *See* J.S. v. R.T.H., 714 A.2d 924 (N.J. 1998) (abuse of neighbors' daughters). If, in such a case, the husband can be sued for committing the sexual abuse, what difference does it make that the husband's wife can be sued for negligent failure to act?

12. ***Threats Posed by Other Relatives and Friends.*** *See* Bell & Hudson, P.C. v. Buhl Realty Co., 462 N.W.2d 851 (Mich. App. 1990) (no duty to prevent brother from

committing a shotgun massacre in a law office); Sierocki v. Hieber, 425 N.W.2d 477 (Mich. Ct. App. 1998) (roommate has no duty to prevent a collision).

2. Protection from Crime

Remsburg v. Docusearch, Inc.

Supreme Court of New Hampshire
816 A.2d 1001 (N.H. 2003)

DALIANIS, J.

... [T]he United States District Court ... certified to us the following ... [question] of law:

... [D]oes a private investigator or information broker who sells information to a client pertaining to a third party have a cognizable duty to that third party with respect to the sale of the information?

.... Docusearch, Inc. and Wing and a Prayer, Inc. (WAAP) jointly own and operate an Internet-based investigation and information service known as Docusearch .com. Daniel Cohn and Kenneth Zeiss each own 50% of each company's stock....

On July 29, 1999, ... Liam Youens contacted Docusearch through its Internet website and requested the date of birth for Amy Lynn Boyer.... Youens provided Docusearch his name, New Hampshire address, and a contact telephone number. He paid the $20 fee by credit card.... The next day, ... Docusearch provided Youens with the birth dates for several Amy Boyers, but none was for the Amy Boyer sought by Youens. In response, Youens e-mailed Docusearch inquiring whether it would be possible to get better results using Boyer's home address, which he provided. Youens gave Docusearch a different contact phone number.

Later that same day, Youens again contacted Docusearch and placed an order for Boyer's social security number (SSN), paying the $45 fee by credit card. On August 2, 1999, Docusearch obtained Boyer's social security number from a credit reporting agency ... and provided it to Youens.... The next day, Youens placed an order with Docusearch for Boyer's employment information, paying the $109 fee by credit card, and giving Docusearch the same phone number he had provided originally.... On August 20, 1999, having received no response to his latest request, Youens placed a second request for Boyer's employment information, again paying the $109 fee by credit card....

With his second request for Boyer's employment information pending, Youens placed yet another order for information with Docusearch on September 6, 1999. This time, he requested a "locate by social security number" search for Boyer. Youens paid the $30 fee by credit card, and received the results of the search — Boyer's home address — on September 7, 1999.

On September 8, 1999, Docusearch informed Youens of Boyer's employment address. Docusearch acquired this address through a subcontractor, Michele

Gambino, who had obtained the information by placing a "pretext" telephone call to Boyer in New Hampshire. Gambino lied about who she was and the purpose of her call in order to convince Boyer to reveal her employment information. Gambino had no contact with Youens, nor did she know why Youens was requesting the information.

On October 15, 1999, Youens drove to Boyer's workplace and fatally shot her as she left work. Youens then shot and killed himself. A subsequent police investigation revealed that Youens kept firearms and ammunition in his bedroom, and maintained a website containing references to stalking and killing Boyer as well as other information and statements related to violence and killing.

. . . .

All persons have a duty to exercise reasonable care not to subject others to an unreasonable risk of harm. . . .

In situations in which the harm is caused by criminal misconduct, however, determining whether a duty exists is complicated by the competing rule "that a private citizen has no general duty to protect others from the criminal attacks of third parties.". . . . This rule is grounded in the fundamental unfairness of holding private citizens responsible for the unanticipated criminal acts of third parties, because "[u] nder all ordinary and normal circumstances, in the absence of any reason to expect the contrary, the actor may reasonably proceed upon the assumption that others will obey the law.". . . .

In certain limited circumstances, however, we have recognized that there are exceptions to the general rule where a duty to exercise reasonable care will arise. . . . We have held that such a duty may arise because: (1) a special relationship exists; (2) special circumstances exist; or (3) the duty has been voluntarily assumed. . . . The special circumstances exception includes situations where there is "an especial temptation and opportunity for criminal misconduct brought about by the defendant.". . . .

Thus, if a private investigator or information broker's (hereinafter "investigator" collectively) disclosure of information to a client creates a foreseeable risk of criminal misconduct against the third person whose information was disclosed, the investigator owes a duty to exercise reasonable care not to subject the third person to an unreasonable risk of harm. In determining whether the risk of criminal misconduct is foreseeable to an investigator, we examine two risks of information disclosure implicated by this case: stalking and identity theft.

It is undisputed that stalkers, in seeking to locate and track a victim, sometimes use an investigator to obtain personal information about the victims. . . .

Public concern about stalking has compelled all fifty States to pass some form of legislation criminalizing stalking. Approximately one million women and 371,000 men are stalked annually in the United States. . . . Stalking is a crime that causes serious psychological harm to the victims, and often results in the victim experiencing post-traumatic stress disorder, anxiety, sleeplessness, and sometimes, suicidal ideations. . . . Not only is stalking itself a crime, but it can lead to more violent crimes, including assault, rape or homicide. . . .

Identity theft, *i.e.*, the use of one person's identity by another, is an increasingly common risk associated with the disclosure of personal information, such as a SSN. . . . A person's SSN has attained the status of a quasi-universal personal identification number. . . . At the same time, however, a person's privacy interest in his or her SSN is recognized by state and federal statutes . . . which prohibits the release of SSNs contained within drivers' license records. . . . "[A]rmed with one's SSN, an unscrupulous individual could obtain a person's welfare benefits or Social Security benefits, order new checks at a new address on that person's checking account, obtain credit cards, or even obtain the person's paycheck." . . .

Like the consequences of stalking, the consequences of identity theft can be severe. The best estimates place the number of victims in excess of 100,000 per year and the dollar loss in excess of $2 billion per year. . . . Victims of identity theft risk the destruction of their good credit histories. This often destroys a victim's ability to obtain credit from any source and may, in some cases, render the victim unemployable or even cause the victim to be incarcerated. . . .

The threats posed by stalking and identity theft lead us to conclude that the risk of criminal misconduct is sufficiently foreseeable so that an investigator has a duty to exercise reasonable care in disclosing a third person's personal information to a client. And we so hold. . . .

Remanded.

Note

1. ***Exception.*** *Remsburg* is an exception to the general rule that there is no duty to protect others from the criminal acts of third parties. A more typical decision is Jones v. Secord, 684 F.3d 1 (1st Cir. 2012). There, the owner of a stolen gun was not held liable for the death of a person who was shot and killed by the thief (the owner's estranged grandson). The court found that by failing to secure the gun the defendant had not created "especial temptation and opportunity for criminal misconduct," particularly in view of the fact that grandson was not known to be in the vicinity and had not visited the camp from which the gun was stolen for more than a decade.

2. ***Criminal Risks to Travelers.*** In McReynolds v. RIU Resorts and Hotels, S.A., 880 N.W.2d 43, 47–48 (Neb. 2016), the court wrote that "travel agents do not owe a general duty to warn travelers of general safety precautions" and have "no duty to disclose information about obvious or apparent dangers." At issue were the dangers posed by a hotel's key system which used a room key bearing the room number and a second key to open the room safe. After the plaintiff's jewelry was stolen from her room safe, she sued her travel company for failure to warn her of the risks that would result from losing both keys. The court rejected the claim, finding that the risks of the system were obvious.

Wolfe v. MBNA America Bank

United State District Court for the Western District of Tennessee
485 F. Supp. 2d 874 (W.D. Tenn. 2007)

DONALD, District Judge.

....

Plaintiff, now a twenty-seven year old male, is a resident of the State of Tennessee.... In or about April 2000, Defendant received a credit account application in Plaintiff's name from a telemarketing company.... The application listed Plaintiff's address as 3557 Frankie Carolyn Drive, Apartment 4, Memphis, Tennessee 38118.... Plaintiff did not reside and had never resided at this address....

Upon receipt of the application, Defendant issued a credit card bearing Plaintiff's name to an unknown and unauthorized individual residing at the address listed on the application.... Plaintiff alleges that Defendant, prior to issuing the card, did not attempt to verify whether the information contained in the credit account application was authentic and accurate.... After receiving the card, the unknown and unauthorized individual charged $864.00 to the credit account, exceeding the account's $500.00 credit limit.... When no payments were made on the account, Defendant, without investigating whether the account was obtained using a stolen identity, declared the account delinquent and transferred the account to NCO Financial Systems, Inc. ("NCO"), a debt collection agency.... Defendant also notified various credit reporting agencies that the account was delinquent....

In order to collect the debt on the delinquent account, NCO hired an attorney, who discovered Plaintiff's actual address.... The attorney, in a letter dated November 29, 2004, notified Plaintiff of the delinquent account and requested payment.... Upon receipt of this letter, Plaintiff contacted the attorney to inquire about the account, but was told that he would receive information about the account in thirty (30) days.... Plaintiff never received any further information....

In January 2005, Plaintiff applied for a job with a bank, but Plaintiff was not hired due to his poor credit score.... Following this denial, Plaintiff contacted Defendant numerous times to dispute the delinquent account but was unable to obtain any "adequate or real explanation" from Defendant.... At some point in time, Defendant mailed a notice of arbitration proceedings to the address listed on the credit account application, which subsequently resulted in an arbitration award against Plaintiff.... Despite Plaintiff notifying Defendant that his identity was stolen, Defendant continues to list the credit account bearing Plaintiff's name as delinquent and has not corrected the information provided to credit reporting agencies regarding the account....

In his Fourth Amended Complaint, Plaintiff asserts that Defendant was negligent and/or grossly negligent in two different factual contexts. First, Plaintiff alleges that Defendant had a *duty to verify* "the accuracy and authenticity of a credit application completed in Plaintiff's name before issuing a credit card.".... Second, Plaintiff alleges that Defendant had a *duty to investigate* "the accuracy and authenticity of a credit application completed in Plaintiff's name . . . before transferring the account to NCO for collection, [and] before falsely reporting Plaintiff's delinquency to various credit reporting agencies.". . . . Plaintiff alleges that Defendant failed to comply with both duties, and thus, is negligent and/or grossly negligent.

. . . Defendant asserts that Plaintiff's negligence and gross negligence claims should be dismissed because Tennessee negligence law does not impose a duty on Defendant to verify the authenticity and accuracy of a credit account application prior to issuing a credit card. Defendant, characterizing Plaintiff's claim as one for the "negligent enablement of identity theft," argues that a duty to verify essentially constitutes a duty to prevent third-party criminal activity. Defendant argues that Tennessee courts have never held that commercial banks have a common law duty to prevent the theft of a non-customer's identity. Defendant further argues that it, like Plaintiff, is a victim of identity theft.

. . . Defendant cites in support of its argument the Supreme Court of South Carolina's decision in Huggins v. Citibank, N.A., 355 S.C. 329, 585 S.E.2d 275 (2003). In *Huggins,* the plaintiff alleged, among other things, that the defendant bank was negligent for issuing a credit card in the plaintiff's name to an unknown and unauthorized person "without any investigation, verification, or corroboration" of the authenticity and accuracy of the credit account application. . . . The defendant argued that under South Carolina negligence law, it had no duty to verify the accuracy and authenticity of the credit account application because plaintiff was technically a non-customer. . . . The South Carolina Supreme Court, despite finding that "it is foreseeable that injury may arise by the negligent issuance of a credit card," ultimately found that no duty to verify existed because "[t]he relationship, if any, between credit card issuers and potential victims of identity theft is far too attenuated to rise to the level of a duty between them.". . . . Noting the similarity between negligence law in Tennessee and South Carolina, Defendant argues that its relationship with Plaintiff, like the parties in *Huggins,* was and is too attenuated to warrant the imposition of a duty to verify.

Upon review, the Court finds the South Carolina Supreme Court's conclusion in *Huggins* to be flawed. In reaching its conclusion, the *Huggins* court relied heavily on the fact that there was no prior business relationship between the parties, that is, the plaintiff was not a customer of the defendant bank. The Court believes that the court's reliance on this fact is misplaced. While the existence of a prior business relationship might have some meaning in the context of a contractual dispute, a prior business relationship has little meaning in the context of negligence law. Instead, to determine whether a duty exists between parties, the Court must examine all relevant circumstances, with emphasis on the foreseeability of the alleged harm. As to the issue of foreseeability, the South Carolina Supreme Court found that "it is foreseeable that injury may arise by the negligent issuance of a credit card" and that such injury "could be prevented if credit card issuers carefully scrutinized credit card applications." The Court agrees with and adopts these findings.

With the alarming increase in identity theft in recent years, commercial banks and credit card issuers have become the first, and often last, line of defense in preventing the devastating damage that identity theft inflicts. Because the injury resulting from the negligent issuance of a credit card is foreseeable and preventable, the Court finds that under Tennessee negligence law, Defendant has a duty to verify the authenticity and accuracy of a credit account application before issuing a credit card. The Court, however, emphasizes that this duty to verify does not impose upon Defendant a duty to prevent all identity theft. The Court recognizes that despite banks utilizing the most reasonable and vigilant verification methods, some criminals will still be able to obtain enough personal information to secure a credit card with a stolen identity. Rather, this duty to verify merely requires Defendant to implement reasonable and cost-effective verification methods that can prevent criminals, in some instances, from obtaining a credit card with a stolen identity. Whether Defendant complied with this duty before issuing a credit card in Plaintiff's name is an issue for the trier of fact. Accordingly, Defendant's motion to dismiss Plaintiff's negligence and gross negligence claims in the first factual context is denied.

.... Addressing the second context or duty, Defendant asserts that Plaintiff's negligence and gross negligence claims relating to Defendant's alleged failure to investigate the authenticity of the credit account prior to declaring the account delinquent and reporting that delinquency to various credit reporting agencies should be dismissed.... [The court concluded that the plaintiff's state law claims relating to Defendant's role as a furnisher of information to credit reporting agencies were preempted by the federal Fair Credit Reporting Act, but that a libel claim was not preempted by the FCRA, and that the plaintiff also stated a claim under the Tennessee Consumer Protection Act.]

....

Defendant's motion to dismiss is granted in part and denied in part.

3. Mental Health Professionals

Peck v. Counseling Service of Addison County, Inc.

Supreme Court of Vermont
499 A.2d 422 (Vt. 1985)

HILL, Justice.

Plaintiffs-appellants appeal from a judgment ... that found ... The Counseling Service of Addison County, Inc. (hereinafter Counseling Service) not liable in negligence ..., and dismissing the plaintiff's cause of action with prejudice....

.... During the night of June 27, 1979, John Peck, age twenty-nine, son of the plaintiffs, set fire to the plaintiffs' barn. The barn, located 130 feet from the plaintiffs' house, was completely destroyed. At the time of this incident, John Peck was an outpatient of the Counseling Service, under the treatment of one of defendant's counselor-psychotherapists. . . . [After a fight with his father,] John told his therapist that he "wanted to get back at his father." In response to a question by the therapist about how he would get back at his father, John stated, "I don't know, I could burn down his barn." After the therapist and John discussed the possible consequences of such an act, John, at the request of the therapist, made a verbal promise not to burn down his father's barn. Believing that John would keep his promise, the therapist did not disclose John's threats to any other staff member . . . or to the plaintiffs.

. . . . Following the trial, the court . . . dismissed the case with prejudice because it determined that under current Vermont law there was no basis to find that the defendant owed a duty to take actions to protect the plaintiffs.

The plaintiffs argue that the defendant, by and through its employees, knew or should have known, in accordance with the prevailing standards of the mental health profession, that John Peck represented an unreasonable risk of harm to them. Plaintiffs further contend that by its failure "to take steps that were reasonably necessary to protect" the plaintiffs, the defendant breached a duty of care owed to them.

Generally, there is no duty to control the conduct of another in order to protect a third person from harm. Restatement (Second) of Torts § 315 (1965). . . .

Defendant contends that the relationship between a community mental health agency and a voluntary outpatient does not give rise to a duty to protect third persons because of the absence of control over the outpatient. . . .

Whether or not there is actual control over an outpatient in a mental health clinic setting similar to that exercised over institutionalized patients, the relationship between a clinical therapist and his or her patient "is sufficient to create a duty to exercise reasonable care to protect a potential victim of another's conduct." Tarasoff v. Regents of the University of California, 551 P.2d 334, 343 (Cal. 1976). Vermont already recognizes the existence of a special relationship between a physician and a patient that imposes certain legal duties on the physician for the benefit of third persons. Physicians, health officials and health institutions are required, in patient cases of venereal and other contagious diseases, to warn others in order to protect the public health. . . . We see no reason why a similar duty to warn should not exist when the "disease" of the patient is a mental illness that poses an analogous risk of harm to others. . . .

. . . . Defendant also argues that a duty to take action . . . should not be imposed . . . because a therapist is no better able than anyone else to predict future violent behavior. . . . This Court recognizes the difficulty of predicting whether "a particular mental patient may pose a danger to himself or others. This factor alone, however, does not justify barring recovery in all situations. The standard of care for [mental] health professionals adequately takes into account the difficult nature of the problem facing [them].". . . .

Defendant states that John's therapist, acting as a reasonably prudent counselor, "concluded in good faith that John Peck would not burn his parent's [sic] barn." The trial court nonetheless found that the therapist was negligent, and did not act as a reasonably prudent counselor, because her good faith belief was based on inadequate information and consultation. Sufficient evidence was presented to the court to support this finding.

Plaintiffs' psychiatric expert testified that, given (1) John's past history of impulsive assaultive behavior, (2) his medical treatment for the control of epilepsy, (3) the possibility of a brain disorder, associated with epilepsy, that increasingly diminished John's capacity for exercising good judgment, and (4) his past alcohol abuse, all of which were known to the therapist, the failure to reveal John's threat was inconsistent with the standards of the mental health profession. The evidence also revealed that at the time of John's threat the therapist was not in possession of John's most recent medical history. The Counseling Service did not have a cross-reference system between its therapists and outside physicians who were treating the medical problems of its patients. Nor did the Counseling Service have any written policy concerning formal intrastaff consultation procedures when a patient presented a serious risk of harm to another. The defendant's own expert testified that a therapist cannot make a reasonable determination of a patient's propensity for carrying out a threatened act of violence without knowledge of the patient's complete medical history.

Our decision today requires only that "the therapist ... exercise 'that reasonable degree of skill, knowledge, and care ordinarily possessed and exercised by members of [that professional specialty] under similar circumstances.' ".... Once a therapist determines, or, based on the standards of the mental health professional community, should have determined that his or her patient poses a serious risk of danger to another, then he or she has the duty to take whatever steps are reasonably necessary to protect the foreseeable victim of that danger. "... [I]n each instance the adequacy of the therapist's conduct must be measured against the traditional negligence standard of the rendition of reasonable care under the circumstances."....

Defendant also argues that the therapist could not lawfully have warned the plaintiffs of John's threat because of the physician-patient privilege against disclosure of confidential information.... We are aware of the crucial role that confidentiality performs between therapist and patient in establishing and maintaining the "tenuous therapeutic alliance.".... Defendant points out that the legislature has specified certain "public policy" exceptions to the physician-patient privilege, *see, e.g.*, 33 V.S.A. §§ 683–684 (Supp. 1984) (report of child abuse), 13 V.S.A. § 4012 (disclosure of gunshot wounds), 18 V.S.A. §§ 1152–1153 (report of abuse of the elderly) and that a therapist's duty to disclose the risk of harm posed by his or her patient to a foreseeable victim is not a recognized legislative exception. Given this, defendant argues that this Court is preempted from finding a duty-to-warn exception to the physician-patient privilege. The statutory exceptions to the physician-patient indicate to this Court, however, that the privilege is not sacrosanct and can properly be waived in the interest of public policy under appropriate circumstances. A mental patient's threat of serious harm to an identified victim is an appropriate circumstance under which the physician-patient privilege may be waived. This exception to the physician-patient privilege is similar to that recognized in the attorney-client relationship when a client informs an attorney of his or her intent to commit a crime. Code of Professional Responsibility, 12 V.S.A., App. IX, DR 4-101(C)(3) (attorney may reveal client's intent to commit a crime). However, "the therapist's obligations to his patient require that he not disclose a confidence unless such disclosure is necessary to avert danger to others, and even then that he do so discretely, and in a fashion that would preserve the privacy of his patient to the fullest extent compatible with the prevention of the threatened danger."....

Cause remanded for entry of judgment consistent with this opinion and the findings of the trial court.

....

BILLINGS, Chief Justice, dissenting.

....

.... It is scientifically recognized that it is impossible to predict future violent behavior. The professional's duty is to the patient, and not to others.... Here the evidence discloses that ... the counselor in good faith did not believe there was any threat to person or property by the patient, and so no duty arises....

The issues here present an important social problem. If the common law requirements of the duty to warn, the foreseeability of harm, and ability to control are not warranted or necessary, that is for the legislature to decide.

Notes

1. ***Tarasoff and the Duties of Mental-Health Professionals.*** The leading decision on the liability of therapists for harm done by their patients is Tarasoff v. Regents of the Univ. of Calif., 551 P.2d 334 (Cal. 1976). Dr. Lawrence Moore, a psychologist, had, according to the complaint, been told by one of his patients, Prosenjit Poddar, that Poddar intended to kill Tatiana Tarasoff. Dr. Moore called the police, who were unable to detain Poddar because he had not committed a crime. Moore did not notify Tatiana (who was then in Brazil) or her parents. After Tatiana returned from Brazil, Poddar killed her. The California Supreme Court held that the "special relationship" between Poddar and Dr. Moore required Moore to take reasonable care to protect Tatiana.

The *Tarasoff* opinion said not only that a doctor who *knows* that a patient would cause harm has a duty to the potential victims, but also that a psychotherapist has a duty to make "reasonable" predictions about the dangerous tendency of his patients and to warn potential victims when appropriate. Because predicting dangerousness is far from easy, California psychotherapists were quite concerned about that aspect of the opinion. The California legislature then enacted a statute which, as later revised, reads as follows.

California Civil Code § 43.92 (Westlaw 2022)

(a) There shall be no monetary liability on the part of, and no cause of action shall arise against, any person who is a psychotherapist ... in failing

> to protect from a patient's threatened violent behavior or failing to predict and protect from a patient's violent behavior except if the patient has communicated to the psychotherapist a serious threat of physical violence against a reasonably identifiable victim or victims.
>
> (b) There shall be no monetary liability on the part of, and no cause of action shall arise against, a psychotherapist who, under the limited circumstances specified in subdivision (a), discharges his or her duty to protect by making reasonable efforts to communicate the threat to the victim or victims and to a law enforcement agency.

What result in *Peck* if Vermont had adopted a statute like California's? What result in *Tarasoff* itself under the California statute?

Restatement, Third, of Torts: Liab. for Physical & Emotional Harm § 41 cmt. g, Reporters' Note (2012) observes:

> Virtually all courts confronting the issue have decided that mental-health professionals owe some affirmative duty to third parties with regard to patients who are recognized as posing dangers. . . . The vast majority of . . . states in which a *Tarasoff* duty has been judicially imposed have subsequently enacted statutes that codify the duty . . . to provide greater clarity or limits to the judicially-imposed duty. . . .
>
> Some courts have declined to adopt a duty beyond warning. . . .
>
> Some courts and statutes require a specific threat by the patient or actual knowledge by the mental-health professional of the patient's danger to another. . . .
>
> Some courts and statutes have limited any warning obligation to those who are specifically identified by the patient. Others couch the limitation as those who are "readily identifiable". . . .
>
> The duty . . . is applicable to all mental-health professionals who act in a relationship with a mental patient.

But see Doe v. Marion, 645 S.E.2d 245 (S.C. 2007) (holding that because there was no specific threat, a molester's psychiatrist had no duty to warn foreseeable victims); Thapar v. Zezulka, 994 S.W.2d 635 (Tex. 1999) (holding that a psychiatrist has no duty to warn a victim or the victim's family because that duty would conflict with a confidentiality statute barring disclosure); Nasser v. Parker, 455 S.E.2d 502 (Va. 1995) (holding that there is no duty unless the defendant has "taken charge" of the patient, which means more than accepting the patient for the purpose of providing prolonged treatment, prescribing medication, and arranging the patient's admission to a hospital); Boynton v. Burglass, 590 So. 2d 446 (Fla. Dist. Ct. App. 1991) (expressly rejecting *Tarasoff*).

2. ***Duty to Prevent Suicide***. What if the threat of harm is not to a third person but only to the well-being of the one making the threat? In Eisel v. Board of Educ., 597 A.2d 447 (Md. 1991), the court, under a *Tarasoff* analysis which recognized the

strong public interest in preventing youth suicide, held that school counselors have a duty to use reasonable means to attempt to prevent suicide when they are on notice of a child or adolescent student's suicidal intent. *See also* Dzung Duy Nguyen v. Massachusetts Inst. of Tech., 96 N.E.3d 128, 142–43 (Mass. 2018) ("Where a university has actual knowledge of a student's suicide attempt that occurred while enrolled at the university or recently before matriculation, or of a student's stated plans or intentions to commit suicide, the university has a duty to take reasonable measures under the circumstances to protect the student from self-harm").

3. ***Lawyers and Their Clients Who Make Threats.*** What if Peck had told his lawyer, rather than his doctor, of his proposal to burn his father's barn? Rule 1.6 of the American Bar Association's Model Rules of Professional Conduct (Westlaw 2022) provides:

> (a) A lawyer shall not reveal information relating to the representation of a client unless the client gives informed consent . . . or the disclosure is permitted by paragraph (b).
>
> (b) A lawyer may reveal information relating to the representation of a client to the extent the lawyer reasonably believes necessary:
>
> (1) to prevent reasonably certain death or substantial bodily harm. . . .

Several states have rules that differ from Model Rule 1.6. For example, Rule 1.05(e) of the Texas Disciplinary Rules of Professional Conduct (Westlaw 2022) provides:

> When a lawyer has confidential information clearly establishing that a client is likely to commit a criminal or fraudulent act that is likely to result in death or substantial bodily harm to a person, the lawyer *shall* reveal the confidential information to the extent reevaluation reasonably appears necessary to prevent the client from committing the criminal or fraudulent act. [Emphasis added.]

The preamble to the Texas ethics rules, like similar language in the ethics codes of other states, indicates that the rules do not set standards for civil liability, and that a "[v]iolation of a rule does not give rise to a private cause of action [or] create a presumption that a legal duty to a client has been breached." There is virtually no authority for saying that *Tarasoff*-type duties apply to lawyers.

4. Creation of a Dangerous Situation

Borrack v. Reed

District Court of Appeal of Florida
53 So. 3d 1253 (Fla. Dist. Ct. App. 2011)

GERBER, J.

.... [The amended complaint alleged: that the parties were dating and had traveled to West Virginia to allow the Plaintiff an opportunity to meet the Defendant's family; that unbeknownst to the Plaintiff, the Defendant planned to play a trick on the Plaintiff to induce her to jump off a very high cliff into a lake; that while hiking up to the top of the cliff, the Plaintiff repeatedly advised the Defendant that she was not comfortable with the climb and was afraid to descend alone; that the Defendant refused to accompany her to the bottom, continuing instead to the top; that the Defendant encouraged her to continue by telling her that the view from the top is something that he used to share with his deceased brother, and now wanted to share with her; that feeling compelled to continue because of the comments made by the Defendant, and being too afraid to descend on her own, the Plaintiff continued to the top of the cliff; that once there she became too frightened to look over the edge and turned to try to descend; that while she was not looking, the Defendant jumped off the cliff into the water below; that when the Plaintiff turned to ask him to leave, he was nowhere to be found; that the Plaintiff yelled to the bottom where the Defendant's nephew was in the water to find out what happened to the Defendant; that the Defendant's nephew responded by stating that he did not know where the Defendant was and that she should jump to find him; and that due to her concern and love for the Defendant, and in an effort to save the Defendant, the Plaintiff jumped off the cliff into the water below and was severely injured when she landed.

The defendant's motion to dismiss argued that the plaintiff failed to state a cause of action for negligence. Specifically, the defendant contended that ... "'[t]rickery' is not negligence."....

The defendant ... explained ...:

> I've never seen a tort called trickery.... Certainly that's not negligence. Tricking is ... pre-thought-out and that would be something in the intentional tort category....

The circuit court ... entered an order granting the defendant's motion to dismiss with prejudice....

This appeal followed....

The primary dispute ... is whether the plaintiff's second amended complaint alleged a set of facts which establish that the defendant created a foreseeable zone of risk and thereby owed a duty of care to the plaintiff pursuant to McCain v. Florida Power Corp., 593 So. 2d 500 (Fla. 1992). In *McCain*, our supreme court held:

> The duty element of negligence focuses on whether the defendant's conduct foreseeably created a broader "zone of risk" that poses a general threat of harm to others....
>
>> Where a defendant's conduct creates a *foreseeable zone of risk*, the law generally will recognize a duty placed upon defendant either to lessen the risk or see that sufficient precautions are taken to protect others from the harm that the risk poses.

... [W]e find that the plaintiff's second amended complaint alleged a set of facts which establish that the defendant created a foreseeable zone of risk and thereby owed a duty of care to the plaintiff. As the plaintiff alleged, the defendant induced the plaintiff to climb to the top edge of a very high cliff despite the plaintiff repeatedly advising the defendant that she was not comfortable with the climb and was afraid to descend alone. That alleged conduct created a foreseeable zone of risk in the form of a fall due to the terrain, gravity, or a combination of both.... As a result, the defendant owed the plaintiff a duty either to lessen the risk or see that sufficient precautions were taken to protect her from the harm which the risk posed.

... [T]he defendant argues that a practical joke is an intentional act and, thus, a practical joke gone awry should be considered an intentional tort.... The supreme court distinguished negligence from an intentional tort as follows:

> Where a reasonable man would believe that a particular result was *substantially certain* to follow, he will be held in the eyes of the law as though he had intended it.... However, the knowledge and appreciation of a *risk*, short of substantial certainty, is not the equivalent of intent. Thus, the distinction between intent and negligence boils down to a matter of degree. Apparently the line has been drawn by the courts at the point where the known danger ceases to be only a foreseeable risk which a reasonable man would avoid (negligence), and become[s] a substantial certainty....

... [T]he plaintiff's characterization of the defendant's alleged conduct in this case does not constitute an intentional tort under the supreme court's "substantially certain" test. The plaintiff has not alleged or implied that the defendant deliberately intended to injure her or engaged in conduct which was substantially certain to result in injury or death....

Second, the defendant argues that the law does not impose a duty for anyone to prevent others from "voluntarily" harming themselves. To support that argument, the defendant cites a Texas case, Rocha v. Faltys, 69 S.W.3d 315 (Tex. App. 2002). In *Rocha,* two fraternity brothers consumed some beer and then went to a local swimming hole. They climbed to the top of a cliff which overlooked the swimming hole. The defendant dove into the water and encouraged Rocha to do the same. Rocha, who was unable to swim, jumped from the cliff and drowned. Rocha's estate sued the defendant for negligence. The defendant moved for summary judgment on the ground that he owed Rocha no duty. The estate argued that the defendant, by taking Rocha to the top of the cliff and encouraging him to jump while he was intoxicated and could not swim, created a dangerous situation, thus giving rise to a duty to prevent Rocha's death.

The trial court granted the defendant's motion for summary judgment, which the appellate court affirmed. The appellate court reasoned:

> It is a basic principle of legal responsibility that individuals should be responsible for their own actions and should not be liable for others' independent misconduct. However, if a party negligently creates a situation, then it becomes his duty to do something about it to prevent injury to others if it reasonably appears or should appear to him that others in the exercise of their lawful rights may be injured thereby.
>
> [The defendant's] act of taking [Rocha] to the top of the cliffs, in and of itself, does not give rise to a legal duty. Simply taking [Rocha], an adult man, to the location where [Rocha] could choose to engage in an allegedly dangerous activity does not constitute negligent creation of a dangerous situation....
>
> .... In holding that [the defendant's] actions did not create a duty, we do not decide whether encouragement could ever give rise to a duty but only that on these facts a duty did not arise.
>
> The "encouragement" alleged to create a duty in the instant case was implicit encouragement at most.... [T]here is no evidence that [the defendant] actively encouraged, urged, pressured, forced, or coerced [Rocha] into jumping from the cliff. Rather, [the defendant] told [Rocha] that he did not have to jump if he did not want to; [Rocha] decided to jump from the cliff. Under these facts we decline to impose a legal duty on [the defendant] for negligently creating a dangerous situation.

69 S.W.3d at 321–22....

We find *Rocha* to be distinguishable.... Here, contrary to the defendant's argument, the plaintiff's second amended complaint never suggests that she "voluntarily" jumped off the cliff. Further, according to the second amended complaint, the defendant allegedly did more than simply taking the plaintiff to the top of the cliff. The defendant allegedly ignored the plaintiff's repeated statements that she was not comfortable with the climb, and he allegedly refused to accompany her to the bottom. The defendant then allegedly tricked the plaintiff into believing that he had fallen into the water and that she should jump in an effort to save him. Such allegations, if true, would constitute evidence that the defendant actively "forced" the plaintiff to climb to the top of the cliff and then "pressured" or "coerced" the plaintiff into jumping off the cliff to save a loved one. Thus, on these allegations, we recognize a legal duty on the defendant for negligently creating a dangerous situation.

....

Reversed and remanded.

[The opinion of MAY, J., concurring specially, has been omitted.]

Note

1. ***Duty to Aid Another Harmed by One's Conduct.*** If a person's actions, whether tortious or innocent, have rendered another helpless or susceptible to harm, the person is under a duty to provide remedial assistance. Thus, if the vehicles of A and B collide, and B fails to stop, leaving A bleeding by the side of the road, B is liable for the aggravation of A's injuries resulting from the loss of blood, regardless of whether B is responsible for the underlying accident and the harm originally inflicted.

In La Raia v. Superior Court, 722 P.2d 286 (Ariz. 1986), a tenant became ill after an employee of the defendant apartment complex sprayed her unit with an improper pesticide. The court held that the defendant's involvement in the accident gave rise to a duty to furnish correct information about the pesticide to medical personnel.

The rule is the same if the harm is caused not by some action on the part of the defendant, but by an instrumentality under the defendant's control. In L.S. Ayres & Co. v. Hicks, 40 N.E.2d 334 (Ind. 1942), a six-year-old boy's fingers got caught in the defendant's escalator. The store was unreasonably slow in stopping the mechanism, which aggravated the injuries. The court held that even though the escalator had not been negligently constructed or operated, the store had an obligation to render aid to the boy once the injury came to its attention.

See Restatement, Third, of Torts: Liab. for Physical & Emotional Harm § 39 (2012); Restatement, Second, of Torts § 322. *See also* Bushnell v. Mott, 254 S.W.3d 451 (Tex. 2008) (the owner of a dog not known to be vicious has a duty to attempt to stop an attack upon learning it has begun); Conant v. Rodriguez, 828 P.2d 425 (N.M. Ct. App. 1992) (an entity which furnished erroneous polygraph results to an employer, leading to plaintiff's discharge, owed a duty to plaintiff to advise the employer of the error).

5. Voluntarily Assumed Duties

Coffee v. McDonnell-Douglas Corp.

Supreme Court of California
503 P.2d 1366 (Cal. 1972)

SULLIVAN, Justice.

In this action for damages for personal injuries defendant McDonnell-Douglas Corporation appeals from a judgment entered upon a jury verdict in favor of plaintiff and from an order denying defendant's motion for a judgment notwithstanding the verdict.

Plaintiff Robert Coffee, after retiring from the United States Air Force in January 1966, applied for a position as a pilot with defendant, a manufacturer of aircraft. Defendant corporation required each of its pilot applicants to undergo a pre-employment physical examination to establish his physical fitness for the job.... [P]laintiff underwent a physical examination at defendant's Long Beach medical clinic. Among other things, the examination consisted of a review of plaintiff's medical history, extensive X-rays, urinalysis, an electrocardiogram and a blood test. Coffee, examined by Dr. Gray, one of defendant's doctor-employees, was told that the examination could not be completed until the results of the X-rays and laboratory tests were received, about one week later. However, Dr. Gray signed the examination form on the day of the examination indicating that Coffee was qualified for duties as a pilot, with the understanding that medical approval would be withdrawn if the laboratory tests or X-rays produced any negative results.

... [P]laintiff was informed by Mr. Heimerdinger, the chief pilot in flight operations for defendant, that he had passed the physical examination and that he was acceptable for employment as a pilot. On August 9, 1966, Coffee began work.

Seven months later, on March 9, 1967, plaintiff collapsed from exhaustion after returning from an extended flight for defendant. He was admitted to the Long Beach Naval Hospital where he remained for approximately 10 days. Dr. Snyder, a hematologist, examined him and found that he had severe anemia, his kidney function was impaired, and that the bone structure of his ribs and skull had deteriorated significantly. Plaintiff's condition was diagnosed as multiple myeloma, a disease commonly referred to as cancer of the bone marrow. Dr. Snyder informed plaintiff that he had three to six months to live unless he responded to drug therapy.

Plaintiff responded favorably to the ensuing medical treatment. Initially he received several blood transfusions. He also began the daily use of drugs which caused nausea and resulting weight loss. Because the drugs prescribed made him more susceptible to infection, he also contracted hepatitis. By the fall of 1967, his condition was described as in a state of remission and the nausea stopped. At the time of the trial in November 1970, his condition was still in remission and he had been able to return to work for defendant.

Plaintiff commenced the instant action against McDonnell-Douglas and its three doctor-employees (Waters, Gray, and Ruetman) alleging that defendants required plaintiff to undergo a pre-employment physical examination to determine whether or not he was physically fit to be a test pilot and that defendants performed the physical examination negligently in that they either "knew or should have known of his true condition [*i.e.*, multiple myeloma] and negligently failed to disclose" it, or that they were so negligent in the performance of the examination that they failed to discover the presence of the disease. As a proximate result of defendants' negligence, plaintiff averred, his "disease progressed and became aggravated and spread because plaintiff was without medical treatment," thereby reducing his life expectancy, lessening his resistance to other diseases, weakening his bone structure and causing loss of wages.

[Plaintiff's evidence showed that, pursuant to McDonnell-Douglas's usual policy, the blood-test report was filed without having been examined by a doctor. An evaluation of the report would have disclosed plaintiff's condition, and while prompt treatment would not have made the condition curable, it would have reduced his suffering.]

....

An employer generally owes no duty to his prospective employees to ascertain whether they are physically fit for the job they seek, but where he assumes such duty, he is liable if he performs it negligently.... The obligation assumed by an employer is derived from the general principle expressed in § 323 of the Restatement, Second, of Torts, that one who voluntarily undertakes to perform an action must do so with due care.[1]

In the case at bench, defendant, in conformity with its policy that all prospective employees undergo a physical examination, required plaintiff to take such an examination in order to ascertain if he was physically fit to perform the duties of a test pilot. Having assumed the duty to examine plaintiff, defendant also assumed the duty to conduct and complete the examination with due care.

Defendant, however, contends that the duty of an employer, within the context of a pre-employment physical examination, is a limited one; that defendant had no duty to *discover* diseased conditions in plaintiff; and, that even if it had the duty to *disclose known* results, defendant's conduct did not constitute a breach of such duty. More specifically, defendant argues, to impose on employers a "duty to discover" would "ignore the purposes" of pre-employment physical examinations and would "place an undue and unreasonable burden on prospective employers screening possible employees."

We agree that defendant did not breach a duty "to disclose" known results of the examination. We have found no evidence in the record establishing that any of the doctor-employees had actual knowledge of the contents of the blood test report showing, among other things, an abnormally high sedimentation rate and thus indicating the presence of an inflammatory condition. Obviously, having no knowledge of the results of the blood test, defendant's doctor-employees who examined plaintiff were at no time under a duty to make a disclosure.

However, we think defendant has misconceived the issue crucial in this case when it asserts that it had no duty "to discover." The question presented here is not whether defendant has assumed the duty "to discover" diseased conditions; rather, the question is whether the relationship between the parties was such that plaintiff was entitled to legal protection against the wrongful conduct of the defendant. Such

1. [Fn. 6:] Restatement, Second, of Torts, § 323, states: "One who undertakes, gratuitously or for consideration, to render services to another which he should recognize as necessary for the protection of the other's person or things, is subject to liability to the other for physical harm resulting from his failure to exercise reasonable care to perform his undertaking, if [¶] (a) his failure to exercise such care increases the risk of such harm, or [¶] (b) the harm is suffered because of the other's reliance upon the undertaking." ....

a relationship was formed here when defendant undertook, although voluntarily, to examine plaintiff so as to ascertain his physical fitness for duties as a pilot.

Defendant insists that the imposition of a duty "to discover" is an "undue burden." However, it has been said that an employer has failed to exercise due care when it fails "to disclose" diseased or dangerous conditions revealed in a physical examination.... Yet, defendant in effect argues that if an employer fails to perform an examination with due care and thereby fails "to discover" the presence of such a condition, he should not be held liable. In other words, defendant's liability would be limited by the commission of its negligent acts. We cannot approve of such a result.

At the same time we do not say that an employer, once having required a prospective employee to submit to a physical examination in order to ascertain his fitness for the job, assumes an absolute obligation to discover any diseased conditions. In our view the proper test is this: whether the employer in such instance is liable for not discovering the disease depends upon whether or not in the light of all of the circumstances he conducted and completed the examination with due care. Included among the relevant circumstances is the purpose of the examination.

In the matter before us, the purpose of the physical examination was to determine plaintiff's physical fitness as a pilot. In order to examine prospective pilots properly, defendant decided it was essential to take a blood sample and subject it to analysis. The blood test report, indicating an inflammatory condition in plaintiff, was never seen by defendant's medical employees because of a corporate procedure allowing the report to be filed without evaluation. The question posed, already answered by the jury in the affirmative, was whether in the exercise of due care, defendant "should have known" of the results of the blood test.... Viewed in this context, the failure "to discover" the inflammatory condition in plaintiff was the consequence of defendant's own negligence.

.... The judgment is affirmed....

Notes

1. ***Acts as Undertakings.*** *See* Union Park Mem. Chapel v. Hutt, 670 So. 2d 64, 66 (Fla. 1996) (a funeral director has no duty to orchestrate a funeral procession, but upon undertaking to do so assumes at least a minimal duty to exercise good judgment to ensure the safety of procession members); Golden Spread Council, Inc. v. Akins, 926 S.W.2d 287 (Tex. 1996) (a council's affirmative act of recommending a scoutmaster created a duty to use reasonable care in light of information the council had received about the scoutmaster's alleged prior misconduct with other boys); Budden v. United States, 963 F.2d 188 (8th Cir. 1992) (the defendant, who provided some weather information in response to a pilot's request, had a duty to provide accurate and complete information); Maussner v. Atlantic City Country Club, 691 A.2d 826 (N.J. Super Ct. 1997) (if a golf course has taken steps to protect golfers from lightning strikes, it must use reasonable care to implement safety precautions). The *Maussner* court wrote:

> [I]f a golf course builds shelters, it must build lightning-proof shelters; if a golf course has an evacuation plan, the evacuation plan must be reasonable and must be posted; if a golf course uses a siren or horn system, the golfers must be able to hear it and must know what the signals mean; and if the golf course uses a weather forecasting system, it must use one that is reasonable under the circumstances.

See generally Restatement, Third, of Torts: Liab. for Physical and Emotional Harm § 43 (2012) (duty based on undertaking).

2. ***Limited Scope of an Undertaking.*** Some undertakings impose no duty to do anything more than the defendant actually did. For example, in *Ex parte BASF Const. Chemicals, LLC*, 153 So. 3d 793, 806 (Ala. 2013), the plaintiff, who slipped and fell on the top floor of a parking deck, sued BASF [the successor in interest to the manufacturer of a product called Sonoguard], alleging that BASF had assumed a broad duty to assure the proper installation of the deck surface. The court rejected that argument, stating:

> BASF [which visited the site from time to time and gave advice] did not assume a duty to provide more advice or assistance to CHP [a subcontractor on the project] than it actually provided. . . . Further, the record does not contain substantial evidence that BASF failed to exercise due care in providing the particular advice and assistance that it did provide . . . or that any such advice or assistance proximately caused the condition that led to Edward Crabtree's fall.

Other cases have held that:

- The scope of any legal duty assumed by a station that inspects a motor vehicle did not extend to injuries suffered by a truck repairer when the truck broke apart while on the repairer's lift, Newton v. Preseau, 236 A.3d 1270 (Vt. 2020);
- A church's adoption of an internal, sexual-harassment and misconduct policy was not an assumption of duty to protect an attendee from sexual abuse, A.H. by next friends C.H. v. Church of God in Christ, Inc., 831 S.E.2d 460, 471-72 (Va. 2019);
- A driver who signaled his intention to yield the right-of-way to a left-turning driver had no duty to ascertain whether it was safe for the left-turning driver to cross all lanes of traffic, and was not liable for injuries to a motorcyclist involved in the resulting collision, Gilmer v. Ellington, 70 Cal. Rptr. 3d 893 (Cal. App. 2008);
- A U.S. attorney's office, which enrolled the decedent in a witness "assistance" program, assumed no duty to protect the decedent from being murdered, Best v. U.S., 522 F. Supp. 2d 252 (D.D.C. 2007);
- A newspaper which stopped delivery of a subscriber's newspaper did not undertake a further legal duty to treat the stop delivery request in confidence,

and therefore was not liable for a burglary of the subscriber's home, Lambeth v. Media General, Inc., 605 S.E.2d 165 (N.C. App. 2004);

- The Postal Service's reassignment of a mail carrier (known by co-workers as "Lester the Molester") to a desk job pending investigation of sexual abuse charges did not assume a duty to protect local children from the mail carrier upon reassignment, LM v. United States, 344 F.3d 695 (7th Cir. 2003);
- An employer's provision of a sleeping facility for its employees did not create a duty to third parties to make sure employees got enough sleep before leaving work in a car, McNeil v. Nabors Drilling USA, Inc., 36 S.W.3d 248 (Tex. App. 2001).

3. ***Narrow Duties Are More Easily Assumed.*** In Jackson v. AEG Live, LLC, 183 Cal. Rptr. 3d 394, 411 (Cal. App. 2015), the court wrote:

> The Jacksons heavily rely on Coffee v. McDonnell–Douglas Corp. [(1972) 8 Cal. 3d 551, *supra*], to support their contention that AEG owed Michael [Jackson] a duty when it undertook to provide medical services to Michael by retaining Dr. Murray as his personal physician. In *Coffee*, . . . the defendant undertook to "examine plaintiff so as to ascertain his physical fitness for duties as a pilot." . . . . The kind of medical examination required in *Coffee* was very specific, while the alleged undertaking of "medical care" is vague and exceptionally broad. Such a broad duty is not only contrary to the case law, but the evidence demonstrates AEG did not undertake Michael's medical care in its entirety. AEG did not prevent Michael from seeing other doctors, and Michael in fact did so during the months leading up to his death. Thus, the trial court properly found there was no evidence that AEG undertook Michael's medical care.

4. ***Contracts That Create Tort Duties to Third Parties.*** Sometimes the defendant owes a contractual duty to one person, and the issue is whether failure to perform that duty creates liability to a third person who was injured as a result. For example, suppose that an architect or engineer owes a client a duty to detect and stop inadequate construction of a building. If the building collapses because of unsafe construction, injuring a passer-by, is the architect or engineer liable to that person? For differing views, see Associated Engineers, Inc. v. Job, 370 F.2d 633 (8th Cir. 1966) (liable); McGovern v. Standish, 357 N.E.2d 1134 (Ill. 1976) (not liable).

See also Affiliated FM Ins. Co. v. LTK Consulting Services, Inc., 243 P.3d 521 (Wash. 2010) (holding, in a suit where an engineering firm's recommended changes for a monorail's electrical grounding system allegedly caused a fire, that the firm owed a duty of reasonable care to a third party, independent of its contractual obligations); *but see* Graham v. Freese & Nichols, Inc., 927 S.W.2d 294 (Tex. App. 1996) (the fact that an engineering firm expressed concerns about safety to a general contractor and issued a stop-order related to the quality of work at the site created no duty to an injured employee of the general contractor).

According to the Restatement:

> An actor who undertakes to render services to another that the actor knows or should know reduce the risk of physical harm to which a third person is exposed has a duty of reasonable care to the third person in conducting the undertaking if:
>
> (a) the failure to exercise reasonable care increases the risk of harm beyond that which existed without the undertaking,
>
> (b) the actor has undertaken to perform a duty owed by the other to the third person, or
>
> (c) the person to whom the services are rendered, the third party, or another relies on the actor's exercising reasonable care in the undertaking.

Restatement, Third, of Torts: Liab. for Physical & Emotional Harm § 43 (2012).

Davis v. Protection One Alarm Monitoring, Inc., 456 F. Supp. 2d 243 (D. Mass. 2006), held that a burglar alarm company under contract with a bank owed a duty of care to injured bank employees.

5. ***Duties to Subjects of Drug Testing.*** A number of cases have held that an entity conducting drug testing of employees or job applicants at the request of an employer owes a duty of care to test subjects. *See* Sharpe v. St. Luke's Hosp., 821 A.2d 1215 (Pa. 2003); Berry v. National Medical Services, Inc., 257 P.3d 287 (Kan. 2011).

6. ***Duties to Subjects of Standardized Testing.*** In Merrick v. Thomas, 522 N.W.2d 402 (Neb. 1994), the court ruled that a merit commission owed a duty of care not only to a sheriff, but also to a job applicant, to score a test accurately.

What if a testing company under contract with a state or school district negligently mis-scores a mandatory test that determines whether a student graduates or advances to the next level? Does the testing company owe a duty only to the state or school district, or also to the adversely affected student? *See* Vincent R. Johnson, *Standardized Tests, Erroneous Scores, and Tort Liability*, 38 Rutgers L.J. 655 (2007) (discussing cases, settlements, and theories of liability to test subjects).

7. ***Contagious Diseases.*** If a doctor gives erroneous advice about a communicable disease to a patient and, as a result, a third person foreseeably contracts the disease, the third person may have a claim against the doctor. *See* DiMarco v. Lynch Homes-Chester County, Inc., 583 A.2d 422 (Pa. 1990) (hepatitis).

8. ***Suppliers of Chattels.*** Suppliers of chattels have a duty to exercise reasonable care to protect others from harm. In Heinz v. Heinz, 653 N.W.2d 334 (Iowa 2002), a farm laborer who was injured when his arm became entangled in a speed jack brought a negligence action against the farmer (his brother). The court held that the farmer was a supplier of a chattel within the meaning of Restatement, Second, of Torts § 392 and therefore owed a duty of care to the laborer with respect to the condition of the chattel.

9. ***Problem: The Auto Club.*** An auto club tow truck fails to locate the disabled vehicle it has been sent to assist. While waiting for assistance, the driver is fatally injured by a drunken driver whose van plows into the disabled car. Is the auto club liable for the death?

Sall v. T's, Inc.

Supreme Court of Kansas
136 P.3d 471 (Kan. 2006)

The opinion of the court was delivered by DAVIS, J.:

Plaintiffs Matthew Patrick Sall (Patrick) . . . and [his parents] Sall . . . brought a negligence action against defendant T's, Inc., d/b/a Smiley's Golf Course (SGC) for injuries Patrick sustained after being struck by lightning while on the grounds of the defendant's golf course. The district court granted summary judgment to SGC, and the Court of Appeals in a split decision affirmed. . . .

. . . Patrick and his friend . . . [Chris] decided to go golfing. However, by that afternoon, the sky had turned stormy.

Thad Borgstadt, the morning manager for SGC, testified that he visually checked the weather every 10 to 15 minutes because that was SGC's policy. At approximately 1:15 p.m., Borgstadt noticed dark clouds in the sky and decided to close the complex.

. . . [T]he complex remained closed at 3 p.m. when Jeff Tull, the afternoon manager, replaced Borgstadt. By 3:50 p.m. Tull noticed the skies were clearing, and radar images on the computer in the pro shop showed the thunderstorms were moving out of the area. In another 5 to 10 minutes, the sun came out and Tull opened SGC to the public at 4 p.m.

. . . . Patrick called SGC to verify that the complex was open. When Patrick's mother questioned him . . . he replied, "Mom . . . they wouldn't be open if it wasn't safe."

Chris estimated they . . . arrived at the first tee shortly before 5 p.m. . . . According to Chris, they discussed whether storms might be moving back into the area. They also discussed the fact that SGC would blow an air horn as a signal to return to the clubhouse in the event of dangerous weather. . . .

By the time Patrick and Chris started putting on the second green, it started raining a little harder. Chris saw a lightning bolt off to the west, but it was far enough away that they were not concerned. . . .

According to Tull, SGC's policies or procedures for inclement weather call for the manager on duty to monitor the local television stations, radar images on the Internet, and visually inspect the weather by stepping outside. SGC also has a weather radio. . . . [Managers check the weather] more frequently when storms are in the area. If the manager determines it is necessary to bring golfers in off the course, the procedure is to sound an air horn.

At approximately 4:50 to 4:55 p.m., . . . an employee informed . . . [Tull that] a television news teaser had just reported that storms were moving back into the area. Tull returned to the computer screen which showed storms to the southwest. . . . Tull walked outside to visually check the weather and noticed dark clouds and lightning. . . . He immediately . . . grabbed the air horn . . . and sounded the horn . . . at approximately 4:57 to 4:58 p.m. . . .

. . . Chris and Patrick heard the air horn. Patrick finished his putt, Chris replaced the flag, and they started walking back to the clubhouse. . . . Chris saw a flash and heard a loud boom. Chris was knocked unconscious. . . . When he came to, he saw Patrick laying face down and unresponsive. Chris returned to the clubhouse for help. . . . When Chris arrived at the clubhouse, he asked someone to call 911. The 911 call was received between 5:16 and 5:17 p.m. Patrick . . . now requires total care.

. . . . [T]he district court . . . determined a business has no duty to protect or warn patrons of lightning because a lightning strike is not foreseeable. . . . Regarding an assumption of duty under Restatement (Second) of Torts § 323 (1964), the judge stated: ". . . I find that the facts in this case are insufficient to invoke the benefits of Section 323." The district court granted SGC's motion for summary judgment.

Restatement (Second) of Torts § 323 — Negligent Performance of Undertaking to Render Services, provides:

> One who undertakes, gratuitously or for consideration, to render services to another which he [or she] should recognize as necessary for the protection of the other's person or things, is subject to liability to the other for physical harm resulting from his [or her] failure to exercise reasonable care to perform his [or her] undertaking, if,
>
> (a) his [or her] failure to exercise such care increases the risk of such harm, or
>
> (b) the harm is suffered because of the other's reliance upon the undertaking.

. . . .

This court recently discussed the requirements for an undertaking under § 323 in South v. McCarter, 119 P.3d 1 (Kan. 2005) and Cunningham v. Braum's Ice Cream & Dairy Stores, 80 P.3d 35 (Kan. 2003).

In *South*, plaintiff Isaac South was injured during a physical altercation with Joshua Mills and James McCarter in the mobile home park where South and McCarter lived with their parents. South's parents brought suit against the mobile home park. . . .

. . . . We found the rental agreement and community guidelines did not impose a duty on management to provide protection to the tenants and, therefore, they could not in themselves demonstrate an undertaking. . . .

The only evidence of any sort of undertaking was a letter that the mobile home park's attorney had sent to McCarter nearly 2 years prior to the altercation banning him from the premises. . . .

We concluded that no undertaking had occurred because there was no indication the purpose of the letter was to protect the residents from McCarter....

In *Cunningham*, the plaintiff customers of the defendant's ice cream store brought a negligence action against the defendant after its employees shooed them out of the store into the path of a tornado. They were injured while driving home when the tornado threw a truck into their car. The defendant's employees were aware at that time that a tornado warning was in effect and had heard reports of a tornado sighting in the area. Additionally, the defendant had an emergency action plan that if... a tornado is sighted, or a Civil Defense warning sounds, anyone not wishing to leave should be directed to the "milk room."....

.... [W]e concluded that because of the capricious nature of tornadoes, it could not be said that the plaintiffs were any safer in the milk room than somewhere else and there was no evidence the plaintiffs relied upon the emergency action plan....

In this case, viewing the facts in a light most favorable to plaintiffs, SGC had a policy or procedures in place which undeniably were for the protection of their patrons in the event of threatening inclement weather....

....

SGC argues a voluntary undertaking never occurred because there was no agreement to provide weather forecasts to Patrick and there was no undertaking to use extraordinary methods of predicting and reporting the approach of inclement weather....

.... Because § 323 allows a voluntarily assumed undertaking, it would not follow that the duty could only arise from an enforceable contractual agreement or promise as SGC suggests. If there is any requirement for a communicated promise, it would flow from the requirement that the plaintiff relied on the undertaking to his or her detriment.

....

If SGC failed to act reasonably in regard to this undertaking, the rule also requires that the failure to exercise such care increases the risk of such harm, or the harm is suffered because of another's reliance upon the undertaking....

> "In most of the cases finding liability, the defendant has made the situation worse, either by increasing the danger, by misleading the plaintiff into the belief that it has been removed, or by depriving him of the possibility of help from other sources....

....

SGC suggests the golfers did not rely on Tull to warn them of lightning because the golfers already saw the lightning....

The Salls contend the evidence shows Patrick and Chris relied on SGC's undertaking because: (1)... Patrick called SGC to verify the complex was open given the weather conditions earlier in the day; (2) Patrick's mother questioned Patrick about the safety of playing that day and Patrick replied, "'Mom, don't worry; they wouldn't be open if it wasn't safe'"; (3) during the course of playing the second hole, Patrick and Chris ... discussed the fact that SGC had a warning system ... and ... would blow the air horn to warn them to come back to the clubhouse if dangerous weather was in the area; (4) Chris ... on at least one occasion [previously] had heard the air horn and returned to the clubhouse because of dangerous weather; and (5) Chris' affidavit stated that both he and Patrick were relying on SGC to blow the air horn to warn them if dangerous weather was moving into the area. The Salls further contend Patrick was harmed because of his reliance on SGC's warning horn because he was struck by lightning approximately 2 to 3 minutes after the horn sounded.

....

There may be a dispute whether Patrick and Chris relied on SGC's warning before returning to the clubhouse because of their own awareness of the weather conditions; however, SGC was in a superior position to determine when it was prudent for golfers to come in for their safety because the managers relied on more than human observation which is all Patrick and Chris could use for their own safety.

....

Patrick may have been comparatively negligent for not heeding the weather conditions that were observable to him; however, SGC's liability would be reduced by Patrick's failure to exercise reasonable care pursuant to ... the comparative fault statute....

.... We conclude ... that material factual issues remain on the issue of whether SGC negligently performed the duty it assumed.... Thus, the summary judgment granted to SGC must be reversed and the case remanded for trial.

Reversed and remanded.

Notes

1. ***Actions That Neither Induce Reliance Nor Increase the Risk of Harm.*** In MacGregor v. Walker, 322 P.3d 706, 710 (Utah 2014), the court held that by establishing a professionally staffed helpline to provide advice to clergy about how to deal with situations involving abuse of parishioners by third persons, a church did not undertake a duty to aid abuse victims. In addition, there was no evidence that the plaintiff, a victim of sexual abuse, had relied on the helpline, or that a clergy member's failure to use the helpline had increased the risk of harm to the plaintiff. The court added that:

> [P]ublic policy would actually disfavor imposing a duty in cases such as this for fear that imposition of a duty would chill efforts to prevent abuse and assist victims. Creation of programs and resources that have the potential to benefit victims of abuse should be encouraged, not discouraged by the threat of potential liability.

2. ***Study Abroad and Voluntary Assumption of Duty.*** How do the rules on voluntary assumption of duty apply to the numerous study abroad programs conducted by American colleges and universities ("program providers")?

[T]here is generally no duty to provide off-campus transportation for college-age students. However, if transportation is provided, care must be exercised to protect students from travel-related injuries. So too, a provider need not tell students what vaccines are recommended for persons traveling to a particular country. But if the provider does so, it must exercise care to ensure that the information is accurate and reliable. There is no rule of law that obliges an international education program to require students to have physicals to ensure that they are medically fit to travel. But if the program provider elects to do so, it must exercise care in administering the tests and in collecting, retaining, and using the data that is assembled....

The point here is that duties that do not otherwise exist may be assumed when providers undertake or promise to undertake certain activities.... In McNeil v. Wagner College, [667 N.Y.S.2d 397 (App. Div. 1998)] a student "slipped on ice and broke her ankle in a town in Austria, which she was visiting as part of an overseas program arranged by the defendant" college. In a subsequent lawsuit..., the student argued, not implausibly, that the program administrator "assumed the duty to act as an interpreter for her in the Austrian hospital and that she suffered nerve damage due to his failure to inform her of the treating physician's recommendation that she undergo immediate surgery." The court found that assuming, *arguendo*, that a duty was voluntarily undertaken, the suit against the college was without merit because the student had "failed to offer evidentiary proof to support her claim that [the administrator] was told of the recommendation of immediate surgery and negligently withheld that information from her." Nevertheless, the threat of assumed-duty liability is clear. The court noted that, aside from the assumed-duty theory, the defendant college "had no obligation to supervise the plaintiff's health care following her accident."

In another medical-emergency case, Fay v. Thiel College, [55 Pa. D. & C. 4th 353 (Ct. Com. Pl. 2001)] a female student became ill while participating in a study abroad program in Peru. After the student "was admitted to a medical clinic, all of the faculty supervisors and all of the other students left on a prescheduled trip that was to last several days, leaving plaintiff alone at the clinic with only a Lutheran missionary... to act as plaintiff's translator." The student subsequently sued the college and others for harm she sustained at the clinic as a result of unnecessary surgery and sexual abuse committed by male personnel.... The defendants contended "that they had no special relationship with plaintiff beyond the fact that plaintiff was a student at Thiel College." They further asserted that "since there was no special relationship between the parties,... defendants did not violate... [the] standard of care in leaving plaintiff alone at the Peruvian medical clinic." The court rejected this argument. The college had required the student to sign a consent form that could be used in an emergency to authorize administration of an anesthetic or surgery. The court found that

> under the terms of the consent form, which assured signatories that the college wanted "to observe the utmost precautions for the welfare of each participant," the "faculty supervisors had a duty to secure whatever treatment is deemed necessary, including the administration of an anesthetic and surgery." As a result, the court concluded that "Thiel College did owe plaintiff a special duty of care as a result of the special relationship that arose . . . pursuant to the consent form" and could be held liable if "the lack of the presence of one or more of the faculty supervisors with plaintiff at the Peruvian medical clinic increased the risk of the male Peruvian doctors unnecessarily performing surgery on plaintiff and/or sexually assaulting plaintiff." . . . .
>
> Suppose . . . for example, that a foreign educational program collects from participants information listing their allergies to medications, but then misplaces the forms, with the result that the information is not available when an injured student who is unconscious needs medical care. . . . [T]he program provider may be liable for harm caused by administration of medication to which the student was allergic. In contrast, if the provider never collected such information in the first place, a court might well hold that there was no duty to do so and that there is no liability for harm caused by administering the medication to which the student was allergic.
>
> Should a program provider gather information about the prior discipline of students who apply to a study abroad program? That information may make it possible for the program provider to anticipate problems that might arise, but it also is likely to expand the provider's exposure to liability. First, cases often hold that when information is collected, the collector has a duty to review the data. Second, if the information that is gathered identifies risks that should be addressed, a court is likely to hold that the failure to do so is negligence. Consequently, it can prudently be urged that unless there is a particular need for personal information relating to program participants, that information should not be solicited.

Vincent R. Johnson, *Americans Abroad: International Education Programs and Tort Liability*, 32 J.C.U.L. 309, 348–55 (2006).

3. ***Promises without Action***. A promise that induces detrimental reliance may constitute an "undertaking" that will serve as the basis for a negligence action. For example, Abresch v. Northwestern Bell Tel. Co., 75 N.W.2d 206 (Minn. 1956), held that although the telephone company has no duty to pass on messages in emergencies, it will be liable if it agrees to relay a request for help and fails to do so. The plaintiff, whose building was burning, had asked the operator to call the fire department. The court pointed out that the victim who relies on the operator's promise to call the fire department will pass up other opportunities to get help.

In Johnson v. Souza, 176 A.2d 797 (N.J. 1961), the defendants failed to take any steps to remove ice on the front steps of their home, although they had been informed of the dangerous condition and had indicated that they would do so. The court held that liability could be imposed if the jury found the injured guest's reliance to be reasonable.

In Pucalik v. Holiday Inns, Inc., 777 F.2d 359 (7th Cir. 1985), the defendant promised its security guards that it would correct unsafe conditions and defects in the security system at its hotel. It never made the promised corrections, and a guard was killed by an intruder. The court upheld a judgment against the hotel.

See also Texas Drydock, Inc. v. Davis, 4 S.W.3d 919 (Tex. App. 1999) (promise to provide non-skid tape for a cherry picker's elevated surfaces); Marsallis v. LaSalle, 94 So. 2d 120 (La. Ct. App. 1957) (promise to confine a cat to determine whether it was rabid).

4. ***Termination of Efforts to Assist.*** Aid, once begun, need not be continued forever; a doctor who administers first-aid to an accident victim and sees the victim taken to a hospital need not continue treating the victim until he or she recovers. However, premature discontinuance of rescue efforts may violate a duty of care, especially if the truncated efforts leave the victim worse off than if no rescue had been attempted. For example, others may have been discouraged from rendering aid, the rescuer may have placed the victim in a position of greater danger or rendered improper assistance, or the victim may have been encouraged by the rescuer to reduce personal efforts to remedy the situation.

In Parvi v. City of Kingston, 362 N.E.2d 960 (N.Y. 1977), city police officers picked up two intoxicated, noisy men. The officers deposited the men on an abandoned golf course near a highway; they wandered onto the highway and were struck by a car. The court held that, once the men were in custody, the officers had a duty to care for their safety.

When beginning and then stopping a rescue leaves the victim worse off than if no rescue had been attempted, the plaintiff's case is strong. What if a would-be rescuer begins rescue efforts and then unreasonably ceases, leaving the victim no worse off than if the rescue had never been attempted? The *Parvi* court, quoting the Restatement, said, "if the actor has succeeded in removing the other from a position of danger to one of safety, he cannot change his position for the worse by unreasonably putting him back into the same peril, or a new one."

Thus, one supposes, a boater who sees a drowning swimmer need not pull the swimmer into the boat, but, having done so, cannot throw him back. That would be unreasonable.

See Brownsville Med. Ctr. v. Gracia, 704 S.W.2d 68 (Tex. App. 1985) (a hospital which began to prepare a child for surgery, but terminated those efforts and transferred the child to another hospital upon learning that the parents lacked financial resources, was held liable for the child's death eight days later without surgery).

If discontinuance of rescue efforts is reasonable, no action will lie. In Bowman v. City of Baton Rouge, 849 So. 2d 622 (La. Ct. App. 2003), the court held that an EMS dispatcher did not owe a duty to continue to interrogate a 911 caller or to send an emergency vehicle after being advised that there was no further emergency.

5. ***Taking Charge of Another***. According to the Restatement:

> (a) An actor who, despite no duty to do so, takes charge of another who reasonably appears to be: (1) imperiled and (2) helpless or unable to protect himself or herself has a duty to exercise reasonable care while the other is within the actor's charge.
>
> (b) An actor who discontinues aid or protection is subject to a duty of reasonable care to refrain from putting the other in a worse position than existed before the actor took charge of the other and, if the other reasonably appears to be in imminent peril of serious bodily harm at the time of termination, to exercise reasonable care with regard to the peril before terminating the rescue.

Restatement, Third, of Torts: Liab. for Phys. & Emotional Harm § 44 (2012).

6. ***Problem: The Ring Buoy***. Emilio, a swimmer, is rendered totally helpless by stomach cramps. Betty, the only other person in sight, throws him a ring-buoy, and pulls him half the distance to shore, then terminates her rescue efforts. If Emilio drowns, is Betty liable for the death?

6. Negligent Entrustment

McKenna v. Straughan

Court of Appeal of California
222 Cal. Rptr. 462 (Ct. App. 1986)

KINTNER, Associate Justice.

. . . . Cherie Straughan, the defendants' daughter, drove her car onto the wrong side of the road and hit [Pamela] McKenna head-on, causing McKenna extensive damages and personal injuries. Cherie was driving under the influence of alcohol at the time and was charged with a felony and convicted of a related criminal charge.

McKenna saw Mrs. Straughan almost every Saturday for several months prior to the accident when McKenna did her hair at the beauty shop. McKenna presented evidence the Straughans knew their daughter Cherie had a serious alcohol problem, had been in and out of eight recovery homes and was still drinking. Cherie lived with her parents since she had wrecked her previous car. Mrs. Straughan knew Cherie had a history of driving while intoxicated. Just before the car was purchased, McKenna had urged the Straughans not to give a car to Cherie because of her drinking problem. Mrs. Straughan told McKenna she and her husband were buying Cherie a car shortly before the accident because they did not want to be bothered driving Cherie to her Alcoholics Anonymous meetings. McKenna said "Why give her another one? That's like giving a six year old a loaded gun and telling them [sic] not to use it." A car was purchased with Cherie as the registered owner and William

Straughan, Cherie's father, as the registered lienholder 10 days before the accident in question.

. . . .

McKenna sued the Straughans, alleging they were negligent in entrusting or supplying the car to Cherie knowing she was an incompetent and unfit driver. . . . McKenna also claimed she was entitled to punitive damages because Cherie voluntarily became intoxicated before driving and because the Straughans recklessly and wantonly supplied the car to Cherie knowing she was an unfit driver. . . .

After hearing, the court granted the Straughans' motion for summary judgment, finding "there [was] no material issue of fact regarding the custody, control or in the required sense, the supplying of the automobile.". . . .

McKenna appeals. . . .

The Straughans argue that . . . McKenna cannot state a cause of action for negligent entrustment because they never owned or controlled the vehicle which Cherie drove at the time of the accident.

. . . . The [trial] Court, apparently . . . decided in favor of the Straughans because liability should not be extended to "an individual who loans money and ends up [as] the lienholder in such a transaction."

The trial court correctly stated the general rule. In a commercial context, acting solely as a lender without more does not subject the lender to liability. . . . Whether there is "more" turns on the facts of a particular case and the application of the criteria laid down in Biakanja v. Irving (1958) 49 Cal. 2d 647, 650, 320 P.2d 16. . . . Those criteria include the foreseeability of harm to the injured party, the degree of certainty that the plaintiff suffered injury, the closeness of the connection between the defendant's conduct and the injury suffered, the moral blame attached to the defendant's conduct and the policy of preventing future harm. . . .

Here, there can be no question on the foreseeability of harm. The plaintiff herself described the risk as being similar to "giving a six year old a loaded gun." There is also no question that McKenna was injured and that absent the Straughans' decision to make a car available to their daughter, Cherie would not have possessed what in her hands was a dangerous instrumentality. The incident occurred 10 days after the Straughans advanced the funds.

In terms of moral responsibility, there is no functional difference between the Straughans giving their daughter the keys to a car or giving her funds specifically to acquire one. Arguably, the Straughans who loaned money to their daughter so she could have permanent use of a car are more culpable than if they had merely allowed her to borrow their car for temporary use. In effect, they gave their daughter a weapon which she was able to use at any and all times regardless of her condition. . . . Imposing potential liability on the Straughans serves the important public policy of protecting the public from intoxicated drivers who cause needless and tragic deaths and injuries on the highways. Our holding has no effect upon the typical financial transaction in which an automobile is financed through a bank or commercial lender since we are not suggesting a lender has an affirmative duty to investigate the driver's condition before advancing funds. . . .

Because we conclude the Straughans' status as lienholder does not preclude their liability on a negligence theory, we reverse the summary judgment to permit a resolution in trial of the factual issues presented.

Notes

1. ***Negligent Enablement.*** In Vince v. Wilson, 561 A.2d 103 (Vt. 1989) the court held that whether a relative, who provided funding for the purchase of a vehicle despite knowledge that the purchaser had no driver's license, had failed the driver's test several times, and had abused alcohol and other drugs was liable for negligent entrustment was for the jury to determine. A similar question was presented as to the liability of the auto sale corporation and the salespersons, because there was evidence that the relative told them that the purchaser lacked a license and had repeatedly failed the test.

But see Zedella v. Gibson, 650 N.E.2d 1000, 1003 (Ill. 1995) (holding that a father's co-signing of a loan for his son to buy a car did not amount to negligent entrustment).

2. ***Negligent Entrustment.*** Section 390 of the Restatement, Second, of Torts provides:

> One who supplies . . . a chattel for the use of another whom the supplier knows or has reason to know to be likely because of his youth, inexperience, or otherwise, to use it in a manner involving unreasonable risk of physical harm to himself and others whom the supplier should expect to share in or be endangered by its use, is subject to liability for physical harm resulting to them.

See Danielle A. *ex rel.* Darryl A. v. Christopher P., 776 N.Y.S.2d 446 (N.Y. Sup. 2004) (paintball gun); Rios v. Smith, 744 N.E.2d 1156 (N.Y. 2001) (all-terrain vehicles); Ross v. Glaser, 559 N.W.2d 331 (Mich. App. 1996) (handgun).

3. ***"Entrusting" a Chattel to Its Owner.*** Some cases hold that to be held liable for negligent entrustment, the defendant must have a superior right to the chattel, and therefore a person with temporary possession of a vehicle cannot be held liable for returning it to its owner. *See* De Blanc v. Jensen, 59 S.W.3d 373 (Tex. App. 2001) (no liability even though the defendants' son had two previous DWIs and the defendant father held a lien on the truck).

7. Statutes Relating to Rescue

Minnesota and Vermont have adopted legislation requiring some persons to render emergency assistance. Here is the Minnesota statute, which combines a duty-to-rescue statute with a "Good Samaritan" immunity statute.

Minnesota Statutes Annotated § 604A.01 (Westlaw 2022)
Good Samaritan Law

Subd. 1. Duty to assist. A person at the scene of an emergency who knows that another person is exposed to or has suffered grave physical harm shall, to the extent that the person can do so without danger or peril to self or others, give reasonable assistance to the exposed person. Reasonable assistance may include obtaining or attempting to obtain aid from law enforcement or medical personnel. A person who violates this subdivision is guilty of a petty misdemeanor.

Subd. 2. General immunity from liability.

(a) A person who, without compensation or the expectation of compensation, renders emergency care, advice, or assistance at the scene of an emergency or during transit to a location where professional medical care can be rendered, is not liable for any civil damages . . . , unless the person acts in a willful and wanton or reckless manner. . . . This subdivision does not apply to a person rendering emergency care, advice, or assistance during the course of regular employment, and receiving compensation or expecting to receive compensation for rendering the care, advice, or assistance.

(b) For the purposes of this section, the scene of an emergency is an area outside the confines of a hospital or other institution that has hospital facilities, or an office of a person licensed to practice one or more of the healing arts. . . .

(c) For the purposes of this section, "person" includes a public or private nonprofit volunteer firefighter, volunteer police officer, volunteer ambulance attendant, volunteer first provider of emergency medical services, volunteer ski patroller, and any partnership, corporation, association, or other entity.

(d) For the purposes of this section, "compensation" does not include payments, reimbursement for expenses, or pension benefits paid to members of volunteer organizations.

(e) For purposes of this section, "emergency care" includes providing emergency medical care by using or providing an automatic external defibrillator,[2] unless the person on whom the device is to be used objects. . . .

Notes

1. ***Scope of the Minnesota Duty to Aid.*** *See* Swenson v. Waseca Mut. Ins. Co., 653 N.W.2d 794 (Minn. Ct. App. 2002) (a motorist who was providing roadside assistance to an injured snowmobiler by attempting to drive her to the hospital was immune from liability for negligent driving under the Good Samaritan law, and

2. Automatic external defibrillators (AEDs) employ a series of small electrical shocks to help restore normal heart rhythms. To encourage the use of such equipment outside of health care facilities, Congress passed the Cardiac Arrest Survival Act of 2000, which, within limits, immunizes from liability for negligence persons who acquire, use, or attempt to use AEDs. *See* 42 U.S.C. § 238q (Westlaw 2022). — Ed.

that protection was not lost by reason of a *de minimis* delay occasioned by planned indirect route to the hospital).

2. ***Vermont Duty to Aid.*** Contrast subdivision 1 of the Minnesota statute, *supra*, with the Vermont law (Vt. Stat. Ann. Tit. 12, § 519(a) (Westlaw 2022)), which provides:

> A person who knows that another is exposed to grave physical harm shall, to the extent that the same can be rendered without danger or peril to himself or without interference with important duties owed to others, give reasonable assistance to the exposed person unless that assistance or care is being provided by others.

3. ***Statutory Duties to Aid and Negligence Per Se.*** If a person violates a statutory duty to render aid, should the person harmed by that failure be permitted to sue the offender for negligence based upon violation of the statute? That is, may a court hold that the statute sets the standard of care for a civil cause of action? Would it make a difference whether the legislation contains a provision similar to one in the Vermont statute which provides, "a person who wilfully violates . . . this section shall be fined not more than $100.00"? Vt. Stat. Ann. Tit. 12, § 519(c) (Westlaw 2022). It might be argued that such a legal obligation was intended to be backed only by a minor fine, not by the risk of a lawsuit for substantial damages. *But see* Restatement, Third, of Torts: Liab. for Physical & Emotional Harm § 38 (2012) ("When a statute requires an actor to act for the protection of another, the court may rely on the statute to decide that an affirmative duty exists and to determine the scope of that duty").

4. ***Doctors and Accident Victims.*** It is widely believed—though it may not be true—that many doctors rendering aid to accident victims have been sued for negligence in rendering that aid. "Good Samaritan" legislation typically bars negligence actions against doctors who furnish help gratuitously in emergencies. *Cf.* Carter v. Reese, 70 N.E.3d 478, 486 (Ohio 2016) (holding that the Ohio Good Samaritan immunity did not apply "only to health care professionals" because the "statute expressly states, 'No person shall be liable in civil damages . . .'").

5. ***Good Samaritan Laws and Compensation.*** The immunities conferred by a Good Samaritan Law are typically unavailable to a person who receives, or expects to receive, some form of compensation for rendering aid. *See* Tobin v. AMR Corp., 637 F. Supp. 2d 406 (N.D. Tex. 2009). In discussing an Illinois statute, the court explained:

> On-duty flight attendants are required to receive training in emergency services, and are not persons who "volunteer their time and talents." They are not "Good Samaritans" as that term is used in the statute; rather, they are professionals performing services within their job duties. They perform such services for compensation, and thus are not entitled to immunity under the Good Samaritan Act.

6. ***Emergency Medical Treatment and Active Labor Act.*** EMTALA is a federal law that requires hospitals receiving Medicare funds to provide appropriate medical screening to all persons who come to an emergency room seeking medical assistance

and to render the services that are necessary to stabilize the patient's condition. Of course, such treatment sometimes gives rise to negligence actions. Under the terms of the statute and its legislative history, "an individual physician cannot be subject to a federal EMTALA claim." Kenyon v. Hospital San Antonio, 2013 WL 210273 (D.P.R.).

7. ***Leaving the Scene***. Many if not all states prohibit those involved in a motor-vehicle accident from leaving the scene. Some of these statutes also require the rendering of assistance to anyone injured in the accident. For example:

Texas Transportation Code § 550.023 (Westlaw 2022)

Duty to Give Information and Render Aid

> The operator of a vehicle involved in an accident resulting in the injury or death of a person or damage to a vehicle that is driven or attended by a person shall:
>
> . . . .
>
> (3) provide any person injured in the accident reasonable assistance, including transporting or making arrangements for transporting the person to a physician or hospital for medical treatment if it is apparent that treatment is necessary, or if the injured person requests the transportation.

C. Abrogation of the General Rule

Soldano v. O'Daniels. The general rule that there is no duty to aid another who is in peril has long been subject to criticism. The numerous exceptions to the rule stand as judicial expressions of disdain for the standard, and there are encroachments on the rule. For example, in Soldano v. O'Daniels, 190 Cal. Rptr. 310 (Ct. App. 1983), a "Good Samaritan," who was seeking to prevent injuries that were threatened to another by a third person, asked a tavern keeper either to call the police or permit him to use the phone to make the call himself. Both requests were refused, and the injuries that were inflicted resulted in the death of the victim. Recognizing the scholarly criticism of the general rule and the fact that today many statutes encourage the rendition of assistance or require the exercise of care under given circumstances, the court held that a cause of action was stated against the tavern. Although the establishment had done nothing to give rise to the threat of harm and stood in no special relationship to either the victim or the aggressor, it was obliged to exercise minimal due care. The court carefully articulated its holding to make clear that the duty imposed was not sweeping, but only a minor abrogation of a morally questionable rule.

Preventing Aid. The *Soldano* court noted that the facts of that suit almost fell within Restatement, Second, of Torts § 327, which provides that an individual who knows that a third person is ready to give aid to another, and negligently prevents the third person from doing so, is subject to liability for harm caused by the absence of the aid. In Maldonado v. Southern Pac. Transp. Co., 629 P.2d 1001 (Ariz. App. 1981), the court explained this provision:

> The actor can prevent a third person from rendering aid to another in many ways including the following: first, by so injuring the third person as to make him incapable of giving aid; second, by interfering with his efforts to give aid; third, by injuring or destroying the usefulness of a thing which the third person is using to give aid or by otherwise preventing him from using it; fourth, by obstructing the third person's access to the other.

Of course, intentional prevention of assistance may also give rise to liability. *See* Restatement, Second, of Torts § 326.

D. The Public-Duty Rule

Governments routinely undertake to protect members of the public from harm. Police and fire protection come immediately to mind; less-obvious examples include weather forecasting (of great importance to the safety of the crews of fishing boats), air-traffic control, the installation and maintenance of traffic lights and signs, and the inspection of food.

The question of how much protection of a particular kind is enough is quintessentially legislative and executive. A city's decision to spend more on traffic-law enforcement instead of buying new fire trucks will save some lives (motorists') at the cost of others (fire victims'). Allowing all of those whose injuries might have been prevented by greater efforts in some safety area to get to a jury against the relevant government agency would soon bankrupt all governments. It would also present factfinders with issues they cannot reasonably be expected to decide: the question whether it was "unreasonable" for a city to spend three times as much on police protection as on fire prevention is not one any sensible society would entrust to juries or judges. It is therefore quite clear that a plaintiff whose only claim is that a government agency should have devoted more resources to preventing the kind of harm the plaintiff suffered has no case.

The inability of the courts to evaluate all government decisions involving safety does not mean, however, that governments can never be liable for conduct relating to safety. If a police officer on the way to interview a suspect drives negligently and runs down the plaintiff, the city will be liable (assuming that municipal immunity has been waived). It will be no defense that tight budgets required the city to hire inexperienced drivers for the police force.

The extreme cases are therefore clear: inadequate performance of specific tasks like driving a car will render a government liable; inadequate decisions about what safety precautions should be taken will not. The difficulties arise in between these extremes, as in the following opinion.

Riss v. City of New York

Court of Appeals of New York
293 N.Y.S.2d 897 (N.Y. 1968)

BREITEL, Judge.

This appeal presents, in a very sympathetic framework, the issue of the liability of a municipality for failure to provide special protection to a member of the public who was repeatedly threatened with personal harm and eventually suffered dire personal injuries for lack of such protection. The facts are amply described in the dissenting opinion. . . .

. . . [This] case involves the provision of a governmental service to protect the public generally from external hazards and particularly to control the activities of criminal wrongdoers. . . . The amount of protection that may be provided is limited by the resources of the community and by a considered legislative-executive decision as to how those resources may be deployed. For the courts to proclaim a new and general duty of protection in the law of tort, even to those who may be the particular seekers of protection based on specific hazards, could and would inevitably determine how the limited police resources of the community should be allocated and without predictable limits. . . .

Before such extension of responsibilities should be dictated by the indirect imposition of tort liabilities, there should be a legislative determination that that should be the scope of public responsibility. . . .

. . . .

When one considers the greatly increased amount of crime committed throughout the cities . . . , it is easy to see the consequences of fixing municipal liability upon a showing of probable need for and request for protection. To be sure these are grave problems at the present time, exciting high priority activity on the part of the national, State and local governments, to which the answers are neither simple, known, or presently within reasonable control. To foist a presumed cure for these problems by judicial innovation of a new kind of liability in tort would be foolhardy indeed and an assumption of judicial wisdom and power not possessed by the courts.

. . . [T]here is no warrant in judicial tradition or in the proper allocation of the powers of governments for the courts, in the absence of legislation, to carve out an area of tort liability for police protection to members of the public. . . .

Accordingly, the order of the Appellate Division affirming the judgment of dismissal should be affirmed.

KEATING, Judge (dissenting).

. . . .

Linda Riss, an attractive young woman, was for more than six months terrorized by a rejected suitor well known to the courts of this State, one Burton Pugach.

This miscreant, masquerading as a respectable attorney, repeatedly threatened to have Linda killed or maimed if she did not yield to him: "If I can't have you, no one else will have you, and when I get through with you, no one else will want you." In fear for her life, she went to those charged by law with the duty of preserving and safeguarding the lives of the citizens and residents of this State. Linda's repeated and almost pathetic pleas for aid were received with little more than indifference. . . . On June 14, 1959 Linda became engaged to another man. At a party held to celebrate the event, she received a phone call warning her that it was her "last chance." Completely distraught, she called the police, begging for help, but was refused. The next day Pugach carried out his dire threats . . . by having a hired thug throw lye in Linda's face. Linda was blinded in one eye, lost a good portion of her vision in the other, and her face was permanently scarred. After the assault the authorities concluded that there was some basis for Linda's fears, and for the next three and one-half years, she was given around-the-clock protection.

No one questions the proposition that the first duty of government is to assure its citizens the opportunity to live in personal security. And no one who reads the record of Linda's ordeal can reach a conclusion other than that the City of New York . . . completely and negligently failed to fulfill this obligation to Linda.

Linda has turned to the courts of this State for redress, asking that the city be held liable in damages for its negligent failure to protect her from harm. With compelling logic, she can point out that, if a stranger, who had absolutely no obligation to aid her, had offered her assistance, and thereafter Burton Pugach was able to injure her as a result of the negligence of the volunteer, the courts would certainly require him to pay damages. (Restatement, 2d, Torts § 323). Why then should the city, whose duties are imposed by law and include the prevention of crime . . . not be responsible? . . . .

Linda's reasoning seems so eminently sensible that surely it must come as a shock to her and to every citizen to hear the city argue and to learn that this court decides that the city has no duty to provide police protection to any given individual. What makes the city's position particularly difficult to understand is that, in conformity to the dictates of the law, Linda did not carry any weapon for self-defense (former Penal Law, § 1897). Thus, by a rather bitter irony she was required to rely for protection on the City of New York which now denies all responsibility to her.

It is not a distortion to summarize the essence of the city's case here in the following language: "Because we owe a duty to everybody, we owe it to nobody." Were it not for the fact that this position has been hallowed by much ancient and revered precedent, we would surely dismiss it as preposterous. . . .

The foremost justification repeatedly urged for the existing rule is the claim that the State and the municipalities will be exposed to limitless liability. . . .

The fear of financial disaster is a myth. The same argument was made a generation ago in opposition to proposals that the State waive its defense of "sovereign immunity." The prophecy proved false then, and it would now. . . . No municipality has gone bankrupt because it has had to respond in damages when a policeman causes injury through carelessly driving a police car or in the thousands of other situations where, by judicial fiat or legislative enactment, the State and its subdivisions have been held liable for the tortious conduct of their employees. Thus, in the past four or five years, New York City has been presented with an average of some 10,000 claims each year. The figure would sound ominous except for the fact the city has been paying out less than $8,000,000 on tort claims each year and this amount includes all those sidewalk defect and snow and ice cases about which the courts fret so often. . . . Certainly this is a slight burden in a budget of more than six billion dollars . . . and of no importance as compared to the injustice of permitting unredressed wrongs to continue to go unrepaired. That Linda Riss should be asked to bear the loss, which should properly fall on the city if we assume, as we must, in the present posture of the case, that her injuries resulted from the city's failure to provide sufficient police to protect Linda is contrary to the most elementary notions of justice.

. . . .

Another variation of the "crushing burden" argument is the contention that, every time a crime is committed, the city will be sued and the claim will be made that it resulted from inadequate police protection. Here . . . too the underlying assumption of the argument is fallacious because it assumes that a strict liability standard is to be imposed and that the courts would prove completely unable to apply general principles of tort liability in a reasonable fashion in the context of actions arising from the negligent acts of police and fire personnel. The argument is also made as if there were no such legal principles as fault, proximate cause or foreseeability, all of which operate to keep liability within reasonable bounds. No one is contending that the police must be at the scene of every potential crime or must provide a personal bodyguard to every person who walks into a police station and claims to have been threatened. They need only act as a reasonable man would under the circumstances. At first there would be a duty to inquire. If the injury indicates nothing to substantiate the alleged threat, the matter may be put aside. . . . If, however, the claims prove to have some basis, appropriate steps would be necessary.

. . . .

It is also contended that liability for inadequate police protection will make the courts the arbiters of decisions by the Police Commissioner in allocating his manpower and his resources. We are not dealing here with a situation where the injury or loss occurred as a result of a conscious choice of policy made by those exercising high administrative responsibility after a complete and thorough deliberation of various alternatives. There was no major policy decision taken by the Police Commissioner to disregard Linda Riss' appeal for help because there was absolutely no manpower available to deal with Pugach. This "garden variety" negligence case arose in the course of "day-by-day operations of government". . . .

More significant, however, is the fundamental flaw in the reasoning behind the argument alleging judicial interference. It is a complete oversimplification of the problem of municipal tort liability. What it ignores is the fact that indirectly courts are reviewing administrative practices in almost every tort case against the State or a municipality, including even decisions of the Police Commissioner. Every time a municipal hospital is held liable for malpractice resulting from inadequate record-keeping, the courts are in effect making a determination that the municipality should have hired or assigned more clerical help or more competent help to medical records or should have done something to improve its record keeping procedures so that the particular injury would not have occurred. Every time a municipality is held liable for a defective sidewalk, it is as if the courts are saying that more money and resources should have been allocated to sidewalk repair, instead of to other public services.

The situation is nowise different in the case of police protection. . . .

. . . .

What has existed until now is that the City of New York and other municipalities have been able to engage in a sort of false bookkeeping in which the real costs of inadequate or incompetent police protection have been hidden by charging the expenditures to the individuals who have sustained often catastrophic losses rather than to the community where it belongs, because the latter had the power to prevent the losses.

. . . . At one time the government was completely immunized from . . . [liability]. This is much less so now, and the imposition of liability has had healthy side effects. In many areas, it has resulted in the adoption of better and more considered procedures just as workmen's compensation resulted in improved industrial safety practices. To visit liability upon the city here will no doubt have similar constructive effects. . . .

. . . [A]lthough "sovereign immunity," by that name, supposedly died . . . it has been revived in a new form. It now goes by the name "public duty."

. . . .

The [public-duty] rule is Judge made and can be judicially modified. By statute, the judicially created doctrine of "sovereign immunity" was destroyed. It was an unrighteous doctrine, carrying as it did the connotation that the government is above the law. Likewise, the law should be purged of all new evasions, which seek to avoid the full implications of the repeal of sovereign immunity.

. . . . A few examples of the actions of the police should suffice to show the true state of the record. Linda Riss received a telephone call from a person who warned Linda that Pugach was arranging to have her beaten up. A detective learned the identity of the caller. . . . When Linda requested that Pugach be arrested, the detective said he could not do that because she had not yet been hurt. The statement was not so. It was and is a crime to conspire to injure someone. True there was no basis to arrest Pugach then, but that was only because the necessary leg work had not been done. No one went to speak to the informant, who might have furnished additional leads. Linda claimed to be receiving telephone calls almost every day. These calls could have been monitored for a few days to obtain evidence against Pugach. Any number of reasonable alternatives presented themselves. . . .

. . . [W]ith actual notice of danger and ample opportunity to confirm and take reasonable remedial steps, a jury could find that the persons involved acted unreasonably and negligently. . . . The order of the Appellate Division should be reversed and a new trial granted.

. . . .

[FULD, C.J., and BURKE, SCILEPPI, BERGAN, and JASEN, JJ., concurred with BREITEL, J.]

Notes

1. ***Inadequate Police and Fire Protection.*** It is still the rule in many states that there is no duty to provide police or fire protection to a particular individual in the absence of facts establishing a "special relationship" between the governmental defendant and the plaintiff. *See* Fisk v. City of Kirkland, 194 P.3d 984 (Wash. 2008) (holding that a "municipality is not liable in tort for negligence for the increased fire damage because of insufficient water pressure for fire suppression purposes"); King v. Northeast Security, Inc., 790 N.E.2d 474, 478–79 (Ind. 2003) (recognizing that a government unit is immune from liability "where a city or state fails to provide adequate police protection to prevent crime" and stating that "[t]o say the governmental entity is immune for acts or omissions in described areas is the functional equivalent of asserting the entity has no duty to anyone in carrying out those activities"); *but see* Am. Jur. 2d Munic. & State Tort Liability § 88, *The Public Duty Doctrine* (2003) (stating that the public-duty rule "provides a defense independent of sovereign immunity").

2. ***Other Public Services.*** The "public-duty rule" has sometimes been applied in contexts not involving police or fire protection. *See* Stone v. N.C. Dept. of Labor, 495 S.E.2d 711 (N.C. 1998) (failure to inspect a plant before a fire); Ohio Dept. of Rehab. and Correction, 728 N.E.2d 428 (Ohio Ct. App. 1999) (release and supervision of a parolee); Stratmeyer v. U.S., 67 F.3d 1340 (7th Cir. 1995) (failure to quarantine a herd of diseased cattle). *But see* Gregory v. Clive, 651 S.E.2d 709 (Ga. 2007) (holding that the doctrine covers only police officers and not building inspectors).

3. ***Firsthand Observation.*** Cases in which a public officer merely knows of a risk of harm to an individual may be distinguished from those where an officer actually witnesses the infliction of harm. In Crosland v. New York Transit Auth., 498 N.E.2d 143 (N.Y. 1986), hoodlums jumped the turnstiles at a subway stop and savagely attacked a group of students, one of whom died. The complaint alleged that several transit authority workers witnessed the incident and did nothing to summon aid. Distinguishing cases in which recovery was denied to persons attacked at stations where no police were present, the court held that a motion to dismiss was properly denied.

4. ***Voluntary Governmental Assumption of Duty.*** In Florence v. Goldberg, 375 N.E.2d 763 (N.Y. 1978), a city was sued by the mother of a first-grader who was struck by a taxicab while returning from school. The complaint alleged that the police department's failure to provide a substitute for a school crossing guard who had called in sick constituted negligence. A crossing guard had been on duty at the intersection for more than two weeks, leading the mother to conclude that she did not need to arrange for someone to provide a similar service. The court stated:

> [W]here a municipality assumes a duty to a particular person or class of persons, it must perform that duty in a nonnegligent manner, notwithstanding that absent its voluntary assumption of that duty, none would have otherwise existed. . . .

See also Schultz v. Foster-Glocester Reg. Sch. Dist., 755 A.2d 153 (R.I. 2000) (allegedly negligent failure to train, supervise, instruct, equip, and treat an injured member of a cheerleading team); Nelson v. Salt Lake City, 919 P.2d 568 (Utah 1996) (allegedly negligent failure by a city to maintain a fence between a park and a river).

5. ***Police Statutory Duties.*** Liability may also be imposed when the police violate a statutory duty. *See* Gonzalez v. Johnson, 581 S.W.3d 529, 535 (Ky. 2019) ("[A]n officer can be the cause-in-fact and legal cause of damages inflicted upon a third party as a result of a negligent pursuit. The duty of care owed to the public at large by pursuing officers is that of due regard in accordance with KRS 189.940.").

6. ***Special Relationships.*** A plaintiff can avoid the obstacle to recovery posed by the public-duty rule by establishing that there was a "special relationship" between the plaintiff and the governmental defendants. The following decision illustrates one type of special-relationship case.

Sorichetti v. City of New York

Court of Appeals of New York
482 N.E.2d 70 (N.Y. 1985)

ALEXANDER, Judge.

This action was commenced against the City of New York (City) by Dina Sorichetti, an infant, and her mother, Josephine Sorichetti, to recover damages resulting from injuries inflicted on Dina by her father, Frank Sorichetti. Plaintiffs' theory of recovery is that the City, through the . . . Police Department, negligently failed to take Frank Sorichetti into custody or otherwise prevent his assault upon his daughter after being informed that he may have violated a Family Court order of protection and that he had threatened to do harm to the infant. Special Term denied a pretrial motion by the City to dismiss the complaint for failure to state a cause of action . . . , and the Appellate Division affirmed. . . .

A jury thereafter returned a verdict in plaintiffs' favor in the amount of $3,000,000 for the infant and $40,000 for the mother. The Appellate Division modified by ordering a new trial on damages unless Dina Sorichetti stipulated to reduce her award to $2,000,000. . . . The infant so stipulated and judgment was entered. . . .

Josephine and Frank Sorichetti were married in 1949, and had three children, the youngest being Dina, who was born in 1969. It appears that Frank drank excessively and that the couple's relationship was quite stormy, with Frank becoming violent and abusive. . . . In January 1975, Josephine obtained an order of protection in Family Court following a particularly violent incident in which her husband had threatened her and punched her in the chest so forcefully as to send her "flying across the room." The order recited that Frank was "forbidden to assault, menace, harass, endanger, threaten or act in a disorderly manner toward" Josephine. By June 1975, Frank's drinking and abusiveness had intensified. Consequently, Josephine moved out of their residence. . . . Upon her return in early July to obtain her personal belongings, Frank attacked her with a butcher knife, cutting her hand, which required suturing, and threatened to kill her and the children. The police were summoned. . . . A second order of protection was issued. . . .

. . . [I]n September 1975, Josephine served divorce papers on . . . Frank [and he] became enraged and proceeded to destroy the contents of their apartment. He broke every piece of furniture, cut up clothes belonging to his wife and Dina, threw the food out of the refrigerator and bent every knife and fork. The police from the 43rd precinct were summoned, but they refused to arrest Frank because "he lived there."

Family Court entered a third order of protection that also ordered Frank Sorichetti to stay away from Josephine's home. During the ensuing months, Frank continued to harass his wife and daughter, following them in the mornings as they walked to Dina's school and threatening that they "were Sorichettis" and were going to "die Sorichettis," and that he was going to "bury them." Josephine reported these incidents to the 43rd precinct. . . .

On November 6, 1975, Josephine and Frank appeared in Family Court where the order of protection was made final for one year. Included in the order was a provision granting Frank visitation privileges with his daughter each weekend from 10:00 a.m. Saturday until 6:00 p.m. Sunday. It was agreed that Dina would be picked up and dropped off at the 43rd precinct. . . . [T]he order also recited that: "[T]he presentation of this Certificate to any Peace Officer shall constitute authority for said Peace Officer to take into custody the person charged with violating the terms of such Order of Protection and bring said person before this Court and otherwise, so far as lies within his power, to aid the Petitioner in securing the protection such Order was intended to afford."

On the following weekend, Josephine delivered Dina to her husband in front of the 43rd precinct at the appointed time. As he walked away with the child, Frank turned to Josephine and shouted, "You, I'm going to kill you." Pointing to his daughter, he said, "You see Dina; you better do the sign of the cross before this weekend is up." He then made the sign of the cross on himself. Josephine understood her husband's statements and actions to be a death threat, and she immediately entered the police station and reported the incident to the officer at the desk. . . .

At 5:30 p.m. the following day, Sunday, Josephine returned to the station house. She was distraught, agitated and crying.... She showed the officer the order of protection and related the threats made the previous morning.... The officer testified that he told Josephine that if "he didn't drop her off in a reasonable time, we would send a radio car out."

The officer referred Josephine to Lieutenant Leon Granello, to whom she detailed the prior events. He dismissed the protective order as "only a piece of paper" that "means nothing" and told Josephine to wait outside until 6:00. At 6:00 p.m., Josephine returned to the Lieutenant who told her, "why don't you wait a few minutes.... Maybe he took her to a movie. He'll be back. Don't worry about it." Josephine made several similar requests, but each time was told "to just wait. We'll just wait."....

.... Josephine ... continued to plead that the officer take immediate action. The Lieutenant again told Josephine "Let's just wait." At 7:00, the Lieutenant told Josephine to leave her phone number and to go home, and that he would call her if Sorichetti showed up. She did as suggested.

.... Between 6:55 and 7:00 p.m., Sorichetti had attacked the infant repeatedly with a fork, a knife and a screwdriver and had attempted to saw off her leg.... The infant plaintiff was hospitalized for 40 days and remains permanently disabled. Frank Sorichetti was convicted of attempted murder, and is currently serving a prison sentence.

....[3]

A municipality cannot be held liable for injuries resulting from a failure to provide adequate police protection absent a special relationship existing between the municipality and the injured party.... In the context of police protection, a different rule "could and would inevitably determine how the limited police resources of the community should be allocated and without predictable limits"....

In several extraordinary instances, a special relationship has been found which imposes a duty on a municipality to provide reasonable police protection to an individual. For example, in Schuster v. City of New York, 5 N.Y.2d 75, 154 N.E.2d 534, the City was held liable when a citizen collaborated with the police in the arrest of a dangerous fugitive and was thereafter denied protection after he received death threats, which were successfully carried out. Similarly, in De Long v. County of Erie (60 N.Y.2d 296, 457 N.E.2d 717 ...), we imposed a special duty of care on a

3. [Fn. 1:] Family Court Act § 168(1) provides: "In any case in which an order of protection or temporary order of protection has been made by the family court, the clerk of the court shall issue a copy of such order to the petitioner and respondent and to any other person affected by the order. The presentation of a copy of an order of protection or temporary order of protection or a warrant or a certificate of warrant to any peace officer, acting pursuant to his special duties, or police officer shall constitute authority for him to arrest a person charged with violating the terms of such order of protection or temporary order of protection and bring such person before the court and, otherwise, so far as lies within his power, to aid in securing the protection such order was intended to afford".

municipality toward a woman who called 911 for police assistance, was told that assistance would be forthcoming, and in reliance on this assurance exposed herself to danger that resulted in her death.

A key element in each of these cases ... is some direct contact between agents of the municipality and the injured party.

In the present case, we hold that a special relationship existed between the City and Dina Sorichetti which arose out of (1) the order of protection; (2) the police department's knowledge of Frank Sorichetti's violent history, gained through and verified both by its actual dealings with him, the existence of the order of protection, and its knowledge of the specific situation in which the infant had been placed; (3) its response to Josephine Sorichetti's pleas for assistance on the day of the assault; and (4) Mrs. Sorichetti's reasonable expectation of police protection.

In enacting Family Court Act § 168, the Legislature intended to encourage police involvement in domestic matters, an area in which the police traditionally have exhibited a reluctance to intervene.... When presented with an order of protection, a police officer is not mandated to make an arrest. Nonetheless, such presentation along with an allegation that the order has been violated, obligates the officer to investigate and take appropriate action.

The issuance of a protective order creates a situation quite unlike that presented in *Riss*, 22 N.Y.2d 579, 240 N.E.2d 860, *supra* in several respects. The order evinces a preincident legislative and judicial determination that its holder should be accorded a reasonable degree of protection from a particular individual. It is presumptive evidence that the individual whose conduct is proscribed has already been found by a court to be a dangerous or violent person and that violations of the order's terms should be treated seriously. Significantly, the class of potential victims to whom a duty to investigate might arise is necessarily limited by the terms of the order.

.... These circumstances are significantly different from those in *Riss*, 22 N.Y.2d 579, 240 N.E.2d 860, *supra* wherein the assailant, who was unknown to the police, was seemingly a citizen in good standing who, up until the attack, had done nothing to indicate a likelihood that he would make good on his threats....

Aside from their awareness of the threatmaker's violent propensity, a critical factor in the creation of a special duty of protection herein is the police officers' conduct toward Josephine.... [T]he police repeatedly told Josephine to "wait awhile longer," never dispelling the notion that they would provide assistance at some reasonable time, until she was finally told at 7:00 to "go home." Josephine, in her helpless and distraught state, had no alternative but to seek the assistance of the police to assure her daughter's safety.... The passage of time was critical inasmuch as the assault did not take place until approximately 6:55.

Thus, in this respect also, this case is unlike *Riss* ... wherein the police made clear to the victim that they would provide no assistance based on the assailant's threats alone.... [W]e hold that a special relationship existed between the police and Josephine and her six-year-old daughter such that the jury could properly consider whether the police conduct satisfied the duty of care owing to Dina.

. . . .

Order affirmed, with costs.

Notes

1. ***Related Cases.*** *Compare Sorichetti with*: Solomon v. City of New York, 489 N.E.2d 1294 (N.Y. 1985) (by promulgating and enforcing regulations prohibiting bicycle riding in an area of a park, where a park patron was struck, the city did not assume a special relationship toward the patron to protect the latter from the prohibited activity); Caldwell v. City of Philadelphia, 517 A.2d 1296 (Pa. Super. Ct. 1986) (officer had no special relationship to an injured pedestrian that created a duty to obtain identification of the motorist who left the scene); Kircher v. City of Jamestown, 543 N.E.2d 443 (N.Y. 1989) (no liability for an officer's failure to call in a witness' report of an abduction as promised, absent direct contact between the victim and the police and justifiable reliance by the victim on assurances of protection that would create a "special relationship"; stating that in *Sorichetti* relaxation of the direct-contact requirement was justified by the existence of the protective order).

2. ***Reliance on Assurances.*** A number of states hold that reliance upon governmental assurances of action will support a claim based on non-action. For example, in City of Rome v. Jordan, 426 S.E.2d 861, 863 (Ga. 1993), the court required the following elements for imposition of a private duty on governmental defendants:

> (1) an explicit assurance by the municipality, through promises or actions, that it would act on behalf of the injured party;
>
> (2) knowledge on the part of the municipality that inaction could lead to harm; and
>
> (3) justifiable and detrimental reliance by the injured party on the municipality's affirmative undertaking.

See also Cuffy v. City of New York, 513 N.Y.S.2d 372 (N.Y. 1987) (same test as in *Rome*, except that direct contact between the city and injured party is also required).

In some cases, the absence of an assurance of help is fatal to the plaintiff's claim. *See* Cummins v. Lewis County, 133 P.3d 458 (Wash. 2006) (no special relationship where a 911 dispatcher did not provide an express assurance that aid would be dispatched); Mullin v. Municipal City of South Bend, 639 N.E.2d 278, 284 (Ind. 1994) (no assurance that an ambulance would be dispatched to a fire immediately).

See also Lauer v. City of N.Y., 733 N.E.2d 184 (N.Y. 2000) (holding that a medical examiner, who failed to correct an erroneous autopsy report about a child that led to a homicide investigation against the child's father, did not have a "special relationship" with the father so as to render the city liable to the father for negligent infliction of emotional distress because the father alleged no personal contact with medical examiner and no other conduct on which he could have relied).

However, there is also authority that:

> a promise and reliance thereon are [not] indispensable elements of a special relationship. Such a relationship has also been found when the conduct of a police officer, in a situation of dependency, results in detrimental reliance on him for protection . . . [by] lulling the injured parties into a false sense of security and perhaps preventing other assistance from being sought.

Souza v. City of Antioch, 62 Cal. Rptr. 2d 909, 918–19 (Cal. Ct. App. 1997) (police had a duty to exercise reasonable care when they took exclusive control of hostage situation).

3. ***Range of Exceptions to the Public Duty Rule.*** In Gonzales v. City of Bozeman, 217 P.3d 487 (Mont. 2009), in rejecting a lack-of-police-protection claim, the court summarized the law in that state:

> There are four recognized situations in which a special relationship has been found: (1) where a statute intended to protect a specific class of persons from a particular type of harm imposes a duty; (2) where the government agent undertakes a specific action to protect a person or property; (3) where government action reasonably induces detrimental reliance by a member of the public; and (4) where the government has actual custody of the plaintiff or of a third person who harms the plaintiff.

4. ***Public Utilities.*** Policy considerations comparable to those described in *Riss* may apply to actions against public utilities, such as electric companies and water companies, for harms caused by the companies' failure to provide services. For example, in Strauss v. Belle Realty Co., 482 N.E.2d 34 (N.Y. 1985), the New York Court of Appeals held that an electric company could not be held liable to someone who fell on stairs that were unlit because of a blackout caused by the company's negligence. The court's main concern seems to have been preventing "crushing exposure to liability." The accident in question took place during a 25-hour blackout of New York City. *Compare* Weinberg v. Dinger, 524 A.2d 366 (N.J. 1987), holding that private water companies which negligently failed to provide water under sufficient pressure to operate fire hydrants could be liable to owners of property that burned.

In some states, statutory tariffs limit a utility's duties to customers. *See* First Assembly of God v. Texas Utilities, 52 S.W.3d 482 (Tex. App. 2001) (holding that a utility company was not liable for fire damages to a church sanctuary that occurred following repairs because the applicable tariff limited liability to cases where the utility's negligence was the "sole proximate cause" of the damages, and here the damages were also caused by an initial lightning strike and bad wiring inside the church).

In many cases, utilities are subject to liability under ordinary negligence principles. *See* Goldberg v. Florida Power & Light Co., 899 So. 2d 1105 (Fla. 2005) (holding that a power company had a "clear duty to warn motorists of the hazardous situation it created by the deactivation of the traffic signal").

5. ***Volunteer Fire Departments.*** The tort liability of volunteer fire departments and their firefighters is governed by statute in many states. *See, e.g.*, Tex. Civ. Prac. & Rem. Code §78.103 (Westlaw 2022) ("A volunteer fire department is . . . liable for damages . . . only to the extent that a county providing the same or similar services would be liable . . . and . . . entitled to the exclusions, exceptions, and defenses applicable to a county under . . . statutory or common law"); *id.* at §78.104 (discussing volunteer firefighters, rather than volunteer fire departments).

6. ***Abrogation of the Public-Duty Rule.*** In Wallace v. Ohio Dept. of Commerce, 773 N.E.2d 1018 (Ohio 2002), the court reviewed the state's prior decisions, which had broadly endorsed the public-duty rule. The court then abrogated the rule in a particular context by holding that the rule was incompatible with the express language of a statutory provision requiring that the state's liability in the Court of Claims be determined "in accordance with the same rules of law applicable to suits between private parties."

See also Coleman v. East Joliet Fire Protection Dist., 46 N.E.3d 741, 757 (Ill. 2016) (abolishing the rule and noting that "the public policy behind the judicially created public duty rule and its special duty exception have largely been supplanted by the legislature's enactment of statutory immunities, rendering the public duty rule and its special duty exception obsolete"); Natrona County v. Blake, 81 P.3d 948 (Wyo. 2003) (noting that "there remain pockets of continued recognition of the public duty rule," but holding that the rule did not bar a wrongful death action against a county arising from a murder perpetrated by an inmate who escaped from a correctional facility).

7. ***Judicial Threat and Legislative Response.*** In Jean v. Commonwealth, 610 N.E.2d 305 (Mass. 1993), the court announced its intention to abolish the public-duty rule at the first opportunity after the end of the legislative session, thereby allowing the legislature time to make appropriate arrangements. The legislature responded that same year by amending the law that waives sovereign immunity.

Massachusetts General Laws 258 §§2–10 (Westlaw 2022)

§2 Public employers shall be liable for injury or loss of property or personal injury or death caused by the negligent or wrongful act or omission of any public employee while acting within the scope of his office or employment, in the same manner and to the same extent as a private individual under like circumstances . . .

§10 The provisions of sections one to eight, inclusive, shall not apply to . . .

(h) any claim based upon the failure to establish a police department or a particular police protection service, or if police protection is provided, for failure to provide adequate police protection, prevent the commission of crimes, investigate, detect or solve crimes, identify or apprehend criminals or suspects, arrest or detain suspects, or enforce any law, but not including

> claims based upon the negligent operation of motor vehicles, negligent protection, supervision or care of persons in custody, or as otherwise provided in clause (1) of subparagraph (j).
>
> . . . .
>
> (j) any claim based on an act or failure to act to prevent or diminish the harmful consequences of a condition or situation, including the violent or tortious conduct of a third person, which is not originally caused by the public employer or any other person acting on behalf of the public employer. This exclusion shall not apply to:
>
> > (1) any claim based upon explicit and specific assurances of safety or assistance, beyond general representations that investigation or assistance will be or has been undertaken, made to the direct victim or a member of his family or household by a public employee, provided that the injury resulted in part from reliance on those assurances. A permit, certificate or report of findings of an investigation or inspection shall not constitute such assurances of safety or assistance. . . .

How would the plaintiffs in *Riss* and *Sorichetti* have fared under the Massachusetts law?

Chapter 10

Limited Duty: Premises Liability

A. The Traditional Categories: Trespassers, Licensees, and Invitees

The early development of the common law was in many respects stridently individualistic. Consistent with that philosophy, the law developed rules which granted possessors of land great scope within which they could do as they pleased, free of most worries of tort liability to those injured by a condition of the property or an activity carried on there.

Three Types of Status. During the late nineteenth and early twentieth centuries, the law developed a rigid system that classified persons on land as "trespassers," "licensees," or "invitees." A person's status determined the duty of care owed by the landowner, or by an occupier of land (such as a tenant), toward that person. This was once the law in every American jurisdiction, and it continues to be the law in many places.

Trespassers—persons present without a privilege or consent of the possessor—were afforded the least protection; licensees—those present with consent or privilege, but often for their own purposes—were entitled to somewhat greater care; and invitees—persons present on the land at the possessor's invitation and often for the possessor's economic benefit—were owed the usual tort duty of reasonable care under the circumstances. In premises-liability litigation, proper categorization of the injured person's status became a question of preeminent importance.

A New Approach. In recent decades, about half of the states have rejected the traditional approach to premises liability in whole or in part. Some of those states hold that possessors ordinarily must exercise reasonable care to protect any entrant on the land from harm. These jurisdictions treat the plaintiff's status as a trespasser, licensee, or invitee as merely one factor to be considered in determining whether the defendant behaved reasonably. Other states have eliminated the distinction between invitees and licensees, and impose a duty of reasonable care to anyone rightfully on the premises.

Second Restatement Versus Third Restatement. The Third Restatement has weighed in on the side of a unitary standard, requiring reasonable care in all cases, except those involving "flagrant trespassers." *See* Restatement, Third, of Torts: Liab. for Physical & Emotional Harm § 51 (2012).

For present purposes, the important point is that different parts of the country embrace divergent views about the structure of the law of premises liability. In roughly half the states, the traditional categories remain critically important. In these jurisdictions, cases still abound with citations to the Restatement, Second, of Torts, which spells out in vivid terms the traditional approach to premises liability. In the remainder of the country, the status categories are much less important. In these jurisdictions, the law is more consistent with the Restatement, Third, of Torts.

This chapter focuses first on the traditional categories of premises liability and then on the abrogation of those rules. It also discusses certain forms of statutory protection for landowners, such as "recreational use statutes," and the special rules applicable to lessors of property who are not in possession.

1. Trespassers

Bonney v. Canadian National Railway Co.

United States Court of Appeals for the First Circuit
800 F.2d 274 (1st Cir. 1986)

LEVIN H. CAMPBELL, Chief Judge.

Plaintiff-appellee Cheryl Bonney brought a tort action seeking damages for the death of her husband, Rodney Bonney, which resulted from his attempt to rescue a 15-year-old trespasser who fell from a railroad bridge under the control of defendant-appellant Canadian National Railway Company (the "Railway"). The Railway now appeals from the judgment entered against it....

The railroad bridge, leased to the Railway, spans the Androscoggin River between Lewiston and Auburn, Maine. The bridge is a concrete and steel structure, approximately 410 feet long, with tracks about 50 feet above the surface of the river. The tracks sit on railroad ties which are spaced several inches apart and which extend about three feet on either side of the tracks. Apart from widely spaced steel supports, there is nothing on the sides of the ties to prevent a pedestrian from falling off the bridge into the river below.

While there is a bridge designed for cars and pedestrians a short distance down the river, residents in the area frequently used the railroad trestle as a shortcut.... The Railway had been aware of this practice for decades. At times, the Railway had placed "No Trespassing" signs on the bridge. The signs, however, were often removed by vandals, and none was posted the day of the accident. In 1969, the Railway made an unsuccessful attempt to secure enforcement of existing Maine laws forbidding trespass on railroad property. Since then, the Railway has made no effort to prevent pedestrian traffic on the bridge.

On the night of April 6, 1981, 15-year-old Jonathan Thibodeau attempted to return from Auburn to his home in Lewiston via the railroad bridge.... The light was so dim that Thibodeau's companion, Mark Sheink, could not see whether anything was written on the trestle. Upon reaching the bridge, Thibodeau told Sheink that he was going to ride his bicycle across the bridge with the tires outside the rails. Sheink warned him not to do so, telling Thibodeau he would die if he attempted such a ride. Nonetheless, Thibodeau rode off ahead. Sheink soon heard a "cathump" and, after a pause, a splash. He then heard Thibodeau's cries for help from the river below.

Sheink ran to a nearby store for help. The first police officer to arrive, Rodney Bonney, swam out in an attempt to rescue Thibodeau. Subsequently, another officer, realizing that Officer Bonney and Thibodeau were in distress, swam out to assist them. Officer Bonney pushed Thibodeau toward the second officer who tried, unsuccessfully, to bring Thibodeau back to shore. Both Thibodeau and Officer Bonney drowned.

. . . .

If . . . defendant violated a duty to Thibodeau, its liability may be extended for the rescuer's benefit, on the theory that defendant's tortious conduct created the situation which invited the rescue attempt, and that the attempt was a foreseeable consequence of defendant's actions. . . .

Under Maine law, . . . a landowner owes no duty of care to a trespasser; its duty is simply to refrain from "wanton, wilful, or reckless acts." . . . The district court ruled that the Railway's "failure to take anything beyond token measures to prevent injury to pedestrians" evinced such a "callous indifference to a known condition of extreme danger to the public" as to violate even the minimum duty owed to trespassers. On appeal, defendant argues that the simple failure to make its premises safe for trespassers does not rise to the level of wanton misconduct forbidden under Maine law. We agree.

In reaching its conclusion that the Railway's failure to act constituted wanton misconduct in this case, the district court relied on a Maine case which defined "wanton misconduct" in the context of an automobile accident as "a reckless disregard of danger to others," Blanchard v. Bass, 153 Me. 354, 358, 139 A.2d 359 (1958), as well as W. Prosser, The Law of Torts § 34, at 184-85 (4th ed. 1971) (defining reckless acts as "highly unreasonable conduct, or an extreme departure from ordinary care, in a situation where a high degree of danger is apparent"). Holding under this standard that the Railway's failure to act displayed "a reckless disregard of danger to others," the court emphasized that the Railway had known "for decades" that the bridge was heavily used by pedestrians of all ages, especially children, and by bicyclists. Witnesses, including five for the railroad, testified that the traffic across the bridge was heavy, from twenty to fifty people on a "busy day," including "winos" and young adults coming from bars at night. Moreover, the court found that the bridge was clearly unsafe for pedestrian use: there were no guardrails, the spaces between the ties were irregular, making it easy to lose one's footing, and protruding between every few ties were large nuts-and-bolts that made walking even more treacherous. . . .

But while we accept the above findings, we do not read Maine case law as supporting a determination that the Railway's "failure to take anything beyond token measures to prevent injury to pedestrians" rose to the level of a "reckless act" violative of a *landowner's* duty towards trespassers. The *Blanchard* definition of "wanton misconduct" was not made in the context of a Maine trespass case, where a defendant normally owes no duty of care to a trespasser. Rather the *Blanchard* definition was tailored to an automobile accident case where the court could properly ask whether defendant's actions in causing a car accident rose to the level of wanton misconduct (or whether he was simply negligent), since defendant had in any event a duty to exercise due care in the operation of his car. Here, the dangerous condition of the bridge being open and obvious, *see infra*, the landowner owed no duty to a trespasser to keep its premises reasonably safe. Absent a duty to act affirmatively, we are reluctant to hold the Railway liable for failure to act under the "reckless disregard of dangers to others" standard in *Blanchard* and Prosser. Applying that standard to trespass cases would, we believe, improperly expand and transform the very limited duty towards trespassers that Maine imposes on landowners.

A trespasser in Maine is deemed to enter at his own risk, and "must take the premises as they are in fact, and he assumes all risk of injury from their condition." . . . Except in special circumstances not applicable here, a landowner is not required to use due care to maintain its premises reasonably safe for the benefit of trespassers. . . . This is particularly true where, as here, the dangerous condition of the land is open and obvious, and fully appreciated by the trespasser. . . .

Moreover, we do not view the particular circumstances of this case (the Railway's long-time knowledge of frequent pedestrian use, the clear dangerousness of the bridge, and the feasibility of making the bridge safer) as differing from those in other trespasser cases so markedly as to have required the Railway to take affirmative measures to prevent injury to trespassers on its bridge. . . .

That it was feasible, as the district court found, for the Railway to have made the bridge safer (by either erecting a barrier gate or installing handrails) does not warrant a finding of liability under Maine law. Even if the effort required of a landowner to make its land less dangerous is minimal, Maine courts have placed the responsibility for protection of trespassers on the person who unlawfully intrudes:

> [W]hat logical reason is there for saying that one, young or old, who is wrongfully upon [the] premises, can hold the owner to the expenditure of any money, or to submission to any degree of inconvenience, for his protection? We can think of none. We think there is no reason except the sentimental one, and that is not the basis of a legal obligation.

Nelson v. Burnham & Morrill Co., 114 Me. 213, 219, 95 A. 1029, 1032 (1915) (emphasis in original).

. . . .

A final issue is whether the Railway owed Bonney an independent duty as a foreseeable rescuer, even though the Railway did not violate any duty to the person Bonney sought to rescue. . . .

Plaintiff argues that this court should . . . recognize an independent duty to rescuers under Maine law on the grounds that "[b]y keeping its bridge in a dangerous condition, (the Railway) created a likely and *foreseeable* risk of harm to potential rescuers who would be called to the scene." (Emphasis added.) We decline to do so. . . .

All American courts of which we know have so far rejected the concept of an independent duty to a rescuer without an underlying tortious act to the person actually placed in peril. . . .

The judgment of the district court is reversed, and the case is remanded with directions to dismiss the complaint.

Note

1. ***Trespassers: The General Rule.*** In states adhering to some form of the "categories," a "landowner owes a trespasser only a duty to refrain from wilful and wanton conduct." In Blakely v. Camp Ondessonk, 38 F.3d 325 (7th Cir. 1994), a teenager sneaked into a Catholic camp for a cliffside beer party and was injured when she fell. The court held that the defendant diocese, which had previously discouraged trespassing, was not liable because it was unaware of the girl's presence and there were no traps or other conditions on the property intended to harm trespassers.

Humphrey v. Twin State Gas & Electric Co.

Supreme Court of Vermont
139 A. 440 (Vt. 1927)

POWERS, J.

[The defendant corporation's electric transmission line was washed out by a flood. Having obtained permission from one Thomas, the defendant effected a temporary repair by stringing its wires on poles and trees across Thomas's wood lot. A wire tie installed by the defendant's servants to hold the line broke, and the line sagged until it touched a barbed wire fence, charging the fence with a deadly electric current. Plaintiff, while hunting on Thomas's land, came in contact with the fence and was severely injured. At trial, the court granted the defendant's motion for a directed verdict. The Supreme Court assumed for purposes of decision that plaintiff was a trespasser.]

. . . .

[Being a trespasser, plaintiff could recover nothing from Thomas for his injuries.]. . . . Thomas owed him no duty to keep the premises safe for his unlawful use. The defendant takes the position that, so far as the plaintiff's rights go, it stands in Thomas's position and can make the same defense that he could; that it owed the plaintiff no duty, and consequently any negligence proved against it is not actionable so far as the plaintiff can assert. Many cases sustaining this doctrine are to be found in the books. . . . However, upon careful consideration, we are unwilling to follow them. Traced to its source, the rule exempting a landowner from liability to a trespasser injured through the condition of the premises, is found to have originated in an over-zealous desire to safeguard the right of ownership as it was regarded under a system of landed estates, long since abandoned, under which the law ascribed a peculiar sanctity to rights therein. Under the feudal system as it existed in Western Europe during the Middle Ages, the act of breaking a man's close was an invasion of exaggerated importance and gravity. It was promptly resented. It was under this system that the action of trespass *quare clausum* developed—beginning as a penal process, and so criminal in essence, and finally becoming a means of redressing a private wrong. Happily, in these more neighborly times, trespasses merely technical in character are usually overlooked or excused, unless accompanied with some claim of right. The object of the law being to safeguard and protect the various rights in land, it is obviously going quite far enough to limit the immunity to the one whose rights have been invaded. Nor does logic or justice require more.

A trespass is an injury to the possession; and, as it is only he whose possession is disturbed who can sue therefor, so it should be that he, alone, could assert the unlawful invasion when suit is brought by an injured trespasser. One should not be allowed "to defend an indefensible act" by showing that the party injured was engaged in doing something which, as to a third person, was unlawful. . . .

Reversed and remanded.

Notes

1. ***Persons Acting for the Possessor's Benefit.*** The protections afforded by the traditional premises-liability limited-duty categories can be invoked only by a possessor or by one who was acting for the benefit of the possessor at the time the hazard was created. *See* Restatement, Second, of Torts §§ 383-86.

2. ***Exceptions to the General Rule.*** Case law presents several exceptions to the rule that an occupier of land has no duty to keep the land safe for trespassers:

(a) ***"Discovered Trespassers."*** Once a landowner discovers someone on the land, a duty arises to take reasonable care for that person's safety, including a duty to warn the trespasser of concealed artificial conditions which create danger. A trespasser is not an outlaw. *See* Sheehan v. St. Paul & Duluth Ry. Co., 76 F. 201 (7th Cir. 1896).

However, in Rhodes v. Illinois Cent. Gulf R.R., 665 N.E.2d 1260, 1268–69 (Ill. 1996), the court held that a duty of reasonable care is owed to a discovered trespasser only if the trespasser is found in "a place of danger." The defendant's employees had discovered the plaintiff's decedent, Rhodes, sleeping in a warming house. Therefore, the trial court erred in ruling that the discovery required the defendant to use reasonable care to protect Rhodes even if he was a trespasser.

(b) ***Constant Trespass on a Limited Area.*** According to §§ 334 and 335 of the Second Restatement, one who knows or should know that trespassers constantly intrude upon a limited area must conduct dangerous activities with reasonable care for the safety of those trespassers, and must take reasonable steps to warn them of dangerous artificial conditions they are unlikely to discover.

In Humphrey v. Glenn, 167 S.W.3d 680 (Mo. 2005), a trespasser driving a four-wheeler was "clotheslined" by a wire cable strung across a private road. Because the defendant tenants knew that trespassers on the road were a "constant" problem, they had a duty to warn the trespasser of the wire cable, which was difficult to see.

(c) ***The Attractive-Nuisance Doctrine.*** It is one thing to say that an adult, or even a teenager, who decides to go onto someone else's land without permission must assume whatever risks that activity entails; it is quite another matter to hold that landowners owe no duty of care to trespassing children, particularly if the dangerous condition is one children are likely to find attractive. The following opinion illustrates the "attractive-nuisance" doctrine.

Banker v. McLaughlin

Supreme Court of Texas
208 S.W.2d 843 (Tex. 1948)

TAYLOR, Justice.

James McLaughlin brought this suit against H. F. Banker to recover damages for the death of his minor son (five years and ten months old.) The trial court awarded judgment in plaintiff's favor on the jury's verdict for $15,200. The Court of Civil Appeals, under the view that the award was excessive, caused a remittitur to be filed which reduced the judgment to $6,000. . . .

The child met his death on June 19, 1945, by drowning in a large hole, or pit, of water on Forest Park Subdivision, a homesite addition which Mr. Banker, the owner . . . was in the process of developing and marketing. . . .

. . . . The pertinent findings were to the effect that the premises (while especially attractive to children) were *dangerous* to children, such as James McLaughlin, Jr.; that children of tender years, as defendant knew or should have known, played about and swam in the pit; *that defendant was negligent* in failing to enclose it prior to June 19, 1945, and in failing to fill it up, or drain it, within a reasonable time; *and that these acts of negligence were proximate causes, respectively, of the child's death; and that plaintiff was not guilty of contributory negligence in not keeping the child away from the pool.*

. . . .

At the time the child was drowned, about 50 families (40 of which had small children) were living in Forest Park Subdivision; and numerous children were living in contiguous group settlements. In response to plaintiff's written request Mr. Banker filed . . . the following admissions: "Defendant . . . does admit that prior to June 19, 1945, some people had bought lots in this subdivision, none of which were located *in the immediate vicinity of the pool of water* . . . ; [that] . . . no warning sign or devices were placed in or near such pit or hole to warn persons of its presence; [and that] H. F. Banker *took no precautions whatsoever to prevent children of immature years from playing about or swimming in said pit or hole.* . . ."

. . . .

The utility of the pool to the owner was negligible after he ceased excavating there for dirt for street grading purposes. His testimony was that the pool was of "no further use" except that "it remained there for the future"; that it would be there as a reservoir for persons "who might purchase the adjoining land"; that it had never "been used for irrigation"; and that "I had nothing to irrigate." He had no cattle or other stock to water there. When asked if he "wanted it for water at the time he built it" his reply was, "I never had occasion to use it"; and that he "let it remain full of water" (that period was "eight or nine months").

Mr. Banker's own testimony indicates also that the expense necessary to be incurred, if any, to eliminate the danger would have been small, if not trivial. As indicated by his filed admissions, he did not endeavor to eliminate the dangerous condition he had created; nor did he erect any warning devices, or any "keep out" signs at the pool, or any "keep off" signs on the premises in its immediate vicinity....

While there was substantial proof of the inherent attractiveness of the place we, under our view of the case as properly one of negligence, *are concerned primarily with the dangerous condition created by petitioner on his open premises* and the fact that the dangerous features of the condition could have been eliminated at small expense without interfering with the owner's marketing of the homesites. The element of attraction is important only in so far as it may mean that the presence of children was to be anticipated.

The excavation was from 5 to 8 feet deep "*at the very shallowest place.*" .... It appears that soon after its use as a dirt supply had been discontinued it filled up with water so that its depth would not be ascertained by children unless (contrary to the nature of children) they are of such mature years and experience that they would measure the depth (as the average adult who could not swim would do) before entering the water.

....

The following features of the facts and circumstances of the case are determinative of the correctness of the action of the Court of Civil Appeals in affirming the trial court's judgment: (a) the place where the condition was maintained was one upon which the possessor knew or should have known that small children would likely frequent the place and play about it; (b) the condition was one of which the possessor knew, or should have known, involved an unreasonable risk of death or serious bodily harm to such children; (c) the child, because of its tender years, did not realize the risk involved in going into the pool; and (d) the utility, if any, to Mr. Banker of eliminating the danger was slight as compared to the probability of injury resulting therefrom. See in this connection, Restatement, Torts, § 339 and 36 A.L.R. p. 294.

....

The Supreme Court of this state took early recognition that the so-called "attractive-nuisance doctrine" had its origin in the turntable cases; and that when children of tender years came upon the premises by virtue of their unusual attractiveness, the legal effect was that of an implied invitation to do so. Such child was regarded, not as a trespasser, but as being rightfully on the premises. We quote from the *Duron* case as follows [7 S.W.2d 869]: "The theory of liability under the attractive nuisance doctrine is that, where the owner maintains a device or machinery on his premises of such an unusually attractive nature as to be especially alluring to children of tender years, *he thereby impliedly invites such children to come upon his premises, and, by reason of such invitation, they are relieved* from being classed as trespassers, but are in the attitude *of being rightfully on the premises.* Under such circumstances, the law places upon the owner of such machinery or device the *duty of exercising ordinary care* to keep such machinery in reasonably safe condition for their protection, if the *facts are such as to raise the issue that the owner knew, or in the exercise of ordinary care ought to have known, that such* children were likely or would probably be attracted by the machinery, and thus be drawn to the premises by such attraction." (Emphasis ours.)

.... Also pertinent is the following excerpt from Prosser on Torts (1941) under the subheading "Trespassing Children"; "Accordingly two-thirds of the American courts have developed a doctrine, which has been sadly miscalled by the name of 'attractive nuisance,' making the occupier of land liable for conditions on it which are highly dangerous to trespassing children. This doctrine, which has aroused endless discussion, is surrounded by no little confusion.... *The better authorities now agree that the element of 'attraction' is important only in so far as it may mean that the trespass is to be anticipated, and that the basis of liability is merely the foreseeability of harm to the child....*" (Emphasis ours.)

....

We ... affirm the judgment of the Court of Civil Appeals....

[The dissent of Justice FOLLEY is omitted.]

Notes

1. ***Children and Known or Obvious Dangers.*** According to Comment j to Restatement, Second, of Torts § 339:

> There are many dangers, such [as] those of fire and water, ... which under ordinary conditions may reasonably be expected to be fully understood and appreciated by any child of an age to be allowed at large. To such conditions the rule stated in this Section ordinarily has no application, in the absence of some other factor creating a special risk that the child will not avoid the danger, such as the fact that the condition is so hidden as not to be readily visible, or a distracting influence which makes it likely that the child will not discover or appreciate it.

In Bonney v. Canadian Natl. Ry. Co., 800 F.2d 274 (1st Cir. 1986) (*supra* p. 584), the court wrote:

> Plaintiff argues that even if the Railway did not have a duty towards adult trespassers to make the bridge safe for pedestrian use, it had a special

> responsibility towards minors who trespass. In Jones v. Billings, 289 A.2d 39 (Me. 1972), the Maine court adopted § 339 of the Restatement (Second) of Torts (1977), which establishes a duty of reasonable care as to highly dangerous conditions on land involving "an unreasonable risk of death or serious bodily harm" *if the trespasser is a child who, because of his youth, fails to discover or appreciate the condition or risk.* But here, even assuming a 15-year-old qualifies as a child for the purposes of § 339, Thibodeau clearly knew and understood the danger of riding his bicycle across the bridge at night. Eight months before, a classmate of his had died after falling off a nearby railroad bridge . . . while bicycling across it; Thibodeau knew of this accident. . . .

See also Kessler v. Mortenson, 16 P.3d 1225 (Utah 2000) (applying the attractive-nuisance doctrine to a case where a six-year-old child was injured by falling through a hole in a floor at a residential construction site).

2. ***Natural Conditions.*** Recognizing that an "attractive nuisance" need neither attract the child onto the property, nor be a "nuisance" (*see* Chapter 20), and that courts often refuse to apply the doctrine to risks created by natural conditions, the Second Restatement (§ 339) eschews the term "attractive nuisance" in favor of the inelegant but descriptive title, "Artificial Conditions Highly Dangerous to Trespassing Children."

2. Licensees and Invitees

Trespassers are easily defined: they are persons on the land without permission and without a privilege. Persons present with the owner's permission or with a privilege to enter are either "licensees" or "invitees." The latter is a confusing term because those invited to enter may well be "licensees" rather than "invitees." According to the Restatement, Second, of Torts § 332 Comment a:

> "Invitee" is a word of art, with a special meaning in the law. . . . A social guest may be cordially invited, and strongly urged to come, but he is not an invitee. . . . Invitees are limited to those persons who enter or remain on land upon an invitation which carries with it an implied representation, assurance, or understanding that reasonable care has been used to prepare the premises, and make them safe for their reception. Such persons fall generally into two classes: (1) those who enter as members of the public for a purpose for which the land is held open to the public; and (2) those who enter for a purpose connected with the business of the possessor. The second class are sometimes called business visitors. There are many visitors, such as customers in shops, who may be placed in either class.

The term "licensee" includes (according to § 330 comment h):

> 1. One whose presence upon the land is solely for his own purposes, in which the possessor has no interest, and to whom the privilege of entering

is extended as a mere personal favor to the individual, whether by express or tacit consent or as a matter of general or local custom.

2. The members of the possessor's household, except boarders or paying guests and servants, who . . . are invitees.

3. Social guests. . . . The explanation usually given by the courts for the classification of social guests as licensees is that there is a common understanding that the guest is expected to take the premises as the possessor himself uses them, and does not expect and is not entitled to expect that they will be prepared for his reception, or that precautions will be taken for his safety. . . . This has not gone without criticism. . . .

Invitees are owed the ordinary duty of reasonable care. While the duty owed to licensees varies somewhat from state to state, the traditional approach is that the possessor owes them a duty to refrain from actively endangering them and to warn them of known latent hazards. Importantly, a possessor has no duty to a licensee to inspect the property to discover unknown dangers.

In Wyckoff v. George C. Fuller Contracting Co., 357 S.W.3d 157 (Tex. App. 2011), the court held that a party guest who fell en route to a wine cellar was a licensee. The court explained that in Texas:

> The duty owed to a licensee is to not injure the licensee by willful, wanton, or grossly negligent conduct and, in cases in which the licensor has actual knowledge of a dangerous condition unknown to the licensee, to use ordinary care to either warn the licensee of the condition or make the condition reasonably safe.

The court rejected the guest's premises liability claim, reasoning as follows:

> Wyckoff alleged the stairway was unreasonably dangerous because it did not have a handrail, contained steps that were irregular, and was not sufficiently lighted. Wyckoff's summary evidence established there were approximately five steps from the top of the wine cellar to the bottom. Standing on the landing at the top of the stairway, it is clear the stairway curves to the right and the width of the steps varies to compensate for the curve. Wyckoff testified that when she entered the stairway, she was aware of the poor lighting and the lack of a handrail. She also testified the steps were uneven. Wyckoff perceived, and thus had actual knowledge of, the allegedly dangerous conditions about which she complains. . . . Therefore, as a matter of law, neither Fuller Contracting [which built the house] nor West [the homeowner] owed a duty to Wyckoff.

Andrushchenko v. Silchuk

Supreme Court of South Dakota
744 N.W.2d 850 (S.D. 2008)

MEIERHENRY, Justice.

Alex and Nataliya Andrushchenko (Andrushchenkos), as guardians *ad litem* of their minor child D.A., and Nataliya Andrushchenko, individually, brought suit against Ivan and Lyuba Silchuk (Silchuks), Metzger Construction, Inc., and M & M Plumbing-HVAC, L.L.C. (M & M) (collectively defendants) for injuries that D.A. sustained from scalding water in the Silchuks' bathtub. The circuit court granted summary judgment to the defendants. . . .

. . . Silchuks invited Andrushchenkos and their three-year-old son, D.A., over to their home for lunch. Early in the visit, D.A. turned on the faucets and flooded the main floor bathroom. Later, the Silchuk children and D.A. went upstairs to play. Mrs. Silchuk went upstairs and saw that D.A. was not playing with the other children. He was playing by himself in another area of the room. She closed the door to the bedroom where the baby was sleeping and rejoined the adults on the main floor. The baby was sleeping in the master bedroom, with access to the master bathroom, which had a whirlpool tub. She did not bring D.A. downstairs with her nor report to his parents that he was playing alone upstairs. Shortly thereafter, the adults heard D.A. scream. They ran upstairs and found him in the bathtub in the master bathroom. He had evidently opened the door of the baby's room and entered the master bathroom. He turned on the hot water and placed toys and other objects in the bathtub. He then either intentionally climbed or accidentally slipped into the bathtub. The hot water caused severe burns. The water in the tub was approximately 160° F. His burns required extensive treatment, including plastic surgery.

Silchuks' water heaters were installed as part of the construction of their home a few months prior to the incident. Metzger Construction, as the general contractor, hired M & M to install the water heaters. M & M claimed it set the thermostats at 125° F.

Andrushchenkos alleged that the defendants were negligent. They claim that Silchuks owed D.A. the duty of ordinary and reasonable care because of his status as an invitee and because of a gratuitous duty undertaken by Mrs. Silchuk to protect D.A.

. . . . As to defendants Silchuks, the circuit court determined that as a social guest D.A. had the status of licensee. Thus, Silchuks only owed a duty to warn of or make safe concealed dangerous conditions known to them at the time D.A. sustained his injuries. The court determined that Andrushchenkos had not produced sufficient evidence to demonstrate that Silchuks knew of any alleged dangerous condition. Similarly, the court rejected Andrushchenkos' gratuitous duty theory. The court based its determination on evidence that Ms. Andrushchenko admitted in her deposition that she had not relinquished her responsibility to supervise D.A. while in . . .

[the Silchuks'] home. The court also found that Andrushchenkos had not presented evidence that Silchuks had agreed to assume the responsibility to supervise D.A.

.... The majority of courts that retain the common law distinctions classify social guests as licensees. *See* Restatement (Second) Torts §§ 330, 332. The general duty owed to licensees is "to warn of concealed, dangerous conditions known to the landowner." .... The rationale for applying a lower standard of care to social guests versus business invitees is that the social guest is invited to the owner's land as a favor and has no reasonable expectation that the owner will make the land safer for the social guest than the owner does for himself. ...

Thus, Silchuks had a duty to warn of any known concealed, dangerous conditions. Silchuks' duty depends on whether they knew of the dangerous condition, and whether a reasonable person would have appreciated the danger the water temperature posed. ... Here, Andrushchenkos failed to provide any affirmative evidence that the Silchuks knew the temperature of the water was excessively hot or that it presented a scalding danger. Andrushchenkos did not dispute that M & M set the thermostats and they were not tampered with after that. We need not determine if the temperature of the water met the requirements of a hidden danger because the facts, viewed in the light most favorable to Andrushchenkos, did not establish that Silchuks knew the water temperature presented a danger about which they had a duty to warn social guests.

.... D.A.'s parents were present during the entire visit and were primarily responsible for the care and supervision of the child. At no time had they relinquished their responsibility. *See Sunnarborg*, 581 N.W.2d at 398–99 ("Generally, when a parent is present, the responsibility to provide for a child's care and safety rests with the parent, and a third party does not stand in a special relationship to the child."); O.L. v. R.L., 62 S.W.3d 469, 475 (Mo. Ct. App. 2001) (it is the "acceptance of the custody and control of a minor child [that] creates a relationship sufficient to support a duty of care.").

The circuit court did not err in granting summary judgment for Silchuks on the gratuitous duty claim.

....

Affirmed.

SABERS, Justice (dissenting).

....

The negligence of Lyuba must be viewed directly and not in comparison to that of D.A.'s mother or father. It is obvious that D.A.'s mother and father were negligent in permitting D.A., an aggressive three-year-old boy, to play by himself for an extended period of time on a separate floor of the house, especially knowing that he liked to turn on water faucets to the point of flooding on a prior occasion.

... Lyuba was aware that D.A. ... had done some damage in her house and she had warned his mother that she would be responsible for any further damage. Lyuba was also aware that D.A.'s mother ignored her warning and left D.A. to play by himself on a separate floor. To an aggressive three-year-old boy, everything is an attractive nuisance, especially if he is left alone on a separate floor for an extended period of time.

All of these facts present genuine issues of material fact as to whether Lyuba was directly negligent to D.A. . . .

The question here is not whether a homeowner is liable to a three-year-old boy when the negligence of the boy's mother is greater than that of the homeowner. . . . This case should be reversed and remanded for trial on this issue.

Notes

1. ***Social Guests.*** Treating social guests as licensees may have originated from a feeling that guests who sue their hosts are ungrateful.

In Carter v. Kinney, 896 S.W.2d 926 (Mo. 1995), the plaintiff slipped on a patch of ice and broke his leg while attending a Bible study session for church members at the defendants' home. Even though the visit was not strictly social, the plaintiff was a mere licensee, for the plaintiff did not enter the defendants' land to afford the defendants any material benefit and the defendants had not thrown their premises open to the public in general.

See Knorpp v. Hale, 981 S.W.2d 469 (Tex. App. 1998) (the boyfriend of a landowner's daughter, who died as a result of injuries sustained while cutting down a tree on the property, was a social guest and thus a licensee, rather than an invitee; he had been invited to attend a bonfire and had not been expecting payment for cutting the tree, which he volunteered to do).

At least one court has decided to treat social guests as invitees. *See* Burrell v. Meads, 569 N.E.2d 637 (Ind. 1991) (treating social guests as licensees "simply does not comport with modern social practices . . . [for it] is customary for possessors to prepare as carefully, if not more carefully, for social guests as for business guests"). As discussed below, a number of states have abolished the legal distinction between invitees and licensees, thus obviating concerns about how social guests are classified.

2. ***Family Members.*** Members of the possessor's family are usually treated as licensees. *But see* McClure v. Rich, 95 S.W.3d 620 (Tex. App. 2003) (holding that there was an issue of material fact as to whether the homeowners' daughter-in-law was an invitee rather than a licensee because there was evidence that the only reason she was on the property was to help the homeowners move into the house, which provided the homeowners with an economic benefit).

3. ***Failure to Object to Entry.*** Unsolicited salespersons and persons loitering at places of business have often been considered licensees, and not trespassers, on the theory that their presence has been consented to by reason of the possessor's failure to object to what is customary in the community. A failure to object to another's entry or remaining on land may constitute consent, at least when the possessor's

lack of willingness could be manifested without considerable trouble or expense. *See generally* Restatement, Second, of Torts § 330 cmts. c–g.

In Currier v. Washman, LLC, 366 P.3d 811, 815 (Or. App. 2016), the plaintiff, while riding a bicycle, was injured when he detoured onto the property of the defendant car wash to avoid an obstruction in the road. The defendant argued that the plaintiff was owed no duty because he was a trespasser. The appellate court held that the defendant's motion for summary judgment was properly denied because:

> Plaintiff presented evidence that defendant did nothing to inform bicyclists that they were unwelcome on the property, particularly to continue to travel around a blocked public way. Plaintiff also produced evidence suggesting that it was the community custom for bicyclists and pedestrians to traverse the parking lots and driveways of stores open for daily business, and customary for bicyclists to assume that they were allowed to do so....

4. ***Premises Liability versus Ordinary Negligence.*** Suppose a social guest is poisoned by a meal negligently prepared by his host. Is the guest's ability to recover limited by his being a "mere licensee"? Almost certainly not: this is an ordinary negligence case, and the fact that the negligence happened to occur on the defendant's property should be irrelevant. The special limited-duty rules for occupiers of land are rules limiting the occupier's duty to keep the land safe, they are not a license to engage in actively negligent behavior. See, for example, Haugh v. Jones & Laughlin Steel Corp., 949 F.2d 914 (7th Cir. 1991), in which the defendant, whose employees negligently injured the plaintiff, sought to invoke a special Indiana rule of limited duty to business invitees. Judge Richard Posner said:

> The argument ... has been immensely confused by [defendant's] insistence on invoking the intricate rules of tort liability of landowners.... The question in the present case, however, is not whether [defendant] provided a safe place for [plaintiff's employer] to perform the services for which it had been hired.... [The negligence of which plaintiff complains is] negligence by employees of [defendant], to which the site of the accident and hence [defendant's] status as a landowner is irrelevant and its duty of care simply the duty that everyone has (*prima facie*) to avoid a careless act that injures another person....

Suppose that the defendant is speeding on an icy road near her house, and that her car goes out of control, slides off the road, and injures two pedestrians—one on the sidewalk and the other, a trespasser, taking a shortcut across the defendant's front lawn. As the case does not involve unsafe conditions on the land, both pedestrians should be able to sue the defendant for ordinary negligence.

5. ***Police, Firefighters, and Rescuers.*** Police officers and firefighters coming onto the defendant's property in the course of their duties are usually on the land for the owner's benefit, but their presence on the property cannot readily be anticipated by the owner. Furthermore, nearly all police officers and firefighters receive medical and disability benefits for on-the-job injuries. And some courts have observed

that the very nature of the plaintiff's occupation requires facing dangers, so that the risks in question have been "assumed." Therefore, the traditional approach has been to treat firefighters and police officers as licensees. *See* Lechuga v. Southern Pac. Transp. Co., 949 F.2d 790 (5th Cir. 1992) (border patrol agent was a licensee); *but see* McDonald v. Highline School Dist. #401, 2010 WL 2479405 (Wash. App. 2010) (following state precedent under which police officers, like firefighters, are invitees).

Allen v. Albright, 43 S.W.3d 643 (Tex. App. 2001), held that a non-professional rescuer was not converted from a licensee into an invitee when a woman whose house had been fire bombed cried for help.

6. ***Licensees Must Prove Actual Notice.*** Under the traditional categories, it is essential for an injured licensee to prove that the possessor had actual notice of the defect that allegedly created a duty to warn or make safe. For example, in City of Denton v. Paper, 376 S.W.3d 762 (Tex. 2012), where a bicyclist was injured when her bike hit a sunken depression in a street, the question was whether the city knew that recent paving had sunk, not simply whether it could sink.

Campbell v. Weathers

Supreme Court of Kansas
111 P.2d 72 (Kan. 1941)

WEDELL, Justice.

. . . .

. . . . Plaintiff had been a customer of the defendant lessee for a number of years. On Sunday morning, June 4, 1939, . . . plaintiff entered the place of business operated by the defendant lessee, as a cigar and lunch business. He spent probably fifteen or twenty minutes in the front part of the building and then started for the toilet [which was located down a dimly lighted hallway in the back part of the building]. He stepped into . . . [an] open trap door in the floor of the hallway [and was injured]. . . .

[The trial court sustained the defendant lessee's demurrer to the evidence, and plaintiff appealed.]

The first issue to be determined is the relationship between plaintiff and the lessee. Was plaintiff a trespasser, a licensee or an invitee? . . . . A part of the answer is contained in the nature of the business the lessee conducted. It is conceded lessee operated a business which was open to the public. . . . Plaintiff had been a customer of the lessee for a number of years. . . . He stopped at the lessee's place of business whenever he was in town. He had used the hallway and toilet on numerous occasions, whenever he was in town, and had never been advised that the toilet was not intended for public use. . . . He saw no signs which warned him not to use the hallway or toilet. . . .

. . . . That the public had a general invitation to be or to become lessee's customers cannot be doubted. . . . Appellant was an invitee not only while in the front part of the place of business where the lunch counter was located but while he was on his way to the toilet. . . . The mere fact appellant had received no special invitation or specific permission on this particular occasion to use the toilet did not convert him into a mere licensee. . . .

Can we say, as a matter of law, in view of the record in this particular case, appellant had no implied invitation to use the toilet simply because he had not made an actual purchase before he was injured? . . . [D]oes the evidence . . . compel such a ruling on the demurrer? We think it does not. . . .

The evidence of lessee's own employee was that the toilet was not regarded as a private toilet. . . . In a densely populated business district such a privilege may have constituted a distinct inducement to bring not only old customers like appellant, but prospective customers into lessee's place of business. . . .

. . . . But we need not rest our conclusion that appellant was an invitee upon the fact that, according to the unqualified evidence, not only customers but everybody was permitted to use the toilet.

. . . . It is common knowledge that business concerns invest huge sums of money in newspaper, radio and other mediums of advertising in order to induce regular and prospective customers to frequent their place[s] of business and to examine their stocks of merchandise. They do not contemplate a sale to every invitee. . . . Shall courts say, as a matter of law, that such guests are not invitees until they actually make a purchase? We think the mere statement of the question compels a negative answer. Manifestly this does not imply that a trespasser or a mere licensee who enters the premises on a personal errand for the advancement of his own interest or benefit is entitled to the protection due to an invitee. . . .

> An invitee is one who is either expressly or impliedly invited onto the premises of another in connection with the business carried on by that other. . . . If one goes into a store with the view of then, or at some other time, doing some business with the store, he is an invitee. . . .

Of course, if it appears that a person had no intention of presently or in the future becoming a customer he could not be held to be an invitee, as there would be no basis for any thought of mutual benefit. . . .

. . . . The order sustaining the demurrer of the lessee is reversed.

Notes

1. ***Business Invitees.*** Many types of business visitors are treated as "invitees" and are entitled to the exercise of reasonable care. *See* Downs v. E.O.M. Entertainment, Inc., 997 So. 2d 125 (La. Ct. App. 2008) (an amusement park patron); Sims v. Giles, 541 S.E.2d 857 (S.C. Ct. App. 2001) (an electric company "meter reader").

2. ***Stretching the Business Invitee Category.*** Some cases apply the business-invitee test broadly by finding a financial benefit to the landowner whenever possible. For instance, New York, Chicago & St. Louis R.R. v. Mushrush, 37 N.E. 954 (Ind. Ct. App. 1894), held that a railroad's duty of reasonable care to its passengers extended

also to those who come to meet passengers or see them off. *See also* McIntosh v. Omaha Public Schools, 544 N.W.2d 502 (Neb. 1996) (a high school student who paid no fee to attend a football clinic was an invitee because "[t]he invitation was of a business nature for the mutual advantage of both parties").

In Freeman v. Eichholz, 705 S.E.2d 919 (Ga. App. 2011), the court held that the plaintiff, who was injured while visiting an inmate at a prison when a chair collapsed, was an invitee because inmate visitation is a tool that may be used to punish or reward prisoners, and thus visitation benefits prison officials and the state penal system.

However, in Sampson v. U. of Texas at Austin, 500 S.W.3d 380, 391 (Tex. 2016), the court found that a law professor who was injured when he tripped on an electrical cord while picking up tickets for a university football game, and who did "not allege that he paid for use of the premises," was a mere licensee.

3. ***Public Invitees.*** A possessor who invites the public onto land owes a duty of reasonable care to any member of the public who accepts the invitation, even though the defendant expected no financial gain. This public-invitee standard may apply to persons injured while attending religious services. *See* Fleischer v. Hebrew Orthodox Congregation, 504 N.E.2d 320 (Ind. Ct. App. 1987).

4. ***Encouragement to Enter.*** Comment d to § 332 of the Restatement, Second, of Torts points out that land has not been held "open to the public" just because the owner permits members of the public to use the land for their own purposes. The owner must indicate in some way that the public is encouraged to use the land:

> When a landowner tacitly permits the boys of the town to play ball on his vacant lot, they are licensees only; but if he installs playground equipment and posts a sign saying that the lot is open free to all children, there is then a public invitation, and those who enter in response to it are invitees.

5. ***Scope of Invitation.*** An invitee whose activities exceed the scope of the invitation may become a trespasser or licensee:

> [O]ne who goes into a shop which occupies part of a building, the rest of which is used as the possessor's residence, is a trespasser if he goes into the residential part of the premises without the shopkeeper's consent; but he is a licensee if the shopkeeper permits him to go to the bathroom, or invites him to pay a social call.

Restatement, Second, of Torts § 332 cmt. l. *See also* Whelan v. Van Atta, 382 S.W.2d 205 (Ky. 1964) (customer given permission to use a toilet became a licensee, and so could not recover for injuries sustained in a fall into an unlit stairwell, since the defendant did not know the light was out); Webb v. Snow, 132 P.2d 114 (Utah 1942) (amusement park patron who was aware that only the west tracks of a ride were open ceased to be a licensee or invitee upon proceeding down the east tracks for the purpose of entreating employees to open them).

6. ***Business Invitees Versus Independent Contractors.*** Some states hold that certain types of business visitors are often not entitled to the exercise of reasonable care on their behalf. In Gonzalez v. Mathis, 493 P.3d 212 (Cal. 2021), the court explained:

> There is a strong presumption under California law that a hirer of an independent contractor delegates to the contractor all responsibility for workplace safety.... This means that a hirer is typically not liable for injuries sustained by an independent contractor or its workers while on the job....
>
> We have nevertheless identified two limited circumstances in which the presumption is overcome. First, ... we held that a hirer may be liable when it retains control over any part of the independent contractor's work and negligently exercises that retained control in a manner that affirmatively contributes to the worker's injury.... Second, ... we held that a landowner who hires an independent contractor may be liable if the landowner knew, or should have known, of a concealed hazard on the property that the contractor did not know of and could not have reasonably discovered....

Id. at 215.

Inkel v. Livingston

Supreme Judicial Court of Maine
869 A.2d 745 (Me. 2005)

LEVY, J.

Leonard R. Inkel appeals from a summary judgment ... in favor of Donald Livingston and Solid Rock Builders....

....

Donald Livingston hired Solid Rock Builders to build an ocean-front home on his property in Cape Neddick. During construction, Livingston lived in a cottage located forty-two feet away from the site of the new house. Livingston invited Inkel and his family to join him and other guests for Easter dinner at his cottage. Inkel, accompanied by his adult son, went outside for a cigarette after dinner. It was approaching dusk, and it was cloudy and raining. As he smoked, Inkel and his son walked toward the shore, in the direction of the new home. There were no lights on in the new home.... [S]ome of the home's walls had been erected, but the construction remained incomplete. Curious about one of its rooms, the two men entered the dimly lit, partially enclosed structure. After walking ten to twenty feet, Inkel fell eight to ten feet through an uncovered chimney hole, suffering injuries. Prior to going outside, Inkel did not inform Livingston that he was going to look at the new house, and Livingston was not actually aware that he was doing so. Livingston was aware, however, that the other guests had gone in and out of the cottage during the dinner.

Inkel brought a negligence action against Livingston and Solid Rock. Both defendants filed motions for summary judgment, which the trial court granted. The court found that Inkel's status was that of an invitee inside the cottage and on the surrounding grounds, but that the scope of Inkel's invitation did not extend, either expressly or impliedly, to the new house....

....

Maine has abolished the common law distinctions between licensees and invitees and, accordingly, under Maine's law of premises liability, a landowner owes a duty of reasonable care to all those lawfully on the land. . . . The determination of a person's legal status as a guest or a trespasser is a question of fact. . . . A person retains his status as a guest "only while he is on the part of the land to which his invitation extends—or in other words, the part of the land upon which the possessor gives him reason to believe that his presence is desired for the purpose for which he has come". . . . [Restatement (Second) of Torts § 332 cmt. 1 (1965)]. Therefore, when a guest enters a part of the possessor's premises "to which there was no express or implied invitation to go, there can be no recovery for resulting injury, even though he is an invitee to other parts of the premises". . . .

Inkel argues that a genuine issue of material fact remains concerning his legal status that should be left to a jury to consider. He contends that the circumstances surrounding his invitation to the cottage create an implied invitation to enter the construction site as well. He points out that he and Livingston were friends; that he had been to Livingston's cottage before for dinner; that the new, partially constructed house was only forty-two feet from the cottage and was the subject of dinner conversation; that the dinner guests did not require Livingston's permission to go in and out of the cottage; and that Livingston was aware that they were doing so. Inkel adds that there were no signs or barriers preventing people from entering the construction site; that the walls were unenclosed; that he had been to the site several times five or six months prior to the accident; and that Livingston, when deposed, "would not say for certain that it would have been improper for Mr. Inkel to come to the construction site [at times when Livingston was away at work] to look at the progress of the construction." Accordingly, he argues that a jury could reasonably have concluded that he had Livingston's implied permission to enter the construction site.

As the trial court found, the undisputed material facts establish that Livingston invited Inkel to the cottage and to the land immediately surrounding it for the limited purpose of having Easter dinner. Inkel's earlier visits to the construction site to salvage doors and windows bore no relation to his Easter dinner invitation. Inkel may have had implied permission to enter and exit the cottage during the dinner to smoke a cigarette on the surrounding grounds. Viewed in a light most favorable to Inkel, however, the record does not establish that he had implied permission to enter the partially constructed new house. The site was not "the part of the land upon which [Livingston gave] him reason to believe that his presence [was] desired for the purpose for which he [had] come."

. . . .

We agree with the trial court's assessment that Inkel exceeded the scope of his invitation when he entered the construction site and, as a trespasser within the confines of the partially constructed house, neither Livingston nor Solid Rock Builders owed him a duty of reasonable care.

The entry is: Judgment affirmed.

CALKINS, J., with whom SAUFLEY, C.J., and DANA, J., join, dissenting.

I respectfully dissent . . . because there is a genuine issue of material fact as to whether Leonard Inkel went beyond the scope of Livingston's invitation to him. . . . My disagreement lies with the Court's conclusion that the record does not support a reasonable inference of an implied permission to Inkel to enter the new structure.

. . . [I]n the absence of any instructions to Inkel not to enter the structure, it was reasonably foreseeable that he would enter it. . . .

Notes

1. ***Other Precedent.*** *See also* Rucker v. Fed. Natl. Mortg. Assn., 2016 WL 4408899, at *3 (Colo. App.) (holding "that 'For Sale' signs, standing alone, do not create an implied representation to strangers to enter the private property of others," and therefore a prospective purchaser's mother was a trespasser, rather than an invitee, for purposes of a premises liability claim against the owner and broker of the house).

2. ***Duty to Discover and Remedy or Warn of Dangerous Conditions.*** A possessor owes a duty to invitees to exercise reasonable care to discover dangerous conditions on the land. However, what an investigation would reveal is often a disputed question of fact. *See* Maddox v. Townsend and Sons, Inc., 639 F.3d 214, 222 (5th Cir. 2011) (unresolved questions of fact precluded summary judgment for a possessor where a deliveryman was injured while sitting on a chain hanging between two metal posts).

3. ***Threats to Invitees Posed by Wild Animals.*** In some states, possessors have only a limited duty to protect business invitees from wild animals. In Hillis v. McCall, 602 S.W.3d 436, 441–44 (Tex. 2020), a case arising from injuries inflicted on a maintenance worker at a bed-and-breakfast by a poisonous spider, the Texas Supreme Court wrote:

> [W]ith certain exceptions, a premises owner generally owes no duty to protect invitees from wild animals on the owner's property. . . . Under this longstanding doctrine of *ferae naturae*, such a duty does not exist "unless the landowner actually reduced indigenous wild animals to [his] possession or control," "introduced nonindigenous animals into the area," or affirmatively "attract[ed] the animals to the property." . . . .
>
> However, courts applying the *ferae naturae* doctrine have long recognized an additional exception to the general no-duty rule, holding that a landowner:
>
>> could be negligent with regard to wild animals found in artificial structures or places where they are not normally found; that is, stores, hotels, apartment houses, or billboards, if the landowner knows or should know of the unreasonable risk of harm posed by an animal on its premises, and cannot expect patrons to realize the danger or guard against it.
>
> . . . [A] property owner who knows or should know of an unreasonable risk that dangerous indoor pests will bite invitees in his particular

> building has a duty to alleviate the danger or warn of it if the invitees neither know nor should know of the heightened risk. This strikes an appropriate balance between protecting invitees and ensuring that the burden placed on landowners is not unduly onerous....

3. Known or Obvious Dangers

Many cases hold that there is no duty to warn an invitee or take other precautions with respect to a known or obvious danger. *See* Nearhood v. Anytime Fitness-Kingsville, 178 So. 3d 623, 627 (La. App. 2015) (a gym owner had no duty disclose a squat machine's dangers to "a sophisticated user" of the machine).

However, there may be a duty to exercise care if there is reason to anticipate harm despite the knowledge or obviousness of the danger. Consequently, if the plaintiff will be distracted by other matters, or will forget because of a lapse of time, or will have visibility blocked, or will find it necessary to encounter the dangerous condition, there is a duty to take precautions to avoid the harm. *See* Restatement, Second, of Torts § 343A.

In some cases, the general no-duty rule governs. For example, in Smrtka v. Boote, 2017 WL 1235471, at *2 (Ohio App.), the patient of a chiropractor was bitten in the doctor's waiting room while trying to pet the head of a dog accompanying another patient. The court affirmed a grant of summary judgment for the doctor because the danger was open and obvious, and there was no evidence that the doctor had superior knowledge about the risk that the dog might bite.

See also Wolfley v. Solectron USA, Inc., 541 F.3d 819 (8th Cir. 2008) (icy parking lot was an open and obvious danger); John Morrell & Co. v. Royal Caribbean Cruises, Ltd., 534 F. Supp. 2d 1345 (S.D. Fla. 2008) (dangers of a dune buggy shore excursion were obvious); Bucki v. Hawkins, 914 A.2d 491 (R.I. 2007) (risk of diving into shallow water at night was open and obvious); Lilya v. Greater Gulf State Fair, Inc., 855 So. 2d 1049 (Ala. 2003) (no duty to warn of possible harm from riding a mechanical bull); Earnsberger v. Griffiths Park Swim Club, 2002 WL 1626126 (Ohio Ct. App.) (a reduction of the spring in a diving board was open and obvious).

In other cases, an exception to the general no-duty-to-warn rule applies. *See* Kentucky River Med. Ctr. v. McIntosh, 319 S.W.3d 385 (Ky. 2010) (it was foreseeable that a paramedic tending to a patient might trip over a curb between the ambulance dock and emergency room doors); Smith v. Wal-Mart Stores, Inc., 967 S.W.2d 198 (Mo. Ct. App. 1998) (store should have anticipated that water on the vestibule floor would cause harm to invitees even if it was open and obvious); Klopp v. Wackenhutt Corp., 824 P.2d 293 (N.M. 1992) (an airline owed a passenger a duty to use ordinary care to protect her from tripping over the base of a security station while she was preoccupied with recovering her jewelry); Ward v. K Mart, 554 N.E.2d 223 (Ill. 1990) (a store's duty encompassed the risk that customers carrying bulky items would collide with a five-foot-tall concrete post near the exit).

Obvious Dangers Under the Third Restatement. The Third Restatement takes the view that the obviousness of a danger does not, by itself, relieve a possessor of the duty to exercise care. *See* Restatement, Third, of Torts: Liab. for Physical & Emotional Harm § 51 cmt. k (2012). This position is discussed in Foster v. Costco Wholesale Corp., 291 P.3d 150 (Nev. 2012). *Foster* held that the fact that a dangerous condition is open and obvious does not automatically shield a landowner from liability but rather bears on (1) whether the landowner exercised reasonable care with respect to that condition and (2) issues of comparative fault.

Warning Signs. Merely posting a warning sign will often be insufficient to fulfill the obligation of due care. In Wilk v. Georges, 514 P.2d 877 (Or. 1973), a nursery erected a sign advising customers to watch their step and disclaiming liability for injuries. The court held that the sign did not preclude an action against the nursery for injuries sustained on a slippery wooden walkway by a woman who was "looking and glancing" at Christmas trees, because a slip-and-fall accident was easily foreseeable despite the sign. *See also* Restatement, Third, of Torts: Liab. for Physical and Emotional Harm § 18(b) (2010):

> Even if the defendant adequately warns of the risk that the defendant's conduct creates, the defendant can fail to exercise reasonable care by failing to adopt further precautions to protect against the risk if it is foreseeable that despite the warning some risk of physical harm will remain.

The Continuing Storm Doctrine. In Rochford v. G.K. Dev., Inc., 845 N.W.2d 715, 718 (Iowa App. 2014), the court held that a "weather event" was "of sufficient significance to qualify for the application of the continuing storm doctrine." As a result, the owner of a mall was temporarily absolved from the duty to remove ice from a sidewalk, because doing so was impractical.

B. Modification of the Traditional Approach

1. Abrogation

Since the late 1960s, many states have repudiated, in whole or in part, the definitive nature of the common-law categories of persons on the land of another. The landmark decision was Rowland v. Christian, 443 P.2d 561 (Cal. 1968). There the court held that although the plaintiff's status as a trespasser, licensee, or invitee may bear on the issue of liability, it is not determinative. In reaching the conclusion that in every case the question is whether reasonable care has been exercised, the court noted that the common-law rules on premises liability ran counter to the fundamental concept that a person should be liable for injuries caused by carelessness. Furthermore, the court found that the categories did not reflect the factors that should control liability in a negligence case, such as: the foreseeability of harm; the certainty that the plaintiff suffered injury; the feasibility of avoiding the harm; the blameworthiness of the defendant's conduct; the policy of preventing future accidents; and the availability of insurance. A majority of the court held that the proper test was whether, in the management of the property, the possessor had acted as a reasonable person would have acted in view of the probability of injury to others.

Split of Authority: Traditional Categories Versus Abrogation. The Reporter's Note to Restatement, Third, of Torts: Liab. for Phys. & Emotional Harm § 51 cmt. a (2012) states:

> Since the Second Restatement was published, 24 states have adopted a unitary standard of reasonable care to at least licensees and invitees. Of those, nine states have extended that duty to all on the land, including trespassers.... Of the 24 jurisdictions that retain the traditional status-based duties, 17 have explicitly considered and rejected reform of their state's law, although several . . . have indicated sympathy for such reform.

The Restatement draft contains a state-by-state chart.

Premises Liability Under the Third Restatement. With an important exception dealing with "flagrant trespassers" (discussed below), the Third Restatement adopts a unified standard of care applicable to all persons on a possessor's land. *See* Restatement, Third, of Torts: Liability for Physical and Emotional Harm § 51 (2012). Contractors who are engaged in work on the land owe the same duties to entrants as the possessor. *See id.* § 49 cmt. f. Family members residing in a possessor's household owe a duty of reasonable care to entrants on the land with respect to risks created by their conduct. *Id.* § 51 cmt. s.

There are no special rules governing firefighters, police officers, or other professional rescuers (*id.* § 51 cmt. m), nor for persons who stray onto private land (*id.* § 51 cmt. o), since all entrants are owed a duty of reasonable care.

Children Under the Third Restatement. As a result of adopting a unitary standard, the Third Restatement contains no special rules governing "known," "constant," or "child" trespassers. *See* Restatement, Third, of Torts: Liab. for Physical & Emotional Harm § 50 (2012). In each instance, a possessor must exercise reasonable care. Although the provisions of the Second Restatement dealing with "attractive nuisance" are superseded, the factors listed in that section (§ 339 of the Second Restatement) might still be relevant to the question of whether reasonable care was exercised in the case of harm to a child. *See* Restatement, Third, of Torts: Liab. for Physical & Emotional Harm § 51 cmt. l (2012).

"Flagrant Trespassers." The sole type of trespasser who is subject to special rules is the "flagrant trespasser." "The only duty a land possessor owes to flagrant trespassers is the duty not to act in an intentional, willful, or wanton manner to cause physical harm." *Id.* § 52. However, even flagrant trespassers are owed a duty of reasonable care if they are imperiled and either helpless or unable to protect themselves. *Id.*

"Flagrant trespasser" is a new category invented by the Third Restatement; the relevant provisions were not a restatement of anything, other than the intuitions of the drafters as to how the law should be configured. The ultimate meaning of the term "flagrant trespasser" has been left to development by the states. The Restatement indicates that a flagrant trespasser (in contrast to an ordinary trespasser) is one whose conduct is so egregious, so atrocious, and so antithetical to the rights of the land possessor that it would be unfair to hold the possessor to a duty of reasonable care. Presumably, a criminal injured during the burglary of a store would qualify as a flagrant trespasser.

2. Recreational Use Statutes

Judicial decisions abolishing the traditional categories have encouraged legislators to protect landowners against some kinds of claims. A particular concern of legislatures has been suits against owners of rural land, often for "failure to warn," by hikers, motorcyclists, and the like who are sometimes trespassers and sometimes licensees who have been permitted, though not invited, to use the land. Most states have enacted "recreational use" statutes in an attempt to protect landowners against the threat of liability. Here is the California version:

California Civil Code § 846 (Westlaw 2022)

An owner of any estate or any other interest in real property, whether possessory or nonpossessory, owes no duty of care to keep the premises safe for entry or use by others for any recreational purpose or to give any warning of hazardous conditions, uses of, structures, or activities on those premises to persons entering for a recreational purpose, except as provided in this section.

A "recreational purpose," as used in this section, includes activities such as fishing, hunting, camping, water sports, hiking, spelunking, sport parachuting, riding, including animal riding, snowmobiling, and all other types of vehicular riding, rock collecting, sightseeing, picnicking, nature study, nature contacting, recreational gardening, gleaning, hang gliding, private noncommercial aviation activities, winter sports, and viewing or enjoying historical, archaeological, scenic, natural, or scientific sites.

An owner of any estate or any other interest in real property, whether possessory or nonpossessory, who gives permission to another for entry or use for the above purpose upon the premises does not thereby (a) extend any assurance that the premises are safe for that purpose, or (b) constitute the person to whom permission has been granted the legal status of an invitee or licensee to whom a duty of care is owed, or (c) assume responsibility for or incur liability for any injury to person or property caused by any act of the person to whom permission has been granted except as provided in this section.

This section does not limit the liability which otherwise exists (a) for willful or malicious failure to guard or warn against a dangerous condition, use, structure or activity; or (b) for injury suffered in any case where permission to enter for the above purpose was granted for a consideration other than the consideration, if any, paid to said landowner by the state, or where consideration has been received from others for the same purpose; or (c) to any persons who are expressly invited rather than merely permitted to come upon the premises by the landowner.

Nothing in this section creates a duty of care or ground of liability for injury to person or property.

Notes

1. ***The Contours of Recreational-Use Immunities.*** An argument available to plaintiffs is that their particular activities were not listed in the statute. *See, e.g.*, Minn. Fire & Cas. Ins. Co. v. Paper Recycling of La Crosse, 627 N.W.2d 527 (Wis. 2001) (crawling through stacks of baled paper at a recycling facility while lighting matches and starting a fire was not a "recreational" activity); Lucero v. Richardson & Richardson, Inc., 39 P.3d 739 (N.M. Ct. App. 2001) (the phrase "or any other recreational purpose" did not extend to organized team sports such as Little League baseball).

However, many statutes cover a broad range of conduct. *See* Kurowski v. Town of Chester, 172 A.3d 522, 526 (N.H. 2017) (attempting to slap the feet of a person using a rope swing before that person hit the water); City of San Antonio v. Peralta, 476 S.W.3d 653, 658 (Tex. App. 2015) (commuting to work on a bicycle on the San Antonio Riverwalk); City of Bellmead v. Torres, 89 S.W.3d 611 (Tex. 2002) (sitting on a swing at a public park).

Duties to invited guests are generally not abrogated by recreational use statutes. *See* Estate of Gordon-Couture v. Brown, 876 A.2d 196 (N.H. 2005) (holding that the state statute did not immunize a landowner from liability for the death of a two-year-old child invited to a birthday party).

In Duffy v. Irons Area Tourist Ass'n, 834 N.W.2d 508, 512 (Mich. App. 2013), the court held that a tourist association, which maintained a trail on which ATVs were used, was not an owner, tenant, or lessee of the trail, and therefore not protected by the state recreational use statute.

2. ***Problem: Thieves and Birdwatchers.*** Suppose that two persons are injured while trespassing on the defendant's rural land. One is a thief, who was on his way to break into the defendant's house; the other is a birdwatcher, who wandered onto the land to get a better look at a woodpecker. Under California law, which plaintiff has the better case?

C. The Demands of Reasonable Care for Possessors

Even if a possessor owes the plaintiff a duty of ordinary care, one must still determine what ordinary care requires. This issue relating to *what* the possessor must do, rather than to *who* may complain, often presents troublesome questions. Sometimes decisions are surprising. For example, Brown v. Dover Downs, Inc., 2011 WL 3907536 (Del. Super. Ct. 2011), *aff'd* 38 A.3d 1254 (Del. 2012), found that "the overwhelming majority of courts that have considered . . . [the] issue have held that innkeepers do not owe their guests a duty to install bathmats").

1. Ill and Injured Invitees

In Hovermale v. Berkeley Springs Moose Lodge, 271 S.E.2d 335 (W. Va. 1980), a Moose Lodge member collapsed to the floor while having a drink and, at the bartender's direction, was taken to his car by two patrons to "sleep it off." The car remained in the parking lot overnight, and the member's body was discovered the following evening. He died of a heart attack a few hours after being placed in the car. In discussing the duty of care owed by the Lodge to the decedent as an invitee, the court wrote:

> [A] possessor of lands open to the public is under a duty to those members of the public who enter in response to its invitation to give them first aid after it knows or has reason to know that they are ill or injured, and to care for them until they can be cared for by others.
>
> . . . .
>
> The rule is not new. In . . . Depue v. Flateau, 100 Minn. 299, 111 N.W. 1 (1907), the . . . plaintiff, who was transacting business during dinner at a farmhouse some distance from his own, fell violently ill and collapsed on the floor. The defendants refused to permit him to stay at their farm and instead, placed him in his wagon and started the horses drawing it toward his home. The plaintiff was found the next morning in an advanced state of ill health due to exposure. The court held that since he was an invitee, the defendants owed him a duty, upon discovering his illness, to exercise reasonable care in their own conduct not to expose him to danger by sending him away from their house. . . .

Restatement, Second, of Torts § 314A provides in part that a possessor of land who holds it open to the public is under a duty to give first aid to an ill or injured member of the public who enters in response to the possessor's invitation. In Winfrey v. GGP Ala Moana LLC, 308 P.3d 891 (Haw. 2013), the court relied on this section. It held that notwithstanding the defendant mall's argument that the plaintiff was a trespasser, the mall had a duty, independent of premises liability law, to give first aid to a patron who had become stuck in a duct after entering it from the roof of the mall, once it learned of the patron's dilemma.

2. Protection Against Crime

As prior chapters suggest, the possessor of land may owe a duty to protect customers (and others) from foreseeable criminal attacks. Thus, in Janice H. v. 696 N. Robertson, LLC, 205 Cal. Rptr. 3d 103, 114 (Cal. App. 2016), the court held that where the managers of a lounge knew that sexual encounters in a unisex restroom stall "could be, or easily become, nonconsensual," the lounge "had a duty to ensure safety by undertaking minimally burdensome security measures, like requiring one of its security guards to remain posted in the restroom area as the club emptied out."

Trammell Crow Central Texas, Ltd. v. Gutierrez

Supreme Court of Texas
267 S.W.3d 9 (2008)

Justice WILLETT . . . :

. . . .

Around 11 o'clock on the night of February 17, 2002, Patrick Robertson, an off-duty policeman, began his shift as a security guard at the Quarry Market, a 53-acre mall in San Antonio. . . . He continued his patrol, heading away from the theater as patrons began exiting the building.

Among those patrons were Luis Gutierrez and his wife Karol Ferman, who had just finished watching a movie . . . Shortly after exiting the building, Karol heard a gunshot. . . . The assailant fired again, hitting Luis in the shoulder and causing him to fall to the ground. . . . Luis suffered four gunshot wounds. . . .

Luis . . . died of his wounds. . . . Luis's mother Maria and Karol, acting for themselves and for Luis's children, filed a civil suit against Trammell Crow, the property manager of the Quarry Market . . . [alleging negligent security at the mall]..

Maria and Karol portrayed the attack as a botched robbery. . . .

Trammell Crow countered that Luis was killed in retaliation for providing the police with information regarding a series of burglaries in which he was involved. . . .

. . . [T]he jury returned a verdict in favor of Maria, Karol, and the children . . . , awarding the plaintiffs over $5 million in damages. Sitting en banc, the court of appeals affirmed in a sharply divided opinion. . . .

. . . . Generally, a person does not have a duty to protect others from third-party criminal acts. However, "[o]ne who controls the premises does have a duty to use ordinary care to protect invitees from criminal acts of third parties if he knows or has reason to know of an unreasonable and foreseeable risk of harm to the invitee." . . . .

. . . Trammell Crow contends that the evidence of previous criminal activity at the mall does not establish that Luis's death was foreseeable.

. . . .

In the two years prior to Luis's death, 227 crimes were reported at the Quarry Market. Of these reported crimes, 203 were property and property-related crimes—mostly thefts, but also a handful of burglaries, auto thefts, and incidents of vandalism. Fourteen "other crimes" occurred—thirteen simple assaults and one incident of weapon possession. The remaining ten crimes, all robberies, were classified as violent crimes—a category that also includes murder, manslaughter, rape, and aggravated assault.

Although . . . the repeated occurrences of theft, vandalism, and simple assaults at the Quarry Market signal that future property crimes are possible, they do not suggest the likelihood of murder. . . . [W]e limit our review to the ten instances of violent crime. . . .

To determine whether the risk of criminal conduct is foreseeable, a court weighs the evidence of prior crimes using five factors: proximity, publicity, recency, frequency, and similarity. . . . Proximity and publicity are not disputed in this case. . . . Therefore, we focus our analysis on the other factors: recency, frequency, and similarity.

. . . . A criminal act is more likely foreseeable if numerous prior crimes are concentrated within a short time span than if few prior crimes are diffused across a long time span. . . . [S]tatistics from the San Antonio area suggest that the Quarry Market has a relatively low rate of violent criminal activity. In 2001, a resident of San Antonio faced a 44,760-to-1 chance of becoming the victim of a violent crime on any given day. In contrast, according to calculations performed by Trammell Crow's expert, the odds of suffering a violent crime on any given day at the Quarry Market during the two years prior to Luis's death were 1,637,630 to 1.

. . . [W]e emphasize that no one ratio or odds calculation conclusively resolves the frequency analysis. . . . Nevertheless, these calculations, performed by a qualified expert, can be used to help a court resolve the difficult question of whether criminal conduct is reasonably foreseeable.

. . . .

In addition to the recency and frequency of past crimes, a court must consider the similarity of the past crimes to the criminal conduct in question. Foreseeability does not require "the exact sequence of events that produced the harm [to] be foreseeable," — rather, previous crimes need only be "sufficiently similar to the crime in question as to place the landowner on notice of the specific danger." . . . .

No one had been murdered at the Quarry Market prior to Luis's shooting, but ten robberies had occurred, many with violent characteristics. One of the incidents is particularly striking — a man exiting the theater at 12:30 a.m. on a Monday morning was approached by a group of strangers, who followed him back into the theater, knocked him down, and stole his valuables before fleeing the scene. However, unlike the attack on Luis, the strangers first accosted the victim; their ultimate aim was to take his property; and they did not use a deadly weapon or seriously injure him.

Of the remaining nine crimes, three involved the use of guns, and another involved an unknown object that could have been a gun. However, none of these weapons were ever fired. . . . Furthermore, no one was seriously injured in any of the nine robberies. Two other differences are noteworthy. First, in six of the nine crimes, the perpetrator made a demand on the victim for property, indicating that the primary purpose of the criminal conduct was to obtain property. There is no evidence that Luis's assailant made any demand, threat, or said anything at all; the assailant simply started shooting. . . .

Considering the five factors together, we cannot conclude that Luis's murder was foreseeable. Trammell Crow had knowledge of violent crimes that were committed at the Quarry Market within a reasonable time prior to Luis's death. Nevertheless, these previous crimes were not sufficiently frequent and similar to give rise to a duty in this case. . . . Even viewing the attack on Luis as a robbery, as we presume the jury did, the circumstances of this attack are extraordinary. The assailant opened fire from behind at long range without making any prior demand. . . . Nothing about the previous robberies committed at the Quarry Market put Trammell Crow on notice that a patron would be murdered as part of a robbery on its premises. Thus, Luis's death was not foreseeable, and Trammell Crow did not have a duty to prevent the attack.

. . . . [W]e reverse the court of appeals' judgment and render a judgment that Respondents take nothing.

[The concurring opinion of Chief Justice JEFFERSON, in which Justices HECHT, BRISTER, and JOHNSON joined, has been omitted.]

Notes

1. ***Other Precedent.*** *See also* Pink v. Rome Youth Hockey Ass'n, Inc., 63 N.E.3d 1148, 1149 (N.Y. 2016). According to the court:

> During the [youth hockey] game, several on-ice fights broke out between the players, who received penalties and in some cases were ejected from the game. . . . The spectators, mostly family members of the players, engaged in yelling and name calling.
>
> . . . . After the game was over, two female spectators got into a fight in the stands and a melee quickly ensued as several others, including plaintiff Raymond Pink, stepped in to break up the fight. Matthew Ricci, the brother of one of the two female spectators involved in the fight, struck plaintiff causing him to sustain a head injury.

In an action against the youth hockey association, the court held that "the criminal assault on plaintiff was not a reasonably foreseeable result of any failure to take preventive measures." It explained that "[w]hile defendant owed a duty to protect spectators from foreseeable criminal conduct, . . . [t]he behavior of the fans, however inappropriate, certainly did not create the risk that failure to eject any specific spectator would result in a criminal assault, particularly since such an assault had never happened before."

2. ***The "Prior Similar Incidents" Rule.*** Some jurisdictions hold that, in the absence of prior similar incidents, an occupier of land is not bound to anticipate the criminal acts of third parties, especially if the assailant was a stranger to both the occupier and the victim and the criminal act resulting in the injury came about precipitately.

In criticizing the "prior similar incidents" rule, in Isaacs v. Huntington Mem. Hosp., 695 P.2d 653 (Cal. 1985), the court said:

> First, the rule leads to results which are contrary to public policy. The rule has the effect of discouraging landowners from taking adequate measures to protect premises which they know are dangerous. This result contravenes the policy of preventing future harm. Moreover, under the rule, the first victim always loses, while subsequent victims are permitted recovery. Such a result is not only unfair, but is inimical to the important policy of compensating injured parties. . . .
>
> Second, a rule which limits evidence of foreseeability to prior similar criminal acts leads to arbitrary results and distinctions. Under this rule, there is uncertainty as to how "similar" the prior incidents must be to satisfy the rule. The rule raises a number of other troubling questions. For example, how close in time do the prior incidents have to be? How near in location must they be? . . . .
>
> Third, the rule erroneously equates foreseeability of a particular act with previous occurrences of similar acts. . . . "The mere fact that a particular kind of an accident has not happened before does not . . . show that such accident is one which might not reasonably have been anticipated." . . . .
>
> Finally, the "prior similar incidents" rule improperly removes too many cases from the jury's consideration. It is well established that foreseeability is ordinarily a question of fact.

3. ***The Significance of the Property Owner's Rules.*** In Mitchell v. Ridgewood E. Apts., LLC, 205 So. 3d 1069, 1080–81 (Miss. 2016), the court held that a property owner's rules and policies did not render third-party criminal acts foreseeable for purposes of negligence liability. Addressing this issue of first impression, the court wrote:

> [W]hile the Guest Policy in the Resident Handbook, which was incorporated by reference into the lease agreement, prohibited alcoholic beverages, loitering in the parking lot, public drunkenness, fighting, disturbances, verbal altercations, threats, or weapons on the grounds and the lease contract permitted Ridgewood East to terminate the lease if a tenant or guest used an illicit drug or engaged in "drug related activity," it cannot be said that by incorporating policies and rules into the lease agreement, Ridgewood East assumed a contractual duty to tenants and guests to prevent any and all violations of the rules, even those of which it had no actual or constructive knowledge.

4. ***Protection of Invitees From the Negligence of Others.*** In Marshall v. Burger King Corp., 856 N.E.2d 1048 (Ill. 2006), a vehicle crashed through the wall of a fast-food restaurant and killed a patron. In an action by the estate of the patron, the court held that the restaurant had a duty to aid or protect customers against unreasonable risks of physical harm posed by the negligent acts of third persons. Of course, whether such an accident is a serious risk depends on the facts. *See* Achtermann v. Bussard, 2007 WL 901642 (Del. Super. Ct.) (restaurant had no duty to protect a customer from a car unforeseeably driven through the front wall).

Boyd v. Racine Currency Exchange, Inc.

Supreme Court of Illinois
306 N.E.2d 39 (Ill. 1973)

RYAN, Justice.

Plaintiff's complaint was dismissed ... for failure to state a cause of action. The appellate court reversed and remanded the cause to the circuit court. ... We granted leave to appeal.

This is a wrongful death action against Racine Currency Exchange and Blanche Murphy to recover damages for the death of plaintiff's decedent during an attempted armed robbery. The facts surrounding that event ... are: The plaintiff's husband, John Boyd, was present in the Racine Currency Exchange on April 27, 1970, for the purpose of transacting business. While he was there, an armed robber entered and placed a pistol to his head and told Blanche Murphy, the teller, to give him the money or open the door or he would kill Boyd. Blanche Murphy was at that time located behind a bulletproof glass window and partition. She did not comply with the demand but instead fell to the floor. The robber then shot Boyd in the head and killed him.

....

It is fundamental that there can be no recovery in tort for negligence unless the defendant has breached a duty owed to the plaintiff. ... The plaintiff contends that a business proprietor has a duty to his invitees to honor criminal demands when failure to do so would subject the invitees to an unreasonable risk. ...

We are aware of only two cases which have discussed issues similar to the one with which we are faced here — whether a person injured during the resistance to a crime is entitled to recover from the person who offered the resistance. In Genovay v. Fox, 50 N.J. Super. 538, 143 A.2d 229, *rev'd on other grounds*, 29 N.J. 436, 149 A.2d 212, a plaintiff who was shot and wounded during the robbery of a bowling alley bar claimed that the proprietor was liable because instead of complying with the criminal demand he stalled the robber and induced resistance by those patrons present. The plaintiff was shot when several patrons attempted to disarm the bandit. The court there balanced the interest of the proprietor in resisting the robbery against the interest of the patrons in not being exposed to bodily harm and held that the complaint stated a cause of action. The court stated: "The value of human life and of the interest of the individual in freedom from serious bodily injury weigh sufficiently heavily in the judicial scales to preclude a determination as a matter of law that they may be disregarded simply because the defendant's activity serves to frustrate the successful accomplishment of a felonious act and to save his property from loss." ... The court held that under the circumstances it was for the jury to determine whether defendant's conduct was reasonable.

In Noll v. Marian, 347 Pa. 213, 32 A.2d 18, the court held that no cause of action existed. The plaintiff was present in a bank when an armed robber entered and announced "It's a holdup. Nobody should move." The bank teller, instead of obeying this order, dropped down out of sight. The gunman then opened fire and wounded the plaintiff. The court held that even though the plaintiff might not have been injured if the teller had stood still, the teller did not act negligently in attempting to save himself and his employer's property.

In Lance v. Senior, 36 Ill. 2d 516, 224 N.E.2d 231, this court noted that foreseeability alone does not result in the imposition of a duty. "The likelihood of injury, the magnitude of the burden of guarding against it and the consequences of placing the burden upon the defendant, must also be taken into account." . . . .

In the present case an analysis of those factors leads to the conclusion that no duty to accede to criminal demands should be imposed. The presence of guards and protective devices do not prevent armed robberies. The presence of armed guards would not have prevented the criminal in this case from either seizing the deceased and using him as a hostage or putting the gun to his head. Apparently nothing would have prevented the injury to the decedent except a complete acquiescence in the robber's demand, and whether acquiescence would have spared the decedent is, at best, speculative. We must also note that the demand of the criminal in this case was to give him the money or open the door. A compliance with this alternate demand would have, in turn, exposed the defendant Murphy to danger of bodily harm.

If a duty is imposed on the Currency Exchange to comply with such a demand the same would only inure to the benefit of the criminal without affording the desired degree of assurance that compliance with the demand will reduce the risk to the invitee. In fact, the consequence of such a holding may well be to encourage the use of hostages for such purposes, thereby generally increasing the risk to invitees upon business premises. If a duty to comply exists, the occupier of the premises would have little choice in determining whether to comply with the criminal demand and surrender the money or to refuse the demand and be held liable in a civil action for damages brought by or on behalf of the hostage. The existence of this dilemma and knowledge of it by those who are disposed to commit such crimes will only grant to them additional leverage to enforce their criminal demands. The only persons who will clearly benefit from the imposition of such a duty are the criminals. In this particular case the result may appear to be harsh and unjust, but, for the protection of the future business invitees, we cannot afford to extend to the criminal another weapon in his arsenal.

For these reasons we hold that the defendants did not owe to the invitee, Boyd, a duty to comply with the demand of the criminal.

Accordingly, the judgment of the appellate court will be reversed, and the judgment of the circuit court of Cook County will be affirmed.

. . . .

[The dissenting opinion of Justice GOLDENHERSH has been omitted.]

Notes

1. ***Other Precedent.*** *See also* Kentucky Fried Chicken v. Superior Ct., 927 P.2d 1260 (Cal. 1997) (no duty to patron to comply with armed robber's unlawful demand); Bence v. Crawford Sav. and Loan Ass'n, 400 N.E.2d 39 (Ill. App. Ct. 1980) (no duty to plaintiff's decedent to activate an electronic door buzzer system to allow robbers to exit); *but see* Helms v. Church's Fried Chicken, Inc., 344 S.E.2d 349 (N.C. Ct. App. 1986) (evidence presented factual issues as to whether an employee, who stated in a loud voice to one customer "when you leave call the police, we are being robbed," negligently increased the risk to customers, precluding summary judgment).

2. ***Problem: Law Students Taken Hostage.*** A gunman takes a classroom full of students hostage at a law school and demands a ransom payment in exchange for their release. Must the law school pay the ransom or do anything else?

3. Duties to Persons Outside the Premises

a. Persons "Invited" onto the Land of Another

Individuals who treat another's property as their own may be held liable if their invitees are injured on that property. For example, in Holiday Inns, Inc. v. Shelburne, 576 So. 2d 322 (Fla. Dist. Ct. App.), *appeal dismissed* 589 So. 2d 291 (Fla. 1991), the court held that the defendants owed a duty of reasonable care not only to patrons who parked on their premises, but also to those who parked on adjacent lots in accordance with the instructions of security guards. *See also* Hopkins v. Fox & Lazo Realtors, 625 A.2d 1110 (N.J. 1993) (real estate broker has a duty to ensure through reasonable inspection and warning the safety of prospective buyers and visitors who tour an open house).

Orthmann v. Apple River Campground, Inc.

United States Court of Appeals for the Seventh Circuit
757 F.2d 909 (7th Cir. 1985)

POSNER, Circuit Judge.

Owen Orthmann, age 19, was rendered a quadriplegic when he dove into the Apple River near the village of Somerset, Wisconsin, and his head struck a rock on the shallow bottom.... Orthmann brought this diversity suit ... against the village and against eight firms that comprise the Floater's Association. Members of the association rent inner tubes for floating down the river to tourists like Orthmann, who was injured when he interrupted his float to go on shore to do some diving. The district judge granted the motion of the members of the Floater's Association ... to dismiss the complaint for failure to state a claim, and the village's motion for summary judgment....

[The court held that the plaintiff's failure to file a notice of claim with the city, as required by statute, precluded any action against it.]

.... [T]he complaint alleges that ... [the remaining] defendants—a campground, a restaurant, and other businesses in Somerset—joined together in a commercial venture (the "Floater's Association") to promote innertubing on the Apple River. On the day of the accident Orthmann rented an inner tube from the campground, where he had camped the night before. The floater is supposed to float down a four-mile stretch of the river and when he comes to the end return on a bus hired by the defendants; the rental fee that Orthmann paid the campground included the bus ride. The defendants own most of the land on both sides of this stretch of the river and take various measures to keep the river clean, such as providing litter bins on the banks. The place where Orthmann dove from, however, was owned not by any of the defendants but by a family named Montbriand. A tree on the property had grown out over the river and kids liked to dive off it, but when Orthmann arrived the queue for the tree was too long and he decided to dive off the bank instead. The water was cloudy, and was reflecting the sun, so that Orthmann couldn't see the bottom, but he was reassured by the fact that he had seen other people dive into the river in the same area without incident.

If the accident had occurred while Orthmann was in the inner tube, there would be no doubt that the complaint should not have been dismissed on the pleadings. One who invites another to engage in a sporting activity for a fee owes him a duty of care. Of course, if the hazard was obvious, or so inseparable a part of the sport that it was a risk assumed by engaging in it, or if the defendants had no reason to know of the hazard (maybe some trespasser had dropped the rock into the river the night before the accident), they might well escape liability....

It is true that only one defendant (the campground) dealt directly with Orthmann, leaving unclear the role of the other seven members of the Floater's Association. But the complaint alleges—not implausibly in light of the name of the association—that floating was a joint venture of the Association's members; and whatever the ultimate truth of this allegation, it is enough to prevent a member from getting the complaint dismissed.... This is not to say that a restaurant which contributed to the cost of a flyer advertising floating, in the hope of getting business from floaters, would be liable as a joint tortfeasor for the torts of the firms actually engaged in renting inner tubes or launching sites. The restaurant would lack the "equal right to a voice in the direction of the enterprise" that is an element of the joint-enterprise doctrine.... But if the restaurant was a joint venturer in floating, it could not escape liability just by not dealing face-to-face with the floater who came to grief....

We can take the analysis a step further, and assert with some confidence that if the defendants (or perhaps just one of them, if they were joint venturers) had owned the Montbriand property, with its popular tree, the complaint would withstand a ... motion [to dismiss]. Although the mere fact that you invite people into a part of your property for a fee does not make them business invitees on the rest of the property, ... we are supposing a situation in which an enterprise trying to make a profit out of floating knows that its customers, while floating down the river, pass by land owned by the enterprise that is conveniently and enticingly fitted with a natural diving board, and that some of these customers land and dive from the tree and the surrounding property. Floating is a summer sport. (Orthmann was injured in July.) A brochure of the Floater's Association shows as one would expect that floaters are young and wear bathing suits. Nothing is more natural than that some of them—maybe many of them—should combine floating with swimming, including diving from a tree invitingly adapted to such use. On these assumptions there would be an implied invitation to the enterprise's customers to use the tree and surrounding land for diving into the river, and the enterprise would be prima facie liable if through its negligence a customer was injured while doing so....

... [E]ven if we could say that Orthmann was negligent as a matter of law, this would not authorize dismissal of the complaint, since contributory negligence is no longer a complete defense in Wisconsin, unless the victim's negligence is greater than the injurer's. Wis. Stat. § 895.045.

....

What makes this case more difficult than our hypothetical variants is that the defendants do not own the property from which Orthmann dove. But according to an affidavit of one of the Montbriands ..., shortly after the accident the defendants came on the Montbriands' land without asking their permission, and cut the tree down. The affidavit also states that the Montbriands had seen the defendants cleaning and maintaining the banks of the river on the Montbriands' land. It is possible to infer that the defendants, though they did not own the Montbriand property, treated it as if they did—the cutting down of the tree after the accident being a dramatic assertion of a right normally associated with ownership or at least (which is all that is necessary, as we are about to see) possession.

This is not to say that the defendants could be held liable, under any tort theory we know, if their customers just strayed onto someone else's property and got injured there. This is not because the defendants could not prevent such injuries; they might be able to prevent them quite cheaply and effectively by a warning sign, just as we have assumed that they might have been able to prevent an accident caused by an object that they were not authorized to remove from the river. It is because the law just has not yet imposed on landowners who invite the public onto their property the duty of inspecting their neighbors' property to see whether any of their customers may be wandering onto it, and endangering themselves by doing so.... Since a landowner has no right to inspect his neighbor's lands, let alone to correct dangerous conditions on them, little would be accomplished, in general, by making him liable for those conditions along with the neighbors. And though one can think of exceptions—cases where the landowner knows of the condition without having gone on his neighbor's land, and can correct it at trivial cost, as with a warning sign—the law has not seen fit to impose such liability. But if the landowner treats the neighbor's property as an integral part of his, the lack of formal title is immaterial. Whoever controls the land is responsible for its safety....

. . . . Suppose an amusement park when it built its parking lot had encroached on a neighbor's land, and a customer of the amusement park was injured by a pothole in the part of the lot that the amusement park actually did not own (not yet having acquired it by operation of the doctrine of adverse possession) or have any right to occupy. The amusement park could not escape liability by pointing out that the hazard was not actually on its property. *See, e.g.*, Merkel v. Safeway Stores, Inc., 77 N.J. Super. 535, 540–41, 187 A.2d 52, 55 (1962), where a grocery store was held liable for an injury resulting from its failure to remove snow and ice from a public sidewalk that "was the means of ingress and egress provided by defendant for its customers." . . . .

. . . [W]hile the judgment in favor of the Village of Somerset is affirmed . . . , the judgment in favor of the other defendants is reversed and the case is remanded for further proceedings consistent with this opinion. . . .

Notes

1. ***Adjacent Highways and Neighboring Premises.*** Courts normally hold that the duties of a possessor leave off at the boundary line of the premises. For example, a nightclub ordinarily has no duty to warn a patron who attended a band performance of the dangers posed by crossing an adjacent highway after the show. *See* Newell v. Montana W., Inc., 154 A.3d 819, 827 (Pa. Super. 2017); *see also* Rhudy v. Bottlecaps Inc., 830 A.2d 402 (Del. 2003) (a business that advertised the availability of nearby free public parking was not liable for harm caused at that location by a robber because the business did not control the lot or increase the risk of harm to patrons parking there); *but see* Mulraney v. Auletto's Catering, 680 A.2d 793 (N.J. 1996) (recognizing a duty to undertake reasonable safeguards to protect customers from dangers posed by crossing an adjoining highway to an area neither owned nor controlled by the proprietor, but which the proprietor knows or should know its customers will use for parking).

2. ***Hazards Farther from the Premises.*** In Mostert v. CBL & Assoc., 741 P.2d 1090 (Wyo. 1987), the court held that a movie theater had a duty to warn departing patrons of the risks posed by a severe storm about which the theater had received notice. The Mosterts "never became aware of the warnings or severity of the storm because they were inside" the defendant's theater, and their daughter drowned when their vehicle was swept away by floodwaters two miles down the road. In his concurrence, Justice Urbigit wrote:

> The night was dark, the rains came; some say a one-in-a-hundred years flood it was to have been. Within the theater, exposed only to make believe of the silver flicks, the audience was unwarned of the anger of nature outside displayed.
>
> Who knew? . . . Theater management knew, but perforce told not one among its paying patrons who otherwise were not to be forewarned. . . .

> One would think that with warning afforded, opportunity to at least listen to the car radio, or telephone to their homes, the life that was lost in a flooded road nearby might have been saved. I see this as a subject for jury review. The issue was not off-premises liability for the theater. I perceive a duty of host to business invitee to communicate his knowledge of facts unknown to the patron of unusual and unexpected exit-time danger. The home of knowledge and needed communication was in the theater, and it was there that the tort occurred, if it did. It simply does not matter whether the clear and obvious danger inculcated in this duty to advise arises from a gunfight adjacent to the north door, a tornado about to arrive, or, as here, flooded conditions on shopping center access roadways.

Compare Mostert with Kuzmicz v. Ivy Hill Park Apts., Inc., 688 A.2d 1018 (N.J. 1997) (landlord did not owe a duty to tenants to protect them from criminal assaults on a city-owned vacant lot located between the complex and a shopping center, either by warning them of the risks of assault on the lot, or by making more exhaustive efforts to mend the fence that separated the complex from the lot, in which a hole allowing passage had been cut).

3. ***Duties to Outsiders.*** What about a possessor's duty to those who have never been on the land at all? Active negligence by the possessor will of course give rise to liability. It is no defense to a negligence claim to say that the negligence took place on the defendant's land, and so a landowner who negligently causes an explosion will be liable to a neighbor whose house is knocked down.

In Salevan v. Wilmington Park, Inc., 72 A.2d 239 (Del. Super. Ct. 1950), a ballpark operator was held liable for injuries to a pedestrian because it had failed to erect a barrier high enough to keep fly balls from regularly being hit into an adjacent street.

4. ***Dangers Posed by Natural Conditions.*** Generally speaking, possessors are said to have no duty to protect their neighbors from dangers arising from natural conditions, so that if rocks fall from a cliff, the possessor is not liable to those on whom they fall. California has gone the other way. In Sprecher v. Adamson Co., 636 P.2d 1121 (Cal. 1981), a landslide shoved some of the defendant's land against that of the plaintiff, who lived downhill from the defendant. The defendant had done nothing to cause the landslide. The California Supreme Court held that "possession alone" creates a duty to exercise care to protect one's neighbors.

5. ***Trees in Urban Areas.*** One fairly widespread exception to the rule of no liability for failure to prevent harm from natural causes involves trees in urban areas. The risk of harm from falling trees in an urban area is large, and urban landowners usually have so few trees that they can be expected to know when they are dangerous and take precautions. Accordingly, the urban landowner who unreasonably fails to have a dead tree or a rotting branch removed will in many states be liable to one on whom the tree falls. *See* Scheckel v. NLI, Inc., 953 N.E.2d 133 (Ind. App. 2011) ("a landowner in a residential or urban community owes a duty to prevent an

unreasonable risk of harm to adjoining property owners or their property resulting from trees growing upon the landowner's property").

Some courts do not distinguish urban trees from rural trees, or trees planted by the defendant (or a preceding owner) from trees which grew naturally, and have applied ordinary negligence principles to all falling-tree cases. *See* Ivancic v. Olmstead, 488 N.E.2d 72 (N.Y. 1985). Factors relevant to determining whether reasonable care has been exercised include the age and size of the tree, its exposure to the wind, the visibility of dead leaves and branches, discolored bark, and the likely proximity and frequency of persons traveling in the vicinity.

6. ***Persons Straying onto Land.*** Possessors may have a duty to anticipate and guard against harm to persons straying a short distance onto private land. Thus, there may be liability for having a dangerous trap near the boundary of the property, such as a concealed pit, against which an entrant cannot exercise self-protection. However, if the condition is not a trap, there is a divergence of opinion as to whether the possessor may be held liable.

In Hayes v. Malkan, 258 N.E.2d 695 (N.Y. 1970), the plaintiff was injured when the car in which he was riding struck a utility pole located on private property a few inches inside the boundary line. Because the dangerous condition was a "visible, sizeable, above-the-surface structure," concerning which travelers could be expected to take precautions, the court held that the complaint against the defendant should have been dismissed. Any other result, the court wrote, would "impose an intolerable burden upon a property owner" by requiring that person "to remove every tree, fence, post, mailbox or name sign located on his property in the vicinity of the highway."

7. ***Streets and Sidewalks.*** At common law, a municipality is normally required to maintain its streets and sidewalks in a reasonably safe condition for the amount and kind of travel which may be fairly expected upon them. *Cf.* Larson v. City of Chicago, 491 N.E.2d 165 (Ill. App. Ct. 1986) (roller skating on a sidewalk was a foreseeable use and therefore a cause of action was stated).

In McDevitt v. Sportsman's Warehouse, Inc., 255 P.3d 1166 (Idaho 2011), the court held that the sidewalk in front of a retail store operated by a tenant in a shopping center was not part of the leased premises, and therefore the tenant owed no duty of care to invitee to ensure that the sidewalk was safe or to warn of hazards.

In Burbach v. Canwest Inv., LLC, 224 P.3d 437 (Colo. App. 2009), the court found that although a city snow removal ordinance imposed on property owners an obligation to remove snow and ice from adjacent public sidewalks, it did not make public sidewalks the "property of" adjacent property owners for purposes of premises liability. Moreover, a property owner's compliance with the obligations imposed by the snow removal ordinance was not a "voluntary" assumption of duties to third persons.

8. *Unreasonable Risk of the Spread of Fire.* An increasing number of cases involve liability for the spread of fires. In Steamfitters Loc. Union No. 602 v. Erie Ins. Exch.,

233 A.3d 59 (Md. 2020), the Maryland Court of Appeals (the State's highest court) wrote:

> [A]lthough no Maryland case discusses a property owner's duty of care in the context of fire spread under conditions similar to the facts of this case, courts in other jurisdictions and treatises have recognized that a property owner has a duty of reasonable care to maintain his or her property in a manner so as not to allow fire to ignite and spread to neighboring properties.
>
> . . . .
>
> Applying the general principles of a property owner's duty of reasonable care . . . which have been similarly applied by other courts, we hold that under the specific facts and circumstances presented in this case, Steamfitters owed its neighbors a common law duty to maintain its property in a manner that would not cause an unreasonable risk of the spread of fire to the neighboring properties. We agree with the [intermediate] Court of Special Appeals that although Steamfitters used its property, including the mulch strip, in a normal or ordinary manner, "there was evidence from which the jury could determine that Steamfitters was aware that hundreds of cigarettes had been discarded in the mulch and that this practice put it on notice that a dangerous practice was occurring on its property, specifically the disposal of cigarettes in a combustible substance." . . . .
>
> The Plaintiffs presented evidence at trial that Steamfitters created the mulched area immediately adjacent to Gordon's property and permitted individuals to linger in the common areas of its property for hours while passing time prior to the commencement of their mandatory training. There was evidence from which a jury could determine that union officials . . . knew or should have known that individuals were carelessly discarding hundreds of cigarette butts in the mulch because they both walked through that area on several occasions in the weeks before the fire. Steamfitters' business manager . . . acknowledged that there were more butts "than there should have been" and that discarding cigarette butts in mulch presents a risk of fire. Despite this knowledge, Steamfitters took no action to prevent the foreseeable risk that a fire might start on its property as a result of individuals' careless acts of habitually discarding cigarette butts in the mulch.

Id. at 75-76.

9. ***Comparative Law Perspective: Building Owners in China.*** From an American perspective, some of the aspects of Chinese Tort Law are surprising. Sometimes the burden of persuasion is placed on the defendant, rather than the plaintiff, and sometimes defendants are supposed to pay something not because they are at fault, but because they have "deep pockets" and it is fair that they should pay something.

In 2005, while Mr. Luo Jiezhi was eating dinner outside an apartment building owned by Lao Xiquan (the Owner), a steel bar fell from above and hit Luo's right wrist causing severe injuries. At the time of the incident, the Owner had a metal structure on the top of the building for drying meat. Luo sued the Owner to recover medical and other expenses. The court relied on Article 126 of China's General Principles of Civil Law (GPCL), which provides that if a building, an installation, or an object placed or hung on a structure collapses, detaches, or falls, the owner or manager of the building is civilly liable for damages caused to another, unless he can prove he was not at fault. The court held for the plaintiff because the Owner failed to produce evidence that he was not at fault.

Chinese scholars say that it is not enough for an owner, in this kind of case, to prove that the owner exercised reasonable care. The owner would have to prove that it was a third party, the plaintiff, or a natural force that caused the plaintiff's injury. If neither the owner nor the plaintiff was at fault, the owner would normally be required to share the plaintiff's loss to the best of his economic ability. The payment is "not absolutely mandatory in nature," but is morally required.

How would a falling object case like this be decided under American law? Would it make a difference whether the place the plaintiff was dining was part of, or outside the boundary line of, the building owner's premises? Would *res ipsa loquitur* apply?

D. Lessors and Lessees

Defining "Possessor." Because possessors of land may be subject to liability for injuries that occur on the land, it is important to precisely identify who qualifies as a possessor. The critical factors are occupation and control, not ownership of the property. According to the Restatement:

> A possessor of land is
>
> (a) a person who occupies the land and controls it;
>
> (b) a person entitled to immediate occupation and control of the land if no other person is a possessor of the land under Subsection (a); or
>
> (c) a person who had occupied the land and controlled it if no other person subsequently became a possessor under Subsection (a) or (c).

Restatement, Third, of Torts: Liab. for Physical & Emotional Harm § 49 (2012).

In Coleman v. Hoffman, 64 P.3d 65 (Wash. Ct. App. 2003), the court held that a mortgagee that merely collected rents after a landlord's default on a loan was not a "mortgagee in possession," and thus, a tenant could not recover for common law premises liability against the mortgagee, absent any other indicia of control that a landlord would normally exhibit, such as leasing, making repairs, paying bills, making management decisions, and receiving and responding to tenant complaints. However, there was sufficient evidence to preclude summary judgment in favor of another mortgagee who exercised control by undertaking plumbing repairs and paying utility bills at the time a child was injured by falling through a rotted balcony railing in a common area.

Matthews v. Amberwood Associates Ltd. Partnership, Inc.

Court of Appeals of Maryland
719 A.2d 119 (Md. 1998)

ELDRIDGE, Judge.

....

Shelly Morton leased apartment A-1.... The apartment building was managed by the defendant Monocle Management, Ltd. and owned by the defendant... [Amberwood]....

...Morton kept her boyfriend's dog, a pit bull named Rampage, in her apartment. Sometimes she kept the dog chained outside, on the grounds of the apartment complex. The dog was not normally aggressive toward persons when Morton was present, but, when she was absent, Rampage would attempt to attack people in his vicinity.... [S]everal employees of the defendants testified about dangerous encounters involving the dog, that the dog was "vicious," and that the incidents involving the dog were reported to the defendants' resident manager or the manager on duty.

...Shanita Matthews and her 16-month-old son Tevin Williams visited Morton.... Morton was called away from the apartment. Shortly after Morton left the apartment, Rampage attacked Tevin. Rampage grabbed Tevin by the neck and was shaking him back and forth. Matthews was unable to free Tevin from Rampage's jaws....

...Tevin died from his injuries.

....

The jury found Amberwood and Monocle liable....

...[T]he Court of Special Appeals reversed..., holding that... the defendants owed no duty to the social invitees of a tenant....

....The plaintiffs contend that Rampage constituted a known dangerous condition upon the property and that the defendants retained control over the presence of the pit bull within the leased premises through the "no pets" clause in the lease. Thus, the plaintiffs argue that the defendants had a duty of care to protect Matthews and her son from that extremely dangerous animal.

...[W]hether a landlord owes a duty to his or her tenants and their guests with respect to dangerous or defective conditions on the property, of which the landlord has notice, depends upon the circumstances presented. In a multi-unit facility, the landlord ordinarily has a duty to maintain the common areas in a reasonably safe condition....

On the other hand, the duty which a landlord owes to a tenant, and the tenant's guests, within the tenant's apartment or other leased premises, is constrained by the general common law principle

> "[t]hat where property is demised, and at the time of the demise it is not a nuisance, and becomes so *only* by the act of the tenant while in his possession, and injury happens during such possession, the owner is not liable. . . ." Owings v. Jones, 9 Md. 108, 117–118 (1856).

. . . . Thus, a landlord is not ordinarily liable to a tenant or guest of a tenant for injuries from a hazardous condition in the leased premises that comes into existence after the tenant has taken possession. . . .

. . . [T]his principle . . . is not absolute and has exceptions. For example, where a landlord agrees to rectify a dangerous condition in the leased premises, and fails to do so, he may be liable for injuries caused by the condition. . . . If a landlord, although not contractually obligated to do so, voluntarily undertakes to rectify a dangerous or defective condition within the leased premises, and does so negligently, the landlord is liable for resulting injuries. . . . Defective or dangerous conditions in the leased premises which violate statutes or ordinances may also be the basis for a negligence action against the landlord. . . .

The principal rationale for the general rule . . . is that the landlord "has parted with control". . . . Moreover, . . . a common thread running through many of our cases involving circumstances in which landlords have been held liable (*i.e.*, common areas, pre-existing defective conditions in the leased premises, a contract under which the landlord and tenant agree that the landlord shall rectify a defective condition) is the landlord's ability to exercise a degree of control over the defective or dangerous condition and to take steps to prevent injuries arising therefrom. . . .

Turning to the case at bar, . . . tenant Morton did not have exclusive control over the leased premises because the lease gave the landlord a degree of control. The landlord retained control over the presence of a dog in the leased premises by virtue of the "no pets" clause in the lease. The lease plainly stated that breach of the "no pets" clause was a "default of the lease."[1] Such a default would enable the landlord to bring a breach of lease action to terminate the tenancy pursuant to . . . the Real Property Article. Even before bringing such an action, the landlord, when it first received notice of the dangerous incidents involving Rampage, could have informed Morton that harboring the pit bull was in violation of her lease, could have told her to get rid of the aggressive animal, and could have threatened legal action if she failed to do so. If the landlord had taken these steps, it would have been likely that Morton would have gotten rid of the pit bull, particularly because she did not own him. . . . The record in this case, however, shows that the landlord did nothing. . . .

In addition to the landlord's control . . . , the foreseeability of the harm supports the imposition of a duty on the landlord. . . . Numerous employees of the defendant testified that they knew of the pit bull, were afraid of the pit bull, witnessed attacks

---

1. [Fn. 4:] At trial a manager employed by the defendants testified that a procedure for the notification of tenants that they were in breach of their lease was in place and that the use of pre-printed forms enabled such notification to be carried out in less than ten minutes.

by the dog, and were unable to carry out their duties, both in the leased premises and in the common areas, because of the presence of the pit bull.

.... The extreme dangerousness of this breed, as it has evolved today, is well recognized. "Pit bulls as a breed are known to be extremely aggressive and have been bred as attack animals." .... The "Pit Bull's massive canine jaws can crush a victim with up to two thousand pounds (2,000) of pressure per square inch — three times that of a German Shepard or Doberman Pinscher." .... *See also* Hearn v. City of Overland Park, ... [772 P.2d 758 (Kan. 1989)] ("pit bull dogs represent a unique public health hazard ... [because] [o]f the 32 known human deaths in the United States due to dog attacks ... [in the period between July 1983 and April 1989], 23 were caused by attacks by pit bull dogs"). ...

We do not hold that a landlord's retention in the lease of some control over particular matters in the leased premises is, standing alone, a sufficient basis to impose a duty upon the landlord which is owed to a guest on the premises. This Court has employed a balancing test to determine whether a duty of reasonable care should be imposed in particular circumstances. ... In the instant case, the various policy considerations that need to be weighed are the general understanding that a tenant is primarily in control of the leased premises and the sanctity of a tenant's home, including her ability generally to do as she sees fit within the privacy thereof, against the public safety concerns of permitting that same tenant to harbor an extremely dangerous animal that will foreseeably endanger individuals inside and outside the walls of the leased premises, the degree of control maintained by the landlord, the landlord's knowledge of the dangerous condition, and the landlord's ability to abate the condition. We ... believe that the balance should be struck on the side of imposing a duty on the landlord which is owed to guests on the premises.

One of the leading cases in this area is Uccello v. Laudenslayer, 44 Cal. App. 3d 504, 118 Cal. Rptr. 741 (1975). There, a tenant's dog inflicted serious injury upon a social guest while the guest was in the kitchen of the leased premises. The California court held "that a duty of care arises when the landlord has actual knowledge of the presence of the dangerous animal and when he has the right to remove the animal by retaking possession of the premises." ....

The New York courts have also addressed the issue. ... In Strunk v. Zoltanski, ... [468 N.E.2d 13 (N.Y. 1984)], the court was faced with a "situation in which the landlord, by leasing the premises to the owner of the dog, could be found ... to have created the very risk which was reasonably foreseeable and which operated to injure the plaintiff." .... Thus, the court held that the landlord was liable because the landlord had an opportunity to act affirmatively prior to letting the property. The *Strunk* court stated, however, that "with respect to the liability of a landlord whose tenant comes into possession of the animal after the premises has been leased," in order to "establish liability it must be shown that the landlord had knowledge of the vicious propensities of the dog and had control of the premises or other capability to remove or confine the animal. ..." ....

[Reversed and remanded with instructions to affirm the judgment of the trial court in relevant part.]

[The dissenting opinion of RODOWSKY, Judge, has been omitted.]

CHASANOW, Judge, dissenting, in which CATHELL, Judge, joins.

.... The legal issue in this case is whether a landlord should have to pay over five million dollars solely because the landlord did not make a futile attempt to evict a tenant whose dog barked and growled at maintenance men trying to enter the dog's residence when its owner was not home.

... [A]ffirming this five million dollar judgment ... may ultimately have severe repercussions for lessees with dogs. Landlords wishing to avoid multimillion dollar lawsuits may be forced to initiate eviction proceedings to terminate leases whenever a tenant's dog acts aggressively toward maintenance personnel who attempt to enter the tenant's dwelling when the tenants are not home....

....

.... I respectfully dissent.

Notes

1. ***Landlords and Pit Bulls.*** See Batra v. Clark, 110 S.W.3d 126 (Tex. App. 2003) (a landlord who did not have actual knowledge of a pit bull's vicious propensities did not owe a duty of care to a neighbor girl).

In Stokes v. Lyddy, 815 A.2d 263 (Conn. App. Ct. 2003), a tenant's pit bull dog escaped from an apartment, left the premises, and bit the plaintiff who was walking on a nearby public sidewalk. The court held that the landlords owed no duty under a theory of premises liability to protect the plaintiff from the attack because it did not occur within any common area under the landlords' control. In addition, the landlords had no duty to keep a dangerous condition on the leased premises from causing harm to persons outside the property because, under the Second Restatement, that kind of liability arises only if at the time of the lease the lessor consented to the activity or knew it would be carried on. In *Stokes*, the tenants did not own a dog when the lease began and did not seek permission from the landlords to keep a dog in the apartment.

2. ***Lessors Not in Possession: General Rule.*** The general rule, that a lessor who has parted with possession is not liable for dangerous conditions on the leased premises, finds broad application. *See, e.g.*, Clauson v. Kempffer, 477 N.W.2d 257 (S.D. 1991) (landlord had no duty to motorcyclist to warn him of a smooth wire fence strung across a road on the leased premises by tenants or to ensure that the fence was safely constructed).

3. ***Short-Term Rentals.*** The general no-duty rule may apply to short-term rentals. Heath-Latson v. Styller, 169 N.E.3d 155 (Mass. 2021), held that the owner of property which was used for short-term rentals did not owe a duty to protect an attendee of

a party from harm caused by a third party. There was no allegation that short-term rentals were correlated with an increase in violent crime or that incidents of violence had previously occurred at the property during rental periods. "[T]he defendant had no control over the premises during the rental period . . . [and] at the start of the rental period the defendant gave Victor [one of the six renters 'sole and exclusive possession of his [r]esidence for the three-day stay, with no visits, monitoring, or supervision by [the defendant].'" *Id.* at 160.

As the notes below indicate, there are several exceptions to the general no-duty rule. *See generally* Restatement, Second, of Torts §§ 355-362.

4. ***Common Areas.*** A lessor may be liable for harm that occurs in a common area that is under the lessor's control. *See* Jackson v. Ray Kruse Constr. Co., 708 S.W.2d 664 (Mo. 1986) (landlord was liable for failing to install parking lot speed bumps to reduce the risk posed by speeding bicyclists).

5. ***Admission of the Public.*** According to Section 359 of the Second Restatement, a lessor may be liable when premises are leased for purposes involving admission of the public, and the lessor has reason to expect that the lessee will admit the public without correcting an unreasonably dangerous situation. In Johnson County Sherriff's Posse, Inc. v. Endsley, 926 S.W.2d 284 (Tex. 1996), the court held that, even assuming the applicability of that section, dirt containing small rocks was, as a matter of law, not an unreasonably dangerous condition for which a rodeo arena lessor could be held liable to a spectator for injuries he sustained when hit in the eye by a rock or clump of dirt kicked into the air by a horse during a barrel race held by tenants.

6. ***Negligent Repairs.*** A landlord or other person who undertakes to make repairs at a leased premises must exercise care in doing so. However, in Pruitt v. Savage, 115 P.3d 1000 (Wash. App. 2005), a neighbor who was struck by a falling garage door while rollerblading at a leased residence could not recover from a property management company. By undertaking several months earlier to check the door with respect to bouncing back if it was opened too hard, the company did not undertake to ensure that the door did not fall at random times long after it had been opened.

7. ***Promised Repairs.*** A landlord who promises to install or repair a lock on a rental apartment to prevent criminal entry, and who fails to do so, may be liable to the tenant for resulting losses. *See* Braitman v. Overlook Terrace Corp., 346 A.2d 76 (N.J. 1975). If a landlord is liable to a tenant for failing to install a lock, should the landlord be liable to a guest of a tenant who is harmed by the same action?

8. ***Concealed Dangers.*** *See* Kinsman v. Unocal Corp., 123 P.3d 931 (Cal. 2005) (holding that "a landowner that hires an independent contractor may be liable to the contractor's employee if . . . the landowner knew, or should have known, of a latent or concealed preexisting hazardous condition on its property" and "the contractor did not know and could not have reasonably discovered this hazardous condition").

9. ***Abrogation.*** Some jurisdictions have abolished the general rule of non-liability of landlords and have substituted instead a reasonable-care standard. For example,

in Pagelsdorf v. Safeco Ins. Co. of Am., 284 N.W.2d 55 (Wis. 1979), the plaintiff, a social guest of a tenant, was injured when he fell through a dry-rotted balcony railing while helping to move furniture. In a suit against the landlord, the court, relying on the same policies which supported its earlier abrogation of the status distinctions relating to the liability of possessors, held that the suit could be maintained because a landlord owes to a tenant or anyone on the premises with the tenant's consent a duty of ordinary care. Presumably, the factors relevant to the issue of liability would include whether the defect was obvious or latent, whether the defendant had access to the premises to inspect or make repairs, and the gravity and likelihood of the threatened harm.

10. ***Duties of Lessors Under the Third Restatement.*** The Third Restatement declines to state a general rule of no liability, and instead simply sets forth the many bases on which a lessor might be liable to those injured on leased premises.

Restatement, Third, of Torts: Liability for Physical and Emotional Harm

§ 53. Duty of Lessor (2012)

Except as provided in § 52 [dealing with duties to flagrant trespassers], a lessor owes to the lessee and all other entrants on the leased premises the following duties:

(a) a duty of reasonable care under § 51 ["General Duty of Land Possessors"] for those portions of the leased premises over which the lessor retains control;

(b) a duty of reasonable care under § 7 ["Duty"] for any risks that are created by the lessor in the condition of the leased premises;

(c) a duty to disclose to the lessee any dangerous condition that satisfies all of the following:

(1) it poses a risk to entrants on the leased premises;

(2) it exists on the leased premises when the lessee takes possession;

(3) it is latent and unknown to the lessee; and

(4) it is known or should be known to the lessor;

(d) a duty of reasonable care for any dangerous condition on the leased premises at the time the lessee takes possession if:

(1) the lease is for a purpose that includes admission of the public; and

(2) the lessor has reason to believe that the lessee will admit persons onto the leased premises without rectifying the dangerous condition;

(e) a duty of reasonable care:

(1) for any contractual undertaking; or

(2) for any voluntary undertaking . . . with regard to the condition of the leased premises;

(f) a duty based on an applicable statute imposing obligations on lessors with regard to the condition of leased premises, unless the court finds that recognition of a tort duty is inconsistent with the statute;

(g) a duty of reasonable care to comply with an applicable implied warranty of habitability; and

(h) a duty of reasonable care to lessees under § 40, Comment m [duties of landlords based on special relationship], as well as any other affirmative duties that may apply. . . .

Chapter 11

Limited Duty: Negligent Infliction of Severe Emotional Distress

No area of tort law is more unsettled than compensation for negligent infliction of emotional distress. The decisions continually restate the criteria for recovery, and there are often substantial differences in the requirements, or their interpretation, from one jurisdiction to the next, and within any one jurisdiction at different times.

The law of negligent infliction of emotional distress must face two special concerns: the need to guarantee the genuineness of claims and the need to limit the scope of liability. Genuineness is a problem here, as it is with all forms of redress for mental harm, because the inner workings of the human mind are difficult to fathom. In the absence of corroboration for the plaintiff's story, there is a substantial risk of falsification. Restricting the scope of liability is important because requiring defendants who are merely negligent (not recklessly or intentionally tortious) to pay for all mental suffering caused by minor lapses could often result in liability disproportionate to fault and exhaust a defendant's resources without regard to whether the most serious claims were compensated. *See* Coward v. Gagne & Son Concrete Blocks, Inc., 238 A.3d 254, 260 (Me. 2020) (discussing the importance of striking "a fair balance between the need to compensate foreseeable psychic injuries and the risk of imposing limitless liability").

If genuineness can be established, and if reasonable lines can be drawn to limit the scope of liability, courts will award compensation, but only if there is proof that the plaintiff suffered serious harm of a type that could reasonably have been anticipated.

A. Serious and Genuine Harm

Lewis v. Westinghouse Electric Corporation

Appellate Court of Illinois
487 N.E.2d 1071 (Ill. App. Ct. 1985)

JIGANTI, Presiding Justice.

... Lucille Lewis sought damages from the defendants, Westinghouse Elevator Co.... and the Chicago Housing Authority (CHA), for the negligent infliction of emotional distress. The defendants moved to dismiss the plaintiff's complaint for failure to state a cause of action. The trial court granted the motion....

The plaintiff is a resident at one of the apartments owned by the defendant CHA. The defendant Westinghouse maintains and services the elevators.... On August 16, 1983, the plaintiff entered the elevator on the first floor and rode it to the 16th floor. As she attempted to exit the elevator, however, the elevator stalled and the doors remained closed. The elevator remained in this position for approximately 40 minutes. The plaintiff alleges that during that time she was in danger of "suffocation and serious physical harm." In addition plaintiff alleges that as a result of the incident she suffered an unstable angina and aggravation of her coronary arteriosclerotic heart disease and hypertension.

... [W]e find that the plaintiff did not have a reasonable fear for her own safety. Whether a fear is reasonable is determined by the objective standard of whether a particular incident would produce fear in the person of ordinary sensibilities.... In this case the elevator merely stalled and the doors failed to open. This is not a case such as Bass v. Nooney Co. (Mo. 1983), 646 S.W.2d 765, where water began to rise in the elevator so that the party reasonably feared drowning. Apprehensive or uncomfortable it may have been for the plaintiff, but, absent something more, the incident in this case was not one which produces fear of suffocation.

... [I]n making that judgment we are mindful of the admonition of the Illinois Supreme Court in a case involving an intentional infliction of emotional distress.... In *Knierim* the court stated that "[i]ndiscriminate allowance of actions for mental anguish would encourage neurotic overreactions to trivial hurts, and the law should aim to toughen the psyche of the citizen rather than pamper it." Knierim v. Izzo (1961), 22 Ill.2d. 73, 85, 174 N.E.2d 157, 164.

.... "[Trial judges ... should] not permit litigation to enter the field of trivialities and mere bad manners." ....

It might be argued that this is not a neurotic overreaction to a trivial hurt since the plaintiff has alleged a resulting physical injury, aggravation of her angina condition. However, the *Knierim* court favorably commented on the case of Slocum v. Food Fair Stores of Florida, Inc. (Fla. 1958), 100 So. 2d 396, in which the plaintiff suffered a heart attack as a result of an aggravation of a preexisting condition. The Florida court found that there was no cause of action because the defendant's conduct must cause distress to a person of "ordinary sensibilities." The finding of the Florida court, in which the Illinois Supreme Court agreed, was that this was not a person of ordinary sensibilities. We judge that to be the situation in this instance.

... [The order of the trial court is affirmed. The dissenting opinion of Justice LINN is omitted.]

Notes

1. ***Severe Distress is Required.*** An independent tort action will lie only if the plaintiff suffers severe emotional distress. *See* Jacobsen v. Allstate Ins. Co., 215 P.3d 649 (Mont. 2009) ("the 'serious or severe' standard ... applies only to independent claims of negligent or intentional infliction of emotional distress," not to claims for parasitic emotional distress damages).

2. ***Ordinary Sensibilities.*** Severity is usually judged by reference to a person of ordinary sensibilities. The "eggshell skull" doctrine (*see* Chapter 7) does not apply to claims seeking compensation for only emotional distress.

3. ***Foreseeability of Severe Distress.*** *Compare Lewis with* Friedman v. Merck & Co., 131 Cal. Rptr. 2d 885 (Ct. App. 2003), where a job applicant, who was a strict, ethical vegan, filed negligence actions against drug test distributors alleging that he suffered serious emotional and subsequent physical injuries when he discovered that a tuberculosis test he took as a condition of employment contained animal products. In rejecting the negligent infliction claim, the court wrote:

> [E]ven if ... defendants, ... knew plaintiff was a strict ethical vegan, it was not reasonably foreseeable that their negligence in responding to the prospective employer's inquiry would likely cause plaintiff to suffer *serious* emotional distress.... Defendants' undertaking was not of a personal nature involving an unavoidable risk of *serious* emotional trauma.... [It was] materially unlike: a physician undertaking to deliver a child; a therapist agreeing to treat a patient; a mortuary contracting to provide burial services; or a doctor telling a patient to advise her husband that she has syphilis....

4. ***Fear of HIV, AIDS, Cancer, or Other Diseases.*** Many courts hold that emotional distress damages for fear of contracting a disease, such as AIDS, can be recovered from a negligent defendant only if the plaintiff was exposed to the disease. *See* Majca v. Beekil, 701 N.E.2d 1084 (Ill. 1998).

Of course the critical question is whether "exposed" means (a) that the defendant had the disease, (b) that the circumstances were such that the disease might have been transmitted, (c) that it is probable that the plaintiff will develop the disease, or (d) that the plaintiff in fact contracted the disease. Courts appear to differ in answering this question. *Compare* Johnson v. West Va. Univ. Hosp., 413 S.E.2d 889 (W. Va. 1991) (where the defendant hospital negligently failed to advise a security officer that an unruly patient had AIDS, and the patient bit the officer after biting himself, the court upheld a $1.9 million award), *with* Potter v. Firestone Tire & Rubber Co., 863

P.2d 795 (Cal. 1993) (damages for fear of cancer in a negligence action are allowed only if the fear stems from a knowledge which is corroborated by reasonable medical and scientific opinion that it is more likely than not that cancer will develop).

In Temple-Inland Forest Products Corp. v. Carter, 993 S.W.2d 88 (Tex. 1999), the court held that workers who were exposed to asbestos, but who did not then have an asbestos-related disease, could not recover damages for fear of developing such a disease in the future.

What if a doctor negligently diagnoses a patient as having AIDS or HIV? *Compare* Chizmar v. Markie, 896 P.2d 196 (Alaska 1995) (permitting recovery of emotional distress damages without proof of physical injury), *with* Heiner v. Moretuzzo, 652 N.E.2d 664 (Ohio 1995) (holding that a patient was not entitled to recovery for emotional distress since she never faced actual physical peril as a result of the alleged negligence).

If recovery for fear of AIDS is permitted even when the plaintiff has not in fact contracted the disease, some courts hold that damages should be limited to the "window of anxiety" that occurs before the plaintiff is able to determine with reasonable medical certainty that there has been no infection. *See* Faya v. Almaraz, 620 A.2d 327 (Md. 1993).

5. ***Ways of Establishing Genuineness.*** In an action for *intentional* infliction of emotional distress (*see* Chapter 2), the genuineness of the plaintiff's claim may be inferred from both the defendant's mental state and the egregious nature of the conduct. The defendant's desire to cause emotional distress or the substantial certainty that distress would result suggests that the plaintiff's claim is not fabricated. Also, it is well known that "extreme and outrageous" conduct is likely to produce in others adverse mental reactions.

In an emotional distress action based on *negligence*, those guarantees of genuineness are not present. The underlying conduct need be only unreasonable (that is, negligent), and intent need not be shown. Not surprisingly, a number of courts have imposed specific requirements that must be met in negligent-emotional-distress cases as a way of excluding claims for which genuineness is hard to determine.

(a) ***The Impact Rule.*** In the early twentieth century, the law generally required a negligent-emotional-distress plaintiff to present evidence of physical impact or injury. Unless the plaintiff suffered such harm, a claim could not succeed.

Most states no longer regard impact as essential. *See* Osborne v. Keeney, 399 S.W.3d 1, 17–18 (Ky. 2012) ("[A]t least forty jurisdictions have either rejected the impact rule or abandoned it"); *but see* Bader v. Johnson, 732 N.E.2d 1212, 1221–22 (Ind. 2000) (adhering to a modified impact rule). However, proof of physical impact or injury is still generally sufficient to secure an award if other requirements are met.

(b) ***Physical Consequences.*** The rigidity of the physical-impact requirement, and its potential for denying recovery in cases where justice appeared to dictate a contrary result, led some courts to seize upon rather trivial impacts, such as a slight jolt, a minor blow, or dust in the eye (*see* W. Page Keeton *et al.*, Prosser and Keeton on Torts (5th ed. 1984)) to justify an award. Many jurisdictions now allow proof of physical consequences or manifestations resulting from emotional distress to substitute for physical impact. However, even this rule can be demanding.

In Elliott v. Elliott, 58 So.3d 878 (Fla. Dist. Ct. App. 2011), the defendant dismembered his mother's corpse, burning it in a barrel, and scattering the remains on the family's farm without disclosing the location of the remains to his siblings. In rejecting the siblings' claim for negligent infliction of emotional distress, the court wrote:

> Medical testimony revealed Mary Ann suffered from stress, insomnia, anxiety, diarrhea, loss of appetite, and hair loss following her mother's death. . . .
>
> Douglas testified he had a "real, real hollow feeling" knowing Martha had not been buried according to her wishes and that it was a horrendous situation trying to keep the family together after Martha's death, mainly because of the continuing legal proceedings. He began having headaches and developed diabetes and sleep apnea after the incident. . . .

The court found that the siblings' physical manifestations did not satisfy the state supreme court's stringent requirements for demonstrable physical injury or illness resulting from negligently inflicted emotional distress. Other courts have found similar evidence of physical consequences to be sufficient.

(c) ***Invasion of Particular Kinds of Rights***. Some courts have awarded compensatory damages for mental anguish unaccompanied by physical injury or physical consequences where the defendant's invasion of a legal right is, by its very nature, likely to provoke serious emotional distress. The cases have frequently involved facts similar to those which, if accompanied by intent, would have been sufficient to state a claim for assault or false imprisonment. *Cf.* Turnage v. Oldham, 346 F. Supp. 3d 1141 (W.D. Tenn. 2018) (detainees colorably alleged that the harm they suffered from the failure by a company to carefully integrate and design a court management system, was reasonably foreseeable, and thus, proximately caused their over-detainments).

Breach of a duty of confidentiality may also be sufficient to support an award of emotional distress damages. *See* Florida Dept. of Corrections v. Abril, 969 So. 2d 201 (Fla. 2007) (involving failure to keep confidential the results of an HIV test).

(d) ***No Special Requirements***. A number of decisions have dispensed altogether with special tests for genuineness, relying instead upon the usual factfinding processes for exposing fraudulent claims, such as cross-examination and jury evaluation of witness demeanor. *See* Jones v. Howard University, Inc., 589 A.2d 419 (D.C. 1991) (holding that a patient who was subjected to x-rays and surgery before being diagnosed as pregnant could recover for serious and verifiable mental distress suffered as a result of her fear that the procedures had injured her or her unborn twins); Folz v. New Mexico, 797 P.2d 246 (N.M. 1990) (holding that a person who witnesses firsthand the fatal injury of a family member can recover for negligent infliction of emotional distress without proof of physical manifestations or physical injuries).

6. ***Attorneys Who Negligently Cause Distress.*** Courts have been reluctant to hold attorneys liable for negligently causing emotional distress to clients. However, liability may be imposed if the lawyer's malpractice results in loss of the client's liberty. *See* Rowell v. Holt, 850 So. 2d 474 (Fla. 2003) (mishandling of a document led to the client's ten-day incarceration).

7. ***Distress Resulting from Property Damage.*** Most courts hold that negligent harm to property, by itself, is an insufficient predicate for an award of emotional-distress damages, at least when the damage occurs outside of the plaintiff's presence. *See* Castillo v. City of Las Vegas, 195 P.3d 870 (N.M. App. 2008) (a sewer backed up onto private property); Birmingham Coal & Coke Co., Inc. v. Johnson, 10 So. 3d 993 (Ala. 2008) (homes damaged by blasting operations); Charlie Stuart Oldsmobile, Inc. v. Smith, 357 N.E.2d 247 (Ind. Ct. App. 1976), *modified on rehearing* 369 N.E.2d 947 (Ind. Ct. App. 1977) (repeated damage to an auto during several attempts to repair); In re Air Crash Disaster Near New Orleans, 764 F.2d 1084 (5th Cir. 1985) (house bulldozed after being doused with jet fuel).

But there is slender authority to the contrary. In Rodrigues v. Hawaii, 472 P.2d 509 (Haw. 1970), a new house was flooded with six inches of water on the day the plaintiffs were to move in, causing extensive damage to the house and furnishings. The flood was allegedly caused by the state's negligence in failing to provide for proper highway drainage. "Mr. Rodrigues reported that he was 'heartbroken' and 'couldn't stand to look at it' and Mrs. Rodrigues testified that she was 'shocked' and cried because they had waited fifteen years to build their own home." The court awarded a modest $2500 for mental suffering. The decision in *Rodrigues* was later superseded by a statute that allows recovery for serious emotional distress arising solely from damage to property or material objects only if it results in "physical injury or mental illness." *See* Haw. Rev. Stat. Ann. § 663-8.9 (Westlaw 2022).

Cases involving mere negligence are distinguishable from intentional torts, and it is not surprising that a large number of courts have awarded mental anguish damages if the defendant intentionally interfered with the plaintiff's chattels or realty. *See, e.g.*, Smith & Gaston Funeral Directors v. Wilson, 79 So. 2d 48 (Ala. 1955) (trespass and desecration of grave site); Grandeson v. International Harvester Credit Corp., 66 So. 2d 317 (La. 1953) (trespassory repossession of refrigerator); Fredeen v. Stride, 525 P.2d 166 (Or. 1974) (conversion of dog).

B. Some Special Cases

One area in which many courts have been willing to award damages for negligently inflicted emotional distress involves the death (or the erroneously reported death) of someone close to the plaintiff. When a funeral director carelessly botches the ceremony, dumping the decedent's remains beside the road, or when a telegraph company carelessly and erroneously informs the plaintiff that a loved one has died, there is reason to conclude that the distress the plaintiff claims is genuine and serious. Furthermore, cases like this seldom give rise to significant financial losses, so limiting recovery to out-of-pocket damages might seriously under-deter misconduct by those responsible for this kind of harm.

Johnson v. New York

Court of Appeals of New York
334 N.E.2d 590 (N.Y. 1975)

BREITEL, Chief Judge.

... [T]he issue is whether the daughter of a patient in a State hospital, falsely advised that the patient, her mother, had died, may recover from the State for emotional harm....

Claimant and her aunt, Nellie Johnson, since deceased, had filed a claim against the State for funeral expenses incurred, emotional harm and punitive damages. The Court of Claims awarded claimant $7,500 for funeral expenses undertaken on the false information, and for emotional harm. It denied her punitive damages, and dismissed the aunt's claim for insufficiency.... The Appellate Division modified, limiting the daughter's award to her pecuniary losses of $1,658.47, and otherwise affirmed as to both claimants. The aunt's estate, unlike the daughter, took no further appeal to this court.

There should be a reversal....

Charles D. Breitel

Claimant's mother, Emma Johnson, had been a patient in the Hudson River State Hospital since 1960. On August 6, 1970, another patient, also named Emma Johnson died. Later that day, the hospital sent a telegram addressed to Nellie Johnson of Albany, claimant's aunt and the sister of the living Emma Johnson. The telegram read:

> [Regret to inform you of death of Emma Johnson. Please notify relatives make burial arrangements have undertaker contact hospital before coming for body. Hospital wishes to study all deaths for scientific reasons. Please wire post mortem consent.
>
> —Hudson River State Hospital]

In accordance with the instructions in the telegram, claimant was notified of her mother's death by her aunt. An undertaker was engaged; the body of the deceased Emma Johnson was released by the hospital and taken to Albany that night. A wake was set for August 11, with burial the next day. In the interim claimant incurred expenses in preparing the body for the funeral, and in notifying other relatives of her mother's death.

On the afternoon of the wake, claimant and her aunt went to the funeral home to view the body. After examining the body, both claimant and her aunt remarked that the mother's appearance had changed. Nellie Johnson also expressed doubt that the corpse was that of her sister Emma. Thereafter the doubts built up, and upon returning that evening for the wake, claimant, in a state of extreme distress, examined the corpse more closely and verified that it was not that of her mother. At this point, claimant became "very, very, hysterical," and had to be helped from the funeral chapel.

The hospital was called, and the mistake confirmed. Claimant's mother was alive and well in another wing of the hospital. . . . Upon the trial it appeared that the hospital had violated its own procedures and with gross carelessness had "pulled" the wrong patient record.

After this incident, claimant did not work in her employment for more than 11 days. She complained of "[r]ecurrent nightmares, terrifying dreams of death, seeing the coffin . . . difficulty in concentrating, irritability, inability to function at work properly, general tenseness and anxiety." Her psychiatrist testified that "She appeared to be somewhat depressed, tremulous. She seemed to be under a considerable amount of pressure. She cried easily when relating events that occurred. I thought that she spoke rather rapidly and obviously perspiring." Both her psychiatrist and that of the State agreed that, as a result of the incident, claimant suffered "excessive anxiety," that is, anxiety neurosis. . . .

. . . . In the absence of contemporaneous or consequential physical injury, courts have been reluctant to permit recovery for negligently caused psychological trauma, with ensuing emotional harm alone. . . . The reasons for the more restrictive rule were best summarized by Prosser . . . : "The temporary emotion of fright, so far from serious that it does no physical harm, is so evanescent a thing, so easily counterfeited, and usually so trivial, that the courts have been quite unwilling to protect the plaintiff against mere negligence, where the elements of extreme outrage and moral blame which have had such weight in the case of the intentional tort are lacking." Contemporaneous or consequential physical harm, coupled with the initial psychological trauma, was, however, thought to provide an index of reliability otherwise absent in a claim for psychological trauma with only psychological consequences.

There have developed, however, two exceptions. The first is the minority rule permitting recovery for emotional harm resulting from negligent transmission by a telegraph company of a message announcing death....

The second exception permits recovery for emotional harm to a close relative resulting from negligent mishandling of a corpse.... Recovery in these cases has ostensibly been grounded on a violation of the relative's quasi-property right in the body.... It has been noted, however, that in this context such a "property right" is little more than a fiction; in reality the personal feelings of the survivors are being protected....

In both the telegraph cases and the corpse mishandling cases, there exists "an especial likelihood of genuine and serious mental distress, arising from the special circumstances, which serves as a guarantee that the claim is not spurious" (p. 330). Prosser notes that "[t]here may perhaps be other such cases" (p. 330; *see* Neiman v. Upper Queens Med. Group, City Ct., 220 N.Y.S.2d 129, 130, in which plaintiff alleged emotional harm due to negligent misinformation by a laboratory that his sperm count indicated sterility; and defendant's motion for judgment on the pleadings was denied). The instant claim provides an example of such a case.

....The consequential funeral expenditures and the serious psychological impact on claimant of a false message informing her of the death of her mother, were all within the "orbit of the danger" and therefore within the "orbit of the duty" for the breach of which a wrongdoer may be held liable (Palsgraf v. Long Is. R.R. Co., 248 N.Y. 339, 343, 162 N.E. 99, 100). Thus, the hospital owed claimant a duty to refrain from such conduct, a duty breached when it negligently sent the false message. The false message and the events flowing from its receipt were the proximate cause of claimant's emotional harm. Hence, claimant is entitled to recover for that harm, especially if supported by objective manifestations of that harm.

.... In this case, ... the injury was inflicted by the hospital directly on claimant by its negligent sending of a false message announcing her mother's death. Claimant was not directly harmed by injury caused to another; she was not a mere eyewitness of or bystander to injury caused to another. Instead, she was the one to whom a duty was directly owed by the hospital, and the one who was directly injured by the hospital's breach of that duty....

Moreover, not only justice but logic compels the further conclusion that if claimant was entitled to recover her pecuniary losses she was also entitled to recover for the emotional harm caused by the same tortious act. The recovery of the funeral expenses stands only because a duty to claimant was breached. Such a duty existing and such a breach of that duty occurring, she is entitled to recover the proven harmful consequences proximately caused by the breach.... [R]ecovery for emotional harm to one subjected directly to the tortious act may not be disallowed so long as the evidence is sufficient to show causation and substantiality of the harm suffered, together with a "guarantee of genuineness"....

Order reversed with costs, and case remitted ... for further proceedings in accordance with the opinion herein.

Notes

1. ***Other Precedent.*** *See also* Wilson v. Ferguson, 747 S.W.2d 499 (Tex. App. 1988) (where a funeral director abandoned a coffin and body at an improperly prepared gravesite, and ignored the family's request for help in correcting the problem, emotional distress damages were awarded without proof of physical injury or physical manifestations).

2. ***Dead Bodies.*** The Restatement, Second, of Torts, § 868, recognizes a tort for interference with dead bodies:

> One who intentionally, recklessly or negligently removes, withholds, mutilates or operates upon the body of a dead person or prevents its proper interment or cremation is subject to liability to a member of the family of the deceased who is entitled to the disposition of the body.

Comment a to § 868 states:

> The technical basis of the cause of action is the interference with the exclusive right of control of the body, which frequently has been called by the courts a "property" or a "quasi-property" right. This does not, however, fit very well into the category of property, since the body ordinarily cannot be sold or transferred, has no utility and can be used only for the one purpose of interment or cremation. In practice the technical right has served as a mere peg upon which to hang damages for the mental distress inflicted upon the survivor; and in reality the cause of action has been exclusively one for the mental distress....

Should liability extend to family members who do not have a right to dispose of the deceased body? In Boorman v. Nevada Mem'l Cremation Soc'y, 236 P.3d 4 (Nev. 2010), the court wrote:

> [A] mortuary voluntarily undertakes a duty to competently prepare the decedent's body for the benefit of the bereaved.... While we must limit liability at some point, and thus conclude that a mortuary's duty does not run to all persons potentially affected by the decedent's passing, such as close friends and distant relatives, we cannot conclude that a mortuary only owes a duty to the person with the right to dispose of the body.
>
> .... [W]e conclude that close family members who are aware of both the death of a loved one and that mortuary services were being performed may

> bring an action for emotional distress resulting from the negligent handling of the deceased's remains.

See also Rader Funeral Home, Inc. v. Chavira, 553 S.W.3d 10 (Tex. App. 2018) (wrong body delivered to decedent's family); Akins Funeral Home, Inc. v. Miller, 878 So. 2d 267 (Ala. 2003) (unwanted cremation); Shipley v. City of New York, 2012 WL 882795 (N.Y. Sup. Ct. 2012) (approving jury awards of $500,000 to each parent in a case involving the mishandling of their child's brain, which was placed on display without authorization).

3. ***Otherwise-Compelling Facts.*** Death cases are not the only ones in which the defendant's misconduct and the plaintiff's suffering are so apparent that recovery seems appealing:

In Hagan v. Coca-Cola Bottling Co., 804 So. 2d 1234 (Fla. 2001), consumers who drank a beverage that appeared to contain a used condom sued for emotional distress based on fear of contracting AIDS. The court held that a plaintiff need not prove the existence of a physical injury in order to recover damages for emotional injuries caused by the consumption of contaminated food or beverage.

The plaintiff in Rowe v. Bennett, 514 A.2d 802 (Me. 1986), sought treatment at a health service for problems in her relationship with her homosexual companion of three years. During the treatment, plaintiff's therapist secretly became emotionally involved with plaintiff's companion, and the two later started living together. The court held that the patient could maintain an action for negligent infliction of mental distress because the plaintiff was "extremely vulnerable" to mental harm.

See also Doe Parents No. 1 v. State Dept. of Educ., 58 P.3d 545 (Haw. 2002) (the action of the state in negligently placing students in an environment where they were left unsupervised with a teacher who was an accused child molester warranted recognition of an exception to the general requirement that a plaintiff seeking redress solely for emotional distress must establish a predicate personal injury).

4. ***Third Restatement and Distress That is "Especially Likely."*** The Third Restatement's rule on "negligent conduct directly inflicting emotional disturbance on another" states that:

> An actor whose negligent conduct causes serious emotional harm to another is subject to liability to the other if the conduct:
>
> (a) places the other in danger of immediate bodily harm and the emotional harm results from the danger; or
>
> (b) occurs in the course of specified categories of activities, undertakings, or relationships in which negligent conduct is especially likely to cause serious emotional harm.

Restatement, Third, of Torts: Liab. for Physical & Emotional Harm § 47 (2012).

5. ***Problem: Mis-Scoring the Bar Exam.*** In May 2003, the National Conference of Bar Examiners announced to bar officials in 48 states that the scores of law students

who took the Multistate Bar Examination in February were being recalculated because one question had been mis-scored as a result of a "keying error." In some jurisdictions, applicants were sent letters saying that the revised scores would be used to determine admission to practice. As a result of the error, some students who had previously been told they had passed had actually failed; some who had been told that they failed actually passed; and others, who had been correctly told that they passed or failed, worried or hoped that they would be told that the result was in fact different. In addition, some test-takers who had passed the bar with scores providing a comfortable margin of safety, worried about the predicament of classmates teetering at the precipice of the necessary minimum. On these facts, does anyone have a claim for negligent infliction of emotional distress?

C. Distress Occasioned by Harm to Another

Two Views: "Zone of Danger" and "Foreseeability." Numerous claims have been brought by bystanders who suffered emotional distress based on witnessing or hearing about injury to another person. In general, the resolution of these cases falls into two categories, the "zone of danger" view and the "foreseeability" view.

In James v. Lieb, 375 N.W.2d 109 (Neb. 1985), a little boy watched his sister being crushed by a garbage truck that was negligently backing up. The court abandoned its earlier adherence to the "zone of danger" view in favor of the "foreseeability" view, explaining:

> Under the "zone of danger" rule followed by this court in . . . [Fournell v. Usher Pest Control Co., 305 N.W.2d 605 (Neb. 1981)], other jurisdictions have allowed bystanders to recover for emotional distress only if they (1) were within a physical "zone of danger," (2) feared for their own safety, and (3) suffered physically manifested mental or physical injuries as a result of this fear. . . . However, other "zone of danger" jurisdictions have allowed bystanders to recover damages for "fear for the safety of another," so long as the plaintiff was also at personal risk. . . . The latter view . . . would allow recovery when a family member is within the zone of danger but his or her emotional distress arises from fear for another's safety.
>
> . . . .
>
> Advocates of the "zone of danger" rule . . . argue that it provides workable, reasonable limits to the liability of a potential defendant. . . .
>
> However, in 1968 the California Supreme Court became the first jurisdiction to abolish the "zone of danger" rule and allow a bystander to recover for negligently inflicted emotional distress in its now landmark decision of Dillon v. Legg, 441 P.2d 912 (Cal. 1968). . . .
>
> While recognizing that "no immutable rule" could establish the defendant's duty for every future case, the [*Dillon*] court suggested the following

> "guidelines" as aids in resolution of bystander claims: (1) Whether plaintiff was located near the scene of the accident as contrasted with one who was a distance away from it. (2) Whether the shock resulted from a direct emotional impact upon plaintiff from the sensory and contemporaneous observance of the accident, as contrasted with learning of the accident from others after its occurrence. (3) Whether plaintiff and the victim were closely related, as contrasted with an absence of any relationship or the presence of only a distant relationship.
>
> .... While these guidelines have also been called arbitrary, ... we believe the *Dillon* approach based upon the reasonable foreseeability of the harm to be a more logical and just method of determining a defendant's liability than the artificial boundaries of recovery drawn by the "zone of danger" rule.

However, in Destefano v. Children's Nat. Med. Ctr., 121 A.3d 59, 72 (D.C. App. 2015), the court re-affirmed and extended its adherence to the zone of danger view. It held that "plaintiffs who enter the zone of danger in a rescue attempt may recover [from the creator of the peril] damages for mental distress, as long as they feared for their own safety, because of the defendant's negligence, while in the zone of danger." In addition, the court determined that "[s]uch plaintiffs can also recover damages for mental distress caused by fear for the safety of an immediate family member who was endangered by the negligent act."

The Foreseeability View. The foreseeability approach to compensation for negligent infliction of severe emotional distress has been interpreted differently by various courts. Some cases hold that the three criteria set out in Dillon v. Legg are flexible guidelines. Other cases treat those same criteria as indispensable prerequisites to recovery.

Regardless of whether the *Dillon* criteria are treated as indispensable or merely useful, courts generally agree that the issue to which they pertain is foreseeability. However, California, the birthplace of *Dillon*, no longer phrases the inquiry in terms of foreseeability. Thing v. La Chusa, 771 P.2d 814 (Cal. 1989), rejected the language of "foreseeability" because of the importance of "certainty in the law" and the need to limit recovery by some means, however arbitrary. Under *Thing*, the plaintiff must be closely related to the victim, present at the scene of the injury, and aware of the injury while it is occurring.

Third Restatement and Bystanders. The Third Restatement's rule on "negligent infliction of emotional disturbance resulting from bodily harm to a third person," states that:

> An actor who negligently causes sudden serious bodily injury to a third person is subject to liability for serious emotional harm caused thereby to a person who:
>
> (a) perceives the event contemporaneously, and
>
> (b) is a close family member of the person suffering the bodily injury.

Restatement, Third, of Torts: Liab. for Physical & Emotional Harm § 48 (2012).

Eskin v. Bartee

Supreme Court of Tennessee
262 S.W.3d 727 (Tenn. 2008)

WILLIAM C. KOCH, JR., J.

....

Marc and Karen Eskin and their three children live in Cordova.... During the 2002–2003 school year, Brendan Eskin, the Eskins' older son, attended the Chimneyrock Elementary School... Brendan Eskin was at school on November 19, 2002. Because Ms. Eskin was going to be unable to pick up her son at the end of the school day, she made arrangements with a neighbor, Jan Durban, to pick him up and to bring him home.

Chimneyrock Elementary maintains an area for students using private transportation to travel to and from school....

.... [A] driver had left his minivan unattended in the right lane. When Alice Bartee arrived at Chimneyrock Elementary, she pulled behind the unattended minivan. She moved her automobile after a school employee directed her to park in front of the minivan. Ms. Bartee lost control of her automobile ... and struck Brendan Eskin. The boy was seriously injured.

Ms. Durban telephoned Ms. Eskin from the scene. She told Ms. Eskin that her automobile had been struck from the rear and that Brendan Eskin had been hurt.... After she hung up, Ms. Eskin gathered up her younger son, Logan Eskin, her daughter, and a child who was visiting Logan Eskin and drove the very short distance to the school.

.... As Ms. Eskin and the children approached the area, she and Logan Eskin saw Brendan Eskin lying on the pavement in a pool of blood.... [H]er son was not being attended to, and he appeared to be lifeless. Both Ms. Eskin and Logan Eskin screamed and tried to run to Brendan Eskin but were restrained. Brendan Eskin sustained permanent brain damage....

... [T]he Eskins filed suit ... against Ms. Bartee.... The complaint alleged that Ms. Eskin and Logan Eskin had been "emotionally traumatized by the event"....

Because Ms. Bartee lacked adequate insurance, the Eskins served a copy of their complaint on USAA, their own insurance carrier, in accordance with Tennessee's uninsured motorist statutes. In July 2005, USAA filed a motion for partial summary judgment.... [T]he accompanying memorandum of law explains that USAA believed it was entitled to a judgment as a matter of law with regard to Ms. Eskin's and Logan Eskin's negligent infliction of emotional distress claims because they had not been present when the accident occurred....

... [T]he trial court filed an order ... granting USAA's motion for summary judgment....

... [T]he Court of Appeals filed an opinion reversing the order of the trial court....

The tort of negligent infliction of emotional distress has emerged as an accepted cause of action within approximately the last half century. Prior to that time, the courts had declined to award damages for mental injuries that were not accompanied by physical injuries because the early common law was "wary of opening the floodgates to fraudulent, frivolous, and perhaps even marginal lawsuits." Today, however, virtually all states recognize the tort of negligent infliction of emotional distress in some form. A majority of these states permit recovery by bystanders who perceive the negligent infliction of physical injury to another person.

Despite the increasing recognition of negligent infliction of emotional distress claims, there is little consensus regarding the elements of the tort. This lack of uniformity arises from lingering concerns about permitting the recovery of damages for purely emotional injuries. Professors Prosser and Keeton cite three of these concerns as follows:

> (1) the problem of permitting legal redress for harm that is often temporary and relatively trivial; (2) the danger that claims of mental harm will be falsified or imagined; and (3) the perceived unfairness of imposing heavy and disproportionate financial burdens upon a defendant, whose conduct was only negligent, for consequence which appear remote from the "wrongful" act.

W. Page Keeton, Prosser and Keeton on the Law of Torts § 54, 360–61 (1984). As a result of these continuing concerns, the courts have recognized a number of principles whose purpose is to assist courts and juries in separating the meritorious and compensable claims from those that are not.

The most frequently adopted principles include: (1) denying recovery for emotional injuries without accompanying bodily harm or other compensable damage to the plaintiff, (2) denying recovery unless the plaintiff is in the "zone of danger," (3) denying recovery unless the plaintiff has "sensory observation" of the event causing the third party's injuries, (4) requiring the existence of a special relationship between the plaintiff and the injured party, and (5) denying recovery unless the injury to the other person is, or is reasonably perceived to be, serious.

A systematic review of decisions of state courts applying these principles prompts three conclusions. First, each state that has recognized the tort of negligent infliction of emotional stress has developed its own set of principles based on the decisions of their courts regarding the most appropriate way to address the concerns identified by Professors Prosser and Keeton. Second, because the life of the law is experience, not logic, many states, over time, have changed the principles or the emphasis given to particular principles. Third, the direction of the development of the law in the United States relating to negligent infliction of emotional distress claims has been to enlarge rather than to restrict the circumstances amenable to the filing of a negligent infliction of emotional distress claim.

The development of the tort of negligent infliction of emotional distress in Tennessee tracks the development of the tort in other states.... [I]t has been neither smooth nor linear....

This case involves plaintiffs who did not actually see or hear the injury-causing accident but who were in sufficient proximity to the accident to be able to arrive at the accident scene quickly before it had significantly changed and before the injured person had been moved. In other words, while the bystanders did not have a sensory perception of the accident as it occurred, they had a direct sensory perception of the accident scene and the results of the accident soon after the accident occurred. In this circumstance, we have determined that it is appropriate and fair to permit recovery of damages for the negligent infliction of emotional distress by plaintiffs who have a close personal relationship with an injured party and who arrive at the scene of the accident while the scene is in essentially the same condition it was in immediately after the accident.

Our decision is premised on two considerations. First, we have historically recognized that it is easily foreseeable that persons who have a close personal relationship with an injured party will suffer serious or severe emotional distress when they see someone "near and dear" to them injured. . . .

The second consideration is the lack of a principled basis to differentiate between a parent who sees or hears the accident that seriously injures or kills his or her child and a parent who sees his or her injured or dead child at the scene shortly after the accident. It defies reason that the mental distress of the latter parent is less than the former parent. Accordingly, other courts have permitted family members who arrived at an accident scene shortly after another family member had been seriously injured or killed to pursue a negligent infliction of emotional distress claim.

When a plaintiff did not witness the injury-producing event, the cause of action for negligent infliction of emotional distress requires proof of the following elements: (1) the actual or apparent death or serious physical injury of another caused by the defendant's negligence, (2) the existence of a close and intimate personal relationship between the plaintiff and the deceased or injured person, (3) the plaintiff's observation of the actual or apparent death or serious physical injury at the scene of the accident before the scene has been materially altered, and (4) the resulting serious or severe emotional injury to the plaintiff caused by the observation of the death or injury. . . .

The required relationship between the plaintiff and the deceased or injured person is not necessarily limited to relationships by blood or marriage. While a parent-child relationship, a spousal relationship, a sibling relationship, or the relationship among immediate family members provides sufficient basis for a claim, other intimate relationships such as engaged parties or step-parents and step-children will also suffice. The burden is on the plaintiff to prove the existence of the close and intimate personal relationship, and the defendant may contest the existence of the relationship.

. . . .

We affirm the judgment of the Court of Appeals reversing the partial summary judgment . . . and remanding the case to the trial court for further proceedings. . . .

Notes

1. ***The Presence and Observation Requirements.*** *Compare Eskin with* Fineran v. Pickett, 465 N.W.2d 662 (Iowa 1991) (denying recovery to parents and sisters who arrived at accident scene within five minutes and witnessed injured bicyclist's unconscious seizure prior to death).

In cases where the primary victim is sexually abused, it seems very unlikely that a close family member who suffers emotional distress will have been present at the time of the injury. *Compare* Haselhorst v. State, 485 N.W.2d 180 (Neb. 1992) (parents permitted to recover from state for distress they suffered upon learning that their foster child had sexually abused their four minor children outside of their presence, where the state negligently placed the 15-year-old foster child with the family without disclosing his history of violence), *with* Schurk v. Christensen, 497 P.2d 937 (Wash. 1972) (denying recovery against neighbors for distress resulting from the neighbors' son's sexual molestation of plaintiffs' daughter outside of their presence, even though neighbors had recommended their son as a babysitter without disclosing his dangerous propensities).

See also Ortiz v. John D. Pittenger Builder, Inc., 889 A.2d 1135 (N.J. Super. Ct. Law Div. 2004) (allowing recovery by a mother and grandmother who observed the fire in which a child burned to death, although they did not actually see the child burning).

In Ko v. Maxim Healthcare Services, Inc., 272 Cal. Rptr. 3d 906, 919 (Ct. App. 2020), a case involving the use of a "nanny cam" that sent real-time images to a cell phone, parents who were "virtually present through modern technology that streamed the audio and video on which they watched" a caregiver physically abuse their two-year-old child stated a claim for negligent infliction of emotional distress.

2. ***The Relationship Requirement.*** In Dunphy v. Gregor, 642 A.2d 372 (N.J. 1994), a woman who was engaged to and cohabiting with an automobile accident victim was held to have a cause of action. Similarly, in Graves v. Estabrook, 818 A.2d 1255 (N.H. 2003), the court held that the fiancee of a motorcyclist who was killed in an accident stated a claim for negligent infliction of emotional distress against the motorist involved in the accident.

However, in Smith v. Toney, 862 N.E.2d 656 (Ind. 2007), the court refused to entertain the emotional distress claim brought by the fiancee of a motorist killed in an auto accident. The court asserted that "[m]ost courts that have considered this issue have disallowed bystander recovery . . . [to] persons engaged to be married or involved in cohabiting but unmarried relationships." The court noted that cases have recognized the "strong state interest in the marriage relationship" and that "drawing the line at marriage for 'bystander' claims of negligent infliction of emotional distress avoids the need to explore the intimate details of a relationship that a claimant asserts is 'analogous' to marriage."

See also Restatement, Third, of Torts: Liab. for Phys. & Emotional Harm § 48 cmt. f (2012) (stating that "[s]ometimes people live functionally in a nuclear family without formal legal family ties. When defining what constitutes a close family relationship, courts should take into account changing practices and social norms and employ a functional approach to determine what constitutes a family").

3. ***Distress Arising From Harm to Animals.*** In Rabideau v. City of Racine, 627 N.W.2d 795 (Wis. 2001), the court held that the owner of a companion dog, who observed a city police officer shoot and kill her dog, was not related to the victim in a way that would support a claim for negligent infliction of emotional distress. *See also* McDougall v. Lamm, 48 A.3d 312 (N.J. 2012) (holding that the owner of a "maltipoo," who saw it shaken to death by a larger dog, could not recover from the larger dog's owner for negligent infliction because "[a]lthough . . . many people form close bonds with their pets, . . . those bonds do not rise to the level of a close familial relationship or intimate, marital-like bond").

4. ***The Zone-of-Danger View.*** The "zone of danger" theory may deny damages in cases that are very sympathetic. *See, e.g.*, Whetham v. Bismarck Hosp., 197 N.W.2d 678 (N.D. 1972) (denying recovery to a mother who watched helplessly from her bed as her newborn child was dropped on a tile floor by a hospital employee, causing the child's skull to fracture); Washington v. John T. Rhines Co., 646 A.2d 345 (D.C. 1994) (dismissing a wife's claim for the mishandling of her husband's corpse because she was not within the zone of danger); Carlson v. Illinois Farmers Ins. Co., 520 N.W.2d 534 (Minn. Ct. App. 1994) (denying recovery to a plaintiff who witnessed the death of her best friend); Boucher v. Dixie Med. Ctr., 850 P.2d 1179 (Utah 1992) (denying recovery to parents who observed their son before and after a coma from which he awakened as a brain-damaged quadriplegic).

In Harper v. Illinois Cent. Gulf R.R., 808 F.2d 1139 (5th Cir. 1987), the court there held that a mother and her son, who were evacuated from their home after a train derailment caused two major explosions over a mile away, were not within the zone of danger since they were "never in any immediate danger of personal injury" and the evacuation was merely a precautionary measure.

In Doe v. SexSearch.com, 551 F.3d 412 (6th Cir. 2008), a man used an online adult dating service to meet a girl who had sex with him, and later proved to be underage. After being prosecuted and convicted, he sued the service on a variety of grounds, alleging in part that the service had caused him emotional distress by negligently failing to remove the underage girl's profile from the database. The court rejected his claim, explaining:

> [U]nder Ohio law, the plaintiff must allege that he was aware of real physical danger to himself or another. . . . Doe's alleged injuries result from embarrassment and harm to social standing and employment prospects; he does not allege that he experienced a dangerous accident or appreciated actual physical peril and, consequently, has not stated a claim for negligent infliction of emotional distress.

In Greene v. Esplanade Venture Partn., 168 N.E.3d 827 (N.Y. 2021), New York's highest court ruled that a grandmother was a member of a child's immediate family, and could pursue a claim for negligent infliction of emotional distress under the state's "zone of danger" rule.

5. ***Primary Victims v. Bystanders.*** Where a claim is based on negligence which directly endangered the plaintiff, rather than someone else, courts generally have little problem with the scope of protection issue. For example, in Jarrett v. Jones, 258 S.W.3d 442 (Mo. 2008), the plaintiff (a driver involved in an accident) suffered emotional distress at watching the death of another person involved in the accident (the daughter of the defendant driver of a different vehicle). The court held that the plaintiff was not a mere bystander and that the limitations applicable to bystander claims did not apply.

See also Hedgepeth v. Whitman Walker Clinic, 22 A.3d 789 (D.C. 2011) (holding that the zone of danger rule did not apply as to preclude an action against a medical clinic that misdiagnosed a patient as being HIV-positive).

However, in some instances, it may be difficult to determine whether the plaintiff is a primary victim, as opposed to someone asserting bystander rights. For example, in Johnson v. Jamaica Hosp., 467 N.E.2d 502 (N.Y. 1984), alleged negligence on the part of a hospital nursery resulted in the abduction of the plaintiff's newborn infant daughter and her absence for four and one-half months. The dissenter argued that the parents were not members of some large, undifferentiated class, and that the mental anguish they suffered was not a mere byproduct of an invasion of the child's rights. Rather, the defendant's negligence directly interfered with the parents' rights to custody of the child, and therefore the parents should have been permitted to sue for their resulting mental suffering. The majority concluded, however, that there was no direct duty running to the parents, and therefore analyzed the case under the "zone of danger" rule applicable to bystanders in that jurisdiction. In denying liability, the majority noted:

> That sound policy reasons support . . . [this] decision is evident here, for to permit recovery by the infant's parents for emotional distress would be to invite open-ended liability for indirect emotional injury suffered by the families in every instance where the very young, or very elderly, or incapacitated persons experience negligent care or treatment.

A useful contrast to *Johnson* is Burgess v. Superior Court, 831 P.2d 1197 (Cal. 1992). The court there held that a mother who suffered emotional distress as a result of negligent injury to her child during labor was not a bystander, but rather a direct victim who could recover for the damages in a professional negligence action without satisfying the criteria of Dillon v. Legg and its progeny. The court wrote:

> Any negligence during delivery which causes injury to the fetus and resultant emotional anguish to the mother . . . breaches a duty owed directly to the mother.
>
> . . . [T]he class of potential plaintiffs in these cases is clearly limited. . . . [T]here is no possibility . . . of unlimited liability presented by these unique cases.

In Perry-Rogers v. Obasaju, 723 N.Y.S.2d 28 (App. Div. 2001), a couple sought damages for emotional harm after their embryo was mistakenly implanted in another woman's uterus. The court held that they stated a viable medical malpractice claim based on breach of a direct legal duty, and therefore it was not necessary to show that, under the zone of danger view, they feared for their personal safety.

6. ***Problem: The Theater Gunman.*** The claim in Soudani v. Century Theaters, Inc., 2016 WL 2956253 (Colo. Dist. Ct.), arose from a shooting at the midnight premiere of a Batman movie, *The Dark Knight Rises*. Panic erupted in Auditorium 9 when a gunman began shooting at patrons, ultimately killing a dozen persons and wounding 70 more. Soon after the shooting began, patrons in Auditorium 16, including the plaintiff, were told simply, "[i]t has been confirmed — police officers have confirmed, shots have been fired, please exit the building." The patrons stampeded toward the exits from Auditorium 16. The plaintiff was trapped in a crowd and feared for her safety, although the shooting may have already stopped before that time. To the plaintiff, "everything started becoming slow motion." She became "very sensitive to everything and just going through the motions." She felt like she was in "[i]ntense and imminent danger," but suffered no physical injury.

In the plaintiff's subsequent lawsuit against the theater company alleging negligent security, the court ruled that Colorado's zone of danger rule had been preempted by a premises liability law which set the applicable legal standard.[1] How would the claim be decided in a state without such a statute? Assume that the statute follows the usual rules governing bystander claims, either the zone of danger view or the foreseeability view.

7. ***Comparative Law Perspective: Emotional Distress Damages in China.*** Chinese tort law recognizes claims for emotional distress when a victim's personal interests are invaded. The law takes a very cautious approach based on the same concerns that United States courts have often expressed related to the scope of liability and frivolous or fraudulent claims. The severity of the plaintiff's emotional distress must be proved.

Unlike American tort law, Chinese tort law makes no distinction between intentional and negligent infliction of emotional distress. If an actor invades the victim's legally protected personal interests causing the victim to suffer severe emotional distress, the victim can recover damages for emotional distress. Personal interests include the rights to life, health, name, image, honor, privacy, dignity, personal freedom, and marriage.

1. "The Court does not opine one way or another whether Ms. Pester was within the zone of danger because the Court concludes as a matter of law (1) that the doctrine of zone of danger relates to whether a legal duty is owed . . . ; and (2) that the premises liability statute abrogated all common law doctrines relating to legal duty, leaving it for a jury to decide whether Cinemark met the duties it owed its invitees. . . ." *Soudani*, at *4

If the injured party is deceased, his or her nearest family members can recover damages against the tortfeasor. Borrowing from the law of wills and estates, the Supreme People's Court interpreted the hierarchy of close family members as follows: (1) Spouse; (2) Parents; (3) Children; (4) Siblings; (5) Grandparents; (6) Grandchildren. Once a family member has successfully made a case for emotional distress damages, he or she will receive compensation regardless of whether the family member was present or within the "zone of danger" at the time the distress occurred, or near the scene at the time of the injury.

In determining the amount of damages for emotional distress, courts consider the following factors: (A) The seriousness of the tortious conduct; (B) The specific circumstances regarding the means, place, and manner of the tortious act; (C) Consequences of the tortious act; (D) Whether the tortfeasor was enriched; (E) The tortfeasor's financial ability to bear the responsibility; and (F) The average standard of living in the area where the court is located.

Chinese judges who decide damages closely follow the local government's guidelines in deciding the amount of compensation. The compensation amount varies depending on each province's prevailing living standard.

In Anhui Province, for example, a plaintiff, who has suffered minor physical harm without disabling injuries, can recover RMB1,000 ($157) to RMB5,000 ($786) in damages for emotional distress. A plaintiff, who has suffered disabling injuries or death, can recover between RMB5,000 ($786) and RMB8,000 ($1,257) in emotional damages. Under exceptional circumstances, the emotional damages award may exceed the above-mentioned scale.

In Chongqing City, damages for emotional distress are capped at RMB10,000 ($1,572) for those who suffer major injuries resulting in severe disabilities or death. A plaintiff who has suffered minor, non-disabling injury, can recover RMB1,000 ($157) to RMB5,000 ($786) in damages for emotional distress depending on any exceptional circumstances.

Shandong Province uses yet another approach, where damages range from RMB1,000 ($157) to RMB3,000 ($471) for ordinary emotional distress, which has interfered with the plaintiff's normal life, work, and study. If the tortfeasor has caused severe emotional distress, which substantially affects the plaintiff's life, work, and study or has driven the plaintiff to commit suicide, the damages increase from RMB3,000($471) to RMB5,000 ($786). If the tortfeasor is a corporation or social organization, the damages for emotional distress increase five to ten times the regular scale.

Occasionally, however, the court may grant more for emotional damages than the amount defined in interpretations by the provincial court. The following case shows how the Beijing court considered factors that were not clearly defined in the law, such as social pressure, media attention, and severe emotional trauma to a high-profile family.

Yan v. Beijing Public Transportation arose from a dispute on a bus in 2005. Yan Jile, a 14-year-old girl, took Bus No. 726 in Beijing with her mother and father, a Qinghua University professor. Zhu Yuqin, the bus conductor, charged RMB 2 ($0.31) for each member of Yan's family. Yan Jile argued that the bus fare should be RMB 1 ($ 0.16). During the dispute, Yan Jile became angry and verbally insulted Zhu Yuqin. In response, Zhu choked Yan twice. By the time Yan's mother stepped forward to intervene, Yan was unresponsive. Despite repeated begging from Yan's family, the bus driver refused to take Yan to the hospital. Instead, Zhu insisted that Yan's family must pay a fine at the main station for refusing to pay the proper bus fare. By the time Yan Jile was transported to the hospital, it was too late. Yan died a few hours after the incident.

Zhu was sentenced to death with a two-year suspension (delay). In a separate trial for civil damages, the trial court followed the interpretation of the high court and granted Yan's family RMB100,000 ($15,720), the highest possible amount in damages for emotional distress. On appeal, the intermediate court unprecedentedly increased the damage award to RMB300,000 ($47,162), the highest amount that any court had ever yet awarded for emotional distress. The court increased the damages for three reasons:

First, as in many other Chinese families, Yan Jile was an only child. Her father was already in his 70s, and it was unlikely the couple would have a second child. Given his age, Yan was more susceptible to this enormous emotional distress than younger parents in a similar situation.

Second, Yan and his wife were present and witnessed Zhu attacking their daughter, who perished in just a few hours. This emotional toll substantially weakened Yan's mental and physical health. He frequently had nightmares, avoided elementary school children, feared seeing his daughter's classmates, and refused to ride a bus again. He testified that even seeing a child's neck on TV would remind him of the horror he experienced. It is unusual for a Chinese court to emphasize a plaintiff's contemporaneous and sensory observations in determining the amount of emotional distress damages. In this case, however, the appellate court made it a crucial factor in granting three times the amount allowed by the guidelines.

Third, the court used the increased award for emotional distress to send a message to all common carriers in the country. Since the tragedy took place during a national holiday, its impact went beyond the local region. Major newspapers and websites nationwide followed the news in an extremely detailed fashion. The public paid close attention to the case because the senior Yan was a 70-year-old professor at Qinghua University, the best engineering school in China. The public was shocked at how such a horrendous crime happened in Beijing, generally viewed as the safest city in the country. Zhu's criminal conduct seriously diminished the public trust in social harmony, which the Communist Party had promised to build and maintain.

If facts similar to those in *Yan* occurred in the United States, who could recover emotional distress? Under what theories of liability? Subject to what limits on compensation?

D. Relationship to Other Actions

1. Loss of Consortium

Lozoya v. Sanchez

Supreme Court of New Mexico
66 P.3d 948 (N.M. 2003)

MINZNER, Justice.

. . . .

This case arises from two automobile collisions in which Ubaldo and Osbaldo Lozoya, father and son, were traveling together. . . . The first of these collisions took place on June 21, 1999. . . . The other vehicle was driven by Defendant Diego Sanchez. . . .

On April 18, 2000, approximately ten months after the first accident, Ubaldo and Osbaldo were involved in another collision. . . . This time, the other vehicle involved was a dump truck operated by Defendant Philip McWaters. . . .

At the time of the first accident, Ubaldo lived in a domestic partnership with Sara Lozoya, although they were not married. They had, however, "been together" for over 30 years. They had three children together. . . . For fifteen years they had lived together in a home that they had purchased. They carried the same last name, and had filed joint tax returns since at least 1997. They were formally married after the first accident, but before the second one [which involved Mr. McWaters], in November 1999.

Ubaldo testified that prior to the accidents, he and Sara had a happy relationship, which included going out dancing, and visiting friends together. Sara testified that they had an intimate relationship, and that they made decisions together. After the first accident, the relationship changed dramatically because Ubaldo became depressed. They could not socialize nearly as much because of the pain that Ubaldo experienced. Ubaldo would stay in bed quite a bit. Their sexual relationship also diminished. After the second accident, the relationship worsened further.

. . . .

Sara brought a loss of consortium claim against both Mr. Sanchez and Mr. McWaters. The district court did not allow the jury to consider such a claim as against Mr. Sanchez, however, because she was not married to Ubaldo at the time. The district court did allow the jury to consider Sara's loss of consortium claim against Mr. McWaters, because Sara and Ubaldo had been married during the interim between the two collisions. The jury did not award Sara damages for this claim because it found that Mr. McWaters was not negligent. Sara claims that the district court erred by not allowing the jury to consider her loss of consortium claim against Mr. Sanchez and his employer.

New Mexico courts did not recognize actions for loss of consortium, spousal or otherwise, until 1994, when this Court decided Romero v. Byers, 117 N.M. 422, 872 P.2d 840 (1994). . . .

> ... [W]e held that it is foreseeable that a surviving spouse would experience emotional distress as a result of injury to or death of a victim of negligent conduct. The law should impose a duty upon the tortfeasor toward that surviving spouse....

While this Court was the last in the nation to recognize that a spouse may bring a cause of action for loss of consortium, ... we were the first in the nation to recognize that a grandparent may bring such a claim in certain circumstances as well. *See* Fernandez v. Walgreen Hastings Co., ... [968 P.2d 774 (N.M. 1998)]. In that case, we ... held that "it can be foreseeable that negligently causing the death of a twenty-two month old child will cause emotional distress to a grandparent who had a close familial relationship with the child." ....

.... Plaintiffs now ask us to decide whether the same rationales that led us to extend a cause of action for loss of consortium in those situations should apply here. At the outset, we note that no other State in the union currently allows unmarried cohabitants to recover for loss of consortium....

Defendants are correct in their assertion that limiting the field of potential claimants to those with a legal relationship to the victim would serve as a convenient and easily applied line-drawing mechanism for courts. This is perhaps the most significant reason that many courts allow only spouses to make a loss of consortium claim.... Defendants point out, "[o]ne would also envision that the injured person has cousins, co-workers, drinking buddies and softball team members who may lose his society, companionship and guidance. For that matter, the dead or injured person may have been having an affair with his married neighbor, who also may suffer a loss of consortium." By only allowing those who are legally married, or familial caretakers to recover, courts would have an easy way for us to dispose of many claims. Ease of administration, however, does not necessarily further the interests of justice.... Of course, the State has a continuing interest in protecting the legal interest of marriage as well....

In Dunphy v. Gregor, 136 N.J. 99, 642 A.2d 372 (1994), the Supreme Court of New Jersey considered whether a woman who was engaged to and cohabited with the victim of an automobile accident could recover against the defendant for negligent infliction of emotional distress ("NIED"). NIED is a claim that is often considered by courts at the same time as a claim for loss of consortium, and the same policies are implicated by broadening the field of potential claimants for each.... The *Dunphy* court observed that a "marital or intimate, familial relationship between the plaintiff and the injured person" was a required basis for recovery on an NIED claim.... When confronted with the same argument made here that a legal relationship provides an easy line-drawing mechanism, the court responded:

> ... [T]he sound assessment of the quality of interpersonal relationships is not beyond a jury's ken and ... courts are capable of dealing with the realities, not simply the legalities, of relationships to assure that resulting emotional injury is genuine and deserving of compensation.

Id. at 378. We agree.... It is appropriate that the finder of fact be allowed to determine, with proper guidance from the court, whether a plaintiff had a sufficient enough relational interest with the victim of a tort to recover for loss of consortium.

Next, Defendants argue that to extend a cause of action for loss of consortium in the present case would be to extend the benefits of marriage to Sara, without requiring her to undertake the burdens of marriage, implying that somehow Sara would be unfairly taking advantage of her position. Specifically, Defendants point out that Sara did not commit to giving her income and property to the community ...; she did not commit to paying Ubaldo's debt ...; she did not commit to leaving a share of her estate to Ubaldo when she dies ...; she did not have to pay income taxes jointly; and she could have left the relationship any time she wanted without going through the process of a divorce.

Defendants are correct in all of these assertions. What Defendants do not recognize is that almost all of these burdens have a corresponding benefit that Sara also did not receive when she was not married to Ubaldo.... We reject any implication that we are enabling Sara to take unfair advantage of the legal system by providing that she may be able to recover for loss of consortium, without paying the "price" of marriage.

... Defendants claim that we would be, in effect, recognizing common law marriage by allowing the claim to proceed.... Our holding today in no way alters this State's nonrecognition of common law marriage. We do think, however, that if a couple were to satisfy the elements of a common law marriage, as it exists in other states, this would be a great indication that the couple would have a significant enough relationship to warrant a claim for loss of consortium.

....

Finally, Defendants argue that allowing unmarried couples to recover for loss of consortium would create an impractical and unworkable cause of action. This would only be true if this Court does not do its duty of providing sufficient guidance to lower courts when determining whether a claim should be allowed. We think that the criteria set forth in *Dunphy* help greatly in this regard. Claimants must prove an "intimate familial relationship" with the victim in order to recover for loss of consortium.... "Persons engaged to be married and living together may foreseeably fall into that category of relationship...."

Of course, not everyone who is engaged to be married, living together, or assuming the roles of husband and wife (common law or not) will be entitled to recover. The claimant must prove a close familial relationship with the victim.... Courts should presume that such a relationship exists if the couple fits into one of the above categories, but a myriad of factors should be considered to determine whether the relationship was significant enough to recover.

> That standard must take into account the duration of the relationship, the degree of mutual dependence, the extent of common contributions to a life

> together, the extent and quality of shared experience, and . . . whether the plaintiff and the injured person were members of the same household, their emotional reliance on each other, the particulars of their day to day relationship, and the manner in which they related to each other in attending to life's mundane requirements.

. . . . By adopting this standard for determining whether an intimate familial relationship exists for loss of consortium purposes, we are putting no additional burden on the finder of fact. Even if the claimant and the victim are actually married, all of this information would need to be weighed when determining the amount of damages anyway. . . .

. . . [W]e think that further limits are appropriate. First, a person can only have an intimate familial relationship with one other person at any one time. That is to say, if a person is married to a different person than the victim of the tort, the claim will be barred. In the case of claims by unmarried cohabitants, the relationship between the claimant and the victim must be demonstrated to be committed and exclusive. . . . Second, the burden of proving that an intimate familial relationship existed will be on the claimant, with a presumption that this exists if the parties were engaged, married, or met the general test for common law marriage. . . .

. . . [W]e cannot deny that Ubaldo and Sara enjoyed a relationship that was very similar, if not identical, to that of the typical married couple, or that a reasonable jury could so find. They had lived together in a house that they owned together for at least fifteen years. They had three children whom they raised together. They carried the same last name, and they generally enjoyed spending time with one another and participating in social events as a couple. Further, their intent to be committed to one another indefinitely is evidenced by their marriage shortly after the first accident, despite Ubaldo's debilitating injuries.

. . . We believe that the evidence presented demonstrates that Sara may be able to present a cognizable claim for loss of consortium. She should therefore be allowed to present this claim to the jury.

. . . . We therefore . . . remand for a new trial. . . .

Note

1. ***Query: Negligent Infliction Versus Loss of Consortium.*** In the case of cohabitants, if actions for both negligent infliction of emotional distress and loss of consortium are permitted, does either action have significant advantages over the other?

2. Breach of Fiduciary Duty

The tort of negligent infliction of emotional distress must be carefully limited, as nearly everyone does things that cause others distress. To take one of countless possible examples, no one but lawyers would gain if the parties to a love affair gone sour could sue for damages, however real the distress they feel. In some cases, however, the existence of a special relationship between the parties may justify imposing a special duty on one of those parties to avoid hurting the other. Consider the following opinion.

F.G. v. MacDonell

Supreme Court of New Jersey
696 A.2d 697 (N.J. 1997)

POLLOCK, J.

. . . .

In 1992, MacDonell was the rector at both All Saints and an affiliated church, St. Luke's Episcopal Church, in Haworth. Harper was the assistant rector at both churches in 1993. In January 1994, following MacDonell's retirement, Harper succeeded MacDonell as rector. F.G. was a parishioner at All Saints in 1992–93.

From April 1992 until the end of 1993, F.G. consulted MacDonell for counseling. Aware that F.G. was vulnerable, MacDonell nonetheless induced her to engage in a sexual relationship with him. . . . [I]t apparently did not involve sexual intercourse.

. . . . The Law Division dismissed Counts I, II, III, and IX, which respectively allege negligent pastoral counseling, negligent infliction of emotional distress, and breach of fiduciary duty by MacDonell, as well as breach of fiduciary duty by Harper. The Appellate Division reversed and remanded the matter to the Law Division. The purpose of the remand was to permit F.G. to prove her claims against defendants for clergy malpractice and breach of their fiduciary duty.

We believe that a claim for breach of fiduciary duty provides the more appropriate form of relief than does clergy malpractice. An action for breach of a clergyman's fiduciary duty permits the parishioner to recover monetary damages without running the risk of entanglement with the free exercise of religion. Consequently, we modify the judgment of the Appellate Division by allowing F.G.'s claim for breach of fiduciary duty against MacDonell, and, subject to a hearing on entanglement with church doctrine, allowing a similar claim against Harper.

. . . .

. . . . The free exercise of religion does not permit members of the clergy to engage in inappropriate sexual conduct with parishioners who seek pastoral counseling.

. . . [T]he record supports the inference that MacDonell's alleged misconduct was not an expression of a sincerely held religious belief, but was an egregious violation of the trust and confidence that F.G. reposed in him.

The First Amendment does not insulate a member of the clergy from actions for breach of fiduciary duty arising out of sexual misconduct that occurs during a time when the clergy member is providing counseling to a parishioner. Thus, without impinging on the First Amendment, courts can resolve a claim that a member of the clergy has committed sexually inappropriate conduct in the course of pastoral counseling.

. . . .

The next question concerns the nature of the duty that defendants owed to F.G. The Appellate Division held that defendants owed F.G. a duty of care, that they breached that duty, and that she could maintain a cause of action for "clergy malpractice." In so concluding, the Appellate Division acknowledged that F.G.'s claim presented an issue of first impression in New Jersey, and that no other court in the United States had yet recognized a clergy-malpractice claim. . . . Deterring other courts has been the concern that a clergy-malpractice claim will entangle courts with the First Amendment's protection of the free exercise of religion. . . .

Several problems inhere in a claim for clergy malpractice. First, such a claim requires definition of the relevant standard of care. Defining that standard could embroil courts in establishing the training, skill, and standards applicable for members of the clergy in a diversity of religions with widely varying beliefs. . . . Furthermore, defining such a standard would require courts to identify the beliefs and practices of the relevant religion and then to determine whether the clergyman had acted in accordance with them. . . . The entanglement could restrain the free exercise of religion.

Concerns about religious entanglement have led some courts also to deny claims for breach of fiduciary duty. . . . We conclude, however, that courts can adjudicate F.G.'s claim for breach of fiduciary duty without becoming entangled in the defendants' free exercise of their religion.

The essence of a fiduciary relationship is that one party places trust and confidence in another who is in a dominant or superior position. A fiduciary relationship arises between two persons when one person is under a duty to act for or give advice for the benefit of another on matters within the scope of their relationship. . . . Trusts and Trustees 2d § 481 (1978) (stating "the exact limits of the term 'fiduciary relation' are impossible of statement. Depending upon the circumstances of the particular case or transaction, certain business, public or social relationships may or may not create or involve a fiduciary character"). The fiduciary's obligations to the dependent party include a duty of loyalty and a duty to exercise reasonable skill and care. Restatement (Second) of Trusts §§ 170, 174 (1959). Accordingly, the fiduciary is liable for harm resulting from a breach of the duties imposed by the existence of such a relationship. Restatement (Second) of Torts § 874 (1979).

Trust and confidence are vital to the counseling relationship between parishioner and pastor. By accepting a parishioner for counseling, a pastor also accepts the responsibility of a fiduciary. Often, parishioners who seek pastoral counseling are troubled and vulnerable. Sometimes, they turn to their pastor in the belief that their religion is the most likely source to sustain them in their time of trouble. The pastor knows, or should know of the parishioner's trust and the pastor's dominant position.

Several jurisdictions have recognized that a clergyman's sexual misconduct with a parishioner constitutes a breach of a fiduciary relationship. . . . We find the rationale of those cases to be persuasive. . . .

Unlike an action for clergy malpractice, an action for breach of fiduciary duty does not require establishing a standard of care and its breach. . . .

. . . . Although MacDonell's ultimate goal in counseling F.G. may have been to help her receive assistance from God, his sexual misconduct violated her legal rights. So viewed, F.G.'s claim does not restrict MacDonell's free exercise of religion.

The Appellate Division also reinstated F.G.'s claim for negligent infliction of emotional distress. We likewise conclude that F.G. may maintain her claim for emotional distress arising from MacDonell's breach of his fiduciary duty to her. Our recognition of F.G.'s claim is consistent with the general rule that a claimant who suffers emotional trauma may recover from the tortfeasor who has caused the claimant distress. . . .

F.G.'s claim against Harper presents additional considerations. Basically, F.G. alleges that she consulted Harper for counseling because of MacDonell's inappropriate physical conduct with her and "the possibility of notifying the parishes of All Saints and St. Lukes" about that conduct. F.G. alleges further that Harper induced F.G. "to give consent to the public disclosure, by letter, of [her] name," by his negligent misrepresentation "that this disclosure was for [her] benefit and part of his pastoral care [of her]." According to F.G., Harper breached his fiduciary duty by "exploiting [her] trust and confidence" through his mischaracterization of MacDonell's conduct and the nature of the relationship between him and F.G.

Our review of those allegations begins with the realization that Harper's alleged breaches occurred in sermons and letters to the congregations. Evaluating those sermons and letters might entangle a court in religious doctrine. The question remains whether, without becoming entangled in religious doctrine, a court can adjudicate Harper's alleged breach of his fiduciary duty to F.G. If the trial court can make such a determination by reference to neutral principles, F.G. may maintain her action against Harper. We conclude that the trial court should conduct a hearing to determine whether it can decide F.G.'s allegations by reference to such principles. . . . If so, F.G. may proceed with her action against Harper.

. . . .

The dissenting opinion of O'HERN, J., which GARIBALDI, J., joined, has been omitted.

Notes

1. ***Breach of Fiduciary Duty.*** Section 874 of the Restatement, Second, of Torts provides that a fiduciary is liable for harm resulting from breach of the fiduciary's duties. The comments refer repeatedly to trustees, agents, guardians, executors, and administrators and direct readers to the Restatement, Second, of Trusts for details. This section was drafted with property cases in mind, not negligent infliction of severe emotional distress.

Some relationships are fiduciary as a matter of law, such as lawyer and client. Other relationships are fiduciary as a matter of fact because there is a bond of trust between the parties, as may be true in the case of brothers who are close. However, most relationships are not fiduciary, but simply ordinary. In that case, they require straight dealing, but neither party is obliged to put the interests of the other first or to demonstrate loyalty to the other. *See* CommScope Credit Union v. Butler & Burke, LLP, 790 S.E.2d 657 (N.C. 2016) (a certified public accounting firm did not owe a fiduciary duty to the credit union the firm was auditing).

2. ***Nonfiduciary Relationships with Clergy.*** Some relationships with clergy are fiduciary; others are not. "Allegations that give rise to only a general clergy-congregant relationship that includes aspects of counseling do not generally impose a fiduciary obligation upon a cleric." Marmelstein v. Kehillat New Hempstead, 892 N.E.2d 375 (N.Y. 2008). In *Marmelstein*, the court found that a woman who had a three-and-one-half-year relationship with a rabbi failed to prove that there was a fiduciary relationship, writing:

> Marmelstein has shown only that she was deceived by Tendler, not that she was so vulnerable as to surrender her will and capacity to determine her own best interests. In the absence of a *prima facie* showing that a fiduciary obligation was owed by Tendler, no cause of action can be maintained for an extended voluntary sexual affair between consenting adults, even if Marmelstein could prove that her acquiescence was obtained through lies, manipulation or other morally opprobrious conduct....

But see Doe v. Liberatore, 478 F. Supp. 2d 742 (M.D. Pa. 2007) (refusing to dismiss a breach of fiduciary duty claim where "a reasonable jury could conclude that Plaintiff was more than a mere parishioner and that ... [a priest] and the Diocesan Defendants exerted an overmastering influence over Plaintiff, or that Plaintiff exhibited weakness, dependence on or justifiable trust in ... [the priest] and the Diocesan Defendants").

3. ***Constitutional Obstacles to Tort Claims against Clergy and Churches.*** *See* DeCorso v. Watchtower Bible and Tract Society of N.Y., Inc., 829 A.2d 38 (Conn. App. 2003). The court held that a religious corporation's alleged acts and omissions in spiritual counseling of a wife, who claimed the corporation's elders had told her to stay in an abusive marriage, were protected by the free exercise and establishment clauses of the First Amendment. The court concluded that it could not consider the wife's negligent infliction of emotional distress count without excessively entangling itself in matters of the Jehovah religion and burdening the free exercise rights of the religious corporation.

4. ***Negligent Hiring and Supervision Claims Against Churches.*** The First Amendment ordinarily will not bar claims based on a religious institution's alleged negligence in failing to prevent foreseeable harm based on sexual assault of a minor or adult parishioner by a member of the clergy. *See* Malicki v. Doe, 814 So. 2d 347 (Fla. 2002).

5. ***Legislative Responses.*** Some states have created civil or criminal liability by legislation for cases involving sexual relations between pastors and parishioners. For example, Tex. Civ. Prac. & Rem. Code § 81.002 (Westlaw 2022) makes a "mental

health services provider" liable to a patient or former patient who suffers physical or emotional injuries as a result of sexual contact between the provider and the patient. The term "mental health services provider" includes a member of the clergy; *id.*, § 81.001(2)(E). *Compare* Minn. Stat. §§ 609.344(l) & 609.345(l) (Westlaw 2022), under which one who is, or who purports to be, a member of the clergy commits criminal sexual conduct by engaging in sexual relations, even if consensual, while providing religious or spiritual advice or counseling. Could a civil cause of action be based on violation of such a criminal enactment? *See generally* Chapter 5, discussing negligence based on violation of statute.

6. ***Ethics in Law Practice: Sexual Relations with Clients.*** The American Bar Association model rule now provides:

Model Rules of Professional Conduct Rule 1.8(j) (Westlaw 2022)

> (j) A lawyer shall not have sexual relations with a client unless a consensual sexual relationship existed between them when the client-lawyer relationship commenced.

The disciplinary standard now applicable in New York is more specific:

N.Y. Rules of Professional Conduct Rule 1.8(j) (Westlaw 2022)

> (1) A lawyer shall not: (i) as a condition of entering into or continuing any professional representation by the lawyer or the lawyer's firm, require or demand sexual relations with any person; (ii) employ coercion, intimidation or undue influence in entering into sexual relations incident to any professional representation by the lawyer or the lawyer's firm; or (iii) in domestic relations matters, enter into sexual relations with a client during the course of the lawyer's representation of the client.
>
> (2) Rule 1.8(j)(1) shall not apply to sexual relations between lawyers and their spouses or to ongoing consensual sexual relationships that predate the initiation of the client-lawyer relationship.

In New York, "sexual relations" is defined as "sexual intercourse or the touching of an intimate part of the lawyer or another person for the purpose of sexual arousal, sexual gratification or sexual abuse." N.Y. Model Rules of Prof'l Conduct R. 1.0(u) (Westlaw 2022). *See also* Calif. Rules of Prof. Conduct 3-120 (Westlaw 2022). States that have not yet enacted ethics rules specifically addressing the issue of lawyer-client sexual relations ordinarily reach similar results on general principles relating to conflict of interest, competence, and the like.

In Stender v. Blessum, 897 N.W.2d 491, 507 (Iowa 2017), the court wrote that, "[o]verwhelmingly, courts have . . . held a sexual relationship alone cannot be the basis for a breach of fiduciary duty or legal malpractice claim, absent some link between the sexual relationship and a wrong committed in the scope of the legal representation." Nevertheless, the court affirmed an award of roughly a half million dollars in compensatory and punitive damages in favor of an aggrieved former client based on assault and battery.

E. Abrogation of Independent Actions Based on Negligence

Boyles v. Kerr

Supreme Court of Texas
855 S.W.2d 593 (Tex. 1993)

PHILLIPS, Chief Justice.

....

On August 10, 1985, Petitioner Dan Boyles, Jr., then seventeen, covertly videotaped nineteen-year-old Respondent Susan Leigh Kerr engaging in sexual intercourse with him.... Kerr testified that she had not had sexual intercourse prior to her relationship with Boyles.

... Boyles arranged with a friend, Karl Broesche, to use the Broesche house for sexual intercourse with Kerr. Broesche suggested videotaping the activity, and Boyles agreed. Broesche and two friends, Ray Widner and John Paul Tamborello, hid a camera in a bedroom before Kerr and Boyles arrived. After setting up the camera, the three videotaped themselves making crude comments and jokes about the activity that was to follow. They left with the camera running, and the ensuing activities were recorded.

Boyles took possession of the tape shortly after it was made, and subsequently showed it on three occasions, each time at a private residence. Although he showed the tape to only ten friends, gossip about the incident soon spread among many of Kerr and Boyles' friends in Houston. Soon many students at Kerr's school, Southwest Texas State University, and Boyles' school, the University of Texas at Austin, also became aware of the story.... After [Kerr] confronted him, Boyles eventually admitted what he had done and surrendered the tape to Kerr. No copies had been made.

Kerr alleges that she suffered humiliation and severe emotional distress.... At social gatherings, friends and even casual acquaintances would approach her and comment about the video, wanting to know "what [she] was going to do" or "why did [she] do it." The tape stigmatized Kerr with the reputation of "porno queen" among some of her friends, and she claimed that the embarrassment and notoriety affected her academic performance.... Eventually, she sought psychological counseling.

Kerr sued Boyles, Broesche, Widner and Tamborello, alleging intentional invasion of privacy, negligent invasion of privacy, and negligent (but not intentional) infliction of emotional distress. Before the case was submitted to the jury, however, Kerr dropped all causes of action except for negligent infliction of emotional distress. The jury returned a verdict for Kerr on that claim, assessing $500,000 in actual damages. The jury also found that all defendants were grossly negligent, awarding an additional $500,000 in punitive damages, $350,000 of which was assessed against Boyles....

Only Boyles appealed to the court of appeals. That court affirmed....

.... Kerr claims that we recognized a broad right to recover for negligently inflicted emotional distress in St. Elizabeth Hospital v. Garrard, 730 S.W.2d 649 (Tex. 1987)....

In *Garrard*, a hospital negligently disposed of the Garrards' stillborn baby in an unmarked, common grave without the plaintiffs' knowledge or consent. The Garrards sued for negligent infliction of emotional distress, without alleging that they suffered any physical injury. This Court nonetheless concluded that they had stated a cause of action. We determined that "Texas first recognized the tort of negligent infliction of mental anguish in Hill v. Kimball, 76 Tex. 210, 13 S.W. 59 (1890)." 730 S.W.2d at 652. This tort, we said, had been administered under traditional tort concepts, subject only to a refinement on the element of damages: the mental suffering is not compensable unless it manifests itself physically. *Id.* After determining that the physical manifestation requirement was arbitrary because it "denies court access to persons with valid claims they could prove if permitted to do so," *id.*, we proceeded to abolish it....

While the holding of *Garrard* was correct, we conclude that its reasoning was based on an erroneous interpretation of Hill v. Kimball, and is out of step with most American jurisdictions. Therefore, we overrule the language of *Garrard* to the extent that it recognizes an independent right to recover for negligently inflicted emotional distress. Instead, mental anguish damages should be compensated only in connection with defendant's breach of some other duty imposed by law....

In *Hill*, a pregnant woman suffered a miscarriage when she witnessed the defendant severely beating two men in her yard. The woman sued for her physical injuries under negligence, claiming that the emotional trauma of witnessing the beatings produced the miscarriage and that the defendant should have reasonably anticipated the danger to her. The Court found that the plaintiff had stated a cause of action. The basis, however, was the physical injury she had suffered, together with her allegation of foreseeability....

.... In other words, the defendant was negligent if he should have known that he was imposing an unreasonable risk of physical injury to the plaintiff, not if he merely should have anticipated that the plaintiff would suffer emotional distress.

Hill, therefore, did not recognize a cause of action for negligent infliction of emotional distress. It merely recognized the right to recover for physical injuries under standard negligence principles, notwithstanding that the physical injury is produced indirectly through emotional trauma. *Garrard* thus did not merely modify *Hill*, but created an entirely new cause of action.

....

By overruling the language of *Garrard*, we hold only that there is no general duty not to negligently inflict emotional distress. Our decision does not affect a claimant's right to recover mental anguish damages caused by defendant's breach of some other legal duty. . . . [The court cited cases dealing with negligent infliction of direct physical injury, wrongful death, battery, failure of telegraph company to timely deliver death message, invasion of privacy, defamation, and negligent handling of corpse.]

Also, our holding does not affect the right of bystanders to recover emotional distress damages suffered as a result of witnessing a serious or fatal accident. Texas has adopted the bystander rules originally promulgated by the California Supreme Court in Dillon v. Legg, [441 P.2d 912, 920 (Cal. 1968)]. . . .

We emphasize that we are not broadening a claimant's right to recover mental anguish damages caused by breach of a particular duty; we leave such right unaffected. . . .

We also are not imposing a requirement that emotional distress manifest itself physically to be compensable. . . .

Most other jurisdictions do not recognize a general duty not to negligently inflict emotional distress. Many limit recovery by requiring proof of a physical manifestation. Others allow recovery where the claimant establishes the breach of some independent duty. A few jurisdictions recognize a general right to recover for negligently inflicted emotional distress, but these jurisdictions are squarely in the minority.

We find the experience in California to be instructive. . . . [T]he California Supreme Court . . . explained as follows:

> [I]t is clear that foreseeability of the injury alone is not a useful "guideline" or a meaningful restriction on the scope of the [negligent infliction of emotional distress] action. The *Dillon* experience confirms, as one commentator observed, that "[f]oreseeability proves too much. . . . Although it may set tolerable limits for most types of physical harm, it provides virtually no limit on liability for nonphysical harm." [citing Rabin, *Tort Recovery for Negligently Inflicted Economic Loss: A Reassessment*, 37 Stan. L. Rev. 1513, 1526 (1985)]. . . . In order to avoid limitless liability out of all proportion to the degree of a defendant's negligence, and against which it is impossible to insure without imposing unacceptable costs on those among whom the risk is spread, the right to recover for negligently caused emotional distress must be limited.

Thing v. La Chusa, [771 P.2d 814, 826–27 (Cal. 1989)].

. . . .

We therefore reverse the judgment of the court of appeals in favor of Kerr on the ground of negligent infliction of emotional distress.

. . . .

Kerr cannot recover based on the cause of action under which she proceeded. It may well be, however, that she failed to assert and preserve alternative causes of action because of her reliance on our holding in *Garrard*. We have broad discretion to remand for a new trial in the interest of justice where it appears that a party may have proceeded under the wrong legal theory. . . . *See generally* Robert W. Calvert, ". . . *In the Interest of Justice*," 4 St. Mary's L.J. 291 (1972). It is even more appropriate where we have also subsequently given formal recognition to a cause of action which might be applicable to the facts of this case. *See* Twyman [v. Twyman, 855 S.W.2d 619 (Tex. 1993)] (expressly recognizing the tort of intentional infliction of emotional distress). We therefore reverse the judgment of the court of appeals and remand this cause to the trial court for a new trial.

GONZALEZ, Justice. [Concurring opinion on rehearing.]

What happened to Ms. Kerr in this case is grossly offensive conduct which no one should tolerate. As such the law should, and does, provide a remedy. However, as a result of the posturing by the dissenting justices, what has been lost in the shuffle is the pivotal role that insurance played in this case.

. . . .

It does not take a rocket scientist to determine why Ms. Kerr's lawyers elected to proceed solely on the tort of negligent infliction of emotional distress. . . .

In Texas, a homeowners policy covers only accidents or careless conduct and excludes intentional acts. Ms. Kerr's lawyers may have believed that if they obtained a judgment declaring that Boyles' conduct came within the rubric of "negligence" (inadvertence or carelessness), they could tap the homeowners policies owned by the parents of Boyles and the other defendants. Thus, this case has a lot to do with a search for a "deep pocket" who can pay. If the purpose of awarding damages is to punish the wrongdoer and deter such conduct in the future, then the individuals responsible for these reprehensible actions are the ones who should suffer, not the people of Texas in the form of higher insurance premiums for home owners.

. . . .

DOGGETT, Justice, dissenting.

. . . .

A young woman was found by a jury to have suffered severe emotional distress when her most intimate act was secretly videotaped and displayed to others. To deny her relief, the majority rewrites Texas law and recants the respect for human dignity affirmed by this court in *St. Elizabeth Hospital*. . . . [T]he majority now declares that in Texas no legal duty necessary to establish negligence arises from nonconsensual, surreptitious videotaping of a woman engaged in sexual intercourse. The rights of Texas women continue to slip away like sand through this majority's fingers.

. . . . In the march to justice, Texas should not fear leadership. But rather than leading, today's majority beats a quick retreat. If every such decision of this court is to be erased from the books as being "out of step," Texas is doomed to last place in legal thinking.

And why the rush to retreat? The majority declares with vigor that "judicial resources" would be "strained," . . . with the insignificant, the trivial, with other mere "intimate" affairs of the heart. 855 S.W.2d at 600. How can anyone view what happened here as just another "instance of rude, insensitive or distasteful behavior"? . . . .

. . . . The law is not irretrievably locked in the days before televisions and videocameras, nor limited to operators of telegraphs and horse-drawn carriages. In refusing to discuss why no duty arises from Boyles' sexual exploitation of Susan Kerr, the majority abdicates its responsibility. Until writings such as today's, our court sought to fulfill its obligation to keep tort law apace with modern times: "The creation of new concepts of duty in tort is historically the province of the judiciary." . . . .

The message of the majority is clear: Don't bother this court to separate injustice from the inconsequential, better to bar both. The cause is now remanded for Susan Kerr to endure the trauma of another trial "in the interest of justice." . . . .

MAUZY and GAMMAGE, JJ., join in this dissenting opinion.

[The supplemental dissenting opinion of Justice DOGGETT on the motion for rehearing, in which Justices GAMMAGE and SPECTOR concurred, has been omitted. The opinion of Justice COOK, concurring and dissenting, has also been omitted.]

Notes

1. ***Query: Outrageous Conduct?*** On the stated facts, could the plaintiff successfully present a claim under the tort of outrage at a new trial?

2. ***Independent Duty.*** In Nelson v. SCI Texas Funeral Services, Inc., 484 S.W.3d 248, 256–57 (Tex. App. 2016), the court held that the plaintiff's "common law, quasi-property right as next of kin and his priority right under the statute [to make funeral arrangements] were sufficient to create a special relationship between himself and SCI, giving rise to a duty on the part of SCI to avoid causing mental anguish" to the plaintiff as the funeral home handling the disposition of his mother's remains.

See also Larsen v. Banner Health System, 81 P.3d 196 (Wyo. 2003). *Larsen* recognized an "independent duty" rule and held that "where a contractual relationship exists for services that carry with them deeply emotional responses in the event of breach, there arises a duty to exercise ordinary care to avoid causing emotional harm." The court found that a mother and daughter, "who were separated for forty-three years because the hospital switched two newborn babies at birth," could maintain a negligence action for purely emotional distress damages.

3. ***Rejection of Negligent Infliction.*** *See* Harris v. Fulton-DeKalb Hosp. Auth., 255 F. Supp. 2d 1347 (N.D. Ga. 2002), *aff'd* 48 Fed. Appx. 742 (11th Cir. 2002) (stating that "Georgia law does not recognize a cause of action for the tort of 'negligent infliction of emotional distress'").

Chapter 12

Limited Duty: Alcohol-Related Injuries

The Eighteenth Amendment to the U.S. Constitution prohibited the "manufacture, sale, or transportation of intoxicating liquors . . . for beverage purposes," and the Twenty-First Amendment repealed the Eighteenth. Needless to say, the history of alcoholic beverages in the United States has been contentious, and the struggle still goes on. Legal issues arising from alcohol-related injuries are frequently the subject of hard-fought litigation and, sometimes, legislative action.

The Common-Law Rule. Traditionally, sellers and donors of alcoholic beverages were not liable to third persons for injuries caused by the drunken behavior of recipients of the alcohol. With little policy analysis, many courts expressed the conclusion of no liability by saying that the proximate cause of the accident was the drinking, not the dispensing, of the intoxicants. *See, e.g.*, Cole v. Rush, 289 P.2d 450 (Cal. 1955). As an application of proximate causation, this approach today seems quite odd; the injuries in question are plainly foreseeable, and they are the sort of thing that can naturally be expected to result from furnishing alcohol to someone who will soon be driving or who has a reputation for spousal abuse. Moreover, there can be more than one proximate cause of harm: the supplier and the imbiber could both be held liable. In doctrinal terms, rules immunizing those who contribute to harm by furnishing alcohol to injurers seem best categorized as rules exempting the defendant from the usual duty to take reasonable safety precautions.

Nevertheless, some decisions continue to talk in terms of proximate causation. For example, in Cook v. MillerCoors, LLC, 872 F. Supp. 2d 1346 (M.D. Fla. 2012), a products liability action alleging failure to warn, defective design, and negligent manufacturing, the court held that even if an alcoholic energy drink could be considered unreasonably dangerous under Florida law, the "voluntary drinking of alcohol is the proximate cause of an injury, rather than the manufacture or sale of those intoxicating beverages." The court ruled that a motorcycle driver's consumption of the alcoholic energy drink was the proximate cause of his passenger's injuries.

Today, the liability of those who furnish alcoholic beverages to persons who become intoxicated and injure themselves or others is a very complicated field, with considerable variation from state to state. Much of the law is statutory.

A. Liability of Sellers

Visibly Intoxicated Patrons and Minors. Sellers of alcohol are often held liable for harm resulting from sales to visibly intoxicated persons and sales to minors. Beyond these two categories, sellers are usually not subject to tort liability. *See* Hall v. Toreros, II, Inc., 626 S.E.2d 861 (N.C. App. 2006) (finding that a restaurant had no duty to prevent an intoxicated patron from driving after he consumed his final drink).

Dram Shop Liability. Most states have adopted "dram shop acts," which make some sellers of alcoholic beverages liable to those injured by the buyer's intoxication. Other states have imposed dram shop liability under common law principles.

No Liability. In a few states, sellers of alcohol are not subject to civil liability. *See* Warr v. JMGM Group, LLC, 70 A.3d 347 (Md. 2013) (bar owners are not subject to dram ship liability); Noone v. Chalet of Wichita, L.L.C., 96 P.3d 674 (Kan. App. 2004) ("reluctantly" enforcing no-duty rules that are increasingly out of step with the "evolving trend of the common law").

The California statute making it a misdemeanor to furnish alcohol "to any habitual or common drunkard or to any obviously intoxicated person" expressly provides that persons who violate the statute are not civilly liable to those injured by the consumer's intoxication. *See* Cal. Bus. & Prof. Code §§ 25602(a)–(b) (Westlaw 2022).

New York General Obligations Law

§ 11-101 (Westlaw 2022)

COMPENSATION FOR INJURY CAUSED BY THE ILLEGAL SALE OF INTOXICATING LIQUOR

1. Any person who shall be injured ... by any intoxicated person, or by reason of the intoxication of any person, ... shall have a right of action against any person who shall, by unlawful selling to or unlawfully assisting in procuring liquor for such intoxicated person, have caused or contributed to such intoxication; and in any such action such person shall have a right to recover actual and exemplary damages.

. . . .

Notes

1. ***Variations on Statutory Dram Shop Liability.***

(a) ***What Is Prohibited?*** Because the New York statute is limited to cases in which the selling was "unlawful" (as, for example, when the defendant sells to a minor or to an obviously intoxicated person), liability under that statute is limited to cases of fairly serious misconduct. *Compare* 235 Ill. Comp. Stat. Ann. 5/6-21 (Westlaw 2022), creating a cause of action for harm done by an intoxicated person against any licensed seller of liquor "who by selling or giving alcoholic liquor ... causes the intoxication." Unlike the New York statute, the Illinois dram shop act limits liability to relatively low dollar amounts, which are adjusted annually according to the Consumer Price Index.

Although the New York statute, unlike those of some states, is not expressly limited to those in the business of selling alcoholic beverages, the courts have tended to construe it as not applying to those who simply give liquor away, even to a minor, and even in a business setting, as when an employer furnishes drinks to its employees. *See* D'Amico v. Christie, 518 N.E.2d 896 (N.Y. 1987). However, the California Supreme Court has held that a statute in that state addressing alcohol provided to an obviously intoxicated minor by certain commercial sellers imposes liability regardless of whether the alcohol is sold or given. *See* Ennabe v. Manosa, 319 P.3d 201, 209 (Cal. 2014).

Decisions vary as to whether dram shop laws impose liability on noncommercial sellers. In McGee v. Alexander, 37 P.3d 800 (Okla. 2001), the court held that a hospital that served alcohol at a golf tournament fund-raising event was a social host, rather than a commercial vendor of alcohol for dram-shop-liability purposes, even though the hospital charged participants a $60 entry fee. In contrast, in Ennabe v. Manosa, 319 P.3d 201 (Cal. 2014), the court held that a party host who allegedly charged a $3 to $5 fee to enter the party was potentially a person who "sold" alcoholic beverages to an obviously intoxicated minor, and was therefore subject to liability for the death of a third person in an auto accident caused by the intoxicated minor.

See also Born v. Mayers, 514 N.W.2d 687 (N.D. 1994) (holding that the state dram shop act creates a cause of action against "any person" who knowingly provides alcoholic beverages to an obviously intoxicated person).

(b) ***When is a Patron Visibly Intoxicated?*** In Robinson Property Group, Ltd. Partnership v. McCalman, 51 So. 3d 946 (Miss. 2011), the court explained that:

> Mississippi's statute commonly called the Dram Shop Act, according to its title, provides "immunity from liability of persons who lawfully furnished or sold intoxicating beverages to one causing damage." The statute includes the following exception:
>
> The limitation of liability provided by this section shall not apply to . . . any holder of an alcoholic beverage, beer or light wine permit, or any agent or employee of such holder when it is shown that the person making a purchase of an alcoholic beverage was at the time of such purchase visibly intoxicated.

The *McCalman* court upheld a finding of liability under the statute because there was evidence to support the jury finding that the patron was visibly intoxicated.

(c) ***Types of Commercial Sellers.*** Is any sale of alcohol by a business entity sufficient to trigger dram shop liability? In some states, a distinction has been drawn between bars and taverns, on one hand, and stores, on the other hand.

For example, Snodgras v. Martin & Bayley, Inc., 204 S.W.3d 638 (Mo. 2006), upheld against a constitutional challenge a statutory dram shop law imposing liability only with respect to on-premises drink consumption, but not with respect to packaged sales. The court reasoned that "unlike the proprietor of a bar or tavern, the seller of packaged liquor is dealing with a single transaction and has less opportunity to observe customers and make judgments about whether they are intoxicated or of age," and therefore the scheme was not irrational.

However, Flores v. Exprezit! Stores 98-Georgia, LLC., 713 S.E.2d 368 (Ga. 2011), rejected such a distinction, finding that because the state statute used "the terms 'sells, furnishes, or serves' alcohol in the disjunctive, it is clear that it was intended to encompass the sale of an alcoholic beverage at places other than the proverbial dram shop." The same court, in an earlier case, Delta Airlines, Inc. v. Townsend, 614 S.E.2d 745 (Ga. 2005), had found that "unlike the clientele of land-based establishments, airline passengers generally do not have direct and immediate access to their vehicles after they deplane," and therefore an airline was not liable under a dram shop statute.

In summary, "[t]oday's dram shop acts commonly include not only bars and liquor stores but also convenience and grocery stores with liquor licenses." Pamela R. Mullis, Driving Toward Justice in a Dram Shop Case, Trial, Feb. 2012, at 32.

(d) ***May the Recipient Sue?*** Courts often hold that a visibly intoxicated patron, who was served in violation of a dram shop law, cannot assert a cause of action under the statute. *See* Been v. MK Enterprise, Inc., 256 P.3d 1040 (Okla. Civ. App. 2011) (finding that a patron who committed various crimes after a tavern and bartender unlawfully served him low-point beer could not state a cause of action).

In states with dram shop laws permitting an injured recipient of alcohol to sue, recovery may be reduced by comparative negligence. *Cf.* Bissett v. DMI, Inc., 717 P.2d 545 (Mont. 1986).

At least one state has held that the enactment of a statutory unlawful conduct defense did not repeal dram shop liability and thereby preclude a claim by an intoxicated patron. In Voss v. Tranquilino, 19 A.3d 470 (N.J. 2011), new legislation provided that a driver convicted of driving while intoxicated in connection with an accident shall have no cause of action for recovery of economic or noneconomic losses. Noting that "[n]owhere in that legislative history was there any suggestion that the statute would affect liability under the Dram Shop Act," the court held that the statute did not bar a driver's claim against the establishment that allegedly served him alcoholic beverages when he was visibly intoxicated prior to the accident.

(e) ***Proportional Liability?*** Traditional rules of joint and several liability have been replaced in many states, in a wide range of circumstances, with principles of proportional liability. (*See* Chapter 17.) It is therefore not surprising that in some states the violator of a dram shop law may be liable only for a portion of the non-patron plaintiff's injuries. *See* F.F.P. Operating Partners, L.P. v. Duenez, 237 S.W.3d 680 (Tex. 2007) (holding that the provisions of the state Proportionate Responsibility Act applied).

2. ***Common-Law Dram Shop Liability.*** In many states, vendors may be subject to liability at common law in addition to, or instead of, liability under dram shop statutes. *See, e.g.*, Klingerman v. SOL Corp., 505 A.2d 474 (Me. 1986) (the personal

representative of a decedent who died of alcoholic poisoning had no cause of action against a tavernkeeper under the dram shop law, but stated a claim for common-law negligence).

Because alcohol wholesalers do not know whether the ultimate purchaser will be intoxicated at the time of the sale at retail, they ordinarily are not subject to liability. *See* Chavez v. Desert Eagle Distributing Co. of N.M., 151 P.3d 77 (N.M. App. 2006) (holding that while the prudence of a retailer's selling alcohol "for twenty-four hours a day as part of a Memorial Day promotion may be debatable," a wholesaler's "actions in selling alcohol to such an establishment does not make the foreseeability of a drunk driving accident anything more than mere speculation," and the wholesaler therefore did not have a duty to a person injured in a resulting accident).

Once a state legislature has entered the field of defining liability for alcohol-related injuries, are courts free to recognize new causes of action? In answering this question, judicial decisions differ widely.

In Reeder v. Daniel, 61 S.W.3d 359 (Tex. 2001), the court held that deference to the legislature was a good reason to hold that an injured guest had no civil cause of action against a host for making alcohol available to guests under the age of eighteen. However, three concurring justices opined that:

> Nothing in the Dram Shop Act itself forecloses common-law liability for an adult who provides alcohol to a minor. . . . If the Legislature wanted to foreclose a cause of action for providing alcohol to persons under eighteen, it could have easily written the law so that it would provide the exclusive remedy for providing alcohol to anyone, regardless of age. . . .

In Craig v. Driscoll, 813 A.2d 1003 (Conn. 2003), the court, by a 3–2 margin, held that the Connecticut Dram Shop Act did not so occupy the field of alcohol-related liability as to preclude new recognition of a common-law cause of action for negligence against the purveyor of alcoholic beverages. However, shortly after the decision in *Craig*, the Connecticut legislature effectively overruled that case by expressly abrogating the common-law dram shop claims. *See* O'Dell v. Kozee, 53 A.3d 178, 197, 307 Conn. 231, 265 (Conn. 2012).

3. ***Dram Shop Liability and Proximate Causation***. In a rare case, a vendor who negligently provides alcohol to a minor who subsequently injures a third person may be saved from liability to the third person by lack of proximate causation. *See* Phan Son Van v. Pena, 990 S.W.2d 751 (Tex. 1999) (holding that gang members' criminal conduct, which involved the rape and murder of two girls, was extraordinary in nature and not the type of harm generally associated with furnishing alcohol to minors, and that therefore the conduct was a superseding cause of the girls' injuries and deaths).

4. ***Sales to Minors***. The unlawful sale of alcohol to a minor may give rise to liability under common law principles. *See* Nunez v. Carrabba's Italian Grill, Inc., 859 N.E.2d 801 (Mass. 2007) (holding that a plaintiff "under the legal drinking age . . . need only establish that the actions of the defendants were negligent. In other words, the

plaintiff must present evidence to show that . . . [the] establishments served him alcoholic beverages knowing, or having reason to know, that he was under twenty-one years of age and, as a consequence, he was injured").

5. ***Casinos and Gambling.*** Does a casino have a duty to refrain from knowingly permitting an invitee to gamble if the patron is visibly intoxicated or under the influence of a narcotic substance? *Compare* GNOC Corp. v. Aboud, 715 F. Supp. 644 (D. N.J. 1989) (yes), *with* Hakimoglu v. Trump Taj Mahal Assoc., 70 F.3d 291 (3d Cir. 1995) (no). *See also* Merrill v. Trump Ind., Inc., 320 F.3d 729 (7th Cir. 2003) (holding that a casino did not owe a duty to a compulsive gambler to prevent him from gambling).

6. ***Controlled Substances.*** A New York statute, N.Y. Gen. Oblig. Law § 11-103 (Westlaw 2022), imposes liability similar to that arising under the state dram shop act for injuries attributable to the illegal sale of controlled substances.

B. Liability of "Social Hosts"

Kelly v. Gwinnell

Supreme Court of New Jersey
476 A.2d 1219 (N.J. 1984)

WILENTZ, C.J.

. . . .

At the trial level, the case was disposed of . . . by summary judgment in favor of the social host. The record . . . discloses that defendant Donald Gwinnell, after driving defendant Joseph Zak home, spent an hour or two at Zak's home before leaving to return to his own home. During that time . . . Gwinnell [allegedly] consumed two or three drinks of scotch on the rocks. Zak accompanied Gwinnell outside to his car, chatted with him, and watched as Gwinnell then drove off to go home. About twenty-five minutes later Zak telephoned Gwinnell's home to make sure Gwinnell had arrived there safely. The phone was answered by Mrs. Gwinnell, who advised Zak that Gwinnell had been involved in a head-on collision. The collision was with an automobile operated by plaintiff, Marie Kelly, who was seriously injured as a result.

. . . . Kelly's expert concluded from . . . [Gwinnell's .286 percent blood alcohol concentration] that Gwinnell had consumed not two or three scotches . . . but the equivalent of thirteen drinks; that while at Zak's home Gwinnell must have been showing unmistakable signs of intoxication; and that in fact he was severely intoxicated while at Zak's residence and at the time of the accident.

Kelly sued Gwinnell and . . . [the Zaks and others]. The Zaks moved for summary judgment, contending that as a matter of law a host is not liable for the negligence of an adult social guest who has become intoxicated while at the host's home. The trial court granted the motion. . . . The Appellate Division affirmed. . . .

The Appellate Division's determination was based on the apparent absence of decisions in this country imposing such liability (except for those that were promptly overruled by the Legislature).... The absence of such determinations is said to reflect a broad consensus that the imposition of liability arising from these social relations is unwise. Certainly this immunization of hosts is not the inevitable result of the law of negligence, for conventional negligence analysis points strongly in exactly the opposite direction. "Negligence is tested by whether the reasonably prudent person at the time and place should recognize and foresee an unreasonable risk or likelihood of harm or danger to others." .... When negligent conduct creates such a risk, setting off foreseeable consequences that lead to plaintiff's injury, the conduct is deemed the proximate cause of the injury....

.... Viewing the facts most favorably to plaintiff (as we must, since the complaint was dismissed on a motion for summary judgment), one could reasonably conclude that the Zaks must have known that their provision of liquor was causing Gwinnell to become drunk, yet they continued to serve him even after he was visibly intoxicated.... A reasonable person in Zak's position could foresee quite clearly that this continued provision of alcohol to Gwinnell was making it more and more likely that Gwinnell would not be able to operate his car carefully... [and] was likely to injure someone as a result of the negligent operation of his car. The usual elements of a cause of action for negligence are clearly present.... [T]he only question remaining is whether a duty exists to prevent such risk or, realistically, whether this Court should impose such a duty.

In most cases the justice of imposing such a duty is so clear that the cause of action in negligence is assumed to exist simply on the basis of the actor's creation of an unreasonable risk of foreseeable harm resulting in injury. In fact, however, more is needed, "more" being the value judgment, based on an analysis of public policy, that the actor owed the injured party a duty of reasonable care.... In Goldberg v. Housing Auth. of Newark, 38 N.J. 578, 583, 186 A.2d 291 (1962), this Court explained that "whether a duty exists is ultimately a question of fairness. The inquiry involves a weighing of the relationship of the parties, the nature of the risk, and the public interest in the proposed solution." ....

When the court determines that a duty exists and liability will be extended, it draws judicial lines based on fairness and policy. In a society where thousands of deaths are caused each year by drunken drivers,[1] where the damage caused by such deaths is regarded increasingly as intolerable, where liquor licensees are prohibited from serving intoxicated adults, and where long-standing criminal sanctions

1. [Fn. 3:] From 1978 to 1982 there were 5,755 highway fatalities in New Jersey. Alcohol was involved in 2,746 or 47.5% of these deaths. Of the 629,118 automobile accident injuries for the same period, 131,160, or 20.5% were alcohol related. The societal cost for New Jersey alcohol-related highway deaths for this period has been estimated as $1,149,516,000.00, based on statistics and documents obtained from the New Jersey Division of Motor Vehicles.... These New Jersey statistics are consistent with nationwide figures....

against drunken driving have recently been significantly strengthened . . . , the imposition of such a duty by the judiciary seems both fair and fully in accord with the State's policy. . . .

The argument is made that the rule imposing liability on licensees is justified because licensees, unlike social hosts, derive a profit from serving liquor. We reject this analysis of the liability's foundation and emphasize that the liability proceeds from the duty of care that accompanies control of the liquor supply. Whatever the motive behind making alcohol available to those who will subsequently drive, the provider has a duty to the public not to create foreseeable, unreasonable risks by this activity.

We therefore hold that a host who serves liquor to an adult social guest, knowing both that the guest is intoxicated and will thereafter be operating a motor vehicle, is liable for injuries inflicted on a third party as a result of the negligent operation of a motor vehicle by the adult guest when such negligence is caused by intoxication. We impose this duty on the host to the third party because we believe that the policy considerations served by its imposition far outweigh those asserted in opposition. While we recognize the concern that our ruling will interfere with accepted standards of social behavior; will intrude on and somewhat diminish the enjoyment, relaxation, and camaraderie that accompany social gatherings at which alcohol is served; and that such gatherings and social relationships are not simply tangential benefits of a civilized society but are regarded by many as important, we believe that the added assurance of just compensation to the victims of drunken driving as well as the added deterrent effect of the rule on such driving outweigh the importance of those other values. . . .

The liability we impose here is analogous to that traditionally imposed on owners of vehicles who lend their cars to persons they know to be intoxicated. . . . If, by lending a car to a drunk, a host becomes liable to third parties injured by the drunken driver's negligence, the same liability should extend to a host who furnishes liquor to a visibly drunken guest who he knows will thereafter drive away.

Some fear has been expressed that the extent of the potential liability may be disproportionate to the fault of the host. . . . [W]e do not believe that the liability is disproportionate when the host's actions, so relatively easily corrected, may result in serious injury or death. . . .

Given the lack of precedent anywhere else in the country, however, we believe it would be unfair to impose this liability retroactively. . . . Homeowners who are social hosts may desire to increase their policy limits; apartment dwellers may want to obtain liability insurance of this kind where perhaps they now have none. . . . We therefore have determined that the liability imposed by this case on social hosts shall be prospective, applicable only to events that occur after the date of this decision. We will, however, apply the doctrine to the parties before us on the usual theory that to do otherwise would not only deprive the plaintiff of any benefit resulting from her own efforts but would also make it less likely that, in the future, individuals will be willing to claim rights, not yet established, that they believe are just.

... [I]f the Legislature differs with us on issues of this kind, it has a clear remedy....

.... Given the facts before us, we decide only that where the social host directly serves the guest and continues to do so even after the guest is visibly intoxicated, knowing that the guest will soon be driving home, the social host may be liable for the consequences of the resulting drunken driving. We are not faced with a party where many guests congregate, nor with guests serving each other, nor with a host busily occupied with other responsibilities and therefore unable to attend to the matter of serving liquor, nor with a drunken host.... We will face those situations when and if they come before us.... The fears expressed by the dissent concerning the vast impact of the decision on the "average citizen's" life are reminiscent of those asserted in opposition to our decisions abolishing husband-wife, parent-child, and generally family immunity.... Some fifteen years have gone by and, as far as we can tell, nothing but good has come as a result of those decisions.

... [T]he dissent's emphasis on the financial impact of an insurance premium increase on the homeowner or the tenant should be measured against the monumental financial losses suffered by society as result of drunken driving. By our decision we not only spread some of that loss so that it need not be borne completely by the victims of this widespread affliction, but, to some extent, reduce the likelihood that the loss will occur in the first place.... Does our society morally approve of the decision to continue to allow the charm of unrestrained social drinking when the cost is the lives of others, sometimes of the guests themselves?

If we but step back and observe ourselves objectively, we will see a phenomenon not of merriment but of cruelty, causing misery to innocent people, tolerated for years despite our knowledge that without fail, out of our extraordinarily high number of deaths caused by automobiles, nearly half have regularly been attributable to drunken driving.... Should we be so concerned about disturbing the customs of those who knowingly supply that which causes the offense, so worried about their inconvenience, as if they were the victims rather than the cause of the carnage?....

We ... reverse the judgment in favor of the defendants Zak and remand the case to the Law Division for proceedings consistent with this opinion.

[The dissenting opinion of GARIBALDI, J., is omitted.]

Notes

1. ***The Legislative Response to*** **Kelly**. New Jersey now has the following statutes:

New Jersey Statutes Annotated
§ 2A:15-5.6–5.8 (Westlaw 2022)

§ 2A:15-5.6 *Exclusive civil remedy for damages in accident involving vehicle resulting from negligent provision of alcoholic beverages by social host to person of legal age....*

a. This act shall be the exclusive civil remedy for personal injury or property damage resulting from the negligent provision of alcoholic beverages by a social host to a person who has attained the legal age to purchase and consume alcoholic beverages.

b. A person who sustains bodily injury or injury to real or personal property as a result of the negligent provision of alcoholic beverages by a social host to a person who has attained the legal age to purchase and consume alcoholic beverages may recover damages from a social host only if:

(1) The social host willfully and knowingly provided alcoholic beverages either: (a) To a person who was visibly intoxicated in the social host's presence; or (b) To a person who was visibly intoxicated under circumstances manifesting reckless disregard of the consequences as affecting the life or property of another; and

(2) The social host provided alcoholic beverages to the visibly intoxicated person under circumstances which created an unreasonable risk of foreseeable harm to the life or property of another, and the social host failed to exercise reasonable care and diligence to avoid the foreseeable risk; and

(3) The injury arose out of an accident caused by the negligent operation of a vehicle by the visibly intoxicated person who was provided alcoholic beverages by a social host.

c. To determine the liability of a social host under subsection b. of this section, if a test to determine the presence of alcohol in the blood indicates a blood alcohol concentration of:

(1) less than 0.10% by weight of alcohol in the blood, there shall be an irrebuttable presumption that the person tested was not visibly intoxicated in the social host's presence and that the social host did not provide alcoholic beverages to the person under circumstances which manifested reckless disregard of the consequences as affecting the life or property of another; or

(2) at least 0.10% but less than 0.15% by weight of alcohol in the blood, there shall be a rebuttable presumption, that the person tested was not visibly intoxicated in the social host's presence and that the social host did not provide alcoholic beverages to the person under circumstances which manifested reckless disregard of the consequences as affecting the life or property of another.

§ 2A:15-5.7 *Limitation of nonliability of social host*

No social host shall be held liable to a person who has attained the legal age to purchase and consume alcoholic beverages for damages suffered as a result of the social host's negligent provision of alcoholic beverages to that person.

§ 2A:15-5.8 *Social hosts or other parties as joint tortfeasors . . .*

. . . [I]n any case where a social host or any other party to a suit instituted pursuant to the provisions of this act is determined to be a joint tortfeasor, the social host or other party shall be responsible for no more than that percentage share of the damages which is equal to the percentage of negligence attributable to the social host or other party.

2. ***Social Hosts Providing Alcohol to Adults.*** Some courts agree with *Kelly*, in whole or in part. *See, e.g.*, McGuiggan v. New England Tel. & Tel. Co., 496 N.E.2d 141 (Mass. 1986) (host may be liable to third parties for injuries caused by the drunken driving of an obviously intoxicated adult guest); Langle v. Kurkul, 510 A.2d 1301 (Vt. 1986) (host may be liable for furnishing alcoholic beverages to a visibly intoxicated person who will drive an automobile or to a minor).

However, other courts have refused to hold social hosts liable for injuries caused by their guests, regardless of how negligent the hosts may have been in furnishing their guests with beverages. *See, e.g.*, Graff v. Beard, 858 S.W.2d 918 (Tex. 1993); Overbaugh v. McKutcheon, 396 S.E.2d 153 (W. Va. 1990).

In some states that have judicially held social hosts liable, the legislature has responded by abolishing liability; see, for example, Cal. Civ. Code § 1714 (Westlaw 2022), which not only abolishes liability based on negligently furnishing alcohol, but also names the California Supreme Court decisions which the legislation was intended to overturn.

3. ***Social Hosts Providing Alcohol to Minors.*** In Pennsylvania, social host liability attaches in cases involving the negligent furnishing of alcoholic beverages to minors, but not to persons of drinking age. *See* Congini by Congini v. Portersville Valve Co., 470 A.2d 515 (Pa. 1983).

4. ***Aiding-and-Abetting Underage Drinking.*** Fassett v. Delta Kappa Epsilon, 807 F.2d 1150 (3d Cir. 1986), was an action following a traffic accident caused by a minor who had become intoxicated at a fraternity party. The court, attempting to discern Pennsylvania law, rejected an argument made by several of the defendants that only those persons who physically hand liquor to a minor can be liable. Instead, liability could attach to anyone whose conduct in "aiding, agreeing or attempting to aid a minor in consuming liquor, did so in substantial fashion." The court refused to dismiss claims against the fraternity's treasurer, whose role in the party consisted of signing the check used to purchase the beverages, against its president, who organized the party, and against the roommates who knowingly allowed their apartment to be used for the party. While the *Fassett* decision may strike the more convivial sort of student as harsh, it may be worth noting that one of the accident victims died and the other was rendered a quadriplegic.

Fassett was a federal court ruling. A later state-court decision made clear that, under Pennsylvania law, a minor cannot be held liable under the social host doctrine for furnishing alcohol to another minor who is subsequently injured. *See* Kapres v. Heller, 640 A.2d 888 (Pa. 1994).

5. ***Splitting the Check***. In Dube v. Lanphear, 868 N.E.2d 619 (Mass. App. Ct. 2007), the court held that companions who paid for the drinks of an allegedly intoxicated friend who intended to drive home were not liable for injuries to a third person in a resulting collision because the companions were not in actual control of the bar's liquor supply or the friend's drinking. The court wrote:

> Sharing a check is not the equivalent of being a host. That the sharing in this instance took the form of rotating payment of the entire bill, rather than equal division of the bill on each occasion, is a distinction that is meaningless . . . [I]t cannot reasonably be argued that the common practice of patronizing eating and drinking establishments with companions, each participant paying a fair share of the charges, imposes social host liability on each member of the group in the event one individual visibly drinks to excess and causes damage afterward.

6. ***Social Host Liability and Proximate Causation***. *See* Nichols v. Dobler, 655 N.W.2d 787 (Mich. Ct. App. 2002) (holding that there was an issue of material fact as to whether a party host's negligence in serving alcohol to a minor proximately caused injuries sustained when the plaintiff was repeatedly hit in the head with a hammer by the minor).

C. Possessors of Property

Del Lago Partners, Inc. v. Smith

Supreme Court of Texas.
307 S.W.3d 762 (Tex. 2010)

Justice WILLETT delivered the opinion of the Court. . . .

This appeal concerns a bar owner's liability for injuries caused when one patron assaulted another during a closing-time melee involving twenty to forty "very intoxicated" customers. The brawl erupted after ninety minutes of recurrent threats, cursing, and shoving by two rival groups of patrons. . . .

Bradley Smith was injured when a fight broke out among customers at the Grandstand Bar, part of the Del Lago resort on the shores of Lake Conroe. . . .

Smith was standing against a wall observing the fight when he saw his friend Forsythe shoved to the floor. Smith knew Forsythe had a heart condition and waded into the scrum to remove him. . . . Before Smith could extricate himself, an unknown person grabbed him and placed him in a headlock. Momentum carried Smith and his attacker into a wall, where Smith's face hit a stud. Smith suffered severe injuries including a skull fracture and brain damage.

Estimates of the fight's duration varied, but most testimony placed it between three and fifteen minutes. Waitress Sweet testified that "it wasn't a quick fight." . . . .

After the fight began, Sweet went to the phone in the bar to call security. Next to the phone was a list of numbers, but none was for security. Sweet called the front desk to get the number. Instead of calling security, the front desk gave the number to Sweet. Instead of immediately calling the number given, Sweet passed it over to a bartender for him to make the call. Once the call was made, the two security guards on duty, Officers Chancellor and Moriarty, responded swiftly, arriving within two to three minutes. Del Lago's loss-prevention officer, Sanchez, also responded and arrived within fifteen to twenty seconds of receiving the call. By the time he arrived, the fight was over.

Smith brought a premises-liability claim against Del Lago. After a nine-day trial involving twenty-one witnesses, the jury sifted through the conflicting evidence and found Del Lago and Smith both negligent, allocating fault at 51–49 percent in favor of Smith. The trial court reduced the jury's actual-damages award by forty-nine percent, and awarded Smith $1,478,283, together with interest and costs. A divided court of appeals affirmed.

Del Lago principally argues that it had no duty to protect Smith from being assaulted by another bar customer. . . .

We have not held that a bar proprietor always or routinely has a duty to protect patrons from other patrons, and do not so hold today. Nor have we held that a duty to protect the clientele necessarily arises when a patron becomes inebriated, or when words are exchanged between patrons that lead to a fight, and do not so hold today.

Generally, a premises owner has no duty to protect invitees from criminal acts by third parties. We have recognized an exception when the owner knows or has reason to know of a risk of harm to invitees that is unreasonable and foreseeable. . . .

In this case, Del Lago observed—but did nothing to reduce—an hour and a half of verbal and physical hostility in the bar. From the moment the wedding party entered, there was palpable and escalating tension. Del Lago continued to serve drunk rivals who were engaged in repeated and aggressive confrontations.

That a fight broke out was no surprise. . . .

We hold that Del Lago had a duty to protect Smith because Del Lago had actual and direct knowledge that a violent brawl was imminent between drunk, belligerent patrons and had ample time and means to defuse the situation. Del Lago's duty arose not because of prior similar criminal conduct but because it was aware of an unreasonable risk of harm at the bar that very night. When a landowner "has *actual* or constructive knowledge of any condition on the premises that poses an unreasonable risk of harm to invitees, he has a duty to take whatever action is reasonably prudent" to reduce or eliminate that risk.

. . . . We do not see the burden of imposing a duty on Del Lago to take reasonable steps to protect patrons of the Grandstand Bar from potentially serious injury as unwarranted in these circumstances. Del Lago is a huge, multi-use facility covering hundreds of acres that provides entertainment and lodging to scores of guests daily. Like any similar facility, it recognized the need to provide private security throughout the resort. It did so through a trained security force.

We do not announce a general rule today. We hold only, on these facts, that during the ninety minutes of recurrent hostilities at the bar, a duty arose on Del Lago's part to use reasonable care to protect the invitees from imminent assaultive conduct. The duty arose because the likelihood and magnitude of the risk to patrons reached the level of an unreasonable risk of harm, the risk was apparent to the property owner, and the risk arose in circumstances where the property owner had readily available opportunities to reduce it.

. . . .

The jury could have found that Del Lago breached its duty because security failed to monitor and intervene during the extended period when the two groups in the bar were becoming more and more intoxicated and antagonistic. Officers Chancellor and Moriarty, the uniformed security personnel on duty that night, testified that they would usually go through the bar five to eight times a night, but they did not have specific recollections of going through the bar that particular evening. . . . .

There was legally sufficient evidence for the jury to conclude that Del Lago bar personnel were fully aware of the events transpiring in the bar and nevertheless unreasonably neglected to notify security. . . .

The jury also could have found negligence on Del Lago's part by finding that bar personnel were not provided with the training and information needed to immediately notify security of an emergency. . . .

Justice Johnson would reverse because Smith was equally aware of the events transpiring at the bar and could have walked away, but instead chose to stay and enter the fray. The jury found Smith contributorily negligent, and Smith, who says he entered the scrum to rescue a friend, does not argue otherwise here. Justice Johnson's view would effectively revive the doctrine of voluntary assumption of the risk as a complete bar to recovery, but the Texas proportionate responsibility statute makes clear that a plaintiff's negligence bars recovery only "if his percentage of responsibility is greater than 50 percent." Here, the jury found that Del Lago's negligence (fifty-one percent) exceeded Smith's (forty-nine percent). We abandoned the assumption-of-the-risk doctrine as a complete defense to tort liability thirty-five years ago, holding that the Legislature's adoption of comparative negligence "evidenced its clear intention to apportion negligence rather than completely bar recovery." A plaintiff's own risky conduct is now absorbed into the allocation of damages through comparative responsibility. . . .

As to causation in fact, generally the test for this element is whether the defendant's act or omission was a substantial factor in causing the injury and without which the injury would not have occurred. The jury could have found, on the lay and expert testimony presented, that a security presence and response in the bar at some point during the ninety minutes that the two antagonistic groups were confronting each other would have defused the situation and prevented the violent brawl at closing time....

The jury also could have reasonably determined that Del Lago's bar and front-desk personnel moved too slowly to notify security after the fight broke out, and that this delay was a proximate cause of Smith's injuries....

Accordingly, we affirm the court of appeals' judgment.

[The dissenting opinions of Justices HECHT, WAINWRIGHT, and JOHNSON have been omitted.]

Notes

1. ***Duties to Protect Invitees.*** As the principal case illustrates, an invitor may have a duty to protect its invitees from alcohol-related injuries.

2. ***Parties Held by One's Children.*** What if the children of a possessor hold a party that gets out of hand and some of the guests are injured? Is the possessor liable? In Dynas v. Nagowski, 762 N.Y.S.2d 745 (App. Div. 2003), the court wrote:

> Landowners have "a duty to control the conduct of third persons on their premises when they have the opportunity to control such persons and are reasonably aware of the need for such control".... Ordinarily, landowners who are not present at the time of the harmful conduct by others and have neither notice of nor control over such conduct are under no duty to protect others from its consequences.

In *Dynas*, the plaintiff's injuries arose from horseplay that got out of hand. The parents were away on a camping trip at the time the party was held by their two adult children. The parents neither requested nor directed that their sons host the party, which was in no way for the parents' benefit. The parents were not involved in the planning of the party and gave no direction concerning the manner in which it was to be conducted, except (according to one witness) to say "keep it small." The court held that it was error not to grant the father's motion for summary judgment in an action by an injured guest because, even if the parents consented to the hosting of the party, the sons were not acting as the agents of the parents with respect to the party, and therefore the father could not be held liable as a principal for the sons' failure to exercise control at the event.

See also Wallace v. Wilson, 575 N.E.2d 1134 (Mass. 1991) (mother was not liable for the assault and battery of third persons at her home caused by teenagers who, with the mother's knowledge, brought beer to a party given by her 17-year-old daughter).

But see Comeau v. Lucas, 455 N.Y.S.2d 871 (App. Div. 1982) (holding that there was an issue of fact as to whether the defendant parents had failed to exercise due care in allowing their 16-year-old daughter to host a party while they were out of the country "despite knowing that beer would be served; that a rock band was engaged; and that many of the guests would be under 18 years of age"; the court further concluded that the daughter was the agent of her parents and was liable for the breach of a duty owed by her parents).

3. ***Ejected Intoxicated Invitees.*** *See* Morris v. Legends Fieldhouse B. and Grill, LLC, 958 N.W.2d 817, 819 (Iowa 2021) (holding that the "defendants owed no continuing legal duty to the intoxicated patron ejected from inside the business after he refused the offer of a cab ride and chose to walk away. The patron was not ordered to leave the parking lot and could have waited there for another ride on that summer evening.").

4. ***Problem: Knowledge of Underage Drinking on One's Property.*** The plaintiff was injured by a car driven by a drunk driver, a minor who became intoxicated at a large gathering of high school students at a party on the defendant's property. The plaintiff alleges that although the defendant did not provide the alcohol, or specifically know that the driver was consuming alcohol, the defendant was present on the property, knew that illegal consumption of alcoholic beverages by underage persons was occurring on the property, and knew that many of the guests had driven cars to the property. If the plaintiff sues the defendant on the theory that the defendant negligently failed to supervise and monitor the activities on the property, does the plaintiff have a strong claim?

D. Other Theories of Liability

The great difficulties of suing a provider of alcohol, in many states, make it desirable for the plaintiff's lawyer to find a basis for a claim that the defendant is responsible on some other ground.

West v. East Tennessee Pioneer Oil Co.

Supreme Court of Tennessee
172 S.W.3d 545 (Tenn. 2005)

WILLIAM M. BARKER, J.

. . . .

The defendant . . . operates an Exxon convenience store. . . .

. . . . Brian Tarver . . . entered the convenience store . . . and the plaintiffs allege that upon entering the store he was obviously intoxicated. There was a large number of customers in the store at the time. . . . Tarver pushed his way to the front of the line and asked the clerk if she would "go get [him] some beer." The clerk, Dorothy Thomas . . . , stated in her deposition that Tarver smelled of beer and staggered as he walked. Thomas refused to sell him beer. . . . After being denied beer, Tarver began cursing loudly, talking to Thomas in a threatening manner, and generally causing a disturbance inside the store. Tarver then managed to pull three crumpled one dollar bills out of his pocket and laid them on the counter. He told Thomas, "we need gas" and then turned to leave. A customer opened the door for Tarver, who staggered out of the store and back toward the gas pump where his car was parked.

A few moments later an alarm began "beeping" inside the store, alerting Thomas that someone was attempting to activate the gasoline pumps outside. . . . Thomas concluded that a customer was having difficulty with the pump. Although the evidence conflicts on this point, Thomas testified that she could not see the pump, so she asked the other employees in the store if someone would "go see who doesn't know what they're doing at the gas pump." Two off-duty employees were at the store: Candice Drinnon ("Drinnon"), who worked at . . . [the Exxon station's] Huddle House restaurant and . . . ice cream counter, and Roy Armani ("Armani"), who worked in the Huddle House. . . .

The accounts . . . differ as to how the events next unfolded. . . .

In any event, Drinnon and Armani came to the aid of the intoxicated Tarver, who could not push the correct button to activate the pump. Drinnon testified that upon approaching Tarver she could tell he had been drinking because she "could smell it on him." Drinnon also states, however, that she and Armani were not fully aware of the degree of Tarver's intoxication until after activating the pump. According to Drinnon, Tarver spoke normally, but, "when we seen him walk away,[we] could tell he was drunk." Drinnon pushed the correct button on the pump and then Thomas, the clerk behind the counter, activated the pump from inside the store which allowed the pump to operate. Tarver then apparently proceeded to operate the nozzle himself, obtaining the gasoline without any further assistance.

Tarver pumped three dollars worth of gasoline, got back into his vehicle, and prepared to leave. Drinnon and Armani watched as Tarver, without turning on his vehicle's headlights, drove off the parking lot and into the wrong lane of traffic . . . , traveling southbound in the northbound lane. . . .

. . . . Tarver managed to travel 2.8 miles from the convenience store before striking the plaintiffs' vehicle head-on. Both of the plaintiffs sustained serious injuries. . . .

During their ensuing investigation, the plaintiffs requested Dr. Jeffrey H. Hodgson, a mechanical engineering professor at the University of Tennessee, to examine the fuel tank of Tarver's vehicle. Based upon the results of his examination, Dr. Hodgson determined that at the time Tarver stopped at the defendant's store his vehicle contained only enough fuel to travel another 1.82 miles. Therefore, without the three dollars worth of gas he obtained at the store, Tarver would have "run out" of gasoline approximately one mile before reaching the accident scene.

On June 1, 2001, the plaintiffs filed suit alleging that the defendant's employees were negligent in selling gasoline to the visibly intoxicated Tarver and assisting him in pumping it into his vehicle. . . .

The defendant filed a motion for summary judgment. . . . Specifically, the defendant contended that it owed no duty of care to the plaintiffs while furnishing gasoline to Tarver and that its employees' actions were not a proximate cause of the accident. The defendant also argued that the tort of negligent entrustment was limited to situations involving a bailment and could not be applied to an outright sale of merchandise from a merchant to a customer. . . .

. . . [T]he trial court entered an order granting summary judgment in favor of the defendant on all three claims. . . . [T]he Court of Appeals affirmed the grant of summary judgment as to the . . . negligent entrustment [theory] of liability, but reversed the trial court on the negligence claim. . . .

We employ a balancing approach to assess whether the risk to the plaintiff is unreasonable and thus gives rise to a duty to act with due care. . . . This Court has held that a risk is unreasonable, "if the foreseeable probability and gravity of harm posed by defendant's conduct outweigh the burden upon defendant to engage in alternative conduct that would have prevented the harm." . . . .

. . . . In our view, the defendant misconstrues the plaintiffs' claims as being based upon a "special relationship" arising from the sale of gasoline to Mr. Tarver (the intoxicated driver). The plaintiffs' allegations do not revolve around any duty of the defendant to control the conduct of a customer. Instead, the claims are predicated on the defendant's employees' affirmative acts in contributing to the creation of a foreseeable and unreasonable risk of harm, *i.e.*, providing mobility to a drunk driver which he otherwise would not have had, thus creating a risk to persons on the roadways. . . .

. . . . Under the facts of this case, we conclude that the acts of the defendant in selling gasoline to an obviously intoxicated driver and/or assisting an obviously intoxicated driver in pumping gasoline into his vehicle created a foreseeable risk to persons on the roadways, including the plaintiffs. It is common knowledge that drunk driving directly results in accidents, injuries, and deaths. As to the possible magnitude of the potential harm posed to the plaintiff, we again need look no further than to the frequency and severity of injuries caused by drunken driving. . . .

We next examine the feasibility of alternative, safer conduct and the burdens associated with such alternative conduct. A safer alternative was readily available and easily feasible — simply refusing to sell gasoline to an obviously intoxicated driver. The clerk at the defendant's store had already refused to sell beer to Mr. Tarver. . . . The relative usefulness and safety of this alternative conduct is obvious. All reasonable persons recognize that refraining from selling gasoline to or assisting intoxicated persons in pumping it into their vehicles will lead to safer roadways.

. . . [W]e conclude that a convenience store employee owes a duty of reasonable care to persons on the roadways, including the plaintiffs, not to sell gasoline to a person whom the employee knows (or reasonably ought to know) to be intoxicated and to be the driver of the motor vehicle. Similarly, a convenience store employee also owes a duty of reasonable care not to assist in providing gasoline (in this case pumping the gasoline) to a person whom the employee knows (or reasonably ought to know) to be intoxicated and to be the driver of the motor vehicle. . . . [Foreseeability] is a question of fact for a jury. . . . We also hasten to point out, as did the Court of Appeals, that by our decision today we do not hold that convenience store employees have a duty to physically restrain or otherwise prevent intoxicated persons from driving.

. . . .

Our conclusion that the defendant owed a duty to the plaintiffs does not completely resolve this case. The plaintiffs at trial still bear the burden of proving the remaining elements of negligence: breach of duty, injury or loss, cause in fact, and proximate cause. . . .

For instance, the jury must determine whether, in consideration of all the facts and circumstances presented, the employees failed to exercise due care resulting in a breach of their duty of care. . . . Another question of fact for the jury is whether the employees' actions can be attributed to the defendant, thus making the defendant vicariously liable for the employees' alleged negligence. . . . Furthermore, the plaintiffs must show that the defendant's employees' acts were the cause in fact of their injuries. While the affidavit from Dr. Hodgson provides probative evidence on this point, the credibility of the witness, the weight given to his testimony and whether this evidence establishes cause in fact are all issues for the jury.

The final element the plaintiffs must prove is proximate cause. . . .

The defendant argues that its employees' actions were not the proximate cause of the plaintiffs' injuries; rather, the injuries were caused solely by the actions of Mr. Tarver. The defendant asserts that its connection to the accident is so tenuous that proximate cause simply does not apply. We note however, "[t]here is no requirement that a cause, to be regarded as the proximate cause of an injury, be the sole cause, the last act, or the one nearest to the injury, provided it is a substantial factor in producing the end result." . . . .

[The court further concluded that "that the plaintiffs have established a prima facie claim of negligent entrustment."]. . . . The judgment of the Court of Appeals on this issue is reversed.

. . . . [T]he judgment of the Court of Appeals is affirmed in part and reversed in part, and the case is remanded. . . .

Notes

1. ***Other Precedent.*** *Compare West with* Moranko v. Downs Racing LP, 118 A.3d 1111 (Pa. Super. 2015). In *Moranko*, the court held, as a matter of first impression, in a wrongful death and survival action arising from a driver's death, that a casino's valet parking service did not have a duty to withhold the driver's automobile keys from him when he was allegedly visibly intoxicated. The court emphasized that the car belonged to the driver and that the case did not involve a claim by a third party injured by the driver.

2. ***Entrustment.*** McKenna v. Straughan, 222 Cal. Rptr. 462 (Ct. App. 1986), *supra* at p. 562, was a case in which furnishing an alcoholic with a car gave rise to an action by a third person based on negligent entrustment. In some jurisdictions, liability under that theory may even extend to cases involving injuries to the person to whom the car was entrusted, and not just to third persons. *See* Casebolt v. Cowan, 829 P.2d 352 (Colo. 1992); *but see* Anderson v. Miller, 559 N.W.2d 29 (Iowa

1997) (concluding that an estate could not recover for entrustment of a vehicle to a drunken driver if the decedent was the driver).

3. ***Assumed Duty and Special Relationship.*** Other possible bases for liability are voluntary assumption of duty or special relationship (*see* Chapter 9), although the cases are disturbingly inconsistent. *Compare* Gushlaw v. Milner, 42 A.3d 1245 (R.I. 2012) (holding that the driver of a motor vehicle, who was an adult but underage drinker, did not have a duty to protect third parties from the tortious conduct of an intoxicated individual, another adult but underage drinker, whom the driver had transported to his parked car), *and* McGee v. Chalfant, 806 P.2d 980 (Kan. 1991) (similar), *with* Leppke v. Segura, 632 P.2d 1057 (Colo. Ct. App. 1981) (imposing liability for jump-starting an intoxicated patron's car), *and* Venetoulias v. O'Brien, 909 S.W.2d 236 (Tex. Ct. App. 1995) (holding that the owner of a bar assumed a duty of care by inducing a patron to drink, taking her keys, and promising to provide a ride).

In Bell v. Hutsell, 955 N.E.2d 1099 (Ill. 2011), the court held that homeowners were not liable for a fatal single-car accident involving an underage guest who became intoxicated at a party at their home. The court rejected an assumed-duty argument, stating:

> [D]efendants' intention to prohibit underage possession and consumption of alcoholic beverages was expressed only to their son, Jonathan. There is no allegation that Jonathan communicated defendants' intention to anyone else. Thus, there are no facts alleged in the complaint that would support an inference of reliance or change of position on the part of any guests attending the party or, for that matter, any "other" person owing them some unarticulated, undefined duty. . . .

4. ***Duties of Employers.*** In Otis Engineering Corp. v. Clark, 668 S.W.2d 307 (Tex. 1983), the court allowed a suit against an employer for injuries sustained by third parties in a highway accident caused by an employee who was sent home drunk. "[W]hen, because of an employee's incapacity, an employer exercises control over the employee, the employer has a duty" to exercise reasonable care to prevent the employee from causing harm to third persons. There was evidence that the employer, having decided to remove the intoxicated employee from the workplace, had alternatives other than to allow the worker to drive home. For example, the employer could have had the employee wait at the nurse's station until he was sober, or could have called the employee's family to come and take him home.

The ruling in *Otis* addressed an employer's liability for allegedly negligent exercise of control. What if an employer *fails* to exercise control? The answer will depend, at least in part, on what is foreseeable. *Compare* Carroll Air Systems, Inc. v. Greenbaum, 629 So. 2d 914 (Fla. Dist. Ct. App. 1993) (a statute barring liability of one who furnishes alcoholic beverages to a person of lawful drinking age did not preclude an employer from being held liable for punitive damages where its fault was not in the furnishing of drinks, but in not preventing an employee from driving away from a meeting in an intoxicated condition), *with* Duge v. Union Pac. R. Co., 71 S.W.3d 358

(Tex. App. 2001) (holding that an employer had no duty to control the actions of an employee who, after being on the job for 27 hours, caused an accident after leaving the workplace because there was "no indication" that the worker was fatigued).

5. ***Public Duty.*** A municipality may be liable for the negligent failure of its police officers to remove from the highway an intoxicated motorist who subsequently causes injuries to other travelers. *See* Irwin v. Town of Ware, 467 N.E.2d 1292 (Mass. 1984). However, in many states, there is ordinarily no cause of action for harm resulting from negligently deficient police protection. *See* Chapter 9 (discussing the public-duty rule) and Chapter 18 (discussing governmental immunities and the discretionary-function rule).

6. ***Intentional Torts.*** A recipient of alcohol (or the recipient's survivors) may also be able to state a claim for battery. *See* Davies v. Butler, 602 P.2d 605 (Nev. 1979), *supra* at p. 150.

7. ***Respondeat Superior.*** An employer may be held liable for drunk driving by an employee within the scope of employment. *See* Hicks v. Korean Airlines Co., 936 N.E.2d 1144 (Ill. Ct. App. 2010) (holding that the state dram shop law did not preempt a claim that an employer was vicariously liable for an employee's intoxicated driving).

8. ***Taking Charge of an Intoxicated Person.*** Garofalo v. Lambda Chi Alpha Frat., 616 N.W.2d 647 (Iowa 2000), suggests that it will be difficult to establish liability for alcohol-related injuries based on "taking charge" of an intoxicated person. In *Garofalo*, a pledge died after consuming excessive quantities of beer and hard liquor. His parents brought a wrongful death action that included claims against a fraternity member who permitted the pledge to lie down on the couch in his room to "sleep it off." The court wrote:

> Reier was not responsible for Garofalo's intoxication. He was not his "big brother." He merely let Garofalo "sleep it off" on his couch. Even if these facts could be stretched to fit the notion of "taking charge," Reier's conduct reveals no breach of that duty. When he left the fraternity house at midnight, Garofalo was intoxicated but conscious. When Reier returned to his room at 3:00 a.m., Garofalo was asleep and snoring. Reier repositioned him on his side, mindful for his safety. When he hurried out the door for an 8:30 a.m. class, Reier glanced at Garofalo, assumed he was asleep and made no attempt to awaken or "revive" him. Although appellants fault this latter omission, we believe the standard urged by appellants is substantially higher than what is required under the Restatement. . . .[2] Given the

---

2. Restatement, Second, of Torts § 324 provides:

One who, being under no duty to do so, takes charge of another who is helpless adequately to aid or protect himself is subject to liability to the other for any bodily harm caused to him by

(a) the failure of the actor to exercise reasonable care to secure the safety of the other while within the actor's charge, or

> gratuitous nature of the undertaking, the rule requires only acting in "good faith and with common decency." . . . .

Compare Garofalo with Wakulich v. Mraz, 785 N.E.2d 843 (Ill. 2003). *Wakulich* held that a complaint by the mother of a 16-year-old girl, who died after drinking a quart of alcohol at the goading of the defendants, stated a cause of action for negligent performance of a voluntary undertaking. The complaint alleged that, after the guest became unconscious, the social hosts placed her in the family room, observed her vomiting profusely, checked on her periodically, did not seek medical attention, and refused to drive her home or to the hospital.

9. ***Drinking and Intentional Torts.*** Fights are a fairly common result of excessive drinking. The victim of an attack by an intoxicated person almost always has a decent battery action, but this action will not do the victim much good if the defendant is judgment-proof. Many otherwise judgment-proof defendants have liability insurance, but that kind of insurance almost always excludes coverage for injuries intentionally inflicted by the insured. In Saba v. Darling, 575 A.2d 1240 (Md. Ct. Spec. App. 1990), the plaintiff dismissed his battery claim after learning that the defendant's insurance would not cover damages for an intentional tort and argued that he had been injured by the defendant's negligence in drinking heavily, as it was foreseeable that heavy drinking could lead to violence. The defendant admitted to a history of fighting when under the influence of alcohol. The court, without much analysis, held that the defendant's conduct, an intentional tort, could not be the subject of a negligence action.

(b) the actor's discontinuing his aid or protection, if by so doing he leaves the other in a worse position than when the actor took charge of him.

Chapter 13

Torts Involving Conception, Pregnancy, Birth, and Adoption

This chapter examines the important, but somewhat confusing, array of tort actions having to do with the birth or adoption of children. Actions relating to unborn children include suits for personal injuries suffered by children prior to birth and for the wrongful death of unborn children. They also include actions for "unwanted pregnancy," in cases of negligence resulting in failed contraception, and for "wrongful birth" and "wrongful life," in cases of negligence which deprives parents of information relevant to abortion of a deformed or impaired fetus. Injuries to unborn children are often accompanied by physical harm to the mother or emotional or economic harm to both parents: these claims will also be discussed.

In considering the cases that follow, it is important to pay close attention to:

(1) who is suing (is the action brought on behalf of the child or by the parents on their own behalf?);

(2) what damages the plaintiff seeks (*e.g.*, costs of medical care, compensation for emotional suffering, or expenses of rearing an unwanted child); and

(3) whether the defendant is alleged to have affirmatively inflicted harm on the child (*e.g.*, by causing a collision with a pregnant woman's vehicle) or deprived the parents of their right not to have children (*e.g.*, through nondisclosure of information relevant to an abortion decision).

Once these matters are clear, it is possible to locate a given set of facts within one or more of the actions dealing with unborn children.

A. Unwanted Pregnancy

McKernan v. Aasheim

Supreme Court of Washington, En Banc
687 P.2d 850 (Wash. 1984)

DIMMICK, Justice.

... Dr. Glen Aasheim performed a sterilization operation known as a tubal ligation upon Karen McKernan. Despite the operation, Karen became pregnant and gave birth to a healthy, normal child.... Karen and her husband James McKernan filed the present lawsuit, alleging [in part] that Dr. Aasheim performed the tubal ligation negligently.... They alleged the following damages:

> an amount equal to the cost of the tubal ligation procedure, and expenses; an amount equal to the cost of the pregnancy and child birth; an amount for pain and suffering associated with the tubal ligation, pregnancy and child birth; an amount for loss of pleasure associated with the tubal ligation, pregnancy and child birth; an amount for the husband's loss of services and consortium associated with the tubal ligation, pregnancy and child birth; *an amount equal to the costs associated with rearing a child, college education, out of pocket expenses and services of parents, and emotional burdens.*

(Italics ours.)

Dr. Aasheim moved for partial summary judgment dismissing that portion of the McKernans' complaint which sought damages for the cost of rearing and educating a normal, healthy child. The trial court granted the motion....

Turning to cases from other jurisdictions, we discover the vast majority of courts have held that no damages may be recovered for the cost of rearing and educating a healthy, normal child born as the result of medical malpractice....

These courts have denied recovery of child-rearing costs for a variety of reasons. Many hold that the benefits of joy, companionship, and affection which a healthy child can provide outweigh the costs of rearing that child.... This view was well expressed in Public Health Trust v. Brown, [388 So. 2d 1084, 1085–86 (Fla. Dist. Ct. App. 1980)]:

> ... [A] parent cannot be said to have been damaged by the birth and rearing of a normal, healthy child ... [I]t is a matter of universally-shared emotion and sentiment that the intangible but all-important, incalculable but invaluable "benefits" of parenthood far outweigh any of the mere monetary burdens involved. Speaking legally, this may be deemed conclusively presumed by the fact that a prospective parent does not abort or subsequently place the "unwanted" child for adoption. On a more practical level, the validity of the principle may be tested simply by asking any parent the purchase price for that particular youngster....

Another common rationale is that recovery of child-rearing costs would be a windfall to the parents and an unreasonable burden on the negligent health care provider.... The Wisconsin Supreme Court put it this way:

> To permit the parents to keep their child and shift the entire cost of its upbringing to a physician who failed to determine or inform them of the fact of pregnancy would be to create a new category of surrogate parent. Every child's smile, every bond of love and affection, every reason for parental pride in a child's achievements, every contribution by the child to the welfare and well-being of the family and parents, is to remain with the mother and father.... On the other hand, every financial cost ... including the costs of food, clothing and education ... would be shifted to the physician who allegedly failed to timely diagnose the fact of pregnancy. We hold that such result would be wholly out of proportion to the culpability involved....

Rieck v. Medical Protective Co., 219 N.W.2d 242 (Wis. 1974).

Still other courts have denied recovery in order to protect the psyche of the child who is the subject of the action:

> Another problem is the possible harm that can be caused to the unwanted child who will one day learn that he not only was not wanted by his or her parents, but was reared by funds supplied by another person. Some authors have referred to such a child as an "emotional bastard" in a realistic, but harsh, attempt to describe the stigma that will attach to him once he learns the true circumstances of his upbringing.

Boone v. Mullendore, *supra* [416 So. 2d 718, 722 (Ala. 1982)]....

Other reasons for denying recovery of child-rearing costs include the speculative nature of the damages ... and the possibility of fraudulent claims....

A minority line of authority permits recovery of the costs of rearing and educating a healthy, normal child. However, only Ohio currently permits full recovery. Bowman v. Davis, 48 Ohio St. 2d 41, 356 N.E.2d 496 (1976). Other courts allow the parents' damage award to be reduced by the value of the benefits conferred by the parent-child relationship....

Courts adopting the "benefits" rule reject the majority rationale that a healthy, normal child is always more benefit than burden. To hold that the birth of a child can never be an injury, they reason, ignores the fact that millions of persons utilize contraceptive devices and methods for the very purpose of avoiding the birth of a child.... Moreover, they note, an individual has a constitutional right to use contraceptive devices and methods to limit the size of his or her family.... Complete denial of child-rearing costs on the theory that the birth of a healthy, normal child can never be an injury would, therefore, impair the parents' constitutional right to forego reproduction....

Another rationale for allowing recovery of child-rearing costs is the perceived need to apply strictly that rule of tort law which holds a tortfeasor liable for all damages which he caused.... At the same time, however, those courts which have adopted the "benefits" rule have refused to apply the avoidable consequences doctrine, holding that both abortion and adoption are unreasonable means of avoiding or minimizing child-rearing damages, as a matter of law.... *But cf.* Sorkin v. Lee, 78 A.D.2d 180, 181–82, 434 N.Y.S.2d 300 (1980) (denying child-rearing costs where parents failed to mitigate damages by obtaining abortion).

To recover under the "benefits" rule, the parents of the unplanned child must prove to the jury that the cost of rearing the child outweighs the benefits of parenthood....

We find some of the above cited reasons for denying recovery of child-rearing costs unpersuasive. To begin with, we cannot agree that the benefits of parenthood always outweigh the costs of rearing a child.... If such were the case, presumably no sterilization operations would be performed. Second, we do not think that recovery may be denied in order to avoid placing an "unreasonable" burden upon health care providers.... It is not our place to deny recovery of certain damages merely in order to insulate health care providers from the shock of big tort judgments. Third, the possibility that some parents might bring fraudulent claims is not a sufficient basis for denying recovery.... We will not presuppose that courts are so ineffectual and the jury system so imperfect that fraudulent claims cannot be distinguished from the legitimate....

Nevertheless, we are convinced that recovery of child-rearing costs must be denied on other grounds.... [W]hen a parent comes before a court alleging that he or she was damaged by the unplanned birth of a child, the only logical method of determining whether such damage has occurred would be to weigh child-rearing costs against the benefits of parenthood. This, of course, is what the "benefits" rule purports to do.

After careful consideration, however, we have come to the conclusion that the "benefits" rule cannot be applied in this state.... [D]amages may not be recovered unless they are established with reasonable certainty.... Perhaps the costs of rearing and educating the child could be determined through use of actuarial tables or similar economic information. But whether these costs are outweighed by the emotional benefits which will be conferred by that child cannot be calculated. The child may turn out to be loving, obedient and attentive, or hostile, unruly and callous. The child may grow up to be President of the United States, or to be an infamous criminal. In short, it is impossible to tell, at an early stage in the child's life, whether its parents have sustained a net loss or net gain.

....

We base our holding that child-rearing costs may not be recovered on yet another ground. Under the "benefits" rule, parents would be obliged to prove their child was more trouble than it was worth. As one court noted:

> an unhandsome, colicky, or otherwise "undesirable" child would provide fewer offsetting benefits, and would therefore presumably be worth more

> monetarily in a "wrongful birth" case. The adoption of that rule would thus engender the unseemly spectacle of parents disparaging the "value" of their children or the degree of their affection for them in open court.... [S]uch a result cannot be countenanced.

....

Moreover, even if the "benefits" rule were not applied, and parents allowed to sue for the full cost of rearing their unplanned child, the simple fact that the parents saw fit to allege their child as a "damage" to them would carry with it the possibility of emotional harm to the child. We are not willing to sweep this ugly possibility under the rug by stating that the parents must be the one to decide whether to risk the emotional well being of their unplanned child.... We therefore hold that to permit recovery of child-rearing costs would violate the public policy of this state. In so holding, we adopt the reasoning of the Arkansas Supreme Court:

> .... Litigation cannot answer every question; every question cannot be answered in terms of dollars and cents. We are also convinced that the damage to the child will be significant; that being an unwanted or "emotional bastard," who will someday learn that its parents did not want it and, in fact, went to court to force someone else to pay for its raising, will be harmful to that child. It will undermine society's need for a strong and healthy family relationship. We have not become so sophisticated a society to dismiss that emotional trauma as nonsense.

Wilbur v. Kerr, 275 Ark. 239, 243–44, 628 S.W.2d 568 (1982).

.... This does not mean, however, that health care providers are immunized from all liability resulting from unsuccessful sterilization operations. The McKernans have alleged damages for the expense, pain and suffering, and loss of consortium associated with the failed tubal ligation, pregnancy and childbirth. Dr. Aasheim has conceded in his brief that these damages, if proven, may be recovered.... We find that these damages may be established with reasonable certainty, and do not invite disparagement of the child involved. Therefore, we agree that they may be recovered if proven.

Affirmed.

Notes

1. ***Terminology.*** Cases like *McKernan*, in which the child is born healthy, are often called "unwanted pregnancy," "wrongful conception," or "wrongful pregnancy" cases. However, in some states, the claim is not a unique cause of action, but simply a form of medical malpractice.

2. ***Child-Rearing Costs.*** Courts remain deeply divided over whether child-rearing costs may be recovered in an unwanted pregnancy case. In Chaffee v. Seslar, 751 N.E.2d 773, 780 nn.7–9 (Ind. Ct. App. 2001), *rev'd* 786 N.E.2d 705 (Ind. 2003), the court summarized American law as follows:

> Four jurisdictions adhere to the full recovery rule. [California, New Mexico, Oregon, and Wisconsin.]. . . .
>
> Five jurisdictions subscribe to the benefits rule. [Arizona, Connecticut, Maryland, Massachusetts, and Minnesota]. . . .
>
> Thirty-one jurisdictions subscribe to the no recovery rule regarding child-rearing expenses, limiting recovery to pregnancy and child-bearing expenses. . . .

In *Chaffee*, the Indiana Supreme Court held that recoverable damages in connection with allegedly negligent sterilization may not include the ordinary costs of raising and educating a normal, healthy child.

Maine has a statute barring recovery of damages for the birth of a healthy child. The relevant section provides:

> No person may maintain a claim for relief or receive an award for damages based on the claim that the birth and rearing of a healthy child resulted in damages to him. A person may maintain a claim for relief based on a failed sterilization procedure resulting in the birth of a healthy child and receive an award of damages for the hospital and medical expenses incurred for the sterilization procedures and pregnancy, the pain and suffering connected with the pregnancy and the loss of earnings by the mother during pregnancy.

24 Maine Rev. Stat. Ann § 2931(2) (Westlaw 2022).

In Doherty v. Merck & Co., Inc., 154 A.3d 1202, 1208 (Me. 2017), the court noted that, "[c]ourts to the present day have continued to recognize the distinction between permanent sterilization and reversible contraception." The court held that the plaintiff's action based on the alleged failure of a manufacturer's birth control drug implant, which resulted in her becoming pregnant, was not an action for a failed "sterilization procedure," and thus not an action permitted under the failed sterilization procedure exception to Maine's statutory bar on actions for damages related to the birth of healthy children.

3. ***Birth Control Devices.*** *See* Miceli v. Ansell, Inc., 23 F. Supp. 2d 929 (N.D. Ind. 1998). In a suit by condom users against a condom manufacturer, alleging strict liability, negligence, and breach of warranty in connection with unwanted pregnancy, the court, addressing an issue of apparent first impression, held that pregnancy may constitute "harm" for purposes of Indiana's products liability statute.

4. ***Deception Relating to Paternity.*** Questions regarding damages can arise in a case where a former wife misrepresents to her former husband that he is the biological father of her child. In Day v. Heller, 653 N.W.2d 475 (Neb. 2002), the court held that public policy barred a former husband's claims for fraud, restitution, and intentional infliction of emotional distress. The court wrote:

> In effect, Robert is saying, "[Adam] . . . is not my son; I want my money back." Robert's fraud and assumpsit causes of action focus on the burdens of

> the parent-child relationship, while ignoring the benefits of the relationship. We do not believe that having a close and loving relationship "imposed" on one because of a misrepresentation of biological fatherhood is the type of "harm" that the law should attempt to remedy.

In addressing the intentional-infliction claim, which it rejected, the *Day* court noted that "other courts have reached conflicting conclusions. . . ."

Pressil v. Gibson, 477 S.W.3d 402, 408-10 (Tex. App. 2015), was a legal malpractice case arising from a medical malpractice case involving unwanted pregnancy. The plaintiff alleged that his former girlfriend surreptitiously arranged for a fertility clinic to impregnate her with sperm from his used condoms. The plaintiff claimed that but for his lawyers' negligence he would have won the underlying medical malpractice action against the clinic. However, in the subsequent suit, the court held that the legal malpractice claim failed because the plaintiff could not have proved damages in the earlier medical malpractice action. As the court explained:

> [I]n Texas, a plaintiff cannot recover damages related to the support and maintenance of a healthy child born as a result of the medical provider's negligence. . . .
>
> . . . [T]he measure of damages available to plaintiffs in wrongful pregnancy cases is limited to the medical expenses associated with the failed procedure that produced the healthy but unwanted child. . . .
>
> . . . Pressil [the plaintiff] did not request damages for the medical expenses associated with any medical procedure. Nor could he have; no medical procedure was performed on him. Moreover, the medical procedure performed on Burnette [plaintiff's former girlfriend] was apparently a rousing success, resulting in the birth of healthy twin boys. The only damages Pressil sought in the Fertility Lawsuit were costs generally associated with the support and maintenance of children, such as mental anguish, loss of opportunity, loss of enjoyment of life, child support, the cost of raising two children, lost earnings, and lost earning capacity. Under prevailing Texas law, none of these damages was recoverable.

B. Wrongful Birth and Wrongful Life

Smith v. Cote

Supreme Court of New Hampshire
513 A.2d 341 (N.H. 1986)

BATCHELDER, Justice.

.... Plaintiff Linda J. Smith became pregnant.... During the course of her pregnancy Linda was under the care of the defendants, physicians who specialize in obstetrics and gynecology....

Linda brought her pregnancy to full term.... [S]he gave birth to a daughter, Heather B. Smith, who is also a plaintiff in this action. Heather was born a victim of congenital rubella syndrome. Today, at age six, Heather suffers from bilateral cataracts, multiple congenital heart defects, motor retardation, and a significant hearing impairment. She is legally blind, and has undergone surgery for her cataracts and heart condition.

.... They allege that Linda contracted rubella early in her pregnancy and that, while she was under the defendants' care, the defendants negligently failed to test for and discover in a timely manner her exposure to the disease. The plaintiffs further contend that the defendants negligently failed to advise Linda of the potential for birth defects in a fetus exposed to rubella, thereby depriving her of the knowledge necessary to [make] an informed decision as to whether to give birth to a potentially impaired child....

The plaintiffs do not allege that the defendants caused Linda to conceive her child or to contract rubella, or that the defendants could have prevented the effects of the disease on the fetus. Rather, the plaintiffs contend that if Linda had known of the risks involved she would have obtained a eugenic abortion.

....

We recognize that the termination of pregnancy involves controversial and divisive social issues. Nonetheless, the Supreme Court of the United States has held that a woman has a constitutionally secured right to terminate a pregnancy. Roe v. Wade, [410 U.S. 113 (1973)].... Today we decide only whether, given the existence of the right of choice recognized in *Roe*, our common law should allow the development of a duty to exercise care in providing information that bears on that choice.

.... A wrongful birth claim is a claim brought by the parents of a child born with severe defects against a physician who negligently fails to inform them, in a timely fashion, of an increased possibility that the mother will give birth to such a child, thereby precluding an informed decision as to whether to have the child.... The parents typically claim damages for their emotional distress and for some or all of the costs of raising the child....

A wrongful life claim, on the other hand, is brought not by the parents of a child born with birth defects, but by or on behalf of the child. The child contends that the defendant physician negligently failed to inform the child's parents of the risk of bearing a defective infant, and hence prevented the parents from choosing to avoid the child's birth.... The child typically claims damages for the extraordinary medical, educational, and institutional costs that it will sustain....

I. Wrongful Birth: Cause of Action

We first must decide whether New Hampshire law recognizes a cause of action for wrongful birth. Although we have never expressly recognized this cause of action, we have considered a similar claim, one for "wrongful conception." In Kingsbury v. Smith, 122 N.H. 237, 442 A.2d 1003 (1982) ... [w]e held that the common law of New Hampshire permitted a claim for wrongful conception, an action "for damages arising from the birth of a child to which a negligently performed sterilization procedure or a negligently filled birth control prescription which fails to prevent conception was a contributing factor." .... We reasoned that failure to recognize a cause of action for wrongful conception would leave "a void in the area of recovery for medical malpractice" that would dilute the standard of professional conduct in the area of family planning....

In this case, the mother contends that her wrongful birth claim fits comfortably within the framework established in *Kingsbury* and is consistent with well established tort principles. The defendants argue that tort principles cannot be extended so as to accommodate wrongful birth, asserting that they did not cause the injury alleged here, and that in any case damages cannot be fairly and accurately ascertained.

The action for wrongful birth occupies a relatively recent place in the history of tort law. Gleitman v. Cosgrove, 49 N.J. 22, 227 A.2d 689 (1967), is the "fountainhead" for debate in cases of this type.... Like the instant case, *Gleitman* involved claims for wrongful birth and wrongful life arising out of the birth of a child suffering from congenital rubella syndrome....

The trial judge dismissed both the wrongful life and the wrongful birth complaints, and the Supreme Court of New Jersey affirmed. The court first disposed of the child's wrongful life claim, holding that the conduct complained of did not give rise to damages cognizable at law. The court explained that it was legally impossible to weigh "the value of life with impairments against the nonexistence of life itself." .... Turning to the parents' wrongful birth claim, the court emphasized the analytical difficulty posed by the dual character of the consequences of the defendants' alleged negligence. On the one hand, the defendants arguably had caused the plaintiffs to incur child rearing costs and to undergo emotional distress. On the other, the birth of the child had conferred the intangible benefits of parenthood on the plaintiffs. The court found that this difficulty made it impossible to determine compensatory damages....

The *Gleitman* court also was troubled by the policy implications of recognizing a cause of action for wrongful birth. According to the court, the parents' complaint sought damages for "the denial of the opportunity to take an embryonic life." ....

The court reasoned that to allow such a claim would be to deny the "sanctity of the single human life," *id.*, and that the child's right to live exceeded and precluded the parents' right not to endure financial and emotional injury.... The court concluded that the wrongful birth complaint was not actionable because the defendants' conduct did not give rise to damages cognizable at law, and that, even if such damages were cognizable, the "countervailing public policy supporting the preciousness of human life" precluded the claim. *Id.*

Gleitman's influence in wrongful birth cases has considerably diminished during the past two decades.... In 1979 the Supreme Court of New Jersey overruled *Gleitman* on the issue of wrongful birth. *See* Berman v. Allan, 80 N.J. 421, 404 A.2d 8 (1979). Today there is "quite general agreement" that some recovery should be permitted in wrongful birth cases....

Two developments help explain the trend toward judicial acceptance of wrongful birth actions. The first is the increased ability of health care professionals to predict and detect the presence of fetal defects. Science's improved capacity to assess risk factors in pregnant women, as well as the development of "sophisticated biochemical and cytogenic tests for assaying amniotic fluid and maternal and fetal blood," have greatly enhanced the importance of reproductive counseling....

Roe v. Wade, 410 U.S. 113 (1973), and its progeny constitute the second development explaining the acceptance of wrongful birth actions.... In *Roe* the Supreme Court held that the constitutional right of privacy encompasses a woman's decision whether to undergo an abortion.... During the first trimester of her pregnancy, a woman may make this decision as she sees fit, free from State interference.... [W]e believe that *Roe* is controlling; we do not hold that our decision would be the same in its absence.

.... Today, as a result of *Roe* and the advances of science, it is possible for prospective parents (1) to know, well in advance of birth, of the risk or presence of congenital defects in the fetus they have conceived; and (2) to decide to terminate the pregnancy on the basis of this knowledge....

With this background in mind, we turn to the first issue before us: whether New Hampshire recognizes a cause of action for wrongful birth....

The first two elements of a negligence action, duty and breach, present no conceptual difficulties here. If the plaintiff establishes that a physician-patient relationship with respect to the pregnancy existed between the defendants and her, it follows that the defendants assumed a duty to use reasonable care in attending and treating her.... Given the decision in Roe v. Wade, we recognize that the "due care" standard ... may have required the defendants to ensure that Linda had an opportunity to make an informed decision regarding the procreative options available to her.... It is a question of fact whether this standard required the defendants, at an appropriate stage of Linda's pregnancy, to test for, diagnose, and disclose her exposure to rubella.... If (1) the applicable standard of care required the defendants to test for and diagnose Linda's rubella infection in a timely manner, and to inform her of the possible effects of the virus on her child's health; and (2) the defendants failed to fulfill this obligation; then the defendants breached their duty of due care.

The third element [of a negligence action], causation, is only slightly more troublesome. The defendants point out that proof that they caused the alleged injury depends on a finding that Linda would have chosen to terminate her pregnancy if she had been fully apprised of the risks of birth defects. The defendants argue that this hypothetical chain of events is too remote to provide the basis for a finding of causation.

We do not agree. No logical obstacle precludes proof of causation in the instant case. Such proof is furnished if the plaintiff can show that, but for the defendants' negligent failure to inform her of the risks of bearing a child with birth defects, she would have obtained an abortion. . . .

We turn to the final element of a negligence action, injury. . . .

. . . . We have long held that difficulty in calculating damages is not a sufficient reason to deny recovery to an injured party. . . . Other courts have recognized that the complexity of the damages calculation in a wrongful birth case is not directly relevant to the validity of the asserted cause of action. . . .

We hold that New Hampshire recognizes a cause of action for wrongful birth. Notwithstanding the disparate views within society on the controversial practice of abortion, we are bound by the law that protects a woman's right to choose to terminate her pregnancy. Our holding today neither encourages nor discourages this practice. . . . We must . . . do our best to effectuate the first principles of our law of negligence: to deter negligent conduct, and to compensate the victims of those who act unreasonably.

II. Wrongful Birth: Damages

We next must decide what elements of damages may be recovered in a wrongful birth action. . . .

A. Tangible Losses

The usual rule of compensatory damages in tort cases requires that the person wronged receive a sum of money that will restore him as nearly as possible to the position he would have been in if the wrong had not been committed. . . . In the present case, if the defendants' failure to advise Linda of the risks of birth defects amounted to negligence, then the reasonably foreseeable result of that negligence was that Linda would incur the expenses involved in raising her daughter. According to the usual rule of damages, then, Linda should recover the entire cost of raising Heather, including both ordinary child-rearing costs and the extraordinary costs attributable to Heather's condition.

However, "few if any jurisdictions appear ready to apply this traditional rule of damages with full vigor in wrongful birth cases." . . . . A special rule of damages has emerged; in most jurisdictions the parents may recover only the extraordinary medical and educational costs attributable to the birth defects. . . . In the present case, in accordance with the rule prevailing elsewhere, Linda seeks to recover, as tangible losses, only her extraordinary costs.

The logic of the "extraordinary costs" rule has been criticized.... The rule in effect divides a plaintiff's pecuniary losses into two categories, ordinary costs and extraordinary costs, and treats the latter category as compensable while ignoring the former category. At first glance, this bifurcation seems difficult to justify.

The disparity is explained, however, by reference to the rule requiring mitigation of tort damages. The "avoidable consequences" rule ... specifies that a plaintiff may not recover damages for "any harm that he could have avoided by the use of reasonable effort or expenditure" after the occurrence of the tort. Rigidly applied, this rule would appear to require wrongful birth plaintiffs to place their children for adoption.... Because of our profound respect for the sanctity of the family, ... we are loathe to sanction the application of the rule in these circumstances. If the rule is not applied, however, wrongful birth plaintiffs may receive windfalls. Hence, a special rule limiting recovery of damages is warranted.

Although the extraordinary costs rule departs from traditional principles of tort damages, it is neither illogical nor unprecedented. The rule represents an application in a tort context of the expectancy rule of damages employed in breach of contracts cases. Wrongful birth plaintiffs typically desire a child (and plan to support it) from the outset.... It is the defendants' duty to help them achieve this goal. When the plaintiffs' expectations are frustrated by the defendants' negligence, the extraordinary costs rule "merely attempts to put plaintiffs in the position they *expected* to be in with defendant's help." ....

.... Accordingly, we hold that a plaintiff in a wrongful birth case may recover the extraordinary medical and educational costs attributable to the child's deformities, but may not recover ordinary child-raising costs.

Three points stand in need of clarification. First, parents may recover extraordinary costs incurred both before and after their child attains majority. Some courts do not permit recovery of postmajority expenses, on the theory that the parents' obligation of support terminates when the child reaches twenty-one.... In New Hampshire, however, parents are required to support their disabled adult offspring....

Second, ... [o]ne court has ruled that parents "cannot recover for services that they have rendered or will render personally to their own child without incurring financial expense." .... We see no reason, however, to treat as noncompensable the burdens imposed on a parent who must devote extraordinary time and effort to caring for a child with birth defects.... We hold that a parent may recover for his or her ministrations to his or her child to the extent that such ministrations:

(1) are made necessary by the child's condition;

(2) clearly exceed those ordinarily rendered by parents of a normal child; and

(3) are reasonably susceptible of valuation....

Third, to the extent that the parent's alleged emotional distress results in tangible pecuniary losses, such as medical expenses or counseling fees, such losses are recoverable. . . .

B. Intangible Losses

Existing damages principles do not resolve the issue whether recovery for emotional distress should be permitted in wrongful birth cases. Emotional distress damages are not uniformly recoverable once a protected interest is shown to have been invaded. . . .

[The court discussed cases which illustrated judicial] . . . reluctance to permit parents of children injured or killed as a result of negligent conduct to recover for their consequent emotional distress. . . . This reluctance . . . [is] founded . . . on a practical consideration: the need to establish a clearly defined limit to the scope of negligence liability in this area. . . .

We also harbor concerns of proportionality. . . . We already have held that a wrongful birth defendant is liable for the pecuniary losses incurred by the parents. Were we additionally to impose liability for parents' emotional distress, we would run the risk of penalizing and overdeterring merely negligent conduct.

We hold that damages for emotional distress are not recoverable in wrongful birth actions. . . .

III. Wrongful Life

The theory of Heather's wrongful life action is as follows: during Linda's pregnancy the defendants owed a duty of care to both Linda and Heather. The defendants breached this duty when they failed to discover Linda's exposure to rubella and failed to advise her of the possible effects of that exposure on her child's health. Had Linda been properly informed, she would have undergone an abortion, and Heather would not have been born. Because Linda was not so informed, Heather must bear the burden of her afflictions for the rest of her life. The defendants' conduct is thus the proximate cause of injury to Heather.

This theory presents a crucial problem, however: the question of injury. . . . In order to recognize Heather's wrongful life action . . . we must determine that the fetal Heather had an interest in avoiding her own birth, that it would have been best *for Heather* if she had not been born.

This premise of the wrongful life action — that the plaintiff's own birth and suffering constitute legal injury — has caused many courts to decline to recognize the claim. . . . As one court has written,

> [w]hether it is better never to have been born at all than to have been born with even gross deficiencies is a mystery more properly to be left to the philosophers and the theologians. Surely the law can assert no competence to resolve the issue. . . .

Moreover, compelling policy reasons militate against recognition of wrongful life claims. The first such reason is our conviction that the courts of this State should not become involved in deciding whether a given person's life is or is not worthwhile. . . .

Our reluctance to decide whether Heather's birth constitutes an injury is not diminished by the evolving "right to die" doctrine. . . . In a right to die case a court may act to protect an individual's right to choose between a natural death and the prolongation of his life by means of extraordinary medical procedures. The court avoids making an objective judgment as to the value of the plaintiff's life; it strives, instead, to protect the individual's subjective will. . . .

The same cannot be said of wrongful life cases. . . . Simply put, the judiciary has an important role to play in protecting the privacy rights of the dying. It has no business declaring that among the living are people who never should have been born.

The second policy reason militating against recognition of Heather's claim is related to the first.

> [L]egal recognition that a disabled life is an injury would harm the interests of those most directly concerned, the handicapped. . . . To characterize the life of a disabled person as an injury would denigrate . . . the handicapped themselves. . . .

The third reason stems from an acknowledgment of the limitations of tort law and the adjudicative process. . . .

In deciding whether to recognize a new tort cause of action, we must consider the "defendant's interest in avoiding an incorrect judgment of liability because of the court's incompetence to determine certain questions raised by application of the announced standard." . . . . Wrongful life claims present problems that cannot be resolved in a "reasonably sensible, even-handed, and fair" manner from case to case. . . . As Chief Justice Weintraub of the Supreme Court of New Jersey recognized nearly twenty years ago, "[t]o recognize a right not to be born is to enter an area in which no one could find his way." . . . .

We decline to recognize a cause of action for wrongful life.

. . . .

Remanded.

KING, C.J., did not sit; SOUTER, J., concurred specially; the others concurred.

SOUTER, Justice, concurring:

. . . . The trial court did not ask whether, or how, a physician with conscientious scruples against abortion, and the testing and counselling that may inform an abortion decision, can discharge his professional obligation without engaging in procedures that his religious or moral principles condemn. To say nothing about this issue could lead to misunderstanding.

. . . I do not understand the court to hold, that a physician can discharge the obligation of due care in such circumstances only by personally ordering such tests and rendering such advice. The court does not hold that some or all physicians must make a choice between rendering services that they morally condemn and leaving their profession in order to escape malpractice exposure. The defensive significance, for example, of timely disclosure of professional limits based on religious or moral scruples, combined with timely referral to other physicians who are not so constrained, is a question open for consideration in any case in which it may be raised....

Notes

1. ***Terminology.*** The distinction between the child's claim and the parents' claim is well established, though not all writers are as careful as the *Smith* court in giving these actions the distinct but misleadingly similar names of "wrongful birth" and "wrongful life."

2. ***Wrongful Birth.*** In wrongful-birth cases, courts often differ as to the elements of damages that may be recovered. *See* Greco v. United States, 893 P.2d 345 (Nev. 1995) (allowing recovery of damages for future extraordinary medical, therapeutic, and custodial costs associated with the child and for emotional damages, but not for loss of companionship); Keel v. Banach, 624 So. 2d 1022 (Ala. 1993) (defining compensable losses to include any medical and hospital expenses incurred as a result of the physician's negligence, physical pain suffered by the mother, loss of consortium, and mental and emotional anguish of the parents). In Tillman v. Goodpasture, 485 P.3d 656 (Kan. 2021), the court held that a statute abolishing wrongful birth causes of action did not violate the plaintiff's rights under the State Constitution.

3. ***Treating Wrongful Birth as Medical Malpractice.*** Some courts have rejected the term "wrongful birth" and treat such claims as just another form of medical malpractice. *See* Bader v. Johnson, 732 N.E.2d 1212 (Ind. 2000). In *Bader*, a physician had failed to inform parents of the results of an ultrasound test that revealed that a fetus would be born with serious birth defects. The court held that the parents stated a cause of action for medical malpractice based on loss of the opportunity and ability to terminate the pregnancy. The court held that the parents could recover (1) hospital and related medical expenses associated with the pregnancy and delivery, (2) costs associated with providing the infant with care and treatment until the child's death at four months of age, (3) lost income, and (4) loss of consortium. However, under Indiana's modified "impact rule" (*see* Chapter 11), only the mother was permitted to recover emotional-distress damages...." The father was "at most... a relative bystander," and therefore not allowed to recover for his emotional distress.

4. ***Causation in Wrongful Birth Cases.*** In Provenzano v. Integrated Genetics, 22 F. Supp. 2d 406 (D. N.J. 1998), the court took a special approach to dealing with the causation requirement. It held that, under New Jersey law, the issue of proximate causation in wrongful birth cases does not conclusively depend upon whether the parents would have aborted a fetus with a birth defect, had they been advised of their option to do so. Rather, proximate cause may be established by evidence demonstrating that the defendant's negligence deprived the parents of their right to accept or reject a parental relationship. Could this approach be endorsed by a

jurisdiction which has rejected the loss-of-a-chance rule in medical malpractice cases? *See* Chapter 7.

5. ***Wrongful Life.*** In Kassama v. Magat, 792 A.2d 1102, 1116–17 (Md. 2002), the court refused to permit a wrongful life claim and summarized the law in other jurisdictions as follows:

> It appears, at this point, that 28 States deny recovery for this kind of action—18 by case law, 10 by statute—but that three, California, New Jersey, and Washington, provide for a limited recovery.

6. ***No Right to be Born Defect Free.*** Paretta v. Medical Officers for Human Reproduction, 760 N.Y.S.2d 639 (Sup. Ct. 2003), was a medical malpractice action alleging that a physician who performed in-vitro fertilization failed to test the egg donor or the father for cystic fibrosis. The court agreed that the claim on behalf of the child was not one for wrongful life because "[h]ere, by contrast, the Parettas maintain that the defendant doctors were actually responsible for Theresa's conception, had a role in her genetic composition, and combined the sperm and egg both of which carried cystic fibrosis." Nonetheless, the court concluded:

> Theresa, ... like any other baby, does not have a protected right to be born free of genetic defects. A conclusion to the contrary, permitting infants to recover against doctors for wrongs allegedly committed during in-vitro fertilization, would give children conceived with the help of modern medical technology more rights and expectations than children conceived without medical assistance. The law does not recognize such a distinction and neither will this Court.

7. ***Wrongful Life and Unwanted Blood Transfusions.*** In DiGeronimo v. Fuchs, 927 N.Y.S.2d 904 (Sup. Ct. 2011), a patient who was a Jehovah's Witness was given a blood transfusion to save her life. Claiming that she had not consented to the procedure, which violated her religious convictions, the patient sued her doctor for medical malpractice. In rejecting the claim, the trial court wrote:

> The plaintiff's argument taken to its logical conclusion is that the doctor should have allowed her (the mother of two children) to die rather than give her an allogenic blood transfusion. Since the plaintiff's transfusion saved her life, this action is analogous to one for "wrongful life" against the doctor. However, there is no cause of action for "wrongful life" in the State of New York.

C. Prenatal Injuries

Farley v. Sartin

Supreme Court of Appeals of West Virginia
466 S.E.2d 522 (W. Va. 1995)

CLECKLEY, Justice.

.... The issue presented to this Court on appeal is whether the plaintiff can maintain a cause of action under West Virginia's wrongful death statute, W. Va. Code, 55-7-5 (1931),[1] for the death of Baby Farley, who was eighteen to twenty-two weeks of gestation and, at best, of questionable viability in light of the evidence presented to the circuit court....

On November 6, 1991, the plaintiff's pregnant wife, Cynthia Farley, was killed in an automobile accident she had with the defendant, Billy R. Sartin, who was driving a tractor trailer owned by the defendant, Lee Sartin Trucking Company, Inc.... [According to the only medical testimony in the record, Baby Farley was neither large enough nor developed enough to survive outside the womb.]

The plaintiff filed a wrongful death action as the Administrator of the Estate of Baby Farley. In response, the defendants filed a motion for summary judgment ... on the basis that Baby Farley was not viable at the time of death; therefore, the defendants argued Baby Farley was not a "person" under the wrongful death statute.... [T]he circuit court granted summary judgment in favor of the defendants.

....

At common law, there was no cause of action for the wrongful death of a person....

Recognizing the problem with this result, the English Parliament passed the Fatal Accidents Act of 1846, commonly referred to as Lord Campbell's Act. 9 & 10 Vict. c. 93 (1846). This Act permitted recovery of damages by the close relatives of a victim who was tortiously killed.

.... Currently, every state has created a cause of action for wrongful death....

.... The common law did not permit recovery for prenatal torts in general, ... and courts remained hesitant to allow wrongful death actions for unborn children....

The argument at common law was that "an unborn child was but a part of the mother, and had no existence or being which could be the subject-matter of injury distinct from the mother, and that an injury to it was but an injury to the mother[.]"....

---

1. In relevant part, W. Va. Code, 55-7-5, states:
"Whenever the death of a person shall be caused by wrongful act, neglect, or default, and the act, neglect or default is such as would (if death had not ensued) have entitled the party injured to maintain an action to recover damages in respect thereof, then, and in every such case, the person who, or the corporation which, would have been liable if death had not ensued, shall be liable to an action for damages, notwithstanding the death of the person injured ..." ....

It was not until 1946 that an American court departed from . . . [this] approach. In Bonbrest v. Kotz, 65 F. Supp. 138 (D. D.C. 1946), the . . . district court determined that logic and justice require "that a child, if born alive and viable[,] . . . should be allowed to maintain an action in the courts for injuries wrongfully committed upon its person while in the womb of its mother." . . . .

. . . [T]oday, every jurisdiction permits recovery for prenatal injuries if a child is born alive. . . .

Despite the fact that recovery generally is allowed for prenatal injuries for a child "born alive," courts disagree upon whether they will permit recovery for injuries causing the death of a child *en ventre sa mere*. Although some jurisdictions do not permit a wrongful death action to be maintained for the death of an unborn child, the majority of jurisdictions now do permit a wrongful death action if the unborn child had reached the point of viability. . . .

In West Virginia, we recognized the right of the survivors of a viable unborn child to recover for wrongful death in Baldwin v. Butcher, 155 W. Va. 431, 184 S.E.2d 428 (1971). . . .

Turning to a cause of action for wrongful death, we confront the issue of whether "viability" is the proper line upon which we should permit a cause of action. With the exception of Georgia, which allows recovery after an unborn child is quick in the womb,[2] and Missouri, which found legislative direction to hold a nonviable child is a "person" under its wrongful death statute, we are not aware of any other cases that permit recovery for injury prior to viability unless there is a live birth. . . . [H]owever, a lack of precedent — standing alone — is an insufficient reason to deny a cause of action. . . .

In jurisdictions where the viability standard is controlling, the tortfeasor remains unaccountable for the full extent of the injuries inflicted by his or her wrongful conduct. In our judgment, justice is denied when a tortfeasor is permitted to walk away with impunity because of the happenstance that the unborn child had not yet reached viability at the time of death. The societal and parental loss is egregious regardless of the state of fetal development. Our concern reflects the fundamental value determination of our society that life — old, young, and prospective — should not be wrongfully taken away. In the absence of legislative direction, the overriding importance of the interest that we have identified merits judicial recognition and protection by imposing the most liberal means of recovery that our law permits.

. . . W. Va. Code, 55-7-5, is remedial in nature and should be liberally construed. . . . In light of our previous interpretation of W. Va. Code, 55-7-5, and the goals and purposes of wrongful death statutes generally, we, therefore, hold that the term "person," as used in this statute . . . encompasses a nonviable unborn child and, thus, permits a cause of action for the tortious death of such child.

2. [Fn. 20:] . . . . ["Quick" means "capable of moving in its mother's womb."]

... [O]ur holding in this case eliminates the need for trial courts to decide what often could be an extremely difficult factual question, *i.e.*, whether the fetus was "viable." ....

Reversed and Remanded.

Notes

1. ***States Permitting a Wrongful Death Action Based on Injury to a Fetus.*** "Thirty-two jurisdictions permit a wrongful-death action on behalf of a viable fetus." Aka v. Jefferson Hosp. Ass'n, Inc., 42 S.W.3d 508 (Ark. 2001); *see also* Castro v. Melchor, 366 P.3d 1058, 1069 (Haw. App. 2016) (finding "compelling reasons to include unborn, viable fetuses as persons under the wrongful death statute").

"Six jurisdictions (Illinois, Louisiana, Missouri, Oklahoma, South Dakota, and West Virginia) now specifically permit wrongful-death actions even where the death of the fetus occurs before the fetus becomes viable." Mack v. Carmack, 79 So.3d 597, 609 (Ala. 2011). *See also* Foster v. de Cholnoky, 2015 WL 5626312 (Conn. Super.) (holding, as a matter of first impression, that a wrongful death action may be brought with respect to a fetus injured *in utero* while nonviable, but born alive, regardless of whether the fetus had reached viability at time of birth).

2. ***States Not Allowing a Wrongful Death Action Based on Injury to a Fetus.*** In Endresz v. Friedberg, 248 N.E.2d 901 (N.Y. 1969), the court embraced the minority view that refuses to permit an action for wrongful death of a fetus, reasoning:

> The considerations of justice which mandate the recovery of damages by an infant, injured in his mother's womb and born deformed through the wrong of a third party, are absent where the fetus, deprived of life while yet unborn, is never faced with the prospect of impaired mental or physical health.
>
> In the latter case, ... proof of pecuniary injury and causation is immeasurably more vague than in suits for prenatal injuries....
>
> Beyond that, since the mother may sue for any injury which she sustained in her own person, including her suffering as a result of the stillbirth, and the father for loss of her services and consortium, an additional award to the "distributees" of the fetus would give its parents an unmerited bounty and would constitute not compensation to the injured but punishment to the wrongdoer....

3. ***Decision to Abort.*** In Williams v. Manchester, 888 N.E.2d 1 (Ill. 2008), a pregnant mother was seriously injured in a collision, but there was no harm to the fetus. The mother decided to abort the fetus based in part on the fact that carrying the fetus to term would have complicated the mother's own recovery from a broken hip and pelvis and because the fetus had been exposed to radiation from x-rays that might have had adverse consequences for the child's later development. A unanimous state supreme court held that the parents could not maintain a wrongful

death action as a result of the termination of the pregnancy because the state wrongful death act required that there must have been an actionable injury to the fetus. On the facts of the case, the fetus was unharmed by the collision and there was no proof of actual harm from the exposure to radiation.

4. ***Pre-Natal Injuries to Children Born Alive.*** Courts have had no trouble allowing recovery when a child who was injured while *en ventre sa mere*[3] is born alive, but with a handicap attributable to the defendant's negligence. *See* Crussell v. Electrolux Home Products, Inc., 499 F. Supp. 2d 1137 (W.D. Ark. 2007) (citing Restatement, Second, of Torts § 869).

Some courts have, however, denied recovery when the negligence injured the mother before the child was conceived, but with consequences that affected the child. Defendants' lawyers in these cases sometimes assert that the defendant cannot "logically" have been negligent toward someone who did not yet exist. However, remember the claims of "DES daughters" discussed in Chapter 7.

5. ***Emotional Distress in Pre-Natal Injury Cases.*** In some instances, harm to a pregnant mother will allow her to commence a personal injury action that will include an award of emotional distress damages relating to the injured fetus. In Smith v. Borello, 804 A.2d 1151 (Md. 2002), the court held, as a matter of first impression in Maryland, that a pregnant woman who sustains a personal injury as the result of a defendant's tortious conduct and who, as part of that injury, suffers the loss of the fetus may recover, in her own action for personal injuries, for any demonstrable emotional distress that accompanies and is attributable to the loss of the fetus.

6. ***Pre-Natal Injuries or Wrongful Death Caused by a Child's Mother.*** Can a mother be held liable to a child for injuries caused by the mother's unsafe conduct during pregnancy? The issue has been addressed by only a handful of cases. *Compare* Remy v. MacDonald, 801 N.E.2d 260 (Mass. 2004) (holding, in connection with a two-car collision, that a mother did not owe a duty to her unborn fetus), *and* Chenault v. Huie, 989 S.W.2d 474 (Tex. App. 1999) (finding no cause of action based on mother's illegal drug use), *with* National Cas. Co. v. Northern Trust Bank of Fla., 807 So. 2d 86 (Fla. Dist. Ct. App. 2001) (holding, in an auto accident case, that a child had cause of action against her mother "up to the limits of the insurance coverage"), *and* Bonte v. Bonte, 616 A.2d 464 (N.H. 1992) (stating a claim based on a mother's alleged negligence in failing to use a crosswalk).

Do not assume that recognition of an action against the child's mother always enlarges the chances of compensation for the child. Proportionate responsibility laws, which abrogate the common law rules on joint and several liability, may allow defendants to partially escape liability by arguing that a portion of the child's harm was caused by the child's mother, and therefore is harm for which the defendant is not responsible. This may be true even if no claim has been asserted by the child against the mother. *See* Chapter 17.

---

3. "[I]n the mother's womb," Black's Law Dictionary (11th ed. 2019).

See also Tesar v. Anderson, 789 N.W.2d 351 (Wis. App. 2010) (holding that public policy did not bar a wrongful death action by a father against a mother's automobile insurer based on the mother's negligent driving that resulted in the stillbirth of their child).

7. ***No-Fault Compensation.*** Virginia has enacted legislation which removes certain infant injuries allegedly caused by medical professionals from the tort system and provides no-fault compensation under a scheme modeled on workers' compensation laws. *See* Va. Code Ann. § 38.2-5002 (Westlaw 2022).

8. ***Pre-Majority Medical Expenses.*** In cases involving pre-natal or post-natal injuries to a child, it is important to determine whether the right to recover compensation for medical expenses belongs to the parents or the child. In Pressey by and through Pressey v. Children's Hosp. Colorado, 2017 WL 929931, at *5 (Colo. App.), a child suffered irreversible brain damage four days after birth based on alleged prior negligence in the administration of medication. The court held that:

> [I]n Colorado, an injury to a minor creates separate causes of action: (1) the parents generally may recover for the child's damages suffered and expenses of the child during minority; (2) the minor may recover expenses the minor actually incurs during minority and for pain and suffering and post-majority impairment of future earning capacity; and (3) an emancipated minor has the right to sue for all damages and expenses....

D. Wrongful Adoption

Burr v. Board of County Commissioners of Stark County

Supreme Court of Ohio
491 N.E.2d 1101 (Ohio 1986)

Appellees Russell H. and Betty J. Burr, filed a "wrongful adoption" civil action against the Board of County Commissioners of Stark County, the Stark County Welfare Department, Logan Burd, its director, and Winifred M. Schaub, a former employee of the department's adoption division.

.... Appellees contacted the adoption division of the Stark County Welfare Department in 1964 expressing their desire to adopt a child. Betty Burr is partially disabled, having earlier lost a leg to polio....

... [A]n employee of appellants telephoned the Burrs and told them a seventeen-month-old boy was available for adoption. At appellants' suggestion, the Burrs met the county caseworker, Schaub, in order to be introduced to the child. During this meeting Schaub [had] told the Burrs the infant was borne by an eighteen-year-old unwed mother, that the mother was living with her parents, that the mother was trying to take care of the child and trying to work during the day, that the grandparents were mean to the child, that the mother was going to Texas for better employment, and that she had surrendered the child to appellants for adoption. Russell Burr testified that Schaub represented to them that the child "... was a nice big, healthy, baby boy" who had been born at the Massillon City Hospital. The Burrs decided to proceed with the adoption....

The Burrs testified that during the ensuing years Patrick suffered from a myriad of physical and mental problems. Physical twitching, speech impediment, poor motor skills, and learning disabilities were among Patrick's more apparent problems.... He was classified as E.M.R. (educable, mentally retarded) and attended special education classes....

... [B]y high school, Patrick was observed to also suffer from hallucinations.... Eventually, Patrick was diagnosed as suffering from Huntington's Disease, a genetically inherited disease which destroys the central nervous system. Movement disorders, delusions and intellectual deterioration are all associated with the disease. The average life expectancy after onset if the disease begins during childhood is 8.5 years. During the course of Patrick's treatment, the Burrs obtained a court order opening the sealed records concerning his background prior to adoption.

.... These previously sealed records revealed that Patrick's mother was actually a thirty-one-year old mental patient at the Massillon State Hospital. Patrick had not been born at Massillon City Hospital, but rather was delivered at the state mental institution. The father's identity was unknown, but he was presumed to also have been a mental patient. Patrick's biological mother shared his low intellectual level and also had a speech impediment. She was diagnosed as having a "mild mental deficiency, idiopathic, with psychotic reactions" and was described as "bovine." The "mean" grandparents, the trip to Texas, voluntary placement, and seemingly all other information regarding Patrick other than his age and sex were fabrications. In fact, prior to adoption, he had been placed in two foster homes.

The records also showed that Patrick suffered a fever at birth, and was known by appellants to be developing slowly.... Although Patrick's biological mother had not been diagnosed as suffering Huntington's Disease, expert testimony established that Patrick's family background and medical profile made him at risk for disease....

In order to recoup Patrick's medical expenses (in excess of $80,000 for the Huntington's Disease treatment alone), together with other damages, the Burrs commenced this "wrongful adoption" action against appellants.

.... The jury returned a verdict in favor of appellees in the sum of $125,000. The court of appeals ... affirmed....

CELEBREZZE, Chief Justice.

....

We deem that in a civil action captioned "Complaint in Fraud ... for Wrongful Adoption," which alleges that adoptive parents were fraudulently misled to their detriment by an adoption agency's material misrepresentations of fact concerning an infant's background and condition, the parents must prove each element of the tort of fraud.

In Cohen v. Lamko, Inc. (1984), 10 Ohio St. 3d 167, 169, 462 N.E.2d 407, we set forth the elements of fraud as:

(a) a representation or, where there is a duty to disclose, concealment of a fact,

(b) which is material to the transaction at hand,

(c) made falsely, with knowledge of its falsity, or with such utter disregard and recklessness as to whether it is true or false that knowledge may be inferred,

(d) with the intent of misleading another into relying upon it,

(e) justifiable reliance upon the representation or concealment, and

(f) a resulting injury proximately caused by the reliance....

... [W]e find that the instant record amply supports the lower courts' decisions that fraud was demonstrated. There was evidence presented that appellants represented to appellees that the infant was a nice, big, healthy baby boy when in fact the welfare agency had test records which indicated ... that the child may have low intelligence and was at risk of disease. Appellants further represented that he was born at the Massillon City Hospital; the working mother was an unwed eighteen-year-old who was living with her parents, could not care for her son and voluntarily signed custody to appellants; that the grandparents were mean to the boy; and that the mother was moving to Texas for better employment.

Each of these untrue statements was found to have been affirmatively made with knowledge of its falsity. The representations were material to the adoption transaction and were obviously made with the intention of misleading the Burrs into relying upon them as fact while making their decision whether to adopt.

Both Mr. and Mrs. Burr testified that had they not been lied to regarding Patrick's history, they never would have adopted him. Hence, had they not relied on the representations, their subsequent damages would never have resulted. In short, appellants knew the history was false, intended reliance, and in fact misled the Burrs to their detriment.

Lastly, we find appellees' reliance was justifiable in this case and that their injuries resulted therefrom....

We find that the judgment and award ($125,000) were appropriate in light of the evidence presented to the jury, medical bills ($81,000), other expenses, and appellees' claimed emotional damage....

... [T]he award appears commensurate with the injuries inflicted and is not so excessive as to be set aside....

We believe it appropriate to comment briefly concerning the breadth of today's decision. In no way do we imply that adoption agencies are guarantors of their placements. Such a view would be tantamount to imposing an untenable contract of insurance that each child adopted would mature to be healthy and happy.... Adoptive parents are in the same position as, and confront risks comparable to those, of natural parents relative to their child's future.... However, just as couples must weigh the risks of becoming natural parents, taking into consideration a host of factors, so too should adoptive parents be allowed to make their decision in an intelligent manner. It is not the mere failure to disclose the risks inherent in the child's background which we hold to be actionable. Rather, it is the deliberate act of misinforming this couple which deprived them of their right to make a sound parenting decision and which led to the compensable injuries....

Judgment affirmed.

Notes

1. ***Query: Finding Relevant Precedent.*** What do the cases in this chapter suggest about how damages should be calculated in a "wrongful adoption" case? Is it relevant whether, as in many states, the law offers the parents the option of annulling the adoption decree?

In Norman v. Xytex Corp., 848 S.E.2d 835, 837 (Ga. 2020), the plaintiffs alleged that a sperm bank sold them human "sperm under false pretenses about the characteristics of its donor, and that the child conceived with that sperm ... [suffered] from a variety of impairments inherited from the sperm donor." The Supreme Court of Georgia held that "claims arising from the very existence of the child are barred, but claims arising from specific impairments caused or exacerbated by defendants' alleged wrongs may proceed, as may other claims that essentially amount to ordinary consumer fraud."

2. ***Culpability in Wrongful-Adoption Cases.*** In other areas of the law, there has sometimes been a tendency to expand the scope of tort liability. For example, once claims for intentional misrepresentation were established, the law began to recognize claims for negligent misrepresentation, too. *See* Chapter 21. In the field of product liability, manufacturers of defective products were once immune from suits for negligence, even though they were liable for deliberately misleading their customers. Today, as discussed in Chapter 15, manufacturers are often liable for injuries caused by their products even if the manufacturers were not at fault. The *Burr* court's attempt in the last paragraph of the opinion to limit the sweep of its decision does not necessarily indicate what the law on this subject will be in future years.

See McKinney v. State, 950 P.2d 461 (Wash. 1998) (recognizing a statutory cause of action for negligent failure to comply with adoption agency reporting requirements relating to disclosure of medical and social information about a child); Mohr v. Commonwealth, 653 N.E.2d 1104 (Mass. 1995) (recognizing liability of an adoption agency for both negligent and intentional misrepresentations); Gibbs v. Ernst, 647 A.2d 882 (Pa. 1994) (holding that traditional common-law causes of action grounded in fraud and negligence applied to adoptions). *See also* Broach-Butts v.

Therapeutic Alternatives, Inc., 191 A.3d 702 (N.J. Super. App. Div. 2018) (holding that a social service agency owed foster parents a duty of reasonable care in placing youth with foster parents, and had a duty to disclose the youth's history of violence prior to placement).

3. ***Wrongful Prolongation of Life.*** In Estate of Taylor v. Muncie Med. Investors, 727 N.E.2d 466 (Ind. Ct. App. 2000), a patient's estate and adult children brought an action against a nursing home for wrongful prolongation of the patient's life, alleging gross negligence, battery, and other claims. The suit accused a nursing home and two physicians of extending the patient's life for 140 days, despite the fact that she had executed a living will and a "do not resuscitate" form. The court held that there was no need to recognize a new cause of action for "wrongful prolongation of life" because the state Health Care Consent Act permitted a cause of action that would have protected the rights of the family.

4. ***Coerced Relinquishment of a Child.*** A different type of "wrongful adoption" issue was raised in Doe v. Archdiocese of Cincinnati, 880 N.E.2d 892 (Ohio 2008). In that case, the plaintiff alleged, on a variety of grounds, that the defendant's agents had coerced her into agreeing to give up for adoption the child she had conceived as the result of a sexual liaison with a priest when she was in high school. The suit, filed decades after the underlying events, was held to be time-barred. If the claim had been timely, what types of damages might have been recovered?

Chapter 14

Strict Liability

Liability without Fault. Defendants are sometimes held liable for injuries despite not having been "at fault" in any sense. When this occurs, the defendants are "strictly liable."

The "strictness" of strict liability lies in the fact that one or more of the usual prerequisites for liability based on fault—typically, proof of unreasonable (or worse) conduct and foreseeability of harm—are dispensed with or modified. As the requirements for recovery become fewer or less formidable, the liability becomes more strict. There are different varieties of strict liability, and not all are equally exacting.

Some authorities have used the term "absolute liability" to refer to the imposition of strict liability under circumstances where the defendant is barred from introducing defenses based on the plaintiff's conduct. *See* Seim v. Garavalia, 306 N.W.2d 806 (Minn. 1981). Other sources employ the "absolute liability" label less precisely.

Policy Basis. Strict liability is sometimes touted as having advantages over negligence as a basis for liability. It has been contended, for example, that strict liability: (1) achieves more-effective deterrence than a negligence standard; (2) increases the likelihood that injured persons will be compensated; (3) may be effectively employed as a device for spreading losses or shifting losses to "deeper pockets"; (4) can be used to ensure that persons who benefit from dangerous activities bear the burden of resulting losses; and (5) is easier to apply than the negligence standard. The merit of these contentions is hotly debated.

Opponents of strict liability often note that relieving plaintiffs of the need to prove fault creates a risk that too many cases will be brought, with the result that the costs of resolving claims may outweigh any advantages gained by a rule of strict liability. It has also been urged that strict liability tends to erode the incentives potential victims otherwise have to exercise care on their own behalf. The weight of this concern depends upon whether a jurisdiction has enacted comparative fault. At common law, assumption of the risk, but not contributory negligence, was a complete defense to a suit for strict liability. Under comparative fault, conduct by a plaintiff amounting to contributory negligence, assumption of the risk, or certain other forms of misconduct may be raised by a defendant to preclude or reduce recovery under a theory of strict liability. *See generally* Chapter 16.

Categories of Strict Liability. One important and recently developed category of strict liability—the liability of manufacturers and other sellers of products for injuries to consumers caused by defects in those products—will be examined in Chapter 15. This Chapter will examine several older forms of strict liability: (1) liability of employers to injured employees under workers' compensation laws; (2) vicarious liability of employers and other principals to those injured by the torts of their employees or agents; (3) liability for harm done by certain kinds of animals kept by the defendant; (4) liability for conducting abnormally dangerous activities; and (5) special rules related to liability for motor vehicles.

A. Employer and Employee

1. Workers' Compensation

Every state has adopted workers' compensation statutes, which require most employers to provide compensation for on-the-job injuries suffered by their employees. In many cases, employers provide for this liability by buying insurance, though large employers often find it cheaper to self-insure.

Recovery under workers' compensation is set by statutory schedules, rather than determined via case-by-case inquiries into the precise amount of harm suffered by the employee. In comparison with tort damages, payments under workers' compensation are usually quite low, especially in cases involving death or serious injury. The thought behind workers' compensation—which was first adopted in most states during the 1910s, following the enactment of statutes in Germany and England in the late 1800s—was to provide employees with the means of paying medical bills and with some measure of compensation for lost wages, not to award recovery for pain and suffering. But an injured worker's right to recover under workers' compensation will often be clear, so the injured person usually need not litigate for years or pay a large portion of any recovery to a lawyer.

In some instances, it is not obvious whether a worker's disability resulted from harm suffered on the job or from some other cause. Recently, claims by former employees for illnesses allegedly caused by on-the-job stress have been much litigated, with mixed results. *See, e.g.*, Roberts v. Waldbaum's, 951 N.Y.S.2d 590 (App. Div. 2012) (holding that a death was compensable under the workers' compensation law because there was evidence that the decedent's fatal heart attack "was triggered by the stress and excitement resulting from the responsibility of running the entire store on Super Bowl Sunday").

Questions can arise about whether the employee was "on the job" at the time of an accident. In what some regarded as a surprising decision, Cooper v. Barnickel Enterprises, Inc., 986 A.2d 38 (N.J. Super. App. Div. 2010), the court held that an employee injured during a five-mile drive to get coffee was eligible for workers' compensation benefits. As the court explained:

> [P]etitioner was an "off-site" employee . . . facing an extended wait to consult with an expert concerning a work-related issue. . . . It cannot be expected

> that he would stand like a statue or remain at the union hall with nothing to do for such a period, particularly when there was no coffee available at the site.... The distance of the coffee shop from respondent's off-site jobsite was reasonable given the rural nature of the community....

Negligence and Recklessness. Workers' compensation is ordinarily an injured employee's exclusive remedy against the employer for failure to exercise care: the statutes bar negligence and recklessness claims relating to injuries arising "in the course of employment." Therefore, although an injured employee may recover from the employer without showing that the employer was negligent, the employee covered by workers' compensation loses the right to sue the employer for negligence. This immunity affords employers with a considerable measure of protection, and will in some cases reduce the employer's incentive to take safety precautions.

Intentional Torts. Workers' compensation laws do not bar suits against an employer for intentional wrongdoing. *See* Fla. Stat. Ann. § 440.11 (Westlaw 2022) (an action may be maintained "[w]hen an employer commits an intentional tort that causes the injury or death of the employee").

Co-Employees. The immunity enjoyed by an employer normally also bars actions against co-employees. *See, e.g.*, La. Rev. Stat. 23:1032 (Westlaw 2022) (barring negligence actions against the "employer, or any principal or any officer, director, stockholder, partner, or employee of such employer or principal"); Tex. Labor Code § 408.001 (Westlaw 2022) (barring suits against the "employer or an agent or employee of the employer").

Third-Parties. Parties outside of the employment relationship do not pay workers' compensation premiums and therefore do not enjoy the benefit of workers' compensation immunity. In cases involving on-the-job accidents, attorneys representing injured workers are assiduous in searching for blameworthy third parties who can be held liable for the injuries. *See* Brown v. Adair, 846 So. 2d 687 (La. 2003) (outside rehabilitation specialists were "third persons" who were not immune from suit).

Employer Participation. In all states except Texas, employers must participate in the workers' compensation system. (In Texas, participation is optional, though it is encouraged by laws providing that a non-participating employer may not raise traditional common-law defenses in a suit by an injured employee). However, even where participation is mandatory, there are exceptions. Employers with less than a certain number of employees may not have to subscribe, and the same is true of certain types of employers (*e.g.*, those employing agricultural workers or domestic help).

The Federal Employees Compensation Act. Federal employees who are injured while performing their duties often have a non-tort remedy under the Federal Employees Compensation Act.

Some law schools offer a separate course on Workers' Compensation Law. The following excerpt from the New York statute shows how workers' compensation is calculated in one state. The schedules typically take into account whether the worker's injury is permanent or temporary and the extent of the injury.

New York Workers' Compensation Law

(Westlaw 2022)

§ 15. Schedule in case of disability

The following schedule of compensation is hereby established:

1. Permanent total disability. In case of total disability adjudged to be permanent sixty-six and two-thirds per centum of the average weekly wages shall be paid to the employee during the continuance of such total disability. Loss of both hands, or both arms, or both feet, or both legs, or both eyes, or of any two thereof shall, in the absence of conclusive proof to the contrary, constitute permanent total disability. In all other cases permanent total disability shall be determined in accordance with the facts....

2. Temporary total disability. In case of temporary total disability, sixty-six and two-thirds per centum of the average weekly wages shall be paid to the employee during the continuance thereof, except as otherwise provided in this chapter.

3. Permanent partial disability. In case of disability partial in character but permanent in quality the compensation shall be sixty-six and two-thirds per centum of the average weekly wages and shall be paid to the employee for the period named in this subdivision, as follows:

	Member lost	Number of weeks' compensation
a.	Arm	312
b.	Leg	288
c.	Hand	244
d.	Foot	205
e.	Eye	160
f.	Thumb	75
g.	First finger	46
h.	Great toe	38
i.	Second finger	30
j.	Third finger	25
k.	Toe other than great	16
l.	Fourth finger	15

m. Loss of hearing. Compensation for the complete loss of the hearing of one ear, for sixty weeks, for the loss of hearing of both ears, for one hundred and fifty weeks.

n. Phalanges. Compensation for the loss of more than one phalange of a digit shall be the same as for loss of the entire digit. Compensation for loss of the first phalange shall be one-half of the compensation for loss of the entire digit.

o. Amputated arm or leg. Compensation for an arm or a leg, if amputated at or above the wrist or ankle, shall be for the proportionate loss of the arm or leg.

p. Binocular vision or per centum of vision. Compensation for loss of binocular vision or for eighty per centum or more of the vision of an eye shall be the same as for loss of the eye.

q. Two or more digits. Compensation for loss or loss of use of two or more digits, or one or more phalanges of two or more digits, of a hand or foot may be proportioned to the loss of use of the hand or foot occasioned thereby but shall not exceed the compensation for loss of a hand or foot.

r. Total loss of use. Compensation for permanent total loss of use of a member shall be the same as for loss of the member.

s. Partial loss or partial loss of use. Compensation for permanent partial loss or loss of use of a member may be for proportionate loss or loss of use of the member. . . .

t. Disfigurement. . . . The board may award proper and equitable compensation for serious facial or head disfigurement, not to exceed twenty thousand dollars, including a disfigurement continuous in length which is partially in the facial area and also extends into the neck region as described in paragraph two hereof.

. . . .

u. Total or partial loss or loss of use of more than one member or parts of members. In any case in which there shall be a loss or loss of use of more than one member or parts of more than one member set forth in paragraphs a to t, both inclusive, of this subdivision, but not amounting to permanent total disability, the board shall award compensation for the loss or loss of use of each such member or part thereof, which awards shall run consecutively.

. . . .

w. Other cases. In all other cases of permanent partial disability, the compensation shall be sixty-six and two-thirds percent of the difference between the injured employee's average weekly wages and his or her wage-earning capacity thereafter in the same employment or otherwise . . . payable during the continuance of such permanent partial disability, but subject to reconsideration of the degree of such impairment by the board on its own motion or upon application of any party in interest.

. . . .

5. Temporary partial disability. In case of temporary partial disability resulting in decrease of earning capacity, the compensation shall be two-thirds of the difference between the injured employee's average weekly wages before the accident and his wage earning capacity after the accident in the same or other employment.

5-a. Determination of wage earning capacity. The wage earning capacity of an injured employee in cases of partial disability shall be determined by his actual earnings, provided, however, that if he has no such actual earnings the board may in the interest of justice fix such wage earning capacity as shall be reasonable, but not in excess of seventy-five per centum of his former full time actual earnings, having due regard to the nature of his injury and his physical impairment.

2. Respondeat Superior

Turning from harms *to* employees to harms inflicted *by* employees, one finds that the doctrine of *respondeat superior* holds employers liable for torts committed by their employees acting in the scope of their employment. This is a form of strict liability because the plaintiff's right to recover against the employer does not depend on a showing that the *employer* was at fault. The plaintiff must, however, show that the employee committed a tort, and in most cases the tort in question is negligence.

In the following case, a court managed to find an employer liable *in tort* for an injury to an employee by applying the doctrine of *respondeat superior* while avoiding the workers' compensation law's denial of a tort cause of action to an employee injured on the job.

Smith v. Lannert

St. Louis Court of Appeals, Missouri
429 S.W.2d 8 (Mo. Ct. App. 1968)

BRADY, Commissioner.

In this action to recover damages for personal injuries allegedly sustained on October 31, 1961, while on Bettendorf-Rapp's premises, plaintiff received a verdict and judgment in the amount of $2,500.00 against Bettendorf-Rapp and the individual defendant. Bettendorf-Rapp was given a judgment in this same amount on its crossclaim against the individual defendant. Both defendants appeal....

.... Plaintiff, who at the time of trial was a 36-year-old married female, was employed as a checker in Bettendorf-Rapp's supermarket at the time of the incident.... On the day this incident occurred plaintiff began work about 9:00 or 9:30 and in the late afternoon of that day went to Lannert to request time for a break to go to the restroom.... She was told to return to work.... Her testimony was Lannert "... told me to get back down to the courtesy checkout and get to work or he would spank me." .... Instead of doing so she asked a coemployee for her purse and upon receiving it started for the ladies' room in the employees' lounge. When she got to the door of the employees' lounge someone grabbed her from behind and pushed her into the lounge. She looked around and saw it was Lannert who then bent her over and struck her three times with his open hand on her buttocks.... The spanking caused red marks....

She went back to the courtesy counter ... and returned to her cash register where she remained for a half hour or so. Her only other conversation with Lannert on this day occurred when he came to check the cash register to see if it balanced. Her testimony was that it did balance and that Lannert told her it was a good thing it did or he would spank her again. Her testimony was that she felt Lannert was trying to joke with her on this occasion but neither she nor Lannert were joking on the earlier occasion when she was struck.

Lannert was called by plaintiff as her witness.... His testimony was that he was not perturbed with plaintiff in any way and thought the incident to be entirely in jest since both he and plaintiff were laughing and "kidding around" at the time. In December of 1961 plaintiff told Bettendorf-Rapp's personnel manager what had happened.

Lannert testified he did not consider himself in the course and scope of his duties when he struck plaintiff. It also appeared it was against company policy to lay hands on any employee and Bettendorf-Rapp had received no complaints about Lannert having ever done so prior to this time....

[The court held that the plaintiff's action was not barred by the State worker's compensation statute because the "accident did not arise 'in the course of' plaintiff's employment for ... she was injured while in the process of disobeying a direct order of her superior and doing an act her employer ... had expressly forbidden her to do."]

There is no dispute but that Lannert was an employee of Bettendorf-Rapp and that he intentionally struck plaintiff.... The issue is whether there is evidence from which the jury could find Lannert "... was within the scope of his employment by Bettendorf-Rapp, Inc." as submitted in that instruction....

The principle of *respondeat superior* underlies the liability of Bettendorf-Rapp, if any exists. As was stated in Haehl v. Wabash R. Co., 119 Mo. 325, 24 S.W. 737 ... "The principal is responsible, not because the servant has acted in his name or under color of his employment, but because the servant was actually engaged in and about his business, and carrying out his purposes.... But if his business is done, or is taking care of itself, and his servant, not being engaged in it, not concerned about it, but impelled by motives that are wholly personal to himself, and simply to gratify his own feeling of resentment, whether provoked or unprovoked, commits an assault upon another, when that has and can have no tendency to promote any purpose in which the principal is interested, and to promote which the servant was employed, then the wrong is the purely personal wrong of the servant, for which he, and he alone, is responsible." In this connection we are cognizant Bettendorf-Rapp may be held responsible for the assault committed by Lannert even though Lannert acted wantonly and contrary to Bettendorf-Rapp's instructions ... provided there is proof the assault was made with intent to promote or further the master's business....

Plaintiff's best evidence shows the employees were entitled to certain rest "breaks" and the jury was entitled to the fair inference these were to be granted at the discretion of the store manager Lannert whom plaintiff's evidence described as having the "full say" over all matters taking place within the store.... [T]he jury could reasonably infer from the evidence Bettendorf-Rapp was interested in maintaining what it deemed to be an adequate work force with which to handle the volume of its business and that this was one of the purposes for which Lannert was employed as store manager. When this inference is considered in the light of Lannert's previous reprimand to plaintiff for taking too much time on an earlier rest break, his refusal to grant permission for another rest break, Lannert's order to plaintiff to return to work, her immediate disobedience of that order, and Lannert's assault upon her following so closely in the sequence of events as to refute any contention but that it was connected therewith, we hold there is evidence from which the jury could find Lannert's act in striking plaintiff was to enforce employee discipline with respect to orders given by the store manager with reference to employee rest breaks, thus promoting Bettendorf-Rapp's purpose of keeping an adequate work force on the floor and maintaining employee discipline.

.... We cannot say as a matter of law Lannert abandoned his duties ... and indulged in the assault as an individual act.

....

The judgment is affirmed.

Notes

1. ***Other Precedent.*** *See also* Rodebush v. Oklahoma Nursing Homes, Ltd., 867 P.2d 1241 (Okla. 1993) (employer held liable for nurse's slapping of an Alzheimer's patient while giving him a bath).

2. ***Respondeat Superior.*** The rule of *respondeat superior*— meaning "let the master answer" or "look to the one higher up"—is a rule of strict, vicarious liability. In the master and servant context, it provides that if an employee commits a tort while acting within the scope of the employment, the employer will be held accountable, even though the employer's conduct is in no way blameworthy. The application of *respondeat superior* hinges on two questions: (1) whether the tortfeasor is an employee (a "servant" in the older jargon), rather than an independent contractor; and (2) whether the tort occurs within the scope of the employment.

3. ***Employees versus Independent Contractors.*** Subject to certain important exceptions dealing with non-delegable duties (discussed *infra*), a principal is not vicariously liable for the torts of an agent who is an independent contractor, rather than an employee. *See* Restatement, Second, of Torts § 409; Restatement, Second, of Agency § 250. *See also* Amaya v. Potter, 94 S.W.3d 856 (Tex. App. 2002) (holding that a repairman temporarily doing work at a garage, who was urged to chase after a stolen vehicle, was not an employee, and therefore *respondeat superior* principles did not apply to an accident resulting from the chase).

(a) ***Terminology.*** Finding the term "equivocal," the current Restatement of Agency "does not use the term 'independent contractor,' except in discussing other material that uses the term." Restatement, Third, of Agency § 1.01 cmt. c (2006). Nevertheless, "independent contractor" terminology is part of the case law in most states and is deeply embedded in the language of practicing lawyers. It is therefore essential to be familiar with the term.

The critical distinction between employees ("servants") and independent contractors is addressed by § 2 of the Restatement, Second, of Agency, which provides:

> (2) A servant is an agent employed by a master to perform service in his affairs whose physical conduct in the performance of the service is controlled or subject to the right to control by the master.
>
> (3) An independent contractor is a person who contracts with another to do something for him but who is not controlled by the other nor subject to the other's right to control with respect to his physical conduct in the performance of the undertaking....

(b) ***Right to Control***. Many decisions have emphasized the importance of the right to control in determining the status of the tortfeasor. *See, e.g.,* Glenmar Cinestate, Inc. v. Farrell, 292 S.E.2d 366 (Va. 1982) (holding a drive-in theater not liable for a death resulting from an off-duty police officer's negligent direction of traffic because the officer was an independent contractor who chose his own methods, and the theater did not reserve the power to direct his activities); Verrett v. Houma Newspapers, Inc., 305 So. 2d 547, 550 (La. Ct. App. 1974) (holding that a carrier delivering newspapers by bicycle was an independent contractor where the publisher did not reserve or retain any right of control over the manner in which the carrier made deliveries).

See also Restatement, Third, of Agency § 2.04 cmt. b (2006) ("*Respondeat superior* is inapplicable when a principal does not have the right to control the actions of the agent..."); *id.* at § 7.07(3) (stating that "an employee is an agent whose principal controls or has the right to control the manner and means of the agent's performance of work, and ... the fact that work is performed gratuitously does not relieve a principal of liability").

(c) ***Other Factors***. However, some cases have minimized the significance of the right to control. In Dias v. Brigham Med. Assoc., 780 N.E.2d 447 (Mass. 2002), the court held that vicarious liability could be imposed on a medical group without proof of its right to control a physician's actions. In interrogatory answers, both the allegedly negligent physician and his medical practice group had indicated that the former was employed by the latter. However, the practice group then sought to escape vicarious liability on the ground that it had no right to control the physician's specific treatment decisions. The court wrote:

> In 1969, ... this court broadened the scope of liability under the theory of *respondeat superior*, and held that an employer need not control the details of an employee's tasks in order to be held liable for the employee's tortious acts. *See* Konick v. Berke, Moore Co., 355 Mass. 463, 467, 468, 245 N.E.2d 750 (1969).... [T]he employer in the *Konick* case was found to be liable for the employee's automobile accident, even though the employer was unable to control the precise manner and means of the employee's driving.... Our *Konick* decision comported with the view of the vast majority of States....
>
> In order to determine whether an employer-employee relationship actually exists, a judge may consider a number of factors.... These factors may

> include, but are not limited to, the method of payment (*e.g.*, whether the employee receives a W-2 form from the employer), and whether the parties themselves believe they have created an employer-employee relationship.... [I]n cases where there is no clear admission of employment, a direction and control analysis may be useful to determine whether the relationship is that of employer-employee as opposed to that of an independent contractor....

In New Jersey:

> A court shall apply the relative nature of the work test if an employer-employee relationship is not found under the control test.... The relative nature of the work test requires a court to examine the "'extent of the economic dependence of the worker upon the business he serves and the relationship of the nature of his work to the operation of that business.'" ... In applying the test, the court should consider whether the employer's goals are served by concluding that the worker is an employee.

Monk v. O'Connell, 2012 WL 4815160 (N.J. Super. App. Div. 2012) (finding that a doctor who worked at a hospital pursuant to a contract between the hospital and a company (EPA) that recruited and supplied emergency room physicians was an employee of EPA under both the control test and the relative nature of work test).

Even courts that talk in terms of a right to control requirement take other factors into account in determining whether *respondeat superior* liability will be imposed. In Limestone Products Distrib., Inc. v. McNamara, 71 S.W.3d 308 (Tex. 2002), the court said that:

> We measure the right to control by considering: (1) the independent nature of the worker's business; (2) the worker's obligation to furnish necessary tools, supplies, and materials to perform the job; (3) the worker's right to control the progress of the work except about final results; (4) the time for which the worker is employed; and (5) the method of payment, whether by unit of time or by the job.

The court concluded that a driver for a limestone supplier was an independent contractor, rather than an employee, at the time of the driver's collision with a motorcyclist. Although the supplier told the driver where to pick up and drop off loads, the supplier merely controlled the end sought to be accomplished. The facts showed that the driver was free to drive any route he wished; the driver did not work regular hours and did not have to visit the supplier's office on a regular basis; the driver used his own truck and paid for gasoline, repairs, and insurance; the supplier paid the driver by the load when he delivered; the driver received no pay if there was no work; the supplier reported the driver's income on IRS 1099 form rather than a W-2 wage-withholding form; the supplier did not pay the driver for vacation, sick leave, or holidays; and the driver paid his own Social Security and federal income taxes.

(d) ***Sources of Compensation***. In some instances, persons will be classified as employees even though they are paid by an outside source or indirectly compensated.

See Riverbend Country Club v. Patterson, 399 S.W.2d 382 (Tex. Civ. App. 1965) (holding a country club liable for injuries caused by a caddy, even though caddies were not required to report for work at a particular time and were paid directly by players, because all caddies registered with and were supervised by a caddy master who controlled the work). *See also* Bishop v. Texas A & M Univ., 35 S.W.3d 605 (Tex. 2000) (holding, in an action based on an accidental stabbing during a school play, that professors who acted as faculty advisors to a drama club were employees rather than volunteers, because, even though they were not separately paid for that activity, service as an advisor to a student organization was considered in determining overall compensation).

4. ***Temporary Servants.*** A person may be held liable for the actions of a "temporary servant." Thus, in some states physicians and nurses who assist in an operation, though employed by the hospital, are held to be temporary servants or agents of the surgeon in charge while the operation is in progress, and liability may be imposed upon the surgeon for their negligent acts under the doctrine of *respondeat superior*. *See* Swierczek v. Lynch, 466 N.W.2d 512, 518 (Neb. 1991).

5. ***Ethics in Law Practice: Lawyers as Independent Contractors.*** A defense attorney hired by an insurer to represent an insured normally is an independent contractor who has discretion regarding the day-to-day details of conducting the defense. Accordingly, an insurer is not vicariously liable for the legal malpractice of an independent attorney whom it selected to defend an insured. *See* State Farm Mut. Auto. Ins. Co. v. Traver, 980 S.W.2d 625 (Tex. 1998).

6. ***Scope of Employment.*** According to the Restatement, Second, of Agency, § 228, the conduct of a servant is within the scope of employment if, but only if:

> (a) it is of the kind he is employed to perform;
>
> (b) it occurs substantially within the authorized time and space limits;
>
> (c) it is actuated, at least in part, by a purpose to serve the master; and
>
> (d) if force is intentionally used by the servant against another, the use of the force is not unexpectable by the master.

Citing § 228, the Supreme Court of South Dakota wrote:

> "[T]his Court [has] adopted a 'foreseeability' test to determine whether an agent's acts were within the scope of employment. . . ." . . . . The "essential focus of inquiry" when determining if an employee's actions were foreseeable and within the scope of their employment is whether the employee's acts were in furtherance of their employment. . . . "[T]he fact that the servant's act is expressly forbidden by the master, or is done in a manner which he has prohibited, is to be considered in determining what the servant has been hired to do, but it is usually not conclusive, and does not in itself prevent the act from being within the scope of employment."

Sheard v. Hattum, 965 N.W.2d 134, 145 (S.D. 2021).

The Restatement, Third, of Agency states a somewhat different test for determining the scope of employment:

> An employee acts within the scope of employment when performing work assigned by the employer or engaging in a course of conduct subject to the employer's control. An employee's act is not within the scope of employment when it occurs within an independent course of conduct not intended by the employee to serve any purpose of the employer.

Restatement, Third, of Agency § 7.07(2) (2006).

(a) ***Off-Duty Conduct.*** "Off-duty" conduct is ordinarily not within the scope of employment. *See* Ginther v. Domino's Pizza, Inc., 93 S.W.3d 300 (Tex. App. 2002) (a pizza delivery driver's actions while driving friends home in a car he used to deliver pizza fell outside the scope of his employment where it was undisputed that the driver's shift had ended and he had left work almost two hours earlier); Burroughs v. Massachusetts, 673 N.E.2d 1217 (Mass. 1996) (an off-duty national guard member who served as a bartender at the armory did so voluntarily and was not within the scope of his employment where the work was uncompensated and there was no evidence that superiors had ordered him to provide the services); Haybeck v. Prodigy Services Co., 944 F. Supp. 326, 331 (S.D.N.Y. 1996), *app. dismissed on other grounds*, 116 F.3d 465 (2d Cir. 1997) (the conduct of an employee of an online service provider, who failed to disclose his HIV status before having sex outside his place of employment with a customer he met in a company "chat room," was not within the scope of employment even if the employee's "conduct arose in part out of his intent to further the business of [his employer]" by encouraging the plaintiff to use more of the employer's services).

(b) ***Violating the Rules.*** As Smith v. Lannert shows, conduct is not "outside the scope of employment" merely because it violates the rules of employment; one who employs drivers cannot escape liability for their negligence merely by prohibiting them from violating traffic laws or otherwise driving carelessly. Sometimes, however, conduct may be found to be so far outside the rules set by an employer as to place that conduct beyond the scope of employment. In Normand v. City of New Orleans, 363 So. 2d 1220 (La. Ct. App. 1978), a park commission employee returned to the zoo after working hours to perform an employment task. After completing the task, and in violation of the commission's rules, the employee took a mother and child into the primate night house, an area off limits to the public. The court held that the employee's conduct was such a significant and unpredictable departure from his employment duties, and was so unrelated to service for his employer, as to remove his conduct from the scope of employment.

(c) ***Business Purpose.*** Conduct that serves no business purpose of the employer ordinarily will not give rise to *respondeat superior* liability. *See* Jones v. Baisch, 40 F.3d 252 (8th Cir. 1994) (leaking of confidential information to friends about a patient's genital herpes was not within the scope of employment). In Minyard Food Stores, Inc. v. Goodman, 80 S.W.3d 573 (Tex. 2002), the court held that a manager was not acting within the scope of his employment when he lied about kissing another employee during a workplace misconduct investigation because the statements were not made "for the accomplishment of the objective for which the employee was employed."

(d) ***Intentional Torts and Scope of Employment.*** It is harder to establish that an intentional tort, as opposed to negligence, is within the scope of employment. *See* Twardy v. Northwest Airlines, Inc., 2001 WL 199567 (N.D. Ill.) (holding that an airline was not liable for a flirtatious flight attendant's smacking, kissing, and dumping water on a passenger).

However, "[i]f the intentional tort is committed in the accomplishment of a duty entrusted to the employee, rather than because of personal animosity, the employer may be liable." GTE Southwest, Inc. v. Bruce, 998 S.W.2d 605 (Tex. 1999) (holding an employer liable for outrageous conduct perpetrated over a two-year period in connection with performance of supervisory duties).

(e) ***Frolic and Detour.*** It is possible for an employee to leave the scope of employment, but later return to it. *See, e.g.*, McNair v. Lend Lease Trucks, Inc., 95 F.3d 325 (4th Cir. 1996) (there was a factual dispute over whether a trucker left the course of his employment by stopping at a lounge and drinking alcohol for over three hours and, if so, whether he returned to the scope of his employment by leaving the lounge and attempting to cross the road to his truck when he was struck by a motorcyclist).

7. ***Broad Interpretation of Scope of Employment.*** In Farmers Ins. Group v. County of Santa Clara, 47 Cal. Rptr. 2d 478, 486–87 (Cal. 1995), the court wrote:

> [A]cts necessary to the comfort, convenience, health, and welfare of the employee while at work, though strictly personal and not acts of service, do not take the employee outside the scope of employment. . . . Moreover, "'where the employee is combining his own business with that of his employer, or attending to both at substantially the same time, no nice inquiry will be made as to which business he was actually engaged in at the time of injury, unless it clearly appears that neither directly nor indirectly could he have been serving his employer.' . . ." . . . .

In *Farmers*, the court held that sexual harassment was not within the scope of employment even though it occurred during work hours in a workplace.

Other courts have declined to follow California's expansive approach to defining the scope of employment. For example, in O'Toole v. Carr, 815 A.2d 471 (N.J. 2003), the court held that a law firm was not responsible for an auto accident involving one of its partners who was en route to a part-time job as a municipal judge, which the plaintiff argued indirectly benefitted the law firm, although no income from the judgeship was paid to the firm. The court wrote:

> [The parties] argue that we should consider the broad articulation of enterprise liability adopted in California, which states that the "'modern and proper basis of vicarious liability of the master is not his control or fault

> but the risks incident to his enterprise.'". . . . In other words, "'[t]he losses caused by the torts of employees, which as a practical matter are sure to occur in the conduct of the employer's enterprise, are placed upon that enterprise itself, as a required cost of doing business.'". . . .
>
> . . . [W]e have thus far declined to adopt that view, retaining instead the Restatement as our vicarious liability standard. . . . Further, even if we were inclined to adopt the broadest view of enterprise liability, it would not alter the outcome in this case. . . . Carr's commutation to his job as a municipal court judge is, as a legal matter, unrelated to his law firm activity. Accordingly, the accident could in no event be considered a risk incident to that enterprise.

8. ***Exoneration of the Agent.*** If the agent is found not to have committed a tort, there is nothing for which the principal can be vicariously liable. *See* H&S Homes, L.L.C. v. McDonald, 978 So. 2d 692 (Ala. 2007).

9. ***Indemnification of an Employer.*** An employer held liable solely on the basis of *respondeat superior* can seek indemnification for the full amount of the judgment from the employee whose actions gave rise to the liability. *See* Chapter 17.

10. ***Vicarious Liability of Partners.*** Relations other than employer-employee can give rise to strict liability for the torts of another. One important example is that a member of a partnership is vicariously liable for torts of another partner within the scope of the partnership business.

John R. v. Oakland Unified School District

Supreme Court of California, En Banc
769 P.2d 948 (Cal. 1989)

ARGUELLES, Justice.

John R. . . . allegedly was sexually molested by his mathematics teacher while he was at the teacher's apartment participating in an officially sanctioned, extracurricular program. The principal question before us is whether the school district that employed the teacher can be held vicariously liable for the teacher's acts under the doctrine of *respondeat superior*. . . .

. . . John R. was a ninth grade student. . . . His mathematics teacher . . . asked John to participate in the school's instructional, work-experience program, under which students received both school credit and monetary payments for assisting teachers by, for example, helping to correct other students' papers. . . .

. . . . Performance of the required work by students at teachers' homes was an option authorized by the district, and the teacher either encouraged or required John to come to his apartment for this purpose. Over the course of many sessions at the teacher's apartment, the teacher sought to develop a close relationship with John as the boy's tutor and counselor, and ultimately endeavored to seduce him. . . . On one occasion . . . , the teacher succeeded in pressuring John into sexual acts. . . .

John A. Arguelles

John's parents, on behalf of their son and on their own behalf, brought suit against the teacher and the district, alleging that the district was vicariously liable for the teacher's acts and directly liable for its own negligence. . . .

The Court of Appeal reversed . . . [a trial court] order sustaining the district's demurrer to those causes of action against it premised on a theory of vicarious liability, reasoning that the facts as pleaded by plaintiffs could allow the trier of fact to find the district responsible for the tort of its employee because the teacher's misconduct, although not within or contemplated by his official duties, was made possible by his use, and abuse, of the official, job-created authority he was given over the boy. We granted review. . . .

. . . . The question before us here is whether an employer (specifically, a school district) can be held liable for a sexual assault committed by an employee (here, a teacher) on another person (particularly, on a student committed to that teacher's supervision). The natural, initial reaction is "No! Of course not!" A more personal escapade less related to an employer's interests is difficult to imagine. But the question is not so easily disposed of. It is closer than might appear upon first examination. . . .

The courts of other jurisdictions and our own Courts of Appeal have struggled in recent years over whether and how to apply the *respondeat superior* doctrine to the sexual assaults or misconduct of employees. The historical and perhaps still prevailing point of view declines to impose vicarious liability in such circumstances. But the other school of thought has its adherents as well. . . .

Plaintiffs urge us to take the approach adopted by the Court of Appeal, which looked not to whether a teacher's sexual abuse of a student is foreseeable in the sense that it is characteristic of the job or broadly incidental to a school district's activities . . . , but rather to the nature of the teacher-student relationship. The essence of their argument is that vicarious liability is appropriate when the tort is a consequence of the employer's conferring of official authority on the employee. That is, plaintiffs would have us impose liability on the employer if: (1) there is an official, job-created, hierarchical relationship by which the employee is given authority over a certain, and possibly limited, class of persons; and (2) there is a sufficient nexus between the exercise of that authority and the commission of the tort that it was foreseeable the authority so conferred might be abused to the detriment of the victim.

We recognize that this theory is not without substance . . . and finds some support in the language of both lines of cases.

. . . .

But although the facts of this case can be made to fit a version of the *respondeat superior* doctrine, we are unpersuaded that they should be or that the doctrine is appropriately invoked here. . . . "The principal justification for the application of the doctrine of *respondeat superior* in any case is the fact that the employer may spread the risk through insurance and carry the cost thereof as part of his costs of doing business." . . . . "Three reasons have been suggested for imposing liability on an enterprise for the risks incident to the enterprise: '(1) [I]t tends to provide a spur toward accident prevention; (2) it tends to provide greater assurance of compensation for accident victims[;] and (3) at the same time it tends to provide reasonable assurance that, like other costs, accident losses will be broadly and equitably distributed among the beneficiaries of the enterprises that entail them.'" . . . . The first of these three considerations just noted plays little role in the allocation of responsibility for the sexual misconduct of employees generally, and with respect to the unique situation of teachers, indicates that untoward consequences could flow from imposing vicarious liability on school districts. Although it is unquestionably important to encourage both the careful selection of these employees and the close monitoring of their conduct, such concerns are, we think, better addressed by holding school districts to the exercise of due care in such matters and subjecting them to liability only for their own direct negligence in that regard. Applying the doctrine of *respondeat superior* to impose, in effect, strict liability in this context would be far too likely to deter districts from encouraging, or even authorizing, extracurricular and/or one-on-one contacts between teachers and students or to induce districts to impose such rigorous controls on activities of this nature that the educational process would be negatively affected. Nor is the second consideration — the assurance of compensation for accident victims — appropriately invoked here. The acts here differ from the normal range of risks for which costs can be spread and insurance sought. . . . The imposition of vicarious liability on school districts for the sexual torts of their employees would tend to make insurance, already a scarce resource, even harder to obtain, and could lead to the diversion of needed funds from the classroom to cover claims.

The only element of the analysis that might point in favor of vicarious liability here is the propriety of spreading the risk of loss among the beneficiaries of the enterprise. School districts and the community at large benefit from the authority placed in teachers to carry out the educational mission, and it can be argued that the consequences of an abuse of that authority should be shared on an equally broad basis. But the connection between the authority conferred on teachers to carry out their instructional duties and the abuse of that authority to indulge in personal, sexual misconduct is simply too attenuated to deem a sexual assault as falling within the range of risks allocable to a teacher's employer. It is not a cost this particular enterprise should bear, and the consequences of imposing liability are unacceptable.

In sum, we believe the Court of Appeal erred in looking mainly to the factual similarities between this case and [White v. County of Orange, 212 Cal. Rptr. 493 (Ct. App. 1985), which imposed liability on a county for a deputy sheriff's threats to rape a motorist] . . . and in failing to consider whether the underlying justifications for the *respondeat superior* doctrine would be served by imposing vicarious liability here. We need not and do not decide whether *White* itself was properly decided or whether the job-created authority theory has any validity in evaluating vicarious liability for the torts of police officers. It suffices here to note that the authority of a police officer over a motorist — bolstered most immediately by his uniform, badge and firearm, and only slightly less so by the prospect of criminal sanctions for disobedience — plainly surpasses that of a teacher over a student. The teacher's authority is different in both degree and kind, and it is simply not great enough to persuade us that vicarious liability should attach here for the teacher's tort. . . .

. . . . The judgment of the Court of Appeal is reversed insofar as it reversed the trial court's order sustaining the district's demurrer to those claims premised on a theory of vicarious liability under the *respondeat superior* doctrine. . . .

[BROUSSARD, J., concurred. LUCAS, C.J., and PANNELLI, J., concurred in a concurring and dissenting opinion by EAGLESON, J., which did not discuss the *respondeat superior* issue and has been omitted.]

MOSK, J., concurring and dissenting.

. . . .

As in *White*, the teacher, by virtue of the exercise of his official authority, was able to perpetrate the sexual assault. That is, through the use of his authority to administer grades, to assign extracurricular work projects, and, significantly, by utilizing the school-approved work experience program, the teacher procured the student's presence in his home facilitating the opportunity for the assault. . . . [W]e [should] focus not on whether the school teacher's sexual activity with a student is either "characteristic" or foreseeable, but rather on whether the assault arose out of the exercise of job-created authority over the plaintiff student. . . .

I would affirm the Court of Appeal judgment in its entirety.

KAUFMAN, J., concurring and dissenting.

.... I would agree it is the rare case in which a sexual assault by a teacher against a student should give rise to liability on the part of his employing school district. Nevertheless, ... this is such a case.

... [T]he courts of this and other jurisdictions have recognized that there are circumstances where an employee's sexual misconduct cannot, in all candor, be deemed so "unusual or startling" that it would be unfair to impose vicarious liability upon the employer....

.... The district affirmatively sanctioned IWE work at teachers' homes as an acceptable feature of the program....

The district did not require that a student obtain the written permission of his parents to participate in the IWE program at the teacher's home, nor did it require that other students or adults be present during the home instruction. In effect, the district sanctioned IWE program virtually guaranteed that the teacher could act with impunity, free from the fear of interruption or discovery, fully assured of complete privacy and secrecy....

The IWE home-instruction program contained none of the usual safeguards incident to most normal extracurricular activities, *i.e.*, a public setting (as opposed to the private seclusion of the teacher's home) and the presence or knowledge of other persons (in contrast to the isolation and secrecy inherent in the IWE program). Such reasonable safeguards would normally act to deter such misconduct, or, failing that, to limit the district's exposure to claims based on vicarious liability.

Indeed, "public policy" militates strongly in favor of vicarious liability in this case. One of the "policy" bases of *respondeat superior* is said to be its tendency to act as a "spur toward accident prevention." .... If that is the case, and incidents of the nature at issue here are, as I believe, a foreseeable result of such ill-advised programs, then the imposition of vicarious liability in this case might ultimately prove to be an inducement, not a deterrent, to well planned and properly executed extracurricular school programs.

... I would allow plaintiffs to proceed against the district on its claims based on vicarious liability....

Notes

1. ***Sexual Abuse by an Employee.*** *See* Lisa M. v. Henry Mayo Newhall Mem. Hosp., 48 Cal. Rptr. 2d 510 (Cal. 1995) (a hospital technician who sexually molested a pregnant patient while performing an ultrasound examination was, as a matter of law, not acting within the scope of employment). *See also* Medlin v. Bass, 398 S.E.2d 460 (N.C. 1990). In refusing to hold a school board liable for a principal's alleged sexual assault of a student, the *Medlin* court wrote:

> While ... [the principal] was exercising authority conferred upon him by ... [the defendant board of education] when he summoned the minor plaintiff to his office to discuss her truancy problem, in proceeding to assault her sexually he was advancing a completely personal objective....

2. ***Ethics in Law Practice: Non-Lawyer Assistants.*** A lawyer may be held liable for the tort of an employee occurring within the scope of the employment. In addition, misconduct by a nonlawyer assistant may subject a lawyer to professional discipline, such as reprimand, suspension, or disbarment. *See, e.g., In re Galbasini*, 786 P.2d 971 (Ariz. 1990) (six-month suspension based on lawyer's failure to supervise employees who engaged in debt collection in the lawyer's name, improperly solicited clients, and failed to communicate with those clients).

3. *Problem: Is the Discipline of Lawyers Related to the Conduct of Subordinates Fault-Based or Strict?*

In the Model Rules of Professional Conduct (Westlaw 2022)—which define standards for attorney discipline, not tort liability—Rule 5.3 provides in part:

> With respect to a nonlawyer employed or retained by or associated with a lawyer:
>
> (a) a partner, and a lawyer who individually or together with other lawyers possesses comparable managerial authority in a law firm shall make reasonable efforts to ensure that the firm has in effect measures giving reasonable assurance that the person's conduct is compatible with the professional obligations of the lawyer;
>
> . . . and
>
> (c) a lawyer shall be responsible for conduct of such a person that would be a violation of the Rules of Professional Conduct if engaged in by a lawyer if:
>
> (1) the lawyer orders or, with the knowledge of the specific conduct, ratifies the conduct involved; or
>
> (2) the lawyer is a partner or has comparable managerial authority in the law firm in which the person is employed, or has direct supervisory authority over the person, and knows of the conduct at a time when its consequences can be avoided or mitigated but fails to take reasonable remedial action.

Does the language of subsection (a) impose strict liability or a fault-based standard? What about subsection (c)?

3. Non-delegable Duties

Courts occasionally speak of non-delegable duties, though it is difficult to predict when this concept will be invoked. The term "non-delegable duty" is more a conclusion (that liability will be imposed) than an aid to analysis. The Second Restatement indicates that a principal will be held vicariously liable for the torts of an independent contractor involving the breach of a non-delegable duty, although it candidly acknowledges that "[f]ew courts have made any attempt to state any general principles as to when the employer's duty cannot be delegated, and it may as yet be impossible to reduce these exceptions to such principles." Restatement, Second, of Torts, note preceding § 416.

Many Varieties. Despite this disclaimer, the Second Restatement attempts to articulate a long list of occasions on which a principal cannot shift responsibility for the proper conduct of work to an independent contractor. This rule applies (but is by no means limited) to cases where the contemplated work requires special precautions (§ 416), is to be done in a public place (§§ 417 and 418), involves the construction or maintenance of buildings in the principal's possession (§ 422) or instrumentalities used in highly dangerous activities (§ 423), is subject to safety requirements imposed by legislation (§ 424), is itself inherently dangerous (§ 427), or involves an "abnormally dangerous" activity (§ 427A). Courts often struggle in attempting to apply these exceptions to the general rule that a principal is not liable for the torts of an independent contractor. Consider how the rules might apply to a study abroad educational program:

> [A] program provider might be subject to a non-delegable duty claim based on hiring a person or company to transport a handicapped student who is confined to a wheelchair or to guide a hike into the mountains on the theory that the transportation or excursion required "special precautions." Similarly, a program provider operating in a dangerous country [*e.g.*, certain countries in the Middle East or in Africa] might be liable for an independent contractor's failure to exercise reasonable care in transporting participants, on the ground that . . . arranging travel for persons in a dangerous country is, by definition, inherently dangerous, in the sense that the risks of harm cannot be eliminated despite the exercise of all reasonable care. The Restatement commentary explains this type of employer liability for the conduct of an independent contractor in these words:
>
> > It is not . . . necessary to the employer's liability that the work be of a kind which cannot be done without a risk of harm to others. . . . It is sufficient that work of any kind involves a risk, recognizable in advance, of physical harm to others which is inherent in the work itself, or normally to be expected in the ordinary course of the usual or prescribed way of doing it, or that the employer has special reason to contemplate such a risk under the particular circumstances under which the work is to be done.

Vincent R. Johnson, *Americans Abroad: International Education Programs and Tort Liability*, 32 J.C. & U.L. 306, 336–37 (2006) (quoting Restatement, Second, of Torts § 427).

Inherently Dangerous Activities. See generally Maldonado v. Gateway Hotel Holdings, L.L.C., 154 S.W.3d 303 (E.D. Mo. 2003) (a boxing match was an inherently dangerous activity, and therefore a hotel was liable for the negligence of an independent contractor in failing to provide post-fight medical monitoring and an ambulance); Beckman v. Butte-Silver Bow Cty., 1 P.3d 348 (Mont. 2000) (trenching is an inherently dangerous activity because the risks of death or serious bodily injury are well-recognized in the construction industry and special precautions are required to prevent a cave-in that could bury a worker); Saiz v. Belen Sch. Dist., 827 P.2d 102 (N.M. 1992) (installation of a high-voltage light system at a football stadium was inherently dangerous work); Huddleston v. Union Rural Elec. Ass'n, 841 P.2d 282 (Colo. 1992) (it was for the jury to determine whether the inherently dangerous activity exception applied to a utility which hired a charter airplane service to fly passengers in winter to the Colorado mountains in an unpressurized plane that was uncertified for flights into icy conditions).

Davis v. Devereux Foundation

Supreme Court of New Jersey
37 A.3d 469 (N.J. 2012)

Justice PATTERSON delivered the opinion of the Court.

.... Roland Davis (Davis) suffered severe burns after he was scalded with boiling water by Charlene McClain (McClain), a resident counselor employed by defendant Devereux Foundation (Devereux). Devereux ... provides services for disabled clients. McClain had no criminal record or prior history of violence. She attributed her act to Davis's previous aggressive behavior toward her, and to her anger about the recent murder of her boyfriend. She was convicted of, and incarcerated for, her assault upon Davis.

Plaintiff, who is Davis's mother and guardian *ad litem*, sued Devereux, its local affiliate ..., and McClain. Barred by the Charitable Immunity Act (CIA) ... from recovering against Devereux on a theory of negligence, plaintiff urges the Court to impose a "non-delegable duty" upon Devereux to protect its residents from the intentional acts of its employees. Plaintiff further contends that McClain was acting within the scope of her employment when she assaulted Davis, and that Devereux should accordingly be held liable pursuant to principles of *respondeat superior*.

... [T]he trial court granted Devereux's motion for summary judgment dismissing all claims. The Appellate Division ... affirmed the trial court's determination that Devereux did not owe Davis a "non-delegable duty,".... However, the Appellate Division reversed the trial court's grant of summary judgment, holding that a reasonable jury could conclude that McClain acted in part within the scope of her employment....

... Devereux conducted a thorough background investigation [of McClain] that revealed no hint of the violent episode to come.

... Davis had a history of aggression toward Devereux staff.... Two such altercations involving McClain occurred shortly before the incident that gave rise to this case.... Davis kicked McClain and "had to be separated from her," prompting McClain to "[lose] her cool"....

The following morning, ... McClain was assigned to serve as Davis's resident counselor for the day. Early that morning, ... McClain put a cup of water in the facility's microwave and heated it. She then scalded Davis with the boiling water as he got out of bed. . . .

. . . .[1]

The doctrine of *respondeat superior* . . . originated in the seventeenth-century common law of England, based upon the concept "that one who would manage his or her affairs through others is obligated to third persons damaged by such others acting in the course of their employment." . . . . The *respondeat superior* standard thus focuses the Court on the relationship between the employee's job responsibilities and his or her tortious conduct.

. . . .

The [non-delegable] duty asserted by plaintiff diverges from traditional concepts of employer liability in two critical respects. First, in contrast to the "scope of employment" standard, which turns on the parameters of the employment relationship, the duty urged here derives from the relationship between the employer and the person to whom the duty is owed. It is imposed because it is of extraordinary importance to the public. . . .

Second, the duty imposed on the employer cannot be satisfied by the employer's exercise of reasonable care. Only the employee's due care can ensure that the employer's duty is satisfied. When such duty is imposed, "the employer's use of care is irrelevant." . . . . Measures taken by the employer to guard against intentional harm by employees — careful review of an applicant's educational and employment history, a thorough background check, probing interviews, meticulous training and exemplary supervision — would offer no defense to liability in the presence of the "non-delegable duty." Once an employee has committed a tortious act, the duty would effectively impose absolute liability upon residential institutions. . . . The duty would thus represent a significant expansion of New Jersey tort law, at the expense of charitable organizations and other providers of essential services to people with developmental disabilities.

. . . . [T]his Court has consistently applied traditional principles of due care and foreseeability to cases involving *in loco parentis* relationships, rather than adopting a "non-delegable" or absolute duty such as that urged by plaintiff here. . . .

. . . . [The court concluded that the non-delegable duty at issue was "not justified by the relationship among the relevant parties, required by the nature of the risk, warranted by the opportunity and ability to exercise care, or grounded in the public policy of our State." Moreover, it found that "imposition of liability for unexpected criminal acts of properly screened, trained and supervised employees would jeopardize charitable institutions that provide critical services for disabled citizens." The court further concluded that "nothing in the language or legislative history of the two relevant statutes — the CIA and DDRA [the Developmentally Disabled Rights Act] — suggests the Legislature's intent that a 'non-delegable duty' be imposed here."]

1. [Fn. 1:] . . . [T]he trial court entered a default judgment against McClain. . . .

.... Existing law already places a duty of reasonable care on Devereux; plaintiff seeks to elevate that duty to one of absolute liability.... There is no evidence that Devereux ignored hints that McClain had a potential for violence, that it condoned or tolerated aggressive behavior by its employees, or that it failed to teach its staff how to deliver respectful and compassionate care. The record reveals no deviation from sound hiring, screening and training practices. It defines no procedures by which an employer in Devereux's situation could anticipate and forestall the harm visited by McClain upon Davis....

.... Non-profit charitable organizations perform an invaluable service to their clients with developmental disabilities and the public as a whole. The imposition of liability upon these organizations for unforeseeable intentional acts of employees such as McClain could jeopardize their continued existence, deter the founding of new providers that could deliver quality services, and increase the cost incurred by residents, families and the State in maintaining residents in institutional care....

Our current state of the law is thus consistent with the decisions of almost every jurisdiction that has addressed this question.

....

We decline to impose a "non-delegable duty" upon Devereux in this case.[2] ....

....

[The court also rejected the plaintiff's respondeat superior claim:] In short, the Court finds that no rational factfinder could construe McClain's premeditated and unprovoked scalding of Davis to be an effort to serve Devereux. As a matter of law, McClain's assault was not within the scope of her employment.... The trial court properly granted summary judgment dismissing plaintiff's claims against Devereux.

... [W]e affirm the Appellate Division's decision insofar as it rejected the imposition of a "non-delegable duty" upon Devereux. We reverse the Appellate Division's decision to the extent that it held that the trial court's grant of summary judgment was error.

Justice HOENS, dissenting.

.... I respectfully dissent.

Much of the basis for the difference between my views and those expressed by the majority arises from the relative infrequency with which this Court has considered the concept of a non-delegable duty. Because it is a concept not often discussed, it is one that has become misunderstood, and therefore improperly analyzed by the majority, leading to an erroneous result....

....

2. [Fn. 10:] ... We do not reach the issue of whether the "non-delegable duty" at issue, were such a duty to be recognized, would be barred by the CIA....

Although the imposition of a non-delegable duty has been a relatively infrequent occurrence, this Court has previously addressed it. *See* Majestic Realty Assocs., Inc. v. Toti Contracting Co., 30 N.J. 425, 436, 153 A.2d 321 (1959). In determining whether the owner of a building, who hired an expert to demolish it, owed the adjoining building's owner a non-delegable duty of care, the Court's approach to the question is instructive. In considering that question, the existence of a duty of care to the adjoining building owner was obvious, and the only question was whether hiring an independent contractor, which under ordinary circumstances would afford the owner a complete shield against liability, discharged that duty of care.... In concluding that it did not, this Court reasoned that there are some duties that simply cannot be delegated away, and concluded that the performance of building demolition created such a risk of injury to the neighbor that it qualified as one of them.... [*See also*] Great Northern Ins. Co. v. Leontarakis, 387 N.J. Super. 583, 592–93, 904 A.2d 846 (App. Div. 2006) (concluding that duty of lateral support owed to adjoining landowner is non-delegable); Marek v. Prof'l Health Servs., Inc., 179 N.J. Super. 433, 441–42, 432 A.2d 538 (App. Div. 1981) (concluding that health care provider had non-delegable duty "to carefully and diligently diagnose within reasonable professional standards any condition or disease positively appearing on [the plaintiff's] chest x-ray" notwithstanding referral to independent contractor radiologist).

... [T]he existence of a non-delegable duty does not equate with the imposition of strict liability on the master, ... nor does it implicate the level of care used by the master in choosing the servant in the first place. Instead, when the servant performs a non-delegable duty, the determination of the master's liability turns on whether the servant used due care in the performance of that duty, not upon whether the master used due care in selecting or training the servant. As a result, if the duty is non-delegable, the employer will be liable to the third party if the employee failed to act with due care regardless of whether the act of the employee was within or outside of the scope of employment....

For affirmance in part; reversal in part—Chief Justice RABNER and Justices LaVECCHIA, ALBIN and PATTERSON and Judge WEFING (temporarily assigned).

For dissent—Justices LONG and HOENS.

Notes

1. ***Negligent Hiring, Training, and Supervision.*** Even if *respondeat superior* is inapplicable and the matter does not involve a non-delegable duty, it may be possible to hold a principal liable for injuries caused by an agent under the doctrine of negligent hiring, training, and supervision. This action requires a showing that the principal had actual or constructive notice of the agent's incompetence and that the injury complained of resulted from that incompetence. *See* Adams v. YMCA of San Antonio, 265 S.W.3d 915 (Tex. 2008) (holding a summer camp operator liable on a negligent hiring, training, and supervision theory to a camper who was sexually abused by a counselor); Ponticas v. K.M.S. Invs., 331 N.W.2d 907 (Minn. 1983)

(liability was imposed because an apartment complex was negligent in investigating the background of a manager who raped a tenant; the manager had a history of violent offenses and was given access to a passkey).

But see Khan v. Houston NFL Holdings LP, 277 Fed. Appx. 503 (5th Cir. 2008) (holding that it was not negligent to hire off-duty police officers as security guards regardless of the fact that the defendant could have made disclosure of the officers' personnel files a condition of employment, which was not an industry practice); Medlin v. Bass, 398 S.E.2d 460 (N.C. 1990) (where a school principal who perpetrated a sexual assault had performed his official duties in a satisfactory manner for 16 years, and the only rumor relating to his sexual tendencies had been investigated and remained unconfirmed, there was no evidence that the defendant Board of Education knew or could have known of the principal's alleged pedophilic tendencies).

Does an employer's liability for negligent hiring end once the employee is discharged? "In many instances it may, but where the employer has created a special relationship whereby his customers admit his employee into their homes, then the employer may be required to give notice or warning to the customers that the employee is no longer employed." Coath v. Jones, 419 A.2d 1249, 1250 (Pa. Super. Ct. 1980).

2. ***Ethics in Law Practice: Malpractice Liability Related to Foreign Outsourcing of Legal Services.*** American law firms increasingly outsource client-related tasks to service providers in foreign countries, such as India, the Philippines, and China. These practices are certain to generate legal malpractice tort claims, for deficiencies in the performance of outsourced work are at least as likely to occur as are the many kinds of professional shortcomings that routinely impair the quality of legal services performed domestically.

Outsourcing law firms are subject to liability under a variety of theories. Some impose liability for the outsourcing firm's own blameworthy conduct (such as claims alleging negligent selection or supervision of the foreign provider). Others impose vicarious liability on the outsourcing law firm for the deficient conduct of the foreign provider (such as under a *respondeat superior* theory when the foreign provider is an employee of the American firm). One theory of vicarious liability that deserves careful consideration is liability for breach of non-delegable duties owed by a law firm to a client:

> The Restatement (Third) of the Law Governing Lawyers states as a simple matter of fact that "[a] firm and its principals are not liable to the client for the acts and omissions of independent contractors except when a contractor is performing the firm's own non-delegable duty to the client." The corresponding Reporter's Note cites a case from one of the nation's most eminent tribunals, the New York Court of Appeals. In Kleeman v. Rheingold [614 N.E.2d 712 (N.Y. 1993)], the highest court of New York ruled that a law firm had a non-delegable duty to its client to exercise care in assuring proper service of legal process and was therefore liable for an independent

contractor's negligent performance of that duty. In terms that might easily be applied to malpractice claims involving foreign outsourcing, Judge Titone explained the analysis of the court:

> ... [A] duty will be deemed non-delegable when "'the responsibility is so important to the community that the employer should not be permitted to transfer it to another'".... This flexible formula recognizes that the "privilege to farm out [work] has its limits" and that those limits are best defined by reference to the gravity of the public policies that are implicated....
>
> .... Manifestly, when an individual retains an attorney to commence an action, timely and accurate service of process is an integral part of the task that the attorney undertakes.... Given the central importance of this duty, our State's attorneys cannot be allowed to evade responsibility for its careful performance by the simple expedient of "farming out" the task to independent contractors.
>
> The existence of an extensive and comprehensive Code of Professional Responsibility that governs the obligations of attorneys to their clients reinforces our conclusion. Under the Code, a lawyer may not "seek, by contract or other means, to ... limit prospectively the lawyer's individual liability to a client for malpractice".... Moreover, the Code forbids lawyers from "[n]eglect[ing] legal matter[s] entrusted to [them]" ..., enjoins them to assist in "secur[ing] and protect[ing] available legal rights" ... and requires them to represent their clients as zealously as the "bounds of the law" permit....
>
> Our conclusion is also supported by the perceptions of the lay public and the average client, who may reasonably assume that all of the tasks associated with the commencement of an action, including its formal initiation through service of process, will be performed either by the attorney or someone acting under the attorney's direction. While it may be a common practice among attorneys to retain outside agencies ... to assist them in effecting service, that custom is not necessarily one of which the general public is aware. Even where a client is expressly made aware that a process serving agency will be retained, it is unlikely that the client will understand or appreciate that the process serving agency's legal status as an "independent contractor" could render the retained attorney immune from liability for the agency's negligence. Under established principles, the client's reasonable expectations and beliefs about who will render a particular service are a significant factor in identifying duties that should be deemed to be "non-delegable"....
>
> .... The responsibility for achieving ... [the goal of timely commencement of legal actions] — and the liability for negligent failures to achieve it — must remain squarely on the shoulders of trained and licensed

> attorneys who, as members of a "learned profession," alone have the necessary knowledge and experience to protect their clients' rights.
>
> .... Saying that a duty is non-delegable is just a different way of saying that the lawyer remains ultimately responsible.

Vincent R. Johnson & Stephen C. Loomis, *Malpractice Liability Related to Foreign Outsourcing of Legal Services* 2 St. Mary's J. Legal Mal. & Ethics 262, 308–11 (2012).

Economic Analysis
Deterrence under Negligence and Strict Liability

Alan Gunn

Will an employer's willingness to take safety precautions depend upon whether the employer is strictly liable for the negligence of its employees or whether the employer is liable only for its own negligence—such as careless hiring of incompetent employees or failure to train or supervise its employees carefully enough? As a first approximation, at least, it may make no difference at all. If one assumes that neither courts nor employers ever make mistakes about negligence, and that damages are set accurately, both strict liability and negligence should give the employer the same incentive to take safety precautions.

To see why strict liability and negligence may be equivalent with respect to safety measures, consider an employer who is deciding whether to spend an additional $1,000 a year in safety training in order to encourage employees to drive more carefully. Suppose that spending the additional $1,000 each year will, on average, prevent one accident every 10 years, and that the cost of the harm done by one accident is either

(1) $12,000, or

(2) $8,000.

If the employer is strictly liable for harm done by its employees, it has an incentive to spend the $1,000 a year to prevent one $12,000 accident every ten years, as the expected annual saving from spending $1,000 a year is $1,200. But the employer would not want to spend $1,000 a year to prevent a one-in-ten chance of an $8,000 accident. The average annual cost of the latter sort of accident is only $800, so the employer will be better off not spending the $1,000 a year on training and paying an average of $800 a year in damages instead.

What if the standard of care is negligence? Again, the employer's incentive is to spend $1,000 a year on training if the expected annual accident cost is $1,200, but not if it is $800. In this case, if the employer does not spend the $1,000 a year to prevent accidents expected to cost $1,200 a year, the employer will be negligent, and therefore liable. (It is unreasonable not to spend $1,000 to prevent harm of $1,200.) If the expected harm from accidents is only $800 a year, the employer will not be found negligent if the $1,000 is not spent, as reasonable care does not require spending $1,000 to save $800. Therefore, under both negligence and strict liability, the employer has the same incentive to take safety precautions.

Two important qualifications to the above discussion are necessary. First, suppose that it is very hard for outsiders — including potential plaintiffs — to get evidence of the inadequacy of an employer's safety precautions. In that case, strict liability will provide the correct incentive, and negligence will not. For instance, suppose that the employer could prevent harm of $1,000 a year by spending $600 a year, and that the employer knows that even if it doesn't spend the money it has a very good chance of convincing juries that it took all "reasonable" precautions. Under a negligence standard, the employer might not spend the $600 in the hope that it will not be held liable for the $1,000 in harm expected to occur.

Second, even if strict liability and negligence create the same incentive to take safety precautions, they differ in another potentially important way: strict liability increases the costs of conducting an activity which will cause injuries even when that activity is carried on with no negligence. For instance, suppose that an employer of truck drivers estimates the average accident cost per trip to be $30 (all borne by outsiders), and suppose that this cost cannot be reduced further by any cost-effective measures the employer can take. If the standard for the employer's liability is negligence, the employer has an incentive to send a driver out even if the trip will earn the employer only $20. Although the expected harm from the trip — $30 — exceeds the employer's benefit — $20 — the harm will fall on someone else. If the employer is strictly liable, it will send the employee out only if the trip will earn more than $30.

Because strict liability — unlike negligence — affects activity levels as well as safety precautions, economists who study tort liability often say that strict liability is efficient, and that negligence is not. This is not always true. Consider the matter (examined further in the next chapter) of strict liability for adverse side effects caused by prescription medicine. If the manufacturer of the medicine is liable for all harm done by the medicine, even though that harm could not have been prevented, the manufacturer's costs will be high, and less of the medicine will be used than if the manufacturer were not liable. If, despite its occasional harmful side-effects, the medicine does a great deal of good by curing disease, any reduction in activity level occasioned by strict liability may do more harm than good. (The harm will fall largely upon those too poor to buy the medicine at a price high enough to cover anticipated liability costs.) The "activity level" case for strict liability ignores the possibility that conducting an activity may provide safety benefits on an overall basis even though it does harm in particular cases.

4. Ostensible or Apparent Agency

Baptist Memorial Hospital System v. Sampson

Supreme Court of Texas
969 S.W.2d 945 (Tex. 1998)

PHILLIPS, Chief Justice, delivered the opinion of the Court.

... Rhea Sampson was bitten on the arm by an unidentified creature that was later identified as a brown recluse spider. By that evening, her arm was swollen and painful, and a friend took her to the Southeast Baptist Hospital emergency room. Dr. Susan Howle, an emergency room physician, examined Sampson, diagnosed an allergic reaction, administered Benadryl and a shot of painkiller, prescribed medication for pain and swelling, and sent her home. Her condition grew worse, and she returned to the Hospital's emergency room by ambulance a little over a day later. This time Dr. Mark Zakula, another emergency room physician, treated her. He administered additional pain medication and released her.... About fourteen hours later, with her condition rapidly deteriorating, Sampson went to another hospital and was admitted to the intensive care ward in septic shock. There, her bite was diagnosed as that of a brown recluse spider, and the proper treatment was administered to save her life. Sampson allegedly continues to have recurrent pain and sensitivity where she was bitten, respiratory difficulties, and extensive scarring.

Sampson sued Drs. Howle and Zakula for medical malpractice. She also sued Baptist Memorial Hospital System ("BMHS").... Sampson ... alleged that the Hospital was vicariously liable for Dr. Zakula's alleged negligence under an ostensible agency theory. Sampson nonsuited Dr. Howle early in the discovery process. The trial court granted BMHS summary judgment on Sampson's claims of vicarious liability.... Sampson appealed....

Both parties agree that BMHS established as a matter of law that Dr. Zakula was not its agent or employee.... Sampson contended that she raised a material fact issue on whether Dr. Zakula was BMHS's ostensible agent. The court of appeals, with one justice dissenting, agreed and reversed the summary judgment....

.... Because an independent contractor has sole control over the means and methods of the work to be accomplished, ... the individual or entity that hires the independent contractor is generally not vicariously liable for the tort or negligence of that person.... Nevertheless, an individual or entity may act in a manner that makes it liable for the conduct of one who is not its agent at all or who, although an agent, has acted outside the scope of his or her authority. Liability may be imposed in this manner under the doctrine of ostensible agency in circumstances when the principal's conduct should equitably prevent it from denying the existence of an agency.[3] .... Ostensible agency in Texas is based on the

3. [Fn. 2:] Many courts use the terms ostensible agency, apparent agency, apparent authority, and agency by estoppel interchangeably. As a practical matter, there is no distinction among

notion of estoppel, that is, a representation by the principal causing justifiable reliance and resulting harm. . . .

. . . [A] hospital may be vicariously liable for the medical malpractice of independent contractor physicians when plaintiffs can establish the elements of ostensible agency. . . .

. . . . As we have explained:

> Apparent authority . . . may arise either from a principal knowingly permitting an agent to hold herself out as having authority or by a principal's actions which lack such ordinary care as to clothe an agent with the indicia of authority, thus leading a reasonably prudent person to believe that the agent has the authority she purports to exercise. . . .
>
> A prerequisite to a proper finding of apparent authority is evidence of conduct by the principal relied upon by the party asserting the estoppel defense which would lead a reasonably prudent person to believe an agent had authority to so act.

. . . . Thus, to establish a hospital's liability for an independent contractor's medical malpractice based on ostensible agency, a plaintiff must show that (1) he or she had a reasonable belief that the physician was the agent or employee of the hospital, (2) such belief was generated by the hospital affirmatively holding out the physician as its agent or employee or knowingly permitting the physician to hold herself out as the hospital's agent or employee, and (3) he or she justifiably relied on the representation of authority. . . .

. . . [W]e reject the suggestion of the court of appeals . . . that we disregard the traditional rules and take "the full leap" of imposing a non-delegable duty on Texas hospitals for the malpractice of emergency room physicians. . . . Imposing such a duty is not necessary to safeguard patients in hospital emergency rooms. A patient injured by a physician's malpractice is not without a remedy. The injured patient ordinarily has a cause of action against the negligent physician, and may retain a direct cause of action against the hospital if the hospital was negligent in the performance of a duty owed directly to the patient. . . .

. . . .

As summary judgment evidence, BMHS offered the affidavit of Dr. Potyka, an emergency room physician, which established that the emergency room doctors are not the actual agents, servants, or employees of the Hospital, and are not subject to the supervision, management, direction, or control of the Hospital when treating patients. Dr. Potyka further stated that when Dr. Zakula treated Sampson, signs were posted in the emergency room notifying patients that the emergency room physicians were independent contractors. Dr. Potyka's affidavit also established that

---

them. . . . Regardless of the term used, the purpose of the doctrine is to prevent injustice and protect those who have been misled. . . .

the Hospital did not collect any fees for emergency room physician services and that the physicians billed the patients directly. BMHS presented copies of signed consent forms as additional summary judgment evidence. During both of Sampson's visits to the Hospital emergency room, before being examined or treated, Sampson signed a "Consent for Diagnosis, Treatment and Hospital Care" form explaining that all physicians at the Hospital are independent contractors who exercise their own professional judgment without control by the Hospital. The consent forms read in part:

> I acknowledge and agree that . . . , Southeast Baptist Hospital, . . . and any Hospital operated as a part of Baptist Memorial Hospital System, is not responsible for the judgment or conduct of any physician who treats or provides a professional service to me, but rather each physician is an independent contractor who is self-employed and is not the agent, servant or employee of the hospital.

To establish her claim of ostensible agency, Sampson offered her own affidavits. In her original affidavit, she stated that although the Hospital directed her to sign several pieces of paper before she was examined, she did not read them and no one explained their contents to her. Her supplemental affidavit stated that she did not recall signing the documents and that she did not, at any time during her visit to the emergency room, see any signs stating that the doctors who work in the emergency room are not employees of the Hospital. Both affidavits state that she did not choose which doctor would treat her and that, at all times, she believed that a physician employed by the hospital was treating her. Based on this record we must determine if Sampson produced sufficient summary judgment evidence to raise a genuine issue of material fact on each element of ostensible agency, thereby defeating BMHS's summary judgment motion.

Even if Sampson's belief that Dr. Zakula was a hospital employee were reasonable, that belief, as we have seen, must be based on or generated by some conduct on the part of the Hospital. . . . The summary judgment proof establishes that the Hospital took no affirmative act to make actual or prospective patients think the emergency room physicians were its agents or employees, and did not fail to take reasonable efforts to disabuse them of such a notion. As a matter of law, on this record, no conduct by the Hospital would lead a reasonable patient to believe that the treating emergency room physicians were hospital employees.

Sampson has failed to raise a fact issue on at least one essential element of her claim. Accordingly, we reverse the judgment of the court of appeals and render judgment that Sampson take nothing.

Notes

1. ***Apparent Authority (Apparent Agency).*** *See* Estate of Cordero *ex rel.* Cordero v. Christ Hosp., 958 A.2d 101 (N.J. Super. A.D. 2008) (holding that the evidence would support a finding that an anesthesiologist acted with apparent authority from a hospital); O'Banner v. McDonald's Corp., 670 N.E.2d 632, 634 (Ill. 1996) (holding that

a restaurant patron who was injured when he slipped and fell in a restaurant's restroom could not recover on "apparent agency" theory from the restaurant franchisor, as patron failed to show that he actually relied on the alleged apparent agency between the franchisee and franchisor in going to the restaurant).

2. ***Manifestations Traceable to the Employer.*** Restatement, Third, of Agency § 2.03 cmt. c (2006), the section on apparent authority, states:

> The doctrine . . . applies to any set of circumstances under which it is reasonable for a third party to believe that an agent has authority, so long as the belief is traceable to manifestations of the principal. . . . A third party's reasonable understanding of the principal's conduct will reflect general business custom, as well as usage that is particular to the principal's industry and prior dealings between the parties. A belief that results solely from the statements or other conduct of the agent, unsupported by any manifestations traceable to the principal, does not create apparent authority unless . . . the agent's conduct has been directed by the principal. An agent's success in misleading the third party as to the existence of actual authority does not in itself make the principal accountable. . . .

3. ***Problem: Stealing a Client.*** A telephone call to a law firm from a prospective client who saw the firm's television ad is routed by the receptionist to an associate, who normally handles such calls. Because the prospective client is disabled, the associate goes to her home to discuss providing representation with respect to prosecution of her personal injury claim. The associate gives the woman one of his law firm business cards, but scratches out the phone number and writes down his cell phone number. He tells the woman that it is best always to call him on his cell phone, and to speak with him personally, to ensure that her case is handled most efficiently. He directs the woman not to bother calling the general phone number for the law firm.

The associate gives the woman a contract to sign. The contract is not the firm's standard contract, but merely a generic form. The form does not contain the name of the law firm. It merely has a blank for the name of the attorney to be filled in, and the associate has written his name in that blank. The client and the associate both sign the contract.

The associate's intent is to "steal" the client from the law firm and to collect the entire fee that results from the representation. No case file for the client is ever established at the law firm, and no one at the firm ever learns of the relationship with the woman. That is not uncommon because many prospective clients are not signed up. Because the associate lacks the resources to hire the necessary experts to assist in the preparation of the case, the matter languishes and important deadlines pass, despite the fact that the woman was seriously harmed and is in pain.

When the woman calls the law firm to complain, she learns that no one in the firm, other than the associate, has ever heard of her case. The firm denies that it has any attorney-client relationship with the woman. The woman sues the law firm for malpractice, alleging that the associate acted with apparent authority and that the law firm is therefore responsible for his bungling of the case. The law firm has never had a problem like this before. What result?

5. The Fellow-Servant Rule

The fellow-servant rule once held that, despite the principle of *respondeat superior*, an employer could not be held liable for harm to an employee that resulted from the conduct of a fellow worker. The injured employee was deemed to have assumed the risk of a co-employee's negligence by reason of having accepted employment during which negligent conduct might occur. The once-significant effect of the harsh fellow-servant rule was greatly diminished by the advent of workers' compensation. To the extent that the rule survives, decisions such as Buckley v. City of New York, 437 N.E.2d 1088 (N.Y. 1982), have refused to apply it on the ground that it is an unsound departure from the policies of deterrence and spreading of losses that are inherent in the rule of *respondeat superior*. Today, the fellow-servant rule plays no significant role in tort litigation.

B. Harm Inflicted by Animals

Wild versus Domestic. A possessor's liability for harm caused by animals frequently depends upon whether the animal is classified as wild or domestic. In the case of harm done by wild animals, liability is usually strict; liability for harm done by domestic animals is normally based on negligence.

Wild Animals (Ferae Naturae). The Third Restatement provides:

> § 22. Wild Animals
>
> (a) An owner or possessor of a wild animal is subject to strict liability for physical harm caused by the wild animal.
>
> (b) A wild animal is an animal that belongs to a category of animals that have not been generally domesticated and that are likely, unless restrained, to cause personal injury.

Restatement, Third, of Torts: Liab. for Physical and Emotional Harm § 22 (2010). According to the commentary:

> The wild-animal definition . . . requires that each of two elements be satisfied: that the category of animals is not generally domesticated and that the category of animals if unrestrained is likely to cause physical injury. For purposes of the first element, the focus is on the status of the category of animals in the United States. . . .

Id. at cmt. b.

Liability under § 22 turns on ownership or possession of the animal, not ownership or possession of the land on which the animal may be present. "Thus, if a customer brings a rattlesnake into a store, it is the customer and not the store owner who is subject to strict liability if the rattlesnake attacks another customer." *Id.* at cmt. e. As to the rules governing harm that ensues following the escape, theft, or return of wild animals, see Comment e.

If the harm caused by a possessor's wild animal is not the result of a dangerous propensity of the species, as where a bear goes to sleep on the highway and is struck by the plaintiff's vehicle, the possessor can be held liable only upon a showing of negligence. *Id.* at cmt. f.

In Tracey v. Solesky, 50 A.3d 1075 (Md. 2012), the Maryland Court of Appeals held that if an owner or other person with the right to control a dog knows or has reason to know that the dog is a pit bull, that person is strictly liable for the damages caused to a plaintiff attacked by the dog. In 2014, the Maryland legislature passed the following statute. Which part of the statute overrules *Tracey*?

Maryland Code, Courts and Judicial Proceedings, § 3-1901

(Westlaw 2022)

§ 3-1901. Actions against dog owners for personal injury or death caused by dog

(a) (1) In an action against an owner of a dog for damages for personal injury or death caused by the dog, evidence that the dog caused the personal injury or death creates a rebuttable presumption that the owner knew or should have known that the dog had vicious or dangerous propensities.

(2) Notwithstanding any other law or rule, in a jury trial, the judge may not rule as a matter of law that the presumption has been rebutted before the jury returns a verdict. . . .

(b) In an action against a person other than an owner of a dog for damages for personal injury or death caused by the dog, the common law of liability relating to attacks by dogs against humans that existed on April 1, 2012, is retained as to the person without regard to the breed or heritage of the dog. . . .

(c) The owner of a dog is liable for any injury, death, or loss to person or property that is caused by the dog, while the dog is running at large, unless the injury, death, or loss was caused to the body or property of a person who was:

(1) Committing or attempting to commit a trespass or other criminal offense on the property of the owner;

(2) Committing or attempting to commit a criminal offense against any person; or

(3) Teasing, tormenting, abusing, or provoking the dog. . . .

(d) This section does not affect:

(1) Any other common law or statutory cause of action; or

(2) Any other common law or statutory defense or immunity.

Domestic Animals. At common law, a possessor of a domestic animal is strictly liable for harm which results from an *abnormally* dangerous propensity of the animal of which the possessor knows or has reason to know. Restatement, Second, of Torts § 509; Restatement, Third, of Torts: Liability for Physical and Emotional Harm § 23 (2010). The emphasis here is on the abnormality of the danger. Many domestic animals, such as bulls and stallions and other breeding animals, are known to have dangerous propensities. But these tendencies are deemed to be ordinary and necessary incidents of civilized life, since these animals are by custom devoted to the service of mankind. Only if a domestic animal poses an *abnormal* danger will strict liability apply.

Absent clear proof that the possessor was on notice of an abnormal danger, a possessor of a domestic animal will be liable only for negligence — which of course requires evidence that harm was foreseeable. *See* Bard v. Jahnke, 848 N.E.2d 463 (N.Y. 2006) (holding that, because the owner of a hornless dairy bull did not have knowledge of the bull's vicious propensities, an injured carpenter could not recover based on strict liability); Labaj v. VanHouten, 322 S.W.3d 416, 424 n.8 (Tex. App. 2010) ("[s]uits for damages caused by known vicious animals are governed by principles of strict liability").

Actual or constructive notice of a domestic animal's dangerousness (whether due to an abnormal propensity or not) is generally a prerequisite to recovery. However, some jurisdictions impose strict liability for unforeseeable dog bites on the theory that the possessor, who enjoys the benefits of having a dog, should also bear the resulting burdens and is in a better position to insure against them. *See* Harris v. Anderson County Sheriff's Office, 673 S.E.2d 423 (S.C. 2009), *supra*, p. 26.

Wandering Livestock and Other Animals. According to the Restatement:

> An owner or possessor of livestock or other animals, except for dogs and cats, that intrude upon the land of another is subject to strict liability for physical harm caused by the intrusion.

Restatement, Third, of Torts: Liability for Physical and Emotional Harm § 21 (2010). In some places, liability may depend upon whether the plaintiff or defendant is required by local law to erect and maintain a fence for the purpose of preventing harm. Some states reject the Restatement's strict liability rule. *Compare Mont. Code Ann. § 27-1-724 (Westlaw 2022) ("a person owning, controlling, or in possession of livestock . . . has no duty to keep livestock from wandering on highways and is not subject to liability for damages to any property or for injury to a person caused by an accident involving a motor vehicle and livestock unless the owner of the livestock or property was grossly negligent or engaged in intentional misconduct"), with* Gibbs v. Jackson, 990 S.W.2d 745 (Tex. 1999) (holding that the keeper of a horse had no statutory or common law duty to prevent the horse from roaming onto a farm-to-market roadway in an area that had not adopted a local stock law). *See also* Liley v. Cedar Springs Ranch Inc., 405 P.3d 817, 822 (Utah App. 2017) ("[m]ere status as a landlord does not make the landlord a possessor or a person in control of the tenant's" livestock, so as to make the landlord liable for negligence).

Limits on Strict Liability. The rules on strict liability for harm caused by animals, as well as the rules on strict liability for abnormally dangerous activity (discussed below), are designed largely to protect innocent third persons. Accordingly, these provisions cannot be invoked for the benefit of trespassers or persons who were seeking to secure some benefit from contact with or proximity to the animal or activity in question. *See* Restatement, Third, of Torts: Liab. for Physical and Emotional Harm § 24(a) (2010). Likewise, strict liability will not be imposed if the defendant maintained ownership or possession of the animal or conducted the activity pursuant to a duty imposed by law. *Id.* at § 24(b). Of course, even if strict-liability principles do not apply, the plaintiff may ordinarily seek to recover for negligence.

Statutory Standards. In many areas, the common law rules relating to harm caused by animals has been supplanted, in part, by statutory standards. *See, e.g.*, Bradacs v. Jiacobone, 625 N.W.2d 108 (Mich. Ct. App. 2001) (holding that a guest's conduct in reaching down to pick up a ball she had dropped some two feet from food being eaten by the homeowner's dog was not "provocation" sufficient to relieve the homeowners of liability under a dog bite statute).

C. Abnormally Dangerous Activities

Strict liability may be imposed for "abnormally dangerous" activities. However, it is often difficult to determine which activities are properly treated as *abnormally* dangerous. The critical question is sometimes whether the conduct in question is ill-suited to the locality. In Yommer v. McKenzie, 257 A.2d 138 (Md. 1969), the court held that the storage of large quantities of gasoline immediately adjacent to a well from which a family drew its water was an activity inappropriate to the locale. It therefore imposed strict liability for leakage that poisoned the plaintiff's water supply.

Assumption of the Risk. A potential plaintiff's assumption of the risk of harm from an abnormally dangerous activity bars recovery for the harm, in whole or in part, depending upon the jurisdiction's adoption of comparative principles. *See* Sheard v. Hattum, 965 N.W.2d 134, 146 (S.D. 2021) (ruling on the issue as a matter of first impression).

Stout v. Warren

Supreme Court of Washington, En Banc
290 P.3d 972 (Wash. 2012)

STEPHENS, J.

Larry Stout was severely injured during his apprehension by a subcontractor of CJ Johnson Bail Bonds (CJ Johnson) and sued the subcontractor, the contractor, and the owners of CJ Johnson. Stout asserts two theories of vicarious liability: (1) the activity is an "abnormally dangerous" one, *see* Restatement (Second) of Torts § 427A (1965), and (2) the activity (a) involves a "special danger" that is "inherent in or normal to the work," *id.* § 427, or (b) poses a "peculiar risk of physical harm," *id.* § 416. The trial court granted summary judgment to the owners of CJ Johnson, determining that vicarious liability does not apply. The Court of Appeals affirmed on different grounds....

... Stout was charged with multiple felonies related to the manufacture of methamphetamine. Bail was set at $50,000, and Stout entered into an agreement with CJ Johnson, a sole proprietorship, which posted the bail bond. Stout failed to appear at two hearings so ... a bench warrant was issued for his arrest and the Pierce County prosecuting attorney's office notified CJ Johnson that it would forfeit its bond.... CJ Johnson entered into a contract with C.C.S.R., a business solely consisting of Michael Golden, to "... [secure the physical custody of Stout and surrender] him ... to" the Pierce County jail.... At some point after C.C.S.R. obtained the contract, Carl Warren contacted Golden, stating that he could apprehend Stout. Golden faxed Warren the necessary paperwork.

On July 16, 2002, Stout left a residence in Pierce County and was traveling down a gravel roadway. As he did so, a 1977 Chevy 4 × 4 pickup truck driven by Warren pulled out and accelerated rapidly toward him. Stout also accelerated to avoid a collision, but Warren rammed the rear end of Stout's 1997 Toyota Corolla, causing it to collide with a tree.... After hitting the tree, Stout was pinned in the vehicle and eventually had to have one leg amputated.

Stout filed an amended complaint for damages ... [against Johnson and others]....

The general rule in Washington is that a principal is not liable for injuries caused by an independent contractor whose services are engaged by the principal.... Two exceptions to this general rule are at issue in the present case: (1) carrying on "an abnormally dangerous activity," *id.* § 427A, and (2) engaging in an activity that is inherently dangerous or poses a "peculiar risk of physical harm," *id.* §§ 416, 427....

Abnormally dangerous activity vicarious liability and peculiar risk vicarious liability are two distinct theories, ... though our case law has not rigorously distinguished between them....

Whether an activity is abnormally dangerous is determined through consideration of six factors. Restatement (Second) of Torts § 520 (1977).[4] The factors consider whether the "dangers and inappropriateness for the locality" of the activity are "so great that, despite any usefulness it may have for the community, [the principal] should be required as a matter of law to pay for any harm it causes, without the need of a finding of negligence." . . . . By contrast, a "peculiar risk of physical harm to others" is one that arises out "of the same character" of "the work to be done" and that "is not a normal, routine matter of customary human activity." *Id.* § 416 & cmt. b, § 413 cmt. b. In particular, a significant distinction between the two theories of vicarious liability is that if the activity is likely to result in harm despite all reasonable care, it is apt to be an abnormally dangerous activity. . . . An abnormally dangerous activity . . . creates strict liability . . . while an activity posing a peculiar risk does not.

. . . .

Fugitive defendant apprehension is not an abnormally dangerous activity. In determining whether an activity is abnormally dangerous, the following factors are to be considered:

> (a) existence of a high degree of risk of some harm to the person, land or chattels of others;
>
> (b) likelihood that the harm that results from it will be great;
>
> (c) inability to eliminate the risk by the exercise of reasonable care;
>
> (d) extent to which the activity is not a matter of common usage;
>
> (e) inappropriateness of the activity to the place where it is carried on; and
>
> (f) extent to which its value to the community is outweighed by its dangerous attributes.

Id. § 520. Though no single factor is either necessary or sufficient, . . . at least one factor among (a), (b), and (c) — the factors addressing whether the activity is "'ultrahazardous'" — must generally be present. . . . And, at least one factor among (d), (e), and (f) must also be present. . . . In addition, consideration of the likelihood of harm and its magnitude "'must be further evaluated in light of factor (c), which speaks of the 'inability to eliminate the risk by the exercise of reasonable care.'" . . . . The relevant "risk" under subsection (c) is the "'high degree of risk'" mentioned in subsection (a); thus, the mere existence of "[s]ome degree of risk" after exercising reasonable care is not sufficient to make subsection (c) weigh in favor of the activity being characterized as abnormally dangerous. . . .

Applying the section 520 factors to fugitive defendant apprehension, it becomes apparent that the activity is not abnormally dangerous. . . . While the record indicates that there is always a risk of *some* harm, it does not demonstrate the requisite

4. [Fn. 2 stated:] The parties did not brief or argue the applicability of the Third Restatement's reformulation of the "abnormally dangerous activity" definition. *See* Restatement (Third) of Torts: Liab. For Physical & Emotional Harm § 20(b) (2010). Accordingly, we do not address it. . . .

"high degree of risk" when reasonable care is exercised — to the contrary, the record suggests that harm infrequently results. In some cases, the magnitude of the harm may be significant, as a fleeing defendant may resort to the use of a deadly weapon to accomplish escape, but there is no showing of a *likelihood* that the harm will be great when reasonable precautions are taken, merely a possibility. Factors (a), (b), and (c) all weigh against treating fugitive defendant apprehension as an abnormally dangerous activity. Absent one of the first three factors, the activity is not "'ultra-hazardous'" and, therefore, cannot be an abnormally dangerous activity. . . .

An activity that is not abnormally dangerous may, nonetheless, pose a peculiar risk of harm and thereby subject a principal to liability for the negligence of its independent contractor. Two sections of the Restatement (Second) of Torts address peculiar risk vicarious liability. Section 416 provides as follows:

> One who employs an independent contractor to do work which the employer should recognize as likely to create during its progress a peculiar risk of physical harm to others unless special precautions are taken, is subject to liability for physical harm caused to them by the failure of the contractor to exercise reasonable care to take such precautions, even though the employer has provided for such precautions in the contract or otherwise.

Similarly, section 427 provides:

> One who employs an independent contractor to do work involving a special danger to others which the employer knows or has reason to know to be inherent in or normal to the work . . . is subject to liability for physical harm caused to such others by the contractor's failure to take reasonable precautions against such danger.

. . . [T]hese sections are two statements of the same principle. . . .

In order for vicarious liability to apply under these sections, (1) the activity itself must pose a risk of physical harm absent special or reasonable precautions (*i.e.*, the risk must be inherent to the activity), (2) the risk must "differ[ ] from the common risks to which persons in general are commonly subjected," . . . (*i.e.*, the risk must be "peculiar" or "special"), (3) the principal must know or have reason to know of the risk, and (4) the harm must arise from the contractor's negligence with respect to the risk that is inherent in the activity. . . . Elements (1) and (2) are properly treated as questions of law.

. . . .

In the context of fugitive defendant apprehension, there is a peculiar risk of harm absent special precautions (*i.e.*, elements (1) and (2) of the peculiar risk exception are satisfied). . . . This risk is twofold. First, there is a risk that the force that the bail bond recovery agent is authorized to employ will be exercised in a negligent or reckless manner causing physical harm. . . . Second, there is a risk that the bail bond recovery agent's negligent actions will cause the fugitive defendant to respond in a manner that causes physical harm to others. For example, if a bail bond recovery agent enters a fugitive defendant's home without identifying himself and fails to secure the fugitive defendant, the fugitive defendant might exercise deadly force in self-defense that causes physical harm to a third party.

The risks peculiar to and inherent in fugitive defendant apprehension differ from common risks to which members of the public are generally subjected. Members of the public are, in general, not subject to the risk of others mistakenly breaking into their homes or mistakenly apprehending them, nor are members of the public generally subject to the risk of being caught in the crossfire between fugitive defendants and those who would recapture them.

In sum, fugitive defendant apprehension is an activity that poses a peculiar risk of physical harm and, therefore, a bail bond company may be vicariously liable for the negligence of its independent contractor bail bond recovery agents.[5]

The Court of Appeals resolved this case under an "exception" to vicarious liability where a third party injured by the conduct of an independent contractor is not "innocent," but instead has "participated" in the dangerous activity that caused him injury. We reject this rule, which amounts to a mistakenly applied theory of assumption of risk. . . . In fact, there is no exception to vicarious liability for inherently dangerous activities based on assumption of risk principles. . . .

. . . . Such an expansive notion would potentially bar suits based on vicarious liability by any plaintiff who engages in conduct that increases the risk of injury. Consider, for example, if a fugitive's mother blocks the door of her home when a bounty hunter tries to enter in pursuit of the fugitive. Is she barred from bringing suit if she is injured when the bounty hunter decides to shoot through the door?

. . . [I]nnocence is not a precondition to asserting a tort claim, even one based on vicarious liability. Injury victims are often far from "innocent" with respect to the causes of their injury; this is comparative fault. There is no support in case law for creating a dual class of third-party plaintiffs: the innocent and the rest. Rather, a plaintiff's culpability, if any, is properly evaluated under settled tort doctrines. . . .[6] . . . .

. . . . We reverse the Court of Appeals.

[The dissenting opinion of Justice OWENS, J., in which Justice J. JOHNSON and C. JOHNSON, concurred, has been omitted.]

---

5. [Fn. 3:] We qualify our holding by noting that only the fugitive apprehension aspect of bail bond recovery is a peculiar risk activity and that there may be cases presenting a question of fact as to whether inherent or peculiar risks exist and are known to one hiring an independent contractor. On this record, we conclude that CJ Johnson is subject to vicarious liability for the actions of its independent contractor in seeking to apprehend Stout.

6. [Fn. 7:] On remand, CJ Johnson may assert assumption of risk or comparative fault, depending on the facts. Moreover, as noted, we are not talking about a strict liability theory if peculiar risk vicarious liability exists, nothing precludes the further consideration of whether the agent's conduct was outside the scope of his authority.

Notes

1. ***Must "Abnormally Dangerous Activities" Be Abnormally Dangerous?*** Consider the two lists that follow: the first list encompasses some activities that have been held (at least by some courts) to subject the person who conducts them to strict liability; the second list includes activities for which liability is based on negligence.

***Strict Liability Activities*:**

- Storing water in a reservoir. (*See* Rylands v. Fletcher, 1 Exch. 265 (1866), *aff'd* Rylands v. Fletcher, L.R. 3 H.L. 330 (1868).)
- Using explosives. (*See, e.g.*, Green v. Ensign-Bickford Co., 595 A.2d 1383 (Conn. App. Ct. 1991).)
- Flying an aircraft (with respect to damage done to objects on the ground when the aircraft comes down). (*See* Restatement, Second, of Torts § 520, but note that many jurisdictions do not follow the Restatement on this point. *See also* Guille v. Swan, 19 Johns 381 (N.Y. 1822) (holding the operator of a balloon liable for damage done to crops when the balloon landed, with no showing that the pilot of the balloon was negligent).)
- Keeping a wild animal as a pet. (See the text earlier in this chapter.)
- Pile driving. (*See* Caporale v. C.W. Blakeslee & Sons, Inc., 175 A.2d 561 (Conn. 1961).)
- Conducting a fireworks display. (*See* Klein v. Pyrodyne Corp., 810 P.2d 917, *modified*, 817 P.2d 1359 (Wash. 1991).)
- Testing rockets. (*See* Smith v. Lockheed Propulsion Co., 56 Cal. Rptr. 128 (Ct. App. 1967) (vibrations damaged plaintiff's well).)
- Dusting crops. (*See* Langan v. Valicopters, Inc., 567 P.2d 218 (Wash. 1977).)
- Disposing of hazardous waste. (*See* Kenney v. Scientific, Inc., 497 A.2d 1310 (N.J. Super. Ct. Law Div. 1985); *contra* Shockley v. Hoechst Celanese Corp., 1993 WL 241179 (4th Cir.).)
- Fumigating a building. (*See* Old Island Fumigation, Inc. v. Barbee, 604 So. 2d 1246 (Fla. Dist. Ct. App. 1992).)

***Activities for Which Liability Is Based on Negligence*:**

- Driving an automobile in a city where small children may run into the street. (*See, e.g.*, Rios v. Sifuentes, 347 N.E.2d 337 (Ill. App. Ct. 1976).)
- Selling explosives. (*See, e.g.*, Allen v. Gornto, 112 S.E.2d 368 (Ga. Ct. App. 1959).)
- Flying an aircraft (with respect to damage done to persons in the aircraft or to persons in other aircraft with which the defendant's aircraft collides). (*See, e.g.*, Farina v. Pan American World Airlines, Inc., 497 N.Y.S.2d 706 (App. Div. 1986) (negligence action by passenger injured in runway accident).)
- Keeping a bull on a farm. (*See* Warren v. Davis, 539 S.W.2d 907 (Tex. Civ. App. 1976) (collision between bull and decedent's automobile).)

- Drilling and operating natural gas wells. (*See* Williams v. Amoco Prod. Co., 734 P.2d 1113 (Kan. 1987).)
- Driving under the influence of alcohol. (*See* Goodwin v. Reilley, 221 Cal. Rptr. 374 (Ct. App. 1985).)
- Hauling steel. (*See* Inland Steel v. Pequignot, 608 N.E.2d 1378 (Ind. Ct. App. 1993).)
- Shipping a flammable toxic chemical by rail. (*See* Indiana Harbor Belt Railroad v. American Cyanamid Co., 916 F.2d 1174 (7th Cir. 1990).)

Some reflection on these examples strongly suggests that despite the Restatement's insistence that strict liability applies to those who engage in "abnormally dangerous" activities (or, as the first Restatement put it, "ultrahazardous" activities), the classification here does not turn primarily on levels of danger. As a practical matter, persons face much more danger from their neighbors' and their own automobiles than from leaking reservoirs or hot-air balloons.

Economic Analysis
Single-Injurer Accidents

Alan Gunn

A better explanation than "abnormal dangerousness" for why some activities are better suited than others for strict liability can be found by considering whether, with respect to a particular activity, the likelihood of an accident turns upon only the defendant's activity level and safety precautions or whether it depends upon the activity levels and safety precautions of both plaintiffs and defendants. In the case of cars striking pedestrians, for instance, the level of accidents depends both on how many people drive and on how many people walk, and upon how careful they are while driving and walking. In other words, both plaintiffs' (pedestrians') and defendants' (drivers') activity levels and safety precautions affect the number of car-pedestrian accidents. By contrast, the amount of harm done to crops from hot-air balloon landings depends almost entirely on the amount of hot-air ballooning that goes on — one would not expect farmers to decide how many beans to plant by taking into account the possibility that errant aviators may alight on their fields.

To put the point somewhat differently, a strict liability standard is appropriate for activities for which the person carrying on the activity is, as a practical matter, the only person in a position realistically to control the amount of harm done by the activity (by taking precautions or by deciding how much of the activity to engage in). A negligence standard, by contrast, is appropriate for activities for which both the potential injurer and the potential victim can take precautions. For instance, when the danger is cars hitting pedestrians, drivers can reduce the chance of harm by not speeding, by keeping a good lookout, and by staying home (especially when the weather is bad). Pedestrians can also affect the likelihood of harm, by refraining from jaywalking, by staying on the sidewalk, and by not walking in dangerous places.

While the analysis above is usually defended by reference to "efficiency" (because the analysis was developed by economists), it also comports with everyday notions of fairness. When the potential problem is damage to a farmer's crops from hot-air balloon landings, one can plausibly say that the balloonist ought to undertake the activity only if willing to compensate those harmed by that activity. This suggests that there is nothing unfair about holding the balloonist strictly liable. But when *A*'s automobile collides at an intersection with *B*'s automobile, one cannot arbitrarily say "this is *A*'s activity, so *A* should be strictly liable"; after all, both *A* and *B* have chosen to engage in an activity that may cause harm to themselves and others. Indeed, it is hard to see how strict liability could be applied to two-car accidents at all, except by holding each driver liable to the other, which would be both unfair and inefficient.

To summarize, strict liability is appropriate for "single-injurer" accidents—accidents for which it is plain that only one of the persons involved was in a position to control the events giving rise to an accident. For that kind of case, strict liability is superior to negligence, for three reasons. First, inquiries into whether someone acted negligently are difficult, and courts will in many cases get it wrong; under strict liability, trials should be much simpler (since the plaintiff's burden will be largely limited to showing causation and damage) and there is less risk that those who should be liable will avoid liability. Second, the increased certainty of liability under a strict liability standard may encourage defendants to settle claims rather than go to court; consequently, the costs of litigation will be reduced. Third, as noted earlier in this chapter, strict liability, unlike negligence, gives potential injurers an incentive to reduce risks by reducing their activity levels, as well as by taking safety precautions. Consider, for instance, a contractor who is about to undertake an excavation project and who must decide whether to do the job quickly, by using dynamite, or slowly, by digging. Suppose that the contractor is quite sure that its employees will be very careful, so that it will not be negligent if it uses dynamite. Suppose also that it knows from experience that there is some chance that blasting, even if very carefully conducted, will cause damage to a neighboring house. Under a negligence standard, the contractor might ignore the risk, figuring that it will not be held liable if harm ensues because it will not be negligent. Under a strict liability standard, the contractor, knowing that it will be held liable if a neighboring house collapses, has an incentive to consider whether some safer but more-expensive method of excavating than blasting might be best.

The analysis above suggests that there will be some cases in which strict liability should not be imposed even on those who engage in an activity which the law characterizes as "abnormally dangerous." Suppose, for instance, that a contractor's blasting has been rattling the walls of neighboring houses all day, and that one of the neighbors stubbornly leaves a Ming vase perched on the edge of a shelf. In this case, the neighbor is in a much better position than the contractor to prevent harm to the vase, so the contractor should not be liable if it falls. On the other hand, if the blasting cracks the neighbor's foundation, the contractor will be liable: the neighbor can hardly be expected to move the house to a safer spot for the duration of the blasting. Consider also the case of the pet bear which falls asleep on the highway and is struck by the plaintiff's car. Here, the plaintiff may have been in a better position than the owner to prevent the harm—maybe the plaintiff was speeding and not keeping a good lookout. A negligence inquiry in cases like this allows imposition of liability on the "cheaper cost avoider." Strict liability typically applies to cases in which it is plain that the "cheaper cost avoider" is the person carrying on the activity.

Note

1. ***Single-Injurer Accidents.*** In Kent v. Gulf States Utilities Co., 418 So. 2d 493 (La. 1982), the transmission of electricity was held not to be a strict-liability activity, in part because it is an everyday occurrence which can be done without a high risk of injury. The court noted that the activities which give rise to strict liability are ones where "the enterpriser is almost invariably the sole cause of the damage and the victim seldom has the ability to protect himself."

Economic Analysis
Tort Liability and Cross-Subsidization

Alan Gunn

Why does it matter whether the cost of an accident properly attributable to a particular activity is borne by that activity or by some other activity? One possible answer rests on concerns of fairness: if *A*'s activity causes harm, it would not be fair, one supposes, to make *B* pay the cost of that harm. But this kind of "fairness" argument carries little weight with many judges, especially when *A* has limited resources, the victim has serious injuries, and *B* has a "deep pocket." In cases like this, many courts employ "risk spreading" to impose liability upon *B* if *B* has some connection, however tenuous, to the accident.

Economists explain the importance of imposing the costs of accidents only upon those whose activities were responsible for the accidents by invoking the concept of cross-subsidization. To illustrate, suppose that automobile manufacturers were held liable for all harms suffered by the owners of their cars—even harms entirely unrelated to driving, as when the owner of a Buick falls down the cellar stairs and suffers serious injuries. What would be wrong with that rule? It would, one supposes, provide a considerable amount of "risk spreading," as the costs of the accident would be borne by all of those who buy cars from General Motors, not just the unfortunate accident victim. And any "unfairness" argument might be countered by announcing the rule in advance, so that General Motors would price its cars so as to take account of the liability.

The case against holding General Motors liable in this hypothetical starts by noting that this kind of liability would make automobiles very expensive. This, by itself, is no argument against liability: there is no basic principle of law or any other discipline which holds that cars should be cheap. The real problem is that holding

General Motors liable for this kind of harm raises the price of cars to a point well beyond the actual costs of producing cars. For instance, if the cost of a particular model of car (*including* the costs of accidents attributable to the car's design) is $20,000, and if an additional cost of $30,000 is imposed for completely unrelated accidents, only those for whom having a car is worth more than $50,000 will buy one. This deprives those for whom having a car would provide $40,000 worth of enjoyment from having that enjoyment, even though the car could be produced at a cost of only $20,000. And this is wasteful, or, as the economists say, "inefficient." The phenomenon described here is called "cross-subsidization" because the liability rule in question causes one activity — driving, in this case — to "subsidize" other activities (anything else that might cause an accident).

A point worth noting about the analysis above is that it assumes that car buyers who would have to pay an extra $30,000 for "insurance" would not get $30,000 worth of insurance benefits from their outlays. This is a very plausible assumption: ordinary insurance markets provide opportunities for most people to get most of the insurance they want at a much lower cost than if that insurance were imposed indirectly by making auto manufacturers liable for all harms to car buyers. Note also that the $30,000 estimate is not excessive; indeed, it is probably much too low. The cost of products-liability insurance for manufacturers of small aircraft runs about $300,000 per plane, and that insurance covers only harm to those injured in plane crashes held to result from defects in the aircraft. Realistically, if car manufacturers were held liable for all injuries to car owners, manufacturing cars would become economically impossible. But cross-subsidization does harm even when the activity that pays the subsidy is only cut back, rather than eliminated entirely.

Cross-subsidization causes harm not only by making the subsidizing activity artificially expensive but also by making the subsidized activity artificially cheap. For example, if automobile manufacturers were held liable for accidents caused by blasting, one result would be that too much blasting would go on; since their liability would be picked up at least in part by the auto companies, contractors contemplating blasting would not face the full costs of their activities and so blasting would be artificially cheap.

Notes

1. ***A Moribund Theory of Liability?*** After reviewing roughly 100 decisions rendered over 35 years, with special emphasis on cases decided after 1980, Professor Gerald W. Boston concluded, in *Strict Liability for Abnormally Dangerous Activity: The Negligence Barrier*, 36 San Diego L. Rev. 597 (1999), that "rarely do plaintiffs succeed in asserting claims for abnormally dangerous activity." He found that "even jurisdictions reflecting the most aggressive application of the doctrine — California, Alaska, and Washington — have indicated a more recent retrenchment." Why? According to Professor Boston: "The answer largely resides in the fact that courts reject strict liability because they conclude that the negligence system can function effectively in enforcing safety concerns associated with the activity."

2. ***Strict Liability by Statute.*** In some areas of the law, strict liability is imposed by statute. For example, in some states, proof of fault is not required in actions based on: harm caused by fires originating on a defendant railroad's rights-of-way (*see, e.g.*, Colo. Rev. Stat. § 40-30-103 (Westlaw 2022); Ohio Rev. Code Ann. § 4963.37 (Westlaw 2022)); and ground damage inflicted by aircraft (*see, e.g.*, Del. Code Ann. tit. 2, § 305 (Westlaw 2022); Vt. Stat. Ann. tit. 5, § 479 (Westlaw 2022)).

Examples of strict liability under federal legislation include water pollution cleanup costs (33 U.S.C. § 1321(f) (Westlaw 2022)) and improper disposal of hazardous waste (42 U.S.C. § 9607 (Westlaw 2022)).

3. ***Third Restatement.*** The most important recent development in the field of abnormally dangerous activities is the Third Restatement's reformulation of the test for defining such activities.

Restatement, Third, of Torts: Liability for Physical and Emotional Harm § 20 (2010)

§ 20 Abnormally Dangerous Activities

(a) An actor who carries on an abnormally dangerous activity is subject to strict liability for physical harm resulting from the activity.

(b) An activity is abnormally dangerous if:

(1) the activity creates a foreseeable and highly significant risk of physical harm even when reasonable care is exercised by all actors; and

(2) the activity is not one of common usage.

Thus far, few cases have grappled with this proposed simplification and reformulation of the rule on abnormally dangerous activities.

D. Other Theories

1. Motor Vehicle Owner Responsibility Laws

In some states, the owner of a motor vehicle is liable by statute for the negligence of one who operates the vehicle with the owner's express or implied consent. *See* N.Y. Veh. & Traf. Law § 388(1) (Westlaw 2022). Under New York law, a plaintiff is not required to identify the driver of the vehicle in order to hold the owner liable, as the driver is presumed to be operating the vehicle with the owner's permission, in the absence of rebuttal evidence. *See* Horvath v. Lindenhurst Auto Salvage, Inc., 104 F.3d 540 (2d Cir. 1997).

The California statute provides:

California Vehicle Code § 17150 (Westlaw 2022)

Every owner of a motor vehicle is liable and responsible for death or injury to person or property resulting from a negligent or wrongful act or omission in the operation of the motor vehicle, in the business of the owner or otherwise, by any person using or operating the same with the permission, express or implied, of the owner.

Note that the statute does not impose very "strict" vicarious liability. The person using the car must have committed a tort, and the car must have been used with consent.

Some states call this type of rule the "dangerous-instrumentality doctrine." *See* Toombs v. Alamo Rent-A-Car, Inc., 833 So. 2d 109 (Fla. 2002).

The Graves Amendment and Rented or Leased Vehicles. In some cases, automobile-related vicarious liability under state law is preempted by federal provisions:

The "Graves Amendment" 49 U.S.C.A. § 30106 (Westlaw 2022)

(a) In general.— An owner of a motor vehicle that rents or leases the vehicle to a person (or an affiliate of the owner) shall not be liable under the law of any State or political subdivision thereof, by reason of being the owner of the vehicle (or an affiliate of the owner), for harm to persons or property that results or arises out of the use, operation, or possession of the vehicle during the period of the rental or lease, if—

(1) the owner (or an affiliate of the owner) is engaged in the trade or business of renting or leasing motor vehicles; and

(2) there is no negligence or criminal wrongdoing on the part of the owner (or an affiliate of the owner). . . .

2. Family Purpose Doctrine

Starr v. Hill

Supreme Court of Tennessee
353 S.W.3d 478 (Tenn. 2011)

SHARON G. LEE, J.

. . . .

On Christmas Eve . . . , Paul B. Hill, Jr. ("Son"), who was sixteen years old, was returning from a holiday shopping trip with his sister and her friend, when the vehicle he was driving collided with another vehicle. Arlene R. Starr ("Plaintiff"), a passenger in the other vehicle, was allegedly injured. She filed suit against Paul B. Hill, Sr., ("Father"), who was the owner of the vehicle, and Son.[7] She asserted that Son's negligent conduct caused the accident and that Father, as the owner of the vehicle, was liable based on the family purpose doctrine. At the time of the accident, Son's parents were divorced, and Father did not live in the same household as Son. Father, as required by the terms of his divorce decree, had purchased the vehicle for

7. [Fn. 1:] Plaintiff later filed a . . . voluntary nonsuit of her claim against Son.

Son when he turned sixteen years old. Father owned and insured the vehicle; Son drove the vehicle.

Father filed a motion for summary judgment, arguing that the family purpose doctrine was not applicable to him because at the time of the accident he did not reside with Son, he provided the vehicle only for the pleasure or comfort of Son, not the family, and he did not have day-to-day control over Son.... The trial court granted Father's motion for summary judgment. The Court of Appeals reversed the trial court, ruling that the family purpose doctrine applied as a matter of law.

....

The family purpose doctrine was first recognized in Tennessee in King v. Smythe, 140 Tenn. 217, 204 S.W. 296 (1918), just ten years after the introduction of the Ford Model T automobile when the automotive industry was still in its infancy. This doctrine imposes vicarious liability on a head of the household for the negligent operation of a motor vehicle by a family member provided that the head of the household maintains the vehicle "for the purpose of providing pleasure or comfort for his or her family," and "the family purpose driver [was] using the motor vehicle at the time of the injury 'in furtherance of that purpose with the permission, either express or implied of the [head of the household] owner.'"....

The doctrine is "a court-created legal fiction" that employs agency principles to hold the owner of the vehicle vicariously liable.... As one learned legal treatise has observed,

> [s]ometimes it is said that the owner would be liable for the negligence of a chauffeur whom he hires to drive his family, and therefore should be liable when he entrusts the same task to a member of his family instead. There is obviously an unblushing element of fiction in this manufactured agency; and it has quite often been recognized, without apology, that the doctrine is an instrument of policy, a transparent device intended to place the liability upon the party most easily held responsible.... While the doctrine is grounded in the law of agency, ... "[t]he law of agency is not confined to business transactions," and when, as happened in that case, a father buys a car "for the pleasure and entertainment of his family, and ... gives his ... son, who is a member of his family, permission to use it for pleasure, ... the son is in the furtherance of this purpose of the father while driving the car for his own pleasure."....

As a matter of public policy, we choose to apply the doctrine to create an incentive for a parent to exercise control over a child's use of the vehicle and to make available another "pocket" from which an injured party may collect compensation.... The need for a responsible adult between the public and a young driver is more compelling today than it was in the early part of the last century. There are a substantially greater number of vehicles on the road than there were ninety years ago, and there is an increased risk of accident. Teen drivers, ages 16–19, are more likely to be involved in a vehicular accident than any other age group.... The family purpose doctrine serves a vital function by providing parents with additional incentive to ensure that their children operate motor vehicles in a safe manner.

The second rationale for the family purpose doctrine—to ensure that innocent members of the public have a source of reasonable compensation—remains a strong reason for its retention despite the enactment of Tennessee's Financial Responsibility Law.... The Financial Responsibility Law requires that the driver of a motor vehicle involved in an accident resulting in death, injury, or property damage of $50 or more submit insurance documentation or other evidence of financial responsibility to the officer investigating the accident.... The Financial Responsibility Law does not require vehicle liability insurance, but the statute contemplates that most drivers will comply with this requirement by purchasing liability insurance....

Although the Financial Responsibility Law may provide innocent victims with some assurance that they will not be totally without recourse in the event they suffer injury, purchase of liability insurance is not required when a vehicle is acquired and the extent of required financial responsibility is only $25,000 for bodily injury to or death of one person, $50,000 for bodily injury to or death of two or more persons in any one accident, and $15,000 for damage to property in any one accident.... The Financial Responsibility Law is an inadequate substitute for the family purpose doctrine.

The family purpose doctrine remains an important component of the tort law of this state and other states,[8] and the underlying principles that prompted adoption of the doctrine in Tennessee in 1918 remain valid reasons for its retention today.

Father and Suzanne Hill ("Mother") separated in August of 2002 and were divorced in October of 2002. Following the separation, Son resided with Mother and his younger sister; Father resided with his parents. The divorce decree, which incorporated a permanent parenting plan and marital dissolution agreement, provided that Mother would be the primary residential parent of Son and his sister, with Father having parenting time on alternate weekends, overnight on Wednesdays, and on various holidays.... Father was required to procure an automobile for each child at age sixteen and pay the automobile insurance.

These facts reflect the changes in our society since the adoption of the family purpose doctrine in 1918. A greater number of divorces, single parent homes, and teenage drivers are an undeniable and pervasive reality of our current life. In 1916, ... the divorce rate was approximately ten percent, whereas by 2008 that rate had increased to almost fifty percent.... While our society has changed, the purpose and essential elements of the family purpose doctrine have remained relatively constant. For the

8. [Fn. 6:] Currently, the doctrine is recognized at common law in ... [Alaska, Arizona, Colorado, Connecticut, Georgia, Kentucky, Nebraska, Nevada, New Mexico, North Carolina, North Dakota, Oregon, South Carolina, Washington, and West Virginia]. In addition, California, Delaware, the District of Columbia, Iowa, Michigan, Minnesota, and New York have statutes that encompass the doctrine....

doctrine to remain viable, it too must change with the times and be interpreted in a manner to effectuate the important policy considerations which support it. The application of the doctrine should not be undermined by the mere fact that a parent is no longer residing in the same physical location as the family member who is driving that parent's motor vehicle. Therefore, the common residency of the owner and driver is not required for the application of the doctrine.

Our review of the common law in Tennessee and elsewhere reveals that the identification of a family member as a head of the household is primarily based on his or her family relationship and duty to support the driver rather than place of residency. . . .

Other jurisdictions addressing the issue have recognized that common residency of the parent and child is not required for the application of the family purpose doctrine. . . . In a case applying Nebraska law, Wiese v. Hjersman, No. 4:04CV3195, 2006 WL 2571372 (D. Neb. 2006), a nine-year-old boy, who was track-riding a motocross bike, struck and injured the plaintiff pedestrian. The plaintiff, relying on the family purpose doctrine, sued the boy's father, who owned the bike. . . . The district court held that the doctrine did "not require the head of household to be the custodial parent, merely the financially responsible parent,". . . . In its ruling, the court quoted . . . from a well-respected legal treatise . . . :

> The dangers of the public from incompetent and financially irresponsible drivers is a menace of such gravity that every precaution is necessary to reduce such perils to the minimum. . . .

Wiese, 2006 WL 2571372, at *6 (quoting 1 Harper & James, *The Law of Torts*, § 8.13, p. 661).

We conclude that in determining whether the owner of a vehicle is to be designated a head of the household for purposes of the family purpose doctrine, appropriate factors to consider include whether there is a family relationship between the owner and the driver and whether the owner has a duty to support the driver. Applying these factors to the case before us, we conclude that Father was a head of the household. . . .

The family purpose doctrine applies only if the vehicle is "maintain[ed] . . . for the purpose of providing pleasure or comfort for [the] family." . . . . This "pleasure or comfort" language became part of the doctrine at a time when vehicles represented a newly available technology and were used primarily for recreation, having not yet become a necessary component of everyday life. Father argues that he provided and maintained the vehicle only for Son's pleasure or comfort, not for the family's pleasure or comfort. Father's interpretation of this requirement is too restrictive. Our case law supports a broader view.

In Gray v. Mitsky, 280 S.W.3d 828 (Tenn. Ct. App. 2008), the plaintiff sued the father of the driver of a car that rear-ended her vehicle. The father, who was the registered owner of the car, testified that he had given his son the car and that his son was not using the car for a family purpose. . . . The son testified that once his father gave him the car, it was the son's alone, that he was completely responsible for it, and that he was not using it for a family purpose. . . . His mother testified that she and the father had cancelled their insurance coverage of the car because it had been given to the son. . . . Nevertheless, the Court of Appeals held that the family purpose doctrine applied, stating that "a driver can be operating a vehicle for a family purpose 'even if the driver is only using the automobile for his own pleasure or convenience.'". . . .

Even though Father may have subjectively intended to give the vehicle just to Son for Son's sole use, in doing so, he provided a benefit to the family unit by providing Son with a source of transportation. At the time of the accident, Son was with his sister on a holiday shopping trip; this was a benefit to the family. There is no genuine issue of material fact as to whether the vehicle was maintained for the purpose of providing pleasure or comfort to the family.

Finally, the doctrine requires that the vehicle be operated with the express or implied consent of the owner. . . . In other words, the owner must have some control over the vehicle's use. . . . The family purpose doctrine is based in part on the factual presumption that the child is subject to parental control. . . .

Other jurisdictions are in accord with Tennessee courts' requirement of this element of control. . . .

Plaintiff's motion for partial summary judgment was supported in part by reference to Father's testimony that "as far as [Father] was concerned, [Son] was permitted to use the car for whatever purpose he wanted to." While this testimony demonstrates that Father relinquished any right he may have had to exercise control over Son's use of the vehicle, it does not establish that at the time of the accident he *had* the right to exercise such control. While Father also testified that he was "jointly going to be dealing with the decision-making related to . . . [Son's] extracurricular activities," the parenting plan provided that decisions regarding the day-to-day care and control of each child would be made by the parent with whom the child was residing. Father testified that "because [Father] did not live with [Son] at [the time of the accident], [Father] relied upon [Mother] to set the parameters of [Son's] driving privileges" and "deferred to Mother to make the day-to-day decisions in the children's lives." The question of whether Son's driving was an extracurricular activity, in which event Father had a right to control Son's use of the vehicle, or a day-to-day activity, in which event Father had no right to control Son's use of the vehicle, is a genuine issue of material fact appropriately addressed by the jury rather than by this Court. Accordingly, we hold that the Court of Appeals erred in granting partial summary judgment in favor of Plaintiff and ruling that the family purpose doctrine applies to Father as a matter of law.

. . . .

. . . . Accordingly, we vacate the Court of Appeals' partial summary judgment in favor of the Plaintiff and remand for trial. . . .

Note

1. ***Other Precedent.*** In Gause v. Smithers, 742 S.E.2d 644, 649 (S.C. 2013), the court held that it was proper for a jury to consider a father's liability for an auto accident caused by his son:

> Gause [the plaintiff] presented evidence that Father was the head of the household and owned, maintained, or provided the Firebird for Son's use. At trial, both Father and Son admitted that Son was living with his parents at the time of the accident. Although Son lived in a broken-down motor home adjacent to Father's home, it was on the same property and Son received electricity from Father's home. Father also stated the Firebird was titled in his name, he paid the property taxes on it, he had a set of keys, and he could have taken the car away from Son if he wanted. Additionally, he acknowledged the Firebird was used by Son for his convenience and general use because he and his wife were tired of having to drive Son around. Accordingly, we find sufficient evidence existed to submit this issue to the jury.

In Anderson v. Lewis, 2017 WL 6419990, at *1-2 (Ga. App.), the plaintiff commenced an action to recover for injuries sustained when her automobile collided with a vehicle owned by Clarence Lewis and driven by his grandson. The court held that the dismissal of the claim against the grandson based on failure to perfect service provided no basis for granting summary judgment to the grandfather, who was being sued under the family purpose doctrine.

Chapter 15

Products Liability

A. Historical Background

At the beginning of the twentieth century, "products liability" as a field of law hardly existed. Indeed, it was then often the case that even someone injured by a product which had been negligently manufactured had no cause of action against the manufacturer. Today, in every state, someone who has been hurt by a defective product can recover, often even without showing negligence, from the product's manufacturer. In many jurisdictions the victim will also have a claim against a nonmanufacturer seller of the product — such as a wholesaler or retailer — again, often without a showing of negligence.

A sketch of the development of the law of products liability from "no liability" to its modern form follows. In this particular case, the history of the law has important practical consequences. For example, the tendency of the law to hold *sellers of products* strictly liable exists because one important source of this body of law has been the law of warranty in sales transactions. Warranties typically apply to sales of goods, but not to the performance of services. Furthermore, it seems quite unlikely that this field, which has undergone extensive change over a very short time, will suddenly stop developing. The lawyer faced with a products-liability case cannot assume that last year's law will determine this year's result. To make reasonably accurate judgments about future developments, the lawyer must have a sense of the way in which the law has grown to its present state.

For clarity of presentation, this sketch of the development of the law is divided into two parts: (1) the development of the law from "no liability" to liability based on negligence, and (2) the fusing of negligence law, contract law, and the academic notion of "enterprise liability" into modern products-liability law.

1. From "No Liability" to Negligence

Winterbottom v. Wright, 152 Eng. Rep. 402 (Exchequer 1842), was an action by a driver of a mail coach who alleged that he had been injured when the coach broke down while he was driving it. The defendant had made a contract with the Postmaster-General of England, by which the defendant agreed to provide the coach in question to the Postmaster-General and to keep it in good repair. The court held that the plaintiff's complaint failed to state a cause of action. The defendant's duty to keep the coach in good repair existed only because of the defendant's contract with the Postmaster-General, and the plaintiff was not a party to that contract. The court thought that, because the defendant's duty to keep the coach in good condition existed only because of the contract, no one but a party to the contract could base a claim on the defendant's failure to do what he had promised.

Winterbottom v. Wright was not a "products liability" case in the modern sense: the plaintiff's complaint was that the defendant had failed to perform a service carefully. Nevertheless, the principle that only a party to a contract can complain when the contract is negligently performed prevented those injured by a defendant's negligence in manufacturing a product from recovering from the manufacturer, save for the very rare case in which the victim was in "privity of contract" with the manufacturer. Suppose, for example, that *A* manufactured a widget and sold it to *B*, a wholesaler, who then resold it to *C*, a retailer, who sold it to the plaintiff, who was hurt because the widget was negligently made. The manufacturer's only contract was with *B*, the wholesaler, who has not been hurt, and so *Winterbottom* barred recovery.

None of this made a bit of sense: the idea that a contract between *A* and *B* can prevent *A* from being liable to a third party if *A* does something dangerous is absurd on its face. And so, almost from the beginning, courts found ways to get around the doctrine of Winterbottom v. Wright in particularly egregious cases. For example, the defendant in Thomas v. Winchester, 6 N.Y. 397 (1852), negligently placed the wrong label on a bottle of poison and sold it to a druggist, who sold it to the plaintiff, who, misled by the label, consumed it. Holding that products "imminently dangerous to the lives of others" were outside the scope of the *Winterbottom* doctrine, the court allowed the action. In 1909, the New York Court of Appeals ruled that a large coffee urn was "imminently dangerous"; Statler v. George A. Ray Mfg. Co., 88 N.E. 1063 (N.Y. 1909).

Judge Benjamin Cardozo's opinion in MacPherson v. Buick Motor Co., 111 N.E. 1050 (N.Y. 1916), in effect held that *Winterbottom* was no longer the law of New York, though Cardozo's opinion purported simply to apply existing law. The plaintiff was injured when the wooden wheel of his Buick automobile collapsed. The Court of Appeals held that the rule of Thomas v. Winchester applied not only to things that are dangerous in themselves, such as poisons, but also to things that are "reasonably certain to place life and limb in peril when negligently made." As the very definition of negligence involves the creation of an unreasonable risk of harm, this reformulation of the Thomas v. Winchester exception to the rule of Winterbottom v. Wright swallowed the rule, and allowed persons injured by a manufacturer's negligence to recover from the manufacturer.

2. From Negligence to Strict Liability

MacPherson was widely followed, and by mid-century, actions against manufacturers for negligence were routinely allowed. Still, the plaintiff injured by a defective product faced serious obstacles to recovery. For one thing, how was the manufacturer's negligence to be shown? And if the manufacturer could not be sued, the victim was out of luck, for the retailer who sold the product would seldom have been negligent, and so could not be liable under *MacPherson*. Current law sometimes allows those injured by product defects to recover against "sellers" of products—which includes not only manufacturers but also wholesalers and retailers—without a showing of negligence. This body of law represents the coming together of three developments:

(1) The doctrine of *res ipsa loquitur*, which often allowed plaintiffs to get to the jury against manufacturers without showing specific negligence;

(2) The law of contract warranty, which allowed purchasers of some products—particularly food—to recover in contract against those who had sold them defectively dangerous products; and

(3) The notion of "enterprise liability," advanced by academic lawyers as a sort of compulsory insurance scheme under which those who profited by making and selling products would be liable to all of those injured by the products. As will be seen, some formulations of enterprise liability are incoherent and almost certainly unwise, but the concept seems to have encouraged a number of judges to take pro-plaintiff positions in particular cases.

***Res Ipsa Loquitur*.** Consider first the doctrine of *res ipsa loquitur*. A plaintiff who is injured when a new machine falls apart the first time it is used often has a decent argument that the builder of the machine was negligent, and this will typically get the plaintiff to the jury against the manufacturer. (Sometimes, however, the defect may have been introduced by the manufacturer of a component part, in which case the liability of the machine's maker under negligence must be based on inadequate inspection, perhaps a less appealing *res ipsa* case than one in which a single manufacturer produced the entire product.) One argument for holding manufacturers (but not all sellers) strictly liable for injuries caused by product defects is that, in most of the cases, the manufacturer's negligence did cause the defect. And the ability of plaintiffs to get to the jury on a *res ipsa* theory makes the adoption of strict liability for manufacturers seem like a small step, rather than a major restructuring of the law.

***Warranty*.** Today's law of products liability sometimes holds all sellers of new products, not just manufacturers, strictly liable. For an explanation of this aspect of the law, it is necessary to turn to the law of sales. If *A* goes to *B*'s restaurant and orders a pie, which turns out to be poisoned, it seems eminently sensible to say that *B* has breached a contract to provide *A* with edible food. This liability—like most of contract liability—is strict, so *B* is liable even if *B* was not negligent (as when *B* bought the pie from Grandma *C*'s Pie Company and had no reason to know that there was anything wrong with the pie). Contract, or "breach of warranty," had therefore long provided a sort of strict liability for sellers of defective products. This was, however, a form of strict liability which operated within a very narrow range, because contract liability could traditionally be disclaimed by agreement, and because many of those injured by product defects were not in privity of contract with the defendant.

For a while, it looked as if strict liability would develop by an expansion of contract, through the use of "implied warranties" that the product in question was fit for use, through restrictions on the ability of sellers and buyers to limit the scope of liability, and through expansion of recovery to those who were not in privity of contract with the defendant. This approach reached its high point in the 1960 case of Henningsen v. Bloomfield Motors, Inc., 161 A.2d 69 (N.J. 1960). Helen Henningsen was injured while driving a new Plymouth which her husband, Claus, had bought from Bloomfield Motors. She claimed that the car went out of control, veered to the right, and struck a brick wall. Finding no evidence of negligence by either Bloomfield or Chrysler, the trial court dismissed the negligence claims, leaving the Henningsens with claims for breach of an implied warranty of merchantability, on which the jury ruled in their favor.

Helen Henningsen's claim had two serious shortcomings as a matter of traditional contract law. First, as it was Claus Henningsen who had bought the car, Helen Henningsen had no contract with anyone. Second, the contract of sale limited the manufacturer's obligation under the warranty to replacing defective parts. Nevertheless, the Supreme Court of New Jersey held that she could recover for breach of warranty. Stressing the fineness of the print in which the warranties were presented, the buyer's inability to negotiate a warranty more favorable than Chrysler's standard warranty, and the "grossly unequal" bargaining power of the manufacturer and the buyer, the court held the disclaimer of liability void and allowed Helen Henningsen to recover.

Section 2-316 of the Uniform Commercial Code allows the sale of goods with no implied warranty that the goods are merchantable, though it requires disclaimers to be clear and, in the case of written disclaimers, conspicuous. If there is a warranty, UCC § 2-318 extends implied warranties beyond the buyer and may prohibit some sellers from limiting liability for personal injury.

Today, warranty law is seldom the preferred basis for personal-injury claims resulting from defective products, for several reasons. First, since goods can be sold "as is" (that is, with no warranty at all), the scope of a law of products liability based on warranty is necessarily quite limited. Second, one version of UCC § 2-318 limits recovery to the purchaser, members of the purchaser's household, or guests of the purchaser; many product claims involve other kinds of plaintiffs. Third, the UCC contains some technical restrictions on recovery for breach of warranty. But perhaps most important is a recognition that a liability which is imposed by the law, and which the parties to an agreement may not modify even if they want to, is not really a contract remedy at all: contract is about enforcing agreements. Nevertheless, the warranty element of the history of products liability has played a major part in shaping the law.

Enterprise Liability. The willingness of the courts to expand liability for injuries attributable to products rests in part on a belief that widespread liability is good social policy. To some extent, this belief may rest on an acceptance of the notion of "enterprise liability," the idea that those carrying on an enterprise should be liable for all the harm done by that enterprise. Thus, it is argued, anyone making a living from the manufacture of automobiles should pay for all harm done by the automobiles in question. This notion had considerable currency in the law schools in the 1930s, '40s, and '50s, and traces of it can be found in judicial opinions.

No court has ever endorsed enterprise liability in its full-blown form, and it is likely that none ever will, for the theory, at least as usually presented, is neither coherent nor practicable. For one thing, the task of identifying "the" activity to be held "responsible" for injuries is unpredictable and arbitrary. Suppose, for instance, that Smith buys a car from General Motors so that she can take a vacation from her strenuous job as a reporter. On her way to the Grand Canyon, she hits a pedestrian, through no fault of Smith, General Motors, or the National Park Service. Is "the" activity that injured the pedestrian "manufacturing automobiles," or "driving," or "being a reporter," or "looking at scenery," or "walking"? "But for" any of these "enterprises," the accident would not have happened. Furthermore, the costs of a real enterprise-liability system would be prohibitive without major changes in the way in which damages are calculated. Even fairly limited personal injuries — such as the loss of an arm or leg — can support a multi-million-dollar verdict. If automobile manufacturers were liable for all injuries involving their products, cars would cost hundreds of thousands of dollars, and the manufacture of cars would cease.

Risk-Spreading and Insurance. One aspect of "enterprise liability theory" often found in judicial opinions is the notion that "risk-spreading" is desirable, and that risk-spreading can be brought about by holding product manufacturers liable in a great many cases. Instead of leaving the loss from an accident to fall on the victim, the manufacturer can pay, and the cost will be reflected in the price of the product. So, instead of the victim's bearing a million-dollar loss, a million customers can pay $1.00 each.

Risk-spreading is often desirable — that is why people buy insurance. It does not follow, however, that risk-spreading is a goal that tort law can sensibly pursue. For one thing, the most expansive possible system of tort liability could not make the private purchase of insurance (or a public equivalent, such as Social Security disability insurance) unnecessary — most people die from causes like sickness, old age, or accidents that are entirely their own fault, causes for which no potential defendant could be found. Whatever "insurance" the tort system provides will therefore be insurance that duplicates coverage many people will buy anyway. In addition, tort damages cover many things for which hardly anyone would buy insurance — pain and suffering and the death of children are examples. Also, those who buy their own insurance and who are also entitled to "tort-insurance" will have, in effect, to buy two policies: their ordinary insurance plus the "policy" they buy whenever they buy a product. These are people who, one presumes, would not buy two policies from an insurance agent, and so one may wonder why it is "good public policy" to make them buy a second, duplicate policy whenever they buy products. If given a choice, few if any buyers would voluntarily buy accident insurance as an optional addition to a product. Since this is so, one may doubt that it is good policy to *make* them buy such insurance. Finally, the "insurance" provided by tort liability is a kind of insurance which may pay claims only after several years of litigation (which the victim is not assured of winning), and which pays as much or more to lawyers, expert witnesses, and others as it does to victims. Nevertheless, the courts are quite fond of the risk-spreading rationale for expanded tort liability.

Justice Roger Traynor's concurring opinion in Escola v. Coca Cola Bottling Co. of Fresno, which follows, is a useful place to begin an examination of modern products-liability law. One thing to ask while reading the opinion is whether the reasons Justice Traynor gives for holding manufacturers liable whenever they sell products with "defects" are limited to that fairly narrow situation. Is the *Escola* concurrence really an argument for products liability, or is it an argument for enterprise liability? Would Justice Traynor favor holding General Motors liable to all pedestrians who are hit by General Motors cars?

Escola v. Coca Cola Bottling Co. of Fresno

Supreme Court of California
150 P.2d 436 (Cal. 1944)

GIBSON, C.J.

[Plaintiff, a waitress, was injured when a bottle of Coca Cola exploded in her hand. She alleged that the defendant, which had bottled and delivered the beverage, was negligent either in failing to detect a defect in the bottle or in putting gas into the bottle at an excessive pressure. At trial, the jury returned a verdict for the plaintiff. The Supreme Court of California ruled that the doctrine of *res ipsa loquitur* allowed the case to go to the jury.]

TRAYNOR, J., concurring

I concur in the judgment, but I believe the manufacturer's negligence should no longer be singled out as the basis of a plaintiff's right to recover in cases like the present one. In my opinion it should now be recognized that a manufacturer incurs an absolute liability when an article that he has placed on the market, knowing that it is to be used without inspection, proves to have a defect that causes injury to human beings. MacPherson v. Buick Motor Co., 217 N.Y. 382, established the principle, recognized by this court, that irrespective of privity of contract, the manufacturer is responsible for an injury caused by such an article to any person who comes in lawful contact with it.... In these cases the source of the manufacturer's liability was his negligence in the manufacturing process or in the inspection of component parts supplied by others. Even if there is no negligence, however, public policy demands that responsibility be fixed wherever it will most effectively reduce the hazards to life and health inherent in defective products that reach the market. It is evident that the manufacturer can anticipate some hazards and guard against the recurrence of others, as the public cannot. Those who suffer injury from defective products are unprepared to meet its consequences. The cost of an injury

Roger J. Traynor

and the loss of time or health may be an overwhelming misfortune to the person injured, and a needless one, for the risk of injury can be insured by the manufacturer and distributed among the public as a cost of doing business. It is to the public interest to discourage the marketing of products having defects that are a menace to the public. If such products nevertheless find their way into the market it is to the public interest to place the responsibility for whatever injury they may cause upon the manufacturer, who, even if he is not negligent in the manufacture of the product, is responsible for its reaching the market. However intermittently such injuries may occur and however haphazardly they may strike, the risk of their occurrence is a constant risk and a general one. Against such a risk there should be general and constant protection and the manufacturer is best situated to afford such protection.

The injury from a defective product does not become a matter of indifference because the defect arises from causes other than the negligence of the manufacturer, such as negligence of a submanufacturer of a component part whose defects could not be revealed by inspection . . . , or unknown causes that even by the device of *res ipsa loquitur* cannot be classified as negligence of the manufacturer. . . . In leaving it to the jury to decide whether the inference has been dispelled, regardless of the evidence against it, the negligence rule approaches the rule of strict liability. It is needlessly circuitous to make negligence the basis of recovery and impose what is in reality liability without negligence. If public policy demands that a manufacturer of goods be responsible for their quality regardless of negligence there is no reason not to fix that responsibility openly.

....

As handicrafts have been replaced by mass production with its great markets and transportation facilities, the close relationship between the producer and consumer of a product has been altered. Manufacturing processes, frequently valuable secrets, are ordinarily either inaccessible to or beyond the ken of the general public. The consumer no longer has means or skill enough to investigate for himself the soundness of a product, even when it is not contained in a sealed package, and his erstwhile vigilance has been lulled by the steady efforts of manufacturers to build up confidence by advertising and marketing devices such as trade-marks.... Consumers no longer approach products warily but accept them on faith, relying on the reputation of the manufacturer or the trade mark.... Manufacturers have sought to justify that faith by increasingly high standards of inspection and a readiness to make good on defective products by way of replacements and refunds.... The manufacturer's obligation to the consumer must keep pace with the changing relationship between them; it cannot be escaped because the marketing of a product has become so complicated as to require one or more intermediaries. Certainly there is greater reason to impose liability on the manufacturer than on the retailer who is but a conduit of a product that he is not himself able to test....

The manufacturer's liability should, of course, be defined in terms of the safety of the product in normal and proper use, and should not extend to injuries that cannot be traced to the product as it reached the market.

Note

1. ***Section 402A***. Justice Traynor's views in *Escola* prevailed in California in Greenman v. Yuba Power Prods., Inc., 377 P.2d 897 (Cal. 1963). Today, all American jurisdictions have adopted some form of strict liability in tort for defective products. A widely accepted starting point for discussing the scope of this liability is § 402A of the Restatement, Second, of Torts. As discussed later, the Restatement, Third, of Torts: Products Liability approaches products liability—especially in "design defect" cases—quite differently. It is important nevertheless to become familiar with the Second Restatement's products-liability provisions, for they reflect the current state of the law in many states and were once the law in virtually all jurisdictions.

Restatement, Second, of Torts § 402A (1965)

Special Liability of Seller of Product for Physical Harm to User or Consumer

(1) One who sells any product in a defective condition unreasonably dangerous to the user or consumer or to his property is subject to liability for physical harm thereby caused to the ultimate user or consumer, or to his property, if

(a) the seller is engaged in the business of selling such a product, and

(b) it is expected to and does reach the user or consumer without substantial change in the condition in which it is sold.

(2) The rule stated in Subsection (1) applies although

(a) the seller has exercised all possible care in the preparation and sale of his product, and

(b) the user or consumer has not bought the product from or entered into any contractual relation with the seller.

. . . .

Comment:

a. . . . The rule stated here [is one of strict liability,] is not exclusive, and does not preclude liability based upon the alternative ground of negligence of the seller, where such negligence can be proved.

. . . .

g. ***Defective condition***. The rule stated in this Section applies only where the product is, at the time it leaves the seller's hands, in a condition not contemplated by the ultimate consumer, which will be unreasonably dangerous to him. The seller is not liable when he delivers the product in a safe condition, and subsequent mishandling or other causes make it harmful by the time it is consumed. The burden of proof that the product was in a defective condition at the time that it left the hands of the particular seller is upon the injured plaintiff. . . .

Safe condition at the time of delivery by the seller . . . include[s] proper packaging, necessary sterilization, and other precautions required to permit the product to remain safe for a normal length of time when handled in a normal manner.

. . . .

i. ***Unreasonably dangerous***. . . . The article sold must be dangerous to an extent beyond that which would be contemplated by the ordinary consumer who purchases it, with the ordinary knowledge common to the community as to its characteristics. Good whiskey is not unreasonably dangerous merely because it will make some people drunk, and is especially dangerous to alcoholics; but bad whiskey, containing a dangerous amount of fuel oil, is unreasonably dangerous. Good tobacco is not unreasonably dangerous merely because the effects of smoking may be harmful;

but tobacco containing something like marijuana may be unreasonably dangerous. Good butter is not unreasonably dangerous merely because, if such be the case, it deposits cholesterol in the arteries and leads to heart attacks; but bad butter, contaminated with poisonous fish oil, is unreasonably dangerous.

. . . .

Notes

1. ***"One Who Sells."*** For purposes of strict liability, manufacturers are normally treated as "sellers," as they sell their products (though not typically to the ultimate consumer). So are wholesalers and retailers of new products. *See also* Oberdorf v. Amazon.com Inc., 930 F.3d 136 (3d Cir. 2019) (holding that the operator of an online marketplace, through which a customer purchased a defective dog collar from a third-party vendor, was a "seller" within the meaning of the Restatement provision limiting strict products liability claims to sellers of products).

2. ***Products Versus Services.*** Some of those who "sell" products in the ordinary sense of the term have been exempted from strict liability on the ground that they are (at least partly) "providers of services," rather than mere "sellers." For example, pharmacies which sold DES or other harmful drugs have been held not subject to strict liability on the ground that pharmacists, as skilled professionals, provide services. *See* Murphy v. E.R. Squibb & Sons, Inc., 710 P.2d 247 (Cal. 1985). Does the fact that the seller is an "expert," and thus in a better position than an ordinary retailer or wholesaler to prevent harm, call for reduced, rather than expanded, liability? In *Murphy*, the court gave the following policy justifications for limiting the liability of pharmacies to negligence:

> If pharmacies were held strictly liable for the drugs they dispense, some of them, to avoid liability, might restrict availability by refusing to dispense drugs which pose even a potentially remote risk of harm, although such medications may be essential to the health or even the survival of patients. Furthermore, . . . the pharmacist [might] select the most expensive product made by an established manufacturer when he has a choice of several brands of the same drug. As [an] amicus brief warns, "Why choose a new company's inexpensive product, which has received excellent reviews in the literature for its quality, over the more expensive product of an established multinational corporation which will certainly have assets available for purpose of indemnification 10, 20, or 30 years down the line?"

See also Bowen v. Niagara Mohawk Power Corp., 590 N.Y.S.2d 628 (App. Div. 1992) (holding sale of electricity was a service, not a product and therefore strict liability would not be imposed where a house was destroyed by a fire caused by a power surge); Cafazzo v. Central Med. Health Services, Inc., 668 A.2d 521 (Pa. 1995) (holding that hospitals and physicians that charge patients for the use of medical devices in connection with providing medical services are not sellers of medical devices and thus may not be held strictly liable for device defects; the primary activity is the provision of medical services).

Several "tests" have emerged for distinguishing "products" from "services." *See* Charles E. Cantu, *A New Look at an Old Conundrum: The Determinative Test for the Hybrid Sales/Service Transaction Under Section 402A of the Restatement (Second) of Torts*, 45 Ark. L. Rev. 913 (1993).

3. ***Blood Shield Laws.*** Several states have provided by statute (sometimes called "blood shield laws") that the sale of blood is a service, thus immunizing blood banks and hospitals against strict liability for hepatitis, AIDS, and other conditions transmitted by blood transfusions. *See, e.g.*, Cal. Health and Safety Code § 1606 (Westlaw 2022).

4. ***Real Estate.*** Courts are divided over "whether section 402A extends to entire buildings." Association of Unit Owners v. Dunning, 69 P.3d 788, 801 (Ore. Ct. App. 2003) (holding that condominium buildings were not "products" within the meaning of a state statute governing product liability actions).

5. ***The Definition of "Defect."*** A shortcoming of the Second Restatement was its attempt to state a single rule governing all unreasonably dangerous products. The Third Restatement does a better job of differentiating the various kinds of product defects. The Third Restatement also reflects a conscious effort to make products liability less strict than its formulation at the time of the Second Restatement.

Restatement, Third, of Torts: Product Liability

(1998)

§ 1. Liability of Commercial Seller or Distributor for Harm Caused by Defective Products

One engaged in the business of selling or otherwise distributing products who sells or distributes a defective product is subject to liability for harm to persons or property caused by the defect.

§ 2. Categories of Product Defect

A product is defective when, at the time of sale or distribution, it contains a manufacturing defect, is defective in design, or is defective because of inadequate instructions or warnings. A product:

(a) contains a manufacturing defect when the product departs from its intended design even though all possible care was exercised in the preparation and marketing of the product;

(b) is defective in design when the foreseeable risks of harm posed by the product could have been reduced or avoided by the adoption of a reasonable alternative design by the seller or other distributor, or a predecessor in the commercial chain of distribution, and the omission of the alternative design renders the product not reasonably safe;

(c) is defective because of inadequate instructions or warnings when the foreseeable risks of harm posed by the product could have been reduced or avoided by the provision of reasonable instructions or warnings by the seller or other distributor, or a predecessor in the commercial chain of distribution, and the omission of the instructions or warnings renders the product not reasonably safe.

Comment:

a. ***Rationale.*** The rules set forth in this Section establish separate standards of liability for manufacturing defects, design defects, and defects based on inadequate instructions or warnings. They are generally applicable to most products. . . .

The rule for manufacturing defects . . . imposes liability whether or not the manufacturer's quality control efforts satisfy standards of reasonableness. . . .

In contrast to manufacturing defects, design defects and defects based on inadequate instructions or warnings are predicated on a different concept of responsibility. In the first place, such defects cannot be determined by reference to the manufacturer's own design or marketing standards because those standards are the very ones that plaintiffs attack as unreasonable. Some sort of independent assessment of advantages and disadvantages, to which some attach the label "risk-utility balancing," is necessary. . . . Many product-related accident costs can be eliminated only by excessively sacrificing product features that make products useful and desirable. Thus, the various trade-offs need to be considered in determining whether accident costs are more fairly and efficiently borne by accident victims, on the one hand, or, on the other hand, by consumers generally through the mechanism of higher product prices attributable to liability costs imposed by courts on product sellers.

Subsections (b) and (c), which impose liability for products that are defectively designed or sold without adequate warnings or instructions and are thus not reasonably safe, achieve the same general objectives as does liability predicated on negligence. . . .

Notes

1. ***Adoption of the Third Restatement.*** Typically, provisions from the Third Restatement are urged for adoption (or resisted) by litigants in pending court cases, and embraced (or rejected) by courts in piecemeal fashion as part of the common-law process of dispute adjudication. However, in some instances, provisions from the Third Restatement have spurred legislative action. For example, a Wisconsin statute now contains language obviously patterned on, but in important respects different from, Restatement, Third, of Torts: Products Liability § 2 (1998). *See* Wis. Stat. Ann. § 895.047(1)(a) (Westlaw 2022).

2. ***Lenient Treatment of Nonmanufacturer Sellers.*** Some decisions have held that nonmanufacturer sellers who are not responsible for defects should not be strictly liable; *e.g.,* Nichols v. Westfield Indus., Ltd., 380 N.W.2d 392 (Iowa 1985). Several

states have adopted legislation to limit the liability of nonmanufacturer sellers to cases in which the sellers were negligent. Other legislation is more complex.

Texas Civil Practice & Remedies Code § 82.003 (Westlaw 2022)

Liability of Nonmanufacturing Sellers.

(a) A seller that did not manufacture a product is not liable for harm caused to the claimant by that product unless the claimant proves:

(1) that the seller participated in the design of the product;

(2) that the seller altered or modified the product and the claimant's harm resulted from that alteration or modification;

(3) that the seller installed the product, or had the product installed, on another product and the claimant's harm resulted from the product's installation onto the assembled product;

(4) that:

(A) the seller exercised substantial control over the content of a warning or instruction that accompanied the product;

(B) the warning or instruction was inadequate; and

(C) the claimant's harm resulted from the inadequacy of the warning or instruction;

(5) that:

(A) the seller made an express factual representation about an aspect of the product;

(B) the representation was incorrect;

(C) the claimant relied on the representation in obtaining or using the product; and

(D) if the aspect of the product had been as represented, the claimant would not have been harmed by the product or would not have suffered the same degree of harm;

(6) that:

(A) the seller actually knew of a defect to the product at the time the seller supplied the product; and

(B) the claimant's harm resulted from the defect; or

(7) that the manufacturer of the product is:

(A) insolvent; or

(B) not subject to the jurisdiction of the court.

3. ***Indemnification of Nonmanufacturer Sellers.*** Some states provide that a nonmanufacturer seller is entitled to indemnity. *See* Tex. Civ. Prac. & Rem. Code § 82.002(a) (Westlaw 2022) ("A manufacturer shall indemnify and hold harmless a

seller against loss arising out of a products liability action, except for any loss caused by the seller's negligence, intentional misconduct, or other act or omission, such as negligently modifying or altering the product, for which the seller is independently liable").

4. ***Selling Another's Product as One's Own.*** Restatement, Third, of Torts: Products Liability § 14 (1998), provides:

> One engaged in the business of selling or otherwise distributing products who sells or distributes as its own a product manufactured by another is subject to the same liability as though the seller or distributor were the product's manufacturer."

The comments to the section explain:

> *b.* . . . To the extent that nonmanufacturers in the chain of distribution are held to the same standards as manufacturers, the rule stated in this Section is of little practical significance. However, many jurisdictions by statute treat nonmanufacturers more leniently. . . . To the extent that a statute specifies responsibilities, the statutory terms control. But to the extent that a statute does not, the rule in this Section states the common-law rule.
>
> *c.* ***Representing oneself as the manufacturer or one for whom the product has been specially manufactured.*** When a commercial seller sells a product manufactured by another under its own trademark or logo, the seller is liable as though it were the manufacturer of the product. This rule applies even if the seller discloses that the product was produced by an identified manufacturer specifically for the seller. . . . The seller's reputation is an implied assurance of the quality of the product, and the seller should be estopped from denying that it stands behind that assurance.
>
> . . . .
>
> *d.* ***Liability of trademark licensors.*** The rule stated in this Section does not, by its terms, apply to the owner of a trademark who licenses a manufacturer to place the licensor's trademark or logo on the manufacturer's product and distribute it as though manufactured by the licensor. In such a case, even if purchasers of the product might assume that the trademark owner was the manufacturer, the licensor does not "sell or distribute as its own a product manufactured by another." . . . .
>
> Trademark licensors are liable for harm caused by defective products distributed under the licensor's trademark or logo when they participate substantially in the design, manufacture, or distribution of the licensee's products. In these circumstances they are treated as sellers of the products bearing their trademarks.

5. ***Long-Term Leases.*** There is now widespread acceptance of the idea that those who lease products on a long-term basis are "sellers," as there is little practical

difference between selling a product and leasing an identical product for a period of several years.

6. ***Used Products.*** The courts are divided about whether to extend strict liability to commercial sellers of used products. The Third Restatement ordinarily limits the liability of a commercial seller of a used product to harms caused by negligence or by the product's failure to comply with a safety statute or regulation. If, however, the seller's marketing practices would cause reasonable buyers to think that the product in question is as good as new, strict liability for a manufacturing defect may be imposed. *See* Restatement, Third, of Torts: Products Liability § 8 (1998).

7. ***Comparative Law Perspective: Strict Products Liability in China.*** In some respects, Chinese products liability law may be more strict than American law because liability may be imposed even if a product is not defective. This point is illustrated by Fang v. Wuyuanjiujun Pharmaceutical Company. In 2003, Fang Liping went to a drug store and purchased forty doses of "Fengqing Wuling Wan," a compound of Chinese herbal medicines supposedly used to treat urinary tract infections. The Inner Mongolia Wuyuanjiujun Pharmaceutical Company (WPC) manufactured the medicine with the approval of the State Drug Administration. Closely following the instructions on the label, Fang took the medicine twice a day, but soon experienced diarrhea and severe abdominal pain. Several weeks later, Fang died in a hospital due to multiple organ failure. An autopsy report showed that the herbal medicine that Fang took was the direct cause of his death. Fang's estate brought a wrongful death action against WPC.

Relying on Article 41 of the Product Quality Law of China (PQL), the trial court ruled the herbal medicine manufactured by WPC not defective. The court emphasized that WPC had complied with state regulations at the time of production. In addition, the defect was not discoverable due to limited scientific and technological capacities.

Nevertheless, in a surprising turn, the court imposed liability by citing Article 132 of the General Principles of Civil Law (GPCL), which provides, "if none of the parties are at fault in causing damage, they may share civil liability according to the actual circumstances." The court reasoned that even though the product was not defective, the autopsy report clearly showed that the herbal medicine manufactured by WPC was the direct cause of Fang's death. Thus, it would therefore be grossly unfair if the plaintiff were not compensated.

On appeal, the court relied on Article 157 of the Supreme People's Court's Notice on the Implementation of the General Principles of Civil Law. Article 157 states "[w]hen two parties engage in an undertaking that benefits one party or both parties, the party that receives the benefit from the other shall provide certain economic compensation to the other who has suffered injuries in the undertaking." The court reasoned that the WPC did benefit from the sales of the medicine and should provide some compensation to the injured party. Therefore, the court ordered the WPC to pay Fang's estate the equivalent of almost $22,000, which was 60% of the damages claimed by the plaintiff.

Under American products liability principles, it is essential for the plaintiff to show that the product that caused harm was defective. Is there any way one could argue, under the facts in *Fang*, that the compounded medicine was defective?

B. Manufacturing Defects

Linden v. CNH America, LLC

United States Court of Appeals for the Eighth Circuit
673 F.3d 829 (8th Cir. 2012)

SHEPHERD, Circuit Judge.

Plaintiff Thomas Lowell Linden, Jr., filed a products liability action against Defendant CNH America, LLC (CNH), based on injuries Linden sustained while operating a CNH-manufactured bulldozer, and a jury returned a verdict in favor of CNH. Linden now appeals, arguing the district court committed reversible error by granting a directed verdict to CNH on his manufacturing defect claim. . . .

. . . . Linden was operating a bulldozer to grade a steep bank in a drainage pond when the bulldozer rolled and Linden was thrown from the safety of the bulldozer's rollover protection system. The bulldozer landed on his legs, causing severe injury.

. . . . In his complaint, Linden alleged the CNH bulldozer incorporated an IMMI seatbelt that was defective in its manufacture, design, and warnings. Because the seatbelt was manufactured more than 10 years earlier, the district court dismissed the claims against IMMI pursuant to the Indiana statute of repose.[1] The court allowed the claims against CNH . . . to proceed. The district court later confirmed that CNH could be held responsible under Iowa law for defects in the seatbelt because the seatbelt was a component part of the bulldozer.

. . . . Linden contends there was sufficient evidence to support a verdict that the seatbelt incorporated by CNH into its bulldozer had three separate manufacturing defects which failed to comport with the intended buckle design: (1) the buckle case was not strengthened by polycarbonate; (2) there was insufficient Ultra Violet (UV) resistant material to protect the buckle casing from UV degradation; and (3) the ejector holder did not fit firmly in the buckle housing. Linden contends that if the jury had been able to consider his theories of manufacturing defect, the verdict likely would have been in his favor.

. . . .

The Supreme Court of Iowa has "adopted the Product Restatement, which provides a product 'contains a manufacturing defect when the product departs from

1. Statutes of repose are discussed in Chapter 19.

its intended design even though all possible care was exercised in the preparation and marketing of the product.'" .... "Courts and the Restatement of Torts distinguish between design defects and manufacturing defects." .... "[T]he distinction is between an unintended configuration [a manufacturing defect], and an intended configuration that may produce unintended and unwanted results [a design defect]." .... As the Restatement explains in its commentary:

> [A] manufacturing defect is a departure from a product unit's design specifications. More distinctly than any other type of defect, manufacturing defects disappoint consumer expectations. Common examples of manufacturing defects are products that are physically flawed, damaged, or incorrectly assembled. In actions against the manufacturer, under prevailing rules concerning allocation of burdens of proof the plaintiff ordinarily bears the burden of establishing that such a defect existed in the product when it left the hands of the manufacturer....

When it took up the directed verdict motion at trial, the district court noted Linden waived his manufacturing defect claim in his written response to the motion. Linden's counsel responded that his filing was in error and then argued that the evidence of a manufacturing defect was "twofold":

> First, there was evidence that ... the ejector holder had a loose fit, and the testimony of the IMMI witness was that it was supposed to have a tight fit. The loose fit can cause it to fail secondary to fatigue. So there was evidence of that.
>
> The second evidence of a manufacturing defect is that apparently IMMI claims that they wanted to put an adequate level of UV protectant in their materials. That's what [CNH expert witness] Mr. Byam said. Our evidence shows that there was not an adequate level of UV protectant in the materials to serve the intended purpose.

....

Linden's counsel never pointed to evidence to support the manufacturing defect theory he now asserts on appeal that the buckle case was not strengthened by polycarbonate. Under these circumstances, any error as to that particular theory of a manufacturing defect is deemed waived....

As to the remaining two theories of manufacturing defect, the district court's assessment of the evidence presented at trial is particularly apt:

> [W]ith regard to UV stabilization, there's no question in this record that IMMI did precisely what they intended to do with the manufacturing process. You're just saying they didn't do enough. That's a design question. That's not an error in manufacturing.
>
> With regard to the ejector holder and whether or not there was a loose fit, the ... total record in this case is that to the extent that there's any loose fit, it's within tolerance. So, again, with regard to that one, it seems to me

> that there's a complete factual failure with regard to a claim for manufacturing defect with regard to the ejector holder and the loose fit.

.... Although Linden attempts to frame these alleged flaws as manufacturing defects, they are properly characterized as design defects. He has not pointed to sufficient evidence in the record that would support his claim that the product manufactured by CNH "departed from its intended design" and did not meet its "design specifications." ....

... [W]e affirm.

Note

1. ***"Manufacturing Defects" Versus "Design Defects."*** Cases involving manufacturing defects are usually simple in principle, though proving that a product was defective when it left the manufacturer's hands may be difficult in practice, especially if many years have passed between the time of manufacture and the accident.

When a plaintiff complains that a product was defective not because something went wrong in the course of making the particular product involved in the accident, but rather because the design of the product should have been better, the case is typically much more difficult than if a manufacturing defect had been involved. Designers of products can never attain perfect safety: knives cut, and cars hurt those with whom they collide. The issue in a "design defect" case is always in some sense whether the product was "safe enough." This requires the factfinder to compare the actual product with a hypothetical product. For instance, someone hurt in an automobile accident may claim that if the car had been designed differently, the injuries would have been less severe. Even if true, this does not necessarily mean that the product was defective: someone injured in the crash of a small, light, fuel-efficient car does not establish the car's defectiveness simply by showing that it was not a Cadillac.

C. Design Defects

Pannu v. Land Rover North America, Inc.

California Court of Appeal
120 Cal. Rptr. 3d 605 (Ct. App. 2011)

PERLUSS, P.J.

Sukhsagar Pannu suffered a severe spinal injury, resulting in quadriplegia, when his Land Rover Discovery (Series 1) sport utility vehicle rolled over following a chain of collisions.... Pannu sued ... [Land Rover] alleging claims ... for strict liability based on defective design.

Following a bench trial, the court entered a judgment for $21,654,000 against Land Rover, finding stability and roof defects in the Discovery had caused Pannu's injury. On appeal Land Rover contends ... the trial court erred as a matter of law in applying the "consumer expectation" test for product liability . . . [and] misapplied the alternative "risk-benefit" test. . . .

. . . Pannu was driving his 1998 Discovery westbound on the 118 Freeway, travelling about 65 miles per hour. Although a light mist had started to fall, the road was dry. Bret Lusis, a teenager driving an Acura Legend at about 75 miles per hour, approached Pannu's vehicle from the rear on the driver's side and collided with the Discovery.[2] The collision forced the Discovery across the freeway toward the far right lane, where it collided with a Chevy Blazer driven by David Beres. . . . Beres saw the Discovery rolling over several times along the right shoulder of the freeway. The Discovery came to a stop on its roof, which was crushed.

. . . Ted Kobayashi, Pannu's accident reconstruction expert, opined the Discovery rolled because of friction between the tire and the roadway. Kobayashi asserted the impacts between the Discovery and the Acura and the Discovery and the Blazer were insufficient to cause the Discovery to roll and, in the absence of a tripping mechanism, he concluded the vehicle rolled as a result of a tire slip . . . Explaining why the roll occurred, he posited that Pannu began a series of five rapid steering maneuvers in an attempt to control his vehicle after it was struck by the Acura. . . .

As a result of the accident, the roof of the Discovery suffered 13 inches of plastic deformation at the A pillar on the driver's side. Elastic deformation, that is the extent of dynamic deformation during the rollover, ranged from 16 to 17 inches of intrusion into the occupant space. To measure the crush-resistance of the Discovery's roof, Pannu's expert, Brian Herbst, performed a drop test on a comparable production Discovery. . . .

. . . Herbst reinforced the roof pillars and roof bows of a second production Discovery with tubular sections of steel and strengthened some of the steel plating on the roof, integrating the additions into the existing support structure of the roof. As Herbst explained, he added approximately 109 pounds of steel tubing, sheet metal and rigid polyurethane foam filling at a cost of $116. The reinforced Discovery was then dropped from the same position as the first Discovery. This time, the roof deformation was limited to three inches at the A pillar, instead of the 16 to 17 inches of deformation suffered by the unreinforced Discovery. Assuming economies of scale and manufacturing, Herbst estimated the true cost of modifying the roof design of the Discovery as approximately $76 and the additional weight to be in the range of 72 pounds.

. . . .

Applying the consumer expectation test to these facts, the [trial] court concluded Land Rover was liable for both stability and roof defects because the Discovery "did not perform as safely as an ordinary consumer would have expected at the time of the accident." . . . .

---

2. [Fn. 1:] Pannu also sued Lusis but settled with him before trial..

Applying the alternate risk-benefit test, the court ruled Pannu had carried his burden of proving the roof and stability design of the vehicle was a substantial factor in causing his injury, and Land Rover had failed to establish the benefits of the design outweighed its inherent risks. . . .

. . . . A design defect exists when the product is built in accordance with its intended specifications, but the design itself is inherently defective. . . .

. . . . The 'consumer expectation test' permits a plaintiff to prove design defect by demonstrating that 'the product failed to perform as safely as an ordinary consumer would expect when used in an intended or reasonably foreseeable manner.' . . . . If the facts permit an inference that the product at issue is one about which consumers may form minimum safety assumptions in the context of a particular accident, then it is enough for a plaintiff, proceeding under the consumer expectation test, to show the circumstances of the accident and 'the objective features of the product which are relevant to an evaluation of its safety' . . . , leaving it to the fact-finder to 'employ "[its] own sense of whether the product meets ordinary expectations as to its safety under the circumstances presented by the evidence."' . . . . Expert testimony as to what consumers ordinarily 'expect' is generally improper. . . .

"The second test for design defect is known as the 'risk-benefit test.' Under this test, products that meet ordinary consumer expectations nevertheless may be defective if the design embodies an 'excessive preventable danger.' . . . . To prove a defect under this test, a plaintiff need only demonstrate that the design proximately caused the injuries. Once proximate cause is demonstrated, the burden shifts to the defendant to establish that the benefits of the challenged design, when balanced against such factors as the feasibility and cost of alternative designs, outweigh its inherent risk of harm. . . . The two tests provide alternative means for a plaintiff to prove design defect and do not serve as defenses . . . to one another. A product may be defective under the consumer expectation test even if the benefits of the design outweigh the risks. . . . On the other hand, a product may be defective if it satisfies consumer expectations but contains an excessively preventable danger in that the risks of the design outweigh its benefits. . . . Whether a plaintiff may proceed under the consumer expectation test or whether design defect must be assessed solely under the risk-benefit test is dependent upon the particular facts in each case."

Land Rover contends the trial court erred in applying the consumer expectation test to the alleged stability and roof defects, arguing the question of defect under the facts of this case is far too complicated to decide based on the perceptions of the ordinary driver. (*See* . . . [Soule v. General Motors Corp., 8 Cal.4th 548, 562, 567 (1994) (because "'[i]n many situations . . . *the consumer would not know what to expect,* because he would have *no idea* how safe the product could be made,'" the consumer expectation test is "reserved for cases in which the *everyday experience* of the product's users permits a conclusion that the product's design violated *minimum* safety assumptions and is thus defective *regardless of expert opinion about the merits of the design*")].) . . .

.... "The critical question, in assessing the applicability of the consumer expectation test, is not whether the product, when considered in isolation, is beyond the ordinary knowledge of the consumer, but whether the product, *in the context of the facts and circumstances of its failure,* is one about which the ordinary consumers can form minimum safety expectations." We concluded the consumer expectation test could properly be applied to the failure of an airbag to deploy in a head-on collision.... [*See also* Campbell v. General Motors Corp., 32 Cal. 3d 112 (1982) (passenger on bus injured during sharp turn could use consumer expectation test to prove absence of "grab bar" was design defect; public transport is matter of common experience and required no expert testimony); Saller v. Crown Cork & Seal Co., Inc. 187 Cal. App. 4th 1220 (2010) (reversing trial court's refusal to instruct on consumer expectation test in claim involving asbestos exposure); Arnold v. Dow Chemical Co., 91 Cal. App. 4th 698, 726 (2001) (home pesticides causing disability was product within common knowledge of consumer, and, therefore, defect could be assessed under consumer expectation theory).]

....

The trial court concluded the rollover here was subject to the consumer expectation test on the ground the vehicle was used as intended, and it was reasonably foreseeable that freeway accidents occur and unpredictable forces can cause a vehicle to "act erratically." Although the trial court's observation about the foreseeability of accidents is undoubtedly true, in our view the applicability of the consumer expectation test to the alleged stability defect under the circumstances of this case is an exceedingly close question.

Moreover, while it might seem easier to conceive of the alleged roof defect falling within the experience of ordinary consumers, the circumstances of this case fall well beyond the examples set forth in *Soule.* Would a reasonable consumer expect the roof of the Discovery to intrude so dramatically on the occupant survivor space in the event of a rollover following multiple collisions at freeway speed? There are few reported California cases on point....

We need not resolve these difficult questions, however. The trial court's alternative finding of strict liability under the risk-benefit test is amply supported by the record and fully justifies the judgment in favor of Pannu.

....

The risk-benefit test for defective product design requires the factfinder to "'consider, among other relevant factors, the gravity of the danger posed by the challenged design, the likelihood that such danger would occur, the mechanical feasibility of a safer alternative design, the financial cost of an improved design, and the adverse consequences to the product and to the consumer that would result from an alternative design.'" .... "In such cases, the jury *must* consider the manufacturer's evidence of competing design considerations ...; and the issue of design defect cannot fairly be resolved by standardless reference to the 'expectations' of an 'ordinary consumer.'". . . . Once the plaintiff has made a *prima facie* showing that his or her injury was caused by the product's defective design, the burden shifts to the defendant to establish that, in light of the relevant factors, the product is not defective. . . . [Barker v. Lull Engineering Co., 20 Cal. 3d 413, 431 (1978).]

. . . . With respect to stability design, Pannu established that the production Discovery would tip under evasive steering maneuvers and that slight modifications to the track width and center of gravity of the vehicle dramatically improved its rollover resistance. Similarly, modest enhancement of the roof support of the production Discovery yielded substantial gains in roof strength. Pannu proved these improvements could be achieved at a modest cost. Land Rover did not rebut any of these showings. Moreover, Land Rover's senior engineer who testified about the design goals of the Discovery acknowledged these modifications were available and could have been made at the time Pannu's vehicle was manufactured. While he also spoke of the specialized needs of sport utility vehicles for high road clearance and traction, he did not state those goals would preclude implementation of these safety-enhancing modifications.[3] This evidence was more than sufficient to establish the Discovery's design presented an "excessive preventable danger" and that "the benefits of the . . . design" did not "outweigh the risk of danger inherent in such design." . . . .

In sum, substantial evidence supports the trial court's findings of strict liability on Pannu's claims of stability and roof defects.

The judgment is affirmed. Pannu is to recover his costs on appeal.

Notes

1. ***Is Design-Defect Liability Strict?*** Since the test for whether a product's design is "good enough" almost necessarily involves an inquiry into the "reasonableness" of the design, it is hard to see why the liability would be called strict liability, rather than negligence liability. However, there are at least three respects in which the liability may be strict.

First, if the risks posed by a product are measured with the benefit of hindsight, the liability is strict. Negligence depends on proof that risks were foreseeable. We know today that asbestos is a very dangerous product, but that was not necessarily foreseeable when asbestos was first placed on the market. In deciding whether to impose liability for harm caused by a product designed to include asbestos, it may make a difference whether the risks are assessed prospectively or retrospectively. The Second Restatement endorsed a retrospective assessment of risk-versus-utility in design defect cases. It focused on risk in fact, not foreseeable risk. Therefore, liability was strict. In contrast, the Third Restatement talks about "foreseeable risks of harm posed by a product" and to that extent does not impose strict liability with respect to design defects.

---

3. [Fn. 13:] Land Rover's ability to credibly rebut this evidence was hampered by the fact it implemented all of these improvements in the successor model, the Discovery Series II.

Second, design-defect liability may be strict if a nonmanufacturer seller, without fault, is held liable for bad design choices that were made by the manufacturer. This is the law in some states. However, as noted earlier, court decisions and statutes in many states protect nonmanufacturer sellers from this kind of liability, at least under some circumstances.

Third, liability for design defects is strict if only strict-liability defenses can be raised. Negligence on the part of the plaintiff is not a defense to a strict liability claim at common law or in comparative negligence states. Insofar as such defenses cannot be raised in a products liability action, the liability is strict. However, about half of the states have adopted comparative fault, which permits such defenses in a strict liability suit. In those states, any difference related to defenses based on the plaintiff's conduct has disappeared.

2. ***Burden of Proof on Design Defectiveness.*** Some courts have gone to considerable lengths to favor plaintiffs in design-defect cases, in part, perhaps, because of a feeling that the adoption of "strict liability" should give plaintiffs something that negligence would not provide. In Barker v. Lull Engineering, 573 P.2d 443 (Cal. 1978), the plaintiff was injured when a high-lift loader tipped over. In reversing a judgment for the defendant, the court wrote:

> [A] product may be found defective in design, so as to subject a manufacturer to strict liability for resulting injuries, under either of two alternative tests . . . [first], if the plaintiff establishes that the product failed to perform as safely as an ordinary consumer would expect when used in an intended or reasonably foreseeable manner[,] . . . [and second], if the plaintiff demonstrates that the product's design proximately caused his injury and the defendant fails to establish, . . . that, on balance, the benefits of the challenged design outweigh the risk of danger inherent in such design.

According to the court:

> Because most of the evidentiary matters which may be relevant to the determination of the adequacy of a product's design under the 'risk-benefit' standard . . . typically . . . involve technical matters peculiarly within the knowledge of the manufacturer, . . . once the plaintiff makes a *prima facie* showing that the injury was proximately caused by the product's design, the burden . . . shift[s] to the defendant to prove . . . that the product is not defective.

The opinion in *Pannu* reflects the fact that California continues to adhere to *Barker* and its rule that after the plaintiff makes a *prima facie* showing that the product's design injured the plaintiff, the burden of proof on defectiveness shifts to the defendant. It is important to note that few states agree with *Barker.* The great majority of courts continue to require the plaintiff to prove that a design was defective. However, purely circumstantial evidence of a defect may support a verdict by the factfinder.

3. ***The Consumer Expectation Test.*** The Third Restatement limits the consumer expectation test to a few special cases. *See* Restatement, Third, of Torts: Products

Liability § 2(b), under which the basic test for design defect is whether a product is not reasonably safe because the manufacturer did not adopt a reasonable alternative design. Comment g to § 2 says:

> Consumer expectations, standing alone, do not take into account whether the proposed alternative design could be implemented at reasonable cost, or whether an alternative design would provide greater overall safety.

The Restatement retains consumer expectations for some special situations. For example, "[w]hether ... a fish bone in a commercially distributed fish chowder constitutes a manufacturing defect ... is best determined by focusing on reasonable consumer expectations," *id.* at cmt. h, so the question whether the presence in a food product of an ingredient that causes harm depends on whether a reasonable consumer would expect to find the ingredient in the product; Restatement, Third, of Torts: Products Liability, § 7. In addition, the Restatement holds sellers of used products strictly liable for manufacturing (and occasionally other) defects in the products only when the seller's marketing practices would cause reasonable buyers to think that the product in question is no riskier than if it were new; *id.*, § 8(b).

Some courts have expressly rejected § 2(b) of the Third Restatement and allow a plaintiff in a design defect case to prove that the product was defective under the consumer expectation test. *See* Tran v. Toyota Motor Corp., 420 F.3d 1310 (11th Cir. 2005) (holding that although "the court's instruction did mention 'the nature and strength of consumer expectations' as one factor in the risk-utility test it directed the jury to apply," the instruction was erroneous under Florida law because it did not "provide for a consumer expectation test as an independent basis for liability"); *see also* Mikolajczyk v. Ford Motor Co., 901 N.E.2d 329 (Ill. 2008) (holding, in a case arising from the collapse of the driver's seat in a rear-end collision, that it was error not to also give the risk-utility instruction requested by the defendant).

Richetta v. Stanley Fastening Systems, L.P.

United States District Court for the Eastern District of Pennsylvania
661 F. Supp. 2d 500 (E.D. Pa. 2009)

GOLDEN, District Judge.

This products liability action is brought by Plaintiffs Bruce Richetta and his wife, Melissa Richetta, against Defendant Stanley Fastening Systems, L.P. ("Stanley"). Plaintiffs allege that Defendant is liable for injuries Bruce Richetta ("Richetta") sustained when a nail gun manufactured by Defendant fell off a ladder and discharged a nail into his body. Plaintiffs are proceeding on a theory of strict liability.[4] In particular, Plaintiffs contend that the nail gun was defectively designed because it did not have a safety switch or trigger lock and that this defect caused Richetta's injuries. ...

4. [Fn. 1:] Plaintiffs also initially alleged negligence and breach of warranty counts. Plaintiffs, however, subsequently withdrew these two counts. ...

Before the Court are two motions for summary judgment, which separately address Plaintiffs' claims for strict liability and punitive damages. . . .

On September 20, 2005, Plaintiff Bruce Richetta was using a Model N80CB-1 pneumatic nail gun manufactured by Defendant Stanley Fastening Systems, L.P. while working at a construction site. . . . The nail gun . . . was manufactured by Defendant in 2001 and purchased by Richetta in 2002. . . . After using the nail gun on site, Richetta — with the intention to continue using the nail gun — laid the gun on top of a six-foot ladder and exited the construction site to retrieve tools. . . . Richetta did not disconnect the air compressor from the nail gun prior to laying the nail gun on the ladder. . . . Upon his return to the construction site, . . . the nail gun fell off the ladder. . . . The "contact trip" of the nail gun then made contact with Richetta, making a loud "bang" sound. The nail gun discharged a nail into the upper chest/collarbone area of his body. . . .

To discharge a nail from a Model N80CB-1 pneumatic nail gun — the nail gun used by Richetta — the nail gun's trigger mechanism must be pulled simultaneously with the touching of the nail gun's "contact trip" against a surface. . . . Plaintiffs do not contend that the gun was defective on the ground that it fired *without* the pulling of the trigger mechanism. Rather, Plaintiffs "concede that something must have depressed the trigger" at the time the nail gun's contact trip made contact with Richetta. . . .

. . . . Defendant may obtain summary judgment by affirmatively demonstrating that Plaintiffs have either no evidence or insufficient evidence to meet their burden at trial. . . .

In [Berrier v. Simplicity Mfg., Inc., 563 F.3d 38 (3d Cir. 2009), . . .], the Third Circuit predicted that the Pennsylvania Supreme Court "would adopt the Restatement (Third) of Torts, §§1 and 2, thereby affording bystanders a cause of action in strict liability." . . . .[5] Until *Berrier*, strict liability claims in Pennsylvania were examined under Section 402A of the Restatement (Second) of Torts.[6] Thus, the Court must assess whether *Berrier*'s prediction applies to the facts of the case *sub judice*, thereby

---

5. [Fn. 4:] Section 1 of the Third Restatement states that "[o]ne engaged in the business of selling or otherwise distributing products who sells or distributes a defective product is subject to liability for harm to persons or property caused by the defect." Restatement (Third) of Torts §1 (1998). Section 2(b) of the Third Restatement states that "[a] product . . . is defective in design when the foreseeable risks of harm posed by the product could have been reduced or avoided by the adoption of a reasonable alternative design by the seller or other distributor, or a predecessor in the commercial chain of distribution, and the omission of the alternative design renders the product not reasonably safe." *Id.* §2(b).

6. [Fn. 5:] Section 402A of the Second Restatement states as follows:

> (1) One who sells any product in a defective condition unreasonably dangerous to the user or consumer or to his property is subject to liability for physical harm thereby caused to the ultimate user or consumer, or to his property, if
>
> (a) the seller is engaged in the business of selling such a product, and
>
> (b) it is expected to and does reach the user or consumer without substantial change in the condition in which it is sold.

rendering Sections 1 and 2 of the Third Restatement the standard by which Plaintiffs' strict liability claim should be evaluated. . . . The differences between the Third Restatement and the Second Restatement are significant, as the Third Restatement emphasizes foreseeable risks of harm while the Second Restatement stresses, among other things, whether the product was being used as intended by an intended user. Indeed, in this case, the debate between the parties under the Second Restatement prior to the *Berrier* decision focused on whether Richetta used the nail gun *as intended* at the time of the accident. . . .[7]

In *Berrier,* the plaintiff parents of a minor child brought a strict liability action against the defendant manufacturer of a riding lawn mower after the minor child's grandfather drove defendant's riding lawn mower in reverse over the minor's leg, causing severe injuries. . . . The plaintiffs argued that the lawn mower was defective because it lacked "back-over" protection, such as a "no mow in reverse" device or roller barriers. . . . The defendant argued — and the district court agreed — that, under Section 402A of the Second Restatement, "Pennsylvania strict products liability law does not permit recovery for injuries to anyone other than the intended user." . . . . The district court therefore concluded that, because the minor "was a bystander and not an intended user of the mower, she could not recover in an action against" the manufacturer. . . . The Third Circuit vacated the district court's decision, holding that the concurring opinion of . . . [a Pennsylvania Supreme Court Justice in an earlier case] foreshadowed Pennsylvania's "adoption of §§ 1 and 2 of the Third Restatement's definition of a cause of action for strict products liability." . . . .

. . . . Plaintiffs' strict liability cause of action will be examined based on the principles articulated in the Third Restatement. . . .

Plaintiffs have presented sufficient evidence for a reasonable jury to conclude that there is a foreseeable risk of inadvertent firings when Defendant's Model N80CB-1 nail guns are left unattended but are still plugged into their respective air compressors. . . . Plaintiffs' expert, Mark Ezra, P.E. ("Ezra"), indicates that "[i]t is not uncommon for construction workers, while performing repetitive work that requires more than one type of hand tool and/or a power tool for the task, to put down their

(2) The rule stated in Subsection (1) applies although

(a) the seller has exercised all possible care in the preparation and sale of his product, and

(b) the user or consumer has not bought the product from or entered into any contractual relation with the seller.

Restatement (Second) of Torts § 402A (1965).

7. [Fn. 6:] There are significant differences between the Third and Second Restatements. By defining "defective in design" in terms of "foreseeable risks of harm," the Third Restatement — unlike the Second Restatement — "does not limit a strict liability cause of action to the 'user or consumer,' and broadly permits any person harmed by a defective product to recover in strict liability.". . . . Additionally, by embracing concepts of foreseeability, the Third Restatement acknowledges that "conceptions borrowed from negligence theory are embedded in strict products liability doctrine in Pennsylvania.". . . .

power tool for a short period of time and leave it connected to its power source." . . . . Richetta also explains that "it is common for workers to walk around the worksite carrying nail guns connected to the air compressor, climb ladders and scaffolding with connected nail guns and to leave the nail guns connected and lay them on top of ladders, on scaffolds, on roofs or on the ground or floor." . . . . Richetta continues: "If nail guns were disconnected, workers would lose time retrieving the air hose and reconnecting it back to the nail gun." . . . Plaintiffs have presented evidence of numerous accidents involving nail gun misfirings. . . .

Additionally, Plaintiffs have presented sufficient evidence for a jury to conclude that a reasonable alternative design, *i.e.*, a trigger lock or safety switch, would prevent the risk of inadvertent firings and injuries. The Comments to the Third Restatement elaborate that, "[i]f . . . the plaintiff introduces expert testimony to establish that a reasonable alternative design could practically have been adopted, a trier of fact may conclude that the product was defective notwithstanding that such a design was not adopted by any manufacturer, or even considered for commercial use, at the time of sale." . . . .

Here, Plaintiffs' expert, Mark Ezra, opines that "[t]he cost of a trigger lock mechanism, allowing the nail gun trigger mechanism to be easily locked in a safe position so that the nail gun could be put down safely by a worker without having to disconnect the air line to the nail gun, is inconsequential." . . . . Further, Matthew Ponko, an engineer employed by Defendant, testified that it was economically and practically feasible for the nail gun used by Richetta to be redesigned to include an on/off or safety switch that would disable the nail gun from firing even though it was plugged in to the air compressor. . . . Robert Olmstead, an engineer formerly employed by Defendant, also testified that it would have been feasible from an engineering standpoint to design and manufacture a gun with an on/off or safety switch that would lock the nail gun's trigger. . . . Thus, a factfinder could conclude that a reasonable alternative design would have prevented the risk of inadvertent firings and injuries.

. . . . Defendant argues that the actual design of the nail gun is safe in the absence of a trigger lock because it provides "the equivalent and indeed, superior type of safety function because the act of unplugging the tool from the air hose while it is not in use or *unattended* deactivates the nailer, making it impossible to discharge a nail." . . . . This feature is emphasized in warnings accompanying the nail gun, which inform the user that the nail gun should be disconnected from the air compressor when not in use. One warning in the manual states that a user of the nail gun should "[n]ever leave a tool unattended with the air attached." . . . . Defendant further contends that the safety superiority of simply unplugging the tool "has been conclusively proven" by Plaintiffs' expert, Mark Ezra, who testified that, had Richetta disconnected the nail gun from the air compressor pursuant to the aforementioned warnings, the accident would not have occurred. . . .

First, the Court disagrees with Defendant's contention that Ezra's testimony conclusively renders, as a matter of law, the product reasonably safe. As noted above,

Plaintiffs' expert has opined in numerous instances that the nail gun's absence of a safety switch mechanism — despite a user's ability to disconnect the air compressor from the nail gun — renders the nail gun unreasonably dangerous because the nail gun's design disregards its foreseeable use by lacking the ability to be left in a state where the nail gun is ready for immediate reuse without the need to reconnect the nail gun to its air supply. . . .

Second, Defendant's argument that the nail gun is safe as a matter of law overemphasizes the effect of the warnings accompanying the nail gun. Under the Third Restatement, "[a] broad range of factors may be considered in determining whether an alternative design is reasonable and whether its omission renders a product not reasonably safe." Restatement (Third) of Torts § 2 cmt. f (1998). These factors include "the magnitude and probability of the foreseeable risks of harm, *the instructions and warnings accompanying the product,* and the nature and strength of consumer expectations regarding the product, including expectations arising from product portrayal and marketing." . . . . Thus, while the warnings accompanying the nail gun (to the extent they are admissible) may be persuasive to a jury in an analysis of these factors, such warnings are not dispositive. Plaintiffs are bringing their strict liability claim pursuant to Section 2(b) of the Third Restatement, not Section 2(c) which addresses whether a product is defective based on inadequate instructions or warnings. The Third Restatement is clear that "[t]he fact that adequate warning was given does not preclude [a plaintiff] from seeking to establish a design defect under Subsection (b)." . . . . Put another way, "when a safer design can reasonably be implemented and risks can reasonably be designed out of a product, adoption of the safer design is required over a warning that leaves a significant residuum of such risks." . . . .

Again, under the Third Restatement, the defect in a particular product must cause harm to the plaintiff for strict liability to apply. . . . To satisfy the proximate cause requirement, a plaintiff must prove that the product's defect "was a substantial factor in causing the injury." . . . . A plaintiff's "negligent conduct is not relevant if the product defect contributed in any way to the harm." . . . However, "where the defense offers evidence to show that the accident occurred *solely* as a result of the plaintiff's conduct, the plaintiff's actions are relevant and admissible to prove causation." . . . .

Plaintiffs have presented enough evidence for a reasonable jury to conclude that the nail gun's lack of a safety lock was a substantial factor in causing Richetta's injuries. . . .

[The court further held that a reasonable jury could not conclude, on the facts of the case, that an award of punitive damages was appropriate.]

An appropriate Order will be docketed.

Notes

1. ***Feasibility of Alternative Design.*** Ordinarily, evidence that a design could have been safer will not get the plaintiff to the jury unless there is also evidence that

the suggested alternative design is technically feasible and practicable in terms of the overall design and operation of the product. In Wilson v. Piper Aircraft Corp., 577 P.2d 1322 (Or. 1978), the plaintiffs alleged that the crash of a small airplane was caused by, among other things, the fact that the plane had a carburetor, rather than a fuel injection system. There was evidence that carburetors generally were more susceptible to icing, and that fuel injection systems were available when the plane was manufactured. However, there was no evidence about what effect the proposed substitution would have had on the airplane's cost, economy of operation, maintenance requirements, overall performance, or safety in other respects. Therefore, the defendant was entitled to a new trial.

In Adamo v. Brown & Williamson Tobacco Corp., 900 N.E.2d 966 (N.Y. 2008), plaintiffs claimed that cigarette companies were "negligent in designing their product, in that they should have used lower levels of tar and nicotine." In rejecting the claim, the court wrote:

> Here, plaintiffs presented evidence from which a jury could find that light cigarettes — cigarettes containing significantly lower levels of tar and nicotine — are "safer" than regular cigarettes, but they did not show that cigarettes from which much of the tar and nicotine has been removed remain "functional." The function of a cigarette is to give pleasure to a smoker; plaintiffs have identified no other function. Plaintiffs made no attempt to prove that smokers find light cigarettes as satisfying as regular cigarettes. . . .
>
> It is not necessary in every product liability case that the plaintiff show the safer product is as acceptable to consumers as the one the defendant sold; but such a showing is necessary where, as here, satisfying the consumer is the only function the product has. . . .

In a few special cases, the Third Restatement relieves the plaintiff of the obligation of establishing a "reasonable alternative design" to recover on a design-defect theory. If the injury in question occurs in a way that common experience suggests must be attributable to a defect, as when a new car explodes, the plaintiff may, in substance, invoke the doctrine of *res ipsa loquitur. See* Restatement, Third, of Torts: Products Liability § 3. A product that does not conform to a safety standard imposed by a government is defective for that reason alone. *See id.*, § 4. And, in a few cases, a product's design may be so "manifestly unreasonable" that sellers will be liable even if no reasonable alternative is available (the Restatement's example is an exploding cigar). *See id.*, § 2, cmt. *e*.

D. Failure to Warn

Lavin v. Conte

Court of Appeals of Michigan
2017 WL 3159682

Per Curiam.

.... Charles Lavin purchased a boat hoist and a canopy frame manufactured and sold by defendant NuCraft. Charles also purchased a vinyl canopy from defendant; defendant did not manufacture the vinyl canopy, but did manufacture and design the canopy frame and the method by which to attach the canopy to the frame. Charles planned to use the hoist and the canopy assembly for a pontoon boat.... Charles assembled the boat hoist on dry land and then transported it into the lake.... Charles also assembled the canopy frame and attached the frame to the boat hoist.

According to Charles,... he, Vanessa, Eduardo Conte, and John Lavin were present.... According to Charles, "[w]e ... brought the pontoon to the lift and put the pontoon on the lift...." Charles stated that at some time in the evening ... the group decided to install the canopy on the boat hoist. Charles continued that the three men retrieved the canopy from the garage, transported it to the dock, and then "cranked the boat up as high as we could with the fabric on it...."

The four individuals then proceeded to attempt to install the canopy on the canopy frame. Vanessa ... was standing on the "seatback,".... Vanessa continued, "I was standing on the seat reaching up holding on to the canvas, and then I wasn't. It was gone out of my hands and I was falling." .... Vanessa fell into the shallow water, severed her spinal cord and was rendered a quadriplegic.

The vinyl canopy did not come with instructions or an assembly sheet. Charles testified that, at some point before the night of the accident, he spoke with Ronald Wiltse, defendant's vice president, regarding the best way to install the canopy. Charles testified as follows:

Q. Okay. Tell me precisely what Ron told you about installation of the frame and canopy.

A.... I asked him if there was any trick ... to lifting the canopy on because I wasn't familiar with it. And he said, no, it's the simplest part. You just get the boat up and get all your stuff on there and install it and just make sure ... there's no wind.

....

Wiltse testified that the vinyl canopy that Charles purchased weighed about 60–70 pounds and was 28-feet long by 126-inches wide. Wiltse testified that defendant included assembly sheets for the frame, but not for the vinyl canopy and defendant did not provide any other instructions on how to install the canopy. Wiltse testified that it was up to the customer to decide how to safely install the vinyl canopy ...

Q. Is it foreseeable that people would try and get on the boats and/or climb on the lift to get the vinyl on top of the framing structure?

A. People are capable of doing anything, you know. That's a wide open question there. . . .

Q. Did you consider how . . . how were people supposed to get the vinyl in the middle of this framing structure without climbing on the boat and/or the boat lift while they're putting the vinyl on?

A. They can do it with ladders on shore. I've done it that way.

Q. Ladders on shore?

A. Ladders on shore, a dock on the side, some people have docks that wrap around. It can be done in a lot of different ways without getting on the boat.

Q. Did you recommend anywhere in the instructions that that's the manner that be used?

A. No.

Q. Did you provide any instruction whatsoever about how to get the vinyl onto the framing structure?

A. No.

. . . .

Wiltse later testified concerning how many customers installed their canopies:

> I think probably for the most part people are probably getting on their boats which . . . we warn the heck out of them . . . it's just something they should not be doing. But . . . if people invested the time or the money into ladders, maybe built a dock around the hoist to prevent that from happening, it would be a much easier way to put it on. . . .

Defendant submitted evidence that the hoist contained the word "danger" and several warnings on stickers stating, "[f]ailure to follow below instructions will result in uncontrolled spindown and possible personal injury and or hoist damage. . . . *Do not* work or play on, around or under hoist with boat in." Additionally, what appears to be a separate sticker states, "Warning . . . SAFETY PRECAUTIONS" and continues, "Do not allow people to occupy your craft or stand on the guideon while hoist is in raised position. CABLE BREAKAGE CAN OCCUR AT ANY TIME." That sticker also states, "Do not work on craft in raised position."

Bartley Eckhardt, a licensed engineer, stated that he "developed a safer alternative design that permits people to install the canopy structure and the canvas while working from ground level." . . . . Asked if any boat hoist manufacturers use a similar design, Eckhardt responded "I did not see a single hoist manufacturer that uses this. They, for all intent[s] and purpose[s], offer the same awful arrangement." Eckhardt testified that he had "several sketches" of his design and submitted them during his deposition.

.... Asked if he performed a cost analysis regarding his design, Eckhardt replied as follows:

> Some, but I quickly realized that whatever subtle differences there are in cost with the structure are safe because the canopy becomes smaller, and so to me, it's an offset. It's a net neutral cost.
>
> ....
>
> The canopy structure is the same conceptually. The telescoping corners are the same. The only difference is you need a little bit more tubing in the corners, and the gusseting arrangement is a little bit different. But in my experience, this adds negligibly to the cost and it's offset by having less canopy material.

.... Asked if he had searched the Internet to inquire whether another manufacture used a design similar to his, Eckhardt stated, "I have, and I don't see anybody that calls for the canopy support to be on the moveable portion....

The trial court granted summary disposition in favor of defendant.... This appeal ensued.

....

Plaintiffs argue that there were issues of fact regarding whether the canopy and lift were defectively designed and whether defendant adequately warned of the dangers posed by the lift and canopy system....

In order to establish a *prima facie* case of negligent design, a plaintiff must show "data or other factual evidence concerning the magnitude of the risks involved, the utility or relative safety of the proposed alternatives, or evidence otherwise concerning the 'unreasonableness' of risks arising from the allegedly defective design.... In product liability actions for production defects,[8] a manufacturer is not liable unless 'the plaintiff establishes that the product was not reasonably safe at the time the specific unit of the product left the control of the manufacturer....'.... A plaintiff must also establish that under 'generally accepted production practices at the time' the allegedly defective product left the control of the defendant, 'a practical and technically feasible alternative production practice was available that would have prevented the harm without significantly impairing the usefulness or desirability of the product to users and without creating equal or greater risk of harm to others.'...."

Here, Eckhardt stated that he had designed a boat hoist that eliminated the potential hazard of a consumer's falling into the water while attempting to install a canopy.... However, an alternative production practice must be available "at the time the specific unit of the product left the control of the manufacturer."....

Plaintiffs presented no evidence that Eckhardt's design existed before 2011, when the subject hoist was manufactured. Moreover, Eckhardt stated that he could find no

---

8. [Fn. 2:] "Production" includes manufacture, design, or labeling. MCL 600.2945(i).

manufacturer that utilized something similar to his design, only one that utilized scaffolding to assist the consumer in installing the canopy. Eckhardt admitted that he had neither performed a cost-utility analysis, nor spoken to manufacturers about the feasibility of the design. Thus, plaintiffs failed to present evidence that Eckhardt's design was "developed," "available," and "economically feasible." ... [T]he trial court properly granted summary disposition as to plaintiffs' design defect theory of negligent design....

The other theory of proving a claim of negligent design involves proving a failure to warn, which "includes the duty to warn about dangers regarding the intended uses of the product, as well as foreseeable misuses." .... However, under MCL 600.2948(2)

> A manufacturer has no duty to warn of a material risk associated with the use of a product if the risk: (1) is obvious, or should be obvious, to a reasonably prudent product user, or (2) is or should be a matter of common knowledge to a person in the same or a similar position as the person upon whose injury or death the claim is based." ....

The trial court did not err in finding that there was no question of fact regarding whether defendant breached its duty to warn about the danger of installing the canopy. The risk at issue in this case was falling from atop the hoisted boat while attempting to install the canopy. This risk was obvious or should have been obvious to a reasonably prudent product user.... Furthermore, it should be a matter of common knowledge to a person in the same or similar position as plaintiffs to understand that there is an inherent risk of falling while installing a canopy from atop a pontoon boat that is elevated on a boat hoist.... The boat was elevated on a hoist and the canopy was heavy and difficult to install. A reasonably prudent user of the canopy would understand the risk of falling that was inherent in attempting to install the canopy while working from atop the boat.

Moreover, even assuming that defendant did have a duty to warn, ... the boat hoist contained stickers warning consumers not to occupy the boat while it was on the hoist. The stickers also warned consumers not to work from the boat.... Accordingly, there were no genuine issues of material fact regarding plaintiffs' failure to warn theory and the trial court did not err in granting summary disposition as to plaintiffs' negligent design claim.

....

Affirmed.

Notes

1. ***Known or Obvious Dangers***. In products liability, as in other areas of the law, there is typically no duty to warn of a known or obvious danger. *See* Coleman v. Cintas Sales Corp., 100 S.W.3d 384 (Tex. App. 2002) (no duty to warn a groundskeeper that a uniform could catch fire because the risk was common knowledge); Bren-Tex Tractor Co, Inc. v. Massey-Ferguson, Inc., 97 S.W.3d 155 (Tex. App. 2002) (the

risk of injury from a rollover in a used tractor that was not equipped with rollover protection system would be recognized by an average user).

However, even on similar facts, courts may differ as to just what dangers are "obvious." *Compare* Lederman v. Pacific Indus., Inc., 119 F.3d 551 (7th Cir. 1997) (there was no duty to warn because a "reasonable adult . . . knowing that the pool was shallow in parts, would have recognized the dangers of diving into such a pool"), *with* Fleck v. KDI Sylvan Pools, Inc., 981 F.2d 107 (3d Cir. 1992) (the danger of jumping into a pool of unknown depth is not open and obvious).

In Liriano v. Hobart, 170 F.3d 264 (2d Cir. 1999), the court held that even if a product's dangers seem obvious, a manufacturer may still need to provide additional warnings. Judge Guido Calabresi wrote for the court:

> [A] warning can do more than exhort its audience to be careful. It can also affect what activities the people warned choose to engage in. . . . And where the function of a warning is to assist the reader in making choices, the value of the warning can lie as much in making known the existence of alternatives as in communicating the fact that a particular choice is dangerous. It follows that the duty to warn is not necessarily obviated merely because a danger is clear.
>
> . . . [A] warning can convey at least two types of messages. One states that a particular place, object, or activity is dangerous. Another explains that people need not risk the danger posed by such a place, object, or activity in order to achieve the purpose for which they might have taken that risk. Thus, a highway sign that says "Danger-Steep Grade" says less than a sign that says "Steep Grade Ahead—Follow Suggested Detour to Avoid Dangerous Areas."
>
> If the hills or mountains responsible for the steep grade are plainly visible, the first sign merely states what a reasonable person would know without having to be warned. The second sign tells drivers what they might not have otherwise known: that there is another road that is flatter and less hazardous. . . . Accordingly, a certain level of obviousness as to the grade of a road might, in principle, eliminate the reason for posting a sign of the first variety. But no matter how patently steep the road, the second kind of sign might still have a beneficial effect. . . .
>
> . . . . Even if most ordinary users may—as a matter of law—know of the risk of using a guardless meat grinder, it does not follow that a sufficient number of them will—as a matter of law—also know that protective guards are available, that using them is a realistic possibility, and that they may ask that such guards be used. It is precisely these last pieces of information that a reasonable manufacturer may have a duty to convey even if the danger of using a grinder were itself deemed obvious.

Some courts hold that the open-and-obvious-danger rule is not controlling in cases where it is alleged that a product has a design defect. In Wright v. Brooke

Group Ltd., 652 N.W.2d 159 (Iowa 2002), the court, embracing the Third Restatement, held that consumer expectations do not constitute an independent standard for judging the defectiveness of product designs and that, therefore, the common knowledge of consumers of the health risk associated with smoking did not necessarily preclude liability in a suit filed against various cigarette manufacturers.

2. ***Rebuttable Presumption Based on Compliance with Government Requirements.*** Many states hold that compliance with government requirements concerning labeling, licensing, or product approval raises a rebuttable presumption that a product is not defective. *See* Perez v. Wyeth Labs. Inc., 734 A.2d 1245 (N.J. 1999) (holding that a rebuttable presumption exists that a manufacturer which complies with FDA labeling and warning requirements has satisfied its duty to warn).

In Goins v. Clorox Co., 926 F.2d 559 (6th Cir. 1991), one woman was killed and another was injured by gases that were emitted when toilet bowl cleaner was mixed with drain cleaner. Because no evidence was offered to rebut the presumption of adequacy that arose with respect to the government-approved labels on the products, summary judgment for the defendants was affirmed. Perhaps the presumption of adequacy could have been rebutted by evidence that, subsequent to the time that government approval had been obtained, new dangers of the products had become known and necessitated additional disclosures to consumers.

A Texas statute addressing the same issue states: "The claimant may rebut the presumption . . . by establishing that . . . (1) the mandatory federal safety standards or regulations applicable to the product were inadequate to protect the public from unreasonable risks of injury or damage; or (2) the manufacturer, before or after marketing the product, withheld or misrepresented information or material relevant to the federal government's or agency's determination of adequacy of the safety standards or regulations at issue in the action." Tex. Civ. Prac. & Rem. Code § 82.008 (Westlaw 2022).

3. ***Excessive Warnings.*** In response to the spate of "failure to warn" cases in recent years, manufacturers have taken to warning consumers of practically anything that the product could possibly do to them. Whether the several pages of detailed warnings that now accompany new products are routinely read by consumers seems most doubtful (do *you* read all the warnings that accompany the products you buy?). An unfortunate side-effect of the mass of warnings now present because of the tort system is that consumers faced with so much to read may read none of the warnings at all, and they may assume that whatever warnings they do read are mere lawyers' boilerplate, not to be taken seriously.

4. ***Warnings Never Read.*** Some courts hold that a plaintiff who admittedly failed to read an allegedly inadequate warning cannot recover under a failure-to-warn theory. Other courts take a contrary position. For example, in Johnson v. Johnson Chem. Co., Inc., 588 N.Y.S.2d 607 (App. Div. 1992), a consumer was injured in an explosion that occurred when she activated a roach "fogger" near a pilot light in her kitchen. The plaintiff had admittedly failed to read the multiple labels on the can

that stated "put out all flames and pilot lights" or words to similar effect. In reversing a grant of summary judgment for the manufacturer, the appellate court wrote:

> It is perhaps difficult to see how a consumer who admittedly does not read the labels on the products he or she uses can reasonably claim to have been injured *because* the text of such label did not give a sufficient warning.
>
> The argument loses its persuasive force, however, once it is understood that the intensity of the language used in the text of a warning is only one of the factors to be considered in deciding whether such warning is adequate. A second factor to be considered is the prominence with which such language is displayed. . . .

5. ***"Heeding" Presumptions in Warning Cases.*** Products-liability cases talk about two different kinds of "heeding" presumptions in warning cases: the first is advantageous to the plaintiff when a warning was not given and the second may be advantageous to the defendant when a warning was given.

(a) *For the Advantage of the Plaintiff.* In some states, the plaintiff in a failure-to-warn case is entitled to a rebuttable presumption that if a warning had been given it would have been heeded. The presumption shifts the burden of proof to the defendant on the issue of causation. The presumption is rebuttable by evidence demonstrating that if a warning had been given it would have been disregarded. If the presumption is not rebutted, the failure to warn is presumed to be a proximate cause of the plaintiff's injuries.

In Coffman v. Keene Corp., 628 A.2d 710, 719 (N.J. 1993), the court adopted a heeding presumption, finding that it was consistent with the strict liability public policies of encouraging product safety and easing the burden of proof for persons injured by defective products. The court noted that a "great many jurisdictions have adopted the heeding presumption in failure-to-warn cases."

See also Bunting v. Sea Ray, Inc., 99 F.3d 887 (8th Cir. 1996) (admitting evidence of a drowned boater's blood alcohol level as relevant to the issue of whether he would have heeded an additional warning).

Some courts say that the plaintiff enjoys a presumption that a warning would have been heeded only in a case where no warning was given, and not in a case where a warning was given but was allegedly inadequate. *See* McLennan v. American Eurocopter Corp., Inc., 245 F.3d 403 (5th Cir. 2001) (Texas law).

(b) *For the Advantage of the Defendant.* Comment j to Restatement, Second, of Torts § 402A provided that:

> Where warning is given, the seller may reasonably assume that it will be read and heeded; and a product bearing such a warning, which is safe for use if it is followed, is not in defective condition, nor is it unreasonably dangerous.

This approach has been rejected by many courts as well as by the Third Restatement, which says:

> Reasonable designs and instructions or warnings both play important roles in the production and distribution of reasonably safe products. In general, when a safer design can reasonably be implemented and risks can reasonably be designed out of a product, adoption of the safer design is required over a warning that leaves a significant residuum of such risks. For example, instructions and warnings may be ineffective because users of the product may not be adequately reached, may be likely to be inattentive, or may be insufficiently motivated to follow the instructions or heed the warnings. . . . Warnings are not . . . a substitute for the provision of a reasonably safe design.

Restatement, Third, of Torts: Products Liability § 2 cmt. l.

In Uniroyal Goodrich Tire Co. v. Martinez, 977 S.W.2d 328 (Tex. 1998), the court, following the Third Restatement, found that the evidence supported the jury's finding that a 16-inch tire that exploded when the plaintiff mechanic attempted to mount it on a 16.5-inch wheel was unreasonably dangerous, even though a prominent warning label attached to the tire warned against mounting it on a 16.5-inch wheel. The facts showed that a redesigned tire would have prevented the accident and that the manufacturer's competitors had previously incorporated the safer design.

6. ***Vaccine-Related Injuries***. Failure to warn was once a principal avenue of recovery for those who sustained injuries from the side effects of vaccines. In an attempt to protect manufacturers of certain vaccines from crushing tort liability, Congress created the National Vaccine Program, 42 U.S.C. §§ 300aa *et seq*. (Westlaw 2022). The Act's no-fault scheme is designed to provide prompt compensation, limited in amount, to victims of vaccine-related injuries. *See* Chapter 1.

7. ***Expert Testimony in Products Liability Cases***. Suits against drug manufacturers have led to huge increases in the costs of some drugs, and in at least one instance have caused the withdrawal of a product from the market. Bendectin, a drug to prevent morning sickness, was withdrawn from the market in 1983. Before its withdrawal, it had been taken by some 30 million pregnant women. The claims in question were that the drug had caused birth defects in the children of those who took it. Although the consensus among scientists was overwhelmingly that Bendectin had not been shown to cause birth defects, and although the manufacturer won most of the cases (in several instances being granted judgment n.o.v. because of the state of the scientific evidence), the potential exposure and the litigation costs made continued production of Bendectin economically senseless. *See generally* Turpin v. Merrell Dow Pharmaceuticals, Inc., 959 F.2d 1349 (6th Cir. 1992).

Many of the pre-1993 Bendectin cases won by the defendant were federal diversity cases in which the plaintiffs were unable to present admissible expert testimony that Bendectin caused birth defects. Under the rule of Frye v. United States, 293 F. 1013 (D.C. Cir. 1923), expert opinion on scientific techniques was admissible only if the techniques were generally accepted in the scientific community. As none of the thirty published studies of Bendectin had found a causal connection between the drug and birth defects, the testimony of the plaintiffs' expert that Bendectin had caused the defects in question was rejected.

In Daubert v. Merrell Dow Pharmaceuticals, Inc., 509 U.S. 579 (1993), the Supreme Court held that the *Frye* doctrine had been overruled by the Federal Rules of Evidence, which allow the admission of "all relevant evidence." The Court vacated a court of appeals decision which had affirmed a grant of summary judgment to the defendant in a Bendectin case. Under *Daubert*, scientific testimony may be admissible even if the expert's conclusion contradicts generally accepted scientific beliefs. Trial judges are, however, supposed to determine whether the "reasoning or methodology underlying the testimony is scientifically valid and . . . whether that reasoning or methodology properly can be applied to the facts in issue" before allowing the testimony.

On remand, the Ninth Circuit upheld the trial court's grant of summary judgment to Merrell Dow; 43 F.3d 1311 (9th Cir. 1995). The court pointed out that the plaintiff's experts had conducted no studies, had published no scientific papers, and had not explained the methods they used to justify their conclusions that the many studies concluding that Bendectin was safe were flawed. Furthermore, even if the plaintiffs could have made a case that Bendectin was capable of causing birth defects, their experts had not offered any serious attempt to show that Bendectin had caused their injuries.

See also Kumho Tire Co. v. Carmichael, 526 U.S. 137 (1999) (holding that *Daubert's* "gatekeeping" obligation applies not only to "scientific" testimony, but to all expert testimony).

In response to *Daubert*, *Kumho*, and other cases, the Federal Rules of Evidence were amended, and now provide:

> A witness who is qualified as an expert by knowledge, skill, experience, training, or education may testify in the form of an opinion or otherwise if:
>
> (a) the expert's scientific, technical, or other specialized knowledge will help the trier of fact to understand the evidence or to determine a fact in issue;
>
> (b) the testimony is based on sufficient facts or data;
>
> (c) the testimony is the product of reliable principles and methods; and
>
> (d) the expert has reliably applied the principles and methods to the facts of the case.

Fed. R. Evid. 702 (Westlaw 2022).

8. ***Prescription Drugs under the Restatement.*** Under the Second Restatement, the analysis of design defect claims relating to prescription drugs focused on Comment k to § 402A, which dealt with "unavoidably unsafe products." Some jurisdictions interpreted Comment k as exempting all prescription drugs from strict liability design defect claims. Other courts interpreted Comment k as providing an

exemption only to those prescription drugs determined on a case-by-case-basis to be "unavoidably dangerous."

Section 6(c) of the Restatement, Third, of Torts: Products Liability adopts a standard for design defects in cases involving prescription drugs and medical devices which few, if any, products will fail to meet:

> A prescription drug or medical device is not reasonably safe due to defective design if the foreseeable risks of harm posed by the drug or medical device are sufficiently great in relation to its foreseeable therapeutic benefits that reasonable health-care providers, knowing of such foreseeable risks and therapeutic benefits, would not prescribe the drug or medical device for any class of patients.

However, as § 6(d) of the Restatement continues to hold drug manufacturers liable for inadequate warnings or instructions, the apparent protections of § 6(c) may be largely illusory.

9. ***"Learned Intermediary" Doctrine.*** The "learned intermediary" doctrine operates as an exception to the manufacturer's duty to warn the ultimate consumer, and shields manufacturers of prescription drugs from liability if they adequately warn the prescribing physicians of dangers. In Alston v. Caraco Pharmaceutical, Inc., 670 F. Supp. 2d 279 (S.D.N.Y. 2009), the court explained:

> For prescription medications . . . , the duty to warn is met by providing information to the prescribing physician, not to the patient directly. . . . As the learned intermediary, it is the role of the physician to "balance the risks against the benefits of various drugs and treatments and to prescribe them and supervise their effects."

"The doctrine extends [only] to prescription drugs because, unlike over-the-counter medications, the patient may obtain the drug only through a physician's prescription, and the use of prescription drugs is generally monitored by a physician." Edwards v. Basel Pharmaceuticals, 933 P.2d 298 (Okla. 1997).

There are at least two exceptions to the learned intermediary doctrine: mass immunizations, because there may be no physician-patient relationship, and warnings required by the FDA to be given directly to the consumer.

The learned intermediary doctrine evolved at a time when prescription drugs were not marketed directly to consumers. That situation has changed dramatically, as prescription drugs are now standard fare for television, newspaper, magazine, and Internet ads. Although ads often urge consumers to "ask your doctor," some courts now hold that the learned intermediary doctrine does not apply to cases of directly marketed prescription drugs. *See* Perez v. Wyeth Labs. Inc., 734 A.2d 1245 (N.J. 1999); *but see* Ebel v. Eli Lilly & Co., 321 F. App'x 350 (5th Cir. 2009) (finding no "overpromotion exception" under Texas law).

10. ***The "Sophisticated User" Doctrine.*** "The sophisticated user doctrine relieves a manufacturer of liability for failing to warn of a product's latent characteristics or

dangers when 'the end user knows or reasonably should know of a product's dangers.'" Carrel v. National Cord & Braid Corp., 852 N.E.2d 100 (Mass. 2006). Depending on the facts, the sophisticated user doctrine can work in somewhat the same fashion as the learned intermediary rule. The plaintiff in *Carrel* was a camper who, while participating in a Boy Scout program, was injured by a bungee cord made by the defendant. The defendant had allegedly breached an implied warranty of merchantability and fitness based on failure to warn of the inability of a new bungee cord to maintain a knot. The court found that the Boy Scouts and a related entity were the relevant "end users" and that it was proper for the trial court to give "sophisticated user" instruction to the jury, which ultimately found against the camper.

11. ***Problem: Drugs for Expectant Mothers.*** You are general counsel to a pharmaceutical company, which has developed a drug that may be taken by millions of pregnant women. Bearing in mind that at least one percent of these women will inevitably give birth to children who are not completely healthy, even if your product is 100-percent safe, would you advise your client to produce the drug? Would it make a difference if use of this drug would save thousands of lives?

12. ***Foreign-Language Warnings.*** Questions arise as to the adequacy of English-language warnings on products purchased or used by non-English speaking consumers. In Farias v. Mr. Heater, Inc., 684 F.3d 1231 (11th Cir. 2012), the court found that the English-language and pictorial warnings accompanying a propane gas heater were adequate as a matter of law, and that the sellers had no obligation to provide Spanish-language warnings absent evidence they had specifically marketed the heater to Spanish-speaking customers in Florida through use of Hispanic media.

13. ***Comparative Law Perspective: Compliance with Chinese Regulatory Standards.*** Whether tort law should defer to administrative regulatory processes depends to a large extent on the soundness of regulatory determinations. Many scholars have little confidence in the Chinese regulatory system, especially after several high-profile scandals in the food and drug industries. Industrial standards in China are equally dubious. For example, in June 2010, a state regulatory agency set the acceptable level for bacteria in milk at 2,000,000/ml, which was four times higher than the standard China set 25 years earlier and 20 times higher than in the United States and European Union. At the same time, the state lowered the nutrition level of milk from 2.95% set in 1986 to 2.8%, which is much lower than the standard in most western countries.

Li v. CSC[9] is one of the rare cases where a Chinese court has overruled state safety standards. In 2006, Li Hualin (Li) purchased a rotary machine from Shuangbai Yufeng (SY) that was manufactured by Chuxiong Shengyuan Company (CSC). A week later, Li started the machine without installing a protection cap and suffered severe injuries to his left leg, which was eventually amputated. Li filed a products liability action against the CSC. At trial, the court ruled for CSC based on its finding

9. Li Hualin v. CSC, available at http://caseshare.cn/full/117561086.html.

that the rotary machine was not defective at the time of production because it met government quality and safety standards. Li appealed, alleging that the CSC failed to provide instructions on the installation and operation of the protection cap, and that such omissions caused his injuries.

Based on Article 46 of the Product Quality Law of China, the appellate court reasoned that whether a product is defective depends on whether the product can cause an unreasonable risk of harm to persons or property. Meeting state or industry standards does not necessarily indicate that the product is not defective. When promulgating safety and quality standards, the state is limited by various factors, such as the development of science and technology and the ability to design safer products. Despite meeting state standards, some products can still be defective. Instruction defects occur when the manufacturer fails to provide accurate instructions on the operation of the product, which tends to cause harm to the product itself or injuries to persons or property. The court believed that for someone like Li, who had no previous experience in operating the machine, it was necessary for the manufacturer to provide an explicit warning of dangers. The court held that the CSC was responsible for the injuries that Li sustained.

In addition, the court found the seller, SY, severally liable for Li's injuries based on Article 18 of the Consumer Protection Law of China (CPL). According to that provision, a seller must ensure that the products or services provided meet applicable safety standards, and must instruct consumers on how to use the product correctly. SY had failed to provide instructions on how to install the protection cap, and therefore was liable in proportion to its fault.

Finally, the court held that Li was contributorily negligent because he failed to exercise reasonable care in the process of assembling the machine. The court therefore allocated the total damages among the three parties according to their fault. CSC, SY, and Li were liable respectively for 30%, 40%, and 30% of the total damages.

E. Damage to Property

1. Harm to the "Product Itself"

Component Parts. Suppose that, because of a manufacturing defect, the brakes of the plaintiff's car wear out prematurely. Unless this failure is covered by a warranty, the plaintiff should have no claim against the manufacturer: the receipt of a product which is not as good as one had hoped is the sort of thing traditionally governed by contract, not tort. But suppose that, because of the failure, the car crashes into the plaintiff's garage, damaging the car, the garage, and the plaintiff. The plaintiff's personal-injury claim is (by today's standards) an everyday tort claim. So, probably, is the claim for damages to the garage. The claim for damages to the car itself is more questionable.

East River Steamship Corp. v. Transamerica Delaval, 476 U.S. 858 (1986), attempted to draw the line between contract and tort in a property-damage case. A defective component of a turbine, which was supplied to purchasers as part of an integral package, damaged only the turbine itself. The plaintiffs sought damages in tort for the cost of repairs and for lost profits because statutes of limitations barred contract claims. After reviewing various approaches that have been used to distinguish strict-liability-in-tort claims from breach-of-contract claims, the court held that a manufacturer has no duty under negligence or strict liability to prevent a product from injuring itself. The court reasoned that economic losses can be insured, that commercial situations generally do not involve large disparities of bargaining power, and that the law of warranty provides sufficient protection for the benefits of the bargain.

Harm to "Other" Property. It is now generally agreed that, in a product-defect case, the plaintiff may not recover damages for economic losses involving harm to the "product itself," but recovery of damages for harm caused to "other" property or persons is allowed. *See* Murray v. Ford Motor Co., 97 S.W.3d 888 (Tex. App. 2003) (in a tort action involving a truck that caught fire, the court allowed recovery of $453.25 in damages to other property, but not for the loss of the truck).

See also Lincoln General Ins. Co. v. Detroit Diesel Corp., 293 S.W.3d 487 (Tenn. 2009) (holding that an insurer could not recover damages in tort from bus and engine manufacturers for damage to a bus resulting from an engine defect that caused a fire); Progressive Ins. Co v. General Motors Corp., 749 N.E.2d 484 (Ind. 2001) (holding that an automobile which caught fire as a result of allegedly defective wiring was to be viewed as a single unit and that therefore there was no damage to "other property" that would support a products-liability claim).

Products That Are Part of a Larger Whole. It is often difficult to determine just what constitutes "other" property as opposed to the "product itself." In Jimenez v. Superior Court, 127 Cal. Rptr. 2d 614 (Cal. 2002), the plaintiff alleged that defective windows installed during construction of their mass-produced homes had caused damage to stucco, dry wall, floor coverings, and other parts of the dwellings, and that those damages constituted harm to "other" property. The defendant window manufacturers, in response, argued that the "product" was the entire house in which their windows were installed. The court disagreed with the manufacturers, holding that applicable rules of law did "not bar a homeowner's recovery in tort for damage that a defective window causes to other parts of the home in which it has been installed."

Tort and Contract. What is the difference between tort and contract? Traditionally, tort covers cases in which the parties cannot be expected to agree in advance about the rules that will apply. For instance, it would be absurd to think that motorists and pedestrians could get together in advance of accidents and agree on who should pay what if someone is hit by a car. Contract, by contrast, applies to cases in which the parties can and do deal in advance: if *A* wants *B*'s house, the way to get it is for *A* to agree to buy the house from *B*, not for *A* to sue *B* on the theory that it would be more "reasonable" for *A* to own the house than for *B* to continue to own it.

2. The Economic Loss Rule(s)

The principle of products liability law that distinguishes harm to "other" property from harm to the "product itself" is part of a larger debate over the extent to which purely economic losses are compensable under tort law. Consider the following excerpt.

Liability for Economic Losses

Vincent R. Johnson[10]

The following sections suggest why the economic loss rule has emerged as an issue of great importance in contemporary tort litigation. They also explain how narrow versions of the rule reflect the role that the economic loss rule plays in defining the boundary line between contract law and torts.

a. The Broad Formulation of Economic Loss Rule

The nature of the common law sometimes produces surprises. Scholars or judges looking back on court decisions occasionally conclude that, even though certain cases did not seem to be related, they are actually proof of a broader rule that is potentially applicable to a wide range of disputes. This is precisely what happened in the late 1990s and early 2000s.

The Broad Formulation of the Rule. Proponents of what could be called the "broad" formulation of the American economic loss rule argued that there is a common law rule which holds that purely economic losses (i.e., monetary losses where there is no personal injury or property damage) cannot be recovered in a tort action for negligence or strict liability (the latter being simply a theory of recovery that sometimes substitutes for negligence). Purely economic losses, the proponents said, are compensable only under contract law principles. Some scholars and courts agreed with these contentions, at least in certain contexts. Many scholars and jurists did not. The issue of whether there is a unified economic loss rule was raised in scores of cases across the country. The resulting decisions were often confused and inconsistent.

The BP Oil Spill ("Deepwater Horizon"). In thinking about whether, under American tort law, there is a broadly applicable economic loss rule, it is important to remember that the potential stakes are huge. Many losses today are purely economic. Consider, for example, the 2010 BP oil spill in the Gulf of Mexico. That oil

10. The material in this section is based substantially on Vincent R. Johnson, Advanced Tort Law: A Problem Approach 6-16 (Carolina Academic Press, 3d ed. 2020) (footnotes omitted).

spill, which was probably caused by negligence (or by activities that would result in strict liability), caused billions of dollars of damages. Most of those losses were purely economic. Of course, some persons suffered personal injuries (*e.g.*, the 11 men killed in an explosion) and others suffered harm to property (*e.g.*, the operators of boats that were damaged when they came into contact with the oil, or the property owners along the coast whose beaches were polluted). However, most of the oil spill claims were for purely economic losses related to the profitability of businesses.

For example, some persons were afraid that seafood from the Gulf had been contaminated, and therefore they did not buy those products. As a result, purely economic losses were suffered by the companies that sell seafood, by the businesses that would have transported or stored those products, and by the workers who were laid off or worked fewer hours because of the diminished demand for seafood.

Similarly, some persons feared that the water along the Gulf coast was contaminated and too dangerous for swimming. They therefore took their vacations elsewhere. As a result, the hotels, restaurants, and stores along the coast had fewer customers and therefore suffered purely economic losses.

In the end, there was no landmark court ruling on the economic loss rule related to the BP oil spill. Under pressure from the Obama Administration and extremely bad publicity, BP voluntarily agreed to pay more than $20 billion in losses. Lawsuits were filed and a global settlement was reached, but disputes emerged over which claims should be paid.

If the tort claims of persons who suffered purely economic losses as a result of the BP oil spill had been decided in court, those plaintiffs might have been barred from recovery by a broad formulation of the economic loss rule. Moreover, if claimants were relegated to contract law remedies, they might have recovered nothing under that theory either. The hotels and restaurants along the coast, for example, presumably had no contracts with BP which would have protected them from economic losses caused by drilling far off shore. It is unlikely that they could have sued BP for breach of contract.

Why did Proponents Think There Was a Rule? Virtually no tort law scholars talked about an "economic loss rule" as late as the early 1990s. Indeed, few persons thought that such a rule existed. So why did some courts and scholars begin to believe that such a rule was part of American common law tort principles? It seems that they were influenced by decisions that courts had made in at least three kinds of cases.

Defective Products. First, in cases involving defective products, courts have long refused to permit recovery under tort principles if the defective product merely harms itself. Only if the product defect causes personal injuries or damages to "other property" can a victim bring an action for negligence (or strict liability).

For example, if, as the result of a defect, a new smart phone catches fire and scorches the plaintiff's skin or burns down the plaintiff's house, the plaintiff can sue in tort to recover compensation for those losses. In contrast, if the defective smart phone simply short circuits and does not work anymore, the plaintiff can recover compensation for economic losses only in a contract action for breach of warranty, not in a tort action for negligence or strict liability.

Similarly:

> [I]f a person buys a can of paint and applies the paint to a door, the person has a potential tort claim . . . if toxic odors from the paint make the plaintiff sick or if the paint eats away at the door and damages that 'other' property. However, if the paint simply fails to adhere to the door effectively and flakes off, or quickly discolors, causing no other damage but making the paint's purchase a waste of money, the buyer's sole avenue for recovery is rooted in contract principles.

The idea behind these types of rulings is that when a plaintiff buys a product, the plaintiff has a chance to decide how much to spend and what features and guarantees should be part of the bargain. Denying a disappointed product purchaser a tort action for negligence in cases involving purely economic losses creates an incentive for consumers to exercise diligence to protect their own interests. They have an incentive to strike a good bargain with sellers and are held to the terms of the bargain they strike. The rulings in cases involving defective products were one bit of evidence that negligence that causes purely economic losses is sometimes not actionable under tort principles.

Traffic Jams. Second, when a driver negligently causes a traffic accident, the individuals who suffer personal injuries or property damages are allowed to commence tort actions to recover damages for physical harm caused by negligence. In contrast, suppose that a traffic accident results in a traffic jam, and that persons do not arrive at work on time and therefore earn less money. Those persons are not allowed to sue the negligent driver to recover their purely economic losses.

A similar point is illustrated by the famous *Kinsman* cases [*see* Chapter 8] which involved two ships that crashed into a bridge on the Buffalo River. In *Kinsman No. 1*, the owners of properties that were flooded when ice formed a dam at the point of the wreckage were allowed to recover compensation under negligence principles for the resulting property damage. In contrast, in *Kinsman No. 2*, the businesses that incurred additional transportation expenses because the wreckage made the river unnavigable were denied compensation. The Second Circuit expressed its decision in *Kinsman No. 2* in opaque language, stating that the losses were too "tenuous and remote." A better, clearer explanation might be to say that recovery was denied in *Kinsman No. 2* because the alleged negligence caused purely economic losses, not personal injuries or property damages. The traffic jam cases and the *Kinsman* decisions were more evidence that seemed to support the idea that there is a broadly applicable economic loss rule.

Key Employees and the Law of Tortious Interference. Third, American cases have generally agreed that interference with the performance of a contract is actionable as a tort only if the interference is intentional (and improper). Negligent interference with a contract is ordinarily not actionable.

Suppose that Person A intentionally induces Person B, who is a key employee of Person C, to breach B's contract with C. Cases like this routinely hold that A is liable to C for purely economic harm caused by B's breach.

In contrast, suppose that Person A negligently injures Person B, a key employee of Person C, by causing an auto accident. On these facts, a court is likely to hold that C cannot sue A for the economic losses that it suffered as a result of A's negligent injury of B. Only intentional interference with contractual rights is actionable as a tort. The decisions in these kinds of cases were more evidence that American tort law does not provide a remedy for negligence that causes purely economic losses.

The Search for a Unified Theory. Relying on these and other bits of scattered precedent, some scholars and jurists argued that there is a unified rule, broadly applicable in American tort law, which means that negligence that causes purely economic losses is never actionable under negligence or strict liability principles. That rule, they said, explains the result in all of these cases. Proponents of a broad rule also insisted that the only avenue of recourse for victims of accidentally caused pure economic loss is under contract principles. This argument was favorably received by critics of American tort law who believed that mid- and late-twentieth century jurists had gone too far in favoring plaintiffs at the expense of businesses.

b. Narrow Formulations of the Economic Loss Rule

Many Exceptions. It soon became clear that if there is a single, broad economic loss rule, it is a rule with many exceptions. For example, lawyers who commit malpractice can be sued for negligently causing purely economic losses (*e.g.*, the failure of a business transaction or a loss of a claim or defense in litigation). Similarly, businesses are routinely held liable for purely economic losses caused by the tort of negligent misrepresentation (*e.g.*, the inability of a lender to collect on a loan made to a company whose financial position was negligently misrepresented). Other exceptions relate to actions for defamation, breach of fiduciary duty, nuisance, loss of consortium, wrongful death, spoliation of evidence, and unreasonable failure to settle a claim within insurance policy limits, all of which may, on appropriate facts, afford recovery for negligence causing purely economic losses. So too, statutory causes of action, even when based on negligence or strict liability principles, usually trump the judicially designed economic loss rule.

Courts sometimes explain the exceptions to the economic loss rule by saying that negligence causing purely economic harm is actionable where there is a "special relationship" between the plaintiff and defendant. However, this line of reasoning cannot justify all of the exceptions, such as the principles allowing recovery of purely economic losses in wrongful death actions or claims against strangers for economic losses caused by spoliation of evidence.

At Odds with Public Policy. Scholars and courts not only identified a long list of exceptions to the supposedly broad economic loss rule, they also argued that an expansive formulation of the rule undercuts the important public policy considerations that shape American tort law. Those policies include the ideas that liability should be based on fault, that tort rules should impose liability to deter conduct that caused unnecessary losses, and that enterprises that benefit from dangerous activities should be forced to internalize the costs of harm arising from those activities.

One Rule or Several. The truth may be that there is not one economic loss rule broadly applicable throughout the field of torts, but rather several more limited rules that govern recovery of economic losses in selected areas of the law. For example, the rules that limit the liability of accountants to third parties for harm caused by negligence, or that save careless drivers from liability to the employer of a person injured in an auto accident, may be fundamentally distinct from the ones that bar compensation in tort for purely economic losses resulting from defective products or misperformance of obligations arising only under contract.

Breach of Purely Contractual Duties. Of course, American jurists have always recognized that there are limits to the negligence theory of tort liability. It is widely agreed, for example, that a breach of a purely contractual duty cannot be the basis of a tort action for negligence. For example, suppose that a newspaper agrees to publish an advertisement, but negligently fails to do so. As a result, the business that paid to have the ad published suffers economic losses. The business can sue the newspaper for breach of contract (subject to the rules that limit recovery of consequential damages), but cannot bring a tort cause of action for negligence.

The Emerging Consensus. A jurisprudential consensus about the economic loss rule has begun to emerge. The consensus holds that there is no unified broadly applicable economic loss rule, but only a narrow economic loss rule that relegates potential plaintiffs to contract remedies when that avenue for redress makes sense. Thus, if there was a contract between the plaintiff and the defendant, and the claim relates to a breach of the contractual obligations, rather than to duties imposed by tort law, the plaintiff can only sue for breach of contract, not under tort law for negligence or strict liability. Similarly, if there was no contract between the plaintiff and defendant, the narrow formulation of the economic loss rule does not bar a tort action.

The Restatement View. The Restatement, Third, of Torts: Liability for Economic Loss (2020) endorses a narrow version of the economic loss rule. Section 3 is entitled "Preclusion of Tort Liability Arising from Contract (Economic Loss Rule)." That section states that "[e]xcept as provided elsewhere in this Restatement, there is no liability in tort for economic loss caused by negligence in the performance or negotiation of a contract between the parties."

c. The Economic Loss Rule Today

Less Confusion, But Confusion Nonetheless. While a consensus in favor of a narrow version of the economic loss rule has started to take hold, there is still much confusion about whether American tort law provides remedies for negligently caused purely economic losses. The jurisprudential ferment is great. Chief Justice Shirley S. Abrahamson of the Supreme Court of Wisconsin noted that the economic loss doctrine was an issue before her state high court or intermediate court forty-seven times in one five-year period. She lamented that at "the current pace, the economic loss doctrine may consume much of tort law if left unchecked."

With more than fifty different American jurisdictions, it will take years for the law to evolve to the point where it is reasonably uniform in dealing with this subject. However, a few points seem clear.

First: Most courts hold that the economic loss rule does not protect a defendant from liability for intentional torts. "In cases where economic losses are deliberately and tortiously inflicted there is little reason to save the defendant from liability, whether under the economic loss rule or otherwise."

Nevertheless, there is so much confusion and litigation relating to the economic loss rule that a defendant might argue, against the great weight of authority, that an intentional tort action should fail because recovery would violate the rule. Thus, counsel for plaintiffs must have a sufficiently clear understanding of the economic loss rule to be able to refute these kinds of bogus arguments.

Second: It is difficult to recover for purely economic losses. The terms and scope of the economic loss rule are the subject of disagreement. However, there is no dispute as to the underlying reality. Recovery in tort actions today for purely economic losses is often difficult to obtain.

Sharyland Water Supply Corp. v. City of Alton

Supreme Court of Texas
354 S.W.3d 407 (Tex. 2011)

Chief Justice JEFFERSON delivered the opinion of the Court.

. . . .

Alton is a municipality. . . . Sharyland Water Supply Corporation is a non-profit rural water supply corporation. . . . Alton and Sharyland entered into a Water Supply Agreement under which Alton conveyed its water system to Sharyland. In exchange, Sharyland provided potable water to Alton residents and maintained the system. . . . Sharyland was responsible for repairing the system and maintaining the lines in conformity with current or future state agency rules and regulations.

In 1994, Alton received federal and local grants to install a sanitary sewer system, consisting of main sewer lines, residential service connections, and yard lines. . . . Alton contracted with . . . [various entities] (collectively, the contractors) to build the sanitary sewer system. In some locations, Alton's sewer main was installed parallel to Sharyland's water main, so that connecting the sewer main to the residential service line (or "stub-out") required that the sewer line cross the water main. Construction was completed in 1999.

Wallace B. Jefferson

A year later, Sharyland sued Alton for breaching the Water Supply Agreement, alleging that Sharyland suffered significant injury because Alton's sanitary sewer residential service connections were negligently installed in violation of state regulations and industry standards.... In particular, Sharyland claimed that the location and proximity of the sewer lines to the water system threatened to contaminate Sharyland's potable water supply.... Sharyland also sued the contractors for negligence and breach of contract, contending it was a third party beneficiary of the contractors' agreement with Alton.

... [Except as noted below, the discussion of the contract law claims is omitted. A jury] found that the contractors' negligence injured Sharyland....

As to the contractors, the court of appeals held that the economic loss rule barred Sharyland's negligence claim....

.... The court of appeals held that Sharyland suffered only economic losses, which it could not recover in its negligence action against the contractors.... It is true that parties may be barred from recovering in negligence or strict liability for purely economic losses. This is often referred to as "the economic loss rule." .... The term is something of a misnomer, however, as

> there is not one economic loss rule broadly applicable throughout the field of torts, but rather several more limited rules that govern recovery of economic losses in selected areas of the law. For example, the rules that limit

> the liability of accountants to third parties for harm caused by negligence or that save careless drivers from liability to the employer of a person injured in an auto accident may be fundamentally distinct from the ones that bar compensation in tort for purely economic losses resulting from defective products or misperformance of obligations arising only under contract.

Vincent R. Johnson, *The Boundary-Line Function of the Economic Loss Rule,* 66 Wash. & Lee L. Rev. 523, 534–35 (2009)....

The economic loss rule was initially formulated to set perimeters in product liability cases.... As we recently described it, "[t]he economic loss rule applies when losses from an occurrence arise from failure of a product and the damage or loss is limited to the product itself." .... In such cases, recovery is generally limited to remedies grounded in contract (or contract-based statutory remedies), rather than tort....

Our earliest articulation of the economic loss rule came in a product liability case. *See* Nobility Homes of Tex., Inc. v. Shivers, 557 S.W.2d 77 (Tex. 1977). In *Nobility Homes*, a mobile-home purchaser sued the manufacturer for defective workmanship and materials.... We held that the plaintiff could "not recover his economic loss under section 402A of the Restatement (Second) of Torts," establishing strict liability for defective products, but that he could "recover such loss under the implied warranties of the Uniform Commercial Code." .... Importantly, we did not hold that economic damages were unavailable, but rather that they were more appropriately recovered through the UCC's thorough commercial-warranty framework....

We reprised this theme... in Mid Continent Aircraft Corp. v. Curry County Spraying Service, Inc., 572 S.W.2d 308, 312–13 (Tex. 1978). Curry bought an overhauled aircraft from Mid Continent and sued after the plane crashed.... We rejected a strict product liability theory in favor of an implied warranty action under the UCC, because Curry's economic loss (damage to the plane itself) was "merely loss of value resulting from a failure of the product to perform according to the contractual bargain...." ....

Subsequently, in Jim Walter Homes, Inc. v. Reed, 711 S.W.2d 617, 618 (Tex. 1986), we examined the difference between contract duties and tort duties arising under contractual relationships. That case involved a claim by homeowners against their builder, and we had to decide whether an independent tort supported an award of exemplary damages against the builder.... Because the injury resulted from negligent construction, we held that such disappointed expectations could "only be characterized as a breach of contract, and breach of contract cannot support recovery of exemplary damages." ...

Relying on the tort and contract distinctions articulated in *Jim Walter Homes*, we again applied the economic loss rule in Southwestern Bell Telephone Co. v. DeLanney, 809 S.W.2d 493 (Tex. 1991). In that case, we considered "whether a cause of action for negligence is stated by an allegation that a telephone company negligently failed to perform its contract to publish a Yellow Pages advertisement." .... We held that, because the plaintiff sought damages for breach of a duty created under contract, as opposed to a duty imposed by law, tort damages were unavailable. . . . [W]e explained that

> [t]he acts of a party may breach duties in tort or contract alone or simultaneously in both. The nature of the injury most often determines which duty or duties are breached. When the injury is only the economic loss to the subject of a contract itself the action sounds in contract alone.

. . . .

We later declined to extend *DeLanney* to a fraudulent inducement claim, even when the claimant suffered only economic losses to the subject of a contract. *See* Formosa Plastics Corp. USA v. Presidio Eng'rs & Contractors, Inc., 960 S.W.2d 41, 46 (Tex. 1998). We reasoned that Texas law has long imposed a duty to refrain from fraudulently inducing a party to enter into a contract, and our prior decisions made it clear that tort damages were not precluded simply because a fraudulent representation caused only an economic loss. . . .

Thus, we have applied the economic loss rule only in cases involving defective products or failure to perform a contract. In both of those situations, we held that the parties' economic losses were more appropriately addressed through statutory warranty actions or common law breach of contract suits than tort claims. Although we applied this rule even to parties not in privity (*e.g.* a remote manufacturer and a consumer [of a defective product]), we have never held that it precludes recovery completely between contractual strangers in a case not involving a defective product—as the court of appeals did here.

The court of appeals relied on a different sort of economic loss rule—one that says that you can never recover economic damages for a tort claim—to reject Sharyland's negligence claim against the contractors. That court analyzed whether Sharyland's claim was one for property damage or for purely economic loss and concluded it was the latter. . . . Because there was no evidence that the sewer lines had contaminated the water supply, the court of appeals reasoned, Sharyland had not suffered property damage, and the economic loss rule precluded a damage award. . . .

There are at least two problems with this analysis. First, it both overstates and oversimplifies the economic loss rule. . . . To say that the economic loss rule "precludes tort claims between parties who are not in contractual privity" and that damages are recoverable only if they are accompanied by "actual physical injury or property damage," . . . overlooks all of the tort claims for which courts have allowed recovery of economic damages even absent physical injury or property damage. . . . Among these are negligent misrepresentation, legal or accounting malpractice, breach of fiduciary duty, fraud, fraudulent inducement, tortious interference with contract, nuisance, wrongful death claims related to loss of support from the decedent, business disparagement, and some statutory causes of action.

Moreover, the question is not whether the economic loss rule should apply where there is no privity of contract (we have already held that it can), but whether it should apply at all in a situation like this. Merely because the sewer was the subject of *a* contract does not mean that a contractual stranger is necessarily barred from suing a contracting party for breach of an independent duty. If that were the case, a party could avoid tort liability to the world simply by entering into a contract with one party.

The court of appeals' blanket statement also expands the rule, deciding a question we have not—whether purely economic losses may ever be recovered in negligence or strict liability cases. This involves a third formulation of the economic loss rule, one that does not lend itself to easy answers or broad pronouncements. *See, e.g.*, Johnson, 66 Wash. & Lee L. Rev. at 527 (noting that outside the realm of product- or contract-related claims, "the operation of the economic loss rule is not well mapped, and whether there is a 'rule' at all is a subject of contention").

This is an area we need not explore today, however, because the court of appeals erred in concluding that Sharyland's water system had not been damaged.... Sharyland's system once complied with the law, and now it does not. Sharyland is contractually obligated to maintain the system in accordance with state law and must either relocate or encase its water lines. These expenses, imposed on Sharyland by the contractors' conduct, were the damages the jury awarded. Costs of repair necessarily imply that the system was damaged, and that was the case here. Sharyland presented evidence that it experiences between 100 and 150 water system leaks each year. A break in the water line threatens contamination. There was evidence ... that approximately 340 locations would require remediation....

The contractors argue that permitting recovery in this case will upend the industry because construction contracts are negotiated based on anticipated risks and liabilities, and allowing parties like Sharyland to recover in tort would skew that analysis. Construction defect cases, however, usually involve parties in a contractual chain who have had the opportunity to allocate risk, unlike the situation faced by Sharyland. While it is impossible to analyze all the situations in which an economic loss rule may apply, it does not govern here. The rule cannot apply to parties without even remote contractual privity, merely because one of those parties had a construction contract with a third party, and when the contracting party causes a loss unrelated to its contract.

....

We reverse the court of appeals' judgment with respect to the contractors, because the economic loss rule does not preclude Sharyland's negligence claim against them....

Notes

1. *Duty Is Still an Issue.* Saying that a cause of action for negligence is not barred by the economic loss rule does not mean that there no other obstacles to the claim. Negligence always requires proof of a breach of duty. A court may well hold that a negligence claim is not viable because the defendant owed no duty to protect the plaintiff from purely economic losses. For example, in Southern California Gas Leak

Cases, 441 P.3d 881 (Cal. 2019), the Supreme Court of California held that a natural gas utility did not owe a duty of care to protect local businesses against purely economic losses that occurred when a storage facility gas leak required the relocation of thousands of persons.

With respect to purely economic losses, the Third Restatement expressly states a baseline no-duty rule. Specifically, "[a]n actor has no general duty to avoid the unintentional infliction of economic loss on another." Restatement, Third, of Torts: Liability for Economic Harm §1 (2020).

However, courts sometimes recognize exceptions to this kind of no-duty rule based on an assessment of relevant policy factors or on other grounds. For example, in Wolfe v. MBNA America Bank, 485 F. Supp. 2d 874 (W.D. Tenn. 2007), the court held that a bank had a duty to a noncustomer not to negligently enable credit card imposter fraud. The harm for which the plaintiff sought recovery was purely economic.

2. *Confused Terminology.* When the term "economic loss rule" is used in connection with a tort claim for purely economic losses, one must always assess carefully what the term means. There are at least three possibilities, probably more.

First, some authorities say that a claim is barred by the economic loss rule when they mean that, on the particular facts, the defendant had no duty under tort law to exercise care to prevent purely economic harm to the plaintiff. Second, other authorities, like the Third Restatement, say that a claim is barred by the economic loss rule because a contract between the parties provides the only legal remedies for the breach of a purely contractual obligation. Third, some authorities use the term economic loss rule to cover both of the preceding situations. Finally, other authorities may mean something else.

F. Defenses

1. State-of-the-Art Defense

Beshada. In Beshada v. Johns-Manville Products Corp., 447 A.2d 539 (N.J. 1982), a product-liability case involving asbestos, the defendant was sued for failing to warn of dangers relating to the product which were allegedly not known when the product was sold. After a careful examination of the differences between strict liability and negligence, and the risk-spreading and accident-avoidance policies that animate strict liability, the court held that it was no defense that the product was as safe as it could have been made, given the technology available at the time. However, *Beshada* has not aged well. The Supreme Court of New Jersey has refused to apply the *Beshada* rule to cases involving drugs. Feldman v. Lederle Labs., 479 A.2d 374 (N.J. 1984), "restricted" the *Beshada* rule "to the circumstances giving rise to its holding" (apparently, that is, to asbestos cases).

Split of Authority on the State-of-the-Art Defense. Other courts are divided on the admissibility of state-of-the-art evidence. Three states take the position that, at least in some circumstances, a manufacturer is charged with a duty to warn of risks without regard to whether the manufacturer knew or reasonably should have known of the risks. *See* In re Haw. Fed. Asbestos Cases, 960 F.2d 806 (9th Cir. 1992) (applying Hawaii law); Jackson v. Nestle-Beich, Inc., 589 N.E.2d 547 (Ill. 1992); Ayers v. Johnson & Johnson Baby Prods. Co., 818 P.2d 1337 (Wash. 1991).

A majority of states permit a state-of-the-art defense. *See, e.g.*, Vassallo v. Baxter Healthcare Corp., 696 N.E.2d 909, 922–23 (Mass. 1998). The Restatement also endorses a state-of-the-art defense. *See* Restatement, Third, of Torts: Products Liability § 2 cmt. a. The Restatement goes on to note that state of the art, in the sense that the defendant's product is the best available at the time of distribution, is not a defense "[if an improved] design could have been practically adopted at the time of sale and if the omission of such a design rendered the product not reasonably safe." *Id.* § 2 cmt d.

In some states, the state-of-the art-defense is embodied in a statute. For example:

FLORIDA STATUTES ANNOTATED § 768.1257 (Westlaw 2022)

> In an action based upon defective design, brought against the manufacturer of a product, the finder of fact shall consider the state of the art of scientific and technical knowledge and other circumstances that existed at the time of manufacture, not at the time of loss or injury.

Economic Analysis

Risk Spreading

Alan Gunn

A few words of elaboration on the *Beshada* court's discussion of "risk spreading" may be in order. If a manufacturer knows before producing a product that sales of the product will generate $5,000,000 in liability, that potential liability will be treated as a "cost" of the product, and the price will be set so as to recover the $5,000,000. If the product cannot be sold at a price that will cover all of its costs, the manufacturer will not produce it. Typically, increasing the price to cover the cost of liability will cause less of the product to be sold than if there were no possible liability. In a sense, then, liabilities predicted when a product is made will be paid, in part, by all of those who buy the product. (In another sense, those who do not buy the product because the price is so high may for that reason bear a burden as well.)

If, as the defendants claimed was the case in *Beshada*, liability is not foreseen when a product is made and sold, the liability, when it is imposed, cannot be passed on to customers in any sense. Suppose, for instance, that Acme Widget Works made and sold Class A widgets years ago, setting prices on the assumption that they could do no harm. It now produces only Class B Widgets, and it has just learned that it will be liable for $5,000,000 in damages caused by Class A widgets. Presumably, the price Acme charges for its Class B widgets is the price that earns it the greatest possible profit on those sales. Its having become liable for $5,000,000 in damages because of Class A widgets does not change the price it will charge for Class B widgets, as changing that price can only reduce its profits (or increase its losses) — recall that the price was set so as to maximize profits on the sale of Class B widgets. To put the point in another way, the manufacturer's liability for harm done by Class A widgets does not increase demand for Class B widgets, and therefore does not enable the manufacturer to sell Class B widgets for a higher price than if it had not been held liable. Therefore, the entire burden of the $5,000,000 liability falls upon Acme (that is, upon its shareholders, creditors, and employees). This is why an unanticipated liability cannot be "passed on" to customers in any sense, as the *Beshada* court recognizes. Note that, in this analysis, "Class A widgets" and "Class B widgets" can be identical products: If a manufacturer learns today that it will be liable for injuries caused by products that it has sold for years, and which it continues to sell, it will price current sales to cover liabilities attributable to the products now being sold, but not liabilities attributable to products sold last year. In other words, knowledge that the manufacturer will be liable for harm done by a product it sold last year does not give the manufacturer the ability to make more money on the products it sells this year.

2. Government Contractor Defense

Under some circumstances, parties who contract with the federal government are immune from products-liability claims. In Boyle v. United Technologies Corp., 487 U.S. 500 (1988), the father of a man who drowned in a Marine helicopter crash sued the craft's manufacturer, alleging that the helicopter had been defectively designed because the escape hatch opened outward, instead of inward, and because the escape hatch handle was obstructed by other equipment. The court found that holding government contractors liable for design defects in military equipment under state products-liability law would conflict with federal policy. Therefore, it concluded, state tort principles are displaced if: (1) the government provides precise specifications; (2) the equipment conforms to those specifications; and (3) the supplier warns the government about dangers of which it knows but of which the government is ignorant. The immunity afforded to government contractors is much more extensive than the legal protection given to other manufacturers whose products comply with government-agency standards. A defendant within the latter group normally enjoys a rebuttable presumption that its product is not defective; a defendant with a product in the former group is wholly immune from liability if the case falls within the terms of the government contractor defense.

Biomaterials Suppliers. The Biomaterials Access Assurance Act of 1998 provides those who supply raw materials to medical device manufacturers with relief from liability should the medical device manufacturer be sued in a product liability action, provided the supplier complied with the terms of its contract with the manufacturer. 21 U.S.C.A. § 1601 (Westlaw 2022).

3. "Misuse" and Other Plaintiff Misconduct

Strictly speaking, there is no such thing as a "misuse" *defense* in products-liability law, but misuse relates to several important issues. Sometimes, showing that the plaintiff "misused" the product amounts to saying that the product was not defective—few products are expected to be completely safe no matter what is done with them—or that the supposed danger was not undisclosed. Occasionally, if the misuse is bizarre enough, a court may rule that the alleged defect was not a "proximate cause" of the plaintiff's injuries. In addition, the best practical way for a seller to defend a products-liability claim may be to show that the accident was in fact the fault of the person who used the product.

Use Not Objectively Foreseeable. A product is not defective if it is reasonably safe for the kind of use that is objectively foreseeable. As explained by one court:

> Essentially, product misuse contemplates two kinds of conduct. One is the use of a product for an improper purpose. "If, for instance, a plaintiff undertakes to use his power saw as a nail clipper and thereby snips his digits, he will not be heard to complain. . . ." . . . . When a plaintiff is injured while using the product for a purpose that is not objectively foreseeable, the injury does not establish that the product is defective.
>
> The other kind of misuse concerns the manner in which the plaintiff used the product. When, for example, the operator of a high-lift forklift is injured while using the forklift on steep, instead of level, terrain, the emphasis should be on the manner, not the purpose, of the misuse. . . . "A product is not in a defective condition when it is safe for normal handling or consumption."
>
> . . . [W]hen misuse is an issue in a design-defect case, the jury should first determine whether the plaintiff used the product for an objectively foreseeable purpose. If the jury finds that the plaintiff's purpose was not foreseeable, the defendant did not breach any duty owed to the plaintiff. If, however, the jury finds that the plaintiff's purpose was foreseeable, it must then decide whether the product was defective.

Jurado v. Western Gear Works, 619 A.2d 1312 (N.J. 1993).

See Kampen v. American Isuzu Motors, Inc., 157 F.3d 306 (5th Cir. 1998) (plaintiff's use of a jack as the sole support for a car, in contravention of two express warnings, was not a reasonably anticipated use).

Is it foreseeable that a metal baseball bat will be used to chip accumulated ice from a sidewalk?

Misuse under Comparative Principles. Whether the plaintiff's negligence should reduce recovery under the law of comparative negligence is a much-litigated question which has received a variety of answers. Some of the decisions turn on the language of the relevant comparative-negligence statute; if the statute speaks of recovery in actions "for negligence" or refers to the defendant's "fault" or "wrongful conduct," courts may be inclined to hold the statute inapplicable to products-liability cases.

In many jurisdictions, comparative negligence has now been replaced by comparative fault (sometimes called comparative causation or proportionate responsibility). Comparative fault rules generally permit a defendant in a strict liability action (including strict products liability) to introduce evidence of the plaintiff's misconduct (often specifically including "product misuse") for the purpose of reducing or precluding recovery by the plaintiff. *See* Chapter 16.

Notes

1. ***Dangerous Fast Food.*** In Pelman v. McDonald's Corp., 237 F. Supp. 2d 512 (S.D.N.Y. 2003), parents brought an action against fast-food corporations and restaurants in connection with their children's over-consumption of fast food. The court wrote:

> [I]n order to state a claim, the Complaint must allege either that the attributes of McDonald's products are so extraordinarily unhealthy that they are outside the reasonable contemplation of the consuming public or that the products are so extraordinarily unhealthy as to be dangerous in their intended use. The Complaint—which merely alleges that the foods contain high levels of cholesterol, fat, salt and sugar, and that the foods are therefore unhealthy—fails to reach this bar. It is well-known that fast food in general, and McDonald's products in particular, contain high levels of cholesterol, fat, salt, and sugar, and that such attributes are bad for one.

2. ***Product Modification After the Sale.*** A recurring problem involves a product which is reasonably safe as sold, but which the buyer modifies, as by removing a safety feature. For example, the defendant in Robinson v. Reed-Prentice Division of Package Machinery Co., 403 N.E.2d 440 (N.Y. 1980), sold a plastic molding machine to Plastic Jewel Parts Co. Plastic Jewel cut a hole in the machine's safety gate, allowing the machine's operator to reach into the mold area to remove the finished product. The operator, whose hand was seriously injured when he reached into the mold area, sued the manufacturer. Holding that "[t]he manufacturer's duty ... does not extend to designing a product that is impossible to abuse or one whose safety features may not be circumvented," the Court of Appeals denied recovery. Judge Jacob D. Fuchsberg's dissent pointed out that the manufacturer knew that the buyer was likely to modify the safety gate and that the plaintiff's experts had testified that the machine could easily have been designed to avoid the dangers that would result from foreseeable modification of the model that was sold.

The Restatement takes the position that cases like *Robinson* should be dealt with by asking whether the product had a defect that proximately caused the plaintiff's injury, rather than by invoking an absolute rule that the manufacturer has no duty to anticipate modifications. *See* Restatement, Third, of Torts: Products Liability, § 2, cmt. p; § 15, cmt. b. Under that approach, a manufacturer who can anticipate a dangerous modification and who can easily make that modification unnecessary or impossible would be liable.

4. Pre-Emption by Federal Law

Article VI of the Constitution provides that the laws of the United States "shall be the supreme Law of the Land; . . . any Thing in the Constitution or Laws of any state to the Contrary notwithstanding." Art. VI, cl. 2. Thus, since our decision in M'Culloch v. Maryland, 17 U.S. (4 Wheat.) 316, 427, 4 L. Ed. 579 (1819), it has been settled that state law that conflicts with federal law is "without effect." Consideration of issues arising under the Supremacy Clause "start[s] with the assumption that the historic police powers of the States [are] not to be superseded by [a] . . . Federal Act unless that [is] the clear and manifest purpose of Congress." Accordingly, "'[t]he purpose of Congress is the ultimate touchstone'" of pre-emption analysis.

Congress' intent may be "explicitly stated in the statute's language or implicitly contained in its structure and purpose." In the absence of an express congressional command, state law is pre-empted if that law actually conflicts with federal law, or if federal law so thoroughly occupies a legislative field "'as to make reasonable the inference that Congress left no room for the States to supplement it.'"

Cipollone v. Liggett Group, Inc., 505 U.S. 504, 516 (1992).

Wyeth v. Levine

Supreme Court of the United States
555 U.S. 555 (2009)

Justice STEVENS delivered the opinion of the Court.

Directly injecting the drug Phenergan into a patient's vein creates a significant risk of catastrophic consequences. A Vermont jury found that petitioner Wyeth, the manufacturer of the drug, had failed to provide an adequate warning of that risk and awarded damages to respondent Diana Levine to compensate her for the amputation of her arm. The warnings on Phenergan's label had been deemed sufficient by the federal Food and Drug Administration (FDA) when it approved Wyeth's new drug application in 1955 and when it later approved changes in the drug's labeling. The question we must decide is whether the FDA's approvals provide Wyeth with a complete defense to Levine's tort claims. We conclude that they do not.

. . . . Phenergan can be administered intramuscularly or intravenously, and it can be administered intravenously through either the "IV-push" method, whereby the drug is injected directly into a patient's vein, or the "IV-drip" method, whereby the drug is introduced into a saline solution in a hanging intravenous bag and slowly descends through a catheter inserted in a patient's vein. The drug is corrosive and causes irreversible gangrene if it enters a patient's artery.

. . . . Although Phenergan's labeling warned of the danger of gangrene and amputation following inadvertent intra-arterial injection, Levine alleged that the labeling was defective because it failed to instruct clinicians to use the IV-drip method of intravenous administration instead of the higher risk IV-push method. . . .

Wyeth filed a motion for summary judgment, arguing that Levine's failure-to-warn claims were pre-empted by federal law. The court found no merit in . . . Wyeth's field pre-emption argument. . . .

. . . [T]he trial judge instructed the jury that it could consider evidence of Wyeth's compliance with FDA requirements but that such compliance did not establish that the warnings were adequate. He also instructed, without objection from Wyeth, that FDA regulations "permit a drug manufacturer to change a product label to add or strengthen a warning about its product without prior FDA approval so long as it later submits the revised warning for review and approval." . . . .

. . . [T]he jury found that Wyeth was negligent . . . [and] that Phenergan was a defective product as a result of inadequate warnings and instructions. . . .

The Vermont Supreme Court affirmed. . . .

. . . . The question presented by the petition is whether the FDA's drug labeling judgments "preempt state law product liability claims premised on the theory that different labeling judgments were necessary to make drugs reasonably safe for use." . . . .

Our answer to that question must be guided by two cornerstones of our pre-emption jurisprudence. First, "the purpose of Congress is the ultimate touchstone in every pre-emption case." . . . . Second, "[i]n all pre-emption cases, and particularly in those in which Congress has 'legislated . . . in a field which the States have traditionally occupied,' . . . we 'start with the assumption that the historic police powers of the States were not to be superseded by the Federal Act unless that was the clear and manifest purpose of Congress.'" . . . .

In order to identify the "purpose of Congress," it is appropriate to briefly review the history of federal regulation of drugs and drug labeling. In 1906, Congress enacted . . . Federal Food and Drugs Act. . . . The Act, which prohibited the manufacture or interstate shipment of adulterated or misbranded drugs, supplemented the protection for consumers already provided by state regulation and common-law liability. In the 1930s, Congress . . . enacted the Federal Food, Drug, and Cosmetic Act (FDCA). . . . The Act's most substantial innovation was its provision for premarket approval of new drugs. It required every manufacturer to submit a new drug application, including reports of investigations and specimens of proposed labeling, to the FDA for review. . . .

In 1962, Congress amended the FDCA and shifted the burden of proof from the FDA to the manufacturer. Before 1962, the agency had to prove harm to keep a drug out of the market, but the amendments required the manufacturer to demonstrate that its drug was "safe for use under the conditions prescribed, recommended, or suggested in the proposed labeling" before it could distribute the drug. . . . In addition, the amendments required the manufacturer to prove the drug's effectiveness. . . .

As it enlarged the FDA's powers to "protect the public health" and "assure the safety, effectiveness, and reliability of drugs," ... Congress took care to preserve state law. The 1962 amendments added a saving clause, indicating that a provision of state law would only be invalidated upon a "direct and positive conflict" with the FDCA.... Consistent with that provision, state common-law suits "continued unabated despite ... FDA regulation." .... And when Congress enacted an express pre-emption provision for medical devices in 1976 ..., it declined to enact such a provision for prescription drugs.

In 2007, after Levine's injury and lawsuit, Congress again amended the FDCA.... For the first time, it granted the FDA statutory authority to require a manufacturer to change its drug label based on safety information that becomes available after a drug's initial approval.... In doing so, however, Congress did not enact a provision in the Senate bill that would have required the FDA to preapprove all changes to drug labels.... Instead, it adopted a rule of construction to make it clear that manufacturers remain responsible for updating their labels....

Wyeth first argues that Levine's state-law claims are pre-empted because it is impossible for it to comply with both the state-law duties underlying those claims and its federal labeling duties.... The FDA's premarket approval of a new drug application includes the approval of the exact text in the proposed label.... Generally speaking, a manufacturer may only change a drug label after the FDA approves a supplemental application. There is, however, an FDA regulation that permits a manufacturer to make certain changes to its label before receiving the agency's approval. Among other things, this "changes being effected" (CBE) regulation provides that if a manufacturer is changing a label to "add or strengthen a contraindication, warning, precaution, or adverse reaction" or to "add or strengthen an instruction about dosage and administration that is intended to increase the safe use of the drug product," it may make the labeling change upon filing its supplemental application with the FDA; it need not wait for FDA approval....

.... Wyeth suggests that the FDA, rather than the manufacturer, bears primary responsibility for drug labeling. Yet through many amendments to the FDCA and to FDA regulations, it has remained a central premise of federal drug regulation that the manufacturer bears responsibility for the content of its label at all times....

Indeed, prior to 2007, the FDA lacked the authority to order manufacturers to revise their labels.... Thus, when the risk of gangrene from IV-push injection of Phenergan became apparent, Wyeth had a duty to provide a warning that adequately described that risk, and the CBE regulation permitted it to provide such a warning before receiving the FDA's approval.

Of course, the FDA retains authority to reject labeling changes made pursuant to the CBE regulation in its review of the manufacturer's supplemental application, just as it retains such authority in reviewing all supplemental applications. But absent clear evidence that the FDA would not have approved a change to Phenergan's label, we will not conclude that it was impossible for Wyeth to comply with both federal and state requirements.

. . . .

Wyeth contends that the FDCA establishes both a floor and a ceiling for drug regulation: Once the FDA has approved a drug's label, a state-law verdict may not deem the label inadequate, regardless of whether there is any evidence that the FDA has considered the stronger warning at issue. The most glaring problem with this argument is that all evidence of Congress' purposes is to the contrary. Building on its 1906 Act, Congress enacted the FDCA to bolster consumer protection against harmful products.... Congress did not provide a federal remedy for consumers harmed by unsafe or ineffective drugs in the 1938 statute or in any subsequent amendment....

If Congress thought state-law suits posed an obstacle to its objectives, it surely would have enacted an express pre-emption provision at some point during the FDCA's 70-year history.... Its silence on the issue, coupled with its certain awareness of the prevalence of state tort litigation, is powerful evidence that Congress did not intend FDA oversight to be the exclusive means of ensuring drug safety and effectiveness. As Justice O'Connor explained in her opinion for a unanimous Court: "The case for federal pre-emption is particularly weak where Congress has indicated its awareness of the operation of state law in a field of federal interest, and has nonetheless decided to stand by both concepts and to tolerate whatever tension there [is] between them."....

... Wyeth nonetheless maintains that, because the FDCA requires the FDA to determine that a drug is safe and effective under the conditions set forth in its labeling, the agency must be presumed to have performed a precise balancing of risks and benefits and to have established a specific labeling standard that leaves no room for different state-law judgments.... Wyeth relies not on any statement by Congress, but instead on the preamble to a 2006 FDA regulation governing the content and format of prescription drug labels.... In that preamble, the FDA declared that the FDCA establishes "both a 'floor' and a 'ceiling,'" so that "FDA approval of labeling ... preempts conflicting or contrary State law." .... It further stated that certain state-law actions, such as those involving failure-to-warn claims, "threaten FDA's statutorily prescribed role as the expert Federal agency responsible for evaluating and regulating drugs." ....

This Court has recognized that an agency regulation with the force of law can pre-empt conflicting state requirements.... We are faced with no such regulation in this case, but rather with an agency's mere assertion that state law is an obstacle to achieving its statutory objectives. Because Congress has not authorized the FDA to pre-empt state law directly ..., the question is what weight we should accord the FDA's opinion.

In prior cases, we have given "some weight" to an agency's views about the impact of tort law on federal objectives when "the subject matter is ... [technical] and the relevant history and background are complex and extensive." .... Even in such cases, however, we have not deferred to an agency's *conclusion* that state law is pre-empted. Rather, we have attended to an agency's explanation of how state law affects the regulatory scheme. While agencies have no special authority to pronounce on pre-emption absent delegation by Congress, they do have a unique understanding of the statutes they administer and an attendant ability to make informed determinations about how state requirements may pose an "obstacle to the accomplishment and execution of the full purposes and objectives of Congress." .... The weight we accord the agency's explanation of state law's impact on the federal scheme depends on its thoroughness, consistency, and persuasiveness....

Under this standard, the FDA's 2006 preamble does not merit deference. When the FDA issued its notice of proposed rulemaking in December 2000, it explained that the rule would "not contain policies that have federalism implications or that preempt State law." .... In 2006, the agency finalized the rule and, without offering States or other interested parties notice or opportunity for comment, articulated a sweeping position on the FDCA's pre-emptive effect in the regulatory preamble. The agency's views on state law are inherently suspect in light of this procedural failure.

.... Further, the preamble is at odds with what evidence we have of Congress' purposes, and it reverses the FDA's own longstanding position without providing a reasoned explanation, including any discussion of how state law has interfered with the FDA's regulation of drug labeling during decades of coexistence....

.... The FDA has limited resources to monitor the 11,000 drugs on the market, and manufacturers have superior access to information about their drugs, especially in the postmarketing phase as new risks emerge. State tort suits uncover unknown drug hazards and provide incentives for drug manufacturers to disclose safety risks promptly. They also serve a distinct compensatory function that may motivate injured persons to come forward with information.... Thus, the FDA long maintained that state law offers an additional, and important, layer of consumer protection that complements FDA regulation. The agency's 2006 preamble represents a dramatic change in position.

Largely based on the FDA's new position, Wyeth argues that this case presents a conflict between state and federal law analogous to the one at issue in Geier [v. American Honda Motor Co., 529 U.S. 861 (2000)]. There, we held that state tort claims premised on Honda's failure to install airbags conflicted with a federal regulation that did not require airbags for all cars. The Department of Transportation (DOT) had promulgated a rule that provided car manufacturers with a range of choices among passive restraint devices.... Rejecting an "all airbag" standard, the agency had called for a gradual phase-in of a mix of passive restraints in order to spur technological development and win consumer acceptance.... Because the plaintiff's claim was that car manufacturers had a duty to install airbags, it presented an obstacle to achieving "the variety and mix of devices that the federal regulation sought."

Wyeth and the dissent contend that the regulatory scheme in this case is nearly identical, but, as we have described, it is quite different. In *Geier,* the DOT conducted a formal rulemaking and then adopted a plan to phase in a mix of passive restraint devices. Examining the rule itself and the DOT's contemporaneous record, which revealed the factors the agency had weighed and the balance it had struck, we determined that state tort suits presented an obstacle to the federal scheme. After conducting our own pre-emption analysis, we considered the agency's explanation of how state law interfered with its regulation, regarding it as further support for our independent conclusion that the plaintiff's tort claim obstructed the federal regime.

By contrast, we have no occasion in this case to consider the pre-emptive effect of a specific agency regulation bearing the force of law. . . .

. . . . Although we recognize that some state-law claims might well frustrate the achievement of congressional objectives, this is not such a case.

. . . [T]he judgment of the Vermont Supreme Court is affirmed.

[The concurring opinions of Justices Thomas and Justice Breyer, and the dissenting opinion of Justice ALITO, with whom THE CHIEF JUSTICE and Justice SCALIA joined, have been omitted.]

Notes

1. ***Pre-emption is Frequently Litigated, Fact-Intensive.*** Pre-emption is a major issue in many products-liability cases, and new decisions by the Supreme Court and lower courts, relating to an ever-increasing number of federal statutes and regulations, are continually being reported. The analysis leading to a particular conclusion is typically fact-intensive, and some decisions seem counter-intuitive.

2. ***Generic Drug Labels.*** Although *Wyeth, supra,* held that federal law did not pre-empt a failure-to-warn claim against the maker of a brand name drug, federal law does expressly pre-empt a failure-to-warn claim against the maker of a generic drug by spelling out exactly how the generic version of the drug should be made and labeled. *See* Drugs. Mut. Pharm. Co., Inc. v. Bartlett, 133 S. Ct. 2466, 2471–72 (2013).

3. ***Tobacco Litigation: Pre-emption and Economic Analysis.*** In Cipollone v. Liggett Group, Inc., 505 U.S. 504 (1992), the Supreme Court held that claims against a cigarette manufacturer were pre-empted by the Public Health Cigarette Smoking Act of 1969 to the extent that the claims were based on the theory that the warnings on cigarette packages should have been stronger. As the act specified the wording that had to be used on the packages, this holding was almost inevitable. However, claims based on "express warranties" (which the plaintiff claimed could be found in the defendant's advertisements) were not pre-empted, and neither were claims based on fraudulent misrepresentation, both in advertising and in statements to government agencies. Following the Supreme Court's decision, the plaintiff decided to drop the suit rather than go through another trial.

Prior to *Cipollone,* the history of tobacco-related tort litigation stretched nearly four decades, during which time the tobacco industry paid not a single adverse monetary award. The major obstacle in many tobacco cases is the argument that recovery is barred, in whole or in part, by contributory negligence or assumption of the risk.

In recent years, many states have sued the tobacco companies for recovery of the costs of providing medical care under Medicaid for smoking-related illnesses. In an attempt to avoid the argument that smokers have brought their illnesses on themselves by using a product which everyone knows can cause harm, the states have claimed that they are victims of various kinds of bad conduct by the tobacco companies, and that they should be allowed to recover even though the defendants would not be liable to the smokers. As a matter of legal doctrine, these cases are highly innovative. For one thing, the claim that states are "injured" because they have had to provide medical care to smokers is questionable. It is clear beyond any doubt that smokers, on the average, incur lower lifetime medical costs than non-smokers, because many smokers die relatively young, before reaching the age at which extremely expensive illnesses such as Alzheimer's disease tend to strike. If everyone were to stop smoking today, total spending on medical care would increase significantly in a few years. (In addition, the Social Security crisis would be greatly worsened if all retirees lived as long as non-smokers typically do.)

Many of the tobacco cases settled for large amounts. At least one of the tobacco cases was "settled" for an amount greater than the plaintiff sought in its complaint: something that does not happen in ordinary tort litigation between persons who are truly adversaries.

G. Policy Issues

Economic Analysis
Liability and Safety

Alan Gunn

A fair number of judicial opinions in products cases say that expansive liability will make the world safer because manufacturers will respond by making safer products. This idea cannot be dismissed out of hand; it is certainly true that one consequence of our society's love of litigation is a pervasive attention to safety. Nevertheless, there are many ways in which increased liability can make the world more dangerous. For one thing, the prospect of liability has certainly discouraged the manufacture of some products, in some cases even leading to the withdrawal of products from the market (small aircraft and Bendectin are two examples). When the products in question make life safer, this is clearly a bad thing. The easiest way to reduce the danger of product-liability suits is to continue making the products one has made for the last thirty years or so: expanded liability undoubtedly discourages innovation, and innovation generally leads to more safety, not less.

Even when a product is not withdrawn, the extra costs associated with "safety features" of questionable value and of insuring against expected liability will make the product less widely available than it would have been if liability were not so widespread. This, too, can increase danger, as when consumers continue to use old, worn-out products rather than buying expensive replacements, or when some consumers forgo buying products that would make them better off. Consider, for example, the middle-aged, overweight man who has a heart attack while shoveling snow, and who would have bought a snowblower but for the several hundred dollars added to the cost of every snowblower by the tort system.

An assumption of many courts, so widely shared that it is usually unstated, is that courts must take an active role in product design because market forces will not do the job. Everyday experience may not bear this out. Consider, for example, automobile safety. Today's cars are much safer than those of even ten years ago. Most of the features that make today's cars safer are features introduced by manufacturers seeking increased safety, not features introduced in response to liability. Anti-lock brakes, all-weather tires, intermittent windshield wipers, and general improvements in the reliability of components are examples. Furthermore, it has been contended that the reluctance of American manufacturers to introduce air bags (which came into fairly widespread use in Europe and Japan earlier) was attributable in part to fears of liability (for example, in the rare cases in which air bags deploy accidentally).

1. Product-Category Liability

One way of making liability even more "strict" than it is now would be to abolish the "defect" requirement entirely, simply making manufacturers of products liable to anyone hurt while using the product. Such a principle has found little, if any, support in the courts. A few courts have, however, held that a jury can decide that a particular product may be defective not because of some feature that might be improved but simply because the dangers of having the product on the market outweigh its utility. For example, in O'Brien v. Muskin Corp., 463 A.2d 298 (N.J. 1983), the plaintiff was injured when he dove into an above-ground swimming pool. The court held that the jury could conclude that the product was so dangerous and of so little utility that it should not have been marketed at all. New Jersey enacted legislation overruling the *O'Brien* decision. *See* N.J. Stat. Ann. § 2A:58 C-1, C-3 (Westlaw 2022).

Handguns and Ammunition. One product which many people consider to carry risks outweighing its utility is the handgun. In response to heavy lobbying by the National Rifle Association, a majority of states have adopted legislation barring actions by crime victims against the manufacturers of guns. *See, e.g.,* Mont. Code Ann. § 27-1-720 (Westlaw 2022); *but see* Cal. Civ. Code § 1714(a) (Westlaw 2022) ("Everyone is responsible . . . for an injury occasioned to another by his or her want of ordinary care or skill in the management of his or her property or person. . . . The design, distribution, or marketing of firearms and ammunition is not exempt from the duty to use ordinary care and skill that is required by this section"). The federal Protection of Lawful Commerce in Arms Act, enacted in 2005, now bars a wide range of civil liability actions against manufacturers, importers, dealers, and other sellers of firearms and ammunition. *See* 15 U.S.C.A. § 7901–03 (Westlaw 2022).

Juries and Undesirable Products. Undesirable products can be prohibited by legislation and by the actions of administrative agencies authorized by statute to bar products. Is allowing juries to decide on a case-by-case basis whether particular products should have been marketed necessary or desirable? Consider the following list of products, none of which is outlawed by legislation or regulation, but all of which are viewed by many people as undesirable: fast automobiles; firearms (especially handguns); alcoholic beverages; cigarettes; motorcycles; mopeds; swimming pools without lifeguards; high-cholesterol food; small automobiles.

It seems likely that most Americans would favor outlawing at least some of these products; many would ban all or most of them if they could. Is there a good reason why a plaintiff injured by one of these products should not have an opportunity to convince a jury that the manufacturer and retailer of the product should have gone into some other line of work?

Product-Category Liability and the Restatement. The Restatement takes a curiously ambivalent approach to product-category liability. In an example using facts like those of the *O'Brien* case, the Restatement says that the plaintiff has failed to establish a design defect because of the uncontradicted expert testimony that no safer alternative design was feasible. *See* Restatement, Third, of Torts: Products Liability § 2 cmt. d, illus. 4. However, in comment e to § 2, the Restatement concludes (using as its example an exploding cigar) that a product can be found defective if its utility is so low and its risk of injury so high that the product should not have been marketed, even though no feasible alternative is possible. Perhaps the distinction between above-ground swimming pools and exploding cigars rests on the fact that many thousands of people purchase and use above-ground pools, while exploding cigars are rare.

Federal Statutory Reform of Products-Liability law. Every state has adopted some legislation relating to aspects of the law of products liability. Many of the statutes respond to particular decisions that the legislature thinks went "too far." Because markets for many products are national, state legislation is unlikely to provide manufacturers with enough protection to cause them to change their activities very much. Bills to reform the law of products liability are introduced in Congress every year; to date, few have passed. Consumer advocates argue that federalizing products liability law would make it easier for highly-paid lobbyists to water-down safety standards.

Chapter 16

Defenses Based on Plaintiff's Conduct

A. Traditional Contributory Negligence

1. In General

"Contributory negligence" is unreasonable conduct on the part of the plaintiff which is a contributing proximate cause of the harm which occurs. At common law, proof of contributory negligence normally constituted a total bar to recovery for negligence, regardless of whether the defendant's fault was greater or less than the plaintiff's. Contributory negligence traditionally did not bar recovery based on reckless or intentional wrongdoing or conduct giving rise to strict liability. Under these rules, the task of categorizing the defendant's culpability took on great importance, for compensation to a negligent plaintiff was awarded on an all-or-nothing basis. As discussed below, the scope and import of a defense based on the plaintiff's unreasonable conduct changed significantly in the last quarter of the twentieth century. Most states adopted some form of "comparative negligence" or "comparative responsibility" system—usually by statute, but sometimes by judicial decision. Under these systems, a victim's negligence will often only reduce, but not eliminate, the victim's recovery against a negligent defendant. *See* note 5, *supra*, at pp. 21–22.

Same Negligence Standard Applies to Plaintiffs and Defendants. The same factors that determine whether the defendant was negligent also determine whether the plaintiff was negligent. *See* Restatement, Third, of Torts: Apportionment of Liab. § 3 (2000).

Anticipating the Negligence of Others. Suppose a potential plaintiff (1) knows that others are likely to act negligently, and (2) takes precautions that are "reasonable" if all others act reasonably also, but which will be insufficient if someone else acts negligently. Is the plaintiff's failure to take greater precautions contributory negligence? In other words, should the plaintiff be entitled to assume, in taking precautions, that everyone else will exercise reasonable care as well, or must the plaintiff's reasonable care be care which anticipates and guards against the negligence of others?

In cases involving traffic accidents, the issue is whether a driver (or pedestrian) can act on the assumption that all other drivers and pedestrians will use reasonable care. Suppose, for instance, that a pedestrian crosses a street without looking for oncoming cars, assuming that they will stop for a red light. If the pedestrian is hit by a driver who runs the light, is the failure to look for traffic contributory negligence? Many judicial opinions simply assume that reasonable care can require anticipating that others will be negligent. This makes sense because it would be highly unrealistic to assess the plaintiff's conduct by reference to a hypothetical world where other persons are never negligent. No one—not even the reasonable prudent person—lives in that kind of world.

2. Imputed Contributory Negligence

Western Union Tel. Co. v. Hoffman

Supreme Court of Texas
15 S.W. 1048 (Tex. 1891)

HENRY, J.

This suit was brought by August Hoffman for himself, and as next friend of his minor son, Kelly Hoffman, to recover damages caused by the neglect of the defendant to deliver the following telegraphic message: "Spring, Texas, August 6, 1889. To Dr. Dutton, Conroe, Texas: Come on first train. Kelly Hoffman broke his arm. [Signed] Henry Hughes." The father of Kelly was away from home when his own son was hurt, and the message was sent by direction of his wife, the mother of the boy. The message was received at Conroe, where Dr. Dutton lived, on the day that it was sent, but was not delivered to him until he inquired for it of the agent of the defendant, on the 15th of the same month. No excuse for the failure to deliver it was offered.

Kelly was 15 years old when he was hurt. His injury was a dislocation of his arm at the elbow. Dr. Dutton was the physician of plaintiff's family, and testified that if the dispatch had been delivered to him he would have responded to it within 24 hours, and would have reset and saved the arm. The testimony shows that the same thing could have been done at any time within a few days after the injury occurred. No other dispatch was sent, and no further effort was made to procure the aid of Dr. Dutton or any other physician. Nothing seems to have been done to remedy the dislocation, and the result followed that, when the wound healed, it left the arm stiff, and permanently disabled. On the 15th day of August—or nine days after the injury occurred—Dr. Dutton happened to be passing by the residence of the parents of the youth, and was seen and called in. He then examined the arm, but did not undertake to treat it. He testified that it was then too late to reset it, and that the attempt to do so would have been attended with great danger to the patient. He was corroborated in this particular by the evidence of another physician.... The defendant pleaded contributory negligence. Upon the verdict of a jury judgment was rendered in favor of the father for $900 and in favor of his son for $4,125....

The only question that we deem it necessary to consider is whether the defense of contributory negligence was made out.... [In view of] the failure to send another message to Dr. Dutton or procure other medical assistance, which would naturally have suggested itself to any person of ordinary prudence and intelligence, we think the evidence clearly shows that the permanent character of the injury must be attributed to a want of proper care upon the part of the parents of the injured boy.... Because of such contributory negligence no verdict should have been rendered in favor of the father of the minor for his own benefit, and the one so rendered should have been set aside upon defendant's motion....

But the negligence of his parents cannot be interposed as a defense to bar a recovery for the benefit of the minor.... The contributory negligence that precludes him from a recovery must be that of the minor himself, and whether it existed or not was a question for the jury to decide, taking into their consideration the age and situation of the minor, and all other circumstances connected with the case.... In the case before us it may be well doubted whether a child 15 years old had sufficient experience or discretion to correctly estimate the consequences of the failure to have his injured arm properly treated, especially when his mental and physical condition caused by the injury are considered.... We think the judgment should be affirmed as to the minor, Kelly Hoffman, and reversed, and the cause be remanded, as to the individual judgment in favor of August Hoffman; and it will be so ordered.

Notes

1. ***Imputed Contributory Negligence.*** Restatement, Third, of Torts: Apportionment of Liab. § 5 adopts a "both ways" rule for imputing negligence to a plaintiff. Generally, if negligence would have been imputed to a person if the person had been a defendant, negligence will also be imputed to the person when that person is a plaintiff. Thus, an employee's negligence will be imputed to the employer (under *respondeat superior*) when the employer is sued by a third person, and the employee's negligence will also be imputed to the employer when the employer is trying to assert a claim against a third person.

Under the "both ways" rule, for purposes of creating a defense in the nature of contributory negligence, a parent's negligence is not imputed to the parent's child (because, at common law, parents are not vicariously liable for the torts of their children); a spouse's negligence is not imputed to the other spouse (because one spouse is not vicariously liable for what another spouse does); and the negligence of the driver of a vehicle is not imputed to a passenger (because drivers are not vicariously liable for the conduct of their passengers).

See Seaborne-Worsley v. Mintiens, 183 A.3d 141 (Md. 2018) (holding that the alleged contributory negligence of a vehicle owner/passenger's husband in parking the vehicle in the travel lane of a parking lot would not be imputed to the owner/passenger).

"When a relationship exists in which imputed plaintiff's negligence would otherwise be appropriate, plaintiff's negligence is not imputed from one party of the relationship to another in a suit between them." *Id.* at cmt. d. Thus, if an employee negligently damages an employer's vehicle, imputed negligence will not bar the employer from suing the employee or reduce the employer's recovery.

2. ***Imputation of Negligence Relating to Wrongful-Death, Survival, and Loss of Consortium.*** In cases involving "derivative claims" for damages resulting from a tort against a third person, the Restatement imputes the negligence of the direct victim to the plaintiff. *See* Restatement, Third, of Torts: Apportionment of Liab. § 6. Many wrongful-death and survival statutes expressly provide for this result.

3. Last Clear Chance

One of the most important limits on the rule of contributory negligence at common law was the doctrine of last clear chance. The doctrine is thought to have originated in Davies v. Mann, 152 Eng. Rep. 588 (1842), an old English case in which, as the Restatement puts it, "the plaintiff left his ass fettered in the highway, and the defendant ran into it." Restatement, Second, of Torts § 479 cmt. a. The doctrine of last clear chance provides that negligence on the part of the plaintiff will not defeat recovery if the defendant (and not the plaintiff), through the exercise of ordinary care, had the last clear chance to avoid the accident. Because, in *Davies*, the defendant driver of the cart, which was traveling too fast when it hit the animal, had the last clear chance to avoid the harm (*e.g.*, by slowing down and taking other evasive measures), the plaintiff's contributory negligence in leaving the animal in the road was disregarded. Full recovery was permitted.

Under last clear chance, once the defendant has discovered the plaintiff's position of peril, the defendant must have sufficient time and ability to avoid the accident. Otherwise, the doctrine does not apply because, in fact, the defendant does not have the last clear chance to avert harm. The great body of precedent which emerged to govern the last-clear-chance doctrine is only of historical interest today. With the rise of comparative negligence and comparative fault, the need for last clear chance as a palliative for the hardships of the all-or-nothing contributory-negligence rule disappeared. Consequently, virtually all jurisdictions have abolished last clear chance. *See* Restatement, Third, of Torts: Apportionment of Liab. § 3 (2000).

Note, however, that in the small number of jurisdictions which have never adopted comparative negligence and comparative fault, the doctrine of last clear chance remains viable. *See, e.g.*, Juvenalis v. District of Columbia, 955 A.2d 187 (D.C. 2008) (doctrine applicable); Eason v. Cleveland Draft House, LLC, 673 S.E.2d 883 (N.C. Ct. App. 2009) (doctrine inapplicable to the facts).

B. Comparative Negligence

Hilen v. Hays

Supreme Court of Kentucky
673 S.W.2d 713 (Ky. 1984)

LEIBSON, Justice.

The appellant, Margie Montgomery Hilen, was severely injured when the automobile in which she was a passenger was driven into the back of another vehicle and overturned. She sued the driver, appellee Keith Hays. There was no question but that the cause of the accident was the driver's negligent operation of the vehicle. There was a factual dispute as to whether the passenger failed to exercise reasonable care for her own safety by riding with a person whom she knew or should have known to be too intoxicated to drive safely.

At the conclusion of the trial the judge directed a verdict as to appellee's negligence and submitted the case to the jury solely on the issue of appellant's contributory negligence. The jury was given the usual instruction that contributory negligence was a complete bar to any recovery. The appellant objected and tendered an instruction based on the doctrine of comparative negligence, which was refused. The jury found for the appellee and this appeal followed. The Court of Appeals affirmed....

The sole issue before us is whether negligence on the part of the appellant contributing to her injury should be a complete bar to any recovery, ... or whether the time has come for us to reject this rule and adopt the doctrine of comparative negligence allocating responsibility for the injury between the parties in proportion to their contributory fault.

... [T]he contributory negligence rule as it applies to this case is court-made law that bears the imprimatur of neither the Kentucky constitution nor the General Assembly.... Prosser states in the Law of Torts, (4th Ed., 1971), p. 434:

> There never has been any essential reason why the change [to comparative negligence] could not be made without a statute by the courts which made the contributory negligence rule in the first place....

Having deference to the doctrine of *stare decisis*, the courts of the several states have been understandably reluctant to abandon contributory negligence as a complete defense notwithstanding the relative merits of the two competing positions. The tendency was to defer consideration of comparative negligence to the legislatures of the several states, although there was no statute mandating the traditional rule and thus no question of separation of powers involved....

So the evolution towards comparative negligence began in the various state legislatures first in a trickle and then in an avalanche. The first comparative negligence statute was enacted in Mississippi in 1910. Wisconsin and Nebraska followed in 1913, South Dakota in 1941, Arkansas in 1957, Maine in 1964. Following a full-scale public debate of the relative merits of comparative negligence in textbooks and treatises, twenty-six more states followed between 1969 and 1983. At present count thirty-two states, Puerto Rico, and the Virgin Islands have adopted comparative negligence or comparative fault by statute.

In addition, between 1975 and the present, courts in nine other states have refused to wait further for their legislatures to act and have adopted comparative negligence by judicial decision. . . .

A comparative negligence bill was introduced at the 1968 session of the Kentucky General Assembly and a similar bill has been introduced in most, if not all, sessions since then. Two bills were introduced in 1984 and neither got out of committee. . . .

In broad outline, *stare decisis* directs us to "stand by" our previous decisions unless there are sound legal reasons to the contrary. . . . But the doctrine of *stare decisis* does not commit us to the sanctification of ancient fallacy. . . .

The common law is not a stagnant pool, but a moving stream. . . . It seeks to purify itself as it flows through time. The common law is our responsibility; the child of the courts. We are responsible for its direction. . . .

A list of the critics of contributory negligence as a complete bar to a plaintiff's recovery reads like a tort hall of fame. . . . In 1953 Prosser wrote:

> The attack upon contributory negligence has been founded upon the obvious injustice of a rule which visits the entire loss caused by the fault of two parties on one of them alone, and that one the injured plaintiff, least able to bear it, and quite possibly much less at fault than the defendant who goes scot-free. No one has ever succeeded in justifying that as a policy, and no one ever will.

. . . .

In Li v. Yellow Cab Co., 13 Cal. 3d 804, 119 Cal. Rptr. 858, 532 P.2d 1226 (1975) [the court stated]:

> The essence of that criticism has been constant and clear: the doctrine is inequitable in its operation because it fails to distribute responsibility in proportion to fault. . . . In a system in which liability is based on fault, the extent of that fault should govern the extent of liability. . . .

Comparative negligence . . . eliminates a windfall for either claimant or defendant as presently exists in our all-or-nothing situation where sometimes claims are barred by contributory negligence and sometimes claims are paid in full regardless of contributory negligence such as in cases involving last clear chance or defendant's willful or wanton negligence. . . .

The answer to the charge that in a comparative negligence system the claimant recovers for his own wrong is that the opposite is true. Even where comparative negligence is applied 100% (the so-called "pure" form of comparative negligence), the claimant who is 95% negligent recovers from the defendant only for that small portion of the injury, 5%, which is fairly attributable to the defendant's fault. In theory, the system is 100% fair.

.... To those who speculate that comparative negligence will cost more money or cause more litigation, we say there are no good economies in an *unjust* law.

....

Having concluded that contributory negligence as a complete defense in Kentucky should give way to comparative negligence, the next question is what form of comparative negligence should be adopted. Although there are variations in the types of comparative negligence, the two basic systems are the "modified" form and the "pure" form, "modified" meaning "limited" and "pure" meaning "complete." Under the "modified" form, with variations depending on the system, the claimant can recover if his percentage of fault is not equal to or greater than that of the defendant(s). Under the "pure" form, the claimant's recovery is reduced by the amount of fault attributable to him, but he may recover regardless of whether his fault is equal to or greater than that of the defendant(s).

Opponents of the "modified" form of comparative negligence argue that this system encourages appeals on the narrow but crucial issue of whether plaintiff's negligence was equal to or greater than defendant's, and further argue that it does not abrogate contributory negligence but "simply shifts the lottery aspect of the rule to a different ground." ....

In eight of the nine states where comparative negligence has been adopted by judicial decision, the courts have opted for the "pure" form. Only West Virginia has held to the contrary....

In contrast to change by the judiciary where pure comparative negligence has been the overwhelming choice, the majority of state legislatures adopting comparative negligence have favored some modified form....

The treatise by Judge Henry Woods, Comparative Fault, ... includes an extensive review of both the legislative and judicial experience of our sister states with comparative negligence. Such a review compels us to conclude that the pure form of comparative negligence is preferable over any of the variety of modified forms that have been suggested....

Henceforth, where contributory negligence has previously been a complete defense, it is supplanted by the doctrine of comparative negligence. In such cases contributory negligence will not bar recovery but shall reduce the total amount of the award in the proportion that the claimant's contributory negligence bears to the total negligence that caused the damages. The trier of fact must consider both negligence and causation in arriving at the proportion that negligence and causation attributable to the claimant bears to the total negligence that was a substantial factor in causing the damages.

....

The final question that remains to be addressed is the application of the present decision to this case and others where contributory negligence is an issue. Other courts that have adopted comparative negligence have all made the doctrine effective to pending cases to some extent. The appellee complains that the rules should not be changed in his case. But unlike contract law the appellee here did not act in reliance on the state of the law at the time of the act, and has no legitimate complaint against the retroactive application of a change. We conclude . . . that the comparative negligence doctrine shall apply to:

1) The present case;

2) All cases tried or retried after the date of filing of this opinion; and

3) All cases pending, including appeals, in which the issue has been preserved.

The decision of the Court of Appeals and the trial court is reversed, and the within action is remanded to the trial court for proceedings in conformity with this opinion.

[The concurring opinion of Justice LEIBSON and the dissenting opinion of Justice VANCE, in which Justice STEPHENSON joined, are omitted.]

Note

1. ***Jurisdictions Not Adopting Comparative Principles.*** Only four states and the District of Columbia retain strict common-law contributory negligence: Alabama (Bergob v. Scrushy, 855 So. 2d 523 (Ala. Civ. App. 2002)); D.C. (Wingfield v. Peoples Drug Store, Inc., 379 A.2d 685, 687 (D.C. 1977)); Maryland (Pippin v. Potomac Electric Power Co., 132 F. Supp. 2d 379, 383 (D. Md. 2001)); North Carolina (Yancey v. Lea, 532 S.E.2d 560, 563 (N.C. Ct. App. 1999)); and Virginia (Litchford v. Hancock, 352 S.E.2d 335, 337 (Va. 1987)).

C. Assumption of the Risk

The second great defense at common law was assumption of the risk. Like contributory negligence, it completely barred recovery by the plaintiff. "In working out the distinction [between contributory negligence and assumption of the risk], the courts . . . arrived at the conclusion that assumption of risk is a matter of knowledge of the danger and intelligent acquiescence in it, and that to the extent that this can be found recovery will be denied; while contributory negligence is a matter of some fault or departure from the standard of reasonable conduct, however unwilling or protesting the plaintiff may be." Masters v. New York Central R. Co., 70 N.E.2d 898, 903 (Ohio 1947).

1. Introduction

Coleman v. Ramada Hotel Operating Co.

United States Court of Appeals for the Seventh Circuit
933 F.2d 470 (7th Cir. 1991)

CUDAHY, Circuit Judge.

Boisterous rough and tumble sports have long been a source of picnic amusement. The three-legged race, the sack hop and the egg toss seldom fail to evoke hearty guffaws. Most of those who participate in such light-hearted antics escape unscathed, but Peggy Coleman was not so lucky. After fracturing her ankle and tearing a ligament during a company-sponsored recreational outing, Coleman filed this personal injury suit against the owner of the grounds where the unfortunate accident took place, Ramada Hotel Operating Company (Ramada). Coleman attributes her injuries to Ramada's alleged negligence in operating an obstacle course as part of the day's entertainment. The district court granted summary judgment in favor of Ramada because it found that Coleman voluntarily assumed the obvious risks inherent in the activity. . . .

. . . . One of the events at the picnic — a "mini olympics" — involved a timed obstacle course. To mount a slide backwards was the first hurdle. Participants were instructed to clamber up the slippery slope of an ordinary playground slide and climb down the stairs on the back of the slide. The slide presented no latent danger. Coleman concedes that the slide was in good repair — it was stable and possessed firm handrails. The only risk, then, was that inherent in the reversal of its normal use.

Of her own volition, Coleman competed in this event. After observing her team member ascend the slide before her, Coleman mounted the chute portion of the slide without incident. Carefully grasping the handrails and treading one step at a time, Coleman descended the ladder portion of the slide. Despite her caution, however, Coleman slipped and fell. . . .

Coleman brought suit against Ramada, charging Ramada with breach of its duty of reasonable care towards her in two distinct ways: first, by failing to warn her of the possibility of injury and, second, by failing to provide safe apparatus for the mini olympics. Ramada moved for summary judgment on both claims.

The district court . . . agreed with Ramada that Illinois imposes no duty to warn of such open and obvious risks. The court relied, however, upon the doctrine of assumption of risk — not the closely-related affirmative defense of contributory negligence — to bar Coleman's second claim, reasoning that any element of negligence in Ramada's decision to include a backward slide in the obstacle course was nullified by Coleman's voluntary choice to engage in an inherently dangerous activity. . . .

[The appeals court held that Ramada was, as a matter of law, not negligent in failing to warn of an obvious danger. It then turned to a discussion of Ramada's assumption-of-the-risk defense to Coleman's claim that Ramada's failure to provide a safer slide presented a negligence question for the factfinder.]

Though distinct in principle, assumption of risk and contributory negligence are often confused and there exists substantial overlap between the two doctrines. Pure assumption of risk consists of voluntary consent to encounter a known risk while pure contributory negligence consists of failure to exercise reasonable care in self-protection. In a large number of real cases, however, the two doctrines are inextricably intertwined. In such cases, the plaintiff's conduct amounts to both assumption of risk and contributory negligence because her acceptance of a known risk is at the same time unreasonable and negligent. . . .

Coleman's conduct . . . appears to fit into both doctrinal pigeonholes, simultaneously constituting assumption of risk and contributory negligence. . . .

This case approaches the paradigmatic instance of assumption of risk: Peggy Coleman elected to take her chances by competing in the mini olympics obstacle course with full knowledge of the hazardous nature of the event. After watching her teammate ascend the first hurdle before her, Coleman mounted the chute portion of the slide and stepped down the ladder, carefully grasping the handrails and treading one step at a time. One who freely chooses to climb up a slide backwards certainly assumes the perils of an inadvertent plunge to the ground. That Coleman was aware of the danger of falling is manifest in the very caution she observed while descending the slide. As Chief Justice Cardozo explained when rejecting the claims of an individual similarly injured by a fall from an amusement park ride aptly termed "The Flopper":

> One who takes part in such a sport accepts the dangers that inhere in it so far as they are obvious and necessary, just as a fencer accepts the risk of a thrust by his antagonist or a spectator at a ball game the chance of contact with the ball.

Murphy v. Steeplechase Amusement Co., 250 N.Y. 479, 482, 166 N.E. 173, 174 (1929). As with "The Flopper," any risks that may have been posed by inclusion of the backwards slide in the obstacle course were overt and inherent in the nature of the activity. Therefore, any misjudgment on Ramada's part in designing the obstacle course was nullified by Coleman's free and informed choice to participate in the event.

Coleman now argues, however, that the doctrine of assumption of risk may be applied only to situations involving an explicit contractual relationship between the parties. Although Illinois courts often proclaim that assumption of risk is limited to cases involving a contractual relationship, they generally construe such a relationship broadly to embrace business invitees. In Provence v. Doolin, 91 Ill. App. 3d at 280, 414 N.E.2d at 793, for example, the Illinois Appellate Court declared that "the defense of assumption of risk is confined to situations where the parties have a contractual or employment relationship" but held that mere payment of a fee for entry upon recreational premises sufficed to create such a contract. The court noted that, although one golfer whose ball strikes and injures another may not assert the defense of assumption of risk, the golf course may raise the defense because of its "contractual relationship" with the injured golfer. . . .

Finally, Coleman asserts that her conduct should not completely bar recovery because it consists solely of secondary implied assumption of risk, a doctrine now merged into the comparative negligence regime. Illinois courts have classified the doctrine of assumption of risk into three categories: express assumption of risk, primary implied assumption of risk and secondary implied assumption of risk. . . . Express assumption of risk demands an explicit agreement while implied assumption of risk infers willingness to accept a known risk from the conduct of the parties. In primary implied assumption of risk, the plaintiff assumes risks inherent in the nature of the activity while in secondary implied assumption of risk, the plaintiff assumes risks that are created by the defendant's negligence. Only the first two of these forms have survived the advent of comparative negligence in Illinois. Because it is deemed functionally similar to contributory negligence, the third category—secondary implied assumption of risk—has been abolished. . . . But Coleman's attempt to squeeze herself into the category of secondary implied assumption of risk is of no avail because any risks that she assumed were intrinsic to the activity itself rather than being the product of any negligence on Ramada's part. Whatever danger Coleman faced in mounting the playground slide backwards stemmed from the nature of the activity and not from Ramada's upkeep of the slide. Thus Coleman's conduct amounts to primary implied assumption of risk, which still operates as a complete bar to recovery.

. . . Coleman's voluntary choice to participate in an inherently risky activity bars her from recovery under Illinois law. Coleman was free to refrain altogether from participation in this hazardous sport had she wished to avert any possible risk of injury. As Chief Justice Cardozo once observed, "The timorous may stay at home." Murphy v. Steeplechase Amusement Co., 250 N.Y. at 483, 166 N.E. at 174. Therefore, the district court's entry of summary judgment in favor of Ramada is

AFFIRMED.

Notes

1. ***Thinking Clearly About Assumption of the Risk.*** Throughout most of America's history, unreasonableness by the plaintiff (contributory negligence) and venturesomeness by the plaintiff (assumption of the risk) were treated as total defenses. It made little difference which label was used to describe the plaintiff's actions; either way the defendant was not liable for negligence. This allowed the courts to be somewhat vague about the contours of assumption of the risk. Furthermore, the doctrine was often invoked in cases in which the real ground of the decision seems to have been that the defendant was not negligent.

The widespread adoption of comparative negligence or comparative fault required courts to rethink the law of assumption of the risk. This was true because, if assumption of the risk was still a complete defense, it would have been possible for defendants to circumvent comparative principles (and the policy favoring liability proportional to fault) in cases in which unreasonable risks were voluntarily assumed. Rather than allege that the plaintiff was careless (comparatively negligent, a partial defense) they would simply have argued that the plaintiff was venturesome in the face of danger (assumption of the risk, a total defense).

A rethinking of assumption of the risk was complicated by the fact that some cases involve the principle of freedom to contract. If a plaintiff expressly, or by necessary implication, agrees to run a risk in exchange for getting something from the defendant, the agreement should be enforced, absent some imperfection such as unconscionability, fraud by the defendant, or some other "public policy" making the agreement unenforceable.

2. ***Three Categories of Assumption of the Risk under Comparative Principles.*** As *Coleman* indicates, there are at least three different categories of assumption of the risk: (1) express assumption of risk, (2) primary implied assumption of risk, and (3) secondary implied assumption of risk. Most states agree that after the adoption of comparative principles, categories (1) and (2) still fully bar liability, and category (3) is a partial defense that is treated the same as comparative negligence. The materials that follow explore these three categories of "assumption of the risk."

3. ***Merger with Comparative Negligence.*** Some states no longer use the language of "assumption of the risk" and talk about the plaintiff's conduct as simply comparative negligence. *See* Shain v. Racine Raiders Football Club, Inc., 726 N.W.2d 346 (Wis. Ct. App. 2006) (stating that "Wisconsin has abolished assumption of risk as an absolute defense, but it is an element of contributory negligence"). In other states, the "assumption of the risk" terminology is still widely used.

2. Express Assumption of the Risk

Gross v. Sweet

Court of Appeals of New York
400 N.E.2d 306 (N.Y. 1979)

FUCHSBERG, Judge.

....

Plaintiff Bruce Gross, wishing to learn how to parachute, enrolled in the Stormville Parachute Center Training School, a facility owned and operated by the defendant William Sweet.... [Despite his having informed defendant that several years earlier an orthopedic pin had been inserted into his leg, he was accepted as a student.] As a prerequisite for admission into the course, Gross had to pay a fee and sign a form entitled "Responsibility Release." He was then given the standard introductory lesson, which consisted of approximately one hour of on-land training, including oral instruction as well as several jumps off a two and a half foot table. Plaintiff then was equipped with a parachute and flown to an altitude of 2,800 feet for his first practice jump. Upon coming in contact with the ground on his descent, plaintiff suffered serious personal injuries.

Jacob D. Fuchsberg

The suit is grounded on negligence, breach of warranty and gross negligence. In the main, plaintiff claims that defendant failed to provide adequate training and safe equipment, violated certain rules and procedures promulgated by the Federal Aviation Administration governing the conduct of parachute jumping schools and failed to warn him sufficiently of the attendant dangers.

Defendant pleaded the release plaintiff had signed and moved for summary judgment, contending that the terms of the release exculpated the defendant from any liability. . . .

. . . . Special Term granted defendant's motion. . . . On plaintiff's appeal from that order, a divided Appellate Division reversed, reinstated the complaint and granted plaintiff's motion to dismiss the affirmative defense. . . .

We begin with the proposition, too well settled to invoke any dispute, that the law frowns upon contracts intended to exculpate a party from the consequences of his own negligence and though, with certain exceptions, they are enforceable, such agreements are subject to close judicial scrutiny. . . . To the extent that agreements purport to grant exemption for liability for willful or grossly negligent acts they have been viewed as wholly void (*see* Restatement, Contracts, § 575, 15 Williston, Contracts [3d Jaeger ed.], § 1750A, p. 141 . . .). And so, here, so much of plaintiff's complaint as contains allegations that defendant was grossly negligent, may not be barred by the release in any event. But we need not explore further this possibility for we conclude the complaint in its entirety withstands the exculpatory agreement.

Nor need we consider plaintiff's request that we ignore the release on the grounds that the special relationship of the parties and the public interest involved forbids its enforcement. While we have, for example, had occasion to invalidate such provisions when they were contained in the contract between a passenger and a common carrier . . . , or in a contract between a customer and a public utility under a duty to furnish telephone service . . . or when imposed by an employer as a condition of employment . . . , the circumstances here do not fit within any of these relationships. And, though we note that a recent statute renders void agreements purporting to exempt from liability for negligence those engaged in a variety of businesses that serve the public (*e.g.*, landlords [General Obligations Law, § 5-321]; caterers [§ 5-322]; building service or maintenance contractors [§ 5-323]; those who maintain garages or parking garages [§ 5-325]; or pools, gymnasiums or places of public amusement or recreation [§ 5-326]), defendant's occupation does not fall within any of these classes either. We also decline, at this point, plaintiff's invitation that we proceed further to consider what effect, if any, the alleged contravention of federal regulations may have on the relationship of the parties or the public interest involved. Such questions need not be reached. . . .

As the cases make clear, the law's reluctance to enforce exculpatory provisions of this nature has resulted in the development of an exacting standard by which courts measure their validity. So, it has been repeatedly emphasized that unless the intention of the parties is expressed in unmistakable language, an exculpatory clause will not be deemed to insulate a party from liability for his own negligent acts. . . . Put another way, it must appear plainly and precisely that the "limitation of liability extends to negligence or other fault of the party attempting to shed his ordinary responsibility". . . .

Not only does this stringent standard require that the drafter of such an agreement make its terms unambiguous, but it mandates that the terms be understandable as well. Thus, a provision that would exempt its drafter from any liability occasioned by his fault should not compel resort to a magnifying glass and lexicon. . . . Of course, this does not imply that only simple or monosyllabic language can be used in such clauses. Rather, what the law demands is that such provisions be clear and coherent. . . .

By and large, if such is the intention of the parties, the fairest course is to provide explicitly that claims based on negligence are included (*see* Ciofalo v. Vic Tanney Gyms, 177 N.E.2d p. 926 [plaintiff "agreed to assume full responsibility for any injuries which might occur to her in or about defendant's premises, 'including but without limitation, any claims for personal injuries resulting from or arising out of the negligence of' the defendant"]). That does not mean that the word "negligence" must be employed for courts to give effect to an exculpatory agreement; however, words conveying a similar import must appear (*see* Theroux v. Kedenburg Racing Assn., 50 Misc. 2d 97, 99, 269 N.Y.S.2d 789, 792, *aff'd*, 28 A.D.2d 960, 282 N.Y.S.2d 930 [agreement provided for release of liability for any injury "regardless of how such injury . . . may arise, and regardless of who is at fault . . . and even if the loss is caused by the neglect or fault of" the defendant]).

We are, of course, cognizant of the fact that the general rule of strict judicial construction has been somewhat liberalized in its application to exoneration clauses in indemnification agreements, which are usually "negotiated at arm's length between ... sophisticated business entities" and which can be viewed as merely "allocating the risk of liability to third parties between themselves, essentially through the employment of insurance".... In such cases, the law, reflecting the economic realities, will recognize an agreement to relieve one party from the consequences of his negligence on the strength of a broadly worded clause framed in less precise language than would normally be required, though even then it must evince the "unmistakable intent of the parties"....

The case before us today obviously does not fit within this exception to the strict legal standard generally employed by the courts of this State under which exculpatory provisions drawn in broad and sweeping language have not been given effect. For example, agreements to release from "any and all responsibility or liability of any nature whatsoever for any loss of property or personal injury occurring on this trip" ... or to "waive claim for any loss to personal property, or for any personal injury while a member of [a] club" ... have not barred claims based on negligence (*see* Bernstein v. Seacliff Beach Club, 35 Misc. 2d 153, 228 N.Y.S.2d 567). Moreover, in Boll v. Sharp & Dohme (281 App. Div. 568, 121 N.Y.S.2d 20, *aff'd*, 307 N.Y. 646, 120 N.E.2d 836 ...), we held not sufficiently unambiguous a release form in which a blood donor was required to agree that defendants were not "in any way responsible for any consequences ... resulting from the giving of such blood or from any of the tests, examinations or procedures incident thereto," and further "release[d] and discharge[d] more [defendants] from all claims and demands whatsoever ... against them or any of them by reason of any matter relative or incident to such donation of blood." .... The donor was thus allowed to sue in negligence for injuries he sustained when, on the completion of the blood donation, he fainted and fell to the floor.

With all this as background, the language of the "Responsibility Release" in the case before us must be viewed as no more explicit than that in *Boll*. In its entirety, it reads: "I, the undersigned, hereby, and by these covenants, do waive any and all claims that I, my heirs, and/or assignees may have against Nathaniel Sweet, the Stormville Parachute Center, the Jumpmaster and the Pilot who shall operate the aircraft when used for the purpose of parachute jumping for any personal injuries or property damage that I may sustain or which may arise out of my learning, practicing or actually jumping from an aircraft. I also assume full responsibility for any damage that I may do or cause while participating in this sport."

Assuming that this language alerted the plaintiff to the dangers inherent in parachute jumping and that he entered into the sport with apprehension of the risks, it does not follow that he was aware of, much less intended to accept, any *enhanced* exposure to injury occasioned by the carelessness of the very persons on which he depended for his safety. Specifically, the release nowhere expresses any intention to exempt the defendant from liability for injury or property damages which may result from his failure to use due care either in his training methods or in his furnishing safe equipment. Thus, whether on a running reading or a careful analysis, the agreement could most reasonably be taken merely as driving home the fact that the defendant was not to bear any responsibility for injuries that ordinarily and inevitably would occur, without any fault of the defendant, to those who participate in such a physically demanding sport.

In short, instead of specifying to prospective students that they would have to abide any consequences attributable to the instructor's own carelessness, the defendant seems to have preferred the use of opaque terminology rather than suffer the possibility of lower enrollment. But, while, with exceptions not pertinent to this case, the law grudgingly accepts the proposition that men may contract away their liability for negligently caused injuries, they may do so only on the condition that their intention be expressed clearly and in "unequivocal terms"....

Accordingly, ... the order of the Appellate Division reversing the grant of summary judgment, reinstating the complaint and dismissing the defense based on the release should be affirmed.

JONES, Judge (dissenting).

... [C]ontracts should not be so construed as to make them meaningless and the intent of the parties is to be drawn from the entire instrument, not from the presence or absence of a particular talismanic word or term....

.... The release ..., if construed as not including claims predicated on negligence, releases nothing and is meaningless and a nullity. A more broadly worded exoneration provision would be difficult to imagine.... [C]laims such as the present ones based on ordinary negligence appear to me to be precisely the claims intended by the parties to be included in the language "any and all claims ... for any personal injuries or property damage that I may sustain or which may arise out of my learning, practicing or actually jumping from an aircraft."

.... Except as to the cause of action predicated on the alleged claim of gross negligence, I would therefore reverse the order of the Appellate Division....

COOKE, C.J., and GABRIELLI and WACHTLER, JJ., concur with FUCHSBERG, J.

JONES, J., dissents and votes to reverse in a separate opinion in which JASEN and MEYER, JJ. concur.

Notes

1. ***The "Express Negligence Doctrine."*** Some courts refer to the rule that a valid pre-accident release must focus the plaintiff's attention on negligence as the "express negligence doctrine." See Ethyl Corp. v. Daniel Constr. Co., 725 S.W.2d 705, 706 (Tex. 1987) (holding that the intent of the parties to exculpate the indemnitee from the consequences of its negligence must be specifically stated within the four corners of the contract).

See also Hyson v. White Water Mt. Resorts, 829 A.2d 827 (Conn. 2003) (holding, in a case in which a woman's snowtube went over a cliff at a point where there was no barrier, that her signed release consenting to inherent risks did not bar an action for negligence because an agreement purporting to release or indemnify another prospectively may not be applied to damages arising from that party's negligence in the absence of express language to that effect); *but see* Chepkevich v. Hidden Valley Resort, L.P., 2 A.3d 1174 (Pa. 2010) (stating that "an exculpatory agreement need not contain the word 'negligence' in order to effectively bar suits arising out of negligence").

2. ***Insufficiently Clear Language.*** *See* Atkins v. Swimwest Family Fitness Ctr., 691 N.W.2d 334 (Wis. 2005) (finding that a swimming facility's release, which stated "I agree to assume all liability for myself without regard to fault," was invalid in part because it never made clear what types of acts the word "fault" encompassed).

Even if a release uses the word "negligence," it may not survive judicial scrutiny. For example, Turnbough v. Ladner, 754 So. 2d 467 (Miss. 1999), involved a negligence claim based on injuries sustained by a scuba-diving student due to the poor planning of a dive by an instructor. The court held that a pre-printed release, which stated that the plaintiff had been thoroughly informed about the risks of decompression sickness and waived liability for injuries resulting from negligence, did not bar an action for harm caused by the instructor's failure to follow basic guidelines. The court wrote:

> The wording of an exculpatory agreement should express as clearly and precisely as possible the *extent* to which a party intends to be absolved from liability. . . . Failing that, we do not sanction broad, general "waiver of negligence" provisions, and strictly construe them against the party asserting them as a defense.

3. ***Releases Void as against Public Policy.*** Occasionally, releases will be declared void as against public policy. In making a determination on the issue, it is appropriate for a court to consider, among other factors: whether the business is generally thought to warrant public regulation; the importance or necessity of the service performed; whether the business holds itself out as willing to serve all comers who fall within established standards; whether the business possesses a decisive advantage in bargaining power; and whether the agreement required the plaintiff to place the plaintiff's person or property under the control of the defendant.

In Copeland v. Healthsouth/Methodist Rehab. Hosp., LP, 565 S.W.3d 260, 274 (Tenn. 2018), the court stated that:

> Although there is no precise rule by which to define sufficient disparity in bargaining power between the parties to invalidate an exculpatory agreement, two key criteria are the importance of the service at issue for the physical or economic well-being of the party signing the agreement and the amount of free choice that party has in seeking alternate services.

The *Copeland* court held that an exculpatory agreement in a contract between a hospital's transportation services provider and a hospital patient was not enforceable against the patient.

In Dalury v. S-K-I, Ltd., 670 A.2d 795 (Vt. 1995), the court held that an exculpatory agreement printed on a form signed by the plaintiff, which purported to release a ski area from "any and all liability for personal injury or property damage resulting from negligence," was void as contrary to public policy. As the court explained:

> The defendants' area is a facility open to the public. They advertise and invite skiers and nonskiers of every level of skiing ability to their premises for the price of a ticket.... Thousands of people ride lifts, buy services, and ski the trails. Each ticket sale may be, for some purposes, a purely private transaction. But when a substantial number of such sales take place as a result of the seller's general invitation to the public to utilize the facilities and services in question, a legitimate public interest arises.
>
> .... Defendants, not recreational skiers, have the expertise and opportunity to foresee and control hazards, and to guard against the negligence of their agents and employees. They alone can properly maintain and inspect their premises, and train their employees in risk management. They alone can insure against risks and effectively spread the cost of insurance among their thousands of customers....
>
> If defendants were permitted to obtain broad waivers of their liability, an important incentive for ski areas to manage risk would be removed with the public bearing the cost of the resulting injuries....

Similarly, in Bagley v. Mt. Bachelor, Inc., 340 P.3d 27, 45 (Or. 2014), the court held that enforcement of an anticipatory release of a ski operator's liability for its own negligence would be unconscionable. It candidly noted that "without potential exposure to liability for their own negligence, ski area operators would lack a commensurate legal incentive to avoid creating unreasonable risks of harm to their business invitees."

Likewise, in Reardon v. Windswept Farm, LLC, 905 A.2d 1156 (Conn. 2006), the court held that a release signed by a horseback riding student was void as against public policy because "there is a reasonable societal expectation that a recreational activity that is under the control of the provider and is open to all individuals, regardless of experience or ability level, will be reasonably safe."

Again, in Berlangieri v. Running Elk Corp., 76 P.3d 1098 (N.M. 2003), the court held that although a liability release executed by a patron clearly expressed the parties' intention that the patron would not hold the lodge liable for its negligent acts, the release was affected by the public interest as expressed in the Equine Liability Act and was unenforceable against a patron who was injured while horseback riding.

However, cases also go the other way. In Winterstein v. Wilcom, 293 A.2d 821 (Md. Ct. Spec. App. 1972), the plaintiff, upon entering a race track to compete in the events, signed a release agreeing not to hold the track liable for harm "due to negligence or any other fault." During the race, plaintiff was injured when his car struck a part that had fallen off of another car. In holding that the release was valid and not against public policy, the court found it particularly significant that car racing was not an "essential" activity and was not heavily regulated by the state.

Rose v. National Tractor Pullers Ass'n, Inc., 33 F. Supp. 2d 757 (D. Wis. 1998), upheld a release and waiver of liability signed by a participant in a tractor pull competition.

4. ***Releases Upheld.*** *Gross* and the cases discussed in the preceding notes illustrate the reluctance of many judges to uphold pre-accident releases. Nevertheless, many courts do uphold releases, especially in cases involving participants in sporting events. If a release is clearly written, if the court is confident that the plaintiff understood what was being signed, and especially if the plaintiff has had some previous experience with the activity, the release may be given effect.

See Nearhood v. Anytime Fitness-Kingsville, 178 So. 3d 623, 627 (La. App. 2015) (the plaintiff, "a sophisticated user of the squat machine" at a gym, assumed the risk of injury by signing a release); Valentino v. Philadelphia Triathlon, LLC, 150 A.3d 483, 493 (Pa. Super. 2016) (a valid liability waiver executed by a triathlon participant, who died during the competition, barred his wife from maintaining a wrongful death action because the decedent's death was not tortious).

In Schoeps v. Whitewater Adventures LLC, 136 Fed. Appx. 966 (9th Cir. 2005), the court concluded that a release signed by a participant in a whitewater rafting trip was not unconscionable or unreasonable. This was true even though the participant "had only a few minutes to decide whether to sign the release" and, if she did not sign, "would have lost her pre-paid ticket price," "could not go with the group on the river and might be stuck without transportation in an isolated area." The release contained no hidden terms and there was no "oppression or lack of meaningful choice" because, before the trip, the participant had been given a brochure stating that the company required all participants to sign liability releases.

See also Michael R. Pfahl, *Enhancing Enforceability of Exculpatory Clauses in Education Abroad Programming Through Examination of Three Pillars*, 46 J.C. & U.L. 93, 96 (2022) (proposing "the adoption of assumption of risk affirmations as a core component accompanying any exculpatory language as well as encouraging discussions of potential dangers to students as a core component of pre-departure orientation programming").

5. *Releases Not Read.* A signed release may be valid even if the plaintiff claims not to have read it. *See* Chauvlier v. Booth Creek Ski Holdings, Inc., 35 P.3d 383 (Wash. Ct. App. 2001) (the release was clear and conspicuous and there was no rush to sign it).

6. ***Parental Waiver of a Child's Cause of Action.*** In Scott v. Pacific W. Mt. Resort, 834 P.2d 6 (Wash. 1992), the plaintiff's parents signed a ski school release for their son. The release provided:

> I hereby hold harmless [the ski school and its owner] and any instructor or chaperon from all claims arising out of the instruction of skiing or in transit to or from the ski area. I accept full responsibility for the cost of treatment for any injury suffered while taking part in the program.

Although the language was found to be sufficiently clear to release a claim for negligence, the agreement was void as against public policy because a parent does not have legal authority to waive a child's future cause of action for injuries resulting from a third party's negligence. Consistent with "[n]umerous cases in other jurisdictions," the court reasoned that "[s]ince a parent generally may not release a child's cause of action after injury [without court approval], it makes little, if any, sense to conclude a parent has the authority to release a child's cause of action prior to an injury."

See also Hojnowski v. Vans Skate Park, 901 A.2d 381 (N.J. 2006) (holding that "public policy . . . prohibits a parent of a minor child from releasing a minor child's potential tort claims arising out of the use of a commercial recreational facility"); *but see* Zivich v. Mentor Soccer Club, Inc., 696 N.E.2d 201, 204–06 (Ohio 1998) (holding that a mother could bind her minor child to an exculpatory agreement immunizing the volunteers and sponsors of a nonprofit soccer organization from liability for negligence).

In Colorado, a decision of the state supreme court holding that parental waiver of a child's future cause of action was invalid was expressly overruled by the legislature. *See* Colo. Rev. Stat. Ann. § 13-22-107 (Westlaw 2022).

7. ***Releases of Gross Negligence or Recklessness.*** In Tayar v. Camelback Ski Corp., Inc., 47 A.3d 1190 (Pa. 2012), the court held that a written release did not bar claims for recklessness arising from a skiing accident. As the court explained:

> [W]ere we to sanction releases for reckless conduct, parties would escape liability for consciously disregarding substantial risks of harm to others. . . . There is near unanimity across jurisdictions that such releases are unenforceable, as such releases would jeopardize the health, safety, and welfare of the people by removing any incentive for parties to adhere to minimal standards of safe conduct. . . .

8. ***Exculpatory Language on the Web or in Brochures.*** In Slotnick v. Club ABC Tours, Inc., 61 A.3d 968 (N.J. Super. Law Div. 2012), the court held that an exculpatory clause on a travel agent's website and on the back of a brochure saved the agent from liability for the negligent acts of service suppliers, regardless of whether the tourist read the clause or "affirmatively agreed to the terms or that the terms were a product of the parties' bargain."

9. ***Ethics in Law Practice: Agreements Limiting Malpractice Liability.*** Can a lawyer include a provision in a retainer agreement whereby the client forfeits any right to sue in the future for malpractice relating to the representation? Almost never. Rule 1.8(h) of the Model Rules of Professional Conduct (Westlaw 2022) provides:

A lawyer shall not:

(1) make an agreement prospectively limiting the lawyer's liability to a client for malpractice unless the client is independently represented in making the agreement; or

(2) settle a claim or potential claim for such liability with an unrepresented client or former client unless that person is advised in writing of the desirability of seeking and is given a reasonable opportunity to seek the advice of independent legal counsel in connection therewith.

An attorney who violates this rule is subject to reprimand, suspension, disbarment, or other sanctions.

3. Primary Implied Assumption of the Risk

Turcotte v. Fell

Court of Appeals of New York
502 N.E.2d 964 (N.Y. 1986)

SIMONS, Judge.

. . . .

Plaintiff Ronald J. Turcotte is a former jockey. Before his injury he had ridden over 22,000 races in his 17-year career and achieved international fame as the jockey aboard "Secretariat" when that horse won the "Triple Crown" races in 1973. On July 13, 1978 plaintiff was injured while riding in the eighth race at Belmont Park, a racetrack owned and operated by defendant New York Racing Association (NYRA). Plaintiff had been assigned the third pole position for the race on a horse named "Flag of Leyte Gulf." Defendant jockey Jeffrey Fell was in the second pole position riding "Small Raja," a horse owned by defendant David P. Reynolds. On the other side of plaintiff, in the fourth position, was the horse "Walter Malone." Seconds after the race began, Turcotte's horse clipped the heels of "Walter Malone" and then tripped and fell, propelling plaintiff to the ground and causing him severe personal injuries which left him a paraplegic.

Plaintiffs, husband and wife, commenced this action against Jeffrey Fell, David P. Reynolds, NYRA and others no longer before the court. . . . [T]hey charge that Fell is liable to them because guilty of common-law negligence and of violating the rules of the New York Racing and Wagering Board regulating "foul riding," that Reynolds is liable for Fell's negligence under the doctrine of *respondeat superior*, and that defendant NYRA is liable because it "negligently failed to water and groom that portion of the racetrack near the starting gate or watered and groomed the same in an improper and careless manner" causing it to be unsafe.

Special Term granted the motions of Fell and Reynolds for summary judgment, holding that Turcotte, by engaging in the sport of horse racing, relieved other participants of any duty of reasonable care with respect to known dangers or risks which inhere in that activity.... NYRA subsequently moved for summary judgment and Special Term denied its motion because it found there were questions of fact concerning NYRA's negligent maintenance of the track. On separate appeals, the Appellate Division affirmed, with one Justice dissenting from the order denying NYRA's motion for summary judgment....

It is fundamental that to recover in a negligence action a plaintiff must establish that the defendant owed him a duty to use reasonable care.... [W]hile the determination of the existence of a duty and the concomitant scope of that duty involve a consideration not only of the wrongfulness of the defendant's action or inaction, they also necessitate an examination of plaintiff's reasonable expectations of the care owed him by others. This is particularly true in professional sporting contests, which by their nature involve an elevated degree of danger. If a participant makes an informed estimate of the risks involved in the activity and willingly undertakes them, then there can be no liability if he is injured as a result of those risks.

Traditionally, the participant's conduct was conveniently analyzed in terms of the defensive doctrine of assumption of risk. With the enactment of the comparative negligence statute, however, assumption of risk is no longer an absolute defense.... Thus, it has become necessary, and quite proper, when measuring a defendant's duty to a plaintiff to consider the risks assumed by the plaintiff.... The shift in analysis is proper because the "doctrine [of assumption of risk] deserves no separate existence (except for *express* assumption of risk) and is simply a confusing way of stating certain no-duty rules"....

The risk assumed has been defined a number of ways but in its most basic sense it "means that the plaintiff, in advance, has given his ... consent to relieve the defendant of an obligation of conduct toward him, and to take his chances of injury from a known risk arising from what the defendant is to do or leave undone. The situation is then the same as where the plaintiff consents to the infliction of what would otherwise be an intentional tort, except that the consent is to run the risk of unintended injury.... The result is that the defendant is relieved of legal duty to the plaintiff; and being under no duty, he cannot be charged with negligence"....

The doctrine has been divided into several categories but as the term applies to sporting events it involves what commentators call "primary" assumption of risk. Risks in this category are incidental to a relationship of free association between the defendant and the plaintiff in the sense that either party is perfectly free to engage in the activity or not as he wishes. Defendant's duty under such circumstances is a duty to exercise care to make the conditions as safe as they appear to be. If the risks of the activity are fully comprehended or perfectly obvious, plaintiff has consented to them and defendant has performed its duty.... Plaintiff's "consent" is not constructive consent; it is actual consent implied from the act of the electing to participate in the activity.... When thus analyzed and applied, assumption of risk is not an absolute defense but a measure of the defendant's duty of care and thus survives the enactment of the comparative-fault statute....

.... It would be a rare thing, indeed, if the election of a professional athlete to participate in a sport at which he makes his living could be said to be involuntary. Plaintiff's participation certainly was not involuntary in this case and thus we are concerned only with the scope of his consent.

.... Some "of the restraints of civilization must accompany every athlete onto the playing field".... [P]articipants do not consent to acts which are reckless or intentional....

Whether a professional athlete should be held ... to have consented to the act or omission of a co-participant which caused his injury involves consideration of a varicty of factors including but not limited to: the ultimate purpose of the game and the method or methods of winning it; the relationship of defendant's conduct to the game's ultimate purpose, especially his conduct with respect to rules and customs whose purpose is to enhance the safety of the participants; and the equipment or animals involved in the playing of the game. The question of whether the consent was an informed one includes consideration of the participant's knowledge and experience in the activity generally. Manifestly a professional athlete is more aware of the dangers of the activity, and presumably more willing to accept them in exchange for a salary, than is an amateur.

In this case plaintiff testified before trial to facts establishing that horse racing is a dangerous activity.... Plaintiff testified that every professional jockey had experiences when he was not able to keep a horse running on a straight line, or a horse would veer, or jump up on its hind legs, or go faster or slower than the jockey indicated. He further acknowledged that horses in a race do not run in prescribed lanes and it is lawful, under the rules of racing, for horses to move out of their starting lane to other parts of the track provided that the horse does not interfere with other horses when doing so. Indeed, during the course of a race, speeding horses lawfully and properly come within inches of other horses and frequently bump each other. Turcotte conceded that there is a fine line between what is lawful and unlawful in the movement of a horse on the track.... Such dangers are inherent in the sport. Because they are recognized as such by plaintiff, the courts below properly held that he consented to relieve defendant Jeffrey Fell of the legal duty to use reasonable care to avoid crossing into his lane of travel.

Plaintiffs nonetheless contend that Fell's alleged violation of 9 NYCRR 4035.2, which prohibits foul riding, is sufficient to sustain their complaint. They assert that the rule is a safety rule and that a participant does not accept or consent to the violation of the rules of a game even though the violation is foreseeable. They rely principally on Hackbart v. Cincinnati Bengals, 601 F.2d 516 [(10th Cir. 1979)], in which the plaintiff was injured when intentionally struck in the neck from behind by an opposing football player after the play was over, and Nabozny v. Barnhill, 31 Ill. App. 3d 212, 334 N.E.2d 258 [(1975)], in which the plaintiff, playing goal tender in a high school soccer match, was injured after picking up the ball in a free kick zone when kicked in the head by player on an opposing team (*see also*, Restatement [Second] of Torts § 50 comment b).

The rules of the sport, however, do not necessarily limit the scope of the professional's consent. Although the foul riding rule is a safety measure, it is not by its terms absolute for it establishes a spectrum of conduct and penalties, depending on whether the violation is careless or willful and whether the contact was the result of mutual fault. As the rule recognizes, bumping and jostling are normal incidents of the sport. They are not, as were the blows in *Nabozny* and *Hackbart*, flagrant infractions unrelated to the normal method of playing the game and done without any competitive purpose. Plaintiff does not claim that Fell intentionally or recklessly bumped him, he claims only that as a result of carelessness, Fell failed to control his mount as the horses raced for the lead and a preferred position on the track. While a participant's "consent" to join in a sporting activity is not a waiver of all rules infractions, nonetheless a professional clearly understands the usual incidents of competition resulting from carelessness, particularly those which result from the customarily accepted method of playing the sport, and accepts them. They are within the known, apparent and foreseeable dangers of the sport and not actionable and thus plaintiffs' complaint against defendant Fell was properly dismissed.

... [T]he dismissal of the complaint against Fell ... mandates dismissal of the complaint against the employer....

The complaint against NYRA should also be dismissed....

NYRA's duty to plaintiff is similarly measured by his position and purpose for being on the track on July 13 and the risks he accepted by being there....

Plaintiffs charge that NYRA was negligent in failing to water the "chute," which leads to the main track, and "overwatering" the main track. Thus, they claim the horses had to run from the dry surface of the chute onto the overly watered, unsafe "cuppy" surface of the main track.[1] Plaintiff testified, however, that "cupping" conditions are common on racetracks and that he had experienced them before at Belmont Park and also at many other tracks. Indeed, he testified that he had never ridden on a track where he had not observed a cupping condition at one time or another. Thus, Turcotte's participation in three prior races at this same track on the day of his injury, his ability to observe the condition of the track before the eighth race and his general knowledge and experience with cupping conditions and their prevalence establish that he was well aware of these conditions and the possible dangers from them and that he accepted the risk.

....

On the appeal by plaintiffs, order affirmed, etc.

On the appeal by defendant NYRA, order reversed, etc.

---

1. [Fn. 2:] "Cuppiness" is the tendency of wet track surface to stick to the underside of a horse's hoof within the shoe.

Notes

1. ***Injuries to Spectators.*** Spectators at athletic events often are held to have assumed the risk of being struck by objects leaving the field. *See, e.g.*, Harting v. Dayton Dragons Professional Baseball Club, L.L.C., 870 N.E.2d 766 (Ohio Ct. App. 2007) (primary assumption of the risk barred recovery even though the spectator was distracted by a mascot); Hurst v. East Coast Hockey League, Inc., 637 S.E.2d 560 (S.C. 2006) (flying puck).

2. ***The "Baseball Rule."*** A number of cases have held that persons holding sporting events have only a limited duty to provide screening.

> [A]t least 12 jurisdictions have adopted the "limited duty rule," which places two important requirements on stadium owners and operators. First, the rule requires stadium owners and operators to provide a sufficient amount of protected seating for those spectators "who may be reasonably anticipated to desire protected seats on an ordinary occasion." Second, it requires stadium owners and operators to provide protection for all spectators located in the most dangerous parts of the stadium, that is, those areas that pose an unduly high risk of injury from foul balls (such as directly behind home plate).

Turner v. Mandalay Sports Entertainment, LLC, 180 P.3d 1172 (Nev. 2008) (there was no great risk of being hit by a foul ball in the concession area); *but see* S. Shore Baseball, LLC v. DeJesus, 11 N.E.3d 903, 907 (Ind. 2014) (refusing to adopt the "Baseball Rule" which limits the duty to provide screening).

New Jersey has addressed the issue of spectator injuries by statute:

New Jersey Baseball Spectator Safety Act of 2006, N.J. Stat. Ann. § 2A:53A-43, *et seq.* (Westlaw 2022)

> § 2A:53A-46
>
> a. Notwithstanding any other provision of law, spectators of professional baseball games are presumed to have knowledge of and to assume the inherent risks of observing professional baseball games. These risks are defined as injuries which result from being struck by a baseball or a baseball bat anywhere on the premises during a professional baseball game.
>
> b. (1) Except as provided in section [2A:53A-47] . . . , the assumption of risk set forth in this section shall be a complete bar to suit. . . .
>
> c. Nothing in this act shall preclude a spectator from bringing an action against another spectator for an injury to person or property resulting from such other spectator's acts or omissions.
>
> § 2A:53A-47
>
> a. Nothing in . . . this act shall prevent or limit the liability of an owner who fails to post and maintain the warning signs required pursuant . . . to this act.

> b. Nothing in . . . this act shall prevent or limit the liability of an owner who fails to provide protection for spectators in the most dangerous sections of the stands. This limited duty may be satisfied by having a net behind home plate.

3. ***Problem: Injured Fans.*** Consider these two hypotheticals:

(1) A baseball stadium serves beer. The spectators get rowdy. The stadium does nothing to calm or protect spectators. A fan for the home team grabs a bat and uses it to beat a fan for the visiting team. Is the owner/operator of the stadium immune from liability under the New Jersey statute?

(2) A pitcher playing at the stadium is heckled by the fans. The pitcher responds by throwing a ball into the stands, which strikes the plaintiff. Is the pitcher, the pitcher's team, or the owner/operator of the stadium immune from liability by reason of the New Jersey statute?

4. ***Injuries to Sports Officials.*** The primary assumption of the risk line of reasoning has been followed in cases involving injuries to sports officials. *See, e.g.*, Wertheim v. U.S. Tennis Ass'n, Inc., 540 N.Y.S.2d 443 (App. Div. 1989) (umpire struck by a tennis ball); Cuesta v. Immaculate Conception Roman Cath. Church, 562 N.Y.S.2d 537 (App. Div. 1990) (umpire struck by a baseball).

5. ***Injuries to Sports Participants.*** Courts have found that primary assumption of the risk bars recovery for many sports-related injuries. *See* Pellham v. Let's Go Tubing, Inc., 398 P.3d 1205, 1209 (Wash. App. 2017) (an inner tube rental company had no duty to warn a renter about a fallen log in the river based on the "doctrine of inherent peril assumption of risk"); Rochford v. Woodloch Pines, Inc., 824 F. Supp. 2d 343 (E.D.N.Y. 2011) (slip-and-fall on a wet outdoor stairway while golfing in the rain); *see also* Wooten v. Caesars Riverboat Casino, LLC, 63 N.E.3d 1069 (Ind. App. 2016) (holding that a golfer's bumping of his golf cart into another golfer's cart was within range of ordinary behavior and did not amount to a breach of duty).

The great weight of authority on injuries to sports participants permits recovery only for reckless or intentional harm. In Marchetti v. Kalish, 559 N.E.2d 699 (Ohio 1990), a girl broke her leg while playing "kick the can," and sued the playmate who had knocked her down. The court held that individuals assume the ordinary risks inherent in recreational and sports activities and cannot recover for any injury unless it can be shown that the other participant's actions were reckless or intentional.

Similarly, in Horvath v. Ish, 979 N.E.2d 1246, 1252 (Ohio 2012), the court held that, as a matter of common law, "skiers . . . cannot recover for an injury unless it can be shown that the other skier's actions were reckless or intentional."

It generally makes no difference that the allegedly negligent conduct violated rules of the sport or of a league, or even a state statute. *See* Reddell v. Johnson, 942 P.2d 200 (Okla. 1997) (voluntary participants in BB gun "war" assumed risk of being shot in the eye, even though the rules of engagement prohibited aiming above the waist);

Jaworski v. Kiernan, 696 A.2d 332 (Conn. 1997) (the only tort duty of a participant in a recreational soccer league was to refrain from reckless or intentional conduct, even though the negligent conduct that caused plaintiff's injuries violated a league rule); Moser v. Ratinoff, 130 Cal. Rptr. 2d 198 (Ct. App. 2003) (primary assumption of the risk barred recovery against a negligent bicyclist who violated statutes).

The policy underlying these cases is that, "[b]y eliminating liability for unintended accidents, the doctrine ensures that the fervor of athletic competition will not be chilled by the constant threat of litigation from every misstep, sharp turn, and sudden stop." Stimson v. Carlson, 14 Cal. Rptr. 2d 670 (Ct. App. 1992) (holding that the risk of being struck by the boom is a fundamental part of sailing, and that failure to call out a course change did not amount to intentional or reckless conduct).

See also Doe v. Moe, 827 N.E.2d 240 (Mass. App. Ct. 2005) (holding that a consensual sexual partner is liable only for injuries wantonly or recklessly inflicted).

6. ***Another Theory: Increasing the Risk of Harm to Participants.*** In Allen v. Dover Co-Recreational Softball League, 807 A.2d 1274 (N.H. 2002), a woman was injured by an errant throw during a co-recreational slow-pitch tournament. The court declined to say that the defendant could be held liable only for reckless or intentional conduct. Rather, the court said, with respect to negligence, "the only duty the defendants had was not to act in an unreasonable manner that would increase or create a risk of injury outside the range of risks that flow from participation." In finding for the defendants, the court wrote in part:

> While the plaintiffs allege that promulgating and enforcing rules that required batting helmets, a larger, softer softball, or a certain male-female ratio would make the game safer, they do not allege that failing to promulgate and enforce such rules created risks outside the risks ordinarily involved in softball and made the game unreasonably dangerous. . . .

In Anand v. Kapoor, 942 N.E.2d 295, 296–97 (N.Y. 2010), the court recognized the rule that a sports participant does not assume the risk of recklessly or intentionally tortious conduct, but held that a golfer had no legal duty to yell "fore" before a shot. As the court explained:

> Kapoor's failure to warn of his intent to strike the ball did not amount to intentional or reckless conduct, and did not unreasonably increase the risks inherent in golf. . . .

7. ***Skier-Responsibility Laws.*** Most states with substantial ski industries have enacted laws limiting the liability of a resort to an injured skier. These laws vary in length and substance, but often provide that a ski resort is not liable for injuries resulting from the inherent risks of skiing. *See* Standish v. Jackson Hole Mt. Resort Corp., 2021 WL 1937253, at *1 (10th Cir.) (finding that a tree stump covered by fresh snow was an inherent risk of skiing for which the Wyoming Recreation Safety Act precludes liability). A number of skier-responsibility statutes attempt to define inherent risks, at least in part. Some states require ski areas to post trail signs in

prominent locations listing the inherent risks of skiing and notifying skiers of the operator's limited liability for injuries to skiers.

In Hughes v. Seven Springs Farm, Inc., 762 A.2d 339 (Pa. 2000), the court held that a skier who was traversing an area at the bottom of the mountain toward the ski lift was engaged in "downhill skiing," and therefore could not recover for injuries sustained when struck by another skier, which was an inherent risk of skiing.

See also Murray v. Great Gorge Resort, Inc., 823 A.2d 101 (N.J. Super. Ct. Law Div. 2003) (the New Jersey act impliedly contemplates that a ski operator will inspect its slopes and trails, at least on a daily basis); Jagger v. Mohawk Mountain Ski Area, Inc., 849 A.2d 813 (Conn. 2004) (holding that negligence by an employee of a ski area operator is not an inherent risk of skiing and that a claim based on such conduct was not barred by the state statute).

Trupia v. Lake George Central School District

Court of Appeals of New York
927 N.E.2d 547 (N.Y. 2010)

Chief Judge LIPPMAN.

While attending a summer program administered by defendants on their premises, the infant plaintiff, Luke Anthony Trupia, rode and ultimately fell from a bannister, injuring himself seriously. The complaint seeks to recover principally upon a theory of negligent supervision; it alleges that at the time of the accident Luke, then not yet 12 years of age, had been left wholly unsupervised.... [The defendants moved to amend their answer, seeking dismissal of the action on the ground that Luke may be deemed to have consented in advance to the risks involved in sliding down a bannister, among them falling from the railing, something which, evidently, had happened to him before. The Supreme Court granted the motion. The Appellate Division reversed and certified a question to the Court of Appeals, asking whether it had erred in doing so.]

....

In 1975, ... the Legislature abolished contributory negligence and assumption of risk as absolute defenses and provided instead that

> "[i]n *any* action to recover damages for personal injury, injury to property, or wrongful death, the culpable conduct attributable to the claimant or to the decedent, *including contributory negligence or assumption of risk, shall not bar recovery,* but the amount of damages otherwise recoverable shall be diminished in the proportion which the culpable conduct attributable to the claimant or decedent bears to the culpable conduct which caused the damages"....

Nonetheless, assumption of risk has survived as a bar to recovery. The theory upon which its retention has been explained and upon which it has been harmonized with the now dominant doctrine of comparative causation is that, by freely assuming a known risk, a plaintiff commensurately negates any duty on the part of the defendant to safeguard him or her from the risk (*see* Turcotte v. Fell, . . . [68 N.Y.2d 432, 438–39 (1986)]. The doctrine, then, is thought of as limiting duty through consent—indeed, it has been described a "principle of no duty" rather than an absolute defense based upon a plaintiff's culpable conduct—and, as thus conceptualized can, at least in theory, coexist with the comparative causation regimen. The reality, however, is that the effect of the doctrine's application is often not different from that which would have obtained by resort to the complete defenses purportedly abandoned with the advent of comparative causation—culpable conduct on the part of a defendant causally related to a plaintiff's harm is rendered nonactionable by reason of culpable conduct on the plaintiff's part that does not entirely account for the complained-of harm. While it may be theoretically satisfying to view such conduct by a plaintiff as signifying consent, in most contexts this is a highly artificial construct and all that is actually involved is a result-oriented application of a complete bar to recovery. Such a renaissance of contributory negligence replete with all its common-law potency is precisely what the comparative negligence statute was enacted to avoid.

The doctrine of assumption of risk does not, and cannot, sit comfortably with comparative causation. In the end, its retention is most persuasively justified not on the ground of doctrinal or practical compatibility, but simply for its utility in "facilitat[ing] free and vigorous participation in athletic activities". . . . We have recognized that athletic and recreative activities possess enormous social value, even while they involve significantly heightened risks, and have employed the notion that these risks may be voluntarily assumed to preserve these beneficial pursuits as against the prohibitive liability to which they would otherwise give rise. We have not applied the doctrine outside of this limited context and it is clear that its application must be closely circumscribed if it is not seriously to undermine and displace the principles of comparative causation . . . that the Legislature has deemed applicable to "*any* action to recover damages for personal injury, injury to property, or wrongful death". . . .

No suitably compelling policy justification has been advanced to permit an assertion of assumption of risk in the present circumstances. The injury-producing activity here at issue, referred to by the parties as "horseplay," is not one that recommends itself as worthy of protection, particularly not in its "free and vigorous" incarnation, and there is, moreover, no nexus between the activity and defendants' auspices, except perhaps negligence. This is, in short, not a case in which the defendant solely by reason of having sponsored or otherwise supported some risk-laden but socially valuable voluntary activity has been called to account in damages.[2]

---

2. [Fn. *:] This does not, of course, mean that the doctrine is applicable wherever these conditions are met; they are threshold conditions only. The doctrine's application will also necessarily depend upon whether, under the particular circumstances, the plaintiff may be said to have freely and knowingly consented to assume the risks of a qualifying activity.

Allowing the defense here would have particularly unfortunate consequences. Little would remain of an educational institution's obligation adequately to supervise . . . the children in its charge . . . if school children could generally be deemed to have consented in advance to risks of their misconduct. Children often act impulsively or without good judgment — that is part of being a child; they do not thereby consent to assume the consequently arising dangers, and it would not be a prudent rule of law that would broadly permit the conclusion that they had done so. If the infant plaintiff's harm is attributable in some measure to his own conduct, and not to negligence on defendants' part, that would be appropriately taken account of within a comparative fault allocation; it is not a predicate upon which an assumption of risk should be permitted to be applied.

We do not hold that children may never assume the risks of activities, such as athletics, in which they freely and knowingly engage, either in or out of school — only that the inference of such an assumption as a ground for exculpation may not be made in their case, or for that matter where adults are concerned, except in the context of pursuits both unusually risky and beneficial that the defendant has in some nonculpable way enabled.

Accordingly, the order of the Appellate Division should be affirmed, with costs, and the certified question answered in the negative.

SMITH, J. (concurring).

This seems to me an extremely easy case. Assumption of risk cannot possibly be a defense here, because it is absurd to say that a 12-year-old boy "assumed the risk" that his teachers would fail to supervise him. That is a risk a great many children would happily assume, but they are not allowed to assume it for the same reason that the duty to supervise exists in the first place: Children are not mature, and it is for adults, not children, to decide how much supervision they need.

The majority makes this point, which is enough to dispose of the case, near the end of its opinion. . . . The rest of the majority opinion is, in my view, an extended dictum, which seems to say that the assumption of risk defense is largely if not entirely limited to cases involving "athletic and recreative activities". . . .

The majority's dictum invites a number of questions that the majority makes no attempt to answer. Most obvious among them: What exactly is "athletic or recreative" activity? Indeed, why was Luke Trupia's chosen activity — sliding down a banister — not "recreative"? He was obviously doing it for fun. The majority says that "athletic and recreative activities possess enormous social value" . . . — a value that presumably does not inhere in banister sliding. But why exactly is sliding down a banister (supposing it to be done by an adult with a taste for such amusement) of less "social value" than sliding down a ski slope or bobsled run? And if the latter activities are more socially valuable than the former, why is the banister slider, who chose the less desirable form of amusement, in a *better* position to recover damages than the skier or bobsledder?

Assumption of risk in tort law is a hard idea to understand, and I do not imply that the majority's understanding of it is necessarily wrong. There may be perfectly good answers to the questions I have asked.... But I think it is a mistake to make sweeping pronouncements in a case that does not require it, while ignoring the questions those sweeping pronouncements raise.

Judges CIPARICK, GRAFFEO and JONES concur with Chief Judge LIPPMAN; Judge SMITH concurs in result in a separate opinion in which Judges READ and PIGOTT concur.

Note

1. ***Comparative Fault and Primary Assumption of the Risk.*** In Pfenning v. Lineman, 947 N.E.2d 392 (Ind. 2011), which involved a golfing injury, the court rejected the primary assumption of risk terminology "to the extent that it suggests that a lack of duty may stem from a plaintiff's incurred risk" because, under the Indiana Comparative Fault Act, "a plaintiff may relieve a defendant of what would otherwise be his or her duty to the plaintiff only by an express consent."

Minnich v. Med-Waste, Inc.

Supreme Court of South Carolina
564 S.E.2d 98 (S.C. 2002)

Justice PLEICONES.

....

Jeffrey Minnich ("Plaintiff") was employed by the Medical University of South Carolina ("MUSC") as a public safety officer. While working in this capacity, Plaintiff assisted in loading medical waste from the premises of MUSC onto a tractor-trailer truck owned by Defendant Med-Waste, Inc. Plaintiff noticed the unoccupied truck begin to roll forward, toward a public street. Plaintiff ran to the truck, jumped inside, and stopped the truck.

Plaintiff alleges he suffered serious injuries, proximately caused by the acts or omissions of the defendants' employees, for which he seeks to recover damages. The defendants assert that Plaintiff's claims are barred by the firefighter's rule. The firefighter's rule is a common law doctrine that precludes a firefighter (and certain other public employees, including police officers) from recovering against a defendant whose negligence caused the firefighter's on-the-job injury.

....

While a number of states have adopted the firefighter's rule in some form, there is no definitive pronouncement from this Court either adopting or rejecting the rule.

....

The common law firefighter's rule originated in the case of Gibson v. Leonard, 143 Ill. 182, 32 N.E. 182 (1892). There, the Illinois Supreme Court held that a firefighter who entered private property in the performance of his job duties was a licensee, and as such, the property owner owed the firefighter a duty only to "refrain from willful or affirmative acts which are injurious." .... Practically, this meant that a firefighter, injured while fighting a blaze on private property, could not recover tort damages from the property owner whose ordinary negligence caused the fire.

A number of courts reason that police officers and firefighters, aware of the risks inherent in their chosen profession, have assumed those risks.... As such, the firefighter or police officer should not be allowed to recover when injured as a result of confronting these known and accepted risks.

A third rationale advanced is public policy. The Supreme Court of Virginia, in Pearson v. Canada Contracting Co., 232 Va. 177, 349 S.E.2d 106, 111 (1986), cited two fundamental policies in support of that state's firefighter's rule: First, injuries to firemen and policemen are compensable through workers' compensation. It follows that liability for their on-the-job injuries is properly borne by the public rather than by individual property owners. Second, firemen and policemen, unlike invitees or licensees, enter at unforeseeable times and at areas not open to the public. In such situations, it is not reasonable to require the level of care that is owed to invitees or licensees.

Still other courts reason that the public fisc pays to train firefighters and police officers on the ways to confront dangerous situations, and compensates them for doing so. If these public employees were permitted to bring suit against the taxpayers whose negligence proximately caused injury, the negligent taxpayer would incur multiple penalties in exchange for the protection provided by firefighters and police officers....

Not only have courts been unable to agree on a consistent rationale for the rule, they have not been able to agree on the proper parameters for the rule. A number of courts which recognize the firefighter's rule as a viable defense to negligence claims allow recovery for willful and wanton conduct resulting in injury. As one court observed, "a tortfeasor who acts wilfully and wantonly is so culpable that the fireman's rule ought not to preclude the injured officer from suing the egregiously culpable wrongdoer." ....

Courts have allowed police officers and firefighters to recover for injuries resulting from an act of negligence unrelated to the specific reason for which the officer or firefighter was originally summoned. As stated by the Supreme Court of New Jersey:

> The core of the "fireman's rule" is that a citizen's ordinary negligence that occasioned the presence of the public safety officer shall not give rise to liability in damages for the injuries sustained by the officer in the course of the response to duty.... The corollary of the rule is that independent and intervening negligent acts that injure the safety officer on duty are not insulated.

Wietecha v. Peoronard, 102 N.J. 591, 510 A.2d 19, 20–21 (1986) . . . (Police officers were injured while investigating a traffic accident when drivers negligently hit parked police cars; officers could pursue action against drivers whose negligence occurred subsequent to officers' presence at the scene). *See also* Terhell v. American Commonwealth Assoc., 172 Cal. App.3d 434, 218 Cal. Rptr. 256, 260 (1985) ("Having an unguarded hole in the roof was not the cause of [the firefighter's] presence at the scene, and the firefighter's rule has never been applied to negligence which did not cause the fire"). According to one commentator, all jurisdictions allow recovery under these circumstances. . . .

More recently, a number of state legislatures have acted to limit or abolish the firefighter's rule. . . . [Citations to statutes from California, Florida, Minnesota, Nevada, New Jersey, New York, and Virginia.]

. . . [In sum, those] jurisdictions which have adopted the firefighter's rule offer no uniform justification therefor, nor do they agree on a consistent application of the rule. The legislatures in many jurisdictions which adhere to the rule have found it necessary to modify or abolish the rule. The rule is riddled with exceptions, and criticism of the rule abounds.

Against this backdrop, we answer the certified question in the negative. South Carolina has never recognized the firefighter's rule, and we find it is not part of this state's common law. . . .

TOAL, C.J., MOORE, WALLER and BURNETT, JJ., concur.

Notes

1. ***The Professional Rescuer's Rule (Firefighter's Rule).*** Under the "professional rescuer's rule," a professional rescuer cannot recover from one who *negligently* creates a crisis for injuries sustained while responding to that crisis. *See* Fordham v. Oldroyd, 171 P.3d 411 (Utah 2007) (adopting the rule). The rule is perhaps best understood as a variety of primary assumption of the risk. Persons who choose to be firefighters ordinarily cannot complain that they are exposed to negligently created risks of injury by fire.

See also Priebe v. Nelson, 140 P.3d 848 (Cal. 2006) (holding that the "veterinarian's rule, an offshoot of the firefighter's rule, . . . [and] yet another application of the doctrine of primary assumption of risk," barred a kennel worker's statutory strict liability claim for dog bite injuries).

The Third Restatement argues that the firefighter's rule requires rethinking. *See* Restatement, Third, of Torts: Liab. for Physical & Emotional Harm § 51 cmt. m (2012).

2. ***Abnormal or Increased Risks.*** Even in states adhering to the firefighter's rule, liability has been imposed if the defendant negligently increased the dangers ordinarily confronted by a firefighter, as by failing to warn of a known hidden peril. *See, e.g.*, Shypulski v. Waldorf Paper Products Co., 45 N.W.2d 549, 553 (Minn. 1951)

(unstable wall); Jenkins v. 313–321 W. 37th Street Corp., 31 N.E.2d 503, 504–05 (N.Y. 1940) (gasoline).

3. ***Intentionally Created Risks.*** Virtually all courts hold that the firefighter's rule does not immunize an intentional or reckless wrongdoer from liability to a professional rescuer. *See* Goodwin v. Hare, 436 S.E.2d 605 (Va. 1993) (holding that the rule is inapplicable to intentional torts, since there is no reason to shift financial losses away from the defendant in cases of injuries or damages intentionally inflicted).

4. ***Abrogation of the Firefighter's Rule.*** As indicated in the principal case, in a number of jurisdictions, the firefighter's rule has been legislatively or judicially repudiated.

4. Secondary Implied Assumption of Risk

Courts differ in their articulation of the elements of secondary implied assumption of the risk. In general, before the doctrine will apply there must be evidence that the plaintiff (1) subjectively appreciated the risk, (2) voluntarily elected to confront it, and (3) (a) manifested a willingness to relieve the defendant of any obligation of care or (b) had no expectation that care would be exercised.

Pachunka v. Rogers Construction, Inc.

Supreme Court of Nebraska
716 N.W.2d 728 (Neb. 2006)

McCORMACK, J.

. . . .

Jerry Pachunka brought the present negligence action against Rogers Construction, Inc., for injuries suffered as a result of a fall while exiting a house built by Rogers Construction. A jury found in favor of Rogers Construction, and Pachunka timely appealed . . .

. . . . Pachunka was employed by Rogers Realty Company as a sales agent. As part of his job duties, Pachunka was required to show model houses built by Rogers Construction to prospective buyers. The houses were in various stages of construction at the time they were shown by Pachunka. On March 23, Pachunka was inspecting a house that was under construction at the time to make sure it was ready for viewing by a potential buyer. . . .

Because of muddy conditions, a walkway made up of excess construction lumber was laid on the ground to provide access to the house. On that particular day, there was also a board angled from the walkway to the front stoop of the house, which stood approximately 16 inches off the ground, creating a ramp up to the stoop. Although there was another entrance through the garage, Pachunka was not provided a key for that entrance. Consequently, in order to enter the house, Pachunka had to either use the ramp or walk through the mud and step up onto the stoop. . . . Pachunka testified that a back condition prevented him from stepping up or down that far; therefore, it was necessary for him to use the ramp, which he used without incident while entering the property. However, while exiting the house on the ramp, Pachunka slipped and fell. . . .

Pachunka filed suit. . . . As part of its defense, Rogers Construction asserted the affirmative defense of assumption of risk. . . . Pachunka made an oral motion to dismiss this defense. Pachunka's motion was denied. Pachunka also requested that the following jury instruction further describing assumption of risk be given to the jury: "A Plaintiff does not assume a risk of harm unless he voluntarily accepts the risk. A Plaintiff's acceptance of a risk is not voluntary if the Defendant's conduct has left Plaintiff no reasonable alternative course." This request was also denied. The court, instead, gave . . . [a different instruction on assumption of risk].

. . . . The jury . . . returned a verdict in favor of Rogers Construction.

Pachunka claims that the trial court erred in submitting the defense of assumption of risk to the jury. Before the defense of assumption of risk is submissible to a jury, the evidence must show that the plaintiff (1) knew of the specific danger, (2) understood the danger, and (3) voluntarily exposed himself or herself to the danger that proximately caused the damage. . . .

Pachunka asserts that Rogers Construction failed to establish that his use of the ramp was voluntary because he was given no reasonable alternative course to using the ramp. We agree.

Assumption of risk is predicated upon the plaintiff's voluntary exposure to the known danger caused by the defendant's negligence. If a plaintiff is deprived of a choice in the matter, the risk is not assumed, even though it may be encountered. . . .

The evidence reflects that Pachunka was required to enter the house as part of his employment and that he was only able to do so through the front door. The evidence further reflects that in order to access the front door, Pachunka had to either use the wooden ramp or step up onto the stoop. However, because of a back problem, it was necessary for Pachunka to use the ramp.

Rogers Construction contends that although Pachunka entered the house through the front, he could have exited the house through the garage and thereby avoided his fall. We have stated that a plaintiff's assumption of risk is not voluntary if the defendant's tortious conduct has left him or her no reasonable alternative course of conduct in order to avert harm to himself or herself. . . . [I]n order to exit through the garage, it would have been necessary for Pachunka to slog through the mud to reach the wooden walkway. But, Rogers Construction testified that the walkway had been built specifically to avoid the mud. We cannot say that this is a reasonable alternative. We therefore conclude that Pachunka did not voluntarily assume the risk of using the ramp and that the court erred by submitting the issue to the jury.

. . . .

We conclude that the trial court erred by submitting the defense of assumption of risk to the jury where the evidence did not establish that the risk was voluntarily assumed.... We therefore reverse the judgment and remand the matter for a new trial consistent with this opinion.

Notes

1. ***"Subjective Appreciation of the Risk."*** For a risk to be assumed, it must be subjectively appreciated. In Castello v. County of Nassau, 636 N.Y.S.2d 817 (App. Div. 1996), a case where the risk presented by a protruding home plate was not concealed, the court held that a softball player consciously assumed that risk by his voluntary participation in a softball game. The player admitted that he knew that the third-base side of home plate had been lowered, and had actually stood in the "ditch" next to the protruding corner of the plate.

See also American Powerlifting Ass'n v. Cotillo, 934 A.2d 27 (Md. 2007) (finding that as a powerlifter with ten years of experience, the plaintiff was aware of and assumed the risk that spotters might negligently fail to catch a lift bar).

2. ***"Choice of Evils" and Lack of Voluntariness.*** If the defendant's conduct has left the plaintiff with no reasonable alternative for averting harm to person or property, the plaintiff's confrontation of danger does not constitute assumption of the risk. A "choice of evils" foisted upon the plaintiff by the defendant is no choice at all.

In Marshall v. Ranne, 511 S.W.2d 255 (Tex. 1974), the court held that the plaintiff did not assume the risk of being injured by the defendant's boar hog. The hog had repeatedly menaced the plaintiff by charging him or holding him "prisoner" in an outhouse. Although the plaintiff could have avoided the hog by staying inside the house, or could have shot the hog, the plaintiff did not assume the risk of being bitten by the hog on the way to his vehicle. The defendant was not entitled to force the plaintiff to surrender his rights to use his real property or to risk criminal liability by shooting the animal. Because the confrontation of the danger was involuntary, there was no assumption of the risk.

See also Rush v. Commercial Realty Co., 145 A. 476 (N.J. 1929). In *Rush*, a tenant fell through a bad floor in a detached privy, landed in the accumulation at the bottom, and had to be extricated by use of a ladder. In finding that the woman had not voluntarily assumed the risk of harm, the court wrote:

> Mrs. Rush had no choice, when impelled by the calls of nature, but to use the facilities placed at her disposal by the landlord, to wit, a privy with a trap door in the floor, poorly maintained.... [S]he was not required to leave the premises and go elsewhere.

See also Caldwell v. Ford Motor Co., 619 S.W.2d 534, 540 (Tenn. Ct. App. 1981) (plaintiff did not assume the risk of injury in removing goods from the bed of a burning truck, for the truck manufacturer had no right to force plaintiff to either confront the fire or let the goods burn).

3. ***Lack of Options Not Attributable to the Defendant.*** If the defendant is not responsible for the plaintiff's lack of alternatives, the plaintiff's choice of a course of action may be deemed voluntary and thus an assumption of the risk. Restatement, Second, of Torts § 496E offers this illustration:

> *A* is injured in an accident, bleeding badly, and in need of immediate medical attention. Having no other means of transportation, he asks *B* to drive him to the hospital, knowing that *B's* car has defective brakes. *A* assumes the risk of injury caused by the brakes.

Similarly, "a plaintiff who is forced to rent a house which is in obvious dangerous condition because he cannot find another dwelling, or cannot afford another, assumes the risk notwithstanding the compulsion under which he is acting." *Id.* at cmt. b.

4. ***Economic Duress and Assumption of the Risk at Work.*** An individual who, in the face of an employer's ultimatum or direction, elects to encounter a known dangerous condition, rather than risk losing the job, does not voluntarily assume the risk of injury. *See* Draper v. Airco, Inc., 580 F.2d 91 (3d Cir. 1978) ("To hold that economic duress of this sort does not vitiate . . . voluntariness . . . would be to ignore reality").

One occasionally finds sweeping statements that the "trend" of authority is that "assumption of risk in the employment setting is no longer valid." Cremeans v. Willmar Henderson Mfg. Co., 566 N.E.2d 1203 (Ohio 1991). These assertions must be carefully scrutinized. *See* Crews v. Hollenbach, 751 A.2d 481 (Md. 2000) (holding that a gas company worker knew and appreciated the risk of confronting a gas leak, and voluntarily assumed the risk).

5. ***No Expectation or Insistence That the Defendant Will Exercise Care.*** Not every knowing and voluntary confrontation of a risk amounts to assumption of the risk. Something more is required. That something is either willingness to relieve the defendant of any obligation to exercise care or lack of a reasonable expectation that care will be exercised. Recall, for example, the case of the pedestrian dashing across a street through busy traffic. That conduct may be comparative negligence, but it is not assumption of the risk. The pedestrian's conduct is not saying "don't worry about me." Indeed, the pedestrian is probably expecting and depending on drivers to exercise greater care than usual to keep harm from occurring.

In many cases, it is easier to talk in terms of "no expectation" that care will be exercised than in terms of "willingness to relieve the defendant" of an obligation to exercise care. Suppose, for example, that a contractor leaves a plank straddling a pit that is in the process of being excavated. If, when no one is around, the plaintiff sees the plank, attempts to walk across it, falls, and is injured, the plaintiff has assumed the risk. It makes more sense to say that the plaintiff had no expectation that care would be exercised to protect him from the known, voluntarily encountered danger, than to say that he consented to relieve the defendant of an obligation to exercise care.

6. ***Preference for Risk as a Complete Defense.*** The Reporter's Note to Restatement, Third, of Torts: Apportionment of Liab. § 2 cmt. i invokes the law of implied-in-fact contracts and rules about the scope of defendants' duties to allow a full defense for cases in which a party "clearly and consciously chooses to confront a risk because of an actual preference for the risk." Otherwise it treats implied assumption of the risk as simply a form of comparative negligence.

7. ***Assumption of the Risk at the Supreme Court.*** In Washington, D.C., at the Supreme Court, there is a basketball court that is used by justices and members of the court staff. Years ago, the court's newsletter, *The Docket Sheet*, described the facilities this way:

> Regulars note the unique structural aspects of the court [which is squeezed into the building above the ceiling of the courtroom and beneath the pitched roof]. The court is the size of a regulation basketball court, and with walls only a foot away from the out-of-bounds stripes, it makes for close quarters. Voices constantly echo off of the walls magnifying the presence of 10 players to stadium levels. Suspended square, plywood boards serve as backboards and vibrate when a "brick" is launched like a clarion call for bad shots. Vent-like protrusions shine light up the walls and towards the ceiling, providing the only sense of Hollywood to a very plain arena. Padding on sharp corners and on the walls provides some protection upon collision.

A sign as one enters the "highest court in the land" reads:

> "All persons use this gym at their own risk. Users assume the risk of the nearness of walls, support columns and stairs to the basketball court."

Is the sign valid? If a user of the court assumes a risk, is this express assumption of the risk, primary implied assumption of the risk, or secondary implied assumption of the risk? Is the bar to liability total or partial?

D. Comparative Fault

The all-or-nothing approach of traditional contributory negligence was an important premise of tort law for more than a century. During that period, other rules were shaped to be consistent with that doctrine—or to react against it. Once contributory negligence began to be supplanted by comparative principles, many questions arose about whether other changes in legal doctrine had to follow. Some of those questions had relatively obvious answers. For example, all courts have held that the doctrine of last clear chance does not survive the adoption of comparative negligence or comparative fault. Other questions have been more subtle, such as whether the endorsement of a comparative approach to accident compensation necessitates changes in the rules on *res ipsa loquitur* (*see* Montgomery Elevator Co. v. Gordon, 619 P.2d 66 (Colo. 1980)), joint and several liability (*see* Chapter 17), liability to rescuers (*see* Altamuro v. Milner Hotel, Inc., 540 F. Supp. 870 (E.D. Pa. 1982)), or superseding causation (*see* Control Techniques, Inc. v. Johnson, 762 N.E.2d 104 (Ind. 2002)). The following case addresses the question of whether, after the adoption of comparative negligence, unreasonable conduct by the plaintiff can be urged as a defense in actions not based on negligence.

Kaneko v. Hilo Coast Processing

Supreme Court of Hawaii
654 P.2d 343 (Haw. 1982)

OGATA, Retired Justice.

....

[Plaintiff, an ironworker, was injured when the steel girt on which he was standing came loose because it had not been fully welded. In the suit which followed, the jury found for the plaintiff on negligence, warranty, and strict products liability theories. The trial court reduced the award in proportion to the contributory negligence of the plaintiff. On appeal, the defendant manufacturer contested only the strict liability finding. The supreme court held that a prefabricated building was a "product" for the purpose of strict products liability. On the cross-appeal, the plaintiff argued that contributory negligence was no defense to strict liability and that therefore the jury award should not have been reduced.]

We now turn to the principal issue raised in Kaneko's cross-appeal, that is, whether the doctrine of comparative negligence should merge with strict products liability.

As is evident from the vast amount of scholarly comment and case law, we are by no means the first to consider this issue. Other jurisdictions which have addressed the problem have reached varied conclusions on differing rationales.

....

The first objection of those in opposition to the merger of strict products liability and comparative negligence is that the two theories are incapable of being reconciled. They argue that there are both conceptual and semantic difficulties in bringing negligence and strict liability concepts together. "The task of merging the two concepts is said to be impossible, that 'apples and oranges' cannot be compared, and that 'oil and water' do not mix, and that strict liability, which is not founded on negligence or fault is inhospitable to comparative principles." Daly v. General Motors Corp., 20 Cal. 3d 725, 734, 575 P.2d 1162, 1167, 144 Cal. Rptr. 380, 385 (1978).

The Supreme Court of South Dakota, in denying that contributory negligence is a defense in strict products liability, stated in Smith v. Smith, 278 N.W.2d 155 (S.D. 1979), that

> Strict liability is an abandonment of the fault concept in product liability cases. No longer are damages to be borne by one who is culpable; rather they are borne by one who markets the defective product. The question of whether the manufacturer or seller is negligent is meaningless under such a concept; liability is imposed irrespectively of his negligence or freedom

> from it. Even though the manufacturer or seller is able to prove beyond all doubt that the defect was not the result of his negligence, it would avail him nothing. We believe it is inconsistent to hold that the user's negligence is material when the seller's is not....

Id. at 160.

On the other hand, courts that favor the merger recognize the conceptual and semantic problems between the two principles, but find they are not incompatible....

In a well reasoned opinion, the California Supreme Court in *Daly, supra*, held that comparative negligence should be merged with strict products liability.... The California Supreme Court's rationale can be summed up with their following statement: "Fixed semantic consistency at this point is less important than the attainment of a just and equitable result. The interweaving of concept and terminology in this area suggests a judicial posture that is flexible rather than doctrinaire."...

In short, those who oppose the merger believe that negligence and strict liability are different theories and therefore are not compatible. Those jurisdictions that are in favor of the merger argue that fairness and equity are more important than semantic consistency.

We believe that the better reasoned view is that comparative negligence is not incompatible with strict products liability. Our adoption of the theory of strict products liability was premised on equity and fairness and our concern for human safety. The interjection of comparative negligence into strict products liability will reduce an injured plaintiff's award by an amount equal to the degree to which he is culpably and contributorily negligent. Such a system will accomplish a fairer and more equitable result....

The second objection to the application of comparative principles in strict products liability cases is that manufacturers will have less incentive to produce safe products. This was the view taken by Justice Mosk in his dissenting opinion in *Daly, supra*.... The majority, however, viewed the concern as "more shadow than substance." The majority supported their view with two points. First, a manufacturer cannot avoid liability merely because a plaintiff has contributed to his own injury. Secondly, the majority argued that a manufacturer cannot assume that the user of a defective product will be blameworthy. Based on these two points, the majority held that "no substantial or significant impairment of the safety incentives of defendant will occur by the adoption of comparative negligence."....

We hold that the majority view in *Daly, supra*, is the better view....

The third major objection to the merger of the two theories is that it will present an impossible task for juries to reconcile the conduct of a plaintiff with the defective product of a defendant.

Some jurisdictions have refused to apply comparative negligence to strict products liability because of a fear of confusing the jury in allocating damages....

....

On the other hand, those courts which have merged the two concepts are not persuaded by the argument that jurors would be unable to undertake a fair apportionment of liability. These courts observe that jurors have no difficulty in apportioning awards when using the maritime doctrine of unseaworthiness, a doctrine similar to strict liability, where plaintiff's misconduct is not an absolute bar to recovery, but may be considered in mitigation of damages as justice requires. . . .

Other jurisdictions which have applied comparative negligence principles to strict products liability have dismissed this issue by simply holding that they find no difficulty for jurors if the two theories are merged.

We . . . hold that jurors will not be confused in determining damages if comparative negligence is merged with strict products liability.

Finding that the major objections of those who oppose the merger of comparative negligence and strict products liability are not persuasive, we conclude that comparative negligence should be judicially merged with strict products liability.

. . . .

The other specifications of error raised in the appeal and the cross-appeal are without merit. We decline to review the merits of the issues raised therein.

[Affirmed.]

Notes

1. ***Negligence as a Defense to Strict Liability.*** Many states now hold that negligence by the plaintiff is a defense, on a pure or modified basis, in actions based on strict liability. This approach is sometimes referred to as "comparative fault," "comparative causation," or "proportionate responsibility."

2. ***Negligence as a Defense to Reckless Conduct.*** Most states also hold that a plaintiff's unreasonable conduct should mitigate a defendant's liability for recklessly inflicted harm.

3. ***Comparisons of Negligence and Intentionally Tortious Conduct.*** States that have adopted comparative fault usually do not include intentionally tortious conduct within the definition of "fault." *See* Whitehead v. Food Max of Miss., Inc., 163 F.3d 265 (5th Cir. 1998). Consequently, a gang member who mugs the plaintiff in a desolate location ordinarily cannot escape or limit liability for battery by arguing that the plaintiff was careless in being alone at the place where the mugging occurred.

However, not all intentional torts are equally blameworthy. A good faith purchaser of stolen goods may be liable for conversion, a child who touches a classmate may have committed a battery, and a home owner who is mistaken about a boundary line may technically be a trespasser (*see* Chapters 1 and 2). In terms of moral culpability, these tortfeasors stand in a very different position than rapists, thieves, violent spouses, or supervisors who victimize disabled employees. If the moral culpability of an intentional tortfeasor is trivial, or lacking altogether, perhaps comparing intentionally tortious conduct with negligence might not be inappropriate.

In Jones v. Thomas, 557 So. 2d 1015 (La. Ct. App. 1990), Thomas punched the plaintiff, Jones, in the face, breaking his jaw. The punch followed a ten-minute harangue by Jones in which he shouted curses, obscenities, and racial slurs at Thomas and threatened to kill Thomas's mother and family. The court ruled that comparative fault principles should be used to reduce the plaintiff's damages "[w]here the words or action of a plaintiff in a civil battery action are sufficient to establish provocation. . . ." The appellate court found the trial court's assignment of 90% of the fault to the plaintiff excessive, however, as the provocation was entirely verbal. The court reduced the plaintiff's fault to 50%.

In addition, if a jurisdiction has adopted comparative fault and abolished joint and several liability (*see* Chapter 17), so that a tortfeasor is to be held liable only for that tortfeasor's percentage of the total fault, it may be necessary to take into account the intentionally tortious conduct of third parties for the purpose of calculating the particular tortfeasor's share of the total fault. *See* Barth v. Coleman, 878 P.2d 319 (N.M. 1994) (bar and bar manager's liability for negligent failure to prevent a fight should have been offset by the percentage of fault attributable to the third-party tortfeasor who intentionally punched the plaintiff in the nose). *But see* Eskin v. Castiglia, 753 A.2d 927, 935 (Conn. 2000) (discussing a state statute prohibiting the apportionment of liability between allegedly negligent tortfeasors and intentional or reckless tortfeasors, among others); Turner v. Jordan, 957 S.W.2d 815 (Tenn. 1997) (holding, in an action by a nurse who was assaulted by mentally ill patient against patient's treating psychiatrist, that the psychiatrist's negligence should not have been compared with the intentional conduct of a nonparty patient in allocating fault).

In Veazey v. Elwood Plantation Associates, Ltd., 650 So. 2d 712 (La. 1994), a tenant, who was raped in her apartment, brought a negligence action against her apartment complex, Southmark. The court wrote:

> First, and foremost, the scope of Southmark's duty to the plaintiff in this case clearly encompassed the exact risk of the occurrence which caused damage to plaintiff. As a general rule, we find that negligent tortfeasors should not be allowed to reduce their fault by the intentional fault of another that they had a duty to prevent. . . .
>
> Second, Southmark, who by definition acted unreasonably under the circumstances in breaching their duty to plaintiff, should not be allowed to benefit at the *innocent* plaintiff's expense by an allocation of fault to the intentional tortfeasor under comparative fault principles. Given the fact that any rational juror will apportion the lion's share of the fault to the intentional tortfeasor when instructed to compare the fault of a negligent tortfeasor and an intentional tortfeasor, application of comparative fault principles in the circumstances presented in this particular case would operate to reduce the incentive of the lessor to protect against the same type of situation occurring again in the future. Such a result is clearly contrary to public policy.

> Third, as Dean Prosser has explained it, intentional wrongdoing "differs from negligence not only in degree but in kind, and in the social condemnation attached to it." .... In our view, this is a correct assessment of the character and nature of the conduct which defendant herein seeks to have the courts compare. Because we believe that intentional torts are of a fundamentally different nature than negligent torts, we find that a true comparison of fault based on an intentional act and fault based on negligence is, in many circumstances, not possible.
>
> In sum, we hold that while Louisiana law is broad enough to allow comparison of fault between intentional tortfeasors and negligent tortfeasors, determination of whether such a comparison should be made must be determined by the trial court on a case by case basis, bearing in mind the public policy concerns discussed herein. We further hold, for the reasons stated herein, that comparison of Southmark's negligence and the rapist's fault in this particular case is not appropriate.... [3]

According to the Restatement, Third, of Torts: Apportionment of Liab. § 1 cmt. c, Reporters' Note:

> Applying comparative responsibility to intentional torts is not the majority rule, but it commands significant support among courts that have addressed the question, especially in cases apportioning damages among defendants. Much of this growing support is in cases involving a comparison of *defendants'* responsibility, not a comparison of a *defendant* with a *plaintiff*....
>
> Some of the support, however, is in cases comparing a *plaintiff's* responsibility with an intentional *defendant's* responsibility....
>
> ... [T]his Restatement does not take a position on whether a plaintiff's negligence is a comparative defense to intentional torts.... This Restatement does, however, apply its system of comparative responsibility to apportion liability among intentional and negligent defendants.

See also Couch v. Red Roof Inns, Inc., 729 S.E.2d 378 (Ga. 2012) (holding that an assailant was partially at fault for purposes of apportioning damages among all wrongdoing parties).

4. ***Some Comparative-Negligence and Comparative-Fault Statutes.*** Here is a small collection of legislation on comparative negligence. Examine each statute with these questions in mind:

---

3. The Louisiana legislature subsequently amended the state's civil code "to require that fault be allocated to all persons causing a plaintiff's injuries ... and to limit liability of each wrongdoer, with certain exceptions, to their percentage of fault." Turner v. Shop Rite, Inc., 149 So.3d 427, 428 (La. Ct. App. 2014).

(1) If the defendant's negligence is 75-percent responsible for an accident causing a $100,000 loss to a plaintiff whose negligence was 25-percent responsible, how much does the defendant have to pay?

(2) Same as (1), except that each party's negligence is equally responsible for the accident.

(3) Same as (1), except that the plaintiff is 90-percent responsible and the defendant 10-percent responsible.

(4) The plaintiff is 40-percent responsible; defendant *A* is 30-percent responsible; and defendant *B* is 30-percent responsible. Plaintiff's loss is $100,000. As a complicating factor, suppose that defendant *B* was not sued because personal jurisdiction could not be obtained.

Do not assume that all of these statutes provide a clear answer to all of the questions raised.

New York Civil Practice Law and Rules § 1411 (Westlaw 2022)

In any action to recover damages for personal injury, injury to property, or wrongful death, the culpable conduct attributable to the claimant or to the decedent, including contributory negligence or assumption of risk, shall not bar recovery, but the amount of damages otherwise recoverable shall be diminished in the proportion which the culpable conduct attributable to the claimant or decedent bears to the culpable conduct which caused the damages.

Wisconsin Statutes Annotated § 895.045(1) (Westlaw 2022)

Contributory negligence does not bar recovery in an action by any person or the person's legal representative to recover damages for negligence resulting in death or in injury to person or property, if that negligence was not greater than the negligence of the person against whom recovery is sought, but any damages allowed shall be diminished in the proportion to the amount of negligence attributed to the person recovering. The negligence of the plaintiff shall be measured separately against the negligence of each person found to be causally negligent. . . .

Uniform Comparative Fault Act §§ 1–2, 12 U.L.A. 123 (Westlaw 2022)

Section 1. [Effect of Contributory Fault]

(a) In an action based on fault seeking to recover damages for injury or death to person or harm to property, any contributory fault chargeable to the claimant diminishes proportionately the amount awarded as compensatory damages for an injury attributable to the claimant's contributory fault, but does not bar recovery. This rule applies whether or not under prior law the claimant's contributory fault constituted a defense or was disregarded under applicable legal doctrines, such as last clear chance.

(b) "Fault" includes acts or omissions that are in any measure negligent or reckless toward the person or property of the actor or others, or that subject a person to strict tort liability. The term also includes breach of warranty, unreasonable assumption of risk not constituting an enforceable express consent, misuse of a product for which the defendant otherwise would be liable, and unreasonable failure to avoid an injury or to mitigate damages. Legal requirements of causal relation apply both to fault as the basis for liability and to contributory fault.

Section 2. [Apportionment of Damages]

(a) In all actions involving fault of more than one party to the action, including third-party defendants and persons who have been released under Section 6, the court, unless otherwise agreed by all parties, shall instruct the jury to answer special interrogatories or, if there is no jury, shall make findings, indicating:

(1) the amount of damages each claimant would be entitled to recover if contributory fault is disregarded; and

(2) the percentage of the total fault of all of the parties to each claim that is allocated to each claimant, defendant, third-party defendant, and person who has been released from liability under Section 6. For this purpose the court may determine that two or more persons are to be treated as a single party.

(b) In determining the percentages of fault, the trier of fact shall consider both the nature of the conduct of each party at fault and the extent of the causal relation between the conduct and the damages claimed.

(c) The court shall determine the award of damages to each claimant in accordance with the findings, subject to any reduction under Section 6, and enter judgment against each party liable on the basis of rules of joint-and-several liability. For purposes of contribution under Sections 4 and 5, the court also shall determine and state in the judgment each party's equitable share of the obligation to each claimant in accordance with the respective percentages of fault.

(d) Upon motion made not later than [one year] after judgment is entered, the court shall determine whether all or part of a party's equitable share of the obligation is uncollectible from that party, and shall reallocate any uncollectible amount among the other parties, including a claimant at fault, according to their respective percentages of fault. The party whose liability is reallocated is nonetheless subject to contribution and to any continuing liability to the claimant on the judgment.

5. ***Apportionment of Liability to Settling Tortfeasors***. There is an important question as to whether liability under a comparative negligence or comparative fault regime should be apportioned to a tortfeasor who has settled with the plaintiff. The

answer necessarily depends on the language of the applicable statute or court decisions. In Ready v. United/Goedecke Services, Inc., 905 N.E.2d 725 (Ill. 2008), the court held that settling tortfeasors were not "defendants" for purposes of apportioning fault under Illinois law.

E. The "Seatbelt Defense"

The non-use of a seatbelt can greatly increase the chances of injury or the extent of damages incurred in an auto accident. However, courts were initially reluctant to recognize a "seatbelt defense." This is understandable. Seatbelts were first widely available in cars in the 1960s, a time when common-law contributory negligence was still the general rule and any finding of fault on the part of the plaintiff could totally bar recovery.

During the subsequent years much has changed. In particular, comparative principles have widely replaced the all-or-nothing approach of contributory negligence. The use of seatbelts has become common, and in many circumstances is legally required.

In general, states fall into two camps. In some jurisdictions, often because of compromises attending the enactment of mandatory-seatbelt-use laws, a defense may not be raised based on the plaintiff's non-use of an available seatbelt. For example, the Illinois statute provides:

Illinois Compiled Statutes Annotated
Chapter 625, 5/12-603.1 (Westlaw 2022)

(a) Each driver and front seat passenger of a motor vehicle . . . shall wear a properly adjusted and fastened seat safety belt. . . .

. . . .

(c) Failure to wear a seat safety belt in violation of this Section shall not be considered evidence of negligence, shall not limit the liability of an insurer, and shall not diminish any recovery for damages arising out of the ownership, maintenance, or operation of a motor vehicle.

(d) A violation of this Section shall be a petty offense and subject to a fine not to exceed $25.

Other states simply treat seatbelt non-use as just one more form of comparative negligence and to that extent recognize the "seatbelt defense." *See* Law v. Superior Court, 755 P.2d 1135 (Ariz. 1988) (jury could consider non-use in apportioning damages due to "fault" of plaintiffs); Ridley v. Safety Kleen Corp., 693 So. 2d 934 (Fla. 1996) (holding that failure to wear seatbelt should be properly raised as an affirmative defense of comparative negligence). The strongest arguments in favor of this position would seem to be that recognizing a seatbelt defense tends to minimize losses by encouraging safe practices, promote individual responsibility, and, where a statute mandates use, fosters respect for the law.

As part of an omnibus "tort reform" package in Texas, the legislature simply deleted the statutory language that previously made seatbelt evidence inadmissible. Subsequently, the Texas Supreme Court held that evidence of use or nonuse of seat belts was admissible for the purpose of apportioning responsibility under the state's proportionate responsibility statute. *See* Nabors Well Services, Ltd. v. Romero, 456 S.W.3d 553 (Tex. 2015).

Under a Colorado law, evidence of seatbelt non-use is admissible to mitigate damages for injuries resulting from an auto accident. According to the statute, "[s]uch mitigation shall be limited to awards for pain and suffering and shall not be used for limiting recovery of economic loss and medical payments." Colo. Rev. Stat. Ann. § 42-4-237(7) (Westlaw 2022). In Pringle v. Valdez, 171 P.3d 624 (Colo. 2007), the court held that "the General Assembly intended 'pain and suffering' as used in this statute to encompass all noneconomic damages, which includes damages for inconvenience, emotional stress, and impairment of the quality of life," but not "damages for physical impairment and disfigurement."

Notes

1. ***Removal of Seatbelts.*** The removal of seatbelts from a vehicle may give rise to a cause of action. Twohig v. Briner, 214 Cal. Rptr. 729 (Ct. App. 1985), held that if the owner or operator of a car removes the seatbelts, a passenger who is thereafter injured may sue on the ground that the owner or operator breached a duty of care by "exposing passengers to increased danger by eliminating their option to 'buckle up'." In some jurisdictions, an automobile owner has a statutory duty to provide seatbelts for the use of occupants. *See, e.g.*, N.Y. Veh. & Traf. Law § 383 (Westlaw 2022).

2. ***Duties to Protect Children in Vehicles.*** *See* Harrison v. Harrison, 733 N.W.2d 451 (Minn. 2007) (holding, in an action on behalf of a child against his parents, that Minnesota's "seat belt gag rule" nevertheless "permits an action to be made against a child's parents for negligent installation and maintenance of a child passenger restraint system"); Dellapenta v. Dellapenta, 838 P.2d 1153 (Wyo. 1992) (holding that parents have a common-law duty to buckle the seatbelts of children dependent on adult care, and may be held liable to an injured child for a breach of that duty).

3. ***Motorcycle Helmets.*** The non-use of motorcycle helmets raises issues similar to those relating to the non-use of seatbelts.

Chapter 17

Joint Tortfeasors

A. Joint and Several Liability

Chapter 16 dealt with the question whether conduct on the part of a plaintiff reduces the amount for which a defendant may be held liable. This chapter is mainly concerned with the different but related question of whether conduct on the part of other actual or potential defendants reduces a particular defendant's exposure to liability. The answer turns, in the first instance, on whether the defendant is subject to "several liability" only or to "joint and several liability."

The law on joint and several liability was once reasonably clear and uniform. Today, however, the law is very much in flux. The rule of joint and several liability still governs many types of litigation. But the rise of comparative principles (comparative negligence and comparative fault), and the consequent jurisprudential focus on the policy of limiting liability in proportion to fault, has caused a vigorous re-examination of the traditional rules. With much success, "tort reform" efforts have sought to eliminate joint and several liability in whole or in part. Before advising a client on questions arising in this field, it is essential to consult local law, particularly acts of the legislature.

1. Definitions

The rule of joint and several liability holds that two or more tortfeasors may be subject to liability for the same harm and may be sued by the plaintiff, together or separately. This does not mean that a plaintiff to whom two tortfeasors (*A* and *B*) are jointly and severally liable for a single judgment can collect in full from each tortfeasor. Rather, the plaintiff can collect in full only once, either all from *A*, or all from *B*, or in part from both. A defendant who pays a disproportionately high amount may be able to recover the excess payment from another tortfeasor under the doctrine—typically statutory—of "contribution." And sometimes a tortfeasor who pays a judgment may be entitled to recover the full amount of the judgment from another; this is called "indemnity." An everyday example of indemnity arises when an employer is held liable for an employee's tort under the doctrine of *respondeat superior*. Although the employer is liable to the plaintiff for the full amount of the judgment, it has, in theory at least, the right to recover that payment from the employee who committed the tort. Contribution and indemnity will be examined later in this chapter.

A useful starting point is American Motorcycle Ass'n v. Superior Ct., 578 P.2d 899 (Cal. 1978). While that decision has been superseded by statute in California, it fairly reflects the common situations in which joint and several liability traditionally arose:

> The "joint and several liability" concept has sometimes caused confusion because the terminology has been used with reference to a number of distinct situations. . . . The terminology originated with respect to tortfeasors who acted in concert to commit a tort, and in that context it reflected the principle . . . that all members of a "conspiracy" or partnership are equally responsible for the acts of each member in furtherance of such conspiracy.
>
> Subsequently, the courts applied the "joint and several liability" terminology to other contexts in which a preexisting relationship between two individuals made it appropriate to hold one individual liable for the act of the other; common examples are instances of vicarious liability between employer and employee or principal and agent, or situations in which joint owners of property owe a common duty to some third party. In these situations, the joint and several liability concept reflects the legal conclusion that one individual may be held liable for the consequences of the negligent act of another.
>
> In the concurrent tortfeasor context, however, the "joint and several liability" label does not express the imposition of any form of vicarious liability, but instead simply embodies the general common law principle, noted above, that a tortfeasor is liable for any injury of which his negligence is *a* proximate cause. Liability attaches to a concurrent tortfeasor in this situation not because he is responsible for the acts of other independent tortfeasors who may also have caused the injury, but because he is responsible for all damage of which his own negligence was a proximate cause. When independent negligent actions of a number of tortfeasors are each a proximate cause of a single injury, each tortfeasor is thus personally liable for the damage sustained, and the injured person may sue one or all of the tortfeasors to obtain a recovery for his injuries; the fact that one of the tortfeasors is impecunious or otherwise immune from suit does not relieve another tortfeasor of his liability for damage which he himself has proximately caused.

Thus, joint and several liability traditionally arose in three situations: first, where persons acting in concert tortiously caused harm to the plaintiff, regardless of whether that harm was divisible (*see, e.g.*, Herman v. Wesgate, 464 N.Y.S.2d 315 (App. Div. 1983), *supra* at p. 439); second, where liability was vicariously imposed on one person for another person's conduct (*see, e.g.*, Smith v. Lannert, 429 S.W.2d 8 (Mo. Ct. App. 1968), *supra* at p. 720); and third, where indivisible harm to the plaintiff was caused by the tortious conduct of two or more actors (*see, e.g.*, *Kinsman No. 1*, 338 F.2d 708 (2d Cir. 1964), *supra* at p. 477).

Although authorities often talk about joint and several liability for negligence, the same rules apply to liability based on intentional, reckless, and strict liability conduct.

2. Divisibility and Apportionment of Harm

Whether harm is divisible may determine whether joint and several liability is imposed in cases not involving concerted action or some other rule imposing vicarious liability (e.g., *respondeat superior*). If, in a particular case, it is unclear whether damages are divisible, who has the burden of proof? Comment h to the Restatement, Third, of Torts: Apportionment of Liab. § 26 (2000) provides that "[a] party alleging that damages are divisible has the burden to prove that they are divisible." As the following opinions show, the burden-of-proof issue may be extremely important and decisions are not always consistent with the Restatement position.

Michie v. Great Lakes Steel Division, National Steel Corp.

United States Court of Appeals for the Sixth Circuit
495 F.2d 213 (6th Cir. 1974)

EDWARDS, Circuit Judge.

This is an interlocutory appeal from a District Judge's denial of a motion to dismiss filed by three corporations which are defendants-appellants herein. . . .

Appellants' motion to dismiss was based upon the contention that each plaintiff individually had failed to meet the requirement of a $10,000 amount in controversy for diversity jurisdiction set forth in 28 U.S.C.A. § 1332 (1970).

. . . . Thirty-seven persons, members of thirteen families residing near LaSalle, Ontario, Canada, have filed a complaint against three corporations which operate seven plants in the United States immediately across the Detroit River from Canada. Plaintiffs claim that pollutants emitted by plants of defendants are noxious in character and that their discharge in the ambient air violates various municipal and state ordinances and laws. They assert that the discharges represent a nuisance and that the pollutants are carried by air currents onto their premises in Canada, thereby damaging their persons and property. Each plaintiff individually claims damages ranging from $11,000 to $35,000 from all three corporate defendants jointly and severally. There is, however, no assertion of joint action or conspiracy on the part of defendants.

. . . .

We believe the principal question presented by this appeal may be phrased thus: Under the law of the State of Michigan, may multiple defendants, whose independent actions of allegedly discharging pollutants into the ambient air thereby allegedly create a nuisance, be jointly and severally liable to multiple plaintiffs for numerous individual injuries which plaintiffs claim to have sustained as a result of said actions, where said pollutants mix in the air so that their separate effects in creating the individual injuries are impossible to analyze.

. . . .

In Maddux v. Donaldson, 362 Mich. 425, 108 N.W.2d 33 the Michigan Supreme Court cites Landers v. East Texas Salt Water Disposal Company, 151 Tex. 251, 248 S.W.2d 731, a pollution case. . . . The court indicated that

> . . . It is clear that there is a manifest unfairness in "putting on the injured party the impossible burden of proving the specific shares of harm done by each. . . . Such results are simply the law's callous dullness to innocent sufferers. One would think that the obvious meanness [sic] of letting wrongdoers go scot free in such cases would cause the courts to think twice and to suspect some fallacy in their rule of law."
>
> . . . .

It is the opinion of this court that the rule of *Maddux*, *supra*, and *Landers*, *supra*, cited therein is the better, and applicable rule in this air pollution case.

. . . .

Like most jurisdictions, Michigan has had great difficulty with the problems posed in tort cases by multiple causes for single or indivisible injuries. . . .

We believe that the issue was decided in the lengthy consideration given by the Michigan court in the *Maddux* case . . . :

> [I]f the triers of the facts conclude that they cannot reasonably make the division of liability between the tort-feasors, this is the point where the road of authority divides. Much ancient authority, not in truth precedent, would say that the case is now over, and that plaintiff shall take nothing. . . . The conclusion is erroneous. . . . When the triers of the facts decide that they cannot make a division of injuries we have, by their own finding, nothing more or less than an indivisible injury, and the precedents as to indivisible injuries will control. They were well summarized in Cooley on Torts in these words: "Where the negligence of two or more persons concur in producing a single, indivisible injury, then such persons are jointly and severally liable, although there was no common duty, common design, or concert action." Maddux v. Donaldson, 362 Mich. 425, 432–433, 108 N.W.2d 33, 36 (1961). . . .

. . . [T]he net effect of Michigan's new rule is to shift the burden of proof as to which one was responsible and to what degree from the injured party to the wrongdoers. The injustice of the old rule is vividly illustrated in an early Michigan case, Frye v. City of Detroit, 256 Mich. 466, 239 N.W. 886 (1932). There a pedestrian was struck by an automobile, thrown in the path of a street car and struck again. Since his widow could not establish which impact killed him, a verdict was directed against her case.

.... Like the District Judge, we believe that the Michigan courts would apply the *Maddux* principles to the case at bar. Under *Maddux*, each plaintiff's complaint should be read as alleging $11,000 or more in damages against each defendant....

As modified [in regard to punitive damages], the judgment of the District Court is affirmed.

Note

1. ***Other Precedent.*** *See* Borman v. Raymark Indus., Inc., 960 F.2d 327 (3d Cir. 1992) (holding an asbestos defendant liable for all damages resulting from decedent's disability because the evidence was too speculative to support a jury charge on apportionment of damages between those caused by cigarette smoking and those caused by asbestos exposure).

Bruckman v. Pena

Colorado Court of Appeals
487 P.2d 566 (Colo. Ct. App. 1971)

DWYER, Judge.

....

Plaintiff was injured on July 21, 1964, when the car in which he was riding collided with a truck driven by the defendant Bruckman and owned by the defendant Armored Motors Service. On June 11, 1965, plaintiff was injured in a second collision and certain injuries he had sustained in the first collision were aggravated. This action was commenced on June 25, 1965, and the only defendants named in the action are the owner and driver of the truck involved in the first collision.

[The jury returned a $50,000 verdict in plaintiff Pena's favor.]

In seeking reversal, defendants assert that the court was in error in one of its instructions to the jury....

.... The first part of the instruction, which is a proper statement of the law applicable to the case, is as follows:

> If you find that after the collision complained of Plaintiff, William Pena, had an injury which aggravated the ailment or disability received in the collision complained of, the Plaintiff is entitled to recover for the injury or pain received in the collision complained of; but he is not entitled to recover for any physical ailment or disability which he may have incurred subsequent to the collision.
>
> Where a subsequent injury occurs which aggravated the condition caused by the collision, it is your duty, if possible, to apportion the amount of disability and pain between that caused by the subsequent injury and that caused by the collision. In addition to this correct statement of the law, the court further instructed the jury: But if you find that the evidence does

> not permit such an apportionment, then the Defendants are liable for the entire disability.

Defendants argue that this last statement in the instruction is in error. . . .

It is the general rule that . . . the burden of proof is upon the plaintiff to establish that the damages he seeks were proximately caused by the negligence of the defendant. In accordance with this general rule, we hold that the instruction is in error because it permits the plaintiffs to recover damages against the defendants for injuries which the plaintiff received subsequent to any act of negligence on the part of the defendants and from causes for which the defendants were in no way responsible. The instruction erroneously places upon the defendants the burden of proving that plaintiff's disability can be apportioned between that caused by the collision here involved and that caused by the subsequent injury in order to limit their liability to the damages proximately caused by their negligence. Counsel for plaintiffs argues that the rules concerning apportionment of disability announced by our Supreme Court in Newbury v. Vogel, 151 Colo. 520, 379 P.2d 811, should also apply here. In *Newbury*, the Court stated:

> We find the law to be that where a pre-existing diseased condition exists, and where after trauma aggravating the condition disability and pain result, and no apportionment of the disability between that caused by the pre-existing condition and that caused by the trauma can be made, in such case, even though a portion of the present and future disability is directly attributable to the pre-existing condition, the defendant, whose act of negligence was the cause of the trauma, is responsible for the entire damage.

The pre-existing condition in the *Newbury* case was of non-traumatic origin, but the rules there announced also apply where the pre-existing condition was caused by trauma. . . . The reasons for the adoption of the *Newbury* rules are not present here. It is one thing to hold a tort-feasor who injures one suffering from a pre-existing condition liable for the entire damage when no apportionment between the pre-existing condition and the damage caused by the defendant can be made, but it is quite another thing to say that a tort-feasor is liable, not only for the damage which he caused, but also for injuries subsequently suffered by the injured person. We hold that the defendants here cannot be held liable for the plaintiff's subsequent injury and this is so whether or not such damage can be apportioned between the two injuries.

The plaintiffs also rely on the case of Maddux v. Donaldson, 362 Mich. 425, 108 N.W.2d 33, 100 A.L.R.2d 1. This case involved a chain-type collision, and plaintiff's injuries resulted from successive impacts which to all intents and purposes were concurrent. The court there held that where independent concurring negligent acts have proximately caused injury and damage which cannot be apportioned between the tort-feasors, each tort-feasor is jointly and severally liable for all of the injury and damage. This rule is not applicable where, as here, the second injury or aggravation of the first injury is attributable to a distinct intervening cause without which the second injury or aggravation would not have occurred.

. . . .

Judgments reversed and cause remanded for a new trial on the issues of damages alone.

Note

1. ***Apportionment Between Tortious and Non-tortious Causes.*** In Murphy v. Implicito, 392 A.2d 678, 688 (N.J. Super. Ct. App. Div. 2007), doctors allegedly exceeded the scope of consent and committed a battery by implanting a "cadaver bone" in the course of an operation. The court wrote:

> [I]f the jury determines that defendants committed a battery, and decides to award more than nominal damages, and it is able to segregate the harm from the use of cadaver bone from the damages flowing from the operation generally, it may award damages solely for the excess harm plaintiff suffered by use of cadaver bone. . . .
>
> . . . . [D]efendants shall bear the burden to segregate the damages caused by the excessive act from those resulting from the surgery in general. While not directly analogous, we liken defendant doctors' obligation here to that of a defendant in a medical malpractice case where the plaintiff's preexisting injuries are aggravated by the doctor's tortious conduct. In such a case, the burden to allocate the plaintiff's damages falls on the defendant.

3. Effect of Comparative Negligence and Comparative Fault

Before the widespread adoption of comparative negligence and comparative fault, joint tortfeasors were nearly always jointly and severally liable for the full amount of the plaintiff's indivisible injuries. For example, if a jury found that a plaintiff's $500,000 injury was caused by both the negligence of another driver and by a defect in the plaintiff's automobile, the other driver and the automobile manufacturer would be jointly and severally liable to the plaintiff for $500,000. This system, like the rule of contributory negligence itself, had the virtue of simplicity and the drawback that a person whose contribution to a misfortune was relatively small might in practice pay all the damages. The adoption of comparative negligence and comparative fault, which necessarily involves juries in assigning percentages of responsibility, has led to pressures to take tortfeasors' percentages of responsibility into account in dividing damages among defendants.

Notes

1. ***Full Compensation Versus Proportionality?*** In American Motorcycle Association v. Superior Court, 578 P.2d 899 (Cal. 1978), a minor who was injured in a motorcycle race sued the sponsors of the event. The sponsors argued that negligence on the part of the minor's parents had contributed to the harm, that the rule of joint

and several liability should be abrogated in light of the state's adoption of comparative negligence, and that the sponsor's liability should be limited to a portion of the total damages corresponding to its share of the total fault. The court declined to abrogate joint and several liability on the ground that doing so would seriously impair the ability of many injured persons to receive full compensation for their injuries because many defendants are judgment-proof. In effect, the court held that the policy of fully compensating victims took priority over the policy of limiting liability in proportion to fault.

2. ***Modification of the Traditional Rules.*** In California and many other states, courts have not had the last word on joint and several liability. In many jurisdictions, the traditional rules have been modified extensively by statute. California abolished joint and several liability for "noneconomic damages," such as damages for pain and suffering, shortly after the American Motorcycle decision. California's "Proposition 51," discussed in detail in Miller v. Stouffer, 11 Cal. Rptr. 2d 454 (Cal. Ct. App. 1992), illustrates this form of liability. Defendants who have caused indivisible harms are jointly and severally liable for harms such as medical expenses and lost wages. For "noneconomic harms" like pain and suffering, however, each defendant is liable only for that defendant's proportionate share of the harm.

Another common modification has been to eliminate joint and several liability for a defendant whose share of the total fault falls below a certain threshold, unless there is compelling evidence of specified types of culpability, such as specific intent to harm others. However, it is important to remember that under the common law rules, there were three bases for joint and several liability. A statutory modification may affect only one or two, but not necessarily all three of those traditional rules. In Reilly v. Anderson, 727 N.W.2d 102 (Iowa 2006), the court held that notwithstanding the state's comparative fault act, under which a defendant is jointly and severally liable for economic damages only if the defendant's share of the fault is 50% or more, a driver and passenger, who acted in concert, were jointly and severally liable for all injuries that occurred when the passenger attempted to steer the vehicle while the driver smoked a marijuana pipe.

Discussing joint and several liability, the Restatement, Third, of Torts: Apportionment of Liab. § 10 cmt. a (2000), states that there is today "no majority rule on this matter," and adds in comment a to § A18 that the number of jurisdictions that retain pure joint and several liability "is dwindling."

3. ***Reformulation of Joint & Several Liability in Texas.*** Here is the Texas statute. How would a statute like this change the traditional rules of joint and several liability?

Texas Civil Practice & Remedies Code §§ 33.002 & 33.013 (Westlaw 2022)

§ 33.002. Applicability

. . . .

(c) This chapter does not apply to . . . a claim for exemplary damages. . . .

§ 33.013. Amount of Liability

(a) Except as provided in Subsection (b), a liable defendant is liable to a claimant only for the percentage of the damages found by the trier of fact equal to that defendant's percentage of responsibility with respect to the personal injury, property damage, death, or other harm for which the damages are allowed.

(b) Notwithstanding Subsection (a), each liable defendant is, in addition to his liability under Subsection (a), jointly and severally liable for the damages recoverable by the claimant under Section 33.012 with respect to a cause of action if:

(1) the percentage of responsibility attributed to the defendant with respect to a cause of action is greater than 50 percent; or

(2) the defendant, with the specific intent to do harm to others, acted in concert with another person to engage in the conduct described in the following provisions of the Penal Code and in so doing proximately caused the damages legally recoverable by the claimant:

(A) Section 19.02 (murder);

(B) Section 19.03 (capital murder);

(C) Section 20.04 (aggravated kidnaping);

(D) Section 22.02 (aggravated assault);

(E) Section 22.011 (sexual assault);

(F) Section 22.021 (aggravated sexual assault);

(G) Section 22.04 (injury to a child, elderly individual, or disabled individual);

(H) Section 32.21 (forgery);

(I) Section 32.43 (commercial bribery);

(J) Section 32.45 (misapplication of fiduciary property or property of financial institution);

(K) Section 32.46 (securing execution of document by deception);

(L) Section 32.47 (fraudulent destruction, removal, or concealment of writing); or

(M) conduct described in Chapter 31 the punishment level for which is a felony of the third degree or higher.

. . . .

(e) . . . Subsection (b)(2) . . . applies only if the claimant proves the defendant acted or failed to act with specific intent to do harm. A defendant acts with specific intent to do harm with respect to the nature of the defendant's conduct and the result of the person's conduct when it is the person's conscious effort or desire to engage in the conduct for the purpose of doing substantial harm to others.

(f) The jury may not be made aware through *voir dire*, introduction into evidence, instruction, or any other means that the conduct to which Subsection (b)(2) refers is defined by the Penal Code.

4. ***Unexpected Result?*** In Lakes of Rosehill Homeowners Assn., Inc. v. Jones, 552 S.W.3d 414 (Tex. App. 2018), the plaintiff alleged that, notwithstanding the Texas statutory provisions quoted above, multiple defendants were jointly and severally liable for harm caused by flooding because "they failed to exercise ordinary care to maintain those portions of the West Ditch on their properties, which resulted in an indivisible injury because defendants' individual responsibility for the injury cannot be apportioned with reasonable certainty." *Id.* at 416. The intermediate appellate court agreed, stating:

> [S]ection 33.013 limits joint and several liability based on a defendant's "percentage of responsibility" as "found by the trier of fact." Tex. Civ. Prac. & Rem. Code Ann. § 33.013(a), (b)(1). If responsibility for the plaintiff's injury cannot be apportioned with reasonable certainty among the defendants and other responsible parties . . . , then by definition the trier of fact cannot find any of them "responsible for a percentage of the harm,"

Id. at 420. The court further noted that:

> As this Court and others have held, "[c]ommon-law joint-and-several-liability rules for partnership, agency, joint venture, and piercing the corporate veil situations survived the enactment of § 33.013 of the Texas Civil Practice and Remedies Code."

Id. Another Texas case makes clear that the relevant provisions of Section 33 did not abolish joint and several liability based on concerted action. *See* Comcast Corp. v. Houston Baseball Partners LLC, 627 S.W.3d 398, 421 (Tex. App. 2021) ("Civil conspiracy is a theory to secure joint and several liability against members of a conspiracy for the harm caused by any one member of the conspiracy").

5. ***Judicial Review of Legislation on Joint and Several Liability.*** Legislative changes to the rules on joint and several liability have sometimes been found to be unconstitutional. *See* Best v. Taylor Machine Works, 689 N.E.2d 1057 (Ill. 1997) (stating that even if a reasonable case could be made for eliminating joint and several liability, that case would apply as strongly to medical-malpractice cases as to others, and therefore the legislature's crafting of different rules for the two kinds of cases violated a state constitutional provision barring "special legislation").

6. ***Problems in Calculating Shares of Fault.*** At first glance, applying comparative principles to the liability of defendants may seem simple: a defendant found to be 40 percent responsible for harm would pay 40 percent of the damages, and so on. In practice, however, things are far from easy. The Restatement, Third, of Torts: Apportionment of Liab., explores questions like the following in detail.

(a) ***Immune Parties***. Suppose that the plaintiff's injuries were caused by the negligence of the plaintiff's employer (not subject to suit because of workers' compensation) and by the defective design of a product. Should the product manufacturer's liability be reduced because of the negligence of the employer? That is, can fault be allocated to an immune party?

According to some courts, the answer is yes. *See* Taylor v. John Crane Inc., 6 Cal. Rptr. 3d 695 (Ct. App. 2003) (holding in an asbestos-exposure case that fault could be allocated to the Navy, even if it was immune from suit); *but see* Jefferson Cty. Commonwealth Attorney's Office v. Kaplan, 65 S.W.3d 916 (Ky. 2001) (holding that fault in a legal malpractice action could not be apportioned to prosecutors who were immune from suit).

(b) ***Intentional Wrongdoers***. What about cases in which some defendants are intentional wrongdoers while others were merely negligent, as when a property owner fails to take reasonable precautions to prevent crimes? Can a portion of the fault be allocated to the intentional wrongdoer? In some instances, the answer is yes, although most states are to the contrary (sometimes because the relevant comparative fault statute does not define intentionally tortious conduct as a type of "fault"). This is a particularly difficult problem when the plaintiff has been negligent, too, as plaintiff's negligence traditionally does not reduce the plaintiff's recovery from an intentional wrongdoer, though it does reduce or eliminate recovery from negligent defendants.

(c) ***Non-Parties***. Should the tortious conduct of persons whom the victim has not sued or of persons who are judgment-proof reduce the amount the plaintiff can recover from others? In some instances, the answer is yes. *See* Tex. Civ. Prac. & Rem. Code §§ 33.003 and 33.004 (Westlaw 2022) (permitting allocation of fault to a designated third party, even if the party has not been joined); Marler v. Scoggins, 105 S.W.3d 596 (Tenn. Ct. App. 2002) (permitting assignment of fault to an unidentified "phantom" driver).

In Staab v. Diocese of St. Cloud, 813 N.W.2d 68 (Minn. 2012), a case involving a wheelchair accident, the court construed a statute which imposes joint and several liability on "a person whose fault is greater than 50 percent." The court held that a jury could allocate fault to the plaintiff's husband, who was not a defendant, and that the defendant diocese, which was only 50% at fault, was liable for only half of the plaintiff's damages.

(d) ***Persons Who Have Settled***. In calculating a defendant's portion of the plaintiff's damages, can fault be apportioned to persons who have settled? In some instances, the answer is yes. *See* Smiley v. Corrigan, 638 N.W.2d 151 (Mich. Ct. App. 2001) (permitting a golf instructor to introduce evidence concerning the fault attributable to a driving range and a fellow patron, both of whom had settled with the plaintiff). Other states are to the contrary.

Questions like these have no settled answers in some jurisdictions.

Economic Analysis
Incentives Relating to Joint and Several Liability

Alan Gunn

At first glance, it may seem that allowing injured persons to recover in full from any defendant who might have prevented the injury will reduce injuries. Absent joint and several liability, a potential defendant might spend less than the optimal amount on injury prevention, knowing that it will be responsible for only a portion of the plaintiff's costs if something goes awry. For example, someone who might expect to be held ten-percent responsible for a $1,000,000 injury might decide to pay no more than $100,000 to prevent the injury. Under a system of joint and several liability, the same potential defendant should be willing to pay much more to prevent the injury, especially if it knows that other potential defendants are likely to be judgment-proof, so that the entire burden will fall on it.

On the other hand, a system that allows joint and several liability encourages plaintiffs to sue as many persons as possible. Potential defendants, knowing this, may assume that much of the financial burden of the harm they cause through their carelessness may be borne by others; when they do, their incentive to exercise care is reduced. Furthermore, the system encourages plaintiffs to draw into litigation all possible defendants who are wealthy or insured, a practice that may deflect attention away from serious wrongdoers and which imposes heavy costs on persons whose connection to the accident was slight, if present at all. For example, it is routine in plane-crash cases for plaintiffs to sue the manufacturer of the airplane involved in the crash, even when it is clear that the crash resulted from gross pilot error.

B. Contribution and Indemnity

Contribution and indemnity are available only from one who is a joint tortfeasor. *See* New Prime, Inc. v. Brandon Balchune Constr., Inc., 2017 WL 6419088, at *10 (M.D. Pa.) ("Without a tort, there can be no tortfeasor, and without a tortfeasor, there can be no right to contribution or indemnity").

Brochner v. Western Insurance Company

Supreme Court of Colorado, En Banc
724 P.2d 1293 (Colo. 1986)

KIRSHBAUM, Justice.

....

The Community Hospital Association (the hospital) . . . granted staff privileges to Dr. Ruben Brochner in October 1964. Brochner performed numerous craniotomies at the hospital over the next few months. In 1965, after reviews of those craniotomies indicated that tissue samples from many of the patients appeared normal, the hospital's executive committee orally required Brochner to obtain consultations before performing craniotomies if the relevant radiographic evidence did not clearly establish pathology....

In March 1968, the hospital's tissue committee received a report that fourteen of twenty-eight tissue samples taken from Brochner's neurosurgery patients were completely normal and that nine of the remaining fourteen samples indicated only low grade disease. An expert testified at trial that one normal tissue of 100 tissue samples was an acceptable ratio and that two normal tissues out of twenty-eight samples would require investigation.

On November 9, 1968, Brochner performed a craniotomy on Esther Cortez which resulted in injury to Cortez. Cortez later filed a civil action against Brochner and the hospital. She alleged that Brochner negligently diagnosed her ..., that the hospital negligently continued Brochner's staff privileges ..., and that the hospital negligently allowed Brochner to perform unnecessary surgery. The claim against Brochner was severed, and trial of the claims against the hospital commenced April 3, 1978. Prior to the conclusion of that trial, Cortez and the hospital agreed to a settlement of $150,000. Sometime later, Cortez reached a settlement of her suit against Brochner, who was uninsured, for an undisclosed sum.

In 1979, the hospital and its subrogee, Western Insurance Company (Western), filed this indemnity action against Brochner, alleging that Brochner's negligence was the active and primary cause of Cortez' injuries while the hospital's negligence was passive and secondary.... [T]he trial court entered judgment for Western and the hospital against Brochner.... The Court of Appeals affirmed....

Brochner first argues that the adoption of the Uniform Contribution Among Tortfeasors Act, §§ 13-50.5-101 to -106, 6 C.R.S. (1985 Supp.) (the Act) abrogated the Colorado common law rule of indemnity to the extent such rule is based upon distinctions between primary and secondary fault. We do not agree that the statute *per se* altered the common law doctrine of indemnity. However, we conclude that existence of the Act sufficiently undermines the historical basis for the rule to require its modification.

The common law of Colorado ... consistently followed the ... rule prohibiting contribution among joint tortfeasors.... Recognizing that strict application of this rule sometimes produces unjust results, a rule permitting indemnity between tortfeasors in certain limited circumstances was also incorporated into this jurisdiction's panoply of common law principles....

Contribution and indemnity are analytically quite distinct concepts. The former is based on the equitable notion that one tortfeasor should not be required to pay sums to an injured party in excess of that tortfeasor's proportionate share of the responsibility for the injuries. The latter is grounded in the legal principle that one joint tortfeasor, as indemnitor, may owe a duty of care to another joint tortfeasor, which duty is unrelated to any duty of care owed by the tortfeasors to the injured party.... When such duty is established, the indemnitor tortfeasor may be liable to the indemnitee tortfeasor for the entire loss experienced by the latter as the result of payments made to the injured party. . . .

. . . . As initially adopted, our rule required the indemnitor's conduct to be the "sole, proximate and primary cause" of the damages suffered by the injured party. . . . However, in Jacobson v. Dahlberg, 171 Colo. 42, 464 P.2d 298 (1970), this court modified the test for indemnity by eliminating the requirement that the indemnitor's conduct be the sole cause of the injured party's damages and adopting a broader standard requiring only that the indemnitor's conduct be the primary cause of such damages. . . .

. . . . [The] difficulties with definitions and applications of the concepts of active, passive, primary and secondary negligence have been the subject of critical discussion by numerous courts and commentators. . . . These difficulties inevitably have produced great variations in judicial decisions, resulting in a severe lack of predictability and often causing as much inequity as the rule was designed to prevent. As the court in *Missouri Pacific R.R. Co.*, 566 S.W.2d 466 [(Mo. 1978)], observed:

> . . . .
>
> We have worked ourselves into a situation where indemnity as between tortfeasors is decided on the basis of which one is guilty of "active" and which one guilty of "passive" negligence. "Passive" wins, "active" loses, no matter how great the proportion of fault may have been of the passive tortfeasor.
>
> . . . .
>
> This is not a sensible way to fix responsibility in indemnity. It comes about by attempting to find a formula by which to excuse one of two joint or concurrent tortfeasors completely when as a practical matter they both are to blame, the true difference between them being only a matter of degree or relativity of fault. With a little ingenuity in phrasing, negligence can be made to be either "active" or "passive" as suits the writer. For example, "driving an automobile with bad brakes" or "running through the stop sign" or "using a defective crane" might be said to be "active" negligence, while "omitting maintenance of brake fluid level" or "neglecting to apply the brakes" or "failing to inspect the crane in order to discover its defectiveness" might be "passive" negligence—these are the same acts or omissions, but the outcome depends not upon the facts, but upon how someone chooses to characterize them.

. . . .

Subsequent to this court's decision in . . . [Ringsby Truck Lines, Inc. v. Bradfield], 193 Colo. 151, 563 P.2d 939 [(1977)], the General Assembly adopted the Act, effective July 1, 1977. This statute abolished the common law prohibition against contribution among joint tortfeasors and established a rule authorizing such contribution based on degrees of relative fault. § 13-50.5-102(6) contains the following provision respecting common law principles defining rights and responsibilities among joint tortfeasors:

> This article does not impair any right [of] indemnity under existing law. Where one tortfeasor is entitled to indemnity from another, the right of the indemnity obligee is for indemnity and not contribution, and the indemnity obligor is not entitled to contribution from the obligee for any portion of his indemnity obligation.

In addition, § 13-50.5-103 provides as follows:

> When there is a disproportion of fault among joint tortfeasors, the relative degrees of fault of the joint tortfeasors shall be used in determining their pro rata shares solely for the purpose of determining their rights of contribution among themselves, each remaining severally liable to the injured person for the whole injury as at common law.

The statute thus recognizes that the remedies of indemnity and contribution are in theory mutually exclusive. . . . [T]he General Assembly's adoption of the principle of contribution among joint tortfeasors invites, if it does not require, reconsideration of the doctrine of indemnity between joint tortfeasors.

Joint tortfeasors are now subject to contribution among themselves based upon their relative degrees of fault. That principle is at odds with the essential characteristic of our present rule of indemnity that, without regard to apportionment of fault, a single tortfeasor may ultimately pay the expense of all injuries sustained by a third party as the result of negligent conduct by two or more tortfeasors. There can be no mistake concerning the intent of the General Assembly to establish the policy of responsibility related to proportionate fault in the context of personal injury litigation. . . . [The court discussed the legislative history.]

. . . . Application of this principle will prove far more certain in varied factual contexts and will consequently promote more predictability than any continued effort to perpetuate ephemeral distinctions based on primary or secondary negligence concepts. For these reasons we conclude that the doctrine of indemnity insofar as it requires one of two joint tortfeasors to reimburse the other for the entire amount paid by the other as damages to a party injured as the result of the negligence of both joint tortfeasors, is no longer viable, and is hereby abolished.

In this case, the trial court found that the hospital acted negligently and that such negligence was independent of Brochner's negligence. . . . As a joint tortfeasor, the hospital has no right to seek indemnity from Brochner; its sole remedy lies in contribution pursuant to the terms of the Act. § 13-50.5-105(1)(b) provides:

> When a release or a covenant not to sue or not to enforce judgment is given in good faith to one of two or more persons liable in tort for the same injury or the same wrongful death:
>
> . . . .
>
> It discharges the tortfeasor to whom it is given from all liability for contribution to any other tortfeasor.

. . . . Because both Brochner and the hospital settled with Cortez after . . . [the effective date of the Act], neither is entitled to contribution from the other.

. . . .

[The discussion of a statute abolishing the doctrine of joint and several liability is omitted.]

The judgment of the Court of Appeals is reversed.

[The dissenting opinion of VOLLACK, J., is omitted.]

Notes

1. ***Indemnity and Contribution Distinguished.*** Indemnity shifts all of the loss from one tortfeasor to another; contribution results in the tortfeasors sharing the loss (sometimes *pro rata*, sometimes in proportion to responsibility). The Restatement, Third, of Torts: Apportionment of Liab. (2000), points out in comment d to § 23 that contribution and indemnity are alternatives. If one defendant is entitled to indemnity from another, the question of contribution does not arise.

The common-law rule, based on the principle that "the law will not aid a wrongdoer," was that contribution was never allowed. This rule has been abolished in every state.

2. ***Cases in Which Indemnity Is Allowed.*** The Restatement takes the position that indemnity is allowed in only three cases: (1) when agreed to by contract between the indemnitor and the indemnitee; (2) when the indemnitee is liable only vicariously for the indemnitor's tort (as when *respondeat superior* makes an employer liable for the negligence of an employee); and (3) when a product seller (*e.g.*, a wholesaler or retailer), not otherwise at fault, is liable for injuries caused by a defect in a product manufactured by the indemnitor. *See* Restatement, Third, of Torts: Apportionment of Liab. § 22.

However, case law supports indemnity in other situations. Examples include an indemnitee whose negligence allowed the indemnitor, an intentional wrongdoer, to harm the plaintiff, as when a store's lax security precautions allow a mugging. More controversially, some decisions allow a tortfeasor whose negligence was "passive" to obtain indemnity from an "actively negligent" defendant — the approach rejected in *Brochner.*

3. ***Indemnity Based on Contract.*** Many cases involving a claim to indemnity based on contract pose little problem. If the contract expressly provides for indemnity, it is likely that the document will be enforced as written. For example, in Churchill Forge, Inc. v. Brown, 61 S.W.3d 368 (Tex. 2001), a lease provision requiring a tenant to reimburse a landlord for losses caused by the negligence of any guest or occupant was held to be valid. However, a contract must be clear if it seeks to indemnify a party for its own active negligence. *See* County of Sacramento v. Valley Healthcare Sys., Inc., 2017 WL 6616589, at *4 (Cal. App.).

4. ***Statutory Indemnity.*** Some indemnity rights are created by statute. *See* Tex. Civ. Prac. & Rem. Code § 82.002 (Westlaw 2022) ("A manufacturer shall indemnify and hold harmless a seller against loss arising out of a products liability action, except for any loss caused by the seller's negligence, intentional misconduct, or other act or omission, such as negligently modifying or altering the product, for which the seller is independently liable"; "'loss' includes court costs and other reasonable expenses, reasonable attorney fees, and any reasonable damages").

5. ***The Satisfaction-of-Claim Requirement.*** Cases sometimes say that contribution or indemnity is available only to one who has extinguished the liability of the person from whom reimbursement is sought. *See* Fetick v. American Cyanamid Co., 38 S.W.3d 415 (Mo. 2001) (a physician who settled claims against him for administering a vaccine that rendered an infant triplegic had no right to contribution from the vaccine manufacturer and distributor who remained defendants in the infant's suit).

6. ***Contribution and Intentional Torts.*** It is generally agreed that an intentional tortfeasor may not obtain contribution. *See, e.g.*, IDA Moorhead Corp. v. Leach, 2016 WL 6647736, at *4 (Ariz. App.) (discussing Arizona law).

7. ***Pro Rata versus Proportional Contribution.*** There are two basic approaches to calculating contribution. The older *pro rata* approach is a rather crude method of counting heads and dividing. If there are three joint tortfeasors, each one bears one-third of the loss, regardless of their respective degrees of fault. Thus, if *A* satisfies a judgment rendered jointly against *A*, *B*, and *C*, *A* can obtain reimbursement for one-third of that amount from *B*, and the same from *C*.

The modern proportional approach is to award contribution in accordance with the tortfeasors' percentages of the total fault. For example, if *A* satisfies a judgment rendered jointly against *A*, *B*, and *C*, and their respective degrees of fault are 85%, 10%, and 5%, *A* can obtain reimbursement from *B* for 10%, and from *C* for 5%, of the amount paid.

Leung v. Verdugo Hills Hospital

Supreme Court of California
282 P.3d 1250 (Cal. 2012)

KENNARD, J.

Six days after his birth, plaintiff [Aidan Ming-Ho Leung] suffered irreversible brain damage. Through his mother as guardian ad litem, he sued his pediatrician and the hospital in which he was born. Before trial, plaintiff and the pediatrician agreed to a settlement of $1 million, the limit of the pediatrician's malpractice insurance policy....

On the hospital's appeal, a major contention was that under the common law "release rule," plaintiff's settlement with the pediatrician also released the nonsettling hospital from liability for plaintiff's economic damages. The Court of Appeal reluctantly agreed. It observed that although this court "has criticized the common law release rule," it "has not abandoned it." Considering itself bound by principles of *stare decisis*, the Court of Appeal then applied the common law release rule to this case, and it reversed that portion of the trial court's judgment awarding plaintiff economic damages against the hospital. We granted plaintiff's petition for review....

Before trial, plaintiff settled with defendant pediatrician for $1 million.... Defendant pediatrician agreed to participate as a defendant at trial, and plaintiff agreed to release him from all claims. The pediatrician petitioned the trial court for a determination that the written settlement agreement met the statutory requirement of having been made in "good faith," seeking to limit his liability to the amount of the settlement. (Code Civ. Proc., § 877 [judicial determination of settlement in good faith discharges the settling party "from all liability for any contribution to any other parties"].)

The trial court denied that motion, as it found the settlement to be "grossly disproportionate to the amount a reasonable person would estimate" the pediatrician's share of liability would be.... Plaintiff and defendant pediatrician nevertheless decided to proceed with the settlement.

At trial,... the jury awarded plaintiff $250,000 in noneconomic damages... [and roughly $15 million in economic damages]. The jury apportioned negligence as follows: 55 percent as to the pediatrician, 40 percent as to the hospital, and 2.5 percent as to each of Aidan's parents. The judgment stated that, subject to a setoff of $1 million, representing the amount of settlement with the pediatrician, the hospital was jointly and severally liable for 95 percent of all economic damages awarded to plaintiff....

....

Under the traditional common law rule, a plaintiff's settlement with, and release from liability of, one joint tortfeasor also releases from liability all other joint tortfeasors.... The common law rule's rationale is that there can be only one compensation for a single injury and because each joint tortfeasor is liable for all of the damage, any joint tortfeasor's payment of compensation in any amount satisfies the plaintiff's entire claim....

The rule, however, can lead to harsh results. An example: A plaintiff might have settled with a joint tortfeasor for a sum far less than the plaintiff's damages because of the tortfeasor's inadequate financial resources.... In an effort to avoid such unjust and inequitable results, California courts held that a plaintiff who settled with one of multiple tortfeasors could, by replacing the word "release" in the settlement agreement with the phrase "covenant not to sue," and by stating that the agreement applied only to the parties to it, preserve the right to obtain additional compensation from the nonsettling joint tortfeasors....

It was against that backdrop... that the California Legislature in 1957 enacted Code of Civil Procedure section 877.... The statute modified the common law release rule by providing that a "good faith" settlement and release of one joint tortfeasor, rather than completely releasing other joint tortfeasors, merely reduces, by the settlement amount, the damages that the plaintiff may recover from the nonsettling joint tortfeasors, and that such a good faith settlement and release discharges the settling tortfeasor from all liability to others. . . . But because the statute governs only good faith settlements, and the trial court here determined that the settlement was not made in good faith . . . , the statute does not apply to this case.

We reject defendant hospital's contention that in enacting Code of Civil Procedure section 877 in 1957, the Legislature signaled an intent to preclude future judicial development of the law pertaining to settlements involving joint tortfeasors, thus preventing us from abrogating the common law release rule. . . .

Here, adherence to the common law release rule would, as a result of plaintiff's settlement with defendant pediatrician for $1 million (the limit of the pediatrician's medical malpractice insurance policy), relieve nonsettling defendant hospital from any liability for plaintiff's economic damages, even though the jury apportioned to the hospital 40 percent of the fault for plaintiff's severe postbirth brain damage. . . . Under the common law release rule, plaintiff . . . would be compensated for only a tiny fraction of his total economic damages, a harsh result.

The rationale for the common law release rule . . . assumes that the amount paid in settlement to a plaintiff in return for releasing one joint tortfeasor from liability always provides full compensation for all of the plaintiff's injuries, and that therefore anything recovered by the plaintiff beyond that amount necessarily constitutes a double or excess recovery. The assumption, however, is unjustified. . . .

In light of the unjust and inequitable results the common law release rule can bring about . . . , we hold that the rule is no longer to be followed in California.

. . . .

In deciding how to apportion liability in a negligence action when a plaintiff's settlement with one of several defendants has been determined by a trial court not to have been made in good faith, we begin with two legal concepts that are central to California negligence law. The first concept is comparative fault, the second is joint and several liability. Under comparative fault, "liability for damage will be borne by those whose negligence caused it in direct proportion to their respective fault." . . . . Under joint and several liability, "each tortfeasor whose negligence is a proximate cause of an indivisible injury remains individually liable for all compensable damages attributable to that injury." . . . .

As has been recognized, "[n]o perfect method exists for apportioning liability among a plaintiff, a settling tortfeasor, and a nonsettling tortfeasor." (Rest. 3d Torts, Apportionment of Liability, § 16, com. c, p. 133.) Three alternative approaches have developed. . . .

Under the first approach, the money paid by the settling tortfeasor is credited against any damages assessed against the nonsettling tortfeasors, who are allowed to seek contribution from the settling tortfeasor for damages they have paid in excess of their equitable shares of liability. (Rest. 2d Torts, § 886A, com. m, p. 343.) We will call this the setoff-with-contribution approach.

Under the second approach, as under the first, nonsettling tortfeasors are entitled to a credit in the amount paid by the settling tortfeasor. But, unlike under the first alternative, nonsettling tortfeasors may not obtain any contribution from the settling tortfeasor. (Rest. 2d Torts, § 886A, com. m, p. 343.) We will call this the setoff-without-contribution approach.

The third approach differs from the first and second by subtracting from the damages assessed against nonsettling tortfeasors the settling tortfeasor's proportionate share of liability, rather than the amount paid in settlement. (Rest. 2d Torts, § 886A, com. m, p. 344.) We will call this the proportionate-share approach.

Which of these three approaches should we apply when, as here, one tortfeasor settles but another does not, and the settlement is judicially determined not to meet Code of Civil Procedure section 877's "good faith" requirement? . . . .

The second approach — setoff *without* contribution by the settling tortfeasor to the nonsettling tortfeasor — is easy to dispose of, as it is not an option here. Although the Legislature has statutorily adopted this apportionment method, it has expressly limited its application to settlements made in good faith. (Code Civ. Proc., §§ 877, 877.6, subd. (c).) . . . .

. . . . Applying the setoff-without-contribution approach to settlements not made in good faith would effectively nullify that statutory provision. . . .

Of the two remaining alternatives — setoff *with* contribution and proportionate share — nonsettling defendant hospital argues that we should adopt the latter. Plaintiff, however, prefers the setoff-with-contribution approach. . . .

Under the setoff-*with*-contribution approach, the settlement has little or no practical effect on the defendants' ultimate liabilities or the plaintiff's ultimate recovery. . . .

With the settlement, under the setoff-*with*-contribution approach, this liability exposure of joint tortfeasors is not affected. In a suit against the nonsettling defendants, the plaintiff may recover damages less the settlement amount and the amount attributable to the plaintiff's own fault. Consistent with the comparative fault principle, the nonsettling tortfeasors may then seek contribution from the settling tortfeasor for any amount they must pay to the plaintiff in excess of their proportionate shares of liability. If in such a contribution action the settling tortfeasor is for any reason unable to fully discharge its share of liability, each nonsettling tortfeasor, consistent with the rule of joint and several liability, remains liable for the difference.

. . . .

Under proportionate-share apportionment [the third approach], the plaintiff's total recovery for economic damages is limited to the settlement amount plus the proportionate shares of the nonsettling tortfeasors. If the settlement payment turns out to be less than the settling tortfeasor's proportionate share, as determined by the trial court or the jury, the plaintiff may not recover the difference from any of the tortfeasors and thus is precluded from obtaining full compensation. . . .

We conclude that the practical implications of the two available apportionment approaches and their consistency or inconsistency with basic tort principles support our adoption of the setoff-with-contribution alternative over the proportionate-share alternative. As explained earlier, setoff-with-contribution apportionment does not change the respective positions of the parties and is fully consistent with both the comparative fault principle and the rule of joint and several liability. In contrast, proportionate-share apportionment alters the parties' positions and would require us to recognize a new exception to our established law of joint and several liability.

. . . .

. . . . Accordingly, we hold that when a settlement with a tortfeasor has judicially been determined not to have been made in good faith (*see* Code Civ. Proc., §§ 877, 877.6, subd. (c)), nonsettling joint tortfeasors remain jointly and severally liable, the amount paid in settlement is credited against any damages awarded against the nonsettling tortfeasors, and the nonsettling tortfeasors are entitled to contribution from the settling tortfeasor for amounts paid in excess of their equitable shares of liability.

. . . .

The judgment of the Court of Appeal is reversed, and the case is remanded to that court for further proceedings consistent with the views expressed in this opinion.

Notes

1. ***Releases and Covenants Not to Sue.*** When a plaintiff enters into a settlement with one or more joint tortfeasors, the agreement is embodied in writing. Traditional wisdom once held that there were two distinct types of settlement documents, a "release" and a "covenant not to sue." A release extinguished the plaintiff's rights against all joint tortfeasors. A covenant not to sue extinguished the plaintiff's rights only against the joint tortfeasor named in the covenant. However, these distinctions are unknown to most tort victims, and there is a risk that an injured person might not correctly understand what rights are given up, even when a document is labeled a "release."

The Restatement, Second, of Torts (§ 885) embraces a sensible position on settlement documents: "A valid release of one tortfeasor . . . does not discharge others liable for the same harm, unless it is agreed that it will discharge them." The intent to reserve rights need not be expressed in writing and can be proved by parol evidence.

Some courts have gone further than the Restatement in attempting to prevent unfairness and uncertainty in the use of settlement documents. For example, in McMillen v. Klingensmith, 467 S.W.2d 193 (Tex. 1971), the court held that a settlement document releases from liability only those tortfeasors named or otherwise specifically identified in the document, and no others. Because the document in *McMillen* named only the driver who caused the accident leading to the plaintiff's injuries, and made no reference to the doctors who were allegedly negligent in treating the plaintiff, the doctors were not released from liability.

Section 4 of the Uniform Contribution Among Tortfeasors Act, which has been adopted in several states, provides that a release by the injured person of one joint tortfeasor

> does not discharge the other tortfeasors unless the release so provides; but reduces the claim against the other tortfeasors in the amount of the consideration paid for the release, or in any amount or proportion by which the release provides that the total claim shall be reduced, if greater than the consideration paid.

(Westlaw 2022).

2. ***Releasing Classes.*** In Duncan v. Cessna Aircraft Co., 665 S.W.2d 414, 419–20 (Tex. 1984), a suit involving multiple defendants, one tortfeasor settled with the plaintiff and obtained a release. Cessna, a second defendant, claimed that because the release purported to discharge "any other corporations or persons whomsoever responsible" for the accident, the document released Cessna from liability. The court held that in a multiple tortfeasor context:

> the mere naming of a general class of tortfeasors in a release does not discharge the liability of each member of that class. A tortfeasor can claim the protection of a release only if the release refers to him by name or with such descriptive particularity that his identity or his connection with the tortious event is not in doubt.

This approach minimizes the risk that a plaintiff will inadvertently release nonsettling wrongdoers.

3. ***What Claims Are Released?*** In Memorial Med. Ctr. of E. Tex. v. Keszler, 943 S.W.2d 433 (Tex. 1997), a physician entered into a settlement in an action he had brought against a hospital after his staff and clinical privileges were revoked. The physician subsequently brought a separate action against the hospital, asserting claims based on toxic exposure during his employment. In addressing whether the release signed as part of the initial settlement barred the later action, the court wrote:

> It is true that to release a claim, the releasing document must "mention" it. . . . But the court of appeals holds a claim is not mentioned unless it is specifically enumerated, stating "We find no mention in the preambles of anything related to appellant's present claims for exposure to ethelyne dioxide gas. . . ."
>
> In this case, the parties agreed that Keszler would release all claims "relating to [Keszler's] relationship with [Memorial]." Keszler's claim of ETO exposure, because it is related to his relationship with Memorial, is

"mentioned" in the releasing document. The court of appeals erred in holding otherwise.

4. ***Release of a Person for Whom Another Is Vicariously Liable.*** Does the release of a tortfeasor for whose conduct another may be held vicariously liable also release the person on whom liability could be vicariously imposed? Many courts say "no," but there is authority to the contrary. *Compare* Miller v. Grand Union Co., 512 S.E.2d 887 (Ga. 1999) (holding that the release of an employee does not release an employer unless the instrument names the employer), *with* Burke v. Webb Boats, Inc., 37 P.3d 811 (Okla. 2001) (release of a boat operator also released the boat owner who could have been held vicariously liable, even though the owner was specifically excluded in the release).

5. ***Contribution from Settling Joint Tortfeasors.*** May contribution be obtained from a joint tortfeasor who settles with the plaintiff? If so, there is little incentive for a defendant to settle, for doing so does not bring an end to the question of the settling defendant's liability. On the other hand, if contribution is not available, other defendants who settle later, or who litigate the case but lose at trial, may be forced to bear a disproportionate part of the total damages paid to the plaintiff.

As the principal case indicates, there are at least three views on this subject, none of which is entirely satisfactory:

(a) Some jurisdictions permit an action for contribution against a settling joint tortfeasor (*see Leung, supra* (dealing with bad-faith settlements)).

(b) Other jurisdictions deny contribution from a settling joint tortfeasor if the settlement is made in good faith (*see Brochner, supra*; *see also Leung, supra* (dealing with good faith settlements));

(c) Still other jurisdictions avoid the issue of contribution by holding that the plaintiff, by settling with a defendant, gives up some portion (determined on a *pro rata* or proportional basis) of the judgment ultimately obtained against non-settling defendants. *See* Tex. Civ. Prac. & Rem. Code § 33.012 (Westlaw 2022) (reduction equal to each settling person's percentage of responsibility, except in certain health care liability claims, as to which different rules apply).

In many states, the issue is controlled by the local version of the Uniform Contribution Among Tortfeasors Act.

Contribution issues do not arise if liability of multiple tortfeasors is several, as a system of several liability makes each tortfeasor liable only for an appropriate share of the plaintiff's damages.

6. ***Contribution for Settling Joint Tortfeasors.*** Many states hold that a tortfeasor who enters into a good faith settlement that extinguishes the liability of another joint tortfeasor may bring an action for contribution. *See* M. Pierre Equip. Co. v. Griffith Consumers Co., 831 A.2d 1036 (D.C. 2003). However, there is authority to the contrary. *See* Charleston Area Med. Ctr., Inc. v. Parke-Davis, 614 S.E.2d 15 (W. Va. 2005)

(holding that "a tortfeasor who negotiates and consummates a settlement with an injured party on behalf of itself before any lawsuit is filed cannot subsequently bring an action seeking contribution from a tortfeasor who was not apprised of and not a party to the settlement negotiations and agreement").

7. ***Contribution Actions Barred by Immunity.*** A person immune from suit by the plaintiff may also be immune from a contribution action by a joint tortfeasor. For example, in Shoemake v. Fogel, Ltd., 826 S.W.2d 933 (Tex. 1992), a child drowned in an apartment complex pool. The court held that the doctrine of parental immunity barred a contribution claim by the complex owners and managers against the child's mother, who was allegedly negligent in supervising the youth. *See also* Slater v. Skyhawk Transp., Inc., 77 F. Supp. 2d 580 (D. N.J. 1999) (holding that workers' compensation laws in New Jersey, Michigan, and Virginia all barred contribution claims against employers by third parties defending against claims by injured employees).

C. Mary Carter Agreements

Elbaor v. Smith

Supreme Court of Texas
845 S.W.2d 240 (Tex. 1992)

GONZALEZ, Justice.

. . . .

Ms. Smith filed [a medical malpractice] suit against D/FW Medical Center, ACH, Drs. Syrquin, Elbaor, Stephens, and Gatmaitan. Sometime before trial, Ms. Smith entered into Mary Carter agreements with Dr. Syrquin, Dr. Stephens, and ACH.[1] The Mary Carter agreements provided for payments to Ms. Smith of $350,000 from Dr. Syrquin, $75,000 from ACH, and $10 from Dr. Stephens. Under the terms of each agreement, the settling defendants were required to participate in the trial of the case. The agreements also contained pay-back provisions whereby Dr. Syrquin and ACH would be reimbursed all or part of the settlement money paid to Ms. Smith out of the recovery against Dr. Elbaor.

Ms. Smith nonsuited her claim against Dr. Gatmaitan and settled and dismissed her claim against D/FW Medical Center. Dr. Elbaor filed a cross claim against Dr. Stephens, Dr. Gatmaitan, Dr. Syrquin, and ACH. He alleged that in the event he was found liable to Ms. Smith, that he was entitled to contribution from these defendants. Furthermore, Dr. Elbaor requested that the trial court hold the Mary Carter agreements void as against public policy, and alternatively, to dismiss the settling

---

1. [Fn. 3:] These agreements acquired their name from a case out of Florida styled Booth v. Mary Carter Paint Co., 202 So. 2d 8, 10–11 (Fla. App. 1967). . . .

Raul Gonzalez

defendants from the suit. The trial court denied this request. The suit proceeded to trial against Dr. Elbaor and the cross defendants.

At trial, the jury found that Ms. Smith's damages totaled $2,253,237.07, of which Dr. Elbaor was responsible for eighty-eight percent, and Dr. Syrquin for twelve percent. After deducting all credits for Dr. Syrquin's percentage of causation and settlements with other defendants, the trial court rendered judgment against Dr. Elbaor for $1,872,848.62.

. . . .

Although the Mary Carter agreements were not entered into evidence, the trial judge was troubled by them and he took remedial measures to mitigate their harmful effects by reapportioning the peremptory challenges, changing the order of proceedings to favor Dr. Elbaor, allowing counsel to explain the agreements to the jury, and instructing the jury regarding the agreements.

During the trial, the settling defendants' attorneys, who sat at the table with Dr. Elbaor's attorneys, vigorously assisted Ms. Smith in pointing the finger of culpability at Dr. Elbaor. This created some odd conflicts of interest and some questionable representations of fact. For example, although Ms. Smith's own experts testified that Dr. Syrquin committed malpractice, her attorney stated during *voir dire* and in her opening statement that Dr. Syrquin's conduct was "heroic" and that Dr. Elbaor's negligence caused Ms. Smith's damages. And during her closing argument, Ms. Smith's attorney urged the jury to find that Dr. Syrquin had not caused

Ms. Smith's damages. This is hardly the kind of statement expected from a plaintiff's lawyer regarding a named defendant. ACH and Drs. Syrquin and Stephens had remained defendants of record, but their attorneys asserted during *voir dire* that Ms. Smith's damages were "devastating," "astoundingly high," and "astronomical." Furthermore, on cross examination they elicited testimony from Ms. Smith favorable to her and requested recovery for pain and mental anguish. The settling defendants' attorneys also abandoned their pleadings on Ms. Smith's contributory negligence, argued that Ms. Smith should be awarded all of her alleged damages, and urged that Dr. Elbaor was 100 percent liable.

....

The term "Mary Carter agreement" has been defined in different ways by various courts and commentators. . . . [2] Today we clarify what we mean by the term "Mary Carter agreement." A Mary Carter agreement exists when the settling defendant retains a financial stake in the plaintiff's recovery *and* remains a party at the trial of the case.[3] This definition comports with both the present majority view and the original understanding of the term.

. . . . The settling defendant, who remains a party, guarantees the plaintiff a minimum payment, which may be offset in whole or in part by an excess judgment recovered at trial. . . . This creates a tremendous incentive for the settling defendant to ensure that the plaintiff succeeds in obtaining a sizable recovery, and thus motivates the defendant to assist greatly in the plaintiff's presentation of the case (as occurred here). Indeed, Mary Carter agreements generally, but not always, contain a clause requiring the settling defendant to participate in the trial on the plaintiff's behalf.

Given this Mary Carter scenario, it is difficult to surmise how these agreements promote settlement. Although the agreements do secure the partial settlement of a lawsuit, they nevertheless nearly always ensure a trial against the non-settling defendant. . . . Thus, "[o]nly a mechanical jurisprudence could characterize Mary

2. [Fn. 13:] The majority of cases and commentators define "Mary Carter agreement" as one in which the settling defendant possesses a financial stake in the outcome of the case and the settling defendant remains a party to the litigation. . . . Many cases also describe other requisite elements of a Mary Carter agreement, such as secrecy. . . . Other cases and commentators argue that a Mary Carter agreement exists any time the settling defendant possesses a financial interest in the plaintiff's recovery. . . .

3. [Fn. 14:] A Mary Carter agreement does not have to expressly state that the settling defendant must participate in the trial. The participation requirement is satisfied by the mere presence of the settling defendant as a party in the case. Obviously, a Mary Carter agreement would not exist if a settling defendant acquires a financial interest in the outcome of the trial and then testifies at trial as a non-party witness. However, Rule 3.04(b) of the Texas Disciplinary Rules of Professional Conduct prohibits a lawyer from paying or offering to pay a witness contingent upon the content of the testimony of the witness or the outcome of the case. Certainly Rule 3.04(b) mandates that an attorney has an ethical duty to refrain from making a settlement contingent, in any way, on the testimony of a witness who was also a settling party.

Carter arrangements as promoting compromise and discouraging litigation — they plainly do just the opposite." . . . .

Many jurisdictions have decided to tolerate the ill effects of Mary Carter agreements, presumably because they believe that the agreements promote settlement. Some have sought to mitigate the agreements' harmful skewing of the trial process by imposing prophylactic protections. Indeed, Texas previously has taken such an approach. . . .[4] These protective measures generally seek to remove the secrecy within which Mary Carter agreements traditionally have been shrouded. . . .

Justice Spears rightly noted in . . . [Scurlock Oil Co. v. Smithwick, 724 S.W.2d 1 (Tex. 1986)] the falsity of the premise upon which the prophylactic protection approach is founded, namely, the promotion of equitable settlements. *Id.* at 8. Mary Carter agreements instead:

> present to the jury a sham of adversity between the plaintiff and one co-defendant, while these parties are actually allied for the purpose of securing a substantial judgment for the plaintiff and, in some cases, exoneration for the settling defendant.

. . . . The agreements pressure the "settling" defendant to alter the character of the suit by contributing discovery material, peremptory challenges, trial tactics, supportive witness examination, and jury influence to the plaintiff's cause. . . . These procedural advantages distort the case presented before a jury that came "to court expecting to see a contest between the plaintiff and the defendants [and] instead see[s] one of the defendants cooperating with the plaintiff." . . . .

Mary Carter agreements not only allow plaintiffs to buy support for their case, they also motivate more culpable defendants to "make a 'good deal' [and thus] end up paying little or nothing in damages." . . . . Remedial measures cannot overcome nor sufficiently alleviate the malignant effects that Mary Carter agreements inflict upon our adversarial system. . . .

. . . . The bottom line is that our public policy favoring fair trials outweighs our public policy favoring partial settlements.

This case typifies the kind of procedural and substantive damage Mary Carter agreements can inflict upon our adversarial system. Thus, we declare them void as violative of sound public policy.

. . . [A] settling defendant may not participate in a trial in which he or she retains a financial interest in the plaintiff's lawsuit. . . . Accordingly, we reverse the judgment of the court of appeals and remand this cause to the trial court for further proceedings consistent with this opinion. . . . [This holding shall be applicable only

---

4. [Fn. 19:] The guidelines provided in . . . [an earlier case] require that Mary Carter agreements: (1) are discoverable; (2) should be fully disclosed "to the trial court before trial or immediately after the agreement is formed"; (3) should be considered by the trial court in allowing jury strikes and ruling on witness examination; and (4) should be fully disclosed to the jury at the start of the trial. . . .

in the present case, to those cases in the judicial pipeline where error has been preserved, and to those actions tried on or after the date of this opinion].

DOGGETT, Justice, dissenting.

....

Although Carole Smith non-suited Dr. Stephens and Dr. Syrquin, they remained as parties because Dr. Elbaor chose to maintain cross-actions against them. The majority remands for perhaps the first trial in Anglo-American jurisprudence in which a named party is denied a right to participate.... The majority denies Dr. Syrquin an opportunity to protect his professional standing by participating at trial. His reputation in the community as a physician has been hereby declared legally worthless, and any effect a jury verdict attributing significant negligence to him may have on hospital privileges, the cost and availability of malpractice insurance, and their patients is completely ignored.... [T]he majority refuses to recognize a central tenet of our judicial system—those called into court should be allowed to answer.

....

The chief problem associated with a Mary Carter agreement is that a hidden alteration of the relationship of some of the parties will give the jury a misleading and incomplete basis for evaluating the evidence. As is true in so many areas of jurisprudence, secrecy is the first enemy of justice. To address this concern, trial judges have appropriately implemented several procedural safeguards that remove the veil of secrecy from such settlements....

In the instant case the trial court took great care to safeguard procedurally the adversarial nature and fairness of its proceedings. Nothing about the agreements now under attack was hidden from anyone.... At *voir dire*, the court informed prospective jury members that ACH and Syrquin, by participating in the trial, could recover all or a portion of the amounts paid in settlement to Smith, depending on the size of the verdict. An additional warning was extended regarding the possibility of witness bias arising from the agreements. The implications of the agreements were also explored by various counsel during *voir dire*.

.... The trial cannot be a "sham of adversity," ... when the jury, as here, is fully aware of this shift in alliances.... So long as at least two parties with antagonistic interests remain, the likelihood that the truth will emerge is not diminished.

Accordingly, most jurisdictions allow Mary Carter agreements when trial courts implement similar procedural safeguards to those adopted here.... In rejecting the full disclosure approach, today's opinion embraces a decidedly minority view accepted in only "a couple of states" that have previously chosen to prohibit such agreements....

.... The elitist view that ordinary people acting as jurors are incapable of determining the facts after full disclosure has once again prevailed....

MAUZY and GAMMAGE, JJ., join in this dissenting opinion.

Notes

1. ***Other Precedent.*** In Rein v. Fog, 2016 WL 4366855, at *8 (N.J. Super. App. Div.), the court explained:

> In general, a Mary Carter agreement has three characteristics: (1) the liability of the settling defendant is limited and the plaintiff is guaranteed a minimum recovery; (2) the settling defendant remains a party to the pending action without disclosing the full agreement to the nonsettling defendants and/or the judge and jury; and (3) if judgment against the nonsettling defendant is for more than the amount of settlement, any money collected will first offset the settlement so that the settling defendant may ultimately pay nothing.

2. ***Ethics in Law Practice: Candor to the Court.*** In Gum v. Dudley, 505 S.E.2d 391 (W. Va. 1997), an attorney who jointly represented a tractor trailer's owner and driver in a wrongful death action arising from an auto accident violated his duty of candor by remaining silent when counsel for a co-defendant stated in response to an inquiry by the court that no parties had entered into a settlement agreement. In fact, the tractor trailer's owner and driver had settled the former's cross-claim against the latter. Counsel was fully aware of the settlement, so his silence constituted a material misrepresentation that no settlement agreement existed. The court referred the matter to the attorney disciplinary authorities for further action.

Chapter 18

Immunities

In the fairly recent past, a tort claim against one's spouse, or by a minor child against a parent, or against a governmental body or a charitable organization, could seldom be brought with success. The defendants in these cases were "immune" from liability for negligence, as well as for most or all other torts. Today, these immunities have been reduced considerably in scope, particularly in the case of spousal and parent-child immunities. Sovereign immunity or governmental immunity still survive in all jurisdictions, but all governmental entities have consented to suit under some circumstances. Charitable immunity also exists in some form in every state, but many claims against charitable enterprises succeed. These topics, as well as the immunities enjoyed by public officials and employees, will be discussed in the following sections.

A. Family Immunities

1. Spousal Immunity

Widespread Abrogation. The common-law notion that "husband and wife are one" gave rise to the doctrine of "spousal immunity," under which tort actions against one's spouse were prohibited. The doctrine even barred actions based on torts committed before the parties were married, so that if *A* negligently ran down *B*, *B*'s tort claim disappeared if *A* and *B* married before it was brought. The notion that husband and wife were the same person, legally, has long lost whatever appeal it once had, and with its decline spousal immunity has withered. The doctrine has no current intellectual or political support. *See* Bozman v. Bozman, 830 A.2d 450 (Md. 2003) ("no less than forty-six States have abrogated the doctrine, either fully or partially, leaving only four States still retaining it"; providing a state-by-state appendix); Lonzo v. Lonzo, 2017 WL 5477053, at *1 (La. App.) (Louisiana statutes provide for spousal immunity in tort cases).

De Facto Immunity for Interspousal Domestic Violence. The widespread abrogation of spousal immunity may be of little practical importance. *See* Jennifer Wriggins, *Interspousal Tort Immunity and Insurance "Family Member Exclusions": Shared Assumptions, Relational and Liberal Feminist Challenges*, 17 Wis. Women's L.J. 251 (2002). Professor Wriggins writes:

> *[D]e facto* interspousal tort immunity persists in the form of insurance exclusions. Insurance companies for decades have included "family member

> exclusions" in homeowner and automobile liability policies. These exclusions provide that family members cannot make claims against the policy. If a wife is injured by her husband, and the wife sues the husband for the injury, the liability policy will not cover the husband for the claim. The injured wife . . . has a choice of bringing a claim against her husband where there is no insurance coverage, and not bringing a claim at all. These provisions are ubiquitous in homeowners liability policies and were widespread in automobile policies until fairly recently. The reason for the exclusions . . . is to protect against collusive suits. Court decisions in both homeowners and automobile contexts have struck some of these exclusions down as against public policy, particularly in the automobile context. An additional common insurance provision, the "intentional acts exclusion," also bars claims for some intentional torts between spouses.
>
> These insurance exclusions have a similar effect to common law interspousal tort immunity. . . . Family member exclusions and intentional act exclusions in individual liability policies guarantee that lawsuits will only rarely be filed for interspousal injury. . . . Despite tort compensation for myriad other harms, both physical and psychic, compensation is simply lacking in the area of injury from domestic violence. . . .

2. Parental Immunity

Suits on Behalf of Unemancipated Minor Children. Like spousal immunity, the once-prevalent doctrine that unemancipated minors could not sue their parents for most torts is fading. However, unlike spousal immunity, parental immunity was based more on solid policy grounds than upon an absurd legal fiction, and so it has shown more staying power. Indeed, an occasional decision has extended the doctrine, in qualified form, to new contexts. *See, e.g.*, Mitchell v. Davis, 598 So. 2d 801 (Ala. 1992) (applying the parental-immunity doctrine to claims of simple negligence against foster parents and governmental agencies acting *in loco parentis*); Squeglia v. Squeglia, 661 A.2d 1007 (Conn. 1995) (holding that parental immunity bars actions based on strict liability, as well as negligence); *but see* Wallace v. Smyth, 786 N.E.2d 980 (Ill. 2002) (holding that a residential child-care facility acting *in loco parentis* could not invoke parental immunity).

Concerns About Collusion. One concern with allowing minors to sue their parents for negligence is that the minor's recovery is likely to benefit the parent, as well as the minor, at least in part. For example, suppose that a father negligently injures his daughter, and that the daughter incurs $5,000 in medical bills as a result. A $5,000 judgment against the father, paid by the father's liability insurer, will in nearly all cases benefit the father rather than the daughter.

Concerns about collusive litigation provide some support for retaining parental immunity. The fear is not so much that actions based on entirely fictitious accidents will be brought—that does happen, but it can happen even with persons who are not related, and who stage an imaginary accident to defraud an insurance company. Rather, the concern is that the prospect of financial benefit to the defendant may cause the defendant to "forget" care that was in fact taken or carelessness on the part of the victim. This may be a real problem, but the "immunity" solution throws out many meritorious claims to bar a few that may be less than solid.

Family Harmony, Parental Discretion, Child Discipline. Some courts have justified parental immunity by invoking a fear that litigation between parent and child would disrupt family harmony. These courts have sometimes allowed the child's action if the parent has died, as a deceased tortfeasor could hardly be angered by litigation. Other justifications for the doctrine involve the need for parents to exercise discretion with respect to child rearing (including discipline) free from concerns about tort liability.

Rousey v. Rousey

District of Columbia Court of Appeals
528 A.2d 416 (D.C. 1987)

TERRY, Associate Judge.

Appellee, Doris Rousey, and her eleven-year-old daughter, Cheryl Rousey, were involved in an automobile accident.... Cheryl sustained injuries, and through her father, Smith Rousey, she brought suit against her mother, alleging ... negligence. Mrs. Rousey, who was insured by Government Employees Insurance Company and represented by its counsel, filed a motion for summary judgment on the ground that parental immunity barred appellant from suing his wife on behalf of their unemancipated daughter. The court granted the motion, and Mr. Rousey appealed to this court.

....

The notion that a parent might be immune from liability for tortious conduct toward his or her child was not recognized in the United States until 1891, when the Supreme Court of Mississippi refused to permit a suit brought by a child against her mother, alleging that the mother had falsely imprisoned the child in an insane asylum. In ordering the suit dismissed, the court said:

> [S]o long as the parent is under obligation to care for, guide, and control, and the child is under reciprocal obligation to aid and comfort and obey, no such action as this can be maintained. The peace of society, and of the families composing society, and a sound public policy, designed to subserve the repose of families and the best interests of society, forbid to the minor child a right to appear in court in the assertion of a claim to civil redress for personal injuries suffered at the hands of the parent.

Hewellette v. George, 68 Miss. 703, 711, 9 So. 885, 887 (1891). Although the court cited no authority for this proposition, courts in all but eight other states followed Mississippi's lead and adopted some form of parental immunity....

Various reasons have been advanced in support of parental immunity, but the reason most frequently cited by the courts has been the need to preserve domestic tranquility and family unity. . . . [T]he courts that have adopted parental immunity have never adequately explained why the immunity applies only to suits in tort and not to suits involving property or contract rights. An action to enforce property or contract rights is surely no less adversarial. . . .

. . . . The courts have also expressed concern that parental discipline and control might be compromised if children were permitted to sue their parents. . . . Others believed that an uncompensated tort contributed to peace in the family and respect for the parent. . . . The absurdity of this reasoning, however, becomes plain when the case involves rape, . . . or a brutal beating, . . . or when the parent-child relationship has been terminated by death before the suit was filed. . . .

Persistent criticism of the doctrine of parental immunity eventually led to its erosion through the creation of various exceptions to it.[1] . . . .

Although the "overwhelming weight of authority" did at one time favor parental immunity, the doctrine began to lose judicial support after a 1963 Wisconsin decision which abolished it entirely except when the allegedly tortious act involved "an exercise of parental authority . . . [or] ordinary parental discretion with respect to the provision of food, clothing, housing, medical and dental services, and other care." Goller v. White, 20 Wis. 2d 402, 413, 122 N.W.2d 193, 198 (1963). In 1977 the American Law Institute completely rejected general tort immunity between parent and child when it published section 895G of the Restatement (Second) of Torts. That section states:

> (1) A parent or child is not immune from tort liability to the other solely by reason of that relationship.
>
> (2) Repudiation of general tort immunity does not establish liability for an act or omission that, because of the parent-child relationship, is otherwise privileged or is not tortious.

Many states have since followed the lead of Goller v. White and the Restatement, so that a substantial majority of states have now abandoned the doctrine in whole or in part. To date eleven states have abrogated it entirely or declined to adopt it; eleven have abrogated it in automobile negligence cases; five have abrogated it in automobile negligence cases in which the parent has liability insurance; and seven have abrogated it except in cases in which the parent's alleged tortious act involves an exercise of parental authority over the child, or ordinary parental discretion with respect to such matters as food, care, and education.

---

1. [Fn. 2:] *See, e.g.*, Dzenutis v. Dzenutis, 200 Conn. 290, 512 A.2d 130 (1986) (no immunity when child's injury arose out of a business activity conducted by the parent away from the home); Hale v. Hale, 312 Ky. 867, 230 S.W.2d 610 (1950) (no immunity when death of either parent or child terminates the parental relationship); Dunlap v. Dunlap, 84 N.H. 352, 150 A. 905 (1930) (no immunity for intentional or reckless infliction of bodily harm).

This trend toward abrogation is attributable, in large part, to the prevalence of liability insurance.... The availability of insurance relieves the parents of direct financial responsibility for injuries sustained by their children, and thus substantially reduces the possibility that an action for damages will disrupt domestic tranquility or family unity. As the Supreme Judicial Court of Massachusetts wrote ... :

> When insurance is involved, the action between parent and child is not truly adversary; both parties seek recovery from the insurance carrier to create a fund for the child's medical care and support without depleting the family's other assets. Far from being a potential source of disharmony, the action is more likely to preserve the family unit in pursuit of a common goal—the easing of family financial difficulties stemming from the child's injuries.

....

Although there is a possibility that parent and child may conspire to defraud the insurance carrier or that the parent may fail to cooperate with the carrier as required under the insurance contract ... that possibility exists to a certain extent in every case; it hardly justifies a "blanket denial of recovery for all minors." ....

> We constantly depend on efficient investigations and on juries and trial judges to sift evidence in order to determine the facts and arrive at proper verdicts. As part of the fact-finding process, these triers of fact must "distinguish the frivolous from the substantial and the fraudulent from the meritorious." .... Experience has shown that the courts are quite adequate for the task.

....

Because there is no controlling precedent on the subject of parental immunity, we need not overrule any prior decisions. Rather, we simply decline to adopt the doctrine of parental immunity as the law of the District of Columbia....

.... We see no reason, moreover, to limit our holding to cases in which the parent-defendant has liability insurance, as some courts have done. There can be no justification for fashioning different rules of law for the insured and the uninsured....

Reversed and remanded.

[The dissenting opinion of Judge BELSON, in which Chief Judge PRYOR joined, is omitted.]

NEBEKER, Associate Judge, dissenting:

....

In declining to adopt parental immunity, the majority disparages the wisdom of the past which championed the family unit, as if a contrary modern view is obviously superior....

.... [P]arental immunity is ... appropriately considered a judicial response to the latter-day attempt to pit child against parent and other family members. I see rejection of this immunity as part of the pandemic course to expand compensation for injury to yet another outer limit.

.... The threat of a tort suit could shackle a parent and prevent the flexibility needed to exercise parental control. As a child progresses through the more intractable stages of adolescence, a parent's fear of being sued must clearly undermine the exercise of parental authority, and thus the family structure. These concerns loom larger as our society grows more litigious.

I fear the majority has thought precious little of the consequences....

I opt for immunity and family unity; so I dissent.

Sepaugh v. LaGrone

Texas Court of Appeals
300 S.W.3d 328 (Tex. App. 2009)

BOB PEMBERTON, Justice.

Marietta Sepaugh, individually and as next friend of her late minor son, Frank LaGrone (Frank), appeals a take-nothing summary judgment on damages claims she had asserted against appellee Paul LaGrone (LaGrone), Frank's father and Sepaugh's ex-husband. Sepaugh sought damages arising from Frank's death in a Christmas Eve 2002 house fire that also killed another of LaGrone's minor sons (Frank's half-brother) and a third child, a friend of the LaGrone children, who was spending the night.... Sepaugh argues that the district court erred in granting summary judgment because parental immunity does not bar her claims....

.... Sepaugh pled theories of negligence and negligence *per se*. Specifically, she alleged that LaGrone had a duty under City of Austin ordinances to have smoke detectors that were audible in all sleeping areas of his home, that he breached this duty, and that such breach was a proximate cause of Frank's death.

... Sepaugh ... asserts four arguments as to why, she contends, parental immunity does not bar her claims. Her first and principal argument is that parental immunity, as a matter of law, does not bar her claims because they are predicated on LaGrone's breach of a duty imposed by city ordinance rather than the sort of discretionary parenting decision that parental immunity protects....

As recognized in Texas today, the affirmative defense of parental immunity operates to shield parents from tort liability to their unemancipated minor children for alleged acts of negligence that "involve a reasonable exercise of parental authority" (*e.g.*, disciplining or supervising a child) or the exercise of "ordinary parental discretion with respect to the care and necessities of the child" that a parent is obligated to furnish. *See* Jilani v. Jilani, 767 S.W.2d 671, 672–73 (Tex. 1988); Felderhoff v. Felderhoff, 473 S.W.2d 928, 933 (Tex. 1971)....

... [T]he modern justification for parental immunity in Texas is stated in terms of preventing the disruption or distortion of parental decision-making within the "wide sphere of reasonable discretion which is necessary ... to provide nurture, care, and discipline for their children" that would otherwise result from the imposition of the negligence "reasonably prudent person" standard of conduct and its attendant economic incentives and disincentives.... As the Texas Supreme Court explained in *Felderhoff*, in rejecting calls to discard parental immunity as "out of date":

> We trust that it is not out of date for the state and its courts to be concerned with the welfare of the family as the most vital unit in our society.... Harmonious family relationships depend on filial and parental love and respect which can neither be created nor preserved by legislatures or courts. The most we can do is to prevent the judicial system from being used to disrupt the wide sphere of reasonable discretion which is necessary in order for parents to properly exercise their responsibility to provide nurture, care, and discipline for their children. These parental duties, which usually include the provision of a home, food, schooling, family chores, medical care, and recreation, could be seriously impaired and retarded if parents were to be held liable to lawsuits by their unemancipated minor children for unintentional errors or ordinary negligence occurring while in the discharge of such parental duties and responsibilities....

.... Relatedly, the parental-immunity defense also reflects a goal of avoiding judicial entanglement with or second-guessing of the myriad religious, cultural, and other personal considerations that come to bear on one's judgments when exercising parental responsibilities....

The elements of the parental-immunity affirmative defense are: (1) the injured party is an unemancipated minor; (2) the defendant is the minor's parent; (3) the minor's alleged injury is a personal injury; (4) the claim is based on the defendant's alleged negligence; and (5) the minor's alleged injury arises from the defendant's "reasonable exercise of parental authority," such as disciplining or supervising a child, or the parent's exercise of "ordinary parental discretion with respect to provisions for the care and necessities of the child" that the parent was required to provide.... Thus, parental immunity does not bar claims predicated on legal duties other than negligence duties, such as contract or property rights.... Similarly, it does not limit the State's enforcement of statutory protections of children, such as those provided under the penal code or family code, or bar suits for intentional torts committed by a parent against his child.... Additionally, the Texas Supreme Court has recognized two "exceptions" to parental immunity permitting child-parent negligence claims for acts and omissions arising from activities it has distinguished from the "essentially parental" acts and decisions that parental immunity is intended to protect: (1) acts "outside a normal family relationship," such as an employer-employee relationship between the parent and child,... and (2) the parent's operation of a motor vehicle....

... [The court cited Texas cases where parental immunity barred negligence claims involving supervision of children who drowned, were left in a room with a loaded gun, or were entrusted with a motor scooter without instructions or a helmet, and where a mother decided to live with her children in an unsecured mobile home "during thunderstorm season" and to remain there with the children when a storm threatened).]

In support of his summary-judgment motion, LaGrone presented evidence that: (1) Frank was an unemancipated minor when he died; (2) LaGrone was Frank's father; (3) Frank died from personal injuries he received in the fire; (4) Sepaugh's claims are based on the allegation that LaGrone's negligence caused Frank's injuries and death; and (5) at the time of the fire, Frank was staying with LaGrone pursuant to the visitation schedule set forth in LaGrone's divorce decree with Sepaugh, during which time the decree required LaGrone to comply with the "duty of care, control, protection, and reasonable discipline" and "duty to provide [Frank] with clothing, food, and shelter." .... Regarding the fifth and last element ... LaGrone contended that his evidence established that Frank's death arose from LaGrone's exercise of parental discretion in providing the child a home and shelter, as he was legally obligated to do during the visitation period.

In response, Sepaugh ... joined issue as to the final element, disputing whether, as a matter of law, Frank's death should be considered to have arisen from LaGrone's exercise of parental discretion in providing Frank a home during the visitation period. Whatever discretion LaGrone possessed in regard to providing Frank a home, Sepaugh urged, was limited by City of Austin ordinances governing smoke detectors in residences. Specifically, Sepaugh referenced provisions of the 1997 Uniform Fire Code that the City had adopted in April 2000 and which were in effect at the time of the fire.... The 1997 Uniform Fire Code provides that existing "dwelling units ... shall be provided with smoke detectors." .... It further requires that "[d]etectors shall sound an alarm audible in all sleeping areas of the dwelling unit where they are located." .... Sepaugh maintained that LaGrone had no discretion, parental or otherwise, to fail to provide or maintain smoke detectors complying with these ordinances....

.... In her briefing, Sepaugh frequently phrases her argument in terms of the fact that she is alleging LaGrone was negligent *per se* in violating the ordinances. To the extent that Sepaugh is suggesting that an allegation of negligence *per se* in itself precludes the application of parental immunity, we reject that notion. Negligence *per se* merely refers to the judicial adoption of a legislatively defined standard of conduct as defining the reasonably prudent person's standard of care.... Consequently, even assuming that negligence *per se* applies here such that the ordinances supply LaGrone's standard of care for purposes of negligence liability, ... parental immunity, if otherwise applicable, would still bar Sepaugh's negligence claims.... What matters instead is whether, as Sepaugh suggests, the Austin smoke-alarm ordinances have the legal effect of reducing the scope of LaGrone's "discretion" in a manner relevant to his parental-immunity defense. We disagree that the ordinances have this effect for two related reasons.

First, regardless of how Sepaugh couches her allegations, it remains that she complains about where and how LaGrone provided a home and shelter for Frank during the child's Christmastime visitation. LaGrone's decision to allow Frank to stay in his house is the sort of "essentially parental" judgment that parental immunity protects. . . . This is so regardless of the existence of any code violations in his house that LaGrone allegedly knew or should have known about. LaGrone's decision that Frank would stay in the house is akin to a parent's opting to stay with his child in a hotel, to take the child camping in the woods, or to allow the child to spend the night at a friend's house—any of which have the potential to expose the child to premises defects or other hazards at that location. . . .

Second, we conclude that Texas precedent does not support Sepaugh's argument. . . . In asserting that the ordinances limit LaGrone's "discretion" in a manner relevant to the parental-immunity defense, Sepaugh relies primarily on language in *Jilani*. . . . In *Jilani*, a mother filed a personal-injury suit on behalf of her three unemancipated minor children seeking damages arising from an automobile accident allegedly caused by their father's (the driver's) negligence. The father obtained summary judgment based on parental immunity, which the court of appeals affirmed. The supreme court reversed. It reasoned that the mother's claims implicated not the "reasonable exercise of parental authority or the exercise of ordinary parental discretion" protected by parental immunity, but the "general obligation the law imposes upon every driver of an automobile . . . an activity not essentially parental." . . . . This was so, the court further held, even though the family had been traveling on vacation and *Felderhoff* had suggested that "recreation" was one of the several parental duties that ordinarily should be beyond the judicial sphere. . . . "Regardless of the purpose of the automobile excursion," according to the *Jilani* court, "this case does not involve the 'reasonable exercise of parental authority or the exercise of parental discretion' as envisioned in *Felderhoff*." *Jilani*, 767 S.W.2d at 673.

Sepaugh views *Jilani* as standing for a general principle that the scope of parental discretion and immunity is limited by "general" statutory or regulatory obligations with which a parent, like other persons, must comply. Consequently, she reasons, LaGrone's parental discretion is limited by Austin city ordinances governing smoke alarms in residences. We disagree that *Jilani* extends so broadly. The *Jilani* court, while perceiving that child-parent automobile negligence claims would not "threaten 'parental authority or discipline' nor . . . risk substituting judicial discretion for parental discretion in the care and rearing of minor children," id., took pains to emphasize that "[o]ur holding today is limited to the facts before us: an automobile tort action brought by an unemancipated minor child against a parent." *Id.*

To date, neither the Texas Supreme Court nor lower Texas courts have extended *Jilani's* rationale beyond the narrow facts to which it was addressed, much less applied it as expansively as Sepaugh proposes. Sepaugh's argument that LaGrone's parental discretion and immunity is limited by the Austin smoke-detector ordinances would seemingly imply that every other conceivable local or municipal regulatory prohibition or requirement—building codes, environmental regulations, watering restrictions, etc.—would have the same effect.[2] Stated another way, it would imply that the Texas Supreme Court in *Jilani* effectively ceded control of future development of common-law negligence principles and their application to parenting decisions to whatever governmental bodies might enact some form of "mandatory" restrictions or regulations. We find no support for that notion in *Jilani* or other Texas precedents addressing parental immunity. It is also inconsistent with the supreme court's view of legislative conduct standards as a basis for negligence liability that is reflected in its application of negligence *per se*. In that context, the court has not categorically adopted or deferred to legislative conduct standards, but engaged in a careful, multi-factor analysis of whether the common law should incorporate those standards as a basis for negligence liability....

Nor do we believe that *Jilani* 's rationale, or the similar reasoning employed in *Felderhoff* regarding parent-child employment relationships, would extend to Sepaugh's complaint regarding the smoke alarms in LaGrone's house.... A complaint that a parent is a bad driver or bad employer, by contrast, has a more attenuated relationship to parental immunity's underlying judicial policies....

Through her argument concerning the Austin smoke-detector ordinances, Sepaugh ultimately advocates a significant expansion of negligence liability for parenting decisions in Texas. We are not at liberty to change Texas law in this manner....

... [W]e affirm the district court's judgment.

[WALDROP, J., concurred.]

J. WOODFIN JONES, Chief Justice, dissenting.

I respectfully dissent.

.... Sepaugh's claims ... are directed specifically to LaGrone's alleged failure to provide a functioning smoke-detection system in the house, as required by City of Austin Ordinance No. 000406-78 (April 6, 2000). A violation of this ordinance is punishable by a fine of up to $2,000, ... and thus is criminal in nature. LaGrone had no discretion, parental or otherwise, to ignore or fail to comply with requirements of the City's ordinance.

The parental-immunity doctrine has been the subject of much recent criticism.... Indeed, as of 2001, eleven states had abrogated the doctrine completely. *See* Herzfeld v. Herzfeld, 781 So.2d 1070, 1073–74 (Fla. 2001). But I am not arguing for that result. I believe the law established by the supreme court in *Felderhoff* and *Jilani* easily supports a refusal to apply the doctrine in the present case. This case is not about a parent negligently allowing his child to engage in illegal or dangerous activity. It is about a parent allegedly violating a mandatory ordinance, which led to the

2. [Fn. 8:] *E.g.*, a personal-injury negligence claim arising from a child's slip-and-fall on a sidewalk made wet by a parent's sprinkler system seemingly could be pled to circumvent parental immunity if couched in terms of the parent's violation of city watering restrictions.

death of the child. The City's criminalization of the act underlying Sepaugh's negligence claim removes any discretionary aspect of LaGrone's conduct.

....

[The appellant filed a motion for reconsideration en banc, which was denied.]

DIANE M. HENSON, Justice, dissenting.

.... The bounds of public policy in protecting parental decision-making should not be stretched to the point that a parent's failure to comply with a city ordinance requiring functioning smoke alarms in a home — an act of negligence endangering not the just the parent's own child but the public at large — is considered the reasonable exercise of ordinary parental discretion and authority.

... I respectfully dissent from the denial of the motion for en banc consideration.

Notes

1. ***Related Material.*** *See generally* Irene Hansen Saba, *Parental Immunity from Liability in Tort: Evolution of a Doctrine in Tennessee*, 36 U. Mem. L. Rev. 829, 849–50 (2006) (describing five categories reflecting the approaches states take to the issue of parental tort liability).

2. ***Aggravated Misconduct.*** In states which have not rejected parental immunity entirely, the trend is to permit actions based on wilful misconduct, even if ordinary negligence is not actionable. *See, e.g.*, Herzfeld v. Herzfeld, 781 So. 2d 1070 (Fla. 2001) (parental immunity does not apply to intentional sexual torts); Doe v. Holt, 418 S.E.2d 511 (N.C. 1992) (actions for rape and sexual molestation are not barred); McGee v. McGee, 936 S.W.2d 360 (Tex. App. 1996) (parental immunity does not preclude actions for intentional or malicious acts, but protects a stepfather from liability for negligently providing alcohol and objectionable materials to a stepson).

3. ***Motor-Vehicle Accidents.*** More than 30 jurisdictions allow a child to sue a parent for negligent driving. The courts have typically reasoned that, since operation of a car is not an act of parental authority or discretion, permitting suit will not interfere with the complex task of providing guidance to a child. Also, the likely presence of automobile insurance reduces the chances that litigation will produce intra-family strife. *See* Md. Code, Courts and Judicial Proceedings, § 5-806(b) (Westlaw 2022) ("The right of action ... by a child or the estate of a child against a parent of the child, for wrongful death, personal injury, or property damage arising out of the operation of a motor vehicle ... may not be restricted by the doctrine of parent-child immunity or by any insurance policy provisions, up to the limits of motor vehicle liability coverage or uninsured motor vehicle coverage").

4. ***Lack of a Significant Parent-Child Relationship.*** In Greenwood v. Anderson, 324 S.W.3d 324, 326–27 (Ark. 2009), the court declined to adopt a proposed exception to parental immunity. As the court explained:

> [A]ppellants urge this court to create a new exception ... in cases where the policies supporting the doctrine will not be advanced because there

> has been no significant relationship developed between the child and the parent-defendant. . . . In this case, appellants contend that appellee was a parent in "only the loosest sense" because he failed to provide significant financial support for the child and spent little of his available time with the child. Appellants' deposition . . . explained that the baby was born on July 17, 2006; appellee left for active duty in the United States Marine Corp on or about August 9, 2006; appellee spent the "majority" of his free time while on leave in November and December with his friends and not the baby; and appellee contributed a total of $100 to the support of the baby. In such a situation, appellants argue, there is no domestic harmony or family tranquility to protect because there was no real "family unit" in existence. . . .
>
> Under appellants' proposed exception, however, every case would require an inquiry into the allegedly negligent parent's relationship with the child to determine whether that relationship is "sufficient" to allow that parent immunity. We find such an approach to be highly subjective and ultimately undesirable. We also note that other jurisdictions have declined to adopt such an approach. . . .

3. Sibling Immunity

Lickteig v. Kolar

Supreme Court of Minnesota
782 N.W.2d 810 (Minn. 2010)

MAGNUSON, Chief Justice.

Appellant Mary Lickteig sued her brother, appellee Robert Kolar, Jr., in the United States District Court for the District of Minnesota for sexual abuse and battery allegedly committed during their childhood, between approximately 1974 and 1977. . . .

Lickteig and Kolar are biological siblings. . . . Lickteig alleged that Kolar sexually abused her for several years. . . . Lickteig also alleged that Kolar sexually abused, raped, and assaulted her older sisters while she was in the same room. Kolar admitted that he sexually abused two of his sisters, but denied Lickteig's allegations against him. . . .

Lickteig sued Kolar in 2007 in federal district court. . . .

. . . . The court concluded that Lickteig did not state a cause of action after determining that . . . the doctrine of intrafamilial immunity barred the action.

. . . . Lickteig appealed to the United States Court of Appeals for the Eighth Circuit, and the Eighth Circuit certified to this court the . . . questions before us. . . .

The second question presented is whether the doctrine of intrafamilial immunity applies to this action between emancipated adult siblings, now living in separate households, where the sexual abuse occurred when both were unemancipated minors living in the same household. . . . [N]o Minnesota appellate court has answered the questions of whether siblings are immune from suits between them or whether the traditional concerns supporting the doctrine apply to claims such as these.

We have addressed the doctrine of intrafamilial immunity in other contexts. We have found unpersuasive the justifications of avoiding disruption of family peace and the proliferation of litigation, and we have abrogated some categories of intrafamilial immunity. See, e.g., Anderson v. Stream, 295 N.W.2d 595, 601 (Minn. 1980) (abrogating parental immunity); Beaudette v. Frana, 285 Minn. 366, 373, 173 N.W.2d 416, 420 (1969) (abrogating interspousal immunity); Balts v. Balts, 273 Minn. 419, 430, 433, 142 N.W.2d 66, 73, 75 (1966) (rejecting immunity for a child in a suit brought by a parent, concluding that "public policy . . . requires that the wrong be righted within the family group by suit or settlement"). In Silesky v. Kelman, we stated, albeit in dictum, that "[s]uits are permitted among unemancipated siblings even though they remain in the [same] family household[,]" citing a Connecticut Supreme Court case that held that no immunity existed between unemancipated minor siblings for a suit involving negligent operation of an automobile. 281 Minn. 431, 435–36, 161 N.W.2d 631, 634 (1968). . . .

The general rule is that the doctrine of intrafamilial immunity does not apply to suits between siblings. The Restatement of Torts, often cited by jurisdictions that have addressed the issue, provides

> [n]one of the justifications that have been advanced in the past for the immunity from tort liability between parent and child . . . has been regarded by any court as sufficient to justify extension of the immunity to other relations of kinship. . . . Thus a brother has no immunity toward his sister.

Restatement (Second) of Torts § 895H cmt. c (1979). Courts that have reached the issue have uniformly rejected extending the doctrine of intrafamilial immunity to actions between unemancipated siblings. . . .

These courts have generally rejected the policy justifications for immunity between siblings, including the concept of family harmony:

> An uncompensated tort is no more apt to promote or preserve peace in the family than is an action between minor brother and sister to recover damages for that tort. Furthermore, the relationship between brother and sister is not complicated by reciprocal rights and obligations of the kind that characterize the relationships of husband and wife and parent and child and that lend some support to the immunities from tort liability that have been recognized in such cases.

Emery, 289 P.2d at 224. In Midkiff v. Midkiff, 201 Va. 829, 113 S.E.2d 875, 877 (1960), the Supreme Court of Virginia rejected policy concerns of family peace as a reason to bar a tort action between siblings because, unlike the husband and wife relationship, there is "no historical or fictional background of legal unity or oneness[,]" nor was the concern of parental discipline and support in the parent/child immunity context present. The Virginia court held that the public policy of family peace does not provide immunity to siblings when they commit torts against each other. . . .

In light of our abrogation of immunity in all other familial contexts, we will not now extend immunity to emancipated siblings where no other court has done so. . . . We hold that the doctrine of intrafamilial immunity does not apply between siblings for a battery tort based on sexual abuse committed when both were unemancipated minors. Therefore, we answer the certified question in the negative.

. . . .

B. Sovereign Immunity and Governmental Immunity

It is useful to be precise in discussing the immunity of governmental entities. The United States of America and the fifty States are sovereigns; local governmental entities are not. For example, municipalities cannot adopt rules of tort liability for themselves or for anyone else. *Cf.* Michigan Coalition for Responsible Gun Owners v. City of Ferndale, 662 N.W.2d 864 (Mich. App. 2003) (holding that a city could not enact and enforce ordinances that made local public buildings gun-free zones).

"Sovereign" Versus "Governmental Immunity." It is important to differentiate the "sovereign immunity" of the federal or state governments from the "governmental immunity" of local governmental entities. *See* City of San Antonio ex rel. City Pub. Serv. Bd. v. Wheelabrator Air Pollution Control, Inc., 381 S.W.3d 597 (Tex. App. 2012) ("Sovereign immunity protects the State, as well as its agencies and officials, from lawsuits for damages and from liability. . . . 'The appurtenant common-law doctrine of governmental immunity similarly protects political subdivisions of the State, including counties, cities, and school districts'"). However, the development of these two different types of immunity (sovereign and governmental) has been confusingly intertwined, and the terms are sometimes used imprecisely.

As explained in Holytz v. City of Milwaukee, 115 N.W.2d 618 (Wis. 1962):

> The rule of sovereign immunity developed . . . from an English doctrine and has been applied in the United States far beyond its original conception. The doctrine expanded to the point where the historical sovereignty of kings was relied upon to support a protective prerogative for municipalities. This, according to Professor Borchard, "is one of the mysteries of legal evolution." . . . . It would seem somewhat anomalous that American courts should have adopted the sovereign immunity theory in the first place since it was based upon the divine right of kings.

The following material focuses first on the immunity of government entities at the federal, state, and local levels, and then on the immunity of government actors (officials and employees) at those same levels.

1. The Federal Tort Claims Act

Negligence May Be Actionable. The Federal Tort Claims Act, now codified in 28 U.S.C.A. §§1346-2680 and in other scattered provisions of the United States Code, defines the extent to which the federal government is liable for its torts. In general, the federal government may be liable "for injury or loss of property, or personal injury or death caused by the negligent or wrongful act or omission of any employee of the Government while acting within the scope of his office or employment, under circumstances where the United States, if a private person, would be liable to the claimant in accordance with the law of the place where the act or omission occurred." 28 U.S.C.A.§1346(b)(1) (Westlaw 2022).

Special Limitations. However, the federal government cannot be sued in state courts, and a jury trial is not available to FTCA claimants. Punitive damages are not allowed. Also, the federal government may not obtain indemnity from an employee when it is liable under the FTCA. *See* U.S. v. Gilman, 347 U.S. 507 (1954). A plaintiff under the FTCA must exhaust administrative remedies, which normally involves presenting a claim to an administrative agency and allowing the agency six months to investigate and render a decision. The FTCA statute of limitations is two years, but a lawsuit must be brought within six-months if an agency denies a claim in writing (rather than allows the claim to languish or renders an oral decision). The amount claimed in the request for administrative relief is the maximum that may be awarded in federal court, unless there is newly discovered evidence that was not available at the time of the administrative claim.

Immunity Applies to Many Intentional Torts. The FTCA contains many exceptions to the waiver of sovereign immunity, some of them explicit, others derived largely from case law. *See* Laurie Higginbotham and Jamal Alsaffar, Navigating the Federal Tort Claims Act, Trial, Oct. 2011, at 14. Generally speaking, the federal government is not liable for intentional torts (assault, battery, false imprisonment, false arrest, malicious prosecution, abuse of process, libel, slander, misrepresentation, deceit, and interference with contract rights), or for torts committed in the course of various governmental functions, such as collecting taxes.

Discretionary-Function Exception to Federal Tort Liability. A broad exception to the FTCA waiver of Federal sovereign immunity is the "discretionary function" exception found in 28 U.S.C.A. §2680(a) (Westlaw 2022). The idea here is that policy-making is not to be challenged in the courts on the ground that the policy in question was "unreasonable"; compare the "public-duty rule" discussed in Chapter 9.

The discretionary-function exception generally covers administrative decisions, regulatory conduct, the design and execution of public works, and other judgmental matters. *See* Monzon v. U.S., 253 F.3d 567 (11th Cir. 2001) (failure to warn individual visitors of the danger of rip currents in the surf near a beach adjacent to a national monument was within the discretionary-function exception). However, the exception does not bar ordinary negligence claims, such as those related to auto accidents or medical malpractice.

In considering the reach of this exception, it is important to differentiate the making of a decision from carrying it out. In Indian Towing Co. v. U.S., 350 U.S. 61, 69 (1955), the court wrote:

> The Coast Guard need not undertake the lighthouse service. But once it exercised its discretion to operate a light . . . , it was obligated to use due care to make certain that the light was kept in good working order. . . . If the Coast Guard failed in its duty and damage was thereby caused . . . , the United States is liable under the [FTCA].

In O'Toole v. U.S., 295 F.3d 1029 (9th Cir. 2002), ranch owners claimed they were being harmed by the Bureau of Indian Affairs's negligent maintenance of irrigation canals downstream. The court said:

> The danger that the discretionary function exception will swallow the FTCA is especially great where the government takes on the role of a private landowner. . . . Every slip and fall, every failure to warn, every inspection and maintenance decision can be couched in terms of policy choices based on allocation of limited resources. As we have noted before in the discretionary function exception context, "[b]udgetary constraints underlie virtually all governmental activity." . . . . Were we to view inadequate funding alone as sufficient to garner the protection of the discretionary function exception, we would read the rule too narrowly and the exception too broadly. Instead, in order to effectuate Congress's intent to compensate individuals harmed by government negligence, the FTCA, as a remedial statute, should be construed liberally, and its exceptions should be read narrowly.

The Feres Doctrine and Active-Duty Military. The *Feres* doctrine bars tort actions involving injuries to active-duty military personnel, and their families, even during peacetime. *See* Feres v. United States, 340 U.S. 135 (1950). However, it does not preclude military-related suits against the government when the injured plaintiff is a civilian.

The history and policy basis of the *Feres* doctrine are discussed by Judge Guido Calabresi in Taber v. Maine, 67 F.3d 1029 (2d Cir. 1995). *Taber* was an off-duty serviceman's action against the federal government based on injuries sustained in an automobile accident with another off-duty serviceman who had been drinking on base. The action was not barred by the *Feres* doctrine because the plaintiff's military status was not sufficiently connected to activity in which he was injured.

2. State Tort Claims Acts

State Tort Claims Acts. Any brief description of the extent to which states have waived sovereign immunity would be quite misleading. The subject is largely statutory, and so variations among jurisdictions are wide.

Some states, such as Pennsylvania, have waived sovereign immunity only in a very narrow range of circumstances. *See* 42 Pa. Consol. Stat. Ann. § 8522 (Westlaw 2022) (listing exceptions to sovereign immunity relating to vehicle liability; professional-medical liability; care, custody or control of personal property; Commonwealth real estate, highways, and sidewalks; potholes and other dangerous conditions; care, custody or control of animals; liquor store sales; national guard activities; and toxoids and vaccines). "Because there is no general provision allowing for a negligence action, plaintiffs would be barred from recovering from a Pennsylvania state college or university based on campus violence." *See* Brett A. Sokolow, *et al.*, *College and University Liability for Violent Campus Attacks*, 34 J.C. & U.L. 319, 339 (2008) (comparing sovereign immunity in Pennsylvania, California, Virginia, and Minnesota).

Discretionary Function Exception. State discretionary functions are normally immune from liability. *See* State Dept. of Corrections v. Cowles, 151 P.3d 353 (Alaska 2006) (establishment of parole conditions); Harrison v. Hardin Cty. Comm. Unit Sch. Dist., 758 N.E.2d 848 (Ill. 2001) (a decision to deny a student's request for early dismissal and tell him to wait for the entire school to be dismissed early because of inclement weather); Texas Dept. of Transp. v. Ramirez, 74 S.W.3d 864 (Tex. 2002) (a roadway median's slope and lack of safety features, such as guardrails); *but see* Texas Dept. of Transp. v. Garrison, 121 S.W.3d 808 (Tex. App. 2003) (stating "once a governmental unit decides to install a particular traffic signal, that decision must be implemented within a reasonable time . . . [and the] implementation of . . . [that] policy decision, unlike the actual decision making, is nondiscretionary").

In New Jersey, a statute provides:

Discretionary Activities

New Jersey Statutes Annotated § 59:2-3 (Westlaw 2022)

> a. A public entity is not liable for an injury resulting from the exercise of judgment or discretion vested in the entity;
>
> b. A public entity is not liable for legislative or judicial action or inaction, or administrative action or inaction of a legislative or judicial nature;
>
> c. A public entity is not liable for the exercise of discretion in determining whether to seek or whether to provide the resources necessary for the purchase of equipment, the construction or maintenance of facilities, the hiring of personnel and, in general, the provision of adequate governmental services;
>
> d. A public entity is not liable for the exercise of discretion when, in the face of competing demands, it determines whether and how to utilize or apply existing resources, including those allocated for equipment, facilities and personnel unless a court concludes that the determination of the public entity was palpably unreasonable. Nothing in this section shall exonerate a public entity for negligence arising out of acts or omissions of its employees in carrying out their ministerial functions.

Under § 59:2-3(d), it is for the jury to determine whether an activity is ministerial, rather than discretionary. *See* Henebema v. Raddi, 2017 WL 6028513, at *2 (N.J. Super. App. Div.).

Notice-of-Claim Requirements. Suits against the government must often comply with strict notice-of-claim requirements. *See, e.g.*, Fairview Ritz Corp. v. Borough of Fairview, 2013 WL 5946986, at *10 (D.N.J.) (holding that trespass and invasion of privacy claims were barred by the New Jersey Tort Claims Act, which provides that the claimant "must file a notice of claim with the entity within ninety days of the accrual of the claim").

Constitutional Restriction. The Eleventh Amendment immunizes states from suit in federal court by United States or foreign citizens.

3. Governmental Immunity of Local Entities

a. Historical Development

As explained by the Supreme Court of Wisconsin in *Holytz v. City of Milwaukee*, 115 N.W.2d 618 (Wis. 1962):

> The concept of municipal immunity from tort claims stems from the English case of Russell v. The Men of Devon (1788), 2 T.R. 667, 100 Eng. Rep. 359. That was a case in which an unincorporated county was relieved of liability for damages which were occasioned by the disrepair of a bridge. One of the grounds advanced in the *Men of Devon* case was that immunity was necessary because the community was an unincorporated one and did not have funds to pay for damages. A second reason advanced was "that it is better that an individual should sustain an injury than that the public should suffer an inconvenience." 100 Eng. Rep., p. 362....
>
> The first case in the United States which adopted the doctrine of the *Men of Devon* case was Mower v. Leicester (1812), 9 Mass. 247, in which immunity was granted even though the county was a corporation and had corporate funds....
>
> The rules surrounding municipal tort immunity have resulted in some highly artificial judicial distinctions. For example, the municipality may be immune or liable depending upon whether we determine that the particular function involved is "proprietary" or "governmental." Our court held in Christian v. New London (1940), 234 Wis. 123, 290 N.W. 621, that a live wire which carried electricity from a municipal electrical utility to a municipal street light was maintained by the city in a proprietary capacity, but a municipal waterworks which supplied water to be used for firefighting was operating in a governmental capacity. Highway Trailer Co. v. Janesville Electric Co. (1925), 187 Wis. 161, 204 N.W. 773. The operation of a municipal hospital, although generally a proprietary activity, may have some of its operations classed as governmental....
>
> There are probably few tenets of American jurisprudence which have been so unanimously berated as the governmental immunity doctrine....

> .... It is almost incredible that in this modern age of comparative sociological enlightenment, and in a republic, the medieval absolutism supposed to be implicit in the maxim, "the King can do no wrong," should exempt the various branches of the government from liability for their torts, and that the entire burden of damage resulting from the wrongful acts of the government should be imposed upon the single individual who suffers the injury, rather than distributed among the entire community constituting the government, where it could be borne without hardship upon any individual, and where it justly belongs....
>
> The immunization of municipalities from tort liability has been chipped away by a number of statutes in this state.... [Citing statutes relating to motor vehicle accidents, judgments against public officers, and highway defects.]
>
> Also, the judiciary has engrafted exceptions on the rule of municipal immunity from tort claims. Municipalities are responsible for negligence occurring in the operation of their proprietary activities.... Municipalities are also responsible for nuisance whether acting in a governmental or proprietary capacity, as long as the municipality and the injured party did not stand in the relationship of governor to governed....
>
> Furthermore, municipalities are responsible for an "attractive nuisance" created in the exercise of a proprietary activity....

Despairing at this confusing state of affairs, the *Holytz* court abolished sovereign and governmental immunity entirely, except for "legislative or judicial or quasi-legislative or quasi-judicial functions," noting that "[i]f the legislature deems it better public policy, it is, of course, free to reinstate immunity." The court explained the broad reach of its decision:

> The case at bar relates specifically to a city; however, we consider that abrogation of the doctrine applies to all public bodies within the state: the state, counties, cities, villages, towns, school districts, sewer districts, drainage districts, and any other political subdivisions of the state....

In response to the *Holytz* decision, the Wisconsin legislature promptly codified the immunity of the state's governmental entities. *See* Javier v. City of Milwaukee, 670 F.3d 823, 828 n.4 (7th Cir. 2012).

b. Local Government Immunity Today

Immunity is Presumed. Today, the governmental immunity of local entities is controlled mainly by state statutes. Thus, a Texas case explained:

> Political subdivisions of the State, such as the City of San Antonio, have governmental immunity from suit unless the Legislature has expressly waived such immunity by statute.... A statute shall not be construed as

> waiving immunity unless the waiver is effected by "clear and unambiguous" language. . . . It has long been recognized that it is the Legislature's sole province to waive immunity from suit. . . . On the other hand, a political subdivision may waive its immunity from liability by entering into a contract with a private party. . . . Only immunity from suit operates as a jurisdictional bar; immunity from liability constitutes an affirmative defense. . . .

City of San Antonio v. Wheelabrator Air Pollution Control, Inc., 381 S.W.3d 597, 601 (Tex. App. 2012).

Damage Caps. Damages against a local governmental entity are sometimes capped by state law. *See* John Tedesco, Damage Claims Hit City One a Day, San Antonio Express-News, Apr. 1, 2012, at A1("[e]ven in cases . . . when a city employee is found to be speeding . . . [a]ccident victims can receive a maximum of $250,000 apiece, no matter how badly they are injured"). Such laws greatly limit governmental liability. In a 12-year period (2000-12), the city of San Antonio, Texas, paid out less than a total of $15.3 million to resolve 5,354 claims stemming from vehicle accidents. *Id.*

Section 1983 Constitutional Torts. A well-known civil rights statute, 42 U.S.C. § 1983 (Westlaw 2022), exposes individual state and local officials acting "under color of" state law to liability for depriving a citizen of federal constitutional or statutory rights. States are immune from suit under § 1983 (*see* Will v. Michigan Dept. of State Police, 491 U.S. 58, 71 (1989)), but municipalities are subject to liability for federal violations if a municipal employee was carrying out an "official policy" or custom of the municipality (*see* Monell v. Department of Soc. Servs., 436 U.S. 658, 663, 690–91 (1978)).

Complexity Reigns. The law on governmental immunity tends to be exceedingly complex. Elusive distinctions abound, inconsistent treatment is commonplace, and arbitrary caps often hurt those who were the most seriously injured. Victims of the tortious conduct of local governmental actors are many times left uncompensated or undercompensated. Potential incentives for safety are ignored. Individuals are sometimes forced to bear costs that should more properly be borne by the citizenry as a whole.

If there is anything to be said for this messy, unsatisfying state of affairs, it is that it provides plenty of work for lawyers. But even that has a downside: the law is so complex that there is an increased risk of committing the type of error that may result in a legal malpractice claim. The handling of governmental liability claims is not for amateurs. Only those who are or intend to become experts in the relevant principles should venture into these legal thickets, which, as the following case illustrates, sometimes involve federal law and constitutional issues, as well as state law.

Parker v. St. Lawrence County Public Health Department

Supreme Court of New York, Appellate Division
954 N.Y.S.2d 259 (App. Div. 2012)

PETERS, P.J.

. . . .

The federal Public Readiness and Emergency Preparedness Act (hereinafter PREP Act) . . . authorizes the Secretary of Health and Human Services to take such action as necessary to respond to a public health emergency. . . . In 2009, in response to an outbreak of the H1N1 influenza virus, the Secretary determined that a public health emergency existed and issued declarations recommending the administration of the influenza antiviral vaccination Peramivir. . . . In response, then Governor Paterson issued an executive order declaring a disaster emergency with respect to the influenza outbreak, which authorized state and local health departments to establish immunization programs. . . .

. . . St. Lawrence County Public Health Department (hereinafter defendant) held a vaccination clinic at defendant Lisbon Central School. . . . Although plaintiff did not execute a parental consent form authorizing the inoculation of her daughter, then a kindergartner, a nurse employed by defendant nonetheless administered a vaccination to the child. Accordingly, plaintiff commenced this action alleging that the administration of the inoculation without consent constituted negligence and resulted in a battery upon her daughter. Defendant moved to dismiss the complaint against it for lack of subject matter jurisdiction on the ground of federal preemption. Supreme Court . . . denied the motion. This appeal by defendant ensued.

. . . .

In determining whether a federal law preempts a state law cause of action, the determinative inquiry is "Congress' intent in enacting the federal statute at issue". . . . Federal preemption "may be either express or implied. . . . Where, as here, a federal law contains an express preemption clause, "[the] 'focus [is] on the plain wording of the clause, which necessarily contains the best evidence of Congress' preemptive intent'". . . .

The preemption clause of the PREP Act provides that, during the effective period of a declaration of a public health emergency, "no State . . . may establish, enforce, or continue in effect with respect to a covered countermeasure any provision of law or legal requirement that (A) is different from, or is in conflict with, any requirement applicable under this section; and (B) relates to the . . . use, . . . dispensing, or administration by qualified persons of the covered countermeasure". . . . In the context of preemption, "[a]bsent other indication, reference to a State's 'requirements' includes its common-law duties". . . . In other words, "[s]ince State regulations can be as effectively exerted through an award of damages as through some form of preventive relief, State common-law tort claims may be preempted along with State statutes and regulations". . . .

... [The PREP Act] provides that "a covered person shall be immune from suit and liability under Federal and State law with respect to all claims for loss caused by, arising out of, relating to, or resulting from the administration to ... an individual of a covered countermeasure".... The "sole exception" to immunity from suit and liability is a federal action for "death or serious physical injury proximately caused by willful misconduct"....[3]

Considering the breadth of the preemption clause together with the sweeping language of the statute's immunity provision, we conclude that Congress intended to preempt all state law tort claims arising from the administration of covered countermeasures by a qualified person pursuant to a declaration by the Secretary, including one based upon a defendant's failure to obtain consent.... Notably, Congress created an alternative administrative remedy—the Countermeasures Injury Compensation Program—for covered injuries stemming from countermeasures taken in response to the declaration of a public health emergency...,[4] as well as a separate federal cause of action for wrongful death or serious physical injury caused by the willful misconduct of covered individuals or entities.... The provision of these exclusive federal remedies further supports our finding of preemption.

.... Plaintiff... asserts that Congress could not have intended to immunize such "radical measures" as administering a vaccination without consent. It is not our role, however, to speculate upon congressional judgments. Rather, we must presume that Congress fully understood that errors in administering a vaccination program may have physical as well as emotional consequences, and determined that such potential tort liability must give way to the need to promptly and efficiently respond to a pandemic or other public health emergency.

... [W]e conclude that plaintiff's state law claims for negligence and battery are preempted by the PREP Act and, inasmuch as the exclusive remedy under the statute is a federal cause of action to be brought in federal court, the complaint must be dismissed for lack of subject matter jurisdiction....

C. Official Immunity

Sovereign immunity and governmental immunity protect *governmental entities* from liability, but it does not shield government officials and employees from liability for their torts, even when they act in furtherance of their duties. Not surprisingly, immunities for various kinds of officials have been developed. Governments

3. [Fn. 4:] Here, there is no dispute concerning whether defendant is a "covered person".... Furthermore, as the complaint seeks damages for unspecified physical and mental injuries suffered by plaintiff's daughter as a result of the administration of the 2009 H1N1 influenza virus vaccine, plaintiff's claim for loss clearly arises out of, and has a causal relationship with, the administration of a covered countermeasure....

4. [Fn. 5:] "'[C]overed injury' means serious physical injury or death"....

could not function if judges could be sued for "negligent" decisions, or if legislators were liable for "unreasonable" votes.

Generally speaking, the more discretion an official or employee has, the more "absolute" that employee's immunity, with judges at the top of the scale. But there are always limits; a judge who sanctions contempt of court by shooting the offender dead will, one supposes, be liable to the decedent's survivors, probably on the ground that the judge's act was not "judicial" in nature. Powerful public employee associations may have the political clout to lobby for broad protection, even for those who perform mainly ministerial duties and exercise little or no discretion.

1. Federal Officials and Employees

Barr v. Matteo, 360 U.S. 564 (1959), was a libel action based on a press release. The suit was commenced by government employees against the acting director of the Office of Rent Stabilization. In a plurality decision, the Supreme Court held that the acting director was absolutely immune from liability. Writing for the plurality, Justice Harlan reasoned that official immunity was needed because government officials

> should be free to exercise their duties unembarrassed by the fear of damage suits in respect of acts done in the course of those duties — suits which would consume time and energies which would otherwise be devoted to governmental service and the threat of which might appreciably inhibit the fearless, vigorous, and effective administration of policies of government.

In subsequent cases, a split of authority developed as to whether federal officials and employees were absolutely immune from personal liability in state common-law tort actions for harm that resulted from all activities within the scope of their employment or only those activities that involved the exercise of discretion. Westfall v. Erwin, 484 U.S. 292 (1988), made clear that the immunity of federal government officials and employees extends only to discretionary acts. Justice Thurgood Marshall wrote for the court:

> The purpose of . . . official immunity is not to protect an erring official, but to insulate the decisionmaking process from the harassment of prospective litigation. . . .
>
> The central purpose of official immunity, promoting effective government, would not be furthered by shielding an official from state-law tort liability without regard to whether the alleged tortious conduct is discretionary in nature. When an official's conduct is not the product of independent judgment, the threat of liability cannot detrimentally inhibit that conduct. . . .

The Westfall Act and Substitution of the Government. Congress then responded to the *Westfall* decision. As described by Judge Reinhard in Pelletier v. Fed. Home Loan Bk. Bd., 968 F.2d 865 (9th Cir. 1992):

> In order to restore immunity to federal employees who perform non-discretionary functions, Congress enacted the FELRTCA [Federal Employees Liability Reform and Tort Compensation Act], popularly known as the Westfall Act. . . . The FELRTCA amended the FTCA to "remove the potential personal liability of Federal employees for common law torts committed within the scope of their employment, and . . . instead provide that the exclusive remedy for such torts is through an action against the United States under the Federal Tort Claims Act." . . . .
>
> Under the FTCA, an individual who has suffered an injury cognizable in tort as a result of the conduct of a federal employee may bring suit against the United States if that employee was "acting within the scope of his office or employment." . . . . The question whether a federal employee whose allegedly tortious conduct is the subject of a lawsuit under the FTCA was "acting within the scope of his office or employment" at the time of the injury is to be answered according to the principles of *respondeat superior* of the state in which the alleged tort occurred. . . .
>
> The FELRTCA accords a right of substitution to any federal employee sued in tort who was "acting within the scope of his office or employment" when the allegedly tortious conduct occurred. . . .

Further:

> The FELRTCA provides that "[u]pon certification by the Attorney General that the defendant employee was acting within the scope of his office or employment at the time of the incident out of which the claim arose . . . the United States shall be substituted as the party defendant."

In Gutierrez de Martinez v. Lamagno, 515 U.S. 417 (1995), the Court held that the Attorney General's scope-of-employment certifications under the Westfall Act are subject to judicial review.

Qualified Immunity for Constitutional Torts. Federal actors are treated differently if a case involves a "constitutional tort," rather than a common-law tort. A *Bivens* action is a court-created tort action against federal employees individually for injuries caused by their constitutional violations. *See* Bivens v. Six Unknown Named Agents of the Fed. Bureau of Narcotics, 403 U.S. 388, 389 (1971). An individual defendant in a *Bivens* action is entitled to assert the defense of qualified immunity. "Qualified immunity is not merely a defense to liability, but a shield from suit . . . [in the sense that a] determination of whether qualified immunity is applicable to any defendant is a matter that is initially determined by the Court as a matter of law." Andrade v. Chojnacki, 65 F. Supp. 2d 431, 452 (W.D. Tex. 1999).

2. State Officials and Employees

Absolute Immunity for Discretionary Acts. At the state level, it is generally agreed that high officials, such as judges, legislators, and top executive officers, enjoy absolute immunity from suit for actions relating to their official duties.

Some states have extended absolute immunity to lesser officials and employees. *See* Dziubak v. Mott, 503 N.W.2d 771 (Minn. 1993) (holding court-appointed public defenders wholly immune from suit for legal malpractice); Miss. Code Ann. § 11-46-7(2) (Westlaw 2022) ("no employee shall be held personally liable for acts or omissions occurring within the course and scope of the employee's duties"); *but see* State v. Second Jud. Dist. Ct., 55 P.3d 420 (Nev. 2002) (refusing to extend absolute quasi-judicial immunity to every state employee involved in supervising foster children).

Qualified Immunity for Discretionary Acts. Lesser state officials typically have only a "qualified" immunity, which may be lost if the plaintiff can prove that the official acted out of malice — dishonestly, without good faith, or for an improper purpose. *See Ex parte Nall & Faulk,* 879 So. 2d 541 (Ala. 2003) (school coaches were entitled to immunity absent evidence that they acted with malice or wilfulness in hitting balls during a practice session).

Any immunity normally extends only to actions within the official's "discretionary" functions, so that an official who negligently runs down a pedestrian on the way to a government meeting will have no immunity at all. *Compare* Quakenbush v. Lackey, 622 N.E.2d 1284 (Ind. 1993) (police officer was not immune from a claim for negligent driving), *with* Ramos v. Tex. Dept. of Pub. Safety, 35 S.W.3d 723 (Tex. App. 2000) (the discretionary duties of an officer administering a driving test continued until the test taker's car was safely parked, and thus the officer was immune from suit for damages caused when the test taker's car lurched forward as the test taker was parking).

See also Harris v. McCray, 867 So. 2d 188 (Miss. 2003) (holding, in a suit where a player suffered heatstroke, that allegedly negligent acts of a high school football coach were discretionary in nature and therefore both the coach and the school district were immune from suit); Aversano v. Palisades Interstate Pkwy. Com'n, 832 A.2d 914 (N.J. Super. Ct. A.D. 2003) (holding that the duty of public parkway police to call a rescue squad, upon receiving a report that a park user had fallen from a cliff, was "ministerial" rather than "discretionary," and therefore the parkway commission and parkway police were not immune from suit).

State Legislation Limiting the Liability of Governmental Employees. Some states have passed laws capping the liability of "public servants." For example:

Texas Civil Practice & Remedies Code § 108.002 (a) & (b) (Westlaw 2022)

(a) Except in an action arising under the constitution or laws of the United States, a public servant is not personally liable for damages in excess of $100,000 arising from personal injury,[5] death, or deprivation of a right, privilege, or immunity if:

(1) the damages are the result of an act or omission by the public servant in the course and scope of the public servant's office, employment,

5. Subsection (b) of the statute contains similar provisions relating to property damage.

or contractual performance for or service on behalf of a state agency, institution, department, or local government; and

(2) for the amount not in excess of $100,000, the public servant is covered:

(A) by the state's obligation to indemnify under Chapter 104;

(B) by a local government's authorization to indemnify under Chapter 102;

(C) by liability or errors and omissions insurance; or

(D) by liability or errors and omissions coverage under an interlocal agreement.

Substitution of the Government. Oregon enacted a statute eliminating causes of action against public employees and agents and substituting a claim against the state as the sole remedy to an aggrieved individual. However, in a medical malpractice action arising from conduct at a state hospital, the Oregon Supreme Court found that the substituted remedy was such an emasculated version of the remedies available at common law that the statute was unconstitutional under the Remedy Clause of the Oregon Constitution. *See* Clarke v. Oregon Health Sciences Univ., 175 P.3d 418 (Or. 2007).

Federal Protection for Teachers with Respect to Student Discipline. The Paul D. Coverdell Teacher Protection Act of 2001, 20 U.S.C.A. § 6731 *et seq.* (Westlaw 2022), with various limits, immunizes teachers at public and private elementary and secondary schools that receive federal funds from liability for negligence based on actions within the scope of the teacher's responsibilities undertaken in "efforts to control, discipline, expel, or suspend a student or maintain order or control in the classroom or school."

The Act's limits on teacher liability "[do] not apply to any misconduct that . . . constitutes a crime of violence . . . or act of international terrorism . . . for which the defendant has been convicted in any court; . . . involves a sexual offense . . . for which the defendant has been convicted in any court; . . . involves misconduct for which the defendant has been found to have violated a Federal or State civil rights law; or . . . where the defendant was under the influence . . . of intoxicating alcohol or any drug at the time of the misconduct." Nothing in the law affects "any State or local law . . . pertaining to the use of corporal punishment."

The Act preempts state law providing less protection to teachers, unless a State has passed legislation electing to have the Act not apply. Suits based on "willful or criminal misconduct, gross negligence, reckless misconduct, or a conscious, flagrant indifference to the rights or safety of the individual harmed by the teacher" may still be maintained.

Under the Act,

> Punitive damages may not be awarded against a teacher in an action brought for harm based on the act or omission of a teacher acting within

the scope of the teacher's employment or responsibilities to a school or governmental entity unless the claimant establishes by clear and convincing evidence that the harm was proximately caused by an act or omission of such teacher that constitutes willful or criminal misconduct, or a conscious, flagrant indifference to the rights or safety of the individual harmed.

....

In any civil action against a teacher, based on an act or omission of a teacher acting within the scope of the teacher's employment or responsibilities to a school or governmental entity ... [a] teacher shall be liable only for the amount of noneconomic loss allocated to that defendant in direct proportion to the percentage of responsibility of that defendant ... for the harm to the claimant with respect to which that defendant is liable.

State Protection for Teachers. Some states have enacted legislation protecting teachers from tort liability. For example:

Texas Education Code § 22.0511 (Westlaw 2022)

(a) A professional employee of a school district is not personally liable for any act that is incident to or within the scope of the duties of the employee's position of employment and that involves the exercise of judgment or discretion on the part of the employee, except in circumstances in which a professional employee uses excessive force in the discipline of students or negligence resulting in bodily injury to students.

(b) This section does not apply to the operation, use, or maintenance of any motor vehicle.

(c) In addition to the immunity provided under this section and under other provisions of state law, an individual is entitled to any immunity and any other protections afforded under the Paul D. Coverdell Teacher Protection Act of 2001....

See Kobza v. Kutac, 109 S.W.3d 89 (Tex. App. 2003) (a high school teacher's act of creating a fake newspaper article about a student as a joke, in an attempt to enhance the learning environment by establishing rapport with the student, was within the scope of her duties and therefore the teacher was immune from a suit for defamation and other claims).

See also MacCabee v. Mollica, 2010 WL 3532089 (Ohio Ct. App.) (holding that a fact issue as to whether a teacher's conduct constituted maliciousness precluded summary judgment on basis of statutory immunity).

A teacher may be entitled not only to immunity but to reimbursement for litigation expenses. *See* Tex. Educ. Code § 22.0517 (Westlaw 2022) ("In an action against a professional employee of a school district involving an act that is incidental to or within the scope of duties of the employee's position of employment and brought against the employee in the employee's individual capacity, the employee is entitled to recover attorney's fees and court costs from the plaintiff if the employee is found immune from liability . . .").

Other Immunities. Some immunities cover persons who are not government officials; witnesses in court proceedings provide an example. *See* Chapter 22.

D. Charitable Immunity

Albritton v. Neighborhood Centers Association for Child Development

Supreme Court of Ohio
466 N.E.2d 867 (Ohio 1984)

[Alfreda Albritton brought an action, on behalf of herself and her minor child, against the Neighborhood Centers Association for Child Development ("NCA"), a nonprofit corporation. The child was injured while participating at no cost in a Head Start day care program run by NCA. Summary judgment was granted in favor of NCA based on the doctrine of charitable immunity. The court of appeals affirmed.]

WILLIAM B. BROWN, Justice.

. . . .

The critical question is whether the doctrine of charitable immunity retains any validity in Ohio today. The origin of the doctrine in the United States is well documented and needs no repetition here. *See* Avellone v. St. John's Hospital . . . [135 N.E.2d 410 (Ohio 1956)], *citing* President & Directors of Georgetown College v. Hughes . . . [130 F.2d 810 (D.C. Cir. 1942)]. Suffice it to say that the rule was originally erroneously adopted in that it derived from *dicta* in two English cases which had already been overruled. Despite such a tenuous inception, the doctrine of charitable immunity spread until it became a concept firmly embedded in American jurisprudence, although not one universally accepted.

However, the "rule" of charitable immunity is, in reality, not a rule at all. In the first place, charitable immunity is an exception to the general principle of liability for tortious conduct. Individuals and entities are ordinarily held responsible for their own legally careless action and for negligent harms inflicted by their agents and employees. . . .

Moreover, . . . the landscape of charitable immunity has been so pockmarked with exceptions as to be virtually unrecognizable. Immunity for hospitals has been abolished. . . . There is no charitable immunity where the injured plaintiff is not a beneficiary of the defendant charity or where the plaintiff is harmed as a result of the charity's negligence in the selection or retention of an employee. . . . Likewise, a charity is liable where it operates a business enterprise for profit not directly related to the purpose for which the organization was established. . . . Finally, there is no immunity where the plaintiff pays for services rendered by the charity. . . . Indeed, the very existence of these manifold exceptions militates strongly against all of the policy arguments advanced in favor of retention of the doctrine.

Furthermore, charitable immunity does not, and has not, existed as a "rule" in the nation as a whole. In other jurisdictions charitable immunity survived only in a welter of conflict founded on a kaleidoscope of result and reasoning.... There is, consequently, no compelling precedential reason for retention of this doctrine.

This court has previously founded its acceptance of charitable immunity on the theory of public policy.... This theory reasons that charities are good and that their purpose, to provide services for intended beneficiaries, should not be defeated by indemnification of tort claimants. As NCA has characterized the rationale, it has been determined that the benefit to society as a whole from protecting charitable organizations outweighs the detriment to any one particular injured individual.

.... A careful review of the competing policies ... convinces this court that ... [charitable immunity] is no longer justified.

In the first place, it is certainly true that a personal injury is no less painful, disabling, costly, or damage producing simply because it was inflicted by a charitable institution rather than by any other party or entity....

... [W]hen an individual is injured or killed through the negligence of a charitable institution there is a strong likelihood that the individual or his or her family will become dependent upon outside support unless recovery may be had.... Such support may be met by governmental assistance or may have to be assumed by another charity.

In addition, a policy exempting a charitable organization from having to compensate for harm caused by it is equivalent to requiring an injured individual to make an unwilling contribution to that organization in the amount of the compensation which would be due him had he been injured by a noncharitable entity.... Such coerced donations are inimical to the whole concept of charitable donation and service....

.... Nowhere is there the slightest evidence that the role of charities has been repressed in the overwhelming majority of jurisdictions which have abolished the rule as opposed to the handful which retain some form of immunity. This reality is independent of the existence of liability insurance. In short, charities continue to operate with very little regard as to whether they are immune from tort liability or not.

.... Jurisdictions which have totally abolished charitable immunity now number well over thirty. Apparently, no state continues to grant absolute immunity to charities. Opinion among legal scholars is virtually unanimous that charitable immunity no longer has any valid reason for existence and must go.... The Restatement of the Law, Torts 2d (1979) 420, § 895E would have the law be that "[o]ne engaged in a charitable, educational, religious or benevolent enterprise or activity is not for that reason immune from tort liability."....

Lastly, NCA contends that if charitable immunity is to be abolished it should be done by the General Assembly and not by the courts.... There is no doubt that charitable immunity was judicially created in Ohio.... [T]his court not only has the power but the duty and responsibility to evaluate an immunity doctrine in light of reason, logic and the actions and functions of the relevant entities in the twentieth century. It is, therefore, the proper province of this court to correct judicially created doctrines if they are no longer grounded in good morals and sound law....

... [C]haritable immunity is hereby abolished. A charitable organization is subject to liability in tort to the same extent as individuals and corporations....

Judgment reversed and cause remanded.

FRANK D. CELEBREZZE, C.J., and SWEENEY, CLIFFORD F. BROWN and JAMES P. CELEBREZZE, JJ., concur.

LOCHER, Justice, dissenting.

....

The many exceptions presented by the majority, contrary to their "exception devouring the rule" characterization, are the result of many decades of thoughtful, patient policy analysis by this court. Exceptions have not gobbled the rule; instead, the rule has adapted to the times and to the needs of charities. Now, in a single stroke, the majority has chosen to abolish all charitable immunity based on a narrow factual pattern concerning a governmentally funded charitable organization. This position is squarely against this court's previous posture of judicial restraint.

... [T]oday's result can only create an expensive bureaucratic tangle. Volunteerism will be chilled and assistance to the hungry and dispossessed will diminish, in exact degree, to sweeten the coffers of the John Street insurance empires. In this tangle the small but sturdy charity which gives aid to the small towns and communities in this state is engulfed and slowly strangled while the few large, structured, and financially viable charities of the larger cities will survive. The committed and dedicated men and women from all walks of life who give service to charity gain in fraternity and spirit by coming to the aid of those in need. Thus not only will the indigent and downtrodden pay the price for today's decision, but the ethical and moral fiber of what gives worth to the lives of so many citizens, and makes this country great, will be diminished.

....

Therefore, I dissent.

HOLMES, Justice, dissenting.

.... I wish to emphasize ... the unreality of subjecting all charities, regardless of size and regardless of services performed, to tort liability to the same extent as individuals and corporations....

There is a great disparity within charitable organizations, some large, serving on a state or national scale; some small, serving a given neighborhood. Some are admittedly of sizable wealth, most are of modest means, receiving all of their revenue from sources such as United Way and other volunteer fundraising efforts. There is sound reason not to apply tort liability in the same manner and degree to all charitable organizations regardless of the nature of the operation.

. . . .

LOCHER, J., concurs in the foregoing dissenting opinion.

Notes

1. ***Charitable Immunity and Gross Negligence.*** Where charitable immunity is recognized, it is unlikely to prevent a suit for conduct worse than negligence. *See* Cowan v. Hospice Support Care, Inc., 603 S.E.2d 916 (Va. 2004) (permitting an action against a hospice for gross negligence).

2. ***The Effect of Liability Insurance.*** The fairly widespread availability of liability insurance has been cited as a reason for doing away with charitable immunity. *See* Tex. Civ. Prac. & Rem. Code §§ 84.001 *et seq.* (Westlaw 2022). The Texas statute conditions selected aspects of immunity on the charity's purchase of liability insurance. *See id.* at 84.007(g).

If the reason for the immunity is to provide an economic benefit to charities, this type of provision makes little sense. Liability insurance is not free; indeed, if insurance companies are to survive they must collect enough money to cover all their liabilities, and more. On an overall basis, the burden of paying for liability insurance cannot possibly be less than the burden of paying judgments.

3. ***Legislative Restoration of Charitable Immunity.*** In many states, immunity for some charitable institutions and their actors has been legislatively restored, at least in part, in recent years. For example, after the New Jersey Supreme Court abolished charitable immunity in Benton v. YMCA, 141 A.2d 298 (N.J. 1958), the state legislature passed the Charitable Immunity Act, reinstating the common-law doctrine as it had been judicially defined. That statute now provides:

New Jersey Statutes Annotated § 2A:53A-7a (Westlaw 2022)

> a. No nonprofit corporation, society or association organized exclusively for religious, charitable or educational purposes or its trustees, directors, officers, employees, agents, servants or volunteers shall, except as is hereinafter set forth, be liable to respond in damages to any person who shall suffer damage from the negligence of any agent or servant of such corporation, society or association, where such person is a beneficiary, to whatever degree, of the works of such nonprofit corporation, society or association; provided, however, that such immunity from liability shall not extend to any person who shall suffer damage from the negligence of such corporation, society, or association or of its agents or servants where such person is one unconcerned in and unrelated to and outside of the benefactions of such corporation, society or association.

> Nothing in this subsection shall be deemed to grant immunity to any health care provider, in the practice of his profession, who is a compensated employee, agent or servant of any nonprofit corporation, society or association organized exclusively for religious, charitable or educational purposes.
>
> b. . . . [Relates to nonprofit hospitals].
>
> c. Nothing in this section shall be deemed to grant immunity to: (1) any trustee, director, officer, employee, agent, servant or volunteer causing damage by a willful, wanton or grossly negligent act of commission or omission, including sexual assault and other crimes of a sexual nature; (2) any trustee, director, officer, employee, agent, servant or volunteer causing damage as the result of the negligent operation of a motor vehicle; or (3) an independent contractor of a nonprofit corporation, society or association organized exclusively for religious, charitable, educational or hospital purposes.

In O'Connell v. State, 795 A.2d 857 (N.J. 2002), the court ruled that a student was a "beneficiary" under the act and was therefore barred from suing a state college for a slip-and-fall accident. The fact that the college received public funds was irrelevant.

4. ***Caps on Damages against Charities.*** In some states, the amount of damages recoverable from a charity has been legislatively capped. *See* Keene v. Brigham and Women's Hosp. Inc., 786 N.E.2d 824 (Mass. 2003) (reducing a $4.1 million malpractice judgment to $20,000).

5. ***State Immunity of Volunteers.*** "[E]ach of the 50 states have passed laws to limit the liability of volunteers in a variety of circumstances." Lomando v. United States, 667 F.3d 363, 378 (3d Cir. 2011). *See, e.g.*, Ark. Code Ann. § 17-95-106 (Westlaw 2022) (retired physicians who provide services at a low-cost medical clinic); La. Rev. Stat. Ann. § 9:2799.5 (Westlaw 2022) (health care providers who provide free services at community clinics); Md. Code Ann., Cts. & Jud. Proc. § 5-425(b) (Westlaw 2022) (professional engineers who, upon request of state officials, volunteer at the scene of an emergency, disaster, or catastrophic event); Tex. Educ. Code § 22.053 (Westlaw 2022) ("A volunteer who is serving as a direct service volunteer of a school district is immune from civil liability to the same extent as a professional employee of a school district . . ."); W. Va. Code § 55-7-19 (Westlaw 2022) (physicians who volunteer for certain athletic events sponsored by a public or private elementary or secondary school).

Some states have passed more broadly applicable statutes that protect volunteers working for a wide range of charities from many types of liability for ordinary negligence occurring within the scope of their duties. *See* Tex. Civ. Prac. & Rem. 84.004 *et seq.* (Westlaw 2022).

6. ***The Federal Volunteer Protection Act.*** A federal statute, the Volunteer Protection Act of 1997, purports to limit the tort liability of those who volunteer their services to nonprofit organizations and governmental bodies. While the act seems at first glance to make many volunteers immune from suit for torts committed within

the scope of their responsibilities, it is so hedged with restrictions and exceptions that it seems largely symbolic. The act confers no immunity for a variety of things, including gross negligence, willful or criminal conduct, reckless misconduct, most motor vehicle accidents, sexual offenses (if the defendant has been convicted), hate crimes, and harms that occurred while the defendant was acting under the influence of "alcohol or any drug." Only volunteers themselves receive protection: the agencies that use their services remain liable. Furthermore, states may enact legislation making the act inapplicable to cases in which all the parties are citizens of that state.

7. ***Immunity for Mediators***. "A substantial number of states extend qualified or absolute immunity to mediators." Robert Rubinson, *Indigency, Secrecy, and Questions of Quality: Minimizing the Risk of "Bad" Mediation for Low-Income Litigants*, 100 Marq. L. Rev. 1353, 1386 (2017).

8. ***Special Immunities for Businesses***. Statutes occasionally immunize businesses from certain types of claims. For example, in Texas:

> An ice skating rink operator may be held liable in negligence for damages for personal injury only if the personal injury is caused by a breach of a duty prescribed in section 760.002 of the Texas Health and Safety Code. Tex. Health & Safety Code Ann. § 760.006(a) ("Except for actions against an operator for gross negligence, malice, or intentional conduct, an operator is not liable in negligence for damages for personal injury, property damage, or death unless the personal injury, property damage, or death is caused by a breach of a duty prescribed in Section 760.002"). Section 760.002 lists the following duties of an ice skating rink operator:
>
> (1) to provide during public skating sessions at least one rink monitor approximately per 200 ice skaters,
>
> (2) to require rink monitors to wear identifying attire, direct and supervise skaters and spectators, and watch for and timely remove foreign objects on the ice skating surface,
>
> (3) to inspect and maintain in good condition the ice skating surface and surrounding floors, railings, boards, and walls,
>
> (4) to inspect and maintain in good mechanical condition ice skating equipment that the operator leases or rents to ice skaters,
>
> (5) to comply with the risk management guidelines for ice skating rinks endorsed by the board of directors of the Ice Skating Institute of America on August 27, 1996,
>
> (6) to post in conspicuous places in the ice skating center the duties of ice skaters and spectators . . . ,
>
> (7) to maintain the stability and legibility of all required signs, symbols, and posted notices, and
>
> (8) to maintain liability insurance of at least $500,000 combined single limits for personal injury, death, or property damage.

Smith v. Moody Gardens, Inc., 336 S.W.3d 816, 819 (Tex. App. 2011).

9. ***Immunities Related to Equine Activities.*** Several states have passed acts governing liability related to equine activities. The Indiana statute provides, with exceptions, that an equine activity sponsor or equine professional is not liable for the injury or death of a participant "resulting from an inherent risk of equine activities." (Ind. Code § 34-31-5-1 (Westlaw 2022).) The act then defines "inherent risks" as including "(2) The unpredictability of an equine's reaction to such things as sound, sudden movement, unfamiliar objects, people, or other animals . . . [and] (5) The potential of a participant to act in a negligent manner that may contribute to injury to the participant or others, such as failing to maintain control over the animal or not acting within the participant's ability." (Ind. Code § 34-6-2-69 (Westlaw 2022).)

In Perry v. Whitley County 4-H Clubs, Inc., 931 N.E.2d 933 (Ind. App. 2010), the court found that:

> [T]he facts viewed most favorably to Perry [the plaintiff] . . . show her injury resulted from inherent risks of equine activities and the 4-H Club was negligent, if at all, only for failing to mitigate those inherent risks. Therefore, the trial court properly concluded the Equine Activity Statute bars Perry's claim and properly granted summary judgment to the 4-H Club.

Chapter 19

Statutes of Limitations

A. Introduction

A tort action must be brought before the applicable statute of limitations expires. When the statutory period begins to run usually depends on whether applicable law follows a "damage rule" or an "occurrence rule."

Damage Rule. In a wide range of circumstances, a tort cause of action accrues, and the statute of limitations period commences, when the plaintiff suffers damage. For example, the relevant statute begins to run:

- when environmental cleanup costs are incurred by a property owner as a result of contamination (Pflanz v. Foster, 888 N.E.2d 756 (Ind. 2008));
- when a credit card holder is denied credit because of an issuer's erroneous negative credit report (Waxler v. Household Credit Servs., Inc., 106 S.W.3d. 277 (Tex. App. 2003));
- when a person rightfully in possession of another's property refuses to return it or acts in a manner inconsistent with the rights of the owner (Grosz v. Museum of Modern Art, 403 Fed. Appx. 575, 577 (2d Cir. 2010)); or
- when use of a keyboard ultimately causes a repetitive stress injury (Dorsey v. Apple Computers, Inc., 936 F. Supp. 89 (E.D.N.Y. 1996)).

Occurrence Rule. In some circumstances, states follow an occurrence rule, rather than a damage rule, and the statute of limitations begins to run at the moment the tortious act or omission occurs, even if damage does not result until a later point in time. For example, courts have held that the statute of limitations began to run:

- when the negligent act or omission constituting medical malpractice took place (Herron v. Anigbo, 897 N.E.2d 444 (Ind. 2008));
- when the touching occurred that was an alleged battery (Kelly v. VinZant, 197 P.3d 803 (Kan. 2008)); or
- when a property appraiser committed a negligent act (Flagstar Bank, F.S.B. v. Airline Union's Mtge. Co., 947 N.E.2d 672 (Ohio 2011)).

See generally Denbo v. DeBray, 968 So. 2d 983 (Ala. 2006) (discussing the differences between a "damage rule" and an "occurrence rule").

Policy Basis. One reason for having statutes of limitations has to do with accuracy of factfinding. Important evidence may be lost if actions are brought long after the events being litigated took place. Witnesses may die or move away, memories will fade, records may be lost or destroyed. Another consideration relates to the welfare of potential defendants. Without statutes of limitations, those whose conduct may or may not have caused someone harm would be put to considerable and often unnecessary expense. For example, records would have to be kept indefinitely, lest some claim arising out of the distant past be brought. Finally, at least for individual defendants, statutes of limitations may provide some peace of mind. Knowledge that one is potentially subject to litigation arising out of anything one did (or was claimed to have done) at any time in the past would be unsettling for many.

As a general rule, statutes of limitations for simple intentional torts are quite short. "This is one reason there have been so few tort suits for domestic violence injuries." Jennifer Wriggins, *Domestic Violence Torts,* 75 S. Cal. L. Rev. 121, 169 (2001). Negligence statutes tend to be somewhat longer, though in some states they are as short as two years. Many states have special statutes of limitations for particular kinds of torts. As an example, consider the following New York statute.

New York C.P.L.R. § 214

(Westlaw 2022)

The following actions must be commenced within three years:

1. an action against a sheriff, constable or other officer for the non-payment of money collected upon an execution;

2. an action to recover upon a liability, penalty or forfeiture created or imposed by statute, except as provided in §§ 213 and 215;

3. an action to recover a chattel or damages for the taking or detaining of a chattel;

4. an action to recover damages for an injury to property except as provided in § 214-c;

5. an action to recover damages for a personal injury except as provided in §§ 214-b, 214-c, and 215;

6. an action to recover damages for malpractice, other than medical, dental or podiatric malpractice, regardless of whether the underlying theory is based on contract or tort; . . . .

Note

1. ***Intentional Torts.*** In New York, as in many states, the statute of limitations for intentional torts is one year. *See* N.Y. C.P.L.R. § 215 (Westlaw 2022). Ordinarily, the victim of an intentional tort knows almost immediately whether there is a claim, so there is little need for a long statute of limitations.

Suppose a physician is sued for failing to disclose the risks of a surgical procedure to a patient. Is this a medical-malpractice claim, for which the New York statute of limitations is two years and six months, or is it a battery, for which the period is one year? In a questionable decision, a New York trial court held that the one-year statute applied. *See* Cox v. Stretton, 352 N.Y.S.2d 834 (Sup. Ct. 1974).

2. ***Difficult Questions.*** In some cases, it is simply not clear which statute of limitations governs. In Goodwin v. Kingsmen Plastering, Inc., 375 P.3d 463 (Or. 2016), the court conducted an exhaustive review of many decades of legislation. The court ultimately held that negligence claims against contractors for property damages arising out of defective installation of synthetic stucco on their home were governed by a two-year statute of limitations for injuries to persons not arising "upon a contract," rather than a six-year statute of limitations for injury to an interest in real property.

B. Tolling the Statute of Limitations

Discovery Rule. The reasons given above for having statutes of limitations suggest that those statutes should be quite short, and that they should begin to run as soon as the potential defendant does the action complained of. Considerations involving prospective plaintiffs cut the other way, however. If a statute of limitations begins to run as soon as the defendant acts negligently or sells a defective product, the statute may run before the plaintiff even knows of the claim, or even before the plaintiff is injured. Consider, for example, a doctor who leaves a sponge inside a patient during an operation, and suppose that the sponge does no harm for years. If the statute of limitations runs from the time of the negligent conduct, the plaintiff's claim may be lost before the plaintiff has any reason to know that there was a claim. Similarly, if a three-year statute of limitations for making a dangerously defective product begins to run when the product is manufactured or sold, a plaintiff injured by the product five years later would have no claim.

The unseemliness of barring actions before damages have occurred and a claim could be commenced has led many courts to hold that statutes of limitations do not begin to run until the plaintiff has been injured. In some cases, the courts have gone even further and held that the running of the statute is "tolled" — suspended — until the plaintiff discovers, or at least should reasonably have discovered, the injury.

For example, in Butler Univ. v. Bahssin, 892 So. 2d 1087 (Fla. Dist. Ct. App. 2004), ballet costumes were donated to a university by the Ballet Russe and misappropriated by a former chairman of the dance department. The university's cause of action against an art dealer did not accrue until the university learned that the art dealer had purchased the costumes from successors of the deceased chairman because the university could not have discovered the loss of the costumes earlier.

The following case illustrates one version of the discovery rule.

Tyson v. Tyson

Supreme Court of Washington, En Banc
727 P.2d 226 (Wash. 1986)

DURHAM, Justice.

The United States District Court for the Western District of Washington has certified the following question of state law to this court: Does the discovery rule, which tolls the statute of limitations until the plaintiff discovers or reasonably should have discovered a cause of action, apply to intentional torts where the victim has blocked the incident from her conscious memory during the entire time of the statute of limitations? We answer that question in the negative.

The plaintiff here alleges that she was the victim of sexual abuse during her childhood. The parties have stipulated to the following facts: Plaintiff Nancy Tyson filed a complaint in the United States District Court . . . , alleging that her father, the defendant Dwight Robert Tyson, committed multiple acts of sexual assault upon her from 1960 through 1969. Plaintiff, whose birthdate is April 20, 1957, was between 3 and 11 years old at the time of the alleged acts, and was 26 years old at the time she filed the complaint. Plaintiff further alleged that the sexual assaults caused her to suppress any memory of the acts and that she did not remember the alleged acts until she entered psychological therapy during 1983. Plaintiff filed the complaint within 1 year of her recollection of the alleged acts.

. . . . RCW 4.16.080(2) provides that, in general, an action for personal injury must be brought within 3 years of the time the cause of action accrued. RCW 4.16.100(1) provides that an action for assault and battery must be brought within 2 years. If the person bringing the action is under the age of 18 years at the time the cause of action accrues, the statute of limitations is tolled until the person becomes 18 years old. RCW 4.16.190. Under a literal reading of the limitation statutes, the cause of action accrues when the alleged wrongful act occurs. Ruth v. Dight, 75 Wash. 2d 660, 665, 453 P.2d 631 (1969). Under these rules, the limitation period in this case expired at the latest on April 20, 1978, or 3 years after plaintiff's 18th birthday. . . .

. . . . The discovery rule provides that a statute of limitations does not begin to run until the plaintiff, using reasonable diligence, would have discovered the cause of action. . . .

Plaintiff claims that the alleged acts of sexual abuse caused her such emotional trauma that she repressed her memory of the events entirely. She asserts that years after the statute of limitations had expired, therapy triggered her knowledge of the abuse and her recognition that the abuse caused emotional problems she was experiencing as an adult. Plaintiff argues that it would be unfair to preclude her claim because she was unable to discover her cause of action during the applicable limitation period.

We recognize that child sexual abuse has devastating impacts on the victim. However, when a person claims emotional injuries resulting from an intentional tort which she has allegedly remembered only after the statute of limitations has expired, we must seriously consider the potential effects on our system of justice.

Statutes of limitation assist the courts in their pursuit of the truth by barring stale claims. A number of evidentiary problems arise from stale claims.... As time passes, evidence becomes less available. For example, the defendant might have had a critical alibi witness, only to find that the witness has died or cannot be located by the time the action is brought. Likewise, witnesses who observed the plaintiff's behavior shortly after the alleged act may no longer be available. Physical evidence is also more likely to be lost when a claim is stale, either because it has been misplaced, or because its significance was not comprehended at the time of the alleged wrong. In addition, the evidence which is available becomes less trustworthy as witnesses' memories fade or are colored by intervening events and experiences. Old claims also are more likely to be spurious than new ones. "With the passing of time, minor grievances may fade away, but they may grow to outlandish proportions, too." .... Thus, stale claims present major evidentiary problems which can seriously undermine the courts' ability to determine the facts. By precluding stale claims, statutes of limitation increase the likelihood that courts will resolve factual issues fairly and accurately.

The discovery rule should be adopted only when the risk of stale claims is outweighed by the unfairness of precluding justified causes of action.... In prior cases where we have applied the discovery rule, there was objective, verifiable evidence of the original wrongful act and the resulting physical injury. This increased the possibility that the fact finder would be able to determine the truth despite the passage of time, and thus diminished the danger of stale claims. For example, in Ruth v. Dight, *supra*, we adopted the discovery rule for a medical malpractice action arising from the presence of a foreign substance left inadvertently in a surgical wound. A hysterectomy was performed on the plaintiff in 1944. For a 22-year period following the surgery, plaintiff suffered recurrent abdominal pain. In 1966, plaintiff underwent an exploratory operation during which a sponge was found in her abdomen. After the sponge was removed, her recovery was normal.... Thus, there was empirical evidence of the occurrence of the alleged act (the initial surgery) and of the resulting harm (discovery of the sponge). In Ohler v. Tacoma Gen. Hosp., 92 Wash. 2d 507, 598 P.2d 1358 (1979), we applied the discovery rule to a products liability action against an incubator manufacturer for blindness due to excessive administration of oxygen to the plaintiff when she was a premature infant. There was evidence that plaintiff was placed in an incubator for about 16 days and given oxygen. Her blindness was an objective manifestation of the resulting injury.... Again, empirical evidence existed of the alleged event and resulting harm. We have also applied the discovery rule to a products liability action for personal injuries resulting from asbestos exposure. Sahlie v. Johns-Manville Sales Corp., 99 Wash. 2d 550, 663 P.2d 473 (1983). There was evidence that the plaintiff had worked around asbestos products for almost 40 years, and he was eventually diagnosed as having asbestosis.... The source of plaintiff's injury, continuous exposure to asbestos products, and the resulting harm, asbestosis, were objectively verifiable.

Because of the availability and trustworthiness of objective, verifiable evidence in the above cases, the claims were neither speculative nor incapable of proof. Since the evidentiary problems which the statute of limitations is designed to prevent did not exist or were reduced, it was reasonable to extend the period for bringing the actions.

.... In contrast, in the present case, no empirical, verifiable evidence exists of the occurrences and resulting harm which plaintiff alleges. Her claim rests on a subjective assertion that wrongful acts occurred and that injuries resulted. There is no objective manifestation of these allegations. Rather, they are based on plaintiff's alleged recollection of a memory long buried in the unconscious which she asserts was triggered by psychological therapy.

It is suggested that the subjectivity of plaintiff's claim can be eliminated at trial through the testimony of witnesses such as family, friends, schoolteachers and treating psychologists. However, none of this testimony would provide objective evidence that the alleged acts occurred. First, witnesses who knew the plaintiff at the time of the alleged events would be testifying from their memories of her emotional condition and behavior during that period. This would require witnesses to attempt to recall events which occurred between 17 and 26 years ago. Witnesses' recollections of memories usually become less reliable in a matter of minutes, much less years. Thus, the more time had passed, the less trustworthy such testimony would be.

Second, the testimony of treating psychologists or psychiatrists would not reduce, much less eliminate, the subjectivity of plaintiff's claim. Psychology and psychiatry are imprecise disciplines. Unlike the biological sciences, their methods of investigation are primarily subjective and most of their findings are not based on physically observable evidence. The fact that plaintiff asserts she discovered the wrongful acts through psychological therapy does not validate their occurrence. Recent studies by certain psychoanalysts have questioned the assumption that the analyst has any special ability to help the subject ascertain the historical truth.... These studies show that the psychoanalytic process can even lead to a distortion of the truth of events in the subject's past life. The analyst's reactions and interpretations may influence the subject's memories or statements about them. The analyst's interpretations of the subject's statements may also be altered by the analyst's own predisposition, expectations, and intention to use them to explain the subject's problems.... While psychoanalysis is certainly of great assistance in treating an individual's emotional problems, the trier of fact in legal proceedings cannot assume that it will produce an accurate account of events in the individual's past.

.... If we applied the discovery rule to ... [actions such as this], the statute of limitations would be effectively eliminated and its purpose ignored. A person would have an unlimited time to bring an action, while the facts became increasingly difficult to determine. The potential for spurious claims would be great and the probability of the court's determining the truth would be unreasonably low.

.... We ... hold that the discovery rule does not apply to an intentional tort claim where the plaintiff has blocked the incident from her conscious memory during the period of the statute of limitations.

DORE, ANDERSEN, CALLOW and GOODLOE, JJ., concur.

GOODLOE, Justice (concurring).

I concur with Justice Durham's majority opinion. I believe the arguments of the dissent are most compelling, however, the end result appears to be subjective judicial policy-making. This is the exclusive province of the Legislature, and the judiciary must not invade it.

PEARSON, Justice (dissenting).

....

Imposition of a statute of limitations generally creates no hardship for plaintiffs because they are aware when they have been wronged. "[W]hen an adult person has a justiciable grievance, he usually knows it and the law affords him ample opportunity to assert it in the courts." .... However, ... in some instances an injured party may not know or be expected to know he has been injured until long after the statute of limitations has cut off his legal remedy. ... In such instances, it is unfair automatically to foreclose a plaintiff's cause of action.

The decision as to whether it is in fact unfair to foreclose a plaintiff's lawsuit involves a balancing test. The court must balance "the harm of being deprived of a remedy versus the harm of being sued." ....

We balanced these harms in *Ruth* and applied the discovery rule. We found that the harm to a surgical patient of being deprived of a remedy outweighed the harm to the defendant surgeon of being sued 22 years after he performed allegedly negligent surgery. Our result was based on "fundamental fairness". ...

The context in *Ruth* was medical malpractice. However, in the 17 years following *Ruth*, both this court and the Court of Appeals have extended the discovery rule to other types of professional malpractice. ... We have also applied the rule in cases of libel, ... products liability, ... and latent disease. ...

.... In attempting to prevent ... injustice, we have never, contrary to the majority's position, required "objective, verifiable evidence" as a prerequisite to application of the rule. Not one of our discovery rule cases has ever imposed such a requirement. Indeed, the nature of available evidence is simply one factor to be considered in balancing the harm to a defendant of being forced to defend a stale claim with the harm to a plaintiff of being deprived of a remedy. Fundamental fairness, not availability of objective evidence, has always been the linchpin of the discovery rule.

....

Just as I am disturbed by the majority's disregard of the rationale of the discovery rule and criticism of mental health professionals, I am also concerned with the summary manner in which it dismisses the enormous problem of child sexual abuse. A single sentence is offered: "We recognize that child sexual abuse has devastating impacts on the victim." . . . .

In reality, the problem warrants a great deal of attention. Indeed, some understanding by this court of the nature of child sexual abuse is essential to our determination of the issue before us. We are asked to determine if fundamental fairness compels us to extend the discovery rule to adults who suffered sexual abuse as children and then repressed that abuse. In reaching our decision, we must understand how and why such repression occurs. It is the repression which gives rise to the need for application of the discovery rule.

Although definitions vary, child sexual abuse can be defined as "contacts or interactions between a child and an adult when the child is being used as an object of gratification for adult sexual needs or desires." . . . . It has been estimated that as much as one-third of the population has experienced some form of child sexual abuse. . . . Much of the sexual abuse of children occurs within the family. . . . In one study of 583 cases of child sexual abuse, the offender was a family member in 47 percent of the cases; otherwise, an acquaintance of the child in 42 percent, and a stranger in only 8 percent. . . . Of this high percentage of cases of abuse among family members, it has been estimated that 75 percent involve incest between father and daughter. . . . Both the high incidence of father/daughter incestuous abuse and the special problems of such incest victims have led to much commentary. . . . Because incestuous abuse is so pervasive and because the instant case involves father/daughter incest, I have focused on this type of sexual abuse.

Incestuous abuse begins, in the average case, when the daughter is 8 or 9 years old, although sexual relations and even intercourse may begin even earlier. . . . In order to ensure his daughter's availability to him and provide a cover for his conduct, the father demands secrecy from the child. Often he frightens her into secrecy with threats of harm. . . . Because the victim is thus sworn to secrecy, she is forced to deal with the situation alone. Because she must cope alone, she is likely to internalize her self-blame, anger, fears, confusion, and sadness resulting from the incest. This internalization results in what has been referred to as "accommodation." . . . . In accommodating herself to an intolerable situation, the victim often "blocks out" her experience for many years. . . . This "blocking out" is a coping mechanism. A victim will cope in this fashion because "some things are literally so difficult to deal with if remembered that your choices are to go crazy or to forget them." . . . .

As the incest victim becomes an adult, she will often begin to exhibit signs of incest trauma. The most common are sexual dysfunction, low self-esteem, poor capacity for self-protection, feelings of isolation, and an inability to form or maintain supportive relationships. . . . At this time, the daughter may know she is injured. However, until such time as she is able to place blame for the incestuous abuse upon her father, it will be impossible for her to realize that his behavior caused her psychological disorders. . . . Often it is only through therapy that the victim is able to recognize the causal link between her father's incestuous conduct and her damages from incest trauma. . . . Once the victim begins to confront her experiences and link her damages with her father's incestuous conduct, she has taken a step as a survivor of childhood incestuous abuse.

The need for maturity of the survivor before she can confront her childhood incest experience results in a general lack of ability to file suit within the statutory period. . . . As has been seen, the maximum age at which an adult survivor of incest may file suit in this state is 21. Since many survivors are simply incapable of discovering a cause of action by the time they are 21 years old, they are effectively denied a legal remedy unless they are given the benefit of the discovery rule.

. . . .

The purpose behind extending the discovery rule to adult survivors of childhood sexual abuse is not to provide a guaranteed remedy to such plaintiffs. The purpose is to provide an *opportunity* for an adult who claims to have been sexually abused as a child to prove not only that she was abused and that the defendant was her abuser, but that her suffering was such that she did not and could not reasonably have discovered all the elements of her cause of action at an earlier time. The policy behind providing this opportunity has been demonstrated: the nature of child sexual abuse, according to extensive expert commentary, is often so secretive, so humiliating, and so devastating that a victim typically represses the events until the abuse is "discovered"—often through psychotherapy, and often well into adulthood.

For these reasons, I dissent. . . .

DOLLIVER, C.J., and UTTER and BRACHENBACH, JJ., concur.

UTTER, Justice (concurring in dissent).

I agree fully with the well-reasoned opinion of Justice Pearson. I write separately to emphasize that the extension of the discovery rule urged by Nancy Tyson is not an issue that should be left to the Legislature. To do so rejects the reasoning adopted by this court in Wyman v. Wallace, 94 Wash. 2d 99, 615 P.2d 452 (1980). It is important for this court to adjust tort law doctrine in response to changes in social values and knowledge. Judicial action is especially appropriate when taken on behalf of individuals who are not organized as a political force and who cannot produce legislative solutions to their problems.

In Wyman v. Wallace, *supra*, we decided that this court does not need to wait for legislative action on matters of common law tort doctrine. We noted in that case that deference to the Legislature is appropriate in some fields; for example, the Legislature is particularly well suited to conduct the fact-finding necessary for economic legislation. . . . However, we concluded that because of its own institutional restraints the Legislature is not always in the best position to modify common law tort doctrine. . . .

This court also has refused to wait for legislative action with respect to application of the statutes of limitations. . . . Under our precedents it is thus within the province of this court to extend the discovery rule to the case of Nancy Tyson.

Increased knowledge and increased public awareness have produced the issue before us. Child abuse has attracted significant attention only since 1962, when the "battered child syndrome" was first defined. Public and professional attention have been directed toward child sexual abuse—incest in particular—for an even shorter period of time.... In fact, mental health therapists and other professionals largely denied the prevalence of incestuous abuse until the 1970s.... It is only in the past decade or so that professionals have documented the damages of incestuous abuse and the "blocking out" that the trauma of the abuse can cause.

This court cannot rely on the Legislature to extend the discovery rule in response to these recent developments. Legislatures rarely reexamine tort law in light of recent changes. Peck, *The Role of the Courts and Legislatures in the Reform of Tort Law*, 48 Minn. L. Rev. 265, 268–70 (1963). Legislators consider so many issues in so little time that only the most compelling needs can be addressed....

This court also cannot rely on tort victims to bring issues of tort reform to the attention of the Legislature. Tort victims do not constitute a well-organized lobbying group. They are not brought together by a common interest in legislation addressed to the future; instead, each plaintiff usually simply desires redress for past injuries. Peck, *Comments on Judicial Creativity*, 69 Iowa L. Rev. 1, 13 (1983).

In this case, especially, we can hardly expect Nancy Tyson to evoke a response from the Legislature. An adult survivor of child sexual abuse cannot elicit the same public support as a child victim. Survivors with experiences similar to those of Nancy may well be reluctant to reveal their painful experiences by lobbying and testifying at legislative hearings. The public agencies and private groups that represent these individuals do not have the resources to launch such a campaign.

....

This court should not hesitate to apply the discovery rule on behalf of adult survivors of child sexual abuse who have repressed their memories during the period of the statute of limitations.... It is particularly appropriate for this court to take action on behalf of a group that cannot obtain representation in the political process....

For these reasons I concur in the dissenting opinion.

Notes

1. ***Legislation***. In response to the decision in *Tyson*, the Washington statute was amended to provide as follows:

WASHINGTON REVISED CODE § 4.16.340 (Westlaw 2022)

> (1) All claims ... based on intentional conduct brought by any person for recovery of damages for injury suffered as a result of childhood sexual abuse shall be commenced within the later of the following periods:
>
> (a) Within three years of the act alleged to have caused the injury or condition;

(b) Within three years of the time the victim discovered or reasonably should have discovered that the injury or condition was caused by said act; or

(c) Within three years of the time the victim discovered that the act caused the injury for which the claim is brought:

Provided, That the time limit for commencement of an action under this section is tolled for a child until the child reaches the age of eighteen years.

2. ***Split of Authority.*** Courts are divided over whether the discovery rule should apply to child-abuse cases. The following rulings are illustrative.

Applicable: Dunlea v. Dappen, 924 P.2d 196 (Haw. 1996); Johnson v. Johnson, 701 F. Supp. 1363 (N.D. Ill. 1988) (Ill. law); Hoult v. Hoult, 792 F. Supp. 143 (D. Mass. 1992) (Mass. law); Sinclair v. Brill, 815 F. Supp. 44 (D. N.H. 1993) (N.H. law); Osland v. Osland, 442 N.W.2d 907 (N.D. 1989).

Inapplicable: Hildebrand v. Hildebrand, 736 F. Supp. 1512 (S.D. Ind. 1990) (Ind. law); Doe v. Maskell, 679 A.2d 1087 (Md. 1996); Lemmerman v. Fealk, 534 N.W.2d 695 (Mich. 1995); Schmidt v. Bishop, 779 F. Supp. 321 (S.D.N.Y. 1991) (N.Y. law); Doe v. Doe, 973 F.2d 237 (4th Cir. 1992) (N.C. law); Bailey v. Lewis, 763 F. Supp. 802 (E.D. Pa. 1991), *aff'd*, 950 F.2d 722 (3d Cir. 1991) (Pa. law); Baye v. Diocese of Rapid City 630 F.3d 757, 760 (8th Cir. 2011) (South Dakota law) S.V. v. R.V., 933 S.W.2d 1 (Tex. 1996).

See also Hyde v. Roman Catholic Bishop of Providence, 139 A.3d 452, 465 (R.I. 2016) (holding that "repressed recollection, in and of itself, is not a viable tolling mechanism against nonperpetrator defendants in childhood sexual abuse cases").

3. ***Liability for Creating False Memories.*** *See* Sawyer v. Midelfort, 595 N.W.2d 423 (Wis. 1999) (permitting a malpractice action by a patient's estate and parents alleging that a psychiatrist and therapist caused the patient to develop false memories of sexual and physical abuse).

4. ***The Discovery Rule and the Continuous-Treatment Exception in Medical-Malpractice Cases.*** The special New York statute of limitations for cases involving medical malpractice provides:

New York Civil Practice Law and Rules § 214-a (Westlaw 2022)

An action for medical, dental or podiatric malpractice must be commenced within two years and six months of the act, omission or failure complained of or last treatment where there is continuous treatment for the same illness, injury or condition which gave rise to the said act, omission or failure; provided, however, that where the action is based upon the discovery of a foreign object in the body of the patient, the action may be commenced within one year of the date of such discovery or of the date of discovery of facts which would reasonably lead to such discovery, whichever is earlier. For purpose[s] of this section, the term "continuous treatment" shall not include examinations undertaken at the request of the patient for the sole purpose of ascertaining the state of the patient's condition. For the purpose of this section, the term "foreign object" shall not include a chemical compound, fixation device or prosthetic aid or device.

The statute bars some malpractice claims before they even arise, as when a doctor's negligence causes no harm to the plaintiff for several years. *See* Goldsmith v. Howmedica, Inc., 491 N.E.2d 1097 (N.Y. 1986) (plaintiff's cause of action accrued in 1973 when a prosthetic device was implanted, not in 1981 when it malfunctioned, and therefore an action commenced in 1983 was barred by a three-year statute of limitations).

Note that the New York statute contains a "continuous treatment" exception. Many states have created this kind of exception for medical malpractice cases by judicial decision. The scope of the exception is often uncertain and is, therefore, the subject of a great deal of litigation.

5. ***"Discovered" vs. "Should Reasonably Have Discovered."*** Discovery rules vary considerably with respect to what the plaintiff must discover to start the statute running. The possibilities include: (1) that the plaintiff has been injured; (2) that the plaintiff has been injured *by the defendant*; (3) facts that would cause a reasonable person to discover the injury.

In Wyckoff v. Mogollon Health All., 307 P.3d 1015, 1018 (Ariz. App. 2013), a case involving toxic mold exposure, the court held that "the cause of action begins to accrue when the claimant experiences physical signs and symptoms of illness, knows that she has been exposed to mold, and knows that mold may present a health hazard."

In Grisham v. Philip Morris U.S.A., Inc., 151 P.3d 1151 (Cal. 2007), the court held that causes of action for physical injuries related to smoking "did not begin to accrue until the physical ailments themselves were, or reasonably should have been, discovered."

6. ***Statutes of Limitations in Sexual Abuse Cases.*** Responding in part to increased allegations of sexual abuse by members of the clergy and others, some states have extended the statutes of limitations applicable to civil actions involving such misconduct. *See* Doe v. Roe, 20 A.3d 787, 788 (Md. 2011) (holding that a statute which lengthened the time for filing an action for sexual abuse of a minor applied retroactively to claims that were not already barred).

Consider the following Illinois statute, which also attempts to address precisely what must be discovered for purposes of triggering the discovery rule.

Illinois Compiled Statutes Annotated Chapter 735, Act 5, § 13-202.2 (Westlaw 2022)

§ 13-202.2. Childhood sexual abuse.

....

(b) ... [A]n action for damages for personal injury based on childhood sexual abuse must be commenced within 20 years of the date the limitation period begins to run under subsection (d) or within 20 years of the date the person abused discovers or through the use of reasonable diligence should discover both (i) that the act of childhood sexual abuse occurred and (ii) that the injury was caused by the childhood sexual abuse. The fact that the person abused discovers or through the use of reasonable diligence should discover that the act of childhood sexual abuse occurred is not, by itself, sufficient to start the discovery period under this subsection (b). Knowledge of the abuse does not constitute discovery of the injury or the causal relationship between any later-discovered injury and the abuse.

. . . .

(d) The limitation periods under subsection (b) do not begin to run before the person abused attains the age of 18 years; and, if at the time the person abused attains the age of 18 years he or she is under other legal disability, the limitation periods under subsection (b) do not begin to run until the removal of the disability.

(d-1) The limitation periods in subsection (b) do not run during a time period when the person abused is subject to threats, intimidation, manipulation, or fraud perpetrated by the abuser or by any person acting in the interest of the abuser. . . .

7. ***"Inherently Undiscoverable."*** Some courts say that a discovery rule will not be applied to a case unless it involves harm of a type that is inherently undiscoverable. *See* Loguidice v. Metro. Life Ins. Co., 336 F.3d 1 (1st Cir. 2003) (refusing to apply a discovery rule because the alleged fraudulent marketing of life insurance as a retirement plan did not involve an inherently unknowable fact; had the plaintiff "looked at the materials in the folder . . . , she would have learned that there was nothing in the folder that could have constituted part of . . . [a] retirement plan").

See also Pero's Steak and Spaghetti House v. Lee, 90 S.W.3d 614 (Tenn. 2002) (holding that the discovery rule did not toll the statute on a claim for conversion in the absence of fraud because the law "presumes that property owners know what their assets are and where they are located").

8. ***Latent-Disease Cases.*** Virtually every jurisdiction applies some form of the discovery rule to latent-disease cases, such as suits resulting from exposure to asbestos, DES, or toxic chemicals. As the U.S. Supreme Court noted in a silicosis case, "no specific date of contact with the [harmful] substances causing the disease can be charged with being the date of injury, inasmuch as the injurious consequences of exposure are the product of a period of time rather than a point of time." Urie v. Thompson, 337 U.S. 163 (1949).

In Childs v. Haussecker, 974 S.W.2d 31 (Tex. 1998), the court noted that requiring the judiciary and defendants to expend their limited resources on premature litigation of speculative claims is neither efficient nor desirable. It held that in the latent occupational disease context, a cause of action does not accrue until a plaintiff's symptoms manifest themselves to a degree or for a duration that would put a reasonable person on notice that he or she suffers from some injury and he or she knows, or in the exercise of reasonable diligence should have known, that the injury is likely work-related.

9. ***Tolling Based on Minority.*** In most jurisdictions, statutes of limitations are tolled while the plaintiff is a minor. Thus, in clergy sexual abuse cases, the applicable statute of limitations typically begins to run only when the victim reaches the age of majority. *See* Doe v. Roman Catholic Archdiocese of Galveston-Houston ex rel. Dinardo, 362 S.W.3d 803 (Tex. App. 2012); Doe v. Archdiocese of Cincinnati, 849 N.E.2d 268 (Ohio 2006).

In Fehrenbach v. O'Malley, 862 N.E.2d 489 (Ohio 2007), the court held that a child's minority also tolled the statute of limitations applicable to the child's parents' derivative loss of consortium claim.

Tort reformers have frequently sought to change the rule on tolling during minority. *See, e.g.,* Iowa Code Ann. § 614.1(9)(b) (Westlaw 2022) (stating that unless a statutory discovery rule applies, a medical malpractice action brought on behalf of a minor who was under the age of eight years when the malpractice occurred shall be commenced no later than the minor's tenth birthday). In some cases, laws extinguishing the rights of minors before they reach majority have been held to be unconstitutional. *See* Sands *ex rel.* Sands v. Green, 156 P.3d 1130 (Alaska 2007).

10. ***Tolling Based on Incompetency.*** Tolling also may occur if the plaintiff is incompetent. For example, in Rivas v. Overlake Hosp. Med. Ctr., 189 P.3d 753 (Wash. 2008), the relevant statute provided for tolling if a person is "incompetent or disabled to such a degree that he or she cannot understand the nature of the proceedings. . . ."

See also Kratz ex rel. Kratz-Spera v. MedSource Community Services, Inc., 139 A.3d 1087, 1094–95 (Md. Spec. App. 2016) ("The tolling exception preserves the legal rights of a mentally incompetent individual until a guardian is appointed; once a guardian is appointed, and gains the requisite knowledge to file a claim on the individual's behalf, the statute begins to run").

11. ***Tolling Based on Fraudulent Concealment.*** The running of the statute is also tolled if the defendant fraudulently conceals the injury. *Cf.* Baye v. Diocese of Rapid City, 630 F.3d 757, 761 (8th Cir. 2011) (holding that fraudulent concealment did not toll the running of the statute of limitations on a claim against a diocese because there was no evidence showing that the diocese knew or should have known about a priest's alleged sexual assault on the plaintiff years earlier).

However, even if fraudulent concealment is proved, it does not extend the period for filing indefinitely. For example, under Texas law, "[t]he estoppel effect of fraudulent concealment ends when a party learns of facts, conditions, or circumstances which would cause a reasonably prudent person to make inquiry, which, if pursued, would lead to discovery of the concealed cause of action." Etan Indus., Inc. v. Lehmann, 359 S.W.3d 620 (Tex. 2011).

12. ***Legal Malpractice and the Continuing-Representation Doctrine.*** Many courts have recognized the "continuing-representation doctrine," which tolls the statute of

limitations in legal malpractice cases while the lawyer continues to represent the plaintiff's interests in the matter in question. According to one court:

> The doctrine "recognizes that a person seeking professional assistance has a right to repose confidence in the professional's ability and good faith, and realistically cannot be expected to question and assess the techniques employed or the manner in which the services are rendered." .... It is not "realistic to say that the client's right of action accrued before he terminated the relationship with the attorney."

Murphy v. Smith, 579 N.E.2d 165 (Mass. 1991). *See also* Jackson Jordan, Inc. v. Leydig, Voit & Mayer, 633 N.E.2d 627 (Ill. 1994) (a law firm was equitably estopped from asserting the statute of limitations as a defense because the firm continually assured the client that its legal position was sound, even after a competitor brought an infringement action).

13. ***Tolling Based on Battered Woman's Syndrome.*** *See* Giovine v. Giovine, 663 A.2d 109 (N.J. Super. Ct. App. Div. 1995) (holding that the statute of limitations may be tolled if the plaintiff establishes that she suffered from battered woman's syndrome).

14. ***Tolling Pursuant to Statute.*** Under California law, no person charged by an accusatory pleading with child abuse may bring a defamation action based on such statements while the charges are pending. The applicable defamation statute of limitations is tolled during that period. *See* Cal. Civ. Code § 48.7(a) (Westlaw 2022).

15. ***Contractual Shortening of the Statute of Limitations.*** Parties may be able to alter the length of the applicable statute of limitations by contract. In Moreno v. Sanchez, 131 Cal. Rptr. 2d 684 (Ct. App. 2003), the court wrote:

> Courts generally enforce parties' agreements for a shorter limitations period than otherwise provided by statute, provided it is reasonable. "Reasonable" in this context means the shortened period nevertheless provides sufficient time to effectively pursue a judicial remedy.

Moreno was an action based on breach of a home inspector's duty of care. The court held that a contractual provision, which provided that a one-year limitations period ran from the date of the inspection (as opposed to when the breach was or should have been discovered), was invalid because it unreasonably deprived the plaintiff of the benefits of the discovery rule.

16. ***Tolling Agreements.*** Parties may enter into a "tolling agreement." A tolling agreement estops the defendant from asserting a statute of limitations defense with respect to the period covered by the agreement. A tolling agreement may be useful when parties are attempting to resolve a claim without the bad publicity that attends a public filing. A tolling agreement can provide more time for negotiations.

17. ***Ethics in Law Practice: Statutes of Limitations and Lawyer Discipline.*** In all jurisdictions, rules of ethics require lawyers to report misconduct by other lawyers. These duties are qualified by a lawyer's obligation to maintain the confidentiality of

client information and are presumably limited by the fact that, in some states, there is a disciplinary statute of limitations. For example, in Texas, the Rules of Disciplinary Procedure provide that:

> No attorney licensed to practice law in Texas may be disciplined for Professional Misconduct occurring more than four years before the time when the allegation of Professional Misconduct is brought to the attention of the Office of Chief Disciplinary Counsel, except in cases in which disbarment or suspension is compulsory. Limitations will not begin to run where fraud or concealment is involved until such Professional Misconduct is discovered or should have been discovered in the exercise of reasonable diligence by the Complainant.

Similarly, a Colorado rule provides that:

> A request for investigation against an attorney shall be filed within five years of the time that the complaining witness discovers or reasonably should have discovered the misconduct. There shall be no statute of limitations for misconduct alleging fraud, conversion, or conviction of a serious crime, or for an offense the discovery of which has been prevented by concealment by the attorney.

See Vincent R. Johnson, Legal Malpractice Litigation and the Duty to Report Misconduct, 1 St. Mary's J. Legal Mal. & Ethics 40, 71 (2011).

C. Statutes of Repose

Modern technology has, on the whole, increased safety considerably; life expectancy today is much greater than it was even thirty years ago, and very much greater than it was in past centuries. Technology has also, however, created situations in which someone's negligence or other tortious conduct may not lead to an injury for many years. Products that will last for decades may inflict injuries long after their manufacture and sale. Toxic substances like asbestos and DES can lead to injuries which manifest themselves long after the plaintiff's exposure to them.

Many states have enacted "statutes of repose" applicable to particular kinds of claims. These statutes resemble statutes of limitations in barring claims after a certain period—generally somewhat longer than the period specified in the statute of limitations—has passed. Unlike statutes of limitations, statutes of repose are not subject to tolling, and they often begin to run when the activity in question, such as the manufacture or sale of the product, takes place, rather than at the time the plaintiff is injured. *See* Stearns v. Metro. Life Ins. Co., 117 N.E.3d 694 (Mass. 2019) (holding that a statute of repose for tort actions arising out of an improvement to real property eliminated all such claims after the established period elapsed, even if the cause of action arose from a disease with an extended latency period).

Statutes of repose have been enacted not only because of the concerns that inspire statutes of limitations, but also in response to complaints by certain kinds of defendants — particularly manufacturers, doctors, and builders — that they are being exposed to crushing liability. These statutes are, therefore, to some extent an arbitrary cutoff on liability for reasons involving more than the difficulties raised by the passage of time.

Some statutes of repose are broadly applicable, such as one in Texas relating to defective products:

Texas Civil Practice & Remedies Code § 16.012 (Westlaw 2022)

> (b) Except as provided by Subsections (c), (d) [involving latent diseases], and (d-1) [involving actions that accrue before the end of the limitations period], a claimant must commence a products liability action against a manufacturer or seller of a product before the end of 15 years after the date of the sale of the product by the defendant.
>
> (c) If a manufacturer or seller expressly warrants in writing that the product has a useful safe life of longer than 15 years, a claimant must commence a products liability action against that manufacturer or seller of the product before the end of the number of years warranted after the date of the sale of the product by that seller.

See Vaughn v. Fedders Corp., 239 Fed. Appx. 27 (5th Cir. 2007) (finding the Texas statute unconstitutional as applied to homeowners who did not have a reasonable period within which to file claims); Fla. Stat. Ann. § 95.031(2)(b)-(d) (Westlaw 2022) (defining statutes of repose applicable to products liability actions).

As with all legislation, the reach of a statute of repose is a matter of interpretation. *See, e.g.*, Hyer v. Pittsburgh Corning Corp., 790 F.2d 30 (4th Cir. 1986) (holding that a six-year statute of repose applied to "injuries," but not to "diseases," caused by exposure to asbestos-containing products); Chrysler Corp. v. Batten, 450 S.E.2d 208 (Ga. 1994) (holding that a statute permitted a negligent-failure-to-warn claim, but not a negligent-design claim). In addition, the statute must apply to the facts of the case at hand. *See, e.g.*, Hickman v. Carven, 784 A.2d 31 (Md. 2001) (desecration of a graveyard was not an "improvement" of realty, and therefore the statute did not bar an action for concealment of the desecration).

Schramm v. Lyon

Supreme Court of Georgia
673 S.E.2d 241 (Ga. 2009)

THOMPSON, Justice.

In 1982, Betty Lyon had her spleen removed as a result of injuries she received in an automobile accident. In September 2004, Lyon developed overwhelming post-splenectomy infection (OPSI), a condition which resulted in significant physical injuries, including the amputation of parts of her arms and legs.

Lyon filed a medical malpractice action on August 29, 2006, against eight physicians and their practices who had treated her in the five years prior to the filing of the action. The complaint as subsequently amended alleged that each doctor failed to advise and warn her about the risk of developing OPSI, failed to inform her of preventative measures she should have taken to reduce the risk of developing OPSI, and failed to prescribe appropriate medications and vaccinations which would have prevented infections that can lead to OPSI.

Three defendants, Doctors Schramm, Barnes and Sharon, each of whom Lyon had first seen prior to August 29, 2001, moved to dismiss the claims against them on the basis of the statute of repose, OCGA § 9-3-71(b), which provides that "in no event may an action for medical malpractice be brought more than five years after the date on which the negligent or wrongful act or omission occurred." The trial court granted the motion, holding that the statute of repose began to run from the date the doctors first provided medical care to Lyon regardless of whether they committed subsequent negligent acts. The Court of Appeals reversed....

Under Georgia law, an action for medical malpractice must be brought within five years from the date on which the negligent or wrongful act or omission occurred.... Unlike cases involving the medical malpractice statute of limitation, see OCGA § 9-3-71(a), our focus in this case is on the date or dates on which appellants may have committed acts of professional negligence.[1] The test for determining when OCGA § 9-3-71(b)'s period of repose begins is based on the determination of when the negligent act causing the injury occurred.

In this case, the complaint alleges and Lyon's experts aver that within the five-year period prior to the filing of the complaint appellants committed separate acts of professional negligence by failing to warn, treat, and advise Lyon when she presented for the treatment of new medical conditions not related to the condition for which she first sought treatment. Accordingly, we agree with the Court of Appeals

1. [Fn. 1:] We agree with the Court of Appeals that this is not a misdiagnosis case.... Lyon did not contract OPSI until September 2004 and she raises no allegation in her complaint that appellants could or should have discovered the infection any sooner. Rather, this case involves appellants' alleged failure to warn Lyon of the dangers related to her post-splenectomy condition and their concomitant failure to advise her of and treat her with available and recommended vaccines which she claims would have prevented the onset of her infection.

that the complaint alleges appellants committed subsequent negligent acts causing new injuries which are subject to separate periods of repose.[2] . . . .

Appellants argue that the statute of repose commenced to run on the date they each first treated Lyon, that any subsequent negligent acts were part of their continuing treatment of Lyon, and therefore, her claims are barred by the five-year statute of repose. We find, and appellants have offered, no legal authority or justification for barring Lyon's claims solely because appellants may also have been negligent at an earlier time. Although chronologically appellants' initial consultation with Lyon may have constituted their first negligent act or omission, OCGA § 9-3-71(b) does not provide that the period of repose commences on the date of the first "negligent . . . act or omission." It provides that the period commences on the date the negligent act or omission occurs, thus establishing the negligent act as the trigger for commencement of the period of repose without purporting to limit the number of separate negligent acts which may act as a trigger. As this Court has recognized, multiple breaches of the standard of care may constitute new and separate instances of professional negligence and more than one negligent act may contribute to a plaintiff's injury. . . . Appellants' argument ignores both these maxims and the allegations of Lyon's complaint specifying that within the five-year period prior to filing her complaint she consulted with appellants for the treatment of new medical conditions and that during the same time period recommended medical protocols for treating post-splenectomy patients had changed. Based on these allegations, the complaint cannot properly be characterized as asserting a single, persistent negligent act as argued by appellants.

Accordingly, we find the statute of repose as to each separate claim of professional negligence began to run within the statutory five-year period and the Court of Appeals in its thorough opinion correctly reversed the trial court's ruling that the claims were barred.

. . . .

Importantly, our holding in this case is not the adoption of the continuing treatment doctrine so as to allow for the tolling of the statute of repose and should not be interpreted as to impose upon physicians a continuing duty to warn patients of risks from an existing condition at each subsequent visit. Instead, it is our recognition that the complaint in this case sufficiently alleges separate and independent acts of professional negligence within the statutory period of repose. Prescribing periods of repose, like periods of limitation, is a legislative function . . . and this Court has consistently rejected attempts to interfere with the legislature's two-year statute of limitation and has not revived the continuing treatment doctrine. . . . Likewise, in this case we reject appellants' invitation to modify the legislatively prescribed five-year statute of repose

2. [Fn. 2:] Because the allegations of the complaint make clear that this is not a continuing treatment case, we need not decide in this appeal whether the continuing treatment doctrine rejected in Young v. Williams, 274 Ga. 845, 560 S.E.2d 690 (2002) is applicable to the statute of repose.

by ruling as a matter of law that the period of repose commences on the occurrence of a defendant's first negligent act. To do so would be inconsistent with the plain language of OCGA § 9-3-71(b) and do nothing to promote the statute's stated goals of eliminating stale claims and stabilizing medical insurance underwriting. . . .

Judgment affirmed.

Notes

1. ***When Does a Repose Statute Begin to Run?*** Anderson v. Wagner, 402 N.E.2d 560 (Ill. 1979), was a case in which the statute of repose may have barred an action before the plaintiffs discovered that they had been injured. The importance of a statute of repose in that kind of case is that the statute overrides the discovery rule. Some repose statutes go further, barring claims even before an injury has occurred. For example, if a products-liability statute of repose bars suits filed more than ten years after the product in question was first sold, someone who buys an eleven-year-old defective product and then sustains an injury has no claim against the manufacturer, even if the claim is filed immediately after the injury. *See* New York C.P.L.R. § 214-a (Westlaw 2022).

See also Brucker v. Mercola, 886 N.E.2d 306 (Ill. 2007) (holding that the repose period applicable to prenatal injuries does not begin to run until the child is born "because liability does not attach until birth and because there is no right to bring a cause of action until birth"). Some states take a different position.

2. ***Revival of Time-Barred Claims.*** Some courts have held that a time-barred claim may be legislatively revived. *See* Hymowitz v. Eli Lilly and Co., 539 N.E.2d 1069 (N.Y. 1989) (DES claims). New York passed a law that revived claims against municipalities by people allegedly sickened while working in and around Ground Zero following the 2001 terror attacks. Joel Stashenko, *N.Y. Opens One-Year Window for Time Barred 9/11 Claims*, www.law.com, Sept. 25, 2009.

However, some states hold that revival of time-barred claims is unconstitutional. See Doe A. v. Diocese of Dallas, 917 N.E.2d 475 (Ill. 2009) (holding, in a case involving sexual abuse, that once a statute of limitations has expired, the defendant has a vested right protected by the state due process clause).

3. ***Laches.*** Only in the rarest of cases will there be no statute of limitations applicable to a tort action. In Haferman v. St. Clare Healthcare Found., Inc., 707 N.W.2d 853 (Wis. 2005), the court concluded that the state legislature had failed to specify a statute of limitations applicable to a medical malpractice claim by a disabled child, and therefore 11-year-old plaintiff's claim for birth-related injuries was not time barred. The court noted that, on appropriate facts, a claim not governed by a statute of limitations might be barred by the equitable doctrine of laches, if the plaintiff unreasonably delayed filing suit and the defendant was prejudiced by the delay.

4. ***Ethics in Law Practice: "Technical" Defenses.*** Is it immoral to assert a "technical" defense, such as a statute of limitations or statute of repose, to assist a client in avoiding payment to a lender, a provider of services, or an injured person to whom

the client, in truth, should be liable? And, if there is a moral issue, is the issue one for the lawyer, or the client, or the lawyer and client jointly? These types of questions have evoked various responses from scholars. In exploring this subject, Professors Thomas L. Shaffer and Robert F. Cochran write:

> [F]ailing to raise . . . [a technical] defense when it is available is probably legal malpractice. To say that, though, is not to say that the lawyer who *refuses* to argue a defense under, say, the statute of limitations, violates the professional rules or is liable for malpractice. The professional rules allow for lawyer conscience. But it is to say that the lawyer who refuses is required to say something to her client about her refusal—not to ignore the issue—and then, if the client insists on making the defense, to withdraw in such a way as not to harm the client's case. The moral issue . . . is whether it is immoral *not* to refuse.

Thomas L. Shaffer & Robert F. Cochran, Jr., *"Technical" Defenses: Ethics, Morals, and the Lawyer as Friend*, 14 Clinical L. Rev. 337, 340 (2007).

Chapter 20

Interference with Possession or Use of Land: Trespass and Nuisance

A defendant's tortious interference with the plaintiff's possession or use of land is actionable, either as "trespass to land" or as "nuisance." Traditionally, the distinction between trespass and nuisance turned upon whether the defendant's misconduct led to a physical invasion of the plaintiff's land. If the defendant intentionally walked across the land or caused rocks to be thrown upon it, the defendant had committed a trespass. If the defendant tortiously interfered with land without physically invading it, as by negligently or intentionally causing foul odors or loud noises to disturb the plaintiff's use of real property, the tort was nuisance.

Neither trespass nor nuisance is an "absolute liability" tort. In order to hold someone liable for either trespass or nuisance, the plaintiff must show that the defendant intentionally interfered with the plaintiff's possession or use of the land, or that the interference was caused by the defendant's failure to exercise care (negligence or recklessness), or that the defendant engaged in an activity—such as blasting—which is subject to strict liability.

It is not enough for the plaintiff simply to show that something the defendant did caused an invasion of the plaintiff's interest in the land. For example, suppose that someone's window has been broken by a baseball hit by a child playing on a nearby lot. Is this a "trespass"? On the limited facts given here, there is no way to tell. If the child was trying to hit the defendant's house there is a trespass, based on an intentional invasion. If the child acted unreasonably in playing ball close to a house, there would also be a trespass, based on negligence or recklessness. But if an intentional, reckless, or negligent invasion cannot be shown, there is no trespass (or any other tort): playing baseball is not a strict-liability activity.

Many authorities speak of trespass to land exclusively as an intentional tort, even though they permit an action for damages when negligence causes harm to land. *See, e.g.*, Snow v. City of Columbia, 409 S.E.2d 797 (S.C. Ct. App. 1991) (trespass would not lie where water from a leaking main caused damage to homeowners, but the issue of the city's negligence in installing and maintaining the main should have been submitted to the jury). Other authorities use the term trespass more expansively. *See* State Farm Fire & Cas. Co. v. White-Rodgers Corp., 77 P.3d 729 (Alaska 2003) (holding that a natural gas explosion that destroyed a house, allegedly as a result of a negligently installed and defective gas control product, was trespass upon real property for purposes of the statute of limitations because the label "'trespass' attaches broadly to any alleged interference with a possessor's property rights").

A brief discussion of trespass was set forth *supra* in Chapter 2.

A. Trespass to Land

The formal name for "trespass to land" is "trespass *quare clausum fregit.*" "*Quare clausum fregit*" (often shortened to "q.c.f.") means "because he broke the close." A "close"[1] is an imaginary barrier around the outside edge of someone's real property. By crossing the property line, an intruder "breaks the close."

Gavcus v. Potts

United States Court of Appeals for the Seventh Circuit
808 F.2d 596 (7th Cir. 1986)

FAIRCHILD, Senior Circuit Judge.

....

Mr. Gavcus died in March of 1981. Lillian Potts was Mr. Gavcus' daughter by a prior marriage and was a residual beneficiary under her father's will. Lillian's family attended his funeral and left several days afterwards after staying with Mrs. Gavcus in her home. The Potts[es] returned to Mrs. Gavcus' home the day after they left and, in her absence, removed a large quantity of silver coins valued at more than $150,000. The deputy who investigated the removal of the coins contacted Mrs. Potts, who later returned the coins to the sheriff's office. A couple of weeks later, Mrs. Gavcus hired an attorney to get the coins back for her. The attorney initiated a proceeding pursuant to ... § 968.20 of the Wisconsin Statutes for return of the coins.... The circuit court determined that the coins belonged to Mrs. Gavcus individually and ordered their return.... Mrs. Gavcus then brought the suit at bar for damages, including the attorney fees she incurred in the prior litigation.

....

Mrs. Gavcus did not claim any physical injury to the real property. The court did allow her to offer evidence of the cost of new locks and the burglar alarm she installed after the removal of the coins, and of the amount of attorney's fees incurred in the earlier litigation. Apparently the district court had some doubt as to the propriety of these items of damage and chose to admit the evidence and submit questions concerning those items in a special verdict, and to address the legal questions after the verdict was returned. The appeal arises from the court's determination that these items were not properly recoverable as damages. The jury had awarded by special verdict $3,126 for the cost of locks and a burglar alarm and $12,000 in attorney's fees.

1. Pronounced like "close" in "please close the door."

Nominal compensatory damages can be awarded when no actual or substantial injury has been alleged or proved, since the law infers some damage from the unauthorized entry of land. Additionally, compensatory damages can be awarded for actual or substantial injury to realty. These latter damages are generally measured by the cost of restoring the property to its former condition or by the change in value before and after the trespass. Consequential damages can also be recovered for a trespass, since a trespasser is liable in damages for all injuries flowing from his trespass which are the natural and proximate result of it. One such compensable result of a trespass is personal injury to the owner of the land. If a trespass causes mental distress, the trespasser is liable in damages for the mental distress and any resulting illness or physical harm. . . .

The installation of locks and a burglar alarm was not a repair of physical damage, and the cost was not recoverable as compensation for injury to property. Mrs. Gavcus' theory is that the trespass had caused an impairment of her sense of security and that the installation became reasonably necessary on account of that impairment.

We reject the theory, however, for two reasons. Impairment of her sense of security would amount, if anything, to a type of emotional distress. Mrs. Gavcus was not prepared to produce medical or other expert testimony on the subject. Judge Gordon ruled that lay evidence would be inadmissible, and Mrs. Gavcus has not argued the ruling was erroneous. Thus there was a failure of proof as to the nature, extent, and causation of any emotional distress, or cost of required treatment.

Second, assuming that she could have proved that the trespass caused increased nervousness, uneasiness, and worry, she cites no authority, nor was any authority found, which shows that the cost of an improvement to property intended to alleviate distress of that type would be properly allowable as damages.

. . . .

[The court held that the attorney's fees in the earlier action were not recoverable in an action for trespass. The fees, it thought, were incurred because of the dispute as to the ownership of the coins, not because of Mrs. Potts's having trespassed in an effort to obtain the coins. Therefore, the prior litigation and the fees incurred in conducting it were not "a natural and proximate result" of Mrs. Potts's trespass.]

. . . .

Both parties agree that the award of punitive damages could not be sustained unless compensatory damages had been awarded. . . .

The judgment appealed from is affirmed.

Notes

1. ***Presumed Damage***. An intentional trespass is actionable even if the plaintiff suffers no actual injury. *See* Smith v. Carbide and Chemicals Corp., 507 F.3d 372 (6th Cir. 2007) (applying Kentucky law in a dispute involving groundwater and surface water).

In Dougherty v. Stepp, 18 N.C. 371 (1835), the defendant entered on the unenclosed land of the plaintiff, with a surveyor and chain carriers, and surveyed a part of it, claiming it as his own, but without marking trees or cutting bushes. The court held that an action for trespass was established: "the law infers some damage; if nothing more, the treading down the grass or herbage, or as here, the shrubbery."

If Hooters and Olive Garden are adjacent restaurants, and employees from Hooters park in spaces leased to Olive Garden despite repeated requests not to do so, an action for trespass will lie regardless of whether damage has been caused. *See* General Mills Restaurants, Inc. v. Texas Wings, Inc., 12 S.W.3d 827 (Tex. App. 2000).

However, some courts reject the presumed damage rule. In Rhodes v. E.I. du Pont de Nemours & Co., 636 F.3d 88, 96 (4th Cir. 2011), an acid (PFOA) dumped by a chemical facility entered the public water supply, was pumped into the plaintiffs' homes, and accumulated in the plaintiffs' blood in measurable amounts. Noting that the plaintiffs had not become ill, the court rejected their trespass claim because they "failed to produce evidence showing that the presence of PFOA in the water supplied to their homes has damaged or interfered with the plaintiffs' possession and use of their property."

2. ***Trespassers and Unforeseeable Harm***. The law has frequently gone to great lengths to hold intentional tortfeasors liable for unforeseeable results. There are many cases in which trespassers have been assessed damages for harm caused by accidentally started fires and other unforeseeable damage to the defendant's land. *See* William L. Prosser, *Transferred Intent*, 45 Tex. L. Rev. 650, 658–61 (1967).

3. ***Mistake***. Many cases of trespass result from disputes over the ownership of land. The defendant's reasonable but mistaken belief that the land belongs to the defendant rather than to someone else does not excuse a trespass. If the law were otherwise, trespass would often not be available to resolve disputes over ownership. Furthermore, the trespasser who removes or destroys part of the real property, such as minerals or trees, is liable to the true owner despite having reasonably believed that the trespasser owned the property.

4. ***Trespass to Airspace***. A defendant need not touch the land in question to be liable for trespass. Thus, building a balcony that overhangs the plaintiff's property is a trespass. In the early days of the common law, the owner's rights in the space above the land were sometimes described by saying, "*cujus est solum, ejus est usque ad coelum*," which means that the landowner owns everything above the surface all the way up to heaven. Until the invention of the airplane, this formulation of the owner's rights did no harm; modern aviation has made change essential.

According to the Restatement, Second, of Torts, §159, flight over land is a trespass only if "it enters into the immediate reaches of the airspace next to the land" or if it "interferes substantially with the . . . use and enjoyment of [the] land." Under United States v. Causby, 328 U.S. 256 (1946), federal legislation and regulations concerning aviation have made airspace at ordinary flying altitudes a "public highway," and federal law now controls the use of that airspace.

To sum up a complex body of law in a sentence, very low flights over someone's land may be a trespass; higher flights which interfere seriously with land use because of noise or repetitiveness may be nuisances; ordinary flying is neither.

See Benjamin D. Mathews, *Potential Tort Liability for Personal Use of Drone Aircraft*, 46 St. Mary's L.J. 573, 592–93 (2015) ("Tort claims for trespass have succeeded at heights of twenty to thirty feet. It is reasonable to infer that flights at a very low level, such as a height of eight feet, will potentially incur liability for trespass, provided the additional elements of the tort are met").

5. ***Termination of Consent or Privilege.*** Rogers v. Board of Road Comm'rs for Kent County, 30 N.W.2d 358 (Mich. 1947), was an action for wrongful death caused by the defendant's failure to remove the anchor posts for a snow fence it had installed on the decedent's land. The defendant had been given permission to erect the fence, on the understanding that it would be taken down at the end of the winter. Plaintiff's decedent died when a mower he was operating struck the anchor post, throwing him into the mower's moving parts. The court held that the defendant's failure to remove the posts was a trespass, citing § 160 of the Restatement, Second, of Torts:

> A trespass may be committed by the continued presence on the land of a structure, chattel or other thing which the actor or his predecessor in legal interest has placed on the land
>
> (a) with the consent of the person then in possession of the land, if the actor fails to remove it after the consent has been effectively terminated, or
>
> (b) pursuant to a privilege conferred on the actor irrespective of the possessor's consent, if the actor fails to remove it after the privilege has been terminated, by the accomplishment of its purpose or otherwise.

See also Montgomery Ward v. Andrews, 736 P.2d 40 (Colo. Ct. App. 1987) (even if the defendant had a statutory or contractual right to enter the premises of a catalog sales agency to repossess secured property, it exceeded its rights and committed a trespass by changing the locks and keeping the keys for ten days).

In Roman Catholic Archbishop of Boston v. Rogers, 39 N.E.3d 736 (Mass. App. 2015), the court held that parishioners of a deconsecrated parish, who maintained an around-the-clock vigil and refused to leave, were trespassers, and permanently enjoined them from entering the church property. The court explained that "[w]hile we acknowledge the defendants' heartfelt beliefs that they are entitled to remain on the premises as an exercise of their freedom of religion, the judge's conclusion that the defendants are trespassers is supported by the evidence."

6. ***Standing.*** Because the action for trespass q.c.f. is intended to protect possession of land, it may ordinarily be maintained only by one currently in possession. *See, e.g,* Russell v. American Real Estate Corp., 89 S.W.3d 204 (Tex. App. 2002) (permitting an action by a tenant at sufferance following foreclosure). However, some authorities permit a person entitled to future possession to sue to protect that interest. In Plotkin v. Club Valencia Condo. Ass'n, 717 P.2d 1027 (Colo. Ct. App. 1986), the owner

of a condominium that was rented to a tenant was deemed to have constructive possession of the unit's balcony and permitted to sue for trespass.

7. ***Trespass by Journalists.*** Is it a trespass for a journalist to accompany law enforcement officers into a private home after a fire? In Florida Publ'g Co. v. Fletcher, 340 So. 2d 914 (Fla. 1976), the court ruled that a journalist has an implied consent, based on custom and usage, to enter private property after a calamity, if invited by officials. Other courts have ruled that journalists accompanying officials may be liable for trespass, and perhaps other torts as well. *See, e.g.*, Berger v. Hanlon, 129 F.3d 505 (9th Cir. 1997), *judgment vacated on other grounds*, 526 U.S. 808 (1999) (a claim for trespass was stated because law enforcement officers conducting a search were not authorized to invite third parties onto the premises for reasons unrelated to law enforcement; *Fletcher* was deemed irrelevant because it involved a "disaster"). *See also* Desnick v. ABC, 44 F.3d 1345, 1351 (7th Cir. 1995) ("there is no journalists' privilege to trespass").

B. Trespass and Private Nuisance

Public Nuisance and Private Nuisance. Nuisance comes in two varieties—"public nuisance" and "private nuisance." This section will compare trespass and "private nuisance," which for present purposes can be thought of as nuisances which affect only the plaintiff, or the plaintiff and a handful of others, as when one's neighbor holds raucous beer parties every weekend with the volume of the music cranked up high. Nuisances not confined in their effects to a few property owners—the wrongful closing of a public road or the pollution of a lake used by many persons for swimming, for example—are "public nuisances," which will be examined in the following section.

"Attractive Nuisance" Distinguished. The "attractive nuisance" doctrine (discussed in Chapter 10) is unrelated to the action for private nuisance. Under the doctrine of attractive nuisance, which is an aspect of the law of premises liability, a landholder may be held liable for injuries to trespassing children caused by highly dangerous artificial conditions on land. *See* Restatement, Second, of Torts § 339. The injury-causing condition need not qualify as a "nuisance" in the sense in which that term is used in this chapter in order for relief to be granted under the attractive nuisance doctrine.

1. Trespass and Nuisance Distinguished

a. The Traditional Distinction

Private nuisance and trespass q.c.f. are closely related, for both involve an impairment of another's interests in land. It has traditionally been said that trespass protects a possessor's right to *exclusive possession* of land, while private nuisance protects the possessor's interest in *use and enjoyment* of the property. Trespass requires entry above, under, or onto the land in question, but typically does not require that the plaintiff suffer actual damages. Private nuisance, in contrast, does not require entry, but substantial harm must be shown.

Since a trespassory invasion may result in serious interference with the enjoyment of land, both trespass and nuisance actions may arise from a physical invasion, as where water is diverted onto a neighbor's property (Humphreys-Mexia Co. v. Arsenaux, 297 S.W. 225 (Tex. 1927)), or an encroaching building is erected on adjacent property (Allen v. Virginia Hill Water Supply Corp., 609 S.W.2d 633 (Tex. Civ. App. 1980)). However, not every intrusion amounts to unreasonable interference. *See* Hennessey v. Pyne, 694 A.2d 691, 695 (R.I. 1997) (a single golf ball, hit by the defendant, was "such an isolated incident" that it was "not the type of conduct that nuisance law is intended to remedy").

Gates v. Rohm and Haas Co., 2008 WL 2977867, *3 (E.D. Pa. 2008), was a case involving airborne vinyl chloride contamination. In discussing the plaintiffs' private nuisance claim, the court explained:

> Where the invading substance is a hazardous chemical, to demonstrate interference with use and enjoyment of the property, a plaintiff must show *either* a physical invasion *or* an invasion by something otherwise perceptible to the senses, but not necessarily physical, like noise or vibrations. . . . [T]he exposure level need not necessarily present a health risk to make out a property damage claim.

Unreasonably loud or persistent noises from sources off the land are a fairly common illustration of a private nuisance that is not a trespass. The Restatement uses "the defendant's dog howl[ing] under the plaintiff's window night after night" as an example of private nuisance. If the dog howls on the plaintiff's land there is a trespass as well. *See* Restatement, Second, of Torts § 821D cmt. e. Odors can be nuisances, as when the defendant raises cows or pigs in a residential area. So can lights, as when the defendant illuminates a residential neighborhood at night with bright lights.

All of the examples of private nuisance given above involved an "invasion" of the plaintiff's property, though not necessarily an invasion by physical objects, as the cases of noise and, perhaps, light[2] show. But there are cases in which the plaintiff's enjoyment of property can be reduced by conduct which never encroaches on the property itself, as when one's neighbor paints his house plaid, or establishes a den of prostitution, or lets junk accumulate on a vacant lot. Some of these activities have been held to be nuisances (either public or private). However, almost anything one can do will annoy some neighbor, and the courts have been reluctant to find

---

2. No opinion is expressed here on the relative merits of the wave theory and the particle theory of light.

non-invasive conduct to be a nuisance except in cases in which the conduct is manifestly undesirable, as in the prostitution example.

b. The Tangible-Mass "Requirement"

Older cases required that something tangible be deposited upon (or enter above or under) the plaintiff's land for a trespass action to lie. Thus, no claim for trespass was stated in cases involving nothing more than smoke, dust, gas, or fumes.

Particulate Trespass. Recent decisions have tended to repudiate the tangible-mass requirement. Many jurisdictions now allow a trespass action for invasions by invisible particles, but only if the plaintiff proves that actual damages have resulted from the invasion. *See* Maddy v. Vulcan Materials Co., 737 F. Supp. 1528 (D. Kan. 1990) (joining the "clear and consistent" case law in other jurisdictions).

Note that, in some jurisdictions, particulate trespass may be actionable without proof of damages. In Stevenson v. E.I. DuPont de Nemours and Co., 327 F.3d 400 (5th Cir. 2003), a case involving the emission of heavy metal particulates, the court opined that Texas courts would so hold and therefore affirmed in part a judgment based on a jury verdict that found that there was no nuisance and no negligence, but that the defendant had committed trespass. "Plaintiffs were not required to show substantial damage to their property" and could recover for diminution in property value.

Permitting an action for particulate trespass helps some plaintiffs by allowing actions that would formerly have been brought in nuisance to take advantage of what may be a longer statute of limitations for trespass.

In Johnson v. Paynesville Farmers Union Co-op. Oil Co., 817 N.W.2d 693, 704 (Minn. 2012), which held that pesticide drift did not constitute trespass on neighboring land used for organic farming, the court declined the plaintiff's "invitation to abandon the traditional distinctions between trespass and nuisance law." According to the court:

> [T]respass claims address tangible invasions of the right to exclusive possession of land, and nuisance claims address invasions of the right to use and enjoyment of land. The Johnsons do not allege that a tangible object invaded their land. The Johnsons' claim is that the Cooperative's actions have prevented them from using their land as an organic farm, not that any action of the Cooperative has prevented the Johnsons from possessing any part of their land. The Johnsons' claim is one for nuisance, not trespass.

Geophysical Trespass. Seismic testing raises difficult questions about the rights of affected owners of land and minerals. What if the test shooting occurs right outside the plaintiff's boundary line and yields valuable information about mineral deposits on the plaintiff's land or impairs the market value of the plaintiff's property? If this type of "interference" is actionable, should the claim be one for trespass or for nuisance? Villarreal v. Grant Geophysical, Inc., 136 S.W.3d 265 (Tex. App. 2004), held that actual physical entry was essential to a claim for geophysical trespass.

2. Significant Harm

Tortious Conduct is Required. An action for private nuisance requires proof that the defendant tortiously (*i.e.*, intentionally, recklessly, negligently, or by strict liability conduct) invaded the plaintiff's interest in land. Absent such evidence of responsibility, no action will lie. For example, in Pesaturo v. Kinne, 20 A.3d 284 (N.H. 2011), the court held that the plaintiff failed to establish a nuisance claim related to a tree with a limb overhanging the plaintiff's property because the plaintiff did not allege that the defendant-neighbor contributed to the existence of the tree on his property.

Aside from tortious conduct on the part of the defendant, the plaintiff must also show that the harm done was significant. Section 821F of the Restatement, Second, of Torts provides:

> There is liability for a nuisance only to those to whom it causes significant harm, of a kind that would be suffered by a normal person in the community or by property in normal condition and used for a normal purpose.

The commentary to the section states:

> c. *Significant Harm.* By significant harm is meant harm of importance, involving more than slight inconvenience or petty annoyance. The law does not concern itself with trifles....
>
> d. *Hypersensitive Persons or Property.* When an invasion involves a detrimental change in the physical condition of land, there is seldom any doubt as to the significant character of the invasion. When, however, it involves only personal discomfort or annoyance, it is sometimes difficult to determine whether the invasion is significant. The standard for the determination of significant character is the standard of normal persons or property in the particular locality....
>
> Thus a hypersensitive nervous invalid cannot found an action for a private nuisance upon ... [conduct that] a normal member of the community would regard ... as unobjectionable or at most a petty annoyance. This is true also when the harm to the plaintiff results only because of the hypersensitive condition of his land or chattels or his abnormal use of them. Thus an ordinary power line supplying electric current for household use does not create a nuisance when it interferes by induction with highly sensitive electrical instruments operating in the vicinity.
>
> On the other hand, when the invasion is of a kind that the normal individual in the community would find definitely annoying or offensive, the fact that those who live in the neighborhood are hardened to it and have no objection will not prevent the plaintiff from maintaining his action. For example, the noise of a boiler factory next door may be a private nuisance even though the plaintiff and others who live in the vicinity are stone deaf and cannot hear it. The deafness of the plaintiff himself will affect the damages that he can recover, but it does not prevent the existence of a genuine

interference with the use and enjoyment of his land as, for example, for the purpose of entertaining guests.

In Langan v. Bellinger, 611 N.Y.S.2d 59 (App. Div. 1994), the court held that the ringing of church bells on an hourly basis, between 8:00 a.m. and 8:00 p.m., and the presentation of carillon concerts at 12 noon and 6:00 p.m., did not constitute a nuisance to a resident of a house 250 feet from the church. An acoustical expert testified that the bells made no more noise than passing automobiles, of which 6,500 went by the resident's property each day, and there were affidavits from 15 village residents that the church bells were pleasant.

Unfounded Fears. Baseless apprehension on the part of the plaintiff will not support a cause of action for nuisance. Recovery was denied in Adkins v. Thomas Solvent Co., 487 N.W.2d 715 (Mich. 1992), because the undisputed testimony showed that the plaintiff's properties were not, and never would be, subject to contamination from the defendant's activities. Likewise, in Union Pac. Resources Co. v. Cooper, 109 S.W.3d 557 (Tex. App. 2003), a nuisance claim was unsuccessful. Although the plaintiff's brother had said "that if they smelled rotten eggs, it was sour gas and they would be sure to die," no sour gas was ever encountered incidental to the defendant's drilling operation.

Interference with Potential Use. For a nuisance to exist, the defendant's conduct need not interfere with the actual, present use of the plaintiff's property; the likelihood of interference with some use to which the property might reasonably be put will suffice. Meat Producers, Inc. v. McFarland, 476 S.W.2d 406, 410 (Tex. Civ. App. 1972), allowed an absentee landlord to recover damages from a cattle feedlot where he produced testimony that the highest and best use of the land was for homesites.

3. Assessing Unreasonableness

A defendant whose conduct has caused significant harm to the plaintiff's use or enjoyment of land will only be liable if the invasion was unreasonable. The reasonableness question is often, but not always, addressed by "balancing" the competing interests of the plaintiff, the defendant, and society as a whole.

Social Value of the Defendant's Conduct. If the defendant's conduct is viewed as necessary or useful to the community, rather than undesirable, it is easier to conclude that the resulting interference is reasonable. Thus, ordinary economic and recreational activities are unlikely to be held nuisances, while the contrary is true of illegal activities causing similar harm.

Some legislation expressly defines certain activities as nuisances. *See* Pope v. City of Houston, 559 S.W.2d 905, 907 (Tex. Civ. App. 1977) ("weeds, brush, [and] rubbish"); Ga. Code Ann. § 41-3-1.1 (Westlaw 2022) ("drug-related activity"); Cal. Health & Safety Code § 11570 (Westlaw 2022) (places "used for . . . unlawfully selling, serving, storing, keeping, manufacturing, or giving away any controlled substance"). Conduct falling within the terms of such enactments is regarded as having minimal social value, provided the enactment is legally valid. A legislative body may not, in the guise of halting injurious conditions, define an otherwise-legal activity as a nuisance, if there is no unreasonable interference with the interests of others. *See* City of Sundown v. Shewmake, 691 S.W.2d 57, 59 (Tex. App. 1985).

Lawfulness Versus Illegality. The defendant's compliance with statutory obligations, while not dispositive, supports a finding of reasonableness. *See* Garland Grain Co. v. D-C Home Owners Improvement Ass'n, 393 S.W.2d 635, 637 (Tex. Civ. App. 1965) (in denying an injunction, the court noted that a cattle feedlot was periodically inspected by the health department).

Violation of a legislative enactment normally supports a finding of unreasonableness, as where the defendant's conduct violates zoning laws.

However, in some instances violation of the law will be disregarded. *See* Luensmann v. Zimmer-Zampese & Assoc., 103 S.W.3d 594 (Tex. App. 2003) (holding that homeowners residing near a raceway were not entitled to permanent injunctive relief limiting drag racing, even though the drag races caused noise in excess of the 85-decibel-level defined in the disorderly conduct statute, because there was evidence that noise from other nearby sources exceeded 85 decibels even before the raceway began operations).

The Defendant's Motive. The defendant's reasons for engaging in an activity may support a nuisance finding if the defendant has done something primarily for the purpose of annoying the plaintiff. The classic example is the "spite fence"—a fence erected only to aggravate a neighbor. *See* Hutcherson v. Alexander, 70 Cal. Rptr. 366, 369 (Ct. App. 1968). However, in cases involving less-egregious conduct, many courts are inclined to treat motives as irrelevant.

Competing Financial Interests. Courts have sometimes taken financial matters into account, by examining the amounts invested in the activity by the plaintiff or the defendant, and by considering the jobs that would be lost if the defendant were enjoined. *See* Boomer v. Atlantic Cement Co., 257 N.E.2d 870 (N.Y. 1970).

Aesthetics. The mere unsightliness of a building will not, by itself, cause the structure to be regarded as a nuisance. Presumably, the reasoning of the courts is not that aesthetic matters are insignificant, but that it would be an unwise expenditure of limited judicial resources to attempt to adjudicate disputes over matters of taste. If, however, other factors suggest that the defendant's conduct unreasonably interferes with the interests of the plaintiff, a court may rely upon aesthetic considerations to bolster a finding of unreasonableness. *See* Tarlton v. Kaufman, 199 P.3d 263 (Mont. 2008) (finding that a jury instruction improperly limited consideration of the unsightliness of a massive fence).

The Defendant's Manner of Operation. If the defendant's manner of operation is normal and customary, and in accordance with sound scientific and technological principles, courts tend to regard any resulting interference as reasonable. Conversely, a defendant's failure to use technically and economically feasible means of avoiding harm to the plaintiff supports a finding that the resulting interference is unreasonable. *See* Restatement, Second, of Torts § 828(c); Guarina v. Bogart, 180 A.2d 557 (Pa. 1962) (a drive-in theater's use of public loudspeakers was enjoined because individual speakers could be installed at a small cost).

The Extent and Character of the Harm. The frequency, duration, and severity of the interference caused by the defendant, and the proximity of the defendant's activities to the site of the disturbance, may be considered by the court in assessing unreasonableness. The number of persons affected by the defendant's conduct is also part of this calculation. *See* Brenteson Wholesale v. Ariz. Public Serv. Co., 803 P.2d 930 (Ariz. Ct. App. 1990) (a utility was entitled to an injunction against use of an airstrip because flights would encroach on the utility's airspace and might result in contact with power lines).

The Appropriateness of the Activities to the Locality. "A nuisance may be merely a right thing in the wrong place, like a pig in the parlor instead of the barnyard." Euclid v. Ambler Realty Co., 272 U.S. 365, 388 (1926). Accordingly, great attention is paid to whether the defendant's activities are suited to the locality. As Prah v. Maretti, 321 N.W.2d 182 (Wis. 1982), *infra*, indicates, it is also appropriate for a court to consider whether the activities allegedly interfered with are themselves suited to the locality.

Who Got There First. The assessment of reasonableness is not simply a question of "who got there first." Therefore, it is no bar to a nuisance action that the offending condition existed before the plaintiff acquired or improved the land. Nevertheless, the fact that the plaintiff "came to the nuisance" is often given substantial weight in the balancing process. *See* Spur Indus. v. Del E. Webb Development Co., 494 P.2d 700 (Ariz. 1972), *infra*.

Prah v. Maretti

Supreme Court of Wisconsin
321 N.W.2d 182 (Wis. 1982)

ABRAHAMSON, Justice.

This appeal . . . was certified to this court by the court of appeals, . . . as presenting an issue of first impression, namely, whether an owner of a solar-heated residence states a claim upon which relief can be granted when he asserts that his neighbor's proposed construction of a residence (which conforms to existing deed restrictions and local ordinances) interferes with his access to an unobstructed path for sunlight across the neighbor's property. This case thus involves a conflict between one landowner (Glenn Prah, the plaintiff) interested in unobstructed access to sunlight across adjoining property as a natural source of energy and an adjoining landowner (Richard D. Maretti, the defendant) interested in the development of his land.

The circuit court concluded that the plaintiff presented no claim upon which relief could be granted. . . . We reverse the judgment of the circuit court and remand the cause to the circuit court for further proceedings.

Shirley S. Abrahamson

... [T]he plaintiff is the owner of a residence, which was constructed during the years 1978–1979. The ... residence has a solar system which includes collectors on the roof to supply energy for heat and hot water and that after the plaintiff built his solar-heated house, the defendant purchased the lot adjacent to and immediately to the south of the plaintiff's lot and commenced planning construction of a home.... [P]laintiff... advised the defendant that if the house were built at the proposed location, defendant's house would substantially and adversely affect the integrity of plaintiff's solar system and could cause plaintiff other damage. Nevertheless, the defendant began construction. The complaint ... demands judgment for injunctive relief and damages.

... Plaintiff's home was the first residence built in the subdivision, and although the plaintiff did not build his house in the center of the lot it was built in accordance with applicable restrictions.... [P]laintiff requested defendant to locate his home an additional several feet away from the plaintiff's lot line, the exact number being disputed. Plaintiff and defendant failed to reach an agreement on the location of defendant's home before defendant started construction. The Architectural Control Committee and the Planning Commission of the City of Muskego approved the defendant's plans for his home, including its location on the lot. After such approval, the defendant apparently changed the grade of the property without prior notice to the Architectural Control Committee.[3] The problem with defendant's proposed construction, as far as the plaintiff's interests are concerned, arises from a combination of the grade and the distance of defendant's home from the defendant's lot line.

....

Although the defendant's obstruction of the plaintiff's access to sunlight appears to fall within the Restatement's broad concept of a private nuisance as a nontrespassory invasion of another's interest in the private use and enjoyment of land, the defendant asserts that he has a right to develop his property in compliance with statutes, ordinances and private covenants without regard to the effect of such development upon the plaintiff's access to sunlight. In essence, the defendant is asking this court to hold that the private nuisance doctrine is not applicable in the instant case and that his right to develop his land is a right which is *per se* superior to his neighbor's interest in access to sunlight. This position is expressed in the maximum "*cujus est solum, ejus est usque ad coelum et ad infernos*," that is, the owner of land owns up to the sky and down to the center of the earth. The rights of the surface owner are, however, not unlimited....

... American courts have afforded some protection to a landowner's interest in access to sunlight. American courts honor express easements to sunlight. American courts initially enforced the English common law doctrine of ancient lights, but later every state which considered the doctrine repudiated it as inconsistent with the needs of a developing country....

Many jurisdictions in this country have protected a landowner from malicious obstruction of access to light (the spite fence cases) under the common law private nuisance doctrine. If an activity is motivated by malice it lacks utility and the harm it causes others outweighs any social values.... This court was reluctant to protect a landowner's interest in sunlight even against a spite fence, only to be overruled by the legislature. Shortly after this court upheld a landowner's right to erect a useless and unsightly sixteen-foot spite fence four feet from his neighbor's windows, ... the legislature enacted a law specifically defining a spite fence as an actionable private nuisance. Thus a landowner's interest in sunlight has been protected in this country by common law private nuisance law at least in the narrow context of the modern American rule invalidating spite fences....

This court's reluctance in the nineteenth and early part of the twentieth century to provide broader protection for a landowner's access to sunlight was premised on three policy considerations. First, the right of landowners to use their property as

3. [Fn. 2:] There appears to be some dispute over ... [whether the defendant built his house at] a grade level not approved by the Board. The specific dispute over this sequence of events is not relevant to this appeal, but suffice it to say that such facts will become relevant to the question of the reasonableness of the defendant's construction in light of our decision that the plaintiff has stated a claim on the issue of private nuisance.

they wished, as long as they did not cause physical damage to a neighbor, was jealously guarded....

Second, sunlight was valued only for aesthetic enjoyment or as illumination. Since artificial light could be used for illumination, loss of sunlight was at most a personal annoyance which was given little, if any, weight by society.

Third, society had significant interest in not restricting or impeding land development.... This court repeatedly emphasized that in the growth period of the nineteenth and early twentieth centuries change is to be expected and is essential to property and that recognition of a right to sunlight would hinder property development....

.... These three policies are no longer fully accepted or applicable. They reflect factual circumstances and social priorities that are now obsolete.

First, society has increasingly regulated the use of land by the landowner for the general welfare....

Second, access to sunlight has taken on a new significance in recent years. In this case the plaintiff seeks to protect access to sunlight, not for aesthetic reasons or as a source of illumination but as a source of energy. Access to sunlight as an energy source is of significance both to the landowner who invests in solar collectors and to a society which has an interest in developing alternative sources of energy.

Third, the policy of favoring unhindered private development in an expanding economy is no longer in harmony with the realities of our society.... The need for easy and rapid development is not as great today as it once was, while our perception of the value of sunlight as a source of energy has increased significantly.

Courts should not implement obsolete policies that have lost their vigor over the course of the years. The law of private nuisance is better suited to resolve landowners' disputes about property development in the 1980s than is a rigid rule which does not recognize a landowner's interest in access to sunlight. As we said in Ballstadt v. Pagel, 202 Wis. 484, 489, 232 N.W. 862 (1930), "What is regarded in law as constituting a nuisance in modern times would no doubt have been tolerated without question in former times." ....

.... Recognition of a nuisance claim for unreasonable obstruction of access to sunlight will not prevent land development or unduly hinder the use of adjoining land. It will promote the reasonable use and enjoyment of land.... That obstruction of access to light might be found to constitute a nuisance in certain circumstances does not mean that it will be or must be found to constitute a nuisance under all circumstances. The result in each case depends on whether the conduct complained of is unreasonable.

....

The circuit court concluded that because the defendant's proposed house was in conformity with zoning regulations, building codes and deed restrictions, the defendant's use of the land was reasonable. This court has concluded that a landowner's compliance with zoning laws does not automatically bar a nuisance claim. Compliance with the law "is not the controlling factor, though it is, of course, entitled to some weight." .... The circuit court also concluded that the plaintiff could have avoided any harm by locating his own house in a better place. Again, plaintiff's ability to avoid the harm is a relevant but not a conclusive factor. *See* §§ 826, 827, 828, Restatement (Second) of Torts (1977).

Furthermore, our examination of the record leads us to conclude that the record does not furnish an adequate basis for the circuit court to apply the proper legal principles on summary judgment. The application of the reasonable use standard in nuisance cases normally requires a full exposition of all underlying facts and circumstances. Too little is known in this case of such matters as the extent of the harm to the plaintiff, the suitability of solar heat in that neighborhood, the availability of remedies to the plaintiff, and the costs to the defendant of avoiding the harm. Summary judgment is not an appropriate procedural vehicle in this case when the circuit court must weigh evidence which has not been presented at trial. ...

For the reasons set forth, we reverse the judgment of the circuit court dismissing the complaint and remand the matter to circuit court for further proceedings not inconsistent with this opinion.

....

[The dissenting opinion of Callow, J., is omitted.]

Winget v. Winn-Dixie Stores, Inc.

Supreme Court of South Carolina
130 S.E.2d 363 (S.C. 1963)

LEWIS, Justice.

Plaintiffs instituted this action for damages alleged to have been sustained from the location and operation by the defendants of a grocery supermarket in such a manner as to constitute a nuisance and for an order perpetually restraining the defendants from using the property where the supermarket was located for a retail grocery business or for any other business purpose. The trial of the case resulted in a judgment in favor of the plaintiffs for the sum of $5,000, actual damages, and a denial by the trial judge of injunctive relief. From the judgment entered in favor of the plaintiffs, the defendants have appealed.

....

The business of the defendants is a lawful one and was located in an area which had been zoned by the City of Sumter for retail business and at a location which the Zoning Board determined to be suitable for a retail grocery. The record shows that every requirement of the municipal authorities was met in establishing the business in question, both in the location and the construction of the building. There is no evidence that the building was constructed in such manner as to interfere with the rights of others. Under such circumstances, it cannot be held that the location of the business in the area in question constituted a nuisance.

The fact, however, that one has been issued a license or permit to conduct a business at a particular location cannot protect the licensee who operates the business in such a manner to constitute a nuisance. . . .

An owner of property even in the conduct of a lawful business thereon is subject to reasonable limitations. In the operation of such business he must not unreasonably interfere with the health or comfort of neighbors or with their right to the enjoyment of their property. . . .

On the other hand, every annoyance or disturbance of a landowner from the use made of property by a neighbor does not constitute a nuisance. The question is not whether plaintiffs have been annoyed or disturbed by the operation of the business in question, but whether there has been an injury to their legal rights. People who live in organized communities must of necessity suffer some inconvenience and annoyance from their neighbors and must submit to annoyances consequent upon the reasonable use of property by others. . . .

Whether a particular use of property is reasonable and whether such use constitutes a nuisance depends largely upon the facts and no definite rule can be laid down for the determination of the question. . . . "What is a reasonable use and whether a particular use is a nuisance cannot be determined by any fixed general rules, but depends upon the facts of each particular case, such as location, character of the neighborhood, nature of the use, extent and frequency of the injury, the effect upon the enjoyment of life, health, and property, and the like. A use of property in one locality and under some circumstances may be lawful and reasonable, which under the other circumstances would be lawful, unreasonable, and a nuisance."

. . . .

In . . . this case, it cannot be properly held that the normal traffic and noise caused by customers going to and from the supermarket would constitute a basis for declaring the operation of the business a nuisance. Of course, the purpose of the business of the defendants is to sell merchandise and in doing so to attract to their store as many customers as possible. It is a natural consequence and incident of the operation of the supermarket that there will be an increase in the number of people visiting the area.

The testimony shows that the store is operated only on week days, opening for business at 8:30 a.m. each day and never closing later than 7:30 p.m. While . . . the operation of the supermarket has caused an increase in the number of people and automobiles coming into the area, there is nothing to show that there was any mass entrance to or exodus from the store at unreasonable hours. On the contrary, the only reasonable inference from the record is that the traffic to and from the business was the normal traffic of patrons visiting such a grocery store over the usual business day. There is no basis for holding that the normal traffic and noise caused by customers going to and from the supermarket constituted a nuisance.

Neither do we think that the operation of trash trucks and street sweepers in connection with the removal of trash and garbage, under the facts here, can form the basis of a finding of a nuisance. The record shows that the trucks of the City of Sumter went upon the premises of the defendants to remove the trash and garbage which accumulated and that the mechanical street sweeper of the City would occasionally sweep the area surrounding the store. There is nothing to indicate that such acts were other than the usual and normal operations of the City in the gathering and removal of trash and garbage. The noise complained of from the usual operation by the City of its trash trucks and mechanical street sweepers could not be charged to the defendants anymore, than, generally, their operation by the City in collecting trash and garbage at any other business establishment could be attributed to those business owners.

However, with regard to other allegations of the complaint, we think that there was some evidence requiring the submission of those issues to the jury for determination. The record shows that the defendants erected fans on their building in connection with the air conditioning equipment. These fans were so directed as to blow against the trees and shrubbery on plaintiffs' property causing some damage and inconvenience. There was also some testimony that, at least, for a while after opening the supermarket, the floodlights on defendants' lot cast a bright glare over the property of plaintiffs until late at night so as to disturb the plaintiffs in the enjoyment of their home, that obnoxious odors were created from the garbage which accumulated at defendants' store, and that paper and trash from the defendants' garbage was permitted to escape onto plaintiffs' lot to an unusual extent. The record gives rise to a reasonable inference that such acts were not normal or necessary incidents of the operation of the business. We think that the foregoing testimony presented a jury issue and that the trial judge properly refused the defendants' motion for a directed verdict.

.... [T]he record shows that the acts which would form any basis for damages because of a nuisance in the operation of the business have been largely, if not entirely, discontinued. It was no doubt for this reason that the court ruled that no grounds existed for the issuance of an injunction. Where the acts complained of as constituting a nuisance have been discontinued and their repetition appeared unlikely, it was proper to refuse to issue an injunction.... "The abatement of a nuisance does not affect the right to recover damages for its past existence." 39 Am. Jur. 389, section 128....

.... It is contended that a new trial should be granted because of the refusal of the trial court to strike the testimony of the witness R.E. Graham relative to depreciation in value of the property of the plaintiffs. The witness Graham was asked to give his opinion as to the value of the plaintiffs' property before and after "the moving in of this Winn-Dixie Corporation." In answer to the question, he testified that the property had depreciated in value from about $12,000 to a value of $8,000 "by reason of the Winn-Dixie moving in this property." . . . .

The testimony of the witness Graham related solely to depreciation in value of plaintiffs' property because of the location in the particular locality of defendants' business and was not based upon the particular manner of operation of the supermarket in question. The testimony was irrelevant to any issue in the case and should have been stricken upon the motion of the defendants. . . .

Reversed and remanded for a new trial.

Note

1. The following opinion approaches the nuisance question in a way that purports to avoid "balancing the equities."

Smith v. Jersey Central Power & Light Co.

Superior Court of New Jersey, Appellate Division
24 A.3d 300 (N.J. Super. Ct. App. Div. 2011)

SKILLMAN, J.A.D. (retired and temporarily assigned on recall).

This is an unusual case involving a nuisance claim based on "neutral-to-earth voltage" (NEV), also called "stray voltage" or "stray current," passing along the ground of a residential property. Plaintiffs, Gary and Eileen Smith, husband and wife, sued defendant, Jersey Central Power & Light Company, because high NEV levels from its electrical distribution system gave them shocks in their backyard. The jury found defendant liable for nuisance and awarded plaintiffs $145,000 for property damage and $50,000 for interference with the use of their property. Plaintiffs appeal. . . .

After returning home from a family vacation . . . , Gary walked barefooted to the hot tub, put his arm into the water to feel the temperature, and felt an electric shock, like "a tingling, hurting sensation," travel up his arm to his chest. The next day, he put his arm in the hot tub again and received an electric shock so strong it felt as though someone had punched him in the chest. He asked Eileen to feel the water. She felt nothing while wearing her shoes, but when she took them off and touched the water, she felt a "tingling sensation, a buzzing sensation," as if she had inserted a fork into a toaster.

An electrician plaintiffs called to investigate the problem found very high levels of electricity in the ground surrounding the hot tub and swing set. The electrician also determined that the source of the problem was not within plaintiffs' house and suggested they call defendant.

Defendant sent investigators to plaintiffs' house, who concluded after extensive testing that the source of the electric shock problem in their backyard was defendant's electrical distribution system, specifically NEV. . . . Suffice it to say that although electricity is distributed to users through electrical wires, all electricity leaving an electrical substation must return to the substation to complete the circuit, and although returning electricity passes mostly through wires, it sometimes goes through the ground when the wires become overloaded. Because electricity seeks the path of least resistance, when the return is through the ground, the electricity will tend to ground to such things as pools, hot tubs, outdoor irrigation systems, faucets, and swing sets.

Although NEV does not ordinarily pose a problem to homeowners, the high level of NEV in the backyards of plaintiffs and some of their neighbors created a significant problem, which was corroborated by defendant's testing. One of defendant's investigators advised plaintiffs to always wear shoes when going outside and not to touch anything metal or wear wet clothing outside their house.

Following the receipt of this advice and fearing for their family's safety, plaintiffs filled in the sandbox, dismantled the swing set and pool in their backyard, and started wearing shoes both inside and outside. They also planned family activities away from the house, and stopped using their backyard. They spent $29,400 to install a second-story fiberglass deck onto their house, so their sons would have a place to play outside without touching the ground.

. . . .

Defendant undertook extensive efforts over a period of several years to correct the problem. The extent to which those efforts succeeded was a contested issue at the trial. . . .

. . . . "The essence of a private nuisance is an unreasonable interference with the use and enjoyment of land." . . . . In determining whether a plaintiff has established an unreasonable interference with the use and enjoyment of land, our courts are guided by the principles set forth in the Restatement (Second) of Torts. . . .

Section 822 of the Restatement states:

> One is subject to liability for a private nuisance if, but only if, his conduct is a legal cause of an invasion of another's interest in the private use and enjoyment of land, and the invasion is either
>
> (a) intentional and unreasonable, or
>
> (b) unintentional and otherwise actionable under the rules controlling liability for negligent or reckless conduct, or for abnormally dangerous conditions or activities.

. . . .

An invasion of a plaintiffs' interest in land is considered "intentional" not only if the defendant "acts for the purpose of causing" an invasion of plaintiffs' interest in the use of his land, *id.* § 825(a), but also if he "knows that [the invasion] is resulting or is substantially certain to result from his conduct," *id.* § 825(b). Even if the defendant's first invasion of plaintiff's land is unintentional, "when the [defendant's] conduct is continued after [he] knows that the invasion is resulting from it, further invasions are intentional." . . . .

"An intentional invasion of [plaintiff's] interest in the use and enjoyment of land is unreasonable if . . . the harm caused by the conduct is serious and the financial burden of compensating for this and similar harm to others would not make the continuation of the conduct not feasible." Restatement (Second) of Torts § 826(b) (1979). This section of the *Restatement* recognizes that "[i]t may sometimes be reasonable to operate an important activity if payment is made for the harm it is causing, but unreasonable to continue it without paying. . . . The action for damages does not seek to stop the activity; it seeks instead to place on the activity the cost of compensating for the harm it causes." *Id.* § 826 cmt. f.

To establish a negligence claim, a plaintiff must show that the defendant's "conduct . . . falls below the standard established by law for the protection of others against unreasonable risk of harm," *id.* § 282, which is generally what "a reasonable man [would do] under like circumstances," *id.* § 283. . . .

It is evident from these sections of the Restatement that the kind of conduct that will support a negligence claim is different from the "unreasonable" interference with the use and enjoyment of land that will support a nuisance claim. A negligence claim is directed solely at the conduct of the defendant; if that conduct is not unreasonable under all the circumstances, it will be found not to have been negligent. *Ibid.* On the other hand, a defendant's conduct may be found to have constituted a nuisance even though the conduct has sufficient social utility to be considered reasonable so long as damages are paid to the party whose use and enjoyment of land has been interfered with by this conduct. . . .

This distinction between causes of action for negligence and nuisance has been recognized in other jurisdictions. In King v. Columbian Carbon Co., 152 F.2d 636 (5th Cir. 1945), the owner of a farm brought a nuisance action against the owner of an adjoining industrial facility that emitted soot and other noxious substances which interfered with the operation of his farm. The farm owner conceded that the industrial facility had not been negligently constructed and was not being negligently operated. Nevertheless, the court concluded that a nuisance action was maintainable. . . .

The discussion of nuisance in Prosser also recognizes that negligence is not an element of this tort:

> [C]onduct may often result in substantial interference, as when a cement factory locates next to a small farmer, without such conduct being unreasonable, and even when defendant is exercising utmost care while utilizing all the technical know-how available. It has often been observed that liability, if imposed in such a case, is liability without fault. But this is a mistake. The harm is intentional. Private property cannot be physically harmed or its value impaired in this way, however socially desirable the conduct, without payment being made for the harm done, if the interference that

> is the consequence of the activity is substantial and considered to be unreasonable.

. . . .

Consistent with these principles, the trial court did not instruct the jury that it had to find defendant negligent in order to impose liability for nuisance. Instead, the court instructed the jury, in language taken almost verbatim from the model jury instruction, Model Jury Charge (Civil), 5.75 (Nuisance) (Dec. 1987), that:

> The word nuisance means an unreasonable interference with the use and the enjoyment of one's land which results in material interference with the ordinary comfort of human existence; that is, annoyance, inconvenience, discomfort, or harm to the person or the property of another. An owner of property has the right to reasonable use of his or her land. In determining what is reasonable you must weigh the utility of the defendant's conduct against the strength of harm suffered by the plaintiff.

. . . .

Therefore, we reject defendant's argument that the jury finding that it was not negligent precluded a finding that it created a nuisance on plaintiffs' property.

. . . .

Affirmed.

Notes

1. ***Intentional Nuisances Only.*** According to § 826(b) of the Restatement, Second, of Torts, the test of unreasonableness based upon the feasibility and fairness of paying damages applies only to intentional invasions of the plaintiff's interest. However, the requirement that the invasion be intentional is easily satisfied, for whenever the defendant is placed on notice by another that conduct is causing harm, continuation of the conduct leads to an "intentional" injury. Intent means simply that the defendant desires to produce the result or is "substantially certain" that it will occur as a result of certain acts. *See* Restatement (Third) of Torts: Liab. for Physical & Emotional Harm § 1 (2010). By limiting the use of the "alternative" test of unreasonableness to intentionally created nuisances, the Restatement ensures that the defendant has the option of ceasing the offending conduct before being held liable for damages under the test. In addition, by establishing that a nuisance was intentionally created, the defense of comparative negligence will become inapplicable.

2. ***Other Precedent.*** *See* Meat Producers, Inc. v. McFarland, 476 S.W.2d 406, 411 (Tex. Civ. App. 1972). In upholding an award of damages, the court reasoned that although the defendant's cattle feedlot was lawful, useful, and appropriately located in a rural area, its continued operation would be unreasonable unless adjoining owners were compensated for the interference with the use of their land.

Economic Analysis
The Coase Theorem and the Law of Nuisance

Alan Gunn

Ronald Coase's article *The Problem of Social Cost*, 3 J. L. & Econ. 1 (1960), is the most-cited article on economics ever written. The article deals with the economic principles underlying the law of nuisance, though it has important implications for other legal issues as well. Whether Coase's approach to nuisance questions is one that courts should adopt is doubtful (the paper is addressed primarily to economists, not courts, and it does not purport to give advice to judges except to suggest that they be explicit when making economic judgments). *The Problem of Social Cost* is discussed here not because it provides a recipe for resolving nuisance disputes but because it clarifies the principles underlying nuisance law.

Coase's article makes three distinct but related points about conflicting uses of land:

(1) Problems of conflicting land use cannot be resolved by labeling one of the uses "the cause" of harm to the other user.

(2) If transactions between neighbors whose uses of land conflict were costless, the parties would negotiate an "efficient" solution to the problem no matter which party's use was protected by law.

(3) In principle, when "transaction costs" make it impossible for the parties to a dispute to negotiate a solution, the law should decide the dispute so that the outcome is that which the parties would have bargained for if there were no transaction costs.

The following discussion elaborates on each of these points.

The Futility of "Cause" as a Guide to the Proper Outcome. In everyday speech, "cause" is often used as a synonym for "ought to be responsible for." Thus, one might say that *A*, whose reckless driving led *A* to run over *B*, has "caused" harm to *B* and so ought to be deterred, or be made to compensate *B*. In the land-use context, it is common to describe a polluter as "causing harm" to the victims of pollution. While the outcomes suggested by these descriptions may well be right, one cannot sensibly *explain* those outcomes by invoking causation. Causation, in the "but for" sense, runs both ways. If defendant's smoking factory makes it impossible for plaintiff to use her house, which sits a block downwind from the factory, *both* defendant's and plaintiff's activities are "causes" (in the but-for sense) of the harm. If defendant had operated a sod farm, rather than a factory, plaintiff's use of her house would have been unimpaired, so defendant's conduct is plainly a "but-for" cause of the harm. But plaintiff's activity is equally a but-for cause of the harm, for if plaintiff had a blast furnace, rather than a house, on her lot, there would have been no harm. Therefore, to call defendant's factory "the cause of the harm" is simply to say that, under these circumstances, plaintiff's use should be preferred. That conclusion may be correct, but one cannot *justify* the conclusion by invoking "causation."

The law has, for the most part, recognized the impossibility of resolving land-use disputes by invoking but-for cause. Lawyers, perhaps more than the economists whom Coase addressed, have always appreciated that so many things are the "but for" cause of any given harm that it makes no sense to say that anyone who has caused harm, in the but-for sense, must be liable. In the case of the house next to the factory, for example, one would expect a court to hold a defendant who regularly produces clouds of smoke in the middle of a residential suburb liable for creating a nuisance. But if the plaintiff built a house in the middle of the industrial part of town, no court would take seriously the plaintiff's argument that the neighboring factories should be enjoined.

A case which nicely illustrates the futility of approaching the problem of incompatible land uses by invoking causation is Fontainebleau Hotel Corp. v. Forty-Five Twenty-Five, Inc., 114 So. 2d 357 (Fla. Dist. Ct. App. 1959). The owners of the Fontainebleau Hotel proposed to add fourteen stories to their hotel. The addition would have cast a shadow over the pool and cabana of the Eden Roc Hotel, which the plaintiffs owned. The plaintiffs sued to enjoin the building of the addition, claiming that it would cause them harm. And so it would; but granting the injunction would have caused the owner of the Fontainebleau harm by denying it the opportunity to enlarge its building. The question in the case, in Coasean terms, was whether the Fontainebleau would be allowed to harm the Eden Roc or whether the Eden Roc would be allowed to harm the Fontainebleau. A principle of "do no harm to your neighbors" does not help to solve the problem. (The court decided the case in favor of the Fontainebleau by invoking "the universal rule—and the custom followed in this state since its inception—that adjoining landowners have an equal right under the law to build to the line of their respective tracts and to such a height as is desired by them. . . .")

Bargaining to Efficient Outcomes. Suppose that the shadow cast by the Fontainebleau Hotel would cause only the most minor inconvenience to the use of the Eden Roc, and that the Fontainebleau would benefit greatly by being able to build the addition. Would it matter a great deal whether the law gave the Eden Roc the right to enjoin the construction? Perhaps not. One might, as a first approximation, guess that the Eden Roc would get an injunction, resulting in great loss to the Fontainebleau and only little benefit to the Eden Roc. But the parties could bargain around this result; for example, the Fontainebleau might pay the Eden Roc $50,000 to let it build its addition. If the addition were worth millions to the Fontainebleau, and the harm from the shadow would cause only a few hundred dollars' worth of harm to the Eden Roc, both parties would benefit by making this deal. Or suppose that the law gave the Fontainebleau the right to build, that the addition would be worth only $100,000 to the Fontainebleau, and that the harm to the Eden Roc would run in the millions. In that case, an efficient outcome could be achieved, despite the law, by the Eden Roc's paying the Fontainebleau not to build.

Coase showed that, in many cases, assignment of the legal right to one party or the other would not determine the ultimate outcome *if transaction costs are zero.*

(Transaction costs are the costs of entering into bargains.) This would occur because, in many cases, the parties could, at no cost, bargain around the outcome supposedly dictated by the legal rule. The principle here extends far beyond disputes between neighbors. If, for example, *A* has a car which *B* would like to own, *B* would not ordinarily seek to have the law changed so that ownership of the car is assigned to him. Instead, he would simply buy the car from *A*.[4]

Coase has been widely misunderstood by lawyers as having said that it doesn't matter who, in cases involving conflicting uses of land, gets the legal right to use the land as desired, because the parties will simply contract around the legal rule. In fact, as Coase fully appreciated, transaction costs will often be so high that bargaining around the rule will not be economically feasible. For example, suppose that smoke from a factory is annoying the owners of 300 houses, and that the factory has a legal right to emit smoke. Suppose further that being free from smoke would be of more value to the homeowners than the ability to pollute is worth to the owner of the factory. A bargain between the homeowners and the factory owner would require, among other things, that the homeowners organize and raise funds to pay the factory to stop polluting. This process would face formidable obstacles (for instance, every homeowner would like to be a "free rider," paying little or nothing in the hope that other homeowners would pay the factory to stop). Even if only two parties are involved, as in the case of the Fontainebleau and the Eden Roc, negotiations may be time-consuming and expensive, as each side argues for the highest or lowest possible price for buying out the other side. (In economic jargon, this is a "bilateral monopoly" problem.) Furthermore, a practice of paying people not to exercise rights to pollute, or to cast shadows, might encourage polluting and shadow-casting by persons hoping to be bought out.

What Should the Law Do? If we cannot often expect, as a practical matter, to see parties bargaining around common-law land-use rules, why did Coase discuss the outcome that would be reached in a world of zero transaction costs? Because he thought that the theoretically correct solution to land-use questions was for the rights to be assigned in such a way that the outcome was the same as if costless bargaining were possible. For example, if the Fontainebleau's shadow would cause great loss to the owners of the Eden Roc, and if the addition would benefit the Fontainebleau very little, a court could enjoin the building of the addition. If, on the other hand, the shadow would be only a minor inconvenience to the Eden Roc, the court might allow the addition. Other ways of reaching these outcomes are possible. For example, if the benefit to the Fontainebleau of an additional fourteen stories were great, and the harm to the Eden Roc small, a rule requiring the

4. One case in which ultimate ownership of the right may depend on which party has the right in the first place is that in which ownership of the right affects one's wealth in an important way. For example, consider a case in which *B* could not afford to buy the car from *A* if *A* had the right, but in which *B* would not sell the car to *A* if *B* had the right. In this case, the right to the car will stay with whichever party it is assigned to.

Fontainebleau to pay damages would be efficient, as it would choose to build and pay the damages.

Coase cited many land-use decisions in support of the view that the courts considered the relative values of different uses in deciding what invasions were actionable. He described a number of cases in which the question whether an activity constituted a nuisance turned not just on what the activity was, but where it was conducted. For example, in Adams v. Ursell, an English case, a fried-fish shop was held to be a nuisance because it was established near houses "of a much better character," but the judge noted that the fish shop, if located elsewhere, might not be a nuisance: "It by no means follows that because a fried-fish shop is a nuisance in one place it is a nuisance in another."

For a lawyer, one of the joys of reading *The Problem of Social Cost* is seeing, time after time, cases in which the courts got it right, while pre-Coase economists would have criticized many of the outcomes as "allowing the defendant to harm the plaintiff." Nevertheless, one may reasonably doubt whether courts can succeed in mimicking the outcomes of cost-free bargaining in making land-use decisions. For one thing, it seems unlikely in the extreme that courts could consistently make accurate evaluations of the costs and benefits to the parties of different outcomes in close cases. With regard to the problem of shadows, for instance, a "rule" allowing construction when the value of the addition to the owner outweighs the harm done by the shadow to the neighbor would be virtually the antithesis of law. One of the major functions of law is making clear to people what their rights are, so that they can get on with their lives. A rule that one may build without fear of liability for shadows does this. So, too, would legislation restricting building heights to a specified limit.

In practice, a system of case-by-case determinations would lead not only to uncertainty but also, one suspects, to decisions based on improper grounds. In the absence of any reliable way of measuring harms and benefits, courts would inevitably resolve disputes according to judges' hunches, political views, or unarticulated beliefs about public policy. Consider, in this regard, the Wisconsin Supreme Court's decision in Prah v. Maretti, 321 N.W.2d 182 (Wis. 1982), *supra*. It is hard to read the opinion without strongly suspecting that the majority believed that solar energy is a "good thing," and that this belief influenced the outcome. Perhaps solar energy is a good thing, or perhaps it is an inefficient form of energy production which wastes resources that might better be used elsewhere. Either way, our system is not one in which judges are supposed to decide cases according to their assumptions about whether solar energy is good or bad.

In the end, the lesson of *The Problem of Social Cost* as applied to nuisance cases may be that there is no alternative to deciding cases not involving physical invasions by asking whether the use in question was an appropriate use of the land, given the surrounding circumstances and relying heavily on traditional notions of what the right to use land means. In traditional trespass cases, as when *A* takes shortcuts across *B*'s property, the only practicable rule is to hold the invasion actionable, despite the theoretical possibility that the result in a particular case is "inefficient" and that transaction costs present obstacles to bargained solutions. We cannot solve land-use problems by holding that every use of land which harms someone else is actionable, but we cannot expect case-by-case cost-benefit analyses to work very well either.

C. Public Nuisance

1. In General

A public nuisance is an unreasonable interference with a right common to the public in general, such as obstruction of a highway, pollution of a stream, or contamination of the air. Facilities and practices prejudicial to health or good morals, such as crack houses or snake handling during religious services, may also qualify as public nuisances. Indeed, even laudable enterprises have occasionally been found to be public nuisances. In Armory Park Neighborhood Association v. Episcopal Community Services, 712 P.2d 914 (Ariz. 1985), the court affirmed a preliminary injunction against continued operation of a soup kitchen. In determining that there was unreasonable interference with the interests of others, the court took into account actions occurring outside of the defendant's premises. The persons being drawn to the soup kitchen had caused property damage to nearby residences and other disturbances.

No Residual Category of Nuisance. Although the term "nuisance" is sometimes used imprecisely by lawyers and judges, there is no actionable tort of nuisance outside of the categories of private and public nuisance. Thus, in Mandell v. Pivnick, 125 A.2d 175 (Conn. Super. Ct. 1956), where the plaintiff was struck by a falling awning, a demurrer to his nuisance complaint was sustained, for "nowhere [did] it appear that he was injured in relation to a right which he enjoy[ed] by reason of his ownership of an interest in land" and there was no allegation "that the installation of the awning was dangerous to the public generally." The court noted that, under a different set of facts, an awning or sign overhanging a public street or sidewalk could constitute a public nuisance, if not properly secured.

Similarities and Differences between Public and Private Nuisance. Actions for public and private nuisance share a number of requirements. Under each tort, the plaintiff must establish: (1) that the harm results from tortious conduct (*i.e.* failure to exercise care, intentional wrongdoing, or a strict-liability activity); (2) that the harm is significant; and (3) that the invasion is unreasonable under the circumstances.

The main difference between public and private nuisance has to do with standing to sue. Anyone with an interest in the land affected by a private nuisance has standing. *See, e.g.*, Graves v. Diehl, 958 S.W.2d 468 (Tex. App. 1997) (purchasers of property under a contract for a deed had a sufficient interest). However, a plaintiff in a public-nuisance case must show an injury "different in kind" from that suffered by members of the public generally or have a legislative grant of standing. These issues are discussed below.

Public Nuisance and Environmental Law. Cases involving environmental issues often contain claims for public nuisance. *See, e.g.*, N.J. Dept. of Envtl. Protection v. Exxon Mobil Corp., 2008 WL 4177038 (Super. Ct. Law Div.) (finding that disposal of toxic waste constituted an abnormally dangerous activity and that the defendant was liable for public nuisance as a matter of law). However, courts are reluctant to allow nuisance principles to be used to second-guess carefully crafted regulatory regimes. *See* North Carolina, ex rel. Cooper v. Tennessee Valley Auth., 615 F.3d 291 (4th Cir. 2010).

2. Public Nuisance and Products Liability

The most dramatic effort to breathe new life into the law of public nuisance has been an array of suits relating to the marketing of mass products, such as cigarettes and guns. Lawyers endeavoring to surmount doctrinal obstacles in other areas of the law (such as the necessity of showing that a product is defective under products-liability law) have argued that certain types of products pose a risk to the welfare of the public in general and are therefore actionable under the law of public nuisance. Needless to say, these efforts have been controversial. Courts have been uncertain whether centuries-old doctrine relating to public nuisance can or should be used to address harm caused in modern society by mass-marketed products. *See* Donald G. Gifford, *Public Nuisance as a Mass Products Liability Tort*, 71 U. Cinn. L. Rev. 743, 747 (2003) (reporting that "states' lawsuits against the tobacco companies were settled before courts could address the viability of public nuisance claims in the context of mass products, but the tobacco settlement . . . inspired states and municipalities and their attorneys to file similar claims against the manufacturers of handguns and lead-pigment").

Judges have been reluctant to use the law of nuisance to address product-related issues. However, there have been startling decisions to the contrary. *See* Ileto v. Glock, Inc., 349 F.3d 1191 (9th Cir. 2003) (holding that victims of a shooting incident perpetrated by an illegal gun purchaser, whose claims rested on the defendants' actions in creating an illegal secondary market, stated claims for public nuisance and negligence under California law against manufacturers, distributors, and dealers of the firearms that were actually fired); City of Cincinnati v. Beretta U.S.A. Corp., 768 N.E.2d 1136 (Ohio 2002) (holding that a city stated a claim for public nuisance against 15 handgun manufacturers, 3 trade associations, and a handgun distributor where it alleged that the defendants manufactured, marketed, distributed, and sold firearms in ways that unreasonably interfered with public health, welfare, and safety in the city).

One significant obstacle that private individuals face in bringing an action for public nuisance, whether in the products-liability field or otherwise, is the harm-different-in-kind requirement.

NAACP v. AcuSport, Inc.

United States District Court for the Eastern District of New York
271 F. Supp. 2d 435 (E.D.N.Y. 2003)

JACK B. WEINSTEIN, Senior District Judge.

Plaintiff, the National Association for the Advancement of Colored People ("NAACP"), is suing for injunctive relief on its own behalf and that of its individual and potential members in the state of New York. The theory is one of public nuisance under New York state law. . . .

The evidence presented at trial demonstrated that defendants are responsible for the creation of a public nuisance and could—voluntarily and through easily implemented changes in marketing and more discriminating control of the sales practices of those to whom they sell their guns—substantially reduce the harm occasioned by the diversion of guns to the illegal market and by the criminal possession and use of those guns. Because, however, plaintiff has failed to demonstrate, as required by New York law, that it has suffered harm different in kind from that suffered by the public at large in the state of New York, the case is dismissed.

. . . .

The law in New York seems to be that public nuisance must be proved by clear and convincing evidence. . . .

Jack B. Weinstein

Since the possibility of a suit brought by a private plaintiff for a public nuisance was first recognized, as early as the sixteenth century, it has been emphasized that no private suit for public nuisance may be brought "unless it be where one man has greater hurt or inconvenience than any other man had, and then he who had more displeasure or hurt, etc., can have an action to recover his damages that he had by reason of this special hurt." Y.B. Mich. 27 Hen. 8, f. 26, pl. 10 (1536), *quoted in* William L. Prosser, *Private Action for Public Nuisance,* 52 Va. L. Rev. 997, 1005 (citing this anonymous case as the breakaway point from the position that public nuisance was a crime and actionable only by the king). A private party bringing an action for public nuisance is acting as a *de facto* private attorney general, suing on behalf of itself as well as the public.

Such a quasi-public action is not appropriate unless the private plaintiff shows some special harm. Prosser succinctly explains this necessity:

> The reasons for the requirement of particular damage have been stated many times. The plaintiff did not and could not represent the king, and the vindication of royal rights was properly left to his duly constituted officers. This is no less true when the rights of the crown have passed to the general public. Defendants are not to be harassed, and the time of the courts taken up, with complaints about public matters from a multitude who claim to have suffered.

Prosser, *supra,* at 1007.

While the special harm required in the anonymous case quoted by Prosser is referred to as "greater" or "more" harm, the case law since that time has consistently recognized that a private plaintiff must show not just that it suffered more harm, but that it suffered some particular harm not shared in common with the rest of the public. *See, e.g.,* Callanan v. Gilman, 107 N.Y. 360, 370 (1887) ("It is the undoubted law that the plaintiffs could not maintain this action without alleging and proving that they sustained special damage from the nuisance, different from that sustained by the general public; in other words, that the damage they sustained was not common to all the public living or doing business in Vesey street and having occasion to use the same."); 532 Madison Ave. Gourmet Foods, Inc. v. Finlandia Ctr., 96 N.Y.2d 280, 294 (2001) ("[I]n that the [harm] was common to an entire community and the plaintiff suffers it only in a greater degree than others, it is not a different kind of harm and the plaintiff cannot recover for the invasion of the public right.") (quoting Restatement of the Law (Second) of Torts § 821C, cmt. h).

As usually stated, the harm must be different in kind, not just in degree. This is true regardless of the form of the relief requested....

Although it is not necessary that the particular harm alleged be exclusive or unique to a single plaintiff, when the class harmed in the same way "becomes so large and general as to include all members of the public who come in contact with the nuisance ... the private action will fail." .... Physical harm, pecuniary loss, or delay and inconvenience suffered by a private plaintiff may satisfy this requirement, but not when they are so widespread as to affect "a whole community, or a very wide area within it." Prosser, *supra,* at 1015.

Some examples illustrate this requirement. New York courts have found that the harm suffered by commercial fishermen as a result of the pollution of the Hudson River was different in kind from that suffered by the public at large. *See* Leo v. General Elec. Co., 538 N.Y.S.2d 844 (App. Div. 1989). The partial obstruction of a sidewalk, although having an effect on the general public's access, affected the owner of neighboring apartment buildings in a peculiar manner. *See* Graceland Corp. v. Consol. Laundries Corp., 180 N.Y.S.2d 644 (App. Div. 1958), *aff'd,* 6 N.Y.2d 900 (1959).

Particular harm was found not to exist where two law firms sought damages for loss resulting when a labor strike forced the closure of the New York City transit system because "every person, firm and corporation conducting [a] business or profession in the City" suffered damage of a similar kind. Burns Jackson Miller Summit & Spitzer v. Lindner, 59 N.Y.2d 314, 334 (1983). As the New York Court of Appeals pointed out in 532 Madison Ave. Gourmet Foods, Inc. v. Finlandia Ctr., Inc., consolidated cases arising out of several construction disasters in Manhattan that resulted in the closure of the affected areas of the City for significant periods of time, "the hot dog vendor and taxi driver suffered the same kind of injury as the plaintiff law firm. Each was impacted in the ability to conduct business, resulting in financial loss." 96 N.Y.2d 280, 294 (2001). The difference in the degree of that injury was irrelevant to determining whether the private plaintiffs had stated claims for public nuisance. *See id.*

The requirement that a private plaintiff suing for public nuisance demonstrate particular harm different from that suffered by the public at large may be criticized on the ground that it inhibits adequate protection of the public when government authorities cannot or will not act. *See, e.g.,* Denise E. Antolini, *Modernizing Public Nuisance: Solving the Paradox of the Special Injury Rule,* 28 Ecology L.Q. 755 (2001). It does cut down potential suits by "busybodies" having no particular interest in abating the nuisance except ideology. It thus stands in somewhat the same shoes as the doctrine of prudence in constitutional Article III standing. New York courts have embraced the doctrine in private suits, preferring in general to rely on public officials such as the Attorney General of the State.

The application of the "harm different in kind" requirement to the facts and issues presented in the instant case . . . is decisive. The court holds that the extensive and severe harm proven by plaintiff to be suffered by the NAACP, its members, and the African-American community in the state of New York is not "different in kind" as that phrase is defined in the case law. It therefore is not necessary to decide precisely who is a member of and represented in the instant action by the NAACP, and therefore whose "injury" should be considered for the purposes of this third element of a private plaintiff's public nuisance action.

African-Americans do suffer greater harm from illegal handguns for complex socio-economic and historical reasons. But to say that they suffer a greater amount of harm is not enough under New York law. In order to show the particular harm necessary to have standing to sue for public nuisance as a private plaintiff, the harm suffered must be different in kind. That is not the case here.

It seems almost offensive that, almost a century and a half, after the freeing of the slaves and formal insistence by the courts of full legal equality, African-Americans feel compelled to argue that they must sue to be specially protected on the streets of New York from guns.... There is an absolute duty on the part of the government to provide equal protection and safety for all its people. Defendants' moral obligation is no narrower.

....

Since plaintiff has not proved all elements of its cause of action ... the case is dismissed....

Notes

1. ***The Remoteness Factor in Public Nuisance.*** In People *ex rel* Spitzer v. Sturm, Ruger & Co., Inc., 761 N.Y.S.2d 192 (App. Div. 2003), the court held that the alleged conduct of handgun manufacturers, in manufacturing, distributing, and marketing handguns in a manner that knowingly placed a disproportionate number of handguns in the possession of people who used them unlawfully, failed to support a claim by the State for common-law public nuisance. The court found that the harm alleged was far too remote from the corporations' otherwise lawful commercial activity to fairly hold the corporations accountable, and that the corporations' lawful commercial activity, having been followed by harm to person and property caused directly and principally by the criminal activity of intervening third parties, could not be considered a proximate cause of such harm. The court said that the legislature was better equipped than the judiciary to address the problems posed by illegal handguns.

2. ***The Federal Protection of Lawful Commerce in Arms Act.*** A federal law enacted in 2005 now bars a wide range of civil liability actions against manufacturers, importers, dealers, and other sellers of firearms and ammunition, including claims based on nuisance. *See* 15 U.S.C.A. § 7901–03 (Westlaw 2022).

3. ***Harm Different in Kind.*** The requirement that the plaintiff's injury differ in kind from the injuries of others means, for example, that an individual may not ordinarily sue to abate an obstruction of a public road (*see* McQueen v. Burkhart, 290 S.W.2d 577 (Tex. Civ. App. 1956)), enjoin the operation of a bawdy house (*see* Coman v. Baker, 179 S.W. 937 (Tex. Civ. App. 1915), *rev'd on other grounds*, 198 S.W. 141 (Tex. 1917)), or close a nude beach (*see* Mark v. Oregon, 974 P.2d 716 (Or. Ct. App. 1999). Were the law otherwise, self-appointed protectors of the public might litigate against many activities they thought undesirable. It is normally the role of government, not busybodies, to keep the highways open and the bawdy houses closed, and to limit nude beaches to appropriate locations.

(a) ***Physical Harm.*** Physical harm to person or property often qualifies as harm different in kind since physical injuries are rarely sustained by a multitude of persons as a result of the same tortious conduct. *See* George v. City of Houston, 465 S.W.2d 387 (Tex. Civ. App. 1971), *rev'd on other grounds*, 479 S.W.2d 257 (Tex. 1972) (child drowned in polluted pond); Prescott v. Leaf River Forest Products, Inc., 740 So. 2d 301 (Miss. 1999) (interference with the condition of land).

In Birke v. Oakwood Worldwide, 87 Cal. Rptr. 3d 602 (Ct. App. 2009), the court held that a public nuisance claim was adequately pleaded because it alleged that secondhand tobacco smoke in an apartment complex's outdoor common areas affected a substantial number of people at the same time and that the five-year old-plaintiff suffered harm different in kind because of her asthma and chronic allergies.

(b) ***Pecuniary Loss.*** Pecuniary losses may also qualify as harm different in kind. *See* Galveston, H. & S.A. Ry. Co. v. De Groff, 118 S.W. 134 (Tex. 1909) (hotel permitted to recover for depreciation in property value and loss of business because of the location of railroad).

(c) ***Difference in Kind Versus Difference in Degree.*** Harm "different in kind" is not equivalent to harm "different in degree." The test is not simply a search for the most seriously injured plaintiffs. Still, the Restatement indicates that magnitude of interference is not entirely irrelevant. Comment c to § 821C of the Restatement, Second, of Torts states:

> Normally there may be no difference in the kind of interference with one who travels a road once a week and one who travels it every day. But if the plaintiff traverses the road a dozen times a day he nearly always has some special reason to do so, and that reason will almost invariably be based upon some special interest of his own, not common to the community. . . . Thus in determining whether there is a difference in the kind of harm, the degree of interference may be a factor of importance that must be considered.

(d) ***Policy.*** In applying a difficult standard such as the "harm different in kind" requirement, it is important to look for guidance to the reasons underlying the rule. Some authorities suggest that the rule is intended to protect the defendant from the multiplicity of suits which would follow if everyone could sue for common harm. This is a weak justification. On the one hand, if the alleged public nuisance does not exist or is not attributable to the defendant, it is unlikely that many persons will go to the trouble and expense of suing the defendant. On the other hand, if a nuisance does exist as a result of the defendant's tortious conduct, there is little reason to protect the defendant from liability, for the law ordinarily holds persons responsible for the consequences of their actions.

A better justification for the "different in kind" requirement is the fact that it tends to ensure that the state will be a party to legal proceedings significantly affecting the public interest. It does this by precluding private individuals, in many instances, from litigating issues relating to rights common to the public in general. Absent the "different in kind" requirement, "the public policy of . . . [the] state on . . . vital matters could be thwarted, without the state having an opportunity to have its side of the controversy presented in a court of justice." Garland Grain Co. v. D-C Home Owners Improvement Ass'n, 393 S.W.2d 635, 640 (Tex. Civ. App. 1965).

Allowing private actions against public nuisances when harm is "different in kind" also performs a "safety valve" function. It permits courts to hear precisely those cases which are unlikely to be championed by the elected representatives of the public—those claims involving atypical injuries which are unlikely to stir enough popular support to secure redress through normal governmental channels.

4. ***Legislative Grants of Standing.*** It is open to the legislature to dispense with the "harm different in kind" requirement, and many have done so, at least in certain contexts. Statutes typically confer standing on particular public officials, and, in some states, on ordinary citizens as well. Consider these provisions:

Florida Statutes Annotated §§ 60.05 and 823.05 (Westlaw 2022)

§ 60.05

(1) When any nuisance as defined in § 823.05 exists, the Attorney General, state attorney, city attorney, county attorney, or any citizen of the county may sue in the name of the state on his or her relation to enjoin the nuisance, the person or persons maintaining it, and the owner or agent of the building or ground on which the nuisance exists. . . .

§ 823.05

Whoever shall erect, establish, continue, or maintain, own or lease any building, booth, tent or place which tends to annoy the community or injure the health of the community, or become manifestly injurious to the morals or manners of the people . . . or any house or place of prostitution, assignation, lewdness or place or building where games of chance are engaged in violation of law or any place where any law of the state is violated, shall be deemed guilty of maintaining a nuisance, and the building, erection, place, tent or booth and the furniture, fixtures and contents are declared a nuisance. All such places or persons shall be abated or enjoined as provided in §§ 60.05 and 60.06 [dealing with the duty and authority of the court].

See also Tex. Civ. Prac. & Rem. Code § 125 (Westlaw 2022).

State ex rel. Hunter v. Johnson & Johnson

Supreme Court of Oklahoma
2021 WL 5191372

Winchester, J.

An opioid drug epidemic exists in the United States. Oklahoma has experienced abuse and misuse of opioid medications . . . and thousands of opioid-related deaths in the past two decades. . . . We also cannot disregard that . . . opioids are currently a vital treatment option for pain. The U.S. Food and Drug Administration ("FDA") has endorsed properly managed medical use of opioids (taken as prescribed) as safe, effective pain management, and rarely addictive. . . .

. . . [T]he State of Oklahoma *ex rel.* Mike Hunter, Attorney General of Oklahoma ("State"), sued three prescription opioid manufacturers and requested that the district court hold opioid manufacturers liable for violating Oklahoma's public nuisance statute. . . . We hold that the district court's expansion of public nuisance law went too far. Oklahoma public nuisance law does not extend to the manufacturing, marketing, and selling of prescription opioids.

. . . .

Since the mid-1990s, Appellant Janssen Pharmaceuticals, Inc. . . . a wholly-owned subsidiary of Appellant Johnson & Johnson (collectively "J&J"), has manufactured, marketed, and sold prescription opioids in Oklahoma. . . .

The State presented evidence that J&J . . . actively promoted the concept that physicians were undertreating pain. Ultimately, the State argued J&J overstated the benefits of opioid use, downplayed the dangers, and failed to disclose the lack of evidence supporting long-term use in the interest of increasing J&J's profits.

J&J no longer promotes any prescription opioids and has not done so for several years. . . . Overall, J&J sold only 3% of all prescription opioids statewide. . . .

. . . . The State settled with the other opioid manufacturers and eventually dismissed all claims against J&J except public nuisance. The district court conducted a 33-day bench trial with the single issue being whether J&J was responsible for creating a public nuisance in the marketing and selling of its opioid products. The district court held J&J liable under Oklahoma's public nuisance statute for conducting "false, misleading, and dangerous marketing campaigns" about prescription opioids. The district court ordered that J&J pay $465 million to fund one year of the State's Abatement Plan, which consisted of the district court appropriating money to 21 government programs for services to combat opioid abuse. The amount of the judgment against J&J was not based on J&J's percentage of prescription opioids sold. The district court also did not take into consideration or grant J&J a set-off for the settlements the State had entered into with the other opioid manufacturers. Instead, the district court held J&J responsible to abate alleged harms done by all opioids, not just opioids manufactured and sold by J&J.

.... This Court has not extended the public nuisance statute to the manufacturing, marketing, and selling of products, and we reject the State's invitation to expand Oklahoma's public nuisance law.

.... However grave the problem of opioid addiction is in Oklahoma, public nuisance law does not provide a remedy for this harm.

....

Public nuisance began as a criminal remedy primarily employed to protect and preserve the rights and property shared by the public. It originated from twelfth-century England where it was a criminal writ to remedy actions or conditions that infringed on royal property or blocked public roads or waterways....

Public nuisance came to cover a large, miscellaneous and diversified group of minor criminal offenses. Restatement (Second) of Torts § 821B cmt. b (Am. Law Inst. 1979). The offenses involved an "interference with the interests of the community at large—interests that were recognized as rights of the general public entitled to protection." *Id.* The Restatement (Second) of Torts explained the interests as follows:

> Interference with the public health, as in the case of keeping diseased animals or the maintenance of a pond breeding malarial mosquitoes; with the public safety, as in the case of the storage of explosives in the midst of a city or the shooting of fireworks in the public streets; with the public morals, as in the case of houses of prostitution or indecent exhibitions; with the public peace, as by loud and disturbing noises; with the public comfort, as in the case of widely disseminated bad odors, dust and smoke; with the public convenience, as by the obstruction of a public highway or a navigable stream; and with a wide variety of other miscellaneous public rights of a similar kind.

Id.

Public nuisance evolved into a common law tort. It covered conduct, performed in a location within the actor's control, which harmed those common rights of the general public.... It has historically been linked to the use of land by the one creating the nuisance.... A public entity that proceeds against the one in control of the nuisance may only seek to abate, at the expense of the one in control of the nuisance. Courts have limited public nuisance claims to these traditional bounds....

Oklahoma's nuisance statute codifies the common law.... It states:

> A nuisance consists in unlawfully doing an act, or omitting to perform a duty, which act or omission either:
>
> First. Annoys, injures or endangers the comfort, repose, health, or safety of others; or
>
> Second. Offends decency; or
>
> Third. Unlawfully interferes with, obstructs or tends to obstruct, or renders dangerous for passage, any lake or navigable river, stream, canal or basin, or any public park, square, street or highway; or

> Fourth. In any way renders other persons insecure in life, or in the use of property, provided, this section shall not apply to preexisting agricultural activities.

50 O.S.2011, §1. The Oklahoma Legislature has long defined public nuisance as a nuisance that contemporaneously affects an entire community or large group of people, but need not damage or annoy equally to all. *Id.* §2.

. . . .

The State's allegations in this case do not fit within Oklahoma nuisance statutes as construed by this Court. The Court applies the nuisance statutes to unlawful conduct that annoys, injures, or endangers the comfort, repose, health, or safety of others. But that conduct has been criminal or property-based conflict. Applying the nuisance statutes to lawful products as the State requests would create unlimited and unprincipled liability for product manufacturers. . . .

The central focus of the State's complaints is that J&J was or should have been aware and that J&J failed to warn of the dangers associated with opioid abuse and addiction in promoting and marketing its opioid products. This classic articulation of tort law duties — to warn of or to make safe — sounds in product-related liability.

Public nuisance and product-related liability are two distinct causes of action, each with boundaries that are not intended to overlap. . . . The Restatement explains as follows:

> Tort suits seeking to recover for public nuisance have occasionally been brought against the makers of products that have caused harm, such as tobacco, firearms, and lead paint. These cases vary in the theory of damages on which they seek recovery, but often involve claims for economic losses the plaintiffs have suffered on account of the defendant's activities; they may include the costs of removing lead paint, for example, or of providing health care to those injured by smoking cigarettes. Liability on such theories has been rejected by most courts, and is excluded by this Section, because the common law of public nuisance is an inapt vehicle for addressing the conduct at issue. Mass harms caused by dangerous products are better addressed through the law of products liability, which has been developed and refined with sensitivity to the various policies at stake.

Restatement (Third) of Torts: Liab. for Econ. Harm §8 cmt. g (Am. Law. Inst. 2020).

. . . [W]e identify three reasons not to extend public nuisance law to envelop J&J's conduct as an opioid manufacturer: (1) the manufacture and distribution of products rarely cause a violation of a public right, (2) a manufacturer does not generally have control of its product once it is sold, and (3) a manufacturer could be held perpetually liable for its products under a nuisance theory. We address each in turn.

. . . .

One factor in rejecting the imposition of liability for public nuisance in this case is that the State has failed to show a violation of a public right. A public nuisance involves a violation of a public right; a public right is more than an aggregate of private rights by a large number of injured people. . . . Rather, a public right is a right to a public good, such as "an indivisible resource shared by the public at large, like air, water, or public rights-of-way." . . . . Unlike an interference with a public resource,

> [t]he manufacture and distribution of products rarely, if ever, causes a violation of a public right as that term has been understood in the law of public nuisance. Products generally are purchased and used by individual consumers, and any harm they cause — even if the use of the product is widespread and the manufacturer's or distributor's conduct is unreasonable — is not an actionable violation of a public right. . . . The sheer number of violations does not transform the harm from individual injury to communal injury.

Donald Gifford, *Public Nuisance as a Mass Products Liability Tort*, 71 U. Cin. L. Rev. 741, 817 (2003); *see also Lead Indus. Ass'n, Inc.*, 951 A.2d at 448, 454 (holding the right of a child to not be poisoned by lead is a nonpublic right). The damages the State seeks are not for a communal injury but are instead more in line with a private tort action for individual injuries sustained from use of a lawful product and in providing medical treatment or preventive treatment to certain, though numerous, individuals.

The State characterizes its suit as an interference with the public right of health. We disagree with the State's characterization. . . . This case does not involve a comparable incident to those in which we have anticipated that an injury to the public health would occur, e.g., diseased animals, pollution in drinking water, or the discharge of sewer on property. . . . Such property-related conditions have no beneficial use and only cause annoyance, injury, or endangerment. In this case, the lawful products, prescription opioids, have a beneficial use in treating pain.

We consider City of Chicago v. Beretta U.S.A. Corp., 213 Ill.2d 351, 821 N.E.2d 1099 (2004), instructive on this issue. In *Beretta*, the City of Chicago and Cook County brought public nuisance claims against manufacturers, distributors, and dealers of handguns. The city and county alleged that the manufacturing defendants knowingly oversupplied the market with their products and marketed their products to appeal to those who intended to use them for criminal purposes. . . . The state and county sought compensation for the abatement of the nuisance, including costs of medical services, law enforcement efforts, and prosecutions for violations of gun control ordinances. . . . The Illinois Supreme Court rejected these claims and sustained the trial court's dismissal of the public nuisance claims. The court acknowledged "[t]he tragic personal consequences of gun violence are inestimable." . . . . However, the state and county failed to show an unreasonable interference with a public right. . . . The Beretta court ultimately concluded that a public right to be free from the threat that others "may defy [criminal] laws would permit nuisance liability to be imposed on an endless list of manufacturers, distributors, and retailers of manufactured products." *Id.* It acknowledged the far-reaching effects of a decision otherwise:

> If there is a public right to be free from the threat that others may use a lawful product to break the law, that right would include the right to drive upon the highways, free from the risk of injury posed by drunk drivers. This public right to safe passage on the highways would provide the basis for public nuisance claims against brewers and distillers, distributing companies, and proprietors of bars, taverns, liquor stores, and restaurants with liquor licenses, all of whom could be said to contribute to an interference with the public right.

.... Similarly, a public right to be free from the threat that others may misuse or abuse prescription opioids — a lawful product — would hold manufacturers, distributors, and prescribers potentially liable for all types of use and misuse of prescription medications....

Another factor in rejecting the imposition of liability for public nuisance in this case is that J&J, as a manufacturer, did not control the instrumentality alleged to constitute the nuisance at the time it occurred. The State asks this Court to broadly extend the application of the nuisance statute, namely to a situation where a manufacturer sold a product (for over 20 years) that was later alleged to constitute a nuisance. A product manufacturer's responsibility is to put a lawful, non-defective product into the market. There is no common law tort duty to monitor how a consumer uses or misuses a product after it is sold. Without control, a manufacturer also cannot remove or abate the nuisance — which is the remedy the State seeks from J&J in this case.

....

Even with its influential marketing, J&J ultimately could not control: (1) how wholesalers distributed its products, (2) how regulations and legislation governed the distribution of its products by prescribers and pharmacies; (3) how doctors prescribed its products, (4) how pharmacies dispersed its products, and (5) how individual patients used its product or how a patient responded to its product, regardless of any warning or instruction given....

Even more, J&J could not control how individuals used other pharmaceutical companies' opioids....

Further, J&J cannot abate the alleged nuisance. The condition, opioid use and addiction, would not cease to exist even if J&J pays for the State's Abatement Plan.... The State's Abatement Plan is not an abatement in that it does not stop the act or omission that constitutes a nuisance....

The final factor in rejecting the imposition of liability for public nuisance in this case is the possibility that J&J could be held continuously liable for its products. Nuisance claims against products manufacturers sidestep any statute of limitations. In this case, the district court held J&J responsible for products that entered the stream of commerce more than 20 years ago....

Extending public nuisance law to the manufacturing, marketing, and selling of products—in this case, opioids—would allow consumers to "convert almost every products liability action into a [public] nuisance claim." . . . .

The common law criminal and property-based limitations have shaped Oklahoma's public nuisance statute. Without these limitations, businesses have no way to know whether they might face nuisance liability for manufacturing, marketing, or selling products, *i.e.*, will a sugar manufacturer or the fast food industry be liable for obesity, will an alcohol manufacturer be liable for psychological harms, or will a car manufacturer be liable for health hazards from lung disease to dementia or for air pollution. . . . We follow the limitations set by this Court for the past 100 years: Oklahoma public nuisance law does not apply to J&J's conduct in manufacturing, marketing, and selling prescription opioids.

. . . This Court defers the policy-making to the legislative and executive branches and rejects the unprecedented expansion of public nuisance law. The district court erred in finding J&J's conduct created a public nuisance.

[The concurring opinion of Kuehn, J., and the dissenting opinion of Edmondson, J., have been omitted.]

Notes

1. ***Other Precedent.*** In People v. Conagra Grocery Products Co., 17 Cal. App. 5th 51 (2017), the "trial court ordered various defendants to pay $1.15 billion into a fund to be used to abate the public nuisance created by interior residential lead paint." After the defendants challenged the trial court's judgment on many grounds, the court of appeals held that "the trial court's judgment must be reversed because substantial evidence does not support causation as to residences built after 1950." It directed "the trial court to hold further proceedings on remand regarding the appointment of a suitable receiver," and rejected "the remainder of defendants' contentions."

2. ***The Issue of Control in Nuisance Actions.*** Unlike the principal case, some courts have minimized the significance of control. *See In re Starlink Corn Products Liability Litig.*, 212 F. Supp. 2d 828 (N.D. Ill. 2002) (holding that corn farmers' allegations that pollen from genetically modified (GMO) corn, which was toxic to insects, drifted across property lines and onto their property were sufficient to support public and private nuisance claims against the GMO corn manufacturer).

D. Remedies in Nuisance Cases

Damages. The damages which may be recovered in an action for public or private nuisance typically provide compensation for a broad range of losses, including physical and emotional harm to persons and damage to tangible property. The former category includes amounts for physical injury, impairment of health, and personal discomfort, annoyance, and inconvenience. Compensation for harm to property may include, among other things, costs of repair, diminished market value, or lost productivity or rent. Punitive damages may be awarded in an egregious case, subject to the usual limitations.

Permanent Versus Temporary Damages. In Schneider Nat. Carriers, Inc. v. Bates, 147 S.W.3d 264 (Tex. 2004), the court wrote:

> We define a permanent nuisance as one that involves "an activity of such a character and existing under such circumstances that it will be presumed to continue indefinitely." . . . .
>
> Conversely, a nuisance is temporary if it is of limited duration. Thus, a nuisance may be considered temporary if it is uncertain if any future injury will occur, or if future injury "is liable to occur only at long intervals." . . . .
>
> . . . . [T]he distinction between temporary and permanent nuisances determines the damages that may be recovered. . . . [I]f a nuisance is temporary, the landowner may recover only lost use and enjoyment (measured in terms of rental value) that has already accrued. Conversely, if a nuisance is permanent, the owner may recover lost market value — a figure that reflects all losses from the injury, including lost rents expected in the future. Because the one claim is included in the other, the two claims are mutually exclusive; a landowner cannot recover both in the same action.

Injunctive Relief. A temporary or permanent injunction may be issued where the plaintiff has no adequate remedy at law. In theory, all nuisance cases in which future harm is threatened should entitle the plaintiff to an injunction, as equity regards every tract of land as being unique. In practice, of course, the courts are reluctant to enjoin the conduct of important activities even if landowners are adversely affected.

In a famous New York case, Boomer v. Atlantic Cement Co., 257 N.E.2d 870 (N.Y. 1970), the defendant's cement plant regularly deposited cement dust on the property of nearby residents. This was held to be a nuisance, and under prior New York decisions someone subject to a nuisance resulting in substantial and permanent damage was entitled to enjoin the nuisance. The court was unwilling to enjoin the plant's operation, and instead required the defendant to pay permanent damages to the plaintiffs. These permanent damages purported to compensate the plaintiffs not only for harm done in the past but also for future harms. Judge Jasen, dissenting, observed that this result had the effect of allowing the defendants to purchase an interest in the plaintiffs' properties — a sort of easement to continue polluting without the plaintiffs' consent.

One need not wait until harm occurs before seeking injunctive relief, though the burden of proving that proposed conduct will constitute a nuisance may be heavy. *See* Sharp v. 251st St. Landfill, Inc., 925 P.2d 546 (Okla. 1996) (neighboring landowners threatened with complete loss of their water supply may apply for injunctive relief without waiting for actual loss).

Self-Help: The Right to Abate a Nuisance. Because resort to the law for monetary or injunctive relief is often slow, expensive, or impractical, authorities recognize that, under appropriate circumstances, an affected individual may act to abate a nuisance without first going to court. This privilege, however, is subject to several qualifications.

First, to encourage the exercise of care by those seeking to take matters into their own hands, the actor is deemed to assume the risk of any mistake about the facts. That the actor honestly and reasonably believed that the condition constituted a nuisance is immaterial to liability if an actual nuisance is not proven.

Second, the means selected to abate the nuisance must not be unnecessarily intrusive or destructive. If the interference with the rights of another exceeds what is warranted by the circumstances, the actor is liable for the excess damage. In addition, entry onto the land of another must be made at a reasonable time and in a reasonable manner, taking into account the degree and extent of the threatened harm and the availability of alternatives. If a request directed to the creator of the nuisance would result in its prompt cessation, a request is prerequisite to self-help. However, if notification is impossible, or if a request has been made and ignored, or if there is reason to believe that the entreaty would be futile, the actor may proceed without making a request.

Third, self-help is permitted only when time is of the essence. Consequently, there is often no right to abate a nuisance which has existed unchanged for a long while. This limitation discourages conduct that would risk a breach of the peace, personal injury, or erroneous interference with property rights under circumstances in which there is time for resort to the courts.

Self-help remedies are allowed, not required. It is no defense to a nuisance action for the defendant to argue that the plaintiff could have used self-help.

Some statutes provide that public representatives may act to halt activities that threaten the health, safety, or welfare of the public without first resorting to legal process.

Spur Industries, Inc. v. Del E. Webb Development Co.

Supreme Court of Arizona, En Banc
494 P.2d 700 (Ariz. 1972)

CAMERON, Vice Chief Justice.

From a judgment permanently enjoining the defendant, Spur Industries, Inc., from operating a cattle feedlot near the plaintiff Del E. Webb Development Company's Sun City, Spur appeals. Webb cross-appeals.... [W]e feel that it is necessary to answer only two questions. They are:

> 1. Where the operation of a business, such as a cattle feedlot is lawful in the first instance, but becomes a nuisance by reason of a nearby residential area, may the feedlot operation be enjoined in an action brought by the developer of the residential area?

2. Assuming that the nuisance may be enjoined, may the developer of a completely new town or urban area in a previously agricultural area be required to indemnify the operator of the feedlot who must move or cease operation because of the presence of the residential area created by the developer?

The facts necessary for a determination of this matter on appeal are as follows. The area in question is located in Maricopa County, Arizona, some 14 to 15 miles west of the urban area of Phoenix. . . .

Farming started in this area about 1911. . . .

In 1956, Spur's predecessors in interest, H. Marion Welborn and the Northside Hay Mill and Trading Company, developed feedlots, about H mile south of Olive Avenue, in an area between the confluence of the usually dry Agua Fria and New Rivers. The area is well suited for cattle feeding and in 1959, there were 25 cattle feeding pens or dairy operations within a 7 mile radius of the location developed by Spur's predecessors. In April and May of 1959, the Northside Hay Mill was feeding between 6,000 and 7,000 head of cattle and Welborn approximately 1,500 head on a combined area of 35 acres.

In May of 1959, Del Webb began to plan the development of an urban area to be known as Sun City. For this purpose, the Marinette and the Santa Fe Ranches, some 20,000 acres of farmland, were purchased for $15,000,000 or $750.00 per acre. This price was considerably less than the price of land located near the urban area of Phoenix, and . . . was a factor influencing the decision to purchase the property in question.

. . . .

By December 1967, Del Webb's property had extended south to Olive Avenue and Spur was within 500 feet of Olive Avenue to the north. . . . Del Webb filed its original complaint alleging that in excess of 1,300 lots in the southwest portion were unfit for development for sale as residential lots because of the operation of the Spur feedlot.

Del Webb's suit complained that the Spur feeding operation was a public nuisance because of the flies and the odor which were drifting or being blown by the prevailing south to north wind over the southern portion of Sun City. At the time of the suit, Spur was feeding between 20,000 and 30,000 head of cattle, and the facts amply support the finding of the trial court that the feed pens had become a nuisance to the people who resided in the southern part of Del Webb's development. The testimony indicated that cattle in a commercial feedlot will produce 35 to 40 pounds of wet manure per day, per head, or over a million pounds of wet manure per day for 30,000 head of cattle, and that despite the admittedly good feedlot management and good housekeeping practices by Spur, the resulting odor and flies produced an annoying if not unhealthy situation as far as the senior citizens of southern Sun City were concerned. There is no doubt that some of the citizens of Sun City were unable to enjoy the outdoor living which Del Webb had advertised and that Del Webb was faced with sales resistance from prospective purchasers as well as strong and persistent complaints from the people who had purchased homes in that area.

... [N]either the citizens of Sun City nor Youngtown are represented in this lawsuit and the suit is solely between Del E. Webb Development Company and Spur Industries, Inc.

....

We have no difficulty ... in agreeing with the conclusion of the trial court that Spur's operation was an enjoinable public nuisance as far as the people in the southern portion of Del Webb's Sun City were concerned.

§ 36-601, subsec. A reads as follows:

> § 36-601. Public nuisances dangerous to public health
>
> A. The following conditions are specifically declared public nuisances dangerous to the public health:
>
> 1. Any condition or place in populous areas which constitutes a breeding place for flies, rodents, mosquitoes and other insects which are capable of carrying and transmitting disease-causing organisms to any person or persons.

By this statute, before an otherwise lawful (and necessary) business may be declared a public nuisance, there must be a "populous" area in which people are injured:

> ... [I]t hardly admits a doubt that, in determining the question as to whether a lawful occupation is so conducted as to constitute a nuisance as a matter of fact, the locality and surroundings are of the first importance.... A business which is not per se a public nuisance may become such by being carried on at a place where the health, comfort, or convenience of a populous neighborhood is affected.... What might amount to a serious nuisance in one locality by reason of the density of the population, or character of the neighborhood affected, may in another place and under different surroundings be deemed proper and unobjectionable....

It is clear that as to the citizens of Sun City, the operation of Spur's feedlot was both a public and a private nuisance. They could have successfully maintained an action to abate the nuisance. Del Webb, having shown a special injury in the loss of sales, had a standing to bring suit to enjoin the nuisance.... The judgment of the trial court permanently enjoining the operation of the feedlot is affirmed.

....

A suit to enjoin a nuisance sounds in equity and the courts have long recognized a special responsibility to the public when acting as a court of equity:

> § 104. Where public interest is involved.
>
> Courts of equity may, and frequently do, go much further both to give and withhold relief in furtherance of the public interest than they are

> accustomed to go when only private interests are involved. Accordingly, the granting or withholding of relief may properly be dependent upon considerations of public interest. . . .

In addition to protecting the public interests, however, courts of equity are concerned with protecting the operator of a lawfully, albeit noxious, business from the result of a knowing and willful encroachment by others near his business.

In the so-called "coming to the nuisance" cases, the courts have held that the residential landowner may not have relief if he knowingly came into a neighborhood reserved for industrial or agricultural endeavors and has been damaged thereby:

> . . . .
>
> People employed in a city who build their homes in suburban areas of the county beyond the limits of a city and zoning regulations do so for a reason. Some do so to avoid the high taxation rate imposed by cities, or to avoid special assessments for street, sewer and water projects. They usually build on improved or hard surface highways, which have been built either at state or county expense and thereby avoid special assessments for these improvements. It may be that they desire to get away from the congestion of traffic, smoke, noise, foul air and the many other annoyances of city life. But with all these advantages in going beyond the area which is zoned and restricted to protect them in their homes, they must be prepared to take the disadvantages. . . .

And:

> . . . [A] party cannot justly call upon the law to make that place suitable for his residence which was not so when he selected it. . . .

Were Webb the only party injured, we would feel justified in holding that the doctrine of "coming to the nuisance" would have been a bar to the relief asked by Webb, and, on the other hand, had Spur located the feedlot near the outskirts of a city and had the city grown toward the feedlot, Spur would have to suffer the cost of abating the nuisance as to those people locating within the growth pattern of the expanding city. . . .

There was no indication in the instant case at the time Spur and its predecessors located in western Maricopa County that a new city would spring up, full-blown, alongside the feeding operation and that the developer of that city would ask the court to order Spur to move because of the new city. Spur is required to move not because of any wrongdoing on the part of Spur, but because of a proper and legitimate regard of the courts for the rights and interests of the public.

Del Webb, on the other hand, is entitled to the relief prayed for (a permanent injunction), not because Webb is blameless, but because of the damage to the people who have been encouraged to purchase homes in Sun City. It does not equitably or legally follow, however, that Webb, being entitled to the injunction, is then free of any liability to Spur if Webb has in fact been the cause of the damage Spur has sustained. It does not seem harsh to require a developer, who has taken advantage of the lesser land values in a rural area as well as the availability of large tracts of land on which to build and develop a new town or city in the area, to indemnify those who are forced to leave as a result.

Having brought people to the nuisance to the foreseeable detriment of Spur, Webb must indemnify Spur for a reasonable amount of the cost of moving or shutting down. It should be noted that this relief to Spur is limited to a case wherein a developer has, with foreseeability, brought into a previously agricultural or industrial area the population which makes necessary the granting of an injunction against a lawful business and for which the business has no adequate relief.

It is therefore the decision of this court that the matter be remanded to the trial court for a hearing upon the damages sustained by the defendant Spur as a reasonable and direct result of the granting of the permanent injunction. Since the result of the appeal may appear novel and both sides have obtained a measure of relief, it is ordered that each side will bear its own costs.

Affirmed in part, reversed in part, and remanded for further proceedings consistent with this opinion.

Notes

1. ***Defenses.*** The defenses which may be asserted in a nuisance action depend upon the nature of the tortious conduct on which the action is based. Thus, a plaintiff may not escape the effect of the defense of comparative negligence by recasting a negligence case as a suit for public or private nuisance predicated on negligent interference.

2. ***Right-to-Farm Laws.*** Every state has passed some type of Right-to-Farm Act. *See* 8 A.L.R. 6th (2005 and supp.). The Texas law provides in part:

Texas Agriculture Code § 251.004 (Westlaw 2022)

> (a) No nuisance action may be brought against an agricultural operation that has lawfully been in operation for one year or more prior to the date on which the action is brought, if the conditions or circumstances complained of as constituting the basis for the nuisance action have existed substantially unchanged since the established date of operation. . . .
>
> (b) A person . . . who violates the provisions of Subsection (a) . . . is liable to the agricultural operator for all costs and expenses incurred in defense of the action, including but not limited to attorney's fees, court costs, travel, and other related incidental expenses incurred in the defense.

3. ***Prescribed-Burn Laws.*** Some states have prescribe-burn statutes. Here is a provision from the Georgia law:

Georgia Code Annotated § 12-6-148(b) (Westlaw 2022)

> No property owner or owner's agent conducting an authorized prescribed burn . . . shall be liable for damages or injury caused by fire or resulting

> smoke unless it is proven that there was gross negligence in starting, controlling, or completing the burn.

In Morgan v. Horton, 707 S.E.2d 144 (Ga. App. 2011), the court held that this provision barred a wrongful death action based in part on nuisance, arising from a highway accident allegedly caused by smoke that reduced visibility. The court found that even if there was some evidence that the defendant landowner was negligent, there was no evidence of gross negligence.

Chapter 21

Misrepresentation

Fraud About Material Matters. This chapter examines claims for harm caused by misrepresentation. Every jurisdiction recognizes an action for fraud (sometimes called "deceit") which is based upon the defendant's having induced the plaintiff to detrimentally rely by intentionally or recklessly misrepresenting a material fact. *See generally* Restatement, Third, of Torts: Liab. for Economic Harm § 9-15 (2020).

A fact is "material" if a reasonable person would attach importance to its existence or nonexistence in determining a course of action, or if the maker of the representation has reason to know that its recipient is likely to regard the matter as important.

Negligent and Strict Liability Misrepresentation. Recovery for misrepresentations made negligently, rather than intentionally or recklessly, is sometimes allowed, particularly in business contexts. However, as discussed below, claims for negligent misrepresentation are in many ways more limited than for fraud. Some jurisdictions also impose strict liability for misrepresentations in very limited circumstances. Thus, even entirely innocent misstatements may be actionable.

This chapter is concerned with all three torts: fraud, negligent misrepresentation, and strict liability for inaccurate statements. By far, the most important of these actions is fraud. Decided cases involving fraud are legion, and the principles governing liability for fraud are extraordinarily well-developed. Because there is no shortage of deceptive conduct in the modern world, these principles are very useful. They enable lawyers to think clearly about the merits of claims alleging that the plaintiff was deceived.

A. Fraud

1. Intentional or Reckless Misrepresentation

Pleading and Proving Fraud. Fraud cases differ procedurally from other tort cases. Under Rule 9(b) of the Federal Rules of Civil Procedure, a complaint alleging fraud must state "with particularity the circumstances constituting fraud" (Westlaw 2022). Most states have a similar requirement. Judge Richard Posner has speculated that the "particularity" requirement may exist because

> Accusations of fraud can do serious damage to the goodwill of a business firm or a professional person. People should be discouraged from tossing

> such accusations into complaints in order to induce advantageous settlements or for other ulterior purposes.

Banker's Trust Co. v. Old Republic Ins. Co., 959 F.2d 677 (7th Cir. 1992). Another reason for requiring particularity may be that, because the governing rules are so intricate, it is impossible to assess the merits of a claim unless the allegedly fraudulent matter is spelled out.

Many jurisdictions say that fraud must be established by "clear and convincing evidence." Some courts hold that the higher standard does not apply to the damage element of fraud.

Securities Fraud. One important kind of fraud (which will not be discussed here) is securities fraud. Unlike common-law fraud, "securities fraud" is based on federal statutes and regulations. In many cases, securities fraud involves conduct that is not fraudulent in the traditional sense.

Deceptive Trade Practices Acts. Every state has enacted some form of statute regulating deceptive trade practices. These laws make it easier for consumers to sue for fraudulent conduct relating to goods or services that may also be actionable under common-law rules. Typically, the statutes permit recovery not only of compensatory damages, but also of attorney's fees and, on appropriate facts, exemplary damages. Consequently, it is sometimes easier to sue under a deceptive trade practice law, and the potential recovery may be larger. Not surprisingly, complaints alleging common-law fraud often also allege a violation of the state deceptive trade practices act.

Words, Conduct, and Silence. An actionable misrepresentation may take any of several forms. Oral and written statements are, of course, the most obvious varieties. For example, in O'Hara v. Western Seven Trees Corp., 142 Cal. Rptr. 487 (Ct. App. 1977), the defendants had represented that an apartment complex was continually patrolled by security guards and was "safe," despite knowing that a rapist had attacked several tenants. The plaintiff, who was subsequently raped, was permitted to recover from the defendants for the physical injuries she sustained.

Conduct may create a misrepresentation, as in the case of the defendant who stacks goods so that the bad ones are hidden. In Cadek v. Great Lakes Dragway, Inc., 58 F.3d 1209 (7th Cir. 1995), a race track owner misrepresented its fire-fighting capability by parking an inoperable fire truck near the place where drivers signed releases.

Silence, too, may be an actionable misrepresentation — but only if there is a duty to speak.

John Doe 1 v. Archdiocese of Milwaukee

Supreme Court of Wisconsin
734 N.W.2d 827 (Wis. 2007)

PATIENCE DRAKE ROGGENSACK, J.

This is a review of an unpublished decision of the court of appeals that affirmed the circuit court's order dismissing the complaints of John Doe 1, John Doe 2, John Doe 3, and Charles Linneman against the Archdiocese of Milwaukee (the Archdiocese). The court of appeals agreed with the circuit court that the claims against the Archdiocese for negligent supervision and fraud relating to the Roman Catholic priests' sexual molestation of children were barred by the statute of limitations. . . .

We conclude that the claims asserted against the Archdiocese for negligent supervision are barred by the statute of limitations. . . . However, we also conclude that the claims of fraud for intentional misrepresentation are independent claims based on the Archdiocese's alleged knowledge of the priests' prior sexual molestation of children and the Archdiocese's intent to deceive children and their families. We further conclude that the date of the accrual of the fraud claims is "when the plaintiffs discovered or, in the exercise of reasonable diligence, should have discovered" that the Archdiocese's alleged fraud was a cause of their injuries. . . . This determination cannot be resolved by a motion to dismiss the complaints. Therefore, we affirm the dismissal of the negligent supervision claims; we reverse the dismissal of the fraud claims; and we remand for further proceedings.

. . . .

A claim for intentional misrepresentation requires proof that:

> (1) the defendant made a factual representation; (2) which was untrue; (3) the defendant either made the representation knowing it was untrue or made it recklessly without caring whether it was true or false; (4) the defendant made the representation with intent to defraud and to induce another to act upon it; and (5) the plaintiff believed the statement to be true and relied on it to his/her detriment.

. . . . The allegations of fraud in the complaints that are before us are of two types: (1) alleged affirmative representations that the priests did not have a history of molesting children and that they were not a danger to children; and (2) alleged failures to disclose the material fact that each priest had a history of sexual molestation of children. Either an affirmative representation or a failure to disclose, when there is a duty to disclose, can support a claim of intentional misrepresentation. . . .

. . . [Wis. Stat.] § 802.03(2), pertaining to pleadings for fraud, states "the circumstances constituting fraud or mistake shall be stated with particularity." We have interpreted this statute to require that "allegations of fraud must specify the particular individuals involved, where and when misrepresentations occurred, and to whom misrepresentations were made." . . . .

As affirmative factual representations, the Doe plaintiffs allege that the Archdiocese represented that it did not know that Widera had a history of molesting children and it did not know he was a danger to children. The Doe plaintiffs allege the Archdiocese did so by its responses to parishioners' letters wherein it affirmed the parishioners' positive comments about Widera's frequent interactions with children. For example, on February 12, 1974, the Vice President of the St. Andrew School Board wrote:

> The children in our school literally follow him (Widera) around, he is so kind and shows so much interest in them.

On February 19, 1974, the Reverend John J. Theisen, Executive Secretary for the Archdiocese, responded:

> We are most happy to hear that you are so pleased with Father Sig Widera. We are happy to hear that he is doing well in the school and shows so much interest in the children.

The Doe plaintiffs' complaints attach and incorporate these letters and other documents showing that Widera was convicted of a violation of Wis. Stat. § 944.17 (1973–74) (sexual perversion) on August 13, 1973. It is alleged that the Archdiocese knew of this conviction when it responded in a reaffirming manner to the parishioners' letters.

The Doe and Linneman complaints also allege that the Archdiocese's act of placing the priests in parishes with unsupervised access to children constituted affirmative representations that the Archdiocese did not know that the priests had a history of sexually molesting children and that the Archdiocese did not know the priests were a danger to children. For example, the Doe plaintiffs' complaints allege:

> 34. By placing Siegfried Widera at St. Andrews in Delavan, the Archdiocese affirmatively represented to minor children and their families at the parish, including [the] Plaintiffs [ ] and their families, that Siegfried Widera did not have a history of molesting children, that Defendant Archdiocese did not know that Siegfried Widera had a history of molesting children and that Defendant Archdiocese did not know that Siegfried Widera was a danger to children.
>
> ....
>
> 36. Particularly, Defendant Archdiocese knew that Siegfried Widera had sexually molested numerous children and that Siegfried Widera was a danger to children before Widera molested ... [Plaintiffs].
>
> ....
>
> 50. Defendant Archdiocese knew that Siegfried Widera had a history of sexually molesting children before Plaintiffs].

.... Similar allegations are made in Linneman's complaint....

We have held that acts can be the equivalent of a representation.... [As we explained in an earlier case:]

> It is not necessary for a person to make oral misrepresentation of fact in order to be guilty of fraudulent conduct. . . .

Courts of other jurisdictions also have recognized that affirmative representations may, under certain circumstances, be made by non-verbal conduct. . . .

Here, all the plaintiffs allege that the Archdiocese's act of placing the priests in parishes where they had unsupervised access to children affirmatively represented to the minor children and their families that the Archdiocese did not know the priests had a history of molesting children and that the Archdiocese did not know the priests were a danger to children. . . . [W]e cannot conclude that such acts as are described in the complaints are not sufficient to constitute an affirmative representation.

The other four elements of intentional misrepresentation were also pled by the plaintiffs. First, the plaintiffs allege that the affirmative representations that the Archdiocese did not know of the priests' history of molestation and that the Archdiocese did not know the priests were a danger to children were untrue. Second, the plaintiffs allege that the Archdiocese knew the representations were untrue when made.[1]

Third, the complaints allege the Archdiocese intended to deceive the plaintiffs and induce them to act on the representations by not telling the parishioners of Widera's criminal conviction of sexually molesting a minor boy and of Becker's history of sexually molesting children.

Fourth, the plaintiffs allege that they relied on such representations because the defendants were in positions of superiority and influence, which caused them to be sexually molested and suffer damages. Therefore, we conclude that the plaintiffs have alleged facts sufficient to state claims for fraud.

. . . .

The complaints also alleged fraud through the Archdiocese's failure to disclose the fact that the priests had histories of sexual abuse of children. In general, silence or a failure to disclose a fact is not an intentional misrepresentation unless the

1. [Fn. 13:] The Doe plaintiffs' complaints state that Widera had been criminally convicted of child molestation and the Archdiocese knew of the conviction. The complaints also state that the Archdiocese received a letter detailing comments of a priest that worked at the parish Widera worked at when criminally convicted. The letter stated that a male grade school teacher who saw Widera "fooling around with the boys of another teacher" told the priest that if Widera "fooled around in the same way with his students, he would punch Father in the face"; that parishioners had come forward after the criminal conviction and reported incidents they had noticed and warnings they gave to their own children. . . .

Linneman alleged that the Archdiocese knew Becker had sexually molested numerous children and that he was a danger to children. . . . The pastor at the church in California asked that Becker be transferred back to Milwaukee. Linneman's complaint also states that the Archdiocese received a report from two parishioners in 1980 that Becker had "an unfortunate incident" with a teenage boy, whereupon the Archdiocese sent Becker to therapy and transferred him to another parish. Linneman's complaint also states the Archdiocese received other complaints from concerned parents regarding Becker's inappropriate behavior with children.

person has a duty to disclose. . . . Therefore, whether non-disclosure can satisfy an element of fraud turns on whether the Archdiocese had a duty to disclose to the plaintiffs the fact that the priests had histories of sexual molestation of children.

Although the question of whether a legal duty exists is a question of law, . . . it is an extremely complex question that may have factual components that make it unsuitable to address on a motion to dismiss. . . . Because we have concluded that the plaintiffs' allegations of affirmative fraudulent misrepresentations are sufficient, we do not address the sufficiency of the plaintiffs' fraudulent misrepresentation claims based on failures to disclose Widera's and Becker's histories of sexually molesting children that were known to the Archdiocese prior to the sexual abuse of the plaintiffs.

. . . .

The decision of the court of appeals is affirmed in part; reversed in part and remanded to the circuit court.

[The opinion of Chief Justice Abrahamson, concurring in part and dissenting in part, in which Justice Bradley joined, is omitted.]

Notes

1. ***Fraud.*** Defined in the Third Restatement. "One who fraudulently makes a material misrepresentation of fact, opinion, intention, or law, for the purpose of inducing another to act or refrain from acting, is subject to liability for economic loss caused by the other's justifiable reliance on the misrepresentation." Restatement, Third, of Torts: Liab. for Economic Harm § 9 (2020).

*2. **Fraud and Non-Pecuniary Injuries.*** Most fraud cases involve losses that are entirely pecuniary, but there is no reason in principle to deny recovery to someone who suffers bodily injury or property damage because of the ***defendant's*** misrepresentations. However, some cases involving misrepresentations seem better characterized as actions for battery (as when the plaintiff is fraudulently induced to consent to harmful contact), or as negligence, than as fraud.

Consider, for example, a case in which the plaintiff is injured when the driver of a car signals to the plaintiff that she can safely pass. If the driver has overlooked an approaching truck and the plaintiff is injured as a result, is the plaintiff's claim one for negligent misrepresentation or is it a simple claim for negligent operation of a motor vehicle?

In many cases, precise characterization of the claim will be unimportant. But suppose the driver is an employee of the federal government. The Federal Tort Claims Act generally allows actions against the government for the negligence of its employees, but it denies recovery for "[a]ny claim arising out of . . . misrepresentation." 28 U.S.C. § 2680(h) (Westlaw 2022). On the facts of the hypothetical above, it seems clear that the policies barring people from suing the government for misrepresentation, but allowing suits for run-of-the-mill motor vehicle accidents, favor recovery.

3. ***Tort, Contract, and Restitution.*** A defendant's fraud can be important for reasons other than providing grounds for a tort action. For example, someone induced by fraud to enter a contract may be excused from performance, and someone whose property has been fraudulently taken by the defendant can recover the property in an action for restitution. *See* Restatement, Third, of Restitution & Unjust Enrichment § 13(1) (2011).

In certain cases, however, a fraud action may give the plaintiff more than could be obtained by avoiding a contract or by restitution. Suppose, for instance, that *D* fraudulently induces *P* to buy Blackacre for $100,000, by telling *P* that Blackacre contains valuable mineral deposits. If Blackacre really contained those deposits, it would be worth $500,000; its actual value is only $20,000. Restitution or rescission of the contract will get *P*'s $100,000 back (if *P* returns the land), but an action for fraud will probably allow *P* to recover the difference between Blackacre's actual value and the $500,000 it would have been worth if the representations had been true.

A tort claim will also be the preferred remedy when the plaintiff was not in privity of contract with the fraudfeasor, or when the plaintiff wants to keep the property in question, or when the plaintiff must sue someone who obtained nothing by making the misrepresentation (as when *A* fraudulently induces *B* to pay $100,000 to *C*, and *B* wants to sue *A* rather than *C*).

In many cases, a complaint will allege claims based on tort, contract, and restitutionary principles. The relief awarded will depend on which claims the plaintiff can establish. If multiple theories of liability are proved, the plaintiff may have to make an "election of remedies" to prevent overcompensation.

Sovereign Pocohontas v. Bond

United States Court of Appeals for the District of Columbia
120 F.2d 39 (D.C. Cir. 1941)

EDGERTON, Associate Judge.

In this action for deceit, the District Court directed a verdict for the defendants. Their alleged misstatements related to the condition of a corporation of which they were officers. There is evidence that they said it was making money, and had made about $800 in the previous quarter and over $3,000 in the preceding year, and that they caused certain financial statements to be sent to plaintiff. Actually the corporation was losing money, and had lost about $86 in the previous quarter and $2,700 in the preceding year, and the financial statements were incorrect.

Defendant Moyer was President, and apparently defendant Bond was Secretary and Treasurer of the corporation. Both were frequently in its office and frequently spoke for it.... There is no evidence that they kept or examined its books, understood bookkeeping, prepared its financial statements, knew whether or not the statements were erroneous, or knew whether or not the corporation had made or was making money. There is evidence that the books were kept by other persons, and no evidence that those persons did not prepare the financial statements.

"The rule is settled that in an action at law where the issue is fraud the party relying upon fraud must show that the misrepresentations asserted were made either with knowledge of their untruth or in reckless disregard of the truth." .... The evidence would, we think, justify an inference that the defendants made untrue statements of objective fact in reckless disregard of the truth. In the absence of evidence tending to show that they were themselves misled by reasonable or merely negligent reliance on what others told them, a corporation's officers may be regarded as acting recklessly when they make glaringly false statements about its current financial history and condition....

Moreover, the evidence would support an inference that the defendants knowingly made untrue statements of subjective fact. They did not say, "We are informed and believe that the company has been making money." Had they done so, it is not likely that the plaintiff would have relied on what they said. Their alleged statements were positive and unqualified. They purported, by clear implication, to know what they were talking about. Where knowledge is possible, one who represents a mere belief as knowledge misrepresents a fact. "Where a party represents a material fact to be true to his personal knowledge, as distinguished from belief or opinion, when he does not know whether it is true or not, and it is actually untrue, he is guilty of falsehood, even if he believes it to be true, and if the statement is thus made with the intention that it shall be acted upon by another, who does so act upon it to his injury, the result is actionable fraud." ....

There was evidence that defendant's statements were made for the purpose of inducing plaintiff to refrain from action to collect a debt which defendants' company owed; that plaintiff did refrain, and also made a further sale to the company, in consequence; and that damage resulted, because the company's condition grew worse and plaintiff was ultimately unable to collect as much as it could have done when the representations were made.... Accordingly it was error to direct a verdict for the defendants.

Reversed.

Notes

1. ***Scienter.*** "*Scienter*"—meaning knowledge of falsity or reckless disregard for the truth—is an element of fraud. According to Restatement, Third, of Torts: Liab. for Economic Harm § 10 (2020):

> A misrepresentation may result in liability only if:
>
> (a) the maker of it knows or believes that it is false;
>
> (b) the maker of it knowingly states or implies a false level of confidence in its accuracy; or
>
> (c) the maker of it knowingly states or implies a basis for the representation that does not exist.

2. ***Facts Supporting Scienter.*** In Jacobs v. Halper, 116 F. Supp. 3d 469, 472 (E.D. Pa. 2015), the dispute arose from the plaintiff's "purchase . . . at a Sotheby's auction of a 1951 Willie Mays New York Giants signed rookie road jersey . . . and a 1950's Willie Mays New York Giants travel bag . . . , which he subsequently learned were inauthentic." Sotheby's argued that the plaintiff's fraud claim failed because he had not alleged facts sufficient to support an inference that Sotheby's acted with knowledge of a false statement or intended to induce reliance. In rejecting those arguments and allowing the claim to go forward, the court pointed out multiple statements in the auction catalog indicating that the memorabilia had been authenticated by a company called Grey Flannel, and the language in Sotheby's contract with Grey Flannel, which required it to provide "cataloguing and condition reports," but made no mention of authentication.

2. Silence and the Duty to Speak

In general, it is still true that "silence is golden." There is ordinarily no duty to disclose information merely because it would be useful, interesting, or important to another person. Thus:

- A reporter had no duty to disclose that he intended to disobey a judge's instruction to the media not to disclose the identity of the plaintiff, a sexual assault victim, who testified following the judge's instruction (Doe v. Associated Press, 331 F.3d 417 (4th Cir. 2003));
- A builder selling a new home had no duty to disclose to the purchaser that a hostile neighbor had raised threatening and abusive objections to the house as an "abominable monolith" (Levine v. The Kramer Group, 807 A.2d 264 (N.J. Super. Ct. App. Div. 2002)); and
- A bank selling a condominium in a neighborhood that had received a "lot of adverse publicity" had no duty to disclose that a toxic waste problem had been recently cleaned up at a nearby school and had caused difficulty selling the unit (Urman v. S. Boston Sav. Bank, 674 N.E.2d 1078, 1080 (Mass. 1997)).

However, there is an important difference between passive non-disclosure and active concealment. In addition, as the following cases and notes illustrate, there are several occasions when there is a duty to speak, in which case non-disclosure will be actionable.

Weintraub v. Krobatsch

Supreme Court of New Jersey
317 A.2d 68 (N.J. 1974)

JACOBS, J.

....

Mrs. Weintraub owned and occupied a six-year-old Englishtown home which she placed in the hands of a real estate broker (The Serafin Agency, Inc.) for sale. The Krobatsches were interested in purchasing the home, examined it while it was illuminated and found it suitable. On June 30, 1971, Mrs. Weintraub, as seller, and the Krobatsches, as purchasers, entered into a contract for the sale of the property for $42,500. The contract provided that the purchasers had inspected the property and were fully satisfied with its physical condition, that no representations had been made and that no responsibility was assumed by the seller as to the present or future condition of the premises. A deposit of $4,250 was sent by the purchasers to the broker to be held in escrow pending the closing of the transaction. The purchasers requested that the seller have the house fumigated and that was done. A fire after the signing of the contract caused damage but the purchasers indicated readiness that there be adjustment at closing.

During the evening of August 25, 1971, prior to closing, the purchasers entered the house, then unoccupied, and as they turned the lights on they were ... "astonished to see roaches literally running in all directions, up the walls, drapes, etc." On the following day their attorney wrote a letter to Mrs. Weintraub ... advising that ... "the presence of vermin in such great quantities, particularly after the exterminator was done, rendered the house as unfit for human habitation at this time and therefore, the contract is rescinded." On September 2, 1971, an exterminator wrote to Mr. Krobatsch advising that he had examined the premises and that "cockroaches were found to have infested the entire house." He said he could eliminate them for a relatively modest charge by two treatments with a twenty-one day interval but that it would be necessary to remove the carpeting "to properly treat all the infested areas."

Mrs. Weintraub rejected the rescission by the purchasers and filed an action in the Law Division joining them and the broker as defendants. Though she originally sought specific performance she later confined her claim to damages in the sum of $4,250, representing the deposit held in escrow by the broker. The broker filed an answer and counterclaim seeking payment of its commission in the sum of $2,550. ... At the argument on the motions it was evident that the purchasers were claiming fraudulent concealment or nondisclosure by the seller as the basis for their rescission. ... [T]heir attorney said: "Your honor, I would point out, and it is in my clients' affidavit, every time that they inspected this house prior to this time every light in the place was illuminated. Now, these insects are nocturnal by nature. ... By keeping the lights on it keeps them out of sight. These sellers had to know they had this problem. You could not live in a house this infested without knowing about it."

. . . . On appeal, the Appellate Division sustained the [Law Division's] summary judgment in Mrs. Weintraub's favor but disagreed with the Law Division's holding that the broker's claim must await trial. . . . [I]t modified the Law Division's judgment to the end that the purchasers were directed to pay not only the sum of $4,250 to Mrs. Weintraub but also the sum of $2,550 to the broker.

. . . .

Mrs. Weintraub . . . relies primarily on cases such as Swinton v. Whitinsville Sav. Bank, 311 Mass. 677, 42 N.E.2d 808, 141 A.L.R. 965 (1942). . . . *Swinton* is pertinent but, as Dean Prosser has noted (Prosser, . . . [Torts 696 (4th ed. 1971)]), it is one of a line of "singularly unappetizing cases" which are surely out of tune with our times.

In *Swinton* the plaintiff purchased a house from the defendant and after he occupied it he found it to be infested with termites. The defendant had made no verbal or written representations but the plaintiff, asserting that the defendant knew of the termites and was under a duty to speak, filed a complaint for damages grounded on fraudulent concealment. The Supreme Judicial Court of Massachusetts sustained a demurrer to the complaint and entered judgment for the defendant. In the course of its opinion, the court acknowledged that "the plaintiff possesses a certain appeal to the moral sense" but concluded that the law has not "reached the point of imposing upon the frailties of human nature a standard so idealistic as this." 42 N.E.2d at 808–809. That was written several decades ago and we are far from certain that it represents views held by the current members of the Massachusetts court. . . . In any event we are certain that it does not represent our sense of justice or fair dealing and it has understandably been rejected in persuasive opinions elsewhere. . . .

In Obde v. Schlemeyer, *supra*, 56 Wash. 2d 449, 353 P.2d 672, the defendants sold an apartment house to the plaintiff. The house was termite infested but that fact was not disclosed by the sellers to the purchasers who later sued for damages alleging fraudulent concealment. The sellers contended that they were under no obligation whatever to speak out and they relied heavily on the decision of the Massachusetts court in *Swinton*. . . . The Supreme Court of Washington flatly rejected their contention, holding that though the parties had dealt at arm's length the sellers were under "a duty to inform the plaintiffs of the termite condition" of which they were fully aware. 353 P.2d at 674; *cf.* Hughes v. Stusser, 68 Wash. 2d 707, 415 P.2d 89, 92 (1966). In the course of its opinion the court quoted approvingly from Dean Keeton's article . . . ["Fraud — Concealment and Non-Disclosure" (1936)] in 15 Tex. L. Rev. 1. There the author first expressed his thought that when Lord Cairns suggested in Peek v. Gurney, L.R. 6 H.L. 377 (1873), that there was no duty to disclose facts, no matter how "morally censurable" (at 403), he was expressing nineteenth century law as shaped by an individualistic philosophy based on freedom of contracts and unconcerned with morals. He then made the following comments which fairly embody a currently acceptable principle on which the holding in *Obde* may be said to be grounded:

> In the present stage of the law, the decisions show a drawing away from this idea, and there can be seen an attempt by many courts to reach a just

> result in so far as possible, but yet maintaining the degree of certainty which the law must have. The statement may often be found that if either party to a contract of sale conceals or suppresses a material fact which he is in good faith bound to disclose then his silence is fraudulent.
>
> The attitude of the courts toward nondisclosure is undergoing a change and contrary to Lord Cairns' famous remark it would seem that the object of the law in these cases should be to impose on parties to the transaction a duty to speak whenever justice, equity, and fair dealing demand it....

... [T]he purchasers here were entitled to withstand the seller's motion for summary judgment. They should have been permitted to proceed with their efforts to establish by testimony that they were equitably entitled to rescind because the house was extensively infested in the manner described by them, the seller was well aware of the infestation, and the seller deliberately concealed or failed to disclose the condition because of the likelihood that it would defeat the transaction. The seller may of course defend factually as well as legally and since the matter is primarily equitable in nature the factual as well as legal disputes will be for the trial judge alone....

If the trial judge finds such deliberate concealment or nondisclosure of the latent infestation not observable by the purchasers on their inspection, he will still be called upon to determine whether, in the light of the full presentation before him, the concealment or nondisclosure was of such significant nature as to justify rescission. Minor conditions which ordinary sellers and purchasers would reasonably disregard as of little or no materiality in the transaction would clearly not call for judicial intervention....

Reversed and Remanded.

Notes

1. ***Concealment.*** *See* Lawson v. Citizens & S. Nat'l Bank, 193 S.E.2d 124 (S.C. 1974) (liability was imposed where a gully was filled with trees and stumps and then covered over with clay and sold to unsuspecting plaintiffs for residential use).

2. ***Reasons for Permitting Non-Disclosure of Material Information.*** Why not simply have a rule that any party to a contemplated transaction must disclose all material information to the other party? One reason is that information is often expensive to acquire. To require everyone having valuable knowledge to give it away free would reduce the incentive to acquire that knowledge in the first place.

3. ***Property Disclosure Laws.*** A majority of states have adopted property disclosure laws which impose on home sellers duties to disclose to buyers a wide range of matters (*e.g.*, asbestos, radon gas, flooding problems, nearby munitions, tree diseases, and deaths on the property). *See, e.g.*, Cal. Civ. Code § 1102.1 *et seq.* (Westlaw 2022). Failure to comply with laws of this kind will normally support an action in tort. *See* Alexander v. McKnight, 9 Cal. Rptr. 2d 453 (Ct. App. 1992) (neighborhood noise problems and nuisances).

While such laws normally expand a seller's disclosure obligations, they have sometimes been interpreted as defining the full extent of a defendant's disclosure obligations. *Cf.* Nobrega v. Edison Glen Assoc., 772 A.2d 368, 374 (N.J. 2001).

4. ***Half-Truths.*** "[O]ne who voluntarily elects to make a partial disclosure is deemed to have assumed the duty to tell the whole truth . . . even though the speaker was under no duty to make the partial disclosure in the first place." Union Pac. Res. Group, Inc. v. Rhone-Poulenc, Inc., 247 F.3d 574, 584 (5th Cir. 2001).

In Thompson v. Best, 478 N.E.2d 79 (Ind. Ct. App. 1985), when the buyer of a house inquired about drainage problems the seller indicated that the house had previously had problems and that there was a sump pump in the basement. The seller failed to disclose that there was also a second sump pump that had to run continuously and that if for any reason it failed to do so the basement would flood. The court held that the seller was subject to liability for fraud and stated: "[a]s soon as Mr. Best introduced Thompson to the fact of the sump pump and the drainage tiles around the house, it was incumbent upon the Bests to *fully* declare any and all problems associated with their function."

See also Columbia/HCA Healthcare Corp. v. Cottey, 72 S.W.3d 735, 744 (Tex. App. 2002) (partial disclosure about a retirement plan was fraudulent because it failed to indicate that the plan could be rescinded at any time); Randi W. v. Muroc Jt. Unified Sch. Dist., 929 P.2d 582 (Cal. 1997) (having volunteered information in letters of recommendation praising an employee's character and personality, defendants were obliged to complete the picture by disclosing material facts regarding charges and complaints of the employee's sexual improprieties).

5. ***Fiduciary and Confidential Relationships.*** A duty to disclose all material facts also arises where the defendant stands in a fiduciary or otherwise trusted relationship to the plaintiff. Such confidential relationships are not limited to purely legal settings, and may be found to exist in situations that are moral, social, domestic, or merely personal. Thus, where the defendant, who was referred to as "uncle" by the plaintiffs and who was the best friend of their deceased father, secured the plaintiffs' signatures on a document which was purportedly a "peace paper" that would prevent other relatives from harassing the plaintiffs, but which secretly deeded the property to the defendant, the court held that a confidential relationship existed and that the deed could be set aside on grounds of fraud. *See* Curl v. Key, 316 S.E.2d 272 (N.C. 1984).

Lawyers and certain other professionals are fiduciaries as a matter of law. Other persons may be fiduciaries as a matter of fact. However, because the law of fiduciary obligations is demanding, courts are reluctant to characterize a non-professional relationship as fiduciary. *See* La Ventana Ranch Owners' Ass'n, Inc. v. Davis, 363 S.W.3d 632 (Tex. App. 2011) (finding no fiduciary relationship between homeowners and members of a homeowners' association architectural committee); *see also* Swenson v. Bender, 764 N.W.2d 596 (Minn. App. 2009) (finding no fiduciary relationship between a doctoral candidate and the online university academic advisor who allegedly stole her ideas).

Fiduciary relationships are distinguished from ordinary arm's-length commercial relationships (such as the typical relationship between a store and its customers). In fiduciary relationships, there are special reasons (such as the necessity of depending on professional expertise) that allow one party to trust another and that oblige the other to act in the best interests of the one who relies. In contrast, in ordinary arm's-length business relationships, parties must safeguard their own interests and cannot trust others to do that for them. In Pellegrini v. Cliffwood-Blue Moon Joint Venture, Inc., 115 S.W.3d 577 (Tex. App. 2003), the court characterized the relationship between a geophysicist contractor and a joint venture as an arm's-length transaction. The joint venture was therefore under no duty to disclose that a particular oil well was not part of the contract and that the geophysicist would earn no royalties therefrom. The geophysicist, the court wrote, "could reasonably be expected to make an investigation, ask questions, draw his own conclusions, and protect his own interests."

In Ho v. University of Texas at Arlington, 984 S.W.2d 672 (Tex. App. 1998), the court held that because there is no fiduciary relationship between students and professors as a matter of law, and no such relationship arose on the facts of the case, a professor did not have an affirmative duty to tell a student that she would not obtain her doctoral degree if she failed part of the oral dissertation. *See also* Brzica v. Trustees of Dartmouth College, 791 A.2d 990 (N.H. 2002) (holding there was no fiduciary relationship between college trustees and alumni requiring the trustees to disclose their intent to use alumni donations to eliminate single-sex fraternities and sororities).

"The fact that one businessman trusts another and relies on another to perform a contract does not give rise to a confidential relationship, because something apart from the transaction between the parties is required." Richter v. Wagner Oil Co., 90 S.W.3d 890, 896 (Tex. App. 2002).

6. ***Subsequently Acquired Information.*** Suppose a defendant tells the plaintiff something the defendant believes to be true. Later, the defendant learns that the statement is no longer true. Failure to correct the statement can be grounds for a fraud action.

For example, in McGrath v. Zenith Radio Corp., 651 F.2d 458 (7th Cir. 1981), the defendants told the plaintiff that he was the "heir apparent" to the presidency of a soon-to-be-acquired subsidiary. Before the plaintiff released his shares of stock to facilitate the acquisition, the defendants learned that there were serious doubts as to whether the plaintiff would ever become president, but failed to disclose that information. In a suit filed by the plaintiff, who was unceremoniously terminated soon after the acquisition, the court upheld a judgment in his favor.

7. ***Information Not Intended to Induce Reliance.*** A defendant who makes a false statement to the plaintiff, not expecting the plaintiff to rely on the statement,

commits fraud by remaining silent after learning that the plaintiff intends to rely. *See* Restatement, Third, of Torts: Liab. for Economic Harm § 13 (2020) (discussing duties to disclose and tacit misrepresentation).

8. ***Facts Basic to the Transaction.*** According to the Second Restatement, § 551, a party has a duty to disclose "facts basic to the transaction," the nondisclosure of which would be "so shocking to the ethical sense of the community, and . . . so extreme and unfair, as to amount to a form of swindling." Restatement, Second, of Torts § 551 and cmt. l. "Thus a seller who knows that his cattle are infected with tick fever . . . is not free to unload them on the buyer and take his money, when he knows that the buyer is not aware of the fact . . . [and] could not easily discover it." *Id.* Liability for nondisclosure of facts basic to the transaction "typically arises from conduct that represents a clear violation of business ethics." Restatement, Third, of Torts: Liab. for Economic Harm § 13 cmt. d (2020).

In Griffith v. Byers Constr. Co., 510 P.2d 198 (Kan. 1973), the court held that there was a duty to disclose to a buyer of a new home the fact that the saline content of the soil (which was part of an abandoned oil field) would not sustain vegetation.

The Restatement rule on facts "basic to the transaction" has been successfully invoked in cases in which:

- An employer failed to disclose a substantial, known risk that the project for which an employee was being hired would be discontinued in the near future; Berger v. Security Pacific Info. Sys., 795 P.2d 1380 (Colo. Ct. App. 1990;
- The purchaser of property and others intended to employ a scheme that would deprive the vendors of their security interest in land; Dewey v. Lutz, 462 N.W.2d 435 (N.D. 1990);
- The seller of cattle failed to disclose that they had not been vaccinated and therefore could never come into the state; Ducheneaux v. Miller, 488 N.W.2d 902 (S.D. 1992).

Note, however, that not only must the fact be basic to the transaction, it must also be reasonable to expect disclosure. *See* Schaller Tel. Co. v. Golden Sky Sys., Inc., 298 F.3d 736 (8th Cir. 2002) (holding that the seller of satellite television services had no reason to expect the buyer to disclose its alleged inability to obtain financing for the transaction).

9. ***Latent Material Facts Not Reasonably Discoverable.*** Even in cases not involving "facts basic to the transaction," there may be a duty to disclose an unknown fact that is material and not reasonably discoverable. This makes sense in light of the reasons underlying the general rule that ordinarily countenances nondisclosure. If the facts are reasonably discoverable, a rule not requiring disclosure creates an incentive for the plaintiffs to protect their own interests by careful investigation and decision making. If, however, the facts are not discoverable, there is nothing to be gained by placing the burden of discovery on the plaintiff: the plaintiff will simply

be relegated to making, and bearing the consequences of, a bad decision. Cognizant of these realities, one court wrote, in a typical opinion:

> Where one party to a contract has . . . knowledge which is not within the fair and reasonable reach of the other party and which he could not discover by the exercise of reasonable diligence . . . he is under a real obligation to speak, and his silence constitutes fraud.

Wolf v. Brungardt, 524 P.2d 726 (Kan. 1974).

10. ***Ethics in Law Practice: Disclosures to Clients and Others.*** When it comes to attorneys and clients, silence is far from golden. Attorneys must use reasonable care to keep clients informed of all material matters and, under certain circumstances, the duty of disclosure is considerably more demanding and sometimes calls for "absolute and perfect candor." *See* Vincent R. Johnson, *"Absolute and Perfect Candor" to Clients,* 34 St. Mary's L.J. 737 (2003).

The rule against half-truths applies with particular force to attorneys and plays an important role in shaping disclosure obligations to clients and others. Thus, one court stated:

> A person must be able to trust a lawyer's word as the lawyer should expect his word to be understood, without having to search for equivocation, hidden meanings, deliberate half-truths or camouflaged escape hatches.
>
> For example, a lawyer cannot state that she was awarded a degree by a university, without mentioning that the degree was later revoked; that she is licensed to practice law, without saying that she is now on inactive status; or that she applied for board certification as a specialist, without indicating that her application was rejected.
>
> However, something is not a half-truth merely because negative information of some sort could be revealed about the speaker that has not yet been disclosed. Rather, a half-truth exists, and additional disclosure is required, only when the undisclosed facts are so directly related to the initial statement, or so pertinent to an understanding of the subject, that the recipient of the initial statement would feel seriously misled about that particular assertion of fact. This nexus requirement is important, for otherwise, the half-truth rule might be read so broadly as to devour both the general rule that countenances silence and the exceptions that impose a duty to speak.

Vincent R. Johnson & Shawn M. Lovorn, *Misrepresentation by Lawyers About Credentials or Experience,* 57 Okla. L. Rev. 529, 549–50 (2004).

3. Statements of Opinion, Prediction, Intention, and Law

It is sometimes said that fraud claims cannot be based on a defendant's expression of an "opinion," as distinct from a statement of "fact." As the following decision shows, this is an overstatement.

Oltmer v. Zamora

Appellate Court of Illinois
418 N.E.2d 506 (Ill. App. Ct. 1981)

GREEN, Justice.

....

Plaintiffs were a married couple who moved from Independence, Missouri, to the Decatur area. Wishing to buy a home in that area, they contacted the defendant Drobisch firm, who sent their agent, defendant Jones, to plaintiffs. She showed plaintiffs several houses and they eventually purchased one of these homes, that house built and owned by the defendants Zamora. The undisputed evidence at trial showed the house to be 13 to 15 inches higher on its south side than on its north side. The evidence upon which the claim of misrepresentation was based was sharply disputed. Taken most favorably to plaintiffs, ... it showed: (1) Juanita Jones was an aunt of Elaine M. Zamora but did not disclose this to plaintiffs; (2) Mrs. Jones disparaged several of the houses which she showed to plaintiffs; (3) Mrs. Jones told plaintiffs that Joseph B. Zamora who built the house was a "very reputable" builder and "one of the best in the area" although she knew he had never built any type of structure before; (4) Mrs. Jones had made several inspections of the house but when told by Mr. Oltmer, during the showing of the house, that he felt like he was "walking uphill," responded that could not be so because the house was new; and (5) when measurements confirmed the existence of the sloping nature of the house, Mrs. Jones suggested to plaintiffs that they attempt to sell it and implied that they do so without informing the purchasers of the problem.

....

Defendants emphasize that [to be liable for the tort of misrepresentation] the representation must be as to matters of fact and not of opinion, citing Parker v. Arthur Murray, Inc. (1973), 10 Ill. App. 3d 1000, 295 N.E.2d 487. There, statements by dance hall proprietors to a customer that he had great potential as a dancer made for the purpose of inducing the customer to contract for lessons were as a matter of law held to be insufficiently factual to constitute the basis of fraud. However, we consider determination of whether a statement which might appear to be an opinion is nevertheless to be treated as a statement of fact is more complicated than *Parker* would indicate. The Restatement spoke to the question in the following manner:

Representation of Opinion Implying Justifying Facts

(1) A statement of opinion as to facts not disclosed and not otherwise known to the recipient may, if it is reasonable to do so, be interpreted by him as an implied statement

(a) that the facts known to the maker are not incompatible with his opinion; or

(b) that he knows facts sufficient to justify him in forming it.

> (2) In determining whether a statement of opinion may reasonably be so interpreted, the recipient's belief as to whether the maker has an adverse interest is important.

Restatement (Second) of Torts § 539 (1965).

The comments to the foregoing state in part . . .

> a. . . . [W]hen land is bought as an investment, a statement, even by the vendor, that a tenant under a long term lease is a good tenant implies that his conduct has been such that it would not be entirely inappropriate to call him a good tenant. Such a representation is therefore fraudulent if the vendor knows that the tenant has rarely paid his rent except under pressure of legal proceedings, since the vendor is giving a materially false picture of the tenant's conduct.
>
> . . . .
>
> c. The habit of vendors to exaggerate the advantages of the bargain that they are offering to make is a well-recognized fact. An intending purchaser may not be justified in relying upon his vendor's statement of the value, quality or other advantages of a thing that he is intending to sell as carrying with it any assurance that the thing is such as to justify a reasonable man in praising it so highly. However, a purchaser is justified in assuming that even his vendor's opinion has some basis of fact and therefore in believing that the vendor knows of nothing which makes his opinion fantastic.

Professor Prosser appears to be in complete agreement. He states:

> . . . . There is quite general agreement that such an assertion is to be implied where the defendant holds himself out or is understood as having special knowledge of the matter which is not available to the plaintiff, so that his opinion becomes in effect an assertion summarizing his knowledge.

Prosser, Torts § 109, at 726 (4th ed. 1971).

Under the theory of the cited text, a statement by Juanita Jones, that Joseph B. Zamora was a reputable builder who was one of the best in the area when he had never built a structure before the house involved here, would be the basis of a cause of action in misrepresentation. Under § 539 of the Restatement (Second) of Torts, and under Prosser, her adverse interest and plaintiffs' unfamiliarity with Zamora, respectively, would be of substantial significance.

The decision in Bergman & Lefkow Insurance Agency v. Flash Cab Co. (1969), 110 Ill. App. 2d 415, 249 N.E.2d 729, is consistent with the texts. An insurance agent assured an official of a taxicab company that a particular insurance carrier was financially sound and capable of carrying their risk. The agent had an interest in the insurance carrier not revealed to the cab company official. Although the statement might appear to have been merely an opinion, it was held to have been a sufficient basis to support a jury determination of fraud after the carrier turned out to have been very unsound financially. . . . In *Bergman & Lefkow Insurance Agency*, the person making the statement had an undisclosed interest adverse to the recipient of the statement. Here there was evidence that Mrs. Jones had an undisclosed interest adverse to plaintiffs. In both cases the jury could have treated the statement in issue as one of fact.

As the tort of misrepresentation involves fraud, the party claiming fraud is required to prove that element by clear and convincing evidence but it may be proved by either direct or circumstantial evidence. . . . That standard requires evidence stronger than that which merely predominates but does not require proof beyond a reasonable doubt. . . . Whether to believe plaintiffs or Mrs. Jones as to whether she made the claimed statement as to Joseph B. Zamora's reputation as a builder was for the jury. Should the plaintiffs be believed, the jury could properly deem that evidence clear and convincing that Mrs. Jones made a misrepresentation that could be treated as one of fact. Such a determination would be supported by the circumstantial evidence that she (1) disparaged other houses, (2) sharply disagreed with Mr. Oltmer's mention of the possibility that the floor sloped, and (3) when the defect in the house was fully established, inferred to plaintiffs that they should attempt to sell the house without revealing the defect. We conclude that the jury could also have found the evidence to be clear and convincing that Mrs. Jones knew of Joseph B. Zamora's lack of previous experience or was culpably ignorant as to whether he had previous experience and that plaintiffs relied upon her statement in purchasing the house and would not have done so had they known of the defect.

. . . .

Reversed and remanded for a new trial.

Notes

1. ***"Puffing."*** A common application of the rule that statements of opinion are not actionable concerns "puffing," or "sales talk." The salesperson who tells a customer that a Prius is "the best car on the market" has not committed a tort, even if she has just read an issue of Consumer Reports excoriating Toyota cars in general and the Prius model in particular.

In Vulcan Metals Co. v. Simmons Mfg. Co., 248 F. 853 (2d Cir. 1918), the court held that a manufacturer's statements that vacuum cleaners were "absolutely perfect even in the smallest detail," "the most economical," and "simple, long-lived, easily operated and effective," and that "perfect satisfaction would result" were not actionable, even if the manufacturer knew that they were not true. However, the privilege to puff does not extend to specific factual claims. The *Vulcan Metals* court held that the plaintiff could recover because the defendant had falsely said that the vacuum cleaners in question had never before been offered for sale.

In re Toyota Motor Corp. Unintended Acceleration Marketing, Sales Practices and Prod. Liab. Litig., 754 F. Supp.2d 1208, 1229 (C.D. Cal. 2010), dealt with tort claims arising from alleged sudden, unintended acceleration of automobiles. The court found that some asserted misrepresentations were actionable and others were not:

> The Court agrees that some of Toyota's alleged statements may fairly be characterized as generalized opinions (*e.g.*, ... ("high quality, reliable, and dependable", "outstanding quality, dependability, and peace of mind")).... These statements constitute "puffing" and are not analogous to the type of opinion that may be construed as actionable under limited circumstances....
>
> However, other statements cited by Plaintiffs have a factual basis and may be proven true or false during discovery. *See, e.g.*, ... (stating to NHTSA [the National Highway Traffic Safety Administration] there was "no evidence of a system or component failure" and "vehicles operated as designed"); ... (stating to NHTSA that no defect trend had emerged ...); ... (telling customer "[i]t is virtually impossible for this type of ... incident to happen."). The foregoing allegations demonstrate Plaintiffs have sufficiently alleged actionable statements....

2. ***Implicit Statements of Fact.*** In Crown Cork & Seal Co. v. Hires Bottling of Chicago, 371 F.2d 256 (7th Cir. 1967), the plaintiff told the defendant's president that bottling equipment the defendant wanted to buy was "first class equipment," and that buying it would be a "very fine move." The defendant, seeking relief from its contractual obligations on the ground that the plaintiff's fraud had induced it to buy the equipment, claimed that the equipment was so bad that the defendant could not use it. The court held that the statements "implied, at least, an assertion of fact that the equipment was capable of producing Hires' goods in marketable condition."

3. ***Exceptions to the No-Reliance-on-Opinion Rule.*** Aside from opinions which carry with them implicit statements of fact, a party may reasonably rely and act upon another's expression of opinion in several situations. *See generally* Restatement, Third, of Torts: Liab. for Economic Harm § 14 (2020).

(a) ***Opinions Stated as Existing Facts.*** Where a party states an opinion in the form of an existing fact, the recipient is entitled to rely on the statement. For example, in Westby v. Gorsuch, 50 P.3d 284 (Wash. Ct. App. 2002), an antique dealer told a seller that a ticket from a survivor of the *Titanic* was worth $500. After purchasing the ticket, the dealer sold it for $100,000. The court affirmed a judgment for the seller, finding unpersuasive the dealer's argument that the misrepresentation did not relate to an existing fact.

(b) ***Opinions Not Honestly Held.*** If a person advances an opinion not honestly or reasonably held, an action may lie. For example, a defendant who told his employees to quote modest figures for additional rent, knowing from several internal memoranda that those were not accurate figures, was held to have made an actionable misrepresentation. *See* Magnaleasing, Inc. v. Staten Is. Mall, 563 F.2d 567 (2d Cir. 1977).

(c) ***Special Reasons to Expect Reliance.*** Recovery has been allowed in certain cases in which the person expressing the opinion had special reason to expect that the recipient would rely upon the statement:

(i) ***Mental Deficiency.*** This rule has found its chief application where the recipient of the communication suffers from a known lack of intelligence, illiteracy, or unusual credulity or gullibility. One who deliberately seeks to take advantage of such special characteristics "cannot be heard to say that the reliance he sought to induce was not justified because his statement was one of opinion and therefore should have been distrusted." Restatement, Second, of Torts § 542 cmt. i.

(ii) ***Opinions of "Disinterested" Persons.*** There is special reason to expect reliance if the speaker purports to be a disinterested party rather than an adversary. In Hanberry v. Hearst Corp., 81 Cal. Rptr. 519 (Ct. App. 1969), the plaintiff slipped and injured herself the first time she wore a new pair of shoes on a vinyl floor. The court permitted an action for negligent misrepresentation against the defendant, which had awarded the shoes its "Good Housekeeping seal of approval" and had said the shoes, were "good ones."

(iii) ***Preventing Investigation.*** If the defendant, after expressing an opinion, uses artifice or trickery to prevent further investigation, and so deprives the plaintiff of other sources of information, there is special reason to expect reliance and an action based on a statement of opinion will lie. *See* Garr v. Alden, 102 N.W. 950 (Mich. 1905) (sale of timber).

(d) ***Fiduciaries and Other Trusted Persons.*** Statements of conclusion or opinion may give rise to liability if a fiduciary or confidential relationship exists. Such a relationship justifies trust and reliance by the plaintiff. This rule has found support in cases involving:

- Attorney and client: Rice v. Press, 94 A.2d 397 (Vt. 1953);
- Partners: Teachout v. Van Hoesen, 40 N.W. 96 (Iowa 1878);
- Insurer and insured: Knox v. Anderson, 297 F.2d 702 (9th Cir. 1961);
- Close friends: Spiess v. Brandt, 41 N.W.2d 561 (Minn. 1950);
- Past business associates: Pulliam v. Gentry, 268 S.W. 557 (Ky. 1925); and
- Husband and wife: In re Estate of Folcher, 135 A.3d 128, 129 (N.J. 2016).

In addition, reliance on opinion is permitted if the speaker has successfully secured the recipient's confidence by stressing common membership in a religious denomination, fraternal order, or social group, or the fact that they were born or lived in the same locality. *See* Restatement, Second, of Torts § 542 cmt. h.

(e) ***Opinions of Persons Purporting to Have Special Knowledge.*** In cases in which specialized knowledge or experience is essential to forming an accurate opinion, courts tend to allow a non-expert who relied on an expert's intentionally false representation of opinion to recover for fraud. For example, according to the Restatement, a jeweler who falsely represents that a diamond is "of the first water," or an antique dealer who falsely claims that a modern imitation is a valuable antique, has committed fraud. Restatement, Second, of Torts § 542 cmt. f.

Tessier v. Rockefeller

Supreme Court of New Hampshire
33 A.3d 1118 (N.H. 2011)

CONBOY, J.

The plaintiff, Lorraine Tessier, . . . brought this action against the defendants, Regina S. Rockefeller and Nixon Peabody, LLP (Nixon Peabody), alleging the following facts. The plaintiff is the wife of Thomas Tessier, an attorney who practiced at the law firm of Christy & Tessier in Manchester. Dr. Frederick Jakobiec hired Attorney Tessier to handle certain estate matters on his behalf. On or about June 26, 2006, Attorney Rockefeller, an attorney employed by the firm of Nixon Peabody, acting on behalf of Dr. Jakobiec, accused Attorney Tessier of misusing and converting substantial assets of the Jakobiec family to his own use.

The plaintiff alleges that Attorney Rockefeller met with Attorney Tessier on numerous occasions and threatened him and, through him, the plaintiff, by demanding an immediate return of the misappropriated assets. Attorney Rockefeller stated to Attorney Tessier that if he repaid the money no further action would be taken against him. If payment was not forthcoming, however, Attorney Rockefeller would report his malfeasance to, among others, the New Hampshire Supreme Court Attorney Discipline Office. She also threatened that criminal proceedings against Attorney Tessier would follow.

As a result of the threats, the plaintiff alleges that she was forced "under duress" to execute a reverse mortgage on, and the release of her homestead interest in, the family home in Manchester and a settlement agreement dated April 2, 2007. She alleges that over the next two years, the defendants "stripped" her and her husband of their individual and joint interests in all of their tangible assets, including a jointly held vacation property in Vermont. Despite the settlement agreement, and without notice to her or her husband, the defendants reported Attorney Tessier's actions to his law partner, the attorney discipline office, and others. In addition, Dr. Jakobiec hired an attorney to bring suit against Attorney Tessier and to foreclose on the mortgage that was the subject of the settlement agreement.

As a result of the defendants' actions, the plaintiff alleges that she suffered severe emotional and physical distress requiring hospitalization. . . .

The defendants moved to dismiss the plaintiff's claims, arguing that she "has not and cannot set forth any legal duty she was owed by the defendants." They argued that Attorney Rockefeller "never met or otherwise communicated with the plaintiff," and, therefore, "it is simply impossible to construct a legal duty Attorney Rockefeller or Nixon Peabody owed to the plaintiff, much less a breach." . . . . The court thereafter ruled that the writ failed to state a cause of action upon which relief may be granted and dismissed it. . . .

. . . . "A representation of the maker's own intention to do or not to do a particular thing is fraudulent if he does not have that intention." Restatement (Second) of

Torts § 530, at 64. "Since a promise necessarily carries with it the implied assertion of an intention to perform it follows that a promise made without such an intention is fraudulent and actionable in deceit.... This is true whether or not the promise is enforceable as a contract." ....

The New Hampshire Rules of Professional Conduct require that "[a] lawyer who knows that another lawyer has committed a violation of the Rules of Professional Conduct that raises a substantial question as to that lawyer's honesty... shall inform the appropriate professional authority." .... Lawyers are deemed to know the Rules of Professional Conduct.... As the writ alleges, "when it appeared that the property of the plaintiff and Attorney Tessier [was] depleted, the defendants... then reported Attorney Tessier's alleged malfeasance to the New Hampshire Supreme Court Attorney Discipline Office, causing him to be suspended from the practice of law and to be the subject of criminal prosecution." These allegations would support a finding that at the time Attorney Rockefeller allegedly promised not to report Attorney Tessier's misconduct, the defendants knew they had the obligation to do so and, thus, had no intention of keeping the promise.

The fact that the alleged misrepresentation was not made directly to the plaintiff does not defeat her cause of action.

> The maker of a fraudulent misrepresentation is subject to liability for pecuniary loss to another who acts in justifiable reliance upon it if the misrepresentation, although not made directly to the other, is made to a third person and the maker intends or has reason to expect that its terms will be repeated or its substance communicated to the other, and that it will influence his conduct in the transaction... involved.

Restatement (Second) of Torts § 533, at 72–73. This rule "is applicable not only when the effect of the misrepresentation is to induce the other to enter into a transaction with the maker, but also when he is induced to enter into a transaction with a third person." ....

.... We read the facts set forth in the writ as alleging that the defendants either intended or had reason to expect that the promises made to Attorney Tessier would be communicated to the plaintiff and would influence her decision to enter into the settlement agreement with Dr. Jakobiec.

"The recipient of a fraudulent misrepresentation can recover against its maker for pecuniary loss resulting from it if... he relies on the misrepresentation in acting... and... his reliance is justifiable." Restatement (Second) of Torts § 537, at 80. Reliance upon a fraudulent misrepresentation is not justifiable unless the matter misrepresented is material....

Whether a reasonable person would have regarded the fact misrepresented to be important in determining her course of action is a question for the jury, unless the court determines that "the fact misrepresented is so obviously unimportant that the jury could not reasonably find that a reasonable [person] would have been influenced by it." .... The plaintiff alleges in her writ that "when faced with the choice of sacrificing her interest in certain of the joint assets of her family which she had accumulated over forty-six (46) years of marriage, or watching professional and criminal action taken against her husband and the exposure of her family to public shame, ridicule and disgrace," she agreed to comply with the defendants' demands against her share of the family assets. We cannot say, as a matter of law, that the alleged fact that the defendants misrepresented that they would not report Attorney Tessier's misconduct if the plaintiff entered into the settlement agreement was so "obviously unimportant" to her course of action as to render her reliance unreasonable. . . .

Because the plaintiff's writ specifies the essential details of the alleged fraud and specifically alleges the defendants' actions, we hold that the plaintiff has stated a claim against the defendants for fraudulent misrepresentation sufficient to withstand a motion to dismiss. . . .

Affirmed in part; reversed in part; and remanded.

Notes

1. ***Statements of Intention.*** In Adams v. Gillig, 92 N.E. 670 (N.Y. 1910), the defendant induced the plaintiff to sell a lot by falsely stating that he would build only single-family dwellings. The very next day he engaged an architect to design a public garage. The court held that while there would have been no liability if the buyer had merely changed his mind as to use of the property after the transaction had been completed, the circumstantial evidence showed that he in fact never intended to use the property for residences and had intentionally deceived the plaintiff by misrepresenting his state of mind. As the court explained:

> Intent is of vital importance in very many transactions. . . . The intent of a person is sometimes difficult to prove, but it is nevertheless a fact and a material and existing fact that must be ascertained in many cases, and, when ascertained, determines the rights of the parties to controversies. The intent of Gillig was a material existing fact in this case, and the plaintiff's reliance upon such fact induced her to enter into a contract that she would not otherwise have entered into. The effect of such false statement by the defendant of his intention cannot be cast aside as immaterial simply because it was possible for him in good faith to have changed his mind or to have sold the property to another who might have a different purpose relating thereto. As the defendant's intention was subject to change in good faith at any time, it was of uncertain value. It was, however, of some value. . . .

See also Graubard Mollen Dannett & Horowitz v. Moskovitz, 653 N.E.2d 1179 (N.Y. 1995) (a law firm stated a claim by alleging that the defendant attorney "represented orally to the partnership that he . . . would act to ensure the future of the firm . . . when he never intended to do so and indeed was even considering the formation of a new partnership").

2. ***Prediction Versus Intention.*** In McElrath v. Electric Inv. Co., 131 N.W. 380 (Minn. 1911), a summer hotel was leased to the plaintiff. The court held that a fraud

action could not be based on an assertion by the defendant that the property "would become an important summer resort," for that prediction rested wholly on conjecture and speculation. However, the defendant's representation that a local traction company intended to extend its line past the property was held to be actionable. What would the result be if the defendant, knowing that the traction company was quite unlikely to extend its line, had predicted that the line would be extended, rather than claiming that the company intended to extend it?

3. ***Prediction Versus Present Status.*** In McConkey v. AON Corp., 804 A.2d 572 (N.J. Super. Ct. App. Div. 2002), the plaintiff sued a company for fraudulently inducing him to leave his former employment by making misstatements that the company was not currently engaged in discussions that could result in a merger or other business combination. Shortly after joining the company, the plaintiff lost his job because of a reduction in force that followed the acquisition of the company by another entity. Finding for the plaintiff, the court noted that, by making inquiries into rumors, he was not asking about "future possibilities concerning the restructuring of the company, but was asking . . . about the present status of the company."

National Conversion Corp. v. Cedar Building Corp.

Court of Appeals of New York
246 N.E.2d 351 (N.Y. 1969)

BREITEL, Judge.

A former tenant of industrial premises sued its landlords for damages in fraud and for breach of warranty. The landlords counterclaimed for subsequent rents and for use and occupation, and also brought a summary proceeding to recover possession which was consolidated with this action. After a trial without a jury the tenant recovered a judgment for $70,086.81 and defendant landlords appeal, the Appellate Division having affirmed, two Justices dissenting.

There is no dispute that the lease contained a false representation that the demised premises were situated in an unrestricted zone. . . .

True, both sides were represented by lawyers. But tenant's testimony is that when it sought an adjournment of the negotiations in order for its lawyer to check whether the premises were located in an unrestricted zone, landlords' lawyer, who was also one of the principals, said that it would not be necessary, that they (landlords) "own the property, and we know the area," that it is in an unrestricted zone, and "We [landlords] guarantee it." . . . . The discussion was resolved only by including the representation in the lease. Tenant contended and proved that it had not actually known of the zoning requirement and had relied on what it was told. This proof, if accepted . . . , made out a classic instance of fraud in the inducement, for landlords intentionally or recklessly made false representations either as to their knowledge of the facts or the facts themselves. . . .

Landlords . . . contend that only a misrepresentation of law rather than of fact is involved and, therefore, that fraud will not lie. There is no longer any doubt that the law has recognized, even in this State, a sharp distinction between a pure opinion of law which may not, except in unusual circumstances, base an action in tort, and a mixed statement of fact as to what the law is or whether it is applicable. . . .

Most important it is that the law has outgrown the over-simple dichotomy between law and fact in the resolution of issues in deceit. It has been said that "a statement as to the law, like a statement as to anything else, may be intended and understood either as one of fact or one of opinion only, according to the circumstances of the case" (Prosser, op. cit., p. 741). The statements in this case, both before the execution of the lease, and in the body of the lease, exemplify ideally an instance in which the statements are not intended or understood merely as an expression of opinion. Landlords said they knew the premises were in an unrestricted district. This meant that they knew, as a fact, that the zoning resolution did not restrict the use of the particular premises, and tenant so understood it. When coupled with the further fact that tenant's lawyer was persuaded not to verify the status of the premises on the landlords' representation, it is equally clear that tenant understood the statement to be one of fact, namely, what the zoning resolution provided by description, map, and requirements as to the area in question. The misrepresented fact, if it is at all necessary to find misrepresented facts, was what the zoning resolution contained by way of description, map, and requirements, hardly opinions as to the law albeit matters to be found in a law.

. . . . "No presumption exists that all men know the law. The maxim 'a man is presumed to know the law,' is a trite, sententious saying, 'by no means universally true.' . . . . If ignorance of the law did not in fact exist, we would not have lawyers to advise and courts to decide what the law is." . . . [I]n the proper circumstances there may indeed be reliance on a fraudulently expressed statement of the law. Arguably, the facts of this case do not require so great a reach, for here the statements were keyed to the underlying data (facts) upon which the applicability of the particular zoning provisions governing the rights of owners and users were to be determined (the law). But, for the reasons indicated, it is not necessary to make the distinction rest on so narrow an analysis.

. . . .

[The discussion of the remaining issues is omitted.]

Accordingly, the order of the Appellate Division should be affirmed, with costs.

Notes

1. ***Statements About Law and Legality.*** The general rule is that an action for misrepresentation cannot be predicated upon statements of law, that is, statements relating to what the law is, what effect it has, or what varieties of conduct are, or are not, legal. The original reasoning underlying this rule seems to have been that because everyone is presumed to know the law, another's statements as to these matters are mere expressions of opinion. Today, the general rule has been extensively eviscerated. Among the exceptions are:

(a) ***Statements Intended as Fact.*** Courts permit an action for misrepresentation to be predicated on a statement of law intended and understood as an assertion of fact (*see National Conversion, supra*; Restatement, Second, of Torts § 525 cmt. d and § 545 cmts. a and b).

In Shafer v. Berger, 131 Cal. Rptr. 2d 777 (Ct. App. 2003), an attorney hired by an insurance company argued that his statement to a third party about limits on insurance coverage was not a representation of fact, but a non-actionable legal opinion. The court rejected that argument, reasoning that to allow counsel for an insurer to hoodwink the opposition into settling for less by deceiving them about the scope of coverage would seriously undermine the justice system.

(b) ***Implicit Statements of Fact.*** Actions are permitted for statements of law that carry with them false implicit statements of fact. In Sorenson v. Gardner, 334 P.2d 471 (Or. 1959), the court allowed an action against the seller of a dwelling, who asserted that the house had been constructed in compliance with code requirements, such as those concerning plumbing, building materials, and the location and size of vents. The statement carried with it assertions as to underlying facts because the recipients were unfamiliar with the relevant data.

The use of qualifying language may prevent an implicit statement of fact from arising from an expression of legal opinion. *See* Restatement, Second, of Torts § 545 cmt. d ("I think that my title to this land is good, but do not take my word for it").

(c) ***Law of Other Jurisdictions.*** Even those who believed that a person could be presumed to know the law never expected persons to know the law of jurisdictions other than their own. Misrepresentation actions may be based on statements concerning the law of states or countries in which the recipient neither resides nor regularly does business. *See* Firemen's Ins. Co. v. Jones, 431 S.W.2d 728 (Ark. 1968).

(d) ***Actionable Statements of Opinion.*** An action for misrepresentation may be based on a statement of law if the statement, though one of opinion, is made under circumstances which render an opinion actionable. *See* Ambrosino v. Rodman & Renshaw, Inc., 635 F. Supp. 968 (N.D. Ill. 1986) (misrepresentation by fiduciary).

4. Justifiable or Reasonable Reliance

Recovery for fraud will be allowed only to a plaintiff whose reliance on the statement in question was "justifiable." However, the plaintiff's reliance need not have been "reasonable" in the usual sense. Many widely practiced forms of fraud depend for their success upon the victim's gullibility (and, often, greed). The victim who gives his life savings to a confidence trickster who claims to have discovered a way to turn lead into gold has behaved quite unreasonably, yet the defendant's talent for finding gullible victims hardly justifies letting the defendant keep the plaintiff's money.

For example, in Behr v. Redmond, 123 Cal. Rptr. 3d 97, 106–07 (Ct. App. 2011), the defendant was found to have fraudulently concealed from his girlfriend the risk of contracting herpes by implying that it was okay to have sex if he was not experiencing an active outbreak. The defendant argued that his girlfriend's reliance on his statements was "unreasonable." Rejecting that argument, the court concluded that "[i]n light of the relationship of intimacy and trust between the parties, . . . [the defendant's] long experience with the disease, and his apparent knowledge about its contagiousness, the jury could reasonably conclude that Behr justifiably relied on Redmond's assurance that it was okay to have sex with him." *See generally* Restatement, Third, of Torts: Liab. for Economic Harm § 11 (2020) (discussing factual causation and justifiable reliance).

Some cases speak of a "reasonable reliance" requirement, or use the terms "reasonable" and "justifiable" interchangeably. In Estate of Lambert v. Fitzgerald, 497 S.W.3d 425, 457 (Tenn. App. 2016), the court held that an investor could not have reasonably relied on an investment opportunity that was too good to be true. The "craziness of the scheme was . . . evident," because "[t]he promises of fantastic returns for the investments, the use of cash only, . . . and the very idea that someone named Ebenezer Bonaparte would, for unexplained reasons, ship $150,000,000.00 of literally dirty cash from South Africa to London [so that it could be cleaned] . . . all scream fraud."

Knowledge of Falsity Precludes Reliance. A party who has learned that a representation is false cannot rely upon it and then sue for misrepresentation. *See* Richter v. Wagner Oil Co., 90 S.W.3d 890, 896 (Tex. App. 2002). Thus, if the falsity of the defendant's statement is obvious to the plaintiff's senses at the time it is made (*e.g.*, the plaintiff sees that the horse has two eyes, not three, as claimed by the defendant), there is no possible action for fraud.

Affirmative Statements and the Duty to Investigate. Ordinarily, if the defendant makes an affirmative representation, the plaintiff may rely upon its truth and need not investigate, so long as the statement is not patently false and there are no danger signals calling for inquiry. For example, in Judd v. Walker, 114 S.W. 979 (Mo. 1908), the court held that the plaintiff could rely upon the defendant's definite statement as to the acreage of land and was not required to measure the property himself, noting that one need not deal "with [one's] fellow man as if he was a thief or a robber."

In Williams v. Rank & Son Buick, Inc., 170 N.W.2d 807 (Wis. 1969), the plaintiff failed to prove that he relied on a salesman's alleged statement that a car had air conditioning because a mere flip of the knob labeled "air" during an hour-and-a-half test drive would have disclosed the falsity of the statement to the plaintiff, who testified that air conditioning was "the main reason he purchased the car."

One possible reading of *Williams* is that a statement that can be checked by the slightest effort—the mere flip of a switch—will be treated as equivalent to a falsehood so obvious that it cannot be actionable. However, the Restatement suggests that cases like *Williams* should not be read broadly, for the general rule permitting reliance on another's affirmative statement "applies not only when an investigation would involve an expenditure of effort and money out of proportion to the magnitude of the transaction, but also when it could be made without any considerable trouble or expense." Restatement, Second, of Torts § 540 cmt. a.

Reliance by Sophisticated Entities. Most courts hold that the rule that a person may rely upon express assurances applies to sophisticated entities, as well as to those less able to protect their own interests. *See* Vmark Software, Inc. v. EMC Corp., 642 N.E.2d 587, 595 n. 11 (Mass. App. Ct. 1994) (computer software licensor and licensee). However, there is authority to the contrary. In Lazard Freres & Co. v. Protective Life Ins. Co., 108 F.3d 1531 (2d Cir. 1997), Judge Guido Calabresi wrote:

> According to Protective, ... Lazard set the whole deal up in such a way that Protective had to rely on Lazard's representations and had to commit itself to purchase the MCC bank debt before it had the opportunity to examine the Scheme Report. It would therefore appear that Protective might have been justified in relying on Lazard's alleged misrepresentations when it orally committed itself to purchase the MCC bank debt. . . .
>
> This conclusion, nevertheless, seems to us to be too simple. As a substantial and sophisticated player in the bank debt market, Protective was under a further duty to protect itself from misrepresentation. It could easily have done so by insisting on an examination of the Scheme Report as a condition of closing. . . .
>
>> [W]here ... a party has been put on notice of the existence of material facts which have not been documented and he nevertheless proceeds with a transaction without securing the available documentation or inserting appropriate language in the agreement for his protection, he may truly be said to have willingly assumed the business risk that the facts may not be as represented. Succinctly put, a party will not be heard to complain that he has been defrauded when it is his own evident lack of due care which is responsible for his predicament.

Danger Signals Requiring Investigation or Action. In Greycas, Inc. v. Proud, 826 F.2d 1560 (7th Cir. 1987), a finance company required the applicant for a loan to supply an opinion letter from an attorney containing assurances that there were no prior liens on the machinery that was to secure the loan. The court held that the company could rely upon the attorney's assurances, even though it would not have been hard for it to conduct its own UCC lien search. However, had the opinion letter disclosed the fact that the attorney was the brother-in-law of the loan applicant, that "might have been a warning signal that [the finance company] ... could ignore only at its peril."

In Sippy v. Cristich, 609 P.2d 204 (Kan. Ct. App. 1980), water stains on the floor and ceiling of a house clearly suggested that the roof leaked. When the buyers inquired, they were repeatedly assured that the stains antedated appropriate repairs to the roof. Since an inspection of the roof would not easily have revealed whether a leak still existed, the buyers were justified in their reliance.

Documentary Disclaimers of Reliance. What if there is language in a contract, order form, or other document stating that the buyer is not relying upon any representations made by the seller? Some courts have held that this language does not automatically preclude an action based on earlier fraudulent statements, but is only one factor for the jury to consider on the reliance issue. Other courts hold that a cause of action is barred, unless the disclaimer clause relates to matters peculiarly within the knowledge of the seller.

Should it make a difference whether the disclaimer consists of a "boilerplate" recitation, as opposed to negotiated language? Or whether it specifically addresses the matter in issue or is general in nature? What if the plaintiff is a sophisticated commercial entity or actually drafted the language? Consider the following case.

Italian Cowboy Partners, Ltd. v. Prudential Ins. Co.

Texas Supreme Court
341 S.W.3d 323 (Tex. 2011)

Justice GREEN delivered the opinion of the Court in which Chief Justice JEFFERSON, Justice WAINWRIGHT, Justice MEDINA, Justice JOHNSON, and Justice LEHRMANN joined.

. . . .

This dispute arose when Jane and Francesco Secchi, owners and operators of a restaurant, Italian Cowboy, terminated the restaurant's lease because of a persistent sewer gas odor. In a suit against the landlord, Prudential Insurance Company of America, and the property manager, Prizm Partners,[2] the Secchis sought to rescind the lease and recover damages for fraud. . . .

. . . . The Secchis began negotiating a potential lease of the vacant restaurant building with Prizm's property management director, Fran Powell.

. . . Powell told the Secchis that the building was practically new and had no problems. In particular, Francesco Secchi testified that Powell told him "the building was in perfect condition, never a problem whatsoever." According to Secchi, Powell also said, "[T]his is my baby and I was here from the first day when they put the first brick until the last one. The size — it's in perfect condition. There is no problem whatsoever. . . . [It is] a perfect building." . . . .

The Secchis began remodeling the property after signing the lease. During this time, the Secchis first heard that a severe odor had plagued Hudson's Grill, the previous tenant. . . .

Upon hearing these statements, Francesco Secchi contacted Powell and specifically asked whether Hudson's Grill had experienced an odor problem. According to Secchi, Powell answered that she had been working with the building "all the time," and that "[n]ever before" had there been a problem — this was the "first time" she heard something was wrong.

. . . .

2. [Fn. 2:] We refer to the respondents collectively as Prudential. . . .

Attempts to remedy the persistent sewer gas odor . . . continued for months. . . .

In hopes that the foul odor would soon be remedied, the Secchis opened Italian Cowboy. The odor persisted, however. . . .

Secchi contacted Powell again later and told her that "the odor was so terrible" that Italian Cowboy "couldn't carry on." Powell then arranged for a smoke test to help identify the odor's source. After the test, Secchi asked Powell if those conducting the test had found anything and "[s]he said no." Yet, Secchi testified that one of the men who conducted the test said, "I found three [smoke] bombs, but those, they're old bombs. They're not our bombs. Those had been put some time ago."

. . . Powell continually denied knowledge of previous odor problems. However, the Secchis soon learned from a former manager of Hudson's Grill . . . that the sewer gas odor was not only present during Hudson's tenancy and that attempts to remedy it at the time were also unsuccessful, but that Powell was aware of the odor at that time. . . .

Upon receiving this information . . . , the Secchis immediately ceased paying rent and closed the restaurant. Italian Cowboy then sued Prudential and Prizm, asserting claims for fraud, including both a theory of fraud in the inducement of the lease, as well as fraud based on later misrepresentations. . . .

The trial court found for Italian Cowboy on all claims. . . .

. . . . The court of appeals . . . reversed. . . .

We turn first to whether the lease contract effectively disclaims reliance on representations made by Prudential, negating an element of Italian Cowboy's fraud claim. . . .

. . . . For more than fifty years, it has been "the rule that a written contract [even] containing a merger clause[3] can [nevertheless] be avoided for antecedent fraud or fraud in its inducement and that the parol evidence rule does not stand in the way of proof of such fraud." . . . . In . . . [Dallas Farm Machinery Co. v. Reaves, 307 S.W.2d 233 (Tex. 1957)], . . . [we stated]:

> The same public policy that in general sanctions the avoidance of a promise obtained by deceit strikes down all attempts to circumvent that policy by means of contractual devices. . . .

Decades later, we recognized an exception to this rule in Schlumberger Technology Corp. v. Swanson, 959 S.W.2d 171 (Tex. 1997), and held that when sophisticated parties represented by counsel disclaim reliance on representations about a specific matter in dispute, such a disclaimer may be binding, conclusively negating the element of reliance in a suit for fraudulent inducement. . . . In other words, fraudulent

3. A "merger clause," also known as "integration clause," is a "contractual provision stating that the contract represents the parties' complete and final agreement and supersedes all informal understandings and oral agreements relating to the subject matter of the contract." Black's Law Dictionary (9th ed. 2009). — Ed.

inducement is almost always grounds to set aside a contract despite a merger clause, but in certain circumstances, it may be possible for a contract's terms to preclude a claim for fraudulent inducement by a clear and specific disclaimer-of-reliance clause. . . .

More recently, in Forest Oil Corp. v. McAllen, 268 S.W.3d 51 (Tex. 2008), we applied our *Schlumberger* analysis to a settlement agreement that was intended to resolve both future and past claims. . . .

Prudential focuses our attention on section 14.18 of the lease contract ("Representations"), suggesting that Italian Cowboy's fraud claim is barred by its agreement that Prudential did not make any representations outside the agreement, *i.e.*, that Italian Cowboy impliedly agreed not to rely on any external representations by agreeing that no external representations were made. . . .

We conclude that the only reasonable interpretation of the contract language at issue here is that the parties to this lease intended nothing more than the provisions of a standard merger clause, and did not intend to include a disclaimer of reliance on representations. . . .

. . . . Prudential and the dissent would have us hold that parties no longer have to disclose known defects if they include a general merger clause in the lease agreement. This is outside a well-settled body of law on the proper legal effect of merger clauses and represents unsound policy. . . .

We have repeatedly held that to disclaim reliance, parties must use clear and unequivocal language. . . . This elevated requirement of precise language helps ensure that parties to a contract—even sophisticated parties represented by able attorneys—understand that the contract's terms disclaim reliance, such that the contract may be binding even if it was induced by fraud. . . .

Because the court of appeals concluded that a binding disclaimer of reliance existed, it did not reach the merits of Italian Cowboy's fraud claims. However, Prudential asserts alternate bases for why Italian Cowboy's fraud claims fail as a matter of law. . . .

Prudential maintains that Italian Cowboy's fraud claims fail as a matter of law because either Powell's representations were statements of opinion . . . , or were not known to be false. . . .

The trial court listed in its findings of fact three actionable representations made during the lease negotiations:

> a. The Secchis were lucky to be able to lease the Premises because the building on the Premises was practically new and was problem-free;
>
> b. No problems had been experienced with the Premises by the prior tenant; [and]
>
> c. The building on the Premises was a perfect restaurant site and that the Secchis could get into the building as a restaurant site for next to nothing.

.... Pure expressions of opinion are not representations of material fact, and thus cannot provide a basis for a fraud claim.... "Whether a statement is an actionable statement of 'fact' or merely one of 'opinion' often depends on the circumstances in which a statement is made." .... Special or one-sided knowledge may help lead to the conclusion that a statement is one of fact, not opinion.... Moreover, even if an expression is an opinion, "[t]here are exceptions to this general rule that an expression of an opinion cannot support an action for fraud." .... One such exception is that "when an opinion is based on past or present facts ... special knowledge establishes a basis for fraud." .... Thus, most simply, "[s]uperior knowledge by one party may also provide the occasion for fraud." ....

Initially, it defies common sense and any plausible meaning of the word "problem" to infer from the first two representations that in Prudential's "opinion," the sewer gas odor was not a problem for Hudson's Grill. A foul odor is obviously problematic to a restaurant. Testimony indicated that Powell herself personally experienced the odor and described it as "almost unbearable" and "ungodly." .... In light of the circumstances, we conclude that the statements concealing the odor "problem" are more properly statements of fact, not pure expressions of opinion.... Similarly, because of the attempts to remedy the odor by Hudson's Grill, known by Powell, combined with testimony that the odor was not remedied before Hudson's Grill closed, Powell's statement that the restaurant site was "perfect" is better characterized as a false statement of fact.... [*Cf.* GJP, Inc. v. Ghosh, 251 S.W.3d 854, 889–90 (Tex. App. 2008)] (determining statements that the vehicle was "in fine running order" and that it had "strong mechanicals" to be factual representations).

Even assuming, however, that Powell's statements are properly considered pure expressions of opinion, Prudential's one-sided knowledge of past facts makes these particular representations actionable under the circumstances.... Powell emphasized to Italian Cowboy that she had been working with the restaurant site since its inception, implying that she had personal knowledge of its entire history from her experience—*i.e.*, if there had been something worth mentioning, she would have known about it and mentioned it. Powell's honest representations about her superior knowledge of the site—such as stating that she "was here from the first day when they put the first brick until the last one"—were so intertwined with her other statements that they are actionable.... The persistent odor problem did not appear until a layer of solidified grease was removed from the grease trap [shortly before the opening], meaning that a reasonable inspection of the premises by Italian Cowboy would not have revealed the problem. Thus, Italian Cowboy did not have access to the same information as Powell.

While it is true that Italian Cowboy could have interviewed the former tenant to inquire about prior problems with the property, we are unwilling to require prospective commercial tenants to undertake this burden simply to ensure that they can later bring claims arising from their reliance on representations about the property made by a lessor with superior, personal knowledge. Rather, commercial tenants are entitled to rely on the fact that a landlord will not actively conceal material information.

Firsthand knowledge—like Powell's—concerning material information—like an odor problem in a restaurant site—is exactly the sort of scenario that demonstrates the sound policy behind the exception allowing an opinion to be actionable under certain circumstances where material information was withheld.

. . . .

We conclude that as a matter of law, Powell's representations were actionable, and legally sufficient evidence existed to demonstrate that they were known to be false when made. Because the court of appeals concluded that Italian Cowboy disclaimed reliance, it never reached Prudential's argument as to the factual sufficiency of the evidence supporting Italian Cowboy's fraud claims. Accordingly, having decided that there is no alternative legal basis to render judgment in favor of Prudential on Italian Cowboy's fraud claims, we remand the case to the court of appeals for further consideration.

[The dissenting opinion of Justice HECHT, in which Justice WILLETT and GUZMAN joined, has been omitted.]

Notes

1. ***Statements Not Communicated to the Plaintiff.*** According to the high court of New York:

> . . . [A] fraud claim requires the plaintiff to have relied upon a misrepresentation by a defendant to his or her detriment. This view is . . . logical insofar as the tort of fraud is intended to protect a party from being induced to act or refrain from acting based on false representations—a situation which does not occur where . . . the misrepresentations were not communicated to, or relied on, by plaintiff. We, therefore, decline to extend the reliance element of fraud to include a claim based on the reliance of a third party, rather than the plaintiff.

Pasternack v. Laboratory Corp. of Am. Holdings, 27 N.Y.3d 817, 829 (N.Y. 2016).

2. ***Time Sequence.*** In determining whether damages were caused by justifiable reliance on a misrepresentation, it is important to consider the sequence of events. Detrimental action that precedes a misstatement obviously was not caused by the misstatement. *See* Wrights v. Red River Fed. Cr. U., 71 S.W.3d 916, 920 (Tex. App. 2002) (where repair work was completed four months before a letter was written, the repairs could not have been done based on any representations in the letter).

3. ***Damages for Fraud.*** Economic damages in a fraud action are often calculated by reference to the bargain that the plaintiff lost (if the plaintiff can prove that there was a bargain, as well as what it was worth) or what the plaintiff paid. Under the benefit-of-the-bargain rule (sometimes called the "contract rule"), the plaintiff receives the difference between the value of the item if it had been as promised and the value of the item as it was received. Under the out-of-pocket rule (sometimes called the "tort rule"), damages are measured by subtracting the value of the item received from the amount paid by the plaintiff.

Regardless of which rule is applied in calculating pecuniary damages, consequential damages may also be recovered for such related losses as physical injury, property damage, harm to reputation, or the costs of completing a project or remedying a problem. See Vmark Software, Inc. v. E.C. Corp., 642 N.E.2d 587 (Mass. App. Ct. 1994) (licensee of misrepresented computer software was entitled to all damages it had suffered as a proximate result, including the cost of computer equipment which it would not have purchased but for the licensor's misleading representations and the cost of hours fruitlessly spent by the licensee's employees trying to make the defective computer system work).

Some courts permit the recovery of emotional distress damages, if that kind of harm was reasonably foreseeable. See Kilduff v. Adams, Inc., 593 A.2d 478 (Conn. 1991).

B. Negligence and Strict Liability

1. Negligent Misrepresentation in Business Transactions

Most American jurisdictions allow some actions for negligent misrepresentation, but only in limited circumstances. The Second Restatement, which influenced the development of negligent misrepresentation law in many states, limited actions for purely economic loss (as opposed to personal injury or property damage) to cases involving the furnishing of "false information for the guidance of others in their business transactions," and also said that liability may be imposed only on those who have a "pecuniary interest" in the transaction in question. *See* Restatement, Second, of Torts § 552.

Under this approach, someone who made a careless mistake in passing information to a friend would not be liable if the friend suffered losses in reliance on the statement. However, an accountant hired to examine the books of a business proposing to borrow money from the accountant's client would certainly be liable to the client for negligently misrepresenting the borrower's financial condition.

In Robinson v. Omer, 952 S.W.2d 423 (Tenn. 1997), an individual who claimed that he had gotten into trouble after being assured by a friend's lawyer that it was perfectly legal to videotape the friend's sexual encounters without the consent of the women involved had no claim against the lawyer for negligent misrepresentation. The misinformation was not supplied "for the guidance of others in their business transactions."

Similarly, in Dinsdale Constr., LLC v. Lumber Specialties, Ltd., 888 N.W.2d 644 (Iowa 2016), the court held that a company which sold building materials and engineering services, and its employee, did not have a pecuniary interest in supplying information to a builder about the structural integrity of a building under construction. Therefore, they could not be held liable for negligent misrepresentation.

However, the Third Restatement omits any requirement that negligent misrepresentation must relate to a business transaction. The Institute found that "cases not involving business transactions sometimes are compelling candidates for liability." Restatement, Third, of Torts: Liab. for Economic Harm § 5 cmt. h (2020). The Third Restatement provides that:

> An actor who, in the course of his or her business, profession, or employment, or in any transaction in which the actor has a pecuniary interest, supplies false information for the guidance of others is subject to liability for pecuniary loss caused to them by their reliance upon the information, if the actor fails to use reasonable care in obtaining or communicating it.

Id. at § 5(1).

For the Benefit of the Recipient. Courts are sometimes reluctant to recognize negligent misrepresentation actions for purely economic harm. For example, in Conway v. Pacific Univ., 924 P.2d 818, 824 (Or. 1996), a professor brought a negligent misrepresentation action against a university based on the university's alleged assurances that poor student evaluations would not affect the professor's prospects for attaining tenure. The court held that the university did not owe the professor a duty to avoid making negligent misrepresentations:

> Conway did not authorize the university to exercise independent judgment in his behalf, by contract or otherwise, thereby placing him in the position of having a right to rely upon the university. Indeed, at the time of the misrepresentations, both parties were acting in their *own* behalf, each for their own benefit, for the purpose of negotiating a renewal of Conway's contract. In that context, then, the university did not have a special responsibility toward Conway to exercise independent judgment in his behalf and to administer, oversee, or otherwise take care of any of his affairs. Consequently, the parties were not in a special relationship giving rise to a duty of care on the university's part to avoid making negligent misrepresentations to Conway.

Silence Versus Affirmative Misstatement. Can silence form the basis for a negligent-misrepresentation action? Some courts answer this question in the affirmative, although there is authority to the contrary. *See* Agrobiotech, Inc. v. Budd, 291 F. Supp. 2d 1186 (D. Nev. 2003) ("silence about material facts basic to the transaction, when combined with a duty to speak, is the functional equivalent of a misrepresentation for 'supplying false information' under Restatement § 552").

Reliance. In actions for negligent misrepresentation, many courts hold that even a sophisticated plaintiff with full access to information can be found to have relied upon a defendant's erroneous statement. *See* Williams Ford, Inc. v. Hartford Courant Co., 657 A.2d 212 (Conn. 1995).

Measure of Damages. Negligent misrepresentation is a narrower cause of action than fraud with respect to the measure of damages. For example, damages may be limited to out-of-pocket losses (as opposed to the benefit-of-the-bargain measure often appropriate for fraud). *See* D.S.A., Inc. v. Hillsboro Indep. Sch. Dist., 973 S.W.2d 662 (Tex. 1998).

Comparative Negligence. The plaintiff's negligence will reduce or eliminate liability that is based on negligent misrepresentation, but not in action for intentional fraud. For example, Gilchrist Timber Co. v. ITT Rayonier, Inc., 696 So. 2d 334 (Fla. 1997), was a suit involving negligent misstatements about zoning restrictions. The court held that the plaintiff's comparative negligence was relevant and that it was appropriate to take into account whether the plaintiff negligently failed to convey to the seller its intent to subdivide the property for residential use and failed to verify the zoning classification set forth in a year-old appraisal contained in materials furnished by the seller.

2. Negligence Causing Physical Harm

If a negligent misrepresentation leads to personal injury or property damage, rather than to the pecuniary loss typical of misrepresentation, the limits discussed above do not come into play. Such cases are sometimes best viewed as ordinary negligence cases, rather than as part of the law of misrepresentation.

3. Strict Liability

A handful of cases allow some plaintiffs to recover for misrepresentations on a strict-liability basis. Here is an example.

Richard v. A. Waldman and Sons, Inc.

Supreme Court of Connecticut
232 A.2d 307 (Conn. 1967)

COTTER, Associate Justice.

. . . .

The parties, by written agreement, contracted for the sale and purchase of a lot together with a building. . . . Nine days after the execution of the agreement, the defendant conveyed the real estate to the plaintiffs by warranty deed containing the usual covenants against encumbrances, except those mentioned in the deed, and thereupon the plaintiffs took possession of the property.

At the time of the closing, the defendant delivered to the plaintiffs a plot plan prepared by a registered engineer and land surveyor. This plan showed a sideyard of twenty feet on the southerly boundary of the lot which was in compliance with the minimum requirements for this lot according to the zoning regulations. . . . A permit had previously been granted for the construction of the building . . . and the survey submitted at the time the defendant made the application indicated that the structure was to be located twenty feet more or less from the southerly property line. Subsequently, a certificate of occupancy was erroneously issued based on the survey submitted by the defendant. Approximately four months after the delivery of the deed to the plaintiffs, the defendant discovered, when it set pins defining the boundaries of the premises, that the southeast corner of the foundation of the plaintiffs' house was only 1.8 feet from the southerly boundary of the lot. At this time, it was found that trespass upon adjoining property occurred in entering and leaving the plaintiffs' back door and stoop. Prior to this discovery, the parties were unaware that there was a violation of the zoning regulations as to sideyard requirements. . . .

The defendant claims that "[a]t most, there was an innocent misrepresentation of fact by the defendant." An innocent misrepresentation may be actionable if the declarant has the means of knowing, ought to know, or has the duty of knowing the truth. 23 Am. Jur. 920, Fraud and Deceit, § 127.

. . . [T]he plaintiffs had reasonable grounds upon which to attribute to the defendant accurate knowledge of what it represented as to the location of the structure on the lot. This was a statement of fact about which the defendant, as a developer of residential real estate, had special means of knowledge, and it was a matter peculiarly relating to its business and one on which the plaintiffs were entitled to rely. . . . The defendant was commercially involved in and responsible for the preliminary and final plans for building and locating the structure which was then constructed on the lot by the defendant in a manner which violated the zoning ordinance. Thereafter, the defendant undertook to provide the plaintiffs with a survey and plot plan which erroneously showed a southerly sideyard of twenty feet. Actual knowledge of the falsity of the representation need not be shown under the circumstances, nor must the plaintiffs allege fraud or bad faith. They have alleged all the facts material to support their claim and demand for damages. It is immaterial whether the wrong which can be legally inferred from the facts arises in contract or in tort. The plaintiffs may seek damages resulting from the defendant's misrepresentation and at the same time retain title to the property. . . . It would be unjust to permit the defendant under these circumstances to "retain the fruits of a bargain induced by" a material misrepresentation upon which the plaintiffs relied. . . .

There is no error.

In this opinion the other judges concurred.

Notes

1. ***Misrepresentations in Sale, Rental, or Exchange Transactions.*** The cases imposing strict liability for inaccurate statements of fact typically involve defendants who sold or leased property. However, the Restatement, Second, of Torts § 552C describes the rule as applying more broadly to "sale, rental or exchange transaction[s]." In some states, a result similar to strict tort liability is achieved by statute. *See, e.g.*, Tex. Bus. & Com. Code Ann. § 27.01 (Westlaw 2022) (dispensing with the need to prove *scienter* in real estate and stock transactions).

As the defendant's misrepresentation of a material fact would allow the plaintiff to rescind the contract in question, the major benefit to plaintiffs of allowing an action "in tort" is to let them keep the property and recover their losses as damages. According to the Second Restatement, damages are limited to the difference between what the plaintiff gave up and what the plaintiff got in exchange. *See* Restatement, Second, of Torts § 552C(2). The Third Restatement does not recognize this form of liability. Restatement, Third, of Torts: Liab. for Economic Harm § 3 cmt. d (2020) ("if a plaintiff was induced to enter into an exchange with the defendant by the defendant's innocent misrepresentation, the plaintiff has recourse under the law of restitution, warranty, and estoppel.").

2. ***Misrepresentations About Products Causing Physical Injuries.*** Another example of liability for innocent misrepresentation is found in the products liability provisions of the Restatement. Under § 402B of the Restatement, Second, of Torts, which has been adopted in several jurisdictions, a seller of goods who, by advertising, labeling, or otherwise, misrepresents to the public a material fact is strictly liable to a consumer for physical injury caused by the erroneous statement. Thus, a seller who incorrectly says that a shampoo is safe for use on hair, that glass is shatterproof, or that rope has a certain strength, will be liable for physical injuries resulting to one who could reasonably have been expected to use the product, even though the victim was not the purchaser of the item and the statement was not made intentionally, recklessly, or negligently.

See Ladd v. Honda Motor Co., Ltd., 939 S.W.2d 83 (Tenn. Ct. App. 1996) (in an action by a boy who became paralyzed when he lost control of an all-terrain vehicle, the court held that a manufacturer's advertisements for an entire product line, and not solely for the model of ATV used by the plaintiff, could provide a basis for liability based on innocent misrepresentation).

Under the Second Restatement, liability is limited to physical harm to a person or property and does not extend to economic loss. As a model provision, § 402B of the Second Restatement has now been replaced:

Restatement, Third, of Torts: Products Liability § 9 (1998)

> One engaged in the business of selling or otherwise distributing products who, in connection with the sale of a product, makes a fraudulent, negligent, or innocent misrepresentation of material fact concerning the product is subject to liability for harm to persons or property caused by the misrepresentation.

C. Liability to Third Parties

Misleading statements made orally are capable of endless repetition, and those embodied in documents may reach many readers. Consequently, it is important to ask which recipients of a statement have a right to sue if they detrimentally rely upon its content. One would expect liability to extend further for fraud than for negligent misrepresentation.

1. Based on Deceit

Foreseeability. A person who intentionally or recklessly perpetrates a fraud may be liable to anyone who suffers losses as a proximate cause of that fraud. That is, in many states, the scope of liability for fraud is defined by foreseeability. *See, e.g.*, Bily v. Arthur Young & Co., 834 P.2d 745, 773 (Cal. 1992) (liability for deceit extends to the class of persons "whom defendant intended or reasonably should have foreseen would rely upon the representation").

Special Reason to Expect Reliance. Some courts have gone to great lengths to indicate that foreseeable reliance is not sufficient to allow an indirect recipient to sue for fraud, and that something more is required. *See* Ernst & Young, L.L.P. v. Pac. Mut. Life Ins. Co., 51 S.W.3d 573 (Tex. 2001) (embracing a reason-to-expect reliance standard that requires more than foreseeability); Restatement, Second, of Torts § 533 & cmt. d ("[I]t is not enough . . . that the maker of the misrepresentation does recognize, or should recognize, the possibility that the third person to whom he makes it may repeat it for the purpose of influencing the conduct of another. He must . . . have information that gives him special reason to expect that it will be communicated to others"); Varwig v. Anderson-Behel Porsche/Audi, Inc., 141 Cal. Rptr. 539 (Ct. App. 1977) (a sales tax exemption certificate gave the seller special reason to know that a car would be resold to a consumer). *See* Restatement, Third, of Torts: Liab. for Economic Harm § 12 cmt. b (2020) ("The principles . . . [of fraud] require more than just foreseeability of a risk that the plaintiff might someday rely on what the defendant says. They require, rather, that the defendant have reason to consider that reliance likely, even if the plaintiff's identity is indistinct").

2. Based on Negligent Misrepresentation

Cases involving negligent misrepresentation pose an increased risk of imposing liability disproportionate to fault if the class of potential plaintiffs is broad. Consequently, recovery by third parties for negligent misrepresentation is more limited than for misrepresentations intentionally or recklessly made.

A distinction must be drawn based on whether the negligent misstatement caused physical harm. If so, liability extends to all foreseeable plaintiffs. In contrast, if purely economic loss (rather than personal injury or property damage) is at issue, different rules apply.

The following case addresses an issue of continuing importance: the liability of accountants to third persons for harm caused by negligent misrepresentation of a company's financial condition. Some of the principles that have guided the resolution of such disputes can be applied to cases of negligent misrepresentation by defendants who are not accountants.

Cast Art Industries, LLC v. KPMG, LLP

Supreme Court of New Jersey
36 A.3d 1049 (N.J. 2012)

Judge WEFING (temporarily assigned) delivered the opinion of the Court.

Following a lengthy trial in this accounting malpractice action, a jury returned a verdict in plaintiffs' favor and awarded damages totaling $31.8 million. . . . [T]he Appellate Division upheld the verdict on liability but vacated the damage award and remanded for a new trial. . . .

Plaintiffs commenced this litigation seeking damages for the losses they said they incurred following the bankruptcy and subsequent liquidation of Cast Art Industries (Cast Art). The business of Cast Art was the production and sale of collectible figurines and giftware. . . . As Cast Art's president, Sherman managed the business. . . .

Papel Giftware (Papel) . . . was in the same line of business as Cast Art, and in the spring of 2000 Cast Art became interested in acquiring Papel. . . . Cast Art lacked the financial ability to complete such a transaction on its own. As a result, it negotiated a loan agreement with PNC Bank (PNC) for $22 million to fund the venture. One of PNC's conditions to advancing the $22 million loan, however, was that it receive audited financial statements of Papel. . . .

Defendant KPMG had audited Papel's financial statements since 1997. . . . KPMG was already in the process of auditing Papel's 1998 and 1999 financial statements when Cast Art and Papel began their merger discussions. . . .

Cast Art obtained copies of the completed 1998 and 1999 audits and provided copies to PNC in satisfaction of its obligation under the loan agreement. Three months later, . . . Cast Art and Papel consummated the merger. Shortly after the merger was finalized, Cast Art began to experience difficulty in collecting some of the accounts receivable that it had believed Papel had had outstanding prior to the merger. Cast Art began its own investigation and learned that the 1998 and 1999 financial statements prepared by Papel were inaccurate and that Papel evidently had engaged regularly in the practice of accelerating revenue.

. . . .

Although Cast Art knew at the time of the merger that Papel was carrying a significant amount of debt, it was unaware of those accounting irregularities until after the merger was complete. The surviving corporation . . . eventually failed.

. . . .

In this litigation, Cast Art alleged that KPMG negligently audited Papel because its audit had not revealed Papel's accounting irregularities. . . . Thus, Cast Art asserted that its losses were caused by KPMG's negligence, and it argued that KPMG should be responsible to make it whole.

.... [T]he dispositive issue is the proper construction of the Accountant Liability Act, N.J.S.A. 2A:53A-25.

The arguments put forth by the parties ... are best understood and analyzed if there is an appreciation of the historical development of the manner in which courts have addressed the issue of an auditor's potential liability to nonclient third parties. Such an appreciation, in turn, requires an understanding of the fundamental nature and purpose of an audit.

> An audit is a systematic, objective examination of a company's financial statements.... The purpose of an audit is to determine if the statements fairly present the financial condition of the company....

Because an auditor's report may be circulated well beyond the borders of its subject, case law has developed three analytical frameworks within which to consider whether and under what circumstances auditors may be held liable for their negligence in conducting an audit. The earliest cases dealing with the question of an auditor's liability to third parties for negligence required the existence of privity or its equivalence as a necessary precondition to holding an auditor liable.

The leading case standing for that principle is Ultramares v. Touche, 255 N.Y. 170, 174 N.E. 441 (1931). The defendant in that case had for several years audited the financial statements of a rubber dealer, Fred Stern & Co. (Stern).... In accordance with its past practice, the defendant audited Stern's records for the year 1923 and at the completion certified that the balance sheet it had prepared from Stern's records "present[ed] a true and correct view" of the company's financial condition.... The plaintiff, a factor,[4] relied on the defendant's audit and advanced significant funds to the company.... Unbeknownst to the defendant auditor, employees of Stern had entered false transactions into the company's records, and in fact Stern was insolvent when the defendant had reported a net worth in excess of $1 million.... The plaintiff factor sued the defendant auditor to recover its losses.... The New York Court of Appeals held the auditor did not owe a duty of care to the factor, and thus the factor could not sue the auditor for negligence.... To impose liability for negligence on an auditor in the absence of privity or an equivalent relationship, wrote Justice Cardozo, "may expose accountants to a liability in an indeterminate amount for an indeterminate time to an indeterminate class." ....

New York, in essence, retains this test although it no longer insists on contractual privity; rather, it requires "some conduct on the part of the accountants linking them" to the parties claiming a loss. Credit Alliance Corp. v. Arthur Andersen & Co., 65 N.Y.2d 536, 493 N.Y.S.2d 435, 483 N.E.2d 110, 118 (1985).

The Restatement (Second) of Torts formulated a somewhat broader test.

> One who, in the course of his business, profession or employment ... supplies false information for the guidance of others in their business transactions,

4. A "factor" is a business organization that lends money on accounts receivable. — Ed.

> is subject to liability for pecuniary loss caused to them by their justifiable reliance upon the information, if he fails to exercise reasonable care or competence in obtaining or communicating the information.

[Restatement (Second) of Torts § 552(1) (1977)].

To forestall the "indeterminate" liability forecast by the *Ultramares* court, subsection (2) of § 552 limits the scope of this potential liability "to those persons, or classes of persons, whom [the accountant] knows and intends will rely on his opinion, or whom he knows his client intends will so rely." . . . .

New Jersey rejected those tests in Rosenblum v. Adler, 93 N.J. 324, 461 A.2d 138 (1983). In that case, the plaintiffs owned and operated two businesses that they sold to Giant Stores Corporation (Giant) and as part of that sale, plaintiffs received stock in Giant. . . . The defendants were partners in Touche Ross & Co., the accounting firm that had audited Giant's financial statements during the relevant time period. . . . The firm had not, however, been directly involved in the negotiations between the plaintiffs and Giant. . . . The Giant stock the plaintiffs received subsequently turned out to be worthless when it was learned that the financial statements prepared by Giant and audited by Touche were false. . . . The plaintiffs sued for their losses, alleging Touche had been negligent in its audit of Giant's books. . . . The defendants responded they could not be held responsible to the plaintiffs, with whom they had had no contractual relationship. The Court rejected that contention with the following statement:

> When the independent auditor furnishes an opinion with no limitation in the certificate as to whom the company may disseminate the financial statements, he has a duty to all those whom that auditor should reasonably foresee as recipients from the company of the statements for its proper business purposes, provided that the recipients rely on the statements pursuant to those business purposes. . . . In those circumstances accounting firms should no longer be permitted to hide within the citadel of privity and avoid liability for their malpractice. . . .

Only a few states adopted this expansive foreseeability test, . . . , and New Jersey has, through the passage of N.J.S.A. 2A:53A-25 in 1995, since abandoned it.

N.J.S.A. 2A:53A-25(b)(2) established preconditions to the imposition of liability on an accountant to a nonclient third party. These preconditions are that the accountant

> (a) knew at the time of the engagement by the client, or agreed with the client after the time of the engagement, that the professional accounting service rendered to the client would be made available to the claimant, who was specifically identified to the accountant in connection with a specified transaction made by the claimant;
>
> (b) knew that the claimant intended to rely upon the professional accounting service in connection with the specified transaction; and

> (c) directly expressed to the claimant, by words or conduct, the accountant's understanding of the claimant's intended reliance on the professional accounting service....

Clearly, KPMG did not know in November 1999, when it agreed to perform this audit, that its work could play a role in a subsequent merger because its agreement predated by several months Cast Art's interest in Papel. Cast Art urges that the statute should not be given such a restrictive interpretation and that the phrase "at the time of the engagement" should be construed to mean "at any time during the period of the engagement." ....

[After a detailed discussion of the statute, the court concluded:] ... In our judgment, a construction of the statute that interprets the phrase "at the time of the engagement" to mean "at the outset of the engagement" is more consonant with the overall intent of the Legislature to narrow the circumstances under which an accountant may be liable to a third party than a construction that interprets the phrase to mean "any time during the engagement."

Several other states have also adopted statutes, modeled on the Uniform Accountancy Act, that limit the scope of an accountant's liability to a nonclient....

We have reviewed these to determine if they might provide some guidance....

Our research has located only three reported cases bearing even tangentially on the issue before us.... None provide any reason to retreat from the conclusions we reached after examining the legislative history of N.J.S.A. 2A:53A-25.

Our conclusion with respect to the proper construction of the Accountant Liability Act is fortified by the nature of an engagement letter, for an auditor's "liability must be defined by the scope of the engagement it entered." .... An auditor is entitled to know at the outset the scope of the work it is being requested to perform and the concomitant risk it is being asked to assume.... [A]t the outset of its engagement with Papel, KPMG was not told that a nonclient would be relying on its work.

....

Because Cast Art failed to establish that KPMG "knew at the time of the engagement by the client" or thereafter agreed that Cast Art could rely on its work in proceeding with this merger, Cast Art failed to satisfy the requisite elements of N.J.S.A. 2A:53A-25(b)(2), and KPMG was entitled to judgment....

The judgment of the Appellate Division is reversed, and the matter is remanded to the trial court for entry of a judgment of dismissal.

Notes

1. ***The New York Near-Privity View.*** In Credit Alliance Corp. v. Arthur Andersen & Co., 483 N.E.2d 110 (N.Y. 1985), New York adhered to a near-privity rule on liability to third parties. *Credit Alliance* is best understood in terms of several earlier decisions of that court.

Glanzer v. Shepard, 135 N.E. 275 (N.Y. 1922), had involved a public weigher which had negligently overstated the weight of a shipment of beans, to the detriment of the purchaser. The court held that because the defendant knew the identity of the plaintiff-purchaser, knew that the plaintiff would rely on the certificate of weight in paying the seller who had arranged for the weighing, and had in fact sent a copy of the certificate to the plaintiff, there should be liability. The purchase by the plaintiff was the "end and aim" of the transaction for "whose benefit and guidance" the information was supplied. The fact and degree of the plaintiff's reliance was no surprise to the defendant.

Jaillet v. Cashman, 139 N.E. 714 (N.Y. 1923), was a case in which a customer in a stockbroker's office had relied to his detriment upon erroneous information the defendant had sent over a ticker. The plaintiff's identity was unknown to the defendant. He was merely one of a potentially vast number of persons who might possibly have been reached by the information. The nature and extent of the transactions in which he intended to rely on the information were also completely unknown to the defendant. The plaintiff's use of the information was not, in any sense, the end or aim of the transaction. The court refused to impose liability.

Between *Glanzer* and *Jaillet* stood a third earlier precedent, Ultramares v. Touche, Niven & Co., 174 N.E. 441 (N.Y. 1931) (discussed in *Cast Art Industries, supra*), a landmark case which involved an accounting firm. In *Ultramares*, Chief Judge Benjamin N. Cardozo, fearful of exposing accountants to liability "in an indeterminate amount for an indeterminate time to an indeterminate class" as a result of momentary carelessness, wrote that a corporation which had lent money to a company on the basis of statements contained in a certified balance sheet could not recover for negligent misrepresentation. While 32 copies of that balance sheet had been supplied (and this would have been enough to establish reason to expect communication and reliance under the deceit count in the complaint, which was permitted to stand), the character of the persons to be reached and influenced and the nature and extent of the contemplated transaction were unknown to the defendant. In short, the scope of the risk of liability was unknown.

Guided by these precedents, the court in *Credit Alliance* decided two appeals, both involving accounting firms. In one, where the audited statements had been passed indirectly to the plaintiff by the audited party, the court held there was no liability. In the other, where the auditors had been in frequent direct communication with the plaintiff, the court held that a cause of action for negligent misrepresentation was stated. The court reasoned that auditors are liable for negligent preparation of financial reports only to those in privity of contract with them, or to those whose relationship with the auditors is "so close as to approach that of privity." For liability to a non-contractual party to attach, (1) the accountants must have been aware that the financial reports were to be used for a particular purpose or purposes; (2) in furtherance of which a known party or parties was intended to rely; and (3) there must be some conduct on the part of the accountants linking them to that party or parties, which evinces the accountants' understanding of the contemplated reliance.

2. ***The Restatement "Intended Beneficiary" View on Liability to Third Parties.*** In Bily v. Arthur Young & Co., 834 P.2d 745 (Cal. 1992), a case addressing the liability of auditors to third parties for negligence, the court noted that, "[m]ost jurisdictions, supported by the weight of commentary . . . , have steered a middle course based in varying degrees on Restatement, Second, of Torts § 552, which generally imposes liability on suppliers of commercial information to third parties who are intended beneficiaries of the information. . . ."

According to § 552 of the Restatement, liability for negligent misrepresentation is limited to losses suffered

> (a) by the person or one of a limited group of persons for whose benefit and guidance . . . [the maker of the statement] intends to supply the information or knows that the recipient intends to supply it; and
>
> (b) through reliance upon it in a transaction that he intends the information to influence or knows that the recipient so intends or in a substantially similar transaction.

Comment h to § 552 further explains:

> In many situations the identity of the person for whose guidance the information is supplied is of no moment to the person who supplies it, although the number and character of the persons to be reached and influenced, and the nature and extent of the transaction for which guidance is furnished may be vitally important. This is true because the risk of liability to which the supplier subjects himself by undertaking to give the information, while it may not be affected by the identity of the person for whose guidance the information is given, is vitally affected by the number and character of the persons, and particularly the nature and extent of the proposed transaction.

See also Restatement, Third, of Torts: Liab. for Economic Harm § 5 (2020) (discussing the scope of liability for negligent misrepresentation).

The *Bily* court distinguished between claims for negligent misrepresentation (which in California are governed by § 552), and ordinary claims for negligence, which in that state may be maintained only by an auditor's client, and not by a third person. The point here is important. Unless the plaintiff shows that the substance of the alleged misstatement was communicated to and relied upon by the plaintiff, the action is not one for misrepresentation, and even more stringent rules may apply.

3. ***Statutes Governing Actions Against Accountants.*** In some states, the liability of accountants to third parties is governed by statute. For example, the Illinois Public Accounting Act provides:

Illinois Compiled Statutes Annotated Chapter 225 § 450 (Westlaw 2022)

> § 30.1. No person . . . or . . . entity licensed . . . under this Act . . . shall be liable to persons not in privity of contract . . . for civil damages resulting from

> acts, omissions, decisions or other conduct in connection with professional services performed by such person . . . or . . . entity, except for:
>
> > (1) such acts, omissions, decisions or conduct that constitute fraud or intentional misrepresentations, or
> >
> > (2) such other acts, omissions, decisions or conduct, if such person, partnership or corporation was aware that a primary intent of the client was for the professional services to benefit or influence the particular person bringing the action; provided, however, for the purposes of this subparagraph (2), if such person . . . or . . . entity (i) identifies in writing to the client those persons who are intended to rely on the services, and (ii) sends a copy of such writing or similar statement to those persons identified in the writing or statement, then such person . . . or . . . entity . . . may be held liable only to such persons intended to so rely, in addition to those persons in privity of contract.

4. ***Errors in Published Works.*** Should liability be imposed if a book contains false factual information which causes injury to a user who relies upon the erroneous information? What if a student following a flawed chemistry text is injured in an explosion? For First Amendment reasons, courts have been extremely reluctant to impose liability. *See, e.g.*, Winter v. G.P. Putnam's Sons, 938 F.2d 1033 (9th Cir. 1991) (no liability for error which caused plaintiffs to eat deadly mushrooms, necessitating liver transplant).

5. ***Ethics in Law Practice: Misrepresentation.*** The ethics codes of most states provide that it is professional misconduct, punishable by disbarment and lesser sanctions, for a lawyer to engage in "conduct involving dishonesty, fraud, deceit or misrepresentation." *See* Model Rules of Professional Conduct Rule 8.4(c) (Westlaw 2022). *See also* Feld's Case, 815 A.2d 383 (N.H. 2002) (an attorney was suspended for one year for knowingly providing false answers to interrogatories in a property dispute).

In Florida B. v. Christensen, 2018 WL 459360, at *2 (Fla.), an attorney was disbarred based in part on conduct that involved misrepresentation. According to the Florida Supreme Court:

> Respondent erroneously advised his clients and provided them with legally meaningless "Official Legal Certifications" purportedly authorizing them to grow and use marijuana, based on determinations made by a physician not licensed to practice medicine in the State of Florida. Several clients who relied upon Respondent's erroneous advice were arrested and criminally prosecuted, and their lives were devastated. . . .

Economic Analysis
Audits and the Cheaper Cost Avoider

Alan Gunn

In evaluating the *Ultramares* doctrine, consider two ways of reducing the risk that some of the several dozen corporations being audited by an accountant will default on large loans. First, the accountant can (at considerable expense) use great care in auditing all of the corporations. Allowing recovery against negligent accountants to all "foreseeable" plaintiffs encourages this approach (and makes auditing quite expensive). Second, lenders could hire their own auditors to check the books of those to whom they propose to lend (with corporations planning to borrow very large amounts getting the closest scrutiny). If, under applicable tort rules, the lender cannot expect recovery against the corporation's own auditors, it has an incentive to protect itself by doing this.

The economic sense behind the New York "near privity" doctrine is that audits performed at the request of the lender can go into the detail appropriate for the transaction in question. Someone planning to lend $100 would not bother with an audit at all, someone planning to lend $5,000,000 would give the books a very careful going over. If, under applicable law, accountants performing any audit are to be liable to any future lender who relies on the audit's results, the accountants cannot know in advance which of the corporations will take out large loans. What, then, should the accountants do? Auditing every corporation on the assumption that it might borrow millions would be extremely expensive. Much of this expense would be borne by corporations which would not in fact borrow heavily.

The above analysis can be summarized by noting that the lender, rather than the accountant performing a routine audit, is often the "cheaper cost avoider" with respect to the risks of making large loans.

Chapter 22

Defamation

Historical Development. Anglo-American tort law has long allowed many of those injured by false, defamatory statements an action for damages. If the statement in question was written, the action is called "libel"; an action based on oral defamation is for "slander." Libel and slander are ancient torts, complete with peculiar and arcane doctrines and terminology. In 1964, the Supreme Court began to "constitutionalize" much of the law of defamation by holding that the First Amendment guarantees of freedom of speech and freedom of the press limit the ability of courts to apply traditional defamation law principles.

A. What Statements Are Defamatory?

1. Harm to Reputation

Not all false statements about the plaintiff give rise to a defamation claim: a statement must injure the plaintiff's reputation to be actionable. Thus, it is often said that the statement must subject the plaintiff to "hatred, ridicule, or contempt." The Restatement, Second, of Torts (§ 559) defines defamatory statements as those that tend "to harm the reputation of [the victim so] as to lower him in the estimation of the community or to deter third persons from associating or dealing with him."

In Jacobus v. Trump, 51 N.Y.S.3d 330, 343 (N.Y. Sup. Ct. 2017), a media commentator brought an action against a presidential candidate and others. The court held that although the intemperate tweets at issue were clearly "intended to belittle and demean plaintiff, any reasonable reading of them makes it 'impossible to conclude that [what defendants said or implied] . . . could subject . . . [plaintiff] to contempt or aversion, induce any unsavory opinion of [her] or reflect adversely upon [her] work,' or otherwise damage her reputation as a partisan political consultant and commentator."

In a society in which people hold widely divergent views about what kind of behavior is proper, it may be difficult to determine whether a particular statement defames the plaintiff. Consider, for example, a false assertion that the plaintiff is a homosexual, or a communist, or has had an abortion. Not many years ago, any of these statements would pretty clearly have been defamatory. Today, the law must pay considerably more attention than in the past to the question of just who it is who will think badly of the plaintiff if the defendant's false statement is believed.

Grant v. Reader's Digest Association, Inc.

United States Court of Appeals for the Second Circuit
151 F.2d 733 (2d Cir. 1945)

L. HAND, Circuit Judge.

This is an appeal from a judgment dismissing a complaint in libel for insufficiency in law upon its face. The complaint alleged that the plaintiff was a Massachusetts lawyer, living in that state; that the defendant, a New York corporation, published a periodical of general circulation, read by lawyers, judges and the general public; and that one issue of the periodical contained an article . . . in which the following passage appeared:

> . . . . In my state the Political Action Committee has hired as its legislative agent one, Sidney S. Grant, who but recently was a legislative representative for the Massachusetts Communist Party.

. . . [A]lthough the words did not say that the plaintiff was a member of the Communist Party, they did say that he had acted on its behalf, and we think that a jury might in addition find that they implied that he was in general sympathy with its objects and methods. The last conclusion does indeed involve the assumption that the Communist Party would not retain as its "legislative representative" a person who was not in general accord with its purposes; but that inference is reasonable and was pretty plainly what the author wished readers to draw from his words. The case therefore turns upon whether it is libelous in New York to write of a lawyer that he has acted as agent of the Communist Party, and is a believer in its aims and methods.

. . . . A man may value his reputation even among those who do not embrace the prevailing moral standards; and it would seem that the jury should be allowed to appraise how far he should be indemnified for the disesteem of such persons. That is the usual rule. Peck v. Tribune Co., . . . [214 U.S. 185]; Restatement of Torts, § 559. . . . [T]he opinions at times seem to make it a condition that to be actionable the words must be such as would so affect "right-thinking people" . . . and it is fairly plain that there must come a point where that is true. As was said in Mawe v. Piggot, Irish Rep. 4 Comm. Law, 54, 62, among those "who were themselves criminal or sympathized with crime," it would expose one "to great odium to represent him as an informer or prosecutor or otherwise aiding in the detection of crime"; yet certainly the words would not be actionable. Be that as it may, in New York if the exception covers more than such a case, it does not go far enough to excuse the utterance at bar. Katapodis v. Brooklyn Spectator, Inc., *supra*, (287 N.Y. 17, 38 N.E.2d 112), following the old case of Moffat v. Cauldwell, 3 Hun. 26, 5 T. & C. 256, held that the imputation of extreme poverty might be actionable; although certainly "right-thinking" people ought not shun, or despise, or otherwise condemn one because he is poor. Indeed, the only declaration of the Court of Appeals (Moore v. Francis, 121 N.Y. 199, 205, 206, 23 N.E. 1127) leaves it still open whether it is not libelous to say that a man is insane. . . . We do not believe, therefore, that we need say whether "right-thinking" people would harbor similar feelings toward a lawyer, because he had been an agent for the

Communist Party, or was a sympathizer with its aims and means. It is enough if there be some, as there certainly are, who would feel so, even though they would be "wrong-thinking" people if they did. . . .

Judgment reversed; cause remanded.

Notes

1. ***The "Whole Publication" Rule.*** In determining whether an article or book is defamatory, the writing must be read as a whole. Thus, a statement that a belly dancer sold her time to lonely old men was held not to be libelous in light of other statements that she did so just to sit with them, to be nice to them, and to talk. *See* James v. Gannett Co., Inc., 353 N.E.2d 834 (N.Y. 1976).

Some courts hold that under the "whole publication" rule, headlines, captions, and illustrations are considered along with the body of the text, and thus an obviously erroneous headline or caption, or an otherwise actionable illustration, may be "cured" by accompanying language which corrects the misconception. *See* Ross v. Columbia Newspapers, Inc., 221 S.E.2d 770 (S.C. 1976) (an erroneous headline that the plaintiff was a suspect in the death of his wife was rendered innocuous by the last sentence of the article, which said that his wife was in serious condition in the hospital).

Where, however, oversized headlines are intentionally published to create a false impression, and the reader is reasonably led to an entirely different conclusion than is supported by the facts recited in the story, the headlines may be considered separately for the purpose of determining whether there has been a defamatory communication. Many newspaper readers read *only* the headlines of most articles, so an absolute rule that headlines alone cannot be defamatory would be much too restrictive.

In Block v. Tanenhaus, 867 F.3d 585, 590 (5th Cir. 2017), a newspaper allegedly quoted a professor in a way that made it appear that he considered slavery "not so bad." The court held that a cause of action was stated because "[i]f, as Block has pleaded, he stated during the interview that slavery was 'not so bad' *except for its involuntariness*, a reasonable jury could determine that the . . . decontextualized quotation falsely portrayed him as communicating that chattel slavery itself was not problematic—exactly the opposite of the point that he says he was making." (Emphasis in opinion.)

2. ***Ambiguous Statements.*** If a statement can be reasonably read in two ways, one of which is defamatory and the other not, most courts hold that the factfinder must determine the sense in which the remark was understood. For example, Belli v. Orlando Daily Newspapers, Inc., 389 F.2d 579 (5th Cir. 1967), held it a jury question whether a prominent lawyer was defamed by a statement that he had "taken" the Florida Bar.

3. ***"Mitior Sensus" and the Innocent Construction Rule.*** In the sixteenth and seventeenth centuries, the courts of England responded to an avalanche of slander suits by adopting the doctrine of "*mitior sensus*," under which statements were

construed as non-defamatory whenever possible. Under this bizarre doctrine, calling someone a forger was not actionable, as it might have meant only that the plaintiff was a metal worker.

The doctrine of *mitior sensus* never had much effect in this country, though some Illinois decisions have taken a somewhat-similar approach, even in libel cases (*mitior sensus* applied only to slander). Some Illinois courts have used a fair amount of ingenuity in finding an innocent construction. Rasky v. Columbia Broadcasting System, Inc., 431 N.E.2d 1055 (Ill. App. Ct. 1981), relied on the dictionary definitions of "landlord" and "slum" to hold that calling someone a "slumlord" might have meant only that he was the landlord of a building located in a slum.

See also Sterling v. Rust Communications, 113 S.W.3d 279 (Mo. Ct. App. 2003) (stating that in determining whether language is defamatory the words must be "stripped of any pleaded innuendo . . . and construed in their most innocent sense" and given their "plain and ordinarily understood meaning").

4. ***Use of Extrinsic Facts to Prove Defamation.*** A statement innocent on its face may be defamatory when considered in the light of other facts. In Cassidy v. Daily Mirror Newspapers, Ltd., [1929] 2 K.B. 331, a newspaper article said that a Mr. Cassidy was engaged to a woman whose picture appeared in the paper. In fact, Cassidy was married, though the paper did not know this, and both Cassidy and the woman gave the paper permission to announce their engagement. The court ruled that the article libeled Cassidy's wife because her acquaintances testified that they inferred from the article that Mrs. Cassidy was not in fact married to Cassidy, with whom she was living.

A written statement defamatory on its face is a "libel *per se*." If knowledge of extrinsic facts turns an apparently harmless written statement into a libel, the statement is a "libel *per quod*." In some jurisdictions, nothing turns on the difference except that the plaintiff in an action for libel *per quod* must establish the extrinsic facts. However, some courts have held that plaintiffs in actions for libel *per quod* (unlike plaintiffs seeking damages for libel *per se*) must prove pecuniary damages in order to recover.

If a statement, on its face, is not defamatory of the plaintiff, the plaintiff may need to plead facts establishing "colloquium" (that the statement referred to the plaintiff), "inducement" (the predicate for the defamatory meaning), or "innuendo" (the defamatory charge). Consider the words "He's dating Gladys." On its face, the statement appears innocent. However, if "he" refers to Reynoldo (colloquium), and if Reynoldo is a Roman Catholic priest (inducement), the statement suggests that Reynoldo is unfaithful to his religion (innuendo).

2. The False Fact Requirement

In Milkovich v. Lorain Journal Co., 497 U.S. 1 (1990), *infra* at p. 1109, a libel action, the Court reiterated its view that statements must be proven false before liability may constitutionally be imposed. A statement devoid of a provably false assertion of fact cannot give rise to liability.

Defamation by Conduct. Some defamation suits are based on conduct, rather than on written or spoken words. For example, courts have found a cause of action stated where the defendant discharged an employee immediately following a polygraph test (Tyler v. Macks Stores of S.C., Inc., 272 S.E.2d 633 (S.C. 1980)), or duped an unwitting plaintiff into being a contestant on a rigged television game show (Morrison v. National Broadcasting Co., 227 N.E.2d 572 (N.Y. 1967)), or dishonored a merchant's checks (Svendsen v. State Bank of Duluth, 65 N.W. 1086 (Minn. 1896)).

However, some courts have declined to recognize a suit for libel or slander based solely on conduct. For example, in Bolton v. Dept. of Human Services, 540 N.W.2d 523, 525–26 (Minn. 1995), a former employee brought an action for defamation based on his former supervisor's accompanying the employee to the exit door, without a spoken word, immediately following the employee's discharge. The court concluded as a matter of law that the plaintiff had not been defamed, stating that:

> In most other states that have allowed an action for defamation by conduct, the behavior has tended to rise to the level of "dramatic pantomime": that is, an interplay of words and conduct that provide a clearly discernible account of the making of a false statement about the aggrieved to a third party.

The *Bolton* court was influenced by the fact that even in a defamation suit based on conduct it is necessary to prove a false statement of fact. It noted the heightened difficulty in a defamatory conduct case of applying legal tests in a suit based on a communication "that can be interpreted by the declarant to have one meaning but to have quite a different one to the recipient."

3. Truth

Who Has the Burden of Proof? Truth is a complete bar to liability for defamation. At common law, the defendant had the burden of proving that the statement was true. However, the Supreme Court has held that, in some cases, allowing the plaintiff to recover damages without showing that the statements in question were false violates the First Amendment; Philadelphia Newspapers, Inc. v. Hepps, 475 U.S. 767 (1986). The *Hepps* rule applies "at least where a newspaper publishes speech of public concern."

In some cases, imposing the burden of proving falsity upon the plaintiff may make it virtually impossible to establish defamation. For example, if the accusation is that the plaintiff short-changes customers whenever it has an opportunity, how can the plaintiff show untruth, as no specific transactions are at issue? Restatement, Second, of Torts § 613 cmt. j.

In one case, a lawyer sued for slander when another lawyer called him "uncivilized, ignorant, and incompetent" in front of his client. *See* Okoli v. Paul Hastings, LLC., No. 152536/2012 (N.Y. Sup. Ct. 2012). In such a case, does it make any difference who has the burden of proof on truth or falsity? (The claim was barred by the judicial proceedings privilege.)

Suits based on broadly stated charges may fail for other reasons. As discussed later in the chapter, statements of opinion that do not imply false facts are not actionable. In Shor Int'l. Corp. v. Eisinger Enterprises, Inc., 2000 WL 1793389 (S.D.N.Y.), statements using the words "shoddy goods and dishonest sales and businesses" were held to be non-actionable expressions of opinion that could not be proven true or false. The court wrote: "referring to all of the defendant's practices as dishonest, as opposed to stating that defendant engaged in dishonest practices on a particular occasion, converts the statement into a hyperbole that cannot be taken as a serious assertion of fact."

Inaccuracies and "Substantial Truth." A trivial inaccuracy in a largely correct account ordinarily will not give rise to liability. Saying that "Jones murdered his wife at 9:15 last night" is not actionable if in fact Jones murdered his wife at 9:30, or even last week.

In Alleman v. Vermilion Publ'g Corp., 316 So. 2d 837 (La. Ct. App. 1975), a "letter to the editor" said that a doctor had refused to see a seriously injured child in a hospital emergency room because the child was "the patient of the doctor on call." According to the doctor, he refused to provide assistance because another doctor had been contacted and was en route to the hospital. The court held that no action would lie because what was said was substantially true; the doctor had declined to treat the child in the emergency room after being requested to do so by his parents.

See also UTV of San Antonio, Inc. v. Ardmore, Inc., 82 S.W.3d 609 (Tex. App. 2002) (holding that a statement that an inspector had found roaches at a daycare center during a follow-up inspection was not more damaging than a more-accurate statement that the inspector had noted allegations by staff members of roaches on a cup, crockpot, and counter, even though no roaches were found on the day of the specific inspection).

Ordinarily, one cannot avoid liability for false, defamatory statements by showing that the plaintiff did something else just as bad. For example, in Kilian v. Doubleday & Co., Inc., 79 A.2d 657 (Pa. 1951), an army officer was falsely accused of permitting the lashing and cursing of prisoners, ordering a badly wounded soldier on a hike, and forcing a fingerless patient to be a stretcher bearer. Those statements were not true, and it was no defense that the officer had been found guilty of permitting different atrocities.

Courts routinely make allowances for the use of technically inaccurate lay terminology. *See* Rouch v. Enquirer & News of Battle Creek, 487 N.W.2d 205 (Mich. 1992) (article using the word "charge" to describe an arrest and booking was not defamatory, even though no formal arraignment had occurred); Rosen v. Capital City Press, 314 So. 2d 511 (La. Ct. App. 1975) (incorrect use of term "narcotics" to encompass depressants and stimulants was not actionable); Restatement, Second, of Torts § 581(A) cmt. f ("A charge of theft may be reasonably interpreted as charging any criminally punishable misappropriation, and its truth may be established by proving the commission of any act of larceny").

In determining whether an inaccuracy is minor and irrelevant, many courts ask whether the "gist" or the "sting" of the defamatory charge is justified. *See* Gustafson v. City of Austin, 110 S.W.3d 652 (Tex. App. 2003) (no action was stated where the gist of an e-mailed statement (namely, that a CPR teacher was no longer a valid heart association CPR instructor and his instructor status had been officially revoked by the association) was not substantially worse than the literal truth (namely, that the teacher was no longer a valid heart association CPR instructor, and while he could still teach CPR courses, the courses were not sanctioned by the heart association)).

In Guccione v. Hustler Magazine, Inc., 800 F.2d 298 (2d Cir. 1986), the plaintiff was accused in 1983 of participating in an ongoing adulterous relationship. In fact, the plaintiff had lived in adultery for 13 of the preceding 17 years, but the adultery had ceased when his wife divorced him. Examining the defamatory language, the court held that the statement could not be read to mean that the marriage and the cohabitation had existed simultaneously for only a moment or brief interval prior to the publication. Rather, the only reasonable construction of the statement was that the marriage and cohabitation had existed simultaneously throughout an undefined span of time that included the period immediately prior to publication. The facts showed this to be substantially true, because the plaintiff's adultery had continued over the course of many years. Because the published statement would not have had a worse effect on the mind of the reader than the truth pertinent to the allegation, the complaint failed to state a claim as a matter of law.

Omissions. A statement about virtually anything is inaccurate in the sense that it is incomplete; there is usually more to be said about any topic. The question whether an accurate statement is defamatory because it omits facts turns upon whether the omissions substantially distort the account or cause it to convey a false meaning.

4. Of and Concerning the Plaintiff

To be actionable, a defamatory statement must refer to the plaintiff. But it is not necessary that the plaintiff be specifically named if other facts, such as an illustration or a verbal description, make it possible for the reader to associate the charge with the plaintiff. *See* Poe v. San Antonio Express-News Corp., 590 S.W.2d 537 (Tex. Civ. App. 1979) (summary judgment was denied because some of the plaintiff's acquaintances might have concluded that he was the "mid-fortyish" teacher who allegedly fondled a 14-year-old girl who was seen rushing from a local high school in tears). The test is whether some recipients of the communication reasonably understood the statement as referring to the plaintiff; the fact that not all recipients, or not even a majority, would have drawn that conclusion does not preclude an action.

"Group Defamation." The defendants in Neiman-Marcus v. Lait, 13 F.R.D. 311 (S.D.N.Y. 1952), published a book which said that

(1) "Some" of the models at a particular store were call girls;

(2) "The salesgirls" were less expensive and "not as snooty as the models";

(3) "Most" of the male sales staff were homosexuals.

The plaintiffs were all nine of Neiman-Marcus's models, fifteen of its twenty-five salesmen, and thirty of its 382 saleswomen. The court held that false accusations against unspecified members of a small group are actionable by each member of the group, and denied the defendants' motion to dismiss the claims of the models and the male salesmen. The female clerks' complaint was dismissed because the group was so large that no reasonable reader could conclude from the accusation that any particular clerk was a prostitute.

See also Prince v. Out Publ'g Inc., 2002 WL 7999 (Cal. App. 2002). In *Prince*, a party-goer sued the publisher of a gay-oriented magazine and others based on an article which referred to illegal drug use and unsafe sex, which included photographs of the plaintiff and others at "circuit parties." The court held that despite the juxtaposition of the photographs and the text, the plaintiff failed to satisfy the "of and concerning" requirement, reasoning:

> The photographs published in the Article establish that there were many people at the party. In addition, the text refers to parties attended by thousands of people. There is nothing in the text of the Article to suggest that the general statements about illegal drug use and unsafe sex apply to plaintiff.

Defamation in Fiction. Many works of fiction contain characters and incidents based on fact, despite the common but wildly unbelievable claim often made at the beginning of novels that no character described has any resemblance to any real person. It is therefore possible for passages in a work of fiction to defame someone.

In Bindrim v. Mitchell, 155 Cal. Rptr. 29 (Ct. App. 1979), the defendant, a novelist, attended "therapy" sessions conducted by the plaintiff, who used a technique called "nude marathon." Later, the defendant wrote a novel describing "nude marathon" sessions conducted by a therapist who used obscene language and did unsavory things. The court upheld a verdict for the plaintiff, ruling that the jury could reasonably have found that readers of the book might think that the incidents it described actually took place at the plaintiff's sessions.

See also Muzikowski v. Paramount Pictures Corp., 322 F.3d 918 (7th Cir. 2003) (holding that a Little League baseball coach stated a claim for defamation based on the movie "Hardball" starring Keanu Reeves, because there were many similarities, though the character had a different name, and, unlike the plaintiff, committed theft and lied about being a licensed securities broker).

A defamatory work of fiction is not actionable unless it contains a plausibly believable false statement of fact. Pring v. Penthouse Int'l, Ltd., 695 F.2d 438 (10th Cir. 1982), reversed a $26.5 million judgment in favor of a former Miss Wyoming, who was a baton twirler, based on a story about a baton-twirling Miss Wyoming who performed astounding sexual feats at a nationally televised beauty pageant. The Tenth Circuit based its decision on the unbelievability of the events in the story (*e.g.*, levitation), ruling that no reasonable reader could have understood the story as describing conduct actually engaged in by the plaintiff.

Entities. An entity, such as a corporation, may be defamed with respect to such institutional characteristics as honesty, efficiency, and credit-worthiness. It is actionable to state falsely that a business has filed for bankruptcy protection. *See* Dun & Bradstreet, Inc. v. Greenmoss Builders, Inc., 472 U.S. 749 (1985).

In Allied Marketing Group, Inc. v. Paramount Pictures Corp., 111 S.W.3d 168 (Tex. App. 2003), the television program *Hard Copy* aired a segment about a sweepstakes scam.

> Paramount intended to use a fictional company name in connection with the . . . segment and thought that "Sweepstakes Clearing House" was a fictional name. However, unknown to Paramount, Allied had been using the name "Sweepstakes Clearinghouse" since 1984 in connection with a direct mail offer business. . . .

The court held that the show's segment on sweepstakes scams was "of and concerning" the sweepstakes company for purposes of the company's defamation action against the television show, because persons who knew the plaintiff could have concluded that the defamatory matter referred to the plaintiff. The court concluded that "[b]ecause the test is based on the reasonable understanding of the viewer of the publication, it is not necessary for the plaintiff to prove that the defendant intended to refer to the plaintiff." The court noted that the program was not an obvious work of fiction.

In Three Amigos SJL Rest., Inc. v. CBS News Inc., 65 N.E.3d 35, 37 (N.Y. 2016), the court held that a statement that a strip club was run by the mafia did not defame the employees of vendors that supplied food, beverages, and talent to the strip club. As the court explained:

> The news broadcast stated that Cheetah's was purportedly used by the Mafia to carry out a larger trafficking scheme. It did not mention any employees of the club or of the management and talent agencies that facilitate its daily operations, let alone the individual plaintiffs in these appeals, who were not identified or pictured in the report. In context, the statement that Cheetah's was "run by the mafia" could not reasonably have been understood to mean that certain unnamed individuals who do not work for Cheetah's but oversee its food, beverage and talent services are members of organized crime. . . .

Defamation of the Dead. Defamation of the dead is not actionable. However, the relatives and friends of a decedent can sometimes state a colorable claim that they have been defamed by statements about the decedent. As the following case shows, the courts have not been eager to accept that argument.

Rose v. Daily Mirror, Inc.

Court of Appeals of New York
31 N.E.2d 182 (N.Y. 1940)

LOUGHRAN, Judge.

The question is whether the complaint in this action states facts sufficient to constitute a cause of action for libel.

The pleading alleges that the plaintiff Anna Rose was the wife of Jack Rose and that the other plaintiffs are their children; that Jack Rose died on May 25, 1939; and that the defendant then published in its newspaper an article of and concerning the deceased Jack Rose wherein he was erroneously identified with one "Baldy Jack Rose," a person described in the article as a self-confessed murderer who had "lived in constant fear that emissaries of the underworld . . . would catch up with him and execute gang vengeance." This article named the respective plaintiffs as the surviving wife and children of the deceased Jack Rose but made no other direct reference to them.

A motion by the defendant for judgment dismissing the complaint was denied by Special Term. The order of the Special Term was reversed and the motion granted by the Appellate Division. . . .

Defendant does not deny that the publication complained of was a libel on the memory of the deceased Jack Rose. Plaintiffs make no claim of any right to recover for that wrong. They stand upon the position that the publication . . . tended to subject them in their own persons to contumely and indignity and was, therefore, a libel upon them. It is true that . . . it has been held that it is a libel to write of a person that a near relative of his was a criminal. . . .

In this State, however, it has long been accepted law that a libel or slander upon the memory of a deceased person which makes no direct reflection upon his relatives gives them no cause of action for defamation. . . .

The judgment should be affirmed, with costs.

FINCH, Judge (dissenting).

. . . . To publish that a man was a notorious criminal, and then to say that one of the plaintiffs was his wife and the others his children and so possessed of his blood, would seem to give them a cause of action for damages, just as much as to say that plaintiff had no proper family origin, i.e., was illegitimate. Shelby v. Sun Printing & Pub. Ass'n, 38 Hun. 474, 476, *affirmed* 109 N.Y. 611, 15 N.E. 895. Either of these charges would cause plaintiffs to be held up to ridicule and contempt. . . .

Mere failure to attribute personal fault or misconduct to plaintiffs does not render the publication of defendant any the less libelous. The charge that the plaintiff is illegitimate is not to attribute fault or misconduct to plaintiff, yet plaintiff has a cause of action. There would seem no distinction between such case and the case at bar.

Plaintiffs are not the widow and children of Baldy Jack Rose, as alleged in the publication in question, and Jack Rose was not the despicable criminal whose shameful career was described. A respectable family whose husband and father has just passed away awakes the next morning to find blazoned forth in a morning newspaper that decedent was a notorious criminal, thus blackening the family and all its members. The slightest effort at verification would have shown the falsity of the story. If the law has reached the result of affording no relief here for the damages suffered, it would seem that the matter should be called to the attention of the Legislature.

It follows that the judgment dismissing the complaint should be reversed.

LEHMAN, C. J., and SEARS and LEWIS, JJ., concur with LOUGHRAN, J.

FINCH, J., dissents in opinion in which RIPPEY and CONWAY, JJ., concur.

Judgment affirmed.

Notes

1. ***Indirect Defamation.*** Is it libelous of a widow to say in an obituary that her husband was a bachelor?

2. ***Statements about Persons Other than the Plaintiff.*** In Sarwer v. Conde Nast Publications, Inc., 654 N.Y.S.2d 768 (App. Div. 1997), the court held that the plaintiff, who was allegedly referred to in a magazine article as a victim of child abuse, did not state a claim for defamation. The statements in the article that were claimed to be defamatory were not about the plaintiff at all, but rather about her family members.

3. ***Comparative Law Perspective: Posthumous Defamation in China.*** One of the unique aspects of Chinese tort law is that it allows close relatives of the dead to sue for emotional damages when an actor inflicts harm to the reputation or privacy of the deceased. Chen v. Wu was a case about posthumous defamation. In 1999, Wu Si published a book entitled Mao's Peasant—Chen Yonggui, which was serialized in the Beijing Youth Daily. Chen, who passed away in 1986, held the office of Vice Premier of the State Council (the central cabinet of the Chinese government) from 1975 to 1980, even though he was illiterate. Rising from a peasant in a remote village in Shanxi Province to becoming a member of the Politburo of the Communist Party of China (CPC), Chen owed his sudden fame primarily to Mao's disastrous policy choices at the peak of the Cultural Revolution.

In the book, Wu portrayed Chen's early life, especially his role during the Japanese occupation from 1937 to 1945. Relying on published articles, including an article by Chen's elder son, Wu claimed that Chen was a member of the "peace maintenance group," a shadowy government established by the Japanese to manage affairs in the occupied areas. After World War II, Chen was arrested and humiliated for his role in aiding the Japanese occupiers. In his application for CPC membership after the war, Chen acknowledged his past involvement in the "peace maintenance group" and sought the CPC's forgiveness. Chen's history was well documented in the Communist Party's archives.

In 2002, Chen Yonggui's son, wife and other close relatives sued Wu for defaming the late Vice Premier because Wu's disclosure of Chen's treasonous past degraded his status as a prominent state official and member of the respected party elite. While the court did not dispute that the author had no intent to smear Chen, it held that Wu cited non-authoritative sources because neither the party nor the government validated personal memoirs or other sources relied upon by Wu.

Despite strong criticism from academia, a court affirmed the trial court's decision that Wu and the publisher were required to issue a public apology and pay RMB20,000 ($3,000) in emotional distress damages.

How would America change if it was unlawful to write true but unflattering things about deceased public officials? Ron Chernow, in his biography of Alexander Hamilton, detailed Hamilton's extramarital affairs. Should Chernow be liable to Hamilton's descendants?

5. Publication

If Smith calls Jones a "dirty rotten liar" and no one else hears the statement, Smith has not slandered Jones. Defamation requires that the statement be heard or read, and understood, by a third person.

Economopoulos v. A. G. Pollard Co.

Supreme Judicial Court of Massachusetts
105 N.E. 896 (Mass. 1914)

This was an action of tort in three counts . . . the third count charging defendant with falsely and maliciously charging plaintiff with larceny by words spoken of plaintiff, as follows: "You have stolen a handkerchief from us and have it in your pocket." There was evidence that a clerk of defendant stated in English to plaintiff, a Greek, that he had stolen a handkerchief, and that a Greek clerk stated to plaintiff in Greek that plaintiff had stolen a handkerchief. There was nothing to show that third persons heard the charge, excepting the floor walker.

. . . .

LORING, J.

. . . [T]he judge was right in directing the jury to find the verdict for the defendant because there was no evidence of publication. . . . There was no evidence that anybody but the plaintiff was present when Carrier spoke to the plaintiff in English. There was no publication of this statement made in English, because on the evidence the words could not have been heard by anyone but the plaintiff. . . .

Nor was there any evidence of publication of the Greek words spoken by Miralos, for although there was evidence that they were spoken in the presence of others, there was no evidence that any one understood them but the plaintiff. . . .

Exceptions overruled.

Notes

1. ***Distributors.*** Ordinarily, one who repeats a defamatory statement is held to have made a publication of the matter. What about libraries, bookstores, printers, and newspaper deliverers who play a role in disseminating falsehoods originated by others? Are they, too, republishers? Ordinarily not. Such distributors are considered to be mere passive conduits and are subject to liability for statements in the materials they make available only if they knew or had reason to know of the defamatory content. *See, e.g.*, Cubby, Inc. v. CompuServe, Inc., 776 F. Supp. 135 (S.D.N.Y. 1991).

Because the publishers of newspapers and magazines exercise editorial control over the content of their publications, they do not qualify as mere distributors and are held to be publishers of any false statements in those works, regardless of where the libel originated. *See* Flowers v. Carville, 266 F. Supp. 2d 1245 (D. Nev. 2003) (stating a cause of action against a publisher who allegedly knew that a book contained false defamatory statements about the plaintiff in connection with her affair with a former President).

2. ***Defamation on the Internet.*** Under the Communications Decency Act of 1996 (47 U.S.C. sec. 230(c)(1) (Westlaw 2022)), "No provider or user of an interactive computer service shall be treated as the publisher or speaker of any information provided by another information content provider." The CDA has been broadly interpreted to bar defamation and other claims against Internet services. *See, e.g.*, Zeran v. America Online, Inc., 129 F.3d 327 (4th Cir. 1997) (the Act barred negligence claims for unreasonable delay in removing defamatory messages, refusal to post retractions of those messages, and failure to screen for similar postings; the court found the "artfully" pled negligence claims to be "indistinguishable" from "garden variety defamation). Of course, the original culpable party who posts defamatory messages on the Internet is subject to liability.

See Schneider v. Amazon.com, 31 P.3d 37 (Wash. Ct. App. 2001) (holding an online bookseller not liable for defamatory comments posted about an author's books).

3. ***Comparative Law Perspective: Defamation on the Internet in China.*** Free speech and free press are values more highly prized in the United States than in China. And public order is more highly prized in China than in the United States. It is therefore not surprising that the law in China dealing with defamation on the Internet differs greatly from the American Communications Decency Act. Article 36 of the Chinese Tort Liability Law (Lawinfochina 2018) provides:

> A network user or network service provider who infringes upon the civil right[s] or interest[s] of another person through [a] network shall assume the tort liability.
>
> Where a network user commits a tort through the network services, the victim of the tort shall be entitled to notify the network service provider to take such necessary measures as deletion, block or disconnection. If, after

being notified, the network service provider fails to take necessary measures in a timely manner, it shall be jointly and severally liable for any additional harm with the network user.

Where a network service provider knows that a network user is infringing upon a civil right or interest of another person through its network services, and fails to take necessary measures, it shall be jointly and severally liable for any additional harm with the network user.

4. ***Anonymous Postings on the Internet.*** Many postings on the Internet are anonymous, and therefore plaintiffs who believe they have been defamed by such comments seek to compel Internet service providers to disclose the identity of the persons who acted anonymously or used pseudonyms. Courts differ in their treatment of these requests. Some states will order disclosure if the plaintiff has a "legitimate, good faith basis" for alleging actionable conduct; other states will compel disclosure if the plaintiff makes a *prima facie* showing that a case for defamation exists; and still other jurisdictions apply a balancing test that weighs the strength of the plaintiff's *prima facie* case against the defendant's First Amendment right to speak anonymously.

5. ***Communications between Agents of the Same Principal.*** There is a substantial conflict as to whether intracompany communications can satisfy the publication element of a defamation claim. Some states follow an agency theory and hold that there is no publication when a corporation, through its agents, is merely communicating with itself. *See* Starr v. Pearle Vision, Inc., 54 F.3d 1548 (10th Cir. 1995) (Oklahoma law). Other states and the Restatement take the contrary position, reasoning that corporate employees remain individuals with distinct personalities and opinions that may be affected by the intra-entity communication of defamatory matter. *See* Restatement, Second, of Torts § 577 cmt. i.

6. ***"Compelled" Self-Publication.*** In general, there is no actionable publication where a defendant communicates a statement directly to a plaintiff, who then repeats it to a third person. Restatement (Second) of Torts § 577, cmt. m. However, a few states hold that the publication requirement is satisfied by facts showing that an employee was "compelled" to publish a defamatory statement by a former employer to a prospective employer under circumstances where that was foreseeable. *See* Kuechle v. Life's Companion P.C.A., Inc., 653 N.W.2d 214 (Minn. App. 2002) (holding that where the plaintiff was told that the defendant had reported her alleged misconduct to the Nurse's Board, the plaintiff had no reasonable means to avoid self-publishing the statement to a new employer, even though she was not asked the reason for her termination).

Most states reject the idea of self-publication. *See* Gonsalves v. Nissan Motor Corp., 58 P.3d 1196 (Haw. 2002). In some states, legislatures have responded to the issue of "compelled self-publication" by passing statutes. Compare the following laws from Colorado and Minnesota:

Colorado Revised Statutes Annotated § 13-25-125.5 (Westlaw 2022)

No action for libel or slander may be brought or maintained unless the party charged with such defamation has published, either orally or in writing, the defamatory statement to a person other than the person making the allegation of libel or slander. Self-publication, either orally or in writing, of the defamatory statement to a third person by the person making such allegation shall not give rise to a claim for libel or slander against the person who originally communicated the defamatory statement.

Minnesota Statutes Annotated § 181.933 (Westlaw 2022)

Subdivision 1. Notice required.

An employee who has been involuntarily terminated may, within fifteen working days following such termination, request in writing that the employer inform the employee of the reason for the termination. Within ten working days following receipt of such request, an employer shall inform the terminated employee in writing of the truthful reason for the termination.

Subdivision 2. Defamation action prohibited.

No communication of the statement furnished by the employer to the employee under subdivision 1 may be made the subject of any action for libel, slander, or defamation by the employee against the employer.

Does the Minnesota provision mean anything more than that one cannot bring a defamation action based on truth?

7. ***Disclosure by the Plaintiff Without Knowledge of the Defamatory Content.*** Some cases involve a plaintiff's unwitting transmission of a defamatory message of whose contents the plaintiff is unaware. Comment *m* to Restatement, Second, of Torts § 577 states: "If the defamed person's transmission of the communication to the third person was made . . . without an awareness of the defamatory nature of the matter and if the circumstances indicated that communication to a third party would be likely, a publication [by the originator to the third person] may properly be held to have occurred." The Restatement offers the following illustrations:

10. A writes a defamatory letter about B and sends it to him through the mails in a sealed envelope. A knows that B is blind and that a member of his family will probably read the letter to him. B receives the letter and his wife reads it to him. A has published a libel.

11. A writes a letter to B accusing him of sexual misconduct. The defamatory matter is written in Latin, though A knows that B has no knowledge of Latin. B takes the letter to a Latin teacher to obtain a translation. A has published a libel.

The blackletter rule stated by § 577 provides that "publication of defamatory matter" means communication of the matter "intentionally or by a negligent act to one other than the person defamed."

8. ***The Single-Publication Rule.*** According to § 577A of the Restatement, Second, of Torts, any one edition of a book or newspaper, or any one radio or television broadcast, is a single publication, with respect to which only one action may be brought for all damages resulting from the publication. This rule prevents the plaintiff from bringing an action every time a book is sold, and in every jurisdiction in which a sale takes place. It also addresses the concern that, if every sale or reading of a book were a publication, there would be no effective statute of limitations in libel cases. However, the rule also eliminates the possibility of hardship to plaintiffs by allowing the collection of all damages in a single case.

Under this rule, if a book is published in 2025, sold at retail in 2026, and resold second-hand in 2027, the statute of limitations begins to run in 2025. However, if a paperback edition of that book is published in 2028, that event is a separate publication for which the statute starts to run in 2028.

In Altschuler v. University of Pa. Law Sch., 1997 WL 129394 (S.D.N.Y. 1997), *aff'd*, 201 F.3d 430 (2d Cir. 1999), the plaintiff asserted that a university had defamed him by putting a false and defamatory grade and other statements on his transcript, which was then released to law firms at various times. In addressing statute of limitations issues, the court wrote:

> The single publication rule does not apply to plaintiff's claims because he does not allege that his law school record and transcript were published to the public in a large, aggregate printing. Rather, he alleges that the law school has allowed professors and administrators to inspect his record "from time to time," and that his transcript has been released to particular law firms where he has applied over a period of time, both before and after his graduation.

The single-publication rule applies to publications on the Internet, because "communications accessible over a public Web site resemble those contained in traditional mass media, only on a far grander scale." Firth v. State, 747 N.Y.S.2d 69, 71 (N.Y. 2002). Does updating the contents of a website constitute a new publication? According to *Firth*:

> The mere addition of unrelated information to a Web site cannot be equated with the repetition of defamatory matter in a separately published edition of a book or newspaper . . . for it is not reasonably inferable that the addition was made either with the intent or the result of communicating the earlier and separate defamatory information to a new audience.

As a practical matter, the statute of limitations for libel in a nationwide publication is that of whatever state has the longest statute of limitations for libel, at least if a substantial number of copies are sold in that state. *See* Keeton v. Hustler Mag., Inc., 465 U.S. 770 (1984), in which the plaintiff sued in New Hampshire because the statute of limitations in every other state had run by the time of the suit.

B. Libel and Slander

Libel and Slander Defined. Written defamation is libel; oral defamation is slander. The law of libel is in some respects harder on the defendant than the law of slander, so it can matter how a case is classified.

Is a radio or television broadcast a libel or a slander, and does the answer depend on whether the person making the remarks in question reads them from a script, or on whether the broadcast is live or recorded, or on whether remarks that are aired also appear on the broadcaster's website? And what about defamation that consists of conduct, rather than words (discussed *supra*).

It was once thought that more people were likely to see a written accusation than to hear a spoken one. However, television and radio certainly changed that. It was also once assumed that a written accusation might be taken more seriously than an oral one, and thus more likely to cause damage. However, a video posted on YouTube may be watched by millions and may cause more harm than most articles.

Restatement, Second, of Torts, § 568 states:

> (1) Libel consists of the publication of defamatory matter by written or printed words, by its embodiment in physical form or by any other form of communication that has the potentially harmful qualities characteristic of written or printed words.
>
> (2) Slander consists of the publication of defamatory matter by spoken words, transitory gestures or by any form of communication other than those stated in Subsection (1).
>
> (3) The area of dissemination, the deliberate and premeditated character of its publication and the persistence of the defamation are factors to be considered in determining whether a publication is a libel rather than a slander.

In addition, § 568A takes the position that, "[b]roadcasting of defamatory matter by means of radio or television is libel, whether or not it is read from a manuscript." However, some states classify broadcast defamation as slander by statute. *See* Rodney A. Smolla, 1 Law of Defamation § 1:14 (2008).

Libel and Slander Per Se. The main difference between libel and slander is that, at common law, a plaintiff in a libel case could more easily recover damages without proof of any injury.[1] For example, in LeBlanc v. Skinner, 2012 WL 6176900, *8 (N.Y. App. Div.), the court wrote:

> While a plaintiff alleging defamation generally must plead and prove that he or she has sustained special damages . . . , any written article is "actionable without alleging special damages if it tends to expose the plaintiff to

---

1. Some states limited this rule to cases in which the libel, on its face, was defamatory of the plaintiff or to certain types of libelous statements.

> public contempt, ridicule, aversion or disgrace, or induce an evil opinion of him in the minds of right-thinking persons, and to deprive him of their friendly intercourse in society". . . . The published allegation that the plaintiff put a severed horse head in a Town Board member's swimming pool constituted defamation *per se* under this standard and, therefore, did not require the plaintiff to plead special damages. . . .

In slander cases, by contrast, the plaintiff ordinarily had to prove special damages, such as lost wages or reduced business income. However, slander is actionable "*per se*,"[2] that is, without proof of damages, if the statement accuses the plaintiff of:

(1) Committing a serious crime;

(2) Having a "loathsome disease" (that is, leprosy or a venereal disease, or perhaps, now, AIDS or SARS);

(3) Being incompetent to practice a chosen business, trade, or profession; or

(4) Engaging in serious sexual misconduct.[3]

Some decisions read these categories strictly. For example, in Bedford v. Spassoff, 520 S.W.3d 901 (Tex. 2017), the court held that a social media posting that a youth baseball organization was supportive of a coach who had engaged in an extramarital affair was not defamatory *per se*. Absent proof of damages, neither the organization nor its president [Spassoff] could establish a *prima facie* defamation claim. As the court explained:

> [In Hancock v. Variyam, 400 S.W.3d 59, 62 (Tex. 2013)], we held statements that a physician lacked veracity and dealt in half-truths were not defamatory per se because they did not injure the physician in his profession by ascribing that he lacked a necessary skill peculiar or unique to the profession of being a physician.
>
> [The] . . . post [in this case] did not accuse Spassoff or the Dodgers of lacking a peculiar or unique skill related to baseball or to running a baseball organization. . . .

See Yonaty v. Mincolla, 945 N.Y.S.2d 774 (App. Div. 2012) (holding that statements falsely describing a person as lesbian, gay, or bisexual does not constitute slander *per se* and that special damages must be proved).

In certain jurisdictions, statutes make particular types of statements actionable as a matter of law. *See* 740 Ill. Comp. Stat. 145/1 (Westlaw 2022) (false accusations of

---

2. Note that this is a different use of the term "*per se*" than was mentioned above in connection with the discussion of "libel *per se*" (as opposed to "libel *per quod*"). *See* p. 1066 n.4 *supra*. Consequently, when the words "*per se*" are used, it is necessary to determine whether the phrase means actionable without proof of special damages as opposed to defamatory of the plaintiff without any need to plead and prove additional facts.

3. In earlier days, this rule was not gender-neutral. Sexually related slander was actionable *per se* only if it imputed unchastity to a woman. Men had to prove damages.

fornication and adultery). Also, at least one state treats libel and slander alike, drawing no distinction based on whether the statement is written or oral. *See* Bryson v. News Am. Pubs., Inc., 672 N.E.2d 1207 (Ill. 1996).

Presumed Damages. Traditionally, in cases involving libel or slander per se, damages were presumed and a jury can make a substantial award of compensatory damages without the type of detailed evidence normally required in tort actions. In arriving at a number for an award of compensatory damages, the factfinder can consider both the nastiness of the defamatory statement and the extent of its dissemination.

In Xiaokang Xu v. Xiaoling Shirley He, 48 N.Y.S.3d 530, 533 (App. Div. 2017), the court approved an award of $5,000 in presumed damages to a plaintiff whose former wife sent a "letter to his employer, calling him an abuser, accusing him of cruel and inhuman treatment, theft of trade secrets, fraud and perjury." The court found that the award did not deviate from reasonable compensation as reflected in other cases (including most recently: in 2007, a $225,000 award for false accusation of sexual abuse of the plaintiff's daughter; in 2009, a $26,800 award for false accusations of criminal conduct; and in 2009, a reduced award of $50,000 for false accusations of improper conduct in public).

The extent to which the common law rules concerning presumed damages survive is a complex question, and the answer is heavily influenced by federal constitutional precedent. As discussed in the following section, the Supreme Court has held that in cases involving matters of "public concern," states may not allow "recovery of presumed or punitive damages when liability is not based on a showing of knowledge of falsity or reckless disregard for the truth"; Gertz v. Robert Welch, Inc., 418 U.S. 323 (1974). However, that limitation does not apply to cases not involving matters of "public concern." *See* Dun & Bradstreet, Inc. v. Greenmoss Builders, Inc., 472 U.S. 749 (1985).

While some states continue to follow the traditional rules on presumed damages, the law in other states restricts a presumed damages recovery to a nominal amount or does not allow recovery of presumed damages. *See* infra pages 1102–08.

C. Constitutional Considerations

At common law, both libel and slander were strict-liability torts. Recall, for example, the *Cassidy* case, [1929] 2 K.B. 331 (at p. 1066 n.4 *supra*), in which the defendant newspaper had no way of knowing that the information it was publishing was false, or even that the plaintiff existed. The Supreme Court has rewritten this aspect of defamation law so that in most if not all cases there is no strict liability. Moreover, in many cases, even a defendant who has negligently published defamatory material cannot be held liable.

The "constitutionalization" of defamation law began with New York Times v. Sullivan, a case which arose at the "intersection of three dominant themes in modern American experience: the power of the federal judiciary, the role of the press as an agent for social change, and the slow and painful struggle of black Americans for legal and social equality." Rodney A. Smolla, Suing The Press: Libel, The Media, & Power 27 (1986). The case involved efforts by southern segregationists to use libel law to levy huge damage awards against the New York Times for running an advertisement supporting Martin Luther King and his struggle for racial justice. The ad, which cost about $4800 and ran in about 650,000 newspapers (fewer than 400 of which were sent to Alabama), contained small factual errors. The plaintiff, a public official not named in the ad, alleged that the errors had defamed him.

In November 1960, the case was tried in an Alabama courtroom with segregated seating. The air was thick with prejudice, as reflected by the judge's reference to "white man's justice" and the repeated use of the word "nigger" by plaintiff's counsel. The atmosphere of racial hatred surrounding the litigation was so intense that the New York Times found it almost impossible to engage a local attorney to represent it. The names and pictures of the jurors were published in the Montgomery papers. When the three-day trial came to an end, television cameras followed the veniremen to the door of the jury room. A verdict for $500,000, the full amount asked for in the complaint, was promptly returned. If the award had been upheld, the effect on the New York Times would have been devastating, for additional suits by other public officials had already been filed throughout Alabama. Exposure of the media to liability under these circumstances threatened to rob the civil rights movement of any support it might find in the press.

The decision in *New York Times v. Sullivan* has transformed the law of libel. The case rendered obsolete hundreds of years of legal development and much of the law of libel in every state. *New York Times* has unquestionably achieved cornerstone status in media law, and there is little evidence that it will be abandoned. It may be the most important tort decision ever rendered by an American court.

There is an interesting footnote to the litigation: T. Eric Embry, the Birmingham lawyer who courageously defended the New York Times at trial, was elected to the Alabama Supreme Court in 1974 and served until 1985.

1. Public Officials and Public Figures

New York Times Co. v. Sullivan

Supreme Court of the United States
376 U.S. 254 (1964)

Mr. Justice BRENNAN delivered the opinion of the Court.

We are required in this case to determine for the first time the extent to which the constitutional protections for speech and press limit a State's power to award damages in a libel action brought by a public official against critics of his official conduct.

Respondent L. B. Sullivan is one of the three elected Commissioners of the City of Montgomery, Alabama. [His duties included supervision of the Police Department.].... He brought this civil libel action against the four individual

William J. Brennan, Jr.

petitioners, who are Negroes and Alabama clergymen, and against petitioner the New York Times Company, a New York corporation which publishes . . . a daily newspaper. A jury in the Circuit Court of Montgomery County awarded him damages of $500,000, the full amount claimed, against all the petitioners, and the Supreme Court of Alabama affirmed. . . .

Respondent's complaint alleged that he had been libeled by statements in a full-page advertisement . . . [relating to the civil rights movement for racial equality.]. . . .

The text appeared over the names of 64 persons, many widely known for their activities in public affairs, religion, trade unions, and the performing arts. . . .

Of the 10 paragraphs of text in the advertisement, the third and a portion of the sixth were the basis of respondent's claim of libel. . . .

It is uncontroverted that some of the statements contained in the two paragraphs were not accurate descriptions of events which occurred in Montgomery. Although Negro students staged a demonstration on the State Capitol steps, they sang the National Anthem and not "My Country, 'Tis of Thee." . . . . Although the police were deployed near the campus in large numbers on three occasions, they did not at any time "ring" the campus, and they were not called to the campus in connection with the demonstration on the State Capitol steps, as the third paragraph implied. Dr. King had not been arrested seven times, but only four; and although he claimed to have been assaulted some years earlier in connection with his arrest for loitering outside a courtroom, one of the officers who made the arrest denied that there was such an assault.

[Respondent was not mentioned by name.] On the premise that the charges in the sixth paragraph could be read as referring to him, respondent was allowed to prove that he had not participated in the events described. . . .

The trial judge submitted the case to the jury under instructions that the statements in the advertisement were "libelous *per se*" and were not privileged, so that petitioners might be held liable if the jury found that they had published the advertisement and that the statements were made "of and concerning" respondent. . . .

Under Alabama law as applied in this case . . . once "libel *per se*" has been established, the defendant has no defense as to stated facts unless he can persuade the jury that they were true in all their particulars. . . .

. . . . The First Amendment, said Judge Learned Hand, "presupposes that right conclusions are more likely to be gathered out of a multitude of tongues, than through any kind of authoritative selection. To many this is, and always will be, folly; but we have staked upon it our all." . . . . Mr. Justice Brandeis, in his concurring opinion in Whitney v. California, [274 U.S. 357], gave the principle its classic formulation:

> Those who won our independence believed . . . that public discussion is a political duty; and that this should be a fundamental principle of American government. They recognized the risks to which all human institutions are subject. But they knew that order cannot be secured merely through fear of punishment for its infractions; that it is hazardous to discourage thought, hope and imagination; that fear breeds repression; that repression breeds hate; that hate menaces stable government; that the path of safety lies in the opportunity to discuss freely supposed grievances and proposed remedies; and that the fitting remedy for evil counsels is good ones. Believing in the power of reason as applied through public discussion, they eschewed silence coerced by law—the argument of force in its worst form. Recognizing the occasional tyrannies of governing majorities, they amended the Constitution so that free speech and assembly should be guaranteed.

Thus we consider this case against the background of a profound national commitment to the principle that debate on public issues should be uninhibited, robust and wide-open, and that it may well include vehement, caustic, and sometimes unpleasantly sharp attacks on government and public officials. . . . The present advertisement, as an expression of grievance and protest, on one of the major public issues of our time, would seem clearly to qualify for the constitutional protection. The question is whether it forfeits that protection by the falsity of some of its factual statements and by its alleged defamation of respondent.

. . . . As Madison said, "Some degree of abuse is inseparable from the proper use of everything; and in no instance is this more true than in that of the press." . . . . In Cantwell v. Connecticut, 310 U.S. 296, the Court declared:

> In the realm of religious faith, and in that of political belief, sharp differences arise. In both fields the tenets of one man may seem the rankest error to his neighbor. To persuade others to his own point of view, the pleader, as we know, at times resorts to exaggeration, to vilification of men who have been, or are, prominent in church or state, and even to false statement. But the people of this nation have ordained in the light of history, that, in spite

> of the probability of excesses and abuses, these liberties are, in the long view, essential to enlightened opinion and right conduct on the part of the citizens of a democracy.

[The] . . . erroneous statement is inevitable in free debate, and . . . it must be protected if the freedoms of expression are to have the "breathing space" that they "need . . . to survive". . . .

If neither factual error nor defamatory content suffices to remove the constitutional shield from criticism of official conduct, the combination of the two elements is no less inadequate. [The Court then considered the history of the Sedition Act of 1798, which made it a crime to publish defamation against high officers of the United States, and reached the conclusion that it was unconstitutional.]

. . . . What a State may not constitutionally bring about by means of a criminal statute is likewise beyond the reach of its civil law of libel. The fear of damage awards under a rule such as that invoked by the Alabama courts here may be markedly more inhibiting than the fear of prosecution under a criminal statute. . . . Presumably a person charged with violation of [a criminal libel] statute enjoys ordinary criminal-law safeguards such as the requirements of an indictment and of proof beyond a reasonable doubt. These safeguards are not available to the defendant in a civil action. The judgment awarded in this case — without the need for any proof of actual pecuniary loss — was one thousand times greater than the maximum fine provided by the Alabama criminal statute, and one hundred times greater than that provided by the Sedition Act. And since there is no double jeopardy limitation applicable to civil lawsuits, this is not the only judgment that may be awarded against petitioners for the same publication. Whether or not a newspaper can survive a succession of such judgments, the pall of fear and timidity imposed upon those who would give voice to public criticism is an atmosphere in which the First Amendment freedoms cannot survive. Plainly the Alabama law of civil libel is "a form of regulation that creates hazards to protected freedoms markedly greater than those that attend reliance upon the criminal law." . . . .

The state rule of law is not saved by its allowance of the defense of truth. . . . A rule compelling the critic of official conduct to guarantee the truth of all his factual assertions — and to do so on pain of libel judgments virtually unlimited in amount — leads to a comparable "self-censorship." Allowance of the defense of truth, with the burden of proving it on the defendant, does not mean that only false speech will be deterred. . . . Under such a rule, would-be critics of official conduct may be deterred from voicing their criticism, even though it is believed to be true and even though it is in fact true, because of doubt whether it can be proved in court or fear of the expense of having to do so. . . . The rule thus dampens the vigor and limits the variety of public debate. It is inconsistent with the First and Fourteenth Amendments.

The constitutional guarantees require, we think, a federal rule that prohibits a public official from recovering damages for a defamatory falsehood relating to his official conduct unless he proves that the statement was made with "actual malice"—that is, with knowledge that it was false or with reckless disregard of whether it was false or not. An oft-cited statement of a like rule, which has been adopted by a number of state courts, is found in the Kansas case of Coleman v. MacLennan, 78 Kan. 711, 98 P. 281 (1908).... On appeal the Supreme Court of Kansas, in an opinion by Justice Burch, reasoned as follows:

> It is of the utmost consequence that the people should discuss the character and qualifications of candidates for their suffrage. The importance to the state and to society of such discussions is so vast, and the advantages derived are so great that they more than counterbalance the inconvenience of private persons whose conduct may be involved, and occasional injury to the reputations of individuals must yield to the public welfare, although at times such injury may be great. The public benefit from publicity is so great and the chance of injury to private character so small that such discussion must be privileged.

....

We hold today that the Constitution delimits a State's power to award damages for libel in actions brought by public officials against critics of their official conduct. Since this is such an action, the rule requiring proof of actual malice is applicable....

... [W]e consider that the proof presented to show actual malice lacks the convincing clarity which the constitutional standard demands, and hence that it would not constitutionally sustain the judgment for respondent under the proper rule of law. The case of the individual petitioners requires little discussion. Even assuming that they could constitutionally be found to have authorized the use of their names on the advertisement, there was no evidence whatever that they were aware of any erroneous statements or were in any way reckless in that regard. The judgment against them is thus without constitutional support.

As to the Times, we similarly conclude that the facts do not support a finding of actual malice. The statement by the Times' Secretary that, apart from the padlocking allegation, he thought the advertisement was "substantially correct," affords no constitutional warrant for the Alabama Supreme Court's conclusion that it was a "cavalier ignoring of the falsity of the advertisement, [from which] the jury could not have but been impressed with the bad faith of The Times, and its maliciousness inferable therefrom." The statement does not indicate malice at the time of the publication; even if the advertisement was not "substantially correct"—although respondent's own proofs tend to show that it was—that opinion was at least a reasonable one, and there was no evidence to impeach the witness' good faith in holding it. The Times' failure to retract upon respondent's demand, although it later retracted upon the demand of Governor Patterson, is likewise not adequate evidence of malice for constitutional purposes. Whether or not a failure to retract may ever constitute such evidence, there are two reasons why it does not here. *First*, the letter written by the Times reflected a reasonable doubt on its part as to whether the advertisement could reasonably be taken to refer to respondent at all. *Second*, it was not a final refusal, since it asked for an explanation on this point—a request that respondent chose to ignore. Nor does the retraction upon the demand of the Governor supply the necessary proof. It may be doubted that a failure to retract which is not itself evidence of malice can retroactively become such by virtue of a retraction subsequently made to another party. But in any event that did not happen here, since the explanation given by the Times' Secretary for the distinction drawn between respondent and the Governor was a reasonable one, the good faith of which was not impeached.

Finally, there is evidence that the Times published the advertisement without checking its accuracy against the news stories in the Times' own files. The mere presence of the stories in the files does not, of course, establish that the Times "knew" the advertisement was false, since the state of mind required for actual malice would have to be brought home to the persons in the Times' organization having responsibility for the publication of the advertisement. With respect to the failure of those persons to make the check, the record shows that they relied upon their knowledge of the good reputation of many of those whose names were listed as sponsors of the advertisement, and upon the letter from A. Philip Randolph, known to them as a responsible individual, certifying that the use of the names was authorized. There was testimony that the persons handling the advertisement saw nothing in it that would render it unacceptable under the Times' policy of rejecting advertisements containing "attacks of a personal character"; their failure to reject it on this ground was not unreasonable. We think the evidence against the Times supports at most a finding of negligence in failing to discover the misstatements, and is constitutionally insufficient to show the recklessness that is required for a finding of actual malice....

We also think the evidence was constitutionally defective in another respect: it was incapable of supporting the jury's finding that the allegedly libelous statements were made "of and concerning" respondent.... There was no reference to respondent in the advertisement, either by name or official position. A number of the allegedly libelous statements ... did not even concern the police.... The statements upon which respondent relies as referring to him are the two allegations that did concern the police or police functions: that "truckloads of police ... ringed the Alabama State College Campus" after the demonstration on the State Capitol steps, and that Dr. King had been "arrested ... seven times." These statements were false only in that the police had been "deployed near" the campus but had not actually "ringed" it and had not gone there in connection with the State Capitol demonstration, and in that Dr. King had been arrested only four times. The ruling that these discrepancies between what was true and what was asserted were sufficient to injure respondent's reputation may itself raise constitutional problems, but we need not consider them here. Although the statements may be taken as referring to the police, they do not on their face make even an oblique reference to respondent as an individual....

.... The present proposition would sidestep this obstacle by transmuting criticism of government, however impersonal it may seem on its face, into personal criticism, and hence potential libel of the officials of whom the government is composed. . . . We hold that such a proposition may not constitutionally be utilized to establish that an otherwise impersonal attack on governmental operations was a libel of an official responsible for those operations. . . .

The judgment of the Supreme Court of Alabama is reversed and the case is remanded to that court for further proceedings not inconsistent with this opinion.

[The concurring opinions of Justices BLACK and GOLDBERG, both of which would have categorically denied any action for defamation to a public official based on public conduct, are omitted. Justice DOUGLAS joined in both concurring opinions.]

Notes

1. ***Harm or Benefit?*** Was there any reason for the jury to presume damage to Sullivan's reputation? Justice Hugo Black, a former Senator from Alabama, noted in his concurring opinion:

> Viewed realistically, this record lends support to an inference that instead of being damaged, Commissioner Sullivan's political, social, and financial prestige has been enhanced by the Times publication.

376 U.S. at 294.

2. ***Failure to Retract.*** As suggested by *New York Times,* a failure to retract is ordinarily insufficient to establish actual malice because the subsequent conduct does not show the defendant's earlier state of mind. However, if there is independent evidence that the reporter knew at the time of the publication that the article was wrong, and later refused to print a retraction, an action will lie. *See* Golden Bear Distrib. Sys. v. Chase Revel, Inc., 708 F.2d 944 (5th Cir. 1983) (the author's notes showed she knew her article was wrong).

3. ***Actual Malice in Reporting.*** In St. Amant v. Thompson, 390 U.S. 727 (1968), the Supreme Court held that relying on a single, perhaps unreliable, source without attempting to verify the accuracy of statements was not "reckless" for purposes of the *New York Times* "actual malice" test. Whether a "reasonable" publisher would have investigated more thoroughly (or at all) is irrelevant. Only defendants who publish with subjective "awareness of probable falsity" are "reckless." The Court observed, however, that a story "based wholly on an unverified anonymous telephone call" or which contains "allegations . . . so improbable that only a reckless man could have put them in circulation" might be actionable.

Under *St. Amant* and subsequent cases, there is ordinarily no obligation on the defendant to talk to the subject of the defamatory communication to obtain that person's version of the events described (Rosenbloom v. Metromedia, Inc., 403 U.S. 29 (1971)) or to endeavor to present an objective picture (New York Times Co. v. Connor, 365 F.2d 567, 576 (5th Cir. 1966)).

Moreover, factual inaccuracies alone do not suffice to prove actual malice (Time, Inc. v. Pape, 401 U.S. 279 (1971)), nor is recklessness established merely by showing that the reporting in question was speculative or even sloppy (Oliver v. Village

Voice, Inc., 417 F. Supp. 235, 238 (S.D.N.Y. 1976)). In Harte-Hanks Communications, Inc. v. Connaughton, 491 U.S. 657 (1989), the Supreme Court explained that "a public figure plaintiff must prove more than an extreme departure from professional standards and . . . a newspaper's motive in publishing a story — whether to promote an opponent's candidacy or to increase its circulation — cannot provide a sufficient basis for finding actual malice."

Even the deliberate alteration of quotations will not prove knowledge of falsity, unless the alteration materially changes the meaning of the quotation alleged to be defamatory. *See* Masson v. New Yorker Mag., Inc., 501 U.S. 496 (1991).

"That a defendant publishes statements anticipating financial gain likewise fails to prove actual malice: a profit motive does not strip communications of constitutional protections." Peter Scalamandre & Sons, Inc. v. Kaufman, 113 F.3d 556, 561 (5th Cir. 1997).

In WJLA-TV v. Levin, 564 S.E.2d 383 (Va. 2002), an orthopedist was accused of sexually assaulting his female patients and using inappropriate medical procedures. The court held that the television station's use of the statements of a physician, which the station knew the physician had retracted, was sufficient to support a jury finding of actual malice. A $2 million award of presumed damages was upheld.

4. ***Focus on State of Mind.*** Because the actual-malice standard makes constitutional protection depend upon the defendant's state of mind, the focus of the litigation often shifts away from the issue of whether the defamatory statement was true or false. When that happens, plaintiffs may find it impossible to clear their names by obtaining rulings on falsity, and the public may never know the truth.

In addition, litigation of the actual-malice issue may be highly disruptive to editorial processes in suits against media defendants. The publisher's state of mind must normally be inferred from circumstantial evidence. Consequently, plaintiffs routinely seek discovery of information about such matters as communications between reporters and editors, facts known but not used in a story, the pressures under which the work was prepared, and the identity and credibility of the defendant's sources.

5. ***"Actual Malice" versus "Express Malice."*** "Actual malice," as defined in *New York Times* and later cases, is a legal term of art which must be clearly distinguished from "express" or "common-law" malice. One may utter true statements, just as easily as those which are false, with spite, ill will, vindictiveness or motives of revenge — that is to say, with express or common-law malice. A showing that the defendant was actuated by bad motives is not, by itself, sufficient to satisfy the actual-malice requirement. Proof of ill will says nothing about whether the defendant knew of, or acted recklessly as to, the falsity of the defamatory statement.

Jury instructions permitting a finding of actual malice merely upon proof of hatred, enmity, desire to injure, or the like are constitutionally defective. In discussing the reasoning underlying this position, the Supreme Court observed in Garrison v. State of Louisiana, 379 U.S. 64, 73–75 (1964), a criminal defamation case:

> [T]he great principles of the Constitution which secure freedom of expression in this area preclude attaching adverse consequences to any except the knowing or reckless falsehood. Debate on public issues will not be uninhibited if the speaker must run the risk that it will be proved in court that he spoke out of hatred; even if he did speak out of hatred, utterances honestly believed contribute to the free interchange of ideas and the ascertainment of truth. Under a rule . . . permitting a finding of [actual] malice based on an intent merely to inflict harm, rather than to inflict harm through falsehood, "it becomes a hazardous matter to speak out against a popular politician, with the result that the dishonest and incompetent will be shielded." . . . . Moreover, "[i]n the case of charges against a popular political figure . . . it may be almost impossible to show freedom from ill-will or selfish political motives."

Of course, in many instances, evidence of express malice may be coupled with facts showing that the defendant lacked an honest belief in the truth of the statements. In those cases, proof of "malice" in the *New York Times* sense allows the action to go forward; proof of common-law malice may encourage the jury to award a large verdict.

6. ***Honest but Erroneous Beliefs.*** The statement of an erroneous belief which is honestly held, and which has some factual grounding, cannot ordinarily be found to have been uttered with actual malice. *See* Peter Scalamandre & Sons, Inc. v. Kaufman, 113 F.3d 556, 562 (5th Cir. 1997) (assertions that the plaintiff conducted "an illegal haul and dump operation" and that the "people of Texas are being poisoned" were shown at trial to be the defendant's honest beliefs and were not so without basis as to constitute reckless disregard for the truth).

7. ***Clear and Convincing Proof of Actual Malice.*** Although other issues in a defamation action are typically governed by the preponderance-of-the-evidence standard, actual malice constitutionally must be established by clear and convincing evidence. *See* Harte-Hanks Communications, Inc. v. Connaughton, 491 U.S. 657, 661 n.2 (1989). This heightened standard of proof applies not only to jury determinations, but to preliminary rulings on motions for summary judgment. *See* Anderson v. Liberty Lobby, Inc., 477 U.S. 242, 255–56 (1986). Consequently, a plaintiff must produce strong evidence of actual malice to survive a defendant's motion for summary disposition — evidence from which actual malice could be found by clear and convincing evidence.

8. ***Judicial Review of Findings on Actual Malice.*** A finding of actual malice is not entitled to the deference usually extended to findings of fact. The question whether the evidence supports a finding of actual malice is a question of law, and in determining whether the constitutional standard is satisfied, the trial court and every reviewing court must consider the factual record in full to ascertain whether there is clear and convincing evidence. *See* Bose Corp. v. Consumers U. of the U.S., Inc., 466 U.S. 485 (1984). Since independent review occurs only when the jury finds for the plaintiff, the rule confers its substantial benefits exclusively on defendants. This

important procedural rule, and the clear-and-convincing-evidence standard, may do more to provide "breathing space" for free expression than the actual-malice standard itself.

9. ***Public Officials***. Not all public employees are subject to the "actual malice" requirement of New York Times v. Sullivan. "It is clear . . . that the 'public official' designation applies at the very least to those among the hierarchy of government employees who have, or appear to the public to have, substantial responsibility for or control over the conduct of governmental affairs." Rosenblatt v. Baer, 383 U.S. 75, 85 (1966). The test is whether the "position in government has such apparent importance that the public has an independent interest in the qualifications and performance of the person who holds it, beyond the general public interest in the qualifications and performance of all governmental employees." *Id.* at 86.

In practice, courts have often viewed the public official category expansively. *See, e.g.*, Hotze v. Miller, 361 S.W.3d 707 (Tex. App. 2012) (physician who served on the state medical board). Police officers of all varieties are routinely classified as public officials. *See* Tomkiewicz v. Detroit News, Inc., 635 N.W.2d 36 (Mich. Ct. App. 2001) (police lieutenant); *but see* Verity v. USA Today, 436 P.3d 653, 663 (Idaho 2019) (holding that "in Idaho a public teacher working in a teaching capacity will rarely, if ever, qualify as a public official").

The Restatement makes clear that the actual-malice rule applies to public officials only if the defamatory statement relates to the official's qualifications. "A statement that the governor drinks himself into a stupor at home every night much more clearly affects his qualifications than a statement that a tax assessor keeps a secret collection of pornographic pictures." Restatement, Second, of Torts § 580A cmt. b.

10. ***Former Public Officials***. A former public official may be subject to the actual-malice standard if the statement relates to official performance while in office. *See* Rosenblatt v. Baer, 383 U.S. 75 (1966).

11. ***Ethics in Law Practice: Criticism of the Judiciary***. Do attorneys enjoy the same free speech rights as members of the general public? Model Rule 8.2 provides that an attorney is not subject to professional discipline (*e.g.*, reprimand, suspension or disbarment), unless a defamatory statement about a judicial officer is made with actual malice:

> A lawyer shall not make a statement that the lawyer knows to be false or with reckless disregard as to its truth or falsity concerning the qualifications or integrity of a judge . . . or of a candidate for election or appointment to judicial . . . office.

Model Rules of Professional Conduct Rule 8.2(a) (Westlaw 2022).

12. ***Public Figures***. The *New York Times* actual-malice requirement was subsequently extended to *public figures* in Curtis Publ'g Co. v. Butts and Associated Press v. Walker, 388 U.S. 130 (1967), and, for a brief time, to cases generally involving *matters of public interest* in Rosenbloom v. Metromedia, Inc., 403 U.S. 29 (1971).

2. Plaintiffs Who Are Not Public Figures

Gertz v. Robert Welch, Inc.

Supreme Court of the United States
418 U.S. 323 (1974)

Mr. Justice POWELL delivered the opinion of the Court.

....

[The family of a youth named Nelson, who was shot and killed by one Nuccio, a police officer later convicted of homicide, retained Elmer Gertz to represent them in civil litigation arising from the death. In this capacity, Gertz attended the coroner's inquest into the boy's death and initiated actions for damages, but he neither discussed Officer Nuccio with the press nor played any part in the criminal proceeding. Notwithstanding petitioner's remote connection with the prosecution of Nuccio, respondent's magazine, an outlet for the views of the John Birch Society, portrayed him as an architect of a plan to "frame" the police officer. Its statements contained serious inaccuracies. The implication that petitioner had a criminal record was false. There was no evidence that he or an organization to which he belonged had taken any part in planning the 1968 demonstrations in Chicago. There was also no basis for the charge that petitioner was a "Leninist" or a "Communist-fronter." And he had never been a member of the "Marxist League for Industrial Democracy" or the "Intercollegiate Socialist Society."]

The managing editor of American Opinion made no effort to verify or substantiate the charges against petitioner. Instead, he appended an editorial introduction stating that the author had "conducted extensive research into the Richard Nuccio Case." ....

[The District Court denied defendant's motion to dismiss petitioner's libel action. After the evidence was in, it "ruled in effect that petitioner was neither a public official nor a public figure," and it submitted the issue of damages to the jury, which awarded $50,000. On further reflection the District Court concluded that the New York Times standard applied and entered judgment for defendant notwithstanding the jury verdict. This action was affirmed by the Court of Appeals for the Seventh Circuit, on the basis of Rosenbloom v. Metromedia, Inc., 403 U.S. 29 (1971).]

The principal issue in this case is whether a newspaper or broadcaster that publishes defamatory falsehoods about an individual who is neither a public official nor a public figure may claim a constitutional privilege against liability for the injury inflicted by those statements....

We begin with the common ground. Under the First Amendment there is no such thing as a false idea. However pernicious an opinion may seem, we depend for its correction not on the conscience of judges and juries but on the competition of other ideas. But there is no constitutional value in false statements of fact. Neither the intentional lie nor the careless error materially advances society's interest in "uninhibited, robust, and wide-open" debate on public issues. . . . They belong to that category of utterances which "are no essential part of any exposition of ideas, and are of such slight social value as a step to truth that any benefit that may be derived from them is clearly outweighed by the social interest in order and morality." . . . .

Although the erroneous statement of fact is not worthy of constitutional protection, it is nevertheless inevitable in free debate. As James Madison pointed out in the Report on the Virginia Resolutions of 1798: "Some degree of abuse is inseparable from the proper use of everything; and in no instance is this more true than in that of the press." . . . . And punishment of error runs the risk of inducing a cautious and restrictive exercise of the constitutionally guaranteed freedoms of speech and press. . . .

The legitimate state interest underlying the law of libel is the compensation of individuals for the harm inflicted on them by defamatory falsehood. We would not lightly require the State to abandon this purpose, for, as Mr. Justice Stewart has reminded us, the individual's right to the protection of his own good name reflects no more than our basic concept of the essential dignity and worth of every human being — a concept at the root of any decent system of ordered liberty. . . .

Some tension necessarily exists between the need for a vigorous and uninhibited press and the legitimate interest in redressing wrongful injury. . . .

The *New York Times* standard defines the level of constitutional protection appropriate to the context of defamation of a public person. Those who, by reason of the notoriety of their achievements or the vigor and success with which they seek the public's attention, are properly classified as public figures and those who hold governmental office may recover for injury to reputation only on clear and convincing proof that the defamatory falsehood was made with knowledge of its falsity or with reckless disregard for the truth. This standard administers an extremely powerful antidote to the inducement to media self-censorship of the common-law rule of strict liability for libel and slander. And it exacts a correspondingly high price from the victims of defamatory falsehood. Plainly many deserving plaintiffs, including some intentionally subjected to injury, will be unable to surmount the barrier of the *New York Times* test. Despite this substantial abridgment of the state law right to compensation for wrongful hurt to one's reputation, the Court has concluded that the protection of the *New York Times* privilege should be available to publishers and broadcasters of defamatory falsehood concerning public officials and public figures. . . . We think that these decisions are correct. . . . For the reasons stated below, we conclude that the state interest in compensating injury to the reputation of private individuals requires that a different rule should obtain with respect to them.

. . . . The first remedy of any victim of defamation is self-help — using available opportunities to contradict the lie or correct the error and thereby to minimize its adverse impact on reputation. Public officials and public figures usually enjoy significantly greater access to the channels of effective communication and hence have a more realistic opportunity to counteract false statements than private individuals normally enjoy. Private individuals are therefore more vulnerable to injury, and the state interest in protecting them is correspondingly greater.

More important . . . , there is a compelling normative consideration underlying the distinction between public and private defamation plaintiffs. An individual who decides to seek governmental office must accept certain necessary consequences of that involvement in public affairs. He runs the risk of closer public scrutiny than might otherwise be the case. . . .

Those classed as public figures stand in a similar position. Hypothetically, it may be possible for someone to become a public figure through no purposeful action of his own, but the instances of truly involuntary public figures must be exceedingly rare. For the most part those who attain this status have assumed roles of especial prominence in the affairs of society. Some occupy positions of such persuasive power and influence that they are deemed public figures for all purposes. More commonly, those classed as public figures have thrust themselves to the forefront of particular public controversies in order to influence the resolution of the issues involved. In either event, they invite attention and comment.

Even if the foregoing generalities do not obtain in every instance, the communications media are entitled to act on the assumption that public officials and public figures have voluntarily exposed themselves to increased risk of injury from defamatory falsehood concerning them. No such assumption is justified with respect to a private individual. He has not accepted public office or assumed an "influential role in ordering society." . . . . He has relinquished no part of his interest in the protection of his own good name, and consequently he has a more compelling call on the courts for redress of injury inflicted by defamatory falsehood. Thus, private individuals are not only more vulnerable to injury than public officials and public figures; they are also more deserving of recovery.

For these reasons we conclude that the States should retain substantial latitude in their efforts to enforce a legal remedy for defamatory falsehood injurious to the reputation of a private individual. The extension of the *New York Times* test proposed by the *Rosenbloom* plurality [*see* note 12 on p. 1091, *supra*] would abridge this legitimate state interest to a degree that we find unacceptable. And it would occasion the additional difficulty of forcing state and federal judges to decide on an *ad hoc* basis which publications address issues of "general or public interest" and which do not—to determine, in the words of Mr. Justice Marshall, "what information is relevant to self-government." . . . . We doubt the wisdom of committing this task to the conscience of judges. Nor does the Constitution require us to draw so thin a line between the drastic alternatives of the *New York Times* privilege and the common law of strict liability for defamatory error. The "public or general interest" test for determining the applicability of the *New York Times* standard to private defamation actions inadequately serves both of the competing values at stake. On the one hand, a private individual whose reputation is injured by defamatory falsehood that does concern an issue of public or general interest has no recourse unless he can meet the rigorous requirements of *New York Times*. This is true despite the factors that distinguish the state interest in compensating private individuals from the analogous interest involved in the context of public persons. On the other hand, a publisher or broadcaster of a defamatory error which a court deems unrelated to an issue of public or general interest may be held liable in damages even if it took every reasonable precaution to ensure the accuracy of its assertions. And liability may far exceed compensation for any actual injury to the plaintiff, for the jury may be permitted to presume damages without proof of loss and even to award punitive damages.

We hold that, so long as they do not impose liability without fault, the States may define for themselves the appropriate standard of liability for a publisher or broadcaster of defamatory falsehood injurious to a private individual. This approach . . . recognizes the strength of the legitimate state interest in compensating private individuals for wrongful injury to reputation, yet shields the press and broadcast media from the rigors of strict liability for defamation. . . .

. . . [W]e endorse this approach in recognition of the strong and legitimate state interest in compensating private individuals for injury to reputation. But this countervailing state interest extends no further than compensation for actual injury. For the reasons stated below, we hold that the States may not permit recovery of presumed or punitive damages, at least when liability is not based on a showing of knowledge of falsity or reckless disregard for the truth.

The common law of defamation is an oddity of tort law, for it allows recovery of purportedly compensatory damages without evidence of actual loss. Under the traditional rules pertaining to actions for libel, the existence of injury is presumed from the fact of publication. Juries may award substantial sums as compensation for supposed damage to reputation without any proof that such harm actually occurred. The largely uncontrolled discretion of juries to award damages where there is no loss unnecessarily compounds the potential of any system of liability for defamatory falsehood to inhibit the vigorous exercise of First Amendment freedoms. Additionally, the doctrine of presumed damages invites juries to punish unpopular opinion rather than to compensate individuals for injury sustained by the publication of a false fact. More to the point, the States have no substantial interest in securing for plaintiffs such as this petitioner gratuitous awards of money damages far in excess of any actual injury.

. . . . It is necessary to restrict defamation plaintiffs who do not prove knowledge of falsity or reckless disregard for the truth to compensation for actual injury. We need not define "actual injury," as trial courts have wide experience in framing appropriate jury instructions in tort actions. Suffice it to say that actual injury is not limited to out-of-pocket loss. Indeed, the more customary types of actual harm inflicted by defamatory falsehood include impairment of reputation and standing in the community, personal humiliation, and mental anguish and suffering. . . . [T]here need be no evidence which assigns an actual dollar value to the injury.

We also find no justification for allowing awards of punitive damages against publishers and broadcasters held liable under state-defined standards of liability for defamation. . . . Like the doctrine of presumed damages, jury discretion to award punitive damages unnecessarily exacerbates the danger of media self-censorship, but, unlike the former rule, punitive damages are wholly irrelevant to the state interest that justifies a negligence standard for private defamation actions. They are not compensation for injury. . . . In short, the private defamation plaintiff who establishes liability under a less demanding standard than that stated by *New York Times* may recover only such damages as are sufficient to compensate him for actual injury.

. . . .

Notwithstanding our refusal to extend the *New York Times* privilege to defamation of private individuals, respondent contends that we should affirm the judgment below on the ground that petitioner is either a public official or a public figure. There is little basis for the former assertion. Several years prior to the present incident, petitioner had served briefly on housing committees appointed by the mayor of Chicago, but at the time of publication he had never held any remunerative governmental position. Respondent admits this but argues that petitioner's appearance at the coroner's inquest rendered him a "*de facto* public official." Our cases recognize no such concept. Respondent's suggestion would sweep all lawyers under the *New York Times* rule as officers of the court and distort the plain meaning of the "public official" category beyond all recognition. We decline to follow it.

Respondent's characterization of petitioner as a public figure raises a different question. . . .

Petitioner has long been active in community and professional affairs. He has served as an officer of local civic groups and of various professional organizations, and he has published several books and articles on legal subjects. Although petitioner was consequently well known in some circles, he had achieved no general fame or notoriety in the community. None of the prospective jurors called at the trial had ever heard of petitioner prior to this litigation, and respondent offered no proof that this response was atypical of the local population. We would not lightly assume that a citizen's participation in community and professional affairs rendered him a public figure for all purposes. Absent clear evidence of general fame or notoriety in the community, and pervasive involvement in the affairs of society, an individual should not be deemed a public personality for all aspects of his life. It is preferable to reduce the public-figure question to a more meaningful context by looking to the nature and extent of an individual's participation in the particular controversy giving rise to the defamation.

In this context it is plain that petitioner was not a public figure. He played a minimal role at the coroner's inquest, and his participation related solely to his representation of a private client. He took no part in the criminal prosecution of Officer Nuccio. Moreover, he never discussed either the criminal or civil litigation with the press and was never quoted as having done so. He plainly did not thrust himself into the vortex of this public issue, nor did he engage the public's attention in an attempt to influence its outcome. We are persuaded that the trial court did not err in refusing to characterize petitioner as a public figure for the purpose of this litigation.

We therefore conclude that the *New York Times* standard is inapplicable to this case and that the trial court erred in entering judgment for respondent. Because the jury was allowed to impose liability without fault and was permitted to presume damages without proof of injury, a new trial is necessary. We reverse and remand for further proceedings in accord with this opinion.

It is so ordered.

[Justice POWELL'S opinion was joined by STEWART, MARSHALL, BLACKMUN and REHNQUIST, JJ. BLACKMUN, J., stated in a concurrence that he found some difficulties with the majority opinion, but that he joined in it to attain a "definitive ruling." BURGER, C.J., dissented in an opinion which indicated that he disapproved of the requirement of negligence for private defamation. DOUGLAS, J., dissented on the basis of his absolute-privilege theory, and would have at least retained the *Rosenbloom* rule. BRENNAN, J., dissented and would have retained the *Rosenbloom* rule. WHITE, J., dissented and would have retained strict liability for private defamation.]

Notes

1. ***Fault as to Falsity in Gertz Cases.*** Virtually all states have accepted *Gertz*'s invitation to require only a showing of negligence in cases brought by private persons suing with respect to matters of public concern. *But see* Poyser v. Peerless, 775 N.E.2d 1101 (Ind. Ct. App. 2002) (requiring actual malice).

2. ***Public Figure Status Is a Question of Law.*** Whether the plaintiff is a public figure for purposes of the defamatory statement is a question of law for the court. In rare cases, the plaintiff will be a public figure for all purposes. However, the key question is simply whether the plaintiff is a public figure with respect to the subject matter of the defamatory statement, that is, a limited purpose public figure. Courts have classified as public figures:

- A woman who "purposefully" disclosed her own rape accusation against an entertainer. McKee v. Cosby, 874 F.3d 54, 62 (1st Cir. 2017).
- A city resident who was the subject of a feature story where he was quoted acknowledging his political actions on behalf of others and his intention to influence government officials. Sparks v. Peaster, 581 S.E.2d 579 (Ga. Ct. App. 2003).
- A restaurant, "for the limited purpose of a food review or reporting on its goods and services." Pegasus v. Reno Newspapers, 57 P.3d 82 (Nev. 2002).
- A Holocaust survivor who authorized a biography. Thomas v. L.A. Times Communications, 45 Fed. Appx. 801 (9th Cir. 2002).
- A security guard who granted a photo shoot and interviews following the explosion of a bomb at an Olympic venue. Atlanta-Journal Constitution v. Jewell, 555 S.E.2d 175 (Ga. Ct. App. 2001).

- A professional football player, with respect to his physical condition, contractual dispute, and retirement. Chuy v. Philadelphia Eagles Football Club, 595 F.2d 1265, 1280 (3d Cir. 1979) (en banc).
- A woman who was the former girlfriend of Elvis Presley and the wife of a retired football star, concerning her marital status and romantic encounters. Brewer v. Memphis Publ'g Co., 626 F.2d 1238, 1255 (5th Cir. 1980).
- A well-known former U.S. Senate candidate. Williams v. Pasma, 656 P.2d 212, 216 (Mont. 1982).
- A Playboy playmate, with respect to allegedly libelous use of a photograph for which she posed. Vitale v. National Lampoon, Inc., 449 F. Supp. 442 (E.D. Pa. 1978).
- A college dean, with respect to a controversy relating to his tenure as dean. Byers v. Southeastern Newspaper Corp., Inc., 288 S.E.2d 698 (Ga. Ct. App. 1982).

However, some decisions have construed "public figure" narrowly. *See, e.g.*, Franklin Prescriptions, Inc. v. New York Times Co., 267 F. Supp. 2d 425 (E.D. Pa. 2003) (holding that a pharmacy, which used the Internet for informational purposes only, and did not take orders over the Internet, was not a limited purpose public figure in the context of a public controversy about online pharmacies making expensive drugs more accessible).

In Lundell Mfg. Co. v. ABC, 98 F.3d 351 (8th Cir. 1996), the court held that a manufacturer of a garbage recycling machine was not a public figure, for although garbage disposal was a matter of public concern, the manufacturer's entry into a contract for the sale of the machine to a county was not the injection of the manufacturer into a controversy for the purpose of influencing a public issue.

3. ***Self-Help***. Are Justice Powell's statements, to the effect that public figures have greater access to avenues of self-help for correcting defamatory falsehoods, still true in the age of the Internet?

4. ***Defamation in Politics***. Political ads often contain extreme characterizations of an opponent's record. These statements are not exempt from liability, but a candidate for public office is a public figure who must prove actual malice in order to recover for defamation. That is a formidable obstacle, but sometimes it can be met.

In Boyce & Isley, PLLC v. Cooper, 568 S.E.2d 893 (N.C. Ct. App. 2002), the successful candidate for attorney general had run a commercial saying that his opponent's law firm had "sued the state" and "charge[d]" the taxpayers an hourly rate of $28,000, "more than a police officer's salary for each hour's work." The ad did not point out that the fee was pursued by the plaintiff's father in a contingent fee class action before the plaintiff joined the firm. The court held that the statements were libelous *per se* because they implied unethical billing practices. Moreover, a claim was stated by all four members of the plaintiff's law firm and the firm itself. Because the successful candidate refused to pull the ad after demands for discontinuance, there was a basis for finding that the defendant acted with actual malice.

In Flowers v. Carville, 310 F.3d 1118 (9th Cir. 2003), the court held that a claim was stated against former presidential advisors based on their repetition of news reports by CNN that tape recordings made by the plaintiff had been "doctored" or "selectively edited." The court acknowledged that the plaintiff, after conducting discovery, might not be able to prove that the defendants acted with actual malice.

5. ***The Economic Realities of Defamation Litigation.*** Plaintiffs in defamation cases against the media face heavy obstacles. For one thing, large media defendants are "repeat players" in defamation litigation. They therefore have an incentive to defend every case to the hilt. A strong defense not only helps to win the case in question, but also to discourage other potential plaintiffs from bringing suit. Furthermore, proof of the kind of injury suffered in a typical defamation case—mental suffering, loss of respect, and so on—may be difficult to establish. Finally, some victims of defamation sue not because they have suffered heavy damages of a measurable sort, but to clear their names. Victims like this may have trouble finding lawyers to handle their cases—which are not easy to litigate—if their recoveries are limited. As a result, many actions by plaintiffs who are not public officials or public figures may not be worth bringing unless the plaintiff expects to be able to prove actual malice, so as to qualify for damages without proof of actual loss. If so, *Gertz* may leave private-figure plaintiffs with less protection than it seems to at first glance.

6. ***Actual Injury versus Special Damages.*** "Actual injury," as defined in *Gertz*, differs from the common-law concept of special damages because "actual injury" includes mental suffering. In Terwilliger v. Wands, 17 N.Y. 54 (1858), a man was orally accused of regularly beating a path to the house of his neighbor for the purpose of having sexual intercourse with her while her husband was in prison. The only injury the man proved was that he was so worked up that he could not attend to business; there was no evidence that anyone treated him differently. The court affirmed a judgment for the defendant because the slander did not fall within the four *per se* categories and there was no proof of special damages. (Note that if the suit had been brought by a woman, or if the accusation had been in writing, there would have been no need to prove special damages under then-applicable law.)

7. ***The "Libel-Proof" Plaintiff.*** Because damages in defamation cases are meant to compensate for harm to the plaintiff's reputation, a plaintiff whose reputation was very bad before a particular defamation occurred may be entitled only to nominal damages. If that is the case, there is a serious question as to whether a court should spend limited judicial resources on hearing the action. For instance, the alleged defamation in Wynberg v. National Enquirer, Inc., 564 F. Supp. 924 (C.D. Cal. 1982), was an accusation that the plaintiff had used his "close personal relationship" with a famous actress (Elizabeth Taylor) for personal gain. The court noted that the plaintiff had been convicted five times for such crimes as contributing to the delinquency of minors, bribery, grand theft, and offering the services of prostitutes to police officers, and that these incidents had been widely publicized. Furthermore, "numerous articles" had discussed the ways in which plaintiff had used his relationship with

the actress for financial gain. Concluding that the plaintiff was libel-proof, the court granted the defendant's motion for summary judgment.

In Davis v. The Tennesseean, 83 S.W.3d 125 (Tenn. Ct. App. 2002), the court held that an inmate, who had been sentenced to 99 years in prison for aiding and abetting a murder, was libel-proof. An article had incorrectly reported that he was the one who shot the tavern owner during the course of a robbery.

See also Lamb v. Rizzo, 242 F. Supp. 2d 1032 (D. Kan. 2003) (holding that a prisoner serving three consecutive life terms for murder and kidnaping was libel-proof).

8. ***Suing Only for Emotional Distress.*** A defamation plaintiff may wish to avoid litigating the issue of damage to reputation, in order to avoid potentially brutal discovery requests, cross-examination, and testimony by others on that issue. In that case, the plaintiff may waive damages to reputation and seek compensation only for emotional distress. For example, in Time, Inc. v. Firestone, 424 U.S. 448 (1976), a libel action arising from an erroneous report about a divorce, then-Justice William H. Rehnquist wrote:

> Petitioner has argued that because respondent withdrew her claim for damages to reputation on the eve of trial, there could be no recovery consistent with *Gertz*. . . . [However, in *Gertz*] we made it clear that States could base awards on elements other than injury to reputation, specifically listing "personal humiliation, and mental anguish and suffering" as examples of injuries which might be compensated consistently with the Constitution upon a showing of fault. Because respondent has decided to forgo recovery for injury to her reputation, she is not prevented from obtaining compensation for such other damages that a defamatory falsehood may have caused her.
>
> . . . . Several witnesses testified to the extent of respondent's anxiety and concern over Time's inaccurately reporting that she had been found guilty of adultery, and she herself took the stand to elaborate on her fears that her young son would be adversely affected by this falsehood when he grew older. The jury decided these injuries should be compensated by an award of $100,000. We have no warrant for re-examining this determination. . . .

9. ***Matters Not of "Public Concern."*** In Dun & Bradstreet, Inc. v. Greenmoss Builders, Inc., 472 U.S. 749 (1985), the Court held that a false and defamatory credit report did not involve a matter of "public concern." State libel law, which allowed the plaintiff to recover presumed and punitive damages without proof of actual malice, did not violate the First Amendment as applied in that case.

Unfortunately, *Dun & Bradstreet* provides little guidance for distinguishing matters of private concern from matters of public concern. Indeed, the Court's application of the law to the facts before it seems counter-intuitive. The credit report had erroneously said that the plaintiff had declared voluntary bankruptcy. Isn't it a matter of public concern whether a business which employs numerous workers and pays taxes is failing? The Court appeared to place weight on the fact that the erroneous credit report was given limited dissemination and that the five subscribers who received the report were contractually precluded from further disseminating its contents. The Court also suggested that the reporting of "objectively verifiable information" deserved less constitutional protection than other kinds of speech, and that market forces gave credit-reporting agencies an incentive to be accurate, "since false credit reporting is of no use to creditors."

It is surprising that *Dun & Bradstreet* drew a distinction between matters of public interest and matters of private concern. In 1971, Rosenbloom v. Metromedia, Inc., 403 U.S. 29, had embraced that distinction in deciding how far to extend the actual-malice standard. However, in 1974, Gertz v. Robert Welch, Inc., 418 U.S. 323, repudiated *Rosenbloom* on the ground that judges should not be called upon to decide what is or is not a matter of public concern. Why was that reasoning not persuasive when *Dun & Bradstreet* was decided in 1985?

Note also that the plurality opinion in *Dun & Bradstreet* was silent on whether the plaintiff in a private-matter action must prove that the defendant acted with some degree of fault as to falsity. Justice White, concurring, thought that *Dun & Bradstreet* had rejected the *Gertz* rule that liability cannot be imposed without fault, as well as the *Gertz* holding on the availability of presumed damages. Justice Brennan, speaking in dissent for four members of the Court, opined that the holding in *Dun & Bradstreet* was narrow and that the parties did not question the requirement of fault to obtain a judgment and actual damages.

10. ***Defining Matters of Public Concern.*** Citing United States Supreme Court decisions, the Texas Supreme Court wrote:

> According to the Supreme Court, speech "deals with matters of public concern when it can 'be fairly considered as relating to any matter of political, social, or other concern to the community.'". . . . Public matters include "a subject of legitimate news interest; that is, a subject of general interest and of value and concern to the public." . . . . Whether "speech addresses a matter of public concern must be determined by [the expression's] content, form, and context . . . as revealed by the whole record." . . . .
>
> Public matters include, among other things, "commission of crime, prosecutions resulting from it, and judicial proceedings arising from the prosecutions." . . . . A report that a corporation and its principal stockholder "had links to organized crime and used some of those links to influence the State's governmental process" was a matter of public concern. Similarly, the "disclosure of misbehavior by public officials is a matter of public interest . . . , especially when it concerns the operation of a police department."

Brady v. Klentzman, 515 S.W.3d 878, 884 (Tex. 2017).

11. ***Summary: Three Categories.*** The Supreme Court's rulings create three categories of defamation cases:

(a) *Actions by Public Officials or Public Figures for Defamation in Respect to Matters of Public Concern (New York Times* controls*).* The plaintiff must prove actual malice. Presumed and punitive damages are not barred by the Constitution.

(b) *Actions by Private Persons for Defamation in Respect to Matters of Public Concern (Gertz,* as modified by *Dun & Bradstreet,* controls*).* The plaintiff must prove that the defendant acted with fault as to the statement's falsity, and recovery is limited to actual injury, unless the plaintiff proves actual malice, in which case, presumed or punitive damages are constitutionally permissible.

(c) *Actions by Anyone for Defamation in Respect to a Matter of Private Concern (Dun & Bradstreet* controls*).* Whether the plaintiff must prove that the defendant acted with fault as to the falsity of the statement has not been decided by the U.S. Supreme Court (states generally require negligence). Presumed and punitive damages may be awarded without proof of actual malice.

3. Presumed Damages Today

W.J.A. v. D.A.

Supreme Court of New Jersey
43 A.3d 1148 (N.J. 2012)

PER CURIAM.

. . . .

In 1998, Dave Adams, an adult, filed a complaint against his uncle, Wayne Anderson, alleging Anderson had sexually assaulted him at various times when Adams was a minor. . . . [Adams's claims were deemed to be barred by the statute of limitations, and Anderson prevailed on a counterclaim for defamation and frivolous litigation.]

. . . .

Adams moved to vacate the judgment against him. . . . [W]hile the motion . . . was pending, Adams created a website on which he recounted the claimed sexual abuse by Anderson . . . , along with allegations of perjury and intimidation of a witness.

Through the site, Adams sought help from anyone who "had similar experiences with [Anderson]" and encouraged visitors to "express [their] feelings on this matter to The F.B.I., The Governor of New Jersey, or The Attorney General of New Jersey." . . . Adams indicated he was "outraged by the justice [he] believed [he] did not get through [the trial] and [he] was desperate for any help [he] could get from anyone." The . . . website indicated that Adams's "[m]ission is to tell all . . . US Citizens about this!" . . . .

. . . Anderson filed a new complaint alleging that Adams's website contained defamatory statements. . . .

. . . Anderson moved for summary judgment. In January 2009, the judge denied the motion, despite finding that Adams's statements were defamatory *per se* because they accused Anderson of having committed a criminal offense and of engaging in serious sexual misconduct. The judge concluded that he could not permit the jury to evaluate the claim without any evidence of cognizable damages. . . .

Anderson appealed and the Appellate Division reversed. . . .

"Damages which may be recovered in an action for defamation are: (1) compensatory or actual, which may be either (a) general or (b) special; (2) punitive or exemplary; and (3) nominal." . . . . Actual damages . . . refers to the real losses flowing from the defamatory statement. It "is not limited to out-of-pocket loss," but includes "impairment to reputation and standing in the community," along with personal humiliation, mental anguish, and suffering to the extent that they flow from the reputational injury. Gertz v. Robert Welch, Inc., . . . [418 U.S. 323, 350 (1974)].

Contained within the notion of actual damages is the doctrine of presumed damages. . . . Presumed damages are a procedural device which permits a plaintiff to obtain a damage award without proving actual harm to his reputation. . . .

Presumed damages apply in libel cases. . . . [S]lander *per se*, like libel, permits the jury to consider presumed damages. . . .[4]

A nominal damages award may be made in a defamation case to a plaintiff who has not proved a compensable loss. . . . Such an award is a "judicial declaration that the plaintiff's right has been violated." . . . .

. . . "Unlike most states, New Jersey accepted the invitation to provide greater protection to speech involving matters of public concern than mandated by the United States Supreme Court's First Amendment jurisprudence." . . . . We thus expanded application of the requirement of proof of actual malice to statements regarding private citizens in matters of public concern.

. . . .

Recently, in *Senna*, . . . [958 A.2d 427 (N.J. 2008)], Justice Albin, writing for the Court, traced the history of the public concern doctrine. . . .

> . . . . When published by a media or media-related defendant, a news story concerning public health and safety, a highly regulated industry, or allegations of criminal or consumer fraud or a substantial regulatory violation will, by definition, involve a matter of public interest or concern. . . . In all other media and non-media cases, to determine whether speech

4. [Fn. 3:] Here, the Appellate Division ruled that the Internet expressions at issue were libel. . . . Other jurisdictions have reached the same conclusion. . . . However, because Adams's allegations against Anderson — repeated acts of child sexual abuse — fall squarely within the slander *per se* category, there is no requirement of special damages regardless of how the Internet is characterized.

> involves a matter of public concern or interest that will trigger the actual-malice standard, a court should consider the content, form, and context of the speech.... Content requires that we look at the nature and importance of the speech. For instance, does the speech in question promote self-government or advance the public's vital interests, or does it predominantly relate to the economic interests of the speaker? Context requires that we look at the identity of the speaker, his ability to exercise due care, and the identity of the targeted audience.
>
> .... Discourse on political subjects and critiques of the government will always fall within the category of protected speech that implicates the actual-malice standard. Public policy and common sense also suggest that the same protections be given to speech concerning significant risks to public health and safety.... On the other hand, there is no great societal benefit or higher free speech value in providing heightened protection for the defamatory and false statements uttered by one business competitor against another. That form of commercial speech, generally, will call for the application of the negligence standard.

.... Adams says this matter is one of public concern; Anderson says it is not. We think Anderson has the better argument. Under *Senna,* the first inquiry is whether Adams is a media or media-related defendant. He clearly is not.... Next, we examine the content and context of Adams's speech. In respect of content, it is evident that Adams's speech does not "promote self-government or advance the public's vital interests," nor does it "predominantly relate to the economic interests of the speaker." .... To be sure, the speech accuses Anderson of engaging in serious criminal conduct, thus qualifying for *per se* treatment. But we have never suggested that such an allegation, in itself, vaults the public concern threshold. Moreover, we note that the allegations never resulted in a criminal prosecution, were remote enough to result in dismissal during civil proceedings, and were found by a jury in an earlier defamation action to be false. An analysis of the context of the speech requires examination of the speaker's status, ability to exercise due care, and targeted audience. That likewise suggests that there is no matter of public concern....

We turn, finally, to the question of the continued vitality of the doctrine of presumed damages in a private citizen/private concern case. Adams argues that it should be cast aside, while Anderson urges that it be retained. The doctrine has been the subject of some scholarly criticism, ... and several other jurisdictions have abolished it in favor of proof of actual injury to reputation in all cases, *see* ... decisions from Arkansas, Kansas, Missouri, New Mexico, and New York]. However, the majority of our sister states have retained the doctrine. *See* ... [decisions from Alabama, Alaska, Connecticut, Illinois, Kentucky, Louisiana, Maine, Mississippi, Nevada, New Hampshire, and South Carolina].... The main criticisms of presumed damages are based on two notions: (1) that the emphasis of modern tort law is injury and that where there is no injury, tort law should not provide a remedy; and (2) that there is no uniform way for a jury to value presumed damages....

We disagree with the first criticism. Under our tort law, it is clear that reparation is not the only focus of the system. Indeed, . . . our law clearly identifies deterrence as an important element. . . . Further, in a defamation case, vindication is a significant part of the analysis. A trial, even one with only nominal damages awarded, will establish that a defendant's allegations against a plaintiff were false. In addition, presumed damage does not mean that no damage occurred. Rather, it operates as a procedural device which relieves a plaintiff from *proving* specific damages.

. . . .

The Supreme Court in *Dun & Bradstreet, supra,* specifically recognized that a state has a legitimate interest, in view of competing First Amendment concerns, in providing an effective remedy for defamation, including the provision of presumed damages for speech that does not involve a matter of public concern. . . . Retention of presumed damages in a private-party/private-concern defamation cause of action exemplifies our common law's respect for the private individual's good name by keeping dignitary loss of one's good name a vital part of damages. . . .

In today's world, one's good name can too easily be harmed through publication of false and defaming statements on the Internet. Indeed, . . . proof of compensatory damages respecting loss of reputation can be difficult if not well-nigh insurmountable. . . . We are not persuaded that the common law of this state need change to require such victims to demonstrate compensatory losses in order to proceed with a cause of action.

. . . .

That said, we acknowledge that the critics' second point — unguided jury evaluation of presumed damages — is fair. Where we part company from them is in their suggestion that that criticism can only be handled by eliminating any use of presumed damages. Indeed, it seems to us that the doctrine of presumed damages continues to have vitality by permitting a plaintiff to survive summary judgment and to obtain nominal damages at trial. That approach sensibly delimits the doctrine of presumed damages by precluding a compensatory award, thus obviating the argument regarding unguided jury verdicts. To receive a compensatory award for reputational loss, a plaintiff will be required to prove actual harm, pecuniary or otherwise, to his reputation through the production of evidence.

Thus, in this case, Anderson proffered no evidence of monetary or other losses to his reputation, and therefore only nominal vindicatory damages appear possible for that claim when it goes to trial. In other words, Anderson may not recover a compensatory award for defamation unless he proves a compensatory loss.

. . . .

The trial court's grant of summary judgment was in error. The judgment of the Appellate Division . . . is affirmed. The matter is remanded for proceedings consistent with this opinion.

Note

1. ***Presumed Damages Today: Three Views.*** As noted above, the Constitution prohibits an award of punitive damages without proof of actual malice in any case involving a matter of public concern. Beyond that important limitation, states currently follow at least three different views on the availability of presumed damages in defamation actions.

(a) ***Libel Per Se and Slander Per Se*** May ***Justify a Substantial Award of Presumed Damages.*** Some states hold that in cases involving libel *per se* or slander *per se*, a jury may award substantial damages without proof of special losses based simply on the nature of the statement and the extent of its dissemination.

(b) ***Libel and Slander Per Se Justify an Award of*** *Nominal* ***Damages.*** Some states, as in the principal case, reject the traditional view of libel *per se* and slander *per se*. They hold that in such a case, a jury may not make a substantial award of presumed damages in the absence of proof of actual damages. Rather, the plaintiff is merely permitted to survive a motion for summary judgment and may obtain an award of nominal damages.

(c) ***Presumed Damages are Not Available.*** Some states hold that presumed damages are no longer available and that, to be successful, a plaintiff must prove *actual* damages. Moreover, as the following case indicates, some states require proof of a particular type of harm, namely harm to reputation.

2. ***Remittitur of Presumed Damages Awards.*** Courts are increasingly reluctant to uphold large presumed damages awards. *See* Eshelman v. Puma Biotechnology, Inc. (4th Cir. 2021) (holding that, under North Carolina law, the district court abused its discretion in denying a corporation's motion for a new trial or remittitur in a defamation case involving an award of more than $15 million in compensatory damages and more than $6 million in punitive damages).

Smith v. Durden

Supreme Court of New Mexico
276 P.3d 943 (N.M. 2012)

SERNA, Justice.

Plaintiff Walter F. Smith, III, a former priest of St. Francis Episcopal Church . . . initiated this defamation action . . . after the publication of a packet of documents which . . . alluded to alleged sexual misconduct involving Plaintiff and minor parishioners. Defendant Will Durden had originally compiled the packet for a presentation before the Standing Committee of the Diocese of the Rio Grande by certain vestry members (lay leaders of the parish) who desired the removal of Plaintiff from his position. . . .

. . . . Over a year after the filing of the complaint, Defendants moved for summary judgment on the ground that Plaintiff failed to establish a cause of action for defamation because he was unable to demonstrate that he had suffered any actual injury to his reputation as a result of the publication of the material by its distribution. Plaintiff responded that falsely accusing a religious leader of pedophilia is always defamatory and that personal humiliation and mental anguish, as defined in the damages instruction for defamation claims (UJI 13-1010 NMRA), qualified as the requisite actual injury. . . .

Plaintiff appealed the district court's grant of summary judgment in favor of Defendants, and the New Mexico Court of Appeals reversed the district court. . . .

. . . [W]e . . . decline to follow *Dun & Bradstreet* on the issue of permitting private plaintiffs in defamation actions concerning private matters to recover for presumed damages. . . . Our current Uniform Jury Instructions, . . . require plaintiffs, irrespective of the plaintiff's and communication's classification as public or private, to prove actual injury to reputation and actual resulting damages.

Numerous other courts have similarly declined to allow presumed damages in defamation cases. . . .

We now take the opportunity to further clarify the state of defamation law in New Mexico, and hold that actual injury to reputation must be shown as part of a plaintiff's *prima facie* case in order to establish liability for defamation. . . .

New Mexico is far from alone in requiring reputational injury to be shown as a prerequisite to recovery. . . .

We conclude that a plaintiff must first establish the *prima facie* case for defamation — which includes proof of actual injury to reputation — before a jury can award damages for mental anguish, humiliation, or any of the other recoverable harms listed in UJI 13-1010. Allowing recovery for such damages without first requiring proof of injury to reputation has been justifiably criticized, as under such an interpretation of defamation, "a plaintiff with a widespread reputation as a local hoodlum can keep that fact from the jury and recover for his mental anguish and personal humiliation if he is negligently and falsely accused of scalping tickets at a football game." . . . .

We note that defamation law in New Mexico will not perfectly align with the Restatement (Second) of Torts (1977) in regard to requisite injury to reputation in defamation actions. The Restatement defines defamatory communication as that which "tends so to harm the reputation of another as to lower him in the estimation of the community or to deter third persons from associating or dealing with him," and specifies that "actual harm to reputation [is] not necessary to make [a] communication defamatory." *Id.* §§ 559A, 559 cmt. d. Although our Uniform Jury Instructions provide a similar definition of defamatory communication to assist the jury in determining whether the communication itself is even "capable of a defamatory meaning" in situations where the statement may not be readily recognized as defamatory . . . , our instructions go on to require proof that the communication was both defamatory . . . and caused actual injury to reputation . . . for the establishment of liability. The Restatement, on the other hand, allows for the recovery of damages for certain defamatory communications without requiring further proof of actual injury to reputation or otherwise. *See* Restatement (Second) of Torts § 570 (identifying, as defamatory communications subject to liability, traditional *per se* categories imputing certain criminal offenses or "loathsome disease[s]," unfitness for work or office, or serious sexual misconduct). Taken together, these provisions suggest that the Restatement allows for recovery without requiring proof of actual injury to reputation under a recognition of defamation *per se*—a theory we view as outmoded by modern defamation jurisprudence. . . .

. . . [W]e acknowledge that "proof of actual damage will be impossible in a great many cases. . . ." . . . . It is undoubtedly the case that "[a] system that restricts recovery to actual loss will be imperfect, but so is any system that attempts to compensate human injury with money." . . . . The interest served by allowing recovery for defamation, however, is the interest of compensating individuals for injury to reputation. . . . Recovery for a mere tendency to injure reputation, or only upon a showing of mental anguish, is not only too speculative where "the tort action for defamation has existed to redress injury to the plaintiff's reputation," . . . , but it inappropriately blends defamation, a tort properly limited by constitutional protections, with other causes of action.

A showing of actual injury to reputation is not so high a barrier to surmount that it limits recovery only to monetary loss and employment termination, however. Injury to reputation may manifest itself in any number of ways. . . . Events indicating an injury to reputation in the present case might include a decline in membership at St. Francis, an unwillingness for parishioners to allow children to participate in parish-related activities, or a decline in general social invitations from fellow parishioners—assuming such evidence could be proved and linked to the defamatory communication. There is no indication that Plaintiff came forward with evidence of any kind to support an argument that his reputation was actually injured by the publication of the anonymous letter.

Because we acknowledge that the requirement to show actual injury to reputation may not have been sufficiently clear prior to this Opinion, however, we remand in order to allow Plaintiff the opportunity to amend his complaint to raise other theories for recovery which may more appropriately provide redress for the injuries he alleges to have suffered. . . .

4. Retraction Statutes

Some states have enacted "retraction statutes," which limit plaintiffs' remedies in some defamation actions if the defendant publishes a retraction. *See* Mathis v. Cannon, 573 S.E.2d 376 (Ga. 2002) (interpreting state statutes as providing that, because the plaintiff did not request the defendant who posted a defamatory Internet message to issue a retraction, punitive damages were not recoverable). Retraction statutes usually apply only to "media defendants," which have received so much in the way of constitutional protection that at least some retraction statutes no longer serve any purpose.

For example, Fla. Stat. Ann. § 770.02 (Westlaw 2022) limits libel plaintiffs' recoveries to actual damages if an erroneous publication or broadcast is properly retracted. The statute applies only if the defendant had "reasonable grounds for believing that the statements . . . were true." Today, with respect to a matter of public concern, *Gertz* holds that a defendant who had reasonable grounds for believing a statement to be true cannot be held liable even if the defendant does not retract. The *Gertz* decision therefore makes the Florida retraction statute pointless in a wide range of cases.

5. "Fact" vs. "Opinion"

One may hold and express an unfavorable *opinion* without becoming liable for defamation, even if airing that opinion harms someone's reputation. However, one cannot insulate a defamatory statement of fact from the law of defamation by casting it as an opinion: "In my opinion, Jones murdered his wife" may be treated as asserting that Jones is a murderer. If so, it is just as actionable as "Jones murdered his wife." However, not all opinions carry with them claims of fact. Recall the discussion in Chapter 21 of how implicit statements of fact are dealt with in the law of misrepresentation.

By the time the following case was decided, all federal circuits and two-thirds of the states had recognized a constitutionally based "opinion" privilege.

Milkovich v. Lorain Journal Co.

Supreme Court of the United States
497 U.S. 1 (1990)

Chief Justice REHNQUIST delivered the opinion of the Court.

. . . . Petitioner Milkovich, now retired, was the wrestling coach at Maple Heights High School in Maple Heights, Ohio. In 1974, his team was involved in an altercation at a home wrestling match with a team from Mentor High School. Several people were injured. In response to the incident, the Ohio High School Athletic Association (OHSAA) held a hearing at which Milkovich and H. Don Scott, the Superintendent of Maple Heights Public Schools, testified. Following the hearing, OHSAA placed the Maple Heights team on probation for a year and declared the team ineligible for the 1975 state tournament. . . . Thereafter, several parents and wrestlers sued OHSAA in the Court of Common Pleas of Franklin County, Ohio, seeking a restraining order against OHSAA's ruling on the grounds that they had been denied due process in the OHSAA proceeding. Both Milkovich and Scott testified in that proceeding. The court overturned OHSAA's probation and ineligibility orders on due process grounds.

William H. Rehnquist

The day after the court rendered its decision, respondent Diadiun's column appeared in the News-Herald. . . . The column bore the heading "Maple beat the law with the 'big lie,'" beneath which appeared Diadiun's photograph and the words "TD Says." The carryover page headline announced ". . . Diadiun says Maple told a lie." The column contained the following passages:

> . . . a lesson was learned (or relearned) yesterday by the student body of Maple Heights High School, and by anyone who attended the Maple-Mentor wrestling meet of last Feb. 8.
>
> A lesson which, sadly, in view of the events of the past year, is well they learned early.
>
> It is simply this: If you get in a jam, lie your way out.
>
> If you're successful enough, and powerful enough, and can sound sincere enough, you stand an excellent chance of making the lie stand up, regardless of what really happened.
>
> The teachers responsible were mainly Maple wrestling coach, Mike Milkovich, and former superintendent of schools, H. Donald Scott.
>
> . . . .
>
> Anyone who attended the meet, whether he be from Maple Heights, Mentor, or impartial observer, knows in his heart that Milkovich and Scott lied at the hearing after each having given his solemn oath to tell the truth.
>
> But they got away with it.

Is that the kind of lesson we want our young people learning from their high school administrators and coaches?

I think not. . . .[5]

[Milkovich commenced a defamation action against respondents in the county court, alleging that the column accused him of committing the crime of perjury, damaged him in his occupation of teacher and coach, and constituted libel *per se*. Ultimately, the trial court granted summary judgment for respondents. The Ohio Court of Appeals affirmed, considering itself bound by the state Supreme Court's determination in Superintendent Scott's separate action against respondents that, as a matter law, the article was constitutionally protected opinion.]

The *Scott* court decided that the proper analysis for determining whether utterances are fact or opinion was set forth in the decision of the United States Court of Appeals for the D.C. Circuit in Ollman v. Evans, [750 F.2d 970 (1984)]. . . . Under that analysis, four factors are considered to ascertain whether, under the "totality of circumstances," a statement is fact or opinion. These factors are: (1) "the specific language used"; (2) "whether the statement is verifiable"; (3) "the general context of the statement"; and (4) "the broader context in which the statement appeared." . . . . The court found that application of the first two factors to the column militated in favor of deeming the challenged passages actionable assertions of fact. . . . That potential outcome was trumped, however, by the court's consideration of the third and fourth factors. With respect to the third factor, the general context, the court explained that "the large caption 'TD Says' . . . would indicate to even the most gullible reader that the article was, in fact, opinion." . . . . As for the fourth factor, the "broader context," the court reasoned that because the article appeared on a sports page — "a traditional haven for cajoling, invective, and hyperbole" — the article would probably be construed as opinion. . . .

Since the latter half of the 16th century, the common law has afforded a cause of action for damage to a person's reputation by the publication of false and defamatory statements. *See* L. Eldredge, Law of Defamation 5 (1978).

In Shakespeare's Othello, Iago says to Othello:

Good name in man and woman, dear my lord.

Is the immediate jewel of their souls.

Who steals my purse steals trash;

'Tis something, nothing;

---

5. [The entire text of the article was set forth in footnote 2. The article included this passage:]

. . . . I was among the 2,000-plus witnesses of the meet at which the trouble broke out, and I also attended the hearing before the OHSAA, so I was in a unique position of being the only non-involved party to observe both the meet itself and the Milkovich-Scott version presented to the board.

Any resemblance between the two occurrences is purely coincidental. . . .

'Twas mine, 'tis his, and has been slave to thousands;
But he that filches from me my good name
Robs me of that which not enriches him,
And makes me poor indeed.

Act III, scene 3. Defamation law developed not only as a means of allowing an individual to vindicate his good name, but also for the purpose of obtaining redress for harm caused by such statements. Eldredge, *supra*, at 5. As the common law developed in this country, apart from the issue of damages, one usually needed only allege an unprivileged publication of false and defamatory matter to state a cause of action for defamation. . . . The common law generally did not place any additional restrictions on the type of statement that could be actionable. Indeed, defamatory communications were deemed actionable regardless of whether they were deemed to be statements of fact or opinion. . . .

However, due to concerns that unduly burdensome defamation laws could stifle valuable public debate, the privilege of "fair comment" was incorporated into the common law as an affirmative defense to an action for defamation. "The principle of 'fair comment' afford[ed] legal immunity for the honest expression of opinion on matters of legitimate public interest when based upon a true or privileged statement of fact." . . . . As this statement implies, comment was generally privileged when it concerned a matter of public concern, was upon true or privileged facts, represented the actual opinion of the speaker, and was not made solely for the purpose of causing harm. . . . Thus under the common law, the privilege of "fair comment" was the device employed to strike the appropriate balance between the need for vigorous public discourse and the need to redress injury to citizens wrought by invidious or irresponsible speech.

. . . .

[The Court discussed its holdings in New York Times Co. v. Sullivan, Curtis Publishing Co. v. Butts, Rosenbloom v. Metromedia, Inc., and Gertz v. Robert Welch, Inc.]

Still later, in Philadelphia Newspapers, Inc. v. Hepps, . . . [475 U.S. 767 (1986)], we held that "the common-law presumption that defamatory speech is false cannot stand when a plaintiff seeks damages against a media defendant for speech of public concern." . . . . In other words, the Court fashioned "a constitutional requirement that the plaintiff bear the burden of showing falsity, as well as fault, before recovering damages." . . . .

We have also recognized constitutional limits on the *type* of speech which may be the subject of state defamation actions. In Greenbelt Cooperative Publishing Assn., Inc. v. Bresler, . . . [398 U.S. 6 (1970)], a real estate developer had engaged in negotiations with a local city council for a zoning variance on certain of his land, while simultaneously negotiating with the city on other land the city wished to purchase from him. A local newspaper published certain articles stating that some people had characterized the developer's negotiating position as "blackmail," and the developer sued for libel. Rejecting a contention that liability could be premised on the notion that the word "blackmail" implied the developer had committed the actual crime of blackmail, we held that "the imposition of liability on such a basis was constitutionally impermissible—that as a matter of constitutional law, the word 'blackmail' in these circumstances was not slander when spoken, and not libel when reported in the Greenbelt News Review." .... Noting that the published reports "were accurate and full," the Court reasoned that "even the most careless reader must have perceived that the word was no more than rhetorical hyperbole, a vigorous epithet used by those who considered [the developer's] negotiating position extremely unreasonable." .... *See also* Hustler Magazine, Inc. v. Falwell, ... [485 U.S. 46, 50 (1988)] (First Amendment precluded recovery under state emotional distress action for ad parody which "could not reasonably have been interpreted as stating actual facts about the public figure involved"); Letter Carriers v. Austin, ... [418 U.S. 264, 284–286 (1974)] (use of the word "traitor" in literary definition of a union "scab" not basis for a defamation action under federal labor law since used "in a loose, figurative sense" and was "merely rhetorical hyperbole, a lusty and imaginative expression of the contempt felt by union members").

The Court has also determined "that in cases raising First Amendment issues ... an appellate court has an obligation to 'make an independent examination of the whole record' in order to make sure that 'the judgment does not constitute a forbidden intrusion on the field of free expression.'"....

Respondents would have us recognize, in addition to the established safeguards discussed above, still another First Amendment-based protection for defamatory statements which are categorized as "opinion" as opposed to "fact." For this proposition they rely principally on the following dictum from our opinion in *Gertz*:

> Under the First Amendment there is no such thing as a false idea. However pernicious an opinion may seem, we depend for its correction not on the conscience of judges and juries but on the competition of other ideas. But there is no constitutional value in false statements of fact....

Judge Friendly appropriately observed that this passage "has become the opening salvo in all arguments for protection from defamation actions on the ground of opinion, even though the case did not remotely concern the question." Cianci v. New Times Publishing Co., 639 F.2d 54, 61 (CA2 1980). Read in context, though, the fair meaning of the passage is to equate the word "opinion" in the second sentence with the word "idea" in the first sentence. Under this view, the language was merely a reiteration of Justice Holmes' classic "marketplace of ideas" concept. *See* Abrams v. United States, 250 U.S. 616, 630 (1919) (Holmes, J., dissenting) ("[T]he ultimate good desired is better reached by free trade in ideas ... the best test of truth is the power of the thought to get itself accepted in the competition of the market").

Thus we do not think this passage from *Gertz* was intended to create a wholesale defamation exemption for anything that might be labeled "opinion." *See Cianci*, *supra*, at 62, n.10 (The "marketplace of ideas" origin of this passage "points strongly to the view that the 'opinions' held to be constitutionally protected were the sort of thing that could be corrected by discussion"). Not only would such an interpretation be contrary to the tenor and context of the passage, but it would also ignore the fact that expressions of "opinion" may often imply an assertion of objective fact.

If a speaker says, "In my opinion John Jones is a liar," he implies a knowledge of facts which lead to the conclusion that Jones told an untruth. Even if the speaker states the facts upon which he bases his opinion, if those facts are either incorrect or incomplete, or if his assessment of them is erroneous, the statement may still imply a false assertion of fact. Simply couching such statements in terms of opinion does not dispel these implications; and the statement, "In my opinion Jones is a liar," can cause as much damage to reputation as the statement, "Jones is a liar." As Judge Friendly aptly stated: "[It] would be destructive of the law of libel if a writer could escape liability for accusations of [defamatory conduct] simply by using, explicitly or implicitly, the words 'I think.'". . . .

Apart from their reliance on the *Gertz* dictum, respondents do not really contend that a statement such as, "In my opinion John Jones is a liar," should be protected by a separate privilege for "opinion" under the First Amendment. But they do contend that in every defamation case the First Amendment mandates an inquiry into whether a statement is "opinion" or "fact," and that only the latter statements may be actionable. They propose that a number of factors developed by the lower courts (in what we hold was a mistaken reliance on the *Gertz* dictum) be considered in deciding which is which. But we think the "'breathing space'" which "'freedoms of expression require in order to survive,'" . . . is adequately secured by existing constitutional doctrine without the creation of an artificial dichotomy between "opinion" and fact.

Foremost, we think *Hepps* stands for the proposition that a statement on matters of public concern must be provable as false before there can be liability under state defamation law, at least in situations, like the present, where a media defendant is involved. Thus, unlike the statement, "In my opinion Mayor Jones is a liar," the statement, "In my opinion Mayor Jones shows his abysmal ignorance by accepting the teachings of Marx and Lenin," would not be actionable. *Hepps* ensures that a statement of opinion relating to matters of public concern which does not contain a provably false factual connotation will receive full constitutional protection.[6]

Next, the *Bresler-Letter Carriers-Falwell* line of cases provides protection for statements that cannot "reasonably [be] interpreted as stating actual facts" about an individual. *Falwell*, 485 U.S., at 50, 108 S. Ct., at 879. This provides assurance that public debate will not suffer for lack of "imaginative expression" or the "rhetorical hyperbole" which has traditionally added much to the discourse of our Nation. . . .

The *New York Times-Butts* and *Gertz* culpability requirements further ensure that debate on public issues remains "uninhibited, robust, and wide-open." New York

6. [Fn. 7:] We note that the issue of falsity relates to the *defamatory* facts implied by a statement. . . .

Times, 376 U.S., at 270, 84 S. Ct., at 720. Thus, where a statement of "opinion" on a matter of public concern reasonably implies false and defamatory facts regarding public figures or officials, those individuals must show that such statements were made with knowledge of their false implications or with reckless disregard of their truth. Similarly, where such a statement involves a private figure on a matter of public concern, a plaintiff must show that the false connotations were made with some level of fault as required by *Gertz*. Finally, the enhanced appellate review required by *Bose Corp.* provides assurance that the foregoing determinations will be made in a manner so as not to "constitute a forbidden intrusion of the field of free expression." . . . .

We are not persuaded that a separate constitutional privilege for "opinion" . . . is required to ensure the freedom of expression guaranteed by the First Amendment. The dispositive question in the present case then becomes whether or not a reasonable factfinder could conclude that the statements in the Diadiun column imply an assertion that petitioner Milkovich perjured himself in a judicial proceeding. We think this question must be answered in the affirmative. As the Ohio Supreme Court itself observed, "the clear impact in some nine sentences and a caption is that [Milkovich] 'lied at the hearing after . . . having given his solemn oath to tell the truth.'" . . . . This is not the sort of loose, figurative or hyperbolic language which would negate the impression that the writer was seriously maintaining petitioner committed the crime of perjury. Nor does the general tenor of the article negate this impression.

We also think the connotation that petitioner committed perjury is sufficiently factual to be susceptible of being proved true or false. A determination of whether petitioner lied in this instance can be made on a core of objective evidence by comparing, *inter alia*, petitioner's testimony before the OHSAA board with his subsequent testimony before the trial court. As the *Scott* court noted regarding the plaintiff in that case, "[w]hether or not H. Don Scott did indeed perjure himself is certainly verifiable by a perjury action with evidence adduced from the transcripts and witnesses present at the hearing. Unlike a subjective assertion the averred defamatory language is an articulation of an objectively verifiable event." . . . . So too with petitioner Milkovich.

. . . . The judgment of the Ohio Court of Appeals is reversed and the case remanded for further proceedings not inconsistent with this opinion.

Reversed.

[WHITE, BLACKMUN, STEVENS, O'CONNOR, SCALIA, and KENNEDY, JJ., joined in the opinion by REHNQUIST, C.J.]

Justice BRENNAN, with whom Justice MARSHALL joins, dissenting.

. . . .

The majority does not rest its decision today on any finding that the statements at issue explicitly state a false and defamatory fact. Nor could it. Diadiun's assumption that Milkovich must have lied at the court hearing is patently conjecture. The majority finds Diadiun's statements actionable, however, because it concludes that these statements imply a factual assertion that Milkovich perjured himself at the judicial proceeding. I disagree. Diadiun not only reveals the facts upon which he is relying but he makes it clear at which point he runs out of facts and is simply guessing. Read in context, the statements cannot reasonably be interpreted as implying such an assertion as fact....

I appreciate this Court's concern with redressing injuries to an individual's reputation. But as long as it is clear to the reader that he is being offered conjecture and not solid information, the danger to reputation is one we have chosen to tolerate in pursuit of "'individual liberty [and] the common quest for truth and the vitality of society as a whole.'"....

.... I respectfully dissent.

Notes

1. ***Actionable Opinions***. The following are examples of statements which, after *Milkovich*, have been held to raise a triable issue relating to implied defamatory facts:

- Repeated accusations by the host of a call-in talk show that a judge was "corrupt"; Bentley v. Bunton, 94 S.W.3d 561 (Tex. 2002);
- Language in the national directory of a professional organization describing the plaintiff attorney as an "ambulance chaser"; Flamm v. American Assoc. of Univ. Women, 201 F.3d 144 (2d Cir. 2000);
- A supervisor's remark to company officials and other employees that "he had reason to believe" that the plaintiff had sabotaged a computer; Staples v. Bangor Hydro-Elec. Co., 629 A.2d 601 (Me. 1993);
- A statement in a story labeled "fiction" which characterized the plaintiff as a "slut"; Bryson v. News Am. Pubs., Inc., 672 N.E.2d 1207 (Ill. 1996).

2. ***Non-Actionable Opinions***. Examples of non-actionable statements include:

- Anonymous comments posted on a newspaper website suggesting that the police department was not properly serving village citizens; Varrenti v. Gannett Co., Inc., 929 N.Y.S.2d 671 (N.Y. Sup. 2011);
- A labor union official describing the union's attorney as "a very poor lawyer"; Sullivan v. Conway, 157 F.3d 1092 (7th Cir. 1998);
- One scholar calling another "a 'crank' for having taken a position that the first scholar considers patently wrongheaded"; Dilworth v. Dudley, 75 F.3d 307, 311 (7th Cir. 1996);
- Referring to the plaintiff as a "lying asshole." Greenhalgh v. Casey, 67 F.3d 299 (6th Cir. 1995).

3. ***Fully Disclosed Facts***. As expressed by one court:

> [A] ... statement of opinion based on fully disclosed facts can be punished only if the stated facts are themselves false and demeaning.... The

> rationale behind this rule is straightforward: When the facts underlying a statement of opinion are disclosed, readers will understand they are getting the author's interpretation of the facts presented; they are therefore unlikely to construe the statement as insinuating the existence of additional, undisclosed facts.

Standing Comm. v. Yagman, 55 F.3d 1430, 1439 (9th Cir. 1995).

4. ***Imprecise Statements That Are Unverifiable.*** A line of cases in Illinois has held that highly unflattering statements were non-actionable statements of opinion because they were not made in any specific factual context and were therefore "too broad, conclusory, and subjective to be objectively verifiable." Schivarelli v. CBS, Inc., 776 N.E.2d 693, 699 (Ill. App. Ct. 2002) ("the evidence seems to indicate that you're cheating the city"); *see also* Dubinsky v. United Airlines Master Exec. Coun., 708 N.E.2d 441 (Ill. App. Ct. 1999) ("crook"); Hopewell v. Vitullo, 701 N.E.2d 99 (Ill App. Ct. 1998) ("fired because of incompetence").

See also Seelig v. Infinity Broad. Corp., 119 Cal. Rptr. 2d 108 (Ct. App. 2002) (holding that the terms "chicken butt," "local loser," and "big shank" were too vague to be capable of being proven true or false).

In Jefferson County Sch. Dist. v. Moody's Investor's Services, Inc., 175 F.3d 848 (10th Cir. 1999), a school district's bond offering did well at first, but then turned sour when, two hours into the sale, Moody's published an article saying that the outlook on the district's obligation debt was "negative" and that the district was under "ongoing financial pressures" because of the state's underfunding of the school finance act. As a result, the district was forced to re-offer the bonds at a higher interest rate, which caused a loss of more than $750,000. The court held that under the circumstances, including the plaintiff's failure to identify a specific false statement, the vagueness of the phrases "negative outlook" and "ongoing financial pressures" rendered them protected expressions of opinion.

5. ***Allowing Readers to Draw Their Own Conclusions.*** In Thomas v. L.A. Times Communications, 45 Fed. Appx. 801 (9th Cir. 2002), the court held that an article that did not accuse a Holocaust survivor of lying, but which merely contained the views of others that conflicted with the survivor's published statements and permitted readers to draw their own conclusions, did not carry defamatory implications and was not actionable.

D. Privileges and Defenses

Even if the elements of a libel or slander cause of action are otherwise satisfied, there will be no liability if the defendant's conduct is privileged. Defamation privileges are generally classified as either qualified or absolute, with the classification determining whether and under what circumstances the privilege will arise or will be lost.

1. Absolute Privileges

Absolute privileges are confined to a few relatively well-defined areas in which it can usually be said that the interests to be advanced by unfettered speech are of such importance as to take complete precedence over any interest society may have in allowing compensation of the defamed individual. An absolute privilege gives a statement within its scope complete immunity from liability, no matter what the defendant knew or why the defendant made the statement.

a. Judicial-Proceedings Privilege

A robust, adversarial litigation process is deemed so essential to the American form of government, and depends so heavily on relevant information being brought into court, that all jurisdictions hold that any statement made during judicial proceedings, which is in any sense pertinent to the issues before the court, is absolutely privileged and may not give rise to liability. *See* Irwin v. Ashurst, 74 P.2d 1127 (Or. 1938) (counsel's statements that plaintiff, a witness, was a "dope fiend," a "lunatic," and "lower than a rattlesnake," held privileged because pertinent to credibility). Any other rule, the courts reason, could deter persons from coming forward with information which, though important to the search for the truth, is not known with certainty to be correct.

Quasi-Judicial Proceedings. The judicial-proceedings privilege applies not only to litigation before courts of general jurisdiction, but to a wide range of public and private hearings involving the exercise of judicial or quasi-judicial powers, as well as the preparation of documents relevant to those proceedings. *See, e.g.*, Henderson v. Wellman, 43 S.W.3d 591 (Tex. App. 2001) (an arbitration hearing is a quasi-judicial proceeding to which the absolute privilege applies); Kelley v. Bonney, 606 A.2d 693 (Conn. 1992) (complaint filed with the state board of education concerning teacher decertification was absolutely privileged).

Pre-Litigation Communications. Statements made before the commencement of judicial proceedings may be absolutely privileged if made in connection with possible litigation and pertinent to that litigation. *See* Mansfield v. Bernabei, 727 S.E.2d 69 (Va. 2012) (draft complaint sent for settlement purposes); Collins v. Red Roof Inns, Inc., 566 S.E.2d 595 (W. Va. 2002) (a letter to an attorney who said that judicial proceedings were imminent); Krishnan v. Law Offices of Preston Henrichson, 83 S.W.3d 295 (Tex. App. 2002) (notice about a potential malpractice claim); Jones v. Clinton, 974 F. Supp. 712 (E.D. Ark. 1997) (statements to media by presidential spokespersons denying an alleged sexual relationship and questioning the plaintiff's motives were absolutely privileged); Hawkins v. Harris, 661 A.2d 284 (N.J. 1995) (statements made by private investigators of a law firm).

Post-Litigation Communications. The judicial-proceedings privilege even provides absolute immunity to certain post-litigation out-of-court statements because an "attorney must be free to discuss with the client the outcome of the litigation, future strategies, if any, and generally respond to inquiries from the client without fear of civil liability." Golden v. Mullen, 693 N.E.2d 385, 390 (Ill. Ct. App. 1998) (holding that the privilege protected a letter to the client, but not a letter to the client's wife).

Statutory Provisions. In some states, the common-law judicial-proceedings privilege has been supplanted by statute. *See* Cal. Civ. Code sec. 47(b) (Westlaw 2022) (providing an absolute privilege for a publication or broadcast made in any legislative, judicial, or other official proceeding authorized by law).

Perjury. One consequence of the judicial-proceedings privilege is that no civil remedy is given to a person harmed by perjury. *See* Cooper v. Parker-Hughey, 894 P.2d 1096 (Okla. 1995).

Note

1. ***Ethics in Law Practice: Treatment of Witnesses and Trial Publicity.*** Although the judicial-proceedings privilege may prevent an attorney from being held civilly liable for defamation of a witness at trial, rules of ethics limit what an attorney can say about a witness. For example, Rule 3.4(e) of the Model Rules of Professional Conduct (Westlaw 2022) provides:

> A lawyer shall not . . . in trial . . . allude to any matter that the lawyer does not reasonably believe is relevant or that will not be supported by admissible evidence. . . .

In addition, attorneys have special obligations with respect to trial publicity. Model Rule 3.6 (a) (Westlaw 2022) provides:

> A lawyer who is participating or has participated in the investigation or litigation of a matter shall not make an extrajudicial statement that the lawyer knows or reasonably should know will be disseminated by means of public communication and will have a substantial likelihood of materially prejudicing an adjudicative proceeding in the matter.

A lawyer who violates either of these rules is subject to professional discipline, including reprimand, suspension, or removal from the bar.

b. Other Absolute Privileges

An absolute privilege applies to pertinent statements during a legislative proceeding. *See* Riddle v. Perry, 40 P.3d 1128 (Utah 2002) (holding that a statement of a legislative witness, which implied that the sponsor of a bill had been bribed, was related to the hearing and therefore absolutely privileged).

Other areas to which courts have applied absolute privileges concern actions of the executive branch, communications between spouses, publications required by law, and communications consented to by the plaintiff.

2. Qualified Privileges

A "qualified privilege" entitles the speaker to some degree of immunity from liability for making false statements, but a qualified privilege will be lost if the speaker abuses that immunity. Unfortunately, the law on when qualified privileges come into play and when they are lost is usually quite ill-defined.

a. Employers and Employees

Many qualified privileges cover communications between persons who have some particular need to discuss the plaintiff's affairs. For example, "an employer has a conditional or qualified privilege that attaches to communications made in the course of an investigation following a report of employee wrongdoing." Randall's Food Markets, Inc. v. Johnson, 891 S.W.2d 640, 646 (Tex. 1995). A former employer's statements made in good faith about a former employee to a state workforce commission are qualifiedly privileged because the speaker and the recipient have a common interest. *See* Patrick v. McGowan, 104 S.W.3d 219 (Tex. App. 2003). In addition, comments by one employee about another employee may enjoy a qualified privilege if they are made at a board of directors' corporate grievance hearing (Hagebak v. Stone, 61 P.3d 201 (N.M. Ct. App. 2002)) or are made to management with respect to the other's job performance (Sheehan v. Anderson, 263 F.3d 159 (3d Cir. 2001)).

However, "the statements must be made in good faith." Kuechle v. Life's Companion P.C.A., Inc., 653 N.W.2d 214 (Minn. Ct. App. 2002). In *Kuechle*, the court held that an employer, who said that an employee had been discharged for allegedly violating a direct order, did not have qualified privilege because the employer made only a cursory investigation of the underlying facts, failed to interview the plaintiff, and ignored a supervisor's statement that she had made a request of the plaintiff, rather than given a direct order.

b. Others

Credit-reporting agencies are usually thought to have a qualified privilege with respect to communications to their subscribers.

Relevant Factors. In theory, a qualified privilege will arise in any situation in which there is good reason for the law to encourage or permit a person to speak or write about someone, even though the speaker is not certain about the accuracy of the information relayed. In determining whether reasons strong enough to justify a privilege exist, courts typically take into account such factors as:

- the relationship, if any, between the publisher and the recipient;
- the risks, if any, posed to the interests of the publisher, the recipient, or others;
- whether the information was solicited or volunteered;
- the relevance of the information to self-protective action by the publisher or the recipient; and
- whether the plaintiff is alleged to have engaged in wrongful conduct.

c. Loss of a Qualified Privilege

A qualified privilege is defeasible in the sense that the law *does* care about what the defendant knew, who the defendant told, and why the defendant made the statement. A qualified privilege will be lost if the defendant acted with common-law "malice" (in the sense of ill-will, spite, vindictiveness, or revenge) in publishing the defamation. Also, excessive publication may cause a privilege to be lost, so that if *A*, who is privileged to say something to *B*, also tells *C*, *A*'s statement to *C* is not privileged.

In addition, at common law, many jurisdictions required the defendant not to be negligent with respect to the accuracy of the statement, and other states said that a qualified privilege was lost if the defendant acted recklessly. The constitutionalization of the law of defamation has made qualified privilege less important than it once was, as in most, if not all cases, libel and slander are no longer strict liability torts. If the plaintiff proves actual malice, there can never be a qualified privilege, because in all jurisdictions a showing of that degree of fault destroys the privilege.

d. Statutes Relating to Former Employees

Statements relating to work present a serious problem for the legal system. Actions based on job recommendations and statements made in connection with the discharge of employees make up a large portion of modern defamation cases. If the plaintiff's employer is asked about the plaintiff's job performance by a prospective new employer, most jurisdictions would say that the employer has a qualified privilege. This may do the employer little good, as qualified privileges can easily be lost, and in any event, the possible existence of a privilege does not prevent a disgruntled employee or former employee from suing. Of course, in certain situations qualified privileges can affect the outcome of cases.

Many employers, fearing defamation suits, have refused to give prospective employers any information about their former employees other than job titles and dates of employment. This harms able employees, who would get good references if employers could comment freely. It may even be dangerous, as when a former employer, fearing litigation, does not disclose a job applicant's history of actual or threatened violence. Many states have tried to encourage disclosure by enacting legislation to make it harder for employees to bring defamation actions. Here is one example.

Kansas Statutes Annotated Chapter 44, Article 1, § 44-119a (Westlaw 2022)

(a) Unless otherwise provided by law, an employer, or an employer's designee, who discloses information about a current or former employee to a prospective employer of the employee shall be qualifiedly immune from civil liability.

(b) Unless otherwise provided by law, an employer who discloses information about a current or former employee to a prospective employer of the employee shall be absolutely immune from civil liability. The immunity applies only to disclosure of the following: (1) date of employment; (2) pay level; (3) job description and duties; (4) wage history.

(c) Unless otherwise provided by law, an employer who responds in writing to a written request concerning a current or former employee from a prospective employer of that employee shall be absolutely immune from civil liability for disclosure of the following information to which an employee may have access:

(1) written employee evaluations which were conducted prior to the employee's separation from the employer and to which an employee shall be given a copy upon request; and

(2) whether the employee was voluntarily or involuntarily released from service and the reasons for the separation....

Note that the Kansas statute covers only information furnished to a prospective employer.

3. The Validity of Releases

Is it possible for a person who provides an employment reference to avoid the risk of being sued for defamation by relying upon a release? To the extent that a release purports to cover knowingly false statements is it void as against public policy? Section 195 of the Restatement, Second, of Contracts says that although one can release another party from liability for negligence, one cannot grant immunity for intentional or reckless torts. In contrast, the Restatement, Second, of Torts § 583 provides that "the consent of another to the publication of defamatory matter concerning him is a complete defense to his action for defamation." The courts are divided on this issue.

4. Other Privileges

The Reporter's Privilege. Section 611 of the Restatement, Second, of Torts provides:

> The publication of defamatory matter concerning another in a report of an official action or proceeding or of a meeting open to the public that deals with a matter of public concern is privileged if the report is accurate and complete or a fair abridgement of the occurrence reported.

Comment i to § 611 indicates that "the purpose of the privilege is to protect those who make available to the public information concerning public events that concern or affect the public interest and that any member of the public could have acquired for himself by attending them." Thus, the "reporter," in essence, acts as a conduit for the information. Because it is important in a democracy that persons perform this function, the privilege exists even if the publisher knows that the words repeated are false. *Id.* § 611 cmt. a.

The reporter's privilege is commonly exercised by newspapers, broadcasters, and others who are in the business of reporting the news to the public, but it extends to any person who makes a report, oral or otherwise, to any other person. For example, an expert witness is privileged to repeat the substance of in-court testimony to journalists waiting on the courthouse steps, provided the events have not been illegitimately orchestrated to create a privilege to "report" defamatory statements first uttered in a privileged forum. *See* Rosenberg v. Helinski, 616 A.2d 866 (Md. 1992).

In Adelson v. Harris, 402 P.3d 665, 670 (Nev. 2017), a case of first impression, the court held that a hyperlink to a court document, that brought statements into an online petition of a political advocacy group, was within the protection of the reporter's privilege.

Statutory Privileges. Other special privileges have been created by statute. For example, Searcy v. Auerbach, 980 F.2d 609 (9th Cir. 1992), turned upon a California law requiring certain persons to report suspected child abuse to a child protective agency, and additionally providing:

> No child care custodian, health practitioner, employee of a child protective agency, or commercial film and photographic print processor who reports a known or suspected instance of child abuse shall be civilly or criminally liable for any report required or authorized by this article.

The court held that the statute did not bar an action for libel against a psychologist who had advised a divorced father (Michael) of his belief that Michael's child had been sexually abused while in the mother's custody. The privilege did not apply because the information reached California authorities only indirectly (Michael disclosed the information to Texas authorities, who in turn shared it with their California counterparts) and because Michael was not a person to whom disclosure of the report was permitted under the act.

The Neutral-Reportage Privilege. In Edwards v. National Audubon Soc'y, Inc., 556 F.2d 113 (2d Cir. 1977), the New York Times reported that a publication of a prominent conservation group had criticized certain scientists as "paid liars" because of their support of the chemical industry in a controversy over the pesticide DDT. In finding for the newspaper, Chief Judge Irving Kaufman said that even if actual malice had been established (which it was not), a constitutional privilege of neutral republication protected the *Times*. The court ruled that the public interest in being informed about on-going controversies justifies creating a privilege to republish allegations made by a responsible organization against a public figure, if the republication is done accurately and neutrally in the context of an existing controversy.

Some courts have rejected the neutral-reportage privilege (*see, e.g.*, Hogan v. Herald Co., 444 N.E.2d 1002 (N.Y. 1982)), and a few have applied it (*see* April v. Reflector-Herald, Inc., 546 N.E.2d 466, 469 (Ohio. Ct. App. 1988) (holding that the privilege applies regardless of whether the plaintiff is a public figure or private person)).

Under a neutral-reportage privilege, it would seem fair to require reporters to place readers clearly on notice that the communication concerns disputed charges and is not an assertion of their truth.

Although the neutral reportage privilege has not been widely endorsed, Professor David Anderson opines:

> If the President of the United States baselessly accused the Vice President of plotting to assassinate him . . . most courts surely would hold that the media could safely report the President's accusation even if they seriously doubted its truth.

Is Libel Law Worth Reforming?, 140 U. Pa. L. Rev. 487, 504 (1991).

Note

1. ***Ethics in Law Practice: Complaints About Lawyers.*** *See* Tex. Gov't Code Ann. T.2, Subt. G, App. A-1 § 15.09 (Westlaw 2022) (creating an absolute privilege relating to complaints to disciplinary authorities about attorney misconduct).

5. SLAPP Suits

Persons who become the subject of unfavorable public attention sometimes respond by "slapping" the disseminator of the information with a suit for defamation. This form of retaliation can undoubtedly chill free expression. Thirty-one states and the District of Columbia have enacted anti-SLAPP (Strategic Lawsuit Against Public Participation) statutes which make it relatively easy to dismiss meritless retaliatory defamation charges. *See* State Anti-SLAPP Laws, Public Participation Project, http://www.anti-slapp.org (2022). However, the laws vary as to whether the exercise of constitutional rights must take place before a governmental forum or must involve a matter of public concern.

In Dove Audio Inc. v. Rosenfeld, Meyer & Susman, 54 Cal. Rptr.2d 830 (Cal. App. 1996), the son of the late actress Audrey Hepburn asked lawyers to look into why one of his mother's charities had received so little in the way of royalties from one of her audio recordings. The lawyers contacted other celebrities who had participated in the recording and their charities, informing them of the problem and stating an intention to file a complaint with the Attorney General. Dove Audio sued the firm for defamation and tortious interference. Finding that the law firm was immune under both the absolute litigation privilege and the SLAPP statute, the court wrote:

> In general terms, a SLAPP suit is "a meritless suit filed primarily to chill the defendant's exercise of First Amendment rights." . . . . Under [Code Civ. Proc.] section 425.16, subdivision (b), "A cause of action against a person arising from any act of that person in furtherance of the person's right of petition or free speech under the United States or California Constitution in connection with a public issue shall be subject to a special motion to

strike, unless the court determines that the plaintiff has established that there is a probability that the plaintiff will prevail on the claim."

Subdivision (e) provides: "As used in this section, 'act in furtherance of a person's right of petition or free speech under the United States or California Constitution in connection with a public issue' includes any written or oral statement or writing made before a legislative, executive, or judicial proceeding, or any other official proceeding authorized by law; any written or oral statement or writing made in connection with an issue under consideration or review by a legislative, executive, or judicial body, or any other official proceeding authorized by law; or any written or oral statement or writing made in a place open to the public or a public forum in connection with an issue of public interest."[7]

. . . .

RM & S's communication raised a question of public interest: whether money designated for charities was being received by those charities. The communication was made in connection with an official proceeding authorized by law, a proposed complaint to the Attorney General seeking an investigation. "The constitutional right to petition . . . includes the basic act of filing litigation or otherwise seeking administrative action." . . . . Just as communications preparatory to or in anticipation of the bringing of an action or other official proceeding are within the protection of the litigation privilege of Civil Code section 47, subdivision (b) . . . , we hold that such statements are equally entitled to the benefits of section 425.16. . . .

. . . . Once the party moving to strike the complaint makes that threshold showing, the burden shifts to the responding plaintiff to establish a probability of prevailing at trial. Appellant did not, and cannot do so in this case. . . . The trial court did not err in granting RM & S's special motion to strike under section 425.16.

In contrast, in Hariri v. Amper, 854 N.Y.S.2d 126 (App. Div. 2008), the court held that an environmental group that was sued for defamation by a landowner, who wanted to operate an airport on his property, could not seek relief under the state SLAPP law because the landowner had never formally requested a zoning variance and was therefore not a "public applicant or permittee."

---

7. The terms of the statute were subsequently enlarged by the legislature.

Comparative Defamation Law: England and the United States

24 U. Miami Intl. & Comp. L. Rev. 1, 4-10 (2016)

Vincent R. Johnson

England and the United States share a common legal tradition that has been shaped by principles dating back at least 800 years to the time of the Magna Carta. Even after the American colonies declared their independence from England in 1776, English law was still widely followed in the new nation unless it was inconsistent with American institutions or new ideas. As late as 1964, American libel law was essentially "identical" to English libel law. This was true, in part, because until the mid-twentieth century, defamation law in both countries was defined "mainly by the common law and decisions of the courts," rather than by statutes, American constitutional principles, or the United Kingdom's recognition of freedoms guaranteed by the European Convention on Human Rights....

However, during the past half century, the paths of England and the United States have significantly diverged in the field of defamation. So great are the differences that in recent decades United States courts have refused to enforce English judgments arising from claims for libel and slander.

In response to what is often called "libel tourism"—the preference of defamation plaintiffs to sue media defendants in England and other countries where they can avoid American constitutional protections for free speech and free press—the United States in 2010 passed a law commonly referred to as the "SPEECH Act." That law prohibits American courts from recognizing or enforcing foreign judgments for libel and slander obtained under laws that do not provide as much protection for speech and press as is afforded by the first amendment of the United States Constitution and by the laws of the state where enforcement is sought. The only exception to this prohibition is if "the party opposing recognition or enforcement of that foreign judgment would have been found liable for defamation by a domestic court" under applicable United States laws.

In light of the SPEECH Act, it is widely assumed that American courts will normally refuse to recognize or enforce English libel and slander judgments against commercial publishers. This is so because United States tribunals have held that American federal and state law "reflects a public policy in favor of a much broader and more protective freedom of the press than ever provided for under English law."

The American refusal to respect English defamation judgments is naturally a source of embarrassment to some English. However, in the United Kingdom, section 9 of Defamation Act 2013 mitigates that problem by including provisions that limit the number of occasions when issues will arise related to recognition of English defamation judgments. Under the 2013 Act, "a court [in England or Wales] does not have jurisdiction to hear and determine an action" against a party not domiciled in the United Kingdom, a Member State of the European Union, or a state that is a contracting party to the Lugano Convention, "unless the court is satisfied that, of all the places in which the statement complained of has been published, England and Wales is clearly the most appropriate place in which to bring an action in respect of the statement." This law is likely to reduce the number of English libel judgments against American publishers and thus minimize the legal friction between the two countries. . . .

Note

1. ***First Amendment Principles Apply to Other Causes of Action.*** Hustler Magazine v. Falwell, 485 U.S. 46 (1988), concerned an obscene parody in which the plaintiff, a public figure, was the principal character. It was presented as fiction, and the event described (an incestuous rendezvous in an out-house) was so outlandish that few if any readers could have believed that it had actually taken place. The jury denied recovery on Falwell's libel claim, finding that the parody could not be taken as describing facts, but it awarded him damages for intentional infliction of emotional distress. Relying on defamation precedent, the Supreme Court reversed, ruling that the First Amendment interest in uninhibited debate on public issues precludes a public figure from recovering against a publisher for intentional infliction of emotional distress unless the publication contained a false statement of fact made with knowledge of its falsity or reckless disregard for its truth.

Chapter 23

Invasion of Privacy

The law of torts protects a person's interest in life, health, property, and reputation. In 1890, Charles Warren and Louis Brandeis argued that it should also protect privacy:

> .... The press is overstepping in every direction the obvious bounds of propriety and of decency. Gossip is no longer the resource of the idle and of the vicious, but has become a trade, which is pursued with industry as well as effrontery.... To occupy the indolent, column upon column is filled with idle gossip, which can only be procured by intrusion upon the domestic circle.

Charles D. Warren & Louis D. Brandeis, *The Right to Privacy*, 4 Harv. L. Rev. 193, 196 (1890).

As a glance at the newspapers sold in supermarket checkout lines shows, the law has done virtually nothing about the problem with which Warren and Brandeis were primarily concerned: the publication in newspapers of information about the personal lives of socially prominent persons.[1] Furthermore, what limited protection the law does afford privacy has not been based upon the principal analogy that Warren and Brandeis proposed: common-law copyright.[2] Nevertheless, the Warren and Brandeis article has become a classic in the sense that it is very often cited—probably more often than it is read. And, in a variety of cases, the law does sometimes afford relief for harms that can be characterized as "invasions of privacy."

Prosser classified the "privacy" torts as involving four distinct kinds of invasions. This chapter will use Prosser's categories, which have become standard. They are:

> ***Public Disclosure of Private Facts.*** This involves the conduct that bothered Warren and Brandeis. While many jurisdictions purport to "recognize" the tort, relatively few cases have allowed recovery. Any action that

---

1. William L. Prosser, *Privacy*, 48 Cal. L. Rev. 383 (1960), claimed that the Warren & Brandeis article was inspired by unwelcome newspaper coverage of the social activities of Warren, a Boston lawyer, and his wife.

2. At common law, the creator of an unpublished work, such as a song or a letter, had a right to prevent the publication of that work. In some cases, this right was used to prevent publications which would have embarrassed the writer. Common-law copyright no longer exists in this country; protection of expression is now exclusively a matter of federal copyright law. Note, however, that the copyright statute recognizes a fair-use doctrine, and that that doctrine has helped to shape the law relating to the right-of-publicity form of invasion of privacy discussed later in this chapter.

allows the award of damages based on dissemination of the truth obviously faces formidable First Amendment obstacles.

Intrusion. In order to obtain private facts to publish, or for other reasons, the defendant may intrude upon the plaintiff's seclusion by peering through windows, tapping the plaintiff's phone, opening the plaintiff's letters, or following the plaintiff closely on the street. Warren and Brandeis did not discuss this aspect of privacy, probably because Boston in 1890 was a considerably more civilized place than it is today, despite the deplorable prevalence of gossip in the Boston papers.

False Light. Warren and Brandeis were concerned with the publication of matters they thought to be none of the reader's business; they did not worry much about distortion. But even accurate information can, because of its context, create a misleading and unfavorable impression, as when a picture of the plaintiff, a bystander, appears in connection with a newspaper article about the arrest of criminals. The harm done by this sort of thing is often similar to that done by defamation. One might think that this subject would have developed as a branch of the law of defamation, but it is sometimes dealt with as an invasion of privacy.

Appropriation of the Plaintiff's Name or Likeness. The healthiest branch of the privacy-tort family is that involving cases in which the defendant uses the plaintiff's name or picture to advertise a product or service, or for other reasons. The plaintiff's right to prevent this—sometimes called the "right of publicity"—is widely recognized. Many of the cases are better seen as involving a "property right" to the plaintiff's identity or public persona than a right to privacy. Indeed, many of the plaintiffs in these cases are celebrities, whose objections are sometimes not to having their names used, but rather to not being paid for the use.

In some states, privacy categories have been set down in statutory form. *See, e.g.*, R.I. Stat. Ann. 9-1-28.1 (Westlaw 2022).

Prosser's four categories can overlap considerably. Suppose, for instance, that a photographer follows the plaintiff, an intensely private person, for days, snapping pictures, and that the pictures are used without the plaintiff's consent to advertise whiskey. This conduct is an appropriation of the plaintiff's likeness; it may put the plaintiff in a false light (as when the plaintiff does not drink); the photographer may have intruded upon the plaintiff's seclusion to get the pictures; and the plaintiff may object to appearing in the press, period. Nevertheless, the categories provide a useful way to organize the cases and statutes.

Constitutional Right of Privacy Distinguished. The tort of invasion of privacy must be clearly distinguished from privacy rights under the United States Constitution. The Constitution limits the power of states to prohibit or regulate certain types of conduct generally involving intimately personal decisions, such as sexual relationships, marriage, child rearing, use of contraceptives, or having an abortion.

Those limitations are referred to, somewhat unfortunately, as the constitutional right of privacy, but they have little to do with the four causes of action described above. Note, however, that other constitutional provisions—particularly freedom of speech and freedom of the press—sometimes play an important role in shaping the contours of the four privacy tort actions.

A. Disclosure of Private Facts

Quoting the Second Restatement, the court in Cowles Publ'g Co. v. State Patrol, 748 P.2d 597, 602 (Wash. 1988), wrote:

> Every individual has some phases of his life and his activities and some facts about himself that he does not expose to the public eye, but keeps entirely to himself or at most reveals only to his family or to close personal friends. Sexual relations, for example, are normally entirely private matters, as are family quarrels, many unpleasant or disgraceful or humiliating illnesses, most intimate personal letters, most details of a man's life in his home, and some of his past history that he would rather forget. When these intimate details of his life are spread before the public gaze in a manner highly offensive to the ordinary reasonable man, there is an actionable invasion of his privacy, unless the matter is one of legitimate public interest.

Sidis v. F-R Publishing Corp.

United States Court of Appeals for the Second Circuit
113 F.2d 806 (2d Cir. 1940)

CLARK, Circuit Judge.

William James Sidis was the unwilling subject of a brief biographical sketch and cartoon printed in The New Yorker weekly magazine. . . . He brought an action in the district court against the publisher, F-R Publishing Corporation. His complaint stated [a] "cause[] of action" [for] violation of his right of privacy. . . . Defendant's motion to dismiss the . . . "cause[] of action" was granted, and plaintiff has filed an appeal. . . .

William James Sidis was a famous child prodigy in 1910. His name and prowess were well known to newspaper readers of the period. At the age of eleven, he lectured to distinguished mathematicians on the subject of Four-Dimensional Bodies. When he was sixteen, he was graduated from Harvard College, amid considerable public attention. Since then, his name has appeared in the press only sporadically, and he has sought to live as unobtrusively as possible. Until the articles objected to appeared in The New Yorker, he had apparently succeeded in his endeavor to avoid the public gaze.

Among The New Yorker's features are brief biographical sketches of current and past personalities. In the latter department, which appears haphazardly under the title of "Where Are They Now?" the article on Sidis was printed with a subtitle "April Fool." The author describes his subject's early accomplishments in mathematics and the wide-spread attention he received, then recounts his general breakdown and the revulsion which Sidis thereafter felt for his former life of fame and study. The unfortunate prodigy is traced over the years that followed, through his attempts to conceal his identity, through his chosen career as an insignificant clerk . . . and through the bizarre ways in which his genius flowered, as in his enthusiasm for collecting streetcar transfers and in his proficiency with an adding machine. The article closes with an account of an interview with Sidis at his present lodgings, "a hall bedroom of Boston's shabby south end." The untidiness of his room, his curious laugh, his manner of speech, and other personal habits are commented upon at length, as is his present interest in the lore of the Okamakammessett Indians. The subtitle is explained by the closing sentence, quoting Sidis as saying "with a grin" that it was strange, "but, you know, I was born on April Fool's Day." Accompanying the biography is a small cartoon showing the genius of eleven years lecturing to a group of astounded professors.

It is not contended that any of the matter printed is untrue. Nor is the manner of the author unfriendly; Sidis today is described as having "a certain childlike charm." But the article is merciless in its dissection of intimate details of its subject's personal life, and this in company with elaborate accounts of Sidis' passion for privacy and the pitiable lengths to which he has gone in order to avoid public scrutiny. The work possesses great reader interest, for it is both amusing and instructive; but it may be fairly described as a ruthless exposure of a once public character, who has since sought and has now been deprived of the seclusion of private life.

. . . [W]e are asked to declare that this exposure transgresses upon plaintiff's right of privacy. . . . The decisions have been carefully analyzed by the court below, and we need not examine them further. None of the cited rulings goes so far as to prevent a newspaper or magazine from publishing the truth about a person, however intimate, revealing, or harmful the truth may be. Nor are there any decided cases that confer such a privilege upon the press. . . .

Warren and Brandeis realized that the interest of the individual in privacy must inevitably conflict with the interest of the public in news. Certain public figures, they conceded, such as holders of public office, must sacrifice their privacy and expose at least part of their lives to public scrutiny as the price of the powers they attain. But even public figures were not to be stripped bare. "In general, then, the matters of which the publication should be repressed may be described as those which concern the private life, habits, acts, and relations of an individual, and have no legitimate connection with his fitness for a public office. . . ." Warren and Brandeis, *supra* at page 1129.

It must be conceded that under the strict standards suggested by these authors plaintiff's right of privacy has been invaded. Sidis today is neither politician, public administrator, nor statesman. Even if he were, some of the personal details revealed were of the sort that Warren and Brandeis believed "all men alike are entitled to keep from popular curiosity."

But despite eminent opinion to the contrary, we are not yet disposed to afford to all of the intimate details of private life an absolute immunity from the prying of the press. Everyone will agree that at some point the public interest in obtaining information becomes dominant over the individual's desire for privacy. Warren and Brandeis were willing to lift the veil somewhat in the case of public officers. We would go further.... At least we would permit limited scrutiny of the "private" life of any person who has achieved, or has had thrust upon him, the questionable and indefinable status of a "public figure." *See* Restatement, Torts, § 867, comments c and d....

William James Sidis was once a public figure. As a child prodigy, he excited both admiration and curiosity. Of him great deeds were expected. In 1910, he was a person about whom the newspapers might display a legitimate intellectual interest, in the sense meant by Warren and Brandeis, as distinguished from a trivial and unseemly curiosity. But the precise motives of the press we regard as unimportant. And even if Sidis had loathed public attention at that time, we think his uncommon achievements and personality would have made the attention permissible. Since then Sidis has cloaked himself in obscurity, but his subsequent history, containing as it did the answer to the question of whether or not he had fulfilled his early promise, was still a matter of public concern. The article in The New Yorker sketched the life of an unusual personality, and it possessed considerable popular news interest.

We express no comment on whether or not the news worthiness of the matter printed will always constitute a complete defense. Revelations may be so intimate and so unwarranted in view of the victim's position as to outrage the community's notions of decency. But when focused upon public characters, truthful comments upon dress, speech, habits, and the ordinary aspects of personality will usually not transgress this line. Regrettably or not, the misfortunes and frailties of neighbors and "public figures" are subjects of considerable interest and discussion of the rest of the population. And when such are the mores of the community, it would be unwise for a court to bar their expression in the newspapers, books, and magazines of the day.

....

Affirmed.

Notes

1. ***Constraints Posed by the Constitution***. Even if *Sidis* had gone the other way, current notions of freedom of speech and of the press as applied to the law of torts would, today, give constitutional protection to the article in question. Indeed, the article would probably not be actionable today even if it contained serious inaccuracies, so long as it was not published with "actual malice" in the sense of knowledge of its falsity or reckless disregard for whether it was true. See the discussion of constitutional protection for defamation in Chapter 22.

At least one state has declined to recognize the private-facts tort because of its potential for conflict with the First Amendment. *See* Hall v. Post, 372 S.E.2d 711 (N.C. 1988); *see also* Doe v. Meth. Hosp., 690 N.E.2d 681 (Ind. 1997) (declining to recognize disclosure actions and noting that "torts involving disclosure of truthful but private facts . . . [encounter] a considerable obstacle in the truth-in-defense provisions of the Indiana Constitution").

2. ***Disclosures Relating to Public Figures.*** Modern constitutional-law developments in defamation suggest that a "disclosure of private facts" case has a serious chance of success only if the facts have nothing to do with the plaintiff's conduct as a public figure or with a matter of legitimate public interest.

The facts of Sidis's life were at least newsworthy, and he had once done things to make himself a public figure, though he later regretted those actions. Compare the situation of a rape victim who does not want her name published. It is hard to see any public interest in publishing the victim's name and impossible to find any "consent" on her part—implied or otherwise—to becoming a public figure. Nevertheless, the Supreme Court held in Cox Broadcasting Corp. v. Cohn, 420 U.S. 469 (1975), that publication of the victim's name—which appeared in official records open to the public—was constitutionally protected. Although disclosure of the identity of a rape victim was prohibited by state law, the Court found that by "placing the information in the public domain on official court records, the state must be presumed to have concluded that the public interest was thereby being served." Interestingly, in reaching a similar conclusion in Florida Star v. B.J.F., 491 U.S. 524, 532 (1989), the Court declined an "invitation to hold broadly that truthful publication may never be punished consistent with the First Amendment."

See also John Doe 2 v. Associated Press, 331 F.3d 417 (4th Cir. 2003) (holding that a reporter was not liable for disclosing the name of a sexual assault victim who testified in open court, even though the judge had instructed reporters not to do so).

3. ***Past Conduct.*** Melvin v. Reid, 297 P. 91 (Cal. Ct. App. 1931), was an action by a former prostitute who, after her acquittal on a murder charge, led a conventional life. The defendants produced a motion picture about her early life. The court held that the plaintiff's activities had ceased to be a matter of public concern and allowed the action to proceed. The California Supreme Court suggested in Forsher v. Bugliosi, 608 P.2d 716 (Cal. 1980), that *Melvin* might come out differently under modern constitutional law. History is, after all, no less deserving than current events of constitutional protection.

The plaintiff in Diaz v. Oakland Tribune, Inc., 188 Cal. Rptr. 762 (Ct. App. 1983), was the president of the student body at her college. The defendant revealed that the plaintiff had once been a man, and had a sex-change operation before going to college. Although the plaintiff had "waived" her right to privacy about her *public* conduct by seeking to become president of the student body, the court held that this did not "warrant that her entire private life be open to public inspection," especially because the "public arena [she] . . . entered . . . is concededly small."

McNamara v. Freedom Newspapers, Inc.

Texas Court of Appeals
802 S.W.2d 901 (Tex. Ct. App. 1991)

BENAVIDES, Justice.

....

The underlying action arises out of the publication by the Newspaper of a photograph taken during a high school soccer game. The photograph in question accurately depicted McNamara and a student from the opposing school running full stride and chasing a soccer ball. The picture further shows McNamara's genitalia which happened to be exposed at the exact moment that the photograph was taken.[3] The photograph was published in conjunction with an article reporting on the soccer game.

....

[McNamara alleged that the defendant invaded his privacy by public disclosure of true private facts.] McNamara argues that the Newspaper could have used one of its other numerous photographs in its article....

The uncontroverted facts in this case establish that the photograph of McNamara was taken by a newspaper photographer for media purposes. The picture accurately depicted a public event and was published as part of a newspaper article describing the game. At the time the photograph was taken, McNamara was voluntarily participating in a spectator sport at a public place. None of the persons involved in the publishing procedure actually noticed that McNamara's genitals were exposed.

We hold that because the published photograph accurately depicts a public, newsworthy event, the First Amendment provides the Newspaper with immunity from liability for damages resulting from its publication of McNamara's photograph....

The trial court's judgment is affirmed.

Notes

1. ***Expectation of Privacy.*** For disclosure to be actionable, there must be a reasonable expectation of privacy. *See* Pontbriand v. Sundlun, 699 A.2d 856 (R.I. 1997) (whether depositors had reasonable expectation of privacy in their bank records and whether disclosure would be offensive to a reasonable person were questions of fact, precluding summary judgment); G.D. v. Kenny, 15 A.3d 300 (N.J. 2011) (holding that a political candidate's former aide did not have a legitimate expectation of privacy in the expunged record of his cocaine conviction and therefore could not successfully assert a disclosure claim).

2. ***Photographs Taken in Public.*** Normally, neither intrusion upon seclusion nor a private-facts claim will lie for using photographs of the plaintiff taken in public.

---

3. [Fn. 1:] The exposure was apparently caused by McNamara's failure to wear the customary athletic supporter.

The plaintiff has voluntarily chosen to appear in a place visible to others, so taking and using the photographs invades no privacy interest. *See* Prince v. Out Publ'g Inc., 30 Media L. Rep. 1289 (Cal. App. 2002) (pictures depicted a party-goer dancing naked from the waist up on an elevated platform); Floyd v. Park Cities People, Inc., 685 S.W.2d 96 (Tex. Ct. App. 1985) (photo of man on a porch published in a newspaper).

However, if the plaintiff is shown in an embarrassing situation encountered accidentally, use of the photograph may be actionable. *See* Daily Times-Democrat Co. v. Graham, 162 So. 2d 474 (Ala. 1964) (publication of a photograph of a woman, taken after a rush of air lifted her skirt in a "Fun House," was actionable); *but see* Neff v. Time, Inc., 406 F. Supp. 858 (C.D. Pa. 1976) (publication of a photograph of a football fan aping at the camera, with his fly open, was permissible).

3. ***Victims.*** Many of the disclosure cases involve victims of crimes or accidents who are photographed in agony or without their clothes on. Unless the pictures create misleading impressions, thus raising a "false light" claim, the plaintiffs nearly always lose.

Anderson v. Fisher Broad. Co., Inc., 712 P.2d 803 (Or. 1986), held that televising pictures of the plaintiff, an accident victim who was bleeding and in pain, was not an invasion of privacy. Compare *Anderson* with Taylor v. KTVB, Inc., 525 P.2d 984 (Idaho 1974), holding that a television station could be held liable for broadcasting a film clip showing plaintiff being arrested and taken from his house in the nude, if it acted with "malice," meaning a purpose of embarrassing or humiliating the plaintiff or recklessness.

4. ***Family Members.*** Some courts have held that family members of decedents have a privacy right in records regarding their deceased relatives. *See* Catsouras v. Department of California Highway Patrol, 104 Cal. Rptr. 3d 352 (Ct. App. 2010) (allowing an action against the California Highway Patrol and two officers who allegedly e-mailed pictures of decedent's corpse to persons not involved in the accident investigation).

5. ***Non-Private Facts.*** In International U. v. Garner, 601 F. Supp. 187 (M.D. Tenn. 1985), employees and union organizers sued police officers who recorded license tag numbers of persons attending union meetings and later disclosed their identity to their employer. The court dismissed a private-facts claim, finding that the information was of legitimate concern to the public and that, in any event, the information was not private because the cars were parked in plain view in front of the meeting hall.

Vassiliades v. Garfinckel's, Brooks Brothers

District of Columbia Court of Appeals
492 A.2d 580 (D.C. 1985)

ROGERS, Associate Judge.

... Mary Vassiliades, sued her plastic surgeon, Csaba Magassy, M.D., and ... [Garfinckel's] for invasion of privacy on several theories because the doctor used "before" and "after" photographs of her cosmetic surgery at a Garfinckel's department store presentation and on a television program promoting the presentation....

.... The jury returned a verdict of $100,000 against Dr. Magassy for the television presentation and a verdict of $250,000 against Dr. Magassy and Garfinckel's jointly for the department store presentation. After a hearing, the trial court granted defendants' motions for judgment notwithstanding the verdicts....

Several months after Mrs. Vassiliades' last postoperative visit, Dr. Magassy was invited by the director of public relations for Garfinckel's to participate in a store promotion during the month of March 1979. He agreed to participate without compensation in a program entitled, "Creams versus Plastic Surgery".... In connection with its promotion and prior to the presentation at Garfinckel's, Garfinckel's arranged to have Dr. Magassy and other participants appear on the "Panorama" television program on WTTG, Channel 5, in Washington, D.C. During his television presentation, Dr. Magassy used slide photographs of several of his patients, including two "before" and two "after" of Mrs. Vassiliades. Although Mrs. Vassiliades' face appeared on the television screen for less than one minute and her name was not mentioned, a former coworker, Beatrice Brooks, recognized her. Mrs. Brooks testified she had not previously known about Mrs. Vassiliades' surgery and after seeing Mrs. Vassiliades' photographs during the television program, she immediately called a friend at work to share this information. The coworker whom Mrs. Brooks called told another employee, Elliott Woo, a neighbor of Mrs. Vassiliades, but he already knew. Three days later Dr. Magassy made a similar presentation at Garfinckel's department store; seventy-nine people were in the audience, but no evidence was presented that anyone there recognized Mrs. Vassiliades' photographs.

Mrs. Vassiliades ... testified that when she learned of the disclosure she was "devastated," "absolutely shocked" and "felt terrible" that everyone at her former office knew about her face-lift. She "went into a terrible depression," and did not want to go out in public anymore. She claimed she virtually went into hiding....

In its Memorandum Opinion and Judgment the trial court held that the right of privacy is not absolute and that, in balancing the individual's right to be let alone and the public's right to know, there are occasions on which the public right must prevail. We agree. We also agree that the precise boundaries of the public interest may be exceedingly difficult to define, that the subject matter of plastic surgery, as the trial court noted, "at a time when many well-known and highly visible men and women were the objects of news articles about face-lifts and other plastic surgery" was of general public interest, and that a professional presentation with photographs would enhance the public interest in the subject. We disagree, however, with the trial court's conclusions that "reasonable minds could not differ in finding the publication [of Mrs. Vassiliades' photographs] to be of legitimate public interest," and that "certainly, the subject of face-lifts and plastic surgery was no longer a subject calculated to generate offense to persons of ordinary sensibilities." We hold Mrs. Vassiliades was entitled to expect photographs of her surgery would not be publicized without her consent.

. . . .

The Restatement, . . . [Second, of Torts] § 652D, recognizes that publicity of a private matter may constitute an invasion of privacy.[4] The drafters contemplated that "any broadcast over the radio, or statement made in an address to a large audience, is sufficient to give publicity" to the private life of a person. *Id.*, comment a. The determinative factor is whether the communication is public as opposed to private. Mrs. Vassiliades offered evidence that, after agonizing over losing her youthful appearance and contemplating plastic surgery for many years, she underwent plastic surgery and kept her surgery secret, telling only family and very intimate friends.

. . . . Publicizing the photographs as part of a presentation on plastic surgery communicated private facts about Mrs. Vassiliades' life. The nature of the publicity ensured that it would reach the public. . . . Thus the fact that Mrs. Vassiliades presented only two witnesses who learned of her plastic surgery from the television show and none who saw the store presentation does not defeat her claim. Nor need her name have been mentioned. . . .

. . . . The trial court found that the photographs were not highly offensive because there was nothing "uncomplimentary or unsavory" about them. Although the photographs may not have been uncomplimentary or unsavory, the issue is whether the publicity of Mrs. Vassialiades' surgery was highly offensive to a reasonable person, a factual question usually given to a jury to determine. . . . "The protection afforded to the plaintiff's interest in his privacy must be relative to the customs of the time and place, to the occupation of the plaintiff and to the habits of his neighbors and fellow citizens." . . . . The jury was instructed that it had to find the publication highly offensive to a reasonable person in order to establish liability. . . . In view of the evidence presented to the jury, we find no basis to conclude that it did not follow the instruction. . . .

Appellees also contend, and the trial court found, that the publicity was protected because there was a legitimate public interest in the publication. It is a defense to a claim of invasion of privacy that the matter publicized is of general public

4. [Fn. 1:] The Restatement, *supra*, § 652D, provides: One who gives publicity to a matter concerning the private life of another is subject to liability to the other for invasion of his privacy, if the matter publicized is of a kind that (a) would be highly offensive to a reasonable person, and (b) is not of legitimate concern to the public.

interest. . . . Moreover, this defense or privilege is not limited to dissemination of news about current events or public affairs, but also protects "information concerning interesting phases of human activity and embraces all issues about which information is needed or appropriate so that that individual may cope with the exigencies of their period." . . . .

Nevertheless, the privilege to publicize matters of legitimate public interest is not absolute. . . . Certain private facts about a person should never be publicized, even if the facts concern matters which are, or relate to persons who are, of legitimate public interest. . . . We thus find persuasive the distinction Mrs. Vassiliades draws between the private fact of her reconstructive surgery and the fact that plastic surgery is a matter of legitimate public interest.

The conflict between the public's right to information and the individual's right to privacy requires a balancing of the competing interests. . . . [U]pon balancing the two interests, we hold that Mrs. Vassiliades had a higher interest to be protected. Although Dr. Magassy and Garfinckel's may well have performed a public service by making the presentations about plastic surgery, and the public undoubtedly has an interest in plastic surgery, it was unnecessary for Dr. Magassy to publicize Mrs. Vassiliades' photographs. Publication of her photographs neither strengthened the impact nor the credibility of the presentations nor otherwise enhanced the public's general awareness of the issues and facts concerning plastic surgery. . . . Dr. Magassy's presentations could have been just as informative by using either photographs of other patients or photographs from medical textbooks. . . . We hold, therefore, that Dr. Magassy invaded Mrs. Vassiliades' privacy by giving publicity to private facts and the trial court erred in granting his motion for a judgment notwithstanding the verdict.

This finding of liability does not compel a like result with respect to Garfinckel's. The undisputed evidence is that Dr. Magassy had unqualifiedly assured Garfinckel's that he had obtained his patients' consent. Clear evidence of consent will insulate a party from liability. . . . Thus, the issue is whether Garfinckel's was justified in relying on Dr. Magassy's oral assurance. Garfinckel's decision to ask Dr. Magassy to participate in its program was based on its understanding that he was a reputable professional. . . . Before the television program, Garfinckel's director . . . asked Dr. Magassy if he had obtained permission from his patients to use the slides. Based on Dr. Magassy's assurance that he had, the director did not inquire about consent prior to the department store presentation. No evidence was presented to suggest that Garfinckel's had any reason to doubt Dr. Magassy's statement.

Under these circumstances, we hold that Garfinckel's was justified in relying on Dr. Magassy's assurances that he had Mrs. Vassiliades' consent and that Mrs. Vassiliades has failed to meet her burden to prove Garfinckel's liability for invasion of her privacy. . . .

A plaintiff whose private life is given publicity may recover damages for the harm to her reputation or interest in privacy resulting from the publicity and also for the "emotional distress or personal humiliation . . . if it is of a kind that normally results from such an invasion and it is normal and reasonable in its extent." Restatement, *supra*, § 652H comment b. Actual harm need not be based on pecuniary loss, and emotional distress may be shown simply by the plaintiff's testimony. . . . Because the damages arising from the tort constitute psychic and emotional harm and the tort is defined in terms of the mores of the community, . . . mental distress lawsuits offer the potential for large verdicts, although little objective evidence is available to test the size of a jury award for mental distress. . . .

Although we hold that Mrs. Vassiliades presented sufficient evidence of an invasion of privacy, it does not necessarily follow that the trial court abused its discretion in ruling that the verdicts were contrary to the weight of the evidence. . . .

The evidence at trial relating to the extent of the injury suffered by Mrs. Vassiliades showed that her photograph was on television for less than 40 seconds, her name was not mentioned and the person in the photograph was referred to only as a patient in her forties. Only one person who saw the television program identified her and that person told one of Mrs. Vassiliades' former coworkers about her surgery. Although most of Mrs. Vassiliades' testimony focused on the television presentation, she also offered evidence that seventy-nine people saw her photograph at the department store presentation. However, her name was not mentioned; only one person at the store presentation knew her, and there was no evidence that anyone recognized her photographs. . . . Mrs. Vassiliades did not offer evidence of the impact of the publicity on the persons who saw her photographs, but only described her own mental and behavioral reactions. Her husband corroborated her behavioral reactions, but no medical evidence was offered to support her claim of severe depression. . . .

. . . [W]e cannot say the trial court's grant of a new trial was so beyond the range of reason as to require reversal. . . .

Accordingly, the judgment is affirmed in part, reversed in part, and the case is remanded for a new trial on damages to be assessed against Dr. Magassy.

[The concurring opinion of Judge Newman, which argued that "judges should be exceedingly reluctant to set aside jury verdicts," has been omitted.]

Notes

1. ***Other Precedent.*** *But see* Judge v. Saltz Plastic Surgery, P.C., 367 P.3d 1006, 1014 (Utah 2016) (because "reasonable minds could differ on whether appearing on television to discuss cosmetic surgery gives rise to a legitimate public interest in viewing explicit photographic documentation of the results of the interviewee's surgery" summary judgment was inappropriate).

2. ***Limited Disclosure and the Publicity Requirement.*** Section 652D of the Restatement defines the private-facts tort as consisting of "giving publicity" to offensive private facts not of legitimate concern to the public. In Yath v. Fairview Clinics, N.P., 767 N.W.2d 34 (Minn. App. 2009), the court addressed the question of whether

posting private information on a social media webpage was "publicity" for purposes of a disclosure action. The court wrote:

> "Publicity," for the purposes of an invasion-of-privacy claim, means that "the matter is made public, by communicating it to the public at large, or to so many persons that the matter must be regarded as substantially certain to become one of public knowledge." . . . [Restatement (Second) of Torts § 652D cmt. a (1977).] In other words, there are two methods to satisfy the publicity element of an invasion-of-privacy claim: the first method is by proving a single communication to the public, and the second method is by proving communication to individuals in such a large number that the information is deemed to have been communicated to the public.

The court found that an unrestricted posting on a social media webpage constituted publicity.

See also Robins v. Conseco Fin. Loan Co., 656 N.W.2d 241 (Minn. Ct. App. 2003) (a lender's disclosure of an applicant's negative credit rating to one person from whom the applicant intended to make a purchase was not publicity); Eddy v. Brown, 715 P.2d 74 (Okla. 1986) (disclosure to a limited number of co-workers that plaintiff was undergoing psychiatric treatment did not amount to "publicity").

In Jergens v. Marias Med. Ctr., 459 P.3d 214 (Mont. 2019), there was no publicity of a supervisor's letter accusing an employee of inflating hours on timesheets where the only two people who confirmed seeing the letter were the employer's hired investigator and an attorney representing a different employee. Note, however, that a small number of cases hold that "[w]hen a special relationship exists, the public can include one person or small groups such as fellow employees, club members, church members, family or neighbors." *See* Pachowitz v. Le Doux, 666 N.W.2d 88, 96 & n.9 (Wis. Ct. App. 2003) (citing cases that have so held; declining to state that disclosure to one person or a small group, as a matter of law, fails to satisfy the publicity requirement; and affirming in relevant part a judgment based on disclosure to one person whom the defendant knew had "loose lips").

3. ***Disclosure of Confidential Information.*** Mere disclosure of confidential information is not necessarily "highly offensive to a reasonable person." *Cf.* Bratt v. IBM, 785 F.2d 352, 359 (1st Cir. 1986) (although revelation that the plaintiff frequently used a confidential open-door process for resolving work-related grievances might have had a negative connotation to some managers, it was "not of such a personal nature that an invasion of privacy" resulted).

4. ***Newsworthiness.*** In Capra v. Thoroughbred Racing Ass'n, 787 F.2d 463, 464–65 (9th Cir. 1986), a man convicted of fixing horse races provided useful testimony for the government, and was thereafter resettled and given a new identity under the federal witness protection program. His wife and son were accorded similar treatment. Organized crime figures allegedly offered large sums of money for information about the husband's new name and whereabouts. After the wife applied to the racing board for licenses (which would have allowed them to purchase and race horses)

in her new name and her son's new name, the board issued a press release disclosing the identity and location of the husband and wife. In a privacy action by the husband, wife, and son, the court applied a three-part standard for newsworthiness:

> On the record before us, a reasonable jury . . . could find that the press release was not newsworthy as to one or more of the plaintiffs. First, the jury must consider the social value of the facts published in light of the public's interest in protecting persons willing to testify. . . . While the federal witness protection program cannot by itself overcome the First Amendment, the program possesses some social values that weigh against unlimited free speech under the general balancing test. . . . Second, the jury must consider the seriousness of the intrusion caused by the publication. Finally, the jury must consider the extent to which parties voluntarily exposed themselves to public notoriety. In this respect, . . . [the husband], who was convicted, his wife . . . , who made the application, and their son Kevin, whose name was placed on the application, are not all similarly situated.

B. Intrusion upon Seclusion

To prevail upon a claim for intrusion upon seclusion, one must establish, first, an intentional interference with one's solitude or seclusion, or prying into one's private affairs or concerns, and second, that the intrusion would be highly offensive to a reasonable person.

Defendant Must Intrude. Intrusion can take many forms. *See, e.g.*, Coalition for an Airline Passengers' Bill of Rights v. Delta Air Lines, Inc., 693 F. Supp. 2d 667 (S.D. Tex. 2010) (hacking into an e-mail account).

In Tompkins v. Cyr, 202 F.3d 770 (5th Cir. 2000), the court held that anti-abortion activists invaded the privacy of an abortion-performing physician and his spouse by engaging in each of the following forms of conduct: watching their house from a car parked on a side street and using binoculars and a camera; using a bull-horn to preach during the demonstrations at the plaintiffs' home; making repeated and harassing phone calls to the plaintiffs; and rattling their gate while they were eating Thanksgiving dinner.

According to Comment b of § 652B of the Restatement, Second, of Torts:

> The invasion may be by physical intrusion into a place in which the plaintiff has secluded himself, as when the defendant forces his way into the plaintiff's room in a hotel or insists over the plaintiff's objection in entering his home. It may also be by the use of the defendant's senses, with or without mechanical aids, to oversee or overhear the plaintiff's private affairs, as by . . . tapping his telephone wires. It may be by some other form of investigation or examination into his private concerns, as by . . . searching his safe or his wallet, examining his private bank account, or compelling him by a

> forged court order to permit an inspection of his personal documents. The intrusion itself makes the defendant subject to liability, even though there is no publication or other use of any kind of the photograph or information outlined.

Something in the Nature of Prying. Not all forms of annoying conduct constitute actionable intrusions. There generally must be something in the nature of prying into the affairs of the plaintiff. In Dwyer v. American Express Co., 652 N.E.2d 1351 (Ill. Ct. App. 1995), American Express cardholders brought suit based on the defendants' practice of renting information regarding cardholder spending habits. The court held that the plaintiffs failed to state an action for intrusion:

> The alleged wrongful actions involve the defendants' practice of renting lists that they have compiled from information contained in their own records. By using the American Express card, a cardholder is voluntarily, and necessarily, giving information to defendants that, if analyzed, will reveal a cardholder's spending habits and shopping preferences. We cannot hold that a defendant has committed an unauthorized intrusion by compiling the information voluntarily given to it and then renting its compilation.

In Ramsdell v. Hartford Hospital, 2019 WL 659344 (Conn. Super. Ct.), the court concluded "that the plaintiff's allegation that the defendants allowed third parties to review confidential information about the plaintiff that was contained in the medical chart of the plaintiff's infant daughter . . . [was] legally insufficient to support a claim of invasion of privacy based on unreasonable intrusion upon the seclusion of another." There was no conduct in the nature of prying.

See also Mayes v. LIN Television of Tex., Inc., 27 Media L. Rep 1214. (N.D. Tex. 1998) (broadcast of a secretly taped phone conversation with a councilperson did not constitute intrusion into seclusion where the station legally obtained the tape, did not record the tape, and the tape had already been disseminated to the public by other media organizations).

Into a Place. In Allstate Ins. Co. v. Ginsberg, 863 So. 2d 156 (Fla. 2003), the court said that for an action to lie there must be intrusion into a *place*. Accordingly, the court held that a supervisor's alleged unwelcome conduct, including physical touching and sexual comments, was not an invasion of privacy.

In Bratt v. Jensen Baird Gardner & Henry, P.A., 2018 WL 4568590, *7 (D. Me.), the court held that an intrusion action could be based on the defendant's absconding with a "box full of digital media" which allegedly belonged to the plaintiff, but was "stored in a trusted family member's home."

Solitude, Seclusion, or Private Affairs. For an action to lie the plaintiff must reasonably expect solitude, seclusion, or privacy of the matter. *See* Sabrah v. Lucent Tech., Inc., 14 NDLR P 14 (N.D. Tex. 1998), *aff'd*, 200 F.3d 815 (5th Cir. 1999) (a claim was stated where the defendant's employee opened several packages of plaintiff's mail, including one labeled "private," and removed their contents); Mauri v. Smith,

929 P.2d 307 (Or. 1996) (allegedly unauthorized entry into an apartment by police officers was actionable); Remsburg v. Docusearch, Inc., 816 A.2d 1001 (N.H. 2003) (stating that "where a person's work address is readily observable by members of the public, the address cannot be private and no intrusion upon seclusion action can be maintained").

In Swerdlick v. Koch, 721 A.2d 849 (R.I. 1998), the court held that a neighbor did not violate the statutory rights of landowners to be secure from unreasonable intrusions upon their physical solitude or seclusion by photographing activities occurring outside the landowners' residence, maintaining a log of arriving delivery trucks, employees, and other vehicles, and repeatedly requesting that the town conduct inspections for alleged zoning violations in connection with the landowners' operation of a business from their home. The conduct all occurred in full public view.

In Tagouma v. Investigative Consultant Services, Inc., 4 A.3d 170 (Pa. Super. 2010), the court held that the plaintiff failed to show that he had an expectation of privacy while praying in public. Therefore, he failed to state a privacy claim against an investigator hired by his employer's workers' compensation carrier, who videotaped him worshiping at an Islamic Center.

Highly Offensive to a Reasonable Person. In Parnoff v. Aquarion Water Co., 204 A.3d 717, 733 (Conn. App. 2019), "the defendants, a water company and its employees, were servicing a hydrant the company had maintained for many decades." A privacy claim for intrusion was rejected because [a]lthough they walked around the plaintiff's property to discover the hydrant, searched in the area of the hydrant for the missing and altered cap, and allegedly accused the plaintiff of stealing water, a reasonable person would not find this conduct to be highly offensive."

Intrusion by Inquiry? *See* Dempsey v. Nat. Enquirer, 702 F. Supp. 927 (D. Maine 1988) (holding that a reporter's repeated and ongoing attempts to interview the plaintiff were insufficient to support an intrusion action); Myrick v. Barron, 820 So. 2d 81 (Ala. 2001) (finding that an investigation, which resulted only in disclosure of information already known by others, could not support a claim under the wrongful intrusion branch of invasion of privacy).

Intrusion Statutes. In some jurisdictions, the cause of action for intrusion is statutory. Nebraska law provides:

NEBRASKA REVISED STATUTES § 20-203 (Westlaw 2022)

> Any person, firm, or corporation that trespasses or intrudes upon any natural person in his or her place of solitude or seclusion, if the intrusion would be highly offensive to a reasonable person, shall be liable for invasion of privacy.

In re Marriage of Tigges

Supreme Court of Iowa
758 N.W.2d 824 (Iowa 2008)

HECHT, Justice.

A husband surreptitiously recorded on videotape his wife's activities in the marital home. The district court entered a judgment for money damages in favor of the wife who claimed the videotaping constituted a tortious invasion of her privacy. The court of appeals affirmed....

.... The long relationship between Jeffrey and Cathy Tigges was plagued by trust issues. Even before their marriage, Jeffrey and Cathy had recorded each other's telephone conversations without the other's knowledge and consent. Apparently undeterred..., they were married on December 31, 1999.

Jeffrey surreptitiously installed recording equipment and recorded Cathy's activities during the marriage in the marital home. The equipment included a video cassette recorder positioned above a ceiling, a camera concealed in an alarm clock located in the bedroom regularly used by Cathy, and a motion sensing "optical eye" installed in the headboard of the bed in that room. Cathy discovered her activities in the bedroom had been recorded when she observed Jeffrey retrieving a cassette from the recorder in August 2006.

.... When she viewed the tape, Cathy discovered it revealed nothing of a graphic or demeaning nature.... [I]t recorded the "comings and goings" from the bedroom she regularly used. Notwithstanding the unremarkable activities recorded on the tape, Cathy suffered damage as a consequence of Jeffrey's actions. She felt violated, fearing Jeffrey had placed, or would place, other hidden cameras in the house.

Jeffrey filed a petition for dissolution of marriage. In her answer, Cathy alleged she was entitled to compensation for Jeffrey's "tortious... violation of her privacy rights"....[5] The district court found Jeffrey had invaded Cathy's privacy and entered judgment in the amount of $22,500.

.... Although this court has never been called upon to decide whether a claim may be brought by one spouse against the other for an invasion of privacy resulting from surreptitious videotaping, the question has been confronted by courts in other jurisdictions. In Miller v. Brooks, 472 S.E.2d 350 (N.C. App. 1996), a wife hired private investigators to install a hidden camera in the bedroom of her estranged husband's separate residence.... The husband discovered the hidden equipment and sued both his wife and her agents who assisted her in its installation.... The trial court granted summary judgment in favor of the defendants.... [T]he North Carolina Court of Appeals noted the expectation of privacy "might, in some cases,

5. [Fn. 2:] Although Iowa Code section 598.3 provides "no cause of action, save for alimony, shall be joined" with a dissolution action, the parties tried the tort claim in the dissolution action without objection and Jeffrey has not raised the joinder question in this appeal.

be less for married persons than for single persons," but that "such is not the case . . . where the spouses were estranged and living separately." . . . . [T]he appellate court reversed the summary judgment, concluding issues of fact remained for trial in the husband's claims against his wife and her agents. . . .

. . . [I]n the case before this court the record is unclear whether Jeffrey installed the equipment and accomplished the recording of Cathy's activities before or after the parties separated. . . . Whether or not Jeffrey and Cathy were residing together in the dwelling at the time, we conclude Cathy had a reasonable expectation that her activities in the bedroom of the home were private when she was alone in that room. Cathy's expectation of privacy at such times is not rendered unreasonable by the fact Jeffrey was her spouse at the time in question, or by the fact that Jeffrey may have been living in the dwelling at that time.

Our conclusion is consistent with the decision reached by the Texas Court of Appeals in Clayton v. Richards, 47 S.W.3d 149 (Tex. App. 2001). In that case, Mrs. Clayton hired Richards to install video equipment in the bedroom shared by Mrs. Clayton and her husband. . . . After discovering the scheme, Mr. Clayton sued his wife and Richards, alleging invasion of his privacy. . . . [T]he Texas Court of Appeals concluded Richards' liability turned on whether Mrs. Clayton's acts were tortious under Texas law. . . . [T]he court observed:

> A spouse shares equal rights in the privacy of the bedroom, and the other spouse relinquishes some of his or her rights to seclusion, solitude, and privacy by entering into marriage, by sharing a bedroom with a spouse, and by entering into ownership of the home with a spouse. *However, nothing in the . . . common law suggests that the right to privacy is limited to unmarried individuals.*
>
> *When a person goes into the privacy of the bedroom, he or she has a right to the expectation of privacy in his or her seclusion. A video recording surreptitiously made in that place of privacy at a time when the individual believes that he or she is in a state of complete privacy could be highly offensive to the ordinary reasonable person.* The video recording of a person without consent in the privacy of his or her bedroom *even when done by the other spouse* could be found to violate his or her rights of privacy.
>
> As a spouse with equal rights to the use and access of the bedroom, it would not be illegal or tortious as an invasion of privacy for a spouse to open the door of the bedroom and view a spouse in bed. It could be argued that a spouse did no more than that by setting up a video camera. . . . It is not generally the role of the courts to supervise privacy between spouses in a mutually shared bedroom. *However, the videotaping of a person without consent or awareness when there is an expectation of privacy goes beyond the rights of a spouse because it may record private matters, which could later be exposed to the public eye. The fact that no later exposure occurs does*

not negate that potential and permit willful intrusion by such technological means into one's personal life in one's bedroom.

....

We find persuasive the courts' characterizations of a spouse's right of privacy in *Miller* and *Clayton.* Cathy did not forfeit through marriage her expectation of privacy as to her activities when she was alone in the bedroom. Accordingly, we conclude Cathy had a reasonable expectation of privacy under the circumstances presented in this case.

.... We have adopted the invasion of privacy principles set out in Restatement (Second) of Torts (1977)....

[W]e focus our analysis in this case on the "intrusion upon seclusion" theory.... Under this theory,

> [o]ne who *intentionally intrudes,* physically or otherwise, upon the solitude or seclusion of another or his private affairs or concerns, is subject to liability to the other for invasion of privacy, if the intrusion would be highly offensive to a reasonable person.[6]

Restatement (Second) of Torts § 652B (emphasis added).

... Jeffrey admitted videotaping her activities in the bedroom and various other rooms in the home. It is undisputed that he covertly installed the video recorder, recorded Cathy's bedroom activities, and attempted to retrieve a cassette from the recorder. We find this conduct clearly constituted an intentional intrusion upon Cathy's privacy.

.... Jeffrey contends the judgment in favor of Cathy must be reversed because the videotaping captured nothing that would be viewed as highly offensive to a reasonable person. He emphasizes the videotape captured nothing of a "private" or "sexual" nature in the bedroom. This contention is without merit, however, because the content of the videotape is not determinative of the question of whether Jeffrey tortiously invaded Cathy's privacy.... The intentional, intrusive, and wrongful nature of Jeffrey's conduct is not excused by the fact that the surreptitious taping recorded no scurrilous or compromising behavior. The wrongfulness of the conduct

6. [Fn. 3:] Restatement section 652B's comments further explain: (a) an intrusion "does *not* depend upon any *publicity* given to the person whose interest is invaded or to his affairs...."; (b) the intrusion may "be by the use of the defendant's senses, *with or without mechanical aids,* to oversee or overhear the plaintiff's private affairs ..."; (c) a defendant is subject to liability "only when he has intruded into a private place, or has otherwise invaded a *private seclusion* that the plaintiff has thrown about his person or affairs.... Even in a public place, however, there may be some matters ... that are not exhibited to the public gaze; and there may still be invasion of privacy when there is intrusion upon these matters."; and (d) there may be no liability "unless the interference with the plaintiff's seclusion is a *substantial one,* of a kind that would be *highly offensive to the ordinary reasonable man,* as the result of conduct to which the *reasonable man would strongly object.*"....

springs not from the specific nature of the recorded activities, but instead from the fact that Cathy's activities were recorded without her knowledge and consent at a time and place and under circumstances in which she had a reasonable expectation of privacy.

Jeffrey also contends Cathy's claim must fail because Cathy effected the only publication of the videotape by permitting her sister to view it. An intrusion upon seclusion "does *not* depend upon any publicity given to the person whose interest is invaded or to his affairs. . . ." . . . . Accordingly, Cathy had no burden to prove the videotape was published to a third party without her consent. We conclude Cathy met her burden to prove Jeffrey's intrusive videotaping would be highly offensive to a reasonable person.

. . . .

Affirmed.

Note

1. ***Copying Address Books.*** In Opperman v. Path, Inc., 87 F. Supp. 3d 1018 (N.D. Cal. 2014), consumers sued the manufacturer of mobile devices and the developers of "apps" that surreptitiously stole and disseminated contact information stored by customers on the devices. The court declined to dismiss the intrusion claim because the plaintiffs had a reasonable expectation of privacy in their address books, and a jury might find that the defendants' copying of the plaintiffs' address books was "highly offensive."

Koeppel v. Speirs

Supreme Court of Iowa
808 N.W.2d 177 (Iowa 2011)

CADY, Chief Justice.

. . . .

Robert Speirs . . . operated his business from an office building . . . He employed Sara Koeppel and Deanna Miller to assist him. . . .

The office included . . . a small unisex bathroom. . . .

. . . Speirs noticed Miller's work performance had deteriorated. He began to suspect she was engaged in conduct detrimental to the operation of his office. In response, Speirs decided to monitor Miller's activities at work using a hidden camera.

. . . .

Speirs claimed that . . . he installed the camera in the reception area of the office to monitor Miller's work station. As a result, he was able to observe the reception area from the monitor in his office. He had no difficulty observing Miller when the equipment was in operation. However, he did not observe any misconduct by Miller and removed the camera from the reception area after approximately ten days. . . .

On December 26, Speirs claimed he found a hypodermic needle in the office parking lot near the spot Miller parked her car. As a result, he installed the camera inside the hollow base of the shelf in the bathroom. He claimed, however, the equipment did not operate after he placed the camera in the bathroom. . . . After unsuccessfully working with the equipment to produce a picture on the monitor, Speirs claimed he unhooked the monitor and receiver and put them in his desk drawer. Nevertheless, he left the camera in the bathroom and claimed he intended to remove it before Koeppel and Miller arrived at work the following day.

The next day, Koeppel discovered the camera in the bathroom. . . .

The police investigation uncovered the monitor and receiver located in Speirs' office. The camera was found in the bathroom but was inoperable due to a dead battery. The investigating officers replaced the battery in the camera, assembled the equipment, and attempted to operate the monitoring system. They eventually observed a "snowy, grainy, foggy" image on the screen of either the legs or arms of the investigating officer who was inside the bathroom. This image appeared only briefly before the monitor displayed a "no signal" message.

Koeppel filed a claim for damages against Speirs. . . . The petition alleged invasion of privacy. . . .

Speirs . . . moved for summary judgment. . . . He claimed the camera did not constitute an intrusion as a matter of law because it did not actually allow him to view or record Koeppel and Miller. . . .

The district court granted Speirs' motion. . . . The court reasoned that . . . the tort of invasion of privacy required proof the equipment had worked and Speirs had viewed the plaintiffs. It concluded the standard required an actual, as opposed to attempted, intrusion.

. . . . The court of appeals . . . reversed. . . . The court of appeals concluded the evidence indicating the camera was operational in the bathroom was sufficient to survive summary judgment on the issue of invasion of privacy. . . .

. . . . Conduct that intrudes on privacy gives rise to liability because it can cause a reasonable person "mental suffering, shame, or humiliation" inconsistent with the general rules of civility and personal autonomy recognized in our society. . . . The importance of privacy has long been considered central to our western notions of freedom. . . .

Importantly, the cause of action for invasion of privacy imposes liability based on a particular method of obtaining information, not the content of the information obtained, or even the use put to the information by the intruder following the intrusion. . . .

. . . . We adopted the definition of invasion of privacy recognized by the Restatement (Second) of Torts, including unreasonable intrusion upon seclusion. . . . This form of invasion of privacy generally requires the plaintiff to establish two elements. The first element requires an intentional intrusion into a matter the plaintiff has a right to expect privacy. . . . The next element requires the act to be "highly offensive to a reasonable person." . . . .

The Restatement . . . give[s] several examples of facts that support a finding of an intrusion. These examples include a newspaper reporter taking the photograph of a woman sick with a rare disease in a hospital room and a private detective in an adjacent building taking intimate photos of activities within another's bedroom. . . .

In this case, the parties do not dispute that placing a camera in a bathroom would be highly objectionable to a reasonable person, nor do they dispute that a bathroom is a place where a reasonable person expects to be left alone. Instead, the parties disagree about the proof necessary to show the act of intrusion occurred. Koeppel primarily argues the installation of the camera in the bathroom with the intent to view is sufficient. . . .

. . . . Courts across the nation are divided on the question whether a person can intrude without actually viewing or recording the victim. Some courts conclude the installation of surveillance equipment in a private place is sufficient to show an intrusion. . . .

On the other hand, other courts have adopted a standard of intrusion requiring a defendant either see or hear another person's private activities. . . .

. . . . The point of disagreement among courts across the nation essentially boils down to whether the harm sought to be remedied by the tort is caused by accessing information from the plaintiff in a private place or by placing mechanisms in a private place that are capable of doing so at the hand of the defendant. . . . [W]e find the . . . secret use of an electronic listening or recording device is abhorrent to the interests sought to be protected by the tort. . . . [T]he comments and illustrations contained in the Restatement (Second) of Torts make no suggestion that the intrusion into solitude or seclusion requires someone to actually see or hear the private information. . . . Finally, the minority rule fails to provide full protection to a victim, while giving too much protection to people who secretly place recording devices in private places. Direct evidence that an actual viewing occurred can be difficult to establish, and a person who is inclined to secretly place a camera in a private area can easily incapacitate the camera when it is not in use so as to minimize any responsibility upon discovery. A plaintiff who learns a camera was placed in a private place should not be forced to live with the uncertainty of whether an actual viewing occurred. . . .

It would be inconsistent with the policy of the tort to find an intrusion when the privacy of the plaintiff could not have been exposed in any way. . . . Accordingly, proof the equipment is functional is an ingredient in the inquiry. . . .

. . . . Under the standard we adopt in this case, a reasonable fact finder could conclude the camera was capable of exposing the plaintiff's activities in the bathroom. . . .

. . . . [W]e agree with Speirs that our law does not recognize a tort of attempted invasion of privacy. . . . However, the act of intrusion is complete once it is discovered by the plaintiff because acquisition of information is not a requirement.... [H]arm from intrusion arises when the plaintiff reasonably believes an intrusion has occurred....

Decision of court of appeals affirmed; district court judgment reversed and remanded.

Notes

1. ***Other Precedent.*** *See also* Carter v. Innisfree Hotel, Inc., 661 So. 2d 1174 (Ala. 1995) (guests who sued a hotel were not required to prove actual identity of the "peeping Tom" or even that anyone had actually spied on them, although the absence of proof of spying might be relevant to the issue of damages).

2. ***Intent Required.*** Intrusion is an intentional tort in virtually all jurisdictions. Thus, the inadvertent viewing of sexual conduct in a bathroom stall is not actionable. *See* Hougum v. Valley Mem. Homes, 574 N.W.2d 812 (1998).

3. ***Telephone Harassment.*** Harassment by numerous phone calls, particularly at unreasonable hours, can support an action for intrusion. *See* Charvat v. NMP, LLC, 656 F.3d 440 (6th Cir. 2011) (31 telemarketing calls over 3 months, 30 of which occurred after the plaintiff expressly requested to be placed on the defendant companies' do-not-call list); *but see* Prukala v. Elle, 11 F. Supp. 3d 443, 449 (M.D. Pa. 2014) (dismissing the plaintiff's intrusion claim because she failed to allege that promotional e-mails sent to her cell phone would be highly offensive to a reasonable person).

4. ***Damage.*** Some courts hold that an intrusion action requires proof of damage. *See* LaMartiniere v. Allstate Ins. Co., 597 So. 2d 1158 (La. Ct. App. 1992) (peeping over a wall to see furniture that had been stored by suspected arsonists was not actionable because it caused no damage); *but see* Sabrina W. v. Willman, 540 N.W.2d 364 (Neb. Ct. App. 1995) (permitting nominal damages).

5. ***Stalking.*** Ordinarily, watching or observing another person in a public place is not tortious. "However, ... surveillance of an individual on public thoroughfares, where such surveillance aims to frighten or torment a person, is an unreasonable intrusion upon a person's privacy." Summers v. Bailey, 55 F.3d 1564 (11th Cir. 1995).

6. ***Information Gathering and Investigative Firms.*** The New York Court of Appeals, applying District of Columbia law, held in Nader v. General Motors Corp., 255 N.E.2d 765 (N.Y. 1970), that gathering information "of a confidential nature" by means that are "unreasonably intrusive" can be an invasion of privacy. The court held that interviewing a noted consumer advocate's acquaintances to obtain personal information was not tortious, nor was causing women to accost him with "illicit proposals." However, allegations of wiretapping and electronic eavesdropping were held to state a cause of action, and keeping the plaintiff under constant surveillance might also be a tort if the surveillance was "overzealous."

In Wolfson v. Lewis, 924 F. Supp. 1413 (E.D. Pa. 1996), the CEO of a health insurer and his family were entitled to a preliminary injunction against television reporters, barring them from violating the family's privacy rights. There was evidence that the reporters had placed the exterior of the family's house under surveillance, with telescopes, zoom lens cameras, and ultra-sensitive microphones; followed the daughter and son-in-law to work and attempted to film them entering a building; followed the family to Florida, where they went for seclusion; and established a surveillance boat in public waters as close as possible to the CEO's house, for the purpose of forcing the CEO to reconsider an earlier decision not to appear on camera for an interview regarding high salaries paid to executives of the insurer.

7. ***Offensiveness***. A privacy action for intrusion, like one for disclosure, will lie only for an invasion that would be highly offensive to a reasonable person. *See* Alderson v. Bonner, 132 P.3d 1261 (Idaho App. 2006) (permitting recovery because even though "standing on another's front porch and looking through a window in the door is not normally offensive," "[w]hen an uninvited man lurks at the front door at night, peering in the window at a young female, with video camera in hand and without announcing his presence, such conduct is objectionable").

In Denton v. Chittenden Bank, 655 A.2d 703 (Vt. 1994), the court held that a supervisor did not commit invasion of privacy when he came to an employee's home during a birthday party for the employee's daughter and asked questions, which were overheard by the employee's family and friends, about the employee's physical condition, his doctor, whether he was taking medication, and when he would be coming back to work. Although the questions were unusual and possibly rude, they would not be highly offensive to a reasonable person.

In *In re Facebook Internet Tracking Litig.*, 263 F. Supp. 3d 836, 846 (N.D. Cal. 2017), Internet users sued a social networking website, alleging intrusion based on the website's practice of embedding "cookies" in users' Internet browsers. The court rejected the claim, reasoning that since these practices "are part of routine Internet functionality and can be easily blocked," they did not constitute a "highly offensive" invasion of the plaintiffs' privacy interests. However, the result was different in *In re Nickelodeon Consumer Priv. Litig.*, 827 F.3d 262, 294 (3d Cir. 2016), which involved cookie tracking on children's websites. The court stated that "a reasonable factfinder could conclude that Viacom's promise not to collect 'ANY personal information' from children itself created an expectation of privacy with respect to browsing activity on the Nickelodeon website." The court reasoned that the same practices "may have encouraged parents to permit their children to browse those websites under false pretenses," and could therefore be found to be highly offensive. Thus, a cause of action for intrusion was stated.

See also Potocnik v. Carlson, 9 F. Supp. 3d 981, 1001 (D. Minn. 2014) (holding that the act of obtaining or disclosing information about the plaintiff from a Department of Vehicle Services database would not be highly offensive to an ordinary, reasonable person).

8. ***The First Amendment and Intrusion***. Intrusion cases rarely raise First Amendment difficulties, for the tort seldom involves speech or other expression. One case

raising free-speech concerns is Miller v. NBC, 232 Cal. Rptr. 668 (Ct. App. 1986). There, a television news crew entered an apartment to film the activities of paramedics called to rescue a man who had suffered a fatal heart attack. The film was used on the nightly news without anyone's consent. In finding that the widow had stated claims for trespass, intrusion, and outrage, the court rejected NBC's argument that liability was precluded by its constitutional right to gather news. It found that "the obligation not to make unauthorized entry into the private premises of individuals . . . does not place an impermissible burden on newsgatherers."

In Shulman v. Group W Productions Co., 955 P.2d 469 (Cal. 1998), the court allowed the plaintiff to get to a jury on an intrusion claim against the employer of a television cameraman, who had videotaped conversations between the plaintiff and a nurse on board a rescue helicopter taking the plaintiff to a hospital after an accident.

9. ***Ethics in Law Practice: Intrusion Upon Seclusion.*** All lawyer ethics codes contain a provision similar to the model rule which provides that it is professional misconduct to "commit a criminal act that reflects adversely on the lawyer's honesty, trustworthiness or fitness as a lawyer in other respects." *See* Model Rules of Professional Conduct R. 8.4(b) (2022). This may be the rule that led to the disbarment of the lawyer discussed in the following article. *See* Carolina Bolado, *Atty Agrees to Disbarment for Filming Women in Restrooms*, Law360, Jan. 18, 2018.

C. False Light

West v. Media General Convergence, Inc.

Supreme Court of Tennessee
53 S.W.3d 640 (Tenn. 2001)

FRANK F. DROWOTA, III, J.

. . . .

This suit arises out of a . . . news report aired by WDEF-TV 12 in Chattanooga about the relationship between the plaintiffs [Charmaine West and First Alternative Probation Counseling, Inc.] and . . . one of the general sessions court judges. Plaintiffs operated a private probation services business, and were referred this business by the general sessions courts. Plaintiffs claim that WDEF-TV defamed them by broadcasting false statements that the plaintiffs' business is illegal. Plaintiff West . . . claims that the defendant invaded her privacy by implying that she had a sexual relationship with one of the general session judges; and that the general sessions judges and the plaintiffs otherwise had a "cozy," and hence improper, relationship.

. . . [T]he District Court for the Eastern District of Tennessee certified to this Court the following question of law: Do the courts of Tennessee recognize the tort of false light invasion of privacy . . . ? . . . .

.... Section 652E of the Restatement (Second) of Torts (1977) defines the tort of false light:

> One who gives publicity to a matter concerning another that places the other before the public in a false light is subject to liability to the other for invasion of his privacy, if
>
> (a) the false light in which the other was placed would be highly offensive to a reasonable person, and
>
> (b) the actor had knowledge of or acted in reckless disregard as to the falsity of the publicized matter and the false light in which the other would be placed.

A majority of jurisdictions addressing false light claims have chosen to recognize false light as a separate actionable tort. Most of these jurisdictions have adopted either the analysis of the tort given by Dean Prosser or the definition provided by the Restatement (Second) of Torts....

A minority of jurisdictions have refused to recognize false light.... Among these jurisdictions, Virginia, New York, and Wisconsin refused to recognize the common law tort of false light because their state legislatures adopted privacy statutes that do not expressly include the tort.

Perhaps the most significant case upholding the minority view is Renwick v. News and Observer Publishing Co., 310 N.C. 312, 312 S.E.2d 405 (1984). In *Renwick,* the Supreme Court of North Carolina expressed two main arguments for not recognizing the tort of false light invasion of privacy in North Carolina. First, the protection provided by false light either duplicates or overlaps the interests already protected by the defamation torts of libel and slander.... Second, "to the extent it would allow recovery beyond that permitted in actions for libel or slander, [recognition of false light] would tend to add to the tension already existing between the First Amendment and the law of torts in cases of this nature." ... *[T]*he North Carolina Supreme Court was unwilling to extend protection to plaintiffs under false light partly because of a concern that recognition of the tort "would reduce judicial efficiency by requiring our courts to consider two claims for the same relief which, if not identical, would not differ significantly." ....

... [W]e agree with the majority of jurisdictions that false light should be recognized as a distinct, actionable tort. While the law of defamation and false light invasion of privacy conceivably overlap in some ways, we conclude that the differences between the two torts warrant their separate recognition....

With respect to the judicial economy concern expressed by the North Carolina Supreme Court, we find that such concerns are outweighed in this instance by the need to maintain the integrity of the right to privacy in this State.... Certainly situations may exist in which persons have had attributed to them certain qualities, characteristics, or beliefs that, while not injurious to their reputation, place those persons in an undesirable false light.[7] However, in situations such as these, victims of invasion of privacy would be without recourse under defamation law. . . .

The Appellant, and likewise the minority view, predict that recognition of the tort will result in unnecessary litigation, even in situations where "positive" or laudatory characteristics are attributed to individuals. We disagree. Such needless litigation is foreclosed by Section 652E (a) of the Restatement (Second) of Torts which imposes liability for false light only if the publicity is highly offensive to a reasonable person. . . .

> Complete and perfect accuracy in published reports concerning any individual is seldom attainable by any reasonable effort, and most minor errors, such as a wrong address for his home, or a mistake in the date when he entered his employment or similar unimportant details of his career, would not in the absence of special circumstances give any serious offense to a reasonable person.

Restatement (Second) of Torts, § 652E cmt. c (1977). Thus, the "highly offensive to a reasonable person" prong of Section 652E deters needless litigation.[8]

. . . .

We must also disagree with the North Carolina Supreme Court that recognition of false light would destabilize current First Amendment protections of speech. . . . In Time, Inc. v. Hill, 385 U.S. 374 (1967), the Court extended the actual malice standard to alleged defamatory statements about matters of public interest.[9] In Gertz v. Robert Welch, Inc., 418 U.S. 323 (1974), the Court held that negligence is a sufficient constitutional standard for defamation claims asserted by a private individual about

---

7. [Fn. 6:] Comment b, Illustration 4 to Section 652E provides such an example:

> A is a democrat. B induces him to sign a petition nominating C for office. A discovers that C is a Republican and demands that B remove his name from the petition. B refuses to do so and continues public circulation of the petition, bearing A's name. B is subject to liability to A for invasion of privacy.

8. [Fn. 7:] Illustrations provided in Section 652E of the Restatement (Second) of Torts, (1977), are helpful in understanding the limits of protection provided by false light. Illustration 9 reads:

> A is the pilot of an airplane flying across the Pacific. The plane develops motor trouble, and A succeeds in landing it after harrowing hours in the air. B Company broadcasts over television a dramatization of the flight, which enacts it in most respects in an accurate manner. Included in the broadcast, however, are scenes, known to B to be false, in which an actor representing A is shown as praying, reassuring passengers, and otherwise conducting himself in a fictitious manner that does not defame him or in any way reflect upon him. Whether this is an invasion of A's privacy depends on whether it is found by the jury that the scenes would be highly objectionable to a reasonable man in A's position.

9. [Fn. 9:] "[T]he constitutional protections for speech and press preclude the application of the New York statute to redress false reports of matters of public interest in the absence of proof that the defendant published the report with knowledge of its falsity or in reckless disregard of the truth." Time, Inc. v. Hill, 385 U.S. at 387–88.

matters of private concern, but the Court has not yet decided which standard applies to false light claims. *See* Cantrell v. Forest City Publishing Co., 419 U.S. 245 (1974).

In light of the uncertain position of the United States Supreme Court with respect to the constitutional standard for false light claims brought by private individuals about matters of private interest, many courts and Section 652E of the Restatement (Second) of Torts adopt actual malice as the standard for all false light claims.... We hold that actual malice is the appropriate standard for false light claims when the plaintiff is a public official or public figure, or when the claim is asserted by a private individual about a matter of public concern. We do not, however, adopt the actual malice standard for false light claims brought by private plaintiffs about matters of private concern. In Memphis Publishing Co. v. Nichols, 569 S.W.2d 412 (Tenn. 1978), this Court adopted negligence as the standard for defamation claims asserted by private individuals about matters of private concern. Our decision to adopt a simple negligence standard in private plaintiff/private matter false light claims is the result of our conclusion that private plaintiffs in false light claims deserve the same heightened protection that private plaintiffs receive in defamation cases. Therefore, when false light invasion of privacy claims are asserted by a private plaintiff regarding a matter of private concern, the plaintiff need only prove that the defendant publisher was negligent in placing the plaintiff in a false light. For all other false light claims, we believe that the actual malice standard achieves the appropriate balance between First Amendment guarantees and privacy interests.

.... Damages are addressed in Section 652H of the Restatement (Second) of Torts (1977), which provides:

> One who has established a cause of action for invasion of his privacy is entitled to recover damages for
>
> (a) the harm to his interest in privacy resulting from the invasion;
>
> (b) his mental distress proved to have been suffered if it is of a kind that normally results from such an invasion; and
>
> (c) special damage of which the invasion is a legal cause.

Consistent with defamation, we emphasize that plaintiffs seeking to recover on false light claims must specifically plead and prove damages allegedly suffered from the invasion of their privacy.... As with defamation, there must be proof of actual damages.... The plaintiff need not prove special damages or out of pocket losses necessarily, as evidence of injury to standing in the community, humiliation, or emotional distress is sufficient....

In addition, for purposes of clarification, this Court adopts Section 652I of the Restatement (Second) of Torts (1977) which recognizes that the right to privacy is a personal right. As such, the right cannot attach to corporations or other business entities, may not be assigned to another, nor may it be asserted by a member of the individual's family, even if brought after the death of the individual. Restatement

(Second) of Torts § 652I cmt. a-c (1977). Therefore, only those persons who have been placed in a false light may recover for invasion of their privacy.

Finally, we recognize that application of different statutes of limitation for false light and defamation cases could undermine the effectiveness of limitations on defamation claims. Therefore, we hold that false light claims are subject to the statutes of limitation that apply to libel and slander. . . .

Having answered the certified question, the Clerk is directed to transmit a copy of this opinion in accordance with Tennessee Supreme Court Rule 23(8). . . .

Notes

1. ***Other Precedent.*** *See* Kolegas v. Heftel Broad. Corp., 607 N.E.2d 201 (Ill. 1992) (holding that a complaint stated a claim for false light based on allegations that the defendants said that the plaintiff and his wife must have been married in a "shotgun wedding," which they were not, and that the plaintiff's wife and child had abnormally large heads as a result of Elephant Man's disease, although their heads were not of abnormal size).

2. ***Publicity Requirement.*** Since "false light" requires "publicity," a newspaper reporter's alleged report to the IRS regarding a village council member's corporation's tax filings did not support the claim. *See* Andrews v. Stallings, 892 P.2d 611 (N.M. Ct. App. 1995).

3. ***False Light and the Constitution.*** Courts routinely hold that constitutional limitations that evolved in the field of defamation apply to false light actions. *See, e.g.*, Stien v. Marriott Ownership Resorts, Inc., 944 P.2d 374 (Utah Ct. App. 1997) (if a statement cannot reasonably be taken as factual, the statement does not amount to false light).

4. ***Implied Falsity.*** Even a hyperbolic utterance may be found to imply a false statement of fact. In S.E. v. Chmerkovskiy, 221 F. Supp. 3d 980, 986-87 (M.D. Tenn. 2016), a celebrity dancer posted a picture of a minor on his social media page with a caption stating, "letting your kid become obese should be considered child abuse." The court held that the minor and her mother stated a claim for false light because the dancer implied that the minor was given unhealthy dietary guidance by her family and was overweight as a result, which the dancer should have known was false since it was allegedly reasonably apparent from the photo that the minor had Down's Syndrome.

5. ***The Supreme Court and False Light.*** Time, Inc. v. Hill, 385 U.S. 374 (1967), was, on its facts,[10] a false-light case; it involved a magazine article about a play, which was based on a crime in which the plaintiffs had been taken hostage for 19 hours. Although the ordeal ended peacefully, the plaintiffs were depicted as having

10. Because *Hill* was brought under the law of New York, which does not recognize a common-law right of privacy, the action was not technically one for false light; it was based on a New York statute.

been subjected to violent and brutal treatment. Noting the differences between false light and defamation, the Court held that both theories required proof of actual malice.

The *Time* decision was reaffirmed in Cantrell v. Forest City Publ'g Co., 419 U.S. 245 (1974), a case in which the survivors of a man killed in the Silver Bridge disaster were portrayed as impoverished, and his widow was described as continually wearing a "mask of non-expression." The Court held that there was adequate evidence of actual malice to support the false-light claim. Though acknowledging that its ruling in Gertz v. Robert Welch, Inc., 418 U.S. 323 (1974), had modified the constitutional standards applicable to defamation actions, the Court found it unnecessary to address whether, in a false-light action by a private person, a state can set the standard for proving fault as to falsity at the level of ordinary negligence. Thus far, the Supreme Court has never resolved the issue, and few of the twenty or so states recognizing false light have said that negligence will suffice.

6. ***Privileges.*** The Restatement, Second, of Torts § 652G provides that the same absolute and conditional privileges that apply to a defamation action (*see* Chapter 22) will also defeat a false-light action.

7. ***False Light versus Defamation.*** There are cases in which a statement is capable of casting a highly offensive false light that is not defamatory. Consider the classic example of an inferior poem, article, or book attributed to a famous author. The author may be highly offended by the misrepresentation, even though the work is not so bad as to subject the author to the hatred, scorn, or ridicule that is the gist of a defamation action.

8. ***Rejection of False Light.*** Would it be desirable to abolish false light and in its stead expand the definition of defamation to encompass those types of statements which traditionally have not been regarded as defamatory, but which nevertheless place the plaintiff in a highly offensive false light?

A number of states have rejected actions for false light. The Texas Supreme Court refused to recognize false light invasion of privacy because defamation encompasses most false light claims and false light "lacks many of the procedural limitations that accompany actions for defamation, thus unacceptably increasing the tension that already exists between free speech constitutional guarantees and tort law." Cain v. Hearst Corp., 878 S.W.2d 577 (Tex. 1994). The court rejected the solution of some jurisdictions—application of the defamation restrictions to false light—because any benefit to protecting nondefamatory false speech was outweighed by the chilling effect on free speech.

In Jews For Jesus, Inc. v. Rapp, 997 So. 2d 1098 (Fla. 2008), an article stated that a woman, who was Jewish, had accepted Christian beliefs. The Florida Supreme Court refused to recognize an action for false light. On remand, the district court of appeal found that Rapp stated a claim for defamation. 1 So. 3d 1284 (Fla. Dist. Ct. App. 4 Dist. 2009).

See also Bilodeau-Allen v. American Media, Inc., 549 F. Supp. 2d 129 (D. Mass. 2008) (declining to recognize an action for false light in a suit based on an article that said that a woman's child was the illegitimate son of a U.S. senator). *But see* Welling v. Weinfeld, 866 N.E.2d 1051 (Ohio 2007) (recognizing false light in a case based on the distribution of handbills that suggested that the neighbors' son might have thrown a rock through a window).

D. Unauthorized Use of the Plaintiff's Name or Picture

1. The "Right of Publicity"

Unauthorized use of the plaintiff's name or likeness is referred to as "appropriation" or interference with the "right of publicity." Some courts have differentiated the two terms, saying that misappropriation involves unauthorized use "to obtain some advantage," while invasion of the right of publicity involves unauthorized use "to obtain a *commercial* advantage." *See* Doe v. TCI Cablevision, 110 S.W.3d 363, 368–69 (Mo. 2003). However, the terms are often used interchangeably.

Statutory Remedies. In some states, there is a statutory remedy for misappropriation. *See* Coton v. Televised Visual X-Ography, Inc., 740 F. Supp. 2d 1299 (M.D. Fla. 2010) (authorizing $25,000 in compensation because, in violation of statute, the plaintiff's self-portrait was placed, without her permission, prominently on the packaging of a DVD for the purpose of marketing a pornographic movie).

Identification of the Plaintiff. There is no liability when the plaintiff's property or a portion of the plaintiff's body (such as a hand or foot) is pictured in a publication, so long as there is nothing to indicate the identity of the plaintiff. Identification may, however, be possible by reason of the clarity of the photograph, the visibility of identifying features, or other circumstances.

In Cohen v. Herbal Concepts, Inc., 472 N.E.2d 307 (N.Y. 1984), a photo of a nude mother and child bathing in a stream was placed in a shampoo ad. The court allowed the question of whether the plaintiffs could be identified to go to the jury, although neither person's face was visible. The court held the identifying features included their hair, bone structure, body contours, stature, posture, and the fact that they were pictured together.

Tanner v. Ebbole

Court of Civil Appeals of Alabama
88 So. 3d 856 (Ala. Civ. App. 2011)

PITTMAN, Judge.

Chassity Greech Ebbole is the proprietor of LA Body Art, a tattoo and body-piercing business.... Paul Averette, Jr., is the proprietor of Demented Needle, LLC, a competing tattoo and body-piercing business.... The complaint asserted slander, libel, and invasion-of-privacy claims.

....

Ebbole alleged that Averette and Demented Needle had invaded her privacy by appropriating a white plaster body cast of her torso, adorning it with satanic symbols, and using it as a mannequin on which to display Demented Needle T-shirts for sale. The evidence established that a local artist had made the body cast and had given it to Averette. Averette adorned the body cast with black roses and drawings of pentagrams, attached black wings and "devil's horns" to it, and displayed Demented Needle T-shirts on it. Although the mannequin did not have a face, or any other features identifying it as a representation of Ebbole, the evidence established that Averette routinely told customers and other individuals who entered the Demented Needle shop that the mannequin was a body cast of Ebbole. Averette even went so far as to tell Danny Pike, when Pike inquired as to Ebbole's whereabouts, that if he "really wanted to talk to [Ebbole, he] could go stand up front and talk to [Ebbole] there... that [Ebbole] was sitting at the front of the shop." When Pike responded that there was no one there, just a mannequin, Averette said, "that's a cast of her body that we use to set spells on her."

.... Ebbole sought recovery... [for] invasion of privacy... [based on] putting the plaintiff in a false light and appropriating some element of the plaintiff's personality for a commercial use. Averette and Demented Needle argue that Ebbole failed to establish either a false-light or a commercial-appropriation invasion-of-privacy claim because, they say, Ebbole did not prove the following facts: (1) that Averette and Demented Needle had wrongfully obtained the body cast from the artist who made it and (2) that the body cast was recognizable as a likeness of Ebbole. We agree that Ebbole failed to prove either of those facts, but we conclude that neither fact was essential to establish her invasion-of-privacy claim.

With respect to the first fact, Averette and Demented Needle point out that, during the trial of this case, Ebbole had a lawsuit pending against the artist who made the body cast to determine the true ownership of the cast. Averette and Demented Needle maintain that, until that lawsuit was resolved, it was impossible to determine whether they had wrongfully obtained the cast. Unlike the tort of conversion, however, which requires proof of "(1) a wrongful taking; (2) an illegal assertion of ownership; (3) an illegal use or misuse of another's property; or (4) a wrongful detention or interference with another's property," ... the tort of invasion of privacy does not require proof of a wrongful *taking* of property or of an illegal assertion of *ownership*. It is sufficient to show an appropriation of some element of the plaintiff's personality for a commercial use. . . .

With respect to the second fact, it was undisputed that no one could tell, just by looking at the body cast, that it was a representation of Ebbole's torso. Nevertheless, it was also undisputed that Averette told anyone who inquired, and even volunteered the information to those who had not inquired, that the mannequin was Ebbole's body cast. Under the circumstances, Ebbole presented sufficient evidence to allow the invasion-of-privacy claim to be submitted to the jury for a factual resolution.

. . . .

[The jury found that the plaintiff was entitled to $1 in compensatory damages from each defendant, and punitive damages in the amount of $100,000 from Averette and $200,000 from Demented Needle, LLC. The appellate court held that punitive damages against the small business were capped at $50,000. The court offered Demented Needle, LLC the option of remitting the excessive punitive damages or a new trial.]

Affirmed.

[The dissenting opinion Judge Moore, dealing with punitive damages has been omitted. Demented Needle, LLC agreed to remit the excessive punitive damages.]

Notes

1. ***Newsworthiness***. New York Civil Rights Law § 51 (Westlaw 2022) provides:

> Any person whose name, portrait, picture or voice is used within this state for advertising purposes or for the purposes of trade without the written consent first obtained . . . may maintain an equitable action . . . to prevent and restrain the use thereof; and may also sue and recover damages for any injuries sustained by reason of such use. . . .

The "right of publicity" conferred by this statute (and by statutes in some other jurisdictions[11]) is protected by similar common-law principles in many states.

Although the New York law does not define the terms "advertising" or "trade," the statute has been consistently construed as not applying to publications concerning newsworthy events or matters of public interest.[12] Accordingly, the right of public-

---

11. There are statutes dealing with interference with the right of publicity in California, Florida, Kentucky, Massachusetts, Nebraska, Nevada, New York, Oklahoma, Rhode Island, Tennessee, Texas, Virginia, and Wisconsin. *See* Restatement, Third, of Unfair Competition § 46 Statutory Note (1995).

12. *Cf.* Restatement, Third, of Unfair Competition § 47 (1995) provides:

> The name, likeness, and other indicia of a person's identity are used "for purposes of trade" under the rule stated in § 46 [Appropriation of The Commercial Value of a Person's Identity: The Right of Publicity] if they are used in advertising the user's goods or services, or are placed on merchandise marketed by the user, or are used in connection with

ity does not prevent the publication of books or articles using the names or pictures of actual people. *See* Meeropol v. Nizer, 560 F.2d 1061 (2d Cir. 1977) (unauthorized biography). Similarly, actual persons and institutions can be given roles in works of fiction. *See* University of Notre Dame du Lac v. Twentieth Century-Fox Film Corp., 207 N.E.2d 508 (N.Y. 1965) (involving a motion picture featuring a preposterous college football game).

In Howell v. New York Post, 612 N.E.2d 699 (N.Y. 1993), a trespassing photographer climbed the wall of a psychiatric facility to photograph a woman who had been involved in a highly publicized child abuse case. In the photograph, which was published on the front page of the Post, the woman was shown walking with the plaintiff, whose hospitalization was otherwise a secret. The court held that the plaintiff could not sue either under the privacy statute or for tortious infliction of emotional distress based on publication of her image.

Similarly, in Finger v. Omni Pubs. Int'l, 566 N.E.2d 141 (N.Y. 1990), the unconsented use of a picture of the plaintiffs and their six children to illustrate a segment about caffeine-enhanced fertility was not actionable even though none of the children had been conceived in the manner suggested by the article. The requisite nexus between the article and the photograph was established because the theme of the article—having a large family—was reflected in the picture. The court wrote:

> [T]he "newsworthiness exception" should be liberally applied . . . not only to reports of political happenings and social trends . . . , and to news stories and articles of consumer interest such as developments in the fashion world . . . , but to matters of scientific and biological interest such as enhanced fertility and *in vitro* fertilization as well. . . . [Q]uestions of "newsworthiness" are better left to reasonable editorial judgment and discretion . . . ; judicial intervention should occur only in those instances where there is "'no real relationship'" between a photograph and an article. . . .

2. ***Uses Incidental to Advertising.*** Interesting questions arise when pictures which have appeared in a publication—as part of a use that does not violate § 51 of the New York law and parallel common-law principles—are used to advertise the publication. The plaintiff in Namath v. Sports Illus., 371 N.Y.S.2d 10 (App. Div. 1975), *aff'd*, 352 N.E.2d 584 (N.Y. 1976), was a professional football player, whose picture was used to illustrate an article in Sports Illustrated on the 1969 Super Bowl game. The magazine then used that picture in advertisements seeking subscriptions to Sports Illustrated. The court held that this use did not violate § 51. It described the use of the picture in the advertisements as "incidental" to advertising the magazine, and pointed out that the pictures were used to illustrate the magazine's quality and content, not to imply that Namath had endorsed it.

---

services rendered by the user. However, use "for purposes of trade" does not ordinarily include the use of a person's identity in news reporting, commentary, entertainment, works of fiction or nonfiction, or in advertising that is incidental to such uses.

3. ***Commercial Use Other than Advertising.*** Advertising is not the only kind of use barred by § 51. For example, marketing clothing or board games with the likeness of a famous person violates that section. *See* Rosemont Ent., Inc. v. Choppy Productions, Inc., 347 N.Y.S.2d 83 (Sup. Ct. 1972), and Rosemont Ent., Inc. v. Urban Sys., Inc., 345 N.Y.S.2d 17 (App. Div. 1973), both involving products exploiting the name of the reclusive billionaire Howard Hughes.

4. ***Non-Commercial Use.*** Common-law rules against appropriation may confer protection against some non-commercial uses of the plaintiff's name or likeness, as where the defendant impersonates the plaintiff to obtain confidential information. *See* Restatement, Second, of Torts § 652C cmt. b.

In Hinish v. Meier & Frank Co., 113 P.2d 438 (Or. 1941), the court found an actionable invasion of privacy where the plaintiff's name had been signed, without his consent, to a telegram urging the governor to veto a bill. Would the result have been the same if the message sent by the defendant had simply stated, "Mr. Hinish, too, opposes the bill," and in fact Hinish did oppose the bill and had expressed his opposition to the defendant? The Oregon Supreme Court, in Humphers v. First Interstate Bank, 696 P.2d 527, 532 (Or. 1985), considered this hypothetical and opined that no action would lie, saying, "The false appropriation, not the potential public exposure of Hinish's actual views, constituted the tort."

5. ***Names.*** In the absence of statute, there is no exclusive right to the use of a personal name. One may change one's name to Tiger Woods, Michelle Obama, or Mother Teresa without risk of liability. However, using a name to appropriate the identity of another, as when one deceptively impersonates an individual, is actionable. Restatement, Second, of Torts § 652C cmt. c.

See also Doe v. TCI Cablevision, 110 S.W.3d 363, 368–69 (Mo. 2003) (although a comic book character did not physically resemble the former professional hockey player Tony Twist, and the publication's story line did not attempt to track Twist's life, both shared the same unusual name and tough-guy persona, and there was sufficient evidence to prove that the defendants intended to use the plaintiff's name as a symbol of his identity to obtain a commercial advantage).

6. ***Businesses That Sell Information About Persons.*** In Remsburg v. Docusearch, Inc., 816 A.2d 1001 (N.H. 2003), the court stated:

> An investigator who sells personal information sells the information for the value of the information itself, not to take advantage of the person's reputation or prestige.... In other words, the benefit derived from the sale in no way relates to the social or commercial standing of the person whose information is sold. Thus, a person whose personal information is sold does not have a cause of action for appropriation against the investigator who sold the information.

In Dwyer v. American Express Co., 652 N.E.2d 1351 (Ill. Ct. App. 1995), a suit by credit cardholders challenging the defendants' practice of renting information regarding cardholder spending habits, the court wrote:

> [P]laintiffs have not stated a claim for tortious appropriation because they have failed to allege the first element. Undeniably, each cardholder's name is valuable to defendants. The more names included on a list, the more that list will be worth. However, a single, random cardholder's name has little or no intrinsic value to defendants (or a merchant). Rather, an individual name has value only when it is associated with one of defendants' lists. Defendants create value by categorizing and aggregating these names. Furthermore, defendants' practices do not deprive any of the cardholders of any value their individual names may possess.

7. ***Benefit to the Defendant.*** According to Restatement, Second, of Torts § 652C Comment c, "In order that there may be liability . . . , the defendant must have appropriated to his own use or benefit the reputation, prestige, social or commercial standing, public interest or other values of the plaintiff's name or likeness."

In Moore v. Big Picture Co., 828 F.2d 270 (5th Cir. 1987), the plaintiff's name was used to fill in a blank on a staffing chart prepared in connection with a contract bid. In response to an appropriation claim, the defendant argued that the name had no particular value and was used only as a symbol for someone with qualifications similar to the plaintiff's. The court acknowledged that it would have been an overstatement for the plaintiff to claim that without his name the contract would not have been awarded. However, testimony showed that the plaintiff was a well-known, highly qualified worker in the field. A judgment for the plaintiff was upheld.

8. ***Statutory Authorization.*** Consent will bar an action for appropriation. The same is true if the transaction in question is authorized by statute. *See* Sloan v. South Carolina Dep't of Pub. Safety, 586 S.E.2d 108 (2003) (a company that purchased driver's license information and photographs pursuant to a fraud-prevention arrangement authorized by statute was not liable for appropriation).

9. ***Appropriating Identity without Name or Likeness.*** Can a phrase be so identified with a person that its mere use constitutes actionable appropriation? In some cases, yes. In Carson v. Here's Johnny Portable Toilets, Inc., 698 F.2d 831 (6th Cir. 1983), the defendant appropriated neither the name nor the likeness of a famous television personality. Rather, in marketing its products, the defendant used the phrase "Here's Johnny"—the words with which the plaintiff was introduced to TV audiences for years on his late-night show. The court held that the use of the phrase was so clearly intended to capitalize on Johnny Carson's identity, notoriety, and achievements that an action would lie. The dissenter, observing that the appropriation action is intended to encourage creative works and to allow those whose achievements have imbued their identities with pecuniary value to profit from their fame, would have disallowed the action since the phrase was neither created by nor spoken by the plaintiff and was, therefore, not a product of his efforts.

2. Deceased Celebrities

An issue of much recent concern is whether the right of publicity survives the death of the person in question. It is hard to imagine an action being brought by the descendants of George Washington, or William Shakespeare, or Attila the Hun for use of the names or likenesses of those persons in advertising. But in the case of celebrities who have died more recently, a carefully exploited image may be the estate's most valuable asset. This kind of asset, if available to all comers, may be less valuable than if its use can be controlled by the decedent's heirs.

Prior Exploitation. In State Ex Rel. Elvis Presley Int'l Mem. Foundation v. Crowell, 733 S.W.2d 89 (Tenn. Ct. App. 1987), a not-for-profit corporation which had been using the name "Elvis Presley" in its corporate title sued another corporation for unfair competition to prevent the defendant corporation from using that name. The court held that under state common law (since modified by statute), the "right of publicity" survived the death of the person in question, at least if the decedent had exploited that right during life, as Presley did. Other courts have embraced different positions on the issue of the descendibility of the right of publicity; some have held that it is not descendible.

No Prior Exploitation. The question of whether a right of publicity not exploited during the decedent's lifetime descends to heirs received a negative answer in Lugosi v. Universal Pictures, 603 P.2d 425 (Cal. 1979).[13] Bela Lugosi, who played Dracula in a well-known motion picture, never sought to cash in on his Dracula image during his lifetime. After Lugosi's death, the owner of the rights to the picture licensed the production of Dracula products which incorporated pictures based on Lugosi's portrayal. The court rejected Lugosi's heirs' claim that this action violated a right of publicity which they had inherited from Lugosi. Because Lugosi himself had not "created" such a right by exploiting his name and image, the right did not exist.

A decision upholding descendibility of the right of publicity without lifetime exploitation is Martin Luther King Ctr. for Soc. Change Inc. v. Am. Heritage Products, Inc., 296 S.E.2d 697, 706 (Ga. 1982). The defendant, without permission, manufactured and sold plastic busts of Dr. King. Rejecting the defendant's argument that commercial exploitation during life was required, the court said:

> The cases which have considered this issue . . . involved entertainers. The net result of following them would be to say that celebrities and public figures have the right of publicity during their lifetimes (as others have the right of privacy), but only those who contract for bubble gum cards, posters and tee shirts have a descendible right of publicity upon their deaths. . . . That we should single out for protection after death those entertainers and athletes who exploit their personae during life, and deny protection after death to those who enjoy public acclamation but did not exploit themselves

---

13. In California, rights relating to a deceased personality are now governed by statute. *See* Cal. Civil Code § 3344.1 (Westlaw 2022).

> during life, puts a premium on exploitation. Having found valid reasons for recognizing the right of publicity during life, we find no reason to protect after death only those who took commercial advantage of their fame.

Persons Playing Fictional Characters. When an actor portrays a fictional character in a motion picture or television production, may the owner of the production license others to use the character's likeness without the actor's consent? Wendt v. Host Int'l, Inc., 125 F.3d 806 (9th Cir. 1997), *rehearing en banc denied*, 197 F.3d 1284 (9th Cir. 1999), says no. George Wendt and John Ratzenberger played "Norm" and "Cliff" on a television show called "Cheers," which was set in a bar. Paramount, which owned the rights to the show, licensed the defendant to create airport bars resembling the bar on the television program. The defendant's bars included robot figures bearing some resemblance to the television characters portrayed by the plaintiffs. The Ninth Circuit ruled that a jury could find that the defendant's use of the robots violated the plaintiffs' right of publicity by appropriating their likenesses if it found that the robots sufficiently resembled Wendt and Ratzenberger. Conceding that they had no rights to the characters, the plaintiffs claimed that the robots' similarities to their own physical characteristics could violate their right of publicity. The court agreed, citing *Lugosi* for the proposition that "an actor . . . does not lose the right to control the commercial exploitation of his . . . likeness by portraying a fictional character," 125 F. 3d at 811. This proposition is certainly true — hiring an actor to play a particular character cannot give a studio the right to use that actor's likeness in any context whatever.

Constitutional Protection of Transformative Appropriation. Can an artist sell sketches of celebrities without becoming liable for appropriation? In Comedy Three Productions, Inc. v. Gary Saderup, Inc., 21 P.3d 797 (Cal. 2001), the court held that an artist faced with a right of publicity challenge to his or her work may assert an affirmative defense that the work is protected by the First Amendment, if the work contains significant transformative elements or the value of the work does not derive primarily from the celebrity's fame. Something more than a mere trivial variation is required. "The artist must have created something recognizably his or her own, in order to qualify for legal protection." Because the defendants' portraits of The Three Stooges contained "no significant transformative or creative contribution," the defendants were liable for violating the plaintiff's right of publicity relating to deceased personalities.

See also Hart v. Electronic Arts, Inc., 717 F.3d 141 (3d Cir. 2013) (holding that the fact that game players could alter the digital avatars of football players did not satisfy the transformative use test so as to protect the game developer from liability for misappropriation).

Actual Malice in Appropriation Cases. In Hoffman v. Capital Cities/ABC, Inc., 255 F.3d 1180 (9th Cir. 2001), a still photograph of the actor Dustin Hoffman in women's clothing from the movie "Tootsie" was used to create a composite computer-generated image that depicted him wearing contemporary designer women's clothes. The altered image was published as part of an article on "Grand Illusions" that featured 16 modified stills from famous movies. The court held that the actor failed to state an action for appropriation. According to the court, the depiction was entitled to full constitutional protection because it was not pure commercial speech. Although the image appeared in a magazine advertising the designer's clothes, it was a "combination of fashion photography, humor, and visual and verbal editorial comment on classic films and famous actors." The use of the image did more than merely propose a commercial transaction. Because the speech in question was fully protected by the Constitution, the plaintiff was required to show that the defendant acted with actual malice, namely that it intended to create a false impression in the mind of readers that when they saw the altered photograph they were seeing the actor's body. Because there were references in the accompanying article that made clear that digital techniques were used to substitute current fashions for clothes worn in the original stills, and the original stills were presented at the end of the article, it was not possible for the plaintiff to prove actual malice. The court noted that in many right-of-publicity cases the question of actual malice does not arise because the challenged use does no more than propose a commercial transaction and does not implicate the First Amendment's protection of expressions of editorial opinion.

Index